# Lecture Notes in Electrical Engineering

Volume 212

For further volumes:
http://www.springer.com/series/7818

Wei Lu · Guoqiang Cai
Weibin Liu · Weiwei Xing
Editors

# Proceedings of the 2012 International Conference on Information Technology and Software Engineering

## Software Engineering & Digital Media Technology

 Springer

*Editors*

Wei Lu
Beijing Jiaotong University
Beijing
People's Republic of China

Guoqiang Cai
Beijing Jiaotong University
Beijing
People's Republic of China

Weibin Liu
Beijing Jiaotong University
Beijing
People's Republic of China

Weiwei Xing
Beijing Jiaotong University
Beijing
People's Republic of China

ISSN 1876-1100        ISSN 1876-1119 (electronic)
ISBN 978-3-662-51186-2    ISBN 978-3-642-34531-9 (eBook)
DOI 10.1007/978-3-642-34531-9
Springer Heidelberg New York Dordrecht London

Printed on acid-free paper

Springer is part of Springer Science+Business Media (www.springer.com)

# Committees

**Honorary Chair**
Yaoxue Zhang, Central South University, China

**General Chairs**
Wei Lu, Beijing Jiaotong University, China
Jianhua Ma, Hosei University, Japan

**Steering Committee Chairs**
Zengqi Sun, Tsinghua University, China
Shi-Kuo Chang, University of Pittsburgh, Knowledge Systems Institute, USA
Mirko Novak, Institute of Computer Science, Czech Academy of Sciences, Czech Republic

**Program Committee Chairs**
Guoqiang Cai, Beijing Jiaotong University, China
Weibin Liu, Beijing Jiaotong University, China

**Organizing Committee Chairs**
Weiwei Xing, Beijing Jiaotong University, China
Qingshan Jiang, Shenzhen Institute of Advanced Technology, Chinese Academy of Science, China
Kin Fun Li, University of Victoria, Canada
Tole Sutikno, Ahmad Dahlan University, Indonesia

**Technical Program Committee Members**
Bin Luo, Nanjing University, China
Charles Clarke, University of Waterloo, Canada
Chih Lai, University of St.Thomas, USA
Chris Price, Aberystwyth University, England
David Levy, University of Sydney, Australia
Hong-Chuan Yang, University of Victoria, Canada

# Preface

The 2012 International Conference on Information Technology and Software Engineering (ITSE2012) was held by Beijing Jiaotong University in Beijing on December 8–10, 2012. The objective of ITSE2012 was to provide a platform for researchers, engineers, academicians as well as industrial professionals from all over the world to present their research results and development activities in Information Technology and Software Engineering. This conference provided opportunities for the delegates to exchange new ideas and application experiences face-to-face, to establish research or business relations and to find global partners for future collaboration.

We have received more than 1,300 papers covering most of the aspects in Information Technology, Software Engineering, Computing Intelligence, Digital Media Technology, Visual Languages and Computing, and etc. All submitted papers have been subject to a strict peer-review process; about 300 of them were selected for presentation at the conference and included in the ITSE2012 Proceedings. We believe the proceedings can provide the readers a broad overview about the latest advances in the fields of Information Technology and Software Engineering.

ITSE2012 has been supported by many professors (see the name list of the committees); we would like to take this opportunity to express our sincere gratitude and highest respect to them. At the same time, we also express our sincere thanks for the support of every delegate.

Wei Lu
Chair of ITSE2012

# Contents

# Part I
# Software Engineering

# Chapter 1
# Detecting Null Dereference with a Game

Jie Chen

**Abstract** As one of the most dangerous and common software vulnerabilities, null dereference often leads to program crashes. In this chapter we propose a human computation method to detect null dereference in a "frog and bug" game. The purpose of the game is to utilize the rich distributed human resource to do the complex science work in a simple and pleasant way. Programs are transformed into visual puzzles first, and then the server collects information from the people playing the game. Finally the recorded metadata is translated back into the positions in the programs where null dereference may happen. The game has shown to be effective.

**Keywords** Null dereference · Human computation · Game

## 1.1 Introduction

Null dereference is a commonly occurring defect that can cause serious software failures. Many automated techniques have been developed to detect this vulnerability [1–5]. Dynamic analysis executes the programs with large sets of test inputs, but it may slow down the software's performance and can rarely test all the possible execution paths. Static analysis requires no real execution and is relatively easier to examine more execution scenarios. However, static tools always report too many false alarms [6].

J. Chen (✉)
National Laboratory for Parallel & Distributed Processing, School of Computer, National University of Defense Technology, 410073 Changsha, P.R. China
e-mail: jchen@nudt.edu.cn

W. Lu et al. (eds.), *Proceedings of the 2012 International Conference on Information Technology and Software Engineering*, Lecture Notes in Electrical Engineering 212, DOI: 10.1007/978-3-642-34531-9_1, © Springer-Verlag Berlin Heidelberg 2013

Unfortunately, the automating effort has limited impact till today. Most of the automated techniques need a lot of interactions with people, and the traditional manual analysis is still widely used in industry. Manual analysis is useful since humans have strong logical reasoning ability and intuition to verify a property or find a counter example. However, the manual process is tedious and time consuming. In this chapter, rather than developing automated approaches, we aim to improve the manual analysis process.

Every day, people from all over the world spend nearly 130 million hours on playing games with their mobile phones [7]. Using this amazing power to solve scientific problems is alluring but challenging. Human computation is known as "games with a purpose" [8] which seeks to elicit useful information from the crowd through funny games. Thus our approach to improve manual analysis is changing the traditional process into an engaging game and utilizing the public to do the null dereference detection work.

In this chapter we introduce an approach which is based on human computation to detect null dereference. It transforms program codes into frog and bug games first, and then shows the games to players connected to the server. Players try to make the frogs represented null to go through the dereference points (eating the bug) by changing initial frog sizes and choosing branch paths. The game is easy and funny that general public can be involved in playing it. The server collects the metadata from the playing process as a by-product, and then translates the information into the positions in the programs where null dereferences may happen. Finally, a null dereference report is generated by the server.

The remainder of this paper is organized as follows. We introduce some preliminaries in Sect. 1.2. Section 1.3 presents our game mechanism. Section 1.4 shows an example. Section. 1.5 concludes the chapter.

## 1.2 Preliminaries

Null dereference error is one kind of dynamic memory errors in languages like C. Programmers can use pointers to manage the dynamic memory space by allocating, freeing, accessing, etc. Dynamic memory errors will happen whenever any of these operations failed.

A null dereference occurs when the application uses a pointer variable to access a memory that it expects the pointer to be valid, but is null. There are two basic situations that cause null dereference. Accessing the allocated memory without checking whether the pointer's value is null may cause null dereference since the allocation may fail and return null. This is represented by Example A in Table 1.1. Null dereference will occur when access the memory that the pointer has been freed. Example B in Table 1.1 shows this process.

According to the first situation, we can extend the null dereference of accessing not-checked memory from allocated by *malloc*() to modified by all function calls.

**Table 1.1** Examples of null dereference

| Example A | Example B |
|---|---|
| *funcA(){* | *funcB(){* |
| ...... | ...... |
| *ptr = malloc(size);* | *free(ptr);* |
| *\*ptr;* | *\*ptr;* |
| ...... | ...... |
| } | } |

In other words, when memory pointers are allocated, modified or returned by any function calls, null dereferences may occur if accessing them without check. Although this principle makes the analysis less precise, it guarantees the soundness and avoids the high cost inter-procedural analysis. For the second situation of null dereference of accessing memory after it has been freed, we extend it to all scenarios which assign null to the memory pointers. It means that if the program accesses a pointer which has been changed to null, there must be a null dereference.

## 1.3 Proposed Approach

Our approach uses a frog and bug game to reflect the program dataflow which only cares about nullness of the pointer variables. It illustrates the actual properties of pointer variables since it is based on the program execution. During the process, we need human insight which is likely to be more effective than any heuristic algorithm.

It is a single-player game. First, a player uses his computer or mobile phone to connect to the game server. Then he begins to play the game as many rounds as possible. In each round, the player is shown a frog and bug puzzle and the objective is to clear all the bugs by eating or dynamite them. What players can do is to change initial frogs' sizes and choose branch paths when the frogs do not know where to go.

One puzzle corresponds to one procedure. As presented in Fig. 1.1, we now explain how to map a program into a frog and bug puzzle. Basic elements in the game are listed in the following:

- *Start and end meadow*: The left meadow is the start boundary and the right one is the end. The boundaries of the puzzle mean the procedure begins and ends in the program.
- *River*: In every puzzle, there are several rivers. One river represents one point variable appears in the procedure. Some are Entrance Rivers that connect with the start meadow, and they represent the point variables which are the arguments of the procedure. The other rivers represent the local pointer variables of the procedure. All the rivers go ahead till the end meadow.

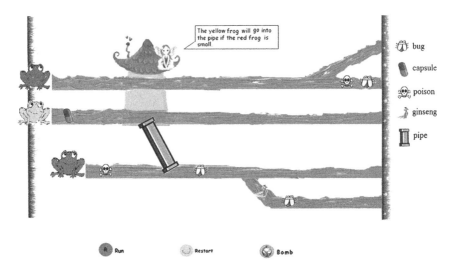

**Fig. 1.1** The interface of a frog and bug puzzle

- *Frog*: It denotes the value of the point variable the river represented, so there is at most one frog in each river. Every frog can be of two different sizes, big or small, which means that the point variable is null or non-null in program execution. Players can initialize the size of frogs in the Entrance Rivers when the frogs are in the start meadow. All frogs jump step by step simultaneously and automatically in their own rivers toward the end meadow. One step means any frog meets a bug, capsule, poison, ginseng, mysterious house, or fork in the river. If a small frog is blocked by a bug, the other frogs do not wait for it and keep jumping.
- *Bug*: The dereference position of a pointer variable in the program is represented by a bug in the river. Players' mission is to clear all the bugs in each puzzle. Only big frogs can eat bugs and then go ahead, while small frogs cannot. Big frogs represent null pointers, so eating a bug means there may be a null dereference.
- *Capsule*: A capsule in a river denotes a program location that frees or assigns null to the pointer variable the river represented. After this program location, the pointer variable becomes null. In the puzzle, a frog will become big size if it eats a capsule. Capsules only work for small frog. A big frog keeps its size no matter how many capsules it eats. If a frog eats a bug after it becomes big by eating a capsule, we can report that there must be a null dereference in the program.
- *Poison*: A poison in a river denotes a program location that assigns a static variable's address to the pointer variable the river represented. After this program location, the pointer variable becomes non-null. In the puzzle, a frog will become small size if it eats a poison. Poisons only work for big frog. A small frog keeps its size no matter how many poisons it eats.

- *Ginseng*: A ginseng in a river denotes a function call that may modify the nullness property of the pointer variable the river represented. After this program position, the property of the pointer variable may change or not. Precise information can only be obtained by inter-procedural analysis which is very expensive. We leave this work to players. In the puzzle, a frog can become small or big size if it eats a ginseng. It asks players whether to change the size of the frog. Then players choose which they like according to the objective of the game. We will report that there may be a null dereference in the program if a frog eats a bug after it becomes big by eating a ginseng.
- *Bomb*: When a small frog meets a bug, it cannot eat the bug. Then players should restart this puzzle. Restarting a puzzle does not influence players' score and will recover all the visual elements except the bugs which have been cleared, since we have obtained the properties of those dereference locations. If players still fail, they should restart the game again and again. After several times, a bomb will appear if all the paths in the puzzle before the bug location have been traveled by any frog. It means that we have achieved 100 % of desired code coverage before the dereference point. The criteria of code coverage can be customized and here we use branch coverage. The bug blocking the small frog will be cleared by pressing the colorized bomb icon and it indicates that the dereference point may be safe under the desired test criteria. Sometimes one bug can be cleared by both big frog and bomb, then we encourage players to use big frog by giving more incentives since we aim to report all the potential null dereference errors.

Besides these basic elements, we should consider assignment statements and branch statements.

Assignment is one of the most important things in pointer analysis since it leads to pointer alias. Here we use a pipe connecting two rivers to denote one assignment. The pipe is oblique and a frog can only go through it from the side near to the start meadow to the other side. For example, when the value of pointer variable *A* is assigned to pointer variable *B*, there is a pipe connecting river *A* (represents pointer *A*) and river *B* (represents pointer *B*). The side of the pipe in river *A* is near to the start meadow, so the frog in river *A* jumps into river *B*. If there is a frog in river *B* before the pipe, it will be replaced by the frog from river *A*.

Branch statements are widely used in almost all programs, since branches make the river networks in the puzzles more complex. There will be a fork in the river if the river represented pointer variable in the branch body is dereferenced or modified that can be visualized by bugs, capsules, poisons or ginsengs. Game does not calculate the value of branch condition. We leave to players the work of deciding which branch path to go. Furthermore, we differentiate branches into two different kinds:

- If the branch condition only contains one or more pointer variables represented by rivers in the puzzle and is about their nullness properties, it lets the forks and all the relative rivers flow into a mysterious house. A fairy is flying on the top right of the mysterious house, telling players how to make the frog jump into the desired river, just like "The red frog will jump into the upper river if the yellow frog is big".

- Otherwise, the game just uses a fork in the river to denote it and asks player which branch path to go.

Loops always exist in programs. However, there is no river cycle in the puzzle, since the game only models the nullness property of pointer variables, not their concrete values or the arithmetic operations of their addresses. Therefore, if there is dereference point in the loop body and it is not safe only when the loop iterates a special number of times, it must be in a conditional branch. Consequently, the game uses the same approach of handling branches to handle loops and going through the loop body once is enough to keep the soundness.

## 1.4 Case Study

The example code in Fig. 1.2 is the objective program we want to analyze. It is a procedure taking two pointer variables as arguments and one pointer as local variable. There are three pointers dereferences at line 7, line 10 and line 14.

According to the mapping mechanism presented previously, we transform the program above into a visual puzzle similar to Fig. 1.1. The only difference is that the bomb icon is gray here since it will become colorized only when frogs traverse all the branches. There are three rivers in the puzzle since there are three pointer variables in the program. Arguments $a$ and $b$ are represented by the red frog and the yellow frog, while the green frog represents the local pointer $d$. A capsule in

**Fig. 1.2** The code of the case study

```
1: main(int *a, int *b){
2:   int c = 2;
3:   b = null;
4:   int *d = &c;
5:   if(a != null)
6:     d = b;
7:   c = *d;
8:   if(rand()){
9:     func(d);
10:     c = *d;
11:   }
12:   else{
13:     a = &c;
14:     c = *a;
15:   }
16:}
```

the middle river and a poison in the under river denote the assignments in line 3 and line 4. Afterwards, the up and middle rivers meet a mysterious house and a pipe because of the branch statements of line 5 and line 6. The yellow frog's direction is decided by the size of the red frog. Line 7 brings a bug. Then another branch makes forks in the up and under rivers. A ginseng and a poison represent the function call in line 9 and the assignment in line 13. Line 10 and 14 are denoted by two bugs.

Let us start to play the game. The game process is showed in Fig. 1.3.

Because the fairy gives us a hint that the yellow frog will go into the pipe if the red frog is small, we set the red frog small and press the Run button to make the frogs jump. Figure 1.3a shows that after the mysterious house, the yellow frog goes through the pipe into the down river and replaces the green frog. Afterwards, the yellow frog eats the bug and meets a fork. We press the down fork, and then the yellow frog eats the ginseng and bug which is represented by Fig. 1.3b. There is still a bug in the up river. Thus, we press the Restart button to play the game again. Restarting a game can recover all the capsules, poisons and ginsengs, but not the bugs which have been eaten, so this time we use the default configuration. When the green frog meets the fork, we choose the up one, and then the Bomb button becomes colorized showed in Fig. 1.3c. We press the Bomb button and the bug in front of the red frog is killed. Afterward, as Fig. 1.3d shows, all the bugs are cleared and all the frogs arrive at the end meadow. The puzzle is completed.

Finally, using the metadata collected from the game, we generate a report that in this program: (1) there must be a null dereference at line 7 when $a! = null$, because the bug is eaten by the yellow frog directly after it eats a capsule; (2) there

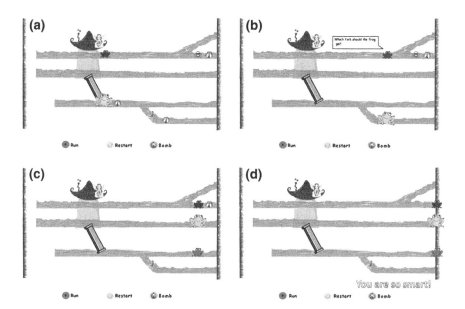

**Fig. 1.3**  The game process of the case study

may be a null dereference at line 10, because the bug is eaten by the frog directly after it eats a ginseng; (3) there cannot be any null dereference in line 14, because the bug is killed by the bomb. This example demonstrates that our game can detect null dereferences and verify a pointer dereference is safe in real programs.

## 1.5  Conclusion

This chapter aims at using crowd-sourcing to do the work of software quality assurance by combing human computation and null dereference detection. Precision and scalability is the major focus of our future work. Inter-procedural analysis will be considered. We are going to implement the game and deploy it on internet. We believe it will show its power to improve the software quality when large amounts of people are involved in playing it.

## References

1. Dillig I, Dillig T, Aiken A (2007) Static error detection using semantic inconsistency inference. In: Proceedings of the 2007 ACM SIGPLAN conference on progress language design and implementation, pp 435–445
2. Hovemeyer D, Pugh W (2007) Finding more null pointer bugs, but not too many. In: Proceedings of 7th ACM SIGPLAN-SIGSOFT workshop on program analysis for software tools and engineering, pp 9–14
3. Hovemeyer D, Spacco J, Pugh W (2005) Evaluating and tuning a static analysis to find null pointer bugs. In: Proceedings of 6th ACM SIGPLAN-SIGSOFT workshop on program analysis for software tools and engineering, pp 13–19
4. Chandra S, Fink SJ, Sridharan M (2009) Snugglebug: a powerful approach to weakest preconditions. In PLDI'09: Proceedings ACM SIGPLAN conference on programming language design and implementation, pp 363–374
5. Nanda MG, Sinha S (2009) Accurate interprocedural null-dereference analysis for Java. In ICSE'09: Proceedings of the 2009 IEEE 31st international conference on software engineering, Washington, USA, pp 133–143
6. Kim Y, Lee J, Han H, Choe KM (2010) Filtering false alarms of buffer overflow analysis using smt solvers. Inf Softw Technol 52(2):210–219
7. International games market data, consulting and publishing, http://www.newzoo.com
8. Von Ahn L (2006) Games with a purpose. IEEE Comput Mag 39(6):96–98

# Chapter 2
# Interactive and Collaborative E-Learning Platform with Integrated Social Software and Learning Management System

Zhao Du, Xiaolong Fu, Can Zhao, Qifeng Liu and Ting Liu

**Abstract** E-learning featured by active participation, interaction and collaboration of learners and educators is becoming more and more important in education both for learners and educators. While learning management system (LMS) is the traditional approach to e-learning which is organized as courses; social software including blogs, wikis, social networking sites, and social bookmarking sites etc. are adopted by many educators to meet their emerging needs in educations. In order to satisfy the needs for participation, interaction, and collaboration of learners and educators in the cognition, construction, and socialization process of learning; we propose an interactive and collaborative e-learning platform which combines the advantages of LMS and social software by integrating social software with LMS. The platform connects course network of users with his/her social network and knowledge network. As a result, it's helpful to users in building their personalized social network and knowledge network during the process of learning.

**Keywords** E-learning · Learning management system · Social software · Social bookmarking sites · Social network sites · Knowledge management · Learning management system

## 2.1 Introduction

Web 2.0, social web, or read/write web has gained increasing popularity in education and brought profound impact to education since the beginning of the new millennium [1, 2]. On one hand, students nowadays are digital natives who

Z. Du (✉) · X. Fu · C. Zhao · Q. Liu · T. Liu
Information Technology Center, Tsinghua University, 100084 Beijing, China
e-mail: dz@cic.tsinghua.edu.cn

W. Lu et al. (eds.), *Proceedings of the 2012 International Conference on Information Technology and Software Engineering*, Lecture Notes in Electrical Engineering 212, DOI: 10.1007/978-3-642-34531-9_2, © Springer-Verlag Berlin Heidelberg 2013

are accustomed to learn in an active learning environment. On the other hand, the world is changing more rapidly than any other period in human history and people are facing an era of knowledge explosion and globalization. As a result, e-learning featured by active participation, interaction and collaboration of learners and educators is becoming more and more important in education both for learners to get better learning experience and for educators to achieve better education effect.

Learning management system is the traditional approach to e-learning. Learning in LMS is organized as courses. It usually serves as the online platform for course syllabus releasing, handouts distribution, assignments management, and course discussion to students, teachers, TAs who are the member of the same course. Although LMS such as Blackboard, Moodle, and Sakai has been used by numerous universities all over the world to support and improve learning of their students [3]; it is primarily designed for course management purpose and has limited impact on pedagogy. The primary limitations of LMS include lack of personalized control for learners over learning process, limited interaction channel and collaboration manner between learners and educators, restricted interaction and collaboration scope within courses. These limitations make LMS not competent for supporting e-learning in the new era which views learning as a self-governed, problem-based and collaborative social process [4].

Recently, social software including blogs, wikis, social networking sites, and social bookmarking sites etc. are gradually adopted by more and more educators to meet their emerging needs in educations. Although there is no common agreed definition for social software, the core features of social software are to facilitate interaction and collaboration among users. Social software represents a shift to more social, personalized, open, dynamic, emergent, and knowledge-pull model for e-learning [5]. It provides learners with the abilities to direct their own problem-solving process, build connections with a wide variety of people and knowledge, and interact and collaborate with other users [6].

Currently, LMS and social software are mostly provided independently by universities and Internet companies to learners and educators. The advantages of this way lie in flexibility and openness. In addition, it's also economic for universities because there is no need for additional investment. These advantages take social software into the sight of learners and educators. Some of them will become loyal users of social software gradually and begin to incorporate t social software into their daily activities including learning. The disadvantages of this way are isolation of information and connections in different systems, lack of specific design in function and UI for educational purposes, and unsustainability of service providing for social software provided by Internet companies. These disadvantages will bring barrier to users especially for students and teachers to whose primary activities are learning and teaching. Based on the considerations above, it's helpful and significant for universities to provide an integrated e-learning platform for students, teachers, alumni and even the public which can support their interaction and collaboration in learning and teaching both on campus and out of campus.

Based on the considerations above, we propose an interactive and collaborative e-learning platform which integrates social software with LMS. The platform provides personalized space for users where they can interact and collaborate with others. The personalized space of users contains their course network, social network and knowledge network. One of the key features of the platform is that it connects course network of users with his/her social network and knowledge network. Therefore, users are able to build their personalized social network and knowledge network during the process of learning. Moreover, it also facilitates interaction and collaboration between users by providing news feed service, recommendation service, and search service.

## 2.2 Interactions and Collaboration in LMS and Social Software

Interactions and collaboration in LMS and social software are different in many aspects. Firstly, the scope and during of interactions and collaboration in LMS are limited to a single course, but there is no limitation for the scope and during of interactions and collaboration in social software. Secondly, interactions and collaboration in LMS are group-oriented, and that in social software are the combination of individual-oriented and group-oriented. Thirdly, the form of interactions and collaboration is relatively simple which is mostly based on text and photos, while the form of interactions and collaboration in social software is much richer which also includes audios and videos. Finally, users can accumulate personalized social network and knowledge network during the process of using social software which is impossible in LMS.

### 2.2.1 Interaction and Collaboration in LMS

The functions of LMS can be viewed from two aspects. The first aspect is to provide online course management service to educators and administrators within the university that hosts the platform. The second aspect is to provide course-based interaction and collaboration service to educators and learners within the hosting university. In the following paragraph, we are going to focus on the features of the interaction and collaboration services that LMS provides to educators and learners.

Interaction and collaboration in LMS is course-based and the relationship between users in a course is temporal and unequal, as described as Fig. 2.1. Learners and educators of the same course can interact and collaborate within the scope of digital space of a common course. Specifically, educators can post course announcement and course material to learners, learners and educators can discuss in the discussion form. Since interaction and collaboration in discussion forum is oriented at all members of a

**Fig. 2.1** Interaction and
collaboration in LMS

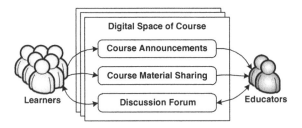

course and mostly based on text and photos, the form and effect of interaction and
collaboration is relatively simple and limited. It's noteworthy that the duration of
interaction and communication is the same as the corresponding course which is
usually one semester. As a result, everything in digital space of a course will be of no
use after the end of the course, and there is no opportunity for users to accumulate
personalized social network and knowledge network.

## 2.2.2 Interaction and Collaboration in Social Software

The key aspects of social software are that it involves shared wider participation in
the creation of information, encourage more active learning, and supports better
group interaction. Therefore, social software can stimulate learner-educator interaction, increase learners' motivation, and fosters a greater sense of community [7].
Social software which is often used in e-learning includes blogs, wikis, social
networking sites, and social bookmarking sites [4].

Difference social software provides different forms of interaction and
collaboration service to users, the relationship between users is permanent and
equal. Social software doesn't have any limitations on duration of group-oriented
interaction and collaboration. Different from LMS, all social software provides
individual-oriented interaction and collaboration; some of them also provide
group-oriented interaction and collaboration, as described as Fig. 2.2. Users can
choose to use individual-oriented or group-oriented interaction and collaboration

**Fig. 2.2** Interaction and
collaboration in social
software

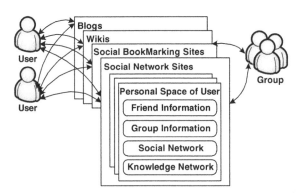

according to their wishes freely. Interactions and collaboration in social software can not only based on text and photos as LMS, but also based on audios and videos as well. During the process of using software, users can build and expand their personalized social network and knowledge network. There is personal space for every user where he/she can read various kinds of information from his/her friends and groups as well as his/her own social network and knowledge network.

## 2.3 Interactions and Collaboration in E-Learning Platform with Integrated Social Software and LMS

Some researchers view the key issue in learning is the support of learning as a cognitive and constructive process [8]. Others view learning as a social process, they stress that the challenge today is not what you know but who you know [9]. The former groups of researcher follow learning theory of behaviourism which focuses on externally observable change, cognitivism which focuses on computational models of the individual mind, or constructivism which presents learners create knowledge as they attempt to understand their experiences; the latter groups of researchers introduce constructivism as a new learning theory which presents learning as a connection/network-forming process [5]. From our point of view, we think learning is a combination of cognitive and constructive process with social process. On one hand, cognitive and constructive are about the aspect of learning process of individual learners; on other hand, social is about the aspects of learning resource and environment of many learners. Therefore, participation, interaction and collaboration in learning are important and helpful in the cognition, construction, and socialization process of learning.

Interactions and collaboration in e-learning platform with integrated social software and LMS can be described as Fig. 2.3. The platform not only combines functions of LMS and social software, but also provides personalized space for each user. The personal space is the place where users can interact and collaborate with others. There are three categories of information and three types of network in personal space of each user. As they can do in LMS, users can participate, interact and collaborate in his/her courses which are organized as course groups in the platform. Besides, users can also read various kinds of information from his/her friends and groups as well as of his/her own within his/her personal space as they can do in social software. The information is flowed to users through the filtering of his/her social network and knowledge network.

The key feature of the platform lies in the connections built between the course network of users and his/her social network and knowledge network, as shown by the dotted line in Fig. 2.3. When users participate in a course, he/she has built permanent group connections with other users who participate in the same course. Furthermore, he/she is also possible to build permanent personal connections with all members of the group. By this way, he/she can build and expand his/her social

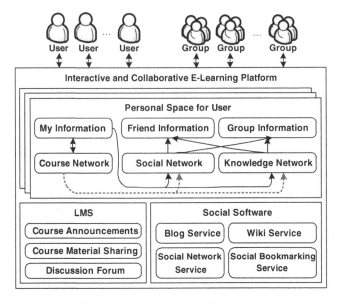

**Fig. 2.3** Interaction and collaboration in e-learning platform

network. At the same time, he/she can create or get useful digital resources. He/she can also make comments on them, add tags to them, share them to other users, and save them as his/her favorite. All additional information of digital resources mentioned above forms the value-added information of original digital resources. The set of original digital resources and their value-added information ultimately constitute knowledge network of users. Social network and knowledge network will provide continuous support for users' learning both inside and outside courses.

## 2.4 Interactive and Collaborative E-Learning Platform

Interactive and collaborative e-learning platform consists of eight parts; these parts can be divided into four layers, as shown in Fig. 2.4. The first and bottom layer is data layer which keeps all data in the platform. Data layer keeps course data, social network data, and knowledge data. The second layer is core services layer which provides all core services in the platform including course services, social software services, and search services. The third layer is information delivery layer which provides various forms of information services to users. Information delivery layer consists of news feed service, relation recommendation service, knowledge recommendation service, and search service. The last and top layer is user interface layer which is the layer users interact with. The platform offers multiple interfaces to its users including web-based interface, mobile-based web interface, and mobile-based app interface.

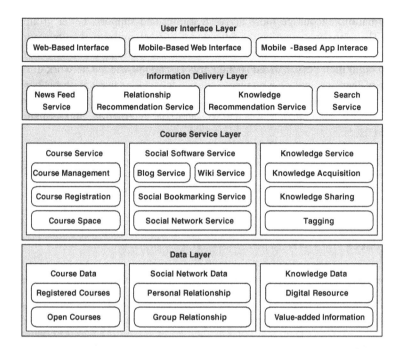

**Fig. 2.4**  Design of interactive and collaborative e-learning platform

The most important layer to facilitate interaction and collaboration between users is information delivery layer. Services in this layer disseminate different types of information to their target users or possible target users. As a result, users will find it's much easier to build their social network and knowledge network. News feed service push information to users using their social network data. Relation recommendation service and knowledge recommendation service provide users with the information of users, groups, and knowledge that they may possibly interested through intelligent analysis of their behaviors. Search service provides a variety of search services to users including course search, user search, and knowledge search. Moreover, users can search in the scope of the whole platform as well as a specific data set.

## 2.5  Conclusions

Since students nowadays are digital natives who are accustomed to learn in an active learning environment, interactive and collaborative e-learning environment beyond traditional LMS is needed by both learners and educators. Under this circumstance, learning is a combination of cognitive and constructive process with social process. Social software involves shared wider participation in the creation of information, encourage more active learning, and supports better group inter-action. Therefore, we combine the advantages of LMS and social software to build an interactive and collaborative e-learning platform. The platform not only helps users to build their personalized social network and knowledge network during the process of learning, but also connects course network of users with his/her social network and knowledge network. It also provides news feed service, recommen-dation service, and search service to facilitate interaction and collaboration between users.

**Acknowledgments** This work is supported by the National Science and Technology Major Project of the Ministry of Science and Technology of China (No. 2009ZX03005-003) and the National Basic Research Program of China (No. 2012CB316000).

# References

1. Ravenscroft A (2009) Social software, web 2.0 and learning: status and implications of an evolving paradigm. J Comput Assist Learn 25(1):1–5
2. Greenhow C, Robelia B, Hughes JE (2009) Learning, teaching, and scholarship in a digital age web 2.0 and classroom research: what path should we take now? Educ Res 38(4):246–259
3. Al-Ajlan A, Zedan H (2008) Why moodle. In: Proceedings of the 12th IEEE international workshop on future trends of distributed computing system (FTDCS'08), 58–64
4. Dalsgarrd C (2006) Social software: e-learning beyond learning management systems. Eur J Open Distance E-Learn
5. Chatti MA, Jarke M, Frosch-Wilke D (2007) The future of e-learning: a shift to knowledge networking and social software. Int J knowl Learn 3(4/5):404–420
6. Mcloughlin C, Mark JWL (2010) Personalized and self regulated learning in the web 2.0 era: international examplars of innovative pedagogy using social software. Aust J Educ Technol 26(1):28–43
7. Minocha S (2009) Role of social software tools in education: a literature review. Educ Train 51(5):353–369
8. Lytras M, Naeve A, Pouloudi A (2005) Knowledge management as a reference theory for e-learning: a conceptual and technological perspective. Int J Distance Educ Technol 3(2):1–12
9. Paavola S, Lipponen L, Hakkarainen K (2002) Epistemological foundations for CSCL: a comparison of three models of innovative knowledge communities. In: Proceedings of the computer-supported collaborative learning 2002 conference, 24–32

# Chapter 3
# Neural Network Based Software Reliability Prediction with the Feed of Testing Process Knowledge

Tian Jie, Zhou Yong and Wang Lina

**Abstract** Software reliability is an important factor for evaluating software quality in the domain of safety-critical software. Traditional software reliability growth models (SRGMs) only uses the failure data produced in a testing process to evaluate the software reliability and its growth. However, the number and severity of the failures uncovered are determined by the effectiveness and efficiency of testing process. Therefore, an unbiased reliability prediction has to take test process knowledge into account. In this paper, we proposed a neural network based reliability prediction method to utilize the testing process metrics to correlate testing process knowledge with failure prediction. The metrics designed in this paper cover information from the system under test (SUT), design of testing, software failure and repair process. The method is validated through the testing process data collected from a real embedded operating system. And the results show a fairly accurate prediction capability.

**Keywords** Software reliability · Testing process · Neural network

T. Jie (✉)
Bei Jing Command College of CPAPF, Beijing, China
e-mail: happyjie717@126.com

Z. Yong
China Machinery TIDI Geotechnical Engineering Co.,Ltd, Wuhan, China

W. Lina
National Key Laboratory of Science and Technology on Aerospace Intelligent Control,
Beijing Aerospace Automatic Control Institute, Beijing, China

W. Lu et al. (eds.), *Proceedings of the 2012 International Conference on Information Technology and Software Engineering*, Lecture Notes in Electrical Engineering 212, DOI: 10.1007/978-3-642-34531-9_3, © Springer-Verlag Berlin Heidelberg 2013

## 3.1 Introduction

Software plays a very important role in our modern life and is used in many applications. It has become the core of many safe-critical systems: communications, monitoring systems, automobiles, airplanes, and so on. All of these applications demand high-quality software. As a critical factor for software quality, software reliability has become more and more important in computer system. Software reliability is defined in ANSI, which is *the probability of failure-free software operation for a specified period of time in a specified environment* [1]. During the last 3 decades, there are many researches around this area, and many software reliability growth models (SRGMs) have been proposed for evaluating software reliability. The basic principle of SRGMs is that computes software reliability through the observed failure data and failure time, and then checks whether the reliability meets the desired requirement. SRGMs can be generally divided into two categories: one is the parametric models, such as nonhomogeneous Poisson process (NHPP) models, Schneidewind models and Musa's Basic execution time model; the other is non-parametric models, which is based on neural network, support vector machine (SVM) and so on. All these proposed models work on software failure data. Through the analysis and test on the collected failure data, we can choose appropriate model to evaluate and predict software reliability.

Failure data is one of the productions of testing process. The number and seriousness of the failures uncovered are determined by the effectiveness and efficiency of testing process. Therefore, we cannot get reliable estimation of the practical reliability only with the failure data. The estimation could be biased toward the low effective or efficient testing. Therefore, an unbiased reliability prediction approach has to take test process knowledge into account. At present, there are some SRGMs have been taken into account relevant factors, such as test coverage. We focus on how to measure and evaluate the testing process to identify more practical factors to feed into the software reliability model to get reliable estimations.

In this paper, we propose a machine learning method to correlate test process knowledge with failure prediction based on neural network. The test metrics used include the information from system under test (SUT), design of testing, software failure and repair process, etc. This method can improve the confidence of software reliability.

The rest of this paper is organized as follows: Sect. 3.2 introduce some related work about software reliability prediction. Section 3.3 describe the proposed method about multi-view analysis of software testing process. In Sect. 3.4, we design the method to predict software reliability based on neural network. Section 3.5 shows the experimental results and finally we conclude this paper in Sect. 3.6.

## 3.2 Related Works

In this section, we first briefly introduce the related works about software testing process in software reliability, and then we introduce some research about neural network based software reliability.

Many studies have indicated that during the software testing process, fault detection rate depends on the test team skills, the program size and software testability factors. Kapur et al. [2] proposed that the fault repair rate can be expressed as a function of testing effort and testing time. Huang et al. [3] pointed out when the testing effort metrics spent on fault detection is not constant, the traditional S-curve may not be suitable for the software failure data. In order to solve this problem, they first evaluated the testing effort function (TEF), and combined the logic testing effort function with the exponential and S-shape software reliability model.

Meanwhile, there are some discussions about software reliability focus on that the execution time cannot be the only measure factors for software failure behavior. In order to improve the accuracy of the prediction, many researchers have taken more factors into account and improved the software reliability models. As the important factor to display the completeness and effectiveness of the testing process, test coverage became a software reliability metrics. Malaiya et al. [4] proposed a logarithm-exponent model, Cai [5] also proposed a test coverage-reliability model (TC-SRM). Their model estimated the failure intensity function based on the testing calendar time and test coverage. However, these models only considered a few classic of test coverage, i.e. code coverage. An and Zhu [6] proposed the concept of integrated test coverage (ITC). They estimated the software reliability though combining multi kinds of test coverage metrics to an integrated parameter.

There are also some researches related to the fault repair process. Schneidewind [7, 8] first modeled the failure repair process. Based on this model, many researchers extended the works.

Since the approaches mentioned above considered the testing process for predict the software reliability. We found that many models depend on a priori assumptions and they have not considered the relationship between the different metrics of the process. In recent years, neural network approach has been used to predict software reliability. This method is more flexible and usable, so we introduce some work about neural network based software reliability.

Karunanithi [9] first used some kind of neural networks to estimate the software reliability. Cai et al. [10] proposed using the recent 50 inter-failure times as the multiple-delayed inputs to predict the next failure time. Tian and Noore [1] proposed a software reliability prediction method based on multiple-delayed-input and single-output.

From existing research, we found the testing process has become an important factor for software reliability, and the neural network can provide a flexible application for predict software reliability. And the multiple-delayed-input and single-output method can help us considering complex factor to prediction. In this paper, we proposed Neural Network based Software Reliability Prediction with the Feed of Testing Process Knowledge. In order to give an accurate prediction, we first analyze the testing process. Furthermore, we will show how to link the testing process factor with the software reliability prediction.

## 3.3 Multi-Perspective Testing Process Analyses

Safety-critical software requires a high reliability. However, in the actual project, we found that using the failure data and failure time to estimate the software reliability is not accuracy. The most important reason is that the testing process directly determines the veracity of the failure data, in addition, the complexity of the system under test (SUT) determine the testability and the number of the potential failure numbers. Testing process is the last stage of software development; we can collect the process data as many as possible. We propose a method which through analyze different perspective on the whole testing process to create a complete comprehensive for software test.

Based on the above understanding, we combine with the characteristic of the software reliability and proposed a method to analyzing the software reliability based on the three perspectives: SUT, Testing process and the Failure data.

In order to analyze the impact of different perspectives on the software reliability, we are following three clues to do the process analysis and the information extraction. For every clue, we first give the information which needs collection, then we give the effect analysis of these information.

### 3.3.1 System Under Test

We choose the SUT as the first perspective because SUT reflect the testability of the system.

As we know, the complexity of SUT determines the testability and the numbers of failures. Generally, we think that the bigger numbers of LOC and McCabe, the more failures will be existed in the system. The relativity of the complexity of SUT and numbers of failures is positive. We choose the LOC and McCabe as the measure index.

### 3.3.2 Testing Process

Testing process is the key factor for the software reliability, because it determines the capability of detecting failures.

In this paper, we take the testing effort, design of the test case and the execution of the test case into account.

In the testing process, we measure the coverage of the test case, including the numbers of the normal test and robust test. Link with the SUT, we also observe the distribution of the test case based on the size and complexity (i.e. McCabe) of the SUT.

In this paper, we choose the number of test cases, execution of test case and test coverage as the measure target. We define the efficiency of the testing as the failure numbers divide the test case numbers. In practice, test case numbers is larger than failure numbers. In order to keep the data consistent, we compute Effective of hundred test cases. Equation 3.1 defines the EoTC:

$$EoTC = \frac{Number\ of\ failure}{NoTC/100}. \tag{3.1}$$

### 3.3.3 Software Failure

Failure is the core factor for the software reliability; we not only collect the failure numbers but also separate the test case which is detecting the failure.

Software failure is the kernel factor of software reliability; it can reflex the situation of the system. In this study, we only concerned about the failure numbers; we will use the knowledge of testing process and SUT to predict failure numbers. In the future work; we will take other factors into account.

Figure 3.1 shows the relationship of the effect factors and software reliability, we divide effects into three perspective based on the three clues. In the figure, blue nodes express the effect factors we will utilize in the software reliability prediction.

## 3.4 Software Reliability Predictions

After we collect the data of the SUT and testing process, we can predict the software failure numbers based on neural network.

### 3.4.1 Neural Network

Neural network can solve following problem: training set contain complex sensor data with noise, and the problems need more symbolic expression.

The characteristics of such problems are: the instance can be expressed as "property-value", and the output of the objective function may be discrete values,

**Fig. 3.1** Multi-perspective of testing process

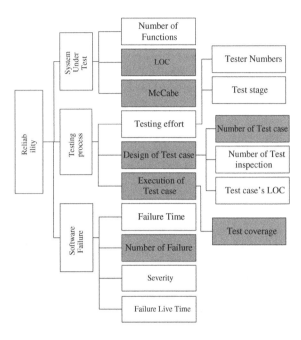

real values or vectors which are contained some discrete property and some real property, the training data may contain errors and so on. These characteristics are very fit for our problems. First, we have a series of process data, and then we use these data to predict the failure numbers. Figure 3.2 give the sketch map of the neurons. *w* is a real constant, which express the weight of the input. *w* determines the input *x* on the neuron of the contribution rate for the output.

Equations 3.2 and 3.3 give the mathematical expression of the neuron.

$$y = f(WA' + b) \tag{3.2}$$

$$y = \sum_{i=1}^{n} w_{ji} x_i + b \tag{3.3}$$

**Fig. 3.2** Neurons: $x_1 \sim x_n$ individual component of the input vector, $w_1 \sim w_n$ weight of each input, b bias, f transfer function, y neuron output

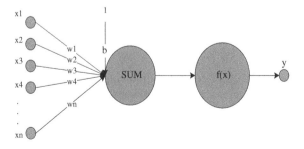

We choose the most commonly used sigmoid function as the activation function. Equation 3.4 give the expression of the sigmoid function.

$$f(a) = \frac{1}{1 + e^{-a}}.$$  (3.4)

### 3.4.2 Design Neural Network

We choose a most common type of neural network architecture which named feed-forward network.

We use the data obtained from the previous section which contains the knowledge of testing process as the input of the neural network. During the training process, we use the Levenberg–Marquardt (LM) algorithm and Gaussian-Newton algorithm to achieve fast convergence. Our work supposes that the ability of testers is stable, and the quality of different test case is equality.

## 3.5 Experiments

### 3.5.1 Data Sets

Our datasets come from a real operating system. We choose kernel module of system as the research data, and the description of the data sets is shown in Table 3.1.

In the experiment, we will partitions the data sets as different modules. In dataset DS1, we use the first 25 modules which cover the 84 % of all modules to training the system. For the dataset DS2, the training data are the first 10 modules coving the 76 % of all modules in DS2. Both of two dataset, the remaining module are used for prediction failure numbers. Through predict the number of failures, we predict the software reliability.

**Table 3.1** Real data sets

| Module | Data | | |
|--------|------|------|------|
| | Description | Number of test case | Number of failure |
| DS1 | Kernel module | 976 | 25 |
| DS2 | Library functions | 725 | 186 |

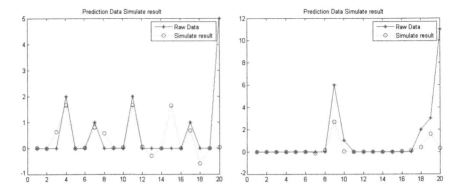

**Fig. 3.3  a** Predict result of DS1. **b** Predict result of DS2

**Fig. 3.4**  Performance of network

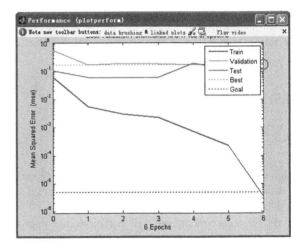

## 3.5.2  Prediction Result

Table 3.1 gives the number of test case and failure numbers in DS1 and DS2. We use first 20 data to train the network, and use last 20 data to predict failure numbers. We compare the reality data and the simulate data, and then compute the mean squared error.

Figure 3.3a shows the predict result of DS1 and Fig. 3.3b give the predict result of DS2. X axis describe the different modules, and y axis give the predict failure numbers of corresponding module.

Figure 3.4 give the performance of neural network. In figure, we can see that when the training reaches the 6th epoch, mean squared error (MSE) is $10^{-1}$. In our experiment, we only predict the failure numbers of the module. In fact, based on the raw data, we can calculate the cumulative of the failure numbers.

## 3.6 Conclusion

In this paper, we proposed a neural network based software reliability method which is depend on the knowledge of software testing process. We first introduce the method, and then we give a real example. This method depends on adequate knowledge of testing process, so we need collect raw data go with the whole testing process. But it can give us a more close to reality result. In the future, we will extract more refined process data, and based on this work, we will predict the cumulative failure numbers.

## References

1. Tian L, Noore A (2005) Evolutionary neural network modeling for software cumulative failure time prediction. Reliab Eng Sys 77:45–51
2. Kapur PK, Goswami DN, Bardhan A, Singh O (2008) Flexible software reliability growth model with testing effort dependent learning process. Appl Math Model 32(7):1298–1307
3. Huang CY, Kuo SY, Lyu MR (2007) An assessment of testing-effort dependent software reliability growth models. IEEE Trans Reliab 56(2):198–211
4. Malaiya YK, Li N, Bieman JM, Karcich R (2002) Software reliability growth with test coverage. IEEE Trans Reliab 51(4):420–426
5. Cai X (2006) Coverage-based testing strategies and reliability modeling for fault-tolerant software systems. Ph.D. thesis, The Chinese University of Hong Kong
6. An J, Zhu J, (2010) Software reliability modeling with integrated test coverage. In: Fourth IEEE international conference on secure software integration and reliability improvement, Singapore
7. Schneidewind NF (2001) Modeling the fault correction process. In: Proceedings of the 12th international symposium on software reliability engineering (ISSRE), Hong Kong, China, 185–190
8. Schneidewind NF (2003) Fault correction profiles. In: Proceedings of the 14th international symposium on software reliability engineering (ISSRE), Denver, USA, 257–267
9. Karunanithi N, Malaiya YK (1992) The scaling problem in neural networks for software reliability prediction. In: Proceedings of the third international IEEE symposium of software reliability engineering, Los Alamitos, CA, 76–82
10. Cai KY, Cai L, Wang WD, Yu ZY, Zhang D (2001) On the neural network approach in software reliability modeling. J Syst Softw 58(1):47–62

# Chapter 4
# Complexity Metrics Significance for Defects: An Empirical View

**Syed Muhammad Ali Shah and Maurizio Morisio**

**Abstract** Software Complexity often seems to be correlated with the defects and this makes difficult to select appropriate complexity metrics that would be effective indicators of defects. The aim of this work is to analyze the relationship of different complexity metrics with the defects for three categories of software projects i.e. large, medium and small. We analyzed 18 complexity metrics and defects from 27,734 software modules of 38 software projects categorized in large, medium and small. In all categories of projects we do not find any strong positive correlation between complexity metrics and defects. However, we cluster the complexity metric values and defects in three categories as high, medium and low. Consequently we observe that for some complexity metrics high complexity results in higher defects. We called these metrics as effective indicators of defects. In the small category of projects we found LCOM as effective indicator, in the medium category of project we found WMC, CBO, RFC, CA, CE, NPM, DAM, MOA, IC, Avg CC as effective indicators of defects and for a large category of projects we found WMC, CBO, RFC, CA, NPM, AMC, Avg CC as effective indicators of defects. The difference shows that complexity metrics relation to defects also varies with the size of projects.

**Keywords** Complexity · Defects · Metrics

S. M. A. Shah (✉) · M. Morisio
Politecnico di Torino, Corso Duca degli Abruzzi, 24 10129 Turin, Italy
e-mail: syed.shah@polito.it

M. Morisio
e-mail: maurizio.morisio@polito.it

W. Lu et al. (eds.), *Proceedings of the 2012 International Conference on Information Technology and Software Engineering*, Lecture Notes in Electrical Engineering 212, DOI: 10.1007/978-3-642-34531-9_4, © Springer-Verlag Berlin Heidelberg 2013

## 4.1 Introduction

For every software product, the quality is critically important. Quality can be characterized by different measures related to defects. However, it is hard to measure defects ahead of time [1]. Therefore, many internal properties are used to predict quality e.g. size and complexity. Size mostly presented in LOC (line of code) as a measure is used in many studies to predict the quality [2, 3], complexity an internal property of software can be measured using different techniques applied to source code and design [4, 5]. The common understanding about the complexity is its positive correlation with the defects. Although the relation is not always linear, it has significant impact. For the complexity measurement, different complexity metrics have been devised in past years [4–8]. Studies showed that the majority of defects are caused by a small portion of the modules [3]. These modules can be identified before time by examining the complexity to reduce the post release and maintainability work. However, it is not straightforward, for the complexity we have different complexity metrics. The selection of appropriate complexity metrics that best relate and indicate with the defects is of concern and requires minimal empirical evaluation for the selection. In this paper, we aim to characterize and compare different complexity metrics for the defects based on different project categories in term of size. Such characterization will help us to identify the complexity metrics with the best ability to indicate the defects in each project category. This observation will not only help us in indicating the complexity metrics having a positive correlation with defects, but also provide a breakthrough for the quality assurance techniques in accessing the projects.

The paper is organized as follows; Sect. 4.2 discussed the related work, Sect. 4.3 presents the research design of the study. Section 4.4 presents the results. Finally, the conclusions are presented in Sect. 4.5.

## 4.2 Related Work

Many studies show an acceptable correlation between complexity metrics and software defect proneness [9–12]. English et al. highlighted the usefulness of the CK metrics for identifying the fault-prone classes [13]. Gyimothy et al. studied the object oriented metrics given by CK for the detection of fault-prone source code of open source Web and e-mail suite called Mozilla. They found that CBO metric seems to be the best in predicting the fault-proneness of classes and DIT metric is untrustworthy, and NOC cannot be used at all for fault-proneness prediction [12]. Yu et al. examined the relationship between the different complexity metrics and the fault-proneness. They used univariate analysis and found that WMC, LOC, CBOout, RFCout LCOM and NOC have a significant relationship with defects but CBOin, RFCin and DIT have no significant relationship [14]. Subramanyam and Krishnan examined the effect of the size along with the WMC, CBO and DIT values on the faults by using multivariate regression analysis for Java and C++ classes. They conclude that size was a good predictor of defects in both languages, but WMC and CBO could be validated only for C++ [11]. Olague et al. studied three OO metrics suites for their ability to predict software quality in terms of fault-proneness: the Chidamber and Kemerer (CK) metrics, Abreu's Metrics for Object-Oriented Design (MOOD), and Bansiya and Davi's Quality Metrics for Object-Oriented Design (QMOOD). They concluded that CK and QMOOD suites contain similar components and produce statistical models that are effective in detecting error-prone classes. They also conclude that class components in the MOOD metrics suite are not good class fault-proneness predictors [15]. However, Nagappan et al. stated that there is no single set of complexity metrics that could act as a universally best defect predictor [16].

From the related work we can extract different implications based on different studies, studying different projects about the relationship of complexity metrics and defect proneness. Hence the results are partial. To study and compare the behavior of complexity metrics indicating defect proneness, it requires an in depth study considering all the complexity metric measures and defects belonging to one project. In addition to generalize the results it requires to take into account many projects having all the metrics available and then analysis should be made collectively. In this way the actual relationship of all the complexity metrics with defect can be understood. Many complexity metrics have been studied in the previous researches [15, 17]. Table 4.1 shows the metrics used in the study.

## 4.3 Research Design

In this section, we present the research question and the data set. One research question is formulated for this research.

*RQ1: Do Complexity Metrics Have an Effect on Defects?*

We selected the last releases of 38 software projects constituting 27,734 modules from the "Promise data repository[1]" having the required metrics freely available for research evaluation purposes [19]. The data set contains 6 proprietary software projects, 15 open source software projects and 17 are academic software projects that were developed by the students. We downloaded the CVS files and found 18 complexity metrics defined in (Sect. 4.2). The values of complexity metrics were available against the defects for every module.

---

[1] http://promisedata.org/

**Table 4.1** The metrics used in the study

The metrics suggested by Chidamber and Kemerer [5] are

**Weighted methods per class (WMC):** WMC is the number of methods defined in each class

**Depth of inheritance tree (DIT):** It is the measure of the number of ancestors of a class

**Number of children (NOC):** It is the measure of a number of direct descendants of the class

**Coupling between objects (CBO):** It is the number of classes coupled to a given class

**Response for a class (RFC):** It is the measure of different methods that can be executed when an object of that class receives a message

**Lack of cohesion in methods (LCOM):** It is the number of pairs of member functions without shared instance variables, minus the number of pairs of member functions with shared instance variables

Henderson Sellers defined one complexity metric [7]

**Lack of cohesion in methods (LCOM3):** According to study [7] LCOM3 is defined as

$$LCOM3 = \frac{\left(\frac{1}{a}\sum_{j=i}^{\square}\mu(A)\right) - m}{1 - m}$$

m—number of methods in a class; a—number of attributes in a class; $\mu(A)$—number of methods that access the attribute A

Bansiya and Davis [6] suggested the following quality metrics suite

**Number of public methods (NPM):** It counts all methods in a class that are declared as public. This metric is also known as Class Interface Size (CIS)

**Data access metric (DAM):** It is the measure of the ratio of the number of private (protected) attributes to the total number of attributes declared in the class

**Measure of aggregation (MOA):** It is the count of the number of class fields whose types are user defined classes

**Measure of functional abstraction (MFA):** It is the ratio of the number of methods inherited by a class to the total number of methods accessible by the member methods of the class

**Cohesion among methods of class (CAM):** It computes the relatedness among methods of a class based upon the parameter list of the methods

**Data access metric (DAM):** It is the measure of the ratio of the number of private (protected) attributes to the total number of attributes declared in the class

**Measure of aggregation (MOA):** It is the count of the number of class fields whose types are user defined classes

**Measure of functional abstraction (MFA):** It is the ratio of the number of methods inherited by a class to the total number of methods accessible by the member methods of the class

**Cohesion among methods of class (CAM):** It computes the relatedness among methods of a class based upon the parameter list of the methods

Tang et al. [18] extended the Chidamber and Kemrer metrics suite focusing on the quality

**Inheritance coupling (IC):** It provides the number of parent classes to which a given class is coupled

**Coupling between methods (CBM):** It measures the number of new/redefined methods to which all the inherited methods are coupled

**Average methods complexity (AMC):** It measures the average method size for each class

Following two metrics were suggested by Martin [8]

**Afferent coupling (Ca):** It is the number of classes that depend upon the measured class

**Efferent coupling (Ce):** It presents the number of classes that the measured class is depended upon

The one metric was suggested by McCabe [4]

**McCabe's cyclomatic complexity (CC).** It is equal to the number of different paths in a method (function) plus one. It is defined as $CC = E - N + P$; where E is the number of edges in the graph, N is the number of nodes of the graph; P is the number of connected components. It is only suitable for the methods; therefore it is converted to the class size metrics, by calculating the arithmetic mean of the CC value in the investigated class

**Table 4.2** Categories of software's in term of size

| Category | No | Average defects | Average size (LoC) |
|---|---|---|---|
| Small (1–60KLoC) | 24 | 52.5 | 17241 |
| Medium (60–300 KLoC) | 7 | 519.14 | 140743 |
| Large (above 300KLoC) | 7 | 508.2 | 427354 |

## 4.4 Results

We carried out the preliminary analysis to identify the three categories of software projects small, medium and large using the K mean clustering algorithm. We found 24 software projects in the small category, 7 software projects in medium and 7 software projects in the large category. The average defects found in the small category of software projects are 52.5, for the medium category of software projects it is 519.14 and 508.2 defects for a large category of software projects. Table 4.2 shows the three categories of software projects i.e. small, medium and large.

### 4.4.1 RQ 1: Do Complexity Metrics Have an Effect on Defects?

We attempted to find the linear correlation between the complexity metrics and defects. We selected Pearson correlation coefficient which best suited to find the linear relation between the two variables. In no case we found the strong correlation among complexity metrics and defects. To study any possible relationship of defects with complexity metrics, we cluster the modules into three categories based on the values, using the K mean clustering algorithm. In order to understand the clusters behavior, we performed the preliminary analysis of the identified clusters for each complexity metric based on the project category. We found three types of behaviors of complexity metrics and grade them as effective, untrustworthy and not useful indicators of defects.

### 4.4.2 Effective Indicators

We extract those complexity metrics where higher values result in higher defects. We called these complexity metrics effective indicators of defects and these metrics exhibit the below phenomenon. Table 4.3 reports the complexity metrics, effective indicators of defects in small, medium and large projects.

$$\text{High Complexity} \rightarrow \text{High Defect}$$

**Table 4.3** Complexity metrics effective indicators of defects

| Project type | Complexity metrics |
|---|---|
| Small | LCOM |
| Medium | WMC, CBO, RFC, CA, CE, NPM, DAM, MOA, IC, Avg CC |
| Large | WMC, CBO, RFC, CA, NPM, AMC |

**Table 4.4** Complexity metrics untrustworthy indicators of defects

| Project type | Complexity metrics |
|---|---|
| Small | WMC, NOC, CBO,RFC, CE, Avg CC |
| Medium | DIT, NOC, LCOM, CBM, AMC |
| Large | DIT, NOC, LCOM, CE, LCOM3, DAM, MOA, MFA, CAM, IC, Avg CC |

### 4.4.3 Untrustworthy Indicators

We classify those complexity metrics that have no fixed criterion of increase in defect with the increase in complexity metric value. We called these complexity metrics untrustworthy indicators of defects. Table 4.4 reports the complexity metric untrustworthy indicator of defects in small, medium and large category of projects. For the untrustworthy indicators we observe two different behaviors of complexity metrics. (a) Medium complexity value resulted in high defects: Medium Complexity → High Defects. (b) High complexity values resulted in high defects but corresponding medium cluster value resulted in lower defects: High Complexity → High Defects, and Medium Complexity → Low Defects.

### 4.4.4 Not Useful Indicators

We classify those complexity metrics where smaller values resulted in high defects, as not useful indicators of defects. Table 4.5 reports the complexity metrics not useful indicator of defects in small, medium and large projects. These complexity metrics exhibit the phenomenon: Low Complexity → High Defects.

### 4.4.5 Hypothesis Testing

For hypothesis testing, we only consider the effective indicator of complexity to verify that the distribution of defects among high, medium and low complexity. We did not perform the analysis on the untrustworthy and not useful indicators because it does not seem to be very meaningful. We take support of statistical hypothesis testing to confirm the difference of defect in three categories of complexity metrics

**Table 4.5** Complexity metrics not useful indicators of defects

| Project type | Complexity metrics |
| --- | --- |
| Small | WMC, DIT, CA, NPM, LCOM3, DAM, MOA, CAM, IC, CBM, AMC |
| Medium | LCOM3, MFA, CAM |
| Large | CBM |

values i.e. high, medium and low. Using statistical techniques, we will test the null hypothesis $H_0$. We will accept and reject it based on the favor of the alternative hypothesis.

- $H_0$: There is no significant difference of defects among high, medium and low complexity of effective indicators.
- $H_1$: There is a significant difference of defects among high, medium and low complexity of effective indicators.

## 4.4.6 Selection of Statistical Test

We first examined the distribution of the samples to choose the appropriate statistical test for the analysis. We applied the Ryan-Joiner test for the normality check and found that for every sample ($p$-value <0.01). The results showed that none of the sample under study has a normal distribution of data. This made us to select the non parametric test for the hypothesis testing. According to the recommendation for not normal samples, we chose non parametric test Kruskal–Wallis test for differences between three or more samples. We compare the defects of high, medium and low complexity cluster of each effective metric. In each category of projects the obtained p value was found less than 0.05 meaning there is a significant difference of defects among high, medium and low complexity value of effective indicators.

## 4.4.7 Threats to Validity

This section discusses the validity threat as classified and proposed by the study [20]. As for construct validity, we collected the CVS logs from the Promise research data repository. Although, we have much confidence in the correctness and accuracy of the provided data but still we have no control to decide that up to which level the data is authentic e.g. how many module's data may be left to record, correctness of the measurement of complexity metric values etc. As for external validity, our findings are based on the large data set of modules i.e. 27,734 of 38 software projects. Although this number is not small but still there can raise some concerns on the generalization of the findings when the projects are categorized into small, medium and large. We have 24 projects from small, 7 projects are from medium and 7 projects are from large categories which are fairly small samples.


## 4.5 Conclusion

The findings have important implications as they are based on the complete set of complexity metrics belonging to one particular project. Similarly 38 such projects were selected which have all the complexity metrics available and then combined to perform the analysis collectively. The artifact of this study is very vital and beneficial for both researchers and practitioners. The primary contribution of this research is the identification of having no linear relation of any complexity metrics with defects. However, based on the complexity metrics high, medium and small value clusters we find that there are some complexity metrics which higher values resulted in a higher number of defects. These complexity metrics are called effective indicators of defects. Consequently the complexity has an effect on defects but not as large as one might expect. The researchers can use the effective complexity metrics for the predicting and estimating of defects and can use in predictive models. The statistical analysis adds confidence that there is a quite significant difference among the defects of effective complexity metrics high, medium and low values. The practitioners can assess their project's quality based on the effective complexity metrics. The categorization of projects is quite useful as it gives practitioners a view to select the appropriate effective complexity metric when assessing their project based on size. We would like to continue our future studies with the same attention considering number of projects to validate the artifacts of this study and thus generalize the effective complexity metrics for small, medium and large projects.


## References

1. Güneş Koru A, Tian J (2003) An empirical comparison and characterization of high defect and high complexity modules. J Syst Softw 67(3):153–163 (Sep 15)
2. Zhang H (2009) An investigation of the relationships between lines of code and defects. ICSM 2009. IEEE international conference on software maintenance. p 274–283
3. Fenton NE, Ohlsson N (2000) Quantitative analysis of faults and failures in a complex software system. Softw Eng IEEE Trans. doi: 10.1109/32.879815. 26(8):797–814
4. McCabe TJ (1976) A complexity measure. Softw Eng IEEE Trans. doi: 10.1109/TSE.1976.233837. SE-2(4):308–320
5. Chidamber SR, Kemerer CF (1994) A metrics suite for object oriented design. Softw Eng IEEE Trans. doi: 10.1109/32.295895. 20(6):476–493
6. Bansiya J, Davis CG (2002) A hierarchical model for object-oriented design quality assessment. Softw Eng IEEE Trans. doi: 10.1109/32.979986. 28(1):4–17
7. Henderson-Sellers B (1996) Object-oriented metrics, measures of complexity. Prentice Hall, NJ

8. Martin R OO Design quality metrics: an analysis of dependencies, presented at the Workshop Pragmatic and Theoretical Directions in Object-Oriented Software Metrics, OOPSLA'94
9. Chidamber SR, Darcy DP, Kemerer CF (1998) Managerial use of metrics for object-oriented software: an exploratory analysis. Softw Eng IEEE Trans. doi: 10.1109/32.707698. 24(8): 629–639
10. Basili VR, Briand LC, Melo WL (1996) A validation of object-oriented design metrics as quality indicators. Softw Eng IEEE Trans. doi: 10.1109/32.544352. 22(10):751–761
11. Subramanyam R, Krishnan MS (2003) Empirical analysis of CK metrics for object-oriented design complexity: implications for software defects. Softw Eng IEEE Trans. doi: 10.1109/TSE.2003.1191795. 29(4):297–310
12. Gyimothy T, Ferenc R, Siket I (2005) Empirical validation of object-oriented metrics on open source software for fault prediction. Softw Eng IEEE Trans. doi: 10.1109/TSE.2005.112. 31(10):897–910
13. English M, Exton C, Rigon I, Cleary B (2009) Fault detection and prediction in an open-source software project. In: Proceedings of the 5th international conference on predictor models in software engineering. Vancouver, British Columbia, Canada: ACM, p 1–11
14. Ping Yu, Systa T, Muller H (2002) Predicting fault-proneness using OO metrics. An industrial case study. In: Proceedings of software maintenance and reengineering, 2002. Sixth European conference on, p 99–107
15. Olague HM, Etzkorn LH, Gholston S, Quattlebaum S (2007) Empirical validation of three software metrics suites to predict fault-proneness of object-oriented classes developed using highly iterative or agile software development processes. Softw Eng IEEE Trans. doi: 10.1109/TSE.2007.1015. 33(6):402–19
16. Nagappan N, Ball T, Zeller A (2006) Mining metrics to predict component failures. In: Proceedings of the 28th international conference on software engineering. Shanghai, China: ACM, p 452–461
17. Catal C, Diri B, Ozumut B (2007) An artificial immune system approach for fault prediction in object-oriented software. In: 2nd International Conference on dependability of computer systems. DepCoS-RELCOMEX'07, p 238–245
18. Tang MH, Kao MH, Chen MH (1999) An empirical study on object-oriented metrics. In: Proceedings of sixth international software metrics symposium, p 242–249
19. Boetticher G, Menzies T, Ostrand T (2007) PROMISE repository of empirical software engineering data [Internet]. Available from: http://promisedata.org/ repository, West Virginia University, Department of Computer Science
20. Wohlin C, Runeson P, Höst M, Ohlsson MC, Regnell B, Wesslen A (2000) Experimentation in software engineering: an introduction. Norwell, Massachusetts. Kluwer Academic Publishers, Dordrecht, USA

Chapter 5
# A Petri Net Based Automatic Executable Code Generation Method for Web Service Composition

Zhijun Ding, Jieqi Liu and Junli Wang

**Abstract** For realizing automatic creation process from formal composition model to executable code, a Petri net based Web services composition model is first presented. Then, an algorithm is designed to automatically generate executed code of Web services composition from Petri net model. Finally, a software tool is realized based on above algorithm, which will make the design of Web services composition more effective.

**Keywords** Petri net · Web services composition · Automatic code generation

## 5.1 Introduction

When the functional requirement in reality becomes more and more complex, the function of single Web service provided would not satisfy the user's demand. Since that, there should be a possibility to combine some existing services together in order to fulfill a more complex function request, that is, the Web services composition problem comes [1]. The standard protocols of Web service such as SOAP, WSDL, UDDI and so on assure the interactions between Web services with one accord. And, if the process of composition between Web services can be achieved by GUI-based tool automatically, the efficiency of developing Web services composition will be highly promoted. The tools such as WebSphere business integration in IBM [2] and BPEL PM Designer in Oracle [3] use the

Z. Ding (✉) · J. Liu · J. Wang
Department of Computer Science and Technology, Tongji University, 201804 Shanghai, China
e-mail: zhijun_ding@outlook.com

W. Lu et al. (eds.), *Proceedings of the 2012 International Conference on Information Technology and Software Engineering*, Lecture Notes in Electrical Engineering 212, DOI: 10.1007/978-3-642-34531-9_5, © Springer-Verlag Berlin Heidelberg 2013

method of process graph to descript the process of Web Service composition, create the special BPEL document, publish the BPEL document to special engine (for example, ODE engine), and at last, run the process composition on a server. On the tool of protégé [4] that is developed by Stanford University, a visualization tool of OWL-S based services composition process logically divides services composition process into a series of standard modules, such as sequence, split, split-join, repeat and so on. This tool transforms the logical composition process of Web services into the augment process of Web services composition process with standard module. All these aforementioned tools make different improvement for Web services composition process in many different aspects. But, due to no formal model, they cannot support the analysis of some important properties, such as reachability, deadlock and so on, which are crucial to the correctness of the composition logic.

Petri net is a formalization method that is well suitable to analyze and verify distributed system, and has been widely used in the design, modeling and analysis of Web services [5] and their composition [6].

Narayanan and McIlraith use Petri net as a tool for model construction, simulation and analysis of DAML-S markups, and then verified the correctness and validity of a composite Web service with reachability analysis method of Petri net [7]. Ding et al. presented a hybrid approach for synthesis Petri nets for modeling and verifying composite Web service. Furthermore, this approach can be used to validate the correctness or soundness of Web Service composition [8]. Hamadi and Benatallah propose a Petri net based algebra for modeling Web service control flows. The model is constructed by step-by-step net refinement, which can support hierarchical modeling for composite service [9].

But these researches merely based on theory, and some problems remain unsolved, such as how to model a Web services composition with Petri net, and how to realize a development tool of Web services composition. For studying and demonstrating an automatic code generation method of Web service composition, we develop a Web services composition code creation tool to model Web services composition by Petri net, achieve the automatic creation process from composition model to executable code, and more meaningfully make it possible to analyze and validate composition logically.

The remainder of this paper is organized as follows. Section 5.2 gives an instance of Web services composition as the whole-length example. Some related definitions of the Petri net model for Web services composition is introduced in Sect. 5.3. Based on the constructed Petri net model for services composition, Sect. 5.4 presents an algorithm to automatically generate executable Web services composition code. Section 5.5 develops a Petri net based Web services composition code creation tool. Finally, the conclusion and future work are presented in Sect. 5.6.

**Table 5.1** Web services and their input, output interfaces

| Web service | Input | Output |
|---|---|---|
| IP2Address | IP address | Location of the machine |
| Weather | Location | Weather information in Chinese |
| Translation | Weather information in Chinese | Weather information in English |

## 5.2 Illustrating Example

Suppose that in an application, it is needed to get the local weather information in English according to a machine's IP address. This application is a complex one, because generally there is no independency Web service on the Web that can fulfill this function. But through some analysis, the issue can be figured out by three sub-issues as follows:

1. How to automatically get current location of the machine?
2. How to get the location's weather?
3. How to translate the weather information into English?

After subdivision the complex application into some simpler applications, it is easier to find their suitable Web services on the Web [10] to figure out the three above issues respectively:

1. Web service *IP2Address*: Queries geographical location according to machine's IP;
2. Web service *Weather*: Queries weather report in Chinese using geographical location;
3. Web service *Translation*: Translates weather report in Chinese into English (Table 5.1).

Because different machine in the internet has different IP address, we can get the geographical location of a machine by *IP2Address* service with the machine's IP address, and *IP2Address* service will use IP address as input and its geographical location as output. Then we can use the geographical location got from *IP2Address* as *Weather* service's input and get the weather information in Chinese by service *Weather*. At last, we use the Chinese weather information got from service *Weather* as the input of service *Translation* to get the final information, the local weather information in English of the machine.

The above process of compositing several simple services to fulfill a complex task is just a process of Web services composition. In a complex Web services composition logic, the composite Web service's properties, such as reachability, deadlock, dead-circulate and so on, are difficult to be analyzed manually. Hence, it is very necessary to build a formal model for analyzing and validating these properties.

## 5.3 Petri Net Model of Web Service

Petri net is a graphical and mathematical tool used for modeling and analyzing systems with concurrency. The mathematical framework behind Petri nets facilitates reasoning about the model generated. Due to the limited space, the definition, terminology of Petri net is referring to Murata [11].

In the Petri net model of Web services composition, we use transition to represent the Web service that will be invoked, place to represent data's source or target, and token to represent the data value assigned about Web service. Each place in this paper has zero or one token. At the same time, for creating executable code by Petri net model, some related information are recorded by added attributes of elements of Petri nets, which are explained as follows.

• Place

Place denotes data's source or target, and it has five attributes: *placeName*, *isALiveToken*, *tokenIsTo*, *inputList*, *outputList*. The meaning of every attribute is stated as below:

1. *placeName*: The name of place, which represents a data's ID in composition code.
2. *isALiveToken*: The value of this attribute is True or False, that True represents the place has one token, and False represents the place has no token.
3. *tokenIsTo*: Parameter number, states which parameter token in this place will transfer to the service represented by transition postset.

For example, let a Web service $S$ has three input parameters a, b and c, it is denoted as S (a, b, c). Then, the parameter number of 'a' is 0, 'b' is 1 and 'c' is 2.

4. *inputList*: The flow relation list from this place's preset to it. If the list is null, the place is an input place, which variable's value represent by the token in this place needs to import from outside.
5. *outputList*: The flow relation list from this place to its postset. If the list is null, the place is an output place, which variable's value represented by the token in this place needs to be exported to outside.

• Transition

A transition represents a Web service, and has four attributes: *WSName*, *isALiveTransition*, *inputList*, *outputList*. The meaning of every attribute is stated as below:

1. *WSName*: The name of service. According to this attribute, a corresponding Web service can be invoked in the process of creating executable code by Petri net model.
2. *isALiveTransition*: The state of this transition, which denotes this transition can be fired or not.

**Fig. 5.1** Petri net model of the illustrating example

**Table 5.2** Initial values of place's attributes

| Place Attribute | IP | Address | Weather | English |
|---|---|---|---|---|
| PlaceName | IP | Address | Weather | English |
| IsALiveToken | False | False | False | False |
| TokenIsTo | 0 | 0 | 0 | −1 |
| InputList | Null | F1 | F3 | F5 |
| OutputList | F0 | F2 | F4 | Null |

**Table 5.3** Initial values of transition's attributes

| Transition Attribute | IP2Address | Weather | Translation |
|---|---|---|---|
| WSName | IP2Address | Weather | Translation |
| IsALiveTransition | False | False | False |
| InputList | F0 | F2 | F4 |
| OutputList | F1 | F3 | F5 |

3. *inputList*: The flow relation list from its preset to this transition.
4. *outputList*: The flow relation list from this transition to its postset.

• Token

Token exists in place. Here we use place's *isALiveToken* data item to represent token's presence.

• Flow relation

Flow relation describe dataflow of Web services composition. It has two attributes: *source* and *target*:

1. *source*: The flow relation's star point, which be a place or transition.
2. *target*: The flow relation's end point, which be a place or transition.

These two values of flow relation can be automatically filled according to the two points linked by this flow relation.

A Petri net model of the Web services composition illustrating example in Sect. 5.2 is shown in Fig. 5.1.

The initial value of attributes of places, transitions and flow relation, respectively are listed in Tables 5.2, 5.3 and 5.4.

**Table 5.4** Initial values of flow relation's attributes

| Flow relation property | F0 | F1 | F2 | F3 | F4 | F5 |
|---|---|---|---|---|---|---|
| Source | IP | IP2Address | Address | Weather | Weather | Translation |
| Target | IP2Address | Address | Weather | Weather | Translation | English |

## 5.4 An Algorithm from Petri net Model to Composition Code

This paper designs the algorithm that automatically creates executable Web services composition code from Petri net model. Base on the Web services composition's Petri net model designed in Sect. 5.3, this algorithm can induct users to create a Code file for saving the Web services composition code. The basic idea is shown as below:

Step 1. Initialize Petri net. If place $p$ has no preset transition, put attribute *isA-LiveToken* of place $p$ to True, write a definite parameter code to Code file;
Step 2. Check all transitions. If all of attribute *isALiveToken* of transition $t$'s presets are True, change $t$'s *isALiveTransition* to True;
Step 3. If $t$'s *isALiveTransition* is True, fire transition $t$, and write code of invoking the Web service represented by transition $t$ to Code file;
Step 4. If there is a transition fired in step 3, turn to step 2, else turn to step 5;
Step 5. Check the places that have no postset, if all of their token states are true, write code of composition service's output, and turn to step 7. Else turn to step 6;
Step 6. The logic of Petri net is wrong. The output state cannot be reached. Turn to step 7;
Step 7. The run of Petri net is over.

Base the Petri net model's data structure defined in Sect. 5.3, for composition service's Petri net model $WSPN = (P, T, F)$, the algorithm for creating composition code in this paper is shown as below:

Step 1. Initiate Petri net, $\forall p \in P$, if $^\bullet p = \Phi$, then $p.isAliveToken$: = True;

Write a definite parameter code to Code file, the code's basic form is shown as below:
**String placename = (data input from outside)**;
//The function of this code is to definite a variable whose value should be got from outside interactively in the running process of the Web services composition code.

Step 2. Check all of transitions,

$\forall t \in T$, if $\forall p \in {}^\bullet t$, and $p.isAliveToken = $ True, then $t.isAliveTransition$: = True;

Step 3. Check all of transitions,

$\forall t \in T$, if $t.isAliveTransition = $ True, then Fire the transition $t$.

Moreover, for $\forall p \in t^\bullet$, $p.isAliveToken$: = True; write following code of invoking the Web service to Code file;

**String placename1 = wsname (String ... placename);**

//Where Placename is a list, placename1 is the value of the attribute *placeName* of *t*'s postset, wsname is the value of attribute *WSName* of transition t. Placename is a list of *placeName* values of *t*'s preset.

Step 4. If there is a transition that has been fired in step 3, turn to step 2, else turn to step 5.

Step 5. Check all of places,

$\forall p \in P$, if $p^\bullet = \Phi$ and $p$.isAliveToken = False, then Petri net model is wrong, else, write code of composition service's output to file as below:

**Print (placename);**

//where placename is value of attribute *placename* of place $p$ satisfying parameter list of property placeName in place that satisfies $p^\bullet = \Phi$ and $p.isAliveToken$ = False and the token state of $p$ is false.

Step 6. Finish the run of Petri net.

## 5.5 Service Composition Code Automatic Generation Tool

Web services composition code automatic generation tool is composed by three parts: Web service local pretreatment, Web service's Petri net model and the generation algorithm of executable code. Architecture of this tool is shown in Fig. 5.2.

The localization pretreatment part treats with the correspondence between local program and Web service, and creates localization JAR to help the automatic generation of executable code for local Web services composition. The Petri net model part uses Petri net to simulate Web service, defines the graphical Petri net

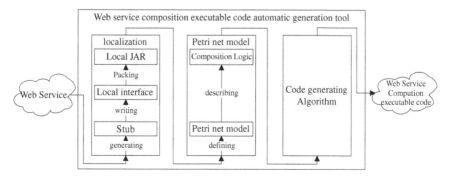

**Fig. 5.2** Tool's system architecture

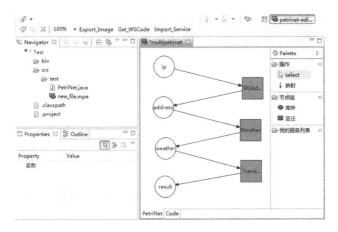

**Fig. 5.3** Petri net model of example

model, and uses the graphical Petri net model editor tool to paint the Web services composition logic visually. The algorithm part automatically generates the executable Web services composition code according to the painted Petri net model in the second part.

The Web service Petri net modeling tool developed in this paper has two interfaces of graphical editor interface and code browse interface. The graphical editor interface base on GEF framework can edit graphical Petri net model, edit properties of Petri net, and also has many assistant functions such as outline view, snap to grid, snap to center line, zoom, delete, undo, redo and other functions. The modeling process strictly observes the syntax of Petri net. Flow relation can only exist between place and transition. And in code browse interface, we can examine the Petri net code model that is synchronous with Petri net graphical model. It can also realize other functions such as copy code, and check the syntax's correctness of model and so on.

The graphical editor can be used to paint Web services composition's Petri net model graph as shown in Fig. 5.1. In the model graph, the parameter represented by the token in place *ip* is inputted from outside (place *ip*'s preset is null). The parameter represented by token in place *result* is the output of the whole composition service (the place *result*'s postset is null). Place *address* is the *IP2Address*'s postset and also the *Weather*'s preset. There is shared data between service Weather and service Translate too. That is, Place *weather* is the Weather's postset, and also the preset of transition *Translate*.

After the visual Petri net model is painted, the daemon of the tool will automatically create the corresponding code model, and the Petri net model of the example is shown in Fig. 5.3.

After running the composition code, user will be reminded to input IP address, just as in Fig. 5.4a. Put the ip: "222.69.212.164" as an input, the composition code will invoke localization interface, and then through stub to exchange with service

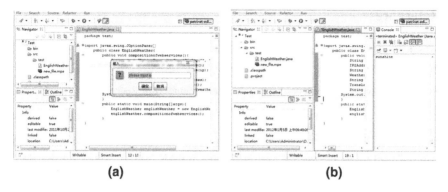

**Fig. 5.4** Running the created composition code. **a** Input interface of running code. **b** Result return from composition code

*IP2Address*. The result got from *IP2Address* will be taken as the input of service *Weather*. Use the same process to invoke services *Weather* and *Translation*. At last, the composition code will return the English weather information at the location of JiaDing that the IP "222.69.212.164" located. The result weather information "sunshine" is shown in Fig. 5.4b.

## 5.6 Conclusion

Web services composition is the one way for effective utilization of Web services. For Web services composition problem, this paper has designed a Web service's Petri net model and a graphical development tool, which can describe the services composition's logic structure in a convenient and shortcut way, use existing analysis means of Petri net to analyze composition service's properties, and design an algorithm to automatically create executable code from model to expedite the development of Web services composition. The experiment results have proven that the methods of this paper are feasible.

**Acknowledgments** This work is partially supported by National Natural Science Foundation of China under Grant No. 61173042 and 61105047, Program for New Century Excellent Talents in University under Grant No. NCET-10-0598, "Shu Guang" Project supported by Shanghai Municipal Education Commission and Shanghai Education Development Foundation under Grant No. 10SG23 Shanghai Rising-Star Program under Grant No. 12QH1402300 and State Key Laboratory of Software Engineering (SKLSE).

# References

1. Schahram D, Wolfgang S (2005) A survey on web services composition. J Web Grid Serv 1(1):1–30
2. Martin K, Jonathan C, Sarah H et al. (2004) BPEL4WS business processes with WebSphere business integration: understanding, modeling, migrating, IBM Redbook
3. Oracle BPEL process manager overview http://www.oracle.com/technetwork/middleware/bpel/overview/index.html
4. Protégé OWL ontology editor http://protege.stanford.edu/plugins/owl/documentation.html
5. Thomas JP, Thomas M, Ghinea G (2003) Modeling of web services flow. In: Proceedings of the 2003 IEEE international conference on E-commerce technology (CEC'03), p 391–399
6. Schlingloff H, Martens A, Schmidt K (2005) Modeling and model checking web services. Electron Notes Theor Comput Sci 126:3–26
7. Narayanan S, McIlraith S (2002) Simulation, verification and automated composition of web services. In: Proceedings of the eleventh international world wide web conference (WWW-11), p 77–88
8. Ding ZJ, Wang JL, Jiang CJ (2008) An approach for synthesis petri nets for modeling and verifying composite web service. J Inf Sci Eng 24(5):1309–1328
9. Hamadi R, Benatallah B (2003) A petri net-based model for web service composition. In: Proceedings of the 14th Australasian database conference database technologies, p 191–200
10. Web Service http://Webservice.Webxml.com.cn
11. Murata T (1989) Petri nets: properties, analysis and applications. Proc IEEE 77(4):541–580

# Chapter 6
# A SPMP Changeability Measurement Model for Reducing Software Development Risk

Sen-Tarng Lai

**Abstract** In software development, it is necessary to face the challenge of plan change. Any plan change always impacts the operations of software development. Plan change not only need to invest extra resource and cost, but also may cause project delay. In plan change process, the affected development documents and plan items should be effectively isolated and completely modified to reduce project failure risk. Therefore, the software project management plan (SPMP) must have high isolation capability and modification flexibility to reduce plan change risk. In this chapter, in order to increase SPMP changeability, discusses the changeable quality factors and proposes a SPMP Changeability Measurement (*SPMPCM*) model. High changeability SPMP can enhance isolation efficiency, modification flexibility to reduce software development risk.

**Keywords** SPMP · Software development risk · Measurement model · Changeability · Software project

## 6.1 Introduction

In software development, change requests are unable to avoid events. Software project is necessary to face the challenge of plan change. For reducing software development risk, software project must overcome the plan change impact [1–3]. Any plan change always affects software development operation. Plan changes not

S.-T. Lai (✉)
Department of Information Technology and Management, Shih Chien University,
No. 70, Dazhi Street, Zhongshan District 104 Taipei City, Taiwan
e-mail: stlai@mail.usc.edu.tw

W. Lu et al. (eds.), *Proceedings of the 2012 International Conference on Information Technology and Software Engineering*, Lecture Notes in Electrical Engineering 212, DOI: 10.1007/978-3-642-34531-9_6, © Springer-Verlag Berlin Heidelberg 2013

only have to invest extra resource and cost, but also may cause project delay [1, 2]. In plan change process [3], affected development documents and planned items unable to effectively isolate and revise, will increase software development risk. For this, software project management plan (SPMP) must have high isolation capability and modification flexibility to reduce plan change risk.

The SPMP is drawn up when the specifications have been signed off by the client. There are many ways to construct an SPMP. One of the best is IEEE standard 1058 [4]. IEEE 1058 SPMP standard defines project organization, management process plans, technical process plans and supporting process plans four major items. SPMP is a critical basis for software development operations. Plan change operations always may affect the SPMP. SPMP should have high isolation capability and modification flexibility to increase changeability and reduce plan changes risk. Therefore, how to increase SPMP changeability is a worthy study issue for reducing software development risk.

Review activities with inspection checklist help collect and quantify SPMP change quality factors. In order to improve and enhance the SPMP changeability, individual factor or measurement should make appropriate combination. Based on the metric combination model, in this paper proposes a SPMP Changeability Measurement (SPMPCM) model. Applying SPMPCM model and rule-based improvement manner, software plan can concretely increase changeability and reduce software development risk. In Sect. 6.2, SPMP major scheme (IEEE std 1058) and of software project failure reason is discussed. In Sect. 6.3, the quality factors of effect of SPMP revision and adjustment capability are listed for illustration. Section 6.4 proposes a SPMP changeability measurement model and a rule-based SPMP changeability improvement manner. In Sect. 6.5, the advantages of SPMPCM model is described again and makes a conclusion for this chapter.

## 6.2 Importance of SPMP

### 6.2.1 Major Configuration Items of SPMP

After the client recognized the requirement, initial version of the SPMP is drawn up and released. Based on the SPMP, software development operation executes with developing schedule, planning works, and meeting each requirement items which proposed by the client. In software development, SPMP has to continuous update and revise with quality improvement, technology enhancement, changed requirements and resource reallocation. IEEE 1058 defined a set of development standard for SPMP [4]. According to IEEE 1058 SPMP standard, four critical chapters are described as follows:

1. Project organization: For all software development personnel, which include internal developers, external communicators and coordinators, have to assign a work role and owing responsibility.

2. Managerial process plans: For control of requirement items, budget, schedule, quality and resource and risk management should have systematic management planning.
3. Technical process plans: Select suitable development models, methodology, tools and technologies, adapting to software and hardware environment.
4. Supporting process plans: Configuration management, testing, quality assurance, reviews and audits, problem solving, subcontractor management and process improvement [5, 6] have to suitable plan.

The SPMP contains budget, schedule, quality, resource and configuration management sub-plans. For each change event impacts, sub-plan should be able to completely and immediately revise or adjust. For keeping the most correct SPMP, in different development phase, the revised SPMP should be released immediately.

## *6.2.2 Critical Factors of Software Project Failure*

According to the Standish group study report which investigated large volume software project, the success rate of software project only approach one-third [7]. And, 80 % failure software projects suffer from some troubled problems which include schedule delay, insufficient budget and incomplete requirements. Plan change usually leads to the situation of schedule delay, insufficient budget and unfinished requirements [8, 9]. Four change events are major reason to cause the software project with high risk [10], describe as follows:

1. Initial period of software development, software system analyst collect incomplete information and defect documents to cause to system requirement specification and user requirement have several differences.
2. In software development process, new technologies and operation environment are innovated continuously. It causes the original plans can not completely match with new technologies and operation environment.
3. In requirement phase, the client proposed many system requirements. However, in software development process, parts of the requirement items will be required to adjust, modify or delete. These change requests will greatly impact to follow up software development operations.
4. Each phase operation of software development needs different resource. Resource allocation may happen to personnel movement, facility delayed delivery, hardware breakdown, equipment failure and obsolete devices. These resource change events may increase software development risk.

Summary the above description, incomplete requirements, technology and environment evolution, client change requests and resource reallocation are four major change events. In software development, change events will be cause different level impacts to software planned items. Change events are also a critical reason of software project failure. For increasing software project success ratio, the SPMP should have high changeability to handle each kinds change events.

## 6.3 Changeability Quality Factors of SPMP

According to McCall's quality factor model description [1] and ISO 9126 quality architecture [11], software quality factors and characteristics have clear hierarchical structure. In ISO 9126, maintainability is a major quality indictor of software maintenance. However, software maintainability is generally focused on development document and source code, but not focused on planning items. In this chapter, plan changeability is regarded as critical capability of plan maintenance. Correctness, completeness, consistency and readability four basic qualities make software planned documents with high flexibility revision and adjustment. Modularity is a necessary characteristic to increase module independence and maintainability. Modularity can also increase plan changeability. Traceability is a critical characteristic to identify cross relationship between planned items. Based on traceability, the planned items affected by change events can be isolated quickly and completely. After plan change, affected schedule and resource should be re-estimated. Clear estimation method [6, 8] can efficiently increase accurate re-estimation. For improving SPMP changeability, basic document quality, modularity, traceability and re-estimation four quality characteristics are discussed as follows:

1. Basic document quality: Four major quality characteristics of planned document described as follows:

   - Correctness, Completeness and Consistency: Incorrect, incomplete or inconsistent planned documents may affect the result of software project revision and adjustment.
   - Readability: Unreadable planned documents may pay more time and effort for software project revision and adjustment.

2. Modularity: Three major factors to affect modularity described as follows:

   - Coupling: For increasing independence, work items should have as low coupling as possible with others work items.
   - Cohesion: For increasing independence, internal subtasks of work items should have as high cohesion as possible.
   - Complexity: Work items with high complexity may reduce the change flexibility for each change events.

3. Traceability: Two major factors to affect the traceability of SPMP described as follows:

   - Internal cross-reference table: The table can easy identify the task inter-relationships in work item.
   - External cross-reference table: The table of work package can easy identify the work item inter-relationships after system break down.

4. Re-estimation: Three factors to affect re-estimation of SPMP described as follows.

- Parameters: Parameters should have clear definition and easy acquisition.
- Formula: Combining simple with accurate estimation formula, the revised work item can quick and accurately re-estimate development effort.
- Transformation: Simple and clear transformation method can easily transfer software development effort to others expenses [8].

## 6.4 Measurement Model and Improvement Manner

### 6.4.1 Changeability Measurement Model

Review activities with inspection checklist can collect the complete SPMP changeability quality factors. Individual factor or measurement can only measure or evaluate the specific quality characteristic. In order to effectively monitor and assess changeability quality defects, measurement and factor should to make appropriate combination [8, 11–14]. Two kind of metric combination models are Linear Combination Model (LCM for short) [11, 12, 14] and Non-Linear Combination Model (NLCM for short) [8, 11, 13]. NLCM has high accuracy measurement than LCM. However, LCM has high flexibility, more extensible and easy formulation than NLCM. In this chapter, LCM is applied to changeability measurement. Major features comparison table between LCM and NLCM shown as Table 6.1.

The different level planning activities have different quality metrics be shown. Therefore, before using the linear combination model, the quality factors must be normalized, and weight values should be acquired from domain expert and senior software engineer. By five combination formulas, basic level quality factors can be combined into four quality characteristic measurements and a SPMP changeability quality indictor. Five equations described as follows:

**Table 6.1** Comparison between LCM and NLCM

| Models features | Linear combination | Non-linear combination |
| --- | --- | --- |
| Accuracy | Middle | High |
| Formula | Simple | Complex |
| Flexibility | High | Low |
| Personnel | Senior software engineer | Senior statistics personnel |
| Data collection | Less | More |

1. Basic Document Quality Measurement (BDQM) is combined with four factors. The formula is shown in Eq. (6.1).

BDQM: Basic document quality measurement
CrF: Correctness factor                          Wcrf: Weight of CrF
CmF: Completeness factor                         Wcmf: Weight of CmF
CnF: Consistency factor                          Wcnf: Weight of CnF
RF: Readability factor                           Wrf: Weight of RF

$$BDQM = W_{crf} * CrF * W_{cmf} * CmF * W_{cnf} * CnF * W_{rf} * RF$$
$$W_{crf} + W_{cmf} + W_{cnf} + W_{rf} = 1 \tag{6.1}$$

2. Planned Item Modularity Measurement (PIMM) is combined with three factors. The formula is shown in Eq. (6.2).

PIMM: Planned item modularity measurement
CU: Coupling factor                              Wcu: Weight of CU
CO: Cohesion factor                              Wco: Weight of CO
CX: Complexity factor                            Wcx: Weight of CX

$$PIMM = W_{cu} * CU * W_{co} * CO + W_{cx} * CX \quad W_{cu} + W_{co} + W_{cx} = 1 \tag{6.2}$$

3. Planned Item Traceability Measurement (PITM) is combined with two factors. The combination formula is shown in Eq. (6.3).

PITM: Planned item traceability measurement
ICRT: Internal cross-reference table             Wicrt: Weight of ICRT
ECRT: External cross-reference table             Wecrt: Weight of ECRT

$$PITM = W_{icrt} * ICRT + W_{ecrt} * ECRT \quad W_{icrt} + W_{ecrt} = 1 \tag{6.3}$$

4. Work Package Re-estimation Measurement (WPRM) is combined with three factors. The formula is shown in Eq. (6.4).

WPRM: Work package re-estimation measurement
PF: Parameter factor                                            Wpf: Weight of PF
FF: Formula factor                                              Wff: Weight of FF
TR: Transformation factor                                       Wtr: Weight of TR

$$WPRM = W_{pf} * PF + W_{ff} * FF + W_{tr} * TR \quad W_{pf} + W_{ff} + W_{tr} = 1 \quad (6.4)$$

Finally, combine BDQM, PIMM, PITM and WPRM four quality measurements into a SPMP Changeability Quality Indictor (SCQI). The combination formula is shown in Eq. (6.5).

SCQI: SPMP changeability quality indictor
BDQM: Basic document quality measurement                        Wqm: Weight of BDQM
PIMM: Planned item modularity measurement                       Wmm: Weight of PIMM
PITM: Planned item traceability measurement                     Wtm: Weight of PITM
WPRM: Work package re-estimation measurement                    Wrm: Weight of WPRM

$$SCQI = W_{qm} * BDQM + W_{mm} * PIMM + W_{tm} * PITM + W_{rm} * WPRM$$
$$W_{qm} + W_{mm} + W_{tm} + W_{rm} = 1 \qquad (6.5)$$

SCQI is generated by three layer combination step. Combination process is called a SPMPCM model. The SPMPCM model architecture is shown in Fig. 6.1.

## 6.4.2 Rule-Based SPMP Changeability Improvement Manner

SCQI is a relative judgment mechanism also is a basis to identify problems or defects of SPMP changeable quality. Therefore, if SCQI does not over the quality threshold, it represents SPMP has high change defect. Based on the combination formulas, high level characteristic measurements mapping to the tasks of planning should be rigorously inspected to identify the problems or defects and propose the corrective action. This paper proposed the rule-based SPMP changeability improvement activity for corrective action, described as follows:

*Rule*1: IF SCQI can not meet the quality threshold

Then according to Eq. (6.5), four high level measurement formulas should be detected.

*Rule* 2: IF BDQM can not meet the quality threshold

**Fig. 6.1** The architecture of
SPMPCM model

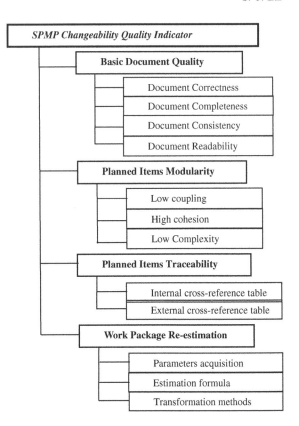

Then according to Eq. (6.1), four low level factors should be analyzed to identify quality defect planned document item.

*Rule* 3: IF PIMM can not meet the quality threshold

Then according to Eq. (6.2), three low level factors should be analyzed to identify quality defect of planned item modularity.

*Rule* 4: IF PITM can not meet the quality threshold

Then according to Eq. (6.3), two low level factors should be analyzed to identify quality defect of planned item traceability.

*Rule* 5: IF WPRM can not meet the quality threshold

Then according to Eq. (6.4), three low level factors should be analyzed to identify quality defect work package re-estimation.

SPMP changeability quality defects can be identified and revised in time. SPMP changeability will be improved and software plan risk can be effectively reduced.

## 6.5 Conclusion

SPMP is the major basis for software project operation and development. However, change events cause that the SPMP has to revise and adjust from time to time. For this, SPMP should have high changeability to reduce plan change risk. For improving changeability of SPMP, the paper proposed a SPMPCM model. High changeability SPMP can quickly and completely handle effects of change events to reduce development risk. The SPMPCM model owns four advantages describe as follows:

- Based on SPMPCM model, SPMP changeability defects can be identified.
- Show the defects reason to help revise SPMP changeability defects.
- Continuously improve SPMP changeability, until software project finish.
- SPMPCM model has clear, simple and high adjustment flexibility formula.

## References

1. ISO/IEC (1988) FCD 9126-1.2: Information technology: software product quality. Part I: quality model
2. Mantel SJ, Meredith JR., Shafer SM, Sutton MM (2011) Project Management in Practice, 4th edn. Wiley, New York
3. Mohan K, Xu P, Ramesh B (2008) Improving the change-management process. CACM 51(5):27–34
4. IEEE std. (1998) 1058–1998, IEEE standard for software project management plans, IEEE, New York
5. Pressman RS (2010) Software engineering: a practitioner's approach. McGraw-Hill, New York
6. Schach SR (2008) Object-oriented software engineering. McGraw-Hill Companies, New York
7. Eveleens JL, Verhoef C (2010) The rise and fall of the chaos report figures. IEEE Softw 27(1):30–36
8. Boehm BW (1981) Software engineering economics. Prentice-Hall, New Jersey
9. Fairley R (1994) Risk management for software projects. IEEE Softw 11(3):57–67
10. Boehm BW (1989) Tutorial: Software risk management. IEEE CS Press, Los Alamitos
11. Galin D (2004) Software quality assurance: from theory to implementation. Pearson Education Limited, England
12. Conte SD, Dunsmore HE, Shen VY (1986) Software engineering metrics and models. Benjamin/Cummings, Menlo Park
13. Fenton NE (1991) Software metrics: a rigorous approach. Chapman & Hall, London
14. Lai ST, Yang CC (1998) A software metric combination model for software reuse. In: Proceedings of 1998 Asia-Pacific software engineering conference, Taiwan, pp 70–77

# Chapter 7
# Timing Sequence Analysis Technology and Application of RVD Software Based on Black Box Testing Environment

Zhenhua Wang, Guofeng Zhang, Zhaohui Chen, Weijin Zhang and Suo Xuhua

**Abstract** Space rendezvous and docking (RVD) is a difficult and critical mission in spacecraft. The navigation and control (GNC) software plays an important role to complete the task. The functions of RVD control software are complex and timing sequence requirement is strict, which has presented extremely high requirements for software testing. This paper introduces FPGA design method and timing sequence analysis technology to capture timing sequence of RVD key data and trace phase relation of uplink and downlink signal. Furthermore, this paper has improved fault trigger and uplink injection method. This testing environment plays an important role in development process of RVD software.

**Keywords** RVD software · Black box testing · Black box testing environment · FPGA design · Timing sequence analysis

Z. Wang (✉) · G. Zhang · Z. Chen · W. Zhang · S. Xuhua
Beijing Institute of Control Engineering, Beijing 100190, China
e-mail: wangzhenhua@bice.org.cn

G. Zhang
e-mail: zhangguofeng@bice.org.cn

Z. Chen
e-mail: chenzhaohui@bice.org.cn

W. Zhang
e-mail: chenzhaohui@bice.org.cn

S. Xuhua
e-mail: suoxuhua@bice.org.cn

Z. Wang · G. Zhang · Z. Chen · W. Zhang · S. Xuhua
Key Laboratory of Space Intelligent Control Technology, Beijing 100190, China

W. Lu et al. (eds.), *Proceedings of the 2012 International Conference on Information Technology and Software Engineering*, Lecture Notes in Electrical Engineering 212, DOI: 10.1007/978-3-642-34531-9_7, © Springer-Verlag Berlin Heidelberg 2013

## 7.1 Introduction

RVD technology of spacecraft is complex and very few countries have mastered the technology. Currently, RVD spacecrafts that come into service include space shuttle of the USA (which has been retired since being launched in 2011), Soyuz manned transport spacecraft of Russia, Progress cargo spacecraft, ATV cargo spacecraft of the EU and HTV cargo spacecraft of Japan [1].

RVD is divided into two main phases, i.e. rendezvous and docking. Rendezvous refers to the process of two spacecrafts on the orbit, i.e. from guiding the tracing spacecraft to access the target spacecraft from a far distance (150–80 km) until satisfying the initial requirements of the two spacecrafts docking mechanisms to perform docking. Docking refers to the process that the two docking mechanisms complete coupling and rigid sealing connection under the condition of the two spacecrafts docking mechanisms are satisfied [2, 3]. During docking process, it is adopted different flying modes and control algorithms when the tracing spacecraft has different distance to the target spacecraft. Spacecraft GNC system is a mission-critical system [4] and its software is extremely complex.

GNC software is the core for docking control. Whether the software is operated normally will affect the reliability of space RVD directly. For the complexity of task, aerospace control software, especial the space RVD software shall has the following features. (1) The software shall have high complexity and timing sequence requirements are strict. (2) The software shall be coupled with the hardware closely and have high performance requirements. (3) The software shall have extremely high reliability and safety.

According to the features of RVD software, validation test focusing on the software shall have the following features. (1) Peripheral interface is varied and timing sequence is complex. (2) It is hard real-time. The software under test is required to have large quantity of tools for support.

## 7.2 Semi-Physical Simulation Testing Environment

Testing Environment is very important in spacecraft software development [5]. Semi-physical test of spacecraft and ground is the most effective way to test spacecraft software. Therefore, we have designed a semi-physical testing environment for the RVD software. As shown in Fig. 7.1, the testing environment includes dynamics simulation computer, telemetry computer, main controlling computer, monitoring computer, integrated interface box, power supply systems and some other parts. Some analogous environments apply to Robot software development etc. [6–8].

Semi-physical simulation testing environment and on-board computer have composed a closed loop and the control software executes on the on-board computer. Through the test of spacecraft and ground running in the testing environment, it can

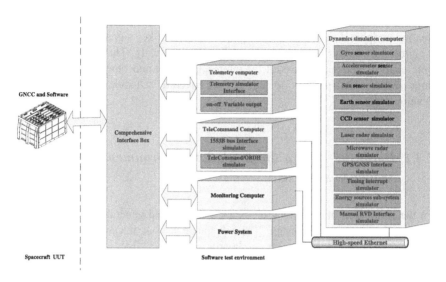

**Fig. 7.1** *Black* structural drawing of box semi-physical simulation testing environment

verify the correctness of spacecraft loaded software and verify the accuracy and completeness of the system plan to provide a dynamic closed loop debugging and testing environment for software application and discover the potential problems in the software as soon as possible. The testing environment is one of the most important conditions for the automatic test [9].

Validation test for RVD software is performed in a semi-physical simulation testing environment, which is a kind of black box testing techniques. This testing environment forms a closed loop to provide orbital dynamics computation simulation by simulating the interfaces of attitude determination sensor (inertial sensors, infrared earth sensors, sun sensors, etc.) and RVD sensors (CCD sensor, laser radar sensor, micro-wave radar sensor, etc.) and simulating information processing remote telemetry, uplink injection and bus communication.

Through semi-physical simulation environment, we can test functions of RVD software. However, we are not only interested in functional testing, but also nonfunction test, such as hard real-time testing. We shall try our best to understand its timing sequence, epical these key data and the conditions that may cause multi-level interrupt and abnormal nesting.

## 7.3 Timing Sequence Analysis Technologies and Application

On the basis of software testing environment based on black box, we have introduced FPGA design, synchronous benchmark treatment and other technique comprehensively. The phase difference relation between the peripheral signals of spacecraft computer and benchmark signals can be obtained through timing sequence analysis capability of testing platform effectively through collecting and treating peripheral signal. Timing sequence relation of key signals we concerns are monitored by analyzing data from interfaces dynamically. Thereby, it could take time analysis and rapid location for interrupt conflict and other abnormal conditions during test process to ensure the overall schedule of the software development.

## 7.3.1 Hardware Design of Simulation Environment Timing Sequence Analysis

To the simulation of peripheral elements, it is adopted generalized FPGA digital input and output board design. The advantage is that it can achieve multiple complex protocol simulation on one board.

On the design of uplink and downlink data setting, FPGA simulation boards are all adopted 100 MHz precise oscillator with high stability. Therefore, the accuracy on time recording can be up to 0.01us. Furthermore, high speed working dominant frequency can reduce the consumed time for data processing to a large content. And then the time accumulation error caused is reduced during operation process of the system. The counting accuracy of sequence circuit is also improved.

The FPGA selected on the board contains 2 million gates, 40 blocks of RAM and 4 clock units, which is completely competent for timing sequence logic simulation with high difficulty and complexity. Through DIP switch, it can switch the procedure content loaded in the board to improve the flexibility of test setting. The setting chip of FPGA has 4 stored procedure areas. The board can have multiple functions by choosing different DIP switch state, which can significantly improve the flexibility of our testing environment.

## 7.3.2 Time Synchronization Technique and Data Integrity Design

The time synchronization is implemented by introducing hardware control cycle signal of on-board computer of spacecraft. This kind of signal is timing interrupt signal of spacecraft GNC software. Therefore, it can be considered as the basis for timing sequence analysis of spacecraft GNC software through recording accurate timestamps of all uplink and downlink signals and control cycle signals.

Moreover, the uplink and downlink data should be kept integrity on the design level. Dynamics software shall visit FPGA once a control cycle to take treatment for uplink and downlink data. Because the dynamics software and spacecraft GNC software are asynchronous, packet loss and packet error may occur. When FPGA is sending uplink data, dynamics software may change the data sent. When FPGA

**Fig. 7.2** Secondary buffer
BUF structure

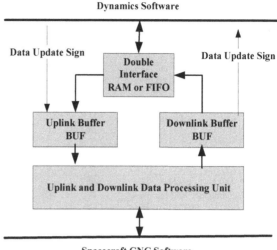

is receiving downlink data, the dynamics software is visiting FPGA obtained data. It is adopted secondary buffer BUF method to ensure the completeness of all kinds of data packets. The structural drawing is shown in Fig. 7.2.

The flow of dynamics software to process uplink data is as following: uplink data processing unit is adopted FPGA to achieve. When the unit is free, it checks the flag of data updating. If there is new data, it will take out the data from the double interface RAM or FIFO to buffer BUF. When the data is taken out, it will clear data and update the flag.

The flow of IP core to check data of FPGA is as following: downlink data treatment unit is adopted FPGA to achieve. After the unit finish receiving data from the spacecraft, it sets the data updating flag and writes the data into the double interface RAM or FIFO. Synchronous design is adopted on the chip PCI9054 bridging FPGA and PCI bus interfaces, which avoids the possibility of data conflicts when EPGA is in reading and writing process and PCI 9054 is in writing and reading process. Figure 7.3 shows dynamics visiting uplink and downlink method.

The flow of FPGA software to process timestamp is as following: after the uplink and downlink channel corresponding counter detects the lower falling edge of control cycle (or on the upper falling edge, which can be set by the host computer software), as the benchmark of time recording, it starts counting. After the FPGA downlink unit receives corresponding data on the spacecraft, it stops counting immediately, records timestamp and calculates phase difference. Meanwhile, it stores the data recorded into the buffer in the FPGA, clears the counter and sets the measuring flag bit of phase difference at "1". When the host computer scans the marked position of the channel is in "1", it reads the data in the buffer area and clears the flag bit. The data is the recorded phase difference of level signal and equivalent weight is 0.01us. The timestamp recording process is shown in Fig. 7.4.

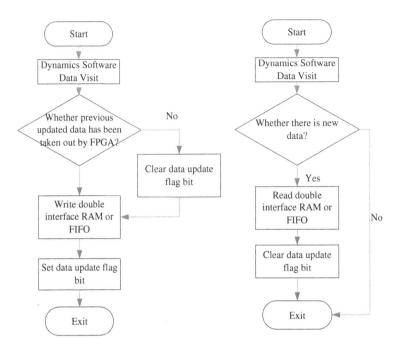

**Fig. 7.3** FPGA and upper computer software data processing flow chart

## 7.3.3 Interfaces Design of Sensor and Actuator

Functional board (laser radar sensor simulator, for instance) in dynamics simulation computer takes judgment for received downlink communication data. There are multiple data areas, A, B, C and D. For each data area, the lowercase letter denotes the identifier of the data area and capital one refers the data area itself. When the frame header of downlink communication data is the identifier "a", the content in the data area "A" is sent. It is similar for the data area "B", "C" and "D". Meanwhile, it can set the response time and interval time for sending uplink data.

Before the functional board enters into normal working mode, it requires the host computer to set parameters for asynchronous communication serial; otherwise it cannot complete the communication work normally. The contents set include the identifiers and contents, response time, interval time, data receiving number and data comparing number of all the four data area.

When the required parameters are set, functional board will be in normal working mode. The host computer can read the downlink communication data in the data buffer area of the board by bus line and read the number, timestamp and other data of some data area (A, B, C or D) at the same time. Timing equivalent weight in the board is 0.01us. Meanwhile, each serial has response switch, and it can be set through the hose computer software. During the process of receiving

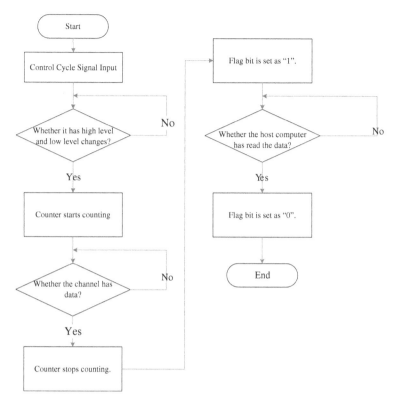

**Fig. 7.4** Timestamp recording process

data, the board will be reset (i.e. the communication process is ended) if time-out (there is no downlink data for a long period).

There is a counter for recording timestamp in serial functional module dedicatedly. When the board checks that there is downlink data in the serial, the counter is triggered to start counting. When data receiving is completed and uplink data is sent, counting is stopped. FPGA will store the recorded data into the internal buffer area, and set the flag bit of receiving completed at "1" when sending the uplink data. After the host computer checks the flag bit, it will read the received data and recorded timestamp in the buffer area.

A worthwhile design, parallel working mode, is adopted on the serial procedure design, i.e. the data collecting and data comparing run simultaneously. After the first byte is received, it will be compared with the first byte in area a, b, c and d immediately. When the downlink data is received completely, data comparison work is also completed at the same time and conclusion can be made rapidly, i.e. whether it is sent from A, B, C, or D. Parallel working mode can make use of circuit resources in FPGA effectively to complete digital logic circuit computation more rapidly than sequential working mode does. Because the receiving function and comparison function are completed nearly at the same time, there is nearly no accumulation error caused by

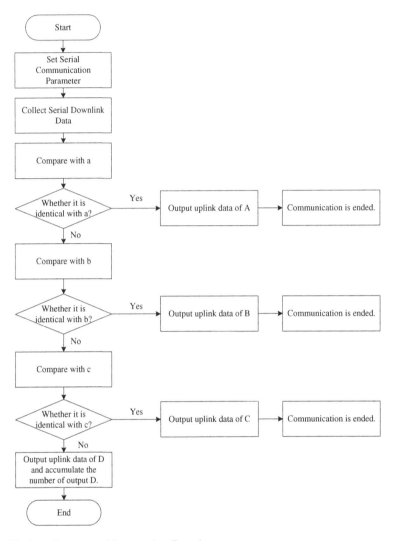

**Fig. 7.5** Asynchronous serial processing flow chart

time-consuming of system computation. Therefore, the timestamp value is extremely accurate. Asynchronies serial procedure is shown in Fig. 7.5.

## 7.3.4 Fault Protection

FPGA on the board can develop max 40 FIFO data buffer areas. During development of FPGA program, a backup storage area is developed for each downlink data storage area. When the host computer does not read the data in time, there is no need to worry about data lost due to being rewritten and covered, because data which is not read in time has been stored in the backup storage area.

When executing serial communication function, if some abnormal case happens suddenly during downlink data sending process, sending process may fail to complete or continue. The functional board will respond as time-out, stop receiving the signal and reset to initial status. In order to avoid affecting the stability and reliability of the board, it shall set time-out and provide response setting interface. The upper bound of time-out should be set by the developer directly.

All connection interfaces of board are set as high resistance mode before initialization. When the user's equipment is connected with the whole system, it should ensure the safety of user's equipment. After the dynamics simulation computer takes initialization to the board, the input and output of board interface can be started.

The board supports hot plug, which strengthen the safety of user's equipment.

### 7.3.5 Application in Spacecraft Software Testing

Accurate phase difference for spacecraft loaded software to sensors, execution mechanisms and other prophetical devices can be obtained through the methodology mentioned above, which can be used to analyze the timing sequence relation of each control cycle to the prophetical devices. Meanwhile, multi-level interrupts concurrent test and nested test of spacecraft GNC software can be implemented by controlling triggering timing sequence of the GNC software external interrupt signal. All those approaches ensure the reliability and security of the GNC software.

An industrial case is given to illustrate the effectiveness of our methodology. In a debugging process, it is discovered the phase relation of sensors is abnormal, and the interrupt control status of the GNC software under execution is also abnormal. During the execution of GNC software, it may be trapped in interrupt occasionally. And the functional board responds a time-out signal. We trace this bug to data area C in a laser radar sensor and find that there occurs a time-out in data sending of the laser radar sensor. The timestamp records reveal that the phase of data sent is abnormal. Through analyzing telemetry data, we discover that counting of the counter trapped in interrupt is increasing, which means that the program has entered trapping interrupt service program.

According to the analysis mentioned above, it reveals that the interrupt timing sequence embedding is unreasonable preliminarily. It has confirmed the correctness of data analysis by using logic analyzer. Figure 7.6 shows the abnormal status captured by logic analyzer.

Causes of the fault: If high level interrupt time is too long, as in the left subfigure of Fig. 7.7, rising edge is impossible to be formed in high level to edge trigger of 82C59 interrupt. It has affected next trigger of the same interrupt, and

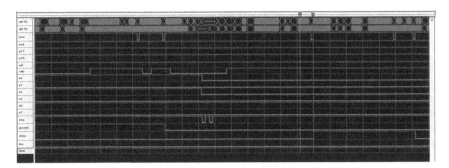

**Fig. 7.6** Software timing sequence captured by logic analyzer

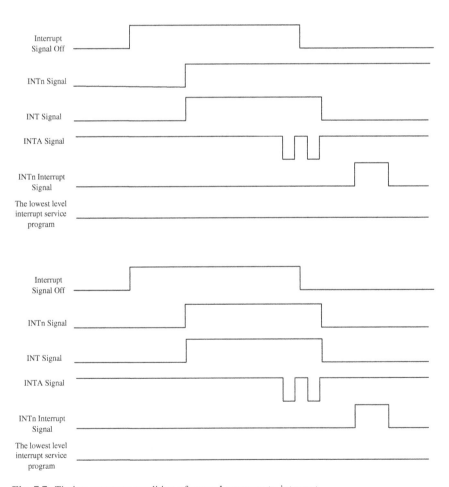

**Fig. 7.7** Timing sequence condition of normal response to interrupt

interrupt lost is caused. Normal and abnormal timing sequence analysis curves are as in Fig. 7.7. The left sub-figure is the abnormal case, while the right one is the normal case.

Through analysis, it prompts the designer to take measures from software or hardware aspects to improve high level length of interrupt request signal. After taking corresponding improvement, the problem does not appear again. Thus, the quality of the aerospace embedded software is improved.

## 7.4 Conclusions

This paper proposed a timing sequence analysis technique based on black box. This technique improved the traditional semi-physical simulation testing. By obtaining time behavior of required uplink and downlink signals, the timing sequence analysis was implemented, which improved the quality of the GNC software for RVD.

Applying this timing analysis technique on GNC software for RVD, the performance testing capability of the semi-physical simulation test environment was improved, and evidences for the reliability design of software were also provided. After taking timing sequence analysis for the testing environment, problem could be located preliminarily. It provided direction to following precise positioning, and saved valuable research and development time.

## References

1. Valin T (2007) Commercial crew and cargo program overview. In: ISS-A new national laboratory special session AIAA aerospace sciences meeting, USA, 11 January 2007
2. Zhang S, Wang Z, Ran L et al (2005) Space RVD measuring technology and engineering application, vol 10. China Astronautic Publishing House, Beijing, pp 1, 18–19 (in Chinese)
3. Zhu R (2007) RVD technology of spacecraft, vol 10. China Machine Press, China, pp 1–3 (in chinese)
4. Sommerville I (2007) Software engineering, 8th edn. Machinery Industry Press, Beijing, pp 44, 45 (Photocopy Edition)
5. Zhu S (2006) Aerospace software engineering practice-the past ten years and the future. Aerosp Control 24(4):66–68 (in chinese)
6. Harris A, Conrad JM (2011) Survey of popular robotics simulators, frameworks, and toolkits. In: The proceedings of IEEE SoutheastCon, Nashville, pp 243–248
7. Harris AC (2010) Design and implementation of an autonomous robotics simulator. In: UNC charlotte MS thesis, May 2011. SSBSE 2nd, Berlin
8. Lindlar F, Windisch A (2010) A search-based approach to functional hardware-in-the-loop testing
9. Chen Jineng (2008) Software testing guide fundamentals, tools and practice, vol 6. Posts& Telecom Press, China, pp 137–139 (in chinese)

# Chapter 8
# Application Research of Two-Dimensional Barcode in Information Construction of Colleges

**Yan Yan, Qifeng Li, Minghua Cao, Haiyan Chen and Jianbin Xue**

**Abstract** The chapter analyzed the main application methods of 2D barcode technology, proposed the application scheme of campus examination information and library management system based on 2D barcode. Use 2D barcode to realize electronic admission certificate and digital management of book lending and borrowing, not only saved the paper resources but also facilitate the automatic collection of information and management. It is a beneficial attempt of 2D barcode in the information construction of colleges.

**Keywords** Two-dimensional barcode · Electronic admission certificate · Digital library management · Identity authentication

## 8.1 Introduction

Barcode technology is known as the most economic and practical automatic identification technology, it has fast recognition ability, highly reliability, flexible and practical [1, 2], which is widely used in transportation, commodity trade, goods management, production line automation, library management, etc. The early used one-dimensional barcode technology, according to different width of distribution of certain direction, is composed by "0" and "1" into a series of

Y. Yan (✉) · M. Cao · H. Chen · J. Xue
School of Computer and Communication, Lanzhou University of Technology, Lanzhou 730050, China
e-mail: yanyan@lut.cn

Q. Li
Combat and training ministry, Public Security Fire Department of Gansu Province, Lanzhou 730000, China

W. Lu et al. (eds.), *Proceedings of the 2012 International Conference on Information Technology and Software Engineering*, Lecture Notes in Electrical Engineering 212, DOI: 10.1007/978-3-642-34531-9_8, © Springer-Verlag Berlin Heidelberg 2013

characters. These binary characters can accurately corresponding to specific information after coding according to certain system agreements. But the information carried by 1D barcode is very limited, more information can only rely on the support of database, and thus the use of 1D barcode has been restricted to some extent. In the 1990s, two-dimensional barcode technology has appeared which has great capacity of data storage, comprehensive coding extent, highly accuracy on recognition, security and many other advantages, and has been recognized as the most effective technology for identification and storage under the development of the Internet of things.

The chapter discussed the main application methods of 2D barcode technology, and proposed application methods of campus examination affairs and library management based on 2D barcode. Using 2D barcode as the carrier to realize electronic admission certificate and digital management of book can not only save the paper cost but also facilitate the automatic input of information and management.

## 8.2 Two-Dimensional Barcode Technology

2D barcode is formed by some black and white figures alternatively on the flat surface according to certain regular pattern. It uses a number of geometric figures according to binary system to represent data, text and other information. In the course of application, information can be gathered and processed automatically by using some image devices or scan equipments.

According to different encoding principle and structure shape, 2D barcode can be divided into Stacked Barcode and Dot Matrix Barcode [3]. Stacked Barcode represent information by laying up height shortened 1D barcode. Code 49, Code 16 K,PDF417 and etc. are the typical formats of this kind. Dot Matrix Barcode arrange the black and white pixels in a rectangular plane space in order to code information. It is a kind of new automatic processing coding system, which builds up on computer image processing technology and combined coding principle. Typical formats such as Code One, Quick Response code (QR Code), Data Matrix and Maxicode are shown in Fig. 8.1.

2D barcode has already been widely applied in documents management, license inspection, vehicle registration, printing propaganda, electronic ticket and many other fields [4]. Especially with the development of mobile communication technology and popularization of the intelligent terminal equipment, mobile 2D barcode service received great favor from the public, and was widely used for various kinds of electronic tickets (such as movie tickets, performance tickets, train tickets, airline tickets, etc.), electronic coupons, conversion voucher of points, electronic guidance of diagnosis and so on [5, 6].

Technically, 2D barcode services can be divided into reading application and scanning application. Reading application use intelligent terminal equipment as the main part, which has 2D barcode reading software on the terminal, gather and

**Fig. 8.1** Different kinds of two-Dimensional barcode. **a** Code 49. **b** Code 16K. **c** PDF417. **d** Code One. **e** QR Code. **f** Data Matrix. **g** Maxicode

analyze 2D barcode images. Typical service models are: connecting internet, business card application, short messaging service (SMS), email application, text applications, etc. The main part of scanning application is the 2D barcode images, which is mainly used for scanning and reading by all kinds of special equipments with 2D barcode reading software. Application of this kind mainly concentrated in business areas, such as electronic tickets, electronic coupons, electronic cards etc.

According to different application patterns, 2D barcode services can be divided into off-line application and on-line application. 2D barcode images stored all the required information (such as business card information, telephone number, e-mail address, etc.) in off-line application, terminal equipments can get all the stored information and realize information entering or quick dial operation only by scanning 2D barcode images. While in on-line application, information stored in 2D barcode images is only the index number, user has to scan a 2D barcode image and get the index number by some client software, and then obtain the detailed information content corresponding to the index number from the network platform database of 2D barcode.

## 8.3 Campus Examination System Based on 2D Barcode

Every year, colleges will hold a large number of examinations, printing various kinds of paper admission tickets will not only need great human resource but also waste a lot of paper resource. If the candidate lost his admission ticket carelessly, he can not participate in the examination. Using 2D barcode to transform the candidates' information and examination arrangement information into electronic admission certificate will not only save paper and manual labor costs but also carry out identity authentication when necessary and avoid exam cheating by replacing the photos of candidates.

## 8.3.1 System Function Design

The system of examination information based on 2D barcode includes two parts. In generation stage, candidates can register his information online (on-line pattern) or go to the educational department to submit personal information (off-line pattern). Educational department will arrange the time, place and seating of examination after sign up through the client software. Finally, electronic admission certificate will be formed through the 2D barcode generation module, and provided to candidates through cell phone platform or the registration web site (shown in Fig. 8.2).

In identification stage, locale identification can use ordinary camera to capture the 2D barcode images, decode by software processing automatically and inquire the information database to contrast user's photo in order to realize identity authentication. In addition, the examination inspection members can use intelligent cell phone with 2D barcode recognition software to scan and land the registration website and check the information of candidates to realize on-line identity authentication [7] (shown in Fig. 8.3).

## 8.3.2 Implementation Method

According to the ideas mentioned above, combined with the main application methods of 2D barcode services, we adopt "website + client software" and "half off-line half on-line" pattern to achieve the examination information platform.

### 8.3.2.1 Registration Website of 2D Barcode Examination System

The registration website for 2D barcode examination system is developed by ASP and SQL technology, which supported the interview of PC and intelligent cell phone. Electronic admission certificate can be downloaded to computer or cell phone, and the embedded information can be decoded by all kinds of recognition

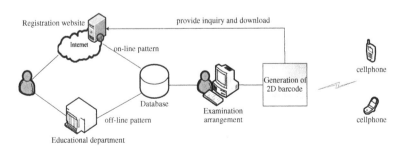

**Fig. 8.2** Generation stage of electronic admission certificate

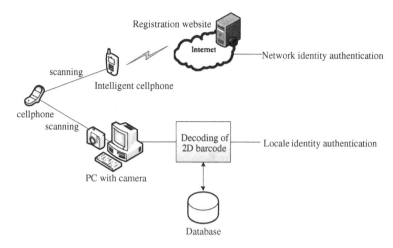

**Fig. 8.3** Identification stage of electronic admission certificate

software of 2D barcode. In order to ensure the security of personal information and prevent tamper or counterfeit the 2D barcode information at the same time, the text content of information has been processed by MD5 encryption algorithm (Figs. 8.4, 8.5).

### 8.3.2.2  Client Software of 2D Barcode Examination System

The client software of 2D barcode examination system is developed by Visual C++ software, mainly to complete off-line information input, examination arrangement,

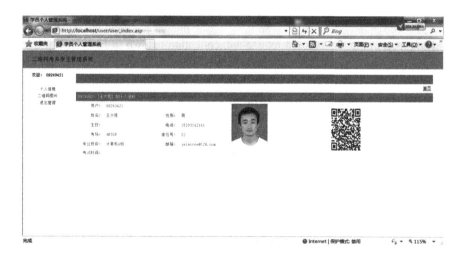

**Fig. 8.4**  Query result on-line

**Fig. 8.5** Decode result from 2D barcode

generation and recognition of 2D barcode and other functions. It is convenient to call EXCEL software to accomplish arrangement of examination, and accord with the habit of official personnel. Encoding process of QR code uses the open source QREncode.dll components, and adds with batch coding function of database and import function of EXCEL.

So far, there has no hand-held terminal and software can rebuild certificate image directly during scanning. In order to ensure the accuracy of identity authentication, while avoiding the problem that 2D barcode can not carry image with high quality, we use two ways to solve this issue. Locale authentication can use PC with ordinary camera to capture the 2D barcode images, decode by recognition software and inquire the database to get user's photo in order to realize identity authentication. On-line authentication use intelligent cell phone with 2D barcode recognition software to scan the barcode images and land the registration website to get user's photo and realize authentication (shown in Figs. 8.6, 8.7).

## 8.4 Digital Library Management System Based on 2D Barcode

Currently, most of the libraries use two kinds of identification system to accomplish book management and user management. When doing the book storage and classification, 1D barcode is used to distinguish different books. But the management of readers using IC card, this phenomenon increased the costs of library management and made the operation complicated.

**Fig. 8.6** Generation of 2D barcode

**Fig. 8.7** Network authentication

## 8.4.1 System Function Design

Digital library management system based on 2D barcode technology mainly includes book information input, user identification, lending and borrowing management and other functions. Library managers can use 2D barcode scanning equipment to recognize one-dimensional or two-dimensional barcode information on books and input the related information into the library management database. They can also generate 2D barcode of book information according to existing database, save it as an image file and print or paste it onto books, so that any user

**Fig. 8.8** Generation of book
2D barcode

along with the circulation of books can use scanning device or 2D barcode reading software to get the content information of books. Setting a related 2D barcode for each book or journal in the information searching function, will help the reader to get the title, author, searching number, locate position and other information about the book. Saving this 2D barcode in the cell phone can be more convenient to find the required books in the library [8].

User management part can use 2D barcode to store the readers' identity information, complete authentication by scanning the personal information of 2D barcode printed on library card or stored in cell phone and comparing with the information in database. Legal users can further scanning the 2D barcode and landing the library management system to check his lending and borrowing records. By the using of SMS, Web and WAP technology, we can also send the information of new book catalog and expiring list of books to the cell phone of users in the form of 2D barcode, offer on-line reading, book reservation, reader communication and other digital library services [9].

## *8.4.2 Realization Method*

The management system of digital library can be realized on the original library website and management software by increasing encoding and decoding modules of 2D barcode and some corresponding data tables. Encoding process of the book

**Fig. 8.9** User authentication

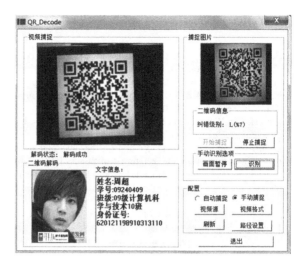

information 2D barcode can still use the open source QREncode.dll components, and the generated barcode can be easily printed by variety of printers and pasted in the books (as shown in Fig. 8.8). User authentication take the off-line mode, image acquisition equipments can be set in the entrance of the library or reading room, which can capture 2D barcode form library card or cell phone, decode the information and pass it into the database, corresponding users' information, certificate photos, lending and borrowing records will be displayed to the screen for authentication or query (shown in Fig. 8.9).

## 8.5 Conclusion

As the key technology in perception layer of Internet of things, 2D barcode and its recognition technology have been considered as the effective way of information collection and object recognition. 2D barcode can be used on different materials, has low production costs and high speed of acquisition and recognition efficiency. This chapter discussed the scheme of examination information system and library management system based on 2D barcode technology, using 2D barcode to carry identity information or specific application information and realize information collection, authentication, media access and other services efficiently. It is a beneficial attempt of 2D barcode technology in the information construction of colleges.

**Acknowledgments** This work is supported by the National Natural Science Foundation of China (61062002, 61265003).

# References

1. Bar code symbology—EAN/UPC—Basic specification (2004) JIS X0507-2004
2. The Educational Foundation of the National Restaurant Association (1996) Bar code
3. Peter L (2011) 2D barcodes the next revolution. J Supply Chain Eur 20(3):28
4. Yang Y, Du X (2008) 2-dimensional bar code service implementation and application. J Inf Commun Technol 1:23–30 (in Chinese)
5. Kato H, Tan KW (2005) 2D barcodes for mobile phones. In: The 2nd international conference on mobile technology, Guangzhou, pp 1–8
6. Chen J, Wang J (2010) Discussion on the development and applications of mobile phone two—dimensional barcode in internet of things. J Telecommun Sci 4:39–43 (in Chinese)
7. Ohbuchi E, Hanaizumi H, Hock LA (2004) Barcode readers using the camera device in mobile phones. In: Proceedings of the 2004 international conference on cyberworlds, Washington, pp 260–265
8. Jiang Z (2011) Application of mobile two-dimensional code in digital library in colleges. J Guangxi Econ Manage Cadre Coll 23(3):98–102 (in Chinese)
9. Zhe Z (2010) On the application of two-dimensional bar code in book borrowing and lending management system. J Changzhou Inst Technolo 23(2):53–55 (in Chinese)

# Chapter 9
# Automatic Test of Space Rendezvous and Docking GNC Software

Zhenhua Wang, Zhaohui Chen, Guofeng Zhang and Hanxiao Zhang

**Abstract** The GNC for the space rendezvous and docking is a complex system. Software testing is the practical methodology to ensure the reliability and robustness of software in industrial domain. Too much effort is taken in software testing because it is extremely high that the reliability and robustness of software on GNC. This chapter proposes an automatic testing methodology towards the software of GNC for the space rendezvous and docking. There are several phases in the process of such methodology: management of test case and test scripts, automatic execution of the testing process, test data interpretation and test defect management. Practical experiments show that the proposed automatic testing methodology significantly improves the software development process efficiently. Therefore, it plays an important role in developing and validating the software on GNC.

**Keywords** Rendezvous and docking (RVD) · GNC software · Automatic test system (ATS) · Data analysis · Defect management

Z. Wang (✉) · Z. Chen · G. Zhang · H. Zhang
Beijing Institute of Control Engineering, Beijing 100190, China
e-mail: wangzhenhua@bice.org.cn

Z. Chen
e-mail: chenzhaohui@bice.org.cn

G. Zhang
e-mail: zhangguofeng@bice.org.cn

H. Zhang
e-mail: zhanghanxiao@bice.org.cn

Z. Wang · Z. Chen · G. Zhang · H. Zhang
Key Laboratory of Space Intelligent Control Technology, Beijing 100190, China

W. Lu et al. (eds.), *Proceedings of the 2012 International Conference on Information Technology and Software Engineering*, Lecture Notes in Electrical Engineering 212, DOI: 10.1007/978-3-642-34531-9_9, © Springer-Verlag Berlin Heidelberg 2013

## 9.1 Introduction

Space RVD process is complex and of great technical difficulties, and It is a mission-critical system [1]. The requirements for guidance navigation control (GNC) software of the RVD system are extremely high. More function points, fault tolerance processing and other complex designs cause that the software size is very large, which propose great challenges to ensure the testing adequate. GNC software plays an important role in the RVD, and it has the characteristics of high safety requirements, hard real-time requirements, high software complexity, close hardware and software connection, complex functionality, rigorous performance requirements and strict timing requirement. It ranges on the software of Class A critical safety. Software testing plays an important role in the software development of GNC. So that engineers should pay serious attention to software testing [2].

Nowadays, the task load of validation testing for rendezvous and docking software increases dramatically while the time and human resources are limited. In such a situation, it is urgent to improve the efficiency of testing and the operational consistency of regression testing.

In the domain of aerospace, NASA, ESA and other organizations have established the relatively complete and systematic system in the field of automatic testing, through long-term development. The American automatic test system (ATS) towards complex multi-system objects has been developed to the third generation, which integrates various test resources, and can automatically realize the function and performance test as well as fault location and diagnosis of the test object. At present, the next ATS (NxTest) is under investigation and development. In the domain of automatic test language: NASA once adopted GOAL (Ground Operations Aerospace Language) [3], and the European Space Agency adopted ETOL (European Test and Operations Language) [4]. In order to adapt to the new development of the automatic test technology, ATLAS Committee and U.S. Department of Defense are jointly developing the new-generation ATLAS test language—ATLAS 2000 [5].

Towards the automatic test, IEEE releases the ATML (Automatic Test Markup Language) [6] system, which is one of the latest achievements in the domain. ATML defines the integrated environment of design data, test strategy and requirements, test procedures, test result management as well as test system realization.

In China, the State Key Laboratory of Software Development Environment of Beihang University proposes an overall framework composed of four suits of software, a functional module and three supporting platforms in accordance with the spacecraft automatic testing system [7]. Standardized automatic test language and common testing environment constitution become the main ideas of automatic test [8].

The techniques and methodologies about automatic testing mentioned above are significant models to design and implement the automatic test system for rendezvous and docking software.

## 9.2  Roadmap

The characteristics under test are involved in varied peripheral interfaces, complicated time sequence, lots of sensors selection and switching, many stages of rendezvous and docking processes, mode conversion relationship conditions, large calculation amount of parts of functions and complex conditions for judging the correctness of operations. Therefore, the test functions of the RVD software shall be treated respectively.

The environmental design principle of automatic test of RVD GNC software is that the purpose of automatic test is to improve test efficiency and ensure test consistency. This requires the combination of automatic test and manual interpretation. Automatic testing is not expected to handle all test function points, and some complex test function point is attacked manually. Because automatic testing itself cost time to develop. While the time and labors are limited. If too many resources are paid on the development of automatic testing, there will be no enough resource to develop the RVD software. Therefore, a reasonable trade-off should be taken up to plan and implement the automatic testing. And then the automatic testing will take its advantages and reveal software defects which are hard to be detected by other approaches [9].

As mentioned above, the test function points should be clarified and then be handled in different manners. From our view, there are two kinds of test function points. The feature of the first class is that their scenarios occur repetitively and the judgments of such points are not complex, mode switch, etc. The second class of test function points always relate with complicated judgments, safety mechanism for rendezvous and docking, etc. Automatic testing is very suitable for the first class of test function points. The second class of test function points can be performed automatically. But human labors should be paid on the judgments of these test function points. According the category of test function points above, the advantages of automatic testing and manual judgment are fully combined, which enhances the test process to ensure the reliability and robustness of the software of RVD.

The main functions of automatic test process management and data processing shall include system management, global configuration, user and authority management, telecommand and telemetry data process, automatic generation and editing of scripts, telecommand sending, data storage and inquiry, data playback, defect management and measurement, automatic generation of test report and other functions, which can be deployed in a distributed system.

## 9.3  Automatic Test Environment

The automatic test system is provided with the functions of automatic generation and execution of test scripts, analysis and interpretation of test data, automatic generation of test report and so on. It is the system integrated with test configuration, automatic execution of test case, test data management and test monitoring, so that the user can realize the software test and completion in time. The requirements of satellite ground test software generalization, automatic and remote control of the test process shall be met, to improve the automation level of software test and enhance the efficiency and coverage rate of software tests.

## 9.3.1 Architecture of ATS

The ATS performs the following critical tasks:

1. Design test cases and auxiliary test cases: Test cases from different versions should be managed uniformly to ease the re-usage of test cases. The management system makes test cases controllable and traceable.
2. Management on test processes of several suits of software under development. Based on the management system, test engineers could select test cases to execute according to the task schedules. They can also name the files storing test data generated from the execution of test cases. If necessary, the test engineers can intervene and control the test execution through a real-time monitoring system running on the network.
3. Record test result. The test data shall be transmitted to the data service center through interfaces. After the data service center receives the data, the data shall be stored and sent to the test monitoring end at the same time. The defects shall be classified in accordance with the interpretation results, and the settlement shall be tracked.
4. Analyze and process comprehensive test data. Query, statistics and analysis can be done on the stored test data. The curves and reports can be generated according to the test engineers' requirements.

## 9.3.2 Automatic Test Process

The dynamic execution and management of automatic testing are implemented by integrating all the test resources through the automatic testing process based on the framework of automatic testing. The test process is shown in Fig. 9.1.

The test flow mainly includes five phases:

1. Test cases generation

The module is required to identify the project code, time, test status setting, input parameter interpretation, instruction, output parameter interpretation, the maximum value of expected parameters, the minimum value of expected parameters and other contents;

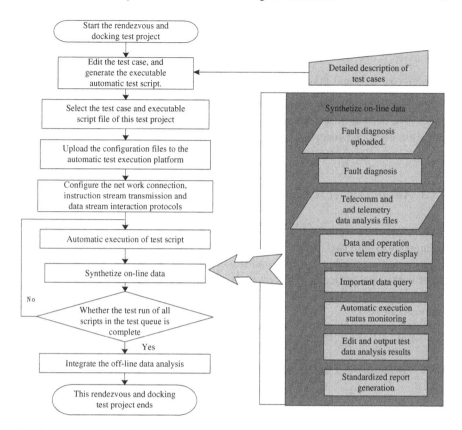

**Fig. 9.1**  Schematic drawing of RVD test flow

2. Automatic execution of control instructions

The test execution process module interprets and executes the script. Based on a certain protocol, when the test script is executed, the corresponding instructions shall be sent to GNC control computer via the dynamics computer, simulation computer and etc. in accordance with time sequencing.

3. Test execution flow management

This phase includes creation, query, configuration and test the process log of the execution flow. The test function items can be decomposed, and test activities shall be arranged in accordance with the test progress. The mapping relations between the function items and the test cases should be established. The configuration of the basic information of projects under test and test process should be maintained.

4. Synthetize test data

Through a distributed framework, the dynamics data, engineering telemetry, high-speed multiplexer data and other data scattered on each piece of test equipment shall be collected on the data server, and then conduct comparison and graphics output analysis of data from different data sources, give the error comparison scope, provide data out-of-tolerance alarm processing.

5. Telemetry data and graphics display

To display the telemetry data through the configuration mode, the software can reflect the current test status by means of various tables, curves, graphics, animation and other forms.

### 9.3.3 Automatic Test Case Management

The tree structure is introduced to organize and manage the test cases, which can be categorized into two types. The nodes in first type represent test collection file folder, which are used to organize and store test cases, and are able to classify and gather the test cases clearly. The rest nodes form test case collection, consisting of multiple contents. Table 9.1 shows the test case and execution script information composition.

### 9.3.4 Automatic Test Flow Management

The automatic test task execution and management module shall complete the integrated dispatching of automatic test process and test task process management,

**Table 9.1** RVD test case and executable script information

| Serial No. | Property | Description |
|---|---|---|
| 1 | Version | Many versions of a test case |
| 2 | Detailed information | Text description of the test case |
| 3 | Test procedures | The specific procedures of the test case include input, output and judgment conditions |
| 4 | Test flow | How the test procedures are conducted, and define the execution process of the test case |
| 5 | Test scrip | Script and script context data, used for completion of initialization, and including the configuration parameters |
| 6 | Appendix | Subsidiary information of the test case, to help the manager have a better understanding |
| 7 | Configuration correlation | Detailed information about which test configurations use the test case |
| 8 | Historical information | History of information addition, deletion and change in the test case |

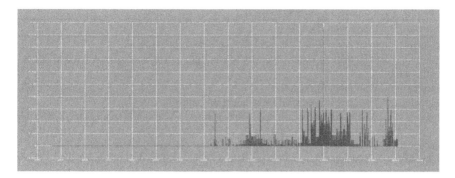

**Fig. 9.2** An off-line variance data analysis in three-machine fault tolerance test (the maximum variance value is about 0.0046)

including: test resource scheduling management engine, test task management engine and automatic test execution engine. The definition of the driving engine shall be described by XML (Extensible Markup Language) language. Each data field shall be marked, and the mark shall interpret the data field. Automatic testing process is implemented by three different engines, test resource scheduling management engine, test task management engine and automatic test execution engine. The test resource scheduling management engine integrates scheduling of various hardware and software and various interface resources of the test platform. The test task management engine schedules of mutual relations and sequencing of test tasks. The automatic test execution engine executes of test cases in the task queue dynamically. The execution coordinates with the test resource management and test task management.

### 9.3.5 Automatic Test Data Analysis

Data analysis is an important part of the test session, can includes on-line analysis and off-line analysis. The on-line analysis monitors the values of some important data variables by setting the fault alarm and threshold value. When the scope of normal value is exceeded, the alarm prompt shall be given.

The off-line data analysis is performed after the experimental test ending. It aims to satisfy some specific requirements. For example: for data analysis of three-machine fault tolerance, see Fig. 9.2.

### 9.3.6 Defect Management in ATS

The defect process management should define different roles and their behaviors in the process. Based on the knowledge processing, the data judgment and fault diagnosis of automatic test system is applied on several spacecraft software under

**Table 9.2** Fault processing judgment way

| Attribute | Description | Details |
|---|---|---|
| Summary | | Brief description of defects, not more than 100 characters |
| Task allocation | | Who shall be responsible for resolving this defect. Can be transferred to others |
| Detected | | Who submits the defect |
| Test date | | The current time shall be automatically filled in |
| Project | | Which project does the defect belong to, can be customized, and configured by the system administrator |
| Functional module | | Which functional module does the defect belong to, can be customized, configured in accordance with the functional module of the project |
| Priority level | Low | Does not affect the test progress |
| | Medium | Can temporarily bypass this defect and continue test |
| | High | Must be resolved as soon as possible. Otherwise, it will cause that the test of some primary services cannot be continued |
| | Emergency | Must be resolved immediately. Otherwise it is impossible to conduct test |
| Severity | Low | Wrongly written characters, unpleasing and other problems |
| | Medium | Some functions cannot be properly realized, but the overall function is not affected |
| | High | Basic and important functions cannot be properly realized, affecting the test progress |
| | Emergency | System crash, system halt, cannot be restored |
| Current state | New | Newly discovered defects, yet to be resolved |
| | Open | Recognized defects, being resolved |
| | Fixed | Fix and submit procedures, untested |
| | Passed | Confirm passed |
| | Refused | This is not a defect, misreport |
| Description | | Detailed description of the defect, including defect procedures, etc. |
| Remarks | | Description of defect resolution process, revised content, etc. |
| Settling time | Settled time | |

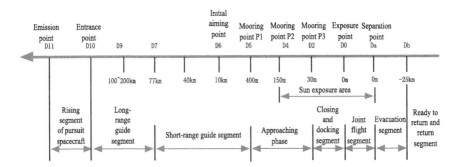

**Fig. 9.3** Schematic drawing of flight phase division of RVD

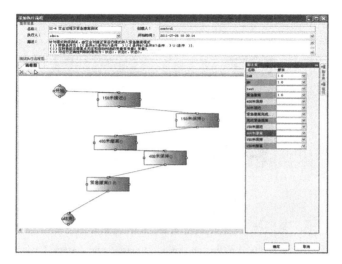

**Fig. 9.4** Automatic test data flow execution flow

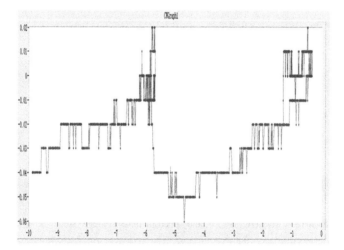

**Fig. 9.5** *Plane curve* of relative position and speed of mass center system Y axis

test synthesizing aerospace software expert system and artificial intelligence techniques. Then data judgment and fault diagnosis can be independent with the test process, which ensures the portability, reusability and sharing of test data diagnostic knowledge. Based on the knowledge processing, the data judgment and fault diagnosis of automatic test system is applied on several spacecraft software under test synthesizing aerospace software expert system and artificial intelligence techniques. Then data judgment and fault diagnosis can be independent with the test process, which ensures the portability, reusability and sharing of test data

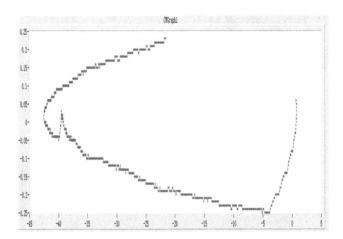

**Fig. 9.6** *Plane curve* of relative position and speed of mass center system Z axis

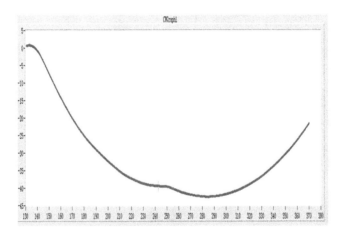

**Fig. 9.7** *Plane curve* of relative position and speed of mass center system XZ

diagnostic knowledge. Thus, open comprehensive diagnostic information architecture can be built. Table 9.2 shows the measuring method of automatic test defect management.

## 9.4 Experimental Results of ATS

Mode conversion is taken as an example to analyze the test content of RVD software on GNC. The test script of automatic test mode conversion shall include (1) judgment of conversion conditions, (2) data flow execution order, (3) monitoring the change of values of important data before and after conversion, (4) automatic judgment of operation correctness before and after conversion, (5) abnormal data and information about alarms on faults.

Figure 9.3 shows the RVD process [10]. Automatic test of emergency evacuation mode conversion, data flow and automatic test dynamic execution monitoring are shown in Fig. 9.4. Under 400 m emergency evacuation retreat mode, plane curve of relative position and speed of mass center system is shown in Figs. 9.5, 9.6 and 9.7.

## 9.5 Conclusions

With the rapid development of aerospace space RVD mission, the automatic testing technique is eagerly required to improve the spacecraft software development efficiency and maintainability.

Base on comprehensive investigation of the spacecraft GNC software characteristics and the test process, we proposed and implemented an automatic GNC software testing approach.

During the test preparation phase, we generalize and summarize the common model, arrange the common test case library. The test case scripts stored in the test case library can be identified by the computer test environment. Therefore, these scripts can be executed without modification or with very few adapted modifications.

During the test execution phase, the automatic test execution engine executes test cases dynamically in the task queue with the coordination between the test resource management and test task management, so as to realize the automatic test process.

During the test data analysis and evaluation phase, the test data generated during the whole test process is stored in the database, which uniforms the test data management and eases the test data analysis. The test data stored in database can be used by several test processes of different spacecraft, which make it easy to share test data between different projects to improve the test efficiency.

The automatic test method and technology introduced in this chapter have played an important role in the specific aerospace software development, which has improved the operating efficiency of the RVD software dramatically. The automatic testing methodology can decrease the randomness caused by long-term manual operation in the testing, so as to solve the problem of poor operational consistency. This automatic methodology can also effectively improve the operation consistency and accuracy during regression testing, which is of great significance to improve the RVD testing capabilities. In addition, as the work is further carried out, we will meet some new problems in the automatic test, which promotes us to conduct further study.

# References

1. Sommerville I (2007) Software engineering, 8th edn. Machinery Industry Press, Beijing, pp 43–44 (photocopy edition)
2. Coauthor of Software Expert Group of China Aerospace Science and Technology Group (2006) Guidelines and specifications for aerospace software engineering technology. March 2006, pp 427–428 (in Chinese)
3. Terry R, Mitchell A (1973) Standard test language-GOAL. The workshop on design automation, New York, Association for computing machinery, 25–27 June, pp 87–96
4. Harrison M, Mclennan M (1998) Effective Tcl/Tk programming. Readings, MA, Addison-Wesley, England
5. IEEE 716-95 (1998) ATLAS 2000 signal and method classification and modeling
6. IEEE Std 1671 (2008) IEEE trial-use standard for automatic test markup language(ATML)for exchanging automatic test equipment and test information via XML. IEEEE standards coordinating committee 20 on test and diagnosis for electric systems
7. Ma S, Yu D (2011) Language and system of spacecraft automatic test. National Defence Industry Press, Beijing, February 2011, pp 10–11 (in Chinese)
8. Jiang T, Yuanwen C, Xiaochen X (2011) Application of next-generation automatic test system in China's aerospace test architecture. Space Control 29(2) (in Chinese)
9. Patton R (2008) Software testing. 2nd edn. Machinery Industry Press, Beijing, March 2008 pp 250–251 (photocopy edition)
10. Zhang S, Wang Z, Ran L et al (2005) Space rendezvous and docking measurement techniques and engineering applications. China Astronautic Publishing House, Beijing, pp 3–5 (in Chinese)

# Chapter 10
# Design and Implementation of Material Supply System Based on B/S and C/S Mixed Mode

**Taiping Mo, Meng Wang, Kefeng Fan and Dan Wang**

**Abstract** In order to improve and optimize the management mode of enterprise production logistics, combined with JIT lean logistics management ideology, the paper established a new logistics distribution mode that when the materials is insufficient, driving materials distribution by sending material requirement instructions directly. Using .NET technical it designs and achieves a Pull-based material supply system which is based on B/S and C/S mixed mode, and the system's modeling, functions as well as the key technologies were described in detail. The system has been put into practice in one assembling industry.

**Keywords** Materials supply system · Production logistics · E-Kanban · JIT

## 10.1 Introduction

In order to cater the flexible and changing morden manufacturing mode, more and more enterprises adopt the Mixed-model assembly line, especially some assembly manufacturing companies [1]. However, this Mixed-model assembly line will inevitably lead logistic of the product line to become complicated and varied. Thus, in order to ensure the running smoothly of the high-speed assembly line, we must adopt one or more of the reasonable material delivery way to achieve the material distribution at the right time, reduce the backlog of materials in the material buffer zone, facilitate the workers' jobs and reduce the dead time of

T. Mo (✉) · M. Wang · K. Fan · D. Wang
School of Electronic Engineering and Automation, Guilin University of Electronic Technology, 541004 Guilin, Guangxi, China
e-mail: wm_zsh@163.com

W. Lu et al. (eds.), *Proceedings of the 2012 International Conference on Information Technology and Software Engineering*, Lecture Notes in Electrical Engineering 212, DOI: 10.1007/978-3-642-34531-9_10, © Springer-Verlag Berlin Heidelberg 2013

the materials in the production process. In the manufacturing shop creating a smooth, agile, low-cost logistics environment to meet the needs of the enterprise flexible manufacturing.

Based on the standardized process, hours of operation, BOM of product, manufacturing enterprises usually create materials delivery plan according to the production plan, and then the logistics management department delivery materials to the material buffer zone in time according to the logistics plan, delivery time, demand quantity, demand station etc. However, sometimes delivery delays due to emergencies reasons would result in material shortages in the material buffer zone and even stopping. In response to these issues, using the just-in-time (JIT) theory of Lean-production methods to analyse the production management process, proposing a new Pull-based materials supply mode to realize the materials in a timely manner supplement. As one kind of the materials distribution modes, it virtually eliminated materials shortage in the materials buffer zone caused by some uncertainties and improved the efficiency of the production of the staff. At the same time, it complied the transmission and monitoring of the production control information and logistics information, ensuring the timely delivery and high service level.

## 10.2 Pull-Based Materials Supply System

Pull-based material supply system: the distribution of materials to be driven by Sending request command of materials through the request materials equipment on the workstation. The Pull-based material supply system usually applies to the materials by package supplying (standard packaging), such as workstations of automobile assembly line. According to the materials consumption sending materials requirements information and then completing materials supply [2].

The entire business process system are as follows: when a material shortage that used by one workstation, the workers on the assembly line operate the request material device to send a single of material requirements, then the information processing side deal it. In accordance with the materials FIFO ingredients rules and the most optimal feeding route to generate the list of ingredient and feeding. In the warehouse, the workers obtain the list of ingredients and based on the list pick material out of the library, meanwhile the system send the response signal for the material which has been distributed, the workers based on the list of feeding send the material to the assembly line buffer area. After material distribution, assembly line workers once again handle the request to material device, to feedback the confirmation message that the material has been distributed. At this point, entire material supply process end.

At the same time, borrow the Kanban management concepts of JIT, the system introduce the E-Kanban as an information transfer medium. In the warehouse, comprehensive monitoring completing materials supply process and through the intuitive and image billboard display request, emergency request, ingredients,

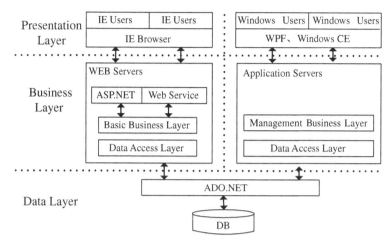

**Fig. 10.1** System architecture design

distribution, delivery confirmation etc. Staging real-time materials information to help materials management staff supervise and control of material warehouse, complying real-time inventory precise control and production of materials timely supply [3].

## 10.3  The Design of Pull-Based Materials Supply System

### 10.3.1  System Architecture Design

Layered model to design the system is divided into presentation layer, business layer and data layer. Presentation layer mainly used to interact with the users. Business layer is responsible for application processing tasks, including dealing the request of presentation layer, connecting and interacting with the database server. Data layer in ADO.NET for interface, mainly handle business layer for the data request. The purpose of this design is for a finer division, to achieve code optimization and reuse. The system uses B/S and C/S mixed mode to system building. It not only plays mature technology of traditional C/S mode and avoids the creation of high price of 3-tier C/S mode, but also gives full play to B/S mode advantages with the Internet technology [4]. Application software architecture is shown in Fig. 10.1. The layers' function and design are as follows:

Presentation layer: as user interface part, it is responsible for the dialogue of the user and the system. It is mainly used for user input and results output. This passage used the Web browser and the client programmer as a user interface.

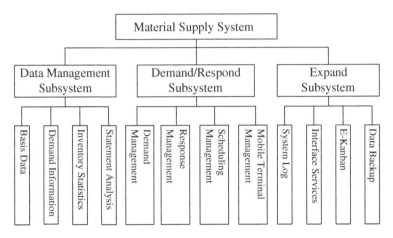

**Fig. 10.2** System function structure chart

Business layer: including business functions and data capabilities, data functions using the data access layer components to interact with data layer. Data access layer use limited data set as model, achieving the operation of data source and creating a method component called a stored procedure. Abstracting the underlying data manipulation, shielding the details of the operation completely, providing unified user interface, so programmers do not need to care about the details of the underlying database.

Data layers: storage of system tables, views, stored procedures, triggers and other database objects to provide data storage.

## 10.3.2 System Features Modular Design

According to the system process and functional requirements of the Pull-based material supply system, the system consists of three functional subsystems. System function structure is shown in Fig. 10.2 shows, each functional subsystem functions are as follows:

### 10.3.2.1 Data Management Subsystem

The system used for data management and maintenance. The basis data module mainly manage and maintain the information of processes, materials, suppliers, user rights, workers request materials and emergency request time. The demand information module mainly manages batching rules, feeding route, task priority and arbitration rules. The inventory statistics module according to the system records data on the assembly line, the amount of materials in real-time statistics in the stock, goods in transit, material buffer area etc., it used as the data source of E-Kanban and the base of storage report. Statement Analysis module is the main statistical analysis of the efficiency of distribution and resource utilization, providing advice from analysis result about buffer stock settings, batching rules, task priority, arbitration rules and resource allocation decisions.

### 10.3.2.2 Demand/Respond Subsystem

The system is responsible for all materials demand and response management. The demand management module mainly realize the display of materials information, demand signal sending, distribution of information receives and display, delivery confirmation information sending. The response management module mainly handles the material requests information, in accordance with the materials FIFO ingredients rules generate the list of ingredients from the large and disorder requests information. Scheduling Management module in accordance with the distribution rules of the system settings as far as possible to optimize the distribution path and increase resource utilization. The mobile terminal management module can be divided into handheld and vehicle-mounted. Handheld terminal used for acquiring and displaying the list of ingredients, sending batching signal. The way to get information can be summarized in two: type-responder and assignment. The responder type means the operator can independently acquire the list. The system arbitration rules determine the ownership when people acquiring the same list at the same time. Assigned type is dominated by the system to obtain the objection, the operator has no right to interfere. Vehicle-mounted terminal acquire feeding information, including vehicle information, the feed line and the destination.

### 10.3.2.3 Expand Subsystem

The system logs module will obtain a copy of the demand/respond operation records, materials delivery and receive records in order to prepare for post-record queries and data analysis. Interface services module is responsible for other systems to exchange data and basic data import, such as the MES system to provide relevant information, thus improving the compatibility of the system. Data Backup module is mainly used for regular backups of system data. E-Kanban module combines computer technology and information processing technology and wireless communication technology with fast response, information sharing, convenient exchange features. It can display real-time state information in the various stages through the whole system operating procedure, and workstation information. The actual production process of material distribution management has good practical value [5]. According to one whole demand/respond operating procedure corresponding database records the update of the status information, the status information changes accordingly on E-Kanban.

## 10.4 The System Implementation Strategy and Major Technical

The system will be obtained via the corporate LAN to connect the assembly line Tablet PC, WEB server, application server, database server clusters, On-board Tablet PC, handheld PDA and storehouse E-Kanban etc. Overall system structure is shown in Fig. 10.3:

In this paper, we use the ASP.NET technology, WPF, three-tier architecture to build the system. It has good overall modularity, high integration, application portability and software reusability advantages. Moreover, the application database management system, business logic and presentation logic, data access and business logic is separate, distributed data management and transaction process, all these ensure the system to be efficient, safe and stable operation [6].

### 10.4.1  WPF Technology

The "Demand End" of system using WPF technology to design the interface aims in building a reasonable, expanding easily, friendly system interface. "Demand End" program interface as shown in Fig. 10.4:

Windows Presentation Foundation (WPF) is a Rich Internet Application (RIA) rich client development technique [7]. The system selected WPF client development techniques, not only meet the high demand of frequent interaction between

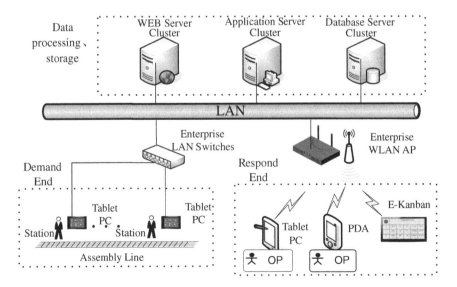

**Fig. 10.3** Overall system structure

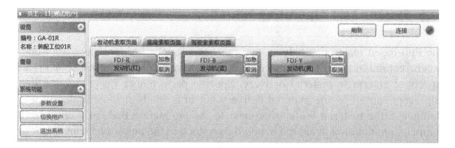

**Fig. 10.4** "Demand End" program interface

user and system, but also meet the needs of future system upgrades and expansions. The system can be easily and seamlessly transplanted to the browser-based application, realize rich internet applications, i.e. RIA applications. RIA is a Web application that combines desktop application and traditional Web application. Using WPF technology and connecting with the server-side Web Service technology closely to improve client experience and enhance the system performance goals.

## 10.4.2 WLAN Technology

Based on comprehensively analyses the disadvantages of the material delivery business processes, such as inflexible of delivery, inefficient of delivery, high probability of transport no-load, the paper presents the specific implementation of the "Demand End" [8]. The system integrate Wireless management philosophy, carry on organic merger to the material delivery business processes, and get the real-time task by wireless equipment (Car Tablet PC, handheld PDA, E-Kanban) on corporate WLAN so that the "Demand End" gets a timely response, avoiding cumbersome document operations, and improve the efficiency of delivery of the material. WLAN as the current rapidly developing emerging information technology, the biggest difference with the ordinary LAN is that it does not use the cables for network wiring and moving communication. It is particularly suitable for the flexible delivery condition and complex manufacturing environment. The practice applying the WLAN technology to the system's material delivery module give full play to the advantages of a WLAN, the support for seamlessly combining wireless solutions and material supply system enables an efficient material delivery strategy.

## 10.5 System Test Operating Situation

The Pull-based material supply system have been applied to a car assembly line, system commissioning preliminary results show a marked improvement of all aspects of enterprise material delivery. Specific performance in: production line stop event caused by the material delivery not in a timely manner basically was eliminated; the material buffer zone next to the production line get a reasonable optimization, not only avoid the material overstock in the buffer and convenient to workers to understand the available material number at any time, avoid production line stop caused by material shortage; materials storage report error is reduced accordingly; the application of the E-Kanban enable the request information to be real-time feedback to batching member, ensure timely access to information, eliminate the response not timely due to human factors.

However, due to the complexity of the production, there are still some problems to be studied and resolved. Firstly, because of the positional uncertainty of material requirement station, further research and analysis is needed to do such as how determine a reasonable delivery path. Secondly, the interaction with the data between material supply system and ERP systems still require human intervention. In addition, how the material supply system's data used in inventory management is the future research directions.

Of course, the enterprise informatization as a huge project, moreover, enterprise material supply system itself is an evolving subject. So it is impossible in a short time to get completely perfect and applying. The implement of the system will be a gradual improvement process.

## 10.6 Conclusion

With information technology rapidly developing, market competition becomes more and more severity. Business logistics management information will be an inevitable road. The Pull-based material supply system is an attempt to combine advanced enterprise management methods and enterprise informatization. The system can resolve many practical problems in production, and provide a Lean logistics distribution mode for the enterprise. Of course, the role of the system is far more than these. With the further optimization of logistics management, a tentative plan to integrate some local suppliers into the system's coverage is put forward. This could send materials request information directly to the supplier and further improve the efficiency of delivery and reduce inventory. As the further application of the system, it will bring more advantages and greatly raise the enterprise logistics management to a new level.

# References

1. Cao Z, Zhu Y (2006) Research on material feeding and its implementation in general assembly line of mixed model automobile. Comput Integr Manuf Syst 12(2):285–291 (in Chinese)
2. Choi W, Lee Y (2002) A dynamic part-feeding system for an automotive assembly line. Comput Ind Eng 43(5):123–134
3. Matta A, Dallery Y, Dimascolo M (2005) Analysis of assembly systems controlled with kanbans. Eur J Oper Res 166(2):310–336
4. Yingsong H, Peng L (2003) Design technology of three-tier architecture on web application based on .NET. Comput Eng 29(8):173–175 (in Chinese)
5. Xuan F, Xiong S, Jiang ZH (2009) Application of E-Kanban in enterprise's logistics management. Logistics Eng Manage 31(10):58–60 (in Chinese)
6. Robinson S, Nagel C (2005) C# Advanced Programming. Tsinghua University Press, Beijing
7. Wang S (2008) Depth analysis WPF programming. Publishing House of Electronics Industry, Beijing
8. Di X, Huang P (2007) Design of material supply system for manufacturing industry based on wireless network. Appl Res Comput 24(12):223–225 (in Chinese)

# Chapter 11
# A Power System Distributed Computing Model Based on SOA

**Ruifeng Zhao, Wei Yan, Jinge Zhang and Fang He**

**Abstract** Aiming at the problem of architectural inflexibility, high maintenance and integration costs of power system distributed computing model based on inter-process communication (PSDCM), a power system distributed computing model based on SOA (PSDCMSOA) is proposed. The characteristic of hierarchical multi-level management and multi-region control pattern and computing node model of power system computing system are analyzed, Ward equivalence method is studied to get equivalence grid of the adjacent power grid, data service is designed to achieve the integration of distributed heterogeneous data, remote communication service is researched to complete data exchange between local node, and then realized the PSDCMSOA. Simulation experiments show that PSDCMSOA can satisfy the requirement of simulating computing of power system effectively.

**Keywords** Power system · Distributed computing · Ward equivalence · Software model · SOA · Data service

R. Zhao (✉) · W. Yan
State Key Laboratory of Power Transmission Equipment and System Security and New Technology, Chongqing University, 400030 Chongqing, China
e-mail: ruifzhao@gmail.com

J. Zhang
School of Software Engineering, Chongqing University, Chongqing, China

F. He
Ziyang Company of Sichuan Electric Power Company, 641300 Ziyang, China

W. Lu et al. (eds.), *Proceedings of the 2012 International Conference on Information Technology and Software Engineering*, Lecture Notes in Electrical Engineering 212, DOI: 10.1007/978-3-642-34531-9_11, © Springer-Verlag Berlin Heidelberg 2013

## 11.1 Introduction

Power grid is one of the fundamental facilities in the modern society, it is important to establish a dependable, stable electrical computation and control system to ensure its security, steady and economic operation. According to the pattern of hierarchical multi-level management and multi-region control, the whole gird is divided into several sub-grids, and each sub-grid holds and maintains its data which is kept secret for other sub-grids except its super control center. Therefore, a contradiction is occurred between the grid management pattern and the use of its data. The traditional simulating computation method which transfers grid's data to a center and computing is not used any more. So distributed computing is an inevitable measure to solve the all-in-one simulation problem for the interconnected power system.

At present, the distributed computing in power industry has not been widely used, most of works in this area are theoretical and algorithm studies [1–3]. Our research team made a detailed analysis from the perspective of software design, abstracted power systems distributed computing node and analyzed the node's behaviors, firstly proposed and developed power system distributed computing model based on inter-process communication (PSDCM) [4]. With the deepening of the application, our research team found that some public infrastructure functions of PSDCM are too complexity, and the maintenance cost is too high.

Service-oriented architecture (SOA) is a set of principles and methodologies for designing and developing software in the form of interoperable services [5]. SOA can promote reuse at the macro (service) level rather than micro (classes) level. It can also simplify interconnection to–and usage of–existing IT (legacy) assets. So, some improvements are made combined with SOA to avoid the problem mentioned in the PSDCM, a power system distributed computing model based on SOA (PSDCMSOA) is proposed to solve the all-in-one simulating computation.

## 11.2 Background Knowledge and Related Work

### 11.2.1 Operation and Management Mechanism of China Power Gird

According to the operation and management mechanism, China power grid is divided into several levels and each level may contains several sub-grids, each sub-grid has a control center to monitor and control its operation. The topology of hierarchical multi-level and multi-region control is shown in Fig. 11.1. In the light of the hierarchy and the role of sub-grid, the power grid is divided into transmission grid, distribution grid, accessing grid and so on, each grid has its own control center.

Under this operation and management mechanism, when a certain level of the grid begins to simulating computation, the total computation tasks should be

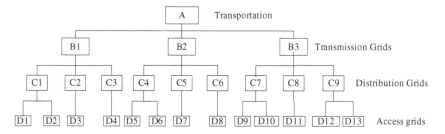

**Fig. 11.1** The topology of hierarchical multi-level and multi-region control

decomposed to its sub-grids due to the data which computation deeded is widely dispersed in each sub-grid, then each sub-grid compute respectively, after all the computation are completed, the results of each sub-region are sent to the superior control center.

## 11.2.2 Computing Node Behavioural Model Abstraction

Combined with the characteristic of China grid, a computing node is abstracted for power system distributed computing which is describe the behavior of each sub-grid in the distributed computing. The computing node model and its behaviors are shown in Fig. 11.2. Several basic behaviors the computing node are simply represented here. The computing node should have an ability to obtain the local and remote computing data, at the same time equivalence data of the adjacent sub-grid should be calculated. Other behaviors are obtainment and respondence of the remote node's data request, communication with the remote node to establish a common computational logic and so on.

**Fig. 11.2** Computing node model

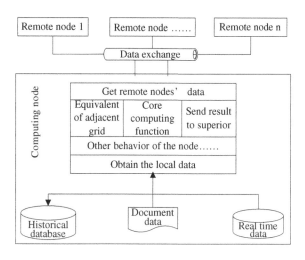

## 11.3 Model of Power System Distributed Computing and Design

### 11.3.1 Architecture of Power System Distributed Computing

According to the analysis of the computing node's behavior, PSDCMSOA mainly composed of five modules: control center (User interface), equivalence of the external grid, data service, remote communication between the different computing nodes and computing function. The architecture of power system distributed computing is given in Fig. 11.3. The various computing functions of power system which are encapsulated in computing service are the key factors of the distributed computing system, control center and remote communication are the infrastructure, the computing data is provided by data service.

### 11.3.2 Equivalence of the External Grid

The data of power system distributed computing are scattered in different sub-grids, and they are kept secret for other sub-girds. Although the power grids are interconnected, the communication networks are not interconnected by different control center of the sub-grid. When a certain sub-grid begins to local computing, the computing data not only need the local's but need its adjacent power grid's data. So this is a significant contradiction.

In order to solve this contradiction Ward Equivalent [6] is employed to achieve data acquisition. The principle of Ward Equivalent is transforming the complex information of external power grids into the equivalent power injection and equivalent impedance of the boundary bus.

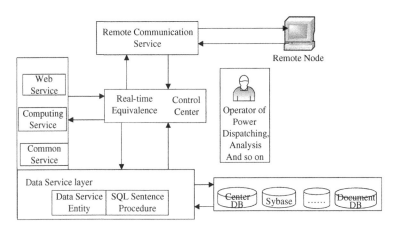

**Fig. 11.3** Architecture of power system distributed computing

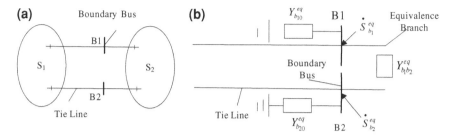

**Fig. 11.4** Ward equivalent model of the two areas power system

### 11.3.2.1 Equivalent of Two Power Grid

The bus is divided into three types, namely, internal system bus set, boundary bus set, external systems bus set, corresponding to a subset of {I}, a subset of {B}, and a subset of {E}. Assuming that the power grid only has two sub-grids system which is shown in Fig. 11.4a, $S_1$ is a bus set of one sub-grid, B = {B1, B2} is the boundary bus set and $S_2$ is a bus set of the other sub-grid. $S_1$ and $S_2$ are external systems for each other.

In light of Ward Equivalent method, the external grid of $S_1$ is equivalent to injection power, branch admittance and ground admittance of the of the boundary buses. The Ward equivalent model of the two areas power system is shown in Fig. 11.4b. Injection power and branch admittance can be obtained by Ward Equivalent as follows.

$$\dot{S}_B^{eq} = -(diag\,[\hat{V}_B])\,Y_{BE}\,Y_{EE}^{-1}\left(\hat{S}_E\big/\hat{V}_E\right) \tag{11.1}$$

$$Y_{BB}^{eq} = -[Y_{BE}]\,[Y_{EE}^{-1}]\,[Y_{EB}] \tag{11.2}$$

### 11.3.2.2 Equivalent of Multi-area Interconnected Power Grid

In the multi-area interconnected power grid, the primary power sub-grid and subordinated sub-grids should be divided from the whole power system for the purpose of equivalent of the power grid. Firstly, the primary sub-grid is determined by the method of master slave relation division, and then merges the equivalent grid of the subordinated grids. The detailed derivation process of equivalent and the graphic description of the multi-grid equivalence are not expressed here. The injection power and branch admittance are given as Formulas (11.3) and (11.4).

$$\dot{S}_{B_3}^{eq} = \dot{S}_{B_3}^{'\,eq} + \dot{S}_{B_3}^{''\,eq} \tag{11.3}$$

$$Y_{b30}^{eq} = Y_{b30}^{'\,eq} + Y_{b30}^{''\,eq} \tag{11.4}$$

## 11.3.3 Data Service

The view of the data service originated from take data as a service for the user, it provides a simple and rapid data access approach [7]. It can integrate various heterogeneous underlying data, including use of SQL statements to query data, data can't obtain by the query statement and some web service data [8]. In each computing node, namely, control center of the dispatching center, the data which is for power system calculation is often obtained from historical database, CIM files, and state data is from real-time data base. Each data base of the computing node may be different, even though the data base is same, its data structure maybe different.

The data services platform is build by Microsoft ADO.NET, in this platform the data service is developed by data entity model, the advantage of this method is that it can access various data source, that is suitable for the requirement of the power system distributed computing. This article is based on the ADO.NET Data Service, using Web services as the access interface to achieve standard data service. The data service provides the data mapping and data parse of the data source, so the difference between data base and non-data base structure can be neglected. All the functions are encapsulated in the data service layer which can provide all the details of data to other applications, this mechanism will be favor of SOA-based solution.

## 11.3.4 Remote Communication Service

The data exchange between local node and remote node and data detection function are encapsulated in the remote communication module which is responsible for monitoring the remote node data exchange request and maintaining the service information of the remote node. In order to meet the different services and ensure the safety and reliability of messaging transfer, factory method pattern is used to build a communications platform structure, multi-thread management strategy, system automatically detect and re-connection strategy, object serialization strategy are used to implement specific communication services.

## 11.3.5 Other Function of the PSDCMSOA

Except some functions and modules mentioned above, there are several other important functions, such as power core calculating service, graph management, control center and so on. Power flow (PF) and state estimation (SE), extended line stability index (ELSI) and so on are encapsulated in the power core calculating service. Control center module is one of the most important functions in power system distributed model which is responsible for scheduling the distributed tasks and providing the user interface. Graph management module shows the wiring diagram of the grid, refreshes the computing result in real-time, and provides an alarm function.

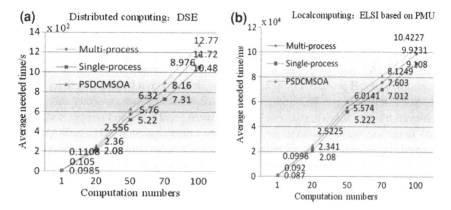

**Fig. 11.5** Comparison of average total time in three software architectures. **a** Test in distributed computing, **b** test in local computing

## 11.4 Experiment Test and Effect Analysis

In order to test whether the computational efficiency of PSDCMSOA can satisfy the actual requirements of practical application, two prototype systems were built based on PSDCMSOA, namely, distributed computing environment and local computing in a signal computer. 24 h run-time data of the PSDCM in dispatch center of Chongqing, Nanan district power supply bureau, Yangjiaping power supply bureau and Sichuan Anyue transformer substation were collected for experiment.

The actual running environment is simulated by the means of the real data, and six experiments about the computational efficiency in different software, different mode of calculation in a simulation environment were done and comparative analysis is expressed as bellow. In the distributed computing pattern, the distributed state estimation (DSE) was used to test in the prototype system based on a single process, PSDCM and PSDCMSOA, and in the local computing ELSI based on PMU was adopted in the different software model which mentioned above. The running time of the same kind of computing in three software architectures under the circumstance that continued computing 100 times without restarting were calculated (does not take into account the idle time of each computing).

After completing 100 computing, in distributed computing environment the accumulated time differences between a single process and PSDCMSOA is 22.9 s, differences between a multi-process and PSDCMSOA is 10.5 s, and in local computing the accumulated time differences 13.147, 4.966 s respectively. The detailed comparison is shown in Fig. 11.5. It clearly can be inferred that the efficiency of proposed the PSDCM can satisfy the application requirements of the power system.

## 11.5 Conclusions

Based on the PSDCM a power system distributed computing model based on SOA (PSDCMSOA) was proposed in this paper. The implementation method and technology of DB process, computing process, and so on in PSDCM were replaced by SOA technology. The integration of distributed heterogeneous data was achieved by data service, data exchange between local node and remote node and data detection was completed by the remote communication service. SOA was adopted in power system distributed computing can reduce the development complexity of PSDCM, enhance architectural flexibility, realize the low coupling, low maintenance and integration costs. The computational efficiency can meet the requirement of power system distributed computing according to the experiment test.

**Acknowledgments** This work is supported by the National Natural Science Foundation of China (Project No. 51177178), the Scientific Research Foundation of the State Key Laboratory of Power Transmission Equipment and System Security and New Technology in China (Project No. 2007DA10512710201) and Doctoral Fund of Ministry of Education of China (Project No. 20090191120019).

## References

1. Liang J, Wang Z, Liu X (2011) Distributed state estimation for discrete-time sensor networks with randomly varying nonlinearities and missing measurements. IEEE Trans Neural Networks 22(3):486–496
2. Korres GN (2011) A distributed multiarea state estimation. IEEE Trans Power Syst 26(1):73–84
3. Contreras J, Losi A, Russo M, Wu FF (2002) Simulation of evaluation of optimization problem solutions in distributed energy management systems. IEEE Trans Power Syst 17(1):57–62
4. Wen J, Luo F, Yan W et al (2009) Electrical distributed computing model based on process communication. Comput Eng Appl 45(1):213–216 (in Chinese)
5. Newcomer E, Lomow G (2005) Understanding SOA with web services, Addison Wesley
6. Wen J, Zhao R, Yan W (2009) Application research on electrical distributed computing bus oriented SOA. Appli Electron Tech 35(10):145–149 (in Chinese)
7. Carey M, Revelistis P, Thatte S et al (2008) Data Service modeling in the aqualogic data services platform. IEEE Congress on Services 2008: part I, Honolulu, Hawaii, USA, 2008:78–80
8. Liu D, Zeng Y, Li G et al (2007) A general model of data service in spatial information grid. IEEE international geoscience and remote sensing symposium, Barcelona, Spain, 2007:1370–1373

# Chapter 12
# Measurability: A Key Problem for Test Systems

**Jing Wang, Qi Zhang and Wei Jiang**

**Abstract** According to the requirement of metrology support of test systems, the concept of measurability, which is a key problem, is firstly put forward by us. The connotation of measurability is explained, and its indexes, which include the quantitative and qualitative aspects, are presented. The relations of measurability and RMS (reliability, maintainability, supportability, testability and security) are analysed. The key problems of measurability are proposed, which include metrology interface, metrology items, modle of design and evaluation, and lengthening of calibration interval.

**Keywords** Measurability · Indexes · RMS Calibration

## 12.1 Introduction

Measurability is a new concept which is put forward to solve the problems of our military equipments and metrology work, and the research to this theory is presently at an early stage. There are little references [1, 2] about measurability of equipment, and people have not reach a consensus about the definition, connotation, indexes and key problems. Aiming at pointing out the research direction for the metrology workers, we proposed some original research about the theory of measurability.

J. Wang (✉) · Q. Zhang · W. Jiang
Mechatronics and Automation School, National University of Defense Technology, 410073
Changsha, China
e-mail: ruohanzi2010@163.com

W. Lu et al. (eds.), *Proceedings of the 2012 International Conference on Information Technology and Software Engineering*, Lecture Notes in Electrical Engineering 212, DOI: 10.1007/978-3-642-34531-9_12, © Springer-Verlag Berlin Heidelberg 2013

## 12.2 The Concept of Measurability

The parameters which affect the function or performance of test systems should be measured or calibrated to ensure the ability of mission implementation. At present, many works have been done about the metrology support of test systems, such as the development of metrology support vehicle, automation of metrology and test system, improvement of metrology approach and so on [3–5]. However, because most of the test systems are not supervised by metrology personal, they are lack of metrology interfaces, and have to be disassembled before calibration. In tackling these questions, we put forward the concept of measurability of test systems.

Measurability is the ability to be measured (calibrated) and conveniently measured (calibrated) which could be further considered as the characteristics to transfer the value truly and well [6, 7]. Measurability is a design characteristic running through the life cycle of equipment which is explained as follows:

At the stage of demonstration, the design indexes of measurability should be explicit and primary designed by metrology personnel according to the RMS of test systems. Science metrology is a legal and compulsory activity, the metrology department should participate in the model selection of measure and instruments of metrology support. At the stage of projection, a model should be established to evaluate the measurability from two aspects (quantitative and quantitative). Furthermore, the feasibility of measurability should be validated and the improvement approaches should be introduced. At the stage of production, the measurability should be transferred to the self–characteristic of the equipment. The interfaces, types of signals and using of values should be universal and standard designed. At the stage of employ, the measurability indexes can be analyzed by the evaluation model. The obtained data can guide the subsequent metrology work for the convenience of recordance and management.

## 12.3 Relations Between Measurability and RMS of Test Systems

Measurability is relevant to RMS for the reasons that they impenetrate each other and reflect the characteristics of test systems. There relations are shown in Fig. 12.1. The real line represents the whole life cycle of a test system, and the dash lines refer to the relations between measurability and RMS.

Firstly, the reliability affects the measurability. There will be more time before fault for systems with high reliability, which lowers the demands of measurability. On the other hand, metrology and calibration can be the methods to evaluate the reliability [8, 9]. If some parameters are out of tolerances when being calibrated, it will be probable that the equipment is not normal and some faults should be detected and isolated.

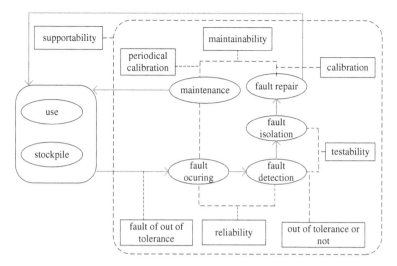

**Fig. 12.1** Relations between measurability and RMS

Secondly, measurability is the important technology sustainments and references of maintainability. The department of different levels can establish the maintenance plan on the basis of calibration data and metrology characteristics. If the equipment is lack of measurability, the accuracy of its parameters will not be assured, and the object of maintenance will be dubious. Therefore, if the equipment is short of maintainability, the metrology can't assure the good technique state. As a summary, the measurability is the base of maintainability.

Thirdly, metrology is a special form of measure (or test), and the metrology is accordance with measure (or test) in the same token. Good testability means that the test system is in a normal state. Besides, good measurability requires that the instruments of the system should be accuracy. That is to say the test systems with high testability may be lack of measurability, and the inverse is not right. Therefore, the early design of measurability and testability can't be ignored by each other.

Fourthly, supportability is the ability that the design characteristic and support resource can satisfy the request of support. At the using stage, it reflects the extent of difficult to ensure the normal running of the equipment. The metrology supportability is one of the supportabilities. So we can say that good measurability is a forceful support for supportability.

## 12.4  Measurability Indexes

In order to analyze the measurability, we put forward some indexes include qualitative and quantitative ones as follows (Fig. 12.2):

The qualitative indexes include:

**Fig. 12.2** Measurability
indexes

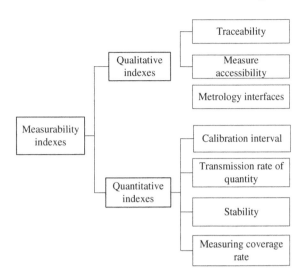

*Traceability*: refers to an unbroken chain of comparisons relating an instrument's measurements to a known standard (library, state or international standard). Traceability is the base of verification and calibration. We should take into account that the self-calibration can't replace the external calibration because of the lack of traceability.

*Measure accessibility*: reflects the level of difficulty to approach the unit under measure. An equipment or system with good measure accessibility requires little assembling moving and can be done at a common environment.

*Metrology interfaces*: includes hardware and software interfaces. At the stage of design and manufacturing, the metrology interfaces should be set to calibrate the test equipments or instruments. The hardware interfaces are those through which the standard signals or the signals being calibrated can be transferred. The software interfaces are the program that can carry out the calibration automatically. The system which can realize the measuring process automatically requires that the structure of the measure (test) software is modularized. Take the automatic test system which is calibrated by calibration program in the host computer as an example, when it's short of measurability software interface, the program will not be able to transfer. In that case, people have to change the test software a lot, and this wastes much more time and money.

*SSG* (standardization, seriation and generalization) of the interfaces and equipment: SSG is the precondition for efficient metrology support. At present, many types of equipments adopt special test instruments whose interfaces are not standard, and the equipments with different types are not compatible which causes difficulty for the metrology work. So at the stage of demonstration and manufacturing, it's commended to choose the general instruments and standard interface protocol.

The quantitative indexes include:

*Number of parameters being calibrated*: total number of parameters which ought to be calibrated according to the requirement of performance. If the number is small, the workload of metrology would be less.

*Transmission rate of the value of quantity*: is defined as the ratio of number of parameters being traced to the total number of the parameters. It reflects the ability to control the technology state of the products.

*Measuring coverage rate*: is defined as the ratio of number of instruments being measured to the total number of instruments. It reflects the ability to implement the metrology support.

*Metrology (verification or calibration) interval*: the time between two consecutive calibrations made on a measure (or test) instrument (or equipment). At the stage of demonstrations, the metrology department should put forward the requirement according to the use frequency, performance, stability and environment conditions. This concept changes the traditional supportable characteristic of metrology work. Furthermore, the manufacture should adjust the calibration intervals opportunely when the equipment is in use.

*Mean time to calibrate*: the ratio of calibration time to the number of parameters being calibrated. It reflects the convenience of metrology, and the capability of support equipments and personnel.

*Repeated calibration rate* of parameters: we define this as

$$1 - \frac{\text{number of parameter types being calibrated}}{\text{number of parameters being calibrated}}$$

In ideal case, the repeated calibration rate is 1.

*Rate of general equipments*: the ratio of number of general equipments to total number of equipments.

## 12.5  Key Problems of Measurability

### 12.5.1 Design and Standardization of Metrology Interface

The metrology interface includes those of test signal, digital signal and calibration software. The metrology interface should not affect the normal use of test systems. It's better to calibrate the parameters on station without portage and disassembly. The metrology interface should also be marked.

For the electric test systems, taking into account the attenuation of signal through transmission, it's advised to take the form of general plug-in, such as Q9, RS232, RS485, IEEE488, ARINC429 and so on.

## 12.5.2 Unitization of Parameters

The target of unitization is given as follows:

1. Making good use of the relations between different parameters. For example, if there are three parameters (voltage, current and resistance) to be calibrated, the resistance can be calibrated by the voltage and current according to the Ohm Law.
2. Making good use of relation between different types of parameters.

The experiments have demonstrated that the parameters in the world are not isolated but affected by each others. There are many such relations in the nature: the higher the temperature is, the longer the mercury is; the microwave impedance can be traced to the length; the length can be traced to the wavelength of light wave; the wavelength can be traced to the time frequency standard; the voltage can be traced to frequency by the Josephson Effect. The new discovery in the field of physics will improve the accuracy of standard.

3. Fo the metrology of different measure ranges, we can reduce it to only one range. Take the instance of a certainty Digital Multimeters, the whole ranges can be calibrated by one point calibration.

## 12.5.3 Determination of Metrology Items

At present, the items to be calibrated are determined by the compulsive verification catalog. The rationality of the catalog is worthy of consideration. In order to assure the metrology support more efficiently, we should determine the metrology items scientifically. In the precondition of satisfaction in the performance of test systems, the metrology items ought to be as less as possible.

## 12.5.4 Model of Measurability Design and Evaluation

The measurability design is the process to adopt some methods to improve the measurability of equipment. The value status of items being calibrated can be obtained and the external standard signal can be transmitted conveniently after measurability design.

When the test system is in use, the model should be built to evaluate the value of measurability indexes. The measurability is the reasonable abstract of different equipments. Because the close relations between testability and measurability, we can find a way to establish the measurability model which is similar to testability.

## 12.5.5 Lengthening of Calibration Interval

The longer the calibration interval is, the less the workload of the metrology personnel. There are two approaches given as follows to prolong the calibration interval:

(1) Improvement of the self calibration or verification. The self calibration and verification are not real metrology because the lack of traceability, but we can prolong the calibration interval by using the instrument of higher accuracy to calibrate the instrument of lower accuracy.
(2) Enhancement of the reliability of parameters.

Reliability is defined as the probability that the parameters will remain in-tolerance through out the established interval [10]. We can see that the reliability is not less important than accuracy. If it is not satisfied, the normal use of the test system is affected by the frequently occurred fault or bias. So if the reliability is high, the calibration interval would be prolonged.

## 12.6 Conclusions

This paper is an original research of measurability. The concept and connotation are discussed and the indexes are proposed. Finally, the key technologies of measurability are analyzed. Because the importance of measurability, we point out that it's essential to take the measurability as either the complementary of RMS for a test systems or a special type of testability. The design of measurability should become the self-conscious behavior of people, and its requirement should be added to the existent laws. The viewpoint in this paper is a guide for the measurability research. We believe that one day the theory of measurability will be mature through the effort of metrology personnel.

## References

1. Dong SL, Tang WZH, Gao WZH (2011) Analysis of key technology in metrology support of aero-equipment. Metrol Test Technol 31(5):45 (in Chinese)
2. Dong SL, Ding Y, Zhang JL, Zeng WP (2011) Analysis and design of metrology of the airboard equipment. Metrol Test Technol 31(3):46
3. Sheppard JW, Kaufman MA (2005) A bayesian approach to diagnosis and prognosis using built-in test instrumentation and measurement. IEEE Trans Comput 54(3):1003
4. GJB2715A-2009 (2009) General terminology of military metrology
5. Gao ZHB, Liang X, Li XSH (2005) Technological research on ATE system calibration. J Electron Meas Instrum 19(2):1 (in Chinese)
6. Eric G (2004) Modeling it both ways: hybrid diagnostic modeling and its application to hierarchical system designs. In: Proceedings of the IEEE AUTOESTCON, IEEE, New York

7. MIL-STD-1839C (2010) Department of defense standard practice: calibration and measurement requirement
8. MIL-HDBK-1839A (2000) Department of defense handbook: calibration and measurement requirement
9. Jing W, Qi Z, Wu S (2012) Analysis of ATE measurability using information flow. Meas Sci Rev 12(4):128
10. MIL-STD-45662A (1998) Calibration system

# Chapter 13
# MBCrawler: A Software Architecture for Micro-Blog Crawler

Gang Lu, Shumei Liu and Kevin Lü

**Abstract** Getting data is the precondition of researching on micro-blogging services. By using Web 2.0 techniques such as AJAX, the contents of micro-blog Web pages are dynamically generated rapidly. That makes it hard for traditional Web page crawler to crawl micro-blog Web pages. Micro-blogging services provide some APIs. Through the APIs, well-structured data can be easily obtained. A software architecture for micro-blogging service crawler, which is named as MBCrawler, is designed basing on the APIs provided by micro-blogging services. The architecture is modular and scalable, so it can fit specific features of different micro-blogging services. SinaMBCrawler, which is a crawler application based on MBCrawler for Sina Weibo, has been developed. It automatically invokes the APIs of Sina Weibo to crawl data. The crawled data is saved into local database.

**Keywords** Social Computing · Micro-blog · Crawler · Twitter

## 13.1 Introduction

As a fast developing and widely used new Web application, micro-blogging service such as Twitter and Sina Weibo, has attracted attention of users, enterprises, governments, and researchers. The first issue comes to researchers is

G. Lu (✉) · S. Liu
College of Information Science and Technology, Beijing University of Chemical Technology, 15 BeiSanhuan East Road, ChaoYang District 100029 Beijing, China
e-mail: sizheng@126.com

K. Lü
Brunel University, Uxbridge UB8 3PH, UK
e-mail: kevin.lu@brunel.ac.uk

W. Lu et al. (eds.), *Proceedings of the 2012 International Conference on Information Technology and Software Engineering*, Lecture Notes in Electrical Engineering 212, DOI: 10.1007/978-3-642-34531-9_13, © Springer-Verlag Berlin Heidelberg 2013

getting data of them. Generally, because of privacy and business reasons, micro-blogging service providers will not provide the data readily.

In 2001, the authors of [1] described the common architecture of a search engine, including the issues about selecting and updating pages, storing, scalability, indexing, ranking, and so on. Nevertheless, being different from traditional Web pages, Web 2.0 techniques such as AJAX (Asynchronous JavaScript and XML) are widely used in micro-blog Web pages, and the contents in micro-blog Web pages change too rapidly and dynamically for web crawlers. Traditional crawlers for static Web pages do not work well to them. Of course, there has been some research on getting web content from AJAX based Web pages [2–6]. However, all of the work is based on the state of the application, and the technique is not that easy to implement. Fortunately, to encourage developers to develop applications about micro-blogging services to make it used as widely as possible, the providers of micro-blogging services publish some APIs. By those APIs, well-formatted data of micro-blogging services can be obtained. Except some work in which Twitter APIs were not used [7], and the work in which the authors did not state how they got the Twitter data [8, 9], most of existing research about Twitter utilizes the provided APIs [10–15].

We can see that Twitter APIs are widely used in the research work on Twitter. We believe that using APIs is the most popular way to get data from micro-blogging services. That provides us the probability of constructing uniform and universal software architecture to utilize the provided APIs, to automatically download and save well-structured data into database. To make it convenient for researchers to obtain data from micro-blogging services, a software architecture named as MBCrawler is proposed. Basing on this software architecture, a crawler using APIs of micro-blogging service with multi threads can be developed. More functions can be added easily along with more APIs are added, and details can be designed to fit different online social network services.

## 13.2 MBCrawler

### 13.2.1 Basic Structure of MBCrawler

Software architecture named as MBCrawler is proposed. This software architecture presents a main framework by which crawlers for micro-blogging services data can be easily designed, developed, and expanded. MBCrawler is designed as multi-threaded, and consists of six components, which are UI, Robots, Data Crawler, Models, Micro-blogging APIs, and Database. The structure of MBCrawler is illustrated in Fig. 13.1.

**Fig. 13.1** Basic Structure of
MBCrawler

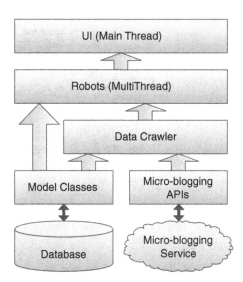

(1) **Database** At the most bottom of MBCrawler is a relational database, in which
    crawled data is stored.
(2) **Model Classes** Each entity like user and status has a database table
    correspondingly. On the other hand, entities appear as Model Classes to the
    upper layers of the architecture. Model Classes provide methods for upper
    layers to manipulate data in database.
(3) **Micro-blogging APIs** Micro-blogging services provide some APIs which
    meet REST (REpresentational State Transfer) requirements. The layer of
    Micro-blogging APIs includes simple wrapped methods of the APIs.
    The methods submit URLs with parameters by HTTP requests, and return the
    result string in the format of XML or JSON.
(4) **Data Crawler** Data Crawler plays a role as a controller between Robots and
    Micro-blogging APIs. It receives commands indicating what data to crawl
    from Robots, and then invokes specific function in Micro-blogging APIs. It
    also transforms the crawled data from the format of XML or JSON into
    instances of certain model class, which will be used by Robots.
(5) **Robots** MBCrawler needs different robots crawl different data in multi-threads
    at the same time. User Relation Robot, User Information Robot, Status Robot,
    and Comment Robot are four main robots, which should be included at least.
    All robots have their own waiting queues, such as queues of users' ID or
    queues of status IDs. The waiting queues are all designed as circular queues to
    crawl the updated data repeatedly.

Generally, a crawler should run continuously. However, some cases may
interrupt its running. For example, the network disconnects, or even the computer
on which the crawler is running has to reboot. As a result, every robot will record
the user ID or status ID before it start to crawl the data. The robots can start from
the last stopped points when they restart.

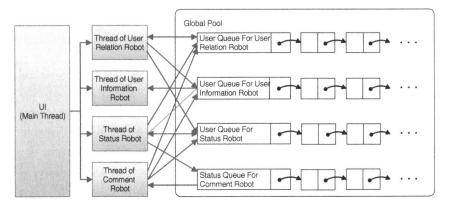

**Fig. 13.2** Multi-threaded robots and their queues

(6) **UI** UI means User Interface. It's the layer of representation, which shows information from the crawler and makes users able to control the program. Necessary options of the program also can be set by UI. Robots can be started, paused, continued, or stopped at any time by the buttons on UI.

## 13.2.2 Multi-Threads Structure of Robots Layer

MBCrawler is multi-threaded. Besides the main thread of UI, more threads with robots working in them is generated, so that different robots can work in parallel. The structure of the multi-threaded robots and their queues is as in Fig. 13.2 shows.

Each robot has its own waiting queue. The queue of Comment Robot is of status IDs, and others are of user IDs.

The arrows between robots and the waiting queues in Fig. 13.2 show the data flow direction between them. Basically, every robot fetches the head item from its own queue to crawl, and then move the item to the end of the queue. By crawling followers and followings IDs of a user, User Relation Robot processes BFS in the social network of micro-blogging service. User Relation Robot will make all waiting queues grow at the same time, by adding new items to them synchronously. User Information Robot does not add new items into any queues. Status Robot adds the ID of the crawled status into the waiting queue of Comment Robot. If it finds new user IDs, it will also add them to the queues of user IDs. Comment Robot also adds commenters' user IDs into the queues of user IDs.

## 13.2.3 Two-Part Queues Management

As it is shown in Sect. 12.2.2, each robot has a waiting queue of user IDs or status IDs. A whole waiting queue is designed as a circular queue, to ensure that every ID

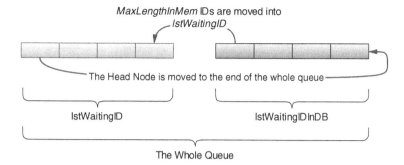

**Fig. 13.3** Structure and working process of a queue

in it will be process repeatedly for information updating. As a result, the queues will grow longer and longer as the crawler works. However, the limited memory of computer cannot contain unlimited queues. To deal with that issue, a queue is departed into two parts. One part is maintained in memory, the other part is stored in disk, namely in database. The two parts are managed by two variable *lstWaitingID* and *lstWaitingIDInDB* respectively.

*lstWaitingID* is a linked list, whose length is limited to *MaxLengthInMem*. *lstWaitingIDInDB* manages the other part of the waiting queue in database. When a robot starts to work, it will create a temporary table in database in order to extend the queue into disk. If the length of the whole queue is longer than *MaxLengthInMem*, new IDs will be added into the temporary table. In this case, IDs in *lstWaitingID* will be moved into *lstWaitingIDInDB* at last. When there is no ID in *lstWaitingID*, the first *MaxLengthInMem* IDs in *lstWaitingIDInDB* will be moved into *lstWaitingID*, as Fig. 13.3 illustrates.

However, if *lstWaitingIDInDB* is too long, and *MaxLengthInMem* is set to a big number, the process of moving *MaxLengthInMem* IDs from *lstWaitingIDInDB* to *lstWaitingID* will take a long time. That may cause the response of database timeout. An alternate way to solve the problem, is adding an additional thread to take the charge of moving IDs between the two parts of the queue, as Fig. 13.4 shows.

As Fig. 13.4 illustrates, a model called *Queue Coordinator* and a queue named *Back Buffer* are added. *Queue Coordinator* fetches IDs from *lstWaitingIDInDB* to *lstWaitingID*. A crawling robot fetches an ID from *lstWaitingID* to crawl. After that, it sends the crawled ID to *Back Buffer*. At the same time, *Queue Coordinator* fetches crawled IDs from *Back Buffer* and pushes them to the back of *lstWaitingIDInDB*. The crawling robot and *Queue Coordinator* work asynchronously in parallel. Of course, each robot needs a *Back Buffer*, but only one *Queue Coordinator* is enough to manage all of the queues.

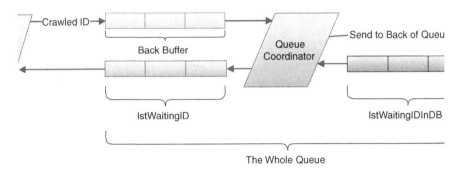

Fig. 13.4 Producer-consumer based queue management

## 13.3 Implementation as SinaMBCrawler

Basing on MBCrawler, a crawler program named as SinaMBCrawler for Sina micro-blog, which is called Sina Weibo, is developed. Sina Weibo is one of the most popular micro-blogging services in China. By SinaMBCrawler, data of Sina Weibo can be crawled into database.

Sina Weibo has some more features than Twitter. For example, users of Sina Weibo can label themselves with no more than 10 words, which can reflect the users' hobbies, profession, and so on. These words are called as tags. As a result, a new robot takes the charge of crawling the data about tags is added, which is named as UserTagRobot.

In our research work, SinaMBCrawler initially was running for months. During that time, it crawled 8,875,141 users' basic information, 55,307,787 user relationship, 1,299,253 tags, 44,958,974 statuses, and 35,546,637 comments. The data is stored in a SQL Server database. However, in that time, SinaMBCrawler was frequently stopped to be modified because of bugs and updates. That makes the data some dirty due to some testing result. So we abandoned that data. From 15:54:46 on May 30th, 2011 to 11:44:26 on January 7th, 2012, a stable version of SinaMBCrawler was running uninterruptedly. The data obtained this time is listed in Table 13.1.

ACR is the abbreviation for Average Crawling Rate, which is different for each robot, because they access different Sina Weibo APIs. For example, only one user's information can be obtained by UserInfoRobot for each invoking the relative API, while at most 5,000 user relationships can be obtained by UserRelationRobot for one time. ACR is also related to the data. For instance, many users don't set their tags, so UserTagRobot can't get their tags. That lowers the ACR of UserTagRobot.

**Table 13.1** Crawled data by a stable version of SinaMBCrawler

| Robot | Data content | Total records | ACR (records/minute) |
|---|---|---|---|
| UserInfoRobot | User information | 6,571,955 | 20 |
| UserRelationRobot | User relationship | 37,902,219 | 118 |
| UserTagRobot | Tag | 1,068,060 | 3 |
| | User owning tags | 8,031,712 | 25 |
| StatusRobot | Status | 32,627,963 | 102 |
| CommentRobot | Comment | 26,884,365 | 84 |

## 13.4  Conclusion and Future Work

Software architecture for micro-blogging services crawler, called MBCrawler, is designed in our work. The whole architecture is designed in levels. By dividing the whole architecture into several levels and applying some simple design patterns, the structure of the architecture is highly modularized and scalable. The different parts of the architecture are loose coupling, and each part is high cohesion. That makes it easy to modify and extend the software.

Basing on MBCrawler, a crawler software for Sina Weibo named as SinaMBCrawler is implemented. Functions and a robot about users' tags are easily added according to Sina Weibo API. Because of the careful design of the architecture, we have easily upgrade SinaMBCrawler according to Sina Weibo API 2.0, in which only JSON format is used and some new properties are added to users, tags, and so on. SinaMBCrawler has been used to crawl a large number of data from Sina Weibo, which is used in our research work.

In summary, comparing to traditional Web page crawlers, MBCrawler mainly has the following features:

1. Because micro-blogging services APIs are the foundation of the design and implementation of MBCrawler, MBCrawler does not need to download Web pages to analyze. It obtains well-structured data by APIs directly. That makes MBCrawler avoid complex technical issues resulted from AJAX.
2. MBCrawler does not store dynamically generated Web pages, but directly stored the well-structured data obtained by APIs into database.
3. Because MBCrawler does not store Web pages, no index module for Web pages is needed. However, the indexing mechanism of the used database can be utilized to enhance the performance of the database.

Nevertheless, there is an important condition for using MBCrawler. To access the APIs, MBCrawler has to act as an application registered at the micro-blogging services provider. Fortunately, it is easy to register applications for it. After that, a unique pair of application ID and secret will be given to access APIs by the application. Because there are access frequency restrictions for an application, in our SinaMBCrawler, we registered five applications for the five robots. As a result, each robot can work as an independent application, and they will not share the same access frequency restriction. That makes SinaMBCrawler work more efficiently.

In the future, MBCrawler can be improved mainly in two aspects. Firstly, a focused module can be designed, to tell the robots what type of data to crawl. For example, the robots can be told to crawl the information of users who are in a specific city, or the statuses including specific words. Secondly, we would like to design a ranking module. It is impossible to crawl the whole user relation graph due to the large scale of it. A ranking module will help the crawler to select more important users to crawl. Additionally, because database is loose-coupled with MBCrawler, it also can be considered that trying some NoSQL databases according to the practice requirements. For example, to research the user relation network, any one of graph databases can be selected to store the network.

**Acknowledgments** This work is supported by the Fundamental Research Funds for the Central Universities grants ZZ1224.

# References

1. Arasu A, Cho J, Garcia-Molina H, Paepcke A, Raghavan S (2001) Searching the web. ACM Trans Internet Technol (TOIT) 1(1):2–43
2. Mesbah A, van Deursen A (2009) Invariant-based automatic testing of AJAX user interfaces. In: Proceedings of the 31st international conference on software engineering, Washington, USA, pp 210–220
3. Xia T (2009) Extracting structured data from Ajax site. In: First international workshop on database technology and applications, pp 259–262
4. Duda C, Frey G, Kossmann D, Matter R, Zhou C (2009) AJAX crawl: making AJAX applications searchable. In: IEEE 25th international conference on data engineering ICDE'09, pp 78–89
5. Peng Z, He N, Jiang C, Li Z, Xu L, Li Y, Ren Y (2012) Graph-based AJAX crawl: mining data from rich internet applications. In: 2012 international conference on computer science and electronics engineering (ICCSEE), vol 3. pp 590–594
6. Mesbah A, van Deursen A, Lenselink S (2012) Crawling ajax-based web applications through dynamic analysis of user interface state changes. ACM Trans Web 6(1):1–30
7. Weng J, Lim E-P, Jiang J, He Q (2010) TwitterRank: finding topic-sensitive influential twitterers. In: Proceedings of the third ACM international conference on web search and data mining, New York, USA, pp 261–270
8. Mendoza M, Poblete B, Castillo C (2010) Twitter under crisis: can we trust what we RT? In: Proceedings of the first workshop on social media analytics, pp 71–79
9. Sriram B, Fuhry D, Demir E, Ferhatosmanoglu H, Demirbas M (2010) Short text classification in twitter to improve information filtering. In: Proceeding of the 33rd international ACM SIGIR conference on research and development in information retrieval, pp 841–842
10. A. for C. M. S. I. G. on Security, Audit, and Control (2007) Why we twitter: understanding microblogging usage and communities. In: Proceedings of the ACM workshop on privacy in the electronic society, Washington, USA
11. Asur S, Huberman BA (2010) Predicting the future with social media. ArXiv 1003:5699
12. Kwak H, Lee C, Park H, Moon S (2010) What is twitter, a social network or a news media? In: Proceedings of the 19th international conference on World wide web, pp 591–600

13. Wu S, Hofman JM, Mason WA, Watts DJ (2011) Who says what to whom on twitter. In: Proceedings of the 20th international conference on World wide web, pp 705–714
14. Bakshy E, Hofman JM, Mason V, Watts DJ (2011) Everyone's an influencer: quantifying influence on twitter. In: Proceedings of the fourth ACM international conference on Web search and data mining, pp 65–74
15. Li R, Lei KH, Khadiwala R, Chang KC-C (2012) TEDAS: a twitter-based event detection and analysis system. In: International conference on data engineering, Los Alamitos, USA, vol 0. pp 1273–1276

# Chapter 14
# Optimization Model of Software Fault Detection

Ye Jun-min, Chen Ying-xiang, Chen Jing-ru and Feng Jia-jie

**Abstract** With the widespread application of software in various fields, considerable attentions are paid on software testing. However, there is still no perfect solution to software fault localization. This paper proposes a fault detection model of a probability-weighted bipartite graph, which based on Bayesian theorem. The model is optimized by Simulated Annealing Algorithm. The experimental results show that this optimized model can reflect real situation by reducing the influence of the priori probability on the experimental results.

**Keywords** Bayesian theorem · Probability-weighted bipartite graph · Software fault detection model · Model optimization

## 14.1 Introduction

The main method about modeling of the fault scenarios and defect location is to gain graph model of question description. There are several efficient approaches, such as fault propagation model [1], Bayesian Network [2–6], MCA algorithm(Max Covering Algorithm) and relevant optimization [7, 8]. In practice, however, the hypothesis is hardly, correct, which leads to great deviation of detection. This paper revises the constructed probability-weighted bipartite graph through learning algorithm to reduce the deviation.

Y. Jun-min · C. Ying-xiang (✉) · C. Jing-ru · F. Jia-jie
School of Computer Science, Central China Normal University, 152 Luoyu Road,
Wuhan, Hubei, China
e-mail: jingru451064@126.com

W. Lu et al. (eds.), *Proceedings of the 2012 International Conference on Information Technology and Software Engineering*, Lecture Notes in Electrical Engineering 212, DOI: 10.1007/978-3-642-34531-9_14, © Springer-Verlag Berlin Heidelberg 2013

## 14.2 Research Foundation

### 14.2.1 The MCA, MCA+ and BSD Algorithm

Algorithm,such as MCA and MCA+ , is based on the idea of greedy that adds faults with the most symptoms into Fault Hypothesis, and rules out all symptoms which can be explained in the symptom set until the set is empty, in other words, all symptoms in the symptom set can be explained by the answer set. The algorithm complexity is $O(|F|*|S|)$, where $|F|$ means the number of fault sets, and $|S|$ means the number of symptom sets. The algorithm complexity of BSD algorithm is $O(|F|*|S|)$, which takes weighted bipartite graph as fault propagation model.

### 14.2.2 Simulated Annealing Algorithm

Simulated Annealing Algorithm (SAA) is a kind of heuristic algorithms, which get the global optimal solution [9] by simulating annealing process of high-temperature object. The algorithm described as Fig. 14.1.

### 14.2.3 Premise of Learning Bayesian Network

Learning Bayesian Network must follow several principles [10]: (1) Simplicity, which requires the topological structure as simple as possible; (2) Accuracy, which requires great degree of fitting with instance-data set, in addition, we can revise the prior probability; (3) Inheritance, namely, it should inherit the topological characteristics of the current network structure

### 14.2.4 Detection Rate and False Detection Rate

Two evaluations-Detection Rate and False Detection Rate should be kept when comparing the experimental results.

**Definition 1** Detection Rate (DR) defined as follow:

$$DR = \frac{|Fr \cap Fs|}{|Fr|} \tag{14.1}$$

**Definition 2** False Detection Rate (FDR) defined as follows:

**Algorithm:** Simulated Annealing Algorithm
**Input:** Initial solution( S), Initial temperature (T), maximum of **K(Kmax )**
**Output:** Approximate optimal solution(ANS)
**Begin**

(1) Set S and T respectively as the initial solution and initial temperature;

(2) When T is small enough, goto (7);

(3) Set K=0 (the number of iterations is zero), and Kmax= a constant number;

(4) Produce neighbor subsets of the solution S (Neighbor(S)) in accordance with specified rules, and get a new state S' as a candidate solution. Then evaluate capabilities of S(C(S)) and S'(C(S'));

(5) If C(S)-C(S')>0, accept solution S' as the next current-solution, otherwise accept S' as the next current-solution in probability. Else if, accept S as the next current-solution;

(6) K=K+1, if K>Kmax, reduce the value of T, goto(2);

Output ANS, which is the current-solution S.

**End**

**Fig. 14.1** Simulated annealing algorithm

$$FDR = \frac{|Fs - Fr|}{|Fs|} \qquad (14.2)$$

Where $Fr$ means the actual fault set, $Fs$ means the fault hypothesis set produced by the foregoing method.

## 14.3  The Software Fault Prediction Model and the Optimization Algorithm

### 14.3.1 The Software Fault Prediction Model

Because of the exponential growth of the complexity of the Bayesian network with the increased number of variables, this paper put forward a method : Learning after simplifying Bayesian Network Structure to Bipartite Graph, which meets the Simplicity and Inheritance principles mentioned in Sect. 14.2.3. According to the Bipartite Graph, we take edge-weight of each edge for learning, videlicet, adjust the prior probability to fit better with instance-data.

Among a large number of graph-learning algorithms, Simulated Annealing Algorithm is characterized by capability of local searching and of avoiding falling into local optimal solution during search [9]. For such character, this paper adopts this learning algorithm.

Here are some prerequisite definitions:

**Definition 3** (probability-weighted bipartite graph, *BG*) *BG = (V, E)*, where *V = {F ∪ S}*, *E = {F × S, Pfs}*. Node set *V* is composed of two disjoint node sets—fault set *F* and symptom set *S*; Edge set *E* contains all directed edge between *F* and *S*, and Pfs is the probability of the directed edge *f- > s*, defined as

$P(f|s).P(f|s)$ is the probability that the already-known symptom s is caused by fault f. According to Beyesian formula, $P(f|s)$ can be defined as:

$$P(f|s) = \frac{P(s|f)P(f)}{p(s)} \qquad (14.3)$$

where

$$P(s) = \sum p(f_i)p(s|f_i) \qquad (14.4)$$

Here are some explanations: (1) $P(f)$ is the prior probability of f given by experts. If there is no $P(f)$, we can simply assume the same priori probability of every fault, and adjust priori probability by learning algorithm; (2) $P(s|f)$ is defined as likelihood in this paper, which means the probability of the already-known symptom s being caused by fault f. When no input, namely, all results are the same each time, $P(s|f) = 1$ if fault f brings about symptom s, otherwise, $P(s|f) = 0$. Because of various options by users, once f makes a mistake, the mistake will last until corrected, however, some options won't display the mistake. In such situation, $P(s|f)$ is the probability of f bringing out s in all options.

In conclusion, $P(f|s)$ represents the probability of f in condition of s.Priori probability assumes the relationship between the fault and symptom, however, such estimated value varying from 0 to 1 is inaccurate even though estimated by experts. It will contribute to large deviation of the experimental results. In order to get more accurate result, we adopt learning algorithm based on Simulated Annealing Algorithm to revise $P(f_i|s_i)$ in weighted bipartite graph.

Taking $F(G)$ as the function, where G is the probability-weighted bipartite graph to be evaluated.Because different symptoms are independent from each other, so are different faults, the weight of every edge is independent of each other in probability-weighted bipartite graph. The weight P(fi|sj) is the probability of observed symptom sj caused by fault fi. Assuming the bipartite graph of the most fitting data is $.\hat{G}.$, the edge weight of the bipartite graph is $\hat{P}(f_i|s_j)$.

**Definition 4** (Function of distance from learning data $\Delta P(G, \hat{G})$)

$$\Delta P(G, \hat{G}) = \sum_{0 < i \le |F|, 0 < j \le |S|} -|P(f_i|s_j) - \hat{P}(f_i|s_j)| \qquad (14.5)$$

where $\Delta P(G, \hat{G})$ represents distance between solution G and the optimal solution $\hat{G}$. The greater $\Delta P(G, \hat{G})$ is, the closer $G$ to $\hat{G}$, the higher the fitting degree.

For the bipartite graph edge weight of the most fitting data is unknown in advance, we can construct a perfectly-fitting Bipartite Graph $\tilde{G}$ by training datas of Bipartite Graph, where $\tilde{P}(f_i|s_j)$ represents the edge-weight in graph $\tilde{G}$, then the $\Delta P(G, \bar{G})$-the degree of fitting between Bipartite graph G to be assessed and the data to be learnt can be defined as follows:

**Definition 5** (Data fitting degree $\Delta P(G, \tilde{G})$)

$$\Delta P(G, \bar{G}) = \sum_{0 < i \le |F|, 0 < j \le |S|} -|P(f_i|s_j) - \bar{P}(f_i|s_j)| \tag{14.6}$$

What needs our attention is that data evaluated by experts will get lost if we only take $\Delta P(G, \tilde{G})$ as evaluation function. It not only wastes expert domain Knowledge, but also may result in overfitting of data, which means the greater deviation of the probability-weighted bipartite graph after learning in actual application. So the following distance function is needed to access the fitting degree between bipartite graph and experts' estimated value

**Definition 6** (Function of distance from experts prediction $Dist(G,G')$)

$$Dist(G, G') = - \sum_{0 < i \le |F|, 0 < j \le |S|} -|P(f_i|s_j) - P'(f_i|s_j) \tag{14.7}$$

where $G$ represents the probability-weighted bipartite graph to be evaluated, $G'$ represents the probability-weighted bipartite graph estimated by experts, $P'(f_i|sj)$ represents edge-weight in $G'$. It's the sum of the absolute difference between $(Dist(G,G'))$ of $P'(f_i|s_j)$ and $P(f_i|s_j)$ that measures the degree of difference between $G$ and $G'$. The greater the $Dist(G,G')$, the smaller the difference, namely, $G$ is more similar to $G'$.

To avoid overfitting, this paper uses Penalty Function $(H(G))$ to represent complexity of $G$.

**Definition 7** (Penalty Function $H(G)$)

$$H(G) = - \sum_{0 < i \le |F|, 0 < j \le |S|} -|P(f_i|s_j) - 0.5| \tag{14.8}$$

In reality, the more certain relationship is more convincing; vaguer relationship is less convincing. So the more accurate fault localization is possible when there is more certain relationship between fault and symptom. The closer $P(f_i|s_j)$ is to 0, the looser the relationship between $s_j$ and $f_i$. On the other hand, the closer $P(f_i|s_j)$ is to 1, the closer the relationship between $s_j$ and fi. And when $P(f_i|s_i)$ is close to 50 %, the vague situation may result from overfitting.

Note, Evaluation Function consists of three parts: the first part describes the degree of fitting with the learning data; the second part describes the degree of fitting with the probability-weighted bipartite graph estimated by experts; the third part is Penalty Function. We define the Evaluation Function on the following basis:

**Definition 8** (Evaluation Function F(G))

$$F(G) = \alpha \Delta(G, \bar{G}) + \beta \, Dist(G, G') - \gamma \, H(G) \tag{14.9}$$

**Algorithm:** Simulated Annealing Algorithm based on learning probability-weighted bipartite graph

**Input:** Initial solution (S), initial temperature (T), maximum of K(Kmax), data for learning

**Output:** Approximate optimal solution(ANS)

**Begin**

        (1) Set S and T respectively as the initial solution and initial temperature;

        (2) When T is small enough, go to (7);

        (3) Set K=0 (the number of iterations is zero), and a constant Kmax, the maximum of K;

        (4) Produce a 01-string whose length is | F | * | S |, the i-th bit represents the modification strategy of the i-th edge-weight, where 1 represents change the weight, and 0 represent the weight remain unchanged. Produce another 01-string whose length equals the number of 1 in the first 01-string, where 0 represents weight reduced by T%, and 1 represents weight increased by T%. If the revised weight is less than 0 or greater than 100%, calculate respectively with 0 and 100%. Take this solution S' as a candidate solution, then evaluate capabilities of F(S) and F(S');

        (5) If F(S)-F(S')>0, accpet solution S' as the next current-solution, otherwise accept S' as the next current-solution in probability . Or else, accept S as the next current-solution;

        (6) K=K+1, if K>Kmax, reduce the value of T, go to (2);

        (7) Return to ANS, which is the current-solution S.

**End**

**Fig. 14.2** Simulated annealing algorithm based on learning probability-weighted bipartite graph

where $\alpha + \beta = 1$, $\alpha$ and $\beta$, which varies from 0 to 1, respectively represents the credibility of the data for learning and of the bipartite graph predicted by experts.

Because of possible errors in the data for learning or lacking confidence about the predicted bipartite graph, we can adjust $\alpha$ and $\beta$ according to actual situations to improve the assessment effect. Especially, when there is no data for learning, namely $\alpha = 0$, accept unconditionally the bipartite graph predicted by experts; when there is no prediction, namely $\beta = 0$, accept unconditionally the adjustment according to the data for learning. $\gamma$ represents delearning rate, when $\gamma = 0$, ignore the probability certainty in the probability-weighted bipartite graph, and when $\gamma$ tends to be infinite accept only certain edge, meanwhile, the probability-weighted bipartite graph degrades into a bipartite graph without weights. $\alpha$, $\beta$, $\gamma$ are determined by the actual situation.

Define abbreviations and acronyms the first time they are used in the text, even after they have been defined in the abstract. Abbreviations such as IEEE, SI, MKS, CGS, sc, dc, and rms do not have to be defined. Do not use abbreviations in the title or heads unless they are unavoidable.

**Fig. 14.3** The comparison of
FDR before and after learning

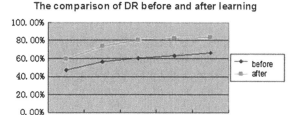

**Fig. 14.4** The comparison of
DR before and after learning

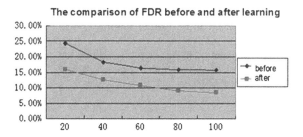

## 14.3.2   The optimization of Software Fault Prediction Model

On the basis of 14.1, this paper proposes an optimized Simulated Annealing
Algorithm based on learning probability-weighted bipartite graph (Fig. 14.2).

Simulated Annealing Algorithm can accept inferior solutions to some degree, so
that it can avoid local optimal solution during search. What's more, this algorithm
can get the solution better fitting the actual data with strong local search ability.

## 14.4   The Experiment and Results

The algorithm tests by simulation data and procedures. 1,000 group simulation
data have been operated, and the Software Fault Location Algorithm proposed in
this paper is evaluated with two principles: Detection Rate (*DR*) and Fault
Detection Rate (*FDR*).

According to the result, the average DR ($\overline{DR}$) is 58.64 % and the average FDR
($\overline{FDR}$) is 18.12 % before learning; the average DR ($\overline{DR}$) is 75.80 % and the
average FDR($\overline{FDR}$) is 11.35 % after learning. The results are shown in the fol-
lowing graphs, x-axis represents the size of the model, namely, the value of $| F | * |
S |$ (Figs. 14.3 and 14.4):

Apparently, the DR increases dramatically and FDR decreases obviously after
learning the probability-weighted bipartite graph. It is illustrated that the optimization prediction model decreases the deviation between fault and symptom.

## 14.5 The Conclusion

In this chapter, we learn the probability-weighted bipartite graph based on Bayesian theorem by Simulated Annealing Algorithm and construct Evaluation Function to estimate the prior probability of bipartite graph, the degree of fitting with actual data, as well as overfitting. The experimental results indicate this optimization algorithm reduces the influence of prior probability after learning the probability-weighted bipartite graph and fits better with actual data. However, because of low learning efficiency, a new algorithm combining genetic algorithms with simulated annealing algorithm is to be studied further. Furthermore, Evaluation Function can be further modified to improve the reliability of the model.

**Acknowledgments** This research is funded by self-determined research funds of CCNU from the colleges' basic research and operation of MOE (CCNU11A02007), CCNU teaching and research project (201116).

## References

1. Yemini SA, Kliger S, Mozes E, Yemini Y, Ohsie D (1996) High speed and robust event correlation. Conununications Mag, IEEE 34(5):82–90
2. Steinder M, Sethi AS(2002) End-to-end service failure diagnosis using belief networks. In: Proceedings of the network operations and management symposium (NOMS), Florence, pp 375–390
3. Steinder M, Sethi AS (2004) Probabilistic fault localization in communication systems using belief networks. IEEE/ACM Trans Networking 12(5):809–822
4. Steinder M, Sethi AS (2003) Probabilistic event-driven fault diagnosis through incremental Hypothesis Updating. In: Proceedings of the IFIP/IEEE Int'l symposium on integrated network management (IM), Colorado Springs
5. Wang KX, Wang SL(2009) Software defect prediction and fault diagnosis based on bayesian network technology. 25(11) (in Chinese)
6. Hu YP,Chen ZP,Lin YP,Li JY (2005) Defect analysis model of bayesian and its application in software testing. J Comput Appl 25(4):31-33 (in Chinese)
7. Huang XH, Zou SH, Chu LW, Cheng SD, Wang WD (2007) Internet services fault management:layering model and algorithm. J Softw 18(10):2584–2594 (in Chinese)
8. Zhang C, Liao JX, Zhu XM (2010) Heuristic fault localization algorithm based on bayesian suspected degree. J Softw 21(10):2610–262 (in Chinese)
9. Hu WC, Cheng ZL, Wang BL (2010) Bayesian classification based on simulated annealing genetic algorithms. Comput Eng 33(9) (in Chinese)
10. Wang RG, Zhang YS, Wang H, Yao HL (2008) Improve MDL principle used for learning bayesian network structure. Comput Eng Appl (in Chinese)

# Chapter 15
# Generic Contract-Regulated Web Service Composition Specification and Verification

**Jie Zhai, Zhiqing Shao, Yi Guo and Haiteng Zhang**

**Abstract** This paper presents a novel formal method to describe contracrt-regulated service composition components using abstract concepts and (semi-) automatically verify the specification. We model web service component behaviours and the contracts based on Tecton language expressed using "concept descriptions", to be used with Violet verification system to prove properties of service composition component. The verified generic contract-regulated composition specification at an abstract level will be used in a variety of instances as BPEL specification without repeating the proof. The main advantage of this method is to improve the reusability of specification and seamlessly integrate behaviour descriptions with contacts.

**Keywords** Generic form · Service composition component · Contract-regulated

## 15.1 Introduction

When services are combined, more attention is paid to regulate the business interactions between them. Human-like activities require more general and sophisticated declarative specifications to describe properties of service compositions with

J. Zhai (✉) · Z. Shao · Y. Guo · H. Zhang
Department of Computer Science and Engineering, ECUST, Shanghai, China
e-mail: zhbzj@ecust.edu.cn

Z. Shao
e-mail: zshao@ecust.edu.cn

Y. Guo
e-mail: yguo1110@ecust.edu.cn

H. Zhang
e-mail: htzhang@ecust.edu.cn

W. Lu et al. (eds.), *Proceedings of the 2012 International Conference on Information Technology and Software Engineering*, Lecture Notes in Electrical Engineering 212, DOI: 10.1007/978-3-642-34531-9_15, © Springer-Verlag Berlin Heidelberg 2013

**Fig. 15.1** Framework of
generic method

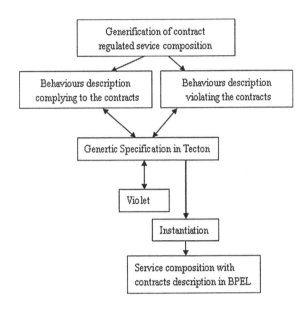

contracts. There're many valuable contributions in the rich literature on the above
domain. However, all proofs are done directly about concrete cases, there will be a
substantial waste of effort. What's more, no language proposed so far seamlessly
integrates behaviour descriptions with contracts.

In this paper, we propose a novel approach towards the verification of service
composition with contracts. The details of this method (see Fig. 15.1) are introduced as follows.

1. Technique with Concepts [1] is also known for Generic technique, it can
   capture the general properties of ordinary services composition and the contracts governing them as generic forms.
2. Further elaboration of generic forms is behaviour descriptions with compliance/
   violations of contracts.
3. Behaviour descriptions are converted into the model [2] of generic service
   composition specification extended to deal with contracts in Tecton [3].
4. Properties of generic specification are verified by Violet [4] system. If some
   properties fail, generic specification must be extended by Extension clauses
   until all properties succeed.
5. After the verification, instead instantiations are written using Concept-instance
   clauses.
6. Instantiations are transformed into BPEL behaviours according to corresponding rules.

The rest of the paper is organised as follows. In Sect. 15.2 we introduce
Tecton language. In Sect. 15.3 we describe the model of generic service compo-
sition with contracts specification. Section 15.4 presents a brief introduction to
Violet. Section 15.5 discusses the method which translates Tecton specification

into BPEL specification. Section 15.6 introduces a motivating example with some typical obligations and violations of contract parties, and presents experimental results of our approach on that example. We conclude in Sect. 15.7.

## 15.2 Tecton

Tecton language mechanisms support for building complex concept descriptions incrementally in concept hierarchies in virtue of two kinds of clauses, uses and refines.

A Tecton definition [3] is a concept description of the form

Tecton definition::=

Definitionconcept-identifier {refines-clause} {;}{uses-clause} {;} {introduces-clause} {;}{generates-clause} {;} {requires-clause}.

At least one of the refines, uses, introduces, generates, or requires clauses must be present. A definition introduces a new description of a set of algebras if neither a refines clause nor a uses clause is present, or (the usual case) it derives a description from previously given descriptions.

A Tecton extension is a concept description of the form:

extension ::=

Extension concept-name {uses-clause} {;}{introduces-clause} {;} {requires-clause}.

At least one of three clauses must be present. An extension is used to introduce new sorts and function identifiers and to state properties about them.

A concept instance is a concept name optionally followed by a clause specifying replacements:

concept-instance ::= concept-name {[with replacement -list]}

concept-name ::= concept-identifier {by concept-identifier}

The concept name part of a concept instance is called the base of the concept instance.

## 15.3 Generic Model

We use generic model [2] (see Fig. 15.2) to describe generic service composition specification with contracts. Data flow transfer between web services by variables. Control flow definite selective state transitions by control process. Once exception happens, fault handle or compensation handle starts up. Status function is made up of name, role, input, output and serv-seq. Concept instance can reuse generic contract-regulated composition specification.

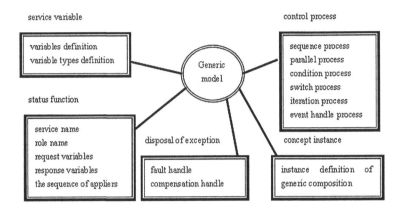

**Fig. 15.2** Model of generic composition specification

**Fig. 15.3** Internal
architecture of Violet system

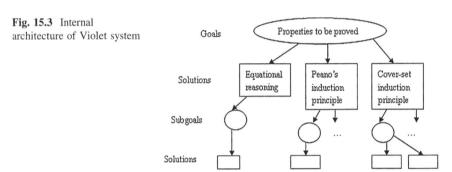

## 15.4 Violet

Violet [4] is a proof system (see Fig. 15.3) based on rewriting techniques for
Tecton definitions. Violet applies three proof methods include equational reasoning, Peano's induction principle and Cover-set induction principle to help the
veri- fication. All equations in the requires clauses of generic model will be looked
on as assistant rules in the verification. These equations are not only behaviour
description fulfilling the contracts but also unwanted behaviour description following certain violations.

## 15.5 Translating Generic Specification into BPEL

BPEL is a high-level XML-based language and a popular and industrial standard
for describing service composition, and provides the infrastructure for describing
the control logic required to coordinate web services participating in a process
flow. The main translator from specification in Tecton to BPEL specification uses
the following rules (see Table 15.1).

**Table 15.1** Translating rules

|  | HSpecification in Tecton | BPEL specification |
|---|---|---|
| Receive message | Status(...,input(),...) | <receive> |
| Send message | Status(...,output(),...) | <reply> |
| Structural activities | Control process(sequence process, swich process, condition process, ...) | <sequence>,<switch>,<while>, ... |
| Data flow | Variable definition/Variable type definition | <variable> |
| Liaison between partners | Status(...,role(),...) | PartnerLinks |
| Trouble Process | Fault handle | <faultHandlers> |
| Event handle | Control process(event handle process) | <eventHandle> |
| Compensation | Compensation handle | <compensationHandler> |

**Fig. 15.4** Interaction between various partners

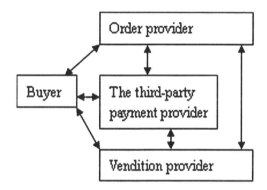

## 15.6 A Motivating Case Study

In this section we put forward to a composition (see Fig. 15.4) of services whose behaviours are regulated by contracts. In the scenario we analyse the participating contract parties comprise: an order provider (*O*), a vendition provider (*V*), a buyer (*B*) and the third-party payment provider (*TPP*). Every partner's obligations are shown in Table 15.2.

## *15.6.1 Generic Model of this Case*

The high-level workflow of the composition is defined as follows: B places an online order provided by O with V and implements online payment based on TPP. The details of behaviours with compliance/violations of the contracts (see Table 15.2) are decribed in Fig. 15.5. Generic specification in Table 15.3 exhibits diverse disposal routes according to each condition in Table 15.4.

**Table 15.2** Obligations of every partner

| Partner | Obligations |
|---|---|
| V | Dispatch goods on time after receiving the notice of the third-party payment platform |
| | Ensure the buyer can receive goods |
| | Goods must match the seller's description |
| TPP | Notice the seller to dispatch goods after receiving the money from the buyer |
| | Send the money to the seller after the buyer confirms payment |
| O | Provide order details |
| B | Online payment for the order on time |
| | If the buyer isn't satisfied with goods, apply for a refund after returning goods |

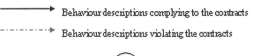

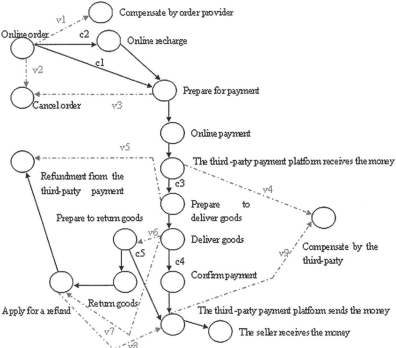

**Fig. 15.5** Behaviour descriptions in the composition

## 15.6.2 Verification by Violet and Translation in BPEL

We propose batch proof method [5] for verifying subgoals of the property of generic specification above underpinned by Violet. If all running paths succeed in various terminating states, we get a conclusion that the specification is complete.

**Table 15.3** Conditions in the composition

| Label | Condition |
|---|---|
| c1 | The account is adequate to pay the order |
| c2 | The account is not adequate to pay the order and the buyer sticks to purchase |
| c3 | The third-party payment platform notices the seller to dispatch goods |
| c4 | The buyer receives goods and is satisfied |
| c5 | The buyer gives up returning goods for some reason |
| v1 | Order provider fails to give correct order details |
| v2 | The account is not adequate to pay the order and the buyer fails to pay |
| v3 | The buyer fails to send payment for some reason |
| v4 | The third-party payment platform fails to notice the seller to dispatch goods |
| v5 | The seller doesn't dispatch goods |
| v6 | Goods the buyer receives can't match the seller's description |
| v7 | The buyer doesn't receive goods |
| v8 | The buyer applies to a refund before returning goods |
| v9 | The third -party payment platform fails to send the money |

**Table 15.4** Generic specification of this case

Definition : order with contracts based on the third -party payment platform

Uses string, order, request-var, response-var, boolean, order-sequences......;

Introduces

      Status(name(string),role(string),input(request-var),output(response-var),serv-seq(order-sequences,order-sequences))→boolean;

Requires(for x: order; s1:order-sequences;......)

(1) Status(name(Online_order),role(seller),......,serv-seq(x-|s1,null))=

    switch

    c1 is true:Status(name(Prepare_for_payment),role(B),..., serv-seq(x-|s1,null))

    c2 is true:Status(name(Online_recharge),role(B),..., serv-seq(x-|s1,null))

    v1 is true:Status(name(Compensate),role(O),..., serv-seq(x-|s1,null))

    v2 is true:Status(name(Cancel_order),role(B),..., serv-seq(s1,null))

...

(6) Status(name(Prepare_to_deliver_goods),role(V),......, serv-seq(x-|s1,null))=

    if v5 is true then Status(name(Refund),role(TPP),......,serv-seq(s1,null))

    else Status(name(Deliver_goods),role(V),......, serv-seq(x-|s1,null))

...

(10) Status(name(Send_ money),role(TPP),......,serv-seq(x-|s1,null))=

    Status(name(Receive_money),role(V),......, serv-seq(s1, singleton (x)))

.../*Note that for brevity, only partial information is shown.*/

Otherwise the specification must be extended. Table 15.5 summarizes some of the findings. Because in Sit5 the path fails, Table 15.6 shows how to extend the specification. After the specification is verified to be complete, an example of instantiation is described in Table 15.7. At last the specification is translated in BPEL as shown in Table 15.8.

**Table 15.5** Verification paths of the property

| Situation | Condition | Terminating state | Satisfaction |
|-----------|-----------|-------------------|--------------|
| Sit1 | c1, c3 and c4 are true | The seller receives the money | Success |
| Sit2 | c2 and v5 are true | Refundment from the third-party | Success |
| Sit5 | C1, c3, v6 and v8 are true | the seller receives the money | Failure |

**Table 15.6** Extension of the specification

Extension : Order with contracts based on the third-party payment platform

...

Requires(for x: order; s1:order-sequences;......)

(1) Status(name(Prepare_to_return_goods),role(B),..., serv-seq(x-|s1,null))=
    Status(name(Apply_for_ refund),role(B),......,serv-seq(x-|s1,null))

**Table 15.7** An example of instantiation

Abbreviation 1: Book Order with contracts based on the third -party payment platform is Order with contracts based on the third -party payment platform [with Book Order as Order, Book Order Sequences as Order Sequences,...]

**Table 15.8** BPEL specification of this case

```
...
<partnerLinks>
      <partnerLink name = "Online_order" partnerLinkType = "Online_orderPLT"
   myRole = "Buyer" partnerRole = "Orderservice"/>
...
<partnerLinks>
   <sequences>
         <receive partnerLink = "Online_order" portType = "Ins:Online_order portType "
                     operation = "SendOrder" variable = "OD" ...>
         ...    /*Note that for brevity, only partial information is shown.*/
```

## 15.7 Conclusion

Contrary to other work [6, 7] focusing on translating concrete BPEL specifications into some formal language verified using the model checker, obviously our generic method can-reduced the need for proof. Furthermore our contribution is to integrate behaviour descriptions with contracts in generic specifications. In the future, we hope to semi-automatically compile the specification in Tecton into BPEL.

**Acknowledgments** The research described in this paper was supported by the National Natural Science Foundation of China under Grant No. 61003126 and the Shanghai Natural Science Foundation of China under Grant No. 09ZR1408400.

# References

1. Musser DR, Shao Z (2002) Concept use or concept refinement: an important distinction in building generic specifications. In Proceedings of the 4th international conference on formal engineering methods. Volume of LNCS 2495, Springer. New York, pp 132–143)
2. Jie Zhai Z, Shao (2011) Specification and verification of generic web service composition. Comput Appl Softw 28(11):64–68 (in Chinese)
3. Musser DR, Shao Z (2003) The Tecton concept description language (revised version). http://www.cs.rpi.edu/~zshao
4. Jie Zhai Z, Shao (2005) The Proof System based on Tecton—Violet. J ECUST 31(2):198–202 (in Chinese)
5. Zhai J, Shao Z (2011) Generic web sevices composition verification based on batch proof method. In ICCIS 2011(3):843–846
6. Lomuscio A, Qu H, Solanki M (2012) Towards verifying contract regulated service compositions. Auton Agent Multi-agent Syst 24:345–373
7. Lomuscio A, Qu H, Raimondi F (2009) MCMAS: a model checker for the verification of multi-agent systems. In: Proceedings of CAV 2009. LNCS (vol 5643). Springer, New York, pp 682–688

# Chapter 16
# Adaptive Random Testing Through Dynamic Partitioning by Localization with Restriction and Enlarged Input Domain

Korosh koochekian sabor and mehran mohsenzadeh

**Abstract** Despite the importance of random testing approach, it is not used itself, but plays a core role in many testing methods. Based on the intuition that evenly distributed test cases have more chance for revealing non-point pattern failure regions, various Adaptive Random Testing (ART) methods have been proposed. A large portion of this methods such as ART with random partitioning by localization have edge preference problem. This problem would decrease the performance of these methods. In this article the enlarged input domain approach is used for decreasing the edge preference in ART through dynamic partitioning by localization with Restriction. Simulations have shown that the failure detection capability of ART through dynamic partitioning by localization with Restriction and enlarged input domain is comparable and usually better than that of other adaptive random testing approaches.

**Keywords** Random testing · Adaptive random testing · Localization · Enlarged input domain

## 16.1 Introduction

It has been widely recognized that exhaustive testing (testing a program with all possible inputs) is not feasible [1]. Different methods for selecting test cases with the aim of improving failure detection capability have been proposed [2–6].

K. k. sabor (✉) · m. mohsenzadeh
Department of Computer Engineering, Science and Research Branch, Islamic Azad University, hesarak 1477893855 Tehran, Iran
e-mail: koorosh.koochekian@gmail.com

m. mohsenzadeh
e-mail: Mohsenzadeh@srbiau.ac.ir

W. Lu et al. (eds.), *Proceedings of the 2012 International Conference on Information Technology and Software Engineering*, Lecture Notes in Electrical Engineering 212, DOI: 10.1007/978-3-642-34531-9_16, © Springer-Verlag Berlin Heidelberg 2013

Random testing is a standard approach for automatic selection of test cases [7, 8]. In random testing test cases are selected randomly until a stopping condition such as detecting a failure, executing predefined number of test cases or ending of a time limitation is met.

As described by Chan et al. in [9] typical failure patterns which happen in programs are block pattern, strip pattern and point pattern. The block pattern in which failures are clustered in one or more continuous areas is the most common case. The strip pattern involves a contiguous area but elongated in one dimension while quite narrow in the other. And lastly the point pattern which involves failures that are distributed in small groups in the input domain.

A simple but effective improvement in random testing is presented in [10, 11]. According to the idea that failures in programs are shaped according to the represented failure patterns the new ART approach uses of the available information about the previously executed test cases location and tries to improve the performance by decreasing the number of executed test cases required to reveal the first failure.

Some of ART methods such as ART through dynamic partitioning by localization have edge preference problem. Edge preference problem happens when the test cases on the boundaries of the input domain have more chance of being selected compared with test cases in the center part of the input domain.

ART through dynamic partitioning localized by restriction integrates the concept of localization into the ART through dynamic partitioning method. Although the localization concept enhances evenly distribution of test cases in ART through dynamic partitioning, it intensifies the edge preference problem.

In this paper we investigate the effect of enlarge input domain for eliminating edge preference in ART through dynamic partitioning localized by restriction.

In this article elements of the input domain are known as failure-causing input, if they produce incorrect outputs. The input domain is denoted by D. The failure rate is calculated as the division of number of failure causing inputs by the total number of inputs in the input domain. F-measure which is defined as number of test cases required for detecting the first failure is used as effectiveness metric. F-Measure is more prominent for testers and is closer to the reality by the reason of that usually when a failure is detected, testing would normally stop and debugging would start.

ART through dynamic partitioning [12] choose the next test case based on the idea that if the test case is selected from the biggest region then it would have more chance of being farthest from the executed test cases. But as it is obvious in Fig. 16.1 this approach would not always leads to the expected result. To overcome to this problem in [13] ART through dynamic partitioning localized by restriction had been proposed.

ART through dynamic partitioning localized by restriction would be executed in two steps, in the first step the test case Generation region would be selected and a restricted region around each nearby previously executed test case will be created, In the second a test case would be selected but it would be executed only if it is outside of all of the restricted regions else it would be discarded and another

**Fig. 16.1** Art through
dynamic partitioning [12]

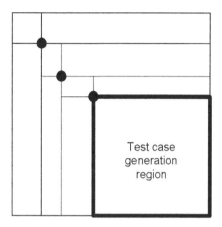

**Fig. 16.2** Art through
dynamic partitioning
localized by restriction

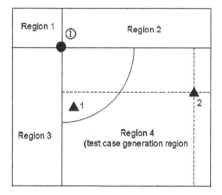

test case would be selected until a test case outside of all the restricted regions found.

It is noteworthy that executed test cases are divided into two categories: nearby executed test cases and far executed test cases. Nearby executed test cases are those which are located in the vertices of the test case generation regions, while the other executed test cases would be classified as far executed test cases. In this method restricted regions would only be created around the nearby executed test cases.

As it is shown in Fig. 16.2 this method resolves the problem in Fig. 16.1 but causes edge preference to occur. As the result the performance would decrease.

The main reason for edge preference is that less nearby previously executed test cases near the boundaries exist. So candidate test cases near the boundaries would have more chance of being selected.

An approach named enlarged input domain for eliminating edge preference has been proposed [14]. In this method the input domain would be enlarged by factor f in each dimension and test cases would be selected from the enlarged input domain but it would only be executed if it is in the original input domain. Figure 16.3 shows the original input domain D and the enlarged input domain $D'$.

**Fig. 16.3** The original input
domain enlarged by factor F
in each dimension [14]

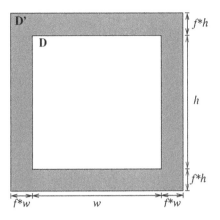

In this paper we would use enlarge input domain method to eliminate edge preference problem in ART through dynamic partitioning localized by restriction. Test cases would be selected from the enlarged input domain and would be used for partitioning input domain, but they will be executed only if they are in the original input domain.

This article is organized as follows In Sect. 16.2 the algorithm of the proposed method named ART through dynamic partitioning localized by restriction and enlarge input domain is presented. In Sect. 16.3, we present our simulation results. Finally, conclusion is presented in Sect. 16.4.

## 16.2 Discussion

Adaptive random testing through dynamic partitioning localized by restriction and enlarge input domain algorithm

1. Enlarge the original input domain by factor f and assume vertexes as $i'_{min}$, $i'_{max}$, $j'_{min}$, $j'_{max}$

2. Initiate the subdomain linked list L with the entire input domain $\{(i'_{min}, j'_{min}, F), (i'_{min}, j'_{max}, F), (i'_{max}, j'_{max}, F), (i'_{max}, j'_{min}, F)\}$ as the only element in it.

3. Choose the last element in the link list L as the test case generation region and set executed test cases set E empty.

4. For all the vertexes of test case generation region if Flag is T add it to nearby executed test cases set E. assume Number of elements in E as l.

5. Create a restricted region around each nearby previously executed test case while a test case which is outside of all the restricted regions not found randomly select test case from the selected region. Assume the founded test case which is outside all of the restricted regions as $c_q$.

**Fig. 16.4** Four region
created by the first non-
failure causing executed test
case

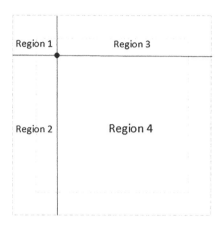

6. If $c_q$ is inside the original input domain Execute it. If it is a failure causing input report the failure and end the algorithm. Else partition the input domain with the executed test case into four regions and add them to the list L. Sort elements in L According to the region size in ascending order. Go to step3. If $c_q$ is not inside the original input domain then do not execute the test case and only partition the input domain with the selected test case into four region. For each region if it is wholly located outside of the original input domain decline it. Else add it to the list L. Sort elements in L According to the region size in ascending order go to step3.

An example for the execution of this algorithm is presented in Figs. 16.4 and 16.5. In these figures the original input domain is shown by the inner dashed line and the enlarged input domain is shown by the outer dashed line. The test cases would be selected from the enlarged input domain. In the first place a test case is randomly selected, it is within the original input domain so it is executed and the enlarged input domain has been partitioned by the executed test case into four regions. These four regions are shown in Fig. 16.4.

In the second pass as it is shown in Fig. 16.5 one test case is randomly selected on the ground that this test case is located in the restricted region it is discarded and the next test case is randomly selected because it is outside of all the restricted regions it is selected as the next test case to be executed. Since the selected test case is outside of the original input domain it is not executed but it has been used for partitioning the enlarged input domain into four regions. Since 3 of these partitions are wholly in the enlarged input domain they are discarded and only one partition which has been left is added to the partitions list.

It is obvious that there are two nearby executed test cases for the third pass in the algorithm. So it can be seen that the edge preference problem would be eliminated.

**Fig. 16.5** Four regions
created by the second test
case which is not in the input
domain

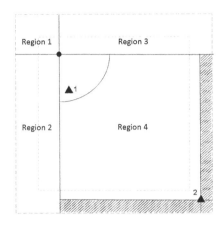

## 16.3 Simulations

In this article a series of simulations in 2-dimensional input space domains with the aim of measuring failure detection capability of the proposed approach has been conducted. In each test run a failure-causing region of the specified size and pattern has been assigned within the input domain. For block pattern a square has been used as failure-causing region. For strip pattern two points on the adjacent borders of the input domain has been randomly selected and have been connected to each other to form a strip with predefined size. For each simulation, 5,000 test runs were executed with failure rate 0.001 and 10, 20, 30 and 40 % as exclusion ratios.

In the first part of experiments the performance of the proposed method has been compared with that of ART through dynamic partitioning localized by restriction and random testing in a 2-dimensional input domain. Line with triangle shows random testing performance, line with diamond shows ART through dynamic partitioning localized by restriction performance and line with square represent proposed method performance. As it can be seen from Fig. 16.6 the performance of both ART through dynamic partitioning localized by restriction and proposed method increases as exclusion ratio increases and both methods have maximum performance when exclusion ratio is equal to 40 %. According to Fig. 16.6 on the ground that when exclusion ratio increases edge preference problem would become more significant and the proposed method eliminates edge preference, performance increase in each step of exclusion ratio grows in the proposed method is more compared with ART through dynamic partitioning localized by restriction.

In the second part of simulations the performance of the proposed method has been compared with that of ART through dynamic partitioning localized by restriction and pure random testing when failure pattern is of strip type.

Line with triangle shows random testing performance, line with diamond shows ART by localization performance and line with square represent proposed method performance. As it can be seen from Fig. 16.7 the performance of both ART

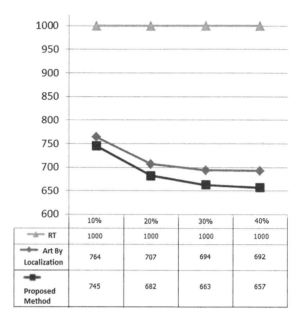

**Fig. 16.6** F-measure of RT and ART through dynamic partitioning localized by restriction and the proposed method in 2D input domain with block failure pattern with diverse exclusion ratios

| | 10% | 20% | 30% | 40% |
|---|---|---|---|---|
| RT | 1000 | 1000 | 1000 | 1000 |
| Art By Localization | 764 | 707 | 694 | 692 |
| Proposed Method | 745 | 682 | 663 | 657 |

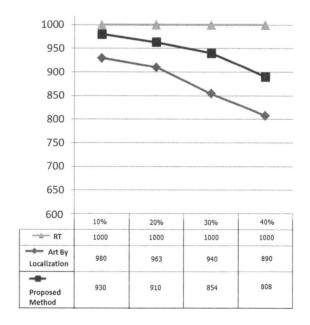

**Fig. 16.7** F-measure of RT and ART through dynamic partitioning localized by restriction and the proposed method in 2D input domain with strip failure pattern with diverse exclusion ratios

| | 10% | 20% | 30% | 40% |
|---|---|---|---|---|
| RT | 1000 | 1000 | 1000 | 1000 |
| Art By Localization | 980 | 963 | 940 | 890 |
| Proposed Method | 930 | 910 | 854 | 808 |

through dynamic partitioning localized by restriction and proposed method increases as exclusion ratio increases and both methods have maximum performance when exclusion ratio is equal to 40 %. According to Fig. 16.7 the proposed method outperforms ART by localization in any exclusion ratio by the reason that it eliminates edge preference in ART through dynamic partitioning localized by restriction.

Intuitively speaking, when the failure pattern is not a point pattern, more evenly spread test cases have a better chance of hitting the failure patterns [15]. Therefore on the ground that in this case ART through dynamic partitioning by localization with restriction would have the same performance compared with random testing, the proposed method would not increase the performance.

## 16.4 Conclusion

In this article a new method for eliminating the edge preference problem in ART through dynamic partitioning localized by restriction has been proposed. According to this combinational method before starting ART through dynamic partitioning localized by distance, input domain would be enlarged by factor f in each dimension and then ART through dynamic partitioning localized by restriction would be executed on the enlarged input domain.

The performance of this combinational method has been compared with ART through dynamic partitioning localized by restriction and pure random testing and it has been observed that as the exclusion ratio grows the performance of the both ART through dynamic partitioning localized by restriction and proposed method increase but this increase is more in the proposed method. Also in all cases the propose method outperforms ART through dynamic partitioning localized by restriction.

According to the empirical results since this combinational method not only eliminates edge preference but also gains benefit from adaptive random testing approach advantages. We recommend testers that if Adaptive random testing through dynamic partitioning localized by restriction is suitable for their goal, to use Adaptive random testing through dynamic partitioning localized by distance and enlarged input domain.

In our future works we would investigate the effect of increase or decrease of factor F in the performance of the method. Also we would investigate the performance of enlarge input domain for eliminating edge preference when it is combined with other adaptive random testing methods.

## References

1. Beizer B (1990) Software testing techniques. Van Nostrand Reinhold, New York
2. Laski JW, Korel B (1983) A data flow oriented program testing strategy. IEEE Trans Softw Eng 9(3):347–354
3. Offutt J, Liu S (1999) Generating test data from SOFL specifications. J Syst Softw 49(1):49–62
4. Offutt J, Liu S, Abdurazik A, Ammann P (2003) Generating test data from state-based specifications. Softw Test Verification Reliab 13(1):25–53

5. Stocks P, Carrington D (1996) A framework for specification-based testing. IEEE Trans Softw Eng 22(11):777–793
6. White LJ, Cohen EI (1980) A domain strategy for computer program testing. IEEE Trans Softw Eng 6(3):247–257
7. Hamlet R (1994) Random testing. Encyclopedia of Software Engineering. Wiley, New York, pp 970–978
8. Loo PS, Tsai WK (1988) Random testing revisited. Inf Softw Technol 30(7):402–417
9. Chan FT, Chen TY, Mak IK, Yu YT (1996) Proportional sampling strategy: guidelines for software testing practitioners. Inf Softw Technol 38:775–782
10. Chen TY, Tse TH, Yu YT (2001) Proportional sampling strategy: a compendium and some insights. J Syst Softw 58:65–81
11. Mak IK (1997) On the effectiveness of random testing. Master's thesis. (Department of Computer Science. The University of Melbourne, Melbourne
12. Chen TY, Eddy G, Merkel R, Wong PK (2004) Adaptive random testing through dynamic partitioning. Accepted to appear in Proceedings of the 4th international conference on quality software (QSIC)
13. Chen TY, Huang DH (2004) Adaptive random testing by localization in Asia-Pacific software engineering conference. pp 1530–1362
14. Mayer J, Schneckenburger C (2006) Adaptive random testing with enlarged input domain. In: Sixth international conference on quality software (QSIC'06) IEEE. pp 251–258
15. Chen TY, leung H, Mak IK (2004) Adaptive random testing. In: 9th Asian computing science conference on computer science. LNC 3321, pp 320–329. Springer, Berlin

# Chapter 17
# Effective Test Case Generation via Concolic Execution

Yan Hu and He Jiang

**Abstract** A concolic execution based testing framework is proposed to generate tests for real-life applications. Concolic execution is a hybrid software analysis technique which combines concrete execution with symbolic execution. It makes some tradeoff between pure static analysis and dynamic analysis. Existing concolic testing tools are mostly targeting programs with sources, and nontrivial dependencies on application development tools are introduced thereby. In our work, we built a concolic execution tool that directly targets program binary. Therefore, it can generate test cases without the presence of program source, and does not incur unnecessary dependances on the application development tools. Depth First Search algorithms are integrated into the test case generation process to explore the test space. Experiments show that concolic execution based test case generation process is effective in both achieving good coverage, and uncovering errors.

**Keywords** Test case generation · Concolic execution · Depth first search · Black-box testing

## 17.1 Introduction

Concolic execution is a hybrid software analysis technique used to find bugs in programs. It is developed as an improvement upon existing random testing techniques [1, 2]. PathCrawler [3], EXE (later extended and renamed Klee) [4], DART

Y. Hu (✉) · H. Jiang
School of Software, Dalian University of Technology, 8th road,
Dalian developement zone, Dalian, China
e-mail: huyan@dlut.edu.cn

W. Lu et al. (eds.), *Proceedings of the 2012 International Conference on Information Technology and Software Engineering*, Lecture Notes in Electrical Engineering 212, DOI: 10.1007/978-3-642-34531-9_17, © Springer-Verlag Berlin Heidelberg 2013

[5] and CUTE [6] is a set of white-box testing tools for programs written in C. The jCute tool is unit testing framework for multithreaded Java programs, which is an extension of CUTE to Java [7].

Concolic execution based testing, a.k.a conclic testing, has been proved by those white box testing tools. Among them, Klee [4] has been applied to large scale applications with the presence of source code. Currently, there still lacks flexible concolic testing tools that could conduct effective blackbox testing. In this chapter, we proposed a blackbox testing technique, which is a concolic testing engine targeting binary programs. The testing tool relies on a dynamic instrumentor to collect program variables information at runtime, and use the collected information to build constraints and solve the constraints. Depth first searching algorithms for input space exploration is designed and evaluated. The coverage effectiveness of two versions of the incorporated DFS algorithm is studied on 3 real world applications.

## 17.2 Preliminaries

Concolic Execution works as an explorer of the program input space. It iteratively inverts some branch condition and solve the new predicate path that represents a program execution path under a new input. Essentially, a concolic testing algorithm can be described by the following steps:

1. Collect all variables from the tested program. Mark the set of input variables, and treat them as symbolic variables.
2. Choose an arbitrary input.
3. Run the tested program in monitored mode with the chosen input. The monitoring of the program can be achieved via static or dynamic instrumentation.
4. Collect the trace log, and symbolically execute the trace to generate the set of symbolic constraints.
5. Negate the last path condition to generate a new condition path. If all condition paths have been negated, then the algorithm terminates.
6. Generate a constraint specification for the new condition path, and send it to a constraint solver. If the solver successfully find a set of symbolic variables values that satisfies the new path constraints, then generate a new input with it.
7. Repeat step 3.

## 17.3 Workflow of the Test Case Generator

In order to generate different inputs, the generator must rely on the program runtime information to make new input generation decisions. To help retrieve the required runtime information, a dynamic instrumentor is used to monitor each

**Fig. 17.1** Test case
generation workflow

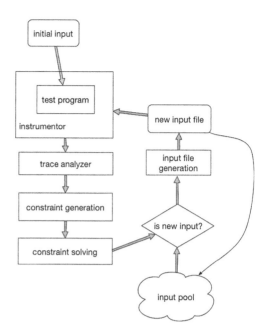

program run. At the start point, an initial input file is supplied to the test program. Various traces are generated after the initial run. Those traces are sent to the trace analyzer, then the trace analyzer uses it's equipped analyses on the traces to get more detailed information about the previous program run. The input information includes conditional program path, and coverage information, and program execution trace, as depicted in Definition 1.

**Definition 1** *(input) the input is a structure <SVS, filename, PP, coverageinfo>.*

- SVS denotes the source variable set.
- Filename means the name of the input data file.
- PP means predicate path. This predicate path is filled only after the input is evaluated, i.e. After the test program has run with the input file, and traces are generated, and analyzed.
- Coverageinfo is a brief description of the customizable coverage information. Various coverage information, like basic lock coverage/line coverage/branch coverage/method coverage, could be used separately, or used as a combined group.

The test case generation process is demonstrated in Fig. 17.1. The initial run triggers the loop of test input generation. After the traces are generated and analyzed, the input variable set and the predicate path will be used as a guidance for generating new input data. The input generation work will done in four phases: One predicate in the predicate path is inverted.

- The new predicate path is used as a model to generate acceptable constraint solver specification.
- The newly generated constraints are solved by the constraint solver. If the satisfying variable set is found, then the input generation will succeed.
- Final input data is generated from the new variable set.

To be effective, not all memory variables are tracked. The instrumentor only monitors the values that are dependent on the source variables. During the program run, the flow of source variable values are monitored by the instrumentor, and all related memory operations and conditional branches are recorded in the form of program traces.

A pool of input data files are maintained. The branch signature is used to identify a certain input. Each time a new input is generated, it will be checked against the current input pool to see if thud input has already existed. If the input is a new one, then it will be added to the input map.

## 17.4 Test Case Generator Implementation

### 17.4.1 Dynamic Instrumentation

Instrumentation is an important part of the test generation process. The test generator relies on instrumenting extra code to generate the data required by the concolic execution engine. As previously stated, we use dynamic instrumentation to collect program data. The popular dynamic instrumentor Valgrind is used as the basis of the dynamic instrumentation process.

First, we need to identify symbolic variables. Program inputs are calculated from those symbolic variables, which can also be called "source variables". The source variables could be declared in several ways:

- Use program annotation to mark which variable should be symbolic.
- Put all the input data in a single file, and read from it.

In this paper, we use the file based symbolic data specification method. With this method, the identification of symbolic variables is simply done via interposition of file operations on a given input file. This work is done with the help of Valgrind system call interposition feature.

Since the program execution flow is determined by those source variables, the analysis records only program operations that are dependent on the source variables. The flow of data is tracked with the help of the dynamic instrumentor.

The tracking procedure is described in Table 17.1. The tracked set is first initialized by adding the variables to which the input file content has been read (line 01). Then as the program runs, process each operation by its type (line 02). Line 03–11 shows how each type of operation is processed.

**Table 17.1** Symbolic data flow tracking

| Procedure: tracking of symbolic data flow parameter: tset—the tracked set of variables |
| --- |
| 01 Init_track_set(tset) |
| 02 For each program operation: |
| 03 If op.type = read: |
| 04 If op.srcopnd is in tracked set: |
| 05 Add op.destOpnd to the tracked set |
| 06 Elif op.type = write: |
| 07 If op.srcOpnd is not in the tracked set: |
| 08 Remove op.destOpnd from the tracked set |
| 09 Elif condition |
| 10 Is tracked(op.condvar) |
| 11 Add the condition to the predicate path |

The tracked data will be used when the dynamic instrumentor is going to record condition path. Each time a conditional operation is met, it is logged into the trace only if the operation is dependant on at least one of the tracked variables in set.

### 17.4.2 The Input Searching Algorithm

The input searching algorithm is described in Table 17.2.

The input search algorithm in Table 17.2 is a depth-first search algorithm with the input pool guidance. We use the boolean valued string of the predicate path to classify input data. All the inputs that generates the same boolean string will be put into the same input category.

A map is used to maintain the predicate path to input group correspondence. The input space is explored in a depth-first manner. As shown in the algorithm, each time a input is selected to generate new inputs, the newly generated inputs are pushed to the top of the input stack one by one (line 20). In each iteration of the outer while loop, one input is poped from the stack (line 08).

In the test generation process, newly generated inputs are not executed until they are popped from the input stack. After the input popped from the stack, the test program runs with the input under the monitor of dynamic instrumentor equipped with customized analyses (line 09). Various logging information, including execution trace and predication path, is recorded. The predication path to input group map forms the actual input pool. With the runtime information acquired, the profits that the new input could gain can be evaluated. E.g. If we care about how the input will affect the coverage capabilities, we can look at the coverage information before and after the program run, to see if how much improvements the input could achieve.

**Table 2** Input searching algorithm

| Algorithm: input search algorithm (depth-first search, DFS) |
| --- |
| 01  Initial_input.file_name <- input file name |
| 02   Run_program(in file)//the traces as well as the predicate path is recorded here |
| 03   Initial_input.predicatePath < - get predicate path of last run |
| 04   PredicatePath_to_inputGroup_map[initial_input.predicate path] = {initial_input} |
| 05   Insert initial_input into the input pool |
| 06   While(input pool is not empty) |
| 07   Begin |
| 08    Input < - inputPool.retrieveFirst() |
| 09      Run_program(input) |
| 10    Path < - getPredicatePath() |
| 11      If PredicatePath_to_inputGroup_map[input] is not null |
| 12             PredicatePath_to_inputGroup_map[input].insert(input) |
| 13      Else |
| 14             PredicatePath_to_inputGroup_map[input] = input |
| 15              For i in 0..path.Len: |
| 16             NewPath < - Invert(path, i) |
| 17             NewVarSet < - SolveThePathConstraint(newPath) |
| 18              If newvarset is not empty: |
| 19                Newinputfile < - generateNewInputFile(newVarSet) |
| 20                InputPool.insertFirst(newInputFile) |
| 21  End |

## 17.4.3 Bounded Depth First Search

Slight changes could be made to the algorithm described in 17.4.2. During the search, we could choose not to try each path condition from start to end (from index 0 to len(path)). We can expand only a certain interval of the path (e.g. from start to start + bound, where start is the index of the first unnegated condition). So that we can gain more flexible control of the search process.

## 17.5  Experiments

### 17.5.1 Experimental Setup

The experimental environment is built on an Laptop with ubuntu Linux 8.04. The benchmarks are a set of C/C++ applications: ld (the GNU linker/loader); js (The javascript interpreter); swfdump (from swftools-0.8.1).

**Fig. 17.2** Coverage statistsic
of ld within 100 iterations (bb
coverage baseline 4,094)

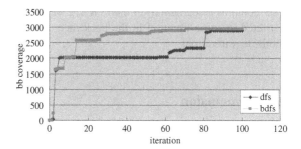

**Fig. 17.3** Coverage statistics
of js within 100 iterations (bb
coverage baseline 6,640)

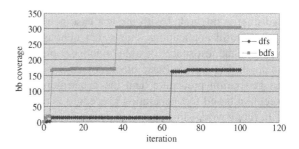

**Fig. 17.4** Coverage statistics
of swfdump within 100
iterations (bb coverage
baseline 2,151)

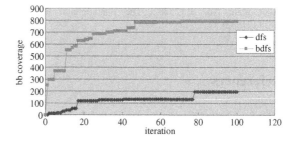

## 17.5.2  Basic Block Coverage Statistics

We run the test generation process until it generates 100 test cases. Each iteration
generates one input. The basic block information is calculated by counting the
basic blocks at binary level. The basic block information is demonstrated in
Figs. 17.2, 17.3, 17.4.

We can see from the experimental results that, bounded depth-first search
outperforms simple depth-first-search in basic block coverage.

## 17.5.3  Coverage of Error

When the target program contains software defects, it should be profitable to add
function-level restrictions to the constraint generation process. Example swfdump

0.8.1 contains a segmentation fault. When we make the constraint generation area restricted to some function in the backtrace of the fault, and the fault was found within less iterations.

## 17.6 Conclusion

In this paper, a test case generation technique based on concolic execution is proposed and evaluated. Standard concolic execution engine is used as the foundation of the test case generation tool. Two versions of depth-first-search algorithm is integrated with the test case generation procedure. The experiments on real-world applications shows that although depth-first-search is effective in exploring the test space, flexible bounds set on the searching depth could improve the depth-first-search. Basic block coverage is used as a criteria to evaluation the test generation procedure, and the experimental results shows that the concolic execution based test generation procedure is effective.

In future works, fine granularity search depth control and function level analysis will be studied.

**Acknowledgments** This work is partially supported by Natual Science Foundation of China under grant No. 61175062; The Fundamental Research Funds for Central Universities (DUT12JS02).

## References

1. Godefroid, P, Michael YL, David M (2007) Automated whitebox fuzz testing (technical report). TR-2007-58. ftp://ftp.research.microsoft.com/pub/tr/TR-2007-58.pdf
2. Godefroid P (2007) Random testing for security: blackbox vs. whitebox fuzzing. In: Proceedings of the 2nd international workshop on random testing. New York
3. Williams N, Bruno M, Patricia M, et al (2005) PathCrawler: automatic generation of path tests by combining static and dynamic analysis. In: Proceedings of the 5th European dependable computing conference, Budapest, Hungary
4. Dawson E, Cristian C, Vijay G, et al (2006) EXE: automatically generating inputs of death. In: Proceedings of the 13th international conference on computer and communications security (CCS 2006). Alexandria
5. Godefroid P, Nils K, Koushik S (2009) DART: directed automated random testing. In: Proceedings of the 2005 ACM SIGPLAN conference on programming language design and implementation. New York
6. Koushik S, Darko M, Gul A (2009) CUTE: a concolic unit testing engine for C. In: Proceedings of the 10th European software engineering conference, New York
7. Koushik S, Gul A (2006) CUTE and jCUTE: concolic unit testing and explicit path model-checking tools. In: Computer aided verification: 18th international conference, CAV 2006, Seattle

# Chapter 18
# An Integrated Method for Rapid Software Development and Effective Process Management

Jyhjong Lin, Chaoyu Lin and Weipang Yang

**Abstract** An integrated method for rapid software development and effective process management is presented in this chapter. The method follows the guidelines suggested by extreme programming that asks less design work for speeding software development. Further, for effective guidance on the development, it directs the construction of system components by imposing a layered specification and construction of these components through its process of development activities where Petri net techniques and Java annotation features are imposed to support such management issues as SCM, traceability, and progress monitoring. Since the method directs a layered development of system components and the management of its development activities is featured in an integrated manner, team productivities can be greatly enhanced by intimate collaborations between development and management staff. For illustration, an example application is presented that directs the development of a software system with business-oriented services.

J. Lin (✉)
Department of Information Management, Ming Chuan University, Taoyuan, Taiwan
e-mail: jlin@mail.mcu.edu.tw

C. Lin · W. Yang
Department of Information Management, National Dong Hwa University, Hualien, Taiwan
e-mail: d9732010@ems.ndhu.edu.tw

W. Yang
e-mail: wpyang@mail.ndhu.edu.tw

W. Lu et al. (eds.), *Proceedings of the 2012 International Conference on Information Technology and Software Engineering*, Lecture Notes in Electrical Engineering 212, DOI: 10.1007/978-3-642-34531-9_18, © Springer-Verlag Berlin Heidelberg 2013

## 18.1 Introduction

Properly identifying required activities and directing the completion of these activities for constructing relevant artifacts/deliverables are key issues for the successful development of a software system. For these needs, it has become a great deal of concerns for a software project team to impose a suitable development method because such a method can help to figure out required activities/artifacts and more importantly can provide information to assist on directing the completion/ construction of these activities/artifacts. Although there are already plenty of software development methods in the literature and also as a common recognition there are no methods that are prefect to employ all sound features for effective development specification and guidance, a desired method that is suitable for a software development project can still be expected with the following features: (1) It can define the structural and dynamic aspects of the development work; (2) It is featured by proper mechanisms to support effective guidance on the development work; (3) The defined activities can be concerned in a leveled manner such that team members can participate in the execution by providing/monitoring respective information about the specification and completion of concerned activities/ artifacts; and (4) It can support rapid development for small- or medium-sized projects by less but effective overhead on completing/constructing defined activities/artifacts; automatic tools should also be generated to facilitate its practical applications.

As mentioned earlier, there are already plenty of software development methods in the literature. In general, they can be divided into three kinds: (1) design-oriented that addresses more analysis/design work such as Rational Unified Process [1, 2], and Spiral model [3, 4]; (2) code- oriented that focuses on code work (e.g., coding and testing) such as Rapid Application Development (RAD) [5] and Extreme Programming (XP) [6, 7]; and (3) compromised ones that employ simplified design and code work through rapid engineering ways [8, 9]. In general, these approaches provide sound mechanisms for development specification and guidance; some drawbacks with respect to the above desired features can still be found among them: (1) For design- or code-oriented models, each one gets an extreme in its concerning spectrums, so the advantages for one kind would become the opposites for the other; (2) For the comprised way that takes advantage of the two extreme kinds, its less overhead on design work and associated rapid engineering way make it good for the rapid development for small- or medium-sized projects. However, such less design work makes it lack sufficient mechanisms for supporting effective guidance on the development work; and (3) Among these existing approaches, they essentially focus on the specification and completion of defined activities; in contrast, few considerations about the management of these tasks can be found in their statements. In our knowledge, however, such management issues should not be negligible since they play a critical role for the success of these tasks.

To address these deficiencies, we presented in our previous chapter [10] a layer-based method that supports rapid software development for small- or medium-sized projects. In the method, less design work is asked for speeding software development. Further, for providing guidance on the development work, it imposes a layered specification and construction of system components on its process of development activities; this makes it easy to direct the development work by means of the execution effects of these activities on system components for realizing desired user requirements. Nonetheless, since the method has not yet addressed those management issues about its process of development activities such as SCM, traceability, and progress monitoring, we expand in this capter the method by imposing Petri nets (PN) [11] and Java annotations [12] on its development process to address these management issues where progress monitoring is specifically discussed for illustration.

This chapter is organized as follows. Section 18.2 presents the method in our previous work where the management issues about its process of development activities are addressed by Petri nets and Java annotations in Sect. 18.3. For illustration, an example application is presented that directs and manages the development of a software system with book publishing services. Finally, Sect. 18.4 has the conclusions.

## 18.2  The Development Method

As shown in Fig. 18.1, the method is layer-based with six steps:

1. **Use case identification**, described in an use case diagram, that clarifies user requirements to be satisfied in the system;
2. **Conceptual components identification**, described in a robustness diagram, that identifies conceptual components with each one playing a specific role in the realization of a desired use case;
3. **Components development order determination**, described in an extended PN process diagram, that determines the development order of those conceptual components in the three layers (Model/View/Control) of the MVC architecture through an iterative process of steps 4–6;
4. **Architectural components specification**, described in two (class and sequence) diagrams, that imposes such architectural considerations as the MVC architecture and relevant supportive design patterns on conceptual components such that formal architectural components can be derived to support the realization of the desired use case;
5. **System components design**, described in two (class and sequence) diagrams, that employs platform specific features into architectural components such that each resultant system component has a specific implementation code on the chosen platform and hence its construction can be easily achieved by a direct transformation from its design work;
6. **System components construction**, described in Java code, that implements and tests platform specific components for realizing the desired use case;

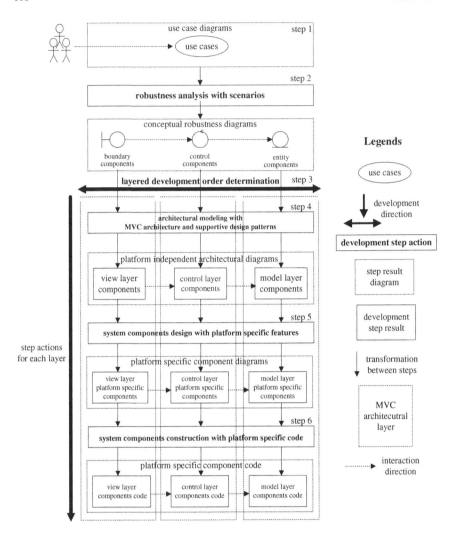

**Fig. 18.1** The architecture-centered development method

Note that steps 4–6 are iterative that proceed the development of system components (via conceptual and architectural versions) under a prescribed order over the three MVC architectural layers and such a layer-based development process is particularly specified in an extended PN process diagram that encompasses formal semantics to support the guidance and management of the development work.

With the method that specifies in step 3 components development order by an extended PN process diagram, Fig. 18.2 shows an example order of components development for the 'share writing experiences' use case in illustrative book publishing services. It is noticed that since this use case focuses on the interactions

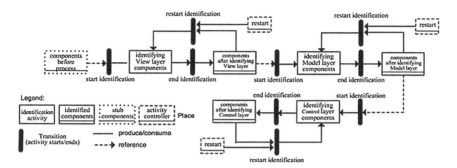

**Fig. 18.2** Development process of system components over the three MVC layers for use case-share writing experiences

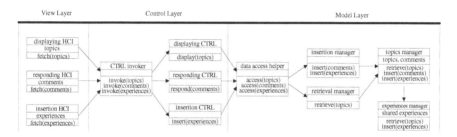

**Fig. 18.3** System components developed through the View -> Model -> Control order

among customers for sharing experiences where interaction and data models play critical roles for its realization, system components can thus be developed through an iterative process with the order View-> Model-> Control to address such characteristics. Figure 18.3 shows the resultant system components after this order of iterative works where supportive Command (CMD) and Data Access Object (DAO) design patterns are used to support effective realization of the desired use case.

## 18.3  The Management of Development Activities

Although the above method provides guidance on the development work by a layered specification and construction of system components, it has not yet addressed those management issues about the development work such as SCM, traceability, and progress monitoring. For this need, we expand herein the method by imposing a management approach with the following three steps:

1. **Components development processes specification**, described in extended PN process diagrams, that specifies those processes of the development work (i.e., specification and construction activities) over the three MVC layers or in each specific MVC layer;

2. **Annotations design**, specified in Java annotations, that describes the managerial mechanisms for addressing those management issues about the above processes of specification and construction activities;
3. **Managements realization**, described in realistic annotation instances, that achieves those management issues about development activities by tracing information revealed from the instances of defined annotations;

Note that with annotations defined in step 2, the step 3 is an iterative process for the three MVC layers; each iteration results in prospective realistic instances of these annotations to realize the management of the development work in a specific MVC layer.

### 18.3.1 Components Development Processes Specification

In addition to the development process over the three MVC layers as shown in Fig. 18.2, it is desired to specify those processes of the development activities in specific MVC layers. In general, this can be achieved by considering the structural and behavioral specification of the system components in each layer to identify any possible sequences about their development. For instance, in Fig. 18.2, the development work for those components in the View layer (i.e., the 'developing View layer components' activity) may be further described by a detailed process of development activities as shown in Fig. 18.4 (i.e., a process for detailed descriptions about the 'developing View layer components' activity in Fig. 18.2). In this detailed process, in particular, three HCI components are developed for displaying experiences, responding comments, and inserting experiences in realizing the use case where they can be focused in parallel due to their independent relationships.

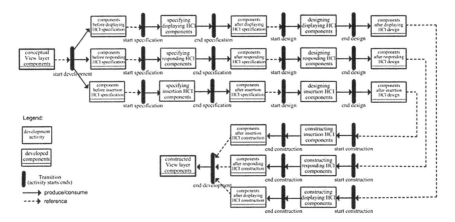

**Fig. 18.4** Development process of system components in the view layer for use case-share writing experiences

## 18.3.2 Annotations Design

With the processes of specification and construction activities over/in MVC layers, the next is to impose adequate managerial mechanisms for desired management issues about these processes of activities. In the context of the management requirements, many issues are commonly desired such as SCM, traceability, and progress monitoring. In our knowledge, among all possible endeavors for addressing these desired management issues, annotation features are recently recognized as suitable mechanisms for their satisfying the core necessity of management requirements—artifacts to be managed can be supplemented with additional information that reveals relevant metadata or comments about the artifacts for management purposes [13]. Therefore, Java annotations are imposed herein to address those management issues about the processes of activities in MVC layers.

In general, annotations are used for defining supplemental information about the processes of activities over the three MVC layers (i.e., defining the structure of the supplemental information for satisfying desired managerial purposes). Thereafter, information about each of these activities (i.e., about how this higher-level activity works for developing components in a specific layer) can then be concluded by collecting realistic information revealed from the instances of these annotations that convey status messages about any detailed processes of lower-level activities in the layer that collaborate to achieve the higher-level activity. For illustration, with the process of activities in Fig. 18.2, the following Java annotation defines supplemental progress information about the three respective activities over the MVC layers for completing the 'share writing experiences' use case.

```
@Target({ElementType.TYPE,ElementType.METHOD})
@Retention(RetentionPolicy.RUNTIME)
public @interface share_writing_experiences {
    Layer layer();/*layer being worked */String component();/*component
    being worked*/
    String developer();/*developer Id */Activity activity();/*activity in the
    work*/
    String startDate();/*activity start date */String endDate();/*activity end
    date*/
    String deadLine();/*activity deadline */String description();/* activity
    description*/}
```

## 18.3.3 Annotations Realization

After annotations for specific processes of such higher-level activities have been defined as above, they can then be used by the managers of these activities to arrange the creation of the instances of these annotations for each activity that is

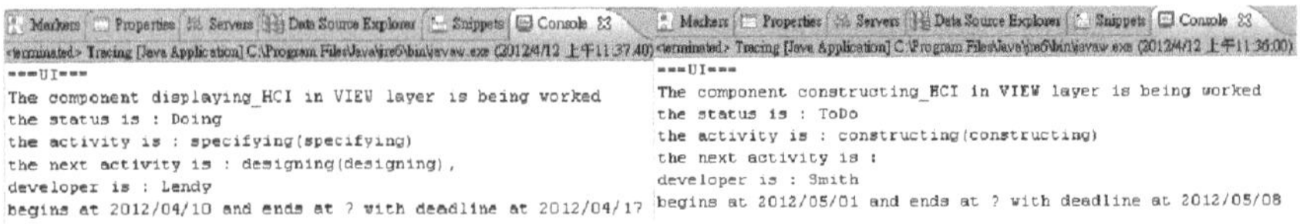

Fig. 18.5  The execution results of the tracing program

actually achieved by a detailed process of lower-level activities. In our example, suppose that the manager of the process of activities in Fig. 18.2 may arrange the creation of the instances of the above annotation for the 'developing View layer components' activity that is actually achieved by those processes of activities in Fig. 18.4. Also, suppose that a developer 'Lendy' is working at the 'specifying_HCI' activity in the outmost process in Fig. 18.4. The manager may ask him to provide information about his working status in a designated period of time (e.g., once per day) by creating the following instance in accordance with the 'share_writing_experiences' annotation:

@share_writing_experiences(
   layer = Layer.VIEW,component = "
   displaying_HCI",developer = "Lendy",
   activity = Activity.specifying, startDate = "2012/04/10", endDate = "",
   deadLine = "2012/04/17",  description = "Specify  the  displaying_HCI
   component")

Meanwhile, in case there is another developer 'Smith' who is going to work at the 'constructing_HCI' activity in the process in Fig. 18.4, he may also be asked to provide information about his to-do work in a designated period of time (e.g., once per week) by creating a new annotation instance as below.

@share_writing_experiences(layer = Layer.VIEW,
   component = "constructing_HCI",developer = "Smith", activity = Activ
   ity.constructing,  startDate = "2012/05/01",  endDate = "",deadLine =
   "2012/05/08", description = "Well prepared for the construction")

Thereafter, while a management requirement for progress monitoring about the outmost process in Fig. 18.4 is desired, a tracing program as below can be executed to trace the above two annotation instances for capturing their provided information. Figure 18.5 shows the execution results of the program that trace the above two instances by capturing their actual parameters.

private static void treatProgress(share_writing_experiences usecase) {
   Layer layer = usecase.layer(); String component = usecase.component();
   String   developer = usecase.developer();   Activity   activity = usecase.
   activity();
   String next = "";
   for (Activity a : activity.next()) {next += a + "(" + a.name() + "),";}

```
String    startDate = usecase.startDate();    String    endDate = usecase.
endDate();
String    deadLine = usecase.deadLine();    String    description = usecase.
description();
String status = ensureStatus(endDate, startDate);
System.out.print("The component " + component + " in " +layer + "
layer is being worked" +
"\nthe    status    is    :" + status + "\nthe    activity    is    :" + activity + "
(" +activity.name() + ")" +
"\nthe    next    activity    is    :    " + next + "\ndeveloper    is    :    " + devel-
oper + "\nbegins at " + startDate +
"and    ends    at" + (endDate.equals("")?"?":endDate) + "with    deadline
at" + deadLine + "\n");}
```

### 18.3.4 Management of Hierarchical Processes of Activities

From the above method, respective processes of activities over the three MVC layers or in each specific MVC layer have been firstly specified. Their prospective annotations and instances are then defined and created for providing information about higher-level activities over the three MVC layers or about lower-level activities in each specific MVC layer. Since these annotation features are specified along such a hierarchical structure of layers, the management of these processes can be achieved by applying annotated information about those activities in the hierarchical structure where (1) the situations of lower-level activities in specific MVC layers are first provided by respective developers and then (2) the status of the higher-level activities over the three MVC layers can be concluded by respective managers from these lower-level situations. Finally, the provided and concluded information can be imposed on the PN process diagrams as those in Figs. 18.2 and 18.4 to achieve desired management requirements. For instance, based on the formal semantics of the PN process diagrams, their reachability graphs can be created to convey the provided or concluded information in their states (i.e., each state has the specific situations of process activities); after then, the graphs can be traversed along their behavioral paths of states to capture the specific situations of concerned activities for satisfying desired management requirements.

## 18.4 Conclusions

In this chapter, we present an integrated method for rapid software development and effective process management. The method follows the guidelines suggested by extreme programming that asks less design work for speeding software development. Further, for effective guidance on the development, it directs the construction of system components by imposing its processes of development activities over/in the three MVC layers where Petri net techniques and Java annotation features are used to support management issues. For illustration, an example application is presented that directs and manages the development of a software system with services for book publishing. More specifically, the 'share writing experiences' use case is illustrated by specifying and managing the development of its components over the MVC layers (with a View -> Model -> Control order) or in each specific layer.

Since the method directs a layered development of system components and the management of its development activities is featured in an integrated hierarchical structure of annotations and instances, team productivities can be greatly enhanced by intimate collaborations between development and management staff.

Currently, we are advancing the method by generating an accompanied CASE tool so that the specification and construction of system components can be supported through those processes of development activities over/in the three MVC layers. In addition, the tool needs to support the management of these activities by featuring integrated annotations and instances in accordance with the hierarchical structure of these activities. In this way, the annotated information can be integrated with those processes of development activities over/in the three MVC layers to achieve desired management requirements.

# References

1. Kruchten P (1999) The rational unified process, Addison Wesley
2. Kruchten P (2000) The rational unified process, Addison Wesley
3. Boehm B (1998) A spiral model of software development and enhancement. IEEE Comput 21(5):61–72
4. Viravna C (1997) Lessons learned from applying the spiral model in the software requirements analysis phase, In: Proceedings of 3th IEEE international symposium on requirements engineering, Japan, p 40
5. Stapleton J (1997) Dynamic systems development method, Addison-Wesley
6. Lindstrom L, Jeffries R (2004) Extreme programming and agile software development methodologies, information systems management
7. Extreme programming: a gentle introduction (2011) http://www.extremeprogramming.org/. Accessed on Jan 2011
8. Armano G, Marchesi M (2000) A rapid development process with UML. ACM SIGAPP Appl Comput Rev 8(1):4–11
9. Wu J (2009) An extended MDA method for user interface modeling and transactions, In: Proceedings of 17th European conference on information systems, pp 1632–1642 June, 2009
10. Lin C, Lin J, Yang W (2011) An architecture-centered method for rapid software development, In: Proceedings of 1st international conference on engineering and technology innovation 2011 (ICETI2011), Kenting, Taiwan, Nov 2011
11. Lin J, Yeh C (2003) An object-oriented software project management model. Int J Comput Appl 10(4):247–262
12. Java annotations (2012) http://docs.oracle.com/javase/1.5.0/docs/guide/language/annotations.html. Accessed Mar 2012
13. Anvik J, Storey M-A (2008) Task articulation in software maintenance: integrating source code annotations with an issue tracking system, In: Proceedings of IEEE international conference on software maintenance, pp 460–461, Oct 2008

# Chapter 19
# A Configuration and Analysis System for Box-Joint Assembly Tooling

Yiwei Wang, Lianyu Zheng and Qingjun Liu

**Abstract** The Box-joint tooling, which can rapidly adapt to the variant products and the modified structures, is a new type of flexible tooling with high reconfigurability. In this paper the reconfigurability of the Box-joint assembly tooling are analyzed in detail, and the configuration and analysis system is developed in the CATIA software. Subsequently the structure and functions of the system are presented, then each module of the system is described in detail. Finally the floorbeams of a certain fuselage are taken as an example to validate the functions of the system. The results indicate that by using this system, workload of tooling designers can be largely reduced, and the design efficiency is siginificantly increased.

**Keywords** Reconfigurable tooling · Box-joint assembly tooling · Tooling configuration · Configuration system

## 19.1 Introduction

The cost of designing, manufacturing and installing for the airplane toolings accounts for 10–20 % of the total cost. The reason for the high cost is that the toolings have the charateristics of customizability and unreusability. The cost of

Y. Wang · L. Zheng (✉) · Q. Liu
School of Mechanical Engineering and Automation, Beihang University, No.37 Xue Yuan Road, HaiDian, Beijing 100191, China
e-mail: lyzheng@buaa.edu.cn

Y. Wang
e-mail: wyw@me.buaa.edu.cr

Q. Liu
e-mail: liugingjun@me.buaa.edu.cn

W. Lu et al. (eds.), *Proceedings of the 2012 International Conference on Information Technology and Software Engineering*, Lecture Notes in Electrical Engineering 212, DOI: 10.1007/978-3-642-34531-9_19, © Springer-Verlag Berlin Heidelberg 2013

redesigning, manufacturing and installing these dedicated fixtures is substantial (e.g. on the order of $100 million/plant/year for automotive manufacturers) [1]. They are bespoke and designed for one aircraft model only. They are permanent structures that are not designed to be moved, reused or altered. When production increases, additional bespoke fixtures are produced to achieve the rates [2]. If production rates decease then it leads to underutilization of the tooling. Due to the complexity of the aircraft structure, the increased assembly operations and the shorten delivery time for the new generation of aircraft products, heavier pressure is brought to the tooling preparation for the model engineering project. Thus the traditional 'rigid' special tooling is unable to meet the needs of multi-model and job-lot production in modern aircraft manufacture, and the problem has become one of the major factors that restrict the development of airplane assembly technology [3]. Therefore, it is necessary to practise reconfigurable flexible tooling technology. A low-cost flexible tooling concept based on Box-Joint is present by Kihlman [4]. In this conception,tooling frameworks areconstructed through a series of standard beams and box-joint components. The joint utilize friction to hold beams together. The whole structrue, easy to adjust and detach, is adapted to requirements of different assembly situations. Box-Joint assembly fixture has broad application prospects in large and small batch assembly, emergency assembly and aircraft maintenance in aircraft product family [5].

## 19.2 Principle and Configurability of Box-Joint Tooling

Box-Joint system is a series of standard beams and joint components that can be combined to form fixtures frameworks. Box-Joint tooling has great reconstruction ability and configurability. Box-Joint is a kind of modular joint which utilize friction to hold two beams and other components together. The joint can not only play the role of connecting beams but also can be used for attaching locators to the framework structure. There are no welds or permanent joints between the connecting parts of the fixture, which makes the beams and the locators easy to adjust.

As show in Fig. 19.1, The joint is made up of fixing plates placed on either side of the beam which are bolted together using standard bolts. A certain amount of preload was exerted to the bolt, and then the two beams is tightened by screws. It is the friction between the two Box-Joint plates that hold the beams in place. When the fixture need to be changed arising from product variant, the screws are simply loosened and the beams are located in their new positions, then screws tighten again. That can achieve rapid reconstruction of the entire assembly frame. The structure of Box-Joint based fixture is basically the same as traditional welding fixture, which include several parts of frame, locators and clamping devices. The difference is that the frame of the former is built of standard beams and Box-Joints.

The reconfigurable ability of Box-Joint based fixture is reflected in the following aspects:

**Fig. 19.1** Box-Joint.
1-Beam1, 2-Bolt, 3-Plate,
4-Beam2, 5-Nut

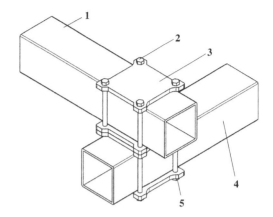

1. Configruable standard parts

Beams, plates, bolts and nuts that fixture used are made in accordance with the specifications series. Taking plates as an example, the side length and the thread holes are parameterized. After that, module series of the plates are established. When a Box-Joint fixture is to be build, the necessary parts is selected from the standard parts library. After the use of the fixture, the parts are dethatched and recycled into the library for reuse. The method improves the utilization percent of parts and reduces the tooling resources redundancy.

2. Configurable Box-Joints

The serialization of plates contributes to a variety of dimension series of Box-Joint, which are adaptive to the square beams with different dimensions. What's more important, a number of Box-Joints with different structures can be evolved through the flexible combination of plates. These Box-Joints can be applied to the fixtures with different connecting requirements such as coplanarity, dissent, orthogonality, skew of two beams in space. The configurability of dimension and structure of Box-Joint greatly enhances the reconfigurability of the assembly fixtures. The features and applications of the Box-Joints in common use are summarized in Table 19.1. When the fixture configuration is being designed, the configurated Box-Joint can be determined automatically according to the number of the beams in need and the spatial relationship among them.

3. Configurable pick-ups(locators)

In the Box-Joint assembly tooling, locators can be classifiled into three types. They are custom, parallel and serial respectively. The internal modules that make up the locators themselves also have the features of interchangeability and configurability, for example, the pogo sticks that make up the serial locators can be used interchangeably in different locators. The locators are fixed on the fixture by basic box-joints, and can be installed, detached and repositioned easily.

**Table 19.1** Features and application instruction of typical box-joints

| Type | Sketch | Box-joint used | Plate/bolt number | Beam number | Instruction |
|------|--------|----------------|-------------------|-------------|-------------|
| Basic |  |  | 2/4 | 1 | Used to constitute the other complex types of box-joint |
| Double box |  |  | 4/4 | 2 | Connect two orthogonal beams in space, for large loads |
| Squeeze box |  |  | 2/4 | 2 | Connect two orthogonal beams in space, for small loads |
| Triple joint |  |  | 12/8 | 3 | Connect three orthogonal beams in space, for large loads |
| Bracket joint |  |  | 8/8 | 3 | Connect bias beams in space, used to form the ribs |
| Turn joint |  |  | 4/4 | 2 | Connect two bias beams in space to enable angular assembly |
| Coplanar joint |  |  | 4/4 | 2 | Connect two beams of coplanar orthogonal in space, for large loads |

## 19.3 Configuration and Analysis System for Box-Joint Assembly Fixture

### 19.3.1 System Structure and Process Model

The system is developed bese on CAA, a secondary development platform which is provied by CATIA. All functions of the system is integrated in CATIA environment. Microsoft Access is used as database platform to manage the tooling resoures and instances. Two develop tools Microsoft Visual C++ 6.0 and Microsoft Visual Basic 6.0 are combinely uesd.

The system structure is divided into three layers which are data layer, business layer and user layer. Data layer stores the information about parts/components library, tooling instance library, composite tooling library, frame module library and tooling knowledge as well as the data about CATIA parametric model. The business layer is the core of the system. It comprise the main function modules that the system implementation, namely, tooling resources management, tooling configuration, tooling performance analysis is and tooling installation planning modules. User layer provides the user interface, mainly the software interface of all the functional modules.

The system process model is shown in Fig. 19.2. The input of whole syetem are product information, fixture working environment information and fixture design specification. Supported by libraries that saved in the database, tooling configuration module configures the assembly tooling using an approach which integrated the method of tooling instance retrieval, composite tooling configuration and modular design. The stability and stiffness of the configured tooling is then analyzed through tooling performance analysis module. After that, the corresponding installation operations are output by installation planning module.

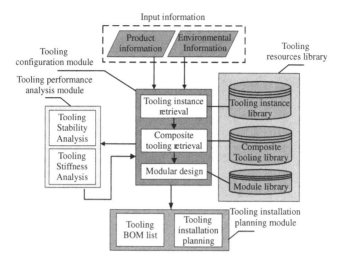

**Fig. 19.2**  Flowchart of the system implementation

## 19.3.2  Function Model of the System

### 19.3.2.1  Tooling Resources Management

Tooling resources management module can effectively manage the required resources for the tooling configuration and the module has the functions of adding, deleting or modifying the resources in the database.The resources contain beams, Box-Joints, locators, frames, tooling instances and so on. The management information includes the tooling instances, the names, the types, the description information and the size information etc. of the components in the tooling instances.

### 19.3.2.2  Tooling Configuration

Focusing on the different conditions in the design, a tooling configuration method that combines three strategies of the instance retrieval, the composite tooling configuration and the modular design is proposed and implemented in the tooling configuration module [6]. The described method can choose relevant configuration strategies according to the different information of assembled parts, thus the designed tooling will be provided with more pertinence and practicability.

Composite tooling is a three-dimensional assembly model as well as a knowledge model which includes parameters, formulas and configuration rules. It is an abstract tooling that abstracted from a series of toolings which have similar function and structure and it embraces all properties and structures of them. When

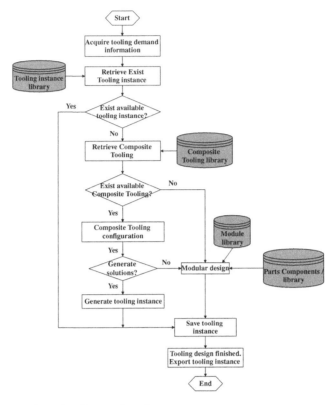

**Fig. 19.3** Flow chart of tooling configuration

product varies within a certain range, the composite tooling can generate tooling solution automatically through solving the configuration rules.

Figure 19.3 is the flowchart of the tooling configuration method. The method integrated three design strategies which are tooling instance retrieval, composite tooling configuration and modular design. The main steps are as follows:

Step 1. Tooling requirement information acquisition. Tooling requirement information, coming from assembly product information, is the fundamental basis of tooling instance retrieval.

Step 2. Tooling instance retrieval. Retrieve tooling instance library according to Tooling requirement information. If available tooling instance is found, modify it according to requirement and then go to step 5. Else retrieve composite tooling library. If the mathed composite tooling exists, go to step 3. Otherwise go to step 4.

Step 3. Solve the configuration rules of the composite tooling. If available solution is generated, go to step5. Otherwise go to step 4.

Step 4. Create a new tooling instance through modular design method according to requirement information.

Step 5. Export tooling instance and save it in the tooling instance library.

### 19.3.2.3 Tooling Performance Analysis

Tooling performance analysis, which determines the validity of the designed tooling, is an important procedure duringtooling design. The system is aimed at analyzing the stability and stiffness of the tooling by using the theory of mechanics of materials and the finite element analysis technique.

### 19.3.2.4 Tooling Installation Planning

The assembly planning module for the tooling installation will output the final data and information of the tooling configuration and analysis system. The tooling model and structures, the schemes and results for the installation and analysis can be presented to the users through documents and videos, including tooling bill of material (BOM), assembly flowchart, assembly process procedures and measurement process procedures.

## 19.4 Instance Validation

Taking the floor-beam of a certain airplane as an example, the validation process of the proposed method in this chapter will be described as follows. The floor-beams are made of 10 longitudinal beams and 5 Latitudinal beams with the distance of 400 mm respectively. The dimensions for the floor-beams are 3 700 mm in length and 2 000 mm in height, and the total weight is 80 kg.

Firstly, enter the tooling configuration module. The main interface of this module is shown in Fig. 19.4a. Press the "Import product" button (Fig. 19.4b) to import the three-dimension model of the floor-beam into CATIA. Then enter the tooling retrieval module. As shown in Fig. 19.4c, the interface includes the areas of obtaining the product information, setting the retrieval conditions, displaying

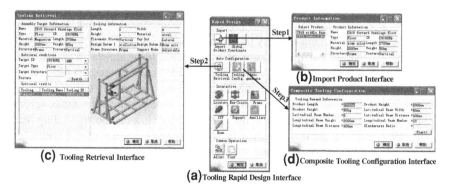

**(c)** Tooling Retrieval Interface   **(d)** Composite Tooling Configuration Interface

**(a)** Tooling Rapid Design Interface

**Fig. 19.4** Main interfaces of tooling configuration module

**Fig. 19.5** Configuration
result of composite tooling

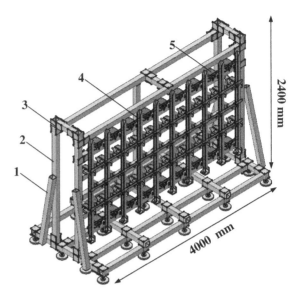

**Fig. 19.6** Interface of
performance analysis and
results

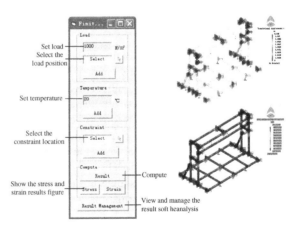

the retrieval results, tooling information and three-dimension model, and so on. When the users choose an assembly part to prepare for assembling, the system will automatically extract the information of the product from the database and the three-dimension model and display them in the related area. In the area of "setting the retrieval conditions", some pre-specified keywords are used in combination to form retrieval conditions, then the retrieval results will be shown by pressing the "retrieval" button. For this instance, the retrieval result is a composite tooling that exists and available, so the interface of the composite tooling configuration is entered. The configuration parameters are presented in Fig. 19.4d. The information demanded for the tooling requirement is still from the assembled parts. Press the "Configurate" button, then the configuration process will be executed automatically. After all the configuration rules are finished, as shown in Fig. 19.5, an assembly tooling instance is acquired without any need of manual interference. After the configuration, enter the tooling performance analysis module. For the fixture with the complex structures, the stiffness is analyzed by the method of finite element analysis. The module and analysis results of the FEA are presented in Fig. 19.6. The maximum stress and maximum strain is 79.4 Mpa and 0.108 mm respectively. The analysis results meet the requirements of stiffness and assembly precision.


## 19.5 Conclusions

Box-joint based assembly tooling is a kind of reconfigurable tooling with good adjustability, configurability and detachability. It is appropriate for the mass and the small batches assembly as well as the airplane emergency assembly and maintenance. Meanwhile the utilization rate of the tooling resources for the airplane assembly can be significantly improved, and the assembly cost for the fixture can be cut down. In this chapter, the developed system for the tooling configuration and analysis of Box-Joint based assembly tooling can configurate the fixture rapidly and generate the tooling instance that meets the tooling requirement, and the stability and stiffness are also analyzed in this system. Finally the installation and scheme documents are output to guide the workers to install the tooling. The developed system is of great significance for promoting the practical application of reconfigurable flexible tooling.


## References

1. Bone GM, Capso D (2003) Vision-guided fixtureless assembly of automotive components. Robot Comput Integr Manuf 19(1):79–87
2. Millar A, Kihlman H (2009) Reconfigurable flexible tooling for aerospace wing assembly. In: Proceedings of SAE aerospace congress and exhibition, Seattle, USA, pp 1–10
3. Guo HJ, Kang XF, Wang L et al (2011) Research on flexible tooling technology for digital assembly of aircraft fuselage. Aeronaut Manuf Technol 22:94–97
4. Helgosson P, Ossbahr G, Tomlinson D (2010) Modular and configurable steel structure for assembly fixtures. In: Proceedings of SAE 2010 aerospace manufacturing and automated fastening conference and exhibition, Wichita, USA, pp 1–14
5. Kihlman H (2005) Affordable automation for airframe assembly: development of key enabling technologies. Department of management and engineering, Linkopings university, Sweden
6. Zheng LY, Ji L (2011) Research and implementation of tooling configuration for product family. Comput Integr Manuf Syst 17(03):585–594 (in Chinese)

# Chapter 20
# A Ranking-Based Approach for Service Composition with Multiple QoS Constraints

Weidong Wang, Wei Lu, Liqiang Wang, Weiwei Xing and Zhao Li

**Abstract** In Web Service Composition (WSC) field, service composition aims at selecting a set of existing services with different Quality of Services (QoS) attributes then compositing them to accomplish a complex task to meet the given user requirements. A grand research challenge of service composition is to select proper service candidates to maximize Quality of Service (QoS). In this paper, we propose a Ranking-Based algorithm of service composition. Specifically we employ the QoS-based model to evaluate QoS parameters, and then select the nearly-optimal execution path of service composition with high-level QoS performance. We evaluated our algorithm using simulation-based comprehensive experiments. The experimental results demonstrate that our approach is more efficient compared to other existing approaches.

**Keywords** Service composition · Service selection · QoS · Utility

W. Wang · W. Lu (✉) · W. Xing · Z. Li
School of Software Engineering, Beijing Jiaotong University, No. 3
Shanyancun Xizhimenwai, Beijing 100044, People's Republic of China
e-mail: luwei@bjtu.edu.cn; 09122448@bjtu.edu.cn

W. Wang
e-mail: 11112094@bjtu.edu.cn

W. Wang · L. Wang
Department of Computer Science, University of Wyoming, Laramie, WY 82071-3315, USA

W. Lu et al. (eds.), *Proceedings of the 2012 International Conference on Information Technology and Software Engineering*, Lecture Notes in Electrical Engineering 212, DOI: 10.1007/978-3-642-34531-9_20, © Springer-Verlag Berlin Heidelberg 2013

## 20.1 Introduction

A single service usually cannot solve a user's complex requirements. We often need to use service composition, which organizes a set of services to one in order to achieve a complex task [1]. How to efficiently and dynamically integrate existing Web services with different Quality of Service (QoS) attributes into a complex service to meet user's requirements has been the research focus in both industry and academia [2, 3]. Usually, QoS-aware service compositions can be transformed into mathematic problems before constructing models and designing algorithms.

One of major research efforts is to select appropriate candidate for each task in the composite web service to obtain the optimal QoS utility and satisfy end-to-end QoS constraints including response time, cost, reliability, and availability [4]. QoS-aware service composition aims at selecting the optimal execution plan to maximize its QoS. This optimization problem can be modeled as multidimensional, multiple-choice knapsack 0–1 problem (MMKP) that has been proved to be an NP-hard problem [5–7]. In order to efficiently solve the problem, several algorithms have been proposed [8–12].The essence of the model is to select a composite service from sets of candidate services to satisfy QoS constrains, and maximize its overall objective function's value.

In this paper, we propose a Ranking-Based approach in support of the end-to-end QoS-aware services. We employ the QoS-based model to evaluate the QoS parameters of each service by considering the relationship of inter-services. Based on this model, we design an algorithm to select the nearly-optimal execution plan to meet user's QoS requirements. We evaluated our algorithm using simulation-based experiments. The experimental results demonstrate that our approach can obtain a nearly-optimal solution that is more efficient compared with other algorithms.

The rest of this paper is organized as follows. Section 20.2 introduces the QoS-based model related to the computation of global QoS attributes and the corresponding algorithm. Section 20.3 presents the performance evaluation and comparison of different algorithms. Section 20.4 concludes this paper and outlines future work.

## 20.2 Ranking-Based Approach for Service Composition

This section describes the process of the service composition through an example shown in Fig. 20.1, where each task may have multiple service candidates. In order to complete the whole task, we need to choose one service for each task from the service candidates. Every candidate item has the same functionality but different QoS. There are several execution plans in this example. For example, in the follow execution plan $<T_A, T_B, T_C, T_E, T_F, T_G, T_H>$, we need to select the candidate service for every task and calculate the overall QoS. The optimal

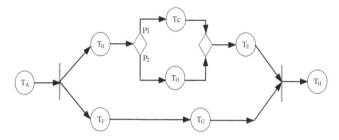

**Fig. 20.1** Example of composite service path

execution plan is the one maximizing the overall QoS to meet the user's requirements. In our study, for example, the number of task is up to 40 and there are 160 candidate items per tasks, and we can describe the user's requirement as follows.

1. Response time $\leq 500$ ms.
2. Execution Time $\leq 1,000$ ms.

### 20.2.1 System Model

Let $q(s, a)$ be QoS Vector. Where $s$ denotes a service and $a$ denotes one of QoS attributes provided by individual Web service. Each service $s$ is related to a QoS vector $q(s, a) = [q(s_1, a), \ldots, q(s_i, a)]$ that contains $i$QoS parameters such as reputation, availability, price, execution time, response time, and usage frequency [13].

Let $S$ be a service class. A service class is a set of candidate services with a common functionalities but different QoS.

Let $s$ denote an individual service in a service class $S$.

Let $U(s, l)$ denote utility function that is determined by system parameters including system load and cost.

In order to evaluate a given service, a utility function can be used to transform all QoS attributes into a single value. A simple additive weighting (SAW) [14] technique is used to normalize values of QoS attributes. There are two steps in applying SAW.

Firstly, we need to normalize the values of the QoS attributes to the same scale because of different measurement metrics used for different QoS attributes. For the positive value, which represents that QoS is improved as the value of QoS attribute is increasing, the attributes need to be maximized as defined in (20.1), while attributes need to be minimized as defined in (20.2) for the negative value, which represents that QoS is weaken as the value of QoS attribute is increasing. $q^{max}(s, a)$ and $q^{min}(s, a)$ are the maximum and minimum values among the service class $S$ and $q(s_i, a)$ is the value of QoS attribute for a selected candidate $s_i$, and $s_i \in S$.

$$q_{norm}^-(s_i, a) = \begin{cases} \frac{q^{max}(s,a) - q(s_i,a)}{q^{max}(S,l) - q^{min}(S,l)} & \text{when: } q^{max}(s,a) - q^{min}(s,a) \neq 0 \\ 1 & \text{when: } q^{max}(s,l) - q^{min}(s,a) = 0 \end{cases} \quad (20.1)$$

$$q_{norm}^+(s_i, a) = \begin{cases} \frac{q(s_i,a) - q(s_i,a)}{q^{max}(s,a) - q^{min}(s,a)} & \text{when: } q^{max}(s,a) - q^{min}(s,a) \neq 0 \\ 1 & \text{when: } q^{max}(s,l) - q^{min}(s,a) = 0 \end{cases} \quad (20.2)$$

We also assign a weight for each QoS attributes mentioned above. The weight of each service is a value between 0 and 1, and the sum of all weights is 1. In our study, QoS attributes are numbered from 1 to 6, such as 1 = price, 2 = usage frequency, 3 = Availability, 4 = execution time, 5 = response time, 6 = reputation.

As Table 20.1 shows, there are three Web services in Task $T_B$. Their values for service price are given by vector $Q_{21} = (95, 75, 80)$. Because price is a positive value, after scaling based on (20.2), we get $q^{max}(s_2, 1) = 95$, $q^{min}(s_2, 1) = 75$. Let S denote the service class of $T_B$. The formula (20.1), (20.2) are used to compute the overall quality score for each Web service, where the superscript "T" denotes vector transpose.

$$q_{norm}(S, 1) = (q_{norm}(s_1, 1), q_{norm}(s_2, 1), q_{norm}(s_3, 1))^T = (1, 0, 0.25)^T$$

Using the same method according to (20.1, 20.2), we get the result as

$$q_{norm}(S, 2) = (q_{norm}(s_1, 2), q_{norm}(s_2, 2), q_{norm}(s_3, 2))^T = (1, 1, 0)^T$$

$$q_{norm}(S, 3) = (q_{norm}(s_1, 3), q_{norm}(s_2, 3), q_{norm}(s_3, 3))^T = (1, 0.33, 0)^T$$

follows. $q_{norm}(S, 4) = (q_{norm}(s_1, 4), q_{norm}(s_2, 4), q_{norm}(s_3, 4))^T = (0, 0.2, 1)^T$

$$q_{norm}(S, 5) = (q_{norm}(s_1, 5), q_{norm}(s_2, 5), q_{norm}(s_3, 5))^T = (0, 1, 0.33)^T$$

$$q_{norm}(S, 6) = (q_{norm}(s_1, 6), q_{norm}(s_2, 6), q_{norm}(s_3, 6))^T = (1, 0, 0.75)^T$$

$$Q_{norm}(S) = (q_{norm}(S, 1), q_{norm}(S, 2), q_{norm}(S, 3), q_{norm}(S, 4), q_{norm}(S_2, 5), q_{norm}(S, 6))$$

$$= \begin{pmatrix} 1 & 1 & 1 & 0 & 0 & 1 \\ 0 & 1 & 0.33 & 0.2 & 1 & 0 \\ 0.25 & 0 & 0 & 1 & 0.33 & 0.75 \end{pmatrix}$$

Secondly, according to the formula (20.3), we summarize the value of $l$-level QoS attributes to a score for QoS attributes, say $R$, which is the sum between the weighted sum of all $n^+$ and the weighted sum of all $n^-$. "+" represents that QoS is improved as

**Table 20.1** QoS attribute values of three candidate services in task $T_B$

| Task | Service Candidate | Reputation | Availability | Price | Execution Time | Response Time | Usage frequency |
|------|-------------------|------------|--------------|-------|----------------|---------------|-----------------|
| $T_B$ | B1 | 0.45 | 0.98 | 95 | 120 | 1 | 0.35 |
| | B2 | 0.25 | 0.96 | 75 | 160 | 4 | 0.35 |
| | B3 | 0.30 | 0.95 | 80 | 170 | 3 | 0.30 |

the value of QoS attribute is increasing. "$-$" represents that QoS is weakened as the value of QoS attribute is increasing. Formula (20.3) is defined below.

$$Score(R) = \sum_{j=1}^{m} w_j^+ * q_{norm}^+(s_i, j) + \sum_{i=m+1}^{n} w_j^- * q_{norm}^-(s_i, j) \qquad (20.3)$$

where $w_i \in [0, 1]$, $\sum_{i=1}^{n} w_i = 1$, and $w_j$ represents the weight of QoS attribute which is provided by the user's experience. In order to compute the score of $Q_i$, we need to use the values of $w_j = [0.12, 0.28, 0.10, 0.30, 0.10, 0.10]$ and $Q_{norm}(S_2)$ and the result is as follows.

$R_{TB1} = 0.12*1 + 0.28*1 + 0.10*1 + 0.10*1 = 0.6$

Using the same method, we get the following result.

$R_{TB2} = 0.473$, $R_{TB3} = 0.438$.

Assuming there are $m$ QoS parameters to be maximized and $n$ QoS parameters to be minimized. We define the utility functions as follows.

$$F_{ij} = \sum_{i=1}^{m} w_x * q_{x(norm)}^+ + \sum_{i=m+1}^{n} w_y * q_{y(norm)}^- \qquad (20.4)$$

where $\sum_{i=1}^{m} w_x + \sum_{i=m+1}^{n} w_y = 1$, and $w_x$ and $w_y$ are the weights for QoS attribute $(0 < w_x, w_y < 1)$.

For a composite service that has $N$ service classes $(S_1, S_2, \ldots, S_N)$ in a process flow plan and with m QoS constraints, we map the service selection problem to a 0–1 multi-dimension multi-choice knapsack problem (MMKP) [15, 16]. In this paper, we extend the algorithm into 0–1 multi-dimension multi-choice knapsack problem simplified with $K$ constraints (MMKP-SK). Formally, the model of MMKP-SK is defined as follows:

$$\text{Maximize p} = \sum_{i=1}^{n} \sum_{j \in S_i} F_{ij} x_{ij} \qquad (20.5)$$

$$\text{Subject to } \sum_{i=1}^{n} \sum_{j \in S_i} q_{ij}^k x_{ij} \le \lfloor Q_{sum}^k \rfloor, \quad k = 1, \ldots, m; \qquad (20.6)$$

$$\lfloor Q_{sum}^k \rfloor = \left\lfloor \sum_{k}^{m} w_k * q_{norm}^k \right\rfloor \le R_c \to R_c^k \qquad (20.7)$$

$$\sum_{j \in S_i} x_{ij} = 1 \qquad (20.8)$$

$$x_{ij} \in \{0, 1\}, \quad i = 1, 2, \ldots, n; \ j \in S_i \qquad (20.9)$$

Each service class $(S_i)$ is mapped to an object item in MMKP-SK. Every candidate service $(s)$ in $S_i$ is mapped to an object in a group in MMKP-SK. The QoS attributes $(q_{ij}^k)$ of each candidate service $(s)$ are mapped to $K$ resources $(R_c^k)$ required by the capability of knapsack in MMKP-SK. $R_c$ is mapped to $R_c^k$ by the given constraints. $Q_{sum}^k$ summarizes the value of all $k$ QoS constraints to a globe one. The utility $(U_{ij})$ of a candidate service is mapped to the profit of knapsack. QoS constraints are considered as the resources to capability of knapsack. If the service $j$ in class $S_i$ is selected, then we have $x_{ij} = 1$, or $x_{ij} = 0$.

The amount of QoS constraints available in the knapsack is $R_c^k = \left( R_c^1, R_c^2 \ldots R_c^k \right)$, and each service has profit $p_{ij}$, and MMKP-SK in this context is to select exactly one service from each service class so as to ensure the total profit $p$ is maximized while the overall QoS constraints are less than the given QoS constraints. According to the MMKP problem, which has been shown to be NP-complete [15], our MMKP-SK algorithm has less time complexity by finding the nearly-optimal execution plan.

## 20.2.2 Algorithm

1. Standardize the utility and simplify QoS constraints.

   We standardize the utility and simplify QoS constraints to a globe one using the approach mentioned in Sect. 20.2.1.

2. Find the feasible solution.

   After the preparation in (20.1) is done, we try to find the feasible solution. According to the flow chart, we first find execution paths for our compositing services. Then we maximize the performance of service composition in each path and get the $Q_{max}$ for QoS attributes. We also minimize the performance of service composition in each path, and get $Q_{min}$ for QoS attributes.

$$\text{d} = \frac{|Q_{max} - Q_{min}|}{\delta}, \quad \delta = 1, 2, 3 \ldots \ldots n \tag{20.10}$$

Let $\{Q_{min}\}$ be QoS level-1, $\{Q_{min} + d\}$ be QoS level-2, $\{Q_{min} + (\delta - 1) * d\}$ be QoS level-$\delta$, and $Q_{max}$ be the top level, as Table 20.2 shows.

**Table 20.2** State of $Q_{sum}$ level for model

| QoS Level | $Q_{sum}$ | $Q_{Li}^1$ | $Q_{Li}^2$ | ...... | $Q_{Li}^k$ |
|---|---|---|---|---|---|
| 1 | $Q_{min}$ | $Q_{L1}^1$ | $Q_{L1}^2$ | ...... | $Q_{L1}^k$ |
| 2 | $Q_{min} + d$ | $Q_{L2}^1$ | $Q_{L2}^2$ | ...... | $Q_{L2}^k$ |
|  |  | ...... |  |  |  |
| $\delta$ | $Q_{min} + (\delta - 1) * d$ | $Q_{L\delta}^1$ | $Q_{L\delta}^2$ | ...... | $Q_{L\delta}^k$ |
| $\delta + 1$ | $Q_{max}$ | $Q_L^1(\delta + 1)$ | $Q_L^2(\delta + 1)$ | ...... | $Q_L^k(\delta + 1)$ |

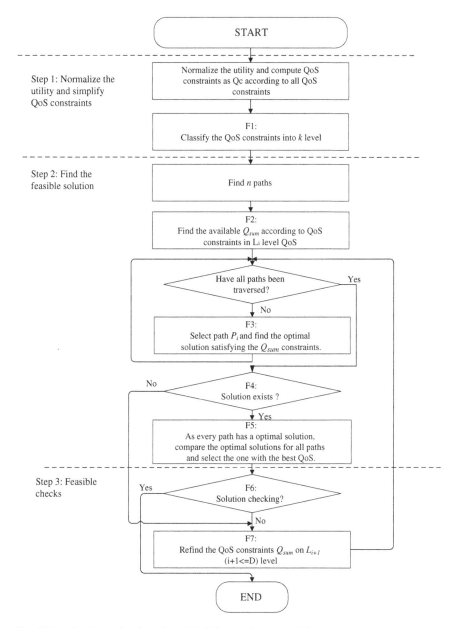

**Fig. 20.2** Algorithm of ranking-based QoS for service composition

We get the normalization value $R_c$ which is specified by users' requirement by step 1. According the Table 20.2, we can find the $Q_{sum}$ nearest to $R_c$ and $Q_{sum} \leq R_c$. Furthermore, in the condition of $Q_{sum}$ we get one optimal solution $X_{sum}$. For the same

**Table 20.3** Functions defined in Ranking-Based Algorithm

| Function | Definition |
|---|---|
| Notations | $R_c$ is normalization value specified by users' requirement. |
| | $Q_{sum}$ is defined by classifying the QoS constraints, and means of QoS constraints in Level $L_j$. |
| | $L_i$ level is the mean of QoS attributes at degree. |
| F1 | $d = \frac{|Q_{max}-Q_{min}|}{\delta}, Q_{sum} = Q_{min} + \delta * d, \delta = 1,2,3...n.$ |
| F2 | $Q_{sum} \leq R_c$ |
| F3 | $f[j, Q_{sum}] = max\{f[j-1, Q_{sum} - Q_j] + P_j(Q_{sum} \geq Q_j)f[j-1, Q_{sum}]\}$ |
| F4 | $X = [X_{sum}^1, X_{sum}^2, ..., X_{sum}^n] \neq \{\}$ |
| F5 | $U_{xi} = Max\{U_{x1}, U_{x2}, ..., U_{xn}\}, X_i \text{ is nearly-optimal solution}$ |
| F6 | $Q_{xi}^k \leq R_c^k$ |
| F7 | $d = \frac{|Q_{max}-Q_{min}|}{\delta}, Q_{sum} = Q_{min} + (\delta+1) * d, \delta = 1,2,3......n$ |

reason, we can also get solutions in the other paths. Let $X = [X_{sum}^1, X_{sum}^2, ..., X_{sum}^n]$ denote the solution set. Comparing results among the $X$, $X_{sum}^i$ is considered as the solution for this problem and its path is the execution path.

3. Solution checking

If the $X_{sum}^i$ is not satisfied for the user's requirement, we can reduce the QoS level and get new $Q_{sum}$ and repeat step 2. Otherwise, no solution may exist. According to all steps mentioned above, we design the algorithm shown in Fig. 20.2. Table 20.3 shows all notions and functions defined.

## 20.3 Experiment

In this section, we present of the result of the simulation experiments to our Ranking-Based algorithm. We perform our experiments on HP 8280 with Intel Core i5-2400 with four CPU at the clock speed of 3.1 GHz and 8 GB RAM. The operation system is Window 7.

In order to simplify the implementation of experiment, we devise the test cases as follows.

1. We randomly generate $k$ dimension vector $Q_{sum}^k$ (k = 3, k = 6), and the constraints vector $Q_c$.
2. We only consider the sequential composition model and ignore service matching problem.

From Fig. 20.3, we know that the CPU computation time goes up when the number of the service increases. When the number of service classes is 20, the number of candidate services is 15. We obtain the solution in 13 ms, which fully meets the user's requirement.

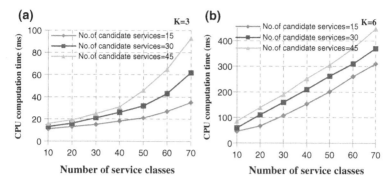

**Fig. 20.3** Algorithm performance

**Fig. 20.4** Approximate
running time under different
constraints

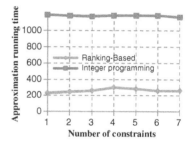

**Fig. 20.5** Approximate ratio
under different constraints

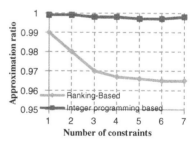

We also compared our algorithm with the Integer programming-based QoS algorithm [16, 17]. As Fig. 20.4 show, when the number of classes is 40 and there are 160 candidate services per class, our algorithm take about 210 ms but the Integer-based algorithm takes more time than 1,000 ms. Moreover, as Fig. 20.5 shows, when the number of classes is also 40 and there are 160 candidate services per class as Fig. 20.4, the globe utility obtained by the Ranking-Based algorithm is close to the optimum utility (i.e. the approximation ratio >96.5 %).

## 20.4 Conclusions

Service composition can integrate existing Web services with different QoS attributes into a complex service to meet user's requirements. In order to select execution plan and proper service candidates to maximize QoS, a critical research challenge is to construct the proper service composition model, and design the efficient algorithm. In this paper, we propose a new Ranking-Based algorithm for service composition. We simplify QoS constraints to a globe one and construct a multiple level table to select the feasible solution for the given requirements. Experimental results demonstrate that our approach is more efficient.

Currently, we are developing a prototype system for complex service composition. In the future work, we will extend our approach to support selecting execution plan and services during runtime.

**Acknowledgments** This research is supported by the National Natural Science Foundation of China (No.61100143, No. 61272353), Fundamental Research Funds for the Central Universities (No.2011JBM023, No. 2012JBM124), and BJTU Hongguoyuan Innovative Talent Program (No.151139522).

## References

1. Casati F, Shan MC (2001) Dynamic and adaptive composition of E-Services. Inf Syst 26(3):143–163
2. Milanovic N, Malek M (2004) Current solutions for web service composition. J IEEE Internet Comput 8(6):51–59
3. Ardagna D, Pernici B (2007) Adaptive service composition in flexible processes. J IEEE Trans Software Eng 33(6):369–384
4. Zeng ZB, Michael R, yu L(2009) A QoS-aware fault tolerant middleware for dependable service composition. In: Proceedings of the IEEE/IFIP International Conference on Dependable Systems and Networks, pp 239–248
5. Alrifai M, Risse T, Dolog P et al (2008) A scalable approach for QoS-based web service selection. In: Proceedings of the 1st international work-shop on quality of service concerns in service oriented architectures. Springer, Berlin, pp 190–199
6. Yu T, Lin KJ (2005) Service selection algorithms for web services with end-to-end QoS constraints. J IseB 3(2):103–125
7. Akbar Md, Rahman MS, Kaykobad M, Manning EG, Shoja GC (2005) Solving the multidimensional multiple-choice knapsack problem by constructing convex hulls. Comput Oper Res 33:1259–1273
8. Rosenberg F, Celikovic P, Michlmayr A, Leitner P, Dustdar S (2009) An End-to-End approach for QoS-aware service composition. In: Proceedings of the IEEE international enterprise distributed object computing conference, pp 151–160
9. Yang Y, Tang S, Xu Y, Zhang W, Fang L (2007) An approach to QoS-aware service selection in dynamic web service compositions. In proceedings of the 3rd international conference on networking and services (icns'07), IEEE Computer Society, Athens, Greece, 19–25 June, pp 18–23
10. Alrifai M, Risse T, Nejdl W (2012) A hybrid approach for efficient web service composition with end-to-to QoS constraints. ACM Trans WEB 6(2)

11. Tong HX, Cao J, Zhang SS, Li ML (2011) A distributed algorithm for web service composition based on service agent model. IEEE Trans Parallel Distrib Syst 22(12):2008–2021
12. Kim T, Palanikumar D, Kousalya G (2011) Optimal WEB service selection and composition using multi objective bees. Algorithm Inf Terdisc J 14(14):3289–3295
13. Dan A et al (2004) Web services on demand: WSLA-driven automated management. IBM syst J 43(1):136–158
14. Hwang CL, Yoon K (1981) Multiple attributes decision making, lecture notes in economics and mathematical systems. Springer, New York
15. Martello S, Toth p (1987) Algorithms for knapsack problems. Ann Discrete Math 31: 70–78
16. Zeng L, Bentallah A, Ngu AHH, Kalagnanam J, Chang H (2004) QoS-aware middleware for web services composition. IEEE Trans Softw Eng IEEE Comput Soc, 30(5):311–327
17. Yu T, Zhang Y, Lin KJ (2007) Efficient algorithms for web services selection with end-to-end QoS constraints. ACM Trans Web 1(1)

# Chapter 21
# Research of Multiple Tenants for Medical Information Service

Jie Liu and Qing Zhu

**Abstract** With the development of Web technology, SaaS-as-a-Service (SaaS) mode which is used as the top-level architecture of cloud computing has become a new concept of software as a service model. How to design efficient and secure system architecture is the key of the application of the SaaS model. This paper starts with the medical information field service, giving the solution of the medical information service platform. This scheme is mainly designed that (multi-tenant) and system security issues can be well designed in SaaS software.

**Keywords** Cloud computing · SaaS · Software as a service · Medical information service · Multiple · Tenants

## 21.1 Introduction

In recent years, the number of diabetic patients increased very fast in China. With the rapid development and maturity of Web 2.0, regardless of diabetic patients or the general population are concerned about the situation of diabetes through the Internet. However, in China, due to the different types of existing diabetes information service platform, scattered resources and information sharing limited, leading the patients to seek care from blindness, medical treatment of intermittent process of treatment and lack of continuity in medical statistics are not standardized. Diabetes medical information service platform is not well play a role.

Facing the problems in the existing platform, compared with the traditional software systems, we should combine with the Software, Service SaaS model [1],

J. Liu (✉) · Q. Zhu
School of Software Engineering, Beijing University of Technology, 100124 Beijing, China
e-mail: liujie023525@sina.com

W. Lu et al. (eds.), *Proceedings of the 2012 International Conference on Information Technology and Software Engineering*, Lecture Notes in Electrical Engineering 212, DOI: 10.1007/978-3-642-34531-9_21, © Springer-Verlag Berlin Heidelberg 2013

provide software services in a low cost and low risk way. SaaS model with its own advantages and the ability of internet spreading quickly build software services to avoid duplication a waste of resources.

At the same time, it enables the software service provider to pay more attention to the quality of software services. In this paper, the actual research project, combined the theory and practice, we analyze the significance of the SaaS model in the diabetes medical information service platform, and discuss the need for and the proposed SaaS applications in the medical services industry.

## 21.2 Advantage of the Medical Information Services Based on SaaS

SaaS is (software as-a-service [2]) referred, it is a mode of delivering software over the Internet, users do not need to purchase software, but leased to the provider of Web-based software to carry out business activities, without the need for software maintenance, service providers, the Chamber of Commerce, discretionary management and maintenance software, for many small businesses, SaaS is the best way for the use of advanced technology, it eliminates the enterprises to purchase, build, and maintenance of infrastructure and application needs.

### 21.2.1 SaaS Service Model

SaaS service providers to build the information technology needs of all network infrastructure and software, hardware, operating platform for SMEs, and it is responsible for the implementation of all pre-and post-maintenance and a range of services. Enterprises don't need to purchase hardware and software, construct of the engine room, the recruit IT person, just simply pre-pay a one-time project implementation costs and regular software rental service fee, they can enjoy the information system via the Internet., There is no basic difference, in effect, between SaaS service model and self-built information systems, but it saves a lot of funds for the purchase of IT products, technology and maintenance to run and easy-to-use information systems, thus greatly reduces the SME information the threshold of risk.

### 21.2.2 SaaS Service Advantage

For medical items in the subject, the advantages of the SaaS model are as follows: From the technical point of view: It no longer needs to arrange the IT and technical persons, meanwhile can get the latest technology to meet their information management needs.

From an investment point of view: only a relatively low investment, not a one-time investment in place, do not take up too much system operation and maintenance funds, thus easing the pressure of inadequate health care funding; without considering the cost of depreciation, and timely access to the latest hardware platforms to get the best solution.

In terms of maintenance and management: taking rented to business management of the platform does not require special maintenance and management person which do not need to pay additional costs for maintenance and management person. Greatly ease the pressure on the human, to enable them to concentrate funds to strengthen the service building and improve the quality of service.

## 21.3 Medical Information Service Model Based on SaaS

### 21.3.1 SaaS Maturity Model

SaaS software to serve multiple tenants, high-performance, configurable, scalable SaaS services characteristic of SaaS maturity model is generally divided into four levels. These models of SaaS maturity are illustrated in Fig. 21.1.

Level 1—Ad-Hoc/Custom

At the first level of maturity, each customer has its own customized version of the hosted application and runs its own instance of the application on the host's servers. Migrating a traditional non-networked or client-server application to this level of SaaS typically requires the least development effort and reduces operating costs by consolidating server hardware and administration.

Level 2—Configurable

The second maturity level provides greater program flexibility through configurable metadata, so that many customers can use separate instances of the same application code. This allows the vendor to meet the different needs of each customer through detailed configuration options, while simplifying maintenance and updating of a common code base.

Level 3—Configurable, Multi-Tenant-Efficient

The third maturity level adds multi-tenancy to the second level, so that a single program instance serves all customers. This approach enables more efficient use of server resources without any apparent difference to the end user, but ultimately is limited in its scalability.

Level 4—Scalable, Configurable, Multi-Tenant-Efficient

At the fourth and final SaaS maturity level, scalability is added through a multi-tier architecture supporting a load-balanced farm of identical application instances, running on a variable number of servers. The system's capacity can be increased or decreased to match demand by adding or removing servers, without the need for any further alteration of application software architecture.

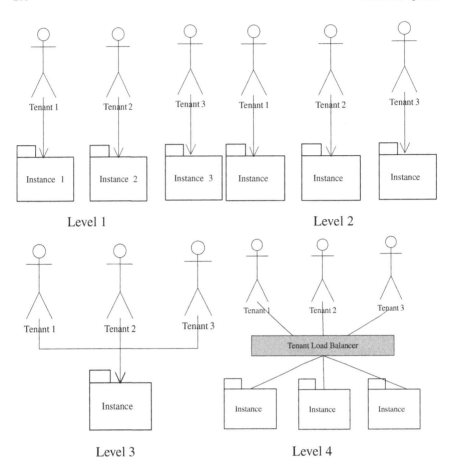

**Fig. 21.1** SaaS maturity model

## 21.3.2 Medical Information Services Strategy

SaaS maturity model, and only reach the third level and above the requirements of SaaS services can be regarded as the true sense of the software as a service. Therefore, the medical information service platform for the construction of multi-tenant model focuses on the shared instance multi-tenant, configurable, scalable, and several other aspects.

### 21.3.2.1 Database Design

In the information systems of the multi-tenant model, the data storage and isolation mode of tenants directly affects the tenants' confidence in the use and data security [3]. SaaS application database has three storage modes (Fig. 21.2).

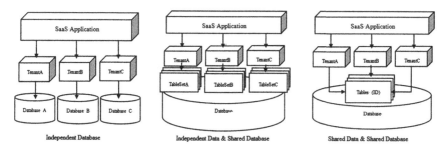

**Fig. 21.2** Database model

1. Independent database schema

Each of the logical relationships among the database instances is independent, but can be deployed on the same hardware. Performance is controlled easily, security and isolation of data are strong but cost is more. This model fits the users whose requirements to performance and independence of data are high.

2. Independent data architecture model of shared database

Each tenant has an mutually exclusive set of tables in which the performance of security, isolation and controllability of data are weaker than that in an entirely independent mode. And cost of the hardware has increased. This model fits the users whose requirements to performance and independence of data within the limited budget are high.

3. Shared data architecture model of shared database

In this mode, the security and isolation of data are accomplished with a particular method in which way the resources of a system are utilized maximally and the most cost-effective; but controllable performance is relatively poor. This model is suitable for users who are sensitive to price.

Isolation and shared strategy of data are key factors to the design of service-oriented database in the SaaS. Meanwhile, the data in the Medical Information Service obeys the medical standardization, consistency of data structures, the identity of data content and other characteristics in high degree, the use of shared data architecture of shared database is more appropriate.

### 21.3.2.2 Multi-Tenant Configuration Design

Under the multi-tenant conditions, the requirements to versatility and universal applicability of SaaS service are higher, and easy-to-use configuration is an important feature of the SaaS model. Configurable designs in the multi-tenant SaaS platform include functional configuration and interface configuration [4], and so forth.

Functional configuration

SaaS services satisfy tenants who have a large number of different functional requirements, SaaS services should be able to support tenants to selectively customize the features they need, and form a complete feature-oriented set, which can truly reflect "on-demand use, on-demand pays "model in SaaS applications.

The decomposition of atomic functions is the basis to realize the functional configuration.

In the process of the decomposition of the atomic functions, decomposition principle, including the atomic function value, not be subdivided, and non-overlapping, non-circular dependencies and systematic integrality, should be obeyed. At the same time, the atomic function is too small and there are some dependencies between all functions in the actual design, but also depending on the type of tenants, scenarios, business logic and habits, the atomic function of integration, the formation of a relatively independent functional package, in accordance with commercial intent, the sales package is divided into a minimum Edition, Standard Edition full version.

Interfacial configuration

The interface of the traditional made-to-order application system can basically meet the needs of users. Among the multi-tenant SaaS applications, the interfaces should change with tenant customization features dynamic interface configuration including the configurable system menu and page content.

### 21.3.2.3 Scalable Design of the Multi-Tenant

The scalability of multi-tenant, simply increase or decrease in the corresponding hardware devices will be able to guaranteed service levels on the basis of no adjustment of the system architecture. The scalability of multi-tenant SaaS system is an important evaluation [5], including the scalability of the application server, database server, storage system, etc. The scalability of the application server makes access and application services equally to more than one application server through the design of certain load balancing mechanism. Access increased considerably, by increasing the application server to ensure that the application layer has good scalability and performance. The scalability of the database by analyzing the characteristics of the applications and data, segmentation data, reading and writing separation methods such as the decentralization of the service pressure to multiple database servers.

## 21.4 SaaS Model Used in the Medical Information Service Platform

The significance of using SaaS model in medical information service platform are as follows:

First, using of the service is simple by SaaS model characteristics [6], thereby it enhances the efficiency in the use of medical information service platform.

Management and use of the platform is not computer professional, computer application technology capacity can not be fully qualified for the large-scale information services software. SaaS platforms, easy-to-use features for the information service platform staff, are familiar with good operability, and laid the foundation for the development of service-oriented software platform.

Using the easy deployment features of SaaS model platform, we can reduce software development costs and hardware costs and maintenance overhead reduction of a great extent by the platform. The traditional software to customer service with a professional is responsible to maintain, therefore, the medical institutions need to be equipped with one or more of the information system engineers to complete the corresponding work under the guidance of the software provider. Platforms in SaaS mode are deployed in the software provider's network server, eliminating the need for the installation and commited of the steps, without installation and maintenance.

Third, the idea of system integration (or service integration), can maximize the integration of existing software system or part of the function, and reduce the secondary development. In the original system, the information service platform for certain applications, these special procedures are discarded rather a pity. However, if you want to be integrated into the software provider of proprietary systems, they have to make the appropriate secondary development, which resulted in waste. The platform under the SaaS model allows system integrators to avoid secondary development of the human and material waste.

## 21.5  Conclusion

In this paper, by doing the research of the structure of the medical information service platform which is based on the SaaS model, describing and analyzing the platform selection and strategy, it takes a good use of the SaaS business mode and the application value in the medical field, and provides a reasonable solution for medical information service.

## References

1. Song F, Wu B, Wang Z, Jia X (2010) Research on laboratory information management system based on SaaS mode. Exp Technol Manage 97–100 (in Chinese)
2. Xu S (2009) SaaS Software as a service Model. Silicon Valley 9 (in Chinese)
3. Hu X, Chen Q, Zhang Z (2011) The study of library information system based on multi-tenant. Libr Inf Serv 112–115 (in Chinese)
4. Ye W (2009) The software revolution of the internet. Publishing House of Electronics Industry, Beijing (in Chinese)
5. Wang Y, Zhang B, Liu Y, Wang D (2010) The modeling tool of saas software, advanced computer control (ICACC). 2nd international conference on 2010. pp 298–302
6. He H (2010) Applications deployment on the SaaS platform, pervasive computing and applications (ICPCA). 5th international conference on 2010. pp 232–237

# Chapter 22
# Automated Generation of Test Cases Based on Path Optimization Algorithm

Ci Liang and Wei Zheng

**Abstract** An automated approach to generate a full set of the test cases is proposed in this paper. The all paths covered optimal algorithm (APCO) for automatically generating test cases based on the CPN model are presented. Taking the scenario of radio blocking center (RBC) handover as an example, the presented method is employed to generate the test cases of this scenario. The results indicate that the test generation approach is fully automatic. Furthermore, the repeatability rate of the generated test cases was reduced compared with the available depth-first search algorithm (DFS), the test cases all the related criterions in "System requirements specification of the CTCS-3 Train Control System" (SRS).

**Keywords** CPN · APCO · Automated test

## 22.1 Introduction

Chinese Train Control System Level 3 (CTCS-3) is continuously marching on the goal of high-speed and high-density. To ensure the high reliability and safe operation of the CTCS-3, applicable and practical test technology is urgently needed. The CTCS-3 is a very complex system and there may be quite a lot of vulnerabilities and flaws in the test cases, which is generated fully by manual

C. Liang (✉) · W. Zheng
National Engineering Research Center of Rail Transportation Operation and Control
System, Beijing Jiaotong University, 10th Floor, Jixiegongcheng Building,
No.3 Shang Yuan Cun 100044 Haidian, Beijing, China
e-mail: liangci321@126.com

W. Zheng
e-mail: wzheng1@bjtu.edu.cn

W. Lu et al. (eds.), *Proceedings of the 2012 International Conference on Information Technology and Software Engineering*, Lecture Notes in Electrical Engineering 212, DOI: 10.1007/978-3-642-34531-9_22, © Springer-Verlag Berlin Heidelberg 2013

generation in China now. In terms of these considerations, the model-based automatic test approaches are becoming a better choice.

From the 1990s, a concept called Formal Description Technique (FDT) was put forward based on system models. Model-based test generation methods are common based on the timed I/O automata (TIOA) [1], the UPPAAL timed automata (UTA) [2, 3], the unified modeling language (UML) [4–6], the finite state automata (FSM) [6, 7], and the colored Petri net (CPN) [8, 9].

In 1995, Uppsala University and Aalborg University jointly put forward the test generation method based on Uppaal timed automata (UTA) [2]. The algorithm of UTA was used to generate traces by Hessel, and the amount of time and space saved by the algorithm obtained in their experiments was 50–58 and 30–35 %, respectively [3]. However, this method could not describe the concurrent behavior of the system, and the generated test cases were on a relatively high level of abstraction, which means the test process could not be truly automated.

Samuel and Joseph [4] proposed to generate the test sequences with UML 2.0 sequence diagrams. They constructed the Sequence Dependency Graph (SDG), and the test sequences were generated from SDG with a traversal algorithm. But the biggest flaw of UML is that there is no definition of any executable metadata model to help the modeling and no hardware support.

Lee put forward the automated conformance test method of the communication security protocol for the train control system based on I/O finite state machine (I/O FSM) [10]. They used the I/O FSM to describe the criterion of the communication security protocol, and then generated a unique I/O (UIO) conformance test sequences. However, the conformance test method based on FSM requires rigorous mathematical assumptions, which, on the contrary, limits the practicality of the system-level test sequences automated generation.

Watanabe and Kudoh [8] presented two methods based on the test generation method of Colored Petri Nets: the Colored Petri Nets Tree (CPT) method and the Colored Petri Net Graph (CPG) method. Compared with FSM-based test case generation method, the results implied that the generated states by using the CPG method was much less than the existing FSM-based method, when the coverage of both methods were the same. But the abstract test cases generated by this method were not conducive to the execution of the test. Therefore, the test process could not be totally automated.

So a new kind of test cases automated generation method is proposed based on Colored Petri Nets (CPN) in this paper. First, researchers establish the model of the system under test with CPN. Then, XML test cases are generated by the proposed all paths covered optimal algorithm (APCO). Finally, the results are be evaluated.

## 22.2 Definitions

Combining with advanced programming language and hierarchical structure of modeling, CPN is able to accomplish the model for the large-scale system and especially suitable for the concurrent, asynchronous, distributed, parallel, or indeterminate system [9]. To facilitate the elaboration of the following sections, the relative concepts are defined in detail on the basis of the CPN theory [8, 11].

**Definition 1** Unstructured CPN is a 9-tuple [11]

$$M = (S, P, T, A, N, C, G, E, I)$$

where, $S$ is a set of non-empty types, called color sets; $P$ is a finite set of places drawn by circles; $T$ is a finite set of transitions including immediate transition drawn by black bars and timed transition drawn by empty boxes color; $A$ is a finite set of arcs such that $P \cap T = P \cap A = T \cap A = 0$; $N$ is a node function, it is defined from $N : \rightarrow P \times T \cup T \times P$; $C$ is a color function; it is defined from $P$ into $S$; $G$ is guard function, it is defined from $T$ into expressions such that $\forall t \in T : [Type(G(t)) = B \land Type(Var(G(t))) \subseteq \sum]$, where $B$ is the Boolean type, $Type(v)$ represents variable type, and $Var(Expr)$ is the set of variables in the expression $Expr$;

$E$ is an arc expression function, it is defined from $A$ into expressions such that $\forall t \in T : [T(E(a)) = C(p)_{MS} \land Type(Var(E(a))) \subseteq \sum]$, where $p$ is a place of $N(a)$; $I$ is an initialization function.

**Definition 2** The test case is a 6-tuple on the basis of CPN models:

$$TC = \{S_{SC}, S_{EC}, I_{IC}, O_{IC}, I_{MC}, O_{MC}\}$$

Where, $I_{IC}$ is the subset of the input interfaceof the test case; $O_{IC}$ is the subset of the output interface; $S_{SC}$ is the subset of the start state of the test case, containing the start state nodes and the conditions; $S_{EC}$ is the subset of the end state, containing the end state nodes and the conditions; $I_{MC}$ is the subset of the output data of the test case, and $I_{MC} \subseteq A$; $O_{MC}$ is the subset of the output data.

**Definition 3** Coverage criteria:

Regarding a variety of coverage criterias described in paper [12], a proper coverage criteria is proposed.

- All-node Coverage Criteria
  When all the generated test cases are executed, they must traverse all the nodes in the CPN model, that is, traversing all the places or transitions, and all the reachable states.
- All-branch Coverage Criteria
  If the generated test cases are executed, they must traverse all the arcs in the CPN model as well as the transfer conditions between all adjacent reachable states.

## 22.3 Automatic Test Generation

The path optimization algorithm proposed in this paper contains the all paths covered optimal algorithm (APCO).

As shown in Fig. 22.1, the test generation method is mainly divided into two stages:

- First stage

The CPN model is built for the object under test, and then the XML file and the reachable graph of the model are obtained. The modeling rules are as follows:

1. The CPN model is established in two layers from top to bottom. The top layer is the interface one. The specific message interactions will not be described in this layer. The second layer is the layer of the scenario function, in which the specific message interactions are all described.
2. In the second layer, there are strict definitions of the input and the output interfaces for the different scenarios. The property of the same interface is unique. It can only be the input or the output, that is, cannot be both input and output at the same time.
3. The message data processing is described with the ML language.
4. All the acts of the judgments are performed in the Guards.
5. The message variable names transferred on the arcs shall be unified.

- Second stage

In this stage, the APCO algorithm is used to generate the test cases on the basis of the established CPN model.

### 22.3.1 Algorithm Description

The APCO algorithm searches all the possible paths between any node in the set of the start state nodes and the corresponding node in the set of the end state nodes, and next, removes the redundant paths, according to the test optimization strategy, to get the most simplified path set which can cover all paths. This algorithm is used to generate test cases as shown in Fig. 22.1.

The APCO algorithm is based on the depth-first search algorithm (DFS) [13], and some improvements are made.

**Fig. 22.1** Frame diagram of the test generation method

```
function Depth Search(Node, Passed Nodes)
    Extend Node, gain Sub Nodes array;
    fori=1 to the length of Sub Nodes
        Passed Nodes of Sub Nodes[i] =Passed Nodes+Sub Nodes [i];
    end for;
    Initialized Output=False and Deep Output=False;
    fori=1 to the length of Sub Nodes
        if Sub Nodes[i] =G
            Output Passed NodesofSub Nodes[i];
            And Output=True;
        else ifSub Nodes [i]is not in Disabled Nodes or Passed Nodes
            Deep Output=Depth Search (Sub Nodes [i], Passed NodesofSub Nodes [i]);
    end for;
    Result=Output or Deep Output;
    if Result=False
        Put Node into DisabledNodes;
    return Results;
end function;
```

**Fig. 22.2** Description of the APCO algorithm

The traditional DFS algorithm has the following disadvantages: (1) It does not take the situation that there may be the nodes of the previous layers in the next layer into account, and this situation will easily lead to an infinite loop; (2) There is the blindness problem that the algorithm cannot skip the invalid node (no path existing between this node and the target node) when it appears.

Compared with the DFS algorithm, the improvements of the APCO algorithm are as follows: First, a public dynamic array named *Disabled Nodes* is created to record all the state nodes that do not conform to the rules, including the invalid nodes. Second, the dynamic array named *Passed Nodes* is created for every state node to record all the state nodes between the initial state node and this node itself. The description of the APCO algorithm is shown as Fig. 22.2.

## 22.3.2 Generation of Test Cases

According to the Definition 2, test cases generation needs the following steps: (1) generation of $S_{SC}$, $S_{EC}$; (2) generation of $I_{IC}$, $O_{IC}$; (3) generation of $I_{MC}$, $O_{MC}$.

### 22.3.2.1 Generation of $S_{SC}$, $S_{EC}$

In the CPN model, there are "In" and "Out" marks in the input and output places of a scenario, and these marks also exist in the corresponding XML file. The places with the "In" property are searched in the XML file, and they correspond to the specified start nodes and conditions. Analogously, the places with the "Out" property are searched in the XML file, and they correspond to the specified end nodes and conditions.Then the repetitive nodes and conditions are removed to get the most concise $S_{SC}$, $S_{EC}$.

### 22.3.2.2 Generation of $I_{IC}$, $O_{IC}$

In order to get the information of the $I_{IC}$ and $O_{IC}$, all the paths from every start state node in the $S_{SC}$ to the corresponding end state node in the $S_{EC}$ are found out by using the APCO algorithm. The generated paths are those with the input and the output interfaces in pairs to avoid the redundancy of the paths and the errors.

### 22.3.2.3 Generation of $I_{MC}$, $O_{MC}$

First, the variable names of the output arcs which begin with the start places must be found out. The variable names are the input message IDs. Next, the relevant variables and their values are added into the $I_{MC}$ according to the message ID.Then the $I_{MC}$ is obtained.

Similarly, the variable names of the input arcs with their terminal pointing to the end places must be found out. The variable names are the output message IDs. Next, the relevant variables and their values are added into the $O_{MC}$ based on the message ID.Then the $O_{MC}$ is obtained.

The $S_{SC}$, $S_{EC}$, $I_{IC}$, $O_{IC}$, $I_{MC}$ and $O_{MC}$ can be obtained via the aforementioned three steps, then the test case set with the executable data are generated, and the XML is the final form of the generated cases. The automated generation software is developed in C++. The software can implement the algorithm aforementioned to generate the test cases.

## 22.4 Application and Analysis of Test Method

The RBC mainly generates the movement authority (MA), line description and temporary speed restriction and other control information which are transmitted to on-board subsystem, receives messages from the on-board subsystem including train data, position reports and acknowledgement, and provides the information for the trackside equipment, train control subsystem and other systems [14].

**Fig. 22.3** The XML instance
of test case 001

```
<?xml version="1.0" encoding="UTF-8"?>
<TestCasesFile>
  <version>1.0</version>
  <testcase_001_description>
    <testcase_number>001</testcase_number>
    <testcase_property>normal</testcase_property>
    <IO_Type>I/O</IO_Type>
    <Interface>JRU</Interface>
    <StartingConditions>LocationReport</StartingConditions>
    <TestDescription>
      <Receive>Message136</Receive>
        <Message136>
          NID_MESSAGE=136
          L_MESSAGE=24
          T_TRAIN=137827
          NID_ENGINE=536586
          NID_PACKET=0
          L_PACKET=114
          Q_SCALE=1
          NID_LRBG=16777215
          D_LRBG=32767
          Q_DIRLRBG=2
          Q_DLRBG=2
          L_DOUBTOVER=32767
          L_DOUBTUNDER=32767
          Q_LENGTH=0
          V_TRAIN=0
          Q_DIRTRAIN=2
          M_MODE=0
          M_LEVEL=3
        </Message136>
      <Send>package131</Send>
    </TestDescription>
    <EndingConditions>HandoverOrder</EndingConditions>
  </testcase_001_description>
  <testcase_002_description>
  ......
  </testcase_002_description>
  ......
</TestCasesFile>
```

## 22.4.1 Generated Test Cases and Sequences

The test cases are generated for "RBC Handing over" scenario as follows:

/ 1 6 7 / 1 5 7 / 6 8 10 12 14 16 18 19 / 6 8 10 12 14 16 17 19 / 6 8 10 12 14 15
17 19 / 6 8 10 12 13 15 17 19 / 6 8 10 11 13 15 17 19 / 6 8 9 11 13 15 17 19 / 6 7
9 11 13 15 17 19 / 18 20 28 29 / 18 20 21 25 27 29 / 18 19 21 25 27 29 / 29 31 35
38 41 / 29 31 34 38 41 /.

These numbers above represent the state nodes. The nodes between a pair of "/"
are the state nodes that one test case contains. It is obvious that 14 cases were
generated for "RBC Handing over" scenario. The generated XML instance of the

test case 001 is shown as Fig. 22.3, including the case version, case number, property (normal/fault), test start and end condition, and the specific values of the message variables required in test, etc.

The above result can be compared with the test cases generated by using the traditional DFS [13]: / 1 6 7 / 1 5 7 / 6 8 10 12 14 16 18 19 / 6 8 10 12 14 16 17 19 / 6 8 10 12 14 15 17 19 / 6 8 10 12 13 15 17 19 / 6 8 10 11 13 15 17 19 / 6 8 9 11 13 15 17 19 / 6 7 9 11 13 15 17 19 / 6 10 12 13 15 17 19 / 6 9 11 13 15 17 19 / 6 12 14 15 17 19 / 18 20 28 29 / 18 20 21 25 27 29 / 18 21 25 27 29 / 18 19 21 25 27 29 / 29 31 35 38 41 / 29 31 34 38 41 / 29 34 38 41 /.

Using the traditional DFS, 19 test sequences are generated and the 10, 11, 12, 15, 19th cases are redundant and unnecessary. Using the approach presented in this paper, the number of generated test cases are reduced from 19 to 14, and cover the standards related to RBC handover in the specification [14, 15].

## 22.5 Conclusion and Future Research

This paper accomplishes the automated generation of test cases in accordance with the coverage criterion in the Definition 3 and the relevant criterions in the specification [14], decrease the repeatability of the test cases to the greatest extent. This approach is able to adapt to the changes of the requirement specifications, and achieve the goal of test automation. The future work is to generate more and impeccable test cases automatically, and inject the fault factors to improve the safety of the train control system.

**Acknowledgments** This paper is supported by the "National High Technology Research and Development Program of China (863 Program)" (2011AA010104), "the Fundamental Research Funds for the Central Universities" (2011JB2004) and "Urban Rail Transit Automation and Control the Beijing Key Laboratory Fund Project".

## References

1. Kaynar DK, LynchN, Segala R (2003) Timed I/O automata: a mathematical framework for modeling and analyzing real-time systems. In: 24th IEEE Int'l real-time system symposium, IEEE Computer Society, Washington, pp 166–177
2. Bahrmann G, Larsen K G, Moiler O (2001) UPPAAL-present and future. In: 40th IEEE conference on decision and control. pp 2881–2886
3. Hessel A, Pettersson P (2004) A test case generation algorithm for real-time systems. In: 4th international conference on quality software. pp 268–273
4. Samuel P, Joseph AT (2008) Test sequence generation from UML sequence diagrams. In: 9th ACIS international conference on software engineering, artificial intelligence, networking, and parallel/distributed computing. pp 879–887

5. Malik QA, Truscan D, Lilius J (2010) Using UML models and formal verification in model-based testing. In: 17th IEEE international conference and workshops on engineering of computer based systems (ECBS). pp 50–56
6. Utting M, Legeard B (2006) Practical model-based testing: a tools approach. Morgan Kaufmann, Elsevier, America
7. Fujiwara S, Bochmarm GV (1991) Test selection based on finite state models. In: IEEE Trans Software Eng 17(6):591–603
8. Watanabe H, Kudoh T (1995) Test suite generation methods for concurrent systems based on colored petri nets. IEEE Software Engineering Conference. pp 242–251
9. Vernez D, Buchs D, Pierrehumbert G (2003) Perspectives in the use of colored petri nets for risk analysis and accident modeling. Saf Sci 41(5):445–463
10. Lee JH, Lee JD, Jung JI (2007) Verification and conformance test generation of communication protocol for railway signaling systems. Comput Stand Interfaces 29(2):143–151
11. Jensen K (1994) An introduction to the theoretical aspects of coloured petri nets. A decade of concurrency reflections and perspectives. Lecture notes in computer science, vol 803. Springer, Berlin, pp 230–272
12. Badban B, Franzle M, Teige T (2006) Test Automation for hybrid systems. In: 3rd international workshop on software quality assurance, pp 14–21
13. Shaffer CA (2011) Data structures and algorithm analysis in C++, 3rd edn. Dover Publications, New York, pp 390–394
14. The Science and Technology Division of the Ministry of Railways and The Transport Bureau of The Ministry of Railways (2008) System requirements specification of the CTCS-3 train control system (v 1.0). The Ministry of Railways of The People's Republic of China, China Railway Publishing House, Beijing, No. 127 (in Chinese)
15. The Science and Technology Division of the Ministry of Railways and The Transport Bureau of The Ministry of Railways (2009) Test cases of the CTCS-3 train control system. The Ministry of Railways of The People's Republic of China, China Railway Publishing House, Beijing, No. 59 (in Chinese)

# Chapter 23
# The Development of Jade Agent for Android Mobile Phones

Yu Weihong and Yan Chen

**Abstract** At present, with the development of mobile applications from the simple calls to data transmission, the contents of mobile applications have become colorful and the requirements to the mobile software will be higher and higher. Especially, as a consequence of the progressive integration between the wireless and wire-line environments, the need of deploying distributed applications such as multi-Agent systems on handheld devices is becoming more and more important. This implementation will make mobile applications more intelligent and proactive but it is very complicated. In this article, Jade-Leap add-on was used to solve the integration of Jade and Android platform. As an example, one Jade Agent for retrieving train running information was successfully developed on Android platform. During the course of research, some problems, such as the communication among Jade Agents, the interactions between Jade Agent and Android Activity, the interactions among Android Activities and so on were addressed and then solved. The application of Agent into mobile platform will make mobile services more intelligent, proactive and interactive, which will meet the personalized needs of mobile phone users.

**Keywords** Jade agent · Jade-leap add-ons · Android platform · System integration

Y. Weihong (✉) · Y. Chen
Transportation and Management College,
DaLian Maritime University, Dalian 116026, China
e-mail: yuwhlx@163.com

Y. Chen
e-mail: dlmu_chenyan@163.com

W. Lu et al. (eds.), *Proceedings of the 2012 International Conference on Information Technology and Software Engineering*, Lecture Notes in Electrical Engineering 212, DOI: 10.1007/978-3-642-34531-9_23, © Springer-Verlag Berlin Heidelberg 2013

## 23.1 Introduction

One of the most widely used mobile OS these days is Android. Android is a Linux-based operating system for mobile devices such as smart phones and tablet computers. It is developed by the Open Handset Alliance, led by Google, and other companies. Its software bunch comprises not only operating system but also middleware and key applications. Android is open source, meaning that manufacturers don't have to pay Google to use it, and that they're free to modify it. This means that it's used in a wide range of hardware varying in price from small budget phones to large-screen high-end handsets.

In 1986, the notion of Agent has been proposed in the book "Society of Mind" written by Minsky who has made many contributions to AI, cognitive psychology, mathematics, computational linguistics, robotics, and optics. Through the development of more than 20 years, the Agent technology has been evolved from theory to implementation. Especially some standard organization, such as FIPA, has played a crucial role in the development of agents' standards and has promoted a number of initiatives and events that contributed to the development of agent technology.

Java Agent Development Framework, or JADE, is a software framework for multi-agent systems. The JADE platform allows the coordination of multiple FIPA-compliant agents and the use of the standard FIPA-ACL communication language in both SL and XML. A JADE platform is composed of agent containers that can be distributed over the network. Agents live in containers which are the Java processes that provide the JADE run-time and all the services needed for hosting and executing agents. There is a special container, called the main container, which represents the bootstrap point of a platform: it is the first container to be launched and all other containers must join to a main container by registering with it.

In the current researches, Jade Agents mainly run on the computers with fixed IP addresses. But with the development of mobile applications from the simple calls to data transmission, the contents of mobile applications have become colorful and the requirements to the mobile software will be higher and higher. Especially, as a consequence of the progressive integration between the wireless and wire-line environments, the need of deploying distributed applications such as multi-Agent systems on handheld devices is becoming more and more important. But it is difficult to implement.

In this article, Jade-Leap add-on will be used to solve the integration of Jade and Android platform. As an example, we develop one Jade Agent for Android platform. This article will elaborate the principles, the methods and the demo, etc.

## 23.2 The Principle and Methods of Developing Jade Agent for Android Platform

### 23.2.1 Bottleneck Issues

*It is difficult to integrate Jade Agent into Android platform. The developers should have a good command of Agent programming mechanisms as well as Android Activity mechanism, Intent mechanism, Broadcast mechanism and so on. Jade and Android are totally different development platforms, especially due to the limitations of hardware normal Jade Agent can not run on mobile devices such as mobile phone or PDA. Therefore, there are some bottleneck issues in the system development:*

1. The complete JADE runtime environment has a memory footprint of some Mbytes that cannot fit the limitations of handheld devices.
2. JADE requires Java 5 (or later) while the majority of handheld devices only support CDC, PersonalJava, or more typically MIDP.
3. Wireless links have different characteristics with respect to fixed network such as high latency, low bandwidth, intermittent connectivity and dynamic IP address assignment that must be taken into account properly.

But fortunately for us, Jade-leap add-on was created to solve these problems and allows deploying JADE agents on handheld devices. For the implementation of deploying Jade Agent to Android phones or other mobile services, we must have a thorough understanding of its principle. In addition to that, during the system development, some interactions must be considered, such as the communications among Jade Agents, the interactions between Jade Agent and Android Activity and the inter-operations among Android Activities.

### 23.2.2 Jade-Leap Add-on and its Execution Mode

*The Jade-Leap add-on is based on Jade but replaces some parts of the JADE kernel and then a modified runtime environment will be formed. This new runtime environment can be shaped in different ways corresponding to the two configurations (CDC and CLDC) of the Java Micro Edition and the Android Dalvik Java Virtual Machine. Therefore, we can use Jade-Leap add-on to deploy Jade Agent to mobile phones or other lightweight devices.*

The JADE runtime environment can be executed in two different modes: "Stand-alone" execution mode and "Split" execution mode.

In the Stand-alone execution mode a complete container is executed on the target device. On the other hand, in the Split execution mode the container is separated into a front-end (meant for running on the embedded device) and a back-end (for running on the host with J2SE) linked together through a permanent connection. The back-end location acts as a dispatcher for message coming and going to other platforms. This execution mode is particularly suited for resource constrained and wireless devices, because it has the following advantages:

1. Split execution is extremely more lightweight.
2. Split execution minimizes the communication over the wireless link.
3. Split execution is faster in the start-up procedure.
4. Split execution can deal with temporary disconnections.

### 23.2.3 The Steps and Methods of Integrating Jade Agent into Android

*For Android project, Jade-Leap add-on provides JadeAndroid.jar for us. This package file includes a lot of jade classes with ad hoc customization for the Android as well as some services oriented Android, such as MicroRuntimeService. During the development, the first step must be including the JadeAndroid.jar library in the classpath of our Android Application project. And then, we can follow the following steps to develop a Jade Agent for Android phones.*

Step 1. Declare MicroRuntimeService in Android Application Project

Consistent with the Android architecture, the Jade runtime is wrapped by an Android service. More specifically, the jadeAndroid.jar library includes two service classes: jade.android.RuntimeService and jade.android.MicroRuntimeService that wrap a full container and a split container, respectively. In this article we use a split container that, in general, is the suggested approach when working with mobile devices. So the MicroRuntimeService should be declared in the Androidmanifest.xml thus it can be identified when the system is running. The function of MicroRuntimeService is to configure the Jade Environment and to start or stop the Jade Runtime when required.

Step 2. Bind MicroRuntimerService with Android Activity

Unlike activities in Android, services run silently in background. Because they have higher priority than inactive activities, it is perfect bind them to the application's component and make the application continue run and response the users' action in the background.

So, now we should bind the MicroRuntimerService which we will use with Android Activity at the application start-ups. The binding function is as below:

context.bindService (new Intent (context, MicroRuntimeService.class), serviceConnection, Context.BIND_AUTO_CREATE);

Step 3. Create a Split Container and Start it

Before this, a main container must be started up and running on a platform server which can be reachable from the android device. The reference codes are as below.

jadeServiceBinder.startAgentContainer("MAIN_HOST", MAIN_PORT, new RuntimeCallback < Void > () {      });

Step 4. Start Jade Agent in the Split Container

Now all set, and we can start our Jade Agent in the Split Container in the following way:

jadeServiceBinder.startAgent("NICK_NAME", "CLASS_NAME", null, new RuntimeCallback < Void > () {        });

Step 5. Implement the Interaction between Jade Agent and Android Activity

1. Transfer information from Android Activity to Jade Agent

To do this, when we start the Agent from the Activity we can pass the application Context and other objects as parameters to Agent. Thus in the Agent setup() method it can retrieve these parameters.

2. Transfer information from Jade Agent to Android Activity

In the Agent code, when you need to notify something to the Activity you can send a broadcast message with the action defined in the Activity, of course some parameters could be included by using the putExtra() method of Intent. In the Activity we should create a custom BroadcastReceiver instance and use the IntentFilter mechanism to receive the broadcast from the Agent.

## 23.3 An Example of Jade Agent for Android

In this article, a distributed multi-agent system for train running information retrieving has been developed. The main idea of this system is that one Jade Agent will be deployed on the user's Android phone; the user will request a train (e.g. the arriving time or departure time at a station) from his Android phone. This request will reach wireless the responder Agent and after finishing the processing of the request, the responder Agent will send a reply with the retrieving results to the requester and the results can be shown on the interface of the user's Android phone.

So, this system comprises two kinds of Agent.

1. Requester Agent

It is deployed and running on the user's Android phone. The user can set the query conditions from the Activity layout and then send the query request to the responder Agent.

2. Responder Agent

It is running on a reachable host with fixed IP addresses. It is responsible for receiving the request from the Android phone and search in the train information database according to the query conditions. After finishing that, it can send the results to the requester Agent.

The framework of the system is shown as Fig. 23.1. The system has been developed under Eclipse. Firstly, we developed the Responder Agent which is a normal Jade Agent and has its CyclicBehaviour to receive and reply message.

**Fig. 23.1** The framework of
the system

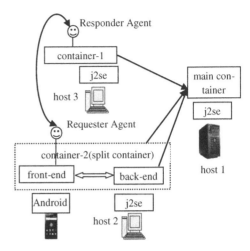

The more difficult part is to develop the Requester Agent which is a Jade Agent for
Android. For that, we created a new Android project and import JadeAndroid.jar.

According to the above principles and methods we made our Requester Agent
successfully work on Android. The running steps and results are as follows:

1. Launch the main container with the JADE GUI using the command: java
   Jade.Boot –gui.
2. Launch a new container and start Responder Agent in it.
3. Run the project as an Android Application, and then we will find a "Train Info"
   icon show on the Android emulator (as illustrated in Fig. 23.2). This is the Jade
   Agent we developed for Android, and it is also the frontend in the split
   execution mode.

**Fig. 23.2** A Jade agent for
android was installed on the
emulator

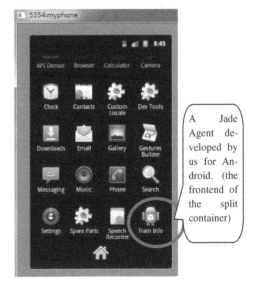

**Fig. 23.3** Input the query criterion

**Fig. 23.4** The change in
Jade platform

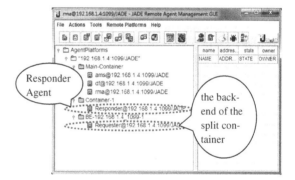

4. Click the"Train Info"icon,the graphical interface will show as Fig. 23.3.

On this interface we can set the query criterion, for example, input "1019" as
the train No. and "hefei" as the name of station. And then, click "Ask" button, we
can find that a new container named "BE" has been added and the Requester
Agent running on it. Actually, "BE" is a split container and Requester is its
backend. This result is shown as Fig. 23.4.

By using the Jade Agent communication mechanism, the Requester will send
the query criterion coming from the Android frontend to the Responder Agent. The
responder Agent will send a reply with the retrieving results to the requester and
finally the results can be shown on the interface of the user's Android phone,
which is shown as Fig. 23.5.

**Fig. 23.5** The result on the
phone screen

## 23.4  Conclusion

In the development of this prototype, JADE-LEAP add-on has been successfully
used to implement a personal agent on Android platform. This framework opens
the way towards any kind of distributed multi-agent systems, in which personal
agents may be smoothly running on mobile devices or other lightweight handle
devices and can communicate wirelessly with agents that may provide various
services available in different places of the city, such as airports, bus stops, train
stations, restaurants and so on. Such application will make mobile services more
intelligent, proactive and interactive, which will meet the personalized needs of
mobile phone users.

# Chapter 24
# Test Case Selection Based on a Spectrum of Complexity Metrics

Bouchaib Falah and Kenneth Magel

**Abstract** Quality continues to be a significant issue for software, and testing is a key activity in ensuring the quality of software. Unfortunately, since testing usually was near the end of software development, it is often rushed and frequently not done well. Thus, this paper suggests an approach that can address some of these issues and examine ways to reduce the software testing costs by selecting test cases based on a Spectrum of Complexity Metrics (SCM). We have developed a comprehensive taxonomy of product metrics based on two dimensions, the product level (class, method, statement) and the characteristics of the product. To evaluate these metrics, we have developed a tool which uses these metrics to target test cases. This tool enables us to identify three sample metric combinations. We have conducted a series of experiments based on three applications. The combinations of metrics were applied to test case selection on each of the applications. To investigate the efficiency of our test case selection, we have created a significant number of mutants using MuJava, and a series of a significant number of seeded errors inserted independently by a third party. Our experiments show that our test case selections discover at least 60 % of seeded errors and mutants. For further evaluation, we compared our approach to the boundary value analysis. Our experiments indicate that our testing approach is highly effective in the detection of the mutants as well as the seeded errors.

B. Falah (✉) · K. Magel
School of Science and Engineering, Al Akhawayn University, Ifrane, Morocco
e-mail: b.falah@aui.ma

K. Magel
e-mail: Kenneth.magel@ndsu.edu

K. Magel
Department of Computer Science, North Dakota State University, Fargo, ND, USA

W. Lu et al. (eds.), *Proceedings of the 2012 International Conference on Information Technology and Software Engineering*, Lecture Notes in Electrical Engineering 212, DOI: 10.1007/978-3-642-34531-9_24, © Springer-Verlag Berlin Heidelberg 2013

**Keywords** Testing · Complexity metrics · Selection test · Mutant · Seeded errors · Boundary value analysis

## 24.1 Introduction

Software testing is the process of determining if a program behaves as expected. It is an intellectually challenging activity aimed at evaluating the capability of a program or system to determine whether or not it meets its requirements. Unfortunately, since testing usually occurs near the end of software development, it is often rushed and frequently not done well.

We propose an approach to reducing significantly the number of test cases needed to reveal the presence of a large percentage of the errors that would be discovered through existing approaches. Our goal is to use no more than twenty percent of the test cases to reveal at least sixty percent of the errors. We deal only with unit testing here although we are working to extend our approach to integration and system testing.

Our approach uses a spectrum of complexity metrics at each of three levels of an application (class, method, and statement), that measure all three dimensions of program complexity (size, data, control).

## 24.2 Related Work

Regression test selection techniques attempt to reduce the cost of software testing by selecting a subset of an existing test suite for execution on a modified program ignoring test cases that cannot or are unlikely to reveal errors caused by or revealed through the specific software changes. To improve the effectiveness of regression test selection, numerous researchers have proposed a variety of test case selection methods. Rothermel et al. [1, 2], Hutchins et al. [3], and Kim and Porter [4] examined different selection test techniques such as minimization, safe, dataflow, control flow, ad hoc and random testing, focusing on their abilities to reduce the cost of testing by decreasing the number of test cases while still detecting the maximum number of defects.

However, there is a critical question facing software engineering today: How do we measure the effectiveness of software testing?

Measurement makes interesting characteristics of products more visible and understandable. Appropriate measurement can identify useful patterns present in the product being measured. Many metrics have been invented. Most of them have been defined and then tested only in a limited environment. The most commonly used metrics for software are the number of lines of source code, LOC (a rough measure of size), and Cyclomatic complexity (a rough measure of control flow).

Chidamber and Kemerer [5] proposed a set of complexity metrics that address many principles of object oriented software production to enhance and improve software development and maintenance. However, their metrics applied to only the method and class levels of complexity.

In recent years, much attention has been directed toward reducing software cost. To this end, software engineers have attempted to find relationships between the characteristics of programs and the complexity of doing programming tasks or achieving desirable properties in the resulting product such as traceability or security. The aim has been to create measures of software complexity to guide efforts to reduce the software costs.

Even though the body of literature dedicated to the development of testing methods has grown, software complexity metrics have not yet gained wide acceptance as useful guides. Only small experiments have been done in this area and the results provide only weak support for the use of complexity metrics. Nonetheless, many researchers continue to develop and create new metrics.

Our work applies a comprehensive suite of complexity metrics to the problem of maximizing the effectiveness of software testing. The frequency with which users of common computer applications encounter serious errors indicates that the industry frequently does an inadequate job of testing before release. However, the problem does not appear to be with the testing process itself. Some software such as that for controlling nuclear reactors is well-tested and has very few errors. Instead, the problem appears to be that the best known methods for testing are too time consuming and complicated to be applied when a project is already running weeks or months behind schedule. Almost always, industry sacrifices best practices in testing to make up some of the time for release.

## 24.3 Spectrum of Complexity Metrics

### 24.3.1 Variety of Metrics

Software metrics usually are considered in one or two of four categories:

- Product: (e.g. lines of code)
- Process: (e.g. test cases produced)
- People: (e.g. inspections participated in)
- Value to the customer: (e.g. requirements completed)

In our work, we concentrated on product metrics as selectors for test cases. Previous work using metrics almost always considered only a small set of metrics which measured only one or two aspects of product complexity.

Our work starts with the development of a comprehensive taxonomy of product metrics. We based this taxonomy on two dimensions: (1) the level of the product to which the metric applies; and (2) the characteristic of product complexity that the metric measures.

The scope of consideration dimension includes the following values: (1) the product's context including other software and hardware with which the product interacts; (2) the entire product; (3) a single subsystem or layer; (4) a single component; (5) a class; (6) a method; (7) a statement.

For the initial uses of this taxonomy reported in this work, we used only (5), (6), and (7) since they appear to be the most relevant scopes for unit testing. Future work may add (3) and (4) as we consider integration testing and (1) and (2) for system testing.

The complexity kind dimension includes the following values: size, control, and data. Each of these values in turn has sub-values.

For size, the sub-values are: (a) number of units (e.g. statements); (b) number of interactions (e.g. number of method calls). For control flow, the sub-values are: (a) number of decisions; (b) nesting depth of decisions. For data, the sub-values are: (a) data usage; (b) data flow.

### 24.3.1.1 Metrics at Statement Level

For each executable statement within a method we had four metrics that emerged from three complexity dimensions:

- Data Dimension: active data values and Data usage values.
- Control Dimension: scope metric.
- Size Dimension: number of operators.

Data Complexity

Data complexity metrics can be divided in two different aspects: data flow and data usage. Data flow is based on the idea that changing the value of any variable will affect the values of the variables that depend upon that variable's value. However, data usage is based on the number of data defined in the unit being considered or the number of data related to that unit. We defined data usage for a statement to be the number of variable values used in that statement plus the number of variables assigned new values in that statement. However, we estimated data flow for each statement in a method by counting how many active data values there are when the method executes. Active data values are counted by determining which variable assignments could still be active when this statement begins execution plus the number of assignments done in this statement. Several testers have chosen testing with data flow because data flow is closely related to Object Oriented cohesion [6–8].

Control Flow

In our work, we used one control flow measure, the scope metric [9]. For each statement we counted the number of control flow statements (if–then-else, select, do-while, etc.) that contain that statement.

Size Complexity

Our size metrics relied on the Halstead Software Science Definition [10]. Halstead's software science is one traditional code complexity measure that approaches the topic of code complexity from a unique perspective. Halstead counted traditional operators, such as + and ‖, and punctuation such as semicolon and (), where parentheses pair counted as just one single operator.

In our work, we counted just traditional operators for simplicity by counting the number of operators used in each statement of the code. Figure 24.1 shows the metrics we used at the statement level. These four metrics are used as roots to derive other complexity metrics that will be used at the method level and class level.

### 24.3.1.2 Metrics at Method Level

Since the method constitutes different statements, we used both the sum of each metric for the statements within that method and the maximum value of each metric for the statements within that method. In addition to the sum and the maximum of these metrics, we used another single level metric that counts the number of other methods within the same module (class) that call this method.

### 24.3.1.3 Metrics at Class Level

At the class level, we used both the sum of each metric for the methods within the class (e.g. Total of Operators) and the maximum value of each metric for the methods within the class (e.g. Max of Operators, Max of Levels, Max of Tot Levels, Max of Tot DU, Max of Tot DF,...). We then added two additional

**Fig. 24.1** Complexity perspective and metrics at statement level

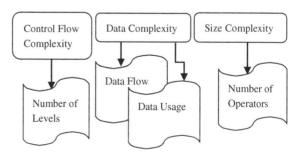

metrics: the in–out degree of that class, which is the number of methods outside of that class that are called by at least one method in that class, and the number of public members within the class. The public members within a class are defined as the public fields and the public methods defined in that class.

Moreover, we proposed that a combination of size, control flow, and data metrics does better than one dimension. This assumption permitted us to use those values with the objective of finding patterns in the entire set of metrics measurements and identifying sample metric combinations to use in our initial evaluation.

Examples of the combinations we proposed are:

$$Oper\ DF\ Combo = \frac{Max\ of\ operators + Max\ of\ DF}{Number\ of\ statements} \tag{24.1}$$

$$Levels\ DU\ Combo = \frac{Max\ of\ Levels + Max\ of\ DU}{Number\ of\ statements} \tag{24.2}$$

$$All\ Combo = \frac{\sum \{Max\ of\ operators\ Max\ of\ Tot\ Levels,\ Max\ of\ Tot\ DU,\ Max\ of\ Tot\ DF\}}{Number\ of\ statements} \tag{24.3}$$

We do not intend to evaluate all possible combinations. That will be a prohibitive number. Other combinations will be given our attention in future work.

## 24.3.2 Test Case Generation Based on Spectrum of Complexity Metrics

It is not enough for us as software engineers to choose a test strategy. Before testing starts, we must also know the minimum number of test cases needed to satisfy the strategy for a given program. This information helps us to plan our testing, not only in terms of generating data for each test case but also in understanding how much time testing is likely to take and what expenses are necessary to deliver the software.

We have developed algorithms for test case generation based on the values calculated from our combinations of spectrum metrics. The aim of the test case generation is to:

- compare the original program with the seeded programs that resulted from the original program after we employed a third party to insert defects manually into our program;
- compare the original program with the mutants after using MuClipse, a popular automatic mutation testing tool that is used in Eclipse, to automatically generate these mutants..

If the test cases were able to differentiate a mutant or a seeded program from the original program, then the mutant/seeded program is said to be killed. Otherwise it is still alive.

The evaluation of our approach was done by calculating the ratio of the number of seeded errors to the number of test cases selected and the ratio of the number of mutants distinguished to the number of test cases selected. The fewer the test cases are, the higher the ratios are and, hence, the more effective our testing strategy is. Our goal is to reduce the number of test cases and the cost of testing and thus, increase the effectiveness of testing. To execute the test cases, we used the procedure pioneered by JUnit of other test case automatic programs.

The test cases are implemented as methods within a new test class associated with the class being tested. An umbrella program then executes each of the test methods against the class being tested and then compares the results to those previously expected.

To reduce the number of test cases, we proposed that our selection testing should be based on our broad spectrum metrics. Our approach is based on the assumption that we should focus on the classes that are more likely to be complex. The targeted classes are more fully tested than the other classes in the application. These classes are determined by the metrics combination mentioned above. Thus, to test an application, we evaluated the metric values of all classes of the application and concentrated our tests on classes with the highest metric values. These classes are likely to be more complex in the application.

Since our SCM tool evaluates each method within each class, the methods with the highest metrics would be our target.

## 24.4 Empirical Study

As a basis for our empirical study, we chose three applications downloaded from sourceforge.net, a popular repository for open source projects: CruiseControl, Blackjack, and CoffeeMaker.

### 24.4.1 Our Approach and Test Cases

We have developed algorithms for test case generation based on the values resulting from our metric combinations (1), (2), and (3) given above.

### 24.4.2 Mutation Testing and Error Seeding

We used two different methods to evaluate testing effectiveness: mutation testing; and error seeding by an independent person. For each class, all methods were tested, but our focus was on the most complex methods. We started with the creation of one test case for each method. Then we ran these test cases on the modified programs and calculated:

- The score of mutants: the number of killed mutants divided by the total number of mutants.
- The detection rate of seeded errors: the number of the detected seeded errors divided by the total number of all seeded errors.

When the score of mutants or the detection rate of the seeded errors was too low, we increased the number of test cases for the complex methods until we got a better score.

## 24.4.3 Evaluation of Our Approach

To assess our approach and show its effectiveness, we compared it with other approaches that have been used in the software engineering discipline. Since Boundary Value Analysis (BVA) is the most widely practiced form of functional testing, we created BVA test cases and ran them on our modified programs in the same way we did for our test cases. In creating BVA test cases, we concentrated our testing efforts on the limits of the boundary of each method within each class subject to test.

The comparison was based on:

- Mutants, by comparing the mutant score divided by the number of test cases.
- Seeded programs, by comparing the detection rate divided by the number of test cases.

Since our regression selection testing approach used three combinations of metrics, the comparison involved evaluating our approach against the boundary value analysis for each combination metric.

In the rest of this paper, we assume that $m$ and $s$ are two real numbers such that:

$$m = \frac{Mutants\ killed\ score}{Number\ of\ test\ cases}$$

$$s = \frac{Percentage\ of\ seeded\ errors\ detected}{Number\ of\ test\ cases}$$

### 24.4.3.1 Mutation Testing Technique

Our approach used the regression selection tests based on the values of the three combination metrics for each class within each application. Tables 24.1, 24.2, and 24.3 provide statistics for every class tested. For each testing class and for each approach, we list:

- The number of test cases created for each class,
- The mutant score, which is the number of mutants killed divided by the total number of mutants
- The number of mutants divided by the total number of test cases.

Based on the statistical results in these tables, we observed that the value of $m$ in our approach is higher than the one in BVA for all testing classes.

### 24.4.3.2  Error Seeding Technique

Error Seeding was done by a third party who intentionally inserted faults in the source code of each of the classes used in this research experiment, for the purpose of monitoring the rate of detection. These faults were inserted according to the top errors usually made by Java programmers [11].

In this technique, we used the same test cases that were used in the mutation testing but with a smaller number for some. Then, we determined the rate of detection obtained for each class by dividing the detected seeded errors by the total number of seeded errors. The experimental results, obtained based on each combination metric, are shown in Tables 24.4, 24.5, and 24.6.

We used a smaller number of test cases in the error seeding technique than in the mutation testing technique. This was due to the fact that we have a smaller number of seeded errors compared to the number of automatic mutants. Based on the experimental results in Tables 24.4 and 24.5, we observed that the values of $s$ for all tested classes in our approach are much higher than for BVA. The results of Table 24.6 show that even though the detection rates for all the classes, except the "Coffee-Maker" class, in both approaches are the same, the values of $s$ in our approach are much higher than for BVA, except for the "Inventory" class, where the value of $s$ is close to the one for BVA. This closeness of the value of $s$ is attributable to the detection rates being the same and the number of test cases being close.

Based on our observation, there are many different data inputs on each method of this class, which makes the number of test cases using BVA technique greater, and thus the value of was lower compared to the one in our approach.

As a summary, our empirical study shows that, using either mutation testing technique or the error seeding testing technique, the rate of mutant score and the rate of detected errors with respect to the number of test cases is a good indicator of the efficiency of our testing approach against the boundary value analysis approach.

**Table 24.1** Comparison on mutants for operators DF combo metric

| Application | Class name | Our approach | | | Boundary value analysis | | |
|---|---|---|---|---|---|---|---|
| | | # of tests | Mutant score (%) | $m$ | # of tests | Mutant score (%) | $m$ |
| Blackjack | Dealer | 3 | 100 | 33 | 6 | 100 | 17 |
| | Hand | 4 | 100 | 25 | 11 | 100 | 9 |
| | User | 6 | 100 | 17 | 14 | 100 | 7 |
| CoffeeMaker | CoffeeMaker | 12 | 100 | 8 | 10 | 21 | 2 |
| | Inventory | 16 | 66 | 4 | 22 | 43 | 2 |
| CruiseControl | CarSimulator | 13 | 100 | 8 | 39 | 100 | 3 |
| | SpeedControl | 8 | 100 | 13 | 19 | 100 | 5 |

**Table 24.2** Comparison on mutant programs for levels DU combo metric

| Application | Class name | Our approach | | | Boundary value analysis | | |
|---|---|---|---|---|---|---|---|
| | | # of tests | Mutant score (%) | *m* | # of tests | Mutant score (%) | *m* |
| Blackjack | Dealer | 3 | 100 | 33 | 6 | 100 | 177 |
| | Hand | 5 | 100 | 25 | 11 | 100 | 9 |
| | LogicalFacade | 18 | 76 | 17 | 32 | 52 | 7 |
| CoffeeMaker | CoffeeMaker | 10 | 100 | 8 | 10 | 21 | 2 |
| | Inventory | 20 | 61 | 4 | 22 | 43 | 2 |
| CruiseControl | CarSimulator | 12 | 100 | 8 | 39 | 100 | 3 |
| | Controller | 10 | 100 | 13 | 45 | 100 | 5 |

**Table 24.3** Comparison on mutant programs for all combo metric

| Application | Class name | Our approach | | | Boundary value analysis | | |
|---|---|---|---|---|---|---|---|
| | | # of tests | Mutant score (%) | *m* | # of tests | Mutant score (%) | *m* |
| Blackjack | Dealer | 3 | 100 | 33 | 6 | 100 | 17 |
| | Hand | 5 | 100 | 20 | 11 | 100 | 9 |
| | User | 6 | 100 | 17 | 14 | 100 | 7 |
| CoffeeMaker | CoffeeMaker | 9 | 100 | 11 | 10 | 21 | 2 |
| | Inventory | 16 | 66 | 4 | 22 | 43 | 2 |
| CruiseControl | CarSimulator | 13 | 100 | 8 | 39 | 100 | 3 |
| | CruiseControl | 4 | 100 | 25 | 16 | 100 | 6 |

**Table 24.4** Comparison on seeded programs for operators DF combo metric

| Application | Class name | Our approach | | | Boundary value analysis | | |
|---|---|---|---|---|---|---|---|
| | | # of tests | Detection rate (%) | *s* | # of tests | Detection rate (%) | *s* |
| Blackjack | Dealer | 2 | 100 | 50 | 6 | 100 | 17 |
| | Hand | 4 | 100 | 25 | 11 | 100 | 9 |
| | User | 6 | 100 | 17 | 14 | 100 | 7 |
| CoffeeMaker | CoffeeMaker | 9 | 100 | 11 | 11 | 66 | 6 |
| | Inventory | 11 | 100 | 9 | 22 | 100 | 5 |
| CruiseControl | CarSimulator | 12 | 100 | 8 | 39 | 100 | 3 |
| | SpeedControl | 8 | 100 | 13 | 19 | 100 | 5 |

**Table 24.5** Comparison on seeded programs for levels DU combo metric

| Application | Class name | Our approach | | | Boundary value analysis | | |
|---|---|---|---|---|---|---|---|
| | | # of tests | Detection rate (%) | $s$ | # of tests | Detection rate (%) | $s$ |
| Blackjack | Dealer | 2 | 100 | 50 | 6 | 100 | 17 |
| | Hand | 4 | 100 | 25 | 11 | 100 | 9 |
| | LogicalFacade | 18 | 100 | 6 | 32 | 100 | 3 |
| CoffeeMaker | CoffeeMaker | 9 | 100 | 11 | 11 | 66 | 6 |
| | Inventory | 14 | 100 | 7 | 22 | 100 | 5 |
| CruiseControl | CarSimulator | 12 | 100 | 8 | 39 | 100 | 3 |
| | Controller | 10 | 100 | 10 | 45 | 100 | 2 |

**Table 24.6** Comparison on seeded programs for all combo metric

| Application | Class name | Our approach | | | Boundary value analysis | | |
|---|---|---|---|---|---|---|---|
| | | # of tests | Detection rate (%) | $s$ | # of tests | Detection rate (%) | $s$ |
| Blackjack | Dealer | 2 | 100 | 50 | 6 | 100 | 17 |
| | Hand | 4 | 100 | 25 | 11 | 100 | 9 |
| | User | 6 | 100 | 17 | 14 | 100 | 7 |
| CoffeeMaker | CoffeeMaker | 9 | 100 | 11 | 11 | 66 | 6 |
| | Inventory | 11 | 100 | 9 | 22 | 100 | 5 |
| CruiseControl | CarSimulator | 12 | 100 | 8 | 39 | 100 | 3 |
| | CruiseControl | 4 | 100 | 25 | 16 | 100 | 6 |

## 24.5  Conclusion and Future Work

Software testing is a crucial element of the software development process. Testing is an intellectually development challenging activity that occurs near the end of software development. Thus, it is often rushed and frequently not done well. Consequently, it is a very costly and time consuming activity.

This paper addresses some of these issues by examining ways to reduce the cost of software unit testing. We developed a methodology to lower the cost of software and evaluate its quality. This methodology consists of creating measures of software complexity that can be used to target test cases where they would be most effective. We started with the development of a comprehensive taxonomy of product metrics. This taxonomy was based on the metric dimension (product level) and the kind dimension (product complexity characteristic).

Since our work considers only unit testing, we used the scope metric dimension values of class, method, and statement. We considered kind dimension values of size, control flow, and data. The three kind dimension values of product complexity have sub-categories. The size has the number of units and the number of interactions. The control flow has the number of decisions and the depth of decisions. The data has the data flow and the data usage.

In our work, we used at least one sub-category from each complexity kind dimension value. For the size, we used the number of units and the number of interactions. For the control flow, we used only number of decisions. For the data, we used data flow and data usage.

Another contribution of this research was the use of summation and maximum to build larger scope metrics from smaller scope metrics. For example, a count of the number of traditional operators is a statement level metric. This count can be used in summation or maximum to derive a method or a class level metric.

These metrics were applied to three simple Java applications. Based on the result of the values of these metrics, we assessed the software defects that need to be found during the testing phase and adjusted schedules or goals consequently. To achieve the reduction of the cost and time of software, we used a selection test that was based on the set of all these complexity metrics. For this reason, we developed an implementation program tool, SCM, which calculates the value of each metric at each scope value (product level) and uses this suite of complexity metrics to target test cases. These calculated values were used to look for patterns in the entire set of metrics measurements that indicate unusual complexity in some part of the Java source code. The resulting patterns allowed us to create three combinations of complexity metrics that were applied effectively to test case selection on each of the independent applications used in this research.

Based on the values of these three combinations for each class, the classes that had the greatest values were our targeted classes. These classes were more fully tested than the other classes in the application. Furthermore, we created more test cases for the methods with the greatest metric values than the other methods within the same class. This methodology allowed us to develop algorithms for test case selection.

To assess the effectiveness of the selection of our test cases, we seeded our targeted classes with automatic defects using MuJava and manual seeded errors done independently by a third party. Then, we ran our test cases on the modified programs.

The effectiveness of our test case generation was evaluated based on the values of the mutant score and the detection rate. To increase the confidence in the quality of object-oriented system testing, we compared our approach with the BVA using mutation testing technique and error seeding technique. The results showed that our approach was more efficient than the BVA approach for all our combination metrics and our specific aim in reducing the cost and time of software was satisfied.

Since the statement, the method, and the class appear the most relevant scopes for unit testing, they were the only scope dimension values used in this paper. So, we plan to produce a comprehensive taxonomy from other kinds of metrics.

# References

1. Graves TL, Harrold MJ, Kim J, Porter A, Rothermel G (2001) An empirical study of regression test selection techniques. ACM Trans Softw Eng Methodol 10(2):184–208
2. Rothermel G, Harrold MJ (1997) A safe, efficient regression test selection technique. ACM Trans Softw Eng Methodol 6(2):173–210
3. Hutchins M, Foster H, Goradia T, Ostrand T (1994) Experiments on the effectiveness of dataflow- and controlflow-based test adequacy criteria. In: Proceedings of the 22nd international conference on software engineering, IEEE, pp 191–200, May 1994
4. Kim J-M, Porter A (2002) A history-based test prioritization technique for regression testing in resource constrained environments. In: Proceedings of the 24th international conference on software engineering
5. Hierons RM (2006) Avoiding coincidental correctness in boundary value analysis. Trans Softw Eng Methodol (TOSEM)
6. Chidamber SR, Keremer CF (1994) A metric suite for object oriented design. IEEE Trans Softw Eng 20(6):476–493
7. Tsui F, Karam O, Iriele S (2008) A test complexity metric based on dataflow testing technique. Internal report supported and funded from PSLSAMP grant
8. Henderson-Sellers B (1996) Object-oriented metrics: measures of complexity. Prentice Hall, Englewood Cliffs
9. Rothermely G, Elbaumz S, Malishevskyy A, Kallakuriz P, Qiuy X (2003) On test suite composition and cost-effective regression testing. 30 Aug 2003
10. Halstead MH (1977) Elements of software science. Elsevier North-Holland, New York
11. Kim S, Clark J, McDermid J (2000) Class mutation: mutation testing for object-oriented programs. OOSS: object-oriented software systems

# Chapter 25
# Web Application Modeling and Anomaly Detection

Huihui Hou and Tongge Xu

**Abstract** Widespread use of Web applications and its distribution and complexity, makes web application performance analysis and anomaly detection become urgent and challenging. Previous web application anomaly detection, was more focused on intrusion detection, and made a lot more sophisticated algorithms and methods, but the performance anomaly detection is mostly achieved with the current monitoring software, which greatly limits the scope of its application. The innovation of this paper is to extract the timing sequence from web logs using stepwise regression method and establish the time consumption model of the server-side, dynamic baseline is also used to determine whether there is an exception, and to analyze whether anomaly is caused by the workload. It's proved the web log records can be obtained via web server with little cost.

**Keywords** Web application · Anomaly detection · Regression · Dynamic baseline

## 25.1 Introduction

The scale and complexity of Web application is increasingly increasing, it is be coming increasingly difficult to discover anomaly manually. The efficient management of Web applications and anomaly detection for the QoS (QOS) requirements is also facing a great challenge.

H. Hou (✉) · T. Xu
Beijing Key Laboratory of Network Technology,School of Computer Science and Engineering, Beihang University, Beijing 100191, China
e-mail: huilela@163.com

T. Xu
e-mail: xutg@buaa.edu.cn

W. Lu et al. (eds.), *Proceedings of the 2012 International Conference on Information Technology and Software Engineering*, Lecture Notes in Electrical Engineering 212, DOI: 10.1007/978-3-642-34531-9_25, © Springer-Verlag Berlin Heidelberg 2013

Anomaly detection [1], the idea was an intrusion detection model first proposed by Denning. Anomaly detection first collects a variety of characteristic parameters of the system during normal operation, such as CPU utilization, memory usage, detection model based on these parameters, and determines the extent to which a behavior "anomaly", namely defining an evaluation function, which is used to calculate the behavior of abnormal indicators and define the anomaly index threshold [2].

The previous Web application anomaly detection is mostly for the intrusion detection, but the anomaly detection in this article focuses on the anomaly detection of performance.

Performance anomalies are mainly caused by the following areas:

*Software for its own reasons*: software updates, re-released, the program exception.

*Container*: containers cannot work properly caused by the exceptions of the container where the operating system.

*Work Load*: exception to produce the bottleneck may be the unreasonable allocation of the server thread pool, the unreasonable distribution of the database thread pool; too many resources occupied by the other processes, hardware resources cannot meet the requirements.

*Services relied on*: including network anomalies, database exception and etc.

*The other reasons* like intrusion.

## 25.2 Related Research

Currently the Anomaly Detection of Web application has a certain sophisticated algorithms and theory at home and abroad. Among the rest, Wang Xiaofeng [2], etc. proposed anomaly detection based on the gap-type variable-length frequent short sequence (GV-Gram) mode for the Web application intrusion exception detection algorithm. It is different from the performance anomaly detection that this article focuses on.

Song Yunkui [3], etc. proposed a performance anomaly detection method based on the service time stamp, marking a relatively stable request service time, and by analyzing the time change to locate performance bottlenecks and analyze possible causes. But its performance parameters obtain at OnceAS monitoring framework ASMF, which has certain limitations.

Ludmila [4] built up resource consumption model according to the regression analysis of the CPU utilization, and combined with the signature of the enterprise applications for automatic anomaly detection and distinguishing between load and program exceptions.

Lots of performance monitoring software, like DiagnoSys, Dirig Application Performance Platform, Quest Central, VERITAS Indepth for J2EE, JDBInsight [5], zabbix etc., the runtime performance indicators can be got to assist the implementation of anomaly detection.

In this paper, it utilized the server request processing time, established the server processing time consumption model by stepwise regression, and detected whether an exception occurs through dynamic baseline analysis method.

## 25.3  Web Application Modeling

### 25.3.1  Transaction

We can interpret the concept of a transaction from different perspectives. For a database, in terms of a transaction, it is a collection containing a set of database operations between transactions. From the perspective of the user session, the transaction is a sequence of Http requests in a user session. Speaking for the client, the response page for a request triggered through the browser explicitly to the server-side is a transaction (the response page, usually consisting of an html page and embedded objects). While for the server-side, the build process of the main Html page is the main reason for the delay in the generation and consumption of resources. Reference [4] elaborated on the similarities and differences of client and server-side transaction.

The transaction discussed in this article is based on the server-side.

### 25.3.2  Parameter Selection and Acquisition

#### 25.3.2.1  Parameter Selection

For a client, request response time is equal to the network transmission time and the request response time of the service system. The Request response time of the service system can be divided into the service time (processing time) and latency time. The service time is time consumed by the system to process a request, not including the time consumed by system administration (such as queuing, scheduling, etc.) time-consuming; latency time is the time experienced by a Web application request from accessing to leaving the system. The latency time reflects the response characteristics of the system. Existing performance testing methods concerned about the latency time, vulnerable to the impact of confounding factors, and does not accurately show the load pressure of the system. However, the processing time is mainly determined by the degree of competition for resources and it is one aspect of the Qos, therefore, it is more suitable for an anomaly detection.

### 25.3.2.2 Data Source

Log on the Web server is generally divided into access log and running log these two categories. Wherein, the access log mainly recorded the access circumstances of each application on the Web server, the server's processing time and the corresponding status information. For the running log, it is mainly recording server running, like startup information.

There are several common web log data models, such as NCSA, extended W3C and IRCache [6] format.

### 25.3.2.3 Data Preprocessing

Due to the presence of local cache, firewall and proxy server, the data in the actual Web access log is often incomplete, redundant or even wrong, which directly affects the subsequent operation and whether the analysis is correct or not, and the strength of operability. In general, Web log preprocessing includes data cleaning, path completion [7] etc.

Data cleaning, reads as follows:

1. Filter the access records with less impact on performance and response time, and like the suffix containing gif, jpeg, jpg, swf, css, map and js in the log.
2. Delete the source and destination IP, request protocol and request method these unrelated fields.
3. Remove the parameters in the URL.

### 25.3.2.4 URL Aggregation

To define a time sequence R which is a finite set $\{(t_i, url_i, sc_i, p_i), (t_j, url_j, sc_j, p_j), \cdots\cdots (t_n, url_n, sc_n, p_n)\}$, satisfying $t_i < t_j < t_n (i = 1, 2, \ldots\ldots, n - 2; j = 2, 3, \ldots\ldots n - 1)$.

We can get a time sequence R through the obtained preprocessing. From the R in accordance with the url aggregation, we can get an access sequence of different transactions $Url_i (\{t_{i1}, sc_{i1}, p_{i1}\}, \ldots, \{t_{ik}, sc_{ik}, p_{ik}\})$, denoted as $Url_i$.

## 25.4 Resource Consumption Model

### 25.4.1 Time Series Segmentation

Adopting time series segmentation algorithm to divide a long time sequence into a number of relatively short sub-sequences, in order to do cluster analysis on these sub-sequences, detect the change points in the time series and create a dynamic model based on the divided time sequence [8].

The time series of Web click stream generally present periodicity, which can be obtained through similarity analysis, and can be also developed based on the apriority knowledge: denoting the observation period as T, in order to observe the laws of the entire cycle, the entire cycle is divided into several fixed-length or variable-length time periods. The length of the time period with the aggregation request rate in a period of time is dynamically adjusted. The time period can be expressed as $(I_1, I_2, I_3 \dots I_n)$.

## 25.4.2 Stepwise Regression Algorithm

Due to the huge number of access log, for each time period $I_i$, obtaining the main transaction set with the stepwise regression method. The variables involved are as follows:

t represents the observation window, L represents the length of the observation window

T represents the time period of the observation, composed of a plurality of observation windows. |T| represents the number of the time window during the observed period of time.

$N_{i,t}$ represents the number of transaction i within the observation window t, where $1 < i < n$.

$\bar{P}_t$ represents the average processing time within the observation window.

$\bar{p}_{i,t}$ represents the average processing time of type i transaction within the observation window.

Pi represents the average processing time of type i transaction, where $1 < i < n$.

Within an observation window, you can get the following formula:

$$\sum_{i=1}^{N} N_{i,t} * \bar{p}_{1,t} = \bar{P}_t * L \qquad (25.1)$$

$$\bar{P}_t = \frac{\sum_{i=1}^{N} N_{i,t} * \bar{p}_{1,t}}{L} \qquad (25.2)$$

where $\bar{p}_{1,t}$ is the average processing time of type i transaction within the time window t, which can be obtained by the formula (25.3).

$$\bar{P}_{1,t} = \frac{\sum_{j=1}^{N_{i,t}} P_{i,j}}{N_{i,t}} \qquad (25.3)$$

For each transaction, we tried to get the solution of the following equation.

$$N_{i,t} * \bar{p}_{1,t} = P_t * L \qquad (25.4)$$

Simultaneously ensure the minimum obtained error:

$$\in_i = \sqrt{\sum_{t \in T} (P'_t - \bar{P}_t)^2} \tag{25.5}$$

$$P'_t = \frac{N_{i,t} * \bar{p}_{i,t}}{L} \tag{25.6}$$

After completion of the above calculation for all transactions, select transaction k ($0 < k < n$) with the smallest mean square to represent.

$$\in_k = \text{Min}_{0 \le i \le N} \in_i \tag{25.7}$$

The operation set is initialized to null. After add k to the empty set, iterate by the above method, and select the next transaction from the residual transaction set to put into the operation set.

Before the new transaction is added into the model, we need to determine whether the regression effect is significant or not through the F test.

$$F = \frac{(n-2)U}{Q} \sim F(1, n-2) \tag{25.8}$$

where $U = \sum_{i=1}^{n} (P'_t - \bar{P}_t)^2$, $Q = (\sum_{i=1}^{n} (\bar{p}_{1,t} - P'_t)^2)$

If $F > F_{1-\alpha}(1, n-2)$, the regression effect is significant and the iteration can be terminated, otherwise, the transaction that cannot be ignored may exist there and the iteration is needed.

### 25.4.3 Dynamic Adjustment of the Transaction Set

Set importance attribute sigAttrj $= 1$ for transaction j in each operation set. Randomly select the transaction with the percentage of $\theta$ in the non-operation set NonOpSet to take statistics of the frequency and processing time. Compare its contribution to the total processing time with that of the transaction in the operation set, if it exceeds a certain threshold, then add it to the operation set and reduce a certain percentage $\gamma$ of its importance property of the corresponding element in the operation set. If its importance property is reduced to that under $\beta$, then adjust it to the non-operation set NonOpSet, so that transaction operable set is automatically updated and adjusted along with the transaction flow change.

The pseudo code can be represented as:

Wherein, RandomSelect(s, $\theta$) represents that selecting the elements with proportion of $\theta$ from the set s.

```
For j in OpSet
sigAttrj=1
RandSet=RandomSelect(NonOpSet, θ)
For k in RandSet
{
    if ∑_{i=1}^{Nik} p_{ki} > min_{j∈OpSet}(∑_{i=1}^{Nij} p_{ji})
{
k→OpSet
        sigAttrj= sigAttrj*γ
        if sigAttrj < β
            j→NonOpSet
    }
}
```

## 25.4.4 Adjust the Acquisition Time Interval

### 25.4.4.1 Aggregation Request Rate of Transaction

The work load is varied with time, and therefore cannot be described by a fixed model, but within a relatively short period of time, it can be regarded as fixed. As the access laws in reality presents cyclical characteristics, the transaction construction model and access time model between cycles can be established, which can be used for carrying out the analysis and judgment of the anomaly.

During the study in this article, it uses an aggregation request rate to represent workload, defines the intensity of the workflow as a vector $(\lambda_1, \lambda_2, \ldots \ldots \lambda_n)$, wherein $\lambda_k$ represents an average request rate of the type k transaction within a specific time window. The aggregation request rate [9] of the transaction is defined as:

$$\lambda = \sum_{n=1}^{N} \lambda_n \tag{25.9}$$

### 25.4.4.2 Adjust the Next Acquisition Time Interval

Calculate the aggregation request rate in interval Ii, denote the number of transactions in interval Ii as n, and denote the number of the transaction j as $\lambda_j$,

$$\lambda(i) = \sum_{j=1}^{n} \lambda_j \tag{25.10}$$

$$\text{if } rate(i) = \frac{\lambda(i)}{\lambda(i-1)} = \alpha, \tag{25.11}$$

$$\text{Then } L(i+1) = f(\alpha) * L(0) \tag{25.12}$$

Control the interval of the $i + 1$th time period through $f(\alpha)$.

## 25.4.5 Calculate the Baseline Value of the Processing Time

### 25.4.5.1 The Baseline Value of the Particular Time Period

1. *Single transaction*

Suppose $P_{ij}$ is the processing time of the $i$th period and the type $j$ transaction in the present cycle, $B_{ij}$ is the baseline value of the processing time of the $I_i$th period until the last cycle under normal conditions. After the $I_i$th period of the present cycle, the new baseline value $B_{ij}$ for the $I_i$th period and the transaction $j$ is updated as follows:

$$B_{ij} = a * P_{ij} + (1 - a) * B_{ij} \quad 0 < a < 1 \tag{25.13}$$

2. *Specific period of time*

Assuming $P_i$ is the total processing time of the $i$th period in the present cycle, $B_i$ is the baseline value of the processing time of the $I_i$th period until the last cycle under normal conditions.

$$B_i = a * P_i + (1 - a) * B_i \quad 0 < a < 1 \tag{25.14}$$

### 25.4.5.2 Determine the Dynamic Threshold

1. *Single transaction*

Suppose $Th_{ij}$ is the threshold for determining whether the processing time is abnormal or not in period $l_i$, the greater the value $B_{ij}$, $Th_{ij}$ should be also greater, that is $B_{ij}$ is proportional to $Th_{ij}$. Set $Th_{ij}$ as a fixed multiples of $B_{ij}$, so as to reflect the characteristics of dynamic baseline. Assuming $K$ is a constant greater than 1.

$$Th_{ij} = K * B_{ij} \tag{25.15}$$

2. *Specific period of time*

Suppose $Th_i$ is the threshold for determining whether the processing time is abnormal or not in period $l_i$, the greater the value $B_i$, $Th_i$ should be also greater, that is $B_i$ is proportional to $Th_i$. Set $Th_i$ as a fixed multiples of $B_i$, so as to reflect the characteristics of dynamic baseline. Assuming $K$ is a constant greater than 1.

$$Th_i = K * B_i \tag{25.16}$$

Wherein, the value of K can be appropriately adjusted according to the correctness of the detection result by the abnormality detection staff. In general, the larger the value of K, the more the phenomenon of abnormal behavior obviously only be easily found. So once the processing time stream is determined to be abnormal, almost can determine the Web application is in an abnormal state, the other hand, if the K value is the smaller, the more the period determined to be abnormal, although most of the exceptions will be determined, the probability of misjudgment also increases.

When the access time for a certain period exceeds a threshold value, this period will be marked as the abnormal period. About this abnormal period, further analysis of the processing time and each transaction of the period are needed to identify the cause of the abnormality.

### 25.4.5.3 Anomaly Analysis and Interpretation

When compared processing time with model threshold, the larger, it is needed to distinguish whether the load is abnormal. When the aggregation request rate is a positive correlation of the processing time, and the abnormal situation can be interpreted, it is determined to be abnormal load, otherwise, to consider determining whether there is a server restart operation during the corresponding period according to the server log. If the abnormal situation can be interpreted, it is judged as a server or program anomaly, and if not, you will need to find other reasons.

When compared processing time with model threshold, the smaller, the adjustment of parameters should be considered to make it smaller error range.

## 25.4.6 Model Training Stage

### 25.4.6.1 Training Data Source

Access logs from a public security system (Web server Tomcat6.0), two weeks of data in total, the data of the first 7 days (267,713) will be as the training data, and the data of the latter 7 days (254,132) will be as the test data. Based on the apriority knowledge, the access laws of the system is in 7 days cycle, take one of the 7 days as an example, and carry out the training process.

In a day, the first sampling interval is set to one hour, to set such a coarse granularity is because that in addition to the duty officer at night, other user's access is relatively less, this parameter should be adjusted with the specificcircumstances. The specific parameter settings as shown in Table 25.1.Where $f(\alpha)$ is the acquisition interval adjustment function, $\sigma$ is the significance level, a is the

**Table 25.1** Parameter settings

| f(α) | σ | a | K | Set |
|------|---|---|---|-----|
| If $\alpha \geq 1$ | $\sigma = 0.1$ | $a = 0.5$ | $K = 2$ | $\theta = 0.5$ |
| $5/\text{floor}(\alpha)$ | | | | $\gamma = 0.5$ |
| If $\alpha < 1$ | | | | $\beta = 0.5$ |
| $5/\text{floor}(\frac{1}{\alpha})$ | | | | |

baseline value adjustment parameter, K is the dynamic threshold adjustment parameter, $\theta, \gamma, \beta$ are respectively the dynamic adjustment parameter set *Set* of the transaction set.

Resource request rate within a day by the end of the training is shown is Fig. 25.1:

Dynamic baseline situation of the processing time within a day by the end of the training is shown in Fig. 25.2:

### 25.4.6.2 Model Testing Phase

Access logs from a public security system (Web server Tomcat6.0), 2 weeks of data in total, the data of the first 7 days (267,713) will be as the training data, and the data of the latter 7 days (254,132) will be as the test data. Based on the apriority knowledge, the access laws of the system is in 7 days cycle, take one of the 7 days as an example, and carry out the testing process.

The processing time generated by the test data is shown below (Fig. 25.3):

Between 15:25 and 15:30, anomaly occurred. You need to check resource load at the time period to determine whether it is abnormal load or not. The options can be checked include the total number of resource load and the proportion of each transaction.

The data showed that in the training phase, the load in this time period is about 423, while the corresponding value in the testing phase is 435, an increase ratio of $(435 - 423)/423 = 0.028$, remains basically stable, the further analysis of the

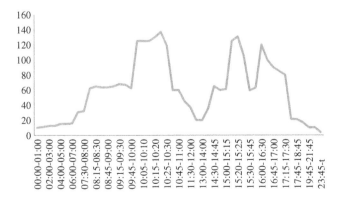

**Fig. 25.1** Resource request rate within a day

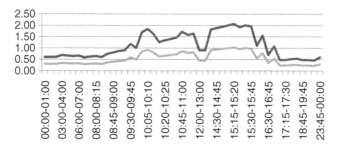

**Fig. 25.2** Dynamic baseline of the processing time within a day after finish the training (the *red* one is dynamic threshold, the *blue* one is baseline)

**Fig. 25.3** The processing time within a day in the test phase (The *purple* Line:is dynamic threshold, the *green* one is value in this cycle, the *red* one is original value)

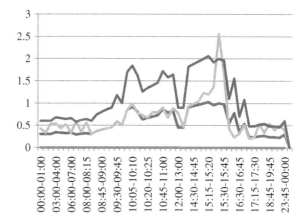

proportion of each transaction is needed. Whether it is due to the high proportion of a transaction (excessive number of requests), causing the time for the server to process the other transactions becomes longer. If the proportion of each transaction compared with that of the previous cycle, no great deviation, you need to consider for reasons other than the load.

## 25.5  Conclusions

In this paper, it establishes the consumption model of the server-side processing time by the preprocessing of Web access log files and the linear regression algorithm of the processing time. It obtains the cycle of consumption of resources according to the apriority knowledge (or similarity analysis).Dynamic baseline method is used to determine whether the specific time period is normal or not, for the abnormal periods, to analyze whether an anomaly is caused by the load, and to distinguish the transaction causing the abnormal load. But due to the limited data sets, the further validation of the model is needed, and the selection for the parameters is worthwhile to continue to analyze and verify.

**Acknowledgments** This work has been supported by Co-Funding Project of Beijing Municipal Educa-tion Commission under Grant No. JD100060630.

# References

1. Denning DE (1987) An intrusion detection model. IEEE Trans Soft Eng 13(2):222–232
2. Wang X (2007) The new technology of anomaly intrusion detection for web applications. Huazhong University of Science and Technology (11). (in Chinese)
3. Song Y, Wang W, Zhang W (2009) Service time signature-based anomaly detection method for multi-tier web applications. Appl Res Comput 26(11):4111–4114, 4118. (in Chinese)
4. Ludmila C, Kivanc O (2009) Automated anomaly detection and performance modelling of enterprise applications. ACM Trans Comput Syst 27(3):1–30
5. Guo J, Liao Y, Behzad P (2004) A survey of J2EE application performance management systems. IEEE international conference on web services (ICWS'04), San Diego, California, USA, 6–9 June 2004
6. NLANR/NSF.IRCache users guide (2004) http://www.ircache.net/,2004
7. Xu Y (2011) Sessions identification in data preprocessing of web log mining. Sci Technol West China 10(4):28–29. 15(in Chinese)
8. Jia P, He H, Liu L et al (2007) Overview of time seriers data mining. Appl Res Comput 27(11):15–18, 29. (in Chinese)
9. Wang Z, Chen Y (2009) AppRAISE: application-level performance management in virtualized server environments. IEEE Trans Netw Serv Manag 6(4):240–25

# Chapter 26
# The Impact of Module Attributes on Project Defect Density

Syed Muhammad Ali Shah and Maurizio Morisio

**Abstract** *Context* Software modules are the basic building blocks of any software project and these modules are engineered differently for different types of projects. Having a diversity of engineering practice, the attributes of these modules should have different impact on projects. *Objective* We studied 54 software projects to analyze the impact of modules attributes on the project's quality in term of defect density (DD). *Results* We found that the module's attributes i.e. very small modules on size and defect free modules have significant impact on the projects DD. The former more percentage resulted in higher projects DD and later more percentage resulted in lower projects DD. The attribute module dependencies have no significant impact on the projects DD. Moreover, we found that projects type (student, open source) having higher DD have more percentage of modules with higher DD, but this trend is not found in the close source projects. We found the significant relationship of projects DD with the module attributes (defect free and very small). *Conclusion* Different module attributes have different impact on projects DD and modules behave differently for different types of projects. This empirical work suggests practitioners and researcher with evidence how module attributes affects the projects DD. The authors recommend some suggestions to take into account during the software construction.

**Keywords** Module · Size · Quality · Defect density

S. M. A. Shah (✉) · M. Morisio
Politecnico di Torino, Corso Duca degli Abruzzi, 24 10129 Torino, Italy
e-mail: syed.shah@polito.it

M. Morisio
e-mail: maurizio.morisio@polito.it

W. Lu et al. (eds.), *Proceedings of the 2012 International Conference on Information Technology and Software Engineering*, Lecture Notes in Electrical Engineering 212, DOI: 10.1007/978-3-642-34531-9_26, © Springer-Verlag Berlin Heidelberg 2013

## 26.1 Introduction

The relationship between size and quality in software projects is highly debated, both at project and module level. Typically a module is intended at the physical level (a file as part of a project), its size measured in LoC, its quality measured in defects or defect density (DD defined as defects/size). In research studies [1, 2], it is found that smaller modules have higher DD compared to the larger modules. Many researchers have made their efforts to highlight different relationship between the size and DD of the modules. For example, in studies [3, 4] it is found that the modules DD increases with the increase in the size of the modules. In studies [1, 2] it is found that the DD decrease with the increase in the size of the modules. However the studies [5, 6] show no significant relation of DD with the size of the modules. In summary the studies show the increase or decrease of DD with size. Although at project level, the consequences of these observations that are proven at module level are not well known. For example if a project is constructed with larger sized modules or small sized modules then what should be the resultant DD of the project. This allows us to devise our research to study the module attributes that have influence on project DD. This paper studies the modules attributes and their effect at project level. The paper is organized as follows; Sect. 26.2 discusses the related work. Section 26.3 presents the design of the study. Section 26.4 presents the results. Finally, discussion and conclusions are presented in Sect. 26.5.

## 26.2 Related Work

Many studies have analyzed modules within a single project. Withrow [3] showed her work by examining the 362 modules of the ADA. She divided the modules into 8 groups based on the module size. She showed that after a certain range of module size (161–250 lines of code) the defects start increasing with the module size. This result also supports the Banker and Kemerer hypothesis [4] where they proposed the optimal module size. The minor size of the module has positive impacts and for greater size, the negative impact starts. Moller and Paulish [7] highlighted that for the module of size smaller than 70 lines of code DD increases significantly and modules that have size greater than the 70 lines of code have similar trends toward DD. Hatton [8] studied 'NASA Goddard' project along with Withrow's data set. He classifies the modules in two categories. For size up to 200 LoC, he suggested that the DD grows logarithmically with the module size and for modules larger than 200 LoC, he observed a quadratic model. Rosenberg [9] has commented on Hatton [8] argument that the observed decrease in DD with rising module sizes is misleading.

Shen et al. [1], worked on three separate releases of an IBM software project by studying 108 modules. They highlighted 24 software modules with size exceeding

500 LoC. They affirm that increases in size did not influence the DD. For the remaining 84 modules, they showed that DD declines as size grows. A study done by Basili and Perricone [2] showed the division of 370 modules into 5 groups based on the module size with increment of 50. They observed the trend of having lower DD of larger module. Fenton and Ohlsson [5] have studied the modules of large telecommunication projects. They selected the modules randomly for the study but did not observe significant dependence of module size with DD. In addition many studies analyzed modules from more than one project. Andersson and Runeson [6] replicated the Fenton and Ohlsson [5] study using the data of three telecommunication projects. They were also not so much successful in finding the significance relation between the number of defects and LoC compared to the original study. El Emam et al. studied three software projects written in C++ and Java. They highlighted that there is a continuous relationship between the class size and faults [10]. Koru et al. [11], studied four large open source projects: Mozilla, Cn3d, JBoss, and Eclipse. They observed that smaller classes are more problematic than larger ones. In particular, for open source software the theory of Relative Defect Proneness (RDP) [12] is postulated about the size defect relationship, stating that "smaller modules are less but proportionally more defects prone compared to larger modules".

In related work we found different types of relationship between the module size and DD. Although these relationships are important to understand, what is still unknown is the impact of these characteristics on the projects DD. For example it would be worth understanding the size or quality of module impact on overall project DD.

## 26.3 Research Design

In this section, we present the research questions and the selected projects on which the analysis is performed. The research questions are formalized from the related work, considering the mostly studied attributes (size, quality, dependencies) at modules level. The overall goal of this work is to understand the effect of module attributes on projects DD and how much it is different for different type of projects. Table 26.1 summarizes the formulated research questions and corresponding hypothesis of the study. We selected the last releases of 54 software projects from the "Promise data repository[1]" [13]. The projects inclusion criterion was the availability of the required metrics (defect per module, no of line of code (LoC) of modules, module dependency metrics) to answer our research questions. The projects did not satisfy the inclusion criteria were excluded. The data set contains 23 close source projects, 15 open source software projects and 17 are academic projects that were developed by the students.

---

[1]  http://promisedata.org/

**Table 26.1** Research questions and hypothesis

**RQ1:** What is the distribution of modules on size in projects?

The goal here is to characterize the modules on size of different projects, and then check the following hypothesis

**RQ2:** What is the distribution of defect free modules in a project?

The aim here is to find the difference in DD of projects by defect free modules, checking the following hypothesis

   H2.1: Projects have the same distribution of defect free modules

   H2.2: Projects with lower DD have a larger percentage of defect free modules

**RQ3**: How modules dependencies affect the projects DD?

The goal here is to find the influence of modules dependencies on the projects DD, checking the following hypothesis

   H3.1: Projects having higher dependencies of modules have higher DD

   H3.2: Projects having lower dependencies of modules have lower DD

**RQ4:** How defect density of modules affects the defect density of projects?

The goal here is to find the difference in DD of projects by modules DD, checking the following hypothesis

   H4.1: Projects with more DD have a larger percentage of modules with higher DD

Notion of Defects: In this work, we consider only post release defects, therefore temporary problems, non defect items like issues, warnings; temporary problems and further enhancements are not included. We believe on the authenticity and reliability of post release defects of the projects available at Promise repository as the data set is publicly available and used in many prior research studies.

Notion of Modules: In this work, the module is assumed to be a smallest unit of functionality i.e. set of declarations and subroutines usually belonging to one file.

Notion of Defect Density: DD is the key object of this study the DD is reported in LoCs on defects. For each project we successively extract and add all the defects related to each module, to obtain the total number of defects in a project. In a similar way (addition of all modules LoC) we calculated the total size of the project in LoC. To obtain the DD per thousand lines of code, we multiply it by 1,000.

For the data analysis we used both graphical representation and the mathematical calculation "percentage". The former gives us the immediate comparison and the later shows weight and the influence to characterize. Where applicable we also used the statistical methods for data analysis.

Concerning RQ1, we carried out the preliminary analysis of three types of projects (student, open source and close source) to categorize the projects in small, medium and large category using the $k$ mean clustering algorithm. Afterward we find the percentage of distribution of very small modules in all categories of projects then we compare the percentage of modules and DD of projects. To find the statistical significant difference between the two groups we used the non parametric test Mann–Whitney. For projects type student, we found 7 small projects, 7 medium and 3 large projects. For projects type open source, we found 6 small, 5 medium and 4 large projects. In projects type close source, we found 14 small, 3 medium and 6 large projects. Table 26.2 shows the three categories of

**Table 26.2** Categories of software's in term of size

| Type | Category | No of projects | Avg size in LoC | Avg DD [KLOC] |
|------|----------|----------------|-----------------|---------------|
| Student | Small | 7 | 4,350 | 4.55 |
| | Medium | 7 | 12,079 | 1.4 |
| | Large | 3 | 40,984 | 1.2 |
| Open source | Small | 6 | 28,639 | 6.15 |
| | Medium | 5 | 114,838 | 5.27 |
| | Large | 4 | 285,061 | 1.22 |
| Close source | Small | 14 | 12,240 | 4.67 |
| | Medium | 3 | 70,784 | 2.38 |
| | Large | 6 | 437,029 | 1.6 |

**Table 26.3** DD of different categories of modules

| Type | Category | Range in Loc | No of module | Avg DD | % of module |
|------|----------|--------------|--------------|--------|-------------|
| Student | V Small | 1–205 | 640 | 7.22 | 67.4 |
| | Small | 206–565 | 204 | 1.6 | 21.4 |
| | Medium | 575–1250 | 78 | 1.15 | 8.2 |
| | Large | 1,347–2,781 | 22 | 0.77 | 2.3 |
| | V Large | 3,211–5,924 | 5 | 1.48 | 0.5 |
| Open source | V Small | 1–283 | 4,732 | 33.2 | 73.6 |
| | Small | 284–850 | 1,207 | 2.86 | 18.7 |
| | Medium | 853–1902 | 329 | 2.06 | 5.1 |
| | Large | 1,940–4,114 | 122 | 1.38 | 1.9 |
| | V Large | 4,202–3,175 | 32 | 0.6 | 0.5 |
| Close source | V Small | 1–132 | 30,179 | 5.6 | 82 |
| | Small | 133–465 | 5,209 | 1.39 | 14.2 |
| | Medium | 466–1263 | 1,065 | 0.77 | 2.9 |
| | Large | 1,266–2,927 | 222 | 0.66 | 0.6 |
| | V Large | 2,928–9,878 | 40 | 0.61 | 0.1 |

software projects i.e. small, medium and large it shows that the large projects in term of size have lower DD in all types. We clustered the modules of each type of projects into 5 categories (very small, small, medium, large, and very large) based on size using the $k$ mean clustering algorithm. We observed that the mean DD of very large modules is less than the DD of other categories of modules.

Table 26.3 reports the DD of very small, small, medium, large and very large modules of each type of project. The preliminary observation shows that in all types of projects there is a smaller percentage of very large modules.

Concerning RQ2: We first extract those modules that are defect free and then find out the percentage of these defect free modules in a project. For the second hypothesis we used a k mean clustering algorithm to cluster the projects based on DD and then performed the analysis observing the DD and percentage of defect free modules.

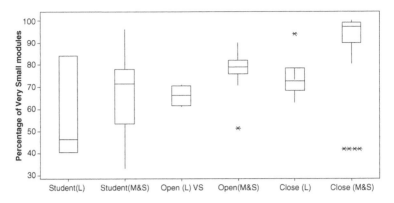

**Fig. 26.1** Percentage of very small modules in projects

Concerning RQ3: To find the module dependencies we used two metrics suggested by Martin[2] to calculate the module dependencies. The metrics we used are:

Afferent Coupling (AC): The number of modules that depend on M.

Efferent Coupling (EC): The number of modules that M depends upon.

We first extracted the dependencies of each module using the above defined two metrics. Afterwards we average the module dependencies of each project to find average module dependencies of a project. Then we performed the analysis observing, how DD of projects is affected by the module dependencies using a statistical measure regression analysis.

Concerning RQ4: For the analysis we consider only top five projects with higher DD. Consequently we observe the distribution of percentage of modules in these projects that have higher DD.

## 26.4 Results

**RQ1: What is the distribution of modules on size in projects?**

From Table 26.3 we found that in all three categories of projects the distribution of modules on size is very different. Hence the distribution of modules on size is very different in all categories of projects; we can reject our hypothesis H1.1, that the projects have not same distribution of modules on size. Considering hypothesis H1.2, we found that very large module have very small percentage in all types of projects. For projects (student, open source) it counts 0.5 %, and for close source projects the percentage is 0.1 %. Hence we can reject our hypothesis H1.2, that the projects have not more percentage of large modules. The secondary observation we obtain is the higher percentage of very small modules in all types

---

[2] http://www.objectmentor.com/resources/articles/oodmetrc.pdf

**Table 26.4** Distribution of very small modules and DD in large sized projects vs. small and medium sized projects

| Type | % of VS modules on large projects | DD of large projects | % of VS modules in small & medium projects | DD of small & medium projects |
|------|------|------|------|------|
| Student | 57 | 1.23 | 67 | 2.98 |
| Open source | 66 | 1.22 | 77.6 | 5.7 |
| Close source | 74.3 | 1.6 | 91.2 | 4.27 |

of projects. It is above 60 %. Figure 26.1 shows the box plots of categories of very small modules in all categories of projects. In all categories of projects, we found the distribution of very small modules of large sized project less than the small and medium sized projects. We notice that there is more variation of percentage of very small module in student projects as compared to open and close source projects.

Afterward we compare the distribution of very small modules and DD of large sized projects, with the distribution of very small modules and DD of small and medium sized projects. Table 26.4 reports the distribution of very small modules and DD of large sized projects compared to small and medium sized projects. It shows that there is a smaller percentage of very small modules in the larger sized projects compared to the small and medium sized projects of all types.

We used Mann–Whitney test to see the significant difference of percentage of very small modules between large sized projects with small and medium sized projects. We obtained $p$ value $= 0.0068$ which is below the significant value 0.05. This confirms that the distribution of very small modules in large projects is different compared to small and medium size project in all types. Recalling Table 26.2 we had observed that large projects have lower DD and hereinafter we found that projects having more percentage of very small modules have higher DD. In particular, when we looked for a comparison between the large sized projects with small and medium sized projects, we found that large projects have a smaller percentage of very small modules and their corresponding DD is also lower than small and medium size projects. Similarly if the projects are constructed by the higher percentage of very small modules then the overall DD of the project is higher. Based on the empirical evidence one might can state that large projects have a smaller percentage of very small modules that would result in lower DD of large projects. However there could be many other factors affecting the DD of larger projects e.g. The larger project is normally taken more seriously, have rigorous testing etc.

**RQ2: What is the distribution of defect free modules in a project?**

We found that the distribution of defect free modules in different types and categories of projects is very different. The difference of distribution allows us to reject our formulated hypothesis H2.1. Table 26.5 reports the distribution of defect free modules in each category of projects by type. Comparing overall by category, it shows that the large projects of all types have a higher number of defect free

**Table 26.5** Distribution of defect free modules and percentage of code of defect free

| Type | Category | % of defect free modules | % of code of defect free modules |
|---|---|---|---|
| Student | Small | 59 | 38.1 |
| | Medium | 70.4 | 41.1 |
| | Large | 78.5 | 56 |
| Open source | Small | 56 | 39.7 |
| | Medium | 54 | 35.4 |
| | Large | 67 | 53.7 |
| Close source | Small | 81.4 | 70.7 |
| | Medium | 75.3 | 55.7 |
| | Large | 87.6 | 75.3 |

modules compared to medium and small category of projects and they make a larger percentage of code size as well. Similarly comparing the defect free modules by type, we found that close source projects have more percentage of defect free modules than open source and student projects. The defect free modules found in close source, open source and student projects are 81, 59 and 69.3 % respectively. Thus it shows that there is more quality attention given to the units of large projects compared to the medium and small sized projects. In addition the close source projects have more percentage of defect free modules compared to open source and student projects. This shows that close source projects have better construction quality.

Concerning hypothesis H2.2, we performed the regression analysis to understand the relationship of defect free modules with the projects DD. For student and open source projects we obtain the $R^2 = 38.4$ and 54.7 % respectively having a partial impact. However for close source projects we obtain $R^2 = 5.9$ % having a very limited impact. To test our hypothesis H2.2 we cluster the projects based on the DD using $k$ means clustering algorithm for all types of projects. Table 26.6 reports the DD and percentage of defect free modules in projects. In all types of projects we found that the projects having a higher percentage of defect free modules have lower DD compared to projects having a smaller percentage of defect free modules. Thus we accept our hypothesis H2.2 that project with lower DD have a larger percentage of the defect free modules.

**RQ3: How modules dependencies affect the projects DD?**

In our data set the module dependency metrics are reported for 36 projects. We answer RQ3 considering those 36 projects, in which there are 17 students, 14 open source and 5 close source projects. Table 26.7 reports the average module dependencies of each category of project along with the DD. Observing the Table 26.7 we can't find any difference of module dependencies and the projects DD in different categories of projects. This makes us to perform our analysis only on the project types, to understand the impact of module dependencies on the projects DD.

**Table 26.6** Projects defect density versus % defect free modules

| Type | No of projects | Defect density | % of defect free |
|---|---|---|---|
| Student | 4 | 5.8 | 41.2 |
| | 5 | 2.3 | 61 |
| | 8 | 1.2 | 84 |
| Open source | 6 | 8.8 | 22.2 |
| | 5 | 4.54 | 58.2 |
| | 4 | 0.5 | 92.7 |
| Close source | 13 | 4.3 | 82.3 |
| | 3 | 4.0 | 56.3 |
| | 7 | 1.93 | 93.28 |

**Table 26.7** Projects module dependencies and DD

| Type | Category | Project | Afferent coupling | Efferent coupling | Defect density |
|---|---|---|---|---|---|
| Student | Small | 7 | 2.5 | 4.0 | 4.55 |
| | Medium | 7 | 4.2 | 3.8 | 1.4 |
| | Large | 3 | 4.7 | 6.1 | 1.2 |
| Open source | Small | 6 | 3.4 | 6.0 | 6.15 |
| | Medium | 5 | 5.3 | 5.0 | 5.27 |
| | Large | 3 | 6.6 | 6.56 | 4.24 |
| Close source | Large | 5 | 2.6 | 12.2 | 1.01 |

Student projects: The obtained $R^2$ value is found to be 27.7 %. There is a positive correlation but it has a limited practical impact. The regression equation is:

$$DD = 3.11 - 1.10\,AC + 0.825\,EC$$

Open source projects: The obtained $R^2$ value is found to be 10.6 % having limited practical impact. The regression equation is:

$$DD = 10.9 - 0.582\,AC - 0.564\,EC$$

Close source projects: The obtained $R^2$ value is found to be 60.5 % having a significant practical impact. The regression equation is:

$$DD = -1.52 + 0.889\,AC + 0.012\,EC$$

Considering all the observation, we do not find any significant impact of modules dependencies on the projects DD in our sample of data. The relationship of module dependencies and DD of projects in type (student, open source) is found to be limited, however considering close source projects there is some practical impact. Thus we cannot accept or reject our formulated hypothesis H3.1 and H3.2.

**RQ4: How defect density of modules affects the defect density of projects?**

To answer the RQ4, we selected top 5 projects from each type that have higher DD. Table 26.8 reports the projects having higher DD in each type. For projects (student, open source) the average percentage of module with higher DD is 51 and

**Table 26.8** Projects with higher DD versus modules with higher DD

| Type | Projects Avg DD | Projects DD | % of modules with higher DD | Avg % of module with higher DD |
|---|---|---|---|---|
| Student | 5.53 | 11.5 | 56 | 51 |
| | | 5.1 | 66.6 | |
| | | 4.8 | 51.2 | |
| | | 3.4 | 45.5 | |
| | | 2.7 | 35.7 | |
| Open source | 10.11 | 15.6 | 50 | 59 |
| | | 13.0 | 91.7 | |
| | | 11.3 | 74.3 | |
| | | 6.1 | 60 | |
| | | 4.4 | 20 | |
| Close source | 6.69 | 8.0 | 35.2 | 19.6 |
| | | 7.2 | 14.7 | |
| | | 6.2 | 21.6 | |
| | | 6.0 | 12.7 | |
| | | 6.0 | 14 | |

59 % respectively. On the contrary for the close source projects the average percentage of module with higher DD is only 19.6 %. Thus our formulated hypothesis is accepted for the students and open source projects that the projects with more DD have the more percentage of modules with higher DD; however the hypothesis H4.1 was not found true in the close source projects.

### 26.4.1 Threats to Validity

We discuss in this section validity threat using the classification proposed by [14].

Internal validity: In this study we only focus our observation towards some basic module attributes like size, quality, dependencies etc., to find their impact on projects DD. However there are many other module attributes that should have an influence on projects DD e.g. testing effort, testers experience and testing techniques etc. We acknowledge all other module attributes but for this study we only focus on the studied ones. Construct validity: In this research, we are dependent on the data logs provided by the *Promise data repository*. Surely, some potential concerns can be raised about the given data set e.g. how many modules may be left, how many defects may be raised and fixed before data collection and how many defects may not be recorded in logs etc. We consider this threat, but as the data set is publicly available and has been used in many previous studies, we believe its authenticity. External validity: In this study our findings are based on a small set of projects i.e. 54 software projects of different nature considering the impact of only a few attributes. Although this number is small but not negligible, this adds to the confidence by presenting some module attributes and their impact on projects DD.

## 26.5  Discussion and Conclusion

This study has two folded outcomes, first how different the internal structural properties of three types (student, opens source, close source) of projects, secondly how module attributes affects the quality (in term of DD) of projects. The results show that the module attributes have some impact on projects DD. We found that the projects have not the same distribution of modules on size. In all types of projects there is a very small percentage of very large modules. The percentage of very small modules are less in large projects compared to medium and small sized projects. The empirical evidence shows that DD of the project increases with more percentage of very small modules (RQ1). The quality of the module has significant impact on the project quality (RQ2). We found that the module dependencies have not significant influence on the projects DD for student and open source projects; however module dependencies have some impact on close source projects DD. Having only 5 close source projects for the analysis does not add much confidence in the results (RQ3). We found that it is not always true that modules with higher DD would result in higher DD of projects as it is found true for student and open source projects but not for close source projects (RQ4). The projects DD can be predicted by using the modules attributes (percentage of very small and defect free modules) as the significant relationship between projects DD and attributes is found (RQ5). Authors want to give some suggestions to practitioners aimed to assess their projects based on our empirical findings.

1. More percentage of very small modules affect negatively to the projects DD.
2. Module compositions have not much effect on projects DD.
3. Modules DD may not always be significant to predict the projects DD.
4. The module attributes (% of very small modules, % of defect free modules) can be used to access the projects DD.

The authors have confidence in these results. These are based on the validated data set of projects that have been used previously and available for research purposes at Promise *Repository*. The artifacts of this study also give direction to the researchers, that different types of projects have different internal structure and their characteristics are quite different from each other. In addition it also shows the importance regarding the previously conducted studies (where mostly the relationship of different module attributes has been shown) but their impact on overall project was unknown. Therefore, we recommend researcher to study more module attributes and their impact on projects. We think that the main limitation of this study is the very few projects and module attributes under study. More attributes like (testing efforts, development process, testing techniques, experience of the team) should be studied to find their impact on the projects DD. As a future work we will expand our research to find another module attributes that have an impact on project DD.

# References

1. Shen VY, Tze-jie Yu, Thebaut SM, Paulsen LR (1985) Identifying error-prone software—an empirical study. IEEE Transactions on Software Engineering SE-11(4):317–24. doi:10.1109/TSE.1985.232222
2. Basili VR, Perricone BT (1984) Software errors and complexity: an empirical investigation. Commun ACM 27(1):42–52
3. Withrow C (1990) Error density and size in Ada software. IEEE Software 7(1):26–30. doi:10.1109/52.43046
4. Banker RD, Kemerer CF (1989) Scale economies in new software development. IEEE Trans Software Eng 15(10):1199–205. doi:10.1109/TSE.1989.559768
5. Fenton NE, Ohlsson N (2000) Quantitative analysis of faults and failures in a complex software system. IEEE Trans Software Eng 26(8):797–814. doi:10.1109/32.879815
6. Andersson C, Runeson P (2007) A replicated quantitative analysis of fault distributions in complex software systems. IEEE Trans Software Eng 33(5):273–86. doi:10.1109/TSE.2007.1005
7. Moller K-H, Paulish DJ (1993) An empirical investigation of software fault distribution. In: Proceedings on first international software metrics symposium, pp 82–90
8. Hatton L (1997) Reexamining the fault density component size connection. IEEE Software 14(2):89–97. doi:10.1109/52.582978
9. Rosenberg J (1997) Some misconceptions about lines of code. In: Proceedings of Fourth international symposium on software metrics, pp 137–42
10. El Emam K, Benlarbi S, Goel N, Melo W, Lounis H, Rai SN (2002) The optimal class size for object-oriented software. IEEE Trans Software Eng 28(5):494–509. doi:10.1109/TSE.2002.1000452
11. Koru AG, Dongsong Zhang, El Emam K, Hongfang Liu (2009) An investigation into the functional form of the size-defect relationship for software modules. IEEE Trans Software Eng 35(2):293–304. doi:10.1109/TSE.2008.90
12. Koru A, Emam KE, Zhang D, Liu H, Mathew D (2008) Theory of relative defect proneness. Empirical Softw Eng 13(5):473–498
13. Boetticher G, Menzies T, Ostrand T (2007) PROMISE repository of empirical software engineering data [Internet]. Available from http://promisedata.org/ repository, West Virginia University, Department of Computer Science
14. Wohlin C, Runeson P, Höst M, Ohlsson MC, Regnell B, Wesslen A (2000) Experimentation in software engineering: an introduction. Kluwer Academic Publishers, Massachusetts

# Chapter 27
# A New Method for Software Reliability Modeling

**Weiyong Huang, Kui Chen, Yuqin Gao and Rong Bao**

**Abstract** In order to improve the forecasting accuracy, a new method for software reliability modeling was proposed by integrating phase-space re-construction, support vector machine (SVM) and improved clone selection algorithm (CSA). Firstly the phase space reconstruction theory was applied to reconstruct data samples. Then SVM was used to construct the forecasting model of software reliability. Finally CSA and the criteria of MAPE (mean absolute percentage error) minimization and RMSE (root mean square error) minimization were introduced to tune automatically the parameter vector of forecasting model. The Experimental results showed that the proposed method has much higher accuracy than ANN method and the model is feasible.

**Keywords** Software reliability modeling · Phase space reconstruction · Support vector machine · Clone selection algorithm

## 27.1 Introduction

As today's software products grow rapidly in size and complexity, the forecast of software reliability plays a critical role in the software development process. So far, more than hundreds of software reliability models have been proposed, including JM, GO, MO, D S-shaped and other analytical model [1]. Because these

W. Huang (✉) · K. Chen · Y. Gao · R. Bao
School of Information and Electrical Engineering, Xuzhou Institute of Technology, NO 1 Fuchun Road, New City, Xuzhou, Jiangsu, China
e-mail: h_weiyong@163.com

W. Lu et al. (eds.), *Proceedings of the 2012 International Conference on Information Technology and Software Engineering*, Lecture Notes in Electrical Engineering 212, DOI: 10.1007/978-3-642-34531-9_27, © Springer-Verlag Berlin Heidelberg 2013

models can not be consistent completely with the actual situation, the forecasting accuracy of software reliability can not be satisfactory.

With the development of machine learning, modeling methods based on data-driven have been attracting a lot of attention, for people do not need to make any assumptions in software process and don't have difficulties in choosing the appropriate models.

At present, the time-series data of software accumulative failure are applied to construct data sample. Although the accumulated data of time-series of software failure can contains all the information of variables involved, the traditional lower dimension coordinate cannot reveal the dynamical characteristics of the complex software system. Takens's theorem of phase space reconstruction proved that the reconstructed system is equivalent of the original dynamic system in the topological sense [2]. Takens's theorem provides the theoretical basis for software reliability modeling.

By using phase space reconstruction to construct dada samples, many method for software reliability modeling based on artificial neural network (ANN) have been proposed [3], but these method needed a large number of samples, had poor reproducibility and high forecasting costs.

As support vector machine (SVM) is a new universal learning method [4], which can effectively solving learning problems with small samples, high dimension and nonlinear relationship, SVM has become a new tool for software reliability modeling.

The theoretical analysis and experimental research showed that the selection of parameter vector of SVM has great significant impact on its performance of regression and forecast. How to select and optimize the parameter vector of SVM became an important issue to be deal with.

Clone selection algorithm (CSA) [5] by Castro according to the theory of immunity in the clone selection mechanism is a new optimization algorithm with heuristic intelligence, which not only has a faster convergence speed in the search range, but also can overcome the problem of premature convergence that many evolutionary computation can not overcome. Clone selection algorithm provides a new way for the selection and optimization of parameter vector of support vector machine with the superior performances over the classical approaches.

In this paper, a new modeling method for software reliability forecast by integrating phase space reconstruction theory, support vector machine and an improved clone selection algorithm was introduced in an attempt to enhance the forecasting accuracy. The Experimental results showed that the proposed method is feasible, and it can yield much lower errors than ANN method.

## 27.2 Principle and Algorithm

### 27.2.1 Principle of Phase Space Reconstruction

Given time series $x(k)$, $k = 1, 2, \ldots, N$, $x$ is observed component, $k$ is time index, $N$ is the number of observations. According to Takens's delay method, the vectors in a reconstructed phase space is formed,

$$X(i) = (x(i), x(i + \tau), x(i + 2\tau), \ldots x(i + (m - 1)\tau)), \ i = 1, 2, \ldots, M \quad (27.1)$$

where $\tau$ is the time delay, m is the embedding dimension, $M = N - (m - 1)\tau$, M is the number of points in the reconstructed phase space.

Takens's theorem proved if embedded dimension $m \geq 2d + 1$ (d is dynamical dimension of original system), the reconstructed phase space can preserve many characteristics of original dynamical system. That is to say, the reconstructed dynamical system is equivalent to the original system in topology sense, and the dynamical characteristics can be recovered in the sense of topological equivalence.

In the reconstructed phase space $R^m$, there exists a mapping $f : R^m \rightarrow R^m$, The transformed form of the reconstructed m-dimensional phase space can be expressed as follows:

$$X(t + 1) = f(X(t)) \quad (27.2)$$

where $X(t)$ are the points in the reconstructed phase space. Formula (27.2) can be expressed as follows:

$$\begin{aligned} &(x(t + \tau), x(t + 2\tau), \ldots, x(t + m\tau)) \\ &= f(x(t), x(t + \tau), \ldots, x(t + (m - 1)\tau)) \end{aligned} \quad (27.3)$$

For the sake of calculating easily and expressing directly, formula (27.3) can be re-written by the follow formula:

$$x(t + m\tau) = F(x(t), x(t + \tau), \cdots, x(t + (m - 1)\tau)) \quad (27.4)$$

where $F(x)$ is a mapping function from d-dimensional space to 1-dimensional real number.

So theoretically, as long as suitable delay time, embedding dimension and approximation function are found, the dynamical behavior of soft system can be described and software reliable modeling can be realized by phase space reconstruction.

### 27.2.2 Principle of SVM

Consider a given data point set G$\{ (x_i, y_i) \}_{i=1}^n$, $x_i$ is input vector, $y_i$ is expected value, $n$ is the total numbers. SVM regression model takes the form:

$$f(\boldsymbol{x}) = \omega \cdot \Phi(x) + b \tag{27.5}$$

Where $\Phi(x)$ is a nonlinear mapping function from the input space to a high dimensional feature space. $\omega$ and $b$ are coefficients.

By introducing $\varepsilon$-insensitive loss function and penalty coefficient C, using the theory of duality, building Lagrange equation, and then adopting Karush-Kuhn-Tucker theorem, the following expression of regression function is achieved:

$$\begin{aligned} f(x) &= \omega \cdot \Phi(x) + b = \sum_{i=1}^{n} (\alpha_i - \alpha_i^*) \Phi(x_i) \cdot \Phi(x) + b \\ &= \sum_{i=1}^{n} (\alpha_i - \alpha_i^*) K(x_i, x) + b \end{aligned} \tag{27.6}$$

where $K(x_i, x)$ is kernel function, which must be positive definite function that satisfies Mercer's condition.

Considering that RBF kernel function could approximate to other forms of kernel function by changing the parameter of RBF kernel function, we selected the following RBF kernel function to make regression analysis.

$$K(\boldsymbol{x}_i, \boldsymbol{x}) = \exp\{ -\|\boldsymbol{x} - \boldsymbol{x}_i\|^2 / 2\sigma^2 \} \tag{27.7}$$

Thus the above SVM's 3 parameters can be described as a vector: $\theta = (\varepsilon, C, \sigma)$, which could be called the parameters vector of SVM. Weather parameter vector of SVM is selected appropriately or not has a decisive influence on the regression performance.

### 27.2.3 Improved Clone Selection Algorithm

The basic principle of clone selection algorithm is that the function to be optimized and its constraints is viewed as antigen, the solution of the problem is viewed as antibody and the affinity between the antibody, antibody-antigen viewed as the objective function of the problem [6]. In order to tune automatically the parameter vector of forecasting model, an improved clone selection algorithm is outlined in the paper. Its block diagram is shown in Fig. 27.1.

### 27.2.4 Software Reliability Modeling Based on Integrating Phase-Space Reconstruction, SVM and CSA

On the basis of phase space reconstruction, a new approach for software reliability modeling was presented in the current paper by integrating support vector machine (SVM) and improved clone selection algorithm (CSA). The block diagram of software reliability modeling is illustrated in Fig. 27.2.

**Fig. 27.1** Block diagram of improved clone selection algorithm

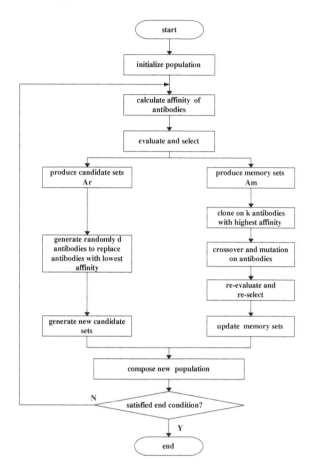

## 27.3  Experiment and Results

The failures data set of real project SYS1 [7] was selected as data source, in which the data is the number of interval failures. In order to improve the speed and the training accuracy, all data were preprocessed: (1) The interval failure data were transformed into the cumulative failure data up to the specified time; (2) All data were normalized by Min − Max method.

After data being normalized, data set can be seen as a time sequence $\{X(t), t = 1, 2, \ldots, n\}$. According to formula (27.1), software reliability models can be described as:

$$X(t) = F[X(t - 1), X(t - 2), \ldots, X(t - p)] \tag{27.8}$$

Therein, $F$ is an unknown nonlinear function, which is realized by SVM in this paper.

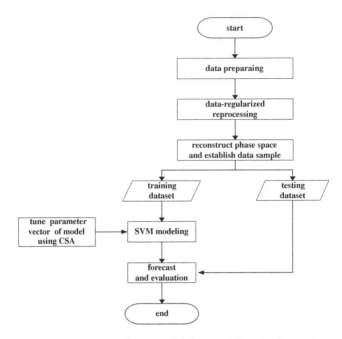

**Fig. 27.2** k Block diagram of software reliability modeling by integrating phase-space reconstruction, SVM and CSA

Although there are many ways for calculating $m$ and $\tau$, no way could not be said to be best. In this paper, optimal embedding dimension $m = 5$ and delay time $\tau = 1$ were obtained by means of experiments. Thus SVM-based forecasting model with multi-input and single-output could be constructed, and input vectors and output vectors of support vector machine could be obtained according to Table 27.1.

To evaluate the algorithm's efficiency and effectiveness, the forecasting performance was evaluated by MAPE (mean absolute percentage error) and RMSE (root mean square error).

Correspondingly, the parameter vector of SVM was also tuned by the criteria of minimum of MAPE and RMSE of the training set at the same time. To ensure that the affinity function is non-negative value, the affinity function was calculated as follows:

**Table 27.1** Structure of input and output vectors

| Sample serial number | Input vectors | Output vectors |
|---|---|---|
| 1 | $X(1), \cdots, X(p-1), X(p)$ | $X(p+1)$ |
| ... | ... | ... |
| $t - p$ | $X(t-p), \cdots, X(t-2), X(t-1)$ | $X(t)$ |
| ... | ... | ... |
| $n - p$ | $X(n-p), \cdots, X(n-2), X(n-1)$ | $X(n)$ |

**Table 27.2** Forecasting error results

|         | SVM    | ANN    |
|---------|--------|--------|
| MAPE/%  | 1.5344 | 3.5685 |
| RMSE/s  | 1.7105 | 2.9058 |

$$J = 100 - [\lambda \cdot MAPE + (1 - \lambda) \cdot RMSE] \tag{27.9}$$

Where, the weighting factor $\lambda$ was used to adjust the importance of these two kinds of errors in the optimal process, $\lambda = 0.5$ in this paper.

According to Table 27.1, all 131 input-output data pairs were divided randomly by the computer program into two parts, 98 sample data being training data set, and the remaining 33 sample data being testing data set. RBF was chosen to be the kernel function of SVM. The parameter vector of SVM was tuned by the CSA automatically. The parameters of the CSA set in this particular example are as follows: Total generation was 100, Initial population size was 100, Length of coding was 22, Clone factor was 10, Suppression threshold was 5, Cross probability was 0.9, and Mutation probability was 0.01.

98 training data were used to train software reliability model. 33 testing data were input into the forecasting model to evaluate its performance. After the output of model was anti-normalized, the final forecasting results were obtained. To avoid attributing the forecasting results to the choice of a particular population and to conduct fair comparison and analysis, we performed the experiment 10 times. According to the calculated results, the forecasting errors of the method proposed were shown in Table 27.2.

In contrast with the traditional approach, the forecasting error of artificial neural network (ANN) method was also listed in Table 27.2.

## 27.4  Conclusions

In this paper a new method for software reliability modeling was introduced by using support vector machine and phase space reconstruction. The optimal parameter vector of model was tuned by clone selection algorithm and the criteria of minimization of MAPE and RMSE simultaneously. The experimental results on public databases SYS1 showed that the forecasting results are more close to the actual value, the forecasting accuracy being obviously superior to the traditional neural network method.

# References

1. Lou JA, Jiang JH, Shuai CY, et al (2010) Software reliability models: a survey. Comput Sci 37(9):13–17. (in Chinese)
2. Packard NH, Crutchfield JP, Farmer JD (1980) Geometry from a time series. Phys Rev Lett 45:712–716
3. Zhang Y, Ren ZH (2010) SVM-based forecasting methods for software fault. J Chinese Comput Syst 31(7):1380–1384 (in Chinese)
4. Vapnik VN (1995) The nature of statistical learning theory. Springer, New York
5. De Castro LN, von Zuben FJ (2002) Learning and optimization using the clonal selection principle. IEEE Trans Evol Comput 6:239–251
6. Bi XJ (2010) Information intelligent processing technology. Publishing House of Electronics Industry, Beijing. (in Chinese)
7. Lyu M (1996) Handbook on software reliability engineering. IEEE Computer Society Press and McGraw-Hill Book Company

# Chapter 28
# The Study on Chinese Speech Recognition Based on Android

Yaping Wang and Baoshan Li

**Abstract** According to Biomimetic Pattern Recognition Theory, this chapter analyses the distribution of different kinds of digit speech in feature space based on Android, and proposes a multi-weight neural network distinction approach. Because this approach takes the inner feature relations of each class of speech samples into full consideration, the neural network constructed can optimal cover each kind of samples. Experiments show the validity of this algorithm.

**Keywords** Android · Biomimetic pattern recognition · Feature extraction · Multi-weight neural

## 28.1 Introduction

Google Android is an operating system which includes middleware, key applications, and software stack for mobile devices [1]. The first Google's Android phone T-Mobile G1 was announced at Guastavino's in New York City unveiled September 23 2008. Over the past years, the market of Google Android continues growing rapidly. Today, many devices install the Android system as the operating system. To developing Android program, the Google Inc provides two kits for the Android development platform: The Android Software Development Kit (SDK) provides necessary tools and libraries for programmers to begin developing applications that run on Android-powered devices [2]. The first Android SDK (m3-rc20a) was

Y. Wang (✉) · B. Li
Information Engineering School, Inner Mongolia University of Science and Technology,
Baotou 014010, China
e-mail: appenwang@163.com

W. Lu et al. (eds.), *Proceedings of the 2012 International Conference on Information Technology and Software Engineering*, Lecture Notes in Electrical Engineering 212, DOI: 10.1007/978-3-642-34531-9_28, © Springer-Verlag Berlin Heidelberg 2013

released on 12 December 2007. Now, the latest version is SDK Tools, Revision 12 was released on July 2011. This version supports Android 2.3.4 and 3.2 Platform developments. The Android Native Development Kit (NDK) is a toolset that lets programmers to embed components that make use of native code in Android applications [3]. The first Android NDK (Android 1.5 NDK, Release 1) was released on June 2009. Now, the latest version of Android NDK, Revision 6 was released on July 2011. This version supports ARM and X86 platforms. Generally, developer does not concern how effective between native code and Dalvik Java code that will causes poor performance of Android.

Speech recognition technology has advanced rapidly in recent years. English digit speech recognition products came to use first among various speech recognition tasks [4]. Research institutions represented by AT&T, Mellon University, and Cambridge University and so on are concentrating on products of large vocabulary speaker-independent English continuous speech recognition and have acquired great achievements. In terms of Chinese speech recognition, large vocabulary speech recognition has also reached a fairly high level [2, 5]. On the contrary, although Chinese digit speech recognition has great application value in many fields such as mobile communication, computer telephonist, phone securities trading and has gained extensive attentions of scientific institutes [6, 7], it develops slowly. English digit speech recognition rate of isolated and connected digit has already reached 99.7 and 99.11 % respectively. However, it is lower than 99 and 95 % for Chinese isolated digit and connected digit respectively by documentary information to the present time. This shows that speech recognition level of Chinese digit is far behind that of English digit.

## 28.2 A Brief Introduction to the Principle of Biomimetic Pattern Recognition Theory

Biomimetic Pattern Recognition (BPR) theory thinks that for any two things in nature which belong to the same class and same source but don't equal to each other completely, and that the difference between them can be gradual but not quintal, there must be at least one gradually changing sequence between them and all the things among the changing sequence belong to this class. Its mathematical description is below.

Suppose that Set A is a point set including all samples class A. Given $x, y \in A$ and $\varepsilon > 0$, there must exist set B which satisfy

$$B = \{x_1 = x, x_2, \ldots, x_{n-1}, x_n = y | \rho(x_m, x_{m+1}) < \varepsilon, \forall m \in [1, n - n], m \in N\} \subset A$$

$$(28.1)$$

This continuity principle existing in same class samples in feature space Rn surpasses the traditional basic supposition which thinks all the information

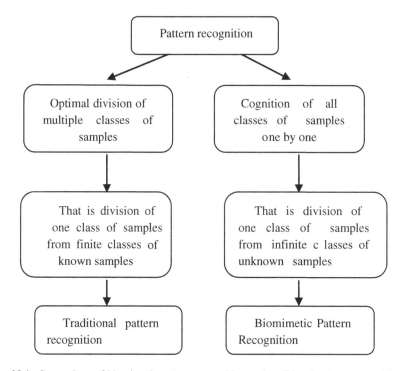

**Fig. 28.1** Comparison of biomimetic pattern recognition and traditional pattern recognition

available is within the training set. Though this continuity principle is an objective discipline that people can intuitively apperceive in objective world, thus it can be empirical knowledge of samples distribution in Biomimetic Pattern Recognition theory and can be used to improve the cognition ability (Fig. 28.1).

After the introduction of the continuity principle of the same class samples in feature space to Biomimetic Pattern Recognition theory, the cognition of one class of thing is essentially analysis and cognition of the shape formed by all samples of this class in feature space. Therefore, unlike the traditional pattern recognition which targets the optimal classification of samples of different classes in feature space, Biomimetic Pattern Recognition theory focuses on the optimal covering of a particular class in feature space. Just because a neuron can be a hyper plane or a hyper surface, it also can be various complex close hyper surface. Thus artificial neural network is an appropriate way to implement Biomimetic Pattern Recognition theory.

## 28.3 The Geometrical Explanation of Multi-Weighted Neuron

When an artificial neuron is considered generally [3], its basic operation formula can be:

$$Y = f[\Phi(x_1, x_2, \ldots, x_n) - \theta] \tag{28.2}$$

Where f is nonlinear output transfer function of neuron, $\theta$ is threshold of neuron, $\Phi(x_1, x_2, \ldots, x_n)$ is the basic operation rule of neuron including all weights. For the neuron of BP, when the transfer function has a hard limiter, the basis of neuron function is:

$$\Phi(x_1, x_2, \ldots, x_n) - \theta = \sum_{i=1}^{n} \omega_i x_i - \theta = 0 \tag{28.3}$$

Here the function of neuron is to set a hyper plane in high dimensional input space. The output is 1 when input lies in one side of the hyper plane, is 0 when input lies in another side of it. This function is usually used in pattern division. As it divides one infinite space into two infinite spaces, it can't divide all classes effectively when there are many classes and their relations are nonlinear. The recognition effects are not optimal in practical application.

For the neuron in RBF network, when the transfer function has a hard limiter, the basis of neuron function is:

$$\Phi(x_1, x_2, \ldots, x_n) - \theta = \left[ \sum_{i=1}^{n} (x_i - \omega_i)^2 \right]^{\frac{1}{2}} = 0 \tag{28.4}$$

This neuron corresponds to a hyper sphere in input space, with $\omega$ as sphere centre, $\theta$ as radius. The output is 1 when input is inside the hyper sphere, is 0 when input is outside of it. It divides an infinite space into a finite space and an infinite space, the division interface is also nonlinear. So RBF neuron is super than hyper plane neural networking when used in pattern classification. RBF neuron is the simplest close hyper surface high rank neuron, it can't change its shape according to the actual distribution information of different pattern, and therefore it has great limits in application.

Although single-weighted neuron can only construct some simple and regular geometrical shape, multi-weighted neuron can describe various complex close hyper surface, namely complex finite spaces.

When the transfer function has a hard limiter, the basis of multi-weighted neuron is:

$$\Phi(X, W_1, W_2, \ldots, W_m) - \theta = 0 \tag{28.5}$$

Where $\Phi(X, W_1, W_2, \ldots, W_m)$ denotes the relation among the input point X and $m$ weights $X, W_1, W_2, \ldots, W_m$. The neuron represents different geometrical shape when $\Phi$ takes different function. Because of its strong nonlinearity and complex close hyper surface, Moreover, its amplitude changing in respective direction when weights change, multi-weighted neuron has perfect performance in pattern recognition.

## 28.4 Speech Processing

### 28.4.1 Subsection Heading

Owing to co-articulation in continuous speech recognition and variability of speech signal, although endpoint detection methods in common use are effective in condition with detection of silence and speech, unvoiced and voiced speech, they are poor in condition with detection of vowel and vowel in voiced speech. Research shows one half of errors come from false endpoint detection, so endpoint detection only by computer couldn't satisfy the requirements of applications. There are abundant information in digit wave, in the other hand, human brain has super image analysis ability and super understanding of speech. By watching the wave and hearing the speech repeatedly, it is easy to find the optimal visual and audio dividing line between digits. This chapter artificially cut continuous speech into single digit speech database of 11 classes, as shown in Table 28.1. This point should be emphasized that this database is essentially different from isolated speech database because it is cut from continuous speech and has the characteristic of continuous speech.

### 28.4.2 Feature Extraction

Firstly, compute MFCC parameters of single digit speech and construct MFCC database of single digit.

Secondly, measure distance by angle between MFCC frames, resample speech data with angle distance threshold $\theta$, delete frames of lower frame angle to compress speech information.

Thirdly, Choose 8 continuous frames that has co-articulation of two phonemes from each digit as representation information of the digit. Construct single digit MFCC database.

**Table 28.1** 11 classes of digits and their Chinese pronunciation

| Digit class | 1 | 2 | 3 | 4 | 5 | 6 | 7 | 8 | 9 | 10 | 11 |
|---|---|---|---|---|---|---|---|---|---|---|---|
| Digit | 1 | 2 | 3 | 4 | 5 | 6 | 7 | 8 | 9 | 10 | 11 |
| Chinese pronunciation | yi | er | san | si | wu | liu | qi | ba | jiu | ling | yao |

## 28.5 Neural Network Construction

According to BPR theory, the distribution of one class of sample in high dimensional space is a complex geometrical body. It is an effective method to realize coving of complex geometrical body by implementing covering of some simple geometrical bodies first, then combining or intersecting simple geometrical bodies. If sample points of pattern is k dimensional manifold in feature space, considering noise disturbance in every direction, the pattern shape in feature space can be topological product of a k dimensional manifold curve and n dimensional hyper sphere (n is dimension of feature space). In order to implement approximately covering through some neurons in practice, some end to end k dimensional simplexes are used to approximate the manifold curve, then to topologically multiply it by n dimensional hyper sphere.

Suppose $S_1, \cdots, S_{k+1}$ are vertexes of k dimensional simplex, then the k +1 weights of multi-weighted neuron can be exclusively decided by $S_1, \cdots, S_{k+1}$, that is:

$$W_1 = \Psi_1(S_1, \cdots, S_{k+1})$$
$$\mathrm{M} \tag{28.7}$$
$$W_{k+1} = \Psi_3(S_1, \cdots, S_{k+1})$$

Thus $\Phi(W_1, \cdots, W_{k+1}, X) = \theta$ can be changed to

$$\Psi(S_1, \cdots, S_{k+1}, X) = \theta \tag{28.8}$$

According to Biomimetic Pattern Recognition theory and high dimensional space geometrical analysis technology, find appropriate $\Psi$ function to satisfy the previous formula when $X = S_i$, $i = 1, \cdots, k + 1$. Therefore, the feature space that this neuron covers is decided by samples $S_1, \cdots, S_{k+1}$. Furthermore, it also fuses the information of $k + 1$ samples.

## 28.6 Experiments and Results

Choose 24 people of different ages and sexes (as shown in Table 28.2), 10 samples per person per digit class, totally 2,640 points as training samples to construct speaker-independent continuous Chinese digit pattern. Choose 7,308 samples of 29 people to test the correction rate (shown in Table 28.3). 24 people within 29 people join in training, 5 people don't. Experiments are done by this algorithm where manifold dimension is 3, $\Psi$ choose triangle function. Experiments results are compared with HMM algorithm in Table 28.4.

**Table 28.2** People who join in construction of neural network pattern

| Age | <20 | 20–30 | 30–40 | 40–50 | 50–60 | >60 |
|---|---|---|---|---|---|---|
| Male | 2 | 2 | 2 | 2 | 2 | 2 |
| Female | 2 | 2 | 2 | 2 | 2 | 2 |

**Table 28.3** Samples to test validity of networks

| Digit class | yi | er | san | si | wu | liu | qi | ba | jiu | ling | yao |
|---|---|---|---|---|---|---|---|---|---|---|---|
| Digit | 534 | 555 | 650 | 950 | 719 | 471 | 1087 | 315 | 888 | 463 | 676 |

**Table 28.4** Comparison of recognition results of multi-weighted neural network and HMM

| Digit | Correct rate of this algorithm (%) | Correct rate of HMM (%) |
|---|---|---|
| yi | 98.7 | 94.9 |
| er | 93.3 | 90.5 |
| san | 98.9 | 97.4 |
| si | 98.1 | 97.0 |
| wu | 97.4 | 97.9 |
| liu | 97.5 | 89.6 |
| qi | 97.0 | 89.0 |
| ba | 99.4 | 94.6 |
| jiu | 97.4 | 93.1 |
| ling | 96.1 | 90.1 |
| yao | 98.5 | 94.8 |
| Average correct rate | 97.4 | 93.6 |

## 28.7  Discussion and Conclusions

1. This algorithm is effective for continuous speech recognition. Its average recognition rate is 97.4 % and higher than HMM algorithm.
2. The complex polyhedron constructed by multi-weighted neural network in high dimensional space can effectively cover samples in feature space.
3. Utilizing prior knowledge to consider the continuity among samples can greatly improve recognition effect.
4. The speech signal disposal method this chapter proposed is feasible.
5. In conclusion, algorithm based on Biomimetic Pattern Recognition and multi-weighted neural network can effectively recognize continuous Chinese digit speech. Experiments also show its validity.

# References

1. Shoujue W (2002) Bionic (Topological) pattern recognition—a new model of pattern recognition theory and its applications. Acta Electronica Sinica, Chinese Institute of Electronics, Beijing, vol 30(10), pp 1417–1420
2. Jia L (2000) Research on large vocabulary mandarin Chinese continuous speech recognition system. Acta Electronica Sinica, Chinese Institute of Electronics, Beijing, vol 28(1), pp 85–91
3. Shoujue W, Bainan W (2002) Analysis and theory of high-dimension space geometry for artificial neural networks. Acta Electronica Sinica, Chinese Institute of Electronics, Beijing, vol 30(1), pp 1–4
4. Rabiner LR, Wilpon G, Soong FK (1989) High performance connected digit recognition using hidden Markov models. IEEE transactions ASSP, IEEE signal processing society, Berlin, Germany, vol 37(8), pp 1214–1225
5. Junlan F, Limin D (1999) Review on Chinese spontaneous speech recognition. Electronic science & technology review, Chinese Institute of Electronics, Beijing, vol 9, pp 3–7
6. Smith J, Jones M Jr, Houghton L et al (1999) Future of health insurance. N Engl J Med 965:325–329
7. Husheng L, Jia L, Runsheng L (2000) High performance digit mandarin speech recognition. J Tsinghua Univ (Sci Technol) 40(1):32–34 (Tsinghua University Beijing, China)

# Chapter 29
# A New Firmware Upgrade Mechanism Designed for Software Defined Radio Based System

**Jianzhuang Li, Cheng Chang, Dongyuan Shi, Wei Xia and Lin Chen**

**Abstract** This paper presents a new firmware upgrade mechanism for Software Defined Radio (SDR) based systems. The mechanism solves many problems existing in firmware on-site upgrade, and makes the upgrade of SDR based systems to be much quicker and easier. A remote upgrade method is used in this mechanism. The software scheme and hardware structure of this mechanism are illustrated. A synchronization mechanism and alternating upgrade strategy are used in the software scheme. In the hardware structure, eight memory sections are allocated to satisfy the requirement of software scheme, and different operation attributes are set for these memory sections. With the implementation of these strategies and settings, this firmware upgrade mechanism becomes safe, secure and reliable.

**Keywords** SDR · Remote upgrade · Firmware upgrade

## 29.1 Introduction

As the Software Defined Radio (SDR) technology has been widely used, firmware upgrades of the systems become possible. The firmware upgrade methods for existing systems are mainly on-site, but for the devices mounted on a high altitude,

J. Li (✉) · C. Chang · D. Shi · W. Xia
School of Electronic Engineering, University of Electronic Science and Technology,
Qingshuihe Campus:No.2006, Xiyuan Ave, West Hi-Tech Zone, Chengdu, Sichuan,
People's Republic of China
e-mail: 201021020510@std.uestc.edu.cn

L. Chen
Regional Military Representative Bureau in Chengdu, No.124, 1st Ring Road,
Chengdu, China
e-mail: liyonghua.student@sina.com

W. Lu et al. (eds.), *Proceedings of the 2012 International Conference on Information Technology and Software Engineering*, Lecture Notes in Electrical Engineering 212, DOI: 10.1007/978-3-642-34531-9_29, © Springer-Verlag Berlin Heidelberg 2013

underground, and other rough terrain, on-site upgrades are extremely difficult, or even impossible. Meanwhile, the devices which need to be upgraded are of great quantity. For these reasons, the upgrade processes are tedious and costly. Therefore, an introduction of remote firmware upgrade mechanism to SDR based systems is of great significance. The SDR based systems are mostly composed of DSP and FPGA [1, 2], so the upgrade of DSP and FPGA is the major work for remote firmware upgrade. However, most of the existing remote upgrade mechanisms are designed for embedded systems [3, 4], and some researches only analyze the upgrade mechanisms for DSP [5, 6].

In view of existing problems in the researches, a safe, secure and reliable remote firmware upgrade mechanism designed for SDR based systems is proposed. Since DSP and FPGA are core chips in these systems, the upgrade of them is mainly discussed in this remote firmware upgrade mechanism. In this paper, the communication mechanism and upgrade package security are firstly introduced. Then the upgrade and loading procedures for DSP and FPGA are explained. At last, a suitable terminal hardware structure is illustrated.

## 29.2 Communication Mechanism and Upgrade Package Security

A sketchy system block diagram is shown in Fig. 29.1. A network based on TCP/IP protocol is used to establish a connection between the authorized work station and terminal. The upgrade packages are transmitted through Internet. By this means, the expense is reduced notably, and the communication between them is relatively in real time. During the upgrade operation, the work station is responsible for transmitting upgrade packages to terminals. When a terminal receives the upgrade packages, it upgrades the program automatically according to the upgrading procedure, and then restarts the system with the loading procedure. The upgrading and loading procedure will be explained in Sect. 29.3.

In order to enhance the security of upgrade packages, an encryption with Advanced Encryption Standard (AES) [7] is used to encode the upgrade packages. Moreover, a digital signature based on SHA-1 algorithm [8] is also applied to the upgrade packages, which improves the security to a higher degree.

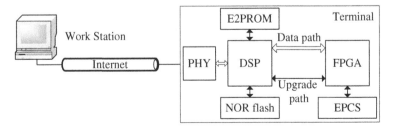

**Fig. 29.1** Framework of remote upgrade system

## 29.3  Upgrading and Loading Procedures for DSP and FPGA

In this section, the safe and reliable procedures for DSP and FPGA are discussed. In these procedures, synchronization mechanism between DSP and FPGA is established to make sure that program upgrading and loading proceed safely and sequentially. Moreover, the alternating upgrade strategy is used in the procedures. This strategy ensures the program presently running in the system is not overwritten. If an upgrade fails, the system can still work at present state. Thus, the cost of upgrading failure is reduced to lowest degree.

### 29.3.1  Upgrading Procedures

Two sets of program are prepared for DSP and FPGA. One is running in the system, and the other is of old version. The upgrading procedures for DSP and FPGA are shown in Fig. 29.2 and have two functions. The first one is to upgrade the program of old version orderly. The second one is to make sure that the program running in the system can be reloaded, when an error occurs during upgrade operation.

The DSP upgrade task and FPGA upgrade block are designed to execute the upgrading procedures. The DSP upgrade task is mainly used to transmit FPGA upgrade program and burn the DSP upgrade program. The FPGA upgrade block is used to receive FPGA upgrade program and burn the new program to specific page according to the received command from DSP.

At the beginning of upgrading procedure, DSP checks the version of program sets and overwrites the DSP program of the old version. Then, it transmits FPGA upgrade program and upgrade page to FPGA. After transmitting finished, a timer in DSP is triggered to check whether the upgrading of FPGA is timeout. A timeout represents the failure of upgrading FPGA. In this circumstance, version information will not be updated. When system restarts, DSP and FPGA will reload the program running in the system before upgrading.

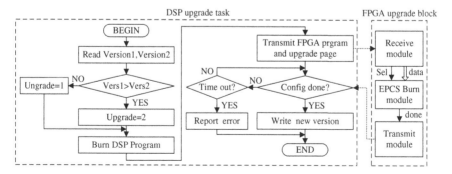

**Fig. 29.2**  Upgrading procedures for DSP and FPGA

## 29.3.2 Loading Procedures

The loading procedures shown in Fig. 29.3 are designed to load DSP and FPGA program orderly and reliably. If an error occurs during upgrade process, the loading procedures can reload the program running in the system. Hardware circuits in the Fig. 29.3 mean that the functions are integrated in chips and processed automatically by hardware circuits.

When DSP powers up, the hardware circuits load boot code automatically [9]. The boot code firstly finds the program of newest version and then sets the corresponding load number. The load number indicates which set of program will be loaded to DSP and FPGA. Next, the load number is transmitted to FPGA. Then the boot code waits until the configuration of FPGA completed. After detecting the completion of FPGA configuration, the boot code checks whether an error occurs in loading FPGA program. If an error occurs, the load number is altered. This means that the programs for DSP and FPGA are changed to the other set.

When FPGA powers up, the hardware circuits load the factory configuration [10]. The factory configuration is designed to select which set of program, application configuration 1 or application configuration 2, will be loaded to FPGA for proper operation. If an error occurs during loading the program, the error state bit, ERR, will be set, and the hardware circuits will load the factory configuration again. Then, the other set of program is loaded to FPGA.

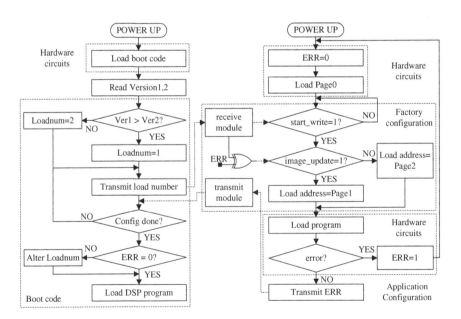

**Fig. 29.3** Loading procedures for DSP and FPGA

## 29.4 Terminal Hardware Structure

### 29.4.1 Hardware Framework

A hardware framework designed for remote firmware upgrading is shown in Fig. 29.1. The cores of the framework are DSP and FPGA. Stratix II series of Altera, for FPGA, and C64x+ series of TI, for DSP, is used in this structure. The EPCSs are dedicated configuration series for Altera's FPGA. The NOR flash is the storage of DSP program, and the E2PROM is used to save key configuration parameters.

### 29.4.2 Memory Sections and Function Description

The memory of EPCS, shown in Fig. 29.4, is divided into three pages: Page0, Page1 and Page2. The corresponding programs are factory configuration, application configuration 1 and application configuration 2, respectively.

When FPGA powers up or an error occurs during loading program, factory configuration will be loaded automatically. In order to enhance the stability of loading program, updating Page0 is prohibited. This setting ensures that factory configuration can be successfully loaded every time. Application configuration 1 and application configuration 2 are designed to execute proper operation of the system. In application configuration 1 and application configuration 2, the FPGA upgrade block which is shown in Fig. 29.2 is included.

As shown in Fig. 29.5, E2PROM and NOR flash are related to DSP program upgrade. Version Section 1 and Version Section 2 locate in E2PROM. These two sections store the version information of program sets. The version information is critical for remote upgrade processing. In order to avoid the information being written or erased by mistake, these sections are physically separated from program sets.

There are three sections in NOR flash: Boot Section, Upgrade Section 1 and Upgrade Section 2. Boot Section stores boot code. The boot code is used to select

**Fig. 29.4** FPGA memory sections

| | EPCS64 |
|---|---|
| Factory configuration | Page0 |
| Application configuration1 | Page1 |
| Application configuration2 | Page2 |
| | ... |

**Fig. 29.5** DSP memory
sections

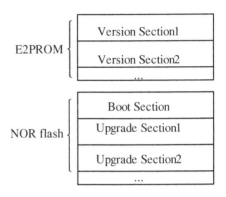

load number and load program to DSP according to this number. Update Section 1 and Update Section 2 store the DSP program sets. The upgrade task shown in Fig. 29.2 is included in DSP program sets.

## 29.5 Conclusion

In this paper, a safe, secure and reliable remote firmware upgrade mechanism is presented to solve the existing firmware upgrade problems in SDR based systems. The synchronization mechanism makes various parts of the system upgrade safely and sequentially. The alternating upgrade strategy reduces the cost of remote firmware upgrade failure to lowest degree. In this upgrade mechanism, different operation attributes are applied to the memory sections. This setting enhances stability of the systems. The remote firmware upgrade mechanism makes the upgrade of SDR based systems much quicker and easier without the constraints of installation location. It reduces the cost of firmware upgrade effectively and can be widely utilized in SDR based systems.

## References

1. Wang XH, Shi XW, Li P et al (2010) Smart antenna design for GPSGLONASS Antijamming. In: Proceedings of the international conferrence on microwave and millimetre wave technology, Chengdu, May 2010, pp 1149–1152
2. Amrita S, Amitabha S (2008) Radio processor: a new reconfigurable architecture for software defined radio. In: International conferrence on computer science and information technology, Singapore Sept 2008, pp 709–713
3. Dai ZC, Ying X (2010) Design of remote upgrade of equipment. In: 2nd international conferrence on information technology and computer science, Kiev June 2010, pp 462–465
4. Li Q, Yan P, He XH (2010) New update method with high-reliability for embedded system software. J Comput Appl 75:2228–2231 (in Chinese)

5. Yang DL, Chen JL, Li C (2006) Research and implementation of software on-line update mechanism for DSP system Electron. Meas Instrum 43:60–63 (in Chinese)
6. Wu HZ, Liu HF, Huang KW Study of boot loader mode for DSP TMS320C6455. Electron Meas Technol 31:155–161 (in Chinese)
7. Cui XD (2009) Design and implementation of AES—based document encryption management system, pp 10–50 (in Chinese)
8. Liu GZ, Huang YJ (2009) Research of digital signature based on SHA-1 and RSA in official document transmission. Comput Eng Des 30:1596–1599 (in Chinese)
9. Allred D (2008) Using the TMS320DM643x bootloader, Texas, May 2008
10. Jose S (2007) Stratix II device handbook, Altera corporation, San Jose, pp 551–716

# Chapter 30
# A Practical Key Management Scheme in Software Layer and Its Applications

An Wang, Zheng Li and Xianwen Yang

**Abstract** In practical application, the conventional key management schemes based on application layer software or tamper-proof hardware have a multiplicity of drawbacks. We propose an idea of managing keys in kernel mode and design a practical key management scheme based on function driver. After comprehensive analysis, our scheme can not only resist the threats of virus and reverse-engineering, but also overcome hardware's shortcomings of high cost and difficulty of upgrade. Moreover, the corruption attack which is troublesome in cryptography can also be resisted.

**Keywords** Cryptography · Driver · Reverse-engineering · Corruption attack

## 30.1 Introduction

Cryptographic products are widely used, such as USB Key, entrance guard card, secure flash disk, and so on [1]. Public key cryptography, including public encryption, authentication protocol, key exchange protocol, electronic cash, and so on, is employed by these products. The management of the private key has become a research hotspot in the fields of computer science. Over the years, a large number of theoretic studies about this topic have been finished, and many theoretical

A. Wang (✉)
Institute for Advanced Study, Tsinghua University, Beijing 100084, China
e-mail: wanganl@tsinghua.edu.cn

Z. Li · X. Yang
Department of Electronic Technology, Information Science and Technology Institute, Zhengzhou 450004, China

W. Lu et al. (eds.), *Proceedings of the 2012 International Conference on Information Technology and Software Engineering*, Lecture Notes in Electrical Engineering 212, DOI: 10.1007/978-3-642-34531-9_30, © Springer-Verlag Berlin Heidelberg 2013

results are achieved [2–4], which make the theory relatively mature. But in practice, there are no such perfect solutions with safety, high-efficiency, and low-cost. In particular, almost nothing can be done to prevent the corruption attack [4].

Early cryptographic products generally placed the keys into the application software with corresponding security mechanisms added. For example, development group FreeOTFE designed a piece of security software to encrypt data stored in a removable storage device in 2004 [5], Sophos company used passwords on the device to make users' ID authentication [6], Gebusia proposed some methods in software encryption for the network file system [7], and so on. But shortly afterwards, attacks on these proposals came one after another [8]: In Windows platform, virus and Trojan horse can change the software's functions, reverse-engineering [9] can pry into their code, hook technology can illegally intercepted message data, loopholes can help the adversary enhance the access authority.

The greatly reduction of the cost of integrated circuits make venders introduce tamper-proof hardware device to implement key management. EMC Company designs a kind of key manager and tokenization [10] to settle the key establishment problem, which uses hardware technology into a synchronous key generator ensuring that every minute it can output a key which is same as another key on the server. Another tamper-proof device, the USB Key [11] which is also widely applied in the fields of banks and e-commerce system, can complete the one-way identity authentication from the USB Key holder to the verifier.

In this paper we present a practical driver-based key management scheme, including user registration, key usage, key update, certificate expiration and other aspects. After a security analysis, we conclude that this scheme has significant advantages in resisting the corruption attack, anti-virus, resistance to reverse-engineering, etc., compared with other conventional schemes.

## 30.2 Key Management Scheme Based on Drivers

Drivers, running in kernel-mode particularly on Windows platforms, have multi-layers structure. Common drivers consist of at least two parts: a Function Driver, which decodes, executes and then transfers (to the lower layers) the request information of applications when communicating with them, and a Bus Driver, which packages the data to make it satisfying the format specification and then transports it. Applications send requests to the devices in the form of I/O Request Packet (IRP) with major function codes giving the purpose of these requests included. Meanwhile, IRPs contain the data, which means one can process it in the function driver if he wants to filter some of the data or make other operations.

Those programs running in kernel-mode can provide the transport of data with a fine protection, as they can successfully avoid the security threat in the upper layer namely the user-mode while they affect none of the data structures of the bus protocols in the lower bus driver layer. So the following statement which is in accordance with reality is widely believed:

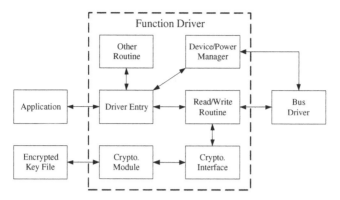

**Fig. 30.1** System structure of function driver

**FACT 1** To implement an attack in software layer, it is much more difficult in the device drivers running in kernel-mode than in the applications of user-mode [1].

## 30.2.1 Design of Function Drivers System Architecture

We propose the key management scheme in software should be implemented in the function driver running in kernel-mode on Windows platforms. Figure 30.1 describes the proposed system architecture of function drivers including some crypto-operations. The function driver plays a role of bridge when the application is communicating with peripheral devices of PCs. And the concrete functions of the different parts in the architecture are listed below:

- Dispatch: This routine deals with the communications between the applications and drivers such as Create, Close, Cleanup, Read, Write, and Device Control.
- Cryptographic Interface: It will receive the requests of crypto-operations when needed. For instance, it runs mutual authentication when enumeration starts, and the encryption/decryptions operations while communicating. And these requests are completed by invocations of the cryptographic module.
- Cryptographic Module: It consists of key management, block cipher algorithm, public-key algorithm, hash function, etc. When a request of encryption, decryption, or authentication is received, a correct key is first obtained by calling key management module, and then participate the operations.
- Furthermore, other routines like PnP, Power, StartIo in the driver collaborating with those ones mentioned above can ensure correctness of drivers' work.

## 30.2.2 Key Management Scheme

The routine of cryptographic module provides the upper-layer routines with cryptographic services. It's easy to implement a cryptographic algorithm, while to manage and store the keys for the cryptographic algorithm properly to keep the whole system's security is a challenge. So we propose the following key management to solve this problem.

### 30.2.2.1 Symbol Explanation

| | |
|---|---|
| T/A | Trusted authority/a user; |
| $ID_A$ | Identification number of user A; |
| $PK_A/SK_A$ | Public/private key of user A; |
| IK_A | The inherent key in the driver of user A; |
| $EKF_A$ | A file storing the encrypted private key $SK_A$; |
| H | Secure hash function; |
| ENC/DEC | Encryption/decryption operation; |
| SIG/VER | Signature/verification operation; |
| $CER_A$ | The certificate of $PK_A$ issued by T; |

### 30.2.2.2 User Registration

When A want to register at T, T first generates public and private key $PK_A$ and $SK_A$ based on the RSA algorithms and records them. Then T produces a so-called inherent key IK_A = $H(ID_A \parallel RN)$ (RN stands for a random number) which is packaged into the driver of A securely (How to implement this in practical? We will discuss it in Sect. 30.2.4) and issues the driver to A. Accordingly, T records IK_A, computes EKF = $ENC_{IK\_A}(SK_A)$ using AES algorithm, and releases the cipher text to A in the form of file. Moreover, with the help of $SK_T$, T computes the signature of $PK_A$, i.e. $SIG_T(PK_A)$, and issues the certification $CER_A$ to A.

### 30.2.2.3 Keys Usage

Figure 30.2 shows the process of cryptographic module when encryption/signature operations are needed in the communications between the driver and applications or devices. First, the routine invokes the key management function to acquire the IK_A and EKF, then sends them to the AES decryption function to restore the private key $SK_A = DEC_{IK\_A}(EKF)$. Finally, the gotten $SK_A$ is provided for the upper encryption/sign requests, which completes the whole service.

**Fig. 30.2** Key management scheme of cryptographic module

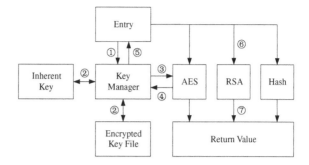

When the public key $PK_A$ is required in computations, the driver can directly extract it from the $CER_A$. However, if the origin and integrity of $PK_A$ can't be ensured, some simple verification and backup schemes should be adopted in local.

### 30.2.2.4 Updating the Keys Online

When A wants to update his public/private keys, he should submit a request which is signed by $SK_A$. After verifying this signature, T regenerates the pair $SK_A$' and $PK_A$', reads IK_A from the database, makes new encrypted key file EKF' = EN-$C_{IK\_A}(SK_A')$ and public-key certificate $CER_A$', computes $SIG_T(EKF', CER_A')$, and sends $(EKF', CER_A', SIG_T(EKF', CER_A'))$ to A through the insecure channel.

When receiving the new EKF' and $CER_A$', A should first verify the signature of them with $PK_T$. Then he updates his former key files to the new ones without making any change of the driver.

### 30.2.2.5 Expiration of the Certificate

When the certificates are out of date, T should update $PK_T/SK_T$ to $PK_T'/SK_T'$. For any user A, T fetches $PK_A$ from the database, issues the new certificate $CER_A$' according to $SK_T'$. Accordingly, T computes $SIG_T(CER_A', PK_T')$ using old keys $SK_T$ and sends $(CER_A', PK_T', SIG_T(CER_A', PK_T'))$ to A through insecure channel.

When A receives the updated certificate, he should verify its signature with the old public key of T $PK_T$, and then overwrite his former certificate file and T's public key file with new ones. Likewise, no change of the driver is needed.

## 30.2.3  Application Examples

The key management scheme of this paper can be used to design a USB Key of mutual authentication whose aim is to make the USB Key's owner or PC's owner ensure the other one's identity. When two legal users want to make some

**Fig. 30.3** Enumeration
process of secure flash disk

interactions, they can execute the protocol of authentication between one user's PC
and the other's USB Key (UK for short). Once the UK is connected to the PC,
it send a request to the PC, which will sequentially cause the cryptographic module
to carry out some procedures such as reading the key file, recovering the key,
signing and so on to finish the authentication mutually. After that, a reversed
course of events, i.e. verifying UK by PC, comprised of verifying the certificate of
UK public key and UK signature, is activated.

Based on the UK above, we can design a secure flash disk. When the USB bus is
not secure, encryption transmission and key exchange protocol are needed. This can
be implemented by Diffie-Hellman protocol to get the session keys additionally
when carrying out a mutual authentication. We can also employ another way to
implement this, such as key transmission by RSA encryption. After established, the
session keys are preserved in the memory for the sake of convenient AES encryp-
tion/decryption. Once the flash disk is unplugged from the PC, memories will be
released and hence the session key becomes invalid. We have implemented this
secure flash disk's driver and hardware on FPGA. The process of authentication, key
establishment, and encryption in enumeration is showed in Fig. 30.3.

## 30.2.4 Some Problems of Implementation

Confidentiality of the inherent key is the most crucial point to the whole scheme.
Hence there must be adequate measures to ensure that. The most common method
of the adversary to access the inherent key is reverse-engineering [9]. To resist
reverse-engineering, the first countermeasure is to shell, which stores the codes in
the disk only after they are encrypted and returns their original states in the
memories only they are to be executed. The shell of the original codes will be run
before the original program through getting the priority of control after loaded into
the memory by the Windows loader, decrypt, then restore to the original state in
execution. By this means, program files can be effectively prevented from illegal
modification and being statically disassembled by an attacker. Towards the details

of the development of the driver, some code-protection techniques can be used to keep the adversary away from understanding the sensitive information from the codes: anti-trace debugging, name obfuscation, control flow obfuscation or deobfuscation, anti-monitoring, and so on.

In computer software layer, to solve the problem of anti-copy is essentially equivalent offering anti-piracy protection. At present, one of the most effective solutions is a binding between the access of program and the machine code which is a unique feature of a computer such as the serial numbers of CPU, hard disks or other main components. In the proposed scheme above, when a user submits a registration request to the trusted authority, his machine code needs to be provided together. As a result, a driver which can only be used on the specified computer is issued from the trusted authority (in essence, a serial number derived from the machine code has been set in the driver). If the driver is copied to another computer, it will not be executed due to the mismatch between its serial number and the machine code. In addition, the machine codes don't require secrecy, and thus they can also be submitted through the network, telephone and other channels.

## 30.3 Security Analysis

An adversary attacking on this scheme, in essence, aims to the user's private key. Some methods such as cryptology analysis, protocol analysis, virus, reverse-engineering, and so on are usually employed to attempt it.

Corruption attack [4] is difficult to resist in the sense of cryptography, because once the user is corrupted by the adversary, his private key is leaked. But in our scheme, even if the adversary gets all of the user's public/private key files, secure device, and even a copy of the driver, he still cannot acquire any useful information or permissions. The "root of trust" in this paper is not a password, a person, or a device, but a driver. So, given that the adversary cannot run the user's driver, the secure flash disk proposed in Sect. 30.2.3 will forever prevent the adversary from the privacy stored in it, even if the corrupted user wishes the adversary to see!

Driver-level virus has come out for a few years although, whose permission and priority is higher than the user-mode application's, its function is quite limited, and also, its development is far more difficult than the normal virus. Currently, most of the driver-level virus modules are not used to actualize destruction and attack, instead, they provide protection for those executable programs sabotaging in the user-level. If these disruptive behaviors merely execute in user-mode, then they have little effect to our key management scheme. Reverse-engineering is effective for the user mode application as a method of attacking, but the countermeasures given in Sect. 30.2.4 provide a good security protection sufficiently for the inherent key.

Compared with conventional application layer key management schemes [5–7] and hardware schemes [10, 11], the proposal scheme is more outstanding against virus, reverse-engineering, which is given in Table 30.1.

**Table 30.1** Security contrast

| Indicator | Conv. SW. scheme | Conv. HW. scheme | Our scheme |
|---|---|---|---|
| Layer | User mode | HW. layer | Kernel mode |
| Root of trust | User's password | Tamper-proof device | Inherent key |
| Permission and priority | Low | Low | High |
| Against corruption | No | No | Yes |
| Against virus | Worse | Better | Better |
| Against reverse engineering | Worse | Better | Better |
| Cost | Lower cost | Higher cost | Lower cost |

## 30.4 Conclusions

Based on a comprehensively study on the kernel-mode programming, the user-mode programming, drivers, reverse-engineering and other technologies, we presents a practical key management scheme in software layer, cites prospects for its application, and address some of the problems in the implementation. And after a security analysis, we conclude that this scheme has significant advantages in resisting the corruption attack, anti-virus, resistance to reverse-engineering, etc., to other traditional schemes implemented in the application layer and hardware. In the future, we will continue furthering the problems discussed in the paper, such as trying to use more advanced means to attack some aspects stated above.

## References

1. Ferguson N, Schneier B, Kohno T (2010) Cryptography engineering: design principles and practical applications. Wiley, London
2. Barker E, Barker W, Burr W, Polk W, Smid M (2007) Recommendation for key management—part 1: general, NIST special publication 800-57, http://csrc.nist.gov/publications/nistpubs/800-57/sp800-57-Part1-revised2_Mar08-2007.pdf
3. Mazieres D, Kaminsky M, Kaashoek MF, Witchel E (1999) Separating key management from file system security. ACM SIGOPS Oper Syst Rev 33(5):124–139
4. Menezes AJ, Van Oorschot PC, Vanstone SA (1997) Handbook of applied cryptography. CRC Press, Boca Raton
5. FreeOTFE develop group (2004) FreeOTFE user manual, http://www.freeotfe.org/user_manual.html
6. Sophos PLC (2009) Data sheet of safe guard removable media, http://www.sophos.com/sophos/ docs/eng/factshts/sophos-safeguard-removablemedia-dsus.pdf
7. Gebusia J (2007) Data encryption on file servers: securing electronic business processes. Vieweg, Germany, pp 38–48
8. Allen JH, Barnum S, Ellison RJ, McGraw G, Mead NR (2008) Software security engineering: a guide for project managers. Addison-Wesley Professional, Boston
9. Foster J (2005) Sockets, shell code, porting, and coding: reverse-engineering exploits and tool coding for security professionals. Syngress, Rockland
10. EMC Corporation (2009) RSA key manager and tokenization, http://www.rsa.com/products/envi-sion/success/10530_MEDFUS_CP_1109.pdf

11. Industrial and commercial bank of China limited (2010) Operating guide of the second generation U-shield, http://www.icbc.com.cn/ICBC/ html/download/dkq/khzsazsc_tdr.doc

# Chapter 31
# CIE: Learner Behavior Modeling Oriented Component Model for Edutainment Game

**Yue Zhang, Zhiqiang Dai and Fang Miao**

**Abstract** Edutainment games with the feature of learner behavior modeling may differ from many aspects, which made it crucial to define all related information according to a unified model. In this paper, we proposed a novel learner behavior modeling oriented component model for edutainment game—CIE, within which the three interrelated components—"Challenge", "Interactive Activity", and "Element" enabled the design team of edutainment game to design, define, and acquire the contents and information which is related to learner behavior modeling. Through the sub-modules such as "sequence of sub-goals" and "difficulty/work-load", the model also provided significant basis for evaluating and analyzing learner behavior qualitatively and quantificationally in a standardized form. The application of the CIE model in the design of an edutainment web game had preliminarily proved its practicality.

**Keywords** Learner · Behavior modeling · Edutainment game · Goal distance

Y. Zhang (✉) · Z. Dai
Department of Digital Media Technology, Information Engineering School,
Communication University of China, DingFuzhuang, ChaoYang, Beijing, China
e-mail: feijisheji@Gmail.com

F. Miao
Department of Communication Engineering, Information Engineering School,
Communication University of China, DingFuzhuang, ChaoYang, Beijing, China
e-mail: miaofang@cuc.edu.cn

W. Lu et al. (eds.), *Proceedings of the 2012 International Conference on Information Technology and Software Engineering*, Lecture Notes in Electrical Engineering 212, DOI: 10.1007/978-3-642-34531-9_31, © Springer-Verlag Berlin Heidelberg 2013

## 31.1 Introduction

As an important feature of edutainment game, adaptivity is quite meaningful for the raise of game play and of learners' learning outcome [1–3], while learner modeling is always a key link to achieve optimal adaptivity [4–6]. Whereas, there hasn't existed a fairly complete and well-targeted information model for the related game content and information which is related to learner behavior modeling within current research of edutainment game [7, 8], which makes it inconvenient to design, define, acquire and calculate the related content and information. In our opinion, the corresponding model should meet the following requirements:

1. Be able to contain the complete information for learner modeling.
2. Be suitable for different types of edutainment games and for different kinds of learner models.
3. Be able to assure the quantificationally analysis and evaluation of learner behavior.
4. Be able to provide the design team of edutainment game sufficient freedom and flexibility to define the game content in different granularities.

Aiming at above requirements, we propose a novel leaner behavior modeling oriented component model for edutainment game—CIE. To meet the requirements with minimal model scale, the model was composed of three components— "Challenge", "Interactive Activity", "Element", while the Challenge component was based on the definition of the Interactive Activity and Element component. We also adopted innovative "resolution + goal" sub-module in the form of "sub-goal sequence" and sub-modules for skill mapping as well as goal distance quantification. Meanwhile, we combined the CIE model closely with the Educator-Researcher-Designer collaborative design architecture for edutainment game which was proposed by us before [9], which integrated the model with an integral design architecture.

## 31.2 The CIE Component Model

The complete process of analyzing and modeling learner behavior within edutainment games could be divided into three stages:

1. The design and definition of game content which directly relates to learner behavior.
2. The recording of behavior related information during game progress.
3. The analysis and evaluation of learner behaviors based on the content and information from preceding two stages.

**Fig. 31.1** The CIE
component model

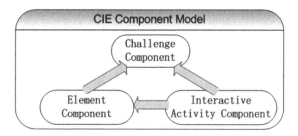

**Fig. 31.2** Composition of
the interactive activity
component

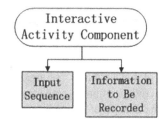

The needed information to be recorded in stage (2) as well as the analysis/evaluation algorithm in stage (3) should also be pre-defined during game design, and all the involved content and information related to each other. Therefore, it's necessary to define them as a unified ensemble.

As shown in Fig. 31.1, the CIE model composed of three components—"Challenge", "Interactive Activity" and "Element", while the definition of the Challenge component was based on the other two components. Each component 1 contained multiple sub-modules. Most of the necessary information for learner behavior modeling within edutainment game had been covered in these three components.

The composition of the Interactive Activity component was shown in Fig. 31.2. The "activity" within our model referred to a fundamental input operation or a sequence of fundamental input operation (such as "drag-and-drop") which had clear meaning in a game. Since the same activity may had different meaning according to different activity targets (i.e. game elements), the Interactive Activity component within our model only involves the information of an activity itself without involving the direct activity targets. Furthermore, the Interactive Activity component was composed of two types of sub-modules. The first type of sub-modules contained the information of the composition of the activity itself and, which corresponded to the antecedent stage (1). The other type contained the information to be recorded during the game progress such as the happening time point or lasting time of an activity, which corresponded to the antecedent stage (2).

The "element" within the CIE model refers not only to all the visible and directly/indirectly interactivable game elements, but also to the invisible elements in an edutainment game. The invisible game elements usually involve some

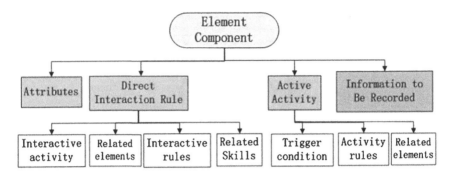

**Fig. 31.3** Composition of the element component

"global attributes" of a game such as the score of the learner. Since the interactive activity within a game mainly directly affect the attributes of game elements, while the change of element attribute could also be induced by pre-defined self-varying rules, the Element component divided the two situations into two sub-modules, so that the effect of interactive activities could be calculated and analysed more precisely. It should be noted that there could exist some game elements which contain certain contents that are not related to challenge resolving directly while still be hoped to be mastered by learners or be helpful indirectly for challenge resolving such as domain knowledge, and certain interactive activities such as reading or summarizing with these elements could be important information for learner behavior modeling at least for qualitative behavior analysis. Therefore, a corresponding "related skills" section was involved within the "direct interaction rule" submodule of the Element component of our model. Besides, it could also be necessary for some edutainment games to record certain information of game elements such as the time point of appearing or disappearing during the game progress, so the "information to be recorded" sub-module was also involved in the Element component (Fig. 31.3).

The "Challenge" component was the most important component of the CIE model, for one of the most primary basis of the analysis and evaluation of learner behavior was the state variation of challenges by each interactive activity. As shown in Fig. 31.4, one of the important innovations of Challenge component was the mixed definition "possible solution + (final) goal" as well as the representation of solution in the form of "sequence of sub-goals". One of the reasons for the structure of this sub-module was the involvement of more than one sub-challenge within a challenge presented to the learner within edutainment games, which also coincided with many problems in reality. The other reason was the requirement of many researchers of edutainment game to provide one or multiple possible solutions for many challenges. Furthermore, each step in a solution could be treated as a sub-goal to achieve. Each sub-goal could be defined in the form of "element state" represented by attributes values or "interactive activity" or their

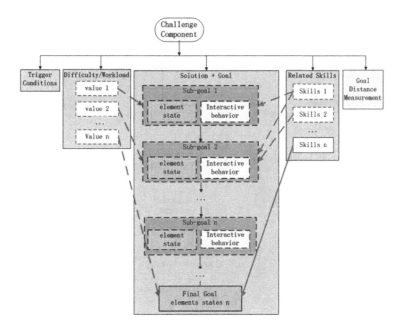

**Fig. 31.4** Composition of the challenge component. The *dashed-line boxes* and *dashed-line arrows* represents optional content and optional corresponding relations

combination, which provided more flexibility. To correlate learner behavior with skills/knowledge, we also defined the "related skills" sub-module in the Challenge component, within which one or more skills could be correlated with each sub-goal or final goal. Besides, the sub-module "difficulty/workload" was another innovative part of our model. It allowed the definition of a value within a pre-defined codomain for each sub-goal of a solution according to its relative difficulty/workload compared with other steps, which enabled better quantifica-tional calculation of the change of goal distance brought by interactive activities since many sub-goals of edutainment games could not be represented by numerical element characters. With the auxiliary mechanism provided by the "difficulty/workload" sub-module, the researchers of edutainment game should be able to define unified quantificational goal distance measurement for each chal-lenge, i.e. the "Goal Distance Measurement" sub-module within the Challenge component, which also provided direct foundation for more flexible and unified learner behavior modeling algorithms. It should be noted that no matter the solution of the challenge, the corresponding relation between sub-goals and skills, or the assigned difficulty/workload values could all be defined with different needed granularities.

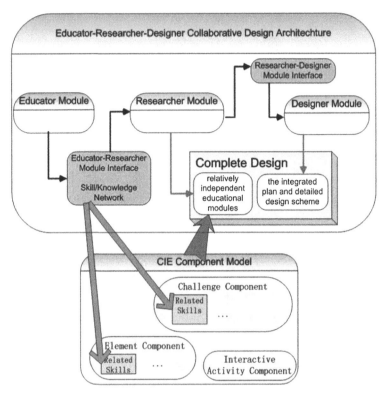

**Fig. 31.5** Combination of the CIE model and the educator-researcher-designer collaborative design architecture

## 31.3 Combination of the CIE Model and the Educator-Researcher-Designer Collaborative Design Architecture for Edutainment Game

To define the component content of the CIE model in the design process of edutainment game more efficiently, we combined the definition process with the Educator-Researcher-Designer collaborative design architecture [9] that we proposed before. The combination of the CIE model and simplified design architecture was shown in Fig. 31.5. The architecture was composed of three successive modules, which corresponded to the educator, researcher of edutainment game and professional game designer of the complete design team. The working result of each module was delivered to the next module by the module interface. As shown in Fig. 31.5, the Educator module was in charge of generating a skill/knowledge network, which is also the source of the skills of the "related skills" sub-module within the Challenge component and the "related Skills" section of the "direct interaction rule" submodule within the Element component of the CIE model. The Researcher module was mainly in charge of

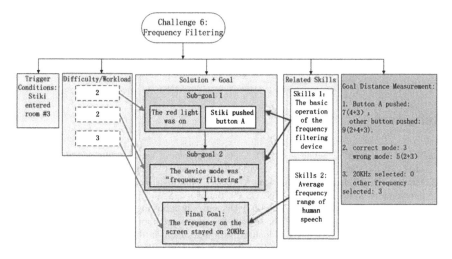

**Fig. 31.6**  An example of a defined challenge component relations

converting the educational material from educator module into optional game contents preliminarily for designer module as well as of designing relatively independently specific educational technical modules, so that the definition of the components of CIE model was involved as part of the Researcher module.

We had applied the CIE component model into the design and development of an auxiliary edutainment web game "The return of Stiki's voice" [10] for the course "Speech Signal Processing". Learner will learn skills and knowledge about speech signal processing in the game through the process of helping a robot named Stiki to recover its speaking function. Although the game is still in production, the design and development work had proved the power and convenience with the unified form to define and acquire needed information as well as with the unified quantificational goal distance measurement brought by the CIE component model, which also made it much more smooth for the programming implementation of the learner behavior modeling module.

We demonstrated a real example of a Challenge component of the CIE model we defined in Fig. 31.6. The value-setting strategy for the "difficulty/workload" sub-module was to select an integer value in the range [1, 5] which represented 5 levels of difficulty for each subgoal, while a default value 3 (medium level of difficulty) would be selected without manual selection.

## 31.4  Conclusion

A standard model for the design, definition and acquirement of needed information related with learner behavior modeling as well as a unified quantificational method for challenge goal distance calculation would be significantly helpful to introducing learner adaptivity into edutainment game, which had also been preliminarily proved by the application of our CIE component model. The future work will focus on more detailed and advanced algorithm for goal distance especially with multiple solutions within the Challenge component.

# References

1. Yolum P, Tumer K, Stone P (2011) Agent programming and adaptive serious games: a survey of the state of the art. In: AAMAS 2011, Taipei, Taiwan, China
2. Michael D, Christina M, Dietrich A (2009) Non-invasive assessment and adaptive interventions in learning games, INCOS'09, Barcelona, Spain
3. Kevin K, Florian M, Cormac H (2007) Dynamically adjusting digital educational games towards learning objectives. In: The seventh framework program in the ICT research priority
4. Thomas A, Cord H (2011) Individualized skill assessment in digital learning games: basic definitions and mathematical formalism, IEEE Trans Learn Technol 4(2) 138–148
5. Valerie J (2011) stealth assessment in computer-based games to support learning, computer games and instruction, 503–523
6. Kickmeie M, Albert D (2010) Micro-adaptivity: protecting immersion in didactically adaptive digital educational games. J Comput Assist Learn 26(2):95–105
7. Mohammad A, Rosella G, Pierpaolo V (2012) Adapting with evidence: the adaptive model and the stimulation plan of TERENCE. Adv Intell Soft Comput 152(2012):75–82
8. Mieke V, Piet D, Piet D (2011) The contribution of learner characteristics in the development of computer-based adaptive learning environments. Comput Hum Behav 27(1):118–1309
9. Zhang Y, Miao F (2011) Educator-researcher-designer collaborative design architecture for edutainment game. In: ICCDA2011, Xian, China
10. Zhang Y, Dai Z, Liu C (2012) Three-layer design model for knowledge summarization module of edutainment game. In: IWET 2012, Shanghai, China

# Part II
# Digital Media Technology

# Chapter 32
# T-Base: A Triangle-Based Iterative Algorithm for Smoothing Quadrilateral Meshes

Gang Mei, John C. Tipper and Nengxiong Xu

**Abstract** We present a novel approach named T-Base for smoothing planar and surface quadrilateral meshes. Our motivation is that the best shape of quadrilateral element—square—can be virtually divided into a pair of equilateral right triangles by any of its diagonals. When move a node to smooth a quadrilateral, it is optimal to make a pair of triangles divided by a diagonal be equilateral right triangles separately. The finally smoothed position is obtained by weighting all individual optimal positions. Three variants are produced according to the determination of weights. Tests by the T-Base are given and compared with Laplacian smoothing: The Vari.1 of T-Base is effectively identical to Laplacian smoothing for planar quad meshes, while Vari.2 is the best. For the quad mesh on underlying parametric surface and interpolation surface, Vari.2 and Vari.1 are best, respectively.

**Keywords** Mesh smoothing · Iterative smoothing · Quad meshes · Laplacian smoothing · Length-weighted

G. Mei (✉) · J. C. Tipper
Institut für Geowissenschaften—Geologie, Albert-Ludwigs-Universität Freiburg,
Albertstreet 23B D-79104 Freiburg im Breisgau, Germany
e-mail: gang.mei@geologie.uni-freiburg.de

J. C. Tipper
e-mail: john.tipper@geologie.uni-freiburg.de

N. Xu
School of Engineering and Technology, China University of Geosciences (Beijing),
Beijing 100083, China
e-mail: xunengxiong@yahoo.com.cn

W. Lu et al. (eds.), *Proceedings of the 2012 International Conference on Information Technology and Software Engineering*, Lecture Notes in Electrical Engineering 212, DOI: 10.1007/978-3-642-34531-9_32, © Springer-Verlag Berlin Heidelberg 2013

## 32.1 Introduction

The quality of meshes is critical to obtain reliable simulation results in finite element analyses. Usually after generating computational meshes, it is necessary to improve the quality of meshes in further. There are two important categories of quality improvement methods. One is called *clear-up* techniques, which alters the connectivity between elements. The other is called *mesh smoothing*, which only relocates the nodes. There are numerous publications on the topic of mesh smoothing. And we just refer some popular and representative ones.

The most popular smoothing methods is Laplacian smoothing [1, 2], which repositions each node at the centroid of its neighbouring nodes in one iteration. The popularity of this method comes from its efficiency and effectiveness. A simpler but more effective method is angle-based approach [3], in which new locations are calculated by conforming specific angle ratios in surrounding polygons.

A geometric element transformation method [4], which is based on a simple geometric transformation, is proposed and applied to polygons. Shimada et al. [5] proposed a method which treats nodes as the centre of bubbles and nodal locations are obtained by deforming bubbles with each other.

A projecting/smoothing method is proposed for smoothing surface meshes [6], where the new position of each free node is obtained by minimizing the mean ratio of all triangles sharing the free node. Based on quadric surface fitting and by combining vertex projecting, curvature estimating and mesh labelling, Wang and Yu [7] proposed a novel method and applied it in biomedical modelling.

A variational method for smoothing surface and volume triangulations is proposed by Jiao [8], where the discrepancies between actual and target elements is reduced by minimizing two energy functions. Also, a general-purpose algorithm called the target-matrix paradigm is introduced in [9], and can be applied to a wide variety of mesh and element types.

To smooth meshes better, two or more basic methods can be combined into a hybrid approach [10–12], i.e., an analytical framework for mesh quality metrics and optimization direction computation in physical and parametric space are proposed for smoothing surface quad meshes in [13].

In this paper we introduce a novel iterative method named T-Base to smooth planar and surface quad meshes. The best shape of a quadrilateral element is square, which can be virtually divided into a pair of equilateral right triangles by any of its diagonals. Hence, when move a node to smooth a quad element, it is optimal to make the two triangles divided the diagonal consisted by the node and its opposite one be equilateral right triangles separately. The final smoothed position is obtained by weighting all the separate optimal positions.

When smooth surface quad meshes, we firstly compute the local coordinates system for each virtual triangle and then calculate the optimal position, and finally obtain the smoothed node by transforming it from local coordinates to the global coordinates and weighting all individual optimal positions.

After generating the optimal smoothed positions, they should be moved again in order to preserve the features of initial surfaces. For quad mesh on parametric surfaces, we project the smoothed node onto the original parametric surface along the normal. For quad mesh on interpolation surfaces, we re-interpolate the smoothed nodes to fit them with the initial surfaces.

The rest of this paper is organized as follows. Section 32.2 describes the details of the T-Base including its three variants for smoothing planar quad meshes. In Sect. 32.3, we simply extend T-Base to smooth surface quad meshes. Then we give several examples in Sect. 32.4 to test the performance of the T-Base and compare it with Laplacian smoothing. Finally, Sect. 32.5 concludes this work.

## 32.2 T-Base for Planar Quad Meshes

The best shape of a quadrilateral element is square, which can be virtually divided into a pair of equilateral right triangles by any of its diagonals. When move a node in order to smooth a quadrilateral, it is optimal to make the two triangles divided by the diagonal consisted with the node and its opposite one be equilateral right triangles separately (Fig. 32.1).

Consider a single quadrilateral element ABCD shown in Fig. 32.1. It is virtually divided into a pair of triangles ABC and CDA. $A^*$'s are the positions to which node A would have to be moved to make ABC and CDA be equilateral right triangles, assuming that nodes B, C and D were fixed. The coordinates of $A^*$ in triangles ABC and CDA are:

$$\begin{cases} X_A^* = X_B + Y_B - Y_C \\ Y_A^* = -X_B + Y_B + X_C \end{cases}, \quad \begin{cases} X_A^* = X_D - Y_D + Y_C \\ Y_A^* = X_D + Y_D - X_C \end{cases} \tag{32.1}$$

Now assume ABCD is part of a quadrilateral mesh. Each node of ABCD—for instance node A—is then shared with several other elements, and $A^*$ can be calculated for each of these. The final position of A—its optimal smoothed position—is obtained by considering all the separately calculated $A^*$'s (Fig. 32.2).

The traditional Laplacian smoothing assumes that the new position of a node should be an average of the positions calculated for it for each of the elements of which it is part (Fig. 32.2). This assumption is not essential, however, and it can be relaxed by making that new position a weighted average of those positions, with the weights being proportional to the lengths of the opposite edges. Then, for node A:

$$X_A = \sum_{i=1}^{2n} \left( w_i \cdot X_{Ai}^* \right), \quad Y_A = \sum_{i=1}^{2n} \left( w_i \cdot Y_{Ai}^* \right), \tag{32.2}$$

where $n$ is the number of elements of which node A is part, and $w_i$ is the weight of the $i$th separate position $A^*$ which can be calculated according to the length $l_i$ of relevant $i$th edge.

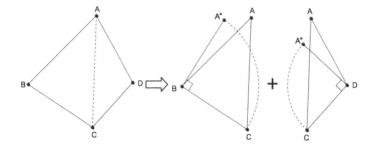

**Fig. 32.1** Smoothing of quad element ABCD based on a pair of virtual triangles

**Fig. 32.2** Node A belongs to 5 quad elements. A$^*$ can be calculated for each triangle separately (*black circles*). Optimal smoothed position for A is produced from all A$^*$s

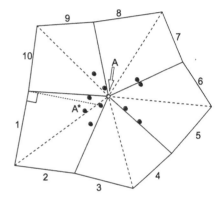

According to the determination of the weights $w_i$, we produce three variants:

**Variant 1**. This variant is termed as the *average* version of the T-Base:

$$w_i = \frac{1}{2n} = l_i^0 \bigg/ \sum_{i=1}^{2n} l_i^0 \tag{32.3}$$

The averaging process is effectively identical to that used in the traditional Laplacian smoothing, which explains why test results obtained using Laplacian smoothing are identical to that of T-Base for planar quad meshes (see Figs. 32.3, 32.4). But the above conclusion is no longer true for surface quadrilateral meshes.

**Variant 2**. This variant is termed as the $(-1/2)$ *inverse-length* version:

$$w_i = \frac{1}{\sqrt{l_i}} \bigg/ \sum_{i=1}^{2n} \frac{1}{\sqrt{l_i}} = l_i^{-1/2} \bigg/ \sum_{i=1}^{2n} l_i^{-1/2} \tag{32.4}$$

**Variant 3**. This variant is termed as the $(-1)$ *inverse-length* version:

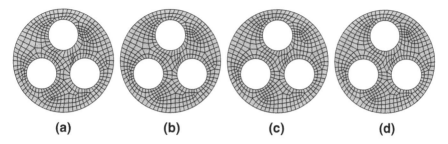

**Fig. 32.3** Test 1 of smoothing planar quad mesh by T-base and Laplacian smoothing (LS). **a** Original. **b** By Vari.1/LS. **c** By Vari.2. **d** By Vari.3

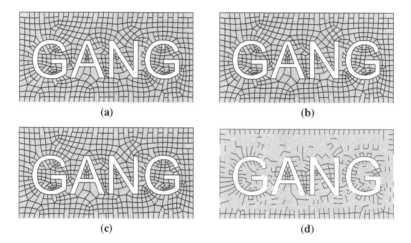

**Fig. 32.4** Test 2 of smoothing planar quad mesh by T-Base and Laplacian smoothing (LS). **a** Original. **b** By Vari.1/LS. **c** By Vari.2. **d** By Vari.3

$$w_i = \frac{1}{l_i} \bigg/ \sum_{i=1}^{2n} \frac{1}{l_i} = l_i^{-1} \bigg/ \sum_{i=1}^{2n} l_i^{-1} \qquad (32.5)$$

The introduction of inverse-length weighting is in many respects advantageous, because high quality elements such as equilateral quadrilateral element or even square generally have nearly or exactly same-length edges. In order to transform quadrilateral elements to be equilateral as more as possible, we let longer edges of an element have less importance in the smoothing than shorter ones.

The disadvantage of inverse-length versions (**Vari.2** and **3**) over the average version (**Vari.1**) is of course that it brings a time penalty, as the weights have to be calculated afresh at each iteration step. This is also the reason why inverse-length versions need more iteration steps to converge than that of the average version.

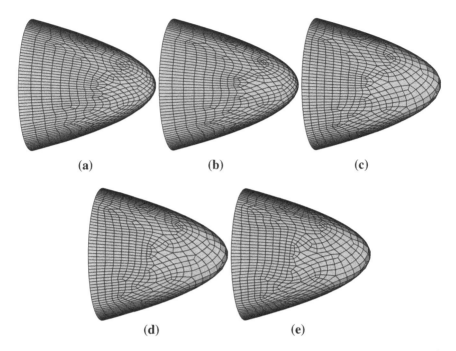

(a)                          (b)                          (c)

(d)                          (e)

**Fig. 32.5** Smoothing results of surface quad mesh on underlying parametric surface. **a** Original.
**b** By LS. **c** By Vari.1. **d** By Vari.2. **e** By Vari.3

The implementation of T-Base for planar quadrilateral meshes is very simple:
(1) search all incident elements for each node; (2) calculate of smoothed positions
of each node by making relevant virtual triangles be equilateral right; and (3)
iterate previous step until a tolerance distance is reached.

## 32.3 T-Base for Surface Quad Meshes

Equation 32.1 computes the optimal position for a virtual triangle in 2D. For
surface quad meshes, we firstly compute the local coordinates system for each
virtual triangle and then calculate the optimal position via Eq. 32.1, and finally
obtain the smoothed nodal position by recovering it to global coordinates and
weighting all $A^*$s.

After obtaining the optimal smoothed positions, updating should be done for
different type of discrete surfaces in order to preserve the shape of initial surfaces.
For quad mesh on parametric surfaces, we compute the normal at each vertex and
then project the smoothed node onto the original parametric surface along the
normal to obtain final position (Fig. 32.5). For quad mesh on interpolation surfaces, we re-interpolate the smoothed nodes to fit them with the initial surfaces
(Fig. 32.6).

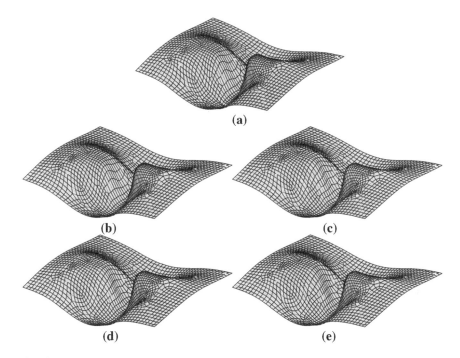

**Fig. 32.6** Smoothing results of surface quad mesh on interpolation surface. **a** Original. **b** By LS. **c** By Vari.1. **d** By Vari.2. **e** By Vari.3

Flow of the T-Base for surface quad meshes is listed in Algorithm 1.

---
**Algorithm 1** T-Base for Smoothing Surface Quad Meshes
---
*Input*: An original surface quad mesh
*Output*: A smoothed surface quad mesh
1: Search the incident elements for each node $v_i$.
2: **while** iterations not terminate **do**
3:   **for** each node $v_i$ **do**
4:     **for** each incident element $Q_j$ $(0 \leq j < n)$ of $v_i$ **do**
5:       Divide $Q_j$ into two triangles and calculate local coordinates separately.
6:       Obtain a pair of $A^*$'s locally and transform them back to global.
7:       Calculate a pair of weights $w$'s in $Q_j$.
8:     **end for**
9:     Obtain optimal smoothed position of $v_i$ :

$$X_A = \sum_{i=1}^{2n}(w_i \cdot X_{Ai}^*)\,, Y_A = \sum_{i=1}^{2n}(w_i \cdot Y_{Ai}^*)\,, Z_A = \sum_{i=1}^{2n}(w_i \cdot Z_{Ai}^*)$$

10:    Update $v_i$ by projecting it to initial parametric surface or re-interpolating.
11:  **end for**
12: **end while**
---

## 32.4 Applications and Discussion

### 32.4.1 Mesh Quality

The simplest way to measure mesh quality is to calculate the distortion values for each of the mesh elements separately, and then to compare the distributions, including mean quality (**MQ**) and mean square error (**MSE**), of those values. For a quad ABCD, we use the measure $\lambda$ [14], shown in Eq. 32.6. The value of $\lambda$ lies between 0 and 1; $\lambda = 0$ when any three nodes are collinear; $\lambda = 1$ when ABCD is square.

$$\lambda = 2\sqrt[4]{\frac{\|AB \times AD\| \cdot \|BC \times BA\| \cdot \|CD \times CB\| \cdot \|DA \times DC\|}{(\|AB\|^2+\|AD\|^2)(\|BC\|^2+\|BA\|^2)(\|CD\|^2+\|CB\|^2)(\|DA\|^2+\|DC\|^2)}}$$

$$(32.6)$$

For a quad element in 3D, it's warped generally. In this paper, we propose a new measurement $\gamma$ in which shape and warpage are taken into account. A quad ABCD can be divided into four triangles: ABC, BCD, CDA and DAB. We firstly calculate the local coordinates system of these triangles and project the original quad element ABCD onto each local coordinates system to obtain four planar quads $ABCD^P$, $BCDA^P$, $CDAB^P$ and $DABC^P$, respectively. Let $\lambda_1$, $\lambda_2$, $\lambda_3$ and $\lambda_4$ denote the $\lambda$ values of the four planar quads, then $\gamma = (\lambda_1 + \lambda_2 + \lambda_3 + \lambda_4)/4$. The value of $\gamma$ also lies between 0 and 1; we specially set $\lambda = 0$ when any three nodes are collinear; $\lambda = 1$ when ABCD is coplanar square. Thus, we have:

$$MQ = \frac{1}{n}\sum_{i=1}^{n}\gamma_i, \quad MSE = \sqrt{\frac{1}{n}\sum_{i=1}^{n}(\gamma_i - MQ)^2}, \qquad (32.7)$$

where $n$ is the number of elements in a quad mesh.

### 32.4.2 Tests of Smoothing Planar Quad Meshes

These two original quad meshes are generated by Q-Morph [15]. Figures 32.3 and 32.4 display the results of the two planar quad meshes by Laplacian smoothing and T-Base. From the comparison of mesh quality listed in Table 32.1, we can learn that Vari.1 is effectively identical to Laplace smoothing, Vari.3 and Vari.2 are better than Vari.1, but Vari.2 is best.

**Convergence** We do not give the algebraic proof of convergence for T-Base in theory. But our tests show that T-Base does converge for planar meshes, and the numbers of iteration steps of Vari.1, 2 and 3 always increases when it converges.

**Table 32.1** Mesh quality results of smoothing planar and surface quad meshes

| Mesh | Algorithm | Element quality (0.0 ~ 1.0) | | | | | MQ | MSE |
|------|-----------|------------------|------------------|------------------|------------------|------------------|------|------|
| | | 0.0 ~ 0.2 (%) | 0.2 ~ 0.4 (%) | 0.4 ~ 0.6 (%) | 0.6 ~ 0.8 (%) | 0.8 ~ 1.0 (%) | | |
| Figure 32.3 | Original | 0.00 | 0.00 | 1.13 | 6.53 | 92.34 | 0.9327 | 0.0860 |
| | Vari.1/LS | 0.00 | 0.00 | 0.00 | 2.93 | 97.07 | 0.9514 | 0.0543 |
| | Vari.2 | 0.00 | 0.00 | 0.00 | 3.15 | 96.85 | 0.9528 | 0.0520 |
| | Vari.3 | 0.00 | 0.00 | 0.00 | 3.60 | 96.40 | 0.9525 | 0.0535 |
| Figure 32.4 | Original | 0.00 | 0.00 | 0.45 | 6.47 | 93.08 | 0.9277 | 0.0781 |
| | Vari.1/LS | 0.00 | 0.00 | 0.30 | 6.47 | 93.23 | 0.9348 | 0.0764 |
| | Vari.2 | 0.00 | 0.00 | 0.45 | 5.86 | 93.69 | 0.9369 | 0.0722 |
| | Vari.3 | 0.00 | 0.00 | 0.90 | 4.81 | 94.29 | 0.9357 | 0.0753 |
| Figure 32.5 | Original | 0.00 | 0.99 | 67.26 | 18.81 | 12.94 | 0.5916 | 0.1457 |
| | LS | 0.00 | 0.00 | 62.45 | 26.03 | 11.53 | 0.6021 | 0.1380 |
| | Vari.1 | 0.00 | 0.00 | 0.64 | 75.74 | 23.62 | 0.7392 | 0.1020 |
| | Vari.2 | 0.00 | 0.00 | 3.18 | 61.10 | 35.71 | 0.7565 | 0.1107 |
| | Vari.3 | 0.14 | 1.13 | 10.04 | 48.30 | 40.38 | 0.7558 | 0.1356 |
| Figure 32.6 | Original | 0.00 | 0.00 | 2.40 | 9.47 | 88.12 | 0.9191 | 0.1020 |
| | LS | 0.00 | 0.00 | 1.98 | 8.01 | 90.01 | 0.9309 | 0.0959 |
| | Vari.1 | 0.00 | 0.00 | 0.14 | 5.70 | 94.16 | 0.945 | 0.0727 |
| | Vari.2 | 0.00 | 0.00 | 0.99 | 5.04 | 93.97 | 0.9447 | 0.0803 |
| | Vari.3 | 0.00 | 0.28 | 1.37 | 4.90 | 93.45 | 0.9434 | 0.0902 |

## 32.4.3 Tests of Smoothing Surface Quad Meshes

We firstly generate the planar meshes in a circular area, and then project it onto the parametric surface $z = 200 - 0.02(x^2 + y^2)$ to obtain the mesh in Fig. 32.5a. The original mesh in Fig. 32.6a is for height interpolation by Kriging method [16]; only z -value/height is interpolated while coordinates $x$ and $y$ are fixed.

Figure 32.5 shows the results of quad meshes on a underlying parametric surface. Noticeably, only Laplacian smoothing converges after 49 iterations. We just let T-Base iterate 49 times as that of Laplacian smoothing. From the comparison of mesh quality in Table 32.1, we can learn that T-Base is better than Laplacian smoothing. In further, Vari.2 is the best, and the Vari.1 is better than Vari.3 since the distribution of element qualities is better than that of Vari.3.

In Fig. 32.6, all optimal smoothed by only Laplacian smoothing or T-Base is generated firstly, and then z -value is re-interpolated by Kriging method. Due to the expensive cost of re-interpolation, we only iterate 10 times. Similar to the quad mesh on parametric surface, T-Base is better than Laplacian smoothing. But Vari.1 is the best, and then the Vari.2, while Vari.3 is the worst.

**Convergence** Only Laplacian smoothing converges for the quad meshes on parametric underlying surface. According to the convergence analysis for planar quad meshes, T-Base needs to iterate more times than Laplacian smoothing, hence, we can firstly record the iteration number of Laplacian smoothing for surface quad meshes, and then set the number from Laplacian smoothing to be the maximum iterations in T-Base. This is the reason we only iterate 49 times in T-Base. When smooth quad meshes on interpolation surface, since re-interpolation is too expensive, we just test the results after a specified-number of iterations. This solution of ending iterations is acceptable and valuable in practical applications.

## 32.5 Conclusion

We present a novel iterative smoothing algorithm called T-Base for planar and surface quad meshes based on virtually dividing a quad element into a pair of triangles by its diagonal. We relocate a node by making all of the incident virtual triangles be equilateral right triangles separately, and then weighting all separate smoothed positions. According to the determination of weights based on length of relevant edges, three variants of T-Base are produced. The T-Base is applied on planar and surface quad meshes, and compared with Laplacian smoothing. The Vari.1 of T-Base is effectively identical to Laplacian smoothing for planar quad meshes, while Vari.2 and 3 are better. For the quad mesh on a underlying parametric surface, Vari.2 is the best; and Vari.1 is the best for the quad mesh on a interpolation surface. Tests also show that T-Base always converges for planar meshes.

**Acknowledgments** This research was supported by the Natural Science Foundation of China (Grant Numbers 40602037 and 40872183) and the Fundamental Research Funds for the Central Universities of China.

## References

1. Field DA (1988) Laplacian smoothing and Delaunay triangulation. Commun Appl Numer Meth 4:709–712
2. Herrman LR (1976) Laplacian-isoparametric grid generation scheme. J Eng Mech EM5:749–756
3. Zhou T, Shimada K (2000) An angle-based approach to two-dimensional mesh smooth-ing. In: Proceedings of 9th international meshing roundtable, pp 373–384
4. Vartziotis D, Wipper J (2009) The geometric element transformation method for mixed mesh smoothing. Eng Comput 25:287–301
5. Shimada K (1997) Anisotropic triangular meshing of parametric surfaces via close packing of ellipsoidal bubbles. In: Proceedings of 6th international meshing roundtable, pp 375–390
6. Escobar JM, Montenegro R, Rodriguez E, Montero G (2011) Simultaneous aligning and smoothing of surface triangulations. Eng Comput 27:17–29
7. Wang J, Yu Z (2009) A novel method for surface mesh smoothing: applications in biomedical modeling. In: Proceedings of 18th international meshing roundtable, pp 195–210
8. Jiao X, Wang D, Zha H (2011) Simple and effective variational optimization of surface and volume triangulations. Eng Comput 27:81–94
9. Knupp PM (2010) Introducing the target-matrix paradigm for mesh optimization via node-movement. In: Proceedings of 19th international meshing roundtable, pp 67–83

10. Canann SA, Tristano JR, Staten ML (1998) An approach to combined Laplacian and optimization-based smoothing for triangular, quadrilateral and quad-dominant meshes. In: Proceedings of 7th international meshing roundtable, pp 479–494
11. Chen Z, Tristano JR, Kwok W (2003) Combined Laplacian and optimization-based smoothing for quadratic mixed surface meshes. In: Proceedings of 12th international meshing roundtable, pp 361–370
12. Freitag LA (1997) On combining Laplacian and optimization-based mesh smoothing techniques. AMD trends in unstructured mesh generation. ASME 220:37–43
13. Shivanna K, Grosland N, Magnotta V (2010) An analytical framework for quadrilateral surface mesh improvement with an underlying triangulated surface definition. In: Proceedings of 19th international meshing roundtable, pp 85–102
14. Hua L (1995) Automatic generation of quadrilateral mesh for arbitrary planar domains. Ph.D. thesis, Dalian University of Technology, China (in Chinese)
15. Owen SJ, Staten ML, Canann SA, Saigal S (1999) Q-Morph: an indirect approach to advancing front quad meshing. Int J Numer Meth Eng 44(9):1317–1340
16. Chiles JP, Delfiner P (2012) Geostatistics: modeling spatial uncertainty, 2nd edn. Wiley-Interscience, New York

# Chapter 33
# A High Efficient Real-Time Look-Ahead NURBS Interpolator

Jianhua Hu, Yunkuan Wang, Hui Wang and Ze Zong

**Abstract** In this paper, a novel non-uniform rational B-spline (NURBS) interpolator is proposed and implemented. This interpolator considers chord errors, feedrate fluctuations and acceleration/deceleration capabilities of the machine. And by introducing the improved S curve Acc/Dec feedrate control algorithm, recursive look-ahead algorithm and dual-port queue, it ensures a high machining accuracy and real-time performance. The advantages of the algorithm were confirmed by the simulation and analyses.

**Keywords** CNC · NURBS · Look-ahead · Parametric interpolator

## 33.1 Introduction

More and more modern CAD/CAM systems adapt parametric curves to represent complex shapes such as dies, vanes, moulds. But most traditional computer numerical control (CNC) systems provide only linear (G01) and circular (G02, G03) interpolators. CAM systems have to divide the curves into a large number of small linear or circular segments to approximate the original curves before sending them to the CNC systems. The CNC systems generate the final trajectories to control the servo. However the traditional interpolator has the following disadvantages:

J. Hu (✉) · Y. Wang · H. Wang
High-tech Innovation Center, Institute of Automation, Chinese Academy of Sciences, Beijing, China
e-mail: hujianhua.jianhua@163.com

Z. Zong
School of Communication and Information Engineering, University of Electronic Science and Technology of China, Chengdu, Sichuan Province, China

W. Lu et al. (eds.), *Proceedings of the 2012 International Conference on Information Technology and Software Engineering*, Lecture Notes in Electrical Engineering 212, DOI: 10.1007/978-3-642-34531-9_33, © Springer-Verlag Berlin Heidelberg 2013

- High accuracy result in shorter segments, hence a large number of data transferred between CAD and CNC systems.
- Motion speed becomes unsmooth because the discontinuous at the junction of two connected line segments.
- Speed discontinuity cause CNC system vibration.

To overcome the drawbacks, various parametric interpolation algorithms have been proposed. Bedi et al. [1] developed a constant parameter increment interpolator for B-Spline curves. Shpitalni et al. [2] proposed the first-order interpolation algorithm based on truncated Taylor's expansion. Yang et al. [3] proposed the second-order Taylor's expansion interpolation algorithm. Yeh et al. [4] developed the speed-controlled interpolator. But all the algorithms didn't consider chord error. Yeh et al. [5] proposed an adaptive interpolation algorithm to generate feedrate according confined chord error. Cheng et al. [6] compared different numerical algorithms and suggested second-order Taylor expansion as a good choice between computation time and geometry precision. Mei Zhang et al. [7] proposed an optimal B-Spline interpolator. But it needed computing VLC and switching point. R.Z. Xu et al. [8] developed a look-ahead interpolation algorithm. But they only considered the situation which the feedrate of the deceleration point is equal to the command feedrate.

In this paper, a real-time acceleration and jerk limited adaptive interpolator with look-ahead module is proposed and implemented. Instead of searching deceleration points off-line, it determines deceleration point by recursively searching the feedrate sensitive points queue on line. And by using an improved S curve Acc/Dec profile algorithm, the calculation time is shortened and the feedrate profile is smoother. Furthermore, the introduction of dual-port queue can improve real-time performance greatly.

## 33.2 NURBS Interpolator

The NURBS interpolator mainly includes two modules: look-ahead module and parameter interpolation module.

### 33.2.1 Look-Ahead Module

The look-ahead module detects the feedrate sensitive points of the curve and removes pseudo deceleration points in order to achieve high-precision machining. It consists of two parts: searching feedrate sensitive points and calculating deceleration points.

### 33.2.1.1 Adaptive Feedrate Respect to Chord Error

In CNC systems, there are two main errors: radial error and chord error. Radial error is mainly caused by rounding off in computation process and can be eliminated with higher computation precision. In modern CNC systems, with more powerful CPU, it is no longer a problem. Chord error is caused by the interpolation and is the main error source. In this paper, a circle approximation is applied to determine the relation between the chord error and the curve feedrate [5].

The approximated chord length is

$$L_i = v_i T_s \tag{33.1}$$

So the chord error $ER_i$ is derived as

$$ER_i = \rho_i - \sqrt{\rho_i^2 - \left(\frac{L_i}{2}\right)^2} \tag{33.2}$$

The speed corresponding to the chord error $ER_i$ is

$$v_l(u_i) = \frac{2}{T_s}\sqrt{\rho_i^2 - (\rho_i - ER_i)^2} \tag{33.3}$$

where $\rho_i = 1/K_i$ is the radius of curvature at parameter $u = u_i$ and the curvature $K_i$ is

$$K_i = \left\|\frac{C_x'(u_i) \cdot C_y''(u_i) - C_y'(u_i) \cdot C_x''(u_i)}{\|C(u_i)\|^3}\right\| \tag{33.4}$$

Assuming the allowed chord is $ER_i$, the feedrate limit can be obtained by

$$v_l(u_i) = \begin{cases} F, & \text{if } \frac{2}{T_s}\sqrt{\rho_i^2 - (\rho_i - ER_i)^2} > F \\ \frac{2}{T_s}\sqrt{\rho_i^2 - (\rho_i - ER_i)^2}, & \text{if } \frac{2}{T_s}\sqrt{\rho_i^2 - (\rho_i - ER_i)^2} \leq F \end{cases} \tag{33.5}$$

where F is the commanded feedrate.

The extreme points of the adaptive feedrate profile are the feedrate sensitive points.

### 33.2.1.2 Improved S Acc/Dec Profile Algorithm

Because the traditional S curve Acc/Dec feedrate control algorithm [9] has complex calculation process, an improved S curve Acc/Dec control algorithm is introduced. First, the threshold feedrate is defined as

$$V_{th} = V_{max} - A_{max}t_m, \tag{33.6}$$

where $V_{max}$ is the command feedrate and $t_m = A_{max}/J$, where J is the maximal jerk.

There are four cases for the improved S curve Acc/Dec algorithm:

Both maximal acceleration and maximal deceleration can be reached ($V_s < V_{th}$, $V_e < V_{th}$).

In this case, there are two possible planning profiles. If the following inequality is satisfied:

$$L \geq \frac{V_{max}^2}{A_{max}} - \frac{1}{2A_{max}}\left(V_s^2 + V_e^2\right) + \frac{1}{2}(2V_{max} + V_s + V_e)t_m \qquad (33.7)$$

The curve is long enough for reaching the maximal feedrate. The parameter can be calculated by normal segments algorithm [9].

If Eq. (33.7) is not satisfied, the curve is very short and would be processed by short segments algorithm [9].

Maximal acceleration can be reached, while maximal deceleration can't be reached ($V_s < V_{th}$, $V_e \geq V_{th}$).

In this case, there are two possible planning profiles. If the following inequality is satisfied:

$$L \geq \frac{1}{2}(V_{max} + V_s)\left(t_m + \frac{V_{max} - V_s}{A_{max}}\right) + 2V_{max}T_5 - JT_5^3 \qquad (33.8)$$

where $T_5$ is

$$T_5 = \sqrt{\frac{V_{max} - V_e}{J}} \qquad (33.9)$$

The curve is long enough for reaching the maximal feedrate. The parameter can be calculated by normal segments algorithm.

If Eq. (33.8) is not satisfied, the curve would be processed by short segments algorithm.

Maximal deceleration can be reached, while maximal acceleration can't be reached ($V_s \geq V_{th}$, $V_e < V_{th}$).

In this case, there are two possible planning profiles. If the following inequality is satisfied:

$$L \geq \frac{1}{2}(V_{max} + V_e)\left(t_m + \frac{V_{max} - V_e}{A_{max}}\right) + 2V_sT_1 - JT_1^3 \qquad (33.10)$$

where

$$T_1 = \sqrt{\frac{V_{max} - V_s}{J}} \qquad (33.11)$$

The curve is long enough for reaching the maximal feedrate. The parameter can be calculated by normal segments algorithm.

If Eq. (33.10) is not satisfied, the curve would be processed by short segments algorithm.

None of maximal acceleration or maximal deceleration can be reached ($V_s \geq V_{th}$, $V_e \geq V_{th}$).

In this case, there are two possible planning profiles. If the following inequality is satisfied:

$$L \geq 2V_s T_1 + JT_1^3 + 2V_{max} T_5 - JT_5^3 \tag{33.12}$$

where

$$T_1 = \sqrt{\frac{V_{max} - V_s}{J}}, T_5 = \sqrt{\frac{V_{max} - V_e}{J}} \tag{33.13}$$

The curve is long enough for reaching the maximal feedrate. The parameter can be calculated by normal segments algorithm.

If Eq. (33.12) is not satisfied, the curve would be processed by short segments algorithm.

### 33.2.1.3 Look-Ahead Algorithm

In the look-ahead module, a series of interpolation parameters (feedrate, u parameter, cumulative chord length) will be calculated step by step using adaptive-feedrate interpolation. The speed sensitive point can be found and actual deceleration point can be determined. The look-ahead algorithm is given as follows:

1. Add the first point of curve as a feedrate sensitive point to the feedrate sensitive queue.
2. Calculate $V_i$ using Eq. (33.5) and $u_{i+1}$ using second-order Taylor's expansion. Once the feedrate sensitive point is founded, add the point to the feedrate sensitive queue and enter the recursive module. If the calculation reaches the end of the curve, go to (3), else go to (2).
3. Add the end point of curve as a feedrate sensitive point to the feedrate sensitive queue.

The recursive module algorithm is described as follows:

1. Calculate the improved S feedrate planning profile between two successive feedrate sensitive points in the feedrate sensitive queue. If the distance is too short for deceleration, go to (2). If the distance is too short for acceleration, go to (3). Otherwise add the planning profile to the interpolation dual-port queue and exit the recursive module.
2. Delete the last but one feedrate sensitive point (pseudo deceleration point) from the queue, and go to (1).
3. Delete the last one feedrate sensitive point (pseudo acceleration point) and go to (1).

## 33.2.2 Interpolation Module

The interpolation module gets the planning profile from look-ahead module and generates command feedrate for CNC machine, the interpolation algorithm is given as follows:

Get planning profile from the dual-port queue and remove the first profile.

Calculate the command feedrate and send it to the CNC machine.

Calculate the next u by second-order Taylor's expansion. If reaching the end point, then interpolation is finished, else go to (1).

## 33.3 Experiment and Analyses

### 33.3.1 Experiment

The interpolator is written in C++ and executed on a personal computer with 2 GHz AMD CPU. The present interpolator is applied to a NURBS parametric curve with two degrees as shown in Fig. 33.1. The control points are {0, 0}, {−150, −150}, {−150, 150}, {0, 0}, {150, −150}, {150, 150} and {0, 0} (mm). The weight vector is {1, 25, 25, 1, 25, 25, 1}. The knot vector is {0, 0, 0, 0.25, 0.5, 0.5, 0.75, 1, 1, 1}. The maximal allowable chord error is $\sigma = 0.1$ μm. The sampling time is $T_s = 0.001$ s. The command feedrate is $F = 200$ mm/s. The maximal acceleration and deceleration is $A_{max} = 1,000$ mm/s$^2$. The maximal jerk is $J = 10,000$ mm/s$^3$.

As Fig. 33.2a and b shown, the variation of jerk falls in the range of CNC system parameters and the acceleration profile is continuous and never exceeds the system limit. From Fig. 33.2 c, it can be seen the feedrate is very smooth. Fig. 33.2d is the resulting chord error; it is constrained under the 0.1 μm.

Figure 33.3 shows the adaptive feedrate and the proposed algorithm feedrate respecting to parameter u. It can be seen the feedrate decreases at the high curvature to improve the contour precision in the proposed algorithm and the feedrate has no fluctuation.

**Fig. 33.1** Example curve

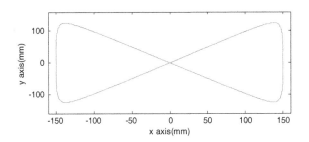

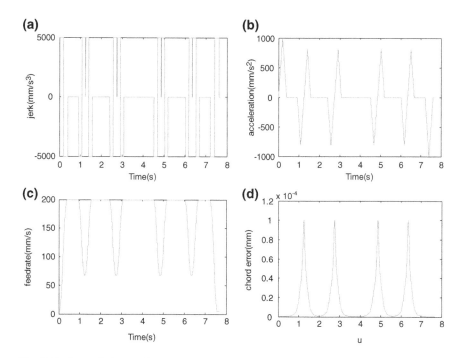

**Fig. 33.2** Interpolation results

**Fig. 33.3** Adaptive feedrate and S Acc/Dec feedrate

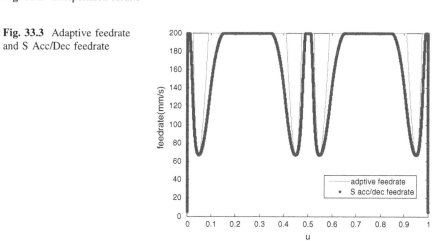

## 33.3.2  Real-Time Performance

In order to realize a real-time command generator, the time consumed by one interpolation must be less than sampling interval of the servo systems. As Table 33.1 shows, the average total time for a step is 0.114 ms. Considering the sampling time is 1 ms, it is feasible to implement this interpolator in real-time application.

**Table 33.1** Machining time

|               | Interpolation steps (ms) | Total time (ms) | Time per step (ms) |
| ------------- | ------------------------ | --------------- | ------------------ |
| Look-ahead    | 7,680                    | 344             | 0.045              |
| Interpolation | 7,680                    | 531             | 0.069              |
| Total         | 7,680                    | 875             | 0.114              |

## 33.4 Conclusions

An efficient real-time look-ahead NURBS interpolator with confined jerk, acceleration and chord error is proposed and implemented. By introducing dual-port queue and improved S Acc/Dec profile algorithm, no pre-processing is needed and the resulting feedrate profile is smooth. Furthermore, the look-ahead module's recursive character can remove pseudo deceleration point and provide the best accuracy. The simulation and real-time performance shows its effectiveness of the proposed interpolator.

## References

1. Bedi S, Ali I, Quan N (1993) Advanced techniques for CNC machines. Trans ASME J Eng Ind 115:329–336
2. Shpitalni M, Koren Y, Lo CC (1994) Real-time curve interpolators. Comput Aided Des 26(11):832–838
3. Yang DCH, Kong T (1994) Parametric interpolator versus linear interpolator for precision CNC machining. Comput Aided Des 26(3):225–234
4. Yeh SS, Hsu PL (1999) The speed-controlled interpolator for machining parametric curves. Comput Aided Des 31(5):349–357
5. Yeh SS, Hs u PL (2002) Adaptive-feedrate interpolation for parametric curves with a confined chord error. Comput Aided Design 34:229–237
6. Cheng MY, Tsai MC, Kuo JC (2002) Real-time NURBS command generators for CNC servo controllers. Int J Mach Tools Manuf 42:801–813
7. Zhang Mei, Yan Wei, Yuan ChunMing, Wang DingKang, Gao XiaoShan (2011) Curve fitting and optimal interpolation on CNC machines based on quadratic B-splines. Sci China Inf Sci 54:1407–1418
8. Xu RZ, Xie L, Li CX, Du DS (2008) Adaptive parametric interpolation scheme with limited acceleration and jerk values for nc machining. Int J Adv Manuf Technol 36:343–354
9. Guo XG (2002) High-speed high-precision interpolation technology for high-speed cutting. Shanghai Jiao Tong University, Shanghai (in Chinese)

# Chapter 34
# A Combinatorial Pruning Algorithm for Voronoi Skeletonization

Hongzhi Liu, Zhonghai Wu, Xing Zhang and D. Frank Hsu

**Abstract** Voronoi skeletons have been used extensively in image processing and analysis due to its fast computation and good properties. However, they are very sensitive to boundary noise which may cause a large number of insignificant branches that need to be pruned. Commonly used measurements of significance can be divided into two types: local and global. Local measurements of significance are context-aware but sensitive to noise. Global measurements of significance are robust to noise but unaware of context information. In this paper, we propose a combinatorial branch pruning algorithm that integrates both local and global measurements. Experimental results show that the proposed method is stable with different shapes and robust to boundary noise.

**Keywords** Voronoi skeleton · Skeleton pruning · Visual significance · Reconstruction significance

H. Liu · X. Zhang
School of Electronics Engineering and Computer Science, Peking University,
100871 Beijing, China
e-mail: liuhzhi@gmail.com

X. Zhang
e-mail: zhx@pku.edu.cn

Z. Wu (✉)
School of Software and Microelectronics, Peking University, 102600 Beijing, China
e-mail: wuzh@pku.edu.cn

D. Frank Hsu
Department of Computer and Information Science, Fordham University,
New York, NY 10023, USA
e-mail: hsu@trill.cis.fordham.edu

W. Lu et al. (eds.), *Proceedings of the 2012 International Conference on Information Technology and Software Engineering*, Lecture Notes in Electrical Engineering 212, DOI: 10.1007/978-3-642-34531-9_34, © Springer-Verlag Berlin Heidelberg 2013

## 34.1 Introduction

Skeleton, defined as the set of centers of all maximal inscribed disks in the shape, is a compact and efficient representation of the shape [1]. It has been used in diverse applications such as object recognition and segmentation, image compression and retrieval, and analysis of scientific and medical images. Since the first definition of skeleton by Blum [1], different methods have been proposed to extract skeletons from 2D shapes. Among these methods, skeletonization based on Voronoi diagram is attractive due to efficiency and it is able to capture the important properties of connectivity as well as Euclidean metrics [2–4]. Voronoi skeleton of a shape is a part of the Voronoi diagram of the sampling points on the shape boundary, which is inside the shape region and excludes the Voronoi edges separating adjacent sampling points [4]. The Voronoi skeleton will converge to the exact skeleton when sampling rate increases.

Voronoi skeletons are extremely sensitive to boundary noise. One way to reduce the effect of noise is to enlarge the sampling step [5]. The accuracy of the approximated skeleton is determined by the selection of sampling points [4]. In discrete space, we can take all the contour pixels as sites to ensure the accuracy of the result. However, this will generate a large number of noisy branches.

Skeleton pruning has been an actively studied problem [5–9]. The main difficulty is lack of standard characterization for the significance of a branch. The original idea of skeleton pruning is to remove the unwanted branches caused by noise or small perturbations and only retain the portion of skeleton arising from the uncorrupted shape [8, 10]. However, it is difficult to identify the uncorrupted shape for a general shape in prior. The significance of a branch is usually evaluated based on a number of factors, including the area of residual and the bending of its corresponding boundary. For example, if removing a branch leads to significant increase of the residual area in the difference between the original shape and the reconstructed shape from the skeleton, this branch is deemed as significant.

There are two types of measurement for the significance of skeleton branches: local and global. Local measurements of significance consider only the information from a small neighborhood around the branch and ignore the global information of the shape. They are often context-aware, but they are also very sensitive to noise and may take some noisy branches as significant ones especially at the thin parts. Global measurements of significance consider the impact of removing a branch on the overall shape of the object. They are robust to noise. But they are unaware of the local context information and may take some significant local deformation as noise.

In this paper, we integrate both local and global measurements of significance by harnessing both of their advantages while avoiding their disadvantages. We define, in Sect. 34.2, a local significance measurement based on visual characteristics, a global significance measurement based on reconstruction characteristics and the combination of both visual and reconstruction significance. Section 34.3

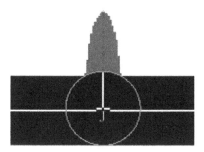

**Fig. 34.1** An example of the residual part of a skeleton branch. J is the junction point and the green circle is the boundary of the maximal disk centered at *J*. The red dash line is the residual part of the branch. The grey region is the residual shape area for the skeleton branch as it can only be reconstructed by this branch

gives the algorithm for skeletonization and pruning which is shown to be stable with different shapes and robust to boundary noise.

## 34.2 Measurement of Branch Significance

### 34.2.1 Local Visual Characteristics

Each skeleton branch corresponds to a sub-part of the object which is attached to the rest of the object at the maximal disk of its adjacent junction point (Fig. 34.1). We can measure the local significance of a branch by its relationship to the maximal disk centered at its adjacent junction point. Different from bending potential ratio [7], which measures the significance by approximating the bending ratio of the corresponding contour segment of a branch, we measure local visual significance by the ratio of residual branch length to the radius of the maximal disk at its adjacent junction point (a measurement of the protrusion ratio of the object part) (Fig. 34.1).

Let $B$ be a branch of skeleton $SK$, $J(B)$ be the junction point at which the branch $B$ attaches to the rest of the skeleton, $D(p)$ be the maximal disk centered at point $p$, $r(p)$ be the radius of $D(p)$.

**Definition 1** Let $l(X)$ be the length of $X$ and $l_{residual}(B)$ be the length of the residual part of the branch $B$ that is outside of $D(J(B))$, i.e.

$$l_{residual}(B) = l(B - B \cap D(J(B)))$$

The *local visual significance* of $B$ is defined as the ratio of $l_{residual}(B)$ to $r(J(B))$, i.e.

$$m_{vs}(B) = l_{residual}(B)/r(J(B)). \tag{34.1}$$

## 34.2.2 Global Reconstruction Characteristics

When we measure the global significance of a branch, we need to have a unified
base for the measurement of all branches. We can take the whole contour length as
the base, and measure the global significance by the ratio of the short contour
segment to the whole contour length [6]. We can also take the whole shape area as
the base and measure the global significance by the ratio of the branch area to the
whole shape area. Area is chosen as the global significance measurement to
measure the global reconstruction significance of a branch in the skeleton
(Fig. 34.1).

**Definition 2** Let $a(g)$ be the area of a region $g$. The reconstruction area of $B$ is the
area of the region that can only be reconstructed by $B$, i.e.

$$a_r(B) = a(\bigcup_{p \in SK} D(p)) - a(\bigcup_{p \in SK-B} D(p))$$

The *global reconstruction significance* of $B$ is defined as the ratio of $a_r(B)$ to
$a_r(SK)$, i.e.

$$m_{rs}(B) = a_r(B)/a_r(SK). \tag{34.2}$$

## 34.2.3 Combination of Visual and Reconstruction Characteristics

We integrate the local visual significance and global reconstruction significance
into one combined significance measurement by using the following formula:

$$m_{cs}(B) = w \cdot e^{f(m_{vs}(B),t_{vs})-1} + (1 - w) \cdot e^{f(m_{rs}(B),t_{rs})-1}, \tag{34.3}$$

where $f(x,t) = \begin{cases} x/t, & x < t \\ 1, & otherwise \end{cases}$, $w$ is a weight to denote trade-off between visual

significance and reconstruction significance, $t_{vs}$ and $t_{rs}$ are the thresholds for visual
significance and reconstruction significance respectively. When $m_{vs}(B)$ (or $m_{rs}(B)$) is
larger than $t_{vs}$(or $t_{rs}$), the branch $B$ is viewed to be significant according to local visual
significance (or global reconstruction significance).

Both local visual significance and global reconstruction significance are
invariant under translation, rotation and scaling. The combined significance is also
invariant under translation, rotation and scaling.

## 34.3 Algorithm for Skeletonization and Pruning

Our algorithm first computes the Voronoi skeleton by using all contour pixels as
sites. Then we prune the skeleton by using the combined significant measurement.

**Algorithm A:**

Set $t_{cs}$ and $t_N$ as a real number and an integer.

Step1. Compute the Voronoi diagram by taking all contour pixels as sites

Step2. Remove the Voronoi edges not wholly contained in the shape, i.e. at least one of its ends is outside of the shape.

Step3. Calculate the combined significance $m_{cs}(B)$ for each branch using Eq. (34.3).

Step4.

> Step4.1. Remove the branch with the lowest combined significance
>
> Step4.2. Update the combined significance for retained branches
>
> Step4.3. If (a) the lowest combined significance is smaller than the threshold $t_{cs}$ OR (b) the number of remaining branches is larger than the threshold $t_N$
> Go to Step 4.1,
> Otherwise STOP.

## 34.3.1 Implementation

The computation of the exact reconstruction area for each branch is a task of high computation cost. Each time we remove a branch, the reconstruction area of other branches may be affected and need to be recalculated. Instead of computing the exact reconstruction area for each branch, we approximate them. For each Voronoi edge, we approximate its reconstruction area by a trapezoid with two bottom edges' length as $2r_i$ and $2r_j$, where $r_i$ and $r_j$ are the radius length of the two maximal disks centered at the two end points.

To calculate the local visual significance and global reconstruction significance of an end branch, we trace back from its end point along the skeleton until it meets the maximal disk centered at the adjacent junction point, and accumulate the length of the path and the reconstruction area by the path.

We separately use the two stop criteria (Step 4.3). If we know the number of branches in prior, we can use it as the stop criterion and ignore the threshold for significance ($t_{cs}$). Otherwise, we recommend using the threshold of significance as the stop criterion.

## 34.3.2 Experiments

To evaluate the performance of the skeletonization and pruning method, we tested and compared it with other existing methods using shapes from MPEG-7 dataset. We first examine the stability of the proposed method for different kinds of objects, and its robustness with boundary noise. Then we compare our method

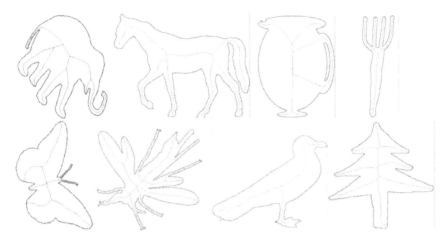

**Fig. 34.2** Results using our approach (*Algorithm A*) for different object shapes in MPEG-7 dataset

**Fig. 34.3** Pruning results using our approach (*Algorithm A*) for shapes with boundary noise in MPEG-7 dataset. **a** are shapes with boundary noise, and **b** are shapes with no noise used for comparison

with two other pruning methods. One is based on discrete curve evolution of shape boundary [11], which is a leading pruning method proposed by Bai et al. [6]. The other is based on the evaluation of chord residual for each Voronoi edge [3].

In all our initial experiments in this paper, the default parameter values are set as follows: $w = 0.5$, $t_{vs} = 1.0$, $t_{rs} = 0.5\,\%$. If we use only significance

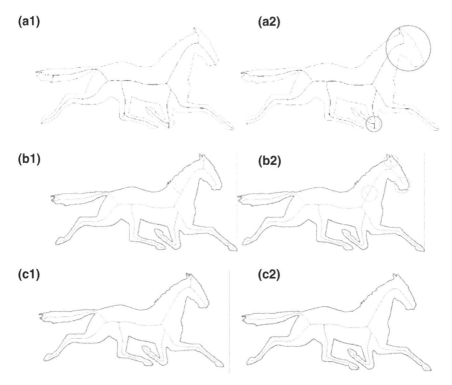

**Fig. 34.4** Comparison between **a** the results by DCE Pruning [6], **b** pruning based on chord residual [3], and **c** ours approach for the same shape. N is a control parameter of DCE pruning, which specify the number of vertices in the simplified boundary polygon [6]. T is the threshold for chord residual [3]. (a1) N = 20, (b1) T = 10.0 , (c1) $t_N$ = 10. (a2) N = 10, (b2) T = 20.0, (c2) $t_N$ = 6

measurement as stop criterion, we set $t_N = 0$ and $t_{cs} = 0.68 \approx (e^0 + e^{-1})/2$ as default value. If we use only branch number as stop criterion, we set $t_{cs}$ as positive infinite.

The results for several selected shapes from MPEG-7 dataset are shown in Figs. 34.2 and 34.3. The results demonstrate that our method is stable for different shapes and robust to boundary noise. Results in Fig. 34.2 are for shapes of different objects. These results show that our method can extract accurate and succinct skeleton for different shapes and it can deal with shapes containing holes correctly. Figure 34.3 contains some results for shapes with boundary noise. The results are clean without the unnecessary branches that may easily be induced by the boundary noise. The results thus have similar skeleton graphs with those generated using shapes with no noise.

Figure 34.4 shows the results for a shape by using DCE pruning [6], pruning based on chord residual [3] and our method (Algorithm A) with different parameters. DCE pruning is good at removing most of noisy branches (Fig. 34.4a1). However, it may remove some significant branches prior to the removal of insignificant ones (the parts indicated by green circles in Fig. 34.4a2). Pruning based on chord residual shortens some significant branches which should keep unchanged, and it can not remove the insignificant ones completely (such as the parts indicated by green circles in Fig. 34.4b2). In contrast, our method ensures removal of the insignificant branches first and it removes the whole of each insignificant branch completely while keeping the significant branches unchanged.


## 34.4 Conclusion and Future Work

In this paper, we present a combinatorial significance measurement for skeleton pruning which integrates both local and global significance measurement. We measure the local significance of a branch by its local visual characteristics, which is context aware. We measure the global significance by global reconstruction characteristics, which is insensitive to noise. The combined significance measurement is invariant under translation, rotation and scaling. Instead of evaluating the significance for each skeleton point, we measure the significance for each branch and remove the whole branch each time. This can avoid the problem of shortening some significant branches while removing insignificant branches caused by pruning skeleton point by point [3]. Experimental results demonstrate that our method is stable with different shapes and robust to boundary noise. More importantly, it ensures the higher priority of removing the insignificant branches. In the future work, we will explore the cases when the weight $w$ is different from 0.5. Moreover, experiments will be conducted using different sets of thresholds for $t_{vs}$, $t_{rs}$ and $t_{cs}$.

**Acknowledgments** This work of Hongzhi Liu and Zhonghai Wu is supported in part by National Key Technology R&D Program of China 2012BAH06B01 and 2012BAH18B04.


## References

1. Blum H (1967) A transformation for extracting new descriptors of shape. Models for the perception of speech and visual form. MIT Press, Cambridge, pp 363–380
2. Fabbri RL, Estrozi F, Costa LF (2002) On Voronoi diagrams and medial axes. J Math Imaging Vis 17:27–40
3. Ogniewicz RL, Kübler O (1995) Hierarchic voronoi skeletons. Pattern Recogn 28(3):343–359
4. Székely G (2008) Voronoi Skeletons. Medial Representations: Mathematics, Algorithms and Applications. 37:191–221
5. Beristain A, Graña M, Gonzalez AI (2012) A pruning algorithm for stable Voronoi skeletons. J Math Imaging Vis 42:225–237
6. Bai X, Latecki LJ, Liu WY (2007) Skeleton pruning by contour partitioning with discrete curve evolution. IEEE Trans Pattern Anal Mach Intell 29(3):449–462

7. Shen W, Bai X, Hu R, Wang HY, Latecki LJ (2011) Skeleton growing and pruning with bending potential ratio. Pattern Recogn 44(2):196–209
8. Ward AD, Hamarneh G (2010) The groupwise medial axis transform for fuzzy skeletonization and pruning. IEEE Trans Pattern Anal Mach Intell 32(6):1084–1096
9. Liu H, Wu Z, Hsu DF, Peterson BS, Xu D (2012) On the generation and pruning of skeletons using generalized Voronoi diagrams. Pattern Recogn Lett. doi:10.1016/j.patrec.2012.07.014
10. Shaked D, Bruckstein AM (1998) Pruning medial axes. Comput Vis Image Underst 69(2):156–169
11. Latecki LJ, Lakämper R (1999) Convexity rule for shape decomposition based on discrete contour evolution. Comput Vis Image Underst 73(3):441–454

# Chapter 35
# Three-Dimensional Geometric Invariant Construction from Images

Xiaodong Wang, Xiao Chen and Shanshan Qu

**Abstract** Geometric invariants have wide applications in computer vision. In most of existing methods, 3D invariants have been obtained from reconstruction, where fundamental matrices between image pairs should be firstly established. Consequently, additional computation errors are introduced during invariants construction. Moreover, it is very time consuming. In this paper, a novel method is proposed to calculate 3D projective invariants from images, without reconstruction. Furthermore, the represented framework is valid even when prior information about corresponding features is not enough for reconstruction. It has been verified in experiments that the proposed method is considerably accurate compared with ground truth, and more efficient compared with reconstruction based methods.

**Keywords** Geometric invariant · Object recognition · Reconstruction

## 35.1 Introduction

Geometric invariants have received growing attentions in the past 20 years [1–5], since they can provide reliable solutions for many applications, such as object recognition and image matching. Theoretically speaking, invariants of geometric configurations are with the property of remaining unchanged under certain kinds of transformations. For example, the separation of two points is invariant under

X. Wang · X. Chen (✉) · S. Qu
Research Institute of Computer Application, China Academy of Engineering Physics,
Mianyang, China
e-mail: derekx.c@gmail.com

W. Lu et al. (eds.), *Proceedings of the 2012 International Conference on Information Technology and Software Engineering*, Lecture Notes in Electrical Engineering 212, DOI: 10.1007/978-3-642-34531-9_35, © Springer-Verlag Berlin Heidelberg 2013

335

Euclidean transformation, but this is not true for similarity transformation. Generally speaking, invariants are derived from geometric configurations in same dimensional space, which implies only 2D invariants are available from image. However, in practice, 3D invariants are more helpful. They can provide more reliable features about objects, especially in the case where 3D surface can not be considered as planes. In most existing methods, 3D invariants have been obtained from reconstructed structure, where fundamental matrices between image pairs should be firstly established. Despite the fact that 3D invariants derived from images directly are more reliable, there are few works to construct 3D projective invariants from multiple images directly.

In this paper, a novel method is proposed to compute 3D projective invariants from images, without reconstructing 3D objects. In our method, the geometric configurations can consist of not only points but also lines. There are, to our knowledge, few works to compute 3D projective invariants of mixed sets of points and lines from images without 3D reconstruction. In [6], this problem has been mentioned in concept, but many details are left unsolved.

## 35.2 Related Works

Projective invariants are functions of certain geometric configurations and they remain unchanged under projective transformation, which is the most general transformation. Projective invariants are well known as effective tools for object recognition, model based object tracking and image matching [7–9]. Invariants are commonly derived from the geometric structures with the same dimension, so large set of lectures so far have been interested in getting 2D invariants from single image [10]. Though it has been indicated that there are no general 3D projective invariants from single view [11], they are available for some special geometric structures and objects with certain property [12–15]. For general geometric configurations, invariants are extracted from the reconstructed 3D structures in most of the proposed algorithms, using the fundamental matrix [16].

It is really an interesting task to compute 3D projective invariants directly from images without reconstruction [17–19]. Computationally, it is reasonable that the invariants which are derived from image features directly are more reliable than those ones which are based on the 3D object structure reconstruction. This is true because the estimation for reconstruction introduces additional error into the process of computing invariants.

Compared to image points, lines are more suitable for computing invariants from multiple views [20, 21]. The fact that computational error should be restrained to enhance the precision of invariant makes lines becoming better choice, because lines can be effectively detected from images with line detection algorithm, and their positions and orientations can be reliably determined by sets of points redundantly. In other words, lines are preferred because comparatively more accurate measurements of their locations can be expected. Furthermore, the redundancy of pixels form lines provides more desirable solutions to the corresponding problem.

Unfortunately, 3D projective invariants from lines are difficult to compute from images directly without additional information, because it is with high complexity. For example, 3D projective invariants from lines can be directly obtained from images with at least six lines in general positions, and nine images are required in this case. So it is not advisable. Methods are proposed to build line invariants in which case lines are in restricted positions [22]. But little work is done to deal with projective invariants of lines in general positions. Other methods are proposed to construct projective invariants from the mixed sets of point and lines in general positions, but fundamental matrix is still necessary [23]. Consequently, this paper is dedicated to the study of constructing 3D projective invariants from mixed configurations of points and lines without reconstruction, in order to achieve the trade-off between the complexity and the accuracy. In this paper, all the points and lines in 3D space are expected to be in general positions, and this means that there are no assumptions such as four 3D points staying in the same plane.

## 35.3  Relation Between 3D Features and Their Image Projections

In computer vision and image processing applications, image point is specified by 2 parameters, namely its horizontal and vertical coordinates. Similarly, 2 values must be provided to locate a line in image. These values and parameters can always be defined as the degree of freedom (DOF). For instance, a point is defined by 3 DOF and a line is by 4 in 3D space. Similarly, the DOF of geometric transformations is defined as the number of independent parameters of the transformation matrices. For example, the 3D projective transformation is expressed by a $4 \times 4$ matrix, in which case there are 15 independent ratios without considering the scaling, so the 3D projective transformation is defined by 15 DOF.

Given a geometric structure consists of points and lines, the relation between points in 3D space and their projections in images can be described as

$$\lambda_i \cdot p_i = C \times P \qquad (35.1)$$

where $C$ is the $3 \times 4$ projective camera model matrix with rank 3, $P_i$ and $p_i$ denote points in space and its projection in image respectively, and $\lambda_i$ is the arbitrary scaling factor which can not be zero.

Given line $L_i$ in 3D space and its image projection $l_i$, $Q_{i1}$ and $Q_{i2}$ are defined as two arbitrary points on $L_i$. Similarly, $q_{i1}$ and $q_{i2}$ are defined as corresponding points on $l_i$. The relations between $Q_{i1}$ and $q_{i1}$, $Q_{i2}$ and $q_{i2}$, can be achieved according to Eq. (35.1). Moreover, $q_{i1}$ and $q_{i2}$ are on the line $l_i$, so there are two equations as following.

$$q_{i1}^T \cdot l_i = 0, \; q_{i2}^T \cdot l_i = 0 \tag{35.2}$$

In this way, two equations about relation between $L_i$ and $l_i$ can be achieved. However, there is still one problem left about the DOF. In our framework, the relation between $L_i$ and $l_i$ are defined by the equations about $Q_{i1}$, $Q_{i2}$ and $l_i$. Totally, 6 DOF is available from $Q_{i1}$ and $Q_{i2}$, and 5 of them are independent without considering the scaling. But $L_i$ is defined by 4 DOF. So, there is a constraint equation about $Q_{i1}$ and $Q_{i2}$. It is a quadratic constraint as following

$$\left| Q_{i1} Q_{i2}^T - Q_{i2} Q_{i1}^T \right| = 0. \tag{35.3}$$

## 35.4 Computing 3D Invariants from Images

In the above section, discussion is focused on the relation construction between 3D feature and their image projections. Now, the detailed description of computing 3D projective invariants from multiple images is given. We will take a geometric configuration as instance, which consists of five points and one line.

Given five points $P_i$ ($i = 1, 2,...,5$) and one line $L_1$ in space, projective invariants can be defined as following [23]

$$I_1 = \frac{|L_1 P_1 P_3||P_1 P_2 P_5 P_4|}{|L_1 P_1 P_2||P_1 P_5 P_3 P_4|} \quad I_2 = \frac{|L_1 P_1 P_4||P_1 P_2 P_3 P_5|}{|L_1 P_1 P_2||P_1 P_5 P_3 P_4|}$$
$$I_3 = \frac{|L_1 P_2 P_4||P_1 P_2 P_3 P_5|}{|L_1 P_1 P_2||P_5 P_2 P_3 P_4|} \quad I_4 = \frac{|L_1 P_2 P_3||P_1 P_2 P_5 P_4|}{|L_1 P_1 P_2||P_5 P_2 P_3 P_4|} \tag{35.4}$$

where $|L_i P_j P_k| = |Q_{i1} Q_{i2} P_j P_k|$ for $Q_{i1}$ and $Q_{i2}$ are two arbitrary points on the line $L_i$ and $|\cdot|$ denotes determinant of the matrix, and the columns are homogeneous coordinates of the corresponding points.

The fifth point can be expressed as a linear combination of the first four points

$$P_5 = aP_1 + bP_2 + cP_3 + dP_4 \tag{35.5}$$

Similarly, the arbitrary two points $Q_{11}$ and $Q_{12}$ on the line $L_1$ can also be considered as the combinations of these four points

$$Q_{11} = a_1 P_1 + b_1 P_2 + c_1 P_3 + d_1 P_4$$
$$Q_{12} = a_2 P_1 + b_2 P_2 + c_2 P_3 + d_2 P_4 \tag{35.6}$$

So the invariants defined by Eq. (35.4) can be rewritten as

$$I_1 = -\frac{(b_1 d_2 - b_2 d_1)c}{(c_1 d_2 - c_2 d_1)b} \; 38; I_2 = \frac{(b_1 c_2 - b_2 c_1)d}{(c_1 d_2 - c_2 d_1)b}$$
$$I_3 = -\frac{(a_1 c_2 - a_2 c_1)d}{(c_1 d_2 - c_2 d_1)a} \; 38; I_4 = \frac{(a_1 d_2 - a_2 d_1)c}{(c_1 d_2 - c_2 d_1)a} \tag{35.7}$$

According to Eqs. (35.1), (35.5) and (35.6), the relation between the points in space and their image measurements can be defined as following

$$\lambda_5 p_5 38; = \lambda_1 a p_1 + \lambda_2 b p_2 + \lambda_3 c p_3 + \lambda_4 d p_4$$
$$\lambda_{11} q_{11} 38; = \lambda_1 a_1 p_1 + \lambda_2 b_1 p_2 + \lambda_3 c_1 p_3 + \lambda_4 d_1 p_4 \qquad (35.8)$$
$$\lambda_{12} q_{12} 38; = \lambda_1 a_2 p_1 + \lambda_2 b_2 p_2 + \lambda_3 c_2 p_3 + \lambda_4 d_2 p_4$$

For the geometric configuration of five points and one line, the distances from the points to the line are respectively measured as $h_i$ and the ratios of them can be described as

$$h_i / h_j = S_i / S_j \qquad (35.9)$$

where $S_k = |q_{11} q_{12} p_k|$ can be viewed as the twice of the triangular area formed by $q_{11}$, $q_{12}$ and $p_k$.

According to Eq. (35.8), $S_k$ can be viewed as the combination of different triangular areas formed by these points. For instance, $S_1$ can be rewritten as

$$\lambda_{11} \lambda_{12} S_1 = 38; \lambda_2 \lambda_3 (b_1 c_2 - b_2 c_1) m_{123}$$
$$38; + \lambda_2 \lambda_4 (b_1 d_2 - b_2 d_1) m_{124} + \lambda_3 \lambda_4 (c_1 d_2 - c_2 d_1) m_{134} \qquad (35.10)$$

where $m_{ijk} = |p_i p_j p_k|$.

There are five points in all, but the fifth point is not independent, which can be expressed as a linear combination of the other four, so $S_5$ is not independent. Totally, three equations similar with Eq. (35.10) can be defined. To eliminate $\lambda_{11}$ and $\lambda_{12}$, the first three equations divide the forth one and then three equations independent of $\lambda_{11}$ and $\lambda_{12}$ are available. In these three equations, there are five outlying parameters named $\lambda_i$ $(i = 1, \ldots, 5)$

According to Eq. (35.8), the triangular areas formed by the fifth point and other two points are measured and they can provide additional relations which can be used to eliminate $\lambda_i$. For instance, the area formed by the first, second and fifth point can be defined as

$$\lambda_5 m_{125} = \lambda_3 c m_{123} + \lambda_4 d m_{124} \qquad (35.11)$$

Similar to Eq. (35.11), other two independent equations can be derived. Now, there are six equations about five unknown parameters $\lambda_i$ in all. Finally, substituting all the $\lambda_i$, the only one equation independent of unknown parameter is available from each image.

$$h_2 h_4 m_{135} I_1 + h_2 h_3 m_{145} I_2 + h_1 h_3 m_{245} I_3$$
$$+ h_1 h_4 m_{235} I_4 + h_1 h_2 m_{345} I_5 + h_3 h_4 m_{125} = 0 \qquad (35.12)$$

where $I_5 = I_1 I_3 - I_2 I_4$ is derived from Eq. (35.3). According to Eq. (35.12), the 3D invariants defined by Eq. (35.4) can be computed directly from image measurements.

It should be mentioned that the 3D reconstruction can not be implemented with the prior corresponding features of five points and one line in multiple images, but the 3D features are still available in our framework. So the proposed method is valid with less prior information, compared with the reconstruction based methods. Furthermore, the accuracy and stability of our method will be shown in the following section.

## 35.5 Experiments

In following subsection, the proposed technique has been evaluated on both synthetic geometric configuration and real object. Experimental results will be given to demonstrate the stability and the accuracy of the presented method. First of all, the synthetic geometric configuration, which consists of five points and one line in general positions, is drawn by OpenGL. The five points are defined by following coordinates, (0,15,6), (2,5,5), (2,0,12), (6,15,5) and (−3,0,5). The line is defined by two points, (5,0,0) and (−5,20,0). Some synthetic pictures are shown in Fig. 35.1. The corresponding features between images are defined by different colors.

The true values of the projective invariants and computed invariants are shown in Table 35.1. $I_a$ denotes the average value of computed invariants.

The differences between computed invariants and true values are list in Table 35.2 to evaluate the accuracy and stability of computed invariants, where $\bar{m}$ and $\sigma$ denote mean value and variance respectively. It is evident that the invariant computed from synthetic image directly is with high accuracy and stability compared with the true values. The experiments are also implemented with the real scene images as shown in Fig. 35.2. The images of cars are taken and the corresponding points and lines are defined by SIFT algorithm [24].

The experimental results prove that the invariants extracted from images directly are more precise than the ones derived from reconstruction based method,

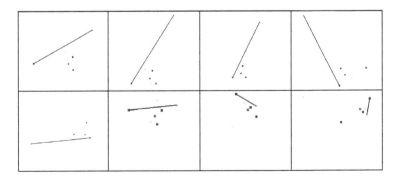

**Fig. 35.1** Synthetic images used in simulated experiments

**Table 35.1**  Computed invariants in simulated experiment

| Group | $I_1$ | $I_2$ | $I_3$ | $I_4$ |
|---|---|---|---|---|
| 1 | 0.3437 | 0.8332 | 0.2413 | 0.1982 |
| 2 | 0.3403 | 0.8276 | 0.2386 | 0.2011 |
| 3 | 0.3394 | 0.8405 | 0.2379 | 0.1987 |
| 4 | 0.3416 | 0.8291 | 0.2402 | 0.1923 |
| 5 | 0.3408 | 0.8328 | 0.2409 | 0.2054 |
| 6 | 0.3419 | 0.8295 | 0.2393 | 0.1922 |
| 7 | 0.3435 | 0.8334 | 0.2392 | 0.1957 |
| 8 | 0.3453 | 0.8321 | 0.2385 | 0.1988 |
| $I_d$ | 0.3421 | 0.8323 | 0.2395 | 0.1978 |
| True values | 0.3429 | 0.8312 | 0.2391 | 0.1973 |

**Table 35.2**  The accuracy and stability of computed invariant

| Group | $d_1$ (%) | $d_2$ (%) | $d_3$ (%) | $d_4$ (%) |
|---|---|---|---|---|
| 1 | 0.23 | 0.24 | 0.92 | 0.46 |
| 2 | 0.76 | 0.43 | 0.21 | 1.93 |
| 3 | 1.02 | 1.12 | 0.50 | 0.71 |
| 4 | 0.38 | 0.25 | 0.46 | 2.53 |
| 5 | 0.61 | 0.19 | 0.75 | 4.11 |
| 6 | 0.29 | 0.20 | 0.08 | 2.58 |
| 7 | 0.17 | 0.26 | 0.04 | 0.81 |
| 8 | 0.69 | 0.11 | 0.25 | 0.76 |
| $\bar{m}$ | 0.52 | 0.35 | 0.40 | 1.74 |
| $\sigma$ | 0.61 | 0.49 | 0.50 | 2.22 |

**Fig. 35.2**  Real images used in experiments

in the case of real scene, as shown in Table 35.3. The fact is that the accurate reconstruction is still considered as a challenge and our proposed algorithm avoids the reconstruction process. Therefore, it is much simpler and working more efficiently.

**Table 35.3** Computed invariants from real images

| Group | $I_1$ | $I_2$ | $I_3$ | $I_4$ |
|---|---|---|---|---|
| 1 | −0.9013 | −0.7977 | 0.168 | 0.7587 |
| 2 | −0.8967 | −0.7457 | 0.1403 | 0.7507 |
| 3 | −0.9024 | −0.7361 | 0.1365 | 0.7529 |
| 4 | −0.7899 | −0.7327 | 0.1399 | 0.7072 |
| 5 | −0.8043 | −0.6992 | 0.1329 | 0.7264 |
| 6 | −0.7851 | −0.6851 | 0.1264 | 0.7185 |
| 7 | −0.8165 | −0.7213 | 0.0951 | 0.6805 |
| 8 | −0.7895 | −0.6838 | 0.1154 | 0.7092 |
| $I_d$ | −0.8357 | −0.7252 | 0.1318 | 0.7255 |
| $I_r$ | −0.7657 | −0.7879 | 0.0985 | 0.6851 |
| $I_h$ | −0.8514 | −0.7456 | 0.1206 | 0.7303 |

## 35.6 Conclusion

Based on the study of existing methods in geometric invariants construction, a general methodology has been proposed to construct projective invariants under geometric configurations of points and lines in this paper. In particular, the numerical solution has been given under the geometric configurations of five points and one line in general space positions. Performances of our proposed algorithm have been intensively investigated, where the invariants calculated from multiple images directly are compared with those extracted from reconstruction based methods. The result show that our calculated invariant is considerably close to the true value. In experiment with synthetic image, projective invariants calculated from images directly are more accurate than those from reconstruction because of the computational bias introduced there. In the case where real scene images are used, since our method requires no reconstruction or fundamental matrix estimation, calculation of invariants is more efficient and with comparable performance.

## References

1. Weiss I (1993) Geometric invariants and object recognition. Int J Comput Vision 10:207–231
2. Wu YH, Hu ZY (2003) The invariant representations of a quadric cone and a twisted cubic. IEEE Trans Pattern Anal Mach Intell 25:1329–1332
3. Begelfor E, Werman M (2006) Affine invariance revisited. IEEE comput soc conf comp vision pattern recognit 2:2087–2094
4. Bayro-Corrochano E, Banarer V (2002) A geometric approach for the theory and applications of 3D projective invariants. J Math Imag Vision 16:131–154
5. Lasenby J, Bayro-Corrochano E, Lasenby AN, Sommer G (1996) A new framework for the formation of invariants and multiple-view constraints in computer vision. International conference on image processing 1:313–316

6. Maybank SJ (1998) Relation between 3D invariants and 2D invariants. Image Vis Comput 16:13–20
7. Sung-Woo L, Bum-Jae Y, Hager GD (1999) Model-based 3D object tracking using projective invariance. IEEE international conference on robotics and automation 2:1589–1594
8. Tico M, Rusu C, Kuosmanen P (1999) A geometric invariant representation for the identification of corresponding points. International conference on image processing 4: 462–466
9. Tsui HT, Zhang ZY, Kong SH (1997) Feature tracking from an image sequence using geometric invariants. IEEE computer society conference on computer vision and pattern recognition 1:244–249
10. Forsyth D, Mundy JL, Zisserman A, Coelho C, Heller A, Rothwell C (1991) Invariant descriptors for 3D object recognition and pose. IEEE Trans Pattern Anal Mach Intell 13: 971–991
11. Moses Y, Ullman S (1998) Generalization to novel views: universal, class-based, and model-based processing. Int J Comput Vision 29:233–253
12. Kyoung Sig R, Bume Jae Y, In So K (1998) 3D object recognition using projective invariant relationship by single-view. IEEE international conference on robotics and automation 4:3394–3399
13. Zhu Y, Seneviratne LD, Earles SWE (1995) A new structure of invariant for 3D point sets from a single view. IEEE international conference on robotics and automation 2:1726–1731
14. Weiss I, Ray M (2001) Model-based recognition of 3D objects from single images. IEEE Trans Pattern Anal Mach Intell 23:116–128
15. Basri R, Moses Y (1999) When is it possible to identify 3D objects from single images using class constraints. Int J Comput Vision 33:95–116
16. Csurka G, Faugeras O (1999) Algebraic and geometric tools to compute projective and permutation invariants. IEEE Trans Pattern Anal Mach Intell 21:58–64
17. Long Q (1995) Invariants of six points and projective reconstruction from three uncalibrated images. IEEE Trans Pattern Anal Mach Intell 17:34–46
18. Schaffalitzky I, Zisserman A, Hartley R, Torr P (2000) A six point solution for structure and motion. Lect Notes Comput Sci 1842:632–648
19. Yan X, Jia-Xiong P, Ming-Yue D, Dong-Hui X (1997) The unique solution of projective invariants of six points from four uncalibrated images. Pattern Recogn 30:513–517
20. Long Q, Kanade T (1997) Affine structure from line correspondences with uncalibrated affine cameras. IEEE Trans Pattern Anal Mach Intell 19:834–845
21. Weng J, Huang TS, Ahuja N (1992) Motion and structure from line correspondences; closed-form solution, uniqueness, and optimization. IEEE Trans Pattern Anal Mach Intell 14:318–336
22. Song BS, Lee KM, Lee SU (2001) Model-based object recognition using geometric invariants of points and lines. Comput Vis Image Underst 84:361–383
23. Lasenby J, Bayro-Corrochano E (1997) Computing 3D projective invariants from points and lines. Lect Notes Comput Sci 1296:82–89
24. Lowe DG (2004) Distinctive image features from scale-invariant keypoints. Int J Comput Vision 60:91–110

# Chapter 36
# A Novel (*k*, *n*) Visual Secret Sharing Scheme Based on Random Grids

Guanshi Zhong and Jianjun Wang

**Abstract** Visual secret sharing (VSS) is a kind of security communication technique. The drawback of the existing (*k*, *n*) VSS schemes is the visual quality of the reconstructed secret image decreases exponentially by increasing *n*. To enhance the visual quality of the revealed secret image, a novel (*k*, *n*) threshold visual secret sharing scheme based on random grids is proposed. The experimental results demonstrate the feasibility of the proposed scheme, and the comparison with previous scheme shows that the result of the proposed scheme is much better.

**Keywords** Visual cryptography · Visual secret sharing · Random grids · Contrast

## 36.1 Introduction

Visual cryptography (VC) was first proposed by Naor and Shamir [1] in 1994. It is a kind of visual secret sharing (VSS) technique which is free of computation during the decoding process. In the (*k*, *n*) VC scheme ($2 \leq k \leq n$), the secret image is encoded into *n* transparencies, called shares, only if at least *k* shares are superimposed together can reveal the secret image, but no information can be obtained by any less than *k* shares. The VC based scheme suffers the pixel expansion problem, which means that the revealed secret image is at least twice

G. Zhong · J. Wang (✉)
Department of Electronic Engineering, Fudan University, Rm. 603,
Henglong Physics Building, 220 Handan Rd, Shanghai, China
e-mail: wangjj@fudan.edu.cn

G. Zhong
e-mail: zhonggshi@163.com

W. Lu et al. (eds.), *Proceedings of the 2012 International Conference on Information Technology and Software Engineering*, Lecture Notes in Electrical Engineering 212, DOI: 10.1007/978-3-642-34531-9_36, © Springer-Verlag Berlin Heidelberg 2013

larger than the original secret image. The other drawback of VC based scheme is that an extra codebook has to be designed.

To solve the aforementioned problems, random grids (RG) introduced by Kafri and Keren [2] in 1987 regains attention of many researchers. Shyu proposed (2, 2) RG-based VSS [3] and (n, n) RG-based VSS scheme [4]. Then Chen and Tsao extended Kafri and Keren's methods to (2, n) and (n, n) VSS schemes [5]. After that Chen and Tsao [6] proposed a (k, n)-threshold VSS (2 ≤ k ≤ n) scheme based on random grids. The main advantage of VSS scheme based on random grids is that it can solve the pixel expansion problem and do not need any codebook designing. However, the visual quality of the reconstructed secret image is still problematic to recognize in either VC or RG based VSS schemes. Therefore, the research to improve the visual quality of VSS scheme is worthwhile.

In this paper, we propose a novel (k, n) RG-based visual secret sharing (RGVSS) scheme aiming at enhancing the visual quality of the revealed secret image, which is measured in terms of contrast.

## 36.2 Related Works

In this section, we briefly give a description of visual secret sharing scheme based on random grids.

The three basic similar algorithms for image encryption by RG were first presented by Kafri and Keren [2]. Firstly, a random grid $R_1$ is generated by randomly selecting each pixel 0 or 1 representing transparent or opaque, respectively. Then the other random grid $R_2$ is created by referring both the secret image $S$ and random grid $R_1$ according to one of the three versions which are summarized in Algorithm 1. Note that *rand_pixel* (0, 1) is a function that returns a binary value 0 or 1 representing a transparent or opaque pixel, respectively.

| **Algorithm 1** *RG(S)* |
| --- |
| **Input**: Secret image $S$ |
| **Output**: Shares $R_1$ and $R_2$ |
| 1. Generate $R_1$ as random grid |
| 2. **For** (each pixel $S(i,j)$) **do** |
| //**Version 1:** |
| **If** $(S(i,j) = 0)$   $R_2(i,j)=R_1(i,j)$ |
| **Else**           $R_2(i,j)=1-R_1(i,j)$ |
| //**Version 2:** |
| **If** $(S(i,j) = 0)$   $R_2(i,j)=R_1(i,j)$ |
| **Else**           $R_2(i,j)=rand\_pixel(0, 1)$ |
| //**Version 3:** |
| **If**$(S(i,j) = 0)$   $R_2(i,j)=rand\_pixel(0, 1)$ |
| **Else**           $R_2(i,j)=1-R_1(i,j)$ |
| 3. **End For** |

| **Algorithm 2** $(k, k)$-*RGVSS(S, k)* |
| --- |
| **Input**: Secret image $S$ and shares number $k$ |
| **Output**: Shares $R_q$ $(1 \le q \le k)$ |
| //1. Create $R_1$, $\tilde{R}_2$ as two random grids |
| $(R_1, \tilde{R}_2 )=RG(S)$ |
| //2. Create $R_2 \sim R_k$ as random grids recursively |
| **For** $q$=2 to $k$-1 |
| $(R_q, \tilde{R}_{q+1} )=RG(\tilde{R}_q )$ |
| **End For** |
| //3. Create $R_k$ as the last random grid |
| $R_k = \tilde{R}_k$ |

Based on Algorithm 1, $(k, k)$-*RGVSS* is proposed in [4] and [5]. The secret $S$ is split into two random grids $R_1$ and $\tilde{R}_2$. Subsequently, $\tilde{R}_2$ is split into two other random grids. Repeat this operation until the number of random grids is $k$. Algorithm 2 presents Chen and Tsao's method [5]. Note that throughout this paper, Algorithm 1 with Version 1 is used.

After the $(k, k)$-*RGVSS* scheme being proposed, Chen and Tsao proposed a $(k, n)$-*RGVSS* scheme of which the kernel is $(k, k)$-*RGVSS* scheme. The $(k, n)$-*RGVSS* scheme comprise three steps:

1. Encode a secret pixel $S(i, j)$ into $k$ sub-pixels $r_1(i, j), \ldots, r_k(i, j)$ by using $(k, k)$-*RGVSS* scheme.
2. The generated $k$ bits are dispatched into $k$ randomly selected random gird pixels
3. Lastly, the $(n - k)$ bits located in the same location $(i, j)$ of the remaining $(n - k)$ random grids are randomly generated.
4. Repeat step (1)–(3) until all secret pixels are processed.

To enhance the visual quality of the revealed secret image, a novel $(k, n)$ RG-based VSS scheme is proposed. In order to formally analyze the properties of random grids, the following definitions are given [3–5].

**Definition 1** (*Average light transmission*) For a certain pixel $s$ in a binary image $S$ whose size is $m \times n$, the probability of pixel color is transparent, say $Prob(s = 0)$, is represented as the light transmission of $s$, denoted as $l(s)$. The light transmission of white (resp. black) pixel is defined as $l(s) = 1$ (resp. $l(s) = 0$). And the average light transmission of $S$ is defined as

$$L(S) = \frac{\sum\limits_{i=1}^{m} \sum\limits_{j=1}^{n} l(S(i,j))}{m \times n} \tag{36.1}$$

**Definition 2** (*Contrast*) The contrast of the reconstructed binary secret image $S^{\Omega}$ with respect to the original secret image $S$ is

$$\alpha = \frac{L(S^{\Omega}[S(0)]) - L(S^{\Omega}[S(1)])}{1 + L(S^{\Omega}[S(1)])} \tag{36.2}$$

where $S^{\Omega} = R_1 \otimes \cdots \otimes R_q = \otimes_{1 \leq q \leq n} R_q$ and $\otimes$ denotes the "OR" operation which represents the superimposition of two random grids pixel by pixel.

## 36.3 Proposed Scheme

### 36.3.1 Algorithm of the Proposed $(k, n)$ RGVSS

The proposed $(k, n)$ RG-based visual secret sharing scheme comprises three phases:

1. Encode a secret pixel $S(i, j)$ into $k$ sub-pixels $r_1(i, j)$, ..., $r_k(i, j)$ by using $(k, k)$-*RGVSS* scheme.
2. Select $(n - k)$ bits independently from $r_q$ $(1 \leq q \leq k)$ at random.
3. Arrange all the $n$ pixels randomly and dispatch them into $R_1(i, j)$, ..., $R_n(i, j)$.
4. Repeat step (1)–(3) until all secret pixels are processed.

The main difference between the proposed $(k, n)$-*RGVSS* scheme and the scheme in [6] is the generation of $(n - k)$ bits. In the proposed scheme, the $(n - k)$ bits are independently and randomly selected from $\{r_1, r_2, ..., r_k\}$ indicating that the elements in $(n - k)$ bits can be repeated, but in the scheme of [6] the remaining $(n - k)$ bits are generated by the function *rand_pixel*(0, 1) which is used to randomly select 0 or 1. Algorithm 3 describes the proposed $(k, n)$-*RGVSS* scheme.

---

**Algorithm 3** $(k, n)$-*RGVSS*$(S, k, n)$

---

**Input**: Secret image $S$, threshold $k$, and shares number $n$
**Output**: Shares $R_q$ $(1 \leq q \leq n)$
1. **For** (each secret pixel $S(i, j)$) **do**
2.          $\{r_1, r_2 ... r_k\} = (k, k)$-*RGVSS* ( $S(i, j)$, $k$ )
3.      **For** (each bit of $(n-k)$ bits) **do**
4.              Select one pixel out of $\{r_1, r_2, ..., r_k\}$ at random
5.      **End For**
6.      Randomly permute all the $n$ bits and dispatch them into
           $R_1(i, j)$, ..., $R_n(i, j)$.
7. **End For**

---

To prove the security properties of the proposed $(k, n)$-*RGVSS* scheme, the following Lemma is presented.

**Lemma 1** [4, 6]. Upon stacking $p$ grid-pixels $b_{i_1}, b_{i_2}, \cdots, b_{i_p}$ generated from secret pixel $s$ in $S$ by Step 3.1 $(p < k)$ to form $b_{i_1 \otimes i_2 \otimes \cdots \otimes i_p} = b_{i_1} \otimes b_{i_2} \otimes \cdots \otimes b_{i_p}$, the stacked result with the light transmission

$$l\left(b_{i_1 \otimes i_2 \otimes ... \otimes i_p}[s(0)]\right) = l\left(b_{i_1 \otimes i_2 \otimes ... \otimes i_p}[s(1)]\right) = (1/2)^p \text{where, } p < k.$$

**Theorem 1** The proposed $(k, n)$-*RGVSS* scheme for binary secret images is as secure as Chen and Tsao's.

*Proof* In $(k, k)$-*RGVSS* scheme, the light transmissions of grid pixels $r_1, r_2, ...,$ and $r_k$ generated from the corresponding secret pixel $s$ in $S$ are 1/2, i.e., $l(r_i[s(0)]) = l(r_i[s(1)]) = 1/2$ $(i = 1, 2, ..., k)$ [5]. Since the $(n - k)$ bits are randomly and independently selected from $\{r_1, r_2 ... r_k\}$, the light transmissions of these grid pixels are the same as that of $r_1, r_2, ...,$ and $r_k$. Therefore, in the proposed $(k, n)$-*RGVSS* scheme, we have

$l(r_i[s(0)]) = l(r_j[s(0)]) = l(r_i[s(1)]) = l(r_j[s(0)]) = 1/2$, where $i \neq j$; $i, j = 1, 2,$ ..., $n$.

By Definition 1, we have
$l(R_i[S(0)]) = l(R_j[S(0)]) = l(R_i[S(1)]) = l(R_j[S(0)]) = 1/2$, where $i \neq j$; $i, j = 1,$
$2, \ldots, n$.

In addition, by Lemma 1, we can get that the light transmission of superimposing any less than $k$ shares is $l(b_{i_1 \otimes i_2 \otimes \ldots \otimes i_p}[s(0)]) = l(b_{i_1 \otimes i_2 \otimes \ldots \otimes i_p}[s(1)])$ $= (1/2)^p$, which indicates that by stacking any less than $k$ shares cannot reveal the secret image. Consequently, the proposed $(k, n)$-RGVSS scheme is secure.     □

### 36.3.2 The Method to Compute the Contrast of Superimposing any $t$ $(k \leq t \leq n)$ Grid-Pixels

Because the elements of $(n - k)$ bits generated by step 2 can be repeated, we denote the number of all different elements in $(n - k)$ bits as $u$, where $1 \leq u \leq min$ $(k, n - k)$. By randomly taking any $t$ grid-pixels out of $n$, we denote the number of all different elements in $t$ grid-pixels as $p$ $(1 \leq p < k)$, and let $P$ be the probability that the $t$ grid-pixels contain all the elements of $\{r_1, r_2 \ldots r_k\}$, $Q_{u,p}$ be the probability that the $t$ grid-pixels do not contain all the elements of $\{r_1, r_2 \ldots r_k\}$ for different $u$ and $p$. Note that

$$P = 1 - \sum_{p=1}^{k-1} \sum_{u=1}^{min(k,n-k)} Q_{u,p}$$

1. Computing $l(b_{i_1 \otimes i_2 \otimes \ldots \otimes i_t}[s(0)])$ and $l(b_{i_1 \otimes i_2 \otimes \ldots \otimes i_t}[s(1)])$, where $i_1, i_2, \cdots, i_t \in \{r_1, r_2, \cdots r_k\}$

**Case 1** $t$ grid-pixels contain all the elements of $\{r_1, r_2 \ldots r_k\}$

Because $(n - k)$ bits are selected from $\{r_1, r_2 \ldots r_k\}$, that is to say, all the $t$ grid-pixels are selected from $\{r_1, r_2 \ldots r_k\}$, and the light transmission of superimposing two identical grid-pixels satisfies that $l(r_i \otimes r_i) = l(r_i)$, thus the light transmissions of superimposing any $t$ grid-pixels which contain all the elements of $\{r_1, r_2 \ldots r_k\}$ are $l(b_{i_1 \otimes i_2 \otimes \ldots \otimes i_t}[s(0)]) = l(b_{r_1 \otimes r_2 \otimes \ldots \otimes r_k}[s(0)]) = 1/2^{k-1}$ and $l(b_{i_1 \otimes i_2 \otimes \ldots \otimes i_t}[s(1)]) = l(b_{r_1 \otimes r_2 \otimes \ldots \otimes r_k}[s(1)]) = 0$, which are the same as that of $(k, k)$-RGVSS scheme [4, 5].

**Case 2** $t$ grid-pixels do not contain all the elements of $\{r_1, r_2 \ldots r_k\}$

Because the light transmission of superimposing two identical grid-pixels satisfies that $l(r_i \otimes r_i) = l(r_i)$, by Lemma 1, the light transmissions of superimposing any $t$ grid-pixels which do not contain all the elements of $\{r_1, r_2 \ldots r_k\}$ are

$$l(b_{i_1 \otimes i_2 \otimes \ldots \otimes i_t}[s(0)]) = l(b_{d_1 \otimes d_2 \otimes \ldots \otimes d_p}[s(0)]) = 1/2^p$$
$$l(b_{i_1 \otimes i_2 \otimes \ldots \otimes i_t}[s(1)]) = l(b_{d_1 \otimes d_2 \otimes \ldots \otimes d_p}[s(1)]) = 1/2^p \cdot$$

where $d_1, d_2, \cdots, d_p \in \{r_1, r_2, \cdots, r_k\}$

2. Computing $Q_{u,p}$

The problem can be considered as that there are $k$ different elements in a set $\{r_1, r_2, \ldots, r_k\}$, and we randomly select one element from the set with replacement and repeat it $n$ times, where $n \geq k$ and the selected $n$ elements contain all the elements in $\{r_1, r_2, \ldots, r_k\}$. Then we randomly select $t$ ($k \leq t \leq n$) elements from the $n$ elements. Therefore there are $C_k^k k^{n-k} C_n^t$ possibilities which we can get the $t$ elements. Afterwards we compute the possibilities of that the $t$ grid-pixels do not contain all the elements of $\{r_1, r_2 \ldots r_k\}$ for different $u$ and $p$, which are denoted as $H_{u,p}$. Thus $Q_{u,p} = H_{u,p}/(C_k^k k^{n-k} C_n^t)$.

3. Computing contrast $\alpha$

By stacking any $t$ grid pixels, the light transmission of $b_{i_1 \otimes i_2 \otimes \ldots \otimes i_t}$ with respect to transparent pixel $s$ in $S$ is

$$
\begin{aligned}
l(b_{i_1 \otimes i_2 \otimes \ldots \otimes i_t}[s(0)]) &= \Pr ob(b_{i_1 \otimes i_2 \otimes \ldots \otimes i_t}[s(0)] = 0 | all\ contain) \\
&\quad + (b_{i_1 \otimes i_2 \otimes \ldots \otimes i_t}[s(0)] = 0 | not\ all\ contain) \\
&= P \times \frac{1}{2^{k-1}} + \sum_{p=1}^{k-1} \sum_{u=1}^{Min(k,n-k)} \left( Q_{u,p} \times \frac{1}{2^p} \right)
\end{aligned}
\tag{36.1}
$$

The light transmission of $b_{i_1 \otimes i_2 \otimes \ldots \otimes i_t}$ with respect to opaque pixel $s$ in $S$ is

$$
\begin{aligned}
l(b_{i_1 \otimes i_2 \otimes \ldots \otimes i_t}[s(1)]) &= \Pr ob(b_{i_1 \otimes i_2 \otimes \ldots \otimes i_t}[s(1)] = 0 | all\ contain) \\
&\quad + \Pr ob(b_{i_1 \otimes i_2 \otimes \ldots \otimes i_t}[s(1)] = 0 | not\ all\ contain) \\
&= P \times 0 + \sum_{p=1}^{k-1} \sum_{u=1}^{Min(k,n-k)} \left( Q_{u,p} \times \frac{1}{2^p} \right)
\end{aligned}
\tag{36.2}
$$

By Definition 1 and 2, the contrast of superimposing any $t$ ($k \leq t \leq n$) grid-pixels is

$$
\alpha = \frac{l(b_{i_1 \otimes i_2 \otimes \ldots \otimes i_t}[s(0)]) - l(b_{i_1 \otimes i_2 \otimes \ldots \otimes i_t}[s(1)])}{1 + l(b_{i_1 \otimes i_2 \otimes \ldots \otimes i_t}[s(1)])} = \frac{P \times \frac{1}{2^{k-1}}}{1 + \sum\limits_{p=1}^{k-1} \sum\limits_{u=1}^{Min(k,n-k)} \left( Q_{u,p} \times \frac{1}{2^p} \right)}
\tag{36.3}
$$

where $P = 1 - \sum\limits_{p=1}^{k-1} \sum\limits_{u=1}^{Min(k,n-k)} Q_{u,p}$

## 36.4 Simulation Results and Discussions

To demonstrate the effectiveness of the proposed $(k, n)$-*RGVSS* scheme, and compare the visual quality of the revealed secret image with Chen and Tsao's scheme [6], a binary secret image Lena with the size of $1,024 \times 1,024$ is encoded for $(k, n) = (3, 5)$. Note that to reconstruct the secret image, we "stack" together the share images with "OR" operation, which is denoted as $\otimes$. Figure 36.1a1–e1 are the results of Chen and Tsao's scheme and Fig. 36.1a2–e2 are the results of the proposed scheme. After being encoded by *RGVSS* scheme for $(k, n) = (3, 5)$, five random grids are generated as meaningless share images. Figure 36.1a1 and a2 show only share1, Fig. 36.1 b1 and b2 show the results of share1 $\otimes$ share2, fig. c1 and c2 show the results of share1 $\otimes$ share2 $\otimes$ share3, fig. d1 and d2 show the results of share1 $\otimes$ share2 $\otimes$ share3 $\otimes$ share4, and Fig. 36.1 e1 and e2 show the results of stacking all the five share images.

From Fig. 36.1, it can be seen that our proposed scheme outperforms Chen and Tsao's scheme. To quantitatively analyze the visual quality, we compute the contrasts of the revealed secret image. Table 36.1 summarizes the contrasts of superimposing any $t$ ($k \le t \le n$) shares for different $(k, n)$, where $2 \le k \le 5$ and $3 \le n \le 6$. To illustrate the enhancement, we define an average enhancement ($AE$) as follows

$$AE = \frac{1}{n - k + 1} \sum_{t=k}^{n} \frac{\alpha_t - \alpha_t'}{\alpha_t'} \times 100 \%$$ (36.1)

where $\alpha_t$ is the contrast of our proposed scheme and $\alpha_t'$ is the contrast of Chen and Tsao's scheme.

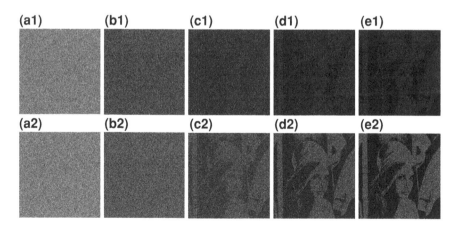

**Fig. 36.1** Comparison of the proposed $(k, n)$-*RGVSS* scheme with Chen and Tsao's scheme for $(k, n) = (3, 5)$. **a1–e1** The results of Chen and Tsao's scheme. **a2–e2** The results of the proposed scheme

**Table 36.1** The contrasts of superimposing any $t$ $(k \le t \le n)$ shares for different $(k, n)$, where $2 \le k \le 6$ and $3 \le n \le 6$

| | Chen and Tsao's | | | | | Ours | | | | | AE (%) |
|---|---|---|---|---|---|---|---|---|---|---|---|
| $(k, n)$ | $t = 2$ | $t = 3$ | $t = 4$ | $t = 5$ | $t = 6$ | $t = 2$ | $t = 3$ | $t = 4$ | $t = 5$ | $t = 6$ | |
| (2, 3) | 1/7 | 1/4 | | | | 2/7 | 1/2 | | | | 100 |
| (2, 4) | 2/29 | 2/17 | 1/8 | | | 7/29 | 7/17 | 1/2 | | | 266 |
| (2, 5) | 2/49 | 2/29 | 3/41 | 1/16 | | 11/49 | 11/29 | 19/41 | 1/2 | | 533 |
| (2, 6) | 1/37 | 1/22 | 4/83 | 4/97 | 1/32 | 8/37 | 4/11 | 37/83 | 47/97 | 1/2 | 960 |
| (3, 4) | 2/35 | 1/8 | | | | 1/9 | 1/4 | | | | 97 |
| (3, 5) | 2/89 | 4/83 | 1/16 | | | 11/140 | 11/64 | 1/4 | | | 269 |
| (3, 6) | 2/179 | 1/42 | 2/65 | 1/32 | | 4/61 | 21/148 | 23/112 | 1/4 | | 563 |
| (4, 5) | 1/42 | 1/16 | | | | 2/43 | 1/8 | | | | 98 |
| (4, 6) | 1/127 | 1/49 | 1/32 | | | 5/177 | 5/67 | 1/8 | | | 275 |
| (5, 6) | 2/197 | 1/32 | | | | 1/50 | 1/16 | | | | 99 |

## 36.5 Conclusions

In this paper, we proposed a novel $(k, n)$-$RGVSS$ scheme. The security of the proposed $(k, n)$-$RGVSS$ scheme is formally proved, and the feasibility is empirically verified. The experimental results show that our scheme outperforms Chen and Tsao's scheme. The contrasts of the proposed scheme are much higher than that of Chen and Tsao's scheme.

**Acknowledgment** This research was partly supported by National Natural Science Foundation of China under Grant No. 61170207.

## References

1. Naor M, Shamir A (1995) Visual cryptography, advances in cryptology—EUROCRYPT'94. Lecture notes in computer science, vol 950, Springer, Berlin, pp 1–12
2. Kafri O, Keren E (1987) Encryption of pictures and shapes by random grids. Opt Lett 12(6):377–379
3. Shyu SJ (2007) Image encryption by random grids. Pattern Recognit 40(3):1014–1031
4. Shyu SJ (2009) Image encryption by multiple random grids. Pattern Recognit 42(7):1582–1596
5. Chen TH, Tsao KH (2009) Visual secret sharing by random grids revisited. Pattern Recognit 42(9):2203–2217
6. Chen TH, Tsao KH (2011) Threshold visual secret sharing by random grids. J Syst Softw 84(7):1197–1208

# Chapter 37
# Web 3D Model Library System Based on Cloud Platform

Mingang Chen, Wenjun Cai, Shida Lu, Luwei Zhang
and Lizhuang Ma

**Abstract** The development of digital content industry needs the support of the online 3D model library. The construction of efficient interaction, stable and reliable model library is the trend of industry. In this paper, we design a web 3D model library system based on the Amazon cloud service platform. It adopted model simplification, model size adaption methods to make the system more efficient interaction. Meanwhile, cloud-based architecture ensured the reliability and scalability of the system.

**Keywords** Web 3D · 3D model library · Collada · Cloud computing

## 37.1 Introduction

As we all know, the production of animation and game is inseparable from the design of 3D virtual scenes and 3D models are the most important component of constructing 3D scenes. Therefore, there have been a few 3D model material

M. Chen (✉) · L. Ma
Department of Computer Science and Technology, Shanghai Jiao Tong University,
Shanghai 200240, China
e-mail: miles_cmg@sjtu.edu.cn

M. Chen
Shanghai Key Laboratory of Computer Software Testing and Evaluating,
Shanghai 201112, China

W. Cai
Autodesk ACRD, Shanghai 201804, China

S. Lu · L. Zhang
Information and Communication Center of SMEPC, Shanghai 200063, China

W. Lu et al. (eds.), *Proceedings of the 2012 International Conference on Information Technology and Software Engineering*, Lecture Notes in Electrical Engineering 212, DOI: 10.1007/978-3-642-34531-9_37, © Springer-Verlag Berlin Heidelberg 2013

library on the web, such as the Google 3D Warehouse and 3D the Export, and 3D kingdom model library.

However, most of the existing online 3D model libraries are still using image-based proxy to display 3D model. In recent years, the panorama technology [1] provides interaction feature for the display of 3D model, but it still cannot provide the functionalities of model rotation at any angle. Google has also launched 3D Warehouse, which provides interactive browsing of 3D models. However, it still has limitations. Firstly, the only interaction is rotation on the horizontal direction and scaling. Secondly, only Google SketchUp model format is supported for.

Web-based 3D model library provide users with model sharing services, and it requires users to contribute new models the library. Such a system is a typical Web 2.0 system. Cloud computing is a new paradigm for Web 2.0 that displaces the current dominant web application. The advantages of web application over cloud like scalability of computing and storage, load balancing, and on demand service drives us to deploy our Web 3D model library application onto the cloud.

In this paper, we design and implement a Web 3D model library based on cloud computing platform. And we propose a front-end efficient Web 3D and back-end reliable cloud computing solutions.

## 37.2 Related Work

### 37.2.1 Web 3D Technology

Nowadays, Web 3D technologies can be broadly divided into two categories, the browser plugin-based approach as well as a small number of systems, which try to integrate the rendering system directly into the browser [2].

Adobe Flash is a multimedia platform for developing content rich Internet applications. Flash has become a popular solution used to add animation and interactivity to web pages. Also, Adobe Flash Player has reached 99 % of the internet users. Therefore, the flash-based technologies are the mainstream Web 3D solution. Away3D is an open source 3D graphics engine, written for the Adobe Flash platform in ActionScript 3, and runs in modern web browsers that utilize Adobe Flash Player. It can be used to render 3D models and perform various other 3D computations. Silverlight is another application framework for writing and running rich Internet applications. It is developed by Microsoft as Flash alternative and is based on the .Net framework. However, users of Silverlight are smaller compared to Flash. So in this paper, Away3D technology is used in the Web 3D model library.

The WebGL solution does not rely on a plugin and it is a cross-platform web standard for a low-level 3D graphics API based on OpenGL ES 2.0, exposed through the HTML5 Canvas element as Document Object Model interfaces. The development of HTML5 greatly promotes the WebGL solution. Further work has been done with the X3DOM project [3], which overcome WebGL limitations by providing an adaptation of the rendering technique. However, WebGL is a low level interface, so it is not fit for the Web 3D model library because of the complex development process.

## 37.2.2 Cloud Computing Services

The Cloud Computing paradigm has gained popularity for hosting applications in recent years, as it provides businesses with pay-as-you-go computation and storage services [4]. A growing number of companies are riding this wave to provide public cloud computing services, such as Amazon AWS, Google AppEngine, Microsoft Azure, and Rackspace CloudServer. These cloud providers offer a variety of options in pricing, performance, and feature set. For instance, some offer platform as a service (PaaS), where a cloud customer builds applications using the APIs provided by the cloud; others offer infrastructure as a service (IaaS), where a customer runs applications inside virtual machines, using the APIs provided by their chosen guest operating systems [5]. In this paper, Amazon AWS is adopted as cloud computing platform for Web 3D model library mainly due to flexibility of services and its great success in the business compared to Google AppEngine, Microsoft Azure.

## 37.3  Web 3D Model Library System Overview

Web 3D model library system adopts the classic three-layer architecture that is data layer, business layer and presentation layer, as shown in Fig. 37.1.

The data layer deployed in Amazon S3 for model files storage. S3 is composed of "buckets" that are geographically distributed across Amazon's multiple data centers in several locations. So S3 is an extremely reliable persistent storage system for model files storage. When the storage capacity of model files is larger than expectation, we can request storage expansion service of S3. Web application servers and models metadata database are deployed in Amazon EC2 mainly provides business logic of the system, such as user's requests, conversion of model formats and model's retrieval etc. Amazon EC2 allows users to deploy scalable resources on demand. The presentation layer in user's browser provides model uploading, downloading, 3D display and interaction functions.

## 37.4  Model Converter and Model Simplifier

Because of the good performance of COLLADA (COLLAborative Design Activity) [6] for model format exchange, some plugins are developed to import and export COLLADA models such as ColladaMaya which is an open source exporter for

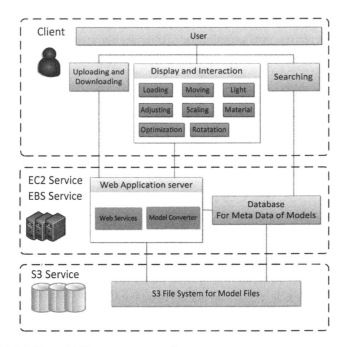

**Fig. 37.1** Web 3D model library system overview

Maya. However, the most model formats in our library are Maya and 3D's Max which are not supported by Away3D directly. In this paper, we design a model conversion service at the server side and any formats of 3D models can be converted to COLLADA model and displayed properly. At the server side, a model converter service runs periodically until meets the request of ending. The task of the service is to get all files in the "NON-COLLADA" file folder one by one and open it in the related modeling software installed COLLADA plugin, then the conversion command script are executed. Then, the converted file will be moved to the "COL-LADA" file folder where model browser can load and display models.

Taking into account complex models is difficult to real-time 3D interaction, so we implement a model simplification service. Because the discussion of model simplification algorithm is beyond the scope of this paper. The interested reader can refer to the work of Michael and Paul [7].

## 37.5 Model Size Automatic Adjustment

When models are just loaded onto the scene, some are too big to be contained by the screen while others are so small that customers have to pay great efforts to zoom them up. So we deeply researched into the perspective projection principle

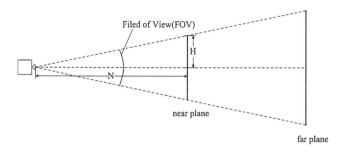

**Fig. 37.2** Illustration of field of view

of Away3D engine and proposed a method to automatically adjust related parameter and display models of various sizes properly.

The perspective projection matrix in Away3D can be found in ActionScript file Camera3D as formula (37.1):

$$
\begin{bmatrix}
\frac{f}{aspect} & 0 & 0 & 0 \\
0 & f & 0 & 0 \\
0 & 0 & -\frac{N+F}{N-F} & \frac{2NF}{N-F} \\
0 & 0 & 1 & 0
\end{bmatrix}
=
\begin{bmatrix}
\frac{N}{W} & 0 & 0 & 0 \\
0 & \frac{N}{H} & 0 & 0 \\
0 & 0 & -\frac{N+F}{N-F} & \frac{2NF}{N-F} \\
0 & 0 & 1 & 0
\end{bmatrix}
\tag{37.1}
$$

where aspect $=$ W/H and $f = 1/\tan(\text{FOV}/2) = N/H$. FOV is illustrated in Fig. 37.2. W and H represent half of the width and height of viewport respectively.

Thus, we grasp the principle of how 3D mesh is projected onto the screen in Away3D engine. When projected onto the screen, a 3D point P(x, y, z) turns into a 2D point, so the width and height of a 3D mesh turns into formula (37.2):

$$
\begin{cases}
ModelWidth = \frac{N}{W}\left(x_{\max} - x_{\min}\right) \\
ModelHeight = \frac{N}{H}\left(y_{\max} - y_{\min}\right)
\end{cases}
\tag{37.2}
$$

where $x_{\max}$ and $x_{\min}$ represents the maximum and minimum X-coordinate value of all points in a model. $y_{\max}$ and $y_{\min}$ are defined similarly. *ModelWidth* and *ModelHeight* have described the bounding box of the model from which we get a general idea of the size of model projected on the screen. With this relationship, we adjust the distance between camera and near plane to a proper value automatically when models are just loaded.

## 37.6  Design of Model Browser

The 3D interaction of the model includes loading, moving, rotating, scaling, changing material and light effect. The model browser is designed more fit for the requirement of the application in Web 3D model library through analyzing and modifying the open source engine files of Away3D.

**Fig. 37.3** Part of
COLLADA file of the
windmill model

```
  1   <?xml version="1.0" encoding="utf-8"?>
  2   <COLLADA xmlns="http://www.collada.org/2005/11/COLLADASchema" version="1.4.1">
  3     <asset>
 14     <library_effects>
234     <library_materials>
235       <material id="ColorEffectROGOBO-material" name="ColorEffectROGOBO-material">
238       <material id="House-material" name="House-material">
241       <material id="Stand-material" name="Stand-material">
244       <material id="Blades-material" name="Blades-material">
247     </library_materials>
248     <library_geometries>
422     <library_images>
433     <library_visual_scenes>
434       <visual_scene id="MaxScene">
435         <node id="node-Scene_Root" name="Scene_Root">
436           <node id="node-House" name="House">
448           <node id="node-Floor" name="Floor">
457           <node id="node-Stand" name="Stand">
468           <node id="node-Blades" name="Blades">
484         </node>
485       </visual_scene>
486     </library_visual_scenes>
487     <scene>
490   </COLLADA>
```

A COLLADA model consists of several nodes and each node has its own information. Figure 37.3 shows the COLLADA file of a windmill model illustrated in Fig. 37.5. There are 4 <node> nodes named "House", "Floor", "Stand" and "Blades" defined within the <library_visual_scenes> node. However, Away3D API only provides access to the whole model rather than nodes. So we modified the model parsing method of Away3D engine and collect data of each node of the model. In the loading process, a Away3D internal class named DAE can be applied to parse the COLLADA file.

In Away3D, we observe the scene and model through Camera3D, an abstract object. So the interaction with camera such as moving, rotating and zooming will realize the effect of interaction with model.

As to the function of light effect, PointLight3D, inherited from general 3D object class, is a Away3D class dealing to light object. To add light effect, we can create an instance of class PointLight3D and add it to the scene. In addition, a color-based fat shading material can be assigned to the model to offer users access to set light and ambient color.

## 37.7 Application of the Web 3D Model Library

The Web 3D model library system is intended to accessible on-line by internet users and provide users good interaction experiences, as shown in Fig. 37.4.

Users can interaction with 3D models such as rotation, scaling and moving in the model browser just using the mouse, as shown in Fig. 37.5.

Figure 37.6 shows the light effects of a model. Interface is designed for user to change the position of light source, light color and ambient color. Figure 37.6a shows a plane model without light effects, and Fig. 37.6b and c are the high light and ambient light effects respectively.

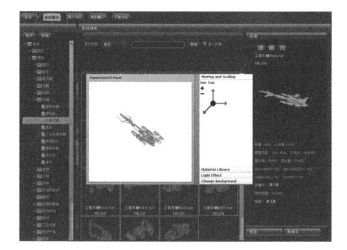

**Fig. 37.4** Web 3D model library system

**Fig. 37.5** The result of 3D model transformation

**Fig. 37.6** The light effects of a model

## 37.8 Conclusion

This paper proposes a web 3D model library solutions and completes system design and implementation. The Web 3D model library is deployed in the Amazon cloud computing platform to ensure the reliability and scalability of the system. We implement a model conversion service to support a variety of model formats in the system. We also design a model size adaptive method to improve user's 3D interaction experience. Our Web 3D design and deployment of solutions can be applied to other web applications, such as online virtual tour and virtual design etc. In the future, we plan to study more efficient model simplification method to improve the speed and effects of model rendering in the web.

**Acknowledgments** This work is funded by Science and Technology Commission of Shanghai Municipality program (NO. 11511500200).

## References

1. Matthew B, David GL (2007) Automatic panoramic image stitching using invariant features. Int J Comput Vision 74(1):59–73
2. Behr J, Eschler P, Jung Y, Zollner M (2009) X3DOM: a DOM-based html5/x3D integration model. In Web3D'09: proceedings of the 14th international conference on 3D web technology. ACM, New York, pp 127–135
3. Behr J, Jung Y, Keil J, Drevensek T, Zoellner M, Eschler P, Fellner D (2010) A scalable architecture for the HTML5/X3D integration model X3DOM. In Web3D'10: proceedings of the 15th international conference on 3D web technology. ACM, Los Angeles, pp 185–194
4. Michael C (2010) Cloud computing and SaaS as new computing platforms. Commun ACM 53(4):27–29
5. Ang L, Yang XW, Srikanth K, Zhang M (2010) CloudCmp: comparing public cloud providers. In: IMC '10 proceedings of the 10th annual conference on internet measurement. ACM, New York, pp 1–14
6. COLLADA. http://www.collada.org
7. Michael G, Paul SH (1997) Surface simplification using quadric error metrics. In: Proceedings of the 24th annual conference on computer graphics and interactive techniques, pp 209–216

# Chapter 38
# A New Framework for Layered Depth Video Coding

Zhu Ting, Dongxiao Li, Wang Lianghao and Ming Zhang

**Abstract** Layered Depth Video (LDV) is recognized as a promising 3D video data representation format in the form of multiple layer texture-plus-depth video from a reference viewpoint. Due to the uncertainty of effective pixel locations in the occlusion layers and the number of total layers, existing video coding standards cannot be directly used for LDV coding. A new framework for LDV coding is presented in this paper. A novel polynomial approximation based prediction tool is proposed for coding of border macroblocks, which contain both effective and blank pixels in the occlusion layers. Precise borders are reconstructed on the decoder side based on analysis of depth discontinuity, which is well preserved by allocating more bits in encoding. Comparing with the state-of-the-art, the proposed method demonstrates improved rate-distortion performance.

**Keywords** Layered depth video (LDV) · Video coding · Border prediction · Polynomial approximation

## 38.1 Introduction

Multi-view video is a set of video sequence which is obtained by capturing the same scene in different viewpoints. It can give audience immerse sense and unique personal experience by reconstructing the real world truthfully. And because 3D video communication system utilizes coding format style of

Z. Ting (✉) · D. Li · W. Lianghao · M. Zhang
Zhejiang Provincial Key Laboratory of Information Network Technology,
Institute of Information and Communication Engineering, Zhejiang University,
Hangzhou 310027, China
e-mail: notlih@sina.com

W. Lu et al. (eds.), *Proceedings of the 2012 International Conference on Information Technology and Software Engineering*, Lecture Notes in Electrical Engineering 212, DOI: 10.1007/978-3-642-34531-9_38, © Springer-Verlag Berlin Heidelberg 2013

"texture + depth + occlusion", it will generate extra augment data quantity. So, 3D video coding efficiency is an imperative factor which influence natural 3D television performance, investigating corresponding multi-view video coding technology is of great significance to implementing of natural 3D system.

Traditional stereo video coding applies existing temporal prediction technology to interview prediction and gain comparatively large compression ratio improvement. Stereo matching and depth image base rendering based on computer vision reduce data size by exploiting geometry relation of different view. But they respectively have some defects, traditional stereo video coding can't fully excavate geometry of mapping relation between texture and depth, and it doesn't support texture warping between different views, stereo matching and DIBR is lack of expression of occlusion information and combination with video coding technology.

In this work, we investigate how to mix two of The above-mentioned technology to decrease data quantity, we first utilize depth sequence provided by MPEG-3D to generate layered depth video, so we get LDV's first layer's texture, first layer's depth, occlusion layers' texture and occlusion layers' depth (maybe separated into several layers).

For first layer's texture and first layer's depth, we use H. 264 compression standard to encode, for occlusion layers' texture and occlusion layers' depth, we first record the Number of Layers (NOL) at each pixel location, and then separate LDV's layers into sequences of same size. For each sequence, we divide macroblock into two parts: border prediction block mode (BPB mode) and not border prediction block mode (NBPB mode). In NBPB mode macroblock, we utilize traditional H. 264 compression tools to encode its residual block, motion vector, intra prediction mode and so forth. In BPB mode macroblock, we propose doing border prediction and polynomial approximation to express the difference of data area and blank area in occlusion layer, for the remaining BPB mode residual block, we still use traditional H. 264 compression tools to encode its residual block, motion vector, intra prediction mode and so forth.

## 38.2 Background

LDV technology can express multi-view video's occlusion information by adding a certain number of layers on back of primary 2D video. Compared with multi-view video format, LDV's merit is that it can describe 3D video's geometry characteristics more intuitively. In 1992, Harvard University [1] firstly apply layered depth image to represent computer generated graphics. In 2004 Zitnick firstly used layered depth image technology in multi-view video's description [2], LDV combined with multi-view video can decrease redundancy between viewpoints caused by different glancing angle at large. Currently, LDV's generation, coding, transmission system consists of following three step.

**Fig. 38.1** Generating LDV from multi-view texture-plus-depth video

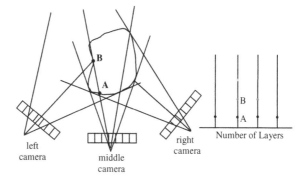

## 38.2.1 LDV Generation

In Fig. 38.1, left camera, middle camera, right camera represent three video cameras that build up a shift sensor arrangement camera array, the absolute location of the three cameras is known, so we know camera external parameters, the camera internal parameters are also known. Take it for example that we get three texture video sequences captured by them and three depth sequences by other means, pixel A appears in three sequences at the same time. To build LDV by the six sequences, we cast every pixel like A in left camera into middle camera by calculating mapping relation from cameras' parameters and pixels' depth value. After the above steps, pixels are divided into two groups, pixels like A are one group, they can merge with pixels in middle camera because they are the same, pixels like B is one group, they are located behind middle camera's coverage. After we cast all pixels from left camera and right camera into middle camera, LDV are generated, we call middle camera and merged pixels like A the first layer, and call pixels like B the occlusion layer. As the screen changes, the number occlusion layers can be up to infinite, but generally, there are not more than three layers in total LDV. In Fig. 38.1, LDV has different number of layers in different pixels, every pixel consists of five data: every layer's Y component, every layer's U component, every layer's V component, every layer's depth value, current pixel's NOL.

## 38.2.2 Compression of LDV

In 1995, Sikora and Makai proposed a method called shape adaptive discrete cosine transform to solve that traditional DCT transform can't be utilized in a block where not every pixel is useful [3, 4]. His algorithm firstly aggregates pixels in left border, and perform vertical transform to rows of different size, then aggregates pixels in up border to perform horizontal transform [5]. Although SA-DCT can do DCT transform to random shape block and enable encoder to predict block information in its original location, but it cannot reconstruct irregular shape by DCT coefficient itself [6, 7].

In 2003, Duan proposed the video object wavelet codec to encode LDI's occlusion data and made comparison with MPEG plus JPEG-LS. In his paper, it also needs to transfer NOL to reconstruct correct border in decoder-term. He mainly compared the two lossless coding tools: win-zip and jpeg-lossless, and concluded that jpeg perform better than win-zip for NOL's coding [8, 9]. He also proposed aggregating occlusion data to reduce LDI's uncertainty and keep data area in one corner of picture before transform coding, and the experiments result highly depends on the accuracy of NOL. One defect of aggregation method is that it can't help macroblock to predict from their adjacent macroblock. Furthermore, since aggregation destroys video frames' inner correlation, it is unsuitable for standard video compression standard like H. 264.

In 2005, Seung-Uk Yoon proposed a structure for LDVs' coding [10]. To make holes in occlusion layer fitted for tradition codec like H. 264, they use first layer's pixels which are located in front of holes to fill in the blank area in occlusion layer, and they use interpolating to preserve block texture's smoothness.

## 38.2.3 View Rendering Based on LDV

View rendering process is operated by casting all pixels in LDV into views that we want to reconstruct. When two pixels are casted into the same location, then the one with low depth value will be rejected. For example, When view rendering process reaches view of left camera, A and B will be casted into different position and be saved in view of left camera at the same time. When view rendering process reaches view of middle camera, A and B will be casted into the same position and B will be rejected because B's location is behind A rightly.

## 38.3 Our Coding Approach

Since 3D video's geometry structure causes occlusion between different view-points, since phenomenon such as illumination change, motion, scene cutover widely exist, occlusion area's size and shape are very uncertain. If this part's information is handled incorrectly, it will do harm to view reconstruction in the end term. For the LDV's rectangle sequence encoding, the coding problem of irregular figure is very important to improve video quality.

In this work, we divide occlusion layer's coding block into two parts, one is border prediction block (BPB) mode macroblock, the other is not border prediction block (NBPB) mode macroblock, NBPB mode macroblock and the first layer's macroblock will be encoded with intra frame prediction and inter frame prediction in H. 264 to reduce redundancy. BPB mode macroblock which is shown in

**Fig. 38.2** Coding framework

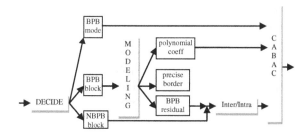

Fig. 38.2 as BPB block will be departed into four parts to encode: the BPB mode value which defines whether this block is BPB mode or not, the precise border of different pixel in one macroblock, the polynomial coefficients which express the difference of luma and chroma between data area and blank area in one macro-block, the BPB mode macroblock's residual block which is get by subtract polynomial reconstruction value from texture, and polynomial coefficients is computed to make it close to blank area's default luma and chroma value. The integral process is showed in Fig. 38.2.

### 38.3.1  The Decision of BPB Mode for Macroblock in Occlusion Layer

We observe that in a LDV's occlusion layer, there are three kind of macroblock: macroblock that include blank area only, macroblock that include both blank area and data area, macroblock that include data area only. For video encoding, macroblock that include an uncertain border between data area and blank area always occupy larger data and are more difficult to reconstruct accurate border only from coded bitstream than other two kind of macroblock. With desire to encode the border and video information in such macroblock more efficiently, we select following algorithm to depart it from others, and call such macroblock BPB mode one. And transfer it in one bit in entropy coding.

$$is\_border = \begin{cases} 1, & if \quad macroblock \ include \ both \ data \ and \ blank \ area \\ 0, & else \end{cases} \tag{38.1}$$

There is one BPB mode macroblock in current location only when $is\_border()$ equals 1. Through the mask, the location of border in one frame can be identified.

In our work, every macroblock in occlusion layer should be identified whether it is BPB mode or not, to decrease data quantity's improvement caused by NOL's increase, we utilize following method to mark the BPB mode macroblock in a layer of high level number.

Through investigate the characteristic of LDV, we can see that if one front layer macroblock's $is\_border()$ is 0, then all macroblock's $is\_border()$ in back layer of it surely will be 0, this is because that if there is data in back layer, there should be data in its front layer too. So we detach such decoding order when decoding a macroblock in a layer of high level number: before decoding the mode value from bitstream, we firstly detect whether current block's front layer is BPB mode, secondly decode one bit as border block mode only if detection result is true. And in the encoding-term, we also encode the mode value bit of one macroblock after detection result show that the front layer macroblock is BPB mode macroblock too.

### 38.3.2 Polynomial Approximation of BPB Mode Macroblock

After obtaining BPB mode in encoder-term, we need to expand the border of data area into blank area properly, the illustrated solution is to combine polynomial approximation and border expansion to give BPB mode macroblock maximized correlation with adjacent macroblock. Through carefully investigating the characteristic of blank area and data area, we firstly determine blank area's default value to be 128, this is because that 128 is more close to all pixel value between 0 and 255, and 128 is also the default value of H. 264s DC intra prediction mode when adjacent pixel is not attainable. After set blank area's data as 128, we propose to use (38.2) to do polynomial approximation for luma value and chroma value of data area.

$$(a,b,c) = \min_{(a,b,c)} \sum_{(x,y)\in macroblock} [pixel(x,y) - (a \cdot x + b \cdot y + c) - 128]^2 \quad (38.2)$$

$(a, b, c)$ represent the two coefficients of first order and the one homogeneous coefficient $(x, y)$ represent the horizontal coordinate and vertical coordinate of pixels in macroblock which are both ranged from 0 to macroblock size. 128 represent the default value of blank area. To utilize the approximation result efficiently, we subtract it from polynomial approximation residual block in (38.2) to make the difference of polynomial reconstruction result and data as close to default blank value as possible.

In ours solution, each BPB mode macroblock will be allocated 12 coefficients: 9 for texture and 3 for depth. All these coefficients are coded by entropy coding, and decoded only when current macroblock is entropy-decoded to be BPB mode macroblock.

Through the up steps, we conclude with information of two parts, one is polynomial coefficient, one is the BPB mode residual block which will be sent into traditional compression tools as intra prediction and inter prediction. In [10], back layer's blank is filled with front layer data, while in the proposed algorithm, we fill the blank with data close to original border, this method's advantage is that it can avoid situation that size of occlusion layer is too small that foreground object texture in front layer data will fall into blank and destruct the correlation built by polynomial approximation.

### 38.3.3 Precise Border's Reconstruction in the Decoder-Term

We usually use existing coding standard or software such as win-zip and JPEG-lossless to encode NOL when reach a irregular figure. But Layered depth image's special data structure and geometry structure enable us to get precise border in the decoder-term more efficiently and more straightforward. In our work, we propose to predict occlusion layer's figure by make full use of the depth information from decoded front layer.

When decoding a BPB mode block from bitstream, we first use decoded polynomial coefficients to get polynomial reconstruction value of all pixels in current macroblock and add it to BPB mode residual block decoded by traditional coding tools' decoding framework. So the reconstruction of all pixels of current macroblock is obtained, its value is ensuring correct by both polynomial coefficients sent by Golomb coding and traditional video coding tools. The only remaining problem is how to obtain the correct border to instruct view synthesis. The border's quality is relevant to output quality of the whole LDV system.

In this work, we propose a new method to predict precise border under instruction of front layer's depth data. Our reconstruct order is from low to high:

Step 1: Reconstruct 1st layer's border when decoding 1st layer's depth map from bitstream. Because 1st layer's border is very simple (there is only one data area in one frame), so it can be get easily and accurately by depth map only.

Step 2: Use 1st layer's reconstructed border as border when decoding 1st layer's texture map.

Step 3: Set $l$ as 1.

Step 4: Reconstruct $(l + 1)$th layer's border from $(l)$th layers' border and depth map reconstructed before when decoding $(l + 1)$th layer's depth map from bitstream.

Step 5: Use reconstructed $(l + 1)$th layer's border as border when decoding 1st layer's texture map.

Step 6: If $l + 1$ is the max NOL, then reconstruction operation finishes. Otherwise add 1 to $l$ and jump to Step 4 to continue.

Considering Step 4 coming to the $(l + 1)$th layer's $j$th row and $i$th column, and $j$ can be any number not more than video's height. Firstly, we detect whether current pixel is belong to a BPB mode macroblock. If detection result is 0, we set current pixel's precise border as 0 to mark it as blank area. Else if detection result is 1, we continue to do the following work. Information about BPB mode is transferred in bitstream and decoded before border's reconstruction. Secondly, we detect all depth jump in $(l)$th layer's $j$th row. This is because of the truth that occlusion occurs only when there is foreground object and background object at the same macroblock, the depth jump we detected in front layer will surely be left border or right border of occlusion figure in back layer. In addition, the detected depth jump's location obviously will not exceed the horizontal coordinate of BPB mode macroblock. Thirdly, we treat all depth jump detected in front layer's $j$th row as a group. For every depth jump in this group, we can get 4 parts of information of current pixel by (38.3): whether this pixel will be both occluded in middle camera and exposed in left camera by current depth jump, whether this pixel will be occluded in left camera by current depth jump, whether this pixel will be both occluded in middle camera and exposed in right camera current depth jump, whether this pixel will be occluded in right camera by current depth jump.

$$is\_l\_s(l+1,i,j,s(l,n,j)) = \begin{cases} 1, & s(l,n,j) \in S\_l(l,j) \\ & and\ cl(s\_l(l,n,j)) < cl(l+1,i,j) < cl(s\_h(l,n,j)) \\ & and\ \exists(l_0 < l+1,i_0,j_0), cm(l_0,i_0,j_0) = cm(l+1,i,j) \\ 0, & else \end{cases}$$

$$not\_l\_s(l+1,i,j,s(l,n,j)) = \begin{cases} 1, & s(l,n,j) \in S\_r(l,j) \\ & and\ cm(l+1,i,j) \geq cm(s\_l(l,n,j)) \\ & and\ cl(l+1,i,j) \leq cl(s\_h(l,n,j)) \\ & and\ \exists(l_0 < l+1,i_0,j_0), cl(l_0,i_0,j_0) = cl(l+1,i,j) \\ 0, & else \end{cases}$$

$$is\_r\_s(l+1,i,j,s(l,n,j)) = \begin{cases} 1, & s(l,n,j) \in S\_r(l,j) \\ & and\ cr(s\_h(l,n,j)) < cr(i,j) < cr(s\_l(l,n,j)) \\ & and\ \exists(l_0 < l+1,i_0,j_0), cm(l_0,i_0,j_0) = cm(l+1,i,j) \\ 0, & else \end{cases}$$

$$not\_r\_s(l+1,i,j,s(l,n,j)) = \begin{cases} 1, & s(l,n,j) \in S\_l(l,j) \\ & and\ cm(l,i,j) \leq cm(s\_l(l,n,j)) \\ & and\ cr(l,i,j) \geq cr(s\_h(l,n,j)) \\ & and\ \exists(l_0 < l+1,i_0,j_0), cr(l_0,i_0,j_0) = cr(l+1,i,j) \\ 0, & else \end{cases}$$

$$(38.3)$$

$(l+1, i, j)$ represent current pixel whose vertical coordinate belong to $(l+1)$th layer's $j$th row and horizontal coordinate belong to a BPB mode macroblock being decoded. $(l_0, i_0, j_0)$ represent one pixel in LDV. $S(l, j)$ is the group of depth jump in $(l)$th layer's $j$th row. $S\_l\ (l, j)$ represent all up depth jump in $S(l, j)$ which show there exist a left border of foreground object. $S\_r\ (l, j)$ represent all down depth jump in $S(l, j)$ which show there exist a right border of foreground object. $s(l, n, j)$ is the nth depth jump in group $S(l, j)$. $s\_h\ (l, n, j)$ is the high depth value one in two pixel belong to $s(l, n, j)$. $s\_l\ (l, n, j)$ is the low depth value one in two pixel belong to $s(l, n, j)$. $cl()$ represent the horizontal coordinate obtained by casting one pixel in LDV into left camera. The camera parameters it used are also transferred in bitstream. The depth value of pixel it used is obtained from decoded depth of macroblock whose layer is frontier than current's and the current macroblock's BPB mode residual block which is decoded before we do precise border reconstruction. $cm()$ represent the horizontal coordinate obtained by casting one pixel in

LDV into middle camera. $cr()$ represent the horizontal coordinate obtained by casting one pixel in LDV into right camera.

Fourthly, we merge current pixel's n sets of information into two parts of information by (38.4): whether current pixel can be seen from left camera and can't be seen from middle camera, whether current pixel can be seen from right camera and can't be seen from middle camera. After we have detect all depth jump, and current pixel's occlusion relation with camera will only be influenced by depth jump detected in front layer (this is because of the truth max disparity in LDV will surely be not more than video's width, and occlusion would only be influenced by depth jump in range of video's max disparity), now we can judge that whether current pixel can be seen from a certain camera from pixel's occlusion relation with n sets of depth jump.

$$
\begin{aligned}
is\_l\_b(l+1,i,j) &= \begin{cases} 1, & \exists n_0, is\_l\_s(l+1,i,j,s(l,n_0,j)) = 1 \\ & and\ \forall n_1, not\_l\_s(l+1,i,j,s(l,n_1,j)) = 0 \\ 0, & else \end{cases} \\
is\_r\_b(l+1,i,j) &= \begin{cases} 1, & \exists n_0, is\_r\_s(l+1,i,j,s(l,n_0,j)) = 1 \\ & and\ \forall n_1, not\_r\_s(l+1,i,j,s(l,n_1,j)) = 0 \\ 0, & else. \end{cases}
\end{aligned}
\tag{38.4}
$$

Fifthly, we compute the precise border of current pixel by (38.5). After (38.4), we merge n sets of information of every pixel into two parts of information. $is\_l\_b()$ is 1 only when current pixel is the occlusion data in (j + 1)th layer seen from left camera, $is\_r\_b()$ is 1 only when current pixel is the occlusion data in (j + 1)th layer seen from right camera. So the precise border is the OR operation result of the two parts of information. In other means, when a pixel in back layer is marked as it can be seen from left camera or right camera and can't be seen from middle camera, it will be separated into data area in current macroblock.

$$
is\_precise\_border(l+1,i,j) = \begin{cases} 1, & is\_l\_b(l+1,i,j) = 1\ or\ is\_r\_b(l+1,i,j) = 1 \\ 0, & else. \end{cases}
\tag{38.5}
$$

Figure 38.3a shows the original border before encoding. Figure 38.3b shows the border reconstruction result of our algorithm. In (38.3), we define two information to show influence between different depth jump in one row: $not\_l\_s()$ and $not\_r\_s()$. The difference between Fig. 38.3b and c show the effect of the two parts of information for precise border's reconstruction. For the reconstruction of border in Fig. 38.3, when the foreground object's shape have a hole-like part, it will also influent the reconstruct process. The left border of hole in front layer's foreground object can create an certain size of data area in back layer, but not all of them can be capture by camera right, actually it's divided into two parts, one is still existing in the back layer, one is obscured by the right border of hole in front layer's foreground object both to right camera and middle camera to become unknown and pull outward of back layer. In Fig. 38.3, the red line spotted area show that it's

**Fig. 38.3** **a** The original border we want to reconstruct. **b** The correct predicted occlusion figure in *back layer*. **c** The incorrect predicted occlusion figure in *back layer*. **d** The front layer texture data in the *rectangle area* in **d**, the foreground object have a special figure that there exist a "hole" in *one horizontal direction* of foreground object, so if we compute the *back layer*'s occlusion width only by depth value's change in one border, we'll get the error in **c** where data should have fallen into front layer because of another border's depth change are regarded as *back layer*'s data. And **b**'s result is right obviously because occlusion's figure should be the same with figure of hole in *front layer*'s foreseen object

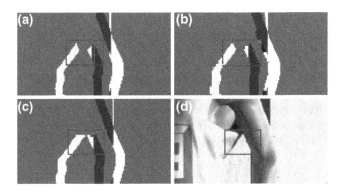

**Fig. 38.4** When we reconstruct *3rd layer*'s border by *2nd layer*'s depth jump, if one side of the depth jump fall into *1st layer*, then we should fill the *2nd layer* with depth value of similar location in *1st layer*

special figure will influent occlusion area's figure both in left camera and in right camera.

Figure 38.4 show a quick algorithm when (38.3) reach a depth jump whose two pixels belong to different layer: we firstly find the lost depth value in similar location of $(l-1)$th layer's or frontier layer's, finally we fill the lost depth value with found one and continue the operation of (38.3). The process can be expressed in Fig. 38.4.

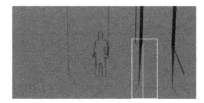

**Fig. 38.5** The *rectangle* show that when reconstructed border is different from encoded sequence's border, block who predict from the pixels in *blank area* will be decoded incorrectly

### 38.3.4 The BPB Mode Residual Block's Disposition

After BPB mode macroblock's residual block is reconstructed in encoder-term's decoding loop or decoder-term, we both can store the whole data reconstructed and the data reconstructed by inter and intra prediction only. Since the two are operated in macroblock level, they will not disturb deblock filter's work. The first one's advantage is that it can make use of correlation of current macroblock and the next one if next one share one common object with current one, its defect is that the precise border in the block will influent inter prediction process for the precise border change largely even when time change by little. And inaccurate prediction by take incorrect border into reference will influent compression ratio. The second one's advantage is that it will do help to inter prediction and intra prediction in term of macroblock pairs located closed in up and down. Its defect is that it consumes extra memory to store the redundant macroblock in decoded pictures other than reconstruction macroblock.

In our work, we use the BPB mode residual block to engage in the following macroblock's inter and intra prediction. This is because that border reconstruction can't operate perfectly all through whole sequence's decoding, sometimes there is reconstruction error of one pixel in reconstructed border, and intra prediction mode usually predict one block by two pixel only, so even there is one pixel's border is reconstructed incorrectly, the whole block predicted by it will be wrong. This situation can be expressed in Fig. 38.5, if we use whole macroblock's reconstruction value to predict the following macroblock, some block of incorrect texture will appear in decoded sequence.

## 38.4 Experimental Result

We use the data sets Undo_Dancer, GT_Fly, Poznan_Hall2 in our experiment which are shown in Table 38.1. We use the 1, 5, 9th viewpoint to give LDV's content as rich as possible. Depth sequence is strictly aligned and obtained by stereo matching or depth camera. We generate a three-level LDV and then render the same view after decoding the three-level LDV.

**Table 38.1** Data sets parameters

| Sequence name | Undo_Dancer | GT_Fly | Poznan_Hall2 |
|---|---|---|---|
| Resolution | 1,920 × 1,088 | 1,920 × 1,088 | 1,920 × 1,088 |
| Format | 4:2:0 | 4:2:0 | 4:2:0 |
| Framerate | 25 fps | 25 fps | 25 fps |
| Bitrate | 626.668 Mbps | 626.668 Mbps | 626.668 Mbps |
| View | 1,5,9 | 1,5,9 | 5,6,7 |
| LDV width | 2,240 | 2,240 | 2,240 |

**Table 38.2** Comparizon of reconstructed view quality

| | | Undo_Dancer | | GT_Fly | | Poznan_ Hall2 | |
|---|---|---|---|---|---|---|---|
| | | LDV coding | JM + BZ2 | LDV coding | JM + BZ2 | LDV coding | JM + BZ2 |
| Bitrate | T/D | 19.3 Mbps | 19.6 Mbps | 13.4 Mbps | 16.2 Mbps | 7.2 Mbps | 8.5 Mbps |
| | NOL | 0 | 0.8 Mbps | 0 | 1.2 Mbps | 0 | 0.8 Mbps |
| Left view texture | | 32.9202 | 32.6711 | 37.9592 | 37.5313 | 34.5591 | 34.2591 |
| Left view depth | | 39.1169 | 38.2982 | 49.1943 | 42.7462 | 33.9983 | 33.5996 |
| Middle view texture | | 36.6155 | 36.5144 | 40.1562 | 39.9966 | 40.9682 | 40.9935 |
| Middle view depth | | 44.2533 | 44.2316 | 54.6105 | 53.8233 | 45.4946 | 45.4511 |
| Right view texture | | 32.9229 | 32.5983 | 38.1613 | 37.757 | 35.7082 | 35.5804 |
| Right view depth | | 41.8731 | 40.2723 | 52.2302 | 46.6365 | 38.3194 | 37.7097 |

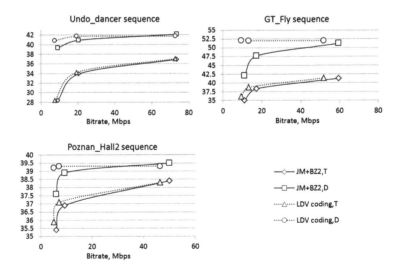

**Fig. 38.6** Our experimental result

In Table 38.2, "LDV coding" represents our experiment result, and "JM + BZ2" means that the contrast group use JM17.2 to encode the texture and depth sequence in LDV's three layers and bzip2 to encode NOL. Table 38.2 shows the comparison of reconstructed view's PSNR. Figure 38.6 shows the RD curve of "LDV coding" and "JM + BZ2".

In our experiment, we choose "IBPIBP" prediction structure and the same QP for our method and contrast group. In addition, first layer's depth map's QP is set different from other's to guarantee reconstructed view's quality.

The sequence we use are used as MPEG-3D standard's designating test sequence, so they have relatively precise depth data and are adaptive for LDV scheme(Poznan_ Hall2's depth map is not accurate enough, so the reconstructed view have some holes). Our work utilizes different viewpoints' spatial correlation so largely improve compression efficiency and decode video's quality.

## 38.5 Conclusions

LDV's generating mainly depends on the accuracy of depth map and actual scene's various kind of situation. After obtaining the right LDV, new method is needed to compress them. Our work propose a new approach to make use of the correlation of front layer's depth value and back layer's occlusion data's figure, the correlation of different kind of macroblock in the special situation where blank and data exists at the same time, and we also select category to give border area high bitrate allocation by encoding the polynomial coefficient apart from other CABAC syntax element. Experiment result show that we not only need to compress NOL, but also get better video quality than traditionally compression standard. There is still some aspect of flaw in our framework, such as the coding of the first layer still occupy large part in our final result, and all these extra data is allocated to serve for avoiding first layer's depth is inaccurate. This is what we should research in further work.

**Acknowledgments** This work was supported in part by the National Natural Science Foundation of China (Grant No. 60802013, 61072081), the National High Technology Research and Development Program (863) of China (Grant No. 2012AA011505), the National Science and Technology Major Project of the Ministry of Science and Technology of China (Grant No. 2009ZX01033-001-007), Key Science and Technology Innovation Team of Zhejiang Province, China (Grant No. 2009R50003) and China Postdoctoral Science Foundation (Grant No. 20110491804).

# References

1. Shade J, Gotler S, He L, Szeliski R (1998) Layered depth image. In: Proceedings ACM SIGGRAPH'98. Orlando, FL, pp 231–242, July 1998
2. Zitnick CL, Kang SB, Uyttendaele M, Winder S, Szeliski R (2004) High-quality video view interpolation using a layered representation. In: ACM Transaction Graphics (SIGGRAPH), pp 600–608
3. Sikor T, Makai B (1995) Shape-adaptive DCT for generic coding of video. IEEE Trans Circuits Syst Video Technol 5(2):59–62
4. Sikora T (1995) Low complexity shape adaptive DCT for coding of arbitrarily shaped image segments. Signal Process Image Commun 7(2):381–395
5. Sikora T, Bauer S, Makai B (1995) Efficiency of shape adaptive transforms for coding of arbitrarily shaped image segments. IEEE Trans Circuits Syst Video Technol 5(6):254–258
6. Sikora T (1997) The MPEG-4 video standard verification model. IEEE Trans Circuits Syst Video Technol 7(2):19–31
7. MPEG-4 Video (1999) MPEG-4 video verification model version 13. 0, ISO/IEC JTC1/SC29/WG11 N2687
8. Duan J, Li J (2003) Compression of the LDI. IEEE Trans Image Process 12(3):365–372
9. ISO/IEC JTC1/SC29/WG11 m12485 (2005) Generation and coding of layered depth images for multi-view video
10. Yoon S, Lee E, Kim S, Ho Y (2005) A framework for multi-view video coding using layered depth images. In: Proceedings of 6th pacific-rim conference on multimedia (PCM 2005), Jeju Island, Korea, pp 431–442

# Chapter 39
# Standard Speaker Selection in Speech Synthesis for Mandarin Tone Learning

Yanlu Xie, Jinsong Zhang and Shuju Shi

**Abstract** The teaching speech chosen to imitate plays a key role in learning Mandarin tone for L2 learners. It has been found that the synthesis teaching speech becomes more acceptable if it is alike the L2 learner's own speech. Voice modification technology can be used to synthesize the teaching speech with both the standard speech of Chinese and the learner's speech. At the same time different standard Chinese speakers will definitely affect the quality of the synthesis speech. The paper studies the selection method of the standard speech of Chinese in the teaching speech synthesis. The speakers' features including MFCC, pitch, rhythm are compared and Gaussian Mixture Model is used to select the most appropriate Chinese speaker. The perceptual experimental results show that the modification with the Chinese speech which is similar to the learner's speech in MFCC gets the best teaching speech both in phonetic and tonal quality.

**Keywords** Mandarin tone · L2 learning · Voice modification · CALL

Y. Xie (✉) · J. Zhang · S. Shi
College of Information Science, Beijing Language and Culture University, Beijing, China
e-mail: xieyanlu@blcu.edu.cn

J. Zhang
e-mail: jinsong.zhang@blcu.edu.cn

S. Shi
e-mail: shujushi0306@gmail.com

J. Zhang
Center for Studies of Chinese as a Second Language,
Beijing Language and Culture University, Beijing, China

W. Lu et al. (eds.), *Proceedings of the 2012 International Conference on Information Technology and Software Engineering*, Lecture Notes in Electrical Engineering 212, DOI: 10.1007/978-3-642-34531-9_39, © Springer-Verlag Berlin Heidelberg 2013

## 39.1 Introduction

Feedback is of great importance in the Computer Aided language learning (CALL) systems. How to improve the efficiency of feedback result has been studied lot in the L2 learning. Some researchers have proved that if the teaching speech is modified from the second language (L2) learners' own voice, the learners will learn easier from the speech [1, 2]. This may be due to the complexity of the human's voice which is full of various information including meaning, language, identity, age and so on. It is easily be interfered by irrelevant factors in the speech when someone learns pronunciation. If the complex variations in the voice are restrict to the variations of something alone, language learners can focus on definite one thing and learn better.

When it comes to tonal languages, with the modified speech based on their own voice, language learners can compare the difference between their own tonal pronunciation and standard tonal pronunciation which also makes it possible for the learners to simply focus on the tone. Through continuous feedback of listening and self-awareness, they can detect and correct their own tone problems.

Mandarin is a tonal language which means that different tones in the speech represent different meanings. At the same time, phonetic quality and tonal quality can be considered independently. The learners whose mother tongue is not tonal will be confused when learning the pronunciation of Mandarin. Previous research showed if the pitch and duration of the speech is adjusted, the learners will be accustomed to the speech better.

Tones in Mandarin are mostly determined by the variation of pitch. Through a phase vocoder Peabody transformed the pitch contour of L2 utterances to match the tonal shapes of native utterances in the learning of Mandarin for learners whose native language is English [3]. In the experiments, the tone classifier results showed the effectiveness of the method. However, the phonetic quality was not given in the paper. Daniel Felps also proposed a voice transformation method to provide a conversion speech of both prosodic and segmental characteristics for correction of foreign-accented in speech learning. Perceptual experiments showed the strong connection between accent and identity [4]. When the prosodic and segmental transformations were performed, the perceived accent was improved while the perceived quality became worse. This may be because the distance between the standard voice and the learners' voice is too big. If the specific standard voice from the speech database is selected to decrease the distance, better result may be got. Ruili Wang provided a method to select golden speakers in L2 learning in CALL. Speakers' gender and speech speed will also affect the interest of the learners [5]. The conclusion showed the specific standard speaker would affect language learning results.

In this paper a new voice modification method is proposed for L2 learning in CALL. The method uses a speech pair of the same Mandarin utterance voiced by the Chinese and Japanese speakers to adjust tone contour of Japanese speakers. Also three kinds of features are applied to compare the similarity of the Japanese and Chinese speakers to select the best one to select the standard speech of Chinese. And the quality of the synthesis speech is also evaluated.

The following is organized as follows: Sect. 39.2 compares the different features in the speech in similarity. Section 39.3 proposes the framework of the voice modification method for tone learning. Section 39.4 gives experimental results and the last part gives the conclusion.

## 39.2 Measurement of the Speech Similar

There are a lot of aspects to measure the similarity between the standard speech and learner's speech. In the previous speech and speaker recognition studies, short time parameters, such as MFCC, PLP, LPCC, are mostly used to measure the speech. Recently supra-segmental features such as pitch, duration and long-term information are also used in the speaker recognition system to improve the system performance. Respectively, different features are used in different tasks. For example, in Ruili Wang's research [5], gender and speech rate information was used to select the standard speech. Also in our previous research it is found Japanese learners are influenced by their mother tongue rhythm while learning Mandarin. So the rhythm information could also distinguish Mandarin voice spoken by Japanese and Chinese. These three kinds of features will also be used to measure the similarity of speech between different Japanese and Chinese speakers.

### 39.2.1 Short Time Parameters

Short time parameters are widely used in speaker recognition. So the similarity of the two speakers (the native speaker and the language learner) can be measured by short time features such as MFCCs.

### 39.2.2 Pitch

The speakers' tonal quality is mainly determined by the variation of pitch. Thus if pitch is used to measure the similarity between the native speakers and learners, better performance might be got in terms of the tonal quality. Also in order to reflect the diversification of pitch, the dynamic and second-order parameters of pitch are also used. The dynamic parameters are calculated as what is done in MFCCs.

### *39.2.3 Rhythm Features*

Since Mandarin is now mostly considered as a syllable-timed language, the rhythm information can also measure the speech which is spoken by Chinese and other speakers [6]. Here four kinds of rhythm features are used to measure the speech of the learners' and the standard who both speak Mandarin. The four rhythm features are %V, $\triangle$V, rPVI, nPVI [7, 8] which show significant distinction between Mandarin data spoken by Mandarin and Japanese speakers in our previous research. The four features are defined as follows.

%V is the mean vowel quantity in a sentence. $\triangle$V is the standard deviation of vowel in a sentence. PVI is the abbreviation of "Pairwise Variability Index" which compares "the level of variability in successive measurements". rPVI is the 'raw PVI' and used for calculation of the consonant intervals. nPVI is the normalized version of the PVI.

$$rPVI = \left[ \sum_{k=1}^{m-1} |d_k - d_{k-1}| / (m-1) \right] \tag{39.1}$$

$$nPVI = 100^* \left[ \sum_{k=1}^{m-1} \left| \frac{d_k - d_{k+1}}{(d_k + d_{k+1})/2} \right| / (m-1) \right] \tag{39.2}$$

Formula (39.1) is for the consonantal raw PVI (rPVI) where m is the number of vocalic or intervocalic intervals in a passage of speech and d is the duration of the $k$th interval.

Formula (39.2) is for the nPVI which is achieved by calculating the duration difference between each pair of successive intervals, then dividing it by the mean duration of the pair, and taking the absolute value. The results for each pair are then summed and divided by the number of differences. The final output is multiplied by 100 to avoid fractional values.

## 39.3 Voice Modification

The framework of voice modification is shown in Fig. 39.1. In the diagram, as a new Mandarin tone learner, his/her pronunciation is compared with that of the speakers in the native speech database. And the most suitable Mandarin speaker is selected as the standard speech to synthesis the teaching speech. The diagram can be mainly divided into two parts.

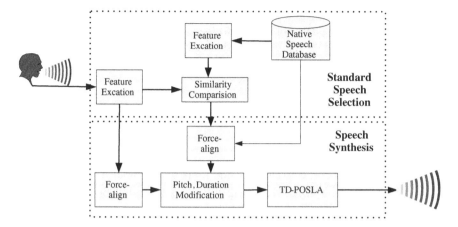

**Fig. 39.1** Diagram of voice modification

## 39.3.1 Standard Speech Selection

The main purpose of this part is to select the most appropriate standard speech of Chinese from the native speech database. As described before, the synthesis speech is achieved based on the combination of both the learners' and the standard speech of same utterance. The better the speech is chosen, the better speech in terms of pronunciation quality and tonal quality may be synthesized.

Firstly, the parameters introduced in Sect. 39.2 are got in the feature extraction module. Then in the similarity comparison module, Gaussian Mixture Model (GMM) is used to compare each speaker. The features of the native speakers are extracted to train GMM for each person. The native speakers' GMMs for different features are trained offline. In the testing process, the same kind of features is got from the learner's speech to calculate the likelihood comparing with the trained GMMs. And the most similar native speaker is selected. Different native speakers may be chosen for the same learner in terms of different features.

## 39.3.2 Speech Synthesis

In this part, the teaching speech is synthesized using the speech of the selected native speakers and the learners.

At the beginning, an automatic speech recognizer is applied to force-align the speech data into phonetic segments. The input utterances voiced by the native speaker and the learner must be exactly the same sentence. So the force-alignment result can be compared between each speech. The duration and the pitch is both modified in every tiny segment in the learner's speech. The adjusted duration is the mean of the two segments and the adjusted pitch is the pitch of the native speaker.

At the related point of the new synthesis speech, the adjusted pitch is added. After the duration and the pitch points are decided, TD-POSLA method is used to synthesize the teaching speech. Since most of acoustic parameters are still from the learner's speech, the semantic content and personality of the synthesis speech is consistent to that of the learner's speech.

## 39.4 Experimental Results

In order to verify the effectiveness of the proposed method, a set of teaching speech is synthesized and the phonetic quality and the tonal quality of the speech are evaluated in the perceptual experiments.

### 39.4.1 Experimental Data

BLCU inter-Chinese speech corpus is used here [9, 10]. In the corpus continuous speech of 3 Japanese speakers' (2 males and 1 female) and 12 Chinese speakers' (6 males and 6 females) are used in the experiments. The corpus is annotated as described in [10]. Each speaker uttered a same sentence set of 301 daily used sentences which are largely used to teach Mandarin.

### 39.4.2 Synthesis of Training Speech

Firstly, MFCCs, Pitch and the rhythm features are extracted from the experimental speech data. Secondly, GMMs are trained using Expectation Maximization (EM) algorithms for each Mandarin speaker. As the amount of the data of three kinds of features is different, the number of mixtures in GMM is also different. The number of mixtures is 32 for MFCCs, and 4 for pitch as well as the four rhythm parameters.

Then the parameters of the three Japanese speakers are compared with the trained GMMs to calculate the likelihood. And the corresponding Mandarin speakers are chosen according to different features comparison result. There are four rhythm features and their results are integrated by the score fusion method to get only one result.

Finally with one Japanese speaker's speech and the selected the Chinese speaker's speech, Praat software is adopted to implement TD-POSLA to synthesis speech [11].

### 39.4.3  Perceptual Experiments

Five graduate students whose native language is Mandarin from the Center for Studies of Chinese as a Second Language in BLCU evaluated the quality of the synthesis speech. The students listened to an utterance and were asked to identify the phonetic quality and the tonal quality of the sentence on a standard MOS scale from 1 (bad) to 5 (excellent). All the students had to assess the voice quality of the Chinese speakers, the Japanese speakers and the synthesis speech. There may be 1–3 kinds of synthesis speech for one Japanese speaker depending on the similarity comparison result of three kinds of features.

### 39.4.4  Experimental Result

Figures 39.2 and 39.3 are the results of perceptual experiments. In the figures M1, M2, F1 refers to the different 2 male and 1 female Japanese speakers. The five columns for each speaker represent the average MOS scores of perceptual experiments. The scores average the results of the 301 daily used sentences given by the five graduate students. The first column CHN refers to the MOS scores of the original Chinese speaker. The second column JPN refers to the scores of the original Japanese speaker. The last three columns MFCC, PITCH and RHYTHM refer to the different MOS scores of the synthesis speech respectively. The last three scores are different because the synthesis speech is achieved based on the same Japanese speech and different Chinese speech. For the MFCC column, the Chinese speech is chosen that is most similar with the Japanese speech in term of the MFCC features. It is the same with PITCH and RHYTHM.

From the two figures, it is found the synthesis speech quality is improved both in the phonetic and the tonal aspects. Since the tone is substituted by the standard speaker's, the tonal quality is improved much more than the phonetic quality. The relative MOS improvement of MFCC based synthesis speech is about 5.4 % in phonetic and 12.6 % in tonal for M1 averaging five students' results.

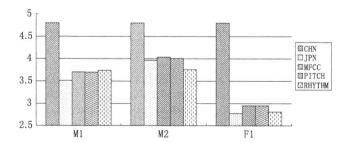

**Fig. 39.2** Perceptual results of phonetic quality

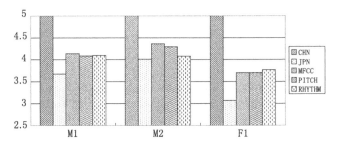

**Fig. 39.3** Perceptual results of tonal quality

Also the worse of the tonal quality of the original Japanese speaker becomes, the better improvement is got in the MOS. For example in the Fig. 39.3, the original Japanese speakers' MOS scores are 3.7, 4.0 and 3.1, and the relative improvement is 12.6, 9.0 and 20.7 % respectively for MFCC column.

## 39.4.5 Discussion

As to the method of selecting the Chinese speaker, it shows no significant difference in the phonetic quality. However, it seems that MFCC selection is better than PITCH and RHYTHM selection. In the Fig. 39.3, for M1 and M2 MFCC performs better than PITCH and RHYTHM. For F1, it is a particular case. The MFCC and PITCH selection choose the same Chinese speaker and the RHYTHM performs a little better than the MFCC and PITCH. This may be due to the fact that the number of Chinese speakers is too smaller in our corpus (only 12 speakers). If there were more speakers, better Chinese speakers might be chosen.

It had been expected that PITCH or RHYTHM might get better performance in selecting standard speech. On the contrary MFCC is better in general. It might because that MFCC reflects most of the acoustic characteristics and some traits of tone as well. The other two kinds of features still remove too much information and the reserved information can not reflect the real tonal contour distribution well.

The quality of speech is also can not compare to that of the standard Chinese in the two figures. This may be that the utterance in 301 daily used sentences is a little long. If the duration and the pitch of the utterance are modified greatly, they may deviate to that of the normal utterance much and PSOLA can not synthesize natural speech. In the future, shorter speech will be selected to verify the hypothesis.

Synthesis speech quality is of great important in the CALL system. Generally there are a lot of standard speakers in the speech database. The above experiments show that if the most appropriate standard speaker is selected, the tonal quality of the synthesis speech could be improved much. It is useful in the next L2 learning experiments.

## 39.5 Conclusions

This paper proposed a new voice modification and standard speech selection method for the learning of Mandarin tone. Through the method, phonetic quality and tonal quality of the synthesis speech are also improved, especially the tonal quality (relative improve 20.7 % in MOS score). Moreover the MFCC feature shows the best standard speech selection performance. Admittedly the number of standard speakers is a little smaller in the corpus. In the future, more speakers will be collected and annotated in the corpus to verify the method. Moreover the L2 learning performance should be evaluated with the synthesis speech and the standard speech.

**Acknowledgments** The research underlying this paper was supported by National Nature Science Foundation of China (61175019) and Youth Independent Research Program Projects of Beijing Language and Culture University (10JBT01).

## References

1. Tang M, Wang C, Seneff S (2001) Voice transformations: from: speech synthesis to mammalian vocalizations. Aalborg, Denmark Eurospeech 2001
2. Probst K, Ke Y, Eskenazi M (2002) Enhancing foreign language tutors-in search of the golden speaker. Speech Commun 37(3-4):161-173
3. Peabody M, Seneff S (2006) Towards automatic tone correction in nonnative mandarin. Chin Spoken Lang Process 2006:602-613
4. Felps D, Bortfeldb H, Gutierrez-Osuna R (2009) Foreign accent conversion in computer assisted pronunciation training. Speech Commun 51(10):920-932
5. Wang R, Lu J (2011) Investigation of golden speakers for second language learners from imitation preference perspective by voice modification. Speech Commun 53(2):175-184
6. Lin H, Wang Q (2007) Mandarin rhythm: an acoustic study. J Chin Linguist Comput 17(3):127-140
7. Ramus F, Nespor M, Mehler J (1999) Correlates of linguistic rhythm in the speech signal. Cognition 72:1-28
8. Grabe E, Low EL (2002) Durational variability in speech and the rhythm class hypothesis. In: Gussenhoven C, Warner N (eds) Laboratory phonology 7. Moutonde Gruyter, New York, pp 515-546
9. Cao W, Zhang J (2009) The establishment of a CAPL inter-chinese corpus and its labeling. In: Proceedings Of NCMMSC (in Chinese)
10. Cao W, Wang D, Zhang J, Xiong Z (2010) Developing a Chinese L2 speech database of Japanese learners with narrow-phonetic labels for computer assisted pronunciation training. Int Speech 2010 1922-1925
11. Boersma P, Weenink D (2010) Praat: doing phonetics by computer. Version 5.1. 44

# Chapter 40
# Separating Algorithm for Quasi-Circle Overlapping Images Based on Improved Hough Transform

Siming Cheng, Kangling Fang and Xinhai Liu

**Abstract** A new separating algorithm for quasi-circle overlapping images based on improved Hough transform is proposed in this paper. This method according to a circle's geometrical property that any point on circumference along the normal direction of the straight line must pass the center of the circle, can extract the central area of the targets, which is used to solve the separating problem of quasi-circle overlapping images. Experiments show that the proposed method can obtain acceptable results.

**Keywords** Quasi-circle objects · Hough transform · Overlapping · Separating

## 40.1 Introduction

Quasi-circle objects can be seen everywhere in nature and life, such as steel bars in iron and steel enterprises, fruits in agricultural production, cells in medical research. Therefore, the research of identification of quasi-circle objects is quite significant in image pattern recognition. Hough transform [1, 2] is a classic method of circle detection. The traditional hough transform has disadvantages of huge computation, occupying a large memory and running slow. Using bar images as example, this paper proposed a separating algorithm for quasi-circle overlapping images based on improved hough transform. The detailed procedure for separating algorithm is explained as follow.

S. Cheng (✉) · K. Fang · X. Liu
College of Information Science and Engineering, Wuhan University of Science and Technology, No. 947 HePing Road, QingShan, Wuhan City, China
e-mail: siming29@126.com

W. Lu et al. (eds.), *Proceedings of the 2012 International Conference on Information Technology and Software Engineering*, Lecture Notes in Electrical Engineering 212, DOI: 10.1007/978-3-642-34531-9_40, © Springer-Verlag Berlin Heidelberg 2013

## 40.2 Image Preprocessing

Noise is produced in the course of collection, transmission and processing. Noise worse the quality of the images, and bring troubles in the follow-up image processing. So, before the separating process, a median filter is used to denoise on the original images.

### 40.2.1 Median Filter

Median filter is a nonlinear filter. Under certain conditions, it can reduce noise and protect the edge details of the image. The principle of median filter is using the median value of the gray value in a sliding window instead of the gray value of the center. The sliding window contains odd points, and the gray values in the window are already sorted.

One-dimensional median filter is defined as follows.

$$y = med\{x_1, x_2, \ldots, x_n\} \tag{40.1}$$

where $x_1, x_2, \ldots, x_n$ are input data, y is output data, n usually is an odd number.

The concept of median filter can be easily extended to two-dimensional. The common shapes of two-dimensional median filtering window are square, circle and cross, etc. In this paper, a $5 \times 5$ sliding window is used to filter. It reduces noise, keeps the edges of the image, and fills the black spots of the bar images.

### 40.2.2 Otsu

After median filtering, binary processing is done to make target area separate from the background area. The most critical technology of image binarization is the selection of optimal threshold. If the threshold is too large, too much target area will be classified as the background area. If the threshold is too small, too much background area is divided into the target area. Currently, the classic automatic threshold calculation methods are bimodal method, iterative method, Otsu method, gray stretch Otsu method and Kirsh operator method [3].

Otsu, proposed by N. Ostu in 1979, is a dynamic threshold method. The basic idea of Otsu is using the image histogram, according to the variance between the target and the background, to dynamically determine the optimal threshold. Set the number of all pixels in the image is N, the gray level is L (0, 1, ..., L−1). The number of the gray value i is $n_i$, then the probability of i is $P_i = \frac{n_i}{N}$. The image is divided into two parts, target area O and background area B with threshold value T, B corresponds to the gray value in [0, T−1] of the pixels, O corresponds to the gray value in [T, L−1] of the pixels.

The probability of background area is

$$w_0 = \sum_{i=0}^{T-1} p_i \qquad (40.2)$$

The probability of target area is

$$w_1 = \sum_{i=T}^{L-1} p_i = 1 - w_0 \qquad (40.3)$$

The mean of background area is

$$u_0 = \sum_{i=0}^{T-1} ip_i/w_0 \qquad (40.4)$$

The mean of target area is

$$u_1 = \sum_{i=T}^{L-1} ip_i/w_1 \qquad (40.5)$$

The mean of the entire image is

$$u = w_0 u_0 + w_1 u_1 \qquad (40.6)$$

The infra- class variance is defined as

$$\sigma^2 = w_0(u0 - u)^2 + w_1(u_1 - u)^2 = w_0 w_1(u_0 - u_1)^2 \qquad (40.7)$$

Make the threshold T traverse each gray level from 0 to 255. When $\sigma^2$ is maximum, the corresponding T is the optimal threshold.

Otsu method uses one-dimensional image gray histogram to determine the segmentation threshold. It is an automatic non-parametric unsupervised threshold selection method. This method is simple to calculate, not affected by the change of contrast and brightness under certain conditions, and able to separate bar area from the background area satisfactorily.

## 40.3 Separation of the Overlapping Bar Image

The end face of bar is similar to round in binary image. Hough transform is a classic method of circle detection. Hough transform implements a mapping from image space to parameter space, the detection problem in the images is transformed to the parameter space, through the simple accumulation in the parameter space to complete the detection task. This paper improved the Hough circle transform algorithm, by using the gradient information of the edges and according to a circle's geometrical property that any point on circumference along the normal direction of the straight line must pass the center of the circle. Hough circle transform in three-dimensional space is converted to two-dimensional space; it implements the separation of the overlapping images.

### 40.3.1 Traditional Hough Circle Transform

In two-dimensional image space, the circle equation can be expressed as

$$(x - a)^2 + (y - b)^2 = r^2 \tag{40.8}$$

where (x, y) is the coordinate of the pixel point on the circumference, (a, b) is center coordinate, r is radius.

Equation (40.8) can be also rewritten as

$$(a - x)^2 + (b - y)^2 = r^2 \tag{40.9}$$

At this time Eq. (40.9) can be regarded as a three-dimensional conical surface in the parameter space $(a, b, r)$. Any circle in the image space is corresponding to a point in the parameter space $(a, b, r)$. Any point in the image space is corresponding to a three-dimensional conical surface in the parameter space $(a, b, r)$. A set$\{(x_i, y_j)\}$ containing all points on the circumferences in the image space is corresponding to the conical surface cluster in the parameter space $(a, b, r)$. If the points in the set are on the same circle, these conical surface clusters will intersect at a point $(a_0, b_0, r_0)$ in the parameter space. In this way, $(a_0, b_0)$ is the center coordinate and $r_0$ is the radius of the circle in the image space.

The steps of traditional Hough transform circle detection are, to appropriately quantify the parameter space for a three-dimensional accumulator $A(a, b, r)$; then to do Hough circle transform for every point in the test image space. That is, calculating the surface in parameter space which is corresponding to this point and plus 1 to the corresponding accumulator. When all points of the image have been transformed, the peak$(a_0, b_0, r_0)$ of the accumulator is the parameters of the circle in the original image space.

In fact, when the parameter space is not more than two-dimensional, the standard Hough transform has desired results. But the parameter space of circle is three-dimensional; the consumption of time and space is very huge when accumulating in the three-dimensional accumulation space. So, it is almost impossible and unrealistic to use the traditional Hough circle transform in practical applications.

**Fig. 40.1** Relationship
between points on
circumference and the center
of circle

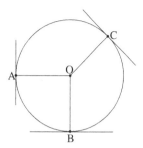

## 40.3.2 Improved Hough Transform for Separating

### 40.3.2.1 The Idea of Algorithm

It will greatly reduce the computing amount by using the gradient information of
the edge [4]. In digital image processing, the first derivative can be used to detect a
point whether belong the edge. The first derivative is approximation based on a
variety of two-dimensional gradient [4]. The gradient of image $f(x, y)$ in $(x, y)$ is
defined as the following direction:

$$\nabla f = \left[G_x, G_y\right]^T = \left[\frac{\partial f}{\partial x}, \frac{\partial f}{\partial y}\right] \qquad (40.10)$$

The direction of gradient is the direction of the maximum change rate of
function $f(x, y)$.

The amplitude of gradient is measured as the size of change rate, its value is
$|\nabla f(x, y)| = \sqrt{(G_x)^2 + (G_y)^2}$.

Let $\theta(x, y)$ present the direction angle of vector $\nabla f$, then $\theta(x, y) = \arctan\left(\frac{G_y}{G_x}\right)$.
Among them, the angle is benchmarked against the x-axis; the direction of the
edge in $(x, y)$ is perpendicular to the gradient direction of this point.

Shown in Fig. 40.1, any point on circumference along the normal direction of
the straight line must pass the center of the circle. So in the ideal situation, the
gradient direction of points on circumference in edge image of the straight line
passes the center of the circle [5].

### 40.3.2.2 Algorithm Steps

According to the improved algorithm, the detailed procedure for separation is
explained in the following steps:

Step 1: Apply median filtering on the original image.
Step 2: Binarize the image to highlight the bar targets.
Step 3: Calculate and record the gradients with Sobel operator.

Step 4: Scan the image from left to right, from top to bottom. As for the edge point P, if the point P satisfies the conditions, seek and record the point M which is $R_{min}$ away from the point P along the normal direction.

Step 5: Seek and record the next point N by stepper one along the normal direction. Determine whether the distance of PN less than the threshold $R_{max}$.

Step 6: If the distance of PN is less than the threshold $R_{max}$, seek the next point by stepper one along the normal direction, otherwise turn to the step 4 to process the next edge point.

Step 7: After all edge points have been transformed, there will be several bar center areas, each area is gathered by a certain number of points.

Step 8: Do areas opening on the image, the overlapping bar will be separated.

## 40.4 Experimental Results and Analysis

In Visual Studio 2010, we program to realize the separating algorithm for quasi-circle overlapping images based on improved Hough transform proposed in this paper. The end face of bars is used as test objects. The four pictures which are shown in Fig. 40.2 shows the basic separation process of the overlapping bar image. Figure 40.2a shows the original bar image. Figure 40.2b shows the result image after doing median filter and binaring by Otsu method. The center areas of bars, which are determined by the improved Hough transform method proposed in this paper, is shown in Fig. 40.2c. The radius of bars is 6–12 pixels. Finally, do area opening on the image, the separation result is shown in Fig. 40.2d. Experiments show that the algorithm can achieve the separation of the overlapping targets, if the overlapping area is less than one-third.

In order to overcome the affection of noises and other factors, to improve the processing speed, and to guarantee the center region as far as possible be concentrated in the center of the bar, several measures have been used in the algorithm.

First, in preprocessing state, median filtering is used to denoise. Because some end face of bars is blue due to oxidation, its pixels will be dimmer when the original image converted to the gray image. If doing binarization directly on the original image without any processing, it will conduct black spots inside the bar, median filtering is also used to fill black spots of bar.

Second, use granulometry technology [5] to get the radius of the bar before separation. Estimate the center of the bar in the case of known radius. Then Hough circle transform in three-dimensional parameter space can be converted to two-dimensional flat space. It will greatly increase the processing speed.

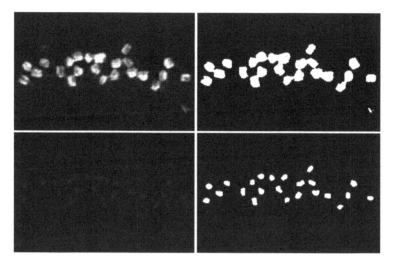

**Fig. 40.2** The separating process of overlapping bar image, **a** Original image. **b** Binary image. **c** Center areas image. **d** Result image

Three, when estimate the center of the bar, set two threshold values based on radius obtained by granulometry, then cumulate by stepper one in the threshold range, not cumulate by stepper one starting from edge point. Thereby, it decreases the computing amount greatly, and the center regions estimated as far as possible are in the center of the bars.

## 40.5 Conclusion

The separating algorithm based on improved Hough transform proposed in this paper, uses to solve the separating problems for overlapping bar image. The algorithm uses granulometry to obtain the radius of bars, combined with improved Hough transform to extract the center areas of the bars, so as to achieve the purpose of separation of overlapping bar image. The algorithm has been successfully used for the separation of overlapping bar image, and is also effective for other quasi-circle overlapping images.

**Acknowledgments**  This work was supported in part by the National Natural Science Foundation of China (Grant No. 60705035).

# References

1. Shu ZL, Qi FH (2003) A novel algorithm for fast circle detection using randomized Hough transform. J Comput Eng 29(6):87–88 (in Chinese)
2. Hallard DH (1981) Generalizing the Hough transform to detect arbitrary shapes. Pattern Recogn 13(2):111–122
3. Liu ZM, Cheng PF (2008) The steel rod automation counting and packaging system based on image discerning. J Hunan Univ Arts Sci (Nature Science Edition) 20(4):82–84 (in Chinese)
4. Qu J, Gan L (2007) The application of grads Hough transformation in circle detection. J East China Jiaotong Univ 24(1):101–103 (in Chinese)
5. You YS, Yu HM (2005) A separating algorithm for overlapping red blood cell images. J Image Graph 10(6):736–740 (in Chinese)

# Chapter 41
# A Video Watermarking Scheme Resistant to Geometric Attacks

Hua Jiang, Tiexin Xu and Xin Wang

**Abstract** This paper presents a new digital video watermarking method based on chaotic scrambling and SVD. The proposed method combined the safe characters of the TD-ERCS chaotic system with the anti-geometric of the singular value decomposition (SVD). Firstly, select the embedded region in the luminance component of the video frame with the help of 2-dimensional chaotic sequence of watermark scrambling produced by TD-ERCS discrete chaotic system. Secondly, making the selected region into sub-blocks to make discrete wavelet transform and making SVD in the low-frequency parts. Finally, by modifying the largest singular value to embed the watermark information. The experimental results indicates that the algorithm is satisfying in performance, watermark can be taken out without the original video sequence, and it also has blind detectability as well as preferable robustness to the common geometric attacks.

**Keywords** Video watermarking · Geometric attacks · Chaotic scrambling · Singular value decomposition · Blind detection

H. Jiang
Network Center, Guilin University of Electronic Technology, 1 Jinji Road Guilin, Guangxi 541004, China
e-mail: jianghua@guet.edu.cn

T. Xu (✉) · X. Wang
School of Computer Science and Engineering, Guilin University of Electronic Technology, 1 Jinji Road Guilin, Guangxi 541004, China
e-mail: fezn_1988@126.com

W. Lu et al. (eds.), *Proceedings of the 2012 International Conference on Information Technology and Software Engineering*, Lecture Notes in Electrical Engineering 212, DOI: 10.1007/978-3-642-34531-9_41, © Springer-Verlag Berlin Heidelberg 2013

## 41.1 Introduction

With the rapid development of the Internet and digital technology, the fields in application of digital media products and technologies are expanded. At the same time, there have been numerous copyright infringements including copying, spreading and distorting that violate the legitimate rights and interests of producers and consumers. Digital watermarking has become a powerful tool to protect copyright and fight against infringements. Among them, the video watermarking has become a hot zone in the field of modern information hidden technology and copyright protection.

In recent years, the singular value decomposition (SVD) watermarking has attracted people's attention. The SVD is an important matrix decomposition in linear algebra. It has very important application value in the field of image processing and statistics [1]. In 2001, Chinese Liu Ruizhen used SVD in digital watermarking system for the first time. Embedding watermark information by modifying singular value of the original image to resist geometric attacks effectively [2]. The algorithm has high robustness though it is of high false alarming rate. There is a high correlation between the needed singular value matrix and extracted watermark. Reference [3] fuses two watermark signals and pseudo-random scrambling pretreatment. Then the video is divided into several scenes and 3-dimensional DWT is made in each scene. Select the binary image as a watermark, watermark information is embedded in the coefficients with good invisibility which pretreated three-dimensional discrete wavelet transform produces. Reference [4] proposed a video watermarking algorithm based on multidimensional scaling and SVD. The method can resist geometric distortion and random noise attack, but the robustness of the time synchronization distortion needs to be improved. Reference [5] takes advantage of the feature points of synchronization frame to recover the attacked digital watermarking video sequences. Rajab proposed a hybrid DWT-SVD blind video watermarking algorithm [6]. First the twice DWT is done in each frame of the video image. Then the $HL_2$ is decomposed by singular value decomposition (SVD), modifying the corresponding singular value with Least Significant Bit (LSB) while embedding watermark.

In order to resist geometric attacks more efficiently, this paper proposed a video watermarking algorithm based on chaotic scrambling and SVD. Select the embedded region in the luminance component of the video frame with the help of 2-dimensional chaotic sequence of watermark scrambling produced by TD-ERCS discrete chaotic system. Making the selected region into sub-blocks to make discrete wavelet transform and making SVD in the low-frequency parts. Finally, by modifying the largest singular value to embed the watermark information. The algorithm has good imperceptibility and robustness to geometric attacks.

## 41.2 Algorithm Overview

### 41.2.1 Watermark Generation

Sheng proposed a cut delay chaotic system of the elliptical reflecting cavity mapping system tangent-delay ellipse reflecting cavity from-map system (TD-ERCS) to produce the chaotic sequence [7]. The experiment shows that the system has a strong resistance to differential cryptanalysis and degradation.

Chaotic system is of many features, such as the good unpredictability of track, the pseudo-random features, extreme sensitive to parameters and initial state. The logistic mapping is commonly used in image encryption algorithm based on chaotic sequences, but the security of low-dimensional chaotic system is not high enough, so high-dimensional chaotic system has gradually become the focus of the image encryption. The chaotic sequence generated by the TD-ERCS chaotic system is extreme sensitive to initial values, a very small error can lead to the watermark unrestored only the correct key can extract the correct watermark information.

The mapping equations are: $x_n = -\frac{2k_{n-1}y_{n-1}+x_{n-1}\left(\mu^2-k_{n-1}^2\right)}{\mu^2+k_{n-1}}$; $k_n = \frac{2k'_{n-m}-k_{n-1}+k_{n-1}k_n'^2-m}{1+2k_{n-1}k'_{n-m}-k_{n-m}'^2}$; $y_n = k_{n-1}(x_n - x_{n-1}) + y_{n-1}$; $k'_{n-m} = -\frac{x_{n-m}}{y_{n-m}}\mu^2$, $n \ge m$. Here, $(x_0, \alpha, \mu, m)$ is the system parameters where $x_0 \in [1, 1]$, $tan \in (-\infty, +\infty)$, $\mu \in (0.05, 1]$, and then $m = 2, 3, 4, 5 \ldots$, Iterative rounds $n = 1, 2, 3, \ldots$ $y_0 = \mu\sqrt{1 - x_0^2}$; $k'_0 = -\frac{x_0}{y_0}\mu^2$; $k_0 = \frac{tan\,\alpha+k'_0}{1-k'_0 tan\,\alpha}$; $k'_n = -\frac{x_n}{y_n}\mu^2$.

Set the parameter of initial seeds can generate two independent non-related 2-dimensional chaotic sequence $\{(x_n, k_n)|n = 1, 2, 3, \ldots\}$, which $x_0$, $\alpha$, $\mu$ and $m$ can be used as keys. Setting a door limit function $signs(X, door)$ by the 2-dimensional chaotic sequence to obtain the corresponding scrambling matrix [8]. The threshold function is set to:

$$signs(X, door)\begin{cases} 1 & x \ge door \\ 0 & x < door \end{cases} \tag{41.1}$$

Here, $x$ is the element of matrix $X$. And then let this chaotic matrix XOR with the watermark matrix to obtain the scrambling watermark image. The chaotic image restore algorithm is the inverse process of the above algorithm. The parameters of TD-ERCS system were $\mu = 0.6$, $x_0 = 0.8$, $\alpha = 0.85$ and $m = 7$. Figure 41.1 is the results of watermark image scrambling generated by a chaotic sequence from TD-ERCS chaotic system.

### 41.2.2 Watermark Embedding

(1) The pretreatment of the watermark. Scrambling the binary watermark with chaotic sequence generated by the TD-ERCS system.

**Fig. 41.1  a** Original
watermark. **b** Watermark
scrambling

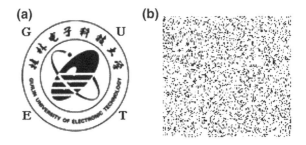

(2) Regard the center of the luminance component of each frame as center, select a $M \times M$ square region as an embedded region.

(3) Make the $M \times M$ square area into sub-blocks, the size of binary watermark image $W$ is $N \times N$, the size of sub-block $Block(i)$ is $K \times K$. That is, $K = M/N$.

(4) Do DWT for $Block(i)$.

(5) Select the low frequency part $LL(i)$ and do SVD. That is, $Block(i) = U(i)S(i)V(i)^T$.

(6) According to the following principles, modify the largest singular value $\lambda(i)$ of diagonal matrix $S(i)$:

$$\lambda(i) = \begin{cases} \lambda(i) - \mathrm{mod}(\lambda(i), Q) - Q/4 & if \; w(i) = 1, \mathrm{mod}(\lambda(i), Q) < \, = Q/4 \\ \lambda(i) = \lambda(i) - \mathrm{mod}(\lambda(i), Q) + 3 \times Q/4 & if \; w(i) = 1, \mathrm{mod}(\lambda(i), Q) > Q/4 \\ \lambda(i) = \lambda(i) - \mathrm{mod}(\lambda(i), Q) + 5 \times Q/4 & if \; w(i) = 1, \mathrm{mod}(\lambda(i), Q) > \, = 3 \times Q/4 \\ \lambda(i) = \lambda(i) - \mathrm{mod}(\lambda(i), Q) + Q/4 & if \; w(i) = 1, \mathrm{mod}(\lambda(i), Q) < 3 \times Q/4 \end{cases}$$

$$(41.2)$$

Here, $\mathrm{mod}(\lambda(i), Q)$ is for the sake of $\lambda(i)$ and $Q$'s remainder. $Q$ is the strength of embedded watermark, $w(i)$ is watermark information to decompose the revised $S'(i)$ Conduct $Block'(i) = U(i) \, S'(i) \, V(i)^T$.

(7) Repeat (4, 5, 6) until watermarks are embedded in all sub-blocks.

### 41.2.3  Watermark Extraction

(1) Regard the center of the luminance component of each frame as center, select a $M \times M$ square region.

(2) Make the $M \times M$ square area into sub-blocks, the size of binary watermark image $W$ is $N \times N$, the size of sub-block $Block(i)$ is $K \times K$. That is, $K = M/N$.

(3) Do IDWT for $Block^*(i)$.

(4) Select the low frequency part $LL(i)$ and do SVD. That is, $Block^*(i) = U^*(i) \, S^*(i) \, V^*(i)^T$.

(5) According to the following principles to judge the largest singular value $\lambda^*(i)$ of the diagonal matrix $S^*(i)$ as follows,

$$w(i) = \begin{cases} 1 & if \ \mathrm{mod}\,(\lambda^*(i), Q) > Q/2 \\ 0 & else \end{cases} \tag{41.3}$$

(6) Repeat (3, 4, 5) until of the watermark is extracted from all blocks.
(7) Binary watermark can be obtained by the chaos scrambling inverse transform of the watermark information.

## 41.3 Experimental Results

### 41.3.1 Experiment Environment

This experiment tests the performance of the proposed algorithm in the Windows XP operating system Matlab 2007 for imperceptibility and robustness. Apply standard video sequence Flower and Salesman for testing. 250 Flower frames and 150 Salesman frames with the same size of $352 \times 288$. The watermark image used in the experiment is the binary image of $32 \times 32$ pixels.

### 41.3.2 Imperceptibility of the Watermark

Figure 41.2 shows the original video image and the watermarked video image. We can see that the human eyes hardly perceive the quality differences between original image and the embedded watermark.

In this paper, two video sequences PSNR are applied for the original and the watermark scrambling to evaluate the invisibility of watermark. Due to a large number of video data, only 1–30 PSNR are extracted. Figure 41.3 shows the PSNR of the watermarked video.

The PSNR value is above 35 in the algorithm to meet the requirements of embedded watermark invisible.

### 41.3.3 Robustness

The robustness of the algorithm is judged by the relevant relationship between the detected watermark and the original watermark. A series of common attacks to watermarked video are conducted in this experiment to test the robustness of the algorithm [9]. The experimental results are shown in Table 41.1.

**Fig. 41.2** Figure shows the original and watermarked frame of flower video. **b** Figure shows the original and watermarked frame of salesman video

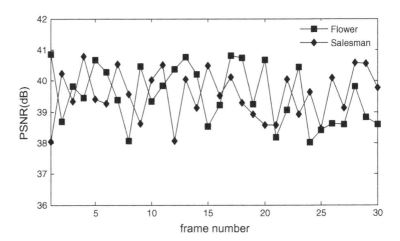

**Fig. 41.3** PSNR of the watermarked video

Normalized correlation function NC (Normalization Correlation) is used to evaluate the robustness of watermark [10]. NC is defined as:

$$NC = \sum_{i=1}^{N} \sum_{j=1}^{M} w(i,j)w^*(i,j) \bigg/ \sum_{i=1}^{N} \sum_{j=1}^{M} (w(i,j))^2 \qquad (41.4)$$

Here, $w(i,j)$ is the original watermark image and $w^*(i,j)$ is the extracted image, $M$ represents the width of the original image, $N$ represents the original image.

**Table 41.1** The average NC for sequences after common attacks

| Attack | Video sequences | |
|---|---|---|
| | Flower | Salesman |
| Random insert 20 % frames | 0.9738 | 0.9689 |
| Random delete 30 % frames | 0.9892 | 0.9916 |
| Crop 25 % | 0.8638 | 0.8527 |
| Rotate 1° | 1.0000 | 1.0000 |
| Rotate 5° | 1.0000 | 1.0000 |
| Rotate 10° | 0.9765 | 0.9682 |
| Rotate 30° | 0.9249 | 0.9153 |
| MPEG-4 compression | 0.9468 | 0.9713 |

**Table 41.2** Random testing of the watermark

| Video sequences | 2 s | 35 s | 82.5 s | 120 s |
|---|---|---|---|---|
| Flower | 0.97 | 0.94 | 0.95 | 0.94 |
| Salesman | 0.94 | 0.92 | 0.93 | 0.94 |

### 41.3.4 Random Testing Analysis

In order to evaluate the improved algorithm meets the requirements of random testing of the watermark or not,in this paper we pick up the watermark from 4 testing points of the two kinds of standard videos which embed the watermark in a random sequence of 2, 35, 82.5, 120 s, and the similarity calculation is applied to the watermark picked up from each testing point. Table 41.2 is the result of random testing of the watermark.

## 41.4 Conclusion

In this paper, a new digital video watermarking method based on chaotic scrambling and SVD is proposed through modifying the largest singular value to embed the watermark information. Combined the advantages of the TD-ERCS chaotic system with singular value decomposition. Watermark detection has blind detectability, meanwhile, watermark can be taken out without the original video sequence and the visual effect can be fully guaranteed after embedding the watermark. According to the simulation result, the algorithm can both meet the imperceptibility of the watermark and show satisfying robustness to the common geometric attacks.

# References

1. Xu G, Wang D (2009) A blind video watermarking algorithm resisting to rotation attack. International conference on computer and communications security, pp 111–114
2. Liu R, Tan T (2002) An SVD-based watermarking scheme for protecting rightful ownership. IEEE Trans Multimedia 14(1):121–128
3. Kim SJ, Lee SH, Moon KS (2004) A new digital video watermarking using the dual watermark images and 3D DWT. In: Proceedings of 2004 IEEE region, pp 291–294
4. Nie X, Qi L, Qin F (2010) Video watermarking based on multi-dimensional scaling and singular value decomposition. J Comput App 30(10):2691–2693 (in Chinese)
5. Yang X, Niu K, Wei P, Wang Y (2007) A video watermark scheme resistant to geometric attacks. Comput Eng 33(8):142–144 (in Chinese)
6. Rajab L, Al-Khatib T, Al-Haj A (2008) Hybrid DWT-SVD video water-marking. In: Proceedings of international conference on innovations in information technology, Al Ain, pp 588–592
7. Sheng L, Sun K, Li C (2004) Study of a discrete chaotic system based on tangent-delay for elliptic reflecting cavity and its properties. Acta Physica Sinica 53(9):2871–2876 (in Chinese)
8. Sun K, Cheng W, Chen Y (2011) Video watermarking algorithm based on chaos and motion vector. App Res Comput 28(8):3046–3048 (in Chinese)
9. Lv A (2009) A novel video watermarking scheme against manifold attacks. J Image Graphic 14(11):2205–2211 (in Chinese)
10. Barni M, Bartolini F, Checcacci N (2005) Watermarking of MPEG-4 video objects multimedia. IEEE Trans 7(1):23–32

# Chapter 42
# A Fast Tracking Algorithm for Multiple-Objects in Occlusions

Zhigang Zhang, Lei Bai and Junqin Huang

**Abstract** Occlusion problem is one of difficult points in moving target tracking, which also is one of key techniques to intelligent vision. Based on moving objects detection, minimum enclosing rectangle of human-body top half area is selected as tracing window, which can eliminate the interference of ground shadow, avoid the disturbing of leg movement, and can reduce the amount of computation. Then color histogram of tracing window is calculated by use of the simplified color space, which combines minimum distance matching is used for target matching under non-occlusion; if occlusion occurs, color histogram matching and trajectory prediction is adopted for target matching, with this method, moving object can be tracked correctly under serious occlusion. The experimental results demonstrate that the algorithm is rapid and robust, it can effectively overcome multi-targets tracking in complex scenarios.

**Keywords** Moving target tracking · Histogram matching · Occlusion · Trajectory prediction

Z. Zhang (✉) · L. Bai
Department of Information Science, Xi'an University of Technology,
No. 5, Jinhua South Road, Xi'an Shaanxi 710048, China
e-mail: zzg@xaut.edu.cn

Z. Zhang
School of Electronics and Information Engineering, Xi'an Jiaotong University,
No. 28, Xianning West Road, Xi'an Shaanxi 710049, China

J. Huang
Xi'an University of Technology Engineering Training Center, No. 58, Yanxiang Road,
Xi'an Shaanxi 710054, China

W. Lu et al. (eds.), *Proceedings of the 2012 International Conference on Information* 401
*Technology and Software Engineering*, Lecture Notes in Electrical Engineering 212,
DOI: 10.1007/978-3-642-34531-9_42, © Springer-Verlag Berlin Heidelberg 2013

## 42.1 Introduction

The task of moving target tracking is to detect moving targets in video sequences, link the same target together and continue updating their location. The characteristics variety of moving target and the complexity of external environment makes big trouble to moving target tracking [1]. Occlusion is one of the difficult problems in accounting moving target tracking, to solve the problem, some scholars put forward many algorithm such as mean-shift algorithm, Kalman filtering algorithm, particle filter algorithm, etc. Mean-shift algorithm describes and matches moving target through its weighted color histogram, which was put forward by Comaniciu [2], it is expanded in the literature [3], some improved algorithms has been presented, for instance, Babu use simple linear weighted mechanism to describe overall target [4], Shen Zhixi puts forward a method to update selective submodel [5], Collins describes target through combining each color component which weight coefficient is different [6], Yongzhong improves mean-shift algorithm by using adaptive integration of multi-characteristic [7], Hong adopts target tracking algorithm based color probability and motion track [8]. Kalman Filter algorithm track moving target through trajectory prediction [9], based which Extend Kalman Filter [10] and Unscented Kalman Filter [11] are developed. Particle Filter algorithm is a kind of probabilistic tracking method, which usually utilizes RGB color histogram [12, 13]. Both gradien histogram and color histogram are used in Particle Filter in literature [14], which enhance the robustness. Most present algorithms can well solve moving target tracking under partial occlusion, but the results are ineffective under severe occlusion.

On the basis of motion detection, this paper select upper half rectangle of Human object as tracing window, in which color histogram of movement pixels is calculated in simplified color space as matching characteristics, it can correct track target correctly under non-occlusion or partial occlusion; When severe occlusion occurs, track prediction are combined with color histogram to track target, which solve target tracking problem well and quickly.

## 42.2 Target Tracking Under Non-occlusion

### 42.2.1 Moving Target Detection and Processing

In this paper human-body motion target is the study object. Moving target detection is the foundation of target tracking, Gaussian Mixture Model is used as the background model to detect motion, which can get the area of human-body target, then math morphologic and close calculations are adopted to create communication area, finally whole human-body area can be obtained.

The area of human who walk upright is rectangular, which aspect ratio is usually about 0.2–0.7. Upper body is the most important part for human moving

**Fig. 42.1** Moving detection
and tracking windows
**a** Moving detection,
**b** Tracking windows

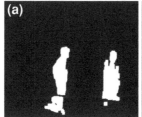

target, therefore, minimum enclosing rectangle of human-body top half area is selected as tracking window, in which there are some important organs such as head, shoulder, and chest. The tracking window not only can eliminate the interference of ground shadow, also can avoid the disturbing of leg movement, moreover, can reduce the amount of computation due to the shrink of tracking window, as shown in Fig. 42.1b.

## 42.2.2  Feature Extraction of Moving Target

Because color characteristics of motion target is stability and insensitive to the change of gesture and shape, color histogram lack sensitivity to partial occlusion and has invariant character for rotation and scale [5], therefore, color histogram of the motion pixels in tracking window is calculated as feature for target matching. Color histogram is defined as joint probability density function (PDF) of three color components, shows as formula (42.1).

$$H(r,g,b) = N_0 P(r,g,b) \tag{42.1}$$

$H(r, g, b)$ represents histogram function, $N_0$ is sum of all pixels within tracking window, $P(r, g, b)$ represents probability distribution of the pixel which color is (r, g, b). In RGB color space, each color component has 256 level, there are $2^{24}$ kinds color, amount of calculation will be very enormous in this color space. Therefore, each color component is compressed from 256 level to 16 level, the total color number is reduced to $2^{12}$, calculation greatly reduced, moreover, only the moving pixel within tracking window is calculated, which can effectively eliminate the interference of background.

## 42.2.3  Track Moving Target

In general, color histogram matching can track the moving target effectively. Euclid distance of color histograms which originated from different tracking windows is used as matching criterion, indicated as formula 42.2. $m$ and $n$ represents respectively two color histograms which steamed from tracking windows of adjacent frame.

$$D(m,n) = \left[ \sum\nolimits_{RGB} (m(r,g,b) - n(r,g,b))^2 \right]^{\frac{1}{2}} \tag{42.2}$$

Obviously, the smaller $D(m, n)$, the more similar two targets are, in practice threshold value of $D(m, n)$ can be defined to judge whether two targets are the same.

When violent turning action or other distraction occur, color histogram matching may be invalid. The interval between adjacent frame is very short, so the shift of same target in adjacent frame is very small. Therefore, minimum distance matching can be utilized: two targets which moving distance is minimum in adjacent frame are likely same human-body, which combines with color histogram matching can accomplish target tracking under non-occlusion.

## 42.3 Target Tracking Under Occlusion

### 42.3.1 Occlusion Appearing

In motion detecting, if the number of targets that ware detected has decreased, then it may be (1) Some target move out of the view field; (2) Occlusion occurred. In this case, if the moving distance less than the threshold, then can identified occlusion appearing, except for that the target move near the border of image. Agglutination of target regions (tracking windows) is the mark of occlusion appearing, as shown in Fig. 42.2.

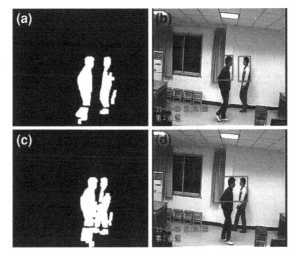

**Fig. 42.2** Occlusion appearing **a** Motion detecting before occlusion, **b** Tracking windows before occlusion, **c** Motion detecting when occlusion, **d** Tracking windows when occlusion

**Fig. 42.3** Target tracking under occlusion **a** Frame 220, **b** Frame 226, **c** Frame 232, **d** Frame 239

## 42.3.2 Processing Occlusion

Target 1 and 2 meets at frame 220, then occlusion emerges, as shown in Fig. 42.3. Previously tracking windows of target 1 and 2 are independent of each (like frame 220), their size recorded as $S_1$ and $S_2$, their color histogram recorded as $D1_{220}$ and $D2_{220}$. Two tracking windows are combined into one bigger tracking window (record as $M$), then select searching window which size is $S_1$ to scan in $M$, and compute the color histogram of searching window (record as $Dt_1$), if $|Dt_1 - D1_{220}| < T$ ($T$ is threshold), it can be confirmed that target 1 is tracked accurately in $M$ (next frame), scanning stop, target 2 will be the same. After that, the following scenario is possible: (1) Both target 1 and 2 are matched successfully, they are tracked accurately; (2) Only one target is matched successfully (for instance target 1), it shows that target 1 is tracked exactly and target 2 is occluded by target 1; (3) Both target 1 and 2 are not matched, it shows that they are occluded by other object, or other grievous disturbance occurs.

To solve occlusion problem, this paper adopts moving trajectory prediction: because human movement is usually at low speed, it can be took as uniform rectilinear motion within few adjacent frames, then motion trail of human satisfy formula (42.3) and (42.4):

$$y = ax + b \tag{42.3}$$

$$D(n, n+1) = D(n+1, n+2) \tag{42.4}$$

Formula (42.3) matches with rectilinear motion, if given the position of the moving target in frame $n$ record as $(x_n, y_n)$, similarly, the position of moving target in frame $n + 1$ record as $(x_{n+1}, y_{n+1})$, then $a$ and $b$ can be obtained through $(x_n, y_n)$ and $(x_{n+1}, y_{n+1})$.

**Table 42.1** Experimental data

| Video clip identifier | Total frame | Tracking correct frame | Tracking fail frame |
|---|---|---|---|
| 1 | 282 | 282 | 0 |
| 2 | 304 | 299 | 5 |
| 3 | 276 | 272 | 4 |
| 4 | 266 | 258 | 8 |
| 5 | 312 | 301 | 11 |
| 6 | 252 | 242 | 10 |
| Total | 1,692 | 1,654 | 38 |
| Ratio | | 97.8 % | 2.2 % |

Formula (42.4) matches with uniform motion, $D(n, n + 1)$ represents the moving distance of a target between frame $n$ and frame $n + 1$, then $D(n + 1, n + 2)$ can be obtained through $D(n, n + 1)$.

Using above method, the position of moving target in current frame can be worked out through the former two frames, which can track the target successfully.

As above, the combination of color histogram matching and moving trajectory prediction can accomplish target tracking under full occlusion.

## 42.4 Experiment Results and Analyses

The algorithm of this paper was developed Based on the VC++ 6.0, hardware environment: CPU Pentium 2.3G, 1 GB RAM, video image: $352 \times 288$, processing speed: 16 ms/frame, which can meet the demands of real time. Shown as in Fig. 42.3, two humans walk at opposite direction, they meet at frame 220, occlusion start occur, terminate at frame 239, all frames can be tracked aright.

Six video clips were tested by using the algorithm of this paper, experimental data is shown in Table 42.1. The results indicate that most frames can be tracked accurately in general, there are few frames fail when moving target swerves sharply or was covered for a long time, but they will be re-tracked correctly after few frames.

## 42.5 Conclusion

This paper select minimum enclosing rectangle of human-body top half area as tracking window based motion detection, shrunken tracking area can reduce the amount of computation and accelerate the matching speed. The combination color histogram matching and minimum distance matching can accomplish target tracking under non-occlusion; when occlusion occur, color histogram matching and trajectory prediction can achieve target tracking, which acquire a better effect even under full occlusion. Experiments have demonstrated that the proposed algorithm has high speed and good robustness, but there is small number frames fail when moving target swerves sharply or was covered for a long time, which is needed to be improved and consummated further.

# References

1. Xue C, Zhu M, Liu C-X (2009) Review of tracking algorithms under occlusions. Chinese J Optics Appl Optics 2(5):388–394 (in Chinese)
2. Comaniciu D, Ramesh V, Meer P (2000) Real-time tracking of non-rigid objects using mean shift. In: Proceedings of IEEE conference on computer vision and pattern recognition. IEEE Computer Society, Hilton Head, SC, USA vol 2, pp 142–149
3. Comaniciu D, Ramesh V, Meer P (2003) Kernel-based object tracking. IEEE Trans Pattern Anal Mach Intell 25(5):564–575
4. Babu RV, Pérez P, Bouthemy P (2007) Robust tracking with motion estimation and local kernel-based color modeling". Image Vis Comput 25(8):1205–1216
5. Shen Z, Yang X, Huang X (2008) Study on target model update method in mean shift algorithm. ACTA Automatica Sinica, 35(5):478–483 (in Chinese)
6. Collins RT, Liu Y, Leordeanu M (2005) Online selection of discriminative tracking features. IEEE Trans Pattern Anal Mach Intell 27(10):1631–1643
7. Yongzhong W, Yan L, Chunhui Z et al (2008) Kernel-based tracking based on adaptive fusion of multiple cues. ACTA Automatica Sinica 34(4):393–399 (in Chinese)
8. Hong L, Ze Yu, Hongbin Z et al (2009) Robust human tracking based on multicue integration and mean-shift. Pattern Recogn Lett 30(9):827–837
9. Wang ZQ, Fan YF, Zhang GL et al (2007) Robust face tracking algorithm with occlusions. SPIE 6786:X1–X10
10. Xiaorong LI, J IL Kov VP (2001) A survey of maneuvering target tracking: part II: ballistic target models. In: Proceedings of 2001 SPIE conference on signal and data processing of small targets. The international society for optical engineering, San Diego, pp 559–581
11. Farina A, Benvenu TID, Ristic B (2002) Tracking aballistic target: comparison of several nonlinear filters. IEEE Trans Aerosp Electron Syst 38(3):854–867
12. Satoh Y, Okatanit, Deguchik (2004) A color-based tracking by Kalman particle filter. In: Proceedings of the 17th international conference on pattern recognition. IEEE computer society, Cambridge, pp 502–505
13. Jia JP, Wang Q, Chai YM (2006) Object tracking by multi-degrees of freedom mean-shift procedure combined with the Kalman particle filter algorithm. In: Proceedings of the 2006 international conference on machine learning and cybernatics. Dalian, pp 3793–3797
14. Zeng W, Zhu G, Chen J, Tang D (2010) Robust tracking algorithm based on multi-feature fusion and particle filter. J Comput App 30(3):643–645 (in Chinese)

# Chapter 43
# An Improved Video Target Tracking Algorithm Based on Particle Filter and Mean-Shift

Zheyi Fan, Mo Li and Zhiwen Liu

**Abstract** A novel tracking algorithm using particle filter algorithm combined with Mean-Shift method is proposed in this paper. To improve the real-time performance, integral histogram is merged into the particle filter tracking framework during building the target template. A Mean-Shift algorithm based on Gabor amplitude spectrum is presented to reduce the influence of similar background interference on the tracking results. Experimental results show that the proposed algorithm is of effectiveness.

**Keywords** Video target tracking · Particle filter · Mean-shift · Integral histogram · Gabor transform

## 43.1 Introduction

Video target tracking is a hot problem in computer vision, and it has been widely applied in robot navigation, video surveillance and human–computer interaction and other relative fields.

Particle filter [1] algorithm and Mean-Shift [2] method are commonly used in target tracking domain. Many studies have been carried on and a lot of achievements have been obtained. In [3], the improved particle filter algorithm and Mean-Shift algorithm are effectively combined, and an effective occlusion detection method based on sub-block is proposed to gain good tracking performance under complex background. In [4], an improved Cam-shift algorithm based on three

Z. Fan (✉) · M. Li · Z. Liu
School of Information and Electronics, Beijing Institute of Technology, Beijing, China
e-mail: funye@bit.edu.cn

W. Lu et al. (eds.), *Proceedings of the 2012 International Conference on Information Technology and Software Engineering*, Lecture Notes in Electrical Engineering 212, DOI: 10.1007/978-3-642-34531-9_43, © Springer-Verlag Berlin Heidelberg 2013

dimensional background weighted histogram in HSV color space is proposed, which effectively overcomes the disturbance of the background color. A tracking method based on sub-block color histogram and particle filter is presented in [5], and the HOG feature is merged into particle filter tracking framework in this paper. In [6], a novel object tracking algorithm based on improved color histogram and particle filter is proposed.

In this paper, an improved tracking method using particle filter algorithm combined with Mean-Shift algorithm is presented. During building the target template, integral histogram is merged into the particle filter tracking framework, and an improved color histogram is proposed. Then a Mean-Shift algorithm based on Gabor amplitude spectrum is presented in this paper.

## 43.2 Particle Filter

Particle filter method is an approximate Bayesian algorithm based on Monte Carlo simulation [7]. The basic idea of particle filter algorithm is that the empirical conditional distribution of system state vector is applied to generate the random sample set and the samples are called particles. Particle weights and particle positions are adjusted continuously by the measured values and the adjusted information is used specially for the correction of the initial empirical conditional distribution.

The steps of traditional particle filter algorithm are as follows

(1) Initialization

The prior probability $p(x_0)$ is used to generate the particle set $\{x_0^i\}_{i=1}^{N_s}$, and the initial particle weight is $1/N_s$.

(2) Updating

Updating of particle weight at time k

$$w_k^i = w_{k-1}^i \, p(z_k|x_k^i) \tag{43.1}$$

The normalized weight is defined as

$$w_k^i = w_k^i \Big/ \sum_{i=1}^{N_s} w_k^i \tag{43.2}$$

The least square estimate criterion of $x$ is defined as

$$\hat{x}_k \approx \sum_{i=1}^{N_s} w_k^i x_k^i \tag{43.3}$$

(3) Re-sampling

Particle re-sampling is adopted to resolve the particle degeneration, and the new particle set is denoted as $\{\tilde{x}_k^j, 1/N_s, j = 1, \ldots N_s\}$.

(4) Prediction

The system equation is used to predict the unknown parameter $x_{k+1}^i$.

(5) $k = k+1$, return to step 2.

## 43.3 Mean-Shift Algorithm

Mean-Shift [8] is a non-parameter estimation algorithm based on data-driven. It is an optimization algorithm by searching the extreme value point of probability density in probability space, the steps of Mean-Shift algorithm are as follows

(1) Establishment of the m order target template $\{\hat{q}_u\}_{u=1,2,\ldots m}$ in the initial frame.
(2) Establishment of the m order candidate template $\{\hat{p}_u\}_{u=1,2,\ldots m}$ in the initial frame.
(3) BH coefficient [9] is used to calculate the similarity of target template and candidate template, the similarity is defined as this

$$\hat{\rho}(y) = \rho(\hat{p}(y), \hat{q}) = \sum_{u=1}^{m} \sqrt{\hat{p}_u(y)\hat{q}_u} \qquad (43.4)$$

(4) Target location

To obtain the maximum value of $\hat{\rho}(y)$, target center $y_0$ in the previous frame is used as the initial position in the current frame. The iterative formula of Mean-Shift algorithm is applied to obtain the new target center $y_1$, the formula is defined as follows

$$y_1 = \frac{\sum_{i=1}^{n} x_i w_i g\left(\left\| \frac{x_i - y_0}{h} \right\|^2\right)}{\sum_{i=1}^{n} w_i g\left(\left\| \frac{x_i - y_0}{h} \right\|^2\right)} \qquad (43.5)$$

where, $x_i$ is the coordinate of pixel point. $w_i$ is the particle weight. $g(\cdot)$ is the Gaussian kernel function, and $h$ is the bandwidth of the kernel function. Particle weight is defined as

$$w_i = \delta[b(x_i) - u]\sqrt{\frac{\hat{q}_u}{\hat{p}_u(y_0)}}, u = 1, 2, \ldots m \qquad (43.6)$$

The tracking method based on Mean-Shift theory has small calculating amount, low complexity and high real-time by avoiding the global search, thus it is widely used in target tracking domain.

## 43.4 An Improved Tracking Method Based on Particle Filter Algorithm and Mean-Shift Algorithm

A target tracking method based on the combined utilization of particle filter algorithm and Mean-Shift method is applied in this paper. Firstly, particle filter method is utilized to estimate the target position, then the estimated target position is used as the initial search center of Mean-Shift algorithm, the steps of the proposed algorithm are given as follows.

### 43.4.1 Initialization

#### 43.4.1.1 The Initialization of Particle State

In the initial frame, the object is obtained by manual selection. The center position of the target is $[x_0, y_0]$. $N$ sample points are sampled in the neighborhood of initial state and initial weight of each sample point is $1/N$.

#### 43.4.1.2 The Establishment of Target Template

In traditional particle filter, kernel color histogram is commonly applied for the establishment of the target template.

Kernel-color histogram[9] has good performance in catching spatial information by endowing the pixels with different distances to the target center with different weights, target template is established as follows

$$\hat{q}_u = C \sum_{i=1}^{N} k\left(\left(||\frac{x_0 - x_i}{h}||^2\right)\right)\delta[b(x_i) - u] \qquad (43.7)$$

where, $x_i$ is the coordinate of pixel point. $b(x_i) : R^2 \rightarrow \{1, 2, \ldots m\}$ is the color stage of the pixel point in H space. N is the number of pixels within the region, u is the index of histogram and m is the order number of histogram.

Although kernel color histogram is an effective means for describing the target, it has problems of large amount of calculation and bad real-time. In addition, during the particle histogram computing process, all the pixels of each particle should be visited and the regions of different particles are partially overlapped. Repeated pixels are calculated for many times, which wastes great time and resources.

Aiming at the above problems, integral histogram is merged into the particle filter tracking framework, and an improved color histogram is proposed in this paper. The basic idea of this proposed algorithm is that each frame is visited to obtain its integral histogram. The image region to be treated is divided into two parts, including the central part and the marginal part. Different calculation methods are applied for the two parts.

Integral histogram [10] is a fast algorithm for computing histograms of all possible small regions in certain region. The basic idea is that the pixels are visited to obtain the integral histogram of any point according to the preset path. And the integral histogram of pixel point is determined by the integral histograms of some points in the anterior path and the color distribution of this pixel point. The integral histogram $IH(i, j)$ is calculated as follows

$$IH(i,j) = IH(i - 1,j) + IH(i,j - 1) - IH(i - 1,j - 1) \qquad (43.8)$$

where $(i, j)$ is the coordinate of pixel point. If $i = 0$ or $j = 0$, then $IH(i, j) = 0$.

Integral histogram is applied specially for particle filter algorithm. To each particle, sub-integral histograms of four corners are extracted from the integral histogram to calculate the common histogram of the particle by three arithmetic operations. Complex histogram calculations of a large number of particles are converted into the addition and subtraction operations of four corners (Fig. 43.1). This method greatly decreases the computing time, and particle histogram is defined as follows

$$H = IH(d) + IH(a) - IH(b) - IH(c) \qquad (43.9)$$

where, $IH$, $H$ are the integral histogram and common histogram.

Integral histogram has some unignorable problems, although it has become a fast method for representing the color distribution of an image. The histogram obtained by integral histogram method only contains the occurring frequencies of colors, therefore, spatial information can not be acquired effectively.

To overcome the lack of spatial information of the integral histogram, the target region is divided into two parts as shown in Fig. 43.2. Part A is located in the marginal part of target region. This part is subjected to noise and background

**Fig. 43.1** The rectangular region of particle

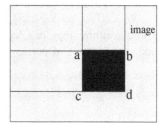

**Fig. 43.2** The target region
division

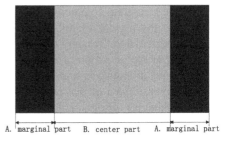

A. marginal part    B. center part    A. marginal part

disturbances, which results in low reliability. Part B is positioned close to the
target center. This part has low interferences caused by noises and occlusion
problems, so the reliability is high, the improved color histogram is summarized as
follows.

(1) The integral histogram of this frame is obtained.
(2) Calculation: Integral histogram method is applied for the center part B. The
    reliability of each pixel in this part is 1.0; to analyze the marginal part A,
    kernel-color histogram is used, and the reliability a is defined as

$$\begin{cases} d = \left(\dfrac{(x - x_0)}{W}\right)^2 + \left(\dfrac{(y - y_0)}{H}\right)^2 \\ a = 1 - d^2 \end{cases} \tag{43.10}$$

(3) Normalization: The results from step 2 are combined and normalized.

The proposed algorithm based on integral histogram and kernel-color histogram
can decrease the computing time and the amount of calculation, so the problem of
bad real time is resolved effectively. Meanwhile, this proposed algorithm can
overcome the lack of spatial information of the integral histogram and the tracking
accuracy is improved. In addition, the pixels in a certain range are endowed with
the same reliabilities, this way can reduce static background interference to some
extent [6]. Therefore, this presented method in this paper has better performance in
describing the target.

### 43.4.2 Target Tracking

#### 43.4.2.1 Target Position Estimation Based on Particle Filter

The algorithm steps in Chap. 2 are applied to estimate the target position. The
updating formula of particle weight is given as follows

$$w_k^i = \frac{1}{\sqrt{2\pi}\sigma} e^{-(1 - \sqrt{1 - \rho(\bar{p}, \bar{q})})^2 / 2\sigma^2} \tag{43.11}$$

### 43.4.2.2 A Mean-Shift Algorithm Based on Gabor Amplitude Spectrum

Traditional Mean-Shift algorithm is an iterative search process on the basis of color histogram. The classified statistics of quantified pixel values is the process to obtain the color histogram. Due to the quantized errors, different pixels with the similar gray values may belong to the same gray level. Therefore, color histogram has a limited ability to distinguish the object from the similar background. It is unable to realize the ideal tracking effect. To improve the searching ability of Mean-Shift under similar background, a Mean-Shift algorithm based on Gabor amplitude spectrum is proposed in this paper.

The basic idea of Gabor transform [11] is to choose a group of filters with different scale parameters and direction parameters to obtain the multi-scale and multi-direction local features of an image. Gabor transform is of strong robustness on the changes of the environment, such as the illumination, pose, expression variation and occlusion, etc. Gabor transform is defined as follows

$$\psi_{u,v}(z) = \frac{\|k_{u,v}\|}{\sigma^2} e^{\left(-\|k_{u,v}\|^2 \|z\|^2 / 2\sigma^2\right)} [e^{ik_{u,v}z} - e^{-\sigma^2/2}] \tag{43.12}$$

where u is the direction of kernel function and v is the scale parameter of kernel function. $z = (x, y)$ is the coordinate of the pixel point. The width of Gaussian window is determined by $k_{u,v}$, and it is given as follows

$$k_{u,v} = k_v e^{j\phi_u} \tag{43.13}$$

Where $k_v = k_{\max}/f_v$ is the sampling scale and $v = \{0, 1, \ldots 3\}$ is the scale labeling. $\phi_u = \pi u/8$ is the sampling direction and $u = \{0, 1, \ldots 7\}$ is the direction labeling.

The Gabor transform on image $I(x, y)$ is obtained by the convolution operation of Gabor function and image I. The process is as follows

$$\begin{cases} J_{u,v}(x, y) = I(x, y) * \psi_{u,v}(x, y) \\ M_{u,v}(x, y) = \sqrt{(\text{Re}(J_{u,v}))^2 + (\text{Im}(J_{u,v}))^2} \end{cases} \tag{43.14}$$

Gabor amplitude spectrum can reflect the energy information of an image. The changes of amplitude spectrum are stable and smooth. And amplitude spectrum would not produce rotary with the position changes. There are no errors of quantitative classification of the gray values because amplitude spectrum is obtained by way of direct calculation of the image region and Gabor template. There is obvious difference in the amplitude spectrum even though under the condition of similar color. Therefore, amplitude spectrum has a strong ability to distinguish the object from the similar background. In addition, Gabor transform is the process of block-convolution operation of the Gabor template and image sub-regions. Therefore, amplitude spectrum can reflect the spatial distribution of pixels to some extent. The steps of the Mean-Shift algorithm based on Gabor amplitude spectrum is summarized as follows

1) Amplitude spectrum of the target template A1 is acquired.
2) Amplitude spectrum of the candidate template A2 is acquired.
3) The new position $y_1$ based on the iterative search of Mean-Shift algorithm is obtained.

$$y_1 = \frac{\sum_{i=1}^n x_i w_i g\left(\left|\left|\frac{x_i - y_0}{h}\right|\right|^2\right)}{\sum_{i=1}^n w_i g\left(\left|\left|\frac{x_i - y_0}{h}\right|\right|^2\right)} \qquad (43.15)$$

where $w_i$ is the ratio of the corresponding pixels in target template and candidate template, the calculation formula is given as

$$w_i = \frac{A1(x_i)}{A2(x_i)} \qquad (43.16)$$

4) If termination condition $||y_1 - y_0|| \le Threshold$ is satisfied, then the iterative process will be stopped. Otherwise, $y_0 \leftarrow y_1$, turn to step 3.

## 43.5 Results

The time consuming results based on traditional color histogram and the improved color histogram proposed in this paper are shown in Table 43.1. The experimental results show that the improved color histogram can greatly decrease the computing time. And the improvement effect becomes more obvious with more particles.

The proposed method in this paper and the traditional Mean-Shift algorithm are applied for an infrared video respectively. The tracking results are shown in Figs. 43.3 and 43.4. The experimental results show that the Mean-Shift algorithm based on Gabor amplitude spectrum can improve the noise immunity and it can still track the object accurately under the similar background to acquire ideal tracking results.

**Table 43.1** The time consuming results

|                             | The number of particles |             |             |
|-----------------------------|-------------------------|-------------|-------------|
|                             | N = 1,000               | N = 2,000   | N = 3,000   |
| Traditional color histogram | 1.48822 s               | 2.9606 s    | 4.6239 s    |
| Improved color histogram    | 1.2694 s                | 1.5060 s    | 1.7408 s    |

**Fig. 43.3** The stimulation results of the proposed mean-shift algorithm. **a** The 110th frame. **b** The 130th frame. **c** The 140th frame

**Fig. 43.4** The stimulation results of the traditional mean-shift algorithm. **a** The 110th frame. **b** The 130th frame. **c** The 140th frame

## 43.6 Conclusion

Aiming at the video moving objects tracking problem, an improved tracking method using particle filter algorithm combined with Mean-Shift method is presented in this paper. Based on the combination of integral histogram and kernel-histogram, an improved color histogram is proposed. Gabor amplitude spectrum is merged into Mean-Shift tracking framework, a Mean-Shift algorithm based on Gabor amplitude spectrum is proposed in this paper. The experimental results show that the proposed algorithm can reduce the influence of time consuming and similar background interference on the tracking results, thus this algorithm has strong robustness and accuracy.

## References

1. Isard M, Blake A (1998) Condensation-conditional density propagation for visual tracking. Int J Comput Vision 29(1):5–28
2. Comaniciu D, Ramesh V, Meer P (2000) Real-time tracking of non-rigid Objects using mean shift. In: Proceedings of the IEEE conference on computer vision and pattern recognition. hilton head island, USA, pp 142–149
3. Ma L, Chang F-L, Qiao Y-Z (2006) Target tracking based on mean shift algorithm and particle filtering algorithm. Pattern Recogn Artif Intell 19(6):787–793 (in Chinese)

4. Birchfield S, Rangarajan S (2005) Spatiograms versus histograms for region-based tracking. IEEE conference on computer vision and pattern recognition, Amsterdam, vol 2, pp 1158–1163

5. Kwok C, Fox D, Meilam (2003) Adaptive real-time particle filters for robot localization. IEEE international conference on robotics and automation, Taiwan, vol 2, pp 2836–2841

6. Liu T, Cheng X-P, Xiang B-K (2010) Improved color-based particle filter algorithm for object tracking. Comput Eng Design 31(8):1750–1752 (in Chinese)

7. Doucet A, Gordon NJ (2001) Sequential Monte Carlo methods in practice. Springer, New York

8. Fukunaga K, Hostetler L (1975) The estimation of the gradient of a density function with application in pattern recognition. IEEE Trans Inf Theor 21(1):32–40

9. Yang JianWei (2010) Research on object tracking using Mean-Shift combined with Kalman filtering [D]. Harbin Institute of Technology, Harbin (in Chinese)

10. Qiu JT, Li YS, Wang CL, Liu Y (2011) Tracking based on integral histogram and particle filter. Acta Photonica Sinica 40(11):1761–1766 (in Chinese)

11. Clausi DA (2005) Huang Deng design-based texture feature fusion using Gabor filters and co-occurrence probabilities. IEEE Trans Image Process 14(7):925–936

# Chapter 44
# Video Content Retrieval System Based on the Contextual Color Features

Lei Niu

**Abstract** Traditional page-oriented Web search engine is usually only concerned with pure text message and when it comes to video, it can only deal with text-form information added manually. To achieve the purpose of more accurately extracting the video information and searching, this system can automatically extract the content features of video files, and quickly find video files according to the keywords describing the features of video content, through the co-ordination between the analyzing process of contextual color features of video files based on OpenCV, and the index-and-search process of feature metadata based on Lucene. It can be verified that this system has the advantages of high efficiency, high accuracy, and ease of use, etc.

**Keywords** Information retrieval · Image processing · Search engine · Contextual video content · HSV

## 44.1 Introduction

It will generate a large amount of information in people's exchange activities with each other. Meanwhile there are vast amounts of audio and video, and other non-text forms of multimedia files generated all the time. People usually have no idea how to deal with it when information is generated like the tide, and it becomes very difficult to obtain information from the flood of information correctly and rapidly. It is this situation has led to the generation of search engines [1, 2].

L. Niu (✉)
School of Computer Science, Beijing University of Posts and Telecommunications,
No 10 XiTuCheng Road, HaiDian, BeiJing 100876, China
e-mail: rayandloyd@gmail.com

W. Lu et al. (eds.), *Proceedings of the 2012 International Conference on Information Technology and Software Engineering*, Lecture Notes in Electrical Engineering 212, DOI: 10.1007/978-3-642-34531-9_44, © Springer-Verlag Berlin Heidelberg 2013

But still there is not much progress in the field of multimedia-oriented search engine, due to the heterogeneity of multimedia files and their huge file size.

In this paper, a content-oriented video file retrieval system based on the color features of characters' clothes is presented. To solve the problems of multimedia files processing, the author will combine the image processing technology and existing full-text search engine technology together, to provide a workable design scheme for video content retrieval. The author will first describe the overall architecture of the system, and then introduce the two main modules of the system—the image processing module and the search engine module, and at last, there will be some experiments to rove the effectiveness of the system.

The outline of the rest of the paper is organized as follows. Section 44.2 describes the overall architecture of the system, and explains the reason why each technology or open source library is selected. Section 44.3 presents the detailed design scheme of the image processing module using OpenCV [3], and Sect. 44.4 presents the detailed design of the search engine module using Lucene [4]. Section 44.5 conducted a series of experiments to prove the effectiveness of the system.

## 44.2 Structure and Process of the Video Content Retrieval System

### 44.2.1 Input and Output of the Whole System

Similar to the traditional page-oriented Web search engine, the system presented in this paper will aim to find where the needed video is stored according to keywords describing the video's content [5]. In order to adapt to people's habits using the traditional page-oriented Web search engine, a string of characters in text form describing the video's content is used as the input of this system [2].

Meanwhile, according to the common ways in which video is used, the location of the video is a must when a program processing it. So, to find the location information of a video from a large number of videos is the goal of this system and a string of characters of the location can be used as the output of this system.

### 44.2.2 Structure and Process of the System

As is shown in Fig. 44.1, the whole system is mainly divided into three parts. The image processing module and the search engine module are responsible for the main processing. The user inputs and obtains the video location he needs. And the process of the system is organized as follows:

- Image processing program fetches one of the video out of the storage system, and then processes it. Then the image processing module transfers the video content information and the video's location information directly got from the storage system to the search engine module.

Fig. 44.1 The structure of the whole system

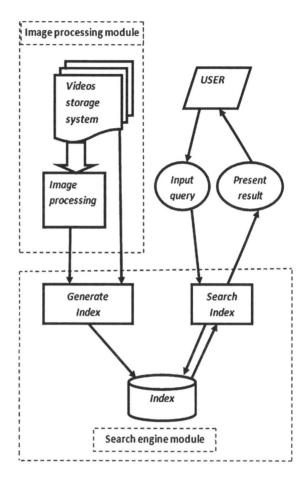

- The index generating program gets the information from the image processing module, and analyzes it. After that, it stores the results of the analysis according to a certain form in the Index for users to search.
- The user input a query which describes the video he needs, and the search program of the search engine module analyzes the query. Then the results of this search request would be returned to the user.

## 44.3 The Image Processing Module

### 44.3.1 OpenCV and People Detect

The author proposes an image processing design scheme to compensate for traditional Web search engine's lack in capabilities handling video files. In order to obtain the video content information, the author uses OpenCV to achieve the goals.

**Fig. 44.2** The process of
image processing module

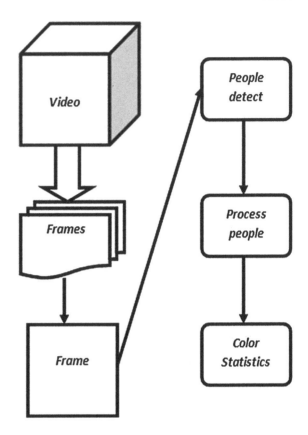

Open Source Computer Vision Library (OpenCV ) is usually used to perform some
advanced processing of the image [3].

We can see from Fig. 44.2 that after cutting a video into frames, which is
completed by OpenCV as pretreatment, the process of extracting content information is divided into three steps—people detect, process people, color statistics.
The people detect function is achieved through the SVM technology [6].

## 44.3.2 The Extraction of Image Contents Based on Contextual Colour Feature

According Fig. 44.2, after obtaining the rectangle with a people body image in it,
we can begin to analyze images according to color information.

At first, the rectangle also contains some background image in addition to
people body, so we have to process this people image to make this system more
accurate. And the author achieves this aim by narrow the rectangle to the center of

the original one, so most of the rectangle can cover the people body part, making most of the pixels of the new rectangle belong to the people's clothes.

Then, we begin the color statistics step, which mainly contains two parts—calculate the pixel color histogram and map the histogram to strings in text form representing the color, for example "red". After that, by comparing some continuous frames' color features, we can get the contextual color information of the video. In the original data structure to store image in OpenCV, the color of the pixels is organized in accordance with RGB color space. The RGB color space is simple and basic, but is not intuitive. Instead the HSV color space is more suitable for this situation [7]. In order to make it easier to map the histogram to string, we will convert each pixel from RGB color space to HSV color space [8].

After that, we obtain a histogram of a people's clothes in HSV color space, and now we will map the histogram to strings according to the hue, saturation, value of each pixel. We obtain the video content information—people's clothes color.

## 44.4 The Search Engine Module

### 44.4.1 Generate the Index

After the image processing, we have the video content information, and we can easily get the video location information as well, both in text form. Then we can build a search engine system to index and search that information.

Lucene is an open source search engine library, and with its help, we can easily build a full-text search engine. As is described in Fig. 44.3, we can see that the whole process of search engine module contains two main parts—generate Index and search Index. When Lucene generates Index, it will first abstract the object to be searched into a data structure called "document", which contains several "fields" [4]. In this system, the author defines two fields—video location and clothes color. Then the Index in the form of the inverted index is established, and user can search from the Index for video of his interest now.

### 44.4.2 Search the Index

After the Index is generated, which means all the information needed for the user to search is prepared; we can now build the search program. The author uses the clothes color field as the search field, and the video location field as the aim field. So, when user inputs a color name, the search program will return a series of video locations where people wearing the above-mentioned color clothes appears. And that is how a search process completes.

**Fig. 44.3** The process of search engine module

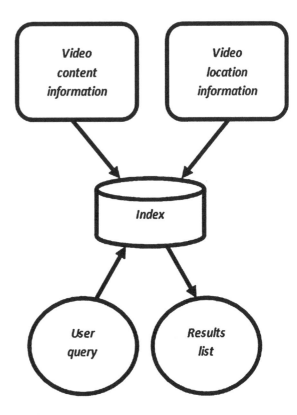

## 44.5 Experiments

### 44.5.1 People Detect Program

Figure 44.4 presents one of the results obtained by running the people detect program (green part). In the figure, we can see that not only the body part is covered, but also some background image such as the wall and the floor. This system intends to count the people's clothes part to obtain the color–based content information, so all the other parts even the arms and legs without clothes will reduce the accuracy of this system.

### 44.5.2 Process People Program

To solve the problem raised above, the progress people program was introduced, expecting to cover the body area as accurate as possible. Figure 44.5 presents one of the results obtained by running the process people program. In the figure, we can see that another smaller rectangle covers an area mostly is clothes. Counting the pixels in the smaller rectangle is more accurate than in the original big one.

**Fig. 44.4** Result of the
people detect program

### 44.5.3  Colour Statistics Program

After the previous work, we now obtain a rectangle in with most of the pixels
belong to the clothes. The color statistics program begins to count the color
information of the rectangle. Table 44.1 presents the sorted statistical result for the
rectangle. According to the table, this program defines this rectangle as yellow,
which means the people in the figure is wearing yellow clothes. This is the color-
based content information of the frame, as well as the video.

### 44.5.4  Video Content Retrieval System

We complete the whole operating mechanism of this entire system from the
previous experiments. For example, if the frame processed is from the video file
E:\video\1.avi, and the system identifies that a people wearing red clothes
appeared in it, then when a user inputs query "a guy in a dark red coats" to the
search program, the video location information "E:\video\1.avi" will be returned
to him quickly.

**Fig. 44.5** Result of the process people program

**Table 44.1** The result of the color statistics program

| Color name | Pixel number |
| --- | --- |
| Yellow | 7,200 |
| White | 890 |
| Blue | 356 |
| Purple | 324 |
| Black | 121 |
| Cyan | 72 |
| Red | 36 |
| Green | 1 |

# References

1. Barroso LA, Dean J (2003) Web search for a planet: the google cluster architecture. IEEE Micro pp 22–28
2. Brin S, Page L (1998) The anatomy of a large-scale hypertextual web search engine. In: Proceedings of WWW7, international world wide web conference committee (IW3C2), pp 107–117
3. Culjak I, Abram D, Pribanic T (2012) A brief introduction to OpenCV, MIPRO, 2012. In: Proceedings of the 35th international convention, pp 1725–1730, 21–25 May 2012
4. http://lucene.apache.org/
5. Markaki OI (2009) Personalization mechanisms for content indexing, search, retrieval and presentation in a multimedia search engine, systems, signals and image processing, 2009. IWSSIP 2009. 16th international conference, pp 1–6, 18–20 June 2009
6. Said Y, Atri M (2011) Human detection based on integral histograms of oriented gradients and SVM, communications, computing and control applications (CCCA), 2011 international conference, pp 1–5, 3–5 Mar 2011
7. Wang J, Zhao W (2010) A method of color space selection for color forest inspection image denoising applications, advanced computer theory and engineering (ICACTE), 2010 3rd international conference, pp V4-207–V4-210, 20–22 Aug 2010
8. http://en.wikipedia.org/wiki/HSL_and_HSV

# Chapter 45
# A Semi-Supervised Active Learning FSVM for Content Based Image Retrieval

Guizhi Li, Changsheng Zhou, Wei Wang and Yahui Liu

**Abstract** Relevance feedback (RF) schemes based on support vector machine (SVM) have been widely used in content-based image retrieval to bridge the semantic gap between low-level visual features and high-level human perception. However, the conventional SVM based RF uses only the labeled images for learning which gives rise to the small sample problem. In this paper, we proposed a method to alleviate the small sample problem in SVM based RF by using semi-supervised active learning algorithm which uses a large amount of unlabeled data together with labeled data to build better models. In relevance feedback, active learning is often used to alleviate the burden of labeling by selecting only the most informative data. In addition, a semi-supervised approach has been developed which employs Nearest-Neighbor technique to label the unlabeled data with a certain degree of uncertainty in its class information. Using these automatically labeled samples, fuzzy support vector machine (FSVM) which takes into account the fuzzy nature of some training samples during its training is trained. We compared our method with standard active SVM based RF on a database of 10,000 images, the experiment results show that our method has a better performance and prove that it is an effective algorithm for CBIR.

**Keywords** Relevance feedback · Image retrieval · FSVM · Semi-supervised

G. Li (✉) · C. Zhou · W. Wang · Y. Liu
Computer Center, Beijing Information and Science and Technology University,
No.12, Xiaoying East Road, Haidian District, Beijing, China
e-mail: lgz403@sina.com

W. Lu et al. (eds.), *Proceedings of the 2012 International Conference on Information*     429
*Technology and Software Engineering*, Lecture Notes in Electrical Engineering 212,
DOI: 10.1007/978-3-642-34531-9_45, © Springer-Verlag Berlin Heidelberg 2013

## 45.1 Introduction

Content-based image retrieval (CBIR) has become one of the most active research areas in multimedia signal processing. It is well known that the performance of content-based image retrieval systems is mainly limited by the semantic gap between low-level features and high-level concepts. Relevance feedback techniques have been widely used in CBIR to bridge the semantic gap between low-level features and high-level semantics [1]. A relevance feedback-based approach allows the user to label the returned images as relevant or irrelevant. Such labeled examples are further used to refine retrieval results by learning techniques.

Many relevance feedback algorithms have been adopted in CBIR systems and demonstrated considerable performance improvement [1–5]. A popular relevance feedback method in CBIR is centered on SVM. However, conventional SVM use only labeled data for training. Labeled instances are often difficult, expensive, or time consuming to obtain, as they require the efforts of experienced human annotators. Therefore, the performance of relevance feedback methods is often constrained by insufficient training samples. To deal with this problem, some works have been done to incorporate the unlabeled data to improve the learning performance [6]. SVM-based active learning has been proposed to carefully select the unseen images that are closest to the SVM decision hyperplane as the most informative images for user feedback [7]. Semi-supervised learning aims to employ unlabeled data to enhance the learning process and improve the retrieval performance [8]. Both semi-supervised learning and active learning can take advantage of the unlabeled data. It is quite natural to combine them to form a more effective method [9].

In this paper, we propose a relevance feedback technique based on FSVM using semi-supervised active learning algorithm for content-based images. SVM active learning is used to alleviate the burden of labeling by selecting only the most informative data. A semi-supervised approach has been developed which uses Nearest-Neighbor technique to label the unlabeled data with a certain degree of uncertainty in its class information. FSVM is trained based on these automatically labeled samples and user labeled samples.

The rest of this paper is organized as follows. Section 45.2 describes the theoretical background of SVM and FSVM. The proposed relevance feedback scheme based on FSVM is presented in Sect. 45.3. Our experimental results are given in Sect 45.4. Finally, Sect. 45.5 gives some concluding remarks of this study.

## 45.2 A Brief Review of SVM and FSVM

### 45.2.1 Support Vector Machines

SVM, proposed by Vapnik [10], is known as an excellent tool for classification and regression problems with a good generalization performance. Its formulation embodies the Structural Risk Minimization principle. By use of kernel function mapping technique, SVM can achieve good ability of classification generalization through small data learning. In the case of pattern recognition, it can be divided into linearly separable case, linearly non-separable case and non-linear case.

In the linearly separable case, consider the following binary classification task. Let $\Omega = \{(x_i, y_i) | i = 1, 2, \ldots N\} \subset R^m \times \{-1, +1\}$ be a set of training examples, where $x_i \in R^m, y_i \in \{-1, +1\}$, $m$ being the dimension of the input space. The goal is to find a decision function $g(x) = \text{sgn}(f(x))$ that accurately predicts the labels of unseen data $(x, y)$, and minimizes the classification error. If $f(x)$ is a linear function:

$$f(x) = w \cdot x + b, \quad \text{for } w \in R^m, b \in R \tag{45.1}$$

Then this gives a classification rule whose decision boundary $\{x | f(x) = 0\}$ is a hyperplane separating the class "+1" and class "-1" from each other. The problem of learning from data can be formulated as finding a set of parameters $(w, b)$ such that $\text{sgn}(w \cdot x_i + b) = y_i$ for all $i \in [1, N]$. And the margin between two classes is:

$$\rho(w, b) = 2/\|w\| \tag{45.2}$$

The optimal separating hyperplane is given by maximizing the margin. Thus, the problem of classification becomes the following optimization problem:

$$\text{Minimize} \quad \Phi(w) = \frac{1}{2} \|w\|^2 \tag{45.3}$$

$$\text{Subject to} \quad y_i((w \cdot x_i) + b) \geq 1, i \in [1, N] \tag{45.4}$$

This constrained optimization problem is solved by introducing Lagrange Multiplier $\alpha_i \geq 0$ and a Lagrangian. The decision function of the SVM is obtained:

$$f(x) = \text{sgn}\left(\sum_{i=1}^{N} \alpha_i y_i (x \cdot x_i) + b\right) \tag{45.5}$$

where $x_i$ represents the support vectors (SVs).

For linearly non-separable cases, one can introduce slack variables $\xi \geq 0$. The constraint of (45.4) is modified to:

$$y_i((w \cdot x_i) + b) \geq 1 - \xi_i, i \in [1, N] \tag{45.6}$$

The generalized optimal separation hyperplane is determined by the vector $w$, which minimizes the following function:

$$\Phi(w, \xi) = \frac{1}{2} \|w\|^2 + C \sum_{i=1}^{N} \xi_i \tag{45.7}$$

subject to the constraint of (45.6).

In the non-linear case where a linear boundary is inappropriate, SVMs can map input vector into a high dimensional feature space. By choosing a non-linear mapping, the SVMs construct an optimal separation hyperplane in this higher dimensional space. $K(x, y)$ is kernel function performing non-linear mapping into feature space. And the kernel version of classification function is given by:

$$f(x) = \text{sgn}\left( \sum_{i=1}^{N} \alpha_i y_i K(x_i, x) + b \right) \tag{45.8}$$

### 45.2.2 Fuzzy Support Vector Machines

FSVM is an extension of SVM that takes into account the different significance of the training samples. For FSVM, each training sample is associated with a fuzzy membership value $\{u_i\}_{i=1}^{n} \in [0, 1]$. The membership value $u_i$ reflects the fidelity of the data; in other words, how confident we are about the actual class information of the data. The higher its value, the more confident we are about its class label. The optimization problem of the FSVM is formulated as follows [11]:

$$\text{Minimize} \quad \Phi(w, \xi) = \frac{1}{2} \|w\|^2 + C \sum_{i=1}^{N} u_i \xi_i 6 \tag{45.9}$$

$$\text{Subject to} \quad y_i((w \cdot x_i) + b) \geq 1 - \xi_i, i \in [1, N] \tag{45.10}$$

It is noted that the error term $\xi_i$ is scaled by the membership value $u_i$. The fuzzy membership values are used to weigh the soft penalty term in the cost function of SVM. The weighted soft penalty term reflects the relative fidelity of the training samples during training. Important samples with larger membership values will have more impact in the FSVM training than those with smaller values.

## 45.3 Semi-Supervised Active Learning FSVM

### 45.3.1 Overview of Our Proposed Framework

In this paper, we propose a unified framework by fusing both unsupervised learning and active learning FSVM for image retrieval. We employ a proportion of unlabeled images in the learning tasks in order to attack the problems of there being insufficient training data. We describe our proposed framework as follows.

1. Given a query image, the system performs the K-NN search using the Euclidean distance for similarity matching. The top $n$ most similar images are returned to the user for feedback.
2. The user labels the $n$ images as either relevant or irrelevant.
3. Train an initial SVM classifier Based on the $n$ labeled images.
4. The SVM active learning is employed by selecting $m$ unlabeled images that are closest to the current SVM separating hyperplane for the user to label.
5. Add the $m$ images to the labeled training set.
6. Use Nearest-neighbor technique to select unlabeled images, assign a label and evaluate the relevance membership of each label in its class.
7. Train a FSVM using a hybrid of the user labeled and automatic labeled images.
8. Repeat steps (4–7) until the user is satisfied with the retrieval results.

### 45.3.2 Nearest-Neighbor Based Unlabeled Image Selection

Nearest-neighbor techniques are effective in all applications where it is difficult to produce a high-level generalization of a class of objects. Relevance learning in content based image retrieval may well fit into this definition, as it is difficult to provide a general model that can be adapted to represent different concepts of similarity [12]. Nearest-neighbor produces a probability density model and attempts to find the basic formation of each class by modeling the data. In this work,we propose to exploit Nearest-neighbor generative model to select the unlabeled images for labeling that have a high probability of belonging to each class. This will enlarge the training data set.

Let us recall that the nearest neighbor ($NN$) classifier is derived from the local estimation of densities in the neighborhood of the test pattern. Such a local density can be written as:

$$p_{NN}(x) = \frac{1/n}{V(\|x - NN(x)\|)} \tag{45.11}$$

where $n$ is the number of training patterns, $x$ is the test image, $NN$ denotes the nearest neighbor of $x$, and $V$ is the volume of the minimal hypersphere centered in $x$, that contains $NN(x)$ (i.e., the radius of the hypersphere is equal to $\|x - NN(x)\|$).Thus, we can compute the local density of relevant images as:

$$p_{NN}^{+}(x) = \frac{1/n}{V(\|x - NN^{+}(x)\|)} \tag{45.12}$$

where $NN^{+}$is the nearest relevant image of $x$. Analogously the local density of non-relevant images can be computed as:

$$p_{NN}^{-}(x) = \frac{1/n}{V(\|x - NN^{-}(x)\|)} \tag{45.13}$$

where $NN^{-}$ is the nearest irrelevant image of $x$.

These densities can be used to estimate fuzzy membership of an unlabeled image in positive class as:

$$u_{NN}^{+}(x) = \frac{p_{NN}^{+}}{p_{NN}^{+} + p_{nn}^{-}} = \frac{\|x - NN^{-}(x)\|}{\|x - NN^{+}(x)\| + \|x - NN^{-}(x)\|} \qquad (45.14)$$

Analogously the degree of relevance of an unlabeled image in negative class is:

$$u_{NN}^{-}(x) = \frac{p_{NN}^{-}}{p_{NN}^{-} + p_{nn}^{+}} = \frac{\|x - NN^{+}(x)\|}{\|x - NN^{-}(x)\| + \|x - NN^{+}(x)\|} \qquad (45.15)$$

We Select $n1$ unlabeled samples with high probability according to Eq. (45.14).These samples are labeled as relevant and added to the training data set. We select $n2$ unlabeled samples with high probability according to Eq. (45.15). These samples are labeled as irrelevant and added to the training data set. In addition, $n1$ and $n2$ values are set according to the distribution of the positive and negative samples in the labeled data.

### 45.3.3 Fuzzy Membership Estimation of the Selected Unlabeled Images

We employ a fuzzy membership function to estimate the class membership of the automatic labeled images. The fuzzy information is then integrated into the FSVM for active learning. Equations (45.14) and (45.15) give the fuzzy membership of the selected unlabeled image in each class. Further, the fuzzy membership function of the unlabeled samples will also depend on a measure of how well the assigned label agrees with the label determined by the trained SVM. A Sigmoid function is employed to estimate the probability. The degree of relevance of the automatic labeled image in each class is:

$$u_{SVM}^{+}(x) == \frac{1}{1 + \exp(-A \times d_{SVM}(x))} \qquad (45.16)$$

$$u_{SVM}^{-}(x) == \frac{1}{1 + \exp(A \times d_{SVM}(x))} \qquad (45.17)$$

where $A$ is a positive constant that can be estimated according to training data, $d_{SVM}(x)$ denote the distance from the automatic labeled image $x$ to the decision boundary of SVM. We combine these two measures to compute the final predicted weight of $x$ as:

$$u^{+(-)}(x) = u_{NN}^{+(-)}(x)u_{SVM}^{+(-)}(x) \qquad (45.18)$$

## 45.4  Experiment Results

The image database used in the experiment contains 10,000 color images of 100 different categories obtained from the Corel Gallery product. In our system, we use two types of visual features: color and texture. Color histogram, color moments, and color auto-correlogram are used as the representation for color features. Gabor wavelet and wavelet moments are used as the texture features representation.

In the experiments, we select 100 query images, one from each category, and evaluate the retrieval quality for a sequence of iterations starting with these initial queries. We perform five feedback iterations in addition to the initial query. At each iteration, active SVM selects 10 images to ask the user to label as relevant or irrelevant, then semi-supervised learning is used to select $n1$ (which is set to 10) and $n2$ (which is computed based on $n1$) unlabeled samples which are respectively labeled as relevant and irrelevant and added to the training data set. After the relevance feedback iterations have finished, the top-k most relevant images were retrieved by SVM to evaluate the retrieval performance. All the measurements are averaged over 100 queries. Precision and recall curve is used to measure the retrieval performance. Precision is defined as the number of retrieved relevant images over the number of total retrieved images. Recall is defined as the number of retrieved relevant images over the total number of relevant images in the database.

We have evaluated the performance of the proposed semi-supervised FSVM (SSFSVM) algorithm and compared with regular active SVM. Figure 45.1 illustrates the precision- recall graphs of the two methods after the last iteration. Each line is plotted with 10 points, each of which shows precision and recall as the number of retrieved images increases from 10 to 100. When the value is 100, since the number of retrieved images is equal to the number of relevant images, the value of precision and recall are the same. From the graph, we can observe that the proposed method outperforms the regular active SVM method in both cases. Our

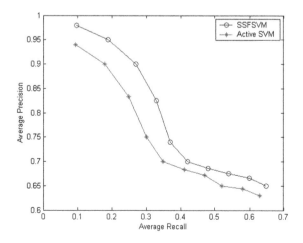

**Fig. 45.1** Average precision-recall graphs

**Fig. 45.2** Precision graphs over the number of iterations

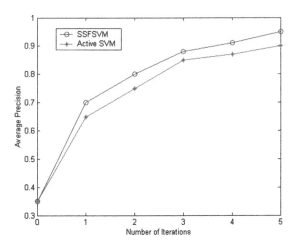

method provides higher recall rate at the same precision level, and higher precision rate at the same recall level.

Figure 45.2 shows the precision graphs of the two approaches over the different iterations. From the graph, we can observe that they produce the same precision for the initial query. Then the precision of our method increase at each iteration and outperform those of the active SVM approach. The improvement mainly lies in the use of unlabeled data for effective learning.

## 45.5 Conclusions

This paper presents a new content-based image retrieval method with relevance feedback technique using semi-supervised active learning algorithm. The approach uses a large amount of unlabeled data to alleviate the small sample problem in SVM based RF. A simple active learning is used to alleviate the burden of labeling by selecting only the most informative data. In addition, a semi-supervised approach has been developed which uses Nearest-Neighbor technique to label the unlabeled data with a certain degree of uncertainty in its class information. Then these automatically labeled samples with user labeled data are used to train FSVM. The experiment results show that our method has a better performance and demonstrate that it is an effective method to improve semantic image retrieval performance.

**Acknowledgments** This work was supported by a grant from general program of science and technology development project of Beijing Municipal Education Commission. (No.51072013).

# References

1. Rui Y, Huang TS, Ortega M et al (1998) Relevance feedback: a power tool for interactive content-base image retrieval. IEEE Trans Circuits Video Technol 8(5):644–655
2. Chandramouli K, Kliegr T et al (2008) Query refinement and user relevance feedback for contextualized image retrieval. In: Proceeding of visual information engineering, pp 453–458
3. Rahman MM, Bhattacharya P, Desai BC (2007) A framework for medical image retrieval using machine learning and statistical similarity matching techniques with relevance feedback. IEEE Trans Inf Technol Biomed 11(1):58–69
4. Muneesawang P, Guan L (2002) Automatic machine interactions for content-based image retrieval using a self-organizing tree map architecture. IEEE Trans Neural Networks 13(4):821–834
5. Liu RJ, Wang YH et al (2008) SVM-Based active feedback in image retrieval using clustering and unlabeled data. Pattern Recogn 41:2645–2655
6. Wang L, Chan KL, Zhang Z (2003) Bootstrapping SVM active learning by incorporating unlabelled images for image retrieval. In: Proceedings IEEE international conference computer vision pattern recognition, pp 629–634
7. Gosselin P, Cord M (2008) Active learning methods for interactive image retrieval. IEEE Trans Image Process 17:1200–1211
8. Lu K, Zhao JD, Cai D (2006) An algorithm for semi-supervised learning in image retrieval. Pattern Recogn 39:717–720
9. Hoi SCH, Lyu MR (2005) A semi-supervised active learning framework for image retrieval. In: Proceedings of the IEEE computer society conference on computer vision and pattern recognition, vol 2, pp 302–309
10. Vapnik VN (1998) Statistical learning theory. Wiley, New York
11. Lin CF, Wang SD (2002) Fuzzy support vector machines. IEEE Trans Neural Networks 13(2):464–471
12. Giacinto G (2007) A nearest-neighbor approach to relevance feedback in content based image retrieval. In: Proceedings of the 6th ACM international conference on image and video retrieval, pp 456–463

# Chapter 46
# Low-Cost Virtual Driving Simulator Design and Its Application

Xingquan Cai and Limei Sun

**Abstract** In this paper, we present one method to develop and design low-cost driving simulator, and this simulator can be used in pilot training, marketing strategy, entertainment, digital education, etc. Firstly, we explore the framework of the driving simulator. The driving simulator is divided into several modules, including loading models, visual simulation, scene interaction, collision detection and audio effects modules, etc. All these modules are designed particularly. Finally, we present the results and the results show that our method is feasible and valid. Our virtual driving simulator has been used in practical projects.

**Keywords** Driving simulation · Loading models · Scene interaction · Cylinder controlling

## 46.1 Introduction

Virtual driving simulator is a kind of equipment of raining-driving which is also a kind of equipment of interactive experience [1]. In China, there is one of the worst traffic conditions in the world. Nearly millions of people were dead because of the traffic accident every year, so it is necessary to train drivers all kinds of conditions. Virtual driving simulator can reproduce all kinds of complicated situation which leads drivers to complete all kinds of training. However, the actual cost is higher on training, and it is hard to reproduce complex conditions of road. Therefore, this

X. Cai (✉) · L. Sun
College of Information Engineering, North China University of Technology,
No.5 Jinyuanzhuang Road, Shijingshan District, Beijing 100144, China
e-mail: xingquancai@126.com

W. Lu et al. (eds.), *Proceedings of the 2012 International Conference on Information Technology and Software Engineering*, Lecture Notes in Electrical Engineering 212, DOI: 10.1007/978-3-642-34531-9_46, © Springer-Verlag Berlin Heidelberg 2013

article mainly research and design a low-cost Virtual Driving Simulator. This system can be used in marketing, entertainment, pilot training and drivers' test, etc.

This paper researches and designs a low-cost and propagable virtual driving simulator particularly. It can be applied to pilot training, drivers' test, marketing and entertainment, etc. The paper explains the framework of virtual driving simulator. And the system can be divided into loading, visual simulation, inter-action, collision detection and audio effects module, and then all the modules are designed particularly. Finally the results and analyses of the experiment are presented.

## 46.2 Related Work

Recent data shows that the study of virtual driving simulator has been began earlier in the United States, Japan, Europe and other developed countries. As to driving simulator, in 2005, Zeng [2] designed a kind of passive low-cost driving simulator. This driving simulator could train new drivers effectively by simulating all different kinds of roads, weather and complicated traffic conditions, moreover, setting up dangerous conditions to train drivers how to deal with risky situations. In 2011, Han [3] designed the armored vehicles to simulate driving training system in 2011. This system was based on the movement rule of armored vehicles, making use of data glove with virtual operating bar to construct the virtual environment of armored vehicles. In 2012, Fu [4] designed and realized a 6-DOF platform virtual driving system. Those simulation systems have their own advantages, but they are not put into production.

There are several other simulators. In 2009, Ma [5] provided high-speed rail simulation system. In 2011, Hu [6] developed Simulation of Tower Crane, Zhang [7] designed tank driving and training simulation system, and Han [8] armored vehicles driving training system, provided.

Virtual Reality technology has been used in our life. So in this paper, we focus on study and design a kind of low-cost virtual driving simulator which can be popularized and can be used for training new drivers and marketing entertainment.

## 46.3 Design and Implementation of Virtual Driving Simulator

### 46.3.1 The Framework of Our System

Virtual driving simulation system includes hardware and software systems. Hardware system simulates real driving environment as far as possible, providing real interoperability. Software system drives hardware system, making virtual driving environment realistic strongly. In this paper the hardware system includes

**Fig. 46.1** Physical
appearance of our driving
simulator

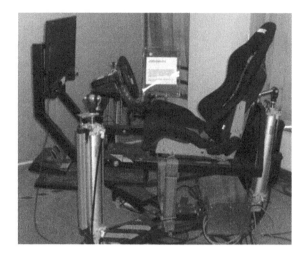

the big screen, dashboard, the components, n-DOF platform, computer, etc. The big screen is responsible for displaying the photos of virtual driving and interaction. The dashboard is responsible for displaying the speed of virtual driving, distance of travel and the remaining oil content, etc. Components include accelerator, the steering wheel, the brake, etc. It is responsible for the control of turning and speed while virtual driving. The n-DOF platform includes four cylinders, and they are responsible for providing the feelings of acceleration, slowing down, turning, uphill, and downhill. Computer installs related software and control systems. It is responsible for the operation of the system. The appearance of simulation system shows in Fig. 46.1.

Software system includes underlying hardware driver and interactive applications. Underlying hardware driver is responsible for driving hardware system. Interactive applications shall be responsible for providing the interface of virtual driving system. The software system is divided into five modules when designing specifically, namely model loading, visual simulation, scene interaction, collision detection and audio effects module, as shown in Fig. 46.2. The man–machine interactive module is divided into four subsystems modules, namely the cylinder control, the steering wheel, the brake and accelerator interaction.

## 46.3.2 Models Loading

Virtual driving simulation system mainly construct virtual environment with strong sense, including driving roads, the surrounding terrain, the surrounding buildings, plants, traffic signs, etc. As a result, a lot of 3D models are needed. The qualities of 3D models affect the authenticity of the system directly, and then influence experience of the users.

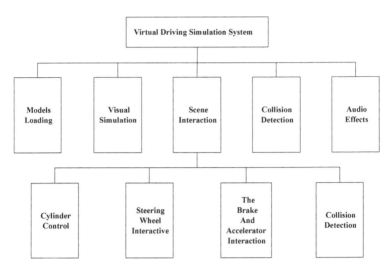

**Fig. 46.2** Framework of our driving simulator system

From the properties of some 3D models, we can conclude that the more the geometric figures of triangle strips, the more fine and realistic the construction of models. Conversely, they are more rough, and false. But if the model of the geometry of the picture is more, loading models will spend more time relatively. This system is designed based on the level of detail control algorithm. On complex virtual scene, the visual important degree of objects is higher from the near viewpoint, the requirements to fine degree of model is higher. On the contrary, the visual important degree of objects is lower from the far viewpoint, the requirements to fine degree of model is lower. So it can not only to ensure the requirements of the authenticity of virtual scene that the user needs, but also can ensure the speed of computer rendering and processing.

### 46.3.3 Visual Simulation

The main purpose of visual simulation module is to provide users the image interface that can be watched. By looking output real-time image information at the screen, users can have personally feeling, realize the natural interaction directly between users and the environment. It mainly includes two aspects, the simulation environment making and simulation environment driving. Simulation environment making is to construct the virtual scene which is similar to the real environment, it mainly includes: model design, texture, special efficiency design, structural scene making, etc. By the production of these aspects, it can construct a three-dimensional scene with lifelike texture and special efficiency. The simulation drive is mainly to be able to mobilize the simulation environment that has been made, making the virtual objects in the scene can simulate real environment.

The simulation driving part mainly includes: model transfer processing, topographical condition processing, distributed interactive, scenario-driven, etc. If it completes these contents, it can represent a real environment, response interactive operation in time.

## 46.3.4 Scene Interaction

The part of scene interaction in the virtual driving simulation system is the hard core. When the user needs to "talk with" the computer, it must use the interactive module. The traditional interactive devices are mainly mouse, keyboard, etc. In order to generate realistic simulation of virtual driving environment, the system adopts the real car interactive equipment, such as the steering wheel, the brake and accelerator, etc. So it can simulate realistic environment preferably.

### 46.3.4.1 Cylinder Control

In order to generate the virtual environment, such as acceleration, slowing down, uphill, downhill, the system adopts n-DOF platform with four cylinders. So it can not only simulate forward and backward, uphill, downhill as the car in the real environment, these are tactile changes from normal operating, but also can rotate with more than a multi-angle and multi-directional, so that it can be used in collision of traffic accidents or deviation scene when turning rapidly, which has more real effect. The part of cylinder control can control the cylinder accelerated speed (that is the rate of the seat), the movement direction of the cylinder, the working state of each cylinder (that is which cylinders working together at the same time), and it can also control the movement of the parameters like the cylinder height. The Fig. 46.3 shows that. Through the real-time control to the cylinder, it can adjust the movement of seat in virtual car, and react all kinds of complicated situations in the process of the virtual driving in real-time.

### 46.3.4.2 Steering Wheel Interactive

In order to simulate the real situation, making the user immersed in the virtual driving better, the system is equipped with a special input device that is used in virtual driving—the steering wheel. It is the same with the steering wheel of a real car, turning the steering wheel can control the direction of virtual car, such as when the driver turns the steering wheel left, virtual car will move to left.

In the module of steering wheel interactive, by binding a control script to the virtual vehicle model to receive the returned information from the steering wheel, and make the corresponding response. The script defines sundry movement states

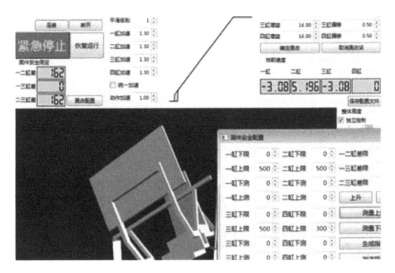

**Fig. 46.3** Cylinder controlling system

of steering wheel. When the user turned the steering wheel, the control script will obtain the current state of the steering wheel, and then the state will be mapped to the virtual vehicle model. So it completed turning interaction.

### 46.3.4.3 The Brake and Accelerator Interaction

Under the seat of the virtual driving simulation system, there are brake, accelerator and clutch. On your right hand you also can see gear with an emergency brake button and forward, backward, left, right and direction control button, etc. So it can control cars in time to simulate real driving cockpit, making the user have authentic feeling, thereby realizing experience closed to real car driving. In addition, the system also constructed the emergency brake button. When meeting emergency situation we can press the button by hand, while pressing the button, the cylinder will stop moving, virtual car also stop and wait for a next command.

When the user hit the brake, the virtual car stopped moving. There is no difference in the true situation. The system controls program to let the virtual car stop moving by capturing brake signal.

## 46.3.5 Collision Detection

The collision between objects often happens when the user driving in the virtual driving simulation system, at this time in order to guarantee the authenticity of the environment, we need to detect the position of the collision which just happened in time and deal with it like in the real environment, or the phenomenon that objects through other collision object will happen, that will lose authenticity.

In this system, we use bounding box method. The method using different cubes surround different objects, then calculate whether the cubes have contact or through each other, if they have, we say that they have a collision. Though the intersection detection between the bounding box, we can find and get rid of those won't intersecting objects as early as possible. Then further detect the bounding box collisions to the overlap part. This can improve the speed of detecting the complex objects. When the object in a collision, we need to simulate real situation after collision happened. Such as when the car crashed into a virtual roadside guardrail, the car should slow down, according to the collision location to change direction and displacement, etc.

### 46.3.6 Audio Effects

In order to react out the actual traffic environment and improve the immersed sense of the system, this system has set up audio effects module. Audio effects module mainly used to simulate the voice in the process of driving cars and the scene special effects in the surrounding. It uses many kinds of realistic sound, including the sound of the engine when starting and driving the car, the sound of urgent brake and collision, the siren of cars and the sound of wind around the car, etc. When the user speeded up, the roar of the engine will enlarge along with the speed increases.

## 46.4 Research

In order to verify the design of the virtual driving simulation system is feasible and effective, we have implemented a verification system. The hardware environment of the verification system includes a big screen, a dashboard, the components, n-DOF platform, computer, etc. The software environment is Inter(R) Core(TM) i5 2.53 GHz CPU, 2 GB ram, ATI Mobility Radeon HD 5470 GRAPHICS CARDS, LCD screen, Windows7, Microsoft Visual Studio 2010, Unity3D, 3DMax.

This system has been fully realized, and has been tested and used. The appearance of the simulator like Fig. 46.1 shows. User can drive under a bridge normally, like it shows in Fig. 46.4a. User can turn the steering wheel to finish it, just as Fig. 46.4b shows. As Fig. 46.4c shows, user can put on the brakes to stop the car quickly in an emergency situation. When the user put on the brakes, the virtual car will produce the fiction between the car tires and the surface and two brake friction marks before stop moving like the real car. In addition, this system can also realize an angle switching in the virtual driving. Figure 46.4d shows the snowing scene in our system.

**Fig. 46.4** Normal situation of a driving virtual car

## 46.5 Conclusions and Future Work

In this paper, we present one method to develop and design low-cost driving simulator, and this simulator can be used in pilot training, marketing strategy, entertainment, digital education, etc. Firstly, we explore the framework of the driving simulator. The driving simulator is divided into several modules, including loading models, visual simulation, scene interaction, collision detection and audio effects modules, etc. All these modules are designed particularly. Finally, we present the results and the results show that our method is feasible and valid. Our virtual driving simulator has been used in practical projects.

As to future work, our research is focus on improving interactive operability, adding driving score, etc.

**Acknowledgments** This work was supported by National Natural Science Foundation of China (No. 51075423), PHR(IHLB) Grant (PHR20100509, PHR201008202), and Funding Project of Beijing Municipal Education Committee (No. KM201010009002).

## References

1. Rekimoto J (2002) An infrastructure for freehand manipulation on interactive surfaces. In: Proceedings of ACM CHI conference pp 113–120
2. Zeng J, Zhang Y, Zhan S (2005) Design and Implementation of low-cost PC-based active and passive driving simulator. J Syst Simul 17(5):1092–1096
3. Han X (2011) The research of armored vehicles virtual reality driving training system technology. Lanzhou University of Technology, Lanzhou

4. Fu Z (2012) Development and application of virtual driving system. East China University of Science and Technology, China
5. Ma C (2009) Design and realization of the trouble-shooting simulation training system for high-speed electric multiple unit. Beijing Jiaotong University, China
6. Hu C (2011) Research on the control simulation of tower crane virtual operating system. Shandong Jianzhu University, China
7. Zhang G (2011) Design for the visual simulation module of a tank driving and training simulation system. Dalian University of Technology, China
9. Han X (2011) The research of armored vehicles virtual reality driving training system technology. Lanzhou University of Technology, Lanzhou

# Chapter 47
# Real-Time Facial Expression Recognition System Based-On Geometric Features

**Qiqiang Zhou and Xiangzhou Wang**

**Abstract** This paper presents a real-time facial expression recognition system based on geometric features. The geometric feature extraction is based on a hybrid method. This method first uses ASM to track the fiducial points coarsely and then applies a method based on threshold segmentation and deformable model to correct the mouth fiducial points due to the incorrect locations in the presence of non-linear image variations such as those caused by large facial expression changes. The geometric features extracted from the fiducial points are classified in one of the seven basic expressions by SVM classifier. The experiment shows the recognition speed can achieve about 12 fps.

**Keywords** Active shape model · Facial expression recognition · Geometric feature extraction · Lip tracking

## 47.1 Introduction

Recognition algorithms can be divided into two major categories: methods based on static images [1–3] and dynamic images [4–7]. The former uses single image of facial expression, considering only the spatial information, and the calculation is relatively simple, but the recognition rate is generally low; the latter uses image sequences, fully taking into account the time and spatial information of facial expression changes, the recognition rate is higher than former, but the calculation

Q. Zhou (✉) · X. Wang
Beijing Institute of Technology, 7th Floor, Building No.6, Beijing 100081, China
e-mail: zhqq299@163.com

W. Lu et al. (eds.), *Proceedings of the 2012 International Conference on Information Technology and Software Engineering*, Lecture Notes in Electrical Engineering 212, DOI: 10.1007/978-3-642-34531-9_47, © Springer-Verlag Berlin Heidelberg 2013
449

is much more complex. Now, most of the facial expression recognition algorithms belong to the latter.

The feature extraction methods are commonly divided into two major categories: texture features and geometric features. The former includes Local Binary mode (LBP) [8], Gabor filter [9] and so on, and the latter include Active Shape Model (ASM) [10], Facial feature lines [11] and so on. Generally, the texture features contain more useful information than geometric features and can achieve higher facial expression recognition rate, but it's time consuming.

In this paper we use geometric features to implement real-time facial expression recognition system. The geometric feature extraction is based on a hybrid method which first uses ASM to track the fiducial points coarsely and then applies a method based on threshold segmentation and deformable model to correct the mouth fiducial points.

The remainder of this paper is organized as follows: Sect. 47.2 describes the framework of the system. Section 47.3 introduces the process of geometric feature extraction in detail. Section 47.4 reports the experimental results and Sect. 47.5 presents the conclusions and future work.

## 47.2  System Description

The proposed system is composed of two parts: training classifier using facial expression database and recognizing facial expression using previously trained classifier from camera or video.

In this system, SVM is used to train classifier and the facial expression database is JAFFE (Japanese Female Facial Expression) [12]. It contains 213 images of ten women of seven expressions including neutral expression. The face is nearly in frontal pose and each expression has 3 or 4 images.

The resolution of captured image from camera or video is 640 * 480 and the system outputs the recognition result in real-time.

## 47.3  Geometric Feature Extraction

The key part of this system is geometric feature extraction and the hybrid method of geometric feature extraction is composed of two steps: (1) locate the fiducial points (eyes, eyebrows and mouth) by ASM fitting, (2) correct mouth fiducial points due to the incorrect locations in the presence of non-linear image variations such as those caused by large facial expression changes. Note that, the neutral expression fiducial points is obtained previously and there are 16 fiducial points, eyes 4 * 2, eyebrow 2 * 2, mouth 4.

**Fig. 47.1** a Correctly
identified, **b** the 16 proposed
points, **c** incorrectly identified

## 47.3.1 Active Shape Model

The Active Shape Model (ASM) is based on Point Distribution Model (PDM)
algorithm, originally proposed by Cootes et al. [13]. ASM is used to search for
features on an object (face in this paper), before searching, it should establish both
the shape model and profile model for each landmark first.

In this paper, we use [14] to search features in face. It has 68 landmarks. The
match results are shown in Fig. 47.1. In Fig. 47.1a, the match result is good and
then the number of fiducial points that are used in the feature extraction process is
reduced 16 (eyes 4 * 2, eyebrow 2 * 2, mouth 4), shown in Fig. 47.1b. Note that,
it doesn't work well on faces at an angle, or with open mouths or other non-neutral
facial expressions such as Fig. 47.1c.

## 47.3.2 Mouth Fiducial Points Correcting

First, we get the mouth rectangle region by the method in [15]. As shown in
Fig. 47.2a, the mouth region is in the scope of the distance of two eyes and 1/3
scope from bottom of face region.

Second, we segment the mouth region by method in [16]. The segment steps are
follows.

1. Calculate the mean value in the mouth rectangle region mean;
2. According the equation:

$$cor = \frac{sqrt\left(\sum_{i=1}^{width} \sum_{j=1}^{height} k(i,j) - mean\right)}{(width * height - 1)} \tag{47.1}$$

Where, width and height are the mouth rectangle region's width and height,
$k(i,j)$ are the pixel value at ith row and jth column, mean is the mean value in 1.

3. Use the mean value and covariance cor to segment the image by threshold.

The segmentation result is shown in Fig. 47.2b, and then we can get the left
mouth corner x1, right mouth corner x2, top lip center x3, bottom lip center x4.

Third, as shown in Fig. 47.2b, the top and bottom lip is easy to be bothered by
the shadow of illumination. To locate the correct location, we use two parabolic

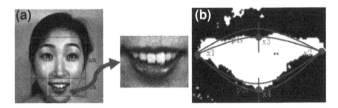

**Fig. 47.2** **a** Mouth region, **b** threshold segmentation

curves to build the mouth outer contour and ASM profile model g and $S_g$ at the top lip center point and the bottom lip center point to locate the right position.

1. The mouth open degree is constrained by the parameter p1, p2, where p1 is for upper lip contour and p2 is for lower lip contour. According to the second step, $p1_0$ and $p2_0$ is determined initially.
2. Set p1 ranging from 0.8 $p1_0$ to 1.2 $p1_0$ and p2 ranging from 0.8 $p2_0$ to 1.2 $p2_0$.
3. According to second step to get the coordinates x3 and x4 and calculate the distance by ASM searching method. The point has minimal distance is the right point.

### 47.3.3 Geometric Features Description

According to Facial Action Code System (FACS ) [17], the features are the same as features described in [18] except the eye features are shown in Fig. 47.3.

All the parameters are calculated as ratios of their current values to their neutral expression values, shown in Table 47.1.

Each input image is scaled to remove the effect of different face size. This is realized by the fact the inner corners of eye are usually unaffected by different expressions. The inner corners of eyes are scaled into 100 pixels for each input image.

**Fig. 47.3** Geometric features

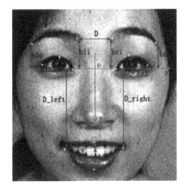

**Table 47.1** Geometric features representation

| Inner brow motion ($r_{binner}$) | Outer brow motion ($r_{outer}$) | Distance of brows ($D_{brow}$) |
|---|---|---|
| $r_{binner} = \dfrac{bi - bi_0}{bi_0}$ <br> If $r_{binner} > 0$, inner brow move up | $r_{outer} = \dfrac{bo - bo_0}{bo_0}$ <br> If $r_{outer} > 0$, outer brow move up | $D_{brow} = \dfrac{D - D_0}{D_0}$ <br> If $D_{brow} < 0$, two brows drawn together |
| Eye height ($r_{eheight}$) <br> $r_{eheight} = \dfrac{(h1+h2)-(h1_0+h2_0)}{h1_0+h2_0}$ <br> If $r_{eheight} > 0$, eye height increase | Eye top lid motion ($r_{top}$) <br> $r_{top} = \dfrac{h1-h1_0}{h1_0}$ <br> If $r_{top} > 0$, eye top lid move up | Eye bottom lid motion ($r_{btm}$) <br> $r_{btm} = \dfrac{h2-h2_0}{h2_0}$ <br> If $r_{btm} > 0$, eye bottom lid move up |
| Lip height ($r_{lheight}$) <br> $r_{lheight} = -\dfrac{(h1+h2)-(h1_0+h2_0)}{h1_0+h2_0}$ <br> If $r_{lheight} > 0$, lip height increases | Lip width ($r_{width}$) <br> $r_{width} = \dfrac{w - w_0}{w_0}$ <br> If $r_{width} > 0$, lip width increases | Left lip corner motion ($r_{left}$) <br> $r_{left} = -\dfrac{D_{left}-D_{left0}}{D_{left0}}$ <br> If $r_{left} > 0$, left lip corner moves up |
| Right lip corner motion($r_{right}$) <br> $r_{right} = -\dfrac{D_{right}-D_{right0}}{D_{right0}}$ <br> If $r_{right} > 0$, right lip corner moves up | Top lip motion($r_{top}$) <br> $r_{top} = -\dfrac{D_{top}-D_{top0}}{D_{top0}}$ <br> If $r_{top} > 0$, top lip moves up | Bottom lip motion($r_{btm}$) <br> $r_{btm} = -\dfrac{D_{btm}-D_{btm0}}{D_{btm0}}$ <br> If $r_{btm} > 0$, bottom lip moves up |

**Fig. 47.4 a** Neutral expression, **b** surprise expression, *note*: *left*-direct ASM method, *right*-hybrid method

**Table 47.2** Recognition rate comparison

| Method | Basic expressions | | | | | | | Average (%) |
|---|---|---|---|---|---|---|---|---|
| | Angry (%) | Disgust (%) | Fear (%) | Happiness (%) | Neutral (%) | Sadness (%) | Surprise (%) | |
| Direct ASM | 70.1 | 62.8 | 69.5 | 65.7 | 89.8 | 61.2 | 65.8 | 69 |
| Hybrid method | 82.3 | 76.5 | 79.7 | 81.1 | 89.3 | 85.2 | 80.3 | 82 |

## 47.4 Experiment

As shown in Fig. 47.4a, when face is with not opening mouth too much, such as neutral expression, both direct ASM method and hybrid method can locate the 16 fiducial points correctly. However, when a person's mouth is widely opened such as surprise or laughing, the direct ASM method fail to locate fiducial points around mouth, which is shown Fig. 47.4b left. The reason is explained in Sect. 47.3; the large facial expressions cause the non-linear image variations, and this result in failure in locating fiducial points around mouth. In my hybrid method, we relocate the mouth region, and get the right fiducial points, as shown in Fig. 47.4b right.

The JAFFE facial expression database is applied to test the recognition rate and the SVM classifier is used to classify the expressions. Here, we use a one-against-all approach to solve the 7-class problem. The kernel type of SVM is POLY and the cost parameter C is 10. We use training sets of 9 women and test set of one woman and get the recognition rate by cross-validation method, the recognition result is shown in Table 47.2. Note that, the neutral expression features of each person in Fig. 47.4 are obtained by calculating each neutral expression image and get the mean value.

From Table 47.2, we can see that, the hybrid method can achieve higher rate than direct ASM method. The reason is obvious that the hybrid method can locate the fiducial points more accurately during the large expressions.

The real-time facial expression system UI is shown in Fig. 47.5. In my computer (Intel Pentium processor dual-core E6600 @ 3.06 GHz, 2GB memory), the resolution of frame from camera or video is 640 * 480, the process time of one frame is 80–90 ms and the recognition speed is about 12 fps, and is nearly real-time recognition speed.

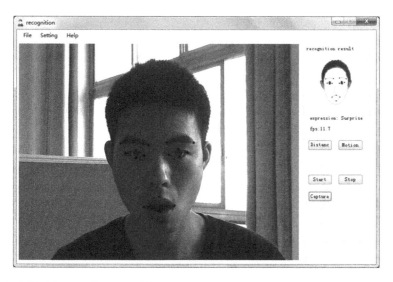

**Fig. 47.5**  Facial expression recognition system

The recognition result is good when in large expression such as mouth opening wide, eyebrow shrink and so on. When in micro expression, this system doesn't work. This is because the fiducial points are relative not enough.

## 47.5  Conclusion and Future Work

In this paper, an automatic facial expression system is presented based on geometric features. A hybrid method is used to locate the landmarks and 16 fiducial points which is chosen to extract the geometric features. The hybrid method first use ASM to locate the fiducial points coarsely, and then a method based on threshold segmentation and deformable model is applied to correct the fiducial points on mouth due to the incorrect locations in the presence of non-linear image variations such as those caused by large facial expression changes. The extracted features are classified one of the seven basic expressions by a one-against-all SVM classifier. The experiment shows its efficiency when all the image sequences are nearly frontal images.

The future work includes tracking more fiducial points, researching the varying posture facial expression recognition, and improving the recognition rate.

# References

1. Dail MN, Garrison Y, Cottrell W (1999) PCA and Gabor for expression recognition UCSD computer science and engineering technical report CS—629, August
2. Lisetti CL, Rumelhart DE (2002). Facial expression recognition using a neural network. In: Proceedings of the 11th international flairs conference, 16–18 May
3. Hong H, Neven H, Von Der Malsburg C (1998) Online facial expression recognition based on personalized galleries. In: Proceedings of third international conference on automatic face and gesture recognition
4. Abboud B, Davoine F, Dang M (2004) Facial expression recognition and synthesis based on an appearance model. Sign Proces Image Commun 19(8):723–740
5. Bartlett MS, Littlewort I, Fasel G, Movellan JR (2003) Real time face detection and expression recognition: development and application to human–computer interaction. In: CVPR workshop on computer vision and pattern recognition for human–computer interaction
6. Lien JJ, Kanade T (1998) Automatic facial expression recognition based on FACS action units. In: Proceedings of FG'98, Nara, 14–16 April
7. Lien JJ-J, Kanade T (1999) Detection, tacking, and classification of action units in facial expression. J Robot Auton Syst (In press)
8. Dubuisson S, Davoine F, Masson M (2002) A solution for facial expression representation and recognition. Sign Proces Image Commun 17(9):657–673
9. Koutlas A, Fotiadis DI (2008) An automatic region based methodology for facial expression recognition. In: Proceedings IEEE SMC, pp 662–666
10. Huang C-L, Huang Y-M (1997) Facial expression recognition using model-based feature extraction and action parameters classification. Vis Commun Image Represent 8(3):278–290
11. Gao Y, Leung M, Hui S, Tananda M (2003) Facial expression recognition from line-based caricatures. IEEE Trans Syst Man Cybern A Syst Hum 33(3):407–412
12. Lyons M, Akamatsu S (1998) Coding facial expressions with gabor wavelets. In: Procedings 3rd international conference automatic face and gesture recognition, pp 200–205
13. Cootes TF, Taylor CJ, Cooper DH, Graham J (1995) Active shape models—their training and application. Comput Vis Image Underst 61(1):38–59
14. Milborrow S, Nicolls F (2008) Locating facial features with an extended active shape model. In: Proceedings of European conference on computer vision, pp 504–513
15. Wenjuan Y, Yaling L, Minghui D (2010) A real-time lip localization and tracking for lip reading, 3rd international conference on advanced computer theory and engineering (ICACTE)
16. Yong-hui et al H (2010) A kind of method about adaptive lip location, computer engineering and application (in Chinese)
17. Ekman P, Friesen WV (1978) Facial action coding system: a technique for the measurement of facial movement. Consulting Psychologists Press, Palo Alto
18. Tian Y, Kanade T, Cohn J (2001) Recognizing action units for facial expression analysis. IEEE Trans Pattern Anal Mach Intell 23(2):97–115

# Chapter 48
# Alignment Error Analysis on Mask and Sensor in Light Field Camera with Attenuating Mask

**Xiubao Zhang, Yushun Fan and Haojiang Gao**

**Abstract** Light Field photography is a new imaging technology which can firstly image then refocus. Camera with attenuating mask is one kind of that. As the key component, the attenuating mask is misalignment with the sensor in practice. The alignment accuracy is one of the key factors affected the image quality on the sensor which determine the sharpness of refocused images in post-processing. Four kinds of typical alignment errors are analyzed in this paper and the error formulas are deduced. Furthermore, a computer simulation model is applied for validation. Additionally, image sharpness evaluation function is applied to analyze the effect of the alignment errors on the sharpness of refocused images quantitatively. At last, alignment error tolerances are given. That is applicable in the camera designing, installing and debugging.

**Keywords** Light field photography · Mask · Refocusing · Alignment error · Image sharpness evaluation function

## 48.1 Introduction

Traditional camera usually focuses on one object plane during imaging, but the objects offfocus will be blurred. Autofocus camera needs complex focusing device and its reliability is poor. The new light field camera can firstly image then

X. Zhang (✉)
Zhongguancun Science Park Haidian District Post-doctoral Workstations Beijing, Northking Technology Co., Ltd Sub-station, Beijing 100089, China
e-mail: xiubaozhang@yahoo.com.cn

Y. Fan
Department of Automation, Tsinghua University, Beijing 100084, China

H. Gao
Beijing Northking Information Technology Co.,Ltd, Beijing 100089, China

W. Lu et al. (eds.), *Proceedings of the 2012 International Conference on Information Technology and Software Engineering*, Lecture Notes in Electrical Engineering 212, DOI: 10.1007/978-3-642-34531-9_48, © Springer-Verlag Berlin Heidelberg 2013

multiply refocus by computing in certain depth of field [1]. By image fusion algorithm, full resolution image in certain depth of field can be obtained [2]. Its structure is simple but reliability is high. According to different imaging manner, the light field camera can be classified into different types, just like micro lens array camera [3], camera arrays [4], "lens-prism" array camera [5], programmable aperture camera [6], camera with attenuating mask [7], and so.

The light filed imaging manner proposed in [7] is based on modulation and demodulation theory. An attenuating mask designed in certain rule is set between lens and sensor in traditional camera to change the transmittance of the light rays for modulating intensity on the sensor [8]. Comparing with traditional camera which can only record intensity information of lights, the light field camera can obtain both intensity and incident angle information. Therefore, it has an ability to refocus after image. In a camera with determined parameters, the mask and the sensor should have a fixed position and alignment error will directly affect the quality of originally obtained image. In other words, it is one of key factors to affect accuracy of the digital refocusing in post-process. But that had not mentioned and analyzed before. Based on research of the imaging principle, the alignment error sources are analyzed in detail, and simulation experiments are performed by applying computer simulation model and refocusing algorithm in this paper.

## 48.2 Principle of Light Field Imaging with Attenuating Mask

As shown in Fig. 48.1, it is similar between light field imaging system with mask and traditional imaging system, except of a patterned mask set between lens and sensor. The distance of the mask and sensor is related to spatial frequency and angle frequency of the light field imaging system.

Assume the distance between lens and sensor is $v$, the distance between mask and sensor is $d$, and the aperture of the lens is $A$.

The frequency of the incident light angle is

$$f_{\theta R} = 1/A \tag{48.1}$$

The frequency of the spatial direction is

$$f_{x0} = 1/(2 \cdot p + 1), \; f_{y0} = 1/(2 \cdot p + 1) \tag{48.2}$$

where $p$ is the number of cosine patterned the mask.

**Fig. 48.1** Sketch map of the structure of the light field camera with attenuating mask

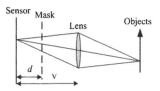

$$\tan \alpha = d/(v - d), \tag{48.3}$$

since $\tan \alpha = f_{\theta R}/f_{x0}$, the distance between mask and sensor is

$$d = v \cdot \tan \alpha/(1 + \tan \alpha). \tag{48.4}$$

Assuming $\varphi = e/d$, $\gamma = 1/\sqrt{\varphi^2 + (1 - \varphi)^2}$, the base frequency in $x$ and $y$ direction is

$$f_x = \gamma \cdot \sqrt{f_{sx}^2 + f_a^2}, \ f_y = \gamma \cdot \sqrt{f_{sy}^2 + f_a^2}. \tag{48.5}$$

The mathematical model of the mask is

$$M(x, y) = \sum_{n_y=-p}^{P} \sum_{n_x=-p}^{P} A \cdot \cos(2\pi n_x f_x x) \cdot \cos(2\pi n_y f_y y), \tag{48.6}$$

where $x$, $y$ is the coordinates of any point in the mask.

## 48.3 Analysis of Alignment Error between Mask and Sensor

As shown in Fig. 48.2, transmittances of the light rays past through the mask are different they are related to the position on the mask.

According to the translation and rotation of the mask along three axes in the space coordinate system, the alignment error can be classified into translation error and angle error. The translation error of the mask along z axis is called distance alignment error. For the periodicity of the position on the mask and the same period along $x$ and $y$ axis, the translation error along the two axes can be classified into one type, we call it translation alignment error. The rotation error of the mask along z axis is called rotation angle error. The rotation error along $x$ and $y$ axis can be classified into one type, we call it tilt angle. The alignment error between mask and sensor is mainly constituted by one or more error types mentioned above.

In the following part, the alignment errors mentioned above will be analyzed in detail and coordinate error formula will be deduced. The established computer

**Fig. 48.2** Sketch map of the mask in space coordinate

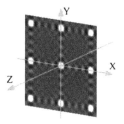

**Fig. 48.3** Sketch map of
**a** the distance alignment
error, and **b** the translation
alignment error

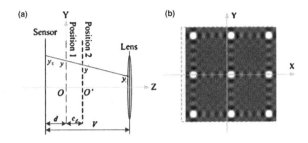

simulation model will be applied to obtain light field images with different values
of different error and the sharp images will be obtained by refocusing computing.

1. Distance alignment error

As shown in Fig. 48.3a, taking one dimension for example, position 1 is the
accurate position of the mask, and position 2 is the error position caused by
translation error $e_d$ along $z$ direction. Along $y$ axis, $y_l$, $y$, $y'$ and $y_s$ are respectively
the intersection coordinates of incident light ray and lens, mask in position 1, mask
in position 2 and sensor. Known $y_l$ and $y_s$,

$$y = y_s - (y_s - y_1) \times d/v. \tag{48.7}$$

Similarly,

$$x = x_s - (x_s - x_1) \times d/v. \tag{48.8}$$

The relationship between $y'$ and $y$, $x'$ and $x$ are

$$y' = y - e_d \cdot (y_s - y_l)V, \ x' = x - e_d \cdot (x_s - x_l)/V. \tag{48.9}$$

2. Translation alignment error

As shown in Fig. 48.3b, there is translation error $e_s$ along $x$ axis, thus the
intersection coordinate is

$$y' = y, \ x' = x + e_s. \tag{48.10}$$

According to the symmetry of the mask, the translation error along $y$ axis can be
deduced similarly.

3. Rotation error

Figure 48.4a is the sketch map of the mask rotated around its origin. In
Fig. 48.4b, the solid line coordinate is the accurate coordinate, and the dotted line
coordinate is the error coordinate with rotation angle $\theta_r$. Coordinate of point A in
the two coordinate system are respectively $(x, y)$ and $(x', y')$.

According to the relationship between the two coordinate systems,

$$y' = y \cdot \cos\theta_r + x \cdot \sin\theta_r, x' = x \cdot \cos\theta_r - y \cdot \sin\theta_r. \tag{48.11}$$

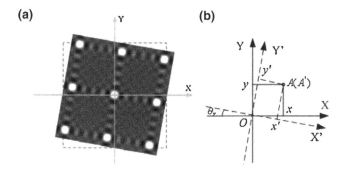

**Fig. 48.4** Sketch map of **a** the rotation error, and **b** coordinate rotation

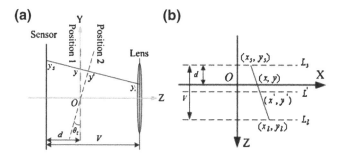

**Fig. 48.5** Sketch map of **a** tilt angle error, and **b** projection of the incident light on the *XOZ* plane

### 4. Tilt angle error

As shown in Fig. 48.5a, position 1 is the accurate position of the mask, and position 2 is the error position with rotation angle $\theta_t$. Along $y$ axis, $y_l$, $y$, $y'$ and $y_s$ are respectively the intersection coordinates of incident light ray and lens, mask in position 1, mask in position 2 and sensor.

Assuming

$$\alpha = \arctan[(y_s - y)/V], \qquad (48.12)$$

in Fig. 48.5b, it can be deduced that

$$y' = y \cdot \cos\alpha/\cos(\alpha - \theta). \qquad (48.13)$$

As shown in Fig. 48.5b, $(x_s, y_s)$, $(x, y)$, $(x', y')$, $(x_l, y_l)$ are respectively the coordinate of the incident light and lens, mask in accurate position, mask in error position with tilt angle and sensor. $L_s$, $L'$, $L$, $L_l$ are respectively lines cross over the intersection point above and parallel to the $x$ axis.

According to the geometric relationship, they can be deduced that

$$\tan\beta = (x_s - x_l)/V,$$ (48.14)

$$x' = x + y \cdot \tan\beta \cdot \cos\alpha \cdot \sin\theta_t/\cos(\alpha - \theta_t).$$ (48.15)

Similarly, the tilt error rotated around $y$ axis can be deduced.

## 48.4 Evaluation of Image Sharpness

Energy spectrum—Entropy is applied in this paper to evaluate the refocused image quantitatively [9].

It is known that, sharpness of image is mainly dependent on high-frequency components in light intensity distribution, but also greatly relate to the level of contrast.

To a image, its Fourier transformation can be expressed as

$$F(u,v) = \sum_{x=1}^{N}\sum_{y=1}^{M} f(x,y) \cdot \exp[-j \cdot 2\pi \cdot [x \cdot u/N + y \cdot v/M]].$$ (48.16)

Normalized energy spectrum of the two-dimensional harmonic component $(u, v)$ in the image is

$$E(u,v) = \left[\operatorname{Re}[F(u,v)]^2 + \operatorname{Im}[F(u,v)]^2\right] \bigg/ \left[\sum_{x=1}^{N}\sum_{y=1}^{M} f(x,y)\right]^2.$$ (48.17)

Entropy of the energy spectrum of the harmonic components is

$$Ek = -\sum_{u=1}^{N}\sum_{v=1}^{M} E(u,v) \cdot \ln(E(u,v)).$$ (48.18)

The greater the entropy value is, the higher the image quality is, in other word, the higher the image sharpness is.

## 48.5 Simulation Experiments

Simulation experiments are performed by applying established computer simulation model and the results are given as follows.

1. Ideal imaging

Figure 48.6 shows human face: Ordinary image and its FFT, light field image obtained by simulation and its FFT and digitally refocused sharp image.

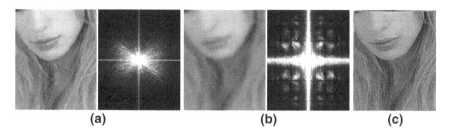

Fig. 48.6 Human face: **a** Ordinary image and its FFT, **b** Light field image and its FFT, and **c** digital refocused image with high sharpness

Fig. 48.7 Refocused images with different relative error of **a** the distance: 1, 10 and 20 %, and **b** the translation: 1, 10, and 20 %

Fig. 48.8 Refocused images with different **a** rotation angle: 0.5°, 1° and 10°, and **b** tilt angle: 0.1°, 1° and 10°

2. Imaging with distance alignment error

When the relative error of the distance $e_d/d$ is 1, 10 and 20 % respectively, the refocused sharp images are shown in Fig. 48.7a.

3. Imaging with translation alignment error

When the relative error of the translation $e_s/d$ is 1, 10 and 20 % respectively, the refocused sharp images are shown in Fig. 48.7b.

4. Imaging with rotation error

When the rotation angle $\theta_r$ is 0.5°, 1° and 10° respectively, the refocused sharp images are shown in Fig. 48.8a.

**Table 48.1** Sharpness evaluation on the refocused images with different translation error

| Error type | Ideal | Distance error | | | Translation error | | |
|---|---|---|---|---|---|---|---|
| Relative error | 0 | 1 % | 10 % | 20 % | 1 % | 10 % | 20 % |
| Sharpness | 0.1725 | 0.1700 | 0.1481 | 0.1414 | 0.1677 | 0.1491 | 0.1346 |

**Table 48.2** Sharpness evaluation on the refocused images with different angle error

| Error type | Ideal | Rotation error | | | Tilt error | | |
|---|---|---|---|---|---|---|---|
| Error value | 0 | 0.5° | 1° | 10° | 0.1° | 1° | 10° |
| Sharpness | 0.1725 | 0.1688 | 0.1551 | 0.1457 | 0.1712 | 0.1402 | 0.0780 |

5. Imaging with tilt error

When the tilt angle $\theta_t$ is 0.5°, 1° and 10° respectively, the refocused sharp images are shown in Fig. 48.8b.

By applying the sharpness evaluation method, the quantitative evaluation on the refocused images with different alignment errors is performed and the results are given in Tables 48.1 and 48.2 as follows.

It is known from Tables 48.1 and 48.2 that the greater the error value is, the worse the sharpness of the refocused image is. By comparing, we can know that distance alignment error and translation alignment error almost have the same affect on the sharpness of the refocused image. But with same values, the tilt error has significantly affect on refocused image than the rotation error. That is mainly related to the camera structure and the mask designing manner.

## 48.6 Conclusion

The alignment error of mask and sensor in light field camera with attenuating mask is detailed analyzed in this paper, and the error formulas are deduced. From simulation experiments, we can know that, there is no significant error in translation error, but there is a major error in the angle error—tilt error. The error tolerance of the alignment can be known that: the relative error of distance alignment is $|e_d/d| \leq 1$ %, the relative error of translation alignment is $|e_s/d| \leq 1$ %, rotation angle error is $|\theta_r| \leq 0.5°$, and tilt angle error is $|\theta_t| \leq 0.1°$.

## References

1. Ng R (2005) Fourier slice photography, ACM Trans Graph 24:735–744
2. Agarwala A, Dontcheva M et al (2004) Interactive digital photomontage, ACM Trans Graph 23(3):294–302

3. Ng R, Levoy M, Brdif M et al (2005) Light field photography with a hand-held plenoptic camera. Stanford University, Stanford (Tech Rep)
4. Wilburn B, Joshi N, Vaish V et al (2005) High performance imaging using large camera arrays, ACM Trans Graph 24(3): 765–776
5. Georgiev T, Zheng KC, Curless B et al (2006) Spatioangular resolution tradeoff in integral photography, Eurographics Symposium on Rendering, 263–272
6. Liang CK, Liu G, Chen HH (2007) Light filed acquisition using programmable aperture camera, ICIP 2007, IEEE, pp 233–236
7. Veeraraghavan A, Raskar R et al (2007) Dappled photography: mask enhanced camera for heterodyned light field and coded aperture refocusing, ACM Trans Graph 26(3):69
8. Zhang X, Yuan Y et al (2009) Computer modeling and simulation of light field camera and digital refocusing with attenuating mask, In: International symposium on photoelectronic detection and imaging 2009, Beijing, 7384: 73842O-1-73842O-9
9. Zhu S, Fang J et al (1999) New kind of energy-spectrum entropy image focusing evaluation function. J Beijing Univ Aeronaut Astronaut 25(6):720–723

# Chapter 49
# Makeup Transfer Using Multi-Example

**Hui Du and Lianqing Shu**

**Abstract** We introduce an individual virtual makeup transfer approach for digital images. Traditional makeup transfer methods focus on the transfer of the whole facial makeup effect, whereas our method can produce high quality individual makeup effect by transferring local makeup effects from multiple examples in different facial component regions. First, we modify the lightness and chroma channels of each facial region of the examples, respectively. Second, we transfer these modified information to corresponding facial region of the target image. Finally, we introduce a hybrid image blending method that allow seamless image composition and combine alpha blending to produce the final result. Experimental results show our method is effective.

**Keywords** Makeup transfer · Multiple examples · Gradient domain image compositing

## 49.1 Introduction

Human has an inherent love of beauty. Since human facial skin does not always look well, people often want to enhance their facial appearance with makeup by using materials such as powder, lipstick. To obtain a perfect makeup effect, a makeup artist must understand users' facial features, which can be eye, lip, cheek and eyebrow. Unfortunately, many people have little professional knowledge of makeup, they have to apply physical makeup to tell whether a makeup solution

H. Du (✉) · L. Shu
New Media College, Zhejiang University of Media and Communications, Zhejiang, China
e-mail: huidu1129@163.com

W. Lu et al. (eds.), *Proceedings of the 2012 International Conference on Information Technology and Software Engineering*, Lecture Notes in Electrical Engineering 212, DOI: 10.1007/978-3-642-34531-9_49, © Springer-Verlag Berlin Heidelberg 2013

adapt to their face. But applying the physical makeup is time-consuming. Amateur users have to modify makeup several times in order to achieve a better result. Therefore, it is a good choice that people can know how they would look with different makeup effect without actually physical makeup. Virtual makeup allows people to try on individual makeup in virtual scene. Currently, people may try on virtual makeup by using makeup software and photo editing software, such as Makeover [1] and Adobe Photoshop. But such virtual makeup software usually only provide many colour types, which are not very intuitive for amateur users. Highly specialized skills and professional knowledge of makeup are necessary in order to obtain perfect makeup by using this kind of software. In addition, using such photo editing software is tedious.

In this paper, we propose an individual makeup style transfer approach. Our approach is to "personalize" the makeup process by transferring various examples' makeup effects to the target face. Previous works toward makeup transfer by Tong et al. [2] and Guo et al. [3] alleviate the burden of users, but their approaches limit to the whole facial makeup transfer. In contrast, besides the whole facial makeup transfer, our individual makeup transfer approach can also transfer local makeup from multiple different examples to the target face. By seamless blending the makeup effects on various regions, we can obtain high quality compositing results. We believe our approach is much more intuitive.

## 49.2 Individual Makeup Transfer

Figure 49.1 shows the flowchart of our approach. In order to achieve the realistic makeup result, our approach consists of three steps: (1) pre-processing; (2) lightness channel processing; (3) hybrid chroma blending. We assume that the target image $T$, which needs to be processed with makeup, and several example images $E_i$ are given. First, we define several facial component regions that represent cheek, eyebrow, eye shadow, lip and residual regions. Next, we warp the example images $E_i$ to align with the target image $T$, convert images to Lab color space, and then process the lightness and chroma channels of the target and examples by using different ways, respectively. Finally, we generate the result from the modified lightness and chroma channels by taking into account the boundary conditions. Each step is discussed in the following sections.

### 49.2.1 Pre-Processing

We divide the whole face into five component regions that represent cheek, eyebrow, eye shadow, lip and other regions (including eye and mouth). In order to obtain high quality result, at first, faces of the target and example images should be aligned because our approach processes makeup transfer pixel by pixel.

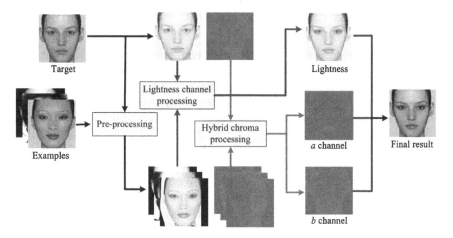

**Fig. 49.1** The flowchart of our makeup transfer approach

**Fig. 49.2** Control points and facial component regions. **a** Control points of the example image, **b** facial component region. Different color represents different component region

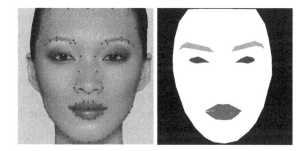

We choose Thin-plate spline (TPS) method [4] to warp the example images to the target image. Here 87 control points are used to face warping. We obtain these control points by using Active shape model method and manually adjusting locations. Then, based on these control points, we divide the target face into five regions that are cheek $S_F$, eyebrow $S_B$, lip $S_L$, eye $S_E$ and mouth region $S_M$. An example of the control points and corresponding facial regions is shown in Fig. 49.2.

Makeup of eye shadow is an important step of eye makeup. Since eye shadow appearance is a soft region, traditional image segmentation methods may not work well to separate the eye shadow region. Here we use closed-form matting method proposed by Levin et al. [5] to separate the eye shadow region from the example images. The alpha mask $S_A$ of the output represents the contribution of the eye shadow from the example image. The eye shadow region $S_{ES}$ is $S_{ES} = \{p \in S_A \setminus S_E\}$, where $p$ represents the pixel.

## 49.2.2 Lightness Channel Processing

Once the example images are aligned to the target image, all images are converted to CIE Lab color space, and we first process each channel respectively, then composite the modified channels to obtain the final result.

Face with makeup often looks smoothing, which means the facial detail after makeup smoothly changes. Recently, He et al. [6] introduced the guided filter that has the edge-preserving smoothing property like the bilateral filter, does not suffer from the gradient reversal artifacts and can be computed efficiently and exactly. Our implementation uses the guided filter to smooth the faces on the lightness channel $L$ because of these above properties. We obtain the smoothed lightness channel that is regarded as the base layer $B$. Then, we subtract the base layer $B$ from the lightness channel to obtain the detail layer $D$, That is

$$D = L - B \tag{49.1}$$

A significant change of facial appearance after makeup is that the luminance of both the eye shadow and the lip regions is changed. Skin in the eye shadow region and most skin in the lip region looks darker, and some skin in the lip region looks lighter since the lip makeup have the effect of adding glossy. Therefore, these makeup effects of the examples should also be smoothly transferred to the target face. Our idea is to add large changes of the example base layers to the target base layer in the eye shadow region $S_{ES}$ and the lip region $S_L$. We adopt a gradient domain editing method that is similar to the mixing gradient method proposed by Pérez et al. [7]. The gradient of the resulting base layer $B_R$ is defined as

$$\nabla B_R = \begin{cases} \nabla B_E & if \|\nabla B_E\| > \beta \\ \nabla B_T & otherwise \end{cases} \tag{49.2}$$

where $\beta$ is a threshold that is 3 in the eye shadow region and 100 in the lip region. $B_E$ and $B_T$ are the base layers of the example and target images, respectively. $\nabla$ denotes the gradient operator. We use Gauss–Seidel method with successive over-relation to solve Poisson equation and obtain the resulting base layer $B_R$.

### 49.2.2.1 Facial Blemish Removing

Inherent skin blemishes such as freckles in the detail layers of the example faces should not be transferred to the target image, because they are not parts of the makeup. We modify the detail layers $D_E$ of the example faces by using gradient domain method to remove the main blemishes. For the cheek region $S_F$, the gradient of the modified example detail layer $D_E^N$ is defined as:

$$\nabla D_E^N = \begin{cases} 0 & if \|\nabla D_E\| > \kappa \\ \nabla D_E & otherwise \end{cases} \tag{49.3}$$

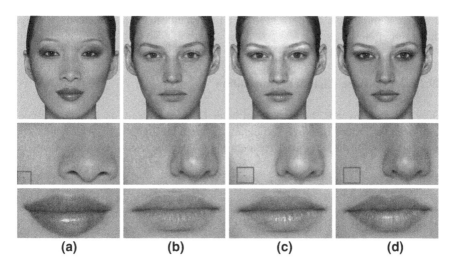

(a)          (b)          (c)          (d)

**Fig. 49.3** Comparison of the whole facial makeup transfer. **a** The example; **b** the target image; **c** the result of Guo et al.'s method; **d** our result. Note the facial blemish of the example is not transferred to the target face, as shown in the red box of the second row

where $\kappa$ is a threshold. The default value of $\kappa$ is 5. After this step, most blemishes of the example cheek region can be removed.

Furthermore, if the eye of the example is double-fold eyelids, the contour of the warped upper eyelid may not match with the target face, and the upper eyelid should not be transferred to the target image in order to avoid artifacts. We again modify the detail layer of the eye shadow region $S_{ES}$ of the example by using the same as the above method. As shown in Fig. 49.3, blemishes of the example facial detail are removed and the upper eyelid of the example does not appear in the result.

### 49.2.2.2 Detail Composition

The resulting details in the cheek region $S_F$, the eyebrow region $S_B$ and the lip region $S_L$ are firstly synthesized. The resulting details in $S_F$ and $S_B$ are obtained by using Guo et al.'s method [3]. In physical makeup procedure, the small detail of the lip is removed and the large detail of the lip is preserved. Therefore, the detail composition in the lip region is different from those of other facial regions. We apply a low pass filter on the detail layer of the target in the lip region in order to remove the small detail and preserve the large detail.

For individual makeup, since the resulting detail in different facial regions may come from different examples, the consistency between the boundaries of different facial regions must be considered. We use seamless cloning method to produce the resulting detail layer $D_R$ in the $S_F$, $S_B$ and $S_L$ regions, respectively. The final detail of the result comes from alpha blending of the above resulting detail and the warped example detail when the target face wants to own makeup in the eye shadow region $S_{ES}$.

### 49.2.2.3 Lightness Channel Composition

Once the base layer $B_R$ and the detail layer $D_R$ of the result are obtained respectively, we sum these two layers to obtain the resulting lightness layer $L_R$. Besides, we again adopt the mixing gradient method between the resulting lightness and the target lightness layers in order to preserve the structure of the target face.

## 49.2.3 Hybrid Chroma Blending

We combine alpha blending with a modified gradient domain method to ensure the chroma consistency at the boundaries between the facial regions except the eye shadow region, and then the chroma in the eye shadow region is processed by using alpha blending based on the warped matted mask.

First, the chroma of the result can be obtained by using the following blending equation in the cheek region $S_F$, the eyebrow region $S_B$ and the lip region $S_L$, respectively:

$$
\begin{aligned}
R_c^i(p) &= \alpha_i E_c^i(p) + (1 - \alpha_i)T_c^i(p) + \mu_i \tilde{F}_c^i(p), \quad i \in \{S_F, S_B, S_L\} \\
\Delta \tilde{F}_c^i &= 0 \text{ over } \Omega, \quad \tilde{F}_c^i|_{\partial\Omega} = (T_c^i - E_c^i)|_{\partial\Omega}
\end{aligned}
\tag{49.4}
$$

where $p$ represents the pixel in the regions, $R_c^i$ is the resulting chroma, $E_c^i$ is the example chroma and $T_c^i$ is the target chroma. $\alpha_i$ is specified by the user on the facial region $S_F$, the eyebrow region $S_B$ and the lip region $S_L$, respectively, $\tilde{F}_c^i$ is the solution of the above Laplace equation. $\Omega$ and $\partial\Omega$ denote the region and the region boundary, respectively. Different from the original seamless cloning, we modify the correction function $\tilde{F}_c^i$ by adding the parameter $\mu$. We define $\mu$ as:

$$
\mu(p) = \max(e^{-\frac{(p-q)^2}{2\sigma^2}})
\tag{49.5}
$$

where $q$ indexes the pixels over the face, the value of $\sigma^2$ is set to *min(width, height)*/20. When $\mu$ closes to 1, namely near the boundary, the result $R_c$ have a good match with the target image.

Second, we use alpha blending method to composite the chroma of the final result in the eye shadow region $S_{ES}$. Up to now, we have obtained the modified lightness and chroma channels, respectively. We composite these three channels to produce the result that makeup effects transferred from different example images.

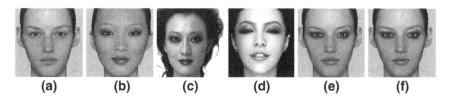

**(a)        (b)        (c)        (d)        (e)        (f)**

**Fig. 49.4**  An example of individual makeup transfer. The cheek makeup effect of the result **f** transfers from the example **d** the eyebrow effect from the example **b** the eye shadow effect from the example **c** and the lip from the example **b**. **e** is the result without lightness layer correction. Note that the upper eyelid of the target image in **f** is preserved

## 49.3 Experimental Results and Discussion

We implement our algorithm using Matlab. Figure 49.3 shows a comparison of our approach with Guo et al.'s approach [3]. In their work, facial blemishes of the example are transferred to the target face. Our method yields results that most facial blemishes of the examples are not transferred because of our blemishes removing step. Our method produces reasonable result that the makeup effect is similar to the example and the texture detail is similar to the target.

Figure 49.4 shows an example of makeup transfer using multi-example. Since we adopt the mixing gradient method to correct the lightness layer we successfully preserve the upper eyelid of the target image. In this example, the makeup effect of the result transfers from three examples. The cheek makeup effect of the result (Fig. 49.4(f)) transfers from the example Fig. 49.4(d), the eyebrow effect comes from the example Fig. 49.4(b), the eye shadow effect transfers from the example Fig. 49.4(c) and the lip effect transfers from the example Fig. 49.4(b).

Our approach can also achieve the result that is similar to image harmonization. In this case, we warp the target image based on the control points and decompose the images. The detail layer and chroma channels of the warped target image are also modified and added to the source image, and then we use seamless cloning method for each channel to yield the compositing result. As shown in Fig. 49.5, compared with seamless cloning, our result has more details in the cloning region.

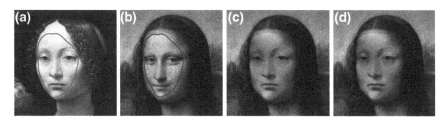

**Fig. 49.5**  Our approach can also achieve the harmonized compositing result. Traditional gradient composition method produces a seamless result (**c**) but has no detail in the cloning region that makes the result unrealistic. In contrast, the detail of the target image can also be incorporated into the result by using our approach (**d**). **a** Source image **b** Target image **c** Seamless cloning **d** Our result

## 49.4 Conclusion

We have presented an individual makeup transfer approach that allows users to create an individual digital makeup of the target image from multiple examples. We use a modified gradient domain method to prevent a visible seam while ensuring that the color style of the significant parts of the blending regions is preserved. Our method can produce good results that most facial blemishes of the examples are not transferred to the target and the consistency between the different makeup styles is achieved; What is more important, to virtual makeup, photo editing skills and makeup knowledge are not required.

However, our approach still suffers from several limitations. For example, the pose difference between the target and the examples should be not large. Large pose difference lead to the bad alignment result that the corresponding detail of the examples may be warped too much. Besides, our approach may produce failure result when the color difference of facial skin between the target and the examples is distinct.

**Acknowledgments** This work is supported by Scientific Research Fund of Zhejiang Provincial Education Department (Y201016221) and Experimental Teaching Demonstration Center of Zhejiang Provincial Animation and Digital Technology.

## References

1. Taaz (2010). http://www.taaz.com
2. Tong WS, Tang CK, Brown MS, Xu YQ (2007) Example-based cosmetic transfer. In: Proceeding of pacific conference on computer graphics and applications, pp 211–218
3. Guo D, Sim T (2009) Digital face makeup by example. In: Proceeding of CVPR
4. Bookstein FL (1989) Principal warps: thin-plate splines and the decomposition of deformations. IEEE Trans Pattern Anal Mach Intell 11(6):567–585
5. Levin A, Lischinski D, Weiss Y (2008) A closed-form solution to natural image matting. IEEE Trans Pattern Anal Mach Intell 30(2):228–242
6. He KM, Sun J, Tang X (2010) Guided image filtering. In: European conference on computer vision
7. Pérez P, Gangnet M, Blake A (2003) Poisson image editing. ACM Trans Graph 22(3):313–318

# Chapter 50
# A Method for Removing Rain from Videos

Gang Liu, Yufen Sun and Xianqiao Chen

**Abstract** Rain streaks in videos change the intensities of pixels and affect the performance of outdoor vision systems. This paper proposes a rain removal method that can recover videos degraded by rain. This method exploits the fact that all rain streaks in a video have similar directions. First a dictionary is learnt for sparse representation of frame differences. Then the gradient distribution of the intensities of the atoms in this dictionary is analyzed to distinguish rain atoms and non-rain atoms. At last, frames are recovered by only using the non-rain atoms to represent frame differences. Experiments on real videos show the effectiveness of this method.

**Keywords** Sparse coding · Dictionary learning · Rain removal · Image rectification

## 50.1 Introduction

Outdoor vision systems process videos shot by outdoor video cameras. In bad weather such as rain or snow, falling water particles are captured by cameras. They change the intensities of pixels in frames. Thus vision algorithms that use local intensity features are hard to acquire correct results. To ensure the performance of outdoor vision systems, researchers should design methods to recover videos shot in bad weather.

G. Liu (✉) · Y. Sun · X. Chen
Intelligent Transportation System Research Center, Wuhan University of Technology,
Wuhan 430063, China
e-mail: liu_gang@whut.edu.cn

W. Lu et al. (eds.), *Proceedings of the 2012 International Conference on Information Technology and Software Engineering*, Lecture Notes in Electrical Engineering 212, DOI: 10.1007/978-3-642-34531-9_50, © Springer-Verlag Berlin Heidelberg 2013

Rain is a familiar bad weather. Recently rain removal from videos has been studied extensively. In a video contains rain, rain streaks appear in different positions with different intensities and different shape. It is hard to detect all rain streaks in a single image. Most existing rain removal methods use the temporal character of rain to detect and remove rain streaks in videos [1–4]. These methods directly utilized the physical characters of rain streaks to distinguish rain streaks from other moving objects. But many physical characters used by these methods, such as lengths and directions of rain streaks, are hard to be calculated reliably. At the same time, these methods pay little attention to successfully recover moving objects occluded by rain streaks. In this paper, we propose a new rain removal method that exploits the fact that all rain streaks in a video have similar directions. But the directions of rain are not calculated from rain streaks in the video. We first perform dictionary learning for sparse representation of frame differences to obtain an atom dictionary. Then the atoms in the dictionary are classified as rain atoms and non-rain atoms based on the gradient distribution of the intensities of the atoms. Finally, sparse coding is performed to represent frame differences using both rain atoms and non-rain atoms. The rain can be removed if we set the coefficients of the rain atoms to zero. Since all computations are performed on frame differences, the method has little influences on the non-rain parts in videos. And the representation ability of non-rain atoms ensures that the intensities in the frame differences caused by object motion or camera motion can be recovered.

In the remainder of this paper, Sect. 50.2 introduces the related work. Section 50.3 describes the new rain removal method. Section 50.4 reports the experimental analysis and last, Sect. 50.5 gives the conclusion.

## 50.2 Related Work

The first video rain removal method is the temporal median filter proposed by Hase et al. [5]. They used the intensity median of a pixel in several frames as the value of the pixel without rain. This method is based on the assumption that each pixel is clear more often than covered by rain. This is true when rain is not heavy.

Similar to the temporal median filter, Zhang et al. [4] found the intensity of a pixel without rain by partitioning the intensities of the pixel in several frames into two clusters. The intensity in the cluster with lower value was identified as the scene intensity. To handle the intensity change caused by object motion, Zhang et al. filtered out false positives by the chromatic property of rain streaks.

Garg and Nayar [3] investigated the appearance model of rain in detail. They used photometric constraint and dynamics model constraint to filter out false positives in candidate rain pixels. The average of the intensities of each rain pixel in two temporal neighbouring frames was considered as background intensity. Brewer and Liu [2] also used the appearance property of rain to assist rain detection.

Barnum et al. [1] proposed the first rain removal method that exploited the global property of rain in frequency space. A parameter model of rain streaks in frequency space was fitted to video for detecting rain streaks. The detected rain pixels were recovered by mixing their intensities in current frame and in an initial estimate of the clear image, which may be the output of any rain removal algorithm, such as a per-pixel temporal median filter.

Kang et al. [6] studied the problem of rain removal from single image. For singe image, all information can be used is the appearance of the rain streaks. Kang et al. first decomposed an image into low-frequency and high-frequency parts using a bilateral filter. Then they generated the sparse representation of the high-frequency part using atoms acquired by dictionary learning. Based on the Histograms of Oriented Gradients (HOG) features [7] of the atoms, the high-frequency part was decomposed into a rain component and a non-rain component. This rain removal method utilizes the direction property of rain. The main advantage of this method is that the scene occluded by rain can be correctly recovered.

From above we can see that existing rain removal methods for videos first use the unique characters of rain streaks to detect rain pixels. Then these pixels are recovered by their intensities in neighbouring frames. But when there exist camera or object motion, the intensities of a pixel in neighbouring frames do not represent the same scene. Thus scene occluded by rain cannot be recovered correctly. In this paper, we combine the temporal property of rain used for videos and the sparse representation used for single image to remove rain from videos.

## 50.3  A Rain Removal Method Based on Sparse Coding

We propose a rain removal method for videos based on temporal and direction properties of rain. The rain pixel candidates are first detected using the temporal property of rain. Then real rain pixels are found out based on the direction property of rain.

### 50.3.1  Generating Rain Candidates

When it is raining, the falling raindrops distribute randomly in the air. It is unlike that a pixel in a frame is always covered by rain streaks even in heavy rain. This temporal property of rain can be used to find rain pixel candidates using frame differences.

Suppose a pixel $i$ in the $k$th frame in a video is covered by a rain streak. If the scene is static and this pixel in the $k + 1$th frame is not covered by rain streak, the intensity difference $I_i^k - I_i^{k+1}$ equals the intensity of the rain streak. Thus in the frame difference, the pixel intensity differences that are greater than zero represent

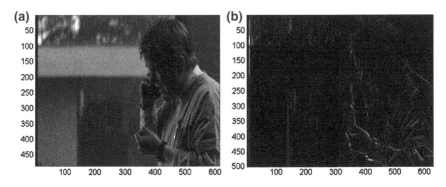

**Fig. 50.1** **a** A frame in a video; **b** the image of rain candidates of the frame in (**a**)

the intensities of rain streaks in $k$-th frame. But when the scene is not static, these differences may be caused by different intensities of the scene. So the pixels with value greater than zero are rain pixel candidates that may contain non-rain pixels.

When a pixel is covered by rain in two consecutive frames, this rain pixel cannot be detected. To ensure that all rain pixels are detected, we treat a pixel as rain candidate as long as its intensity is not the least in several consecutive frames. The rain candidates of a frame form an image. Figure 50.1 shows the image of rain candidates for a frame in a video used in [3]. In this example, we use eleven consecutive frames to detect rain candidates for the middle frame. When the rain is not heavy, fewer frames are enough for rain detection.

### 50.3.2 Dictionary Learning and Partition

As shown in Fig. 50.1b, the real rain pixels in the candidates form patches in similar directions. But the shape of these patches is complex. It is hard to reliably calculate the direction of each patch. If these patches are decomposed into simpler atoms, then the directions of atoms can be used to represent the directions of patches.

We use patches in the images of rain candidate to learn a redundant dictionary for sparse representation of the images. The learning process is to solve the following optimization problem:

$$\min_{\mathbf{D} \in R^{m \times p}} \frac{1}{n} \sum_{i=1}^{n} \min_{\alpha^i} \left[ \frac{1}{2} \|\mathbf{x}^i - \mathbf{D}\alpha^i\|_2^2 + \psi(\alpha^i) \right], \tag{50.1}$$

where $m$ is the number of pixels in a patch, $\mathbf{x}^i \in R^m$ is the $i$th patch in the image, $n$ is the number of patches in the image, $\mathbf{D} \in R^{m \times p}$ is a dictionary that contains $p$ atoms, $\alpha^i \in R^p$ denotes the sparse coefficients of $\mathbf{x}^i$ with respect to $\mathbf{D}$, and $\psi(\alpha^i)$ is a sparsity-inducing regularizer. If $\mathbf{x}^i$ is a square patch, then there are

**Fig. 50.2** The dictionary
learnt from the patches
extracted from the image in
Fig. 50.1b

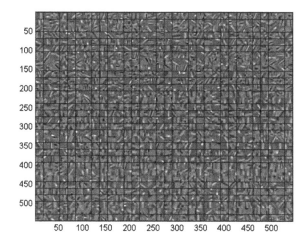

$(mm - \sqrt{m} + 1) \times (nn - \sqrt{m} + 1)$ patches in a $mm \times nn$ image. We apply the
dictionary learning algorithm proposed by Mairal et al. [8] to solve Eq. (50.1) to
obtain the dictionary **D**. For the image shown in Fig. 50.1, the learnt dictionary is
illustrated in Fig. 50.2.

In the sparse representation of a patch of rain streak, the contents in the atoms
with non-zero coefficients will be similar to the rain streak. Since the rain streaks
in a video have similar directions, the intensity gradient distributions of these
atoms will be similar, too. We use the CENsus Transform hISTogram
(CENTRIST) descriptor [9] to encode the gradient distribution information of the
atoms. The $k$-means clustering algorithm is performed to partition all atoms in the
dictionary into several clusters based on their CENTRIST descriptors. The most
compact cluster is identified as the cluster of rain atoms. Figure 50.3 is the clustering results of the atoms in Fig. 50.2. The atoms are partitioned into four clusters,
and the first cluster consists of rain atoms.

### 50.3.3 Sparse Coding and Rain Removal

We use all atoms in the learnt dictionary to generate a sparse representation of the
rain candidate image. The sparse coding process is to solve the following optimization problem:

$$\min_{\alpha \in R^p} \|x - D\alpha\|_2^2 \quad \text{s.t.} \quad \|\alpha\|_0 \leq L, \tag{50.2}$$

The coefficient vector $\alpha$ for a patch x in the image can be acquired by solving
Eq. (50.2) using the OMP (Orthogonal Matching Pursuit) algorithm [10]. If we set
the components of $\alpha$ corresponding to the rain atoms to zero, the rain streaks will
be removed from the image. Figure 50.4 shows the rain removal result of the rain

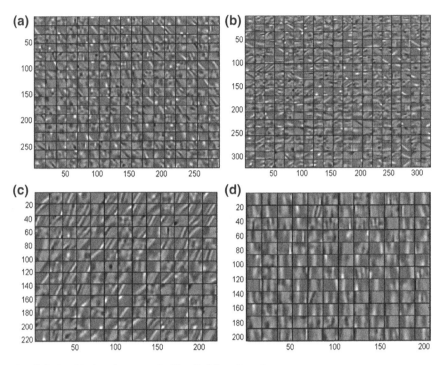

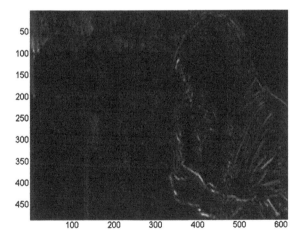

**Fig. 50.3** Partitioning the atoms in Fig. 50.2 into four clusters

**Fig. 50.4** Rain removal
result of the image in
Fig. 50.1b

candidate image in Fig. 50.1b. To remove rain from Fig. 50.1a, we subtract
Fig. 50.1b from Fig. 50.1a, and then add Fig. 50.4 to Fig. 50.1a. The result is
shown in Fig. 50.5.

**Fig. 50.5** Rain removal
result of the frame in
Fig. 50.1a

## 50.4 Experimental Analysis

We perform experimental analysis on the video provided by Garg and Nayar [3]. For each test gray-scale frame, the patch size is $16 \times 16$, the dictionary size is 1,024, and the number of training iterations is 100. The size of each frame in the video is $500 \times 630$. Thus there are $(500 - 16 + 1) \times (630 - 16 + 1) = 298,275$ patches in each frame.

Since the directions of rain streaks in a video are similar, the rain atoms learnt from one frame can be used to extract rain streaks in other frames. In our experiments, we perform dictionary learning only once for a video.

Figure 50.6 compares the rain removal result of our method and the result of the method proposed by Garg and Nayar in [3]. The rain streaks are removed in both results. And the moving hand in Fig. 50.6a is clearer than in Fig. 50.6b. Thus our method is more effective to recover moving objects.

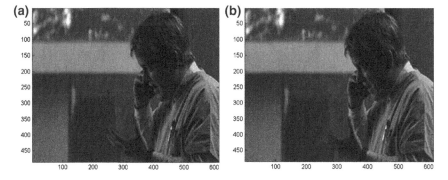

**Fig. 50.6** **a** Rain removal result of our method; **b** the result obtained by Garg and Nayar

## 50.5 Conclusion

A rain removal method that uses the temporal and direction properties of rain streaks is proposed in this paper. Based on the temporal property of rain, rain pixel candidates are generated by comparing the intensities of a pixel in different frames. The direction property of rain is used to find real rain pixels in these candidates. Sparse coding and dictionary learning algorithms are used to reliably calculate the direction of rain. Based on the representation ability of non-rain atoms, this method can recover moving objects. Our experimental analysis shows the effectiveness of this method.

**Acknowledgments** This work was supported by the National Natural Science Foundation of China (51179146) and the Fundamental Research Funds for the Central Universities (2012-IV-041).

## References

1. Barnum PC, Narasimhan S, Kanade T (2010) Analysis of rain and snow in frequency space. Int J Comput Vis 86(2–3):256–274
2. Brewer N, Liu NJ (2008) Using the shape characteristics of rain to identify and remove rain from video. In: Lecture notes in computer science, vol 5342/2008. Springer, Berlin, pp 451–458
3. Garg K, Nayar SK (2004) Detection and removal of rain from videos. In: Proceedings of the international conference on computer vision and pattern recognition, IEEE, pp 528–535
4. Zhang XP, Li H, Qi YY, Leow WK, Ng TK (2006) Rain removal in video by combining temporal and chromatic properties. In: Proceedings of the international conference on multimedia and expo, IEEE, pp 461–464
5. Hase H, Miyake K, Yoneda M (1999) Real-time snowfall noise elimination. In: Proceedings of the international conference on image processing, IEEE, pp 406–409
6. Kang LW, Lin CW, Fu YH (2012) Automatic single-image-based rain streaks removal via image decomposition. IEEE Trans Image Process (TIP) 21(4):1742–1755
7. Dalal N, Triggs B (2005) Histograms of oriented gradients for human detection. In: Proceedings of the IEEE computer society conference on computer vision and pattern recognition (CVPR), pp 886–893
8. Mairal J, Bach F, Ponce J, Sapiro G (2010) Online learning for matrix factorization and sparse coding. J Mach Learn Res 11:19–60
9. Wu J, Rehg JM (2011) CENTRIST: a visual descriptor for scene categorization. IEEE Trans Pattern Anal Mach Intell 33(8):1489–1501
10. Mallat SG, Zhang Z (1993) Matching pursuits with time-frequency dictionaries. IEEE Trans Signal Process 41(12):3397–3415

# Chapter 51
# Chaos System and YCbCr Color Space Based Semi-Fragile Watermarking Algorithm for Color Images

Zhenzhen Zhang, Jianjun Hou, Zhaohong Li and Zhengchao Yang

**Abstract** For identifying the content integrity of color images, a semi-fragile watermarking algorithm is proposed. First, the color image was converted from RGB color space to YCbCr color space, then the watermark was obtained by iterating the chaos system from the initial value which depends on a grayscale image, a watermarking key and the low coefficients of Y component. According to the invariant properties of discrete cosine transform (DCT) coefficients before and after joint photographic experts group (JPEG) compression, the watermark was embedded into the intermediate-frequency DCT coefficients of Y component. Experimental results show that the proposed algorithm is not only robust against JPEG lossy compression, with zero false alarm ratio when quality factor (QF) of JPEG compression is higher than 40, but also sensitive to tampers with a detection ratio above 0.9.

**Keywords** Semi-fragile watermarking · Color images · Chaos mapping · Integrity authentication · JPEG

## 51.1 Introduction

In today's digital age, it is easy and simple to tamper digital images and create visually convincing digital image forgeries by using photo editing software such as Photoshop and ACD-See, which makes people pay more and more attention to the

Z. Zhang (✉) · J. Hou · Z. Li · Z. Yang
School of Electronic and Information, Beijing Jiaotong University,
No 3 Shang Yuan Cun, Hai Dian District, Beijing, China
e-mail: 11111053@bjtu.edu.cn

W. Lu et al. (eds.), *Proceedings of the 2012 International Conference on Information Technology and Software Engineering*, Lecture Notes in Electrical Engineering 212, DOI: 10.1007/978-3-642-34531-9_51, © Springer-Verlag Berlin Heidelberg 2013

content integrity authentication of digital images. Semi-fragile watermark is an effective method to verify the content integrity of a digital image. It can not only checkout whether the image content has been altered or not, but also resist reasonable image processing operations. At present, many algorithms are proposed for the authentication of grayscale images [1–6], while fewer algorithms have been developed for color images [7–9]. The algorithm in Ref. [10] proved that the robustness of the watermark which was embedded in the blue channel of the RGB color space was poor. Cheng et al. [11] embedded the watermark in red, green and blue channels simultaneously, the algorithm got a strong robustness, but the computational complexity was high. Ling et al. [12] developed a robust watermarking algorithm aiming for copyright protection. This algorithm transformed the color image to the YCbCr color space, embedded the watermark in the DCT intermediate frequency coefficients of luminance Y, which made it have strong robustness to JPEG lossy robustness. But it was a non-blind detection algorithm which needed information of the original image when extracting the watermark.

On the other hand, as a result of the popularity of JPEG compression, anti-JPEG compression is always an important research aspect of semi-fragile watermark. Algorithms in Refs. [13, 14] are semi-fragile watermarking algorithms against JPEG compression, but the robustness to JPEG compression is not strong because the degree of the acceptable JPEG compression cannot be preset and the false alarm ratio is high.

In this paper, a semi-fragile watermarking algorithm for color images based on block-independent is proposed. The algorithm transforms the original image data from RGB space to YCbCr space, and divides luminance of Y into non-overlapping blocks, and embeds the watermark in the DCT intermediate frequency coefficients of luminance Y. The results of the experiment show that the proposed algorithm has a strong robustness to JPEG compression, and can localize the tampers accurately.

The subsequent of this paper is structured as follows. The watermark embedding and extraction methods are described in Sects. 51.2 and 51.3. In Sect. 51.4, the experimental results are demonstrated. Section 51.5 concludes this paper.

## 51.2 Watermark Embedding

The embedding of the watermark requires two main steps: obtaining the watermark by utilizing chaos mapping and embedding the watermark into the original image. In this section, the embedding steps of the watermark will be described in detail. Figure 51.1 depicts the algorithm for watermark embedding.

The steps of watermark embedding:

1. Transform the original image $I$ from RGB color space to YCbCr color space by using the formula (51.1):

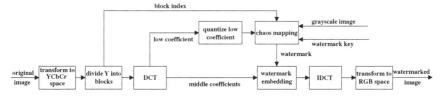

**Fig. 51.1**  Algorithm for watermark embedding

$$
\begin{pmatrix} Y \\ Cb \\ Cr \end{pmatrix} = \begin{pmatrix} 0.256862 \\ -0.148234 \\ 0.439231 \end{pmatrix} \boldsymbol{R} + \begin{pmatrix} 0.504245 \\ -0.290997 \\ -0.367758 \end{pmatrix} \boldsymbol{G} + \begin{pmatrix} 0.097999 \\ 0.439231 \\ -0.071473 \end{pmatrix} \boldsymbol{B} + \begin{pmatrix} 16 \\ 128 \\ 128 \end{pmatrix}
$$
(51.1)

2. A grayscale image $G$ which is the same size of the original image is used as a key. Divide $G$ into $\gamma$ non-overlapping blocks with size of $8 \times 8$ pixels. Get the pixel value of the position (2,1) in each block, and denote it as $G_p$, $p = 1, 2, \ldots, \gamma$, where $p$ represents the block index. Divide luminance $Y$ into $\gamma$ non-overlapping blocks with size of $8 \times 8$ pixels.

3. Do DCT to each $8 \times 8$ block of $Y$, and denote it as $Y_p$. Take out one low frequency coefficient of $Y_p$, and denote it as $L_p$. According to Ref. [1], quantize $L_p$ with pre-quantized step $Q'_m(v)$, then we get the pre-quantized low frequency coefficient $\dot{L}_p = IntegerRound\left(\frac{L_p}{Q'_m(v)}\right) \cdot Q'_m(v)$, where $Q'_m(v) > Q_m(v)$, $Q_m(v)$ is the quantization matrix of JPEG compression with QF $= 50$, which is shown in Table 51.1.

4. Calculate the mean value and the maximum value of the absolute values of $\dot{L}_p$ and $G_p$, and denote them as $L_{pmean}$ and $L_{pMax}$ respectively. Obtain the initial value $x_{p0}$ of logistic chaos mapping by using the watermark key $k$.

$$
x_{p0} = \frac{1}{2}\left(\frac{L_{pmean}}{L_{pMax}} + k\right), \quad k \in (0, 1)
$$
(51.2)

**Table 51.1**  Quantization matrix of JPEG compression with QF $= 50$

| 16 | 11 | 10 | 16 | 24  | 40  | 51  | 61  |
|----|----|----|----|-----|-----|-----|-----|
| 12 | 12 | 14 | 19 | 26  | 58  | 60  | 55  |
| 14 | 13 | 16 | 24 | 40  | 57  | 69  | 56  |
| 14 | 17 | 22 | 29 | 51  | 87  | 80  | 62  |
| 18 | 22 | 37 | 56 | 68  | 109 | 103 | 77  |
| 24 | 35 | 55 | 64 | 81  | 104 | 113 | 92  |
| 49 | 64 | 78 | 87 | 103 | 121 | 120 | 101 |
| 72 | 92 | 95 | 98 | 112 | 100 | 103 | 99  |

Logistic mapping is very sensitive to initial value and its iteration equation is shown as formula (51.3).

$$x_{n+1} = \alpha x_n(1 - x_n), \; \alpha \in [0, 4], \; x_n \in [0, 1] \tag{51.3}$$

When $\alpha = 4$, the mean value of logistic chaos sequence is 0.5. Therefore, it is available to change real value sequence $x_0, x_1, \ldots, x_n$ to binary sequence (0 or 1) $b_0, b_1, \ldots, b_n$ by using the threshold function $q(x)$,

$$q(x) = \begin{cases} 1 & x \geq 0.5 \\ 1 & x < 0.5 \end{cases} \tag{51.4}$$

Substitute $x_{p0}$ into (51.3), after $T = p \times 30$ times iteration, we get a sequence with length of $T$. By using the threshold function $q(x)$, a binary sequence $b_{p1}, b_{p2}, \ldots, b_{pT}$ is gained. Take the last $n$ bits of the sequence $b_{p1}, b_{p2}, \ldots, b_{pT}$ as the watermark, which are denoted as $W_{p1}, W_{p2}, \ldots, W_{pn}$, $n$ is the length of the watermark of each block.

5. Embed the watermark into the DCT intermediate frequency coefficients of $Y_p$. Choose $n$ middle coefficients in each block, and denote them as $M_p(i)$, $i = 1, 2, \ldots, n$.

$$M'_p(i) = IntegerRound\left(\frac{M_p(i)}{Q'_m(v)}\right) \tag{51.5}$$

where, $Q'_m(v)$ is the pre-quantized step corresponds to $M_p(i)$, the embedding equation is shown as Eq. (51.6).

$$\dot{M}_p(i) = \begin{cases} M'_p(i)Q'_m(v), & LSB\left(M'_p(i)\right) = W_{pi} \\ \left\{M'_p(i) + sgn\left(\frac{M_p(i)}{Q'_m(v)} - M'_p(i)\right)\right\} \cdot Q'_m(v) & LSB\left(M'_p(i)\right) \neq W_{pi} \end{cases} \tag{51.6}$$

where, $sgn(x)$ is the sign function,

$$sgn(x) = \begin{cases} 1, & x > 0 \\ 0, & x = 0 \\ -1, & x < 0 \end{cases} \tag{51.7}$$

6. Deal with all the blocks with the same operations (51.1–51.5). Replace the low frequency coefficients and the intermediate frequency coefficients of $Y_p$ with the new low frequency coefficients $\dot{L}_p$ and intermediate frequency coefficients $\dot{M}_p(i)$, $i = 1, 2, \ldots, n$. Then do IDCT to $Y_p$ and finally the new luminance $Y_w$ is obtained. Transform the image from YCbCr color space to RGB color space, by using Eq. (51.8), and then the watermarked image $I_w$ is achieved.

$$\begin{pmatrix} R \\ G \\ B \end{pmatrix} = \begin{pmatrix} 1.164 \\ 1.164 \\ 1.164 \end{pmatrix} \times (Y - 16) + \begin{pmatrix} 0 \\ -0.392 \\ 2.017 \end{pmatrix} \times (Cb - 128) + \begin{pmatrix} 1.596 \\ -0.813 \\ 0 \end{pmatrix} \times (Cr - 128)$$

$$(51.8)$$

7. Embed the watermark repeatedly, until the difference meet the requirement of embedding effectiveness, the difference consists of two parts, one part is the difference between the DCT low frequency coefficients of the luminance component of $I_w$ and $\dot{L}_p$, the other one is the difference between the DCT intermediate frequency coefficients of the luminance component of $I_w$ and $\dot{M}_p(i)$, $i = 1, 2, \ldots, n$.

## 51.3 Watermark Extraction

(1) Deal with the watermarked image $I_w$ with the same steps (1)–(4) as Sect. 51.2, we get $\gamma$ groups of watermark, which is denoted as $\dot{W}_p$, $p = 1, 2, \ldots, \gamma$.
(2) Extract the DCT intermediate frequency coefficients of each block of the watermarked image $I_w$, and denote them as $M_{wp}(i)$, $i = 1, 2, \ldots n$, $n$ is the length of watermark embedded in each block. Calculate the LSBs of $M_{wp}(i)$, which is denoted as $\tilde{W}_p$,

$$\tilde{W}_p = LSB\left(M'_{wp}(i)\right), \; i = 1, 2, \ldots, n \tag{51.9}$$

$$M'_{wp}(i) = IntegerRound\left(\frac{M_{wp}(i)}{Q'_m(v)}\right) \tag{51.10}$$

(3) Compare $\dot{W}_p$ with $\tilde{W}_p$ block by block, if $\dot{W}_p = \tilde{W}_p$ it indicates that the content integrity of the image block is reliable; otherwise, $\dot{W}_p \neq \tilde{W}_p$, we consider that the image block has been altered by malicious attacks.

## 51.4 Experimental Results

In order to test the validity of the proposed algorithm, 10 color images with size of $576 \times 720$ pixels are test. The length of the watermark embedded in each block is 4. The watermark is embedded into positions (1, 8), (2, 7), (3, 6) and (4, 5) of DCT intermediate frequency coefficients of each $Y$ component block. Moreover, the watermark key is $k = 0.3$, $\alpha = 4$, the acceptable JPEG compression is $Q_m = Q_{50}$.

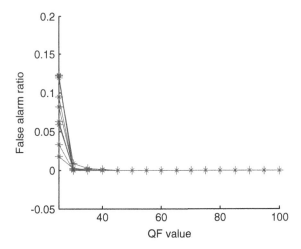

**Fig. 51.2** QF-false alarm
ratio under cropping attack

## 51.4.1 Robustness to JPEG Lossy Compression

Figures 51.2 and 51.3 shows the QF-false alarm ratio curves of the tested color images after different attacks including cropping and copying, The QF of JPEG compression is increased 5 each step from 25 to 100. The attack against images in Fig. 51.2 is cropping the left top quarter of the image; in Fig. 51.3 the attack is copying part of the image (multiple of 8 × 8) to another part of the same image.

Figures 51.2 and 51.3 show that the false alarm ratio of the ten images is equal to 0 when QF ≥ 40, which indicates that the algorithm has strong robustness to JPEG lossy compression.

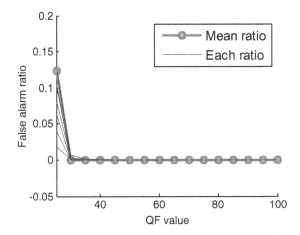

**Fig. 51.3** QF-false alarm ratio under copying attack

**Table 51.2** Comparing results on false alarm ratio with references

| JPEG QF | Proposed scheme | Reference [4] | Reference [5] | Reference [6] | Reference [7] | Reference [8] | Reference [9] |
|---------|-----------------|---------------|---------------|---------------|---------------|---------------|---------------|
| 90 | 0 | 0.009 | 0.0219 | 0.049 | 0.0212 | 0.04 | / |
| 60 | 0 | / | / | / | 0.1286 | 0.22 | 0.0211 |
| 50 | 0 | 0.255 | 0.081 | 0.199 | / | 0.28 | 0.0291 |

QF-false alarm ratio reflects the robustness of the algorithm to JPEG lossy compression. Table 51.2 shows the comparing results on false alarm ratio with Refs. [4–9].

These results indicate that the proposed scheme has a stronger robustness against JPEG lossy compression than Refs. [4–9].

## 51.4.2 The Sensitivity to Tampers and Locating Capability

In this section, we present the QF-detection ratio curves of the tested color images which experience identical attacks as in Sect. 51.4.1. Figures 51.4 and 51.5 show the QF-detection ratio curves of the ten color images after cropping attack and copying attack respectively.

Figures 51.4 and 51.5 clearly show that the detection ratio of the proposed algorithm is very high to different QF values and different images. Theoretically, the detection ratio is 0.9375. The ten QF-detection curves in Fig. 51.4 coincide to a straight line, the reason for this is that the cropping area of each image is identical and the pixel values of the cropping area are changed to 255.

Figures 51.6, 51.7, 51.8 and 51.9 illustrates the sensitivity to tampers and locating capability of the proposed algorithm vividly.

**Fig. 51.4** QF-detection ratio under cropping attack

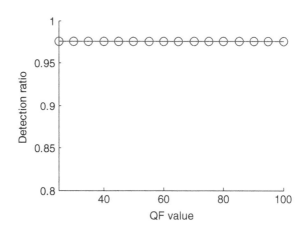

**Fig. 51.5** QF-detection ratio
under copying attack

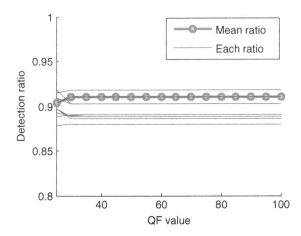

**Fig. 51.6** Original image

Figure 51.6 is the original image, Fig. 51.7 is the watermarked image, Fig. 51.8 is the watermarked image after tampering which replacing the year 2009 by 2005, Fig. 51.9 is the image after detection, the tampered area is marked by black blocks. The experimental results show that the proposed algorithm can locate the tamper area accurately.

## 51.5 Conclusion

An effective semi-fragile watermarking algorithm for identifying the content integrity of color images is presented. The algorithm is based on DCT domain, and embeds the watermark in the DCT intermediate frequency coefficients of $8 \times 8$ blocks of luminance Y. Compared to Refs. [4–9], the proposed algorithm has

**Fig. 51.7** Watermarked image

**Fig. 51.8** Tampered image

**Fig. 51.9** Image after detection

stronger robustness to JPEG lossy compression, and allows to preset the acceptable degree of JPEG compression in advance. The scheme can localize the tampers accurately, with a high detection ratio above 0.9.

# References

1. Li ZH, Hou JJ (2007) Semi-fragile water marking technique based on JPEG invariant and chaotic maps. Comput Eng Appl 43(32):40–43 (in Chinese)
2. Wang XQ, Wang J, Peng H (2009) A semi-fragile image watermarking resisting to JPEG compression. In: International conference on management of e-Commerce and e-Government (ICMECG), pp 498–502
3. Ping WW, Memon N (2001) Secret and public key image watermarking schemes for image authentication and ownership verification. IEEE Trans Image Process 10(10):1593–1601
4. Li CH, Lu ZD (2004) An image digital watermarking based on support vector machine. J Image Graphics 11(9):1322–1326 (in Chinese)
5. Gao GY (2010) A blind grayscale watermark algorithm based on chaos and mixed transform domain. In: International conference on computer and automation engineering, pp 658–662
6. Song W (2010) Research on several digital image watermarking algorithms. Doctoral dissertation, Beijing Jiaotong University, pp 45–49 (in Chinese)
7. Huang CY, Gong Q, Huang QL (2010) Color image watermarking algorithm based on two dimension chaotic encryption. Comput Technol Dev (2):141–144,236 (in Chinese)
8. Liu KC, Chou CH (2009) Robust and transparent watermarking scheme for colour images. IET Image Process 3:228–242
9. Thorat CG, Jadhav BD (2010) A blind digital watermark technique for color image wavelet transform and SIFT. Procedia Comput Sci 2:236–241
10. Pan G, Wu ZH, Lu B (2003) A bi-image watermarking method based on 2D-DCT. J Eng Graphics 3:118–125 (in Chinese)
11. Cheng WD, Huang JW, Liu HM (2002) A color image watermarking algorithm based on 3D-DCT. Acta Electronica Sinica 19(12A):1778–1781 (in Chinese)
12. Ling HF, Lu ZD, Yang SY (2005) 2-Dimention color image digital watermarking technique based on YCbCr color space. Mini Micro Syst 26(3):482–484 (in Chinese)
13. Li CT (2004) Digital fragile watermarking scheme for authentication of JPEG images. IEEE Proc Vision Image Sign Process 151(6):460–466
14. Yang SY, Lu ZD, Zou FH (2004) A novel semi-fragile watermarking technique for image authentication. Int Conf Sign Process (3):2282–2285

# Chapter 52
# Sparse Representation Based Gender Recognition Algorithm

**Longfei Cui, Ming Zhu, Rui Liu and Wenke Zhang**

**Abstract** Gender recognition is using the feature extracted from the training sets to identify the gender of a test sample. To achieve this propose, we should grip the difference between the features of male and female. Here, Gabor and LBP are used to get features of face image. The relationship between the feature of training sets and test samples is much more than distance or projection. By analyzing the mathematic essence of sparse representation between images, a test sample can be viewed as the linear combination of training samples and based on this theory, the sparse representation algorithm of gender recognition is proposed. Finally, some experiments on gender recognition verified the efficacy of the proposed algorithm.

**Keywords** Spare representation · Gender recognition · Gabor · LBP

## 52.1 Introduction

Gender recognition is a fundamental aspect of demographic classification, and has a high application potential in areas such as surveillance, identity authentication, human–computer interaction, access control, video indexing and dynamic marketing surveys.

It's difficult for computer to classify gender only based on facial image analysis. The mainly reason is that the inherent variability of human face due to different image formation process in terms of image quality and photometry, geometry,

L. Cui (✉) · M. Zhu · R. Liu · W. Zhang
University of Science and Technology of China, Hefei, Anhui, China
e-mail: cuilong@mail.ustc.edu.cn

W. Lu et al. (eds.), *Proceedings of the 2012 International Conference on Information Technology and Software Engineering*, Lecture Notes in Electrical Engineering 212, DOI: 10.1007/978-3-642-34531-9_52, © Springer-Verlag Berlin Heidelberg 2013

occlusion etc. Some surveys addressed these challenges and possible solution in with respect to face recognition [1] and facial expression recognition [2] is also presented in details. Mäkinen and Raisamo [3] we had provided guidelines to carry out classification experiments and also present a systematic study on gender classification with automatically detected and aligned faces [4]. So far, different methods have been proposed for gender classification using gait [5], iris[6], and hand shape [7]. However, almost every method mentioned above is not able to take full use of the features.

By analyzing the way of how the features constitute an image, we proposed a new method for gender classification in this paper which is based on spare matrix. Also, our system utilizes Gabor and LBP to get the feature to increase gender classification accuracy.

## 52.2 Proposed Approach

In our mind, how to get the feature is not more important than how to use it. So in our approach as shown in Fig. 52.1, our first task is to get the feature. It can mainly be divided into two steps. Firstly, we use Gabor transform to get the multi-resolution image set of the source image. Secondly, we use LBP operator to get the features.

After we get the features of the training set, we can use them to classify the gender of the test image. The concrete steps are as follows:

Firstly, get the feature of the test image. Secondly, calculate the sparse representation of the test image feature. Then by the spares vector of the male sets and the female sets, reconstruct the man image and the woman image separately. Last by measuring the distance of the source image to the man image and he woman image reconstructed, finish the classification.

### 52.2.1 Feature Extraction

#### 52.2.1.1 Gabor Transform

Gabor transform is an effective time–frequency analysis method. Our idea is to use multi-scale, multi-directional Gabor filter to decompose the input face image. The filter is defined as follows [8]:

$$\Psi_{u,v}(z) = \frac{\left\| k_{u,v} \right\|^2}{\sigma^2} e^{-\frac{\left\| k_{u,v} \right\|^2 |z|^2}{2\sigma^2}} [e^{ik_{u,v}z} - e^{-\frac{\sigma^2}{2}}] \qquad (52.1)$$

where $u$ and $v$ define the orientation and scale of the Gabor kernels, $z = (x, y)$, $\|\cdot\|$ denotes the norm operator, and the wave vector $k_{u,v}$ is defined as follows:

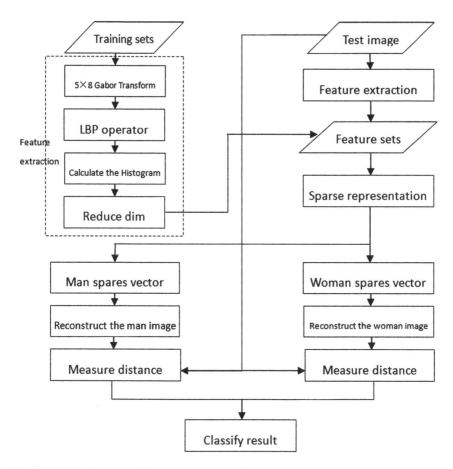

**Fig. 52.1** Main flowchart of the proposed approach

$$k_{u,v} = \begin{pmatrix} k_v \cos \phi_u \\ k_v \sin \phi_u \end{pmatrix} \tag{52.2}$$

where $k_v = \frac{k_{Max}}{\lambda}$, $\phi_u = u\frac{\pi}{8}$, and $\lambda$ is the spacing factor between kernels in the frequency domain. Let $I(x,y)$ be the gray level distribution of an image, the convolution of image $I$ and a Gabor kernel $\Psi_{u,v}$ is defined as follows:

$$G_{u,v}(z) = I(z) \otimes \Psi_{u,v}(z) \tag{52.3}$$

where $z = (x,y)$, $\otimes$ denotes the convolution operator, and $G_{u,v}(z)$ is the convolution result corresponding to the Gabor kernel at orientation $u$ and scale $v$. Here, we set 8 orientations as $u \in \{0,1,2,3,4,5,6,7\}$ and 5 scale as $v = \{0,1,2,3\}$. Then we only retain the amplitude part of the result for the next step. Therefore, we could get 40 Gabor amplitude sets $S_{u,v} = \{|G_{u,v}(z)|\}$ of every face image.

### 52.2.1.2 Local Binary Pattern

LBP [9] operator labels the pixels of an image by threshold the $3 \times 3$ neighborhood of each pixel with the center value and considering the result as a binary number:

$$S(f_p - f_c) = \begin{cases} 1 & f_p \geq f_c \\ 0 & f_p \leq f_c \end{cases} \tag{52.4}$$

Where $f_c$ is the center value and $f_p$ are the neighboring values around. Then the LBP value at the center pixel is:

$$LBP(f_c) = \sum_{p=0}^{7} S(f_p - f_c)2^p \tag{52.5}$$

Then the LBP operator is applied on very Gabor amplitude image to get the preliminary feature. There are mainly 3 steps to finish it as illustrated in Fig. 52.1.

1. *Generating LBP Face Image*: At the beginning Gabor amplitude image is represented using LBP operator, the LBP operator is applied in the Gabor amplitude image using the Eq. (52.5).
2. *Histogram of LBP*: Divide each piece of LBP images into $k \times k$ non-overlapping rectangular region of the $R_0, R_1, \ldots, R_{m-1}$ ($m = k \times k$). Each histogram of the rectangular area can form a L-levels histogram sequence. The jth rectangular area in a LBP image histogram sequence H can be expressed as

$$H_{u,v,j} = \{h_{u,v,0,j}, \ldots, h_{u,v,L-1,j}\} \tag{52.6}$$

where

$$h_{u,v,i,j} = \sum_{x,y} I(f(x,y) = i) \cdot I(x,y) \in R_j) \tag{52.7}$$

$f(x, y)$ is the gray level of the point $(x, y)$ in the image; $i = 0, 1, \ldots, L - 1$; $j = 0, 1, \ldots, m - 1$ and the function I is defined as following

$$I(A) = \begin{cases} 1 & A \text{ is ture} \\ 0 & A \text{ is false} \end{cases} \tag{52.8}$$

3. *Concatenated LBP Histogram*: These all LBP histograms are concatenated to get a spatially combined LBP histogram. So we can get a global face feature for each given face image shown as following:

$$V = \{H_{0,0,0}, \ldots, H_{0,0,m-1}, H_{0,1,0}, \ldots, H_{0,1,m-1}, \ldots, H_{7,4,m-1}\} \tag{52.9}$$

### 52.2.1.3 Principal Component Analysis

Suppose m as mentioned above is the block num of each LBP image divided. Then the dimension of the feature vector in formula (52.9) can be calculated as

$5 \times 8 \times 59\,\text{m} = 2,360\,\text{m}$. To cope with this problem, we are willing to use Principal Component Analysis (PCA) to reduce dimension The approach is presented as follows:

Suppose, in the training set, there are p images labeled as male and q images labeled as female, and $M^i_{u,v,j}$ $(i = 1,\ldots p)$ is the $H_{u,v,j}$ of the image labeled male while $W^i_{u,v,j}$ $(i = 1,\ldots q)$ is ones labeled female.

First, we compute the means for the two class:

$$M_{u,v,j} = (\sum_{i=1}^{p} M^i_{u,v,j})^T, \; W_{u,v,j} = (\sum_{i=1}^{q} W^i_{u,v,j})^T \qquad (52.10)$$

Second, calculate the projection direction matrix:

$$D_{u,v,j} = (\frac{M_{u,v,j}}{p} - \frac{W_{u,v,j}}{q})/\left\|\frac{M_{u,v,j}}{p} - \frac{W_{u,v,j}}{q}\right\| \qquad (52.11)$$

Then, map each histogram $H_{u,v,j}$ into a single value, the mapping formula is shown here:

$$f_{u,v,j} = H_{u,v,j}D^T_{u,v,j} \qquad (52.12)$$

Finally, all the single values are fitted to form the feature vector:

$$F = \{f_{0,0,0},\ldots,f_{0,0,m-1},f_{0,1,0},\ldots,f_{0,1,m-1},\ldots,f_{7,4,m-1}\} \qquad (52.13)$$

### 52.2.2 Classifier Construction

In this section, we will use the feature F of all the training samples to construct a over-complete dictionary. Then we will compute the sparse representation of every input face with respect to the entire training set. With the coefficient of each input image, we can further identify its gender so that the classifier is completely constructed.

#### 52.2.2.1 Over-Complete Dictionary

The basic idea of sparse representation is to find suitable sparse representation of the signals based on over-complete dictionary. To apply the theory of sparse representation to image processing, how we shall construct effective image signal sparse representation dictionary is crucial. Over-complete dictionary is to chose the suitable training sample set which should contain as much as possible the information structure of all the database. Thus sparse representation of the gender test images is to find a linear combination of the training set of images. By finding the sparsest solution of the input images, we can get effective description of the relevance of information between the internal structure and characteristics of gender identity in sparse.

Now suppose $C = \{M, W\}$ express the input image belonging to the label of man and woman and the feature vector of the image of each class calculated in Eq. (52.13) is $F_m$ and $F_w$ respectively. Obviously, the dimension of them is 59 m. The number of the sample images of man and woman is $N_m$ and $N_w$ respectively. For all the man images, we can get $F_{m,i} \in R^{59m}$, $(i = 1, \ldots N_m - 1)$. The $F = \{F_{m,i}, (i = 1, \ldots N_m - 1)\}$ is the over-complete dictionary, and the matrix form is $D_M = [F_{m,1}, \ldots F_{m,N_m}] \in R^{59m \times N_m}$. So one test image $T_m$ of man can be disassembled as a linear combination of the training set of images:

$$T_m = \sum_{i=1}^{N_m} F_{m,i}\alpha_{m,i} = D_m \Phi_m \tag{52.14}$$

where, $\Phi_m = [\alpha_1, \ldots \alpha_{N_m}]^T$.

It's the same with the class of the woman.

Actually, it's impossible to know the class of the test image belonging to. So we should use both classes to construct to over-complete dictionary, which is defined as following:

$$D = [D_m, D_W] = [F_{m,1}, \ldots, F_{m,N_m}, F_{w,1}, \ldots, F_{w,N_w}] \tag{52.15}$$

and the Eq. (52.14) will be:

$$T = D\Phi + \theta \tag{2.16}$$

where, $\Phi = [\Phi_m^T, \Phi_w^T]^T$, $\theta$ is the noise.

### 52.2.2.2 Sparse Representation

Now suppose we get a over-complete dictionary $D$ through Eq. (52.15), and the element of $D$ is linear independent. Then the sparsest representation will be the solution to the optimization problem:

$$(P_0) : \min_{\Phi} \|\Phi\|_1 \text{ subject to } \|\theta\|_2 \le \delta \tag{52.17}$$

This can be cast as solving a corresponding convex optimization in Lagrangian form [10]:

$$(P_1) : \min_{\Phi} \|\Phi\|_1 + \lambda \|T - D\Phi\|_2^2 \tag{2.18}$$

When get the sparse vector $\Phi = [\Phi_m^T, \Phi_w^T]^T$, we can reconstruct $T_m$, $T_w$ of the test sample $T$ trough $\Phi_m$, $\Phi_w$ respectively, as Fig. 52.2 showed. Then by comparing the distance between $T$ and $T_m$ to that of $T$ and $T_m$, the finally class of test sample $T$ is determined.

**Fig. 52.2  a** Sample $T$.
**b** Sparse representation.
**c** Reconstructed $T_m$.
**d** Reconstructed $T_w$

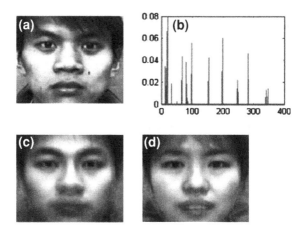

### 52.2.2.3  Data Refine

As analyzed above, because the over-complete dictionary relies on the training sets, so the sparse representation based classifier is training sample sensitive. To keep the completeness of the dictionary, we used data retraining to refine data the training set. The entire process is summarized as Algorithm 2.1.

**Algorithm 2.1:**

> **Input**: Face image database $I$, including $I_m$ and $I_w$.
> **Output**: Over-complete dictionary F, the test sets $T$.
>
> 1: Randomly chose $3N/2$ images of $I$ as training sets $I'$. The rest is $T$.
> 2: Randomly chose $N/2$ images of $I'$ as training sets $I'_{train}$, the rest is $I'_{test}$.
> 3: Compute the feature $F_{I'_{train}}$ of $I'_{train}$.
> 4: Construct $F_{I'_{train}}$ to dictionary $D''_{I'_{train}}$.
> 5: According to $D''_{I'_{train}}$, classify $I'_{test}$, add the error classed samples to $D''_{I'_{train}}$, now signed as $D'_{I'_{train}}$.
> 6: Count the different number $n$ of $D'_{I'_{train}}$ and $N$, randomly chose $n$ images from the rest of training sets $I'_{train}$, adding in $D'_{I'_{train}}$ now signed as F.

## 52.3  Experiments

The performance of gender classification using proposed method s evaluated with images from the CAS-PEAL database. This database contains 30,864 facial images of 1,040 individuals with 9 different poses. In this work, we collect 1,040 mug-shot face images out of which 595 faces are male and rest 445 are female face.

**Table 52.1** Classification accuracy with different number of over-complete dictionary

| Number of dictionary | Classification accuracy | | |
|---|---|---|---|
| | Overall (%) | Male (%) | Female (%) |
| 200 | 93.09 | 93.53 | 92.46 |
| 400 | 95.50 | 95.95 | 94.69 |
| 600 | 95.91 | 95.93 | 95.86 |

**Table 52.2** Classification accuracy with other method

| Methods classification accuracy (feature + classifier) | Classification accuracy Overall (%) |
|---|---|
| Gray + SVM [11] | 89.90 |
| Gabor + SVM [11] | 90.30 |
| LBP + SVM [11] | 92.90 |
| Proposed gabor + LBP + sparse | 95.50 |

Before the facial images are available for feature extraction, they have to be pre-processed. The eye coordinates of each image are first manually located. Then the image is cropped by the eye coordinates and normalized to the size of $130 \times 150$ pixels. Every image is partitioned into $10 \times 10$ sub-blocks to generate spatially combined LBP histogram feature vector as discussed in Sect. 52.1. For each pose we pick 200 images of male and female respectively for training and the rest are used for test.

Our experiments shows increasing the number of over-complete dictionary can enhance the performance. However, it increases the length of feature vector and requires extra bit of processing. The classification performance in respect to different number of over-complete dictionary is shown with Table 52.1. Performance of the proposed method in comparison other state of the art methods is shown in Table 52.2.

## 52.4 Conclusions

This paper describes a new gender classifier based on sparse representation of local face. First, we utilized Gabor and LBP to get the features, and then we use PCA to reduce the dimensionality of the feature. Second, a new gender classifier is proposed based on the sparse representation differences between male and female faces. To evaluate the proposed method, we had finished the experiment on the CAS-PEAL database and got promising results.

**Acknowledgments** This work was supported by the Pilot project of Chinese Academy of Sciences "Network video transmission and control" project under Contract XDA06030900, and the National science and technology support plan "Enhanced search system architecture, key technology and standardized test research" under Contract 2011BAH11B01.

# References

1. Zhao W, Chellappa R, hillips. PJ (2003) Face recognition: a literature survey. ACM Comput Surv 35(4):399–458
2. Fasel B, Luettin J (2003) Automatic facial expression analysis: a survey. Pattern Recogn 36(1):259–275
3. Makinen E, Raisamo R (2008) An experimental comparison of gender classification methods. Pattern Recogn Lett 29(10):1544–1556
4. Makinen E, Raisamo R (2008) Evaluation of gender classification methods with automatically detected and aligned faces. IEEE Trans Pattern Anal Mach Intell 30:541–547
5. Shan C, Gong S, McOwan PW (2007) Learning gender from human gaits and faces. In: IEEE conference on advanced video and signal based surveillance, doi: 10.1109/AVSS.2007.4425362
6. Thomas V, Chawla NV, Bowyer KW, Flynn PJ (2007) Learning to predict gender from iris images. In: IEEE conference on biometrics: theory, applications, and systems, doi:10.1109/BTAS.2007.4401911
7. Amayeh G, Bebis G, Nicolescu M (2008) Gender classification from hand shape. IEEE Comput Vis Pattern Recogn Workshop. doi:10.1109/CVPRW.2008.4563122
8. Liu C, Wechsler H (2002) Gabor feature based classification using the enhanced fisher linear discriminant model for face recognition. IEEE Trans Image Process 11:467–476
9. Ahonen T, Hadid A, Pietikainen (2006) Face description with local binary patterns: application to face recognition. IEEE Trans Pattern Anal Mach Intell 28(12):2037–2041
10. Donoho DL, Elad M, Temlyakov VN (2006) Stable recovery of sparse overcomplete representations in the presence of noise. IEEE Trans Inf Theory 52:6–18
11. Xia B, Sun H, Lu B (2008) Multi-view gender Classification based on local gabor binary mapping pattern and support vector machines. In: IEEE conference on international joint conference on neural networks, doi: 10.1109/IJCNN.2008.4634279

# Chapter 53
# Region-Based Image Annotation Using Gaussian Mixture Model

Xin Luo and Kenji Kita

**Abstract**  A number of image annotation information for a training image is available only at the image level, but not at the region level. However, an image contains several regions and each region may represent different semantic meaning. In this paper, a region based samples learning approach to image annotation using Gaussian mixture model (GMM) is presented, which make use of coordinate and color feature in image region to compute GMM of each region, by samples learning to achieve automatic annotation of each image semantic purpose. The experiments over Corel images have shown that this approach is effective for image annotation.

**Keywords**  Region · Image annotation · Gaussian mixture model (GMM)

## 53.1 Introduction

In recent years, Content-Based Image Retrieval (CBIR) has attracted significant interest amongst the computer vision community [1]. CBIR systems use low-level features automatically extracted from image regions, such as color and texture, to search for images relevant to a query. However, although there are many

X. Luo (✉)
School of Computer Science and Technology, Donghua University, No 2999 North people Road, Songjiang District, Shanghai 201620, China
e-mail: xin@dhu.edu.cn

K. Kita
Faculty and School of Engineering, The University of Tokushima, 2–24 Shinkura-cho, Tokushima 770-8501, Japan

W. Lu et al. (eds.), *Proceedings of the 2012 International Conference on Information Technology and Software Engineering*, Lecture Notes in Electrical Engineering 212, DOI: 10.1007/978-3-642-34531-9_53, © Springer-Verlag Berlin Heidelberg 2013

sophisticated algorithms to describe color, shape and texture features approaches, these algorithms do not satisfied and comfort to human perception. Consequently, in the approach of CBIR, there exists a "Semantic Gap" between low-level visual features and high-level concepts [2]. Thus, to narrow the gap for image retrieval is a very challenging problem yet to be solved [3].

At the present time, many of the papers on image retrieval make reference to the problem of the semantic gap. Whether in papers by researchers of content based techniques who believe they may be providing a bridge to the semantics or by professional searchers frustrated by the inability of systems to accommodate their queries, the semantic gap appears as a recurring issue in their endeavours. Automatic image annotation is considered to be one of the effective methods to bridging the image semantic gap.

A number of image annotation information for a training image is available only at the image level, but not at the region level. However, an image contains several regions and each region may represent different semantic meaning. In this paper, we present a method for automatic image annotation based on Gaussian Mixture Model (GMM) by region-based color and coordinate of matching. The proposed method consists of two phases: In the first phase, the image is partitioned into disjoint, connected regions with color features and XY coordinate. Each region or valid combinations of neighbouring regions constitute potential objects. In the second phase, we modelled a training dataset through GMM to have a stable annotation result. Gaussian parameters are computed through Expectation Maximization on the training dataset. Our approach takes into account the relational spatial semantics among objects in the images which affects the quality of the retrieval results. Representation of spatial relations semantics among objects are important as it can convey important information about the image and to further increase the confidence in image understanding contribute to richer querying and retrieval facilities. The experiments over Corel images have shown that this approach is effective for image annotation.

The rest of this paper is organized as follows. Section 53.2 reviews the related work. In Sect. 53.3, we formulate image annotation as a supervised learning problem in the GMM setting. Section 53.4 describes the extensive experiments we have performed and provides the results. Finally, we conclude in Sect. 53.5.

## 53.2 Related Works

In this section, we provide a review of previous works in manual image annotation and automatic image annotation.

## 53.2.1 Manual Image Annotation

One conventional and common ways to describe the image in high level is using the manual annotation. Examples include Photoblog, Fotopages, Flickr and etc. Manual image annotation approaches can be categorized into two types. The most common approach is tagging, which allows the users to annotate images with a chosen set of keywords from a controlled or uncontrolled vocabulary. Another approach is browsing, which requires users to sequentially browse a group of images and judge their relevance to a pre-defined keyword.

Since keywords are selected based on human determination of the semantic content of images, manual annotation of image content is considered a "best case" in terms of accuracy. However, manual image annotation can be a tedious and labor-intensive process [4]. In addition, manual annotation may also introduce retrieval errors due to users forgetting what descriptors they used when annotating their images after a lengthy period of time. And until now, there are few studies available on quantitatively analyzing and optimizing the efficiency of the manual image annotation process. So, researchers are moving toward automatically automatic extraction of the image semantic content.

## 53.2.2 Semi/Automatic Image Annotation

Automatic image annotation, which aims to automatically detect the visual keywords from image content, have attracted a lot of attention from researchers in the last decade. These automatic annotation approaches have achieved notable success recently. For instance, Ref. [5] proposed an annotation model called cross-media relevance model which directly computed the probability of annotations given an image. The ALIPR system [6] uses advanced statistical learning techniques to provide fully automatic and real-time annotation for digital pictures.

However, most of the methods discussed are only able to retrieve similar images which have the whole semantics and does not indicate which part of the image gives rise to which words, so it is not explicitly object recognition. Usually, an image contains several regions. Since each region may have different contents and represent different semantic meaning, it is intuitive to divide an image into regions and extract visual features from each region. Reference [7] presented a novel Asymmetrical Support Vector Machine-based MIL algorithm (ASVM-MIL) for region-based image annotation. Reference [8] implements a cross-media relevance model. The model in learns the joint probability of associating words to image features from training sets and uses it to generate the probability of associating a word to a given query image. In [9] to use continuous probability density functions to describe the process of generating blob features, hoping to avoid the loss of information related to quantization and achieve substantially better retrieval performance on the same dataset.

Region-based image annotation even though the region semantics can be captured but then the extraction of spatial relational semantic descriptors is often neglected. If do not take into account the relational spatial semantics among objects in the images which affects the result of the automatic annotation. Representation of spatial relations semantics among objects are important as it can convey important information about the image and to further increase the confidence in image understanding.

## 53.3 Region-Based Image Annotation Using Gaussian Mixture Model

In this section, we present a Gaussian Mixture Model (GMM) algorithm for region-based image annotation.

### 53.3.1 Gaussian Mixture Model

Mixture models are a type of density models which that comprise a number of component functions, usually Gaussian. The GMM probability density function can be defined as a weighted sum of Gaussian as:

$$P(\vec{x}|\lambda) = \sum_{i=1}^{M} w_i \cdot g(\vec{x}|\vec{\mu}_i, \sum_i)  \qquad (53.1)$$

Where $\vec{x}$ is a D-dimensional feature vector, $w_i, i = 1, \ldots, M$, are the mixture weight parameter of the $i$th Gaussian component and $g(\vec{x}|\vec{\mu}_i, \sum_i), i = 1, \ldots, M$ are the normal distribution of $i$th component densities. Each component density is a D-variate Gaussian function of the form,

$$g(x|\mu_i, \sum_i) = \frac{1}{\sqrt{(2\pi)^D |\sum_i|}} \exp\left\{ -\frac{1}{2}(\vec{x} - \vec{\mu}_i)^T \sum_i^{-1} (\vec{x} - \vec{\mu}_i) \right\}  \qquad (53.2)$$

With mean vector $\vec{\mu}_i$ and covariance matrix $\sum_i$. The mixture weights satisfy the constraint that $\sum_{i=1}^{M} w_i = 1$.

The complete Gaussian mixture density is parameterized by the mean vectors, covariance matrices and mixture weights from all component densities. These parameters are collectively represented by the notation.

$$\lambda = \left\{ p_i, \vec{\mu}_i, \sum_i \right\}  \qquad i = 1, \ldots, M$$

Given a collection of training vectors, maximum likelihood model parameters are estimated using the iterative Expectation–Maximization (EM) algorithm. The EM algorithm iteratively refines the GMM parameters to monotonically increase the likelihood of the estimated model for the observed feature vectors, i.e., for iterations $k$ and $k+1$, $p(X|\lambda^{(k+1)}) > p(X|\lambda^{(k)})$. Generally, five iterations are sufficient for parameter convergence.

Usually, the feature vectors of $\vec{x}$ are assumed independent, so the log likelihood of a model $\lambda$ for a sequence of feature vectors, $\vec{x} = (\vec{x}_1, \vec{x}_2, \ldots, \vec{x}_N)$, is computed as

$$\log P(\vec{x}|\lambda) = \sum_{n=1}^{N} \log \left( \sum_{i=1}^{M} w_i \cdot g(\vec{x}|\vec{\mu}_i, \sum_i) \right). \tag{53.3}$$

## 53.3.2 Algorithm of Automatic Image Semantic Annotation

Images semantic annotation used by GMM algorithm as following:

The first step: training dataset of GMM. Firstly, we choose the representational image for region segmentation, and adding corresponding keywords for every region by hands. Secondly, classify each region by keywords, and extract 5-d feature vector according to XY coordinate and LUV color feature. In the mean time, according to the variances of each dimension's variance and normalization of XY coordinate and color value.

As shown in the left of Fig. 53.1, the original image was segmented for 6 regions and every region added some keywords, such as cloud, sky, tree, mountain, river, grassland and so on, according to the eigenvector of region to compute the GMM of every keywords.

The second step: Image semantic automatic annotation. According to the same method of the first step, we segment al the target images and extract feature vector of each region, then use Eq. (53.3) to compute GMM logarithm likelihood function of each region, refer to GMM keyword in first step, the maximum logarithm value corresponding keyword as semantic of this region.

As shown in the right of Fig. 53.1, firstly, segment images, and compute feature vector of each region. Secondly, compare logarithm likelihood function between feature vector and studied keywords, then the maximum value is annotated to image, the image shown is annotated semantic of sky, cloud and forest.

## 53.4 Experiments and Evaluation

In order to evaluate efficiency of the method, we select 500 representative color images to evaluate it, 400 images apply to GMM study and 100 images apply to GMM semantic evaluation.

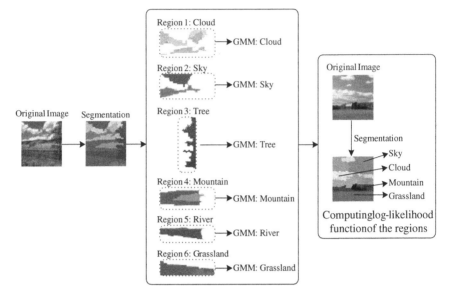

**Fig. 53.1** Flowchart of automatic semantic using GMM

We use mean shift algorithm method [10] to segment images to automatic edge, owing to neighbourhood unions only use color feature, an average of 12 regions of a images. Then we mark every region with keywords for 400 images of GMM study, the content of keywords have 67, and conclude sea, hills, forest, trees, rocks and so on. Most regions have a secondary keyword, but a part of regions have many secondary keywords according to the content.

For study image regions(total regions are 4,873), according to XY coordinates and LUV color feature value of each neighbourhood unions, generative 5-d feature vector, and classification of the feature vector according to keywords, then compute GMM logarithm likelihood function use Eq. (53.3).

As same as compute the logarithm likelihood function of 100 images region, total 1,267 images regions, then select in a similar way of study images' GMM logarithm likelihood function of the keyword as the keyword of images corresponding region. For each images regions, select descending order of the top five keywords as candidate keywords. Table 53.1 shows regions additional semantic of a segmented image, according to each region, we select the maximum semantic of GMM logarithm likelihood function as the best semantic of the regions. Consequently, image automatic additional semantic conclude "sea", "tree", "forest", "house".

To evaluate efficiency of the method, we used to compare manual additional keywords with automatic additional keywords, and compute an average accurate rate of this method. The compare content conclude the accurate rate of the top five candidate keywords which alter the quantity K of Gaussian distribution, the average accurate rate of additional semantic under Gaussian distribution maximum quantity is 32,16 and 8 respectively:

**Table 53.1** Annotation results and the logarithm likelihood function of the sample image provided by GMM

| Original image | | | Segmentation image | |
|---|---|---|---|---|
| Region No. | Semantic-1 | Semantic-2 | Semantic-3 | Semantic-4 | Semantic-5 |
| 0 | Sea | Cloud | Grassland | Sky | River |
| | 37.75092003 | 32.20198372 | 25.79201927 | 18.20392092 | 12.28273923 |
| 1 | Tree | Rock | Mountain | Cloud | House |
| | 41.20274381 | 36.18273017 | 27.201602739 | 14.37012525 | 10.33892074 |
| 2 | Grassland | River | Field | Mountain | Grass |
| | 28.92038017 | 25.02730291 | 16.81002835 | 13.72910028 | 7.82019039 |
| 3 | House | Tree | Rock | Stone | Water |
| | 65.82071402 | 58.28032031 | 49.01928302 | 44.72035809 | 37.90837105 |

**Fig. 53.2** Average annotation precision for *top* 5 keywords used K = 32, K = 16 and K = 8 by GMM

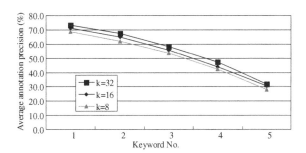

As shown in Fig. 53.2, the accurate rate of best semantic above 70 % in the top candidate five semantic, and with the increase of comprehensive parameters, the accurate rate has the trend of ascent. To analysis in manual additional semantic, too little study samples is the main reason of leading cause the accurate rate of automatic semantic, such as "sun", "rock", "road", these samples almost exceed 5,000, and accurate rate is higher, even above 80 %. Consequently, the adequacy of study samples is necessary to the proposed method, and will bring the automatic additional effect.

Besides, on the premise of enough study samples, the accurate rate of additional semantic of "cloud", "sea" can above 95 %, the leading cause of the study data we used are coordinate and color feature, because of they are change smaller, and can reach superior study effect under the same position and same color feature.

## 53.5 Conclusion

In this paper, we had proposed a method of image semantic annotation based on Gaussian mixture model. Firstly, image segmentation, extract XY coordinates and LUV color feature of each image region. Secondly, compute natural logarithm function of each region by Gaussian mixture model, then establish relations between image regions and candidate keywords. We proposed the Gaussian mixture model realize image regions automatic semantic annotation. The future work emphases on feature extraction in optimization region, especially reflect feature extraction of region semantic, and increase the accuracy of semantic matching.

**Acknowledgments** This research was partially supported by "the Fundamental Research Funds for the Central Universities".

## References

1. Luo X, Shishibori M, Ren F, Kita K (2007) Incorporate feature space transformation to content-based image retrieval with relevance feedback. Int J Innovative Comput Inf Control (IJICIC) 3(5):1237–1250
2. Liu Y, Zhang D, Lu G, Wei-Ying M (2007) A survey of content-based image retrieval with high-level semantics. Pattern Recognit 40(1):262–282
3. Chang CY, Wang HY, Li CF (2009) Semantic analysis of real world images using support vector machine. Expert Syst Appl: Int J 36(7):10560–10569
4. Yan R, Natsev A, Campbell M (2007) An efficient manual image annotation approach based on tagging and browsing. In: Proceedings multimedia information retrieval workshop, ACM Multimedia, pp 13–20
5. Jeon J, Lavrenko V, Manmatha R (2003) Automatic image annotation and retrieval using cross-media relevance models. In: Proceedings of the 26th annual international ACM SIGIR conference on Research and development in information retrieval, pp 119–126
6. Li J, Wang JZ (2006) Real-time computerized annotation of pictures. In: Proceedings of ACM international conference on Multimedia, pp 911–920
7. Yang C, Dong M, Hua J (2006) Region-based image annotation using asymmetrical support vector machine-based multiple-instance learning. In: Proceedings of the IEEE international conference on computer vision and pattern recognition
8. Jeon J, Laverenko V, Manmatha R (2003) Automatic image annotation and retrieval using crossmedia relevance models. In: Proceedings of international ACM conference on research and development in information retrieval
9. Lavrenko V, Manmatha R, Jeon J (2003) A model for learning the semantics of pictures. In: Proceedings of the 16th conference on advances in neural information processing systems NIPS
10. Comaniciu D, Meer P (1997) Robust analysis of feature space: color image segmentation. In: Proceedings of IEEE Conference on Computer Vision and Pattern Recognition pp 105–112

# Chapter 54
# Web-Based Multi-Dimensional Medical Image Collaborative Annotation System

**Gaihong Yu, Dianfu Ma, Hualei Shen and Yonggang Huang**

**Abstract** Medical image annotation is playing an increasingly important role in clinical diagnosis and medical research. Existing medical image annotation is faced with many demands and challenges. (1) The emergence and sharp increasing speed of multi-dimensional medical images. (2) Image annotation includes not only text annotation, but also graphical annotation, clinical diagnostic information and image content features information. (3) Uneven distribution of medical resources, which makes difficult to aggregate group intelligence from a much larger scale of distributed experts. Most of the present study is texted based within hospitals on single images annotation. It is difficult to organize and manage unstructured medical image annotation and collaborative sharing information. This paper dedicated to the research on collaborative web-based multi-dimensional medical image annotation and retrieval in order to address these problems, overcome the shortcoming of traditional thin client and facilitate medical experts in different locations to exchange views and comments,. It proposed (1) a system architecture that provides authoring, storing, querying, and exchanging of annotations, and supports web-based collaboration. (2) 2D multi-frame and 3D medical image collaborative annotation data model. (3) Collaborative annotation mechanisms.

**Keywords** Medical image · Annotation · Data model · Collaborative

G. Yu (✉) · D. Ma · H. Shen · Y. Huang
State Key Laboratory of Software Development Environment, Beihang University,
100191 Beijing, China
e-mail: yugh@act.buaa.edu.cn

W. Lu et al. (eds.), *Proceedings of the 2012 International Conference on Information Technology and Software Engineering*, Lecture Notes in Electrical Engineering 212, DOI: 10.1007/978-3-642-34531-9_54, © Springer-Verlag Berlin Heidelberg 2013

## 54.1 Introduction

In-depth development of modern imaging and image processing technology makes medical images rapidly expanding in recent years. Images can be used for clinical, teaching and research. For example, early in 2002, only University Hospital of Geneva radiation department generated 12,000 pieces of images every day [1]. The total amount of image data produced in United States and European Union gets thousands of TB annually. In China a medium-sized hospital produced about 1–6 TB image data annually and hospitals across the country produce about 2 PB each year. Bill Ziegler, IBM's global vice president, forecasts that in 5–10 years 30 % of the global storage will be used to store medical image data.

Medical image annotation and mark is the core of medical research whether for clinical trials or scientific researches. Traditional image annotation of PACS systems is text-based, which is difficult for organizing, managing and sharing unstructured medical image annotation information. The standard storage format of medical images is DICOM, but there is no standard data model for medical images annotation. Using appropriate method to represent the image annotation and markup, share image data and knowledge has been the bottleneck for researchers. Image annotation includes not only the graphical annotation, such as rectangles, polylines, irregular graphics, as well as clinical diagnostic information, feature information of image content. Therefore, establishment of an effective model for storage and management of annotation data is critical. So above analysis, this paper gives a new multi-dimensional medical image annotation model which integrated graphics, text, and the underlying characteristics. We only need to extract features of the label the region where we are interested in the disease, which can greatly reduce the time and improve the space efficiency.

Some of complex image annotation data often requires experts and doctors to synchronously diagnose and collaborative operation on the interest annotation image data sets. So they can get better analysis through sharing knowledge and experience. In order to facilitate diagnosis and research, exchanging and sharing medical experts' diagnosis opinions and comments in different locations is very meaningful. But now diagnostic systems are installed within hospitals, which is difficult to concentrate the wisdom of experts around between the hospitals. Collaborative systems technology is relatively mature, such as based on message delivery, and service-based transfer etc. This paper gives an effective collaborative annotation mechanism.

## 54.2 Related Work

Present paper and related work about medical image label model is very enough. Professor Wang Fu sheng proposed a single-frame medical images marked model CAM [2] when he did research in Siemens in 2008. Stanford University Daniel and others gave an ontology-based annotation model, AIM model [3].

In order to obtain an accurate marked regional characteristic, an effective feature extraction algorithm is very important. Recent feature extraction algorithm research contains follows. Harris corner detection algorithm [4] is a classic image feature extraction algorithm. Corner is robust for image translation, image rotation and image noise, but cannot adapt to changes in image scale. In recent years, some scale-invariant feature points are extracted from feature point extraction algorithm, such as Harris-Laplacian, Patch-Duplets algorithm, Laplacian algorithm and SIFT algorithm. And the first four algorithms are based on Harris corner point and extended to scale space. Such algorithms have robustness, but high computational complexity and poor performance in real-time, not suitable for Web-based operation to extract the features. Scale-invariant feature transform (SIFT) algorithm is published in 1999 by David Lowe [5], perfectly summarized in 2004 [6]. It is a computer vision algorithm which is used to detect and describe the localized features in image. It finds the extreme points in the spatial scale, and extracted its location, scale, rotation invariant. This algorithm imports the image pyramid structure into scale space in order to reduce the amount of computation. At the same time it used BBF algorithm to speed up the search process, achieved good results on 128-dimensional feature vector space. This article uses ROI-based SIFT feature extraction.

In this paper, after we label the interest region, we can extract the ROI features. SIFT features extracted the following four steps [7, 8]: Construct the scale space, detect the extreme points, gain the scale invariance; Feature point filter and precise positioning, excluding unstable feature points; Extract feature descriptor at feature points to determine the main direction of the key points; Generate feature descriptors and find match points by using feature descriptors. Through the above four steps, finally we get SIFT local feature descriptors which not sensitive to illumination changes, scale changes and rotation.

At present, there appears some medical image collaborative visualization system, the DIAGNOSIS systems [9], Disney system [10] and Common Object Request Broker Architecture-based (CORBA) medical image collaborative visualization system [11]. These system are adopted a collaborative model of sharing event which: (1) need to backup an image data set in each collaborative client. (2) Each collaborative client needs operating the event to achieve the same state. This collaborative mechanism is inadequate for it needs to transfer large image data sets to each collaborative client before the collaborative session. (1) On the one hand, it requires high network bandwidth to transmit image data to each collaborative client. (2) On the other hand, each collaborative client needs to install a professional collaborative visualization customer. SOA technology is mature, we can build SOA-based collaborative mechanisms, which all operating service are called and executed on the server, and the server pushes result status to each collaborative client. This greatly increases the speed of collaborative and save collaborative cost.

## 54.3 System Architecture and Functions

WEB-based multi-dimensional medical image collaborative annotation system (MICAS), the diagram is shown in Fig. 54.1.

MICAS is divided into server and client side. System client provides users a Web-based GUI, including user register module, image web annotation module, features extract module, collaborative annotation, and annotation image retrieval. The server contains two layers: data layer and service layer. The data layer contains three databases: source DICOM image database, annotation user database and annotation data database which using MIAM data model. The service layer includes DICOM image rendering service, annotation operation service, feature extract service, annotation recommend service, collaborative framework service and retrieval service.

Its main functions are as follows:

1. DICOM image rendering service: It contains Muti-2D frame images rendering and 3D medical image rendering. We can directly open ".dcm" files through the internet.
2. Web-based Image Annotation: we provide kinds of graphical annotation shapes including rectangle, circle, ellipse, line, polyline, etc. Users can add sematic annotation that contains diagnostic information, study date and doctor name. And we can extract the features of ROI using the SIFT algorithm. These data is very important for annotation image retrieval and collaboration.
3. Annotation retrieval module: In order to improve the precision and resolve describe difficulties, the retrieval module include three patterns. First, a simple search method just uses keywords and sematic information such as the time marked by the user. Second, retrieval based on SIFT features which can find a

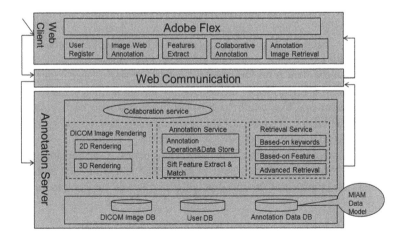

**Fig. 54.1** MICAS architecture

similar images by using ROI features. Third, integrate the keywords and image features for retrieval.

4. Collaborative service: experts in different locations can access the system at the same time, diagnose the same cases. They can see the others' opinions and can audio and video collaborative so as to help diagnosing.

5. Annotation data management service: the source DICOM data is organized by AUDR and the annotation image data is organized by MIAM annotation data model, which contains four parts of annotation data, graphical data, sematic data, features data and collaborative data. And we need a user database to manage user data for safety consideration.

## 54.4  Collaborative Image Annotation Data Model

Now in hospitals, medical image data are stored in DICOM format, including image data and image header files. The image data contain single-frame data, 3D image data and 2D multi-frame data (Fig. 54.2). The header file information called "head Info" contains basic information of the patient and image.

We proposed a Medical Imaging collaborative Annotation data Model (MIAM) as Fig. 54.3 depicts. In the model, each root node, as DICOM, represents an annotation data and the meaning of each child nodes are explained respectively. Each DICOM node contains image header file information, as head Info, and one or more User Annotation Space, as UAS. For 3D images, we first need to label the interested view of 3D image called View of Interest (VOI). And each view has different interested frames called Slice of Interest (SOI). We can organize different SOI into groups, as Group of Interest (GOI), which can be used to identify a disease. And for each single-frame image, we just need to mark the different regions of interest ROI. Each ROI contains graphical annotations, semantic annotations, feature extractions and collaborative comments.

Based on the above analysis, we give the formal definition of medical image collaborative annotation model Medical Image Annotation Model for collaboration (MIAM):

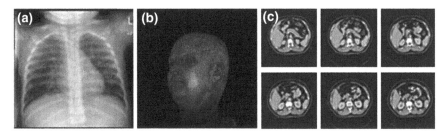

**Fig. 54.2**  Image data. **a** Single-frame **b** 3D image **c** 2D Multi-frame

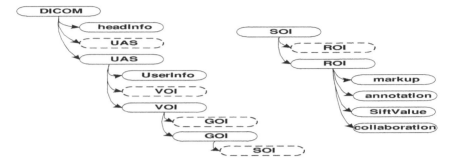

**Fig. 54.3** Description of image annotation data model MIAM

**Definition 1:**

$$MIAM = (H, U) \tag{1}$$

H, head Info, denotes the basic information collection of medical image. This information is contained in the head files of DICOM data and can be obtained by parsing the DICOM data. The patients' information include patient number, name, ID number, gender, age, date of birth. The images information includes check date, hospital, hospital Code, Image, position, clinical, sharer, image type (CT, MR, DR etc.), shooting site etc. U represents the collection of UAS. The system allows more than one user visit it at the same time, and a user can have more than one annotation space, so we allow more than one UAS node. Each UAS is determined by annotation state of the current. U is defined as Definition 2.

**Definition 2:**

$$U = (D, V, G, R) \tag{2}$$

In definition 2, U represents the current UAS. D is basic information of the user and can be obtained from User Info. It contains username, password, real name, role, company, address, mobile, telephone, fax, email, title, description, collaborative group of the annotation user. V represents VOI. G is the group of interested frames GOI, R represents ROI and can be obtained by the user operation and feature extraction, collaborative diagnosis. r, an element of R, is defined as definition 3:

**Definition 3:**

$$r = (M, A, S, C) \tag{3}$$

According definition 3, each **r** represents a ROI, where M is the graphical annotation information called markup, a graphical notation information, such as lines, rectangles, polylines. A contains the diagnosis of semantic information, such as diagnostic information "pleurisy". S means the regional SIFT feature characteristics of ROI. C represents the collaborative diagnosis/reviews/comments and visibility settings etc.

## 54.5  Collaborative Annotation Mechanisms

In this section, we will present the collaborative annotation model, framework, and collaborative operation flow and design.

### 54.5.1  Collaborative Annotation Model

Collaborative annotation model is as Fig. 54.4. This collaborative annotation model uses server push technology and mechanism of sharing the event result.

In this model, the primary client, as in Fig. 54.4 Client A, who execute annotation on the medical image sent this operation event to the server. On the server side, server calls the corresponding medical image annotation service according to the operation event type. The service returns medical image annotation results. Collaboration servers will distribute the results to every collaborative client, Fig. 54.4 Client B and C. The client can be Notebook computers or mobile phones, just need a browser and internet. Various collaborative clients receive the results and achieve the same label status through front show.

### 54.5.2  Collaborative Annotation Framework

Collaborative annotation framework [12, 13], as Fig. 54.5 shows, is divided into three levels: collaboration client layer, collaboration server layer, and annotation image server layer.

With web 2.0 [14, 15] technology development, rich client side technologies are increasingly being used to build Web applications. In order to provide better interactivity and user interface, we adopt Flex technology to build a collaborative client.

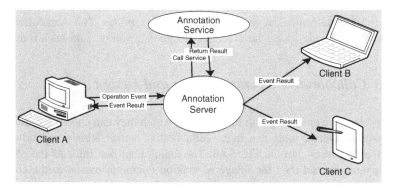

**Fig. 54.4** Collaborative annotation model

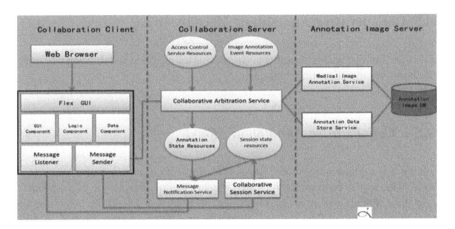

**Fig. 54.5** Collaborative annotation frameworks

Collaborative client layer contains a Flex-based user interface to demonstrate the collaborative annotation results and user interaction. And users can do interoperability of medical imaging through the user interface. Logic modules and data modules are used to maintain the logic operation and annotation data of the client. The message listener and sender modules are used for receiving collaborative notification messages and sending operating messages.

Collaborative server layer consists of three core services: collaborative arbitration service, message notification service, and collaborative session service. We manage collaborative session by using collaborative session service, and client can join or leave a collaborative session under the management of this service. Collaborative arbitration services are very important. It determines the acceptance of collaborative client interaction events, and calls the corresponding image annotation service. Message notification service distribute message to the collaborative client.

The image server layer includes medical image annotation services and annotation data store service. The image annotation service can perform the image visualization operations and generate visualization results. And collaborative client can annotate medical image by the image services. The Annotation data store service provide access interface for image data storage and management.

### 54.5.3 Collaborative Operation Flow and Design

In the system, we create a group for each user which they can choose the user they want to communicate with. And in the collaborative conversation group, all clients operating processes show in Fig. 54.6. The main client first initiates the collaborative operation, and then the image annotation operation passed to the collaborative arbitration service. Collaborative arbitration services analysis annotation operation message, check the legality of the operation, then map the operating

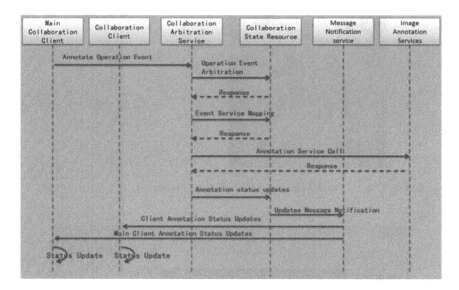

**Fig. 54.6**   Collaborative operation flow

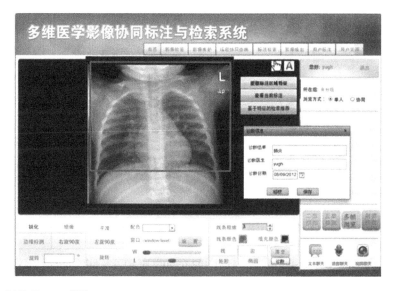

**Fig. 54.7**   System GUI

event to the corresponding Web Service [12, 13]. The Web Service returns the collaboration state resources which including the current label shape, size, location, and the feature values of the marked region, as well as the label image state and view state. All collaborative clients in the collaborative session get status updates, through message notification service and finally update the local state and collaboration servers consistent.

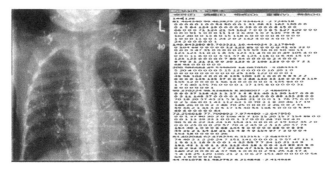

**Fig. 54.8** SIFT feature of ROI. **a** feature results **b** feature results.txt

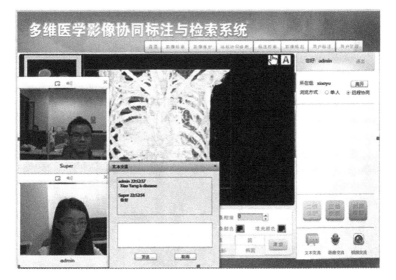

**Fig. 54.9** Collaboration results

## 54.6 System Results and GUI

This part simply gives the system GUI, the feature of ROI results and collaborative results.

In the System, as shown in Fig. 54.7, we can choose the annotation shape, line style, line color etc. Then can add sematic annotation as "diagnose information" window shows, which including diagnostic results, doctor, and date. On the right side, we can see extract feature button, see the current annotation button, annotation recommend button. And we can see the collaborative operation zone.

Figure 54.8 shows the SIFT feature of ROI. Figure 54.8a shows the intercepted part feature extraction results which the end of the arrow represents the location of the feature points, the direction of the arrow represents the direction of the feature points, the segment length represents the scale of the feature points. And in Fig. 54.8b shows the result is saved as a text file in order to store into the database.

Figure 54.9 shows collaborative annotation, which including audio and text communication.

## 54.7 Conclusions and Future Work

The most import of the research is that gives a new online medical application diagnostic form and architecture. This paper completes the following aspects:

1. We propose a new scenarios and system architecture about medical image collaborative annotation.
2. In order to solve the problem of effective organization and management of unstructured medical image annotation data, we propose a collaborative medical image annotation data model (MIAM).
3. In order to facilitate experts in different locations to access the system at the same time, diagnose the same cases, we give a collaborative mechanism to improve the speed, saving the cost of collaboration.

In future, in order to improve the retrieval accuracy of the region of interest, we use SIFT features and sematic annotation together.

**Acknowledgments**   This work was funded by National Science and Technology Major Research Plan of China (grant number 2010ZX01042-002-001) and State Key Laboratory of Software Development Environment (grant number SKLSDE-2010ZX-08). The authors would also like to appreciate all those who took part in the groups and experiments.

## References

1. Shibata T, Suzuki M, Kato T (2004) 3D retrieval system based on cognitive level. In: Proceedings of the 2004 International conference on cyber worlds IEEE
2. Wang F, Rabsch C, Liu P (2008) Native web browser enabled SVG-based collaborative multimedia annotation for medical images. In: proceedings of the IEEE 24th international conference on data engineering, ICDE 2008, April, pp 1219–1228
3. Rubin DL, Rodriguez C, Shah P, Beaulieu C (2008) Ipad: semantic annotation and markup of radiological images, AMIA annu symposium proceedings, pp 626–630
4. Kman P, Friesen WV (1978) Facial action coding system. Consulting Psychologists Press, Palo Alto
5. Lowe DG (1999) Object recognition from local scale-invariant features. In: Proceedings of the 7th international conference on computer vision, Greece, pp 1150–1157
6. Lowe DG (2004) Distinctive image features from scale-invariant key points. Int J Comput Vision 60(2):91–110
7. Zhao H (2007) Research on image registration algorithm based on point features. Shangdong University, Shangdong (in Chinese)

8. David G, Lowe (2004) Distinctive image features from scale-invariant key points. Int J Comput Vision 60(2):91–110
9. Mougiakakou SG, Valavanis IK, Mouravliansky NA, Nikita KS, Nikita A (2009) Diagnosis: A telematics-enabled system for medical image archiving, management, and diagnosis assistance. IEEE Trans Instrum Meas 58(7):2113–2120
10. Alberola C, Cárdenes R, Martín v, Martín M, Rodríguez-Florido M, Ruiz-Alzola J(2000) Disnei: A collaborative environment for medical images analysis and visualization. In medical image computing and computer-assisted intervention, 3rd international conference, Pittsburgh
11. J. Chun and J. Son, "A CORBA-based telemedicine system for medical image analysis and modeling", In the 14th IEEE symposium on computer-based medical systems, 2002, pp. 53–58
12. Papazoglou MP, Traverso P, Dustdar S, Leymann F (2003) Service-oriented computing. Commun ACM 46:25–28
13. Newcomer E, Lomow G (2004) Understanding SOA with web services (independent technology guides). Addison-wesley professional
14. Oreilly T (2007) What is web 2.0: design patterns and business models for the next generation of software. SSRN library
15. Anderson v (2007) What is web 2.0? ideas, technologies and implications for education. JISC Technology and Standards Watch

# Chapter 55
# Real-Time Simulation and Visualization of Buoy in Irregular Wave

**Xiufeng Zhang, Yong Yin, Guixin Zhan and Hongxiang Ren**

**Abstract** Buoys and other navigational aid marks are very important references to the ship's pilots. Based on ship sea-keeping theory and the strip theory of ships in irregular waves heaving and pitching of the coupled equations of motions, we can obtain the motion mathematical model of the buoys in irregular wave. The particle system algorithm was applied to simulate the different waves of the sea level when the beacons or buoys by the impact of waves and spray occur, resulting in waves around the real-time effect, to achieve a buoy and around spray visualization, and to make visual system more realistic in the Marine Simulator.

**Keywords** Marine simulator · Visual system · Buoys · Particle system · Strip theory

## 55.1 Introduction

The buoy is a floating object that has certain shape, size and color, and it is an essential navigation aid facility to moored ships and sailing ship. The buoy is movable, but it is anchored at a special point by chain. So it moves with a certain circle under wind, current and wave. The position of buoy is not fixed. They are used for navigation. In the actual sea, buoy will move with six degrees of freedom under the waves, that is, surge, sway, heave, roll, pitch and yaw. And at the same time,

X. Zhang (✉) · Y. Yin · G. Zhan · H. Ren
Navigation College of Dalian Maritime University, Dalian Liaoning 116026, China
e-mail: zxfdmu@163.com

Y. Yin
e-mail: bushyin_dmu@263.net

W. Lu et al. (eds.), *Proceedings of the 2012 International Conference on Information Technology and Software Engineering*, Lecture Notes in Electrical Engineering 212, DOI: 10.1007/978-3-642-34531-9_55, © Springer-Verlag Berlin Heidelberg 2013

spray will produced around the buoy. Using the statistical analysis methods, Yun [1] puts forward buoy movement spectrum characteristics under the wind and the wave. And it was used to design a kind of buoy and optimized its movement feature in wave. Mingquan et al. [2, 3] studied the performance of a three-chain mooring system in a wave tank. The buoy is moored by three chains. The experimental results show that the motions of the buoy can satisfy the limitation from the equipments and the mooring forces is smaller. In Ref. [3], the added-mass,damping coefficients and motion responses of a buoy are calculated by the three-dimensional potential theory. And then the motions of the buoy and the forces of the chain of both water depths under the extreme sea state are simulated in the time domain in terms of the Cummins' equations of six-degree.It is useful for the design of the buoy and the mooring chains.

ShaoChun [4] analysis and simulates the cylindrical buoy, the results can give improvement suggestions; effectively improve the stability of the cylindrical buoy. Above literatures studied kinematic analysis, calculation and simulation of buoy, not including visualization. Yong et al. [5] displayed buoy in the visual of Marine simulator in order to help the navigation marks, but the detail is not perfect.

This paper studies and improves the visual effect of buoy in the Marine Simulator to make the scene realism, based on the ship sea-keeping theory, by the influence of the regular wave, and build motion model, using the method of particle system real-time simulate its surrounding spray, and achieve movement model of the buoy in waves and around the visualization of spray.

## 55.2 Buoy Motion Mathematical Models

Based on the ship sea-keeping theory, according to Newton's second law dynamics, combining with the ship movement differential equations, create buoy heave and pitch movement differential equations.

Then, determine respectively the non-dimension coefficients of differential equations, and then substitute into above equation groups. Finally, solve the heave amplitude and pitch amplitude of buoy under regular wave. They are special solutions. So buoy movement function with time respectively can be gotten. And the data are transferred to the viewing system real time to show.

### 55.2.1 Coordinate System

According to Ship sea-keeping principle, build the earth coordinate system, the buoy movement coordinate system and the balance moving with ship coordinate system, they are shown as Fig. 55.1.

**Fig. 55.1** Coordinate system

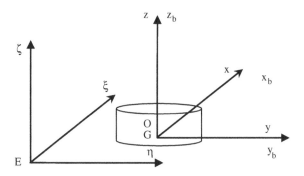

1. The earth coordinate system E $- \xi\eta\zeta$

Build the fixed earth coordinate system E $- \xi\eta\zeta$. The original point E is chosen a point at the sea surface or in the sea. Buoy gravity center is chosen as original point in the earth coordinate system in this paper. Coordinate plane E$\xi\eta$ is overlap with static water plane. Axis E$\xi$ points the North, and E$\eta$ points the East, E$\zeta$ points upwards.

2. The buoy moving coordinate system $G - x_b y_b z_b$

The original point of Moving coordinate system is chosen at buoy gravity center $G$. Axis $Gx_b$ is parallel with keel and point to bow, $Gy_b$ is vertical to middle longitudinal plane and point to starboard, $Gz_b$ is vertical to $Gx_b$ and in the middle longitudinal plane and point upwards.

3. The balance moving with ship coordinate system $O - xyz$

When ship navigates in still water, coordinate system $O - xyz$ moves with ship, $Oxy$ is in still water. When ship is sway in waves, $O - xyz$ is not sway with ship. It is different from in still water. In this paper, assume that buoy is moored by chain, and $O$ and $G$ is the same point. Forwards speed is set to 0 m/s, $u$ is ignored in motion equations.

## 55.2.2 Moving Analysis and Equations

The buoy is affected by gravity, floating force, mooring force, wind force and wave force and so on. The buoy motion is very complex. As buoy is a radical symmetrical object, we assume that the buoy is only affected in regular head sea. That is, the encounter wave angle is zero ignoring surge, sway, roll and yaw.

According Newton Second dynamics Law and Linear wave theory, buoy motion mathematical model is built in regular wave as the following Eq. (55.1).

$$\begin{cases} m\ddot{z} = F \\ I_{yy}\ddot{\theta} = M \end{cases} \tag{55.1}$$

Where, $F$ and $M$ are hydrodynamic force and moment, $m$ is mass of buoy, and $m = \rho \nabla$. $\rho$ is density of sea water. $\nabla$ is occupy water volume. $I_{yy}$ is inertial moment of buoy. $z$ and $\theta$ are heave displacement and pitch angle. So Eq. (55.1) can be written as Eq. (55.2):

$$\begin{cases} (m + A_{11})\ddot{z} + A_{12}\dot{z} + A_{13}z + A_{14}\ddot{\theta} + A_{15}\dot{\theta} + A_{16}\theta = F_{zc}\cos\omega_e t - F_{zs}\sin\omega_e t \\ (I_{yy} + A_{21})\ddot{\theta} + A_{22}\dot{\theta} + A_{23}\theta + A_{24}\ddot{z} + A_{25}\dot{z} + A_{26}z = M_{\theta c}\cos\omega_e t - M_{\theta s}\sin\omega_e t \end{cases}$$

(55.2)

Where, $\omega_e$ is encounter frequency. $\omega_e = \omega(1 - \frac{V\cos\mu}{g})$, $\omega$ is wave circle frequency. $V$ is the velocity of ship, $\mu$ is wave direction, $g$ is gravity accelerate. $F_{zc}, F_{zs}, M_{\theta c}, M_{\theta s}$ are force or moment real coefficient and imaginary coefficient, $t$ is time.

In the force equation, Where, $A_{11}$, $A_{12}$, and $A_{13}$ is hydro-acceleration, velocity and displacement coefficients about heave motion. $A_{14}$, $A_{15}$ and $A_{16}$ is hydro-acceleration, velocity and displacement coefficients about pitch motion.

In the moment equation, Where, $A_{21}$, $A_{22}$ and $A_{23}$ is hydro-acceleration, velocity and displacement coefficients about pitch motion. $A_{24}$, $A_{25}$ and $A_{26}$ is hydro-acceleration, velocity and displacement coefficients about heave motion [6].

According to strip theory methods, all no-dimensional coefficients are gotten as following expression groups (55.3) (55.4) and (55.5).

$$\begin{cases} A_{11} = \int_L m'dx, A_{12} = \int_L N'dx, A_{13} = 2\rho g \int_L y_w dx, A_{14} = -\int_L m'xdx \\ A_{15} = -\int_L N'xdx, A_{16} = -2\rho g \int_L y_w xdx \end{cases}$$

(55.3)

$$\begin{cases} A_{21} = \int_L m'x^2 dx, A_{22} = \int_L N'x^2 dx, A_{23} = 2\rho g \int_L y_w x^2 dx, A_{24} = -\int_L m'xdx \\ A_{25} = -\int_L N'xdx, A_{26} = -2\rho g \int_L y_w xdx \end{cases}$$

(55.4)

$$\begin{cases} F_{zc} = 2\rho g \zeta_a \int_L y_w e^{-KT^*}\cos(Kx)dx, F_{zs} = 2\rho g \zeta_a \int_L y_w e^{-KT^*}\sin(Kx)dx \\ M_{\theta c} = -2\rho g \zeta_a \int_L y_w x e^{-KT^*}\cos(Kx)dx, M_{\theta s} = -2\rho g \zeta_a \int_L y_w x e^{-KT^*}\sin(Kx)dx. \end{cases}$$

(55.5)

### 55.2.3 Hydrodynamic Coefficients

Assume that, the maximal height of buoy is $h = 6$ m, the height of cylinder is $h_B = 1$ m, the diameter is $d = 2.4$ m, the mean draft is $T^* = 0.5$ m, $g = 9.8$ m/s$^2$. Real buoy is shown as Fig. 55.2.

Using ship sea-keeping strip theory, the coefficients in the Eq. (55.2) are calculated [6, 7]. Heave added mass and heave damping coefficient with encounter frequency are shown as Figs. 55.3 and 55.4. And the others are ignored here.

**Fig. 55.2** Real buoy in the sea

**Fig. 55.3** Heave added mass

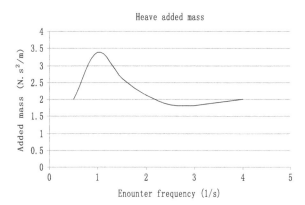

**Fig. 55.4** Heave damping coefficient

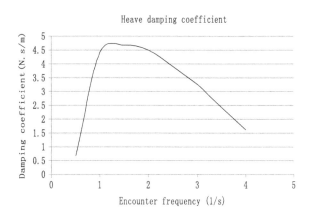

## 55.2.4 Wave Energy Spectrum and Wave Force or Moment

Irregular wave energy spectrums are used in fully developed long crest waves. We assume that the slight wave is two dimensional waves. Linear wave theory has been proved that two dimensional irregular waves by an infinite number of different amplitude and wavelength of the unit linear superposition of regular waves (wave phase of the unit rule is random). Consider the full developed irregular waves; the wave height of a fixed point can be expressed as [8]:

$$\zeta(t) = \sum_{i=1}^{\infty} \zeta_{ai} \cos(\omega_i t + \varepsilon_i) \qquad (55.6)$$

Where $\omega_i$ is the $i$th circular frequency of wave component. $\varepsilon_i$ is phase, is a random variable, it is evenly distributed between 0 and $2\pi$.

For a stationary random process, wave is expressed by spectral analysis of the characteristics of irregular waves. Many typical wave spectrums have been published. For example: P-M spectrum, JONSWAP spectrum, ITTC recommended spectrum and the spectrum for the Chinese coast.

We can know from the definition of wave spectrum density function:

$$S_\zeta(\omega) = \frac{\sum\limits_{\omega}^{\omega+d\omega} \frac{1}{2}\zeta_{a_n}^2}{d\omega} \qquad (55.7)$$

Where $\zeta_{a_n}$ is a regular wave amplitude, $S_\zeta(\omega)$ is wave energy density, $\omega$ is some frequency, $d\omega$ is frequency differential segment. According to the definition of wave energy spectrum, in a small discrete intervals, regular wave amplitude may be gained. One of regular amplitude is shown as formula (55.8).

$$\zeta_{a_i} = \sqrt{2S_\zeta(\hat{\omega}_i)\Delta\omega_i} \qquad (55.8)$$

When a finite number of regular waves, then the irregular wave surface equation are shown as followed.

$$\zeta(t) = \sum_{i=1}^{N} \sqrt{2S_\zeta(\hat{\omega}_i)\Delta\omega} \cos(\tilde{\omega}_i t + \varepsilon_i) \qquad (55.9)$$

Where $\hat{\omega}_i = \frac{(\omega_{i-1}+\omega_i)}{2}$, $\tilde{\omega}_i$ is the $i$th expression frequency regular wave. $\Delta\omega$ is average frequency spacing.

Irregular wave can be divided into multiple regular wave, for any one regular wave is concerned, in the heave disturbing force calculation, we assume that ship is rest, and the waves move slowly. The wave disturbing force equals to any instantaneous extra buoyancy. Thus, we can calculate the wave force or moment as expressions groups (55.5).

**Fig. 55.5**  Spray viewing effect

## 55.3  The Visualization of Buoy and Spray Around It

The sea state level determines the corresponding wave height $H$, wave period $T$ and wavelength $\lambda$. When the wave meets the buoy, white spray can be produced around it with waves bump on the buoy. The numbers and sizes of the spray around the buoy are decided by sea state.

Particle system is a typical algorithm based on a dynamic stochastic growth model, is a kind of process model. Particle system is dynamic, accompanied by the passage of time, the particle system adds constantly new particles, removes the old. In this paper, the particle positions and the values of life change with the time constantly. The dynamic and random of irregular objects are reflected fully [9]. We state a particle structure. The structure is briefly described some defines of the basic particles properties, including: the velocity, the motion direction, the position coordinates, and dilute alpha value. Spray effects are shown under the fifth sea states as Fig. 55.5. We can see that, it shows a vivid visual effect.

## 55.4  Summarize

Based on the sea-keeping theory, the mathematical model of buoy including pitch and heave motion is built, and the motion rule is analyzed under irregular wave. Using particle system algorithm, draw and rendering real time the buoy and the spray around it, realize visualization for the buoy and its spray, making the buoy display more realistically in maritime simulator for the screw training to provide more realistic visual reference.

**Acknowledgments** This paper is supported by National Key Basic Research Development Project "973" (2009CB320805), National Nature Science Foundation of China under Grant No. 51109020 and the Fundamental Research Funds for the Central Universities No. 2012TD002.

# References

1. Yun Z (2002) Movement feature analysis of buoy in wave [J]. Ocean Technol 21(3):5–7 (in Chinese)
2. Quan-ming M, Min G, Zhan-ming Y, De-cai Z (2003) Experiment study on motions of a moored buoy in waves [J]. Shipbuilding China 44(z):359–366 (in Chinese)
3. Quanming M, Min G, Zhanming Y, Chuxue L (2003) Estimation of buoy motions and chain forces in extreme sea state [J]. J Ship Mech (5):21–27 (in Chinese)
4. Shao-chun Q, Kun Z, Ying-min W (2010) Analysis and simulation of spar buoy motion [J]. J Comput Simul 27(6):363–367 (in Chinese)
5. Yong Y, Yi-cheng J, Hong-xiang R, Xiu-feng Z, Xiu-wen L, Jun-sheng R (2009) Research on evaluation method and key technologies of full mission navigation simulation system [J]. J Syst Simul 21(21):6910–6914 (in Chinese)
6. Teillant B, Gilloteaux JC, Ringwood JV Optimal damping profile for a Heaving Buoy wave energy converter [C]. International offshore and polar engineering conference proceedings vol 1. pp 477–485. ISSN 1098-6189
7. Journée JMJ (1993) Hydromechanic coefficients for calculating time domain motions of cutter suction dredges by Cummins equations [R]. Report 968, March 1993, Delft University of Technology, Ship Hydromechanics Laboratory, Mekelweg 2, 2628 CD Delft, The Netherlands
8. Yaosen TAO (1996) Ship Sea-keeping [M]. Shanghai Jiaotong University Press, Shanghai (in Chinese)
9. Monen T, Kont kanen J (2003) The second order particle system [J]. J WSCG 11(1): 1213–6972

# Chapter 56
# License Plate Location Based on Projection Method and Genetic Algorithm

Xin-Yan Cao, Ya-Juan Song and Tan Xu

**Abstract** License plate recognition is an important part of the Intelligent Transportation Systems. The key technologies of the license plate recognition license are plate location, character segmentation and character recognition, which license plate location technology is the core technology of the three technologies. There are two problems of license plate location algorithm, one is complex background interference; another is conditions such as weather, light image quality and difficult to locate. In this paper, the license plate location method based on projection and genetic algorithm method combination for these two issues. Projection method has the features of simple, rapid and easy to implement. The genetic algorithm has efficient, parallel, adaptive characteristics. For the case of this article, we can quickly find the global optimum, and to combine these two methods. To a certain extent it is good solution to these two problems, the versatility of the algorithm greatly enhance the advantages into full play, the positioning accuracy is improved.

**Keywords** License plate location · Artificial neural network · Genetic algorithm

X.-Y. Cao (✉)
College of Electronic Information Engineering, University of Changchun,
Changchun, Jilin Province, China
e-mail: ccdxcaoxinyan@yahoo.com.cn

Y.-J. Song
School of Communication Engineering, Jilin University, Changchun,
Jilin Province, China
e-mail: yajuansong@sohu.com

T. Xu
College of Computer Science and Technology, University of Changchun,
Changchun, Jilin Province, China

W. Lu et al. (eds.), *Proceedings of the 2012 International Conference on Information Technology and Software Engineering*, Lecture Notes in Electrical Engineering 212, DOI: 10.1007/978-3-642-34531-9_56, © Springer-Verlag Berlin Heidelberg 2013

## 56.1 Introduction

License plate recognition applications has used in the field of vehicle automation management, it include no parking but fee, parking management, multi-purpose toll collection system, as well as a variety of illegal vehicle monitoring. As the complexity of the image background as well as the uncertainty of the image quality, there are still many technical difficulties not been good solution in the license plate recognition. License plate location, character segmentation, character recognition are the three key technologies of the license plate recognition systems, and license plate positioning technology is the primary key technologies in the three technologies.

License plate positioning method is based on the license plate of the following characteristics: in case of plate tilt has no angle, the ratio of the license plate approximation is to a fixed value; License plate background color and license plate character color contrast. The rich texture of the plate area with the surrounding. The color characteristics of China license plate has four types of colors: blue and white, black and yellow, black and white, black and white license plate. License plate in China is rectangular shape, border, character within a rectangular border interval fixed. Based on these characteristics, the domestic and foreign scholars have proposed a variety of license plate location method: artificial neural network, with its strong anti-noise, fault-tolerant, adaptive ability to get a wide range of applications [1] in the license plate location. Reference [2] describes the use of mathematical morphology morphological operations weakening the non license plate area of noise to the license plate location, and characteristics of the license plate area and easy to extract. Reference [3] quickly locate a license plate based on color features, the algorithm take full advantage of the relatively fixed characteristics of the license plate color license plate location. Reference [4] based on the color value of the license plate location method. The license plate area has a unique texture features and statistical laws, and these characteristics are not sensitive to light and tilt. Reference [5] based on the co-occurrence matrix texture description. Since wavelet analysis has overcome many of the weaknesses of the Fourier analysis Ref. [6] proposed a discrete binary wavelet transform based on the use of image wavelet decomposition of different characteristics of each sub-band image to select a different threshold to obtain better denoising effect for edge detection using wavelet multi-resolution analysis methods, the final positioning of the plate [7] apply genetic algorithms to extract the key points of the license plate area [8] proposed to use the multiscale filtering technology to get the image texture features to find the license plate area. License plate positioning algorithm has two problems: First, complex background interference, second, weather, light conditions often make the image quality and difficult to locate. For these two issues, this paper proposes a combined license plate positioning method based on the projection method and the genetic algorithm. To some extent, it is a good solution to these two issues, and greatly improve the versatility of the algorithm.

## 56.2 Left and Right Borders Location Based on Projection Method

As the characters of the license plate region image pixel gray value to be larger than its surrounding, so that the gradation value of the pixels on the same column accumulation as the ordinate, i.e. the input image is a size for the i × j of the matrix F, the matrix summing each element of each column, of F, the size of the one-dimensional matrix of 1 × j G, can be represented by the formula (56.1) is formed. Based on a priori knowledge, license plate at the bottom of the image, one-third of the line from the image, that round (i/3) start (round rounded).

$$G(j) = \sum_{k=round(i/3)}^{i} F(k,j) \qquad (56.1)$$

Where, G index as abscissa, each element value of G as the ordinate, to draw out the image—the column scanning FIG, because the left and right sides of the vehicle image is substantially symmetrical, so the column scan also showed a certain degree of symmetry, As shown in Fig. 56.1.

Tests show that the column scanning diagram of an edge image showing certain symmetries, first calculate the average of all of the elements in the matrix G, in order to facilitate handling, and the matrix G is smaller than the elements of this average zero, referred to as G', and then drawn out of the line scan, shown in Fig. 56.2.

Based on the characteristics of the car image, in the image of the license plate area, due to the presence of characters and license plate border, this part of the richly textured, gray-scale variations in the lights as well as the left and right edges of the part of the car, there are also some gray change, but no dramatic changes in the license plate area, while in other regions of the image gray flat, fewer changes based on these characteristics, the columns of the image scan showed the following characteristics: a zero value in the license plate area on both sides of depression, and the value of zero sag length substantially equal. In the middle of the two depressions, grayscale rapid change. Column scan around is roughly symmetrical. In the picture there many zero-value sag exists.

According to the left and right borders of the license plate of the column scan positioning algorithm is:

Step 1: In G 'to find a connected a region of zero, if the length of the area is greater than 20, the center position of this region are marked either. The figure may be more qualified with zero area, they need a tag.

Step 2: Followed statistical gray change, two marks within every gradation change between the two markers are recorded as one transition.

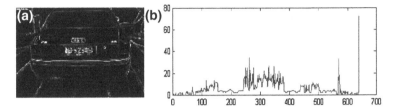

**Fig. 56.1** **a** Edge image. **b** Column scan diagram

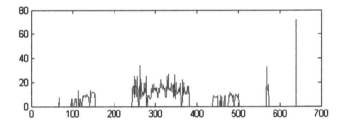

**Fig. 56.2** Column scan after treatment

**Fig. 56.3** *Left* and *right*
boundary of the plate
positioning effect diagram

Step 3: Compared markers between the number of transitions, the jump the maximum number of times is the area for the license plate area, then the location of the first non-zero value in this region to the last non-zero value of the position is the license plate of the left and right borders.

As shown in Fig. 56.3, the tests showed that after positioning the image retains all the information of the license plate area while filtering out the majority of redundant information, so that, use the genetic algorithm in positioning the upper and lower boundaries, the search range is greatly reduced, and improve the running speed.

## 56.3 Upper and Lower Borders Location Based on Genetic Algorithm

Left and right the license plate image boundary position in the license plate area has a rich texture features than other areas, basically less changed in other regions, texture, and texture as the fitness function of the design of the characteristic quantities.

### 56.3.1 Filter

Usually two interference will seriously affect the positioning results in the process of using genetic algorithms to locate car around the heat sink; car scene is released in the body of reflection and light are released in the body mottled light, edge detection, the performance of these interference for a large number of straight lines and the density of different spots, for this situation, the designed three operator, specifically for straight and isolated points in the filtered image, the following operator:

Operator $T_1$ for detecting a width of more than two pixels of a straight line, the threshold value 3.

$$T_1 = \begin{bmatrix} -1 & -1 & -1 \\ 1 & 1 & 1 \end{bmatrix} \tag{56.1}$$

For detecting a width of one pixel linear operator $T_2$, the threshold value of 6

$$T_2 = \begin{bmatrix} -1 & -1 & -1 \\ 2 & 2 & 2 \\ -1 & -1 & -1 \end{bmatrix} \tag{56.2}$$

Operator $T_3$, used to detect the isolated points, the threshold value of 8.

$$T_3 = \begin{bmatrix} -1 & -1 & -1 \\ -1 & 8 & -1 \\ -1 & -1 & -1 \end{bmatrix} \tag{56.3}$$

Three templates, respectively, superimposed on the image, so that the operator is moved on the image, the calculated value is greater than or equal to the threshold value, as to detect the target, and the target is removed, and Fig. 56.4 is a filtering effect.

Chart analysis showed that filtered figure straight lines and spots disappeared, although it will not completely filter out interference, and the license plate part will loss some information, but the texture feature of the license plate basic preserved. The test proved that this method is very effective, and the residual interference will not affect positioning result, after that the accurate rate significantly increased after such processing.

**Fig. 56.4** Comparison
diagram before and after filter

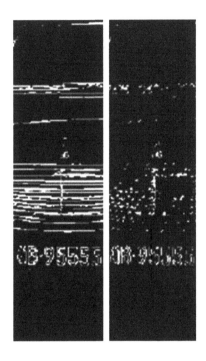

## 56.3.2 Algorithm to Construct

Figure 56.5 is a left and right boundary positioning license plate image, and its size is m × n, corresponding to the size of m × n matrix W. Then the length of the plates is n, According to the a priori knowledge of license plate, aspect ratio is about 3 to 1, and n/3 is the width of the license plate. Randomly it will generate a certain number of points, these points in the interval [1, m] within one correspondence with the elements of the first column of the matrix W, $x_1$, $x_2$, ... $x_k$, It expressed, assuming that one point xi rectangular is the upper left corner points, with n as the length of the rectangle, and form a rectangular area of n/3 as the width of the rectangle, this rectangular region is to be the search area, and calculate the value of T in this region, referred to as of Ti, each point corresponding to an rectangular area, to calculate the value of T for each region, referred to as $T_1$, $T_2$ ... $T_k$. [1, m] is the populations of individual ranges, $x_1$, $x_2$, ... $x_k$ is the population of individuals, k is the number of individuals, $T_1$, $T_2$ ... $T_k$ is the objective function value corresponding to each individual. The purpose is to find the maximum objective function value of the individual, then with this individual corresponding to the rectangle is a plate area, the points corresponding to the individual points in the upper left corner is the license plate. As in the car in the image, the plate area is generally located in the image in the lower portion, so, at the one-third of the image search down, i.e. the individual ranges [m/3, m].

**Fig. 56.5** Images after the
*left* and *right* borders of the
license plate

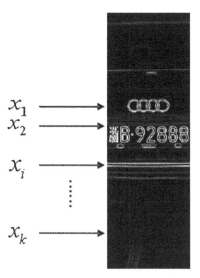

$$x_1 \longrightarrow$$
$$x_2 \longrightarrow$$

$$x_i \longrightarrow$$

$$\vdots$$

$$x_k \longrightarrow$$

## 56.3.3 Parameter Optimization

The choice of parameters in the genetic algorithm is very critical to the performance. The different parameters will greatly influent genetic algorithm, it will
impact to the convergence of the algorithm. Typically, the crossover probability
range of 0.4 to 0.99, the mutation probability ranges from 0.0001 to 0.1 and
population size is selected between 10 and 200 according to the actual situation.
Apply Gray code encoding, random traverse and sampling, single-point crossover.
Sort-based fitness assignment, linear sorting, selection pressure is 2. Binary code
string length is 20, the number of individuals 10, evolution algebra 10, crossover
probability of 0.7, uniform mutation, the mutation probability of 0.035.

## 56.4 Simulation and Results Analysis

Although in some cases, with two hidden layer neural network may bring
additional benefits, but the increase in the number of hidden layer makes the
network more complex, increase the computing workload and will require more
samples number, so that the network's training cycle is longer. Symbols identify
the problem, with one hidden layer neural network has enough.

The test sample source is taken with an ordinary digital camera photos and
images collected in the network, a total of 100. Among them, the minimum size of
the image is 297 × 228, the maximum image size of 800 × 560, with complex
background, various features of the glare interference and fuzzy. 97 pictures can
accurately locate the three images which can not be accurately positioned, is an

**Fig. 56.6** Effect diagram of
license plate location

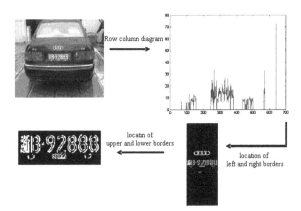

image by local light interference can result in poor image quality, the other two
because of the interference of the noise texture. Figure 56.5 is part of the
localization effect.

In the positioning time, and each time the calculation of the objective function,
are in a rectangle, the width of the rectangular frame is directly affect the calculation speed, before the use of genetic algorithms will reduce the width of the
original image to 40 pixels wide, so that the objective function of the calculation is
in a smaller rectangle, and the computation speed is greatly improved. Secondly,
in order to avoid the loss of license plate information, each extraction plate
upwardly to take on more the width of 10 pixels down to take on more of the width
of the five pixels, the excess portion will be removed together in the removal of the
license plate upper and lower borders. This algorithm is for the image after edge
extraction operation, but if operating directly on the edge image, there will
be some of the relatively low intensity of the texture of the positioning result cause
interference, the solution is first edge extraction of the image, and then the edge
image binarization, binary image pixel values 0 and 1, and then use a genetic
algorithm to calculate.

## 56.5  Conclusion

Using the left and right borders of the projection method positioning license plate,
due to the car image with the left and right symmetry, even in the case of more
complex background interference accurately locate the license plate of the left and
right borders, so that filter out most of the interference image into a low-noise
image on this basis, using genetic algorithm for positioning the upper and lower
boundaries of the license plate to the license plate area can quickly search, in the
case of population size and evolution algebra less. License plate location method
based on projection and genetic algorithm take full advantage of the efficiency of a

simple projection method and genetic algorithm, for good positioning in the complex background, the image of poor quality, license target, positioning accuracy markedly improved.

# References

1. Fei L (2007) The research on license plate recognition system based on artificial neural network [D]. North University of China. (in Chinese)
2. Yaqin L, Lingchao W (2005) A method of license plate location based on morphology [J]. Comput Eng 2(3):224–226
3. Wei W, Jirong C, Jingye X (2006) Fast license plate localization based on color features [J]. Comput Eng Appl 2006(1):226–229
4. Jin-jun W, Shu-xin D (2006) Vehicle license plate locating based on binary color Image [J]. J Highw Transp Res Dev 23(4):135–138
5. Haralick RM, Shanmagam K, Dinstein I (1973) Textural features for image classification [J]. IEEE Trans Syst Man Cybern 3:610–621
6. Dashun Q, Minghui L (2005) Algorithm research on the detection and orientation of vehicle-license-plate image based on wavelet [J]. Tech Inf Water Transp 2:91–93
7. Xiang-quan S, Yuan-ling H, Meng-bo C (2000) Application of genetic algorithm in license plate location [J]. J Highw Transp Res Andk Dev 17(2):33–36
8. Jun X, Sidan D, Duntang G, Qinhong S (2004) Locating car license plate under various illumination conditions using genetic algorithm. Signal processing, 2004 proceedings ICSP apos 04 2004 7th international conference, pp 2502–2505

# Chapter 57
# Image Segmentation Based on Edge Growth

**Xiuyan Cao, Weili Ding, Shuo Hu and Liancheng Su**

**Abstract** We propose a novel approach for solving the over-segmentation problem in image segmentation. Rather than focusing on clustering gray pixels in the image data, our approach aims at extracting salient regions based on edges information. We treat image segmentation as an edge linking problem and propose a novel process, *edge growth*, for segmenting the image. The edge growth process is starting from the breakpoints and then prolongs the edge chains based on its local structure until there is another breakpoint or edges. We have applied this approach to segmenting static images without tuning any parameters. The experimental result shows the effective of our proposed algorithm.

**Keywords** Image segmentation · Edge detection · Breakpoints · Edge Growth

## 57.1 Introduction

Image segmentation is an essential step for image analysis and understanding, which can be applied in several practical problems such as medical research, intelligent recognition, 3D reconstruction and image retrieval/compression. An ideal segmentation algorithm should cluster pixels into salient regions which corresponding to individual surfaces, objects or nature parts of objects.

X. Cao (✉) · W. Ding · S. Hu · L. Su
Institute of Electrical Engineering, Yanshan University, No 438 He Bei Road,
Qinhuangdao City, China
e-mail: xiuyan86@gmail.com

W. Ding
e-mail: weiye51@ysu.edu.cn

W. Lu et al. (eds.), *Proceedings of the 2012 International Conference on Information Technology and Software Engineering*, Lecture Notes in Electrical Engineering 212, DOI: 10.1007/978-3-642-34531-9_57, © Springer-Verlag Berlin Heidelberg 2013

**Fig. 57.1** Segmentation results with four classical algorithms. **a** wateshed. **b** Meanshift. **c** N-cuts

Image segmentation is an old and recurrent problem in computer vision. Various algorithms have been proposed to cope with this problem. Generally, The proposed classical algorithms including watershed [1, 2], mean shift [3–5], region-growing [6, 7], and superpixel [8, 9] are based on region, which start from the gray pixel, and cluster the pixels with similar value into different regions. As shown in Fig. 57.1, the Watershed algorithm is fast and easy to extend to n-dimensional images, but it may leads to under-segmentation in the absence of boundary cues (see Fig. 57.1b), and the result depend on the threshold; Mean shift is an effective clustering iterative algorithm, but it also creates under-segmentation and unmeaning regions because of the lacking compactness constraint; Super-pixel algorithms based on graph cut [9] and geometric flows are proposed in recent years, which can divide an image into many small regions. however most of the regions in Fig. 57.1d are not corresponding an independent part or object, and the long runtime is another disadvantage of these algorithms.

The other kind of algorithms is based on edges [10–13], which attain the segmentation goal by linking the edges into a series of closed boundary. For example, Chen and Sun [12] present a new edge-based interactive image segmentation method based the edge image which is generated with the edge detector; Takumi Uemura and Gou Koutaki [10] propose an algorithm by using their proposed boundary code method, which is more accurately than existing methods in images those have a narrow elongated object, shading and blurring. However, this kind of methods are not rich compared with the region based method, but it is more attractive because it can attain a more meaningful result and avoid the threshold problem.

In this paper, we propose an effective algorithm to divide the image into a series meaningful region by using the edge information. Our method is starting from the breakpoints which caused by the canny detector, and then the edge chains are grown at the breakpoints with the proposed criterions to achieve the goal of edge linking. Finally, two adjacent closed regions with similar color will be merged into one region.

Section 57.2 gives the global procedure of the proposed algorithm; Sect. 57.3 describes the key steps of the proposed algorithm; Sect. 57.4 comments on the experimental results in detail and Sect. 57.5 concludes the paper.

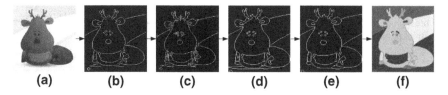

**Fig. 57.2** The process of our proposed algorithm. **a** input image; **b** edge detection; **c** breakpoints detection; **d** edge growth; **e** region merging; **d** segmentation result

## 57.2 Segmentation Process

As shown in Fig. 57.2, the process of our algorithm mainly contains four steps:

1. **Edge Detection**. We choose canny detector to obtain the edges in the image because of its excellent linking ability for edges with low contrast.
2. **Breakpoints Detection**. As shown in Fig. 57.2c, there are a lot of breakpoints (the green crosses), so the boundary of the toy is not closed. In order to remove them, we extract breakpoints with the algorithm described in Sect. 57.3.1 and extract a set of edge chains which connected with the breakpoints.
3. **Edge Growth**. If the edge chain connected with the breakpoint is prolonged based on a certain criterion, all edges will be closed and the salient region will be segmented. Based on this idea, we propose our algorithm in Sect. 57.3.2, and the closed regions are labeled after edge growth (see Fig. 57.2d).
4. **Region Merging**. Because the unreasonable regions are still exist after edge growth (e.g. the regions in the head of the toy), we merge them based on the color similarity (See the detailed algorithm in Sect. 57.3.3), and the final labeled image is shown in Fig. 57.2f.

## 57.3 Key Steps in Segmentation

### 57.3.1 Breakpoint Detection

For a non-zero pixel (the gray pixel in Fig. 57.3) in the edge map and its 3-by-3 neighborhood whose label is shown in Fig. 57.3a, we define

$$f(x) = \sum_{j=1}^{8} (a_j - b_j), \qquad (57.1)$$

Where $a = [x(1), x(2), x(3), x(6), x(9), x(8), x(7), x(4)]$, $b = [x(2), x(3), x(6), x(9), x(8), x(7), x(4), x(1)]$ and $x(i) = \{0, 1\}, (i = 1 \ldots 9)$ is the value of each pixel in the 3-by-3 neighborhood matrix. Based on the previous study [14], the non-zero pixel is a breakpoint (See Fig. 57.3b) when $f(x) = 2$.

Fig. 57.3 8-neighborhood of a breakpoint. **a** The label; **b** Breakpoints

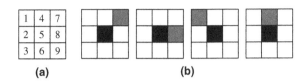

(a)                                         (b)

## 57.3.2 Edge Growth

Given a breakpoint $P$ we consider its local structure in a sliding window $(M \times M)$. As shown in Fig. 57.4, the edge will be grown at the breakpoint based on two cases:

1. Other breakpoints such as $P_1, P_2, \ldots, P_n$, (Fig. 57.4a) are existed in the window:

   First, the total gradient of each route (four routes in Fig. 57.4a) from $P$ to $P_i$ will be computed by

$$G = \sum_{i=1}^{n-1} \left( (Gr(x_{i+1}, y_{i+1}) - Gr(x_i, y_i))^2 + (Gr(x_i, y_{i+i}) - Gr(x_i, y_i))^2 \right)^{1/2} \quad (57.2)$$

Where $G$ is the grayscale, $(x, y)$ is the coordinates of the route, $Gr(x, y)$ is the gray value;

Then the route with the maximum value of $G$ will be chosen as the final linking route (the black route in Fig. 57.4a), and the edge will be linked in the sliding window finally.

2. No other breakpoints are existed in the window (Fig. 57.4.b):

   In this case, we map the edges connected with $P$ (the gray pixels in Fig. 57.4b) to its symmetric positions(the black pixels in Fig. 57.4b) in the sliding window and update $P$. Then above step will be repeated until $P$ meets the image boundary or other edges.

## 57.3.3 Region Merging

After edge growth, the edge map will be segmented into many closed regions. For an added edge with a certain length, we compute the average gray value of its two adjacent regions which labeled as $i$ and $j$, and defined them as $G_i$ and $G_j$. If their absolute difference is smaller than the predefined threshold $T$, this edge will be deleted in edge map $B$.

$$G_{i/j} = \frac{1}{m} \sum_{k=1}^{m} Gr(x_k, y_k) \quad (57.3)$$

Where $Gr$ is the grayscale image, $Gr(x_k, y_k)$ is the $k$th pixel's gray value of the closed region $i$ or $j$, and $m$ is the total numbers of pixels.

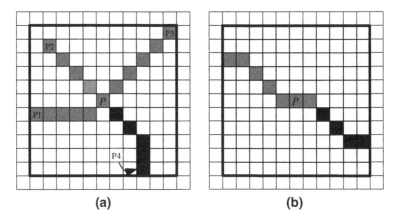

**Fig. 57.4**  Edge Growth method, the *black* boxes are the sliding window. **a** $P_4$ is the final point linked to $P$, the final linking route (*black*); **b** original edge (*gray*), the mapping part (*black*)

**Fig. 57.5**  Time cost (in seconds) requires by our algorithm for the processing of 72 images

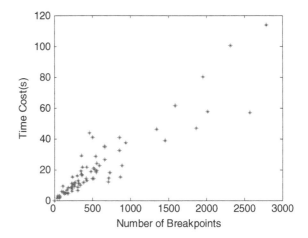

## 57.4  Experiment

Figure 57.5 gives the computation time of all 72 images. In our experiments, all results are implemented on Intel Core 2 Duo CPU 2.8 GHz with Matlab 2008a. We can see that the computation time is approximately proportional to the number of breakpoints, and 91.54 % images require a time less than 40 s.

Figure 57.6 shows some qualitative results of our algorithm in a part of chosen nature images which contain highly geometrical contents. We can see that the results are close with the human vision system and nearly all regions are segmented completely, and the regions connected with low contrast edges are also extracted well. Specifically, the regions in the traffic sign image and the road

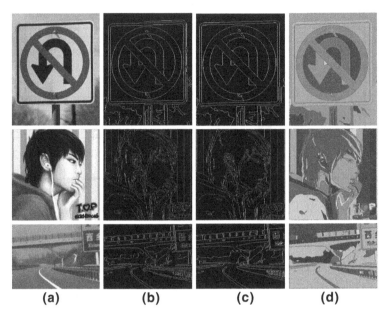

**(a)**              **(b)**              **(c)**              **(d)**

**Fig. 57.6** Segmentation result. **a** input image; **b** edge map; **c** edge growth; **d** labeled segments

image are meaningful enough to the further image understanding such as shape analysis, object identification and 3D reconstruction.

Figure 57.7 shows a comparison of various classical algorithms and our proposed algorithm. As shown in the figure, the improved Watershed algorithm leads to under-segmentation because it depends much on the gray level information. For instance, the whole image was segmented into just two parts and some detailed regions such as the trees and the road sign were lost in the road image, and the cylinder is not segmented from the background in the second image; Mean shift algorithm cluster a lot of crushing and unmeaning regions(See the small regions in the human image) and need to set different parameters for different image; N-cuts algorithm divided an complete region into a lot of irregular regions, and the results around the edges with low contrast are not satisfied. Compared with the above algorithms, our algorithm gives a more encouraging result because the shadow of the person, the cylinder and the traffic signs are all segmented completely. In addition, the runtime of N-cuts is much longer than ours, as shown in Fig. 57.7.

## 57.5 Conclusion

In this paper, we proposed a novel method to segment image by using the edges information. Our approach avoids the problem in threshold setting and seed selection, and the segmentation regions are more practical significance. However,

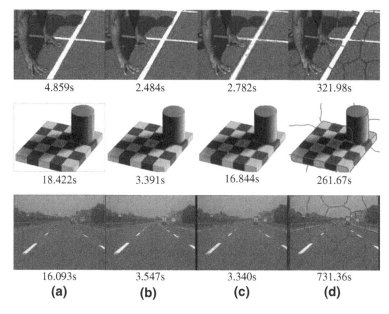

4.859s          2.484s          2.782s          321.98s

18.422s         3.391s          16.844s         261.67s

16.093s         3.547s          3.340s          731.36s
**(a)**         **(b)**         **(c)**         **(d)**

**Fig. 57.7** A comparison of four image segment methods. **a** proposed algorithm; **b** Watershed; **c** Mean Shift; **d** N-cuts

there are still many regions are over-segmentation. The main reasons are: (1) noise interference. Canny operator takes noises as a lot of short edges, which will affect the segmentation result; (2) Errors during edge growth, Though most of edge chains can be linked or grown in a right way based on our algorithm, some edge chains whose shape is a curve will be prolonged in a wrong way. So our work was just beginning. It should be studied further to solve the above problems.

**Acknowledgments** The research was supported by NSFC (61005034, 60905046) and the natural science foundation of Hebei Province (F2012203185, F2012203182).

# References

1. Vincent L, Soille P (1991) Watersheds in digital spaces: an efficient algorithm based on immersion simulations. IEEE Trans Pattern Anal Mach Intell 13(6):583–598
2. Beucher S, Lantue C (1979) Use of watersheds in contour detection. In: Proceedings Int'l Workshop Image Processing Real-Time Edge and Motion Detection/Estimation
3. Edoardo A, Roberto P, Orazio G (2007) Fuzzy C-Means segmentation on brain MR slices corrupted by RF-inhomogeneity. Lect Notes Comput Sci 4578:378–384
4. Zhou HY, Gerald S, Shi CM (2008) A mean shift based fuzzy c-means algorithm for image segmentation. Proceedings of the 30th annual international conference of the ieee engineering in medicine and biology society, Personalized Healthcare through Technology, pp 3091–3094
5. Comaniciu D, Meer P (2002) Mean shift: a robust approach toward feature space analysis. IEEE Trans Pattern Anal Mach Intell 24(5):603–619

6. Ren X, Malik J (2003) Learning a classification model for segmentation. In: Proceedings IEEE Int'l Conference Computer Vision, pp 10–17
7. Yu S, Shi J (2003) Multiclass spectral clustering. Proc IEEE Int'l Conf Computer Vision 1:313–319
8. Levinshtein A, Stere A, Kutulakos N (2009) Turbo pixels: fast superpixels using geometric flows. IEEE Int'l Conf Comput Vision 31:2290–2297
9. Shi J, Malik J (2000) Normalized cuts and image segmentation. IEEE Trans Pattern Anal Mach Intell 22(8):888–905
10. Uemura T, Koutaki G, Uchimura K (2011) Image segmentation based on Edge detection using boundary code. ICCV 7:6073–6083
11. Lin CH, Chen CC (2010) Image segmentation based on edge detection and region growing for thinprep-cervical smear. Pattern Recognit Artif Intell 24(7):1061–1089
12. Chen Q, Sun QS, Xia DS (2010) A new edge-based interactive image segmentation method. The international society for optical engineering, international conference on image processing and pattern recognition in industrial engineering, p 7820
13. Lindeberg T, Li MX (1997) Segmentation and classification of edges using minimum description length approximation and complementary junction cues. Comput Vis Image Underst 67(1):88–98
14. Kovesi PD (2008) http://www.csse.uwa.edu.au/~pk/Research/MatlabFns/index.html

# Chapter 58
# The Study on Network Three Dimensional GIS Terrain Data Transmission Methods Based on the Terrain Features

**Dong Wei and Lijuan Niu**

**Abstract** This paper presents an algorithm for massive terrain data transmission by network in the network three dimensional GIS. First of all, use the 8 neighborhood to calculate the terrain feature points. Secondly, setting the threshold by the slope rate of the change to extract the data points which are reflected terrain trends and terrain undulation. The points extracted by the two methods above were transferred to the client through the network, and then after those points interpolated, those points were used to reconstruct three dimensional terrain in client. This network three dimensional GIS terrain data transmission method based on the terrain features can reduce the burden of network data transmission to provide a technical support to solve the network transmission the network three dimensional GIS massive spatial data.

**Keywords** Terrain feature points · Slope rate of the change · Interpolation

## 58.1 Introduction

Two dimensional geographic information system is essentially based on a system of abstract symbols, can not give primitive feelings of nature [1]. Compared to the universal two dimensional GIS, three dimensional GIS can more accurately express the reality. Three dimensional GIS is not only able to express the plane relationships among space objects, but also can describe and express the vertical relationships [2]. From two dimensional GIS to three dimensional GIS, space

D. Wei (✉) · L. Niu
Shenyang University of Technology, Shen Liao Road 111, Shenyang, China
e-mail: dongweisut@126.com

W. Lu et al. (eds.), *Proceedings of the 2012 International Conference on Information Technology and Software Engineering*, Lecture Notes in Electrical Engineering 212, DOI: 10.1007/978-3-642-34531-9_58, © Springer-Verlag Berlin Heidelberg 2013

dimensions increased only one, but it can accommodate almost all of the space information, and can break out the conventional two dimensional representations forms of bondage, which give more choices for better insight and understanding of the real world [3]. However, more complex problems will appear, one of which is that the number of three dimensional terrain data significantly increased.

Along with the development of network of three dimensional geographic information system and continuously refined three dimensional terrain models, the resulting triangle mesh data has become increasingly sophisticated. In order to express realistic three dimensional terrain, more and more triangles are needed which require for high computer capacity and high processing speed. The general network three dimension GIS system use of the organization and scheduling of data [4], the three dimensional space data storage management [5], spatial data processing in LOD [6], client and server design caches [7] and other methods to achieve the large number of three dimensional terrain data transmission. However such methods generating terrain models on the server side, when a user makes a request, server need to not only transfer the terrain data to the client but the large number of topological relations also need to be transferred to the client. In this case, the network load is very heavy. So how to reduce the massive three dimensional terrain data for network transmission has become a hot research direction of the Network Geographic Information system [8].

Three dimensional terrain display needs to consider two aspects, the accuracy of three dimensional terrain model and server processing time. Based on the above situation, research some of massive three dimensional terrain data transmission methods. In the permission, reduce the amount of terrain data to achieve three dimensional terrain data transmission.

## 58.2 Arithmetic Descriptions

### 58.2.1 Algorithm Principle

According to the geomorphologic situation, the terrain is divided into terraces, plains, hills, mountains [9]. Characteristics of terrain elements: on the spatial distribution characteristics of terrain on the surface of a control point, line or area [10]. These control points are called terrain feature points. Terrain features can be divided into peak, depression, saddle, foot of the mountain, the ridge and valley point. Non-characteristic element are the distribute in each terrain unit which is designed to meet the sampling points and measuring the density of points. These points are mainly used to aid reconstruction of the terrain [10].

Feature point mainly reflects the information about these terrain features elements, in order to reflect changes in terrain trends and terrain undulation consideration should also be given to the terrain of the slope gradient and the slope rate of the change at the two important parameters. Slope gradient is the first order

**Fig. 58.1** The 3 * 3 window

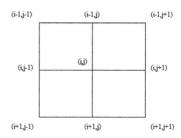

differential equation of the terrain curved surface, can represent the ratio of elevation change accompanied by distance. The slope of the rate of change is the second derivative equation of the terrain surface, to further characterize the changes of the slope, which reflects the complexity of the terrain.

Using slope rate of the change can extract the terrain data points which can reflect terrain trend and terrain undulation. Those extracted terrain data points and the terrain feature points are collectively referred to the key points. Through the above method a large number of terrain data can reduce to an appropriate quantity to transmission. In order to avoid transmitting a lot of topological relationship, the key points transported to client, and then create the topological relationship on client. The terrain data points' topological relationship can use interpolation algorithm and triangulation to establish. Because of the regular grid DEM data files are adopted, using interpolation algorithm to reconstruct three dimensional terrain.

## 58.2.2 Algorithm Design

### 58.2.2.1 The Extraction of the Characteristics of the Terrain Elements

The study uses the DEM data files which are provided by the USGS. Terrain feature points can be identified by its 8 neighborhood grid points. Specific methods are as follows:

Have a 3 * 3 window as shown in the Fig. 58.1, if $\left(Z_{i,j-1} - Z_{i,j}\right)\left(Z_{i,j+1} - Z_{i,j}\right) > 0$:

1. when the $Z_{i,j+1} > Z_{i,j}$, the VR $(i,j) = -1$;
2. when the $Z_{i,j+1} < Z_{i,j}$, the VR $(i,j) = 1$.

If $\left(Z_{i-1,j} - Z_{i,j}\right)\left(Z_{i+1,j} - Z_{i,j}\right) > 0$:

3. when the $Z_{i+1,j} > Z_{i,j}$, the VR $(i,j) = -1$;
4. when the $Z_{i+1,j} < Z_{i,j}$, the VR $(i,j) = 1$.

If 1 and 4 or 2 and 3 to set up, the VR $(i,j) = 2$.
If the above conditions are not true, the VR $(i,j) = 0$.

$$VR\ (i,\ j) = \begin{cases} -1, & \text{Valley point} \\ 1, & \text{represent a ridge point} \\ 2, & \text{saddle point} \\ 0, & \text{other points} \end{cases}$$

Using the above algorithm we can get the valley, the ridge point, saddle point, and other terrain feature points.

### 58.2.2.2 Using the Slope and Slope Rate of the Change to Extract the Terrain Data Points

The DEM data files which we used are downloaded from the USGS. So we use the direct method [11] to calculated the slope of each data points. It is mainly use the grid point on the center and its eight neighborhood grid points to calculate their difference in elevation and then calculate the center grid point's slope.

The slope of the rate of change is based on the direct method. Slope of the rate of change formula is expressed as:

$$\frac{d\beta_i}{dg} = \begin{cases} \frac{\beta_i - \beta_0}{g} \\ \frac{\beta_i - \beta_0}{\sqrt{2}g} \end{cases}$$

After using the above method to calculate the slope rate of the change, based on the slope rate of the change to set a certain threshold value. Through the test can get a corresponding threshold value, when the slope of the rate above the threshold value, extract this point as the key point.

### 58.2.2.3 Interpolation Algorithm of Reconstruction of Three Dimensional Terrain

Need to transfer data include two categories: One kind is the key points which are extracted from terrain. The other kind is the number of rows, number of columns, starting point coordinates and the grid interval distance which are the basic information to restore the three dimensional topography provided by the header files of the DEM data. In this paper, the basic idea of using the terrain feature points to restore the three dimensional the terrain:

1. According to Download DEM data header files to provide the basic information of the terrain, you can calculate the specific location of the X-axis and Y axis of each grid point, then set the Z-axis value (elevation value) is 0.
2. Comparing the information (the X axis and Y-axis value) of the key points with the information of each grid point (X-axis and Y-axis value). If the information are same, we can determine the location of the key point of the terrain is the grid point. Then add the key point's elevation information to the grid point.

If the key point and the grid point do not match, continue to compare the information to the next grid point. Until all of the key points matched successfully. Put all of the key points' elevation information inserted into the corresponding grid node.

3. After Complete all terrain feature points matching, the rest of the terrain points which are not the key points use the interpolation to get their height information. The interpolation algorithm main idea is: Seek out the eight neighborhood points which the elevation information are not equal to 0, use those points' elevation information to calculated their average elevation information, and then insert the average elevation information into the center grid point. And then implement all of the grid elevation interpolation.

4. The DEM data files which we used are downloaded from the USGS. Use the triangulation network model to implement three dimensional terrain modeling. Parsing and reading the header file of the downloaded DEM files can be calculated the position coordinate for each grid point, the number of rows, the number of columns and the number of data of each line. Using the key points and the interpolation to calculated the other grid points' elevation information, and then constructed triangulation. Finally implement the three dimensional terrain modeling.

## 58.3  Algorithm Analyses

### 58.3.1  Experimental Results and Experimental Analysis

The experimental results shown in Fig. 58.2. Figure 58.2a analyzed the head file of the DEM data file which is downloaded from the USGS. And then use all of terrain data points to generated three dimensional terrain. Figure 58.2b is used the extracted terrain feature points and the interpolation algorithm to reconstruction the three dimensional terrain. It can be seen in the ridge, valley, saddle, etc. regions the expression are correct (for example, Fig. 58.2b, the annotation a), but in some transitional regions the expression have biggish errors (for example, Fig. 58.2b, the annotation b). This is because of the terrain feature points can not reflect terrain trend and terrain undulation. Figure 58.2c is used the terrain data points which are extracted by the slope rate of the change and the interpolation algorithm to reconstruction the three dimensional terrain. It can be seen in the ridge, valley, saddle, etc. regions the expression have biggish errors (for example, Fig. 58.2c, the annotation a), but in transitional regions the expression are correct (for example, Fig. 58.2c, the annotation b). This is because the extracted data points can not accurately reflect the terrain control points. Figure 58.2d is combined the terrain feature points and the terrain data points which are extracted by the slope rate of the change with the interpolation algorithm to reconstruction the three dimensional terrain. This method combines the advantages of the above two

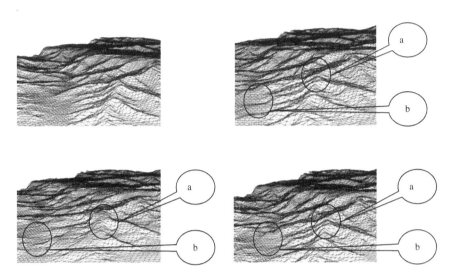

**Fig. 58.2** The experimental results

**Table 58.1** Three dimensional terrain analysis table

| Three dimensional terrain data types | Threshold (slope rate of the change) | Total number of data points |
|---|---|---|
| All of data points in the source file | – | 92600 |
| The extracted terrain feature point | – | 25592 |
| The data points extracted by use of the slope rate of the change | 0.005 | 27250 |
| The key points | 0.15 | 34009 |

algorithms. It can be seen in the ridge, valley, saddle, etc. regions the expression are correct (for example, Fig. 58.2d, the annotation a), in transitional regions the expression are barely noticeable difference (for example, Fig. 58.2d, the annotation b).

The threshold value and amount of data which attained by the above methods of 3 d terrain reconstruction was described in Table 58.1.

## 58.3.2 Error Analysis

The profile method and the check point method are the usual methods to evaluated DEM accuracy [12]. Use check point method to check error. Calculated the error between the interpolated elevation and the real elevation for every point, and then calculated the average error [13].

**Table 58.2** Elevation error

| Slope classification | Slope | The number of data point | DEM grid spacing | Points elevation error (m) |
|---|---|---|---|---|
| Plain to slightly inclined slope | <2° | 23850 | 30 | 4.653 |
| Slow tilt slope | 2°–5° | 16180 | 30 | 4.651 |
| Slope | 5°–5° | 48056 | 30 | 6.538 |
| Steep slope | 15°–25° | 1848 | 30 | 10.905 |
| Acute slope | ≥25° | 30 | 30 | 9.394 |

**Table 58.3** Error classification and error analysis

| Error number | Error range (m) | The number of points |
|---|---|---|
| 1 | Within 5 | 87210 |
| 2 | More than 5 less than 10 | 4557 |
| 3 | More than 10 less than 20 | 787 |
| 4 | More than 20 | 46 |

According to the slope classification which provided by the International Cartographic Association the slope is divided into seven grades: Plain to slightly inclined slope (<2°), slow tilt slope (2°–5°), slope (5°–15°), steep slope(15°–25°), acute slope (25°–35°), acute and steep (35°–55°), vertical slope (>55°) [14]. All types of slopes error results shown in Table 58.2.

Figure out all of the network's average elevation error is 6.224 m.

Through the test, the errors can be divided into 4 categories. The number of data point in each type of error is shown in Table 58.3. It can be seen from Table 58.3 that the vast majority of grid points of error control within 5 m. So extract the key points and the use the interpolation method to reconstructed the three dimensional terrain is feasible.

Through experiment can get the maximum error is 28.989 m.

## 58.4 Summary

Using the slope rate of the change to extracted terrain data points and using the 8 neighborhood algorithm to extracted terrain feature points. Transmitted those key points to the client through network. On the client using the interpolation algorithm to reconstructed the topological relationship between the terrain data. Finally reconstructed the three dimensional terrain. This algorithm has the advantages of less computational complexity and is also easy to achieve with the good result.

# References

1. Xiao YB, Zhong ES, Liu JY, Song GF (2001) A discussion on basic problems of 3D GIS. J Image Graph 1006–8961:842–849 (in Chinese)
2. Shi JS, Liu JZ (2005) Development stage of 3D GIS technology. Surv Mapp Sci 1009–2307: 110–117 (in Chinese)
3. Zhu Q (2004) 3D geographic information systems reviewed. World Geogr Inf 1672–1586: 8–12 (in Chinese)
4. Wang EQ, Li YC, Xue YL, Xiao JC, Liu XL, Liu L (2008) The study of grid data of network 3D image map organization methods. Sci Surv Mapp 1009–2307:26–30 (in Chinese)
5. Li ZM, Yu ZW (2008) Terrain data object storage mode and its declustering method. Acta Geodaetica Et Cartographic Sinica 1001–1595:489–495 (in Chinese)
6. Hu HT, Zhu XY, Zhu Q (2003) Web-based 3D geo-information release: research and implementation. Bull Surv Mapp 0494–0911:27–31 (in Chinese)
7. Wang J, Deng KY (2009) The research on massive data storage and 3D visualization under network environment. Geomat Spat Inf Technol 672–5867:28–31 (in Chinese)
8. Gao XW, Wang P, Wang CQ (2006) Design and realization of the 3D-GIS based on the internet. Remote Sens Inf 1000–3177:77–81 (in Chinese)
9. Li JZ (1982) The first exploration on the quantity index of the basic form of the China landform. Acta Geogr Sinica 37(1):17–25 (in Chinese)
10. Zhou QM, Liu XJ (2005) Digital terrain analysis. China Social Sciences Publishing House, Beijing (in Chinese)
11. Hu C (1998) The improvements of direct method to calculate the terrain slope. Jiang Su Surv Mapp 21(2):28–31 (in Chinese)
12. Zhou XH, Yao YQ, Zhao JX (2005) Research on interpolation and the assessing accuracy of DEM. Sci Surv Mapp 30(5):86–88 (in Chinese)
13. Lan Y, Wang MH, Liu SH, Dai XMA (2009) Study on building DEM based on point-by-point interpolation algorithm. Sci Surv Mapp 1009–2307:214–217 (in Chinese)
14. Chen G, He ZW, Yang B (2010) Spatial association rules data mining research on terrain feature and mountain climate change. Geogr Geo-Inf Sci 1672–0504:37–41 (in Chinese)

# Chapter 59
# Distorted Document Image Rectification Based on Inflection Detection and Heterogeneous Registration

**Lijing Tong, Quanyao Peng, Guoliang Zhan and Yifan Li**

**Abstract** To get better document image quality and Optical Character Recognition (OCR) rate, a warped document image correction method based on inflection point detection and heterogeneous registration strategies is proposed. This method mosaics two distorted images of the same document from different viewpoints. Firstly, two inflection points are detected from one image based on the inflection point detection method, which includes steps of image binarization and morphological dilation, text line extraction and characteristic point detection, curve fitting and inflection point determining. Then the two inflection points are registered in the other image base on heterogeneous registration strategies. At last, image mosaics are done for the two images, and the best mosaiced image is selected by OCR recognition results. For the best mosaiced image, the distortions are mostly removed and the OCR results are improved markedly. Experimental results show that the proposed method can resolve the issue of document image distortion more effectively.

**Keywords** Image registration · Image mosaic · Inflection point detection · Curve fitting · Document image distortion

## 59.1 Introduction

Along with the appearance of cheap and convenient modern devices (such as digital cell phones, PDAs, video cameras), document images are getting more and more popular. However, geometric distortions often appear when the documents

L. Tong (✉) · Q. Peng · G. Zhan · Y. Li
Institution of Information Engineering, North China University of Technology,
Beijing, China
e-mail: tong_lijing@163.com

W. Lu et al. (eds.), *Proceedings of the 2012 International Conference on Information Technology and Software Engineering*, Lecture Notes in Electrical Engineering 212, DOI: 10.1007/978-3-642-34531-9_59, © Springer-Verlag Berlin Heidelberg 2013

are captured which usually causes non-planar geometric shapes such as spine curves, rolling curves and so on. And the geometric distortions make significant problems for further analysis and recognition processes. Therefore, the restoration of geometric distortions is an important preprocessing step to make further processes more effective and successful.

Previously, the geometric rectification problem out of various binding curves, rolling curves and folds has been studied extensively and the proposed methods can be divided into two categories: 3D-based shape manipulation techniques and purely 2D-based image processing techniques.

In the former techniques, in order to get the information of the surface shape, many 3D-based methods introduced special setups such as structured lighting, laser scans or other setups [1–3]. In these methods, the captured 3D model was supposed to be mapped to a plane to obtain the restored image, or they tried to reconstruct the surface shape. However, 3D-based methods usually acquire additional devices, which make it inconvenient for most of the people to process images.

As to the 2D-based methods, Miao Ligang et al. proposed a novel morphology based radial lens correction method for document images captured with hand-held cameras [4]. But this method is limited to correct document image caused by various degrees of lens distortions.

In another work, Bukhari et al. presented a new approach for document image dewarping with curled text lines information that was extracted with a modified active contour model based on ridges [5]. Luo Sanding et al. proposed a method based on text lines for efficient calibration of document images [6]. However, these methods are mainly for English document image correction.

Shape-from-shading formulation is another way to restoration the warped images. Zhang et al. used a shape-from-shading formulation to reconstruct the 3-D shape of the document's surface [7]. This technique requires lighting knowledge, which in most of the cases is unknown.

In Gatos's approach, a novel segmentation-based technique for restoration of arbitrarily warped document images was presented according to the word rotation and translation [8]. Song Lili's approach was an improvement of Gatos's [9]. Nikolaos Stamatopoulos et al. proposed a goal-oriented rectification methodology to compensate for undesirable document image distortions [10].These text line-based methods without amendments of the text centerlines are vulnerable to the impact of the error text lines, and are not applicable to document with pictures.

In addition, Kluzner and Tzadok proposed a method to compute a global, polynomial transformation-based correction for the page distortion [11]. However, it is based on the supposition that 70 % of the words in the book are recurring terms.

We also have already proposed a distorted document image rectification method based on image registration. However, the feature points were selected by hand and there was only one registration strategy in that rectification system [12].

In order to recover and recognize the warped document images in an even better fashion, in this paper, we propose a distorted document image correction method based on inflection point detection method and heterogeneous image registration

**Fig. 59.1** Image from left viewpoint

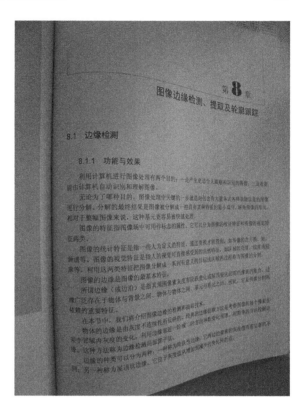

strategies, which uses image mosaic technology for recognizing and rectifying the warped document images. For two images (one is the primary image, the other is the auxiliary image) of the same warped document page from left and right viewpoints, e.g. Figs. 59.1 and 59.2, the general procedure is as follows: (i) inflection point detection for a warped document page, (ii) image registration based on the inflection point and heterogeneous strategies; (iii) image mosaicing, (iv) determining and outputting the best correction result by recognition rate returned by Optical Character Recognition (OCR) software.

## 59.2 Inflection Point Detection Method

### 59.2.1 Binarization and Morphological Dilation

The first step of the image processing for inflection point detection is grizzling. For the each pixels' red, green and blue value, $R$, $G$ and $B$, the image pixel's gray value, $H$, is calculated as:

**Fig. 59.2** Image from right viewpoint

$$H = 0.299R + 0.587G + 0.114B \tag{59.1}$$

Binarization processing is a necessary preprocessing step for morphological dilation [13]. Here, Niblack algorithm is selected as the local binarization threshold calculation method [14]. First, an $n * n$ window is chosen centered with the point $(x, y)$. Secondly, the mean value, $\psi(x, y)$, and the mean variance, $\varphi(x, y)$, are calculated. Then, the threshold of the centre point, $f(x, y)$, is calculated by (59.2).

$$f(x, y) = \psi(x, y) - 0.2\phi(x, y) \tag{59.2}$$

Morphology dilation is a necessary step for text line extraction. It can be done by expending black pixels to their adjacent pixels in the binarized image.

### 59.2.2 Text Line Extraction and Characteristic Point Detection

After morphological dilation, the text lines are extracted. The method of the text line extraction is as follows.

**Fig. 59.3** An extracted text line

Step 1: The image is scanned by columns, if a black pixel is found, the vertical coordinate of this pixel is noted as $y_1$.

Step 2: The scanning is continued vertically until a white pixel is found.

Step 3: The vertical coordinate of this white pixel is noted as $y_2$.

Step 4: The vertical coordinate of the text line pixel, i.e. $y_3$, should be the average value of the continuous black pixels as (59.3):

$$y_3 = \frac{y_1 + y_2 + 1}{2} \tag{59.3}$$

An example of an extracted text line is shown in Fig. 59.3.

In order to calculate correct curve fitting result, the text line segments of other rows and the noise text line segments should be deleted from the current text line. Only pixels near the average y-axis coordinate are the characteristic points and should be reserved. For every pixel $(x_i, y_i)$ in an extracted text line set $S$, the characteristic point detection algorithm is presented as follows.

Firstly, the average y-axis coordinate can be calculated as:

$$M = \frac{\sum_{i=1}^{n} y_i}{n} \tag{59.4}$$

Then for an adaptive parameter $K$, a deviation threshold can be calculated as:

$$N = K\sqrt{\sum_{i=1}^{n} (y_i - M)^2} \tag{59.5}$$

Finally, for the pixels which y-axis coordinate is between $M - N$ and $M + N$ are reserved as set $T(x_i, y_i)$, i.e.,

$$\{T(x_i, y_i) | M - N < y_i < M + N (x_i, y_i) \in S\} \tag{59.6}$$

Here, the parameter $K$ in (59.5) is adaptive. In the beginning, $K$ is 0. For a demanded sample point number $L$, $K$ is increased until the number of the points in set $T(x, y)$ is more than $L$.

The characteristic points detected from Fig. 59.3 by this algorithm is presented in Fig. 59.4.

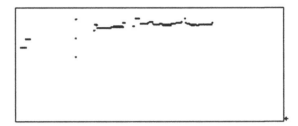

**Fig. 59.4** Characteristic sample point detected

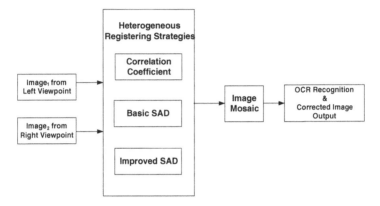

**Fig. 59.5** Heterogeneous registration model

## 59.2.3 Curve Fitting and Inflection Point Determining

For the characteristic points, curve fitting is performed by:

$$y = ax^2 + bx + c \tag{59.7}$$

After curve fitting, parameter $a$ is determined. If $a > 0$, the minimal y-axis coordinate pixel in set $T$ is determined as the inflection point. Otherwise, the maximal y-axis coordinate pixel is determined as the inflection point.

## 59.3 Heterogeneous Registration Strategies

To mosaic two images, image registration should be done based on the feature points at the inflection point's position. However, not in all cases, a registration method can get the correct results. Hence, we propose heterogeneous registration strategy model for image mosaic. The best mosaiced image is determined and output by the OCR software module.

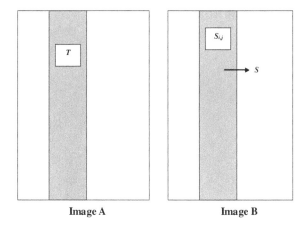

**Fig. 59.6** Mask matching between two images

Image A          Image B

In this paper, we proposed a rectifying system based on 3 different registration strategies. Figure 59.5 is our heterogeneous registration strategy system model.

### 59.3.1 Correlation Coefficient Registration Method

As shown in Fig. 59.6, image $A$ and image $B$ have a vertical overlap region (shaded area). Image $A$ contains a template block $T$. The shaded area in image $B$ represents the search area $S$. Template $T$ moves on the search area $S$, and the search area covered by the template is the sub-graph $S_{i,\ j}$. $(i,\ j)$ is the upper-left corner coordinate of the sub-graph $S_{i,\ j}$. The size of $T$ is $X \times Y$.

The cross-correlation similarity measure equation is as follows [15]:

$$R(i,j) = \frac{\sum_{x=1}^{X}\sum_{y=1}^{Y}\left[s_{i,j}(x,y) * T(x,y)\right]}{\sqrt{\sum_{x=1}^{X}\sum_{y=1}^{Y}\left[s_{i,j}(x,y)\right]^2}\sqrt{\sum_{x=1}^{X}\sum_{y=1}^{Y}\left[T(x,y)\right]^2}} \tag{59.8}$$

According to Schwarz inequality: point $(i, j)$ is the best matched point when $R(i, j)$ get the maximum value during the template moving.

### 59.3.2 Basic SAD Registration Method

SAD means Sum of Absolute Difference [16]. Like the Fig. 59.6, the absolute error is normally defined as:

$$\|E(i,j)\| = \sum_{x=1}^{X}\sum_{y=1}^{Y}\left|S_{i,j}(x,y) - T(x,y)\right| \tag{59.9}$$

**Fig. 59.7** Two reference
points

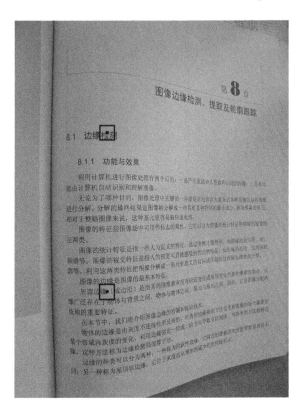

The best matching point is the Point $(i, j)$ when $E(i, j)$ get the minimum value
during the template moving.

### 59.3.3 Improved SAD Registration Method

SAD is not robust always, especially when the two images has different illumination. To make the SAD more robust, we improved SAD method for image
registration, i.e. normalizing the gray windows of the template $T$ and the sub-graph
$S_{i, j}$ before the SAD is performed.

Given that the left end point of the gray histogram of $T$ is $a$, the peak point is $b$,
the right end point is $c$, and the left end point of the gray histogram of $S_{i, j}$ is $d$, the
peak point is $e$, the right end point is $f$, for the gray value $M$ in $S_{i, j}$, the normalized
value $g(x, y)$ is calculated as:

$$g(x,y) = \begin{cases} a + (M - d) \times (b - a)/(e - d); & M \le e \\ c - (f - M) \times (c - b)/(f - e); & M > e \end{cases} \quad (59.10)$$

**Fig. 59.8** Mosaiced image based on basic SAD

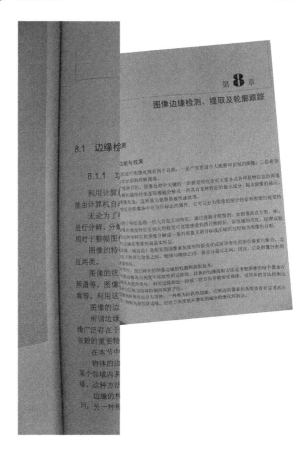

After normalization, the registration point is calculated as the basic SAD method according to (59.9).

## 59.4 Experiment and Test Results

A lot of warped document image tests demonstrated that this method can deal with the problem of the distorted document recognition effectively. An actual example is shown in Figs. 59.7, 59.8, 59.9.

Two reference points are selected in Fig. 59.7 based on the inflection point detection method. Figure 59.8 is a wrong mosaiced image from Figs. 59.2 and 59.7 based on basic SAD. Figure 59.9 is the correct mosaiced image from Figs. 59.2 and 59.7 based on correlation coefficient and improved SAD. After OCR recognition feedback, the heterogeneous registration system output the Fig. 59.9 as the distorted document image rectifying result. The comparison of OCR results on entire images is shown in Table 59.1.

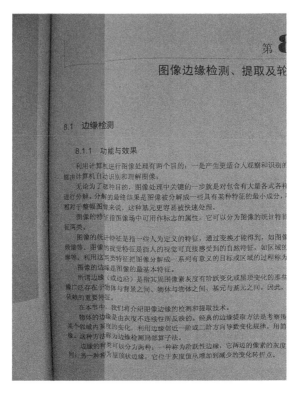

**Fig. 59.9** Mosaiced image based on correlation coefficient and improved SAD

**Table 59.1** Comparison of OCR results

| Image | Figure 59.1 | Figure 59.2 | Figure 59.8 | Figure 59.9 |
| --- | --- | --- | --- | --- |
| OCR rate of entire image (%) | 48.5 | 86.1 | 55.8 | 97.6 |

## 59.5 Conclusions

This paper presents a distorted document image rectification method based on inflection point detection method and heterogeneous image registration strategies. This method mosaics two images, which are photographed from different viewpoints for the same distorted document page, with several different image registration methods at the inflection point position. Experimental results show that our proposed method can effectively solve the issue of the document image distortion.

**Acknowledgments** This research is funded by Funding Project for Academic Human Resources Development (PHR201107107, PHR20110865) in Institutions of Higher Learning under the Jurisdiction of Beijing Municipality, and the 11th Five-year Key Technology R&D Program (2009BAI71B02) of China.

# References

1. Brown MS, Seales WB (2004) Image restoration of arbitrarily warped documents. In: Proceedings of IEEE symposium of pattern analysis and machine intelligence (TPAMI 04). doi: 10.1109/TPAMI.2004.87
2. Chua KB, Zhang L, Zhang Y, Tan CL (2005) A fast and stable approach for restoration of warped document images. In: Proceedings of IEEE symposium of document analysis and recognition (ICDAR 05). doi: 10.1109/ICDAR.2005.8
3. Li Z (2006) Restoring warped document images using shape-from-shading and surface interpolation. In: Proceedings of IEEE symposium pattern recognition (ICPR 06). doi: 10.1109/ICPR.2006.997
4. Miao LG, Chang J (2010) A mathematic morphology approach for radial lens correction of document image. In: Proceedings of 2010 international conference on computer design and applications (ICCDA). doi: 10.1109/ICCDA.2010.5540729
5. Bukhari SS, Shafait F, Breuel TM (2009) Dewarping of document images using coupled-snakes. In: Proceedings of 3rd international workshop on camera-based document analysis and recognition, Part 1, pp 34–41
6. Luo SD, Fang XM, Zhao C, Luo YS (2011) Text line based correction of distorted document images. In: Proceedings of 2011 IEEE 10th international conference on trust, security and privacy in computing and communications. doi: 10.1109/TrustCom.2011.206
7. Zhang L, Yip AM, Brown MS, Tan CL (2009) A unified framework for document restoration using in painting and shape-from-shading. J Pattern Recognit 42(11):2961–2978
8. Gatos B, Pratikakis I, Ntirogiannis K (2007) Segmentation based recovery of arbitrarily warped document images. In: Proceedings of international conference on document analysis and recognition. doi: 10.1109/ICDAR.2007.4377063
9. Song L, Wu Y, Sun B (2010) New document image distortion correction method. J Comput Appl 30(12):3317–3320 (in Chinese)
10. Stamatopoulos N, Gatos B, Pratikakis I, Perantonis SJ (2011) Goal-oriented rectification of camera-based document images. IEEE Trans Image Process 20(4):910–920
11. Kluzner V, Tzadok A (2011) Page curling correction for scanned books using local distortion information. In: Proceedings of 2011 international conference on document analysis and recognition (ICDAR). doi: 10.1109/ICDAR.2011.182
12. Tong L, Zhang Y, Zhao H (2011) A warped document image mosaicing method based on registration and TRS transform. In: Proceedings of computer and information science. doi: 10.1109/ICIS.2011.34
13. Su B, Lu S, Tan CL (2011) Combination of document image binarization techniques. In: Proceedings of IEEE symposium of document analysis and recognition (ICDAR 11). doi: 10.1109/ICDAR.2011.14
14. Tong L, Chen K, Zhang Y, Fu X, Duan J (2009) Document image binarization based on NFCM. In: Proceedings of IEEE symposium of image and signal processing (CISP 09). doi: 10.1109/CISP.2009.5305330
15. Wang WT, Li YL, Zhao QL (2012) A new approach to automatic feature based registration of multi-sensor remote sensing images. In: Proceedings of 2012 2nd international conference on remote sensing, environment and transportation engineering (RSETE). doi: 10.1109/RSETE.2012.6260357
16. Kokiopoulou E, Zervos M, Kressner D, Paragios N (2011) Optimal similarity registration of volumetric images. In: Proceedings of IEEE conference on computer vision and pattern recognition (CVPR). doi: 10.1109/CVPR.2011.5995337

# Chapter 60
# Target Recognition and Tracking Method Based on Multiple Templates in Complex Scenes

Zhifeng Gao, Bo Wang, Mingjie Dong and Yongsheng Shi

**Abstract** Image matching is a key technology in target recognition and tracking systems. This paper presents a method based on multi-template replacement strategy. The proposed method can ensure the resolution and accuracy of target recognition regardless of distance and field of view, and uses the idea of the Bayesian classifier. The problem of target recognition is converted into solving the Bayesian class posterior probability. This method was found to have high real-time performance and high target recognition accuracy.

**Keywords** Bayesian classifier · Image processing · Multiple templates · Offline training

## 60.1 Introduction

With the development of image processing, target recognition and tracking technologies have been widely used in medicine, public safety, transportation, and the military. In particular, image-guided weapons using target automatic recognition and tracking technology can achieve fire-and-forget performance and high shooting accuracy. Therefore, image processing is a potential area for research and has practical value.

Most traditional target recognition algorithms are based on global features of the target image, such as Fourier descriptors [1], various moment invariants [2, 3],

Z. Gao (✉) · B. Wang · M. Dong · Y. Shi
School of Automation, Beijing Institute of Technology, No 5, Zhongguancun South Street, Haidian District, 100081 Beijing, China
e-mail: gzf@bit.edu.cn

W. Lu et al. (eds.), *Proceedings of the 2012 International Conference on Information Technology and Software Engineering*, Lecture Notes in Electrical Engineering 212, DOI: 10.1007/978-3-642-34531-9_60, © Springer-Verlag Berlin Heidelberg 2013

histogram, and the target edge, contour, and texture. However, when a target has missing information, recognition technology based on global features cannot effectively describe and track the target. Therefore, difficulties arise in addressing complex scenes such as imperceptible targets, posture changes, or partial occlusion. The target recognition method based on local features can solve this problem. We select the appropriate feature point descriptors to describe the local image region feature around each point. The feature points can be matched based on the descriptors. Common descriptors have algorithms such as SIFT [4, 5], GLOH [6], SURF [7]. In these algorithms, building and matching the descriptors require considerable computing power. Most image processing systems use embedded processors, and have limited computing speed and capacity. Thus, heavy computation for image processing or real-time tracking of computing is unfavorable.

The present study uses an image classification method based on Bayesian classifier, which converts the image feature-matching problem into a feature classification problem [8]. The most time-consuming local feature vector calculation can be conducted via offline training. Using the joint distribution of the conditional probability of local area in the training phase, the online feature classification can be classified under the Bayesian classification theory [9]. This method reduces the calculation of online target recognition stage, and can meet real-time tracking requirements.

This article also uses a target tracking method based on multi-template replacement strategy. This strategy can address the great difference in scale of the actual target image and the template image. In addition, the method has stable identification and tracking capabilities.

## 60.2 Bayesian Classifier Theory

With the formula, Bayesian classifier can calculate the posterior probability of the object from the priori probability. The posterior probability is that the object belongs to a particular class, the class with maximum posterior probability. Assuming that $m$ classes $\{c_1, c_2, \ldots, c_M\}$ are present, the classifier first calculates the posterior probability $P(c_i|x)$ of the $N$-dimensional Eigenvectors $x = [x_1, x_2, \ldots, x_N]^T$ that belong to each category label $c_i(i = 1,2,\ldots,M)$. The largest class $c_i$ of $P(c_i|x)$ is the maximum posteriori assumption. The Bayesian formula is as follows:

$$P(c_i|x) = \frac{P(x|c_i)P(c_i)}{P(x)} \tag{60.1}$$

We assume that the naive Bayesian classifier is a conditional independence between the components of the eigenvectors. It can estimate the necessary parameters by a small amount of training data, thus greatly reducing the computing scale and complexity. At this point, the class conditional probability $P(x|c_i)$ can be simplified as:

$$P(x|c_i) = \prod_{k=1}^{N} P(x_k|c_i) \tag{60.2}$$

The valuation of probability $P(x_1|c_i), P(x_2|c_i), \ldots, P(x_n|c_i)$ can be obtained from the training samples.

In the application of feature point classification, several binary comparison operators within the local area contain the intrinsic relationship. Satisfying the above conditional independence assumptions is therefore difficult. We then choose semi-naive Bayesian classification model [10], which relaxes the conditional independence assumption of the naive Bayesian classifier. It not only retains the efficiency of the naive Bayesian classifier, but also considers the correlation between the parts of the property. $N$-dimensional eigenvector $x = [x_1, x_2, \ldots, x_N]^T$ is divided into $S$ sub-eigenvectors; each sub-vector contains $R = N/S$ binary characteristic components. We assume that it is independent from the different sub-eigenvector. Each binary characteristic component of the sub-eigenvector has correlation. Each sub-vector is defined as a fern, represented by the symbol $F_k$. Calculating the joint distribution $P(F_k|C = c_i)$ of each fern corresponding class conditional probability, we can get the classification expression based on semi-Naive Bayesian classification model:

$$P(x|c_i) = \prod_{k=1}^{S} P(F_k|c_i) \tag{60.3}$$

Where $F_k = \{x_{\sigma(k,1)}, x_{\sigma(k,2)}, \ldots, x_{\sigma(k,R)}\}$, $k = 1, 2, \ldots, S$ is the $k$-fern, $\sigma(k, j)$ is the random function with the range $1, \ldots, N$.

The semi-Bayesian classifier algorithm improves the efficiency of the algorithm in addition to greatly reducing the amount of storage, thus making it conducive to engineering applications.

## 60.3  Extraction of Feature Points

To extract feature points, we used a simple and efficient corner detection algorithm published by Rosten and Drummond: FAST corner detection [11]. In grayscale images, if a sufficient number of consecutive pixels are in the neighborhood around a pixel, and all their gray values are greater than or less than the gray value of the middle point, the middle point can be defined as the candidate corner.

The detection method is shown in Fig. 60.1. The circle around the detection point c should be verified, and the longest arc should be located. If the gray value of all points in the arc meets the following formula, then, we can determine that point $C$ is the corner.

$$|I(x) - I(c)| > t \tag{60.4}$$

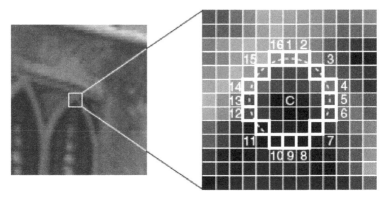

**Fig. 60.1** FAST corner detection

Where $I(c)$ is the gray scale value of $C$-point, $I(x)$ is the gray value of the point on the arc, and t is a threshold of the grayscale difference to the point.

Threshold $t$ is selected as 9. The algorithm is termed FAST-9 corner detection algorithm; research [12] has demonstrated that the FAST-9 algorithm achieves the best balance in terms of repeatability and speed.

The algorithm adds noise and affine transformation to the template image, and generates a sample set consisting of n deformable templates. It then extracts multi-scale FAST-9 corners in each image of the sample set, and records the number of repetitions of each corner. Finally, a certain number of repetitive maximum corner points are selected as stable feature points in the next offline classifier training and online feature recognition operations.

## 60.4 Offline Training

Each stable feature point $k_i$ in camera images is regarded as a class $c_i(i = 1,2,...,M)$. Offline training aims to record several samples, and to get each class $c_i$ required by the semi-naive Bayesian classifiers and the class conditional probability $P(F_M|C = c_i)$ for all ferns.

Based on the template image, we can produce training image samples that set with the number of N around each feature point via random affine transformation. The $S * R$ pixels are randomly selected: the R binary eigenvalue component $x_j$ in S-ferns of class $c_i$. The number of training samples of the classifier is taken as 10,000. The joint distribution of the conditional probability of feature points must be obtained to complete offline training.

## 60.5  RANSAC Method to Eliminate Error Matching

After obtaining the joint distribution of the conditional probability of feature points, the classification model in Eq. (60.3) can be used to classify real-time input image feature points to achieve feature matching. Figure 60.2 shows the classification results of the template image and the target image. Local feature matching is effective by using semi-Naive Bayesian classifier. Most feature points get the right match, but error matching is inevitable. Other measures are needed to remove errors; we thus use the RANSAC method.

Random sample consensus method (RANSAC) was first proposed by Fischler and Bolles. It is widely used as a robust method to eliminate mismatch [13]. It is a non-deterministic algorithm based on a sample data set containing abnormal data. It also calculates the mathematical model parameters of the data through an iterative approach, then gets the valid sample data. The algorithm works as follows:

1. A model that is applicable to the hypothetical inlier points is chosen. All unknown parameters can be calculated from the inlier points. This paper selected a homography model.
2. The model in 1 is used to test all other data. If a point is applied to the model, then this point is the inlier.
3. If enough points can be classified as inliers, the estimated model is reasonable. Then, all assumption inlier points, not only the initial inlier points, are used to re-estimate the model.
4. Finally, the model is evaluated with the error of estimating inlier points.

The above process is repeated a certain number of times. The generation model of each time is either discarded because the inlier points are too few, or selected because it is better than the existing model.

Figure 60.3 shows the result of mismatched removed after RANSAC.

**Fig. 60.2** Feature classification results by Bayesian classifier

**Fig. 60.3** Mismatch
excluding results

## 60.6 Multi-Template Replacement Strategy

When the camera searches the target, in the case of complex background or target distance, problems are encountered. For example, the image of the target in the field of view is very small and unclear; the resolution is low. Accurate identification becomes difficult because the target is the sole source of information. To solve this problem, this paper proposed a multi-template replacement strategy. In the early stages of the study, we used a smaller-scale template of the target, and made the template image, including the surrounding landscape, as far as possible.

As the target becomes nearer, its image becomes bigger and clearer. On the other hand, if the target increases to a certain extent, it replaces another large-scale template. The field of view covered by the new template is smaller, but the target is clearer. This multi-template replacement strategy based on scale information can solve the problem of long-range guided target tracking, and improve its accuracy.

As shown in Fig. 60.4, three template images from far and near are selected. In the three pictures, the field of view decreases, the image contains less information, and the target (the ship) becomes clearer.

## 60.7 Experimental Results and Analysis

The experiment used a high simulation sand table in which a model ship was used as the target. The target templates are shown in Fig. 60.4. The algorithm identifies the target by matching the features of the target image and the template image. A closer distance results in a larger target. The algorithm can automatically change the template image, and effectively track the target. Replacement of the template

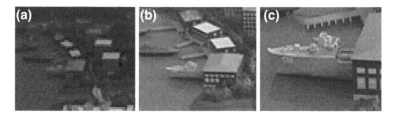

**Fig. 60.4** Three templates from far and near: **a** the template with the farthest distance, **b** the template with the halfway distance, **c** the template with the nearest distance

**Fig. 60.5** Results of target identifying and tracking: **a** identify the target with the first template, **b** identify the target with the second template, **c** identify the target with the second template, **d** identify the target with the third template

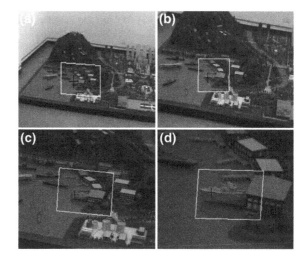

and tracking results are shown in Fig. 60.5. Regardless of the target distance, whether far or near, the algorithm can accurately identify and track the target in real time. The algorithm is proven to have target identification and tracking ability in scenes of perspective transformation, image rotation, or target partial occlusion. Therefore, it is able to meet real-time requirements.

## 60.8  Conclusion

A target recognition and tracking method based on multi-templates is proposed. The method uses a different scale multi-template replacement strategy, and uses Bayesian classifiers to organize target features. The proposed method is proven to have high robustness and real-time performance, and has significant effects in target recognition and tracking.

# References

1. Crimmings TR (1982) A complete set of Fourier descriptors for two-dimensional shapes. IEEE Trans Syst Man Cybernet SMC 12(6):845–855
2. Hu MK (1962) Visual pattern recognition by moment invariants. IRE Trans Inf Theory 8:179–187
3. Flusser J, Suk T (1993) Pattern recognition by affine moment invariants. Pattern Recogn 26(1):167–174
4. Lowe DG (2004) Distinctive image features from scale-invariant keypoints. Int J Comput Vision 60(2):91–110
5. Lowe DG (1999) Object recognition from local scale-invariant features. In: International conference on computer vision, Corfu, Greece, pp 1150–1155
6. Mikolajczyk K, Schmid CA (2005) Performance evaluation of local descriptors. IEEE Trans Pattern Anal Mach Intell 27(10):1615–1630
7. Bay H, Tuytelaars T (2008) SURF: speeded up robust features. Comput Vis Image Underst 110(3):346–359
8. Lepetit V, Fua P (2006) Keypoint recognition using randomized trees. IEEE Trans Pattern Anal Mach Intell 28(9):1465–1479
9. Dong LY, Yuan SM, Liu GY (2007) Image classification based on Bayesian classifier. J Jilin University 45(2):249–253
10. Zheng F, Webb G (2005) A comparative study of semi-naive Bayes methods in classification learning. In: Proceedings of the fourth Australasian data mining conference (AusDM05), pp 141–156
11. Rosten E, Durmmond T (2006) Machine learning for high speed corner detection. In: 9th European conference on computer vision, vol 3951(1), pp 430-443
12. Rosten E, Porter R, Drummond T (2008) Faster and better: a machine learning approach to corner detection. IEEE Trans Pattern Anal Mach Intell 32(1):105–119
13. Fisehler MA, Bolles RC (1981) Random sample consensus: a paradigm for model fitting with applications to image analysis and automated cartography. Commun ACM 24(6):381–395

# Chapter 61
# A Framework of Static Hand Shape Recognition System

Shufen Zhang, Liling Ma and Junzheng Wang

**Abstract** The Shape Context is not rotation-invariant as the gesture features, and the computational cost is expensive. In this paper, a novel method named as Shape Context based on the key points is proposed. The contour points with larger curvature are looked as key points, and the direction of the key point is described as x-axis direction, then Shape Context feature histogram is calculated. These make features translation, scaling and rotation invariant and reduce the time complexity. Meanwhile, the experiments show the method is effective and efficiency in the real-time system.

**Keywords** Hand gesture · Shape context · Invariant · Recognition

## 61.1 Introduction

With the development of technology, the human–computer interaction (HCI) has drawn more and more attention. There are many substitutions for mouse and keyboard, such as head, face, hand, arms or body motion recognition, which are nature and intuitive ways for human. And the technology is mainly divided into sensor-based and vision-based, however, the sensor-based techniques get information using sensors that is not convenience and expensive. So more researchers tend to the vision-based techniques, and there are many related literatures published.

S. Zhang (✉) · L. Ma · J. Wang
School of Automation, Beijing Institute of Technology, 100081 Beijing, China
e-mail: zsf87917@163.com

W. Lu et al. (eds.), *Proceedings of the 2012 International Conference on Information Technology and Software Engineering*, Lecture Notes in Electrical Engineering 212, DOI: 10.1007/978-3-642-34531-9_61, © Springer-Verlag Berlin Heidelberg 2013

There are many applications using HCI system introduced in papers [1, 2], and they can be divided into the three-dimensional(3D) and the two-dimensional (2D) way. Ali Erol et al. [2] reviewed pose estimation systems aiming to capture the real 3D motion of the hand, which is more complicated than the 2D approach. Since 3D needs complicated processes, it is difficult to work in real-time using usual hardware. Therefore, the majority of researchers adopt the 2D approach to meet the requirement of real-time and low computational complexity in the relatively low-precision systems. There are many samples. Sören Lenman et al. [3] showed a overview of HCI using the hand gesture for remote home applications control, which is the outline of the system. Hosub Yoon et al. [4] described a algorithm used for controlling a robot, which has the additional limits of a moving camera, moving objects, various face orientations, and unfixed illuminations. And a system can handle intermittent motion of the camera was proposed by Singh et al. [5], which revealed a robust combining of the motion and color cues using the motion history image. In 2010, Chen et al. [6] developed a real-time human–robot interaction with hand gesture recognition that could be constructed combining color and shape cues, nevertheless, it is restricted to wearing the red glove. In order to get rid of the limit, Choi et al. [7] presented a hand shape recognition system using distance transform and shape decomposition. And the system can work in real-time, however, it can not bear the palm rotation angle too large, that is to say the feature extraction is not rotation invariant.

Sangineto et al. [8] presented a model based approach to articulated hand detection which split this variability problem by separately searching for simple angle models in the input image. This paper supplies a way to detects hands in cluttered backgrounds and various illuminations, and the detection is the first step to the whole recognition system. Porta et al. [9] discussed several techniques including head tracking, face/facial expression recognition, eye tracking, gesture recognition and so on, and the gestures distinguish static and dynamic. It showed the applications in simulating a mouse click event and drawing characters. The HCI will be more complicated, but convenient, natural for us. Several articles imply the development direction of HCI, for example, the multimodal human–computer interaction (MMHCI) system to audio–visual speech recognition [10].

In this paper, a real-time HCI for robot with naked-hand gesture recognition in real time was shown. The rest of the paper is organized as follows: in Sect. 61.2, we introduce some simple background about Shape Context. Next the whole procedure for an image is presented in Sect. 61.3. Especially an efficient rotation invariance algorithm is included. The experimental results are summarized in Sect. 61.4. At last, we conclude in Sect. 61.5.

## 61.2 Related Works

Many papers about computer vision about hand gesture recognition have been published in the past years [11–14]. There are many methods, and they can be classified into model-based methods and model-less methods [7]. The model-based methods recognize hand shapes by comparing input images with a hand model which is well-described 3D model. As mentioned above, it can't reach the requirement of real-time. In contrast, the model-less methods recognize hand shapes by comparing input images or feature values computed from the input images with a database containing 2D template images, feature values related to various hand shapes. Further, it depends on the situation of the applications. And hand segmentation, feature extraction and classification are the critical steps of the processes.

Shape context proposed by Belongie [15], is a successful method for shape recognition. It is has been widely used in many applications: character recognition from license plate images, horse recognition, Gait Recognition, SAR images and so on [16–18]. Since the shape is represented by the points of the contour, the relationship between points can be described by the distance and the angle, and the distribution is called log-polar histogram. Suppose the number of total points is $N$ and one of points is $p_i$, then the distribution of the positions of $N - 1$ remaining points relative to $p_i$: the distance and the angle are quantized into $s$ bins and $t$ bins respectively, then there is $K = s * t$ bins in the histogram:

$$h_i(k) = \#\{q \neq p_i : (q - p_i) \in bin(k)\} \tag{61.1}$$

The collection of shape context for every point in the shape is a redundant and powerful descriptor for the shape.

Suppose one point $p_i$ on the first shape and a point $q_j$ on the second shape, the $\chi^2$ test statistic is used to measure their similarity.

$$C_{ij} \equiv C(p_i, q_j) = \frac{1}{2} \sum_{k=1}^{K} \frac{[h_i(k) - h_j(k)]^2}{h_i(k) + h_j(k)} \tag{61.2}$$

where $h_i(k)$ and $h_j(k)$ denote the $k$-bin normalized histogram at $p_i$ and $q_j$ respectively. By finding the minimizing the total costs of the distance between all pairs of points $p_i$ on the first shape and $q_j$, on the second shape with constraint that the matching be one-to-one.

## 61.3 The Vision System Description

The hand gesture acquired by monocular camera and the image is processed and classified by a person computer. Then the result triggers the robot or entertainment games.

The operational flowchart of the system is shown in Fig. 61.1.

### 61.3.1 Preprocessing of the System

The purpose of hand tracking was tracking a moving area as a region of interest. It could input the result of extracted background with Camshift algorithm [19].

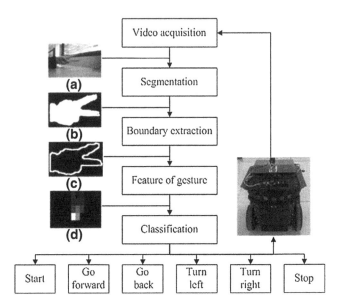

**Fig. 61.1** The operational flowchart of the system

Color features are widely used in skin detection [20, 21], and it is well known method in computer vision. An efficient skin color detection approach should be able to segment the skin color from the intricate background. The primary steps for skin detection in an image using color information are: choose a suitable color space, model the skin and non-skin pixels using a suitable distribution and classify the pixels of the image. In the literature, there are studies using normalized RGB, HSV (or HSI), YCbCr (or YCgCr) and so on. And the existing skin color model methods can be roughly classified into three categories, namely, threshold selection method, parametric methods, and the nonparametric methods [20]. However, the skin color distribution varies distinctly under various illuminations and for different people. Therefore, it is difficult to segment the whole skin area with explicitly threshold and the parametric methods in the actual practice, which results in the wrong recognition rate of the system.

So in our system, we perform the skin detection on an H–S projection of the HSV space (see [21] for more details), which is one of typical nonparametric method estimating the skin color distribution from the training data. Besides, the HSV color space is an intuitive color space, so it approximates the way humans perceive and interpret colors. And a shadow will not lead to a great modification in this color space. We get a probability image through the skin detection, so to get the binary image we use a threshold value. The binary image as it is shown in Fig. 61.1b, and Fig. 61.1a is the original image.

The result of segmentation is no perfect, and the noise in the background and the object can affect the contour of hand. Hence, morphological filtering is used to obtain a complete shape of hand by dilation and erosion operations. There are some skin-like region in the original image, and we detect the maximize area as the region of interest. The canny edge-detection is utilized. Because we get multiple-pixel-wide edges through the edge detector, an edge thinning algorithm named as connectivity preserved edge thinning algorithm is employed in our system [22]. We can get acceptable single-pixel-wide edges with lower computing cost. Figure 61.1c shows, the edge map of the original image.

Next we extract the boundary of the object in the edge image after these processes. As we know, the edge image consists of white pixels as the object, and the black pixels as the background. So we get the points of hand boundary by sliding the eight-connectivity (see [6] for more detail).

### 61.3.2  The Improved Shape Context Descriptor and Recognition

Shape context is invariant to translation and scaling as the gesture features, however, it is not invariant to rotation and the computational cost is expensive. In order to meet the requirements of real-time interaction and rotation invariant, the algorithm needs to be improved. The main idea of the improvements is: the contour points with larger curvature are extracted as "interest points", for every interest point we calculate the oriented Shape Context feature histogram and take the orientation of interest point as x-axis. The steps of the procedure are as follow:

(1) Extract extreme points using the curvature function and these points are "interest points", which looks like the corner points of the object, shown as Fig. 61.2a. And the equations are as follows using the adjacent three points:

$$k = \frac{\dot{x}_i \ddot{y}_i - \dot{y}_i \ddot{x}_i}{(\dot{x}_i^2 + \dot{y}_i^2)^{3/2}} \tag{61.3}$$

$$\begin{cases} \dot{x}_i = (x_{i+1} - x_{i-1})/2, & \ddot{x}_i = x_{i+1} + x_{i-1} - 2x_i \\ \dot{y}_i = (y_{i+1} - y_{i-1})/2, & \ddot{y}_i = y_{i+1} + y_{i-1} - 2y_i \end{cases} \tag{61.4}$$

(2) Get the centroid of the shape and take it as the center of rotation. For every interest point, we rotate the whole object and let this point to the zero orientation (x-axis) using the Eq. (61.5), the objects would then all in roughly the same direction. Figure 61 2b shows one of the key point rotated into the x-axis.

$$\begin{cases} x_i' = x_i \cos\theta + y_i \sin\theta \\ y_i' = y_i \cos\theta - x_i \sin\theta \end{cases} \tag{61.5}$$

(3) Calculate the log-polar histogram according to Eq. (61.1). Figure 61.2c shows the histogram of the shape at one of interest points.

S. Zhang et al.

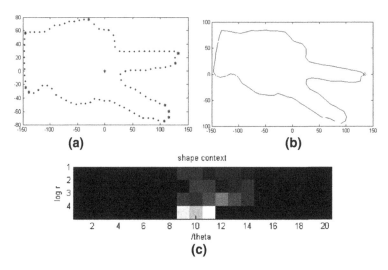

**Fig. 61.2** The procedure of feature extract

The complexity of the SC histograms for a shape is $O(N^2)$. In our system, getting the curvatures of the whole shape is $O(N)$, and the sorting algorithm is $O(N^2)$, and one SC histogram is $O(N)$, that is the complexity is $O(N^2)$. However, the process of recognition not needs the matching, and the complexity of matching time is $O(N^3)$. The complexity is just $O(K^2)$, where $K$ is the number of the interest points much smaller than $N$.

In our system, since it is not necessary to match the points of the hand, we just need to find the similar gesture. We compared one feature histogram of interest point from the identifying gesture with all the feature histograms of interest points from the reference gestures. We found the nearest one and identified the identifying gesture belonged to that one.

## 61.4 Experiments

We defined 6 classes in the system and got the images at different environments under restrictive conditions that the palm faced to the camera. Some examples of the images are shown in Fig. 61.3. There was skin-like region on the background, like the door or desk in the images, and we needed to change model of skin depending on the illumination, and the classification rate is shown in Table 61.1. We used 35 images of each class, and we get the average recognition rate is 89 %.

We used UP-VoyagerII robot as the platform. Our system captured the image including user's hand gesture by CCD camera. The image was processed as mentioned above, and the user's hand gesture could be transformed into proper instruction. At last, the instruction triggered correct action for the mobile robot.

**Fig. 61.3** The predefine hand gestures and parts of samples

**Table 61.1** The confusion matrix of the 6 hand shapes

| Lables | 0 | 1 | 2 | 3 | 4 | 5 |
| --- | --- | --- | --- | --- | --- | --- |
| 0 | 28 | 0 | 2 | 0 | 1 | 1 |
| 1 | 0 | 32 | 0 | 3 | 0 | 3 |
| 2 | 3 | 0 | 32 | 0 | 0 | 0 |
| 3 | 1 | 1 | 0 | 32 | 0 | 1 |
| 4 | 0 | 1 | 0 | 0 | 32 | 0 |
| 5 | 3 | 1 | 1 | 0 | 2 | 31 |
| Recognition rate (%) | 80 | 91 | 91 | 91 | 91 | 89 |

The relevant parameters chose as follows: hysteresis threshold values used 100 and 150 in canny edge-detection, the histogram of shape context is 4 * 20 bins and the number of interest points is 10 and the frame rate is 20 fps. The time processing an image is about 0.06 s.

## 61.5 Conclusion and Future Works

In this paper, we focus on static gesture recognition in the different environment. The key to recognition is to extract the characteristics of the different gestures, and this paper is mainly to improve the shape context approach. The improved shape context is invariant to translation, scaling and rotation. Besides, experimental results show that the method can work effectively and can reach the requirement of real-time.

But there are some shortcomings, the samples of skin needs to collect in different environment, and the system can not work normally if there are one more hands or faces regions bigger than the gesture hand. So it needs more researches in the future.

# References

1. Pavlovic VI, Sharma R, Huang TS (1997) Visual interpretation of hand gestures for human–computer interaction: a review. IEEE Trans Pattern Anal Mach Intell 19:677–695
2. Erol A, Bebis G, Nicolescu M, Boyle RD, Twombly X (2007) Vision-based hand pose estimation: a review. Comput Vis Image Underst 108:52–73
3. Lenman S, Bretzner L, Thuresson B (2002) Computer vision based hand gesture interfaces for human–computer interaction, CID, Centre for User Oriented IT Design NADA, Department of Numerical Analysis and Computer Science KTH (Royal Institute of Technology)
4. Yoon H, Kim D, Chi S, Cho Y (2006) A robust human head detection method for human tracking. In: IEEE/RSJ international conference on intelligent robots and systems, Beijing
5. Singh R. Seth B, Desai UB (2006) A real-time framework for vision based human robot interaction. In: IEEE/RSJ international conference on intelligent robots and systems, Beijing
6. Chen K, Chien C, Chang W, Teng J (2010) An integrated color and hand gesture recognition approach for an autonomous mobile robot. In: 3rd international congress on image and signal processing (CISP), Yantai
7. Choi J, Park H, Park J (2011) Hand shape recognition using distance transform and shape decomposition. In: 18th IEEE international conference on image processing (ICIP), Brussels
8. Sangineto E, Cupelli M (2012) Real-time viewpoint-invariant hand localization with cluttered backgrounds. Image Vis Comput 30:26–37
9. Porta M (2002) Vision-based user interfaces: methods and applications. Int J Hum Comput Stud 57:27–73
10. Jaimes A, Sebe N (2007) Multimodal human–computer interaction: a survey. Comput Vis Image Underst 108:116–134
11. Xiong W, Toh KA, Yau WY, Jiang X (2005) Model-guided deformable hand shape recognition without positioning aids. Pattern Recogn 38:1651–1664
12. Kumar A, Zhang D (2006) Personal recognition using hand shape and texture. IEEE Trans Image Process 15:2454–2461
13. Feng ZQ, Yang B, Chen YH, Zheng YW, Xu T, Li Y, Xu T, Zhu DL (2011) Features extraction from hand images based on new detection operators. Pattern Recogn 44:1089–1105
14. Duta N (2009) A survey of biometric technology based on hand shape. Pattern Recogn 42:2797–2806
15. Belongie S, Malik J, Puzicha J (2002) Shape matching and object recognition using shape contexts. IEEE Trans Pattern Anal Mach Intell 24:509–522
16. Tepper M, Acevedo D, Goussies N, Jacobo J, Mejail M (2009) A decision step for shape context matching. In: 16th IEEE international conference on image processing (ICIP), Cairo
17. Zhai Y, Jia Y, QI C (2009) Gait recognition based on multi-resolution regional shape context. In: Chinese conference on pattern recognition, Nanjing
18. Wei Z, Jie W, Jian G (2011) An efficient SAR target recognition algorithm based on contour and shape context. In: 3rd international Asia-Pacific conference on synthetic aperture radar (APSAR), Seoul

19. Avidan S (2005) 01467482. In: IEEE computer society conference on computer vision and pattern recognition
20. Kakumanu P, Makrogiannis S, Bourbakis N (2007) A survey of skin-color modeling and detection methods. Pattern Recogn 40:1106–1122
21. Vezhnevets V, Sazonov V, Andreeva A (2003) A survey on pixel-based skin color detection techniques. GraphiCon
22. Yu-Song T, Zhou X-M (2004) Connectivity preserved edge thinning algorithm. J Natl University Def Technol 4(26):51–56 (in Chinese)

# Chapter 62
# Face Recognition Using Semi-Supervised Sparse Discriminant Neighborhood Preserving Embedding

Feng Li

**Abstract** A semi-supervised dimensionality reduction algorithm called semi-supervised sparse discriminant neighborhood preserving embedding (SSDNPE) is proposed, which fuse supervised linear discriminant information and unsupervised information of sparse reconstruction and neighborhood with the way of trade-off parameter, inheriting advantages of sparsity preserving projections (SPP), linear discriminative analysis (LDA) and neighborhood preserving embedding (NPE). Experiments operated on Yale, UMIST and AR face dataset show the algorithm is more efficient.

**Keywords** Dimensionality reduction · Sparsity preserving projecting · Linear discriminative analysis · Neighbourhood preserving embedding · Fusion

## 62.1 Introduction

Face recognition is computer applications for automatically identifying. High-dimensional face images are often difficult to do with. Therefore, dimensionality reduction is required. Nowadays researchers have developed numerous dimensionality reduction algorithms. Dimensionality reduction aims at mapping high-dimensional data to a lower dimensional space while preserving the intrinsic geometry of data samples by eliminating noises. The past 20 years has witnessed growing development in dimensionality reduction techniques for face recognition, including include Eigen faces [1], a method employing principal component analysis (PCA) [2] on face images; Fisher faces [3], a method employing linear

F. Li (✉)
School of Computer Science and Technology, Huaqiao University, Xiamen, China
e-mail: fengli502@gmail.com

W. Lu et al. (eds.), *Proceedings of the 2012 International Conference on Information Technology and Software Engineering*, Lecture Notes in Electrical Engineering 212, DOI: 10.1007/978-3-642-34531-9_62, © Springer-Verlag Berlin Heidelberg 2013

discriminative analysis (LDA) [4] on face images; Laplacianfaces [5] a method employing Locality Preserving Projection (LPP) [6] for face representation; neighborhood preserving embedding (NPE) [7] methods for face analysis and recognition. NPE is another linear dimensionality reduction technique proposed by He et al. It is the linearization of the locally linear embedding (LLE) [8] algorithm, which aims at finding a low-dimensional embedding that optimally preserves the local neighborhood structure on the original data manifold.

Since local structure seems to be more important than global structure, NPE usually outperforms PCA and LDA which aim at preserving the global Euclidean structure. However, there are many unlabeled samples that contain plenty of useful discriminant information in practical face recognition. How to make use of them is important for face recognition. Under the background, semi-supervised dimensionality reduction is proposed, which not only make use of unsupervised information contained in many unlabeled samples but also mine exploit fully supervised information implicated labeled samples. On the basic of NPE, Wei et al. [9] proposed neighborhood preserving based semi-supervised dimensionality reduction (NPSSDR). The algorithm not only preserves the must-link and cannot-link constraints but also preserves the local neighborhood structure of input data in the low dimensional embedding subspace by the regularization way, which makes NPSSDR easy to get into collapse in local structure.

Recently sparse learning has been applied in machine learning [10]. Sparsity preserving projections (SPP) [11] for dimensionality reduction is proposed. As a new unsupervised dimensionality reduction algorithm, SPP contains better discriminating classification information. In contrast to PCA, SPP has obvious superiority in preserving nonlinear structure of data, especially classification robustness in face images.

As a supervised dimensionality reduction algorithm, LDA is the common dimensionality reduction algorithm, which aims to find an optimal linear transformation to maximum class discrimination by minimizing the within-class distance and maximizing the between-class distance simultaneously. Motivated SPP and LDA, a semi-supervised sparse discriminant neighborhood preserving embedding (SSDNPE) for face recognition is proposed in the paper. The algorithm inosculates SPP, LDA and NPE with trade-off parameters in the process of dimensionality reduction for face recognition. Experiments based on Yale, UMIST and AR face dataset demonstrate better classification performance of our proposed SSDNPE.

## 62.2 Relational Markov Networks Review

### 62.2.1 Sparity Preserving Projections (SPP)

SPP aims to preserving the sparse reconstruction relations of high-dimensional spatial data in the process of dimensionality reduction [7]. Let $X = \{x_1, x_2, x_3, \ldots, x_n\}$ be the matrix of training samples and let $s_i = [s_{i1}, \ldots, s_{ii-1}, 0, s_{ii+1}, s_{im}]^T \in R^m$ be reconstruction coefficient of sparse $x_i$:

$$x_i = s_{i1}x_1 + \ldots + s_{ii-1}x_{i-1} + s_{ii-1}x_{i+1} + s_{im}x_m \tag{62.1}$$

Let T be the matrix of sparse preserving projection and let be the projection point of sparse reconstruction of high-dimensional, then the objective function of sparse preserving projection is defined by [7]:

$$\min_T \sum_{i=1}^{m} ||T^T x_i - T^T X s_i||^2 \tag{62.2}$$

A constrained condition of $T^T X X^T T = I$ is introduced, Eq. (62.2) can be further transformed into:

$$\min_T \frac{T^T X (I - S - S^T + S^T S) X^T T}{T^T X X^T T} \tag{62.3}$$

Equation (62.3) can be transformed equivalently:

$$\max_T \frac{T^T X S_\alpha X^T T}{T^T X X^T T} \tag{62.4}$$

where $S_\alpha = S + S^T - S^T S$.

### 62.2.2 Linear Discriminant Analysis (LDA)

The objective function of LDA problem is listed as follows:

$$\max_T \frac{T^T S_b T}{T^T S_w T} \tag{62.5}$$

where $S_b$ and $S_w$ are the between-class and within-class scatter matrices, namely

$$S_b = \frac{1}{N} \sum_{i=1}^{c} C_i (\bar{x}_i - \bar{x})(\bar{x}_i - \bar{x})^T \tag{62.6}$$

$$S_w = \frac{1}{N} \sum_{i=1}^{C} \sum_{j=1}^{C_i} (x_{ij} - \bar{x}_i)(x_{ij} - \bar{x}_i)^T \tag{62.7}$$

where $\bar{x} = \frac{1}{N} \sum_{i=1}^{N} x_i$ is the mean of samples, $\bar{x}_i = \frac{1}{C_i} \sum_{i=1}^{C_i} x_{ij}$ is the mean of the class $C_i$.

### 62.2.3 Neighborhood Preserving Embedding (NPE)

Let $X = \{x_1, \ldots, x_n\} \in R^{d \times n}$ NPE is the linearization of LLE. Linearization assumes that for $Y = T^T X = \{y_1, \ldots, y_n\} \in R^{l \times n} (l < d)$, where $T = [t_1, \ldots, t_n]$ is the transformation matrix with its columns as the projective vectors. There are some following main steps of NPE:

(1) Firstly, constructing an adjacency graph $G$. Let $G$ denotes a graph with $m$ nodes. The $i$-th node corresponds to the data point $x_i$. $K$-nearest neighbors and $\varepsilon$neighborhood are two way to construct the adjacency. In many real world applications, it is difficult to choose $K$ or $\varepsilon$. In this work, we adopt the KNN method to construct the adjacency graph.

(2) Secondly, computing the weights. We compute weights on the edges in the adjacency graph $G$. Let W denote the weight matrix with $W_{i,j}$. The weights on the edges can be computed by minimizing the following objective function:

$$\max_{T} \frac{T^T X M X^T T}{T^T X X^T T} \tag{62.8}$$

where $M = (I - W)^T (I - W)$ and $I = diag(1, \ldots, 1)$.

(3) Finally, computing the Projections. We compute the linear projections. Solve the following generalized eigenvector problem:

$$XMX^T a = \lambda XX^T a \tag{62.9}$$

## 62.3 Semi-Supervised Neighborhood Preserving Embedding (SNPE)

### 62.3.1 Movtivated Idea

NPE, SPP and LDA have their own advantages and disadvantages. As unsupervised dimensionality reduction algorithms, NPE aims at finding a low-dimensional embedding that optimally preserves the local neighborhood structure on the original data manifold. NPE usually outperforms PCA and LDA which aim at preserving the global Euclidean structure. NPE employs a nearest neighbor search in the low-dimensional space to yield results to that in the high-dimensional image space as similar as possible. The projections of SPP are sought such that the sparse reconstructive weights can be best preserved. SPP is shown to outperform PCA, LPP and NPE on all the data sets used here, and is very simple to perform like PCA by avoiding the difficulty of parameter selection as in LPP and NPE. Since it remains unclear how to define the locality theoretically for many locality-based algorithms like LPP and NPE, SPP can be considered as an alternative to them. But SPP is sensitive to large variations in pose as many whole-pattern.

LDA is a popular statistical supervised dimensionality reduction technology, it seeks discriminant projection directions by maximizing the ratio of the between-class scatter matrix to the within class scatter matrix and has great classification. However, like other supervised dimensionality reduction algorithms, LDA is easy to reduce into the over-learning problem.

Therefore, to fuse NEP, LDA and SPP will not only inherit their advantages and overcome their shortcomings.

### 62.3.2 Objective Function

Introducing Eq. (62.4), (62.5) and (62.8) with the trade-off parameter $\alpha$ and $\beta$, we define following objective function:

$$\max_{T} \frac{T^T(\varphi S_b + \beta XS_\alpha X^T + (1 - \varphi - \beta)XMX^T)T}{T^T(\varphi S_w + (1 - \varphi)XX^T)T} \tag{62.10}$$

### 62.3.3 Algorithm Steps

**Input:** training samples $X = \{x_1, x_2, x_3, \ldots, x_n\}$, $x_i \in R^{d \times n}$, trade-off parameter $\varphi(0 \leq \varphi \leq 1)$ and $\beta(0 \leq \beta \leq 1)$.
**Output:** projecting matrix $T^{d \times r}(r < d)$.

**Steps:**

(1) According to Eq. (62.2), calculate the sparse reconstructive matrix $S$ and obtain $S_\alpha$.
(2) For $x_i \in X$, construct adjacency graph $W$ with $K$-nearest neighbors way and obtain $M$.
(3) According to Eq. (62.10), calculate generalized eigenvector problem:

$$X(\alpha S_b + \beta XS_\alpha X^T + (1 - \alpha - \beta)XMX^T)X^T t_i = \lambda_i(\alpha S_w + (1 - \alpha)XX^T)t_i \quad \text{and}$$

obtain $T = [t_1, \ldots, t_r] \in R^{d \times r}(r < d)$.

## 62.4 Experiments

### 62.4.1 Experimental Databases

In the paper we select Yale, UMIST and AR face dataset as experimental data. Their descriptions are given as follows:

(1) Yale face database contains 165 face images of 15 individuals. There are 11 images per subject, and these 11 images are, respectively, under the following different facial expression or configuration: center-light, wearing glasses, happy, left-light, wearing no glasses, normal, right-light, sad, sleepy, surprised and wink. Samples of a group of face in Yale are showed in Fig. 62.1.

(2) UMIST face Database consists of 564 images of 20 people. Each covers a range of poses from profile to frontal views. Samples of a group of face in UMIST are showed in Fig. 62.2.

(3) AR face database consists of over 4,000 face images of 126 individuals. For each individual, 26 pictures were taken in two sessions separated by two week and each section contains 13 images. These images include front view of faces with different expressions, illuminations and occlusions. Samples of a group of face in AR are showed in Fig. 62.3.

### 62.4.2 Experimental Setup

For some high-dimensional data, the matrix is sometime singular since the training sample size is much smaller than the feature dimensions. To address this problem, the training set can be first projected into a PCA subspace with the radio of PCA is setted to 1. In order to evaluate the performance of SNPE, SPP, NPE and NPSSDR are compared with our proposed algorithm and the simplest nearest neighbor classifier is adopted. All the experiments were repeated 40 times and average classification accuracy rates are gotten. Specific parameter settings of these algorithms are shown in Table 62.1.

Where BaseLine denotes the simplest nearest neighbor classifier without dimensionality reduction.

### 62.4.3 Experimental Results

L face images as training samples from every group face are randomly selected and remains are tested samples. The number of feature dimension increases gradually with certain increment. Results of algorithms under feature dimension number are shown in Figs. 62.4, 62.5, 62.6, 62.7, 62.8, and 62.9.

From above experimental results, we can draw following conclusion:

**Fig. 62.1** Samples of one group of face in Yale

**Fig. 62.2** Samples of one group of face in UMIST

**Fig. 62.3** Samples of one group of face in AR

**Table 62.1** Specific parameter settings of each algorithm

| Algorithm | Parameter settings |
|---|---|
| Baseline | No |
| SPP | No |
| NPE | $k = 7$ |
| LDA | No |
| SSDNPE | $\varphi = 0.2, \beta = 0.3, k = 7$ |

(1) Although SPP has power robustness on face images, the performance than SPP when the number of training samples is most poor. This demonstrates that the certain number of training samples is required for SPP. LDA outperform SPP and NPE under small training samples, which illuminates that the performance of supervised dimensionality reduction is more than unsupervised dimensionality reduction.

(2) SSDNPE is superior to SPP, NPE and LDA, which demonstrate that the SSDNPE fuse efficiently their feature information.

**Fig. 62.4** Recognition rate versus number of dimension on yale when $L = 3$

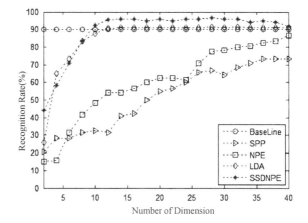

**Fig. 62.5** Recognition rate
versus number of dimension
on yale when $L = 6$

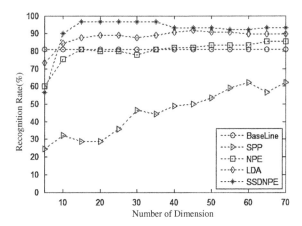

**Fig. 62.6** Recognition rate
versus number of dimension
on AR when $L = 5$

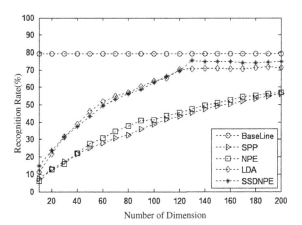

**Fig. 62.7** Recognition rate
vs. number of dimension on
AR when $L = 10$

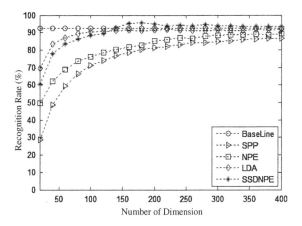

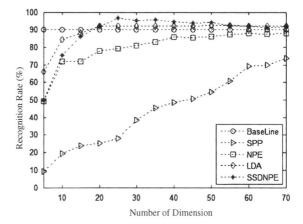

**Fig. 62.8** Recognition rate vs. number of dimension on UMIST when $L = 4$

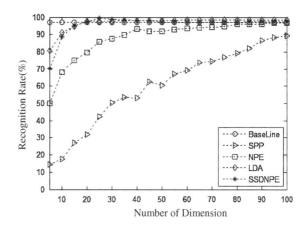

**Fig. 62.9** Recognition rate vs. number of dimension on UMIST when $L = 8$

## 62.5  Conclusion

In this paper, we proposed a dimensionality reduction algorithm for face recognition, called semi-supervised sparse discriminant neighborhood preserving embedding (SSDNPE). On the basic of SPP, LDA and NPE, the algorithm fuses supervised linear discriminant information and unsupervised information of sparse reconstruction and neighborhood, inheriting advantages of SPP, LDA and NPE and overcoming their disadvantages. Experiment results on real face databases show, in contrast to SPP, LDA, NPE and NPSDDR, SSDNPE has more classification performance. However, SSDNPE must transform feature matrices to vectors, ignoring spatial relation of pixels in face images. Tensor SSDNPE is the future study work.

# References

1. Turk M, Pentland A (1991) Eigenfaces for recognition. J Cogn Neurosci 3(1):71–86
2. Hotelling H (1933) Analysis of a complex of statistical variables into principal components. J Edu Psychol 24(6):417–441
3. Belhumeur PN, Hespanha JP, Kriengman DJ (1997) Eigenfaces vs fisher faces: recognition using class specific linear projection. IEEE Trans Pattern Anal Mach Intell 19(7):711–720
4. Fisher RA (1936) The use of multiple measurements in taxonomic problems. Ann Eug 7(2):179–188
5. He XF, Yan SC, Hu YX, Niyogi P, Zhang HJ (2005) Laplacianfaces.IEEE Trans Pattern Anal Mach Intell 27(3):328–340
6. He XF, Niyogi P (2003) Locality preserving projections. In: Proceedings of the conference on advances in neural information processing systems
7. He XF, Cai D, Yan SC, Zhang HJ (2005) Neighborhood preserving embedding. IEEE Int Conf Comput Vision (ICCV) 1208–1213
8. Roweis ST, Saul LK (2000) Nonlinear dimensionality reduction by locally linear embedding. 290(5500):2323–2326
9. Wei J, Peng H (2008) neighborhood preserving based semi-supervised dimensionality reduction. Electron Lett 44(20):1190–1191
10. Wright J, Yang A, Sastry S, Ma Y (2009) Robust face recognition via sparse representation. IEEE Trans Pattern Anal Mach Intell 31(2):210–227
11. Qiao L, Chen S, Tan X (2010) Sparsity preserving projections with applications to face recognition. Pattern Recogn 43(1):331–341

# Chapter 63
# ODTMIS: An On-Demand Transmission Based Medical Image System for Movable Analysis

**Sujun Sun, Dianfu Ma, Hualei Shen and Yongwang Zhao**

**Abstract** Flexibility and timeliness of medical image analysis offered by mobile devices is useful in bedside patient attendance and emergency situations. However, movable management and collaboratively processing for mobile devices with low storage and processing capabilities and usually in poor network environment is still one of the biggest challenges to support this. Consequently, this paper presents an on-demand transmission based medical image system-ODTMIS. It gives functions of medical image management, dynamic browsing and collaborative processing for multi-terminals. ODTMIS only transmits data needed to represent the medical image in resolution and quality suitable for the device while accessing or collaboratively processing, which reduces transmitted image size and increases overall performance. Moreover, it can be available at the present of Web-browsers conveniently. Finally, the paper evaluates the prototype system using several kinds of medical data sets, which demonstrates the good performance of ODTMIS.

**Keywords** Movable analysis · Medical image management · Dynamic browsing · On-demand transmission · Collaborative processing · Web-based

## 63.1 Introduction

The idea for accessing, viewing and processing of medical image outside the radiology reading room spread among the scientists for several years. It becomes increasingly important with the rapid growth of mobile devices, such as laptops,

S. Sun (✉) · D. Ma · H. Shen · Y. Zhao
School of Computer Science & Engineering of Beihang University,
Xueyuan Rd. 37 100191 Haidian District, Beijing, China
e-mail: sujun.sun.my@gmail.com

W. Lu et al. (eds.), *Proceedings of the 2012 International Conference on Information Technology and Software Engineering*, Lecture Notes in Electrical Engineering 212, DOI: 10.1007/978-3-642-34531-9_63, © Springer-Verlag Berlin Heidelberg 2013

PDAs or mobile phones. Typically the flexibility and timeliness of medical image analysis offered by mobile devices is useful in bedside patient attendance and emergency situations. Medical workers can participate in diagnosis wherever they are, which provides great convenience for emergency and saves a lot of time.

Traditional Picture Archiving and Communication System (PACS)-like systems, like DIAGNOSIS [1] and diSNei [2], providing powerful functions to help physicians diagnose, but these systems need special client tools. It will limit the clients to access the same server and share resources without using it, which will take the client processor a lot when processing. For mobile devices with low storage and processing capabilities, it's far more unacceptable to install such tools.

However, as Web-based applications provide cross-platform compatibility in most cases, it will be a reasonable solution to eliminate the defects of the traditional PACS-like systems. Current Web-based medical image systems have been equipped with different technologies and advancements to support different medical services. Some of these advances have improved medical imaging systems remarkably. For example, collaborative systems improve the communication between physicians, and telemedicine provides remote and ubiquitous access to medical services. There are some applications and systems that have provided remote accessibility and collaboration all together, like TeleInViVo [3], CoMed [4]. However, they do not have the ability to manage medical images and give few image processing choices, which can also obviously help doctors to well diagnose diseases. Other Web-based medical image systems like N_CMAM [5], MIFAS [6] gives functions for image access, graphic mark-up, 3D reconstruction and visualization functions, which help medical workers diagnose effectively to some extent.

However, to our best knowledge all of these systems think little of the differences between terminals, they transmit same data size while different terminals accessing the same image. It wastes bandwidth and increases processing burden for mobile devices with low storage and processing capabilities and low resolution displays, and also increase transmission delay especially in poor network environment. What's more, it may lead to terminal equipment breakdown to reveal a high resolution image while accessing or collaboratively processing. Therefor how to transfer images to different terminals for viewing effectively is a key issue and also a challenge for Web-based medical image processing systems.

To address the above issues, we propose ODTMIS: An on-demand transmission based medical image system for universal management and collaborative processing through Web. It takes the terminal differences into account while the visualization and processing of medical image. ODTMIS only transmits data needed to represent the medical image in resolution and quality suitable for the device while accessing or collaboratively processing (We call this on-demand transmission). It reduces the transmitted image size and increases the overall performance, which eliminate limitations deriving from network bandwidth and cross-platform and is of great advantage for mobile devices with low storage and processing capabilities and low resolution displays.

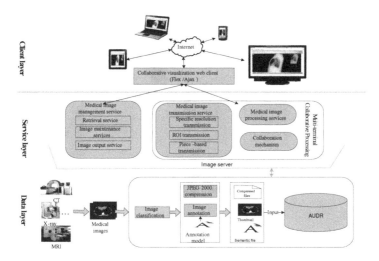

**Fig. 63.1** Architecture of ODTMIS

The organization of the rest of the paper is as follows: Sect. 63.2 gives the architecture and design of ODTMIS. Functions of ODTMIS are described in Sect. 63.3. In Sect. 63.4, the experimental results are presented. Conclusion is in Sect. 63.5.

## 63.2 Architecture and Design

Figure 63.1 presents the architecture. As can be observed, the entire system can be logically divided into three layers and functionally divided into three subsystems. The three layers are data layer, service layer, and client layer, which are respectively used for data storage, data management, data processing and visualization. The three subsystems are medical image management subsystem (MIMS), medical image transmission subsystem (MITS), and multi-terminal collaborative processing subsystem (MCPS).

MIMS, as shown in Fig. 63.2, uses Advanced Unstructured Data Repository (AUDR) [7] to index image. MIMS comprises JPEG format thumbnails storage and JPEG2000 [8] compressed images storage. JPEG format thumbnails are mainly used for quickly scanning by Web-browsers after retrieving. JPEG2000 compressed images are for on-demand transmission for high resolution medical images which is difficult to be displayed for mobile devices with low storage and processing capabilities and low resolution displays. The reason we adopt it is that JPEG2000 has many excellent features, like lossless and lossy compression/ decompression, ROI, random stream access. And our transmission service allows HTTP connection rather than JPIP, which needs special client and takes more

**Fig. 63.2** Medical image
management

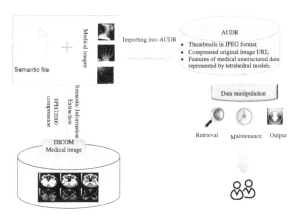

processor resources. This paper gives three main aspects for medical image online management, including medical image retrieve, maintenance and essential information output for diagnosis.

MITS is the core of transmitting appropriate image to different terminals using on-demand transmission. It supports specific resolution and ROI transmission. On-demand transmission mainly uses the random stream access feature of JPEG2000. It extracts data interested or needed to represent the medical image in resolution and quality suitable for the device from the compressed medical image while accessing or collaboratively processing. Figure 63.3 shows the transmission process. The first request is about file information with the response containing image height and width, and DWT-Level, and the second is image data request, which transfer the interest data. The main process is as follows: ExtURLResolver analyses the request, then call the JPEG2000 related API given in Scalable Trans Frame to get what the client want, finally the resolver gives response to the client.

MCPS includes remote processing services and collaborative mechanism, and uses on-demand transmission to achieve the purpose of collaborative processing among different terminals. We adopt publish-subscribe [9] model to achieve collaborative processing among terminals. And in the execution procedure, the collaborative terminals request results which are suitable for themselves in resolution and quality. When a user accesses to medical server to process a medical image, each operation of the user changes the state of message service in the server and result of the operated image is saved as a JPEG2000 format picture, called result image. And immediately, this changed state triggers synchronization event of terminals which are in the same collaborative session. Then, the users calculate the best image size for them and request the result through on-demand transmission service, after that a collaborative operation is accomplished, and the next operation can be taken by any user who received the permission.

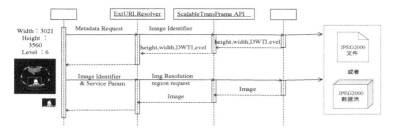

**Fig. 63.3** Transmission process of data request

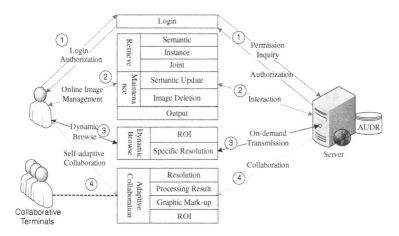

**Fig. 63.4** Functions map

## 63.3 Main Functions

In this section, we present the main functions of ODTMIS. Figure 63.4 shows the function map of the whole system. The functions are mainly divided into four parts: login, image management, dynamic browsing and self-adaptive collaboration. Dynamic browsing uses on-demand transmission to make the client view every resolution level (JPEG2000 permits) they want. Self-adaptive collaboration deals with the collaborative operation between different terminals, and makes the data transmitted suitable for their own resolution.

Figure 63.5 shows the functions of medical image management. There are three ways to retrieve data in ODTMIS: semantic retrieval, instance retrieval and joint retrieval. Semantic retrieval uses basic and semantic features to find images. Instance retrieval uses existing image to help doctors find similar images. Joint retrieval mainly combines both semantic and instance retrieval. Image maintenance allows medical works to edit or add essential information about an image. Finally, "output" organizes information related to a medical image and output it to a word document when necessary. The first one is about retrieve, which allows

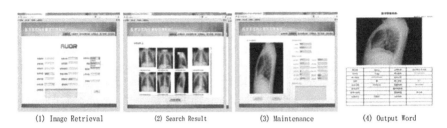

(1) Image Retrieval          (2) Search Result          (3) Maintenance          (4) Output Word

**Fig. 63.5** Image management

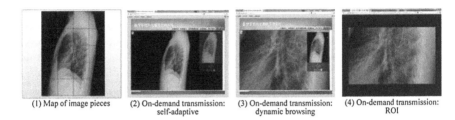

(1) Map of image pieces    (2) On-demand transmission:    (3) On-demand transmission:    (4) On-demand transmission:
                                  self-adaptive                  dynamic browsing                  ROI

**Fig. 63.6** Image transmission

user to upload instance image. The second picture shows the search results. The third means image maintenance, and the last one is output word document.

Figure 63.6 shows the dynamic browsing. The first picture shows the map of pieces. You can set to $64 \times 64$, $128 \times 128$, $256 \times 256$ or others appropriate. The second picture show the result of image transmission right to the terminal, and the last two separately refer to dynamic browsing and ROI.

In ODTMIS, Medical image self-adaptive collaboration functions include:

1. Adaptive display, which use on-demand transmission to transmit image size just needed.
2. Find edges, which can find edge of an organ in an image.
3. Add noise, which can add noise to an image.
4. Smooth, which can smooth an image.
5. Sharpen, which can highlight the key area of the image.
6. LUT, which can display the different issues more outstandingly.
7. Window/Level, which can help doctors obtain clinically useful information from medical images.
8. Rotation, which can rotate an image in a two dimensional space.
9. Graphic mark-up, which allows doctors to graphically mark lesions.

The initialization UI is shown in Fig. 63.7 picture (1). You can hide the menu on the right by click the "Hide" button on the left to give more space for image display. Picture (2) and (3) in Fig. 63.7 show the collaboratively Window/Level result. Picture (4) and (5) present the effects of collaborative LUT processing and

| (1) Initialization | (2) Collaborative Window/Level for Tablet Computer | (3) Collaborative Window/Level for Mobile Phone | (4) Collaborative LUT and Graphic Mark-up for Tablet Computer | (5) Collaborative LUT and Graphic Mark-up for Mobile Phone |

**Fig. 63.7**  Collaborative functions

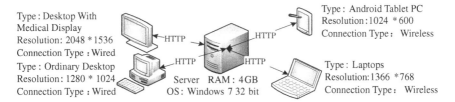

**Fig. 63.8**  Experiment environment

graphic mark-up among different terminals. All processing results above can be properly displayed according to the terminal resolution, which minimizes data size transmitted and lessen terminal processing burden.

## 63.4  Experiments and Results

To evaluate ODTMIS, we have performed experiments on various medical data with many repeated tests. The experiment environment is shown in Fig. 63.8. We use four types of terminal with wired and wireless connection type. Most of image data involved are from the hospitals which are partners of our laboratory, such as Perking University Third Hospital (PUTH) in China. Therefore, these real medical data could be very convincing for evaluating the performance of ODTMIS.

The experiment and results of the system are as follows:

Figure 63.9 picture (1) shows the result of various terminals access an image with size 1,2841 KB and resolution 2,374 × 2,766 using PNG as output format considering different image size and output format have no effect on the transmission trend. "Width" and "Height" represent the horizontal and vertical resolution of terminals. "Data Transferred" represents data size transmitted. Green line with squares and red with dots are used to distinguish on-demand and all at once transmission. Star is the XY plane projection of "Data Transferred" to facilitate data comparison.

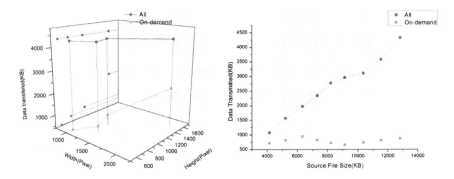

**Fig. 63.9** Experiment result

Obviously, image amount transmitted by "on-demand transmission" varies with terminal resolution and won't exceed "All at once transmission" at worst. Therefore, for small mobile terminals and poor network, "on-demand transmission" transmits much less image and makes more reasonable use of bandwidth.

Figure 63.9 picture (2) shows the data transmission result of a desktop with resolution 1,280 × 1,024 using PNG as output format. It is obvious that, in this situation, data amount transmitted by "on-demand transmission" hardly increases with the increase of original image size, while "All at once transmission" is almost proportional to the increase of original image size.

## 63.5 Conclusion

We present ODTMIS, which provides a Web-based environment for physicians located in different sites or using various terminals to process and analyze medical images collaboratively. Meanwhile, ODTMIS also provides functions of medical image management including retrieve, maintenance and information output.

In ODTMIS, we adopt publish-subscribe model to achieve collaborative processing. In order to enhance the performance among different terminals, on-demand transmission method is used to minimize data transmitted and lessen terminal burden. Furthermore, all of the functions provided by ODTMIS are based on Web service technology. It can be easily accessed as long as users have a general Web-browser with Internet connection.

**Acknowledgments** This work was funded by the National Major Research Plan of Infrastructure Software (grant number 2010ZX01042-002-001) and National Natural Science Foundation of China (NSFC) (grant number 61003017).

# References

1. Mougiakakou SG, Valavanis I (2006) Diagnosis: a telematics enabled system for medical image archiving, management and diagnosis assistance. International workshop on imaging systems and techniques, pp 43–48
2. Alberola-Lopez C et al (2000) DiSNei: a collaborative environment for medical images analysis and visualization. Int Conf Med Image Comput Assist Interv 3:814–823
3. Coleman J, Goettsch A et al (1996) TeleInViVo$^{TM}$: towards collaborative volume visualization environments. Comput Graphics 20(6):801–811
4. Sung MY, Kim MS, Kim EJ, Yoo JH, Sung MW (2000) CoMed: a real-time collaborative medicine system. Int J Med Inf 57(2–3):117–126
5. Wang V, Rabsch C, Liu P (2008) Native web browser enabled SVG-based collaborative multimedia annotation for medical images. In: Proceedings of the IEEE 24th international conference on data engineering, ICDE 2008, April, pp 1219–1228
6. Yang CT, Chen CH et al (2008) MIFAS: Medical image file accessing system in co-allocation data grids. IEEE Asia–Pacific services computing conference, pp 769–774
7. Liu XL et al (2011) AUDR: an advanced unstructured data repository. In: 6th international conference on pervasive computing and applications, IEEE press, pp 462–469
8. Skodras A, Christopoulos C, Ebrahimi T (2001) The JPEG2000 still image compression standard. IEEE signal processing magazine, pp 36–58
9. Balderson J, Ent P, Heider J (2009) Professional adobe flex 3. Wiley Publishing, pp 870–894 (in Chinese)

# Chapter 64
# Ship Target Segmentation in ISAR Images

Wang Jun and Wan Dongdong

**Abstract** For problem of ship target segmentation, this paper firstly uses CFAR algorithms, which is based on K-distribution, to segment ISAR images, then applies morphological image processing, to improve segmentation results. Morphological algorithm can not only effectively filter out noise, but also retain original image information. The final step is to remove non-target area. Segmentation experimental results show that the methods given in this article can be effective on ship target segmentation.

**Keywords** SAR/ISAR · CFAR algorithm · Image segmentation · Morphological methods

## 64.1 Introduction

Synthetic aperture radar (SAR) or inverse synthetic aperture radar (ISAR) as an advanced and active microwave remote sensing, with its advantages of all-weather, all-time detection, is increasingly becoming important. It is mainly used for battlefield reconnaissance, marine detection, camouflage identification and discovery of false targets in the military field; in the marine detection, SAR/ISAR can all-time all-weather detection ships on the sea, which is based on reflective

W. Jun (✉) · W. Dongdong
BUAA Electronic and Information Engineering Institute, Beijing, China
e-mail: wangj203@buaa.edu.cn

W. Dongdong
e-mail: wandongd@163.com

W. Lu et al. (eds.), *Proceedings of the 2012 International Conference on Information Technology and Software Engineering*, Lecture Notes in Electrical Engineering 212, DOI: 10.1007/978-3-642-34531-9_64, © Springer-Verlag Berlin Heidelberg 2013

properties of ship target itself and its wake characteristics, and through extracting characteristics of ship targets in SAR/ISAR images to identify ship target.

Image segmentation of ship targets at sea, especially the combat ship target, has been a hot issue at home and abroad, because it is an important foundation and prerequisite for reliable capture at sea and recognition of ship targets.

So far, people have proposed a lot of segmentation methods based on SAR images. Some methods firstly use filtering to reduce speckle noise, and then use a similar approach with optical image to SAR images. For multi-view case, these methods can get better results, but in strong noise case, it will result in loss of detail characteristics of images. In addition, one kind of methods is used in many cases, which is that making use of statistical properties of SAR image to segment images. Such as, MUM, which is based on matrix characteristics, segments SAR image into small pieces, and then calculate the first order and second order statistics of every region. This method will not get inaccurate second-order statistical properties if the initial partition is too small, while bigger initial partition will lead to lower partition details.

In [1], for SAR images, the author constructed an approach based on Markov Random Field (MRF) and morphological operations, which is high precision, but slow in segmentation, the algorithm may fall into local optimization. In [2], according to inherent multiplicative spot noise of SAR images, the probable competing networks for SAR images segmentation takes advantage of pixel space adjacency relationship, but don't consider intensity information. In [3], combining with SAR images and wavelet transform which has characteristics of multi-resolution analysis, the author uses wavelet transform to extract texture characteristics information of SAR images for segmentation. In [4], based on active contour, it gives integrated active contour model, which is adapted in SAR images segmentation, by edges and regional co-song movement to achieve SAR images segmentation. In [5], the author uses space matrix of SAR image as the vaccine of immune algorithm, and uses immune algorithm to search the partition result, and converge to the optimal.

So far, SAR image segmentation algorithms [6] still include sea ice segmentation algorithm, which applies data mining; unsupervised segmentation algorithm based on Poisson distribution; optimized edge detection algorithm; maximum likelihood region growing and simulated annealing to a combination of segmentation algorithm and so on. These methods, some are based on assumption that, others are based on gray information [7]. Although there are a variety of methods, but we still need to analyze characteristics of ship images.

This article firstly uses local window CFAR algorithm for target detection for SAR image, which is based on K-distribution and sea clutter model, and then use mathematical morphology operations method for image segmentation processing, and finally clean the non-target area of pixels to obtain final segmentation results.

## 64.2  Principle and Methods

### 64.2.1  Local Window CFAR Algorithm Based on K Distribution

Two-parameter CFAR target detection algorithm [8] is based on the assumption that background clutter is obeyed on Gaussian distribution, and this algorithm uses local sliding window to adapt to localized changes of background clutter. However Gaussian distribution model for two-parameter CFAR algorithm is not suitable to describe sea clutter, in most cases, sea clutter shows distribution characteristics of a long tail, K-distribution model [9] will better describe grass and other ground clutter and sea clutter.

For SAR images of uneven sea background, Jin song has proposed a new algorithm, which uses local sliding window concept of two-parameter CFAR algorithm to combine with K-distribution CFAR algorithm.

The algorithm uses local sliding window to detect each image pixel, and defines two local sliding windows around it: protective window and background window. The background window is used for background clutter statistics in order to estimate target detection threshold. The purpose of protective window is to prevent the target pixel leaking into the background window to affect the statistical validity of background clutter.

Because ship is in any direction, sliding window is square. The window size is selected based on experience. In general, the side length of protective window is taken as two times as the size of a large ship targets in the image.

For each pixel to be detected in the image, perform the following steps.

1. Statistical calculate the intensity of pixels in background window, respectively, to estimate the mean and and variance [10].

$$E(x) = \frac{1}{N} \sum_{i=1}^{N} x_i \qquad (64.1)$$

$$Var(x) = \frac{1}{N} \sum_{i=1}^{N} x_i^2 - \left( \frac{1}{N} \sum_{i=1}^{N} x_i \right)^2 \qquad (64.2)$$

Where: $x_i$ is the pixel intensity; $N$ is total number of pixels of background window.

2. Calculate the mean and shape parameter of K distribution probability density function.

K-distribution probability density function of sea clutter in SAR images can be written as [11]:

$$p(x) = \frac{2}{x\Gamma(v)\Gamma(L)} \left( \frac{Lvx}{\mu} \right)^{\frac{L+v}{2}} K_{v-L} \left( 2\sqrt{\frac{Lvx}{\mu}} \right) \qquad (64.3)$$

Where: $x$ is the pixel intensity $(x > 0)$; $\mu$ is the mean; $v$ is shape parameter; $L$ is the looks of SAR image; $\Gamma(\bullet)$ is Gamma function; $K_{v-L}$ is $v - L$ order correction of the Bessel function.

The relationship between shape parameter and statistical variance of K-distribution can defined as:

$$Var(x) = \left[\left(1 + \frac{1}{v}\right)\left(1 + \frac{1}{L}\right) - 1\right]\mu^2 \qquad (64.4)$$

Therefore, we can easily get K-distribution mean and shape parameters based on the calculation in first step, that is, with Eq. (64.1) and (64.2) to get estimates, as K-distribution of the mean and variance, respectively, and then substitute into Eq. (64.4), which can be anti-solve the shape parameter, so we can get a complete mathematical expression of the K-distribution.

3. Solve false alarm probability equation to calculate the target detection threshold.

Based on K-distribution probability density function in second step, solvie the equation of false alarm probability

$$1 - P_{fa} = \int_{0}^{I_c} p(x)dx \qquad (64.5)$$

From Eq. (64.5), we can get detection threshold $I_c$. Where $P_{fa}$ is false alarm probability, its value is $10^{-7} \sim 10^{-9}$ in general.

To solve the Eq. (64.5), we need to integral to calculate distribution function $F(x)$ of K-distribution [12]. Because the calculation is so complicated, we use commonly the approximate formula

$$F(x) = \frac{\lambda + \alpha - 1}{(\lambda - \alpha + 1)(\lambda + \alpha + 1)} t^{\lambda+1} K_\alpha(t)_1 F_2\left(1; \frac{\lambda - \alpha + 3}{2}, \frac{\lambda + \alpha + 1}{2}; \frac{t^2}{4}\right) +$$
$$\frac{1}{(\lambda - \alpha + 1)(\lambda + \alpha + 1)} t^{\lambda+2} K_{\alpha-1}(t)_1 F_2\left(1; \frac{\lambda - \alpha + 3}{2}, \frac{\lambda + \alpha + 3}{2}; \frac{t^2}{4}\right)$$

Where: $t = 2\sqrt{\frac{Lvx}{u}}$; $\alpha = v - L$; $\lambda = v + L - 1$ $F_2(a; b; c; z) = \sum_{k=0}^{+\infty} \frac{\Gamma(b)\Gamma(c)\Gamma(a+k)}{\Gamma(a)\Gamma(b+k)\Gamma(c+k)} \frac{z^k}{k!}$

is generalized hyper-geometric function.

4. Target detection decision

Based on detection threshold $I_c$ in third step, judge to be detected pixels whether are target pixels. The decision rule of target is

$$X_T \underset{\leq}{\overset{>}{\phantom{=}}} I_c \qquad (64.6)$$

When $X_T > I_c$, it is target; when $X_T \leq I_c$, it is background.

## 64.2.2 SAR Image Segmentation Based on Mathematical Morphology

Mathematical morphology [13] is a science which has a rigorous mathematical theory that is based on morphology concept, and has been successfully used in image processing and pattern recognition. Morphological operations is an important image processing method, including erosion, dilation, opening operation and closing operation of four kinds of basic operations, it can filter, segment, feature extraction and edge detection on binary image.

Dilation is "extended" or "thicker" operation in the binary image. A is be dilate by B, denoted by $A \oplus B$, which is defined as $A \oplus B = \left\{ z | (\hat{B})_z \cap A \neq \emptyset \right\}$, where $\emptyset$ is empty set, B is the structural element. Dilation is a collection which is composed of origin location of all structural elements, where the mapping and translation of B overlaps at least some parts of A.

Erosion "shrinkage" or "refine" the object in the binary image. A is eroded by B which is labelled as $A \ominus B$, defined as $A \ominus B = \left\{ z | (B)_z \cap A^c \neq \emptyset \right\}$. In other words, A being eroded by B is a collection of origin positions of all structural elements, where the translation of B do not overlap with background of A.

A is opened by B that can be credited for $A \circ B$, it is the results that A is eroded by B and then be dilated by B: $A \circ B = (A \ominus B) \oplus B$. Morphological opening operation completely deletes the area of object that can't contain structural elements, and smooth the contours of object, disconnects the narrow connection, remove the small prominent part.

A is be closed by B that can be credited for $A \cdot B$ it is the result of erosion after first dilation: $A \cdot B = \{A \oplus B\} \ominus B$. Morphological closing operator will smooth the outline of object, but different to opening operation, closing operation will connect the narrow gap together to form a slender curved mouth, and fill small holes of structure elements.

This paper will select closing operation for image processing, basing on ship detection results and actual characteristics,

## 64.2.3 Segmentation Processes

Summarizing the above analysis, segmentation processes of ship targets that is based on SAR/ISAR images can be described as follows [14]:

1. Detect and reduce vertical stripes of image. These stripes that only have a few pixels wide are related to image features, they may be generated by multiple reflections of internal movement of ships or from a moving sea level.
2. Smooth image noise with a low-pass filter.
3. Use CFAR algorithm that is based on K distribution of local window to threshold segment on the smoothed image.

**Fig. 64.1** Image
segmentation process flow
chart

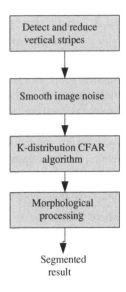

4. Morphological processing after image threshold segmentation.
5. Use geometric clustering algorithm to remove the non-target point within the target area (Fig. 64.1).

## 64.3 Experiment Results and Analysis

This article uses the algorithm to do segmentation experiments for been given ISAR images of ship. The experimental results are shown in Fig. 64.2. Forming the original ISAR image based on the given image data, as shown in Fig. 64.2a, for image partition of ship target on sea, we firstly need to separate ship target from background clutter, since sea clutter is the main interference source for sea targets, so it is necessary to understand and analyze the statistical characteristics of sea clutter. This paper selects K-distribution model as a model of sea clutter, because K-distribution compared to other distribution, has a complete theoretical basis, provide accurate background sea clutter distribution model, and reflect better complex sea of ship targets. According to K-distribution model, using the CFAR algorithm to calculate target detection threshold, and do not apply it for threshold segmentation, but according to the threshold to reduce the vertical stripes, as shown in Fig. 64 2b. Since ISAR images with speckle noise, in order to smooth the image, lee filter is used to remove noise from images, as shown in Fig 64.2c. Apply the threshold to the smoothed image to distinguish target with background, the results is a binary image, as shown in Fig. 64.2d. In order to get better segmentation results, apply morphological closing operation to the segmented image, as shown in Fig. 64.2e. After morphological processing, the effect of target area is

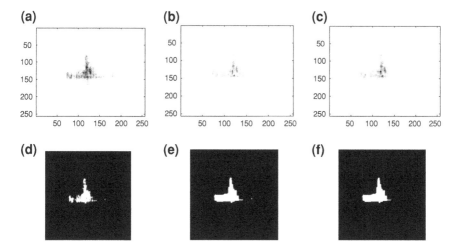

**Fig. 64.2** Segmentation processing. (**a**) Original ISAR image, (**b**) unstreaked image, (**c**) smoothed image, (**d**) threshold image, (**e**) morphological processing image, (**f**) segmented image

better, but there are still individual non-target area, apply geometric clustering method. Firstly label regions of target image, and then remove the non-target area according to marks, the final segmentation results, is shown in Fig. 64 2f.

## 64.4  Conclusion

Image segmentation is the key for image processing and image analysis [15]. Segmentation results are good or not that have a direct impact on image understanding. Especially for interpretation of ship target, image segmentation plays an important role to further target identification. For problem of ship target segmentation, this paper firstly uses CFAR algorithms based on K-distribution to segment ISAR images, so target area in these images are separated from background clutter. Then this article applies morphological image processing, to improve segmentation results. Morphological algorithm can not only effectively filter out noise, but also retain the original image information. The final step is to remove non-target area. ISAR images segmentation experimental results show that methods given in this article can be effective on the ship target segmentation, the results were satisfactory.

# References

1. Weiping Ni, Weidong Yan, Bianhui (2011) SAR image segmentation based on MRF model and morphological operation. Optics Control 18(1):32–36 (in Chinese)
2. Xiaorong X, Yangning Z, Rongchun Z, Duan F (2004) SAR image segmentation based on wavelet transform. Comput Eng 30(7):11–12 (in Chinese)
3. Ruihui P, Xiangwei W, Yongsheng L (2011) An integrated active contour-based SAR imaging segmentation method. J Astron 32(7):1605–0611 (in Chinese)
4. Bo H, Fulong M, Li-cheng J (2007) Research on immune algorithm based method for SAR image segmentation. J Electron Info Technol 29(2):375–378 (in Chinese)
5. Jiongsong Z, OuYang Y, Minhui Z (2006) SAR image of marine target detection. Ocean Press, Beijing (in Chinese)
6. Panfei LEI, Qinghe SU, Gangyi Y (2011) Research on detection of ship target from SAR image. Imaging Technol (4):40–45 (in Chinese)
7. Han X, Li J, Sun M (2005) Research of ship targets segmentation algorithms in SAR image. Microelectron Comput 22(6):41–47 (in Chinese)
8. Song Jianshe, Zheng YongAn (2008) SAR image understanding and application. Science Press, Beijing (in Chinese)
9. Pastina C, Spina C (2009) Multi-feature based automatic recognition of ship targets in ISAR. IET Radar Sonar Navig 3(4):406–423
10. Musman S, Kerr D, Bachmann C (1996) Automatic recognition of ISAR ship images. IEEE Trans Aerosp Electron Syst 32(4):1392–1404
11. LEE J-S, Jurkevich I (1989) Segmentation of SAR images. IEEE Trans Geosci Remote Sensing 27(6):674–679
12. Lemarechal R, Fjortoft R, Marthon P (1998) SAR images segmentation by morphorlogical methods. SPIE 3497:111–121
13. Estable S, Teufel F, Ullmanu T (2009) Detection and classification of offshore artificial objects in TerraSAR-X images: first outcomes of the DeMarine-DEKO project. IEEE
14. Ei-Zarrt A, Ziou D, Wang S, Jiang Q (2002) Segmentation of SAR images. Pattern Recogniton 35:713–724
15. Migliaccio M, Gamberdella A, Nunziata F (2008) Ship detection over single-look complex SAR images. IEEE of International Symposium

# Chapter 65
# The Study of Target Tracking Method in Video Surveillance

Guoqiang Wang, Lan Wang and Jingquan Wang

**Abstract** In intelligent video surveillance, the theories of Particle Filter and Mean-shift are the most classic in target tracking algorithm. But, Particle Filter algorithm exists degradation phenomena, large amount of calculation and some other disadvantages. Although Mean-shift algorithm has less calculation, it will result in tracking lost when it encounters occlusion. In allusion to the problems mentioned above, this paper adopts a method that Mean-shift is embedded to tracking framework of Particle Filter, when it encounters occlusion, the algorithm switches to Particle Filter for continuing tracking, and uses resampling methods to suppress the particle degradation phenomena. And when it encounters noncon-clusion, it uses Mean-shift algorithm to improve the tracking real-time and robustness. The results show that the adopted algorithm has more real-time and robustness than any single traditional algorithm.

**Keywords** Target tracking · Particle filter · Mean-shift

## 65.1 Introduction

Object Tracking is a hot research in the field of computer vision. Object tracking technology in the video image can be applied to many fields, such as video surveillance, biomedical, traffic control [1] and so on. It fuses the advanced

G. Wang (✉) · L. Wang · J. Wang
Electric Engineer College of Heilongjiang University, Harbin, China
e-mail: wangguoqiang@hlju.edu.cn

L. Wang
e-mail: 3jia3jia@163.com

J. Wang
e-mail: wjq0451@126.com

W. Lu et al. (eds.), *Proceedings of the 2012 International Conference on Information Technology and Software Engineering*, Lecture Notes in Electrical Engineering 212, DOI: 10.1007/978-3-642-34531-9_65, © Springer-Verlag Berlin Heidelberg 2013

technology and research related to the field, such as image processing, pattern recognition, artificial intelligence, automatic control and computer application technology, and has broad apply foreground and practical value. Presently, most attention for tracking algorithm can be roughly divided into two categories: the algorithms based on stochastic model and based on determined data [2].

The tracking based on stochastic model is a target state estimation algorithm. Particle Filter is the most representative type of algorithms. Particle Filter algorithm can handle nonlinear situations on occlusion and background interference. However, it has large amount of calculation and degradation phenomena, and therefore, its widespread use is by restricted. In general principle, resampling [3] is used to solve degradation issues, but resampling can make loss of diversity of particle. Mean-shift is a tracking algorithm based on determined data. It has optimization features of rapid convergent. This feature allows tracking with high real-time, but at the same time, when it encounters occlusion, it can not guarantee tracking robustness, so as to result in tracking failure. In allusion to the problems mentioned above, this paper adopts a method that Mean-shift is embedded to tracking framework of Particle Filter, when it encounters occlusion, the algorithm switches to Particle Filter for continuing tracking, and uses resampling methods to suppress the particle degradation phenomena. And when it encounters nonconclusion, it uses Mean-shift algorithm to improve the tracking real-time and robustness.

## 65.2 Conventional Algorithms

### 65.2.1 The Principle of Particle Filter

The Particle Filter is a statistical filtering method by based on non-parametric Monte Carlo method and the recursive Bayesian [4]. It is applied to non-Gaussian background and nonlinear stochastic systems represented by any state-space model, and precision can approximate the optimal estimation. It is a very effective method to calculate posterior probability [5] from non-Gaussian to nonlinear observer data.

Here's the basic idea: firstly, target state needs random sampling. Next, the weights of samples need to be calculated. In the end, weights of random samples are used to represent estimated value of target state. This algorithm is that using approximate solution of updating a posterior probability density recursive an approximate Bayesian solution. According to the theory of Monte Carlo, when the number of particles is large, the accuracy is approximating to optimal estimation, but, at the same time, calculation also increases significantly.

The basic flow of Particle Filters in target tracking [6] is as follows.

### 65.2.1.1 State Transition Model

The system state transition is particle propagation–refers to the update process of the time of the target state. Take solving Posterior probability of the target state at time k as an example, particle propagation obeys the first-order auto-regressive process (ARP) equation.

$$x_k = Ax_{k-1} + Bw_{k-1} \qquad (65.1)$$

Which, $\{x_k, k \in N\}$ represents target state at time k, $w_{k-1}$ is normalized noise; A and B are constants. The second-order ARP model can be expressed as follows:

$$x_k = Ax_{k-2} + Bw_{k-1} + Cw_{k-1}. \qquad (65.2)$$

### 65.2.1.2 Particle Update

After the particles spread, it is needed to observe the degree of similarity between target state represented each particle and the true state of target. Particles of closing to true state of target are given larger weights, on the contrary, smaller weights. In frame k, all the particles are $x_k\left((x,y)_k^T, w_k\right), x_k^i\left((x_i,y_i)_k^T, w_k^i\right)$ indicates that the positional parameters of the particles. In the current frame, weights of updating the particle are:

$$w_k^i = w_{k-1}^i p\left(z_k | x_k^i\right). \qquad (65.3)$$

### 65.2.1.3 Take Representation of Weighted Sum of Particle Weighted to Determine the Final Location of the Target

$$x^{new} = \sum x_k^i w_k^i \qquad (65.4)$$

After determining the location of the target, the particles may be degradation, so as to resampling.

### 65.2.1.4 Resampling

Resampling is a way to reduce the particle deprivation. The idea is to resampling for the probability density function of the particles and the corresponding weights to increase the number of larger weights particles. Therefore, the particles of larger weights are repeatedly copied, and particle of smaller weights may be discarded for improving tracking validity.

## 65.2.2 The Principle of Mean-Shift

Mean-shift theory [7, 8] is a fast pattern matching algorithm based on the non-parametric kernel density estimation, and its essence is a process that continuous iterative search for optimal solutions. Applied to target tracking, it needs to use target detection or manually to determine the tracking target, then calculate the histogram distribution of weighted target window of the kernel function. Use the same method to calculate the histogram distribution of the current frame corresponding to the target candidate model window. Target model and target candidate model make use of Bhattacharyya coefficient between two histograms as their similarity. Following the principle of the largest coefficient, target window moves along biggest of increasing density in the direction until the actual location. Its essence is that Mean-shift vector is calculated, and it makes use of the vector to iteratively update the center position of kernel function window. Assume that location of given particle S is, and continuous iteration to find its new location.is defined as follows:

$$y_{new} = \frac{\sum_{i=1}^{m}\left(x_i w_i g\left(\frac{\|y_0 - c_0\|^2}{h^2}\right)\right)}{\sum_{i=1}^{m}\left(w_i g\left(\frac{\|y_0 - c_0\|^2}{h^2}\right)\right)} \tag{65.5}$$

Where: $x_i$ is ith pixel coordinates; $w_i$ is weighted vector of the particle; $g(\cdot)$ is Gaussian kernel function; h is bandwidth of the kernel function. At $\|y_{new} - y_0\| < T$, it needs to set the threshold T for determining iteration stop condition. When particles move to a local optimum position, iterative process stops. But the particles can not be globally optimal. It will result in tracking lost when it encounters occlusion and any distractions in the background.

## 65.3 The Improved Algorithm

In target tracking area, the theory of Particle Filter and Mean-shift are the most classical algorithms. They have their own advantages and weaknesses, but at the same time, there is a strong complementarity in them. The Mean-shift algorithm has less calculation and it is easy to do real-time tracking. Through iteration, it can quickly converge to the local maximum of the probability density function. But it will result in tracking lost when it encounters occlusion and any distractions in the background.

   In the non-linear, non-Gaussian system status and under occlusion, Particle Filter can also be a good tracking [9]. But it exists particles degradation phenomena. When selected particles are too many, real-time tracking can not be guaranteed. When selected particles are too fewer, tracking results are inaccurate. Therefore, this paper adopts a method that Mean-shift is embedded to tracking framework of Particle Filter. Its purposes is to make candidate regions of these particles closer to target template for a more stable tracking results and more accuracy. At the same time, it can solve problems that Mean-shift algorithm fails on occlusion. Through reasonable means to combine these two algorithms, the effect can be better than any single algorithm.

According to above, it is given that the steps of improved target tracking algorithm combined by the Mean-shift and Particle Filter algorithm are as follows:

Step1: **Initialization.** Chosen t = 0, in the initial frame, tracked target needs to be selected to manually, and the number of particles S = 100 in this experiment;

Step2: **Resampling.** S particles are sorted by weights $w_i^t$. Substitute particles derived by large weighted particles for smaller weighted particles to solve the problem of particle degradation;

Step3: **Prediction.** Use the state transition equation $x_t = Ax_{t-1} + Bw_{t-1}$, and change the state of each particle;

Step4: **Occlusion Judgment.** Set the similarity threshold $\varepsilon$ to judge whether is on occlusion. If the similarity is less than the threshold $\varepsilon$, the goal is on occlusion, and perform five). Otherwise, perform Mean-shift tracking. This step is used to solve the event of failure when Mean-shift encounters occlusion;

Step5: **Weight Updating.** In the current frame, update the weights of the particles and normalized implementation;

Step6: **Calculate the new target location.** Which, in step 4, $\varepsilon$ is self-set threshold, its selection has a great influence on the effect of tracking. Its setting is based on concrete scenario to easily switch between two tracking algorithms, normally, value is ranging from 0.8 to 0.9 to meet the requirements.

## 65.4 Experimental Results and Analysis

Development environment of the algorithm in this paper combines Visual C++6.0 with OPENCV [10] library. The machine configuration is a Pentium D 2.8G, 2 GB of memory, Windows XP Processional as operating system, video size in pixels: 320 × 240, 30/s for frame rate, and the initial window are manual calibration. In order to verify the validity of the algorithm, the experiment uses proposed algorithm in this paper to track a video. At the same time, on this video tracking using Mean-shift and Particle Filter algorithm for tracking the same video to reach comparative results. The experimental results are as shown below. From left to right are video images in frame 117, 178, 261.

In Fig. 65.1, it shows the Mean-shift tracking results. We can see from it, Mean-shift algorithm is invalid for the tracking target on occlusion. In frame 261,

**Fig. 65.1** Tracking results of Mean-shift algorithm

**Fig. 65.2** Tracking results of Particle Filter

it also fails to re-locate the tracking target to result in tracking completely lost. In Fig. 65.2, it shows the particle filter tracking results. Compared with the Mean-shift algorithm, when it encounters occlusion, the particle filter can more accurately track the target for lost target. However, the algorithm has large amount of calculation and video frame rate greatly reduces on using it. The video frame rate is reduced to 4/s, and is far below 25/s in Mean-shift algorithm. In Fig. 65.3, it shows the tracking result of the improved algorithm. Compared with the first two results, the improved algorithm can very accurately track the target, when it encounters occlusion. And it will not happen target lost, at the same time, its frame rate can reach 20/s. It can enhance real-time.

**Fig. 65.3** Tracking results of the improved algorithm in this paper

## 65.5  Conclusions

This paper use a simple way to embed Mean-shift algorithm to the framework of the particle filter algorithm. Its purpose is that it full plays their respective advantages and mutually compensate for their shortcomings. So real-time of algorithm has been improved. The experiments show that the algorithm can track the target more accurately and stably for the target on occlusion and the target of fast motion; And it overcomes the shortcomings that Mean-shift algorithm can track the loss and be restored, and the particle filter algorithm has large amount of calculation. It has a more real-time and robustness. In future work, it needs to combine more information to enhance the robustness of the algorithm, and study how to use this algorithm to realize real-time tracking of multiple objectives.

## References

1. Yilmaz A, Javed O, Shah M (2006) Object tracking: a survey. ACM Comput Surv 38(4): 13–57
2. Commaniciu D, Ramesh V, Merr P (2003) Kernel-based object tracking. IEEE Trans Pattern Anal Mach Intell 25(5):564–577
3. Maskel S, 1 S Arulampalam, T Clapp. A tu-torial on particle filters for on-line non-lin-ear non-Gaussian bayesian tracking[J]. IEEE Tran. Signal Processing, 2002,55(2):174-188
4. Gordon NJ, Salmond DJ, SmithAF M (1993) Novel approach to nonlinear/non-Gaussian Bayesian state estimation. IEEE Proceedings 140(2):107–113
5. Li XJ, Li LF (2011) Particle filter tracking algorithms based on the posterior probability measure. Applied optics, 32(4):646-651.(in Chinese)
6. Wang YR, Liu JF, Liu GJ (2009) Human motion tracking based on particle filter regional combination. ACTA AUTOMATICA SINICA, 35(11):1387-1393.(in Chinese)
7. Yang C, Duraiswami R, Davis L (2005) Efficient mean-shift tracking via a new similarity measure.IEEE Conf on Comp Vision and Patt Recog, 176-183
8. Comaniciu D, Ramesh V, Meer P (2000) Real-time tracking of non-rigid objects using mean shift.IEEE Conference on Computer Vision and Pattern recognition. 2:142-149
9. Xia KH, Xu HL (2005) The key technology and application of Particle Filtering. Electron Opt and Control, 25(6):1-4.(in Chinese)
10. Liu R, Shi YQ (2007) OpenCV tutorial—Expo Basics. Beijing University of Aeronautics and Astronautics Press, Beijing (in Chinese)

# Chapter 66
# Inner-Knuckle-Print Recognition Based on Improved LBP

**Ming Liu, Yongmei Tian and Yinghui Ma**

**Abstract** A new approach for inner-knuckle-print (IKP) recognition is proposed. The approach is based on the local binary pattern (LBP) features. In our algorithm, straight line neighbourhood is used to calculate the LBP features, so that more distinctive IKP features can be obtained. Moreover, as the LBP feature for each IKP sample, 59 binary images are extracted, and then matched by using a cross-correlation-based algorithm, which is developed to calculate the similarity between the IKP samples. The experiments on a finger image database which includes 2,000 images from 100 different individuals show the good performance of the proposed approach.

**Keywords** Biometrics · Personal authentication · Local binary pattern

## 66.1 Introduction

Recently, the image pattern of the knuckle surface has been found to be unique and can be used in personal authentication systems [1]. The pattern of the inner surface of the knuckle is shown in Fig. 66.1. Compared with other biological characteristics, IKP has some advantages such as prominent line feature and rich information content, so it attracts more and more attention.

M. Liu (✉) · Y. Tian
College of Electronic and Information Engineering, Hebei University,
Baoding 071002, China
e-mail: yongmeitian999@163.com

Y. Ma
Environmental Management College of China, Qinhuangdao 066000, China
e-mail: myh-4wd@163.com

W. Lu et al. (eds.), *Proceedings of the 2012 International Conference on Information Technology and Software Engineering*, Lecture Notes in Electrical Engineering 212, DOI: 10.1007/978-3-642-34531-9_66, © Springer-Verlag Berlin Heidelberg 2013

**Fig. 66.1** Examples of the IKPs

In 2004, Li et al. [2] extracted four IKP ROIs and a palmprint ROI simulta-neously from the image of the whole hand, and then identify a person on the basis of the fusion of the information provided by the IKPs and the palmprint. Gabor transform was used to extract line features in their algorithm. Ribaric et al. [3] presented a new IKP recognition approach on the basis of the eigenfinger features and eigenpalm features. In their algorithm, the IKP ROIs were also extracted from the image of the whole hand. Luo et al. [4] proposed to detect line features of the IKP by Radon transform and singular value decomposition. Nanni et al. [5] developed an IKP recognition method on the basis of tokenized pseudo-random numbers and user specific knuckle features. A contactless palmprint and knuckle print recognition system was reported [6]. In Ref. [7], the difficulty of matching the line features of the IKP was considered, and the binary line image was projected to the horizontal axis.

However, some important issues in IKP recognition need to be solved yet. First, interference such as different intensity of light or dry skin conditions can reduce the effect of recognition. Second, the previous methods usually extract the line features. So we can delve into extraction methods for local IKP features, which can extract more local features with rotation invariance and translation invariance.

Local Binary Pattern (LBP) is a simple and efficient operator to describe local features, proposed by Ojala [8]. firstly. LBP has monotonic transformation invariance and rotation invariance. Therefore, it is low sensitivity to light and rotation. LBP has been adapted to many applications, such as texture classification, face recognition, and shape localization.

Therefore, we proposed a new approach based on LBP for IKP recognition; moreover, we improved LBP as follows: First, we optimized the neighbors for LBP operator according to characteristics owned by IKP. Second, we improved the algorithm in the feature extraction and matching stage. All in all, the proposed method can take full advantage of the spatial location of the feature points, and can solve the problem of translation displacement accurately.

## 66.2 IKP Recognition Based on Traditional LBP

LBP code is a binary representation of the orbicular neighborhood of a pixel [8]. It can be calculated by the following formula:

Histogram for each region

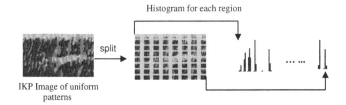

IKP Image of uniform
patterns

**Fig. 66.2**  The framework of the traditional LBP

$$LBP_{P,R}(q) = \sum_{p=0}^{P-1} s(g_p - g_q)2^p, \quad s(x) = \begin{cases} 1, & x \geq 0 \\ 0, & x < 0 \end{cases} \quad (66.1)$$

where $g_q$ represents the gray value of a pixel $q$, $g_p(p = 0, \ldots, P - 1)$ denote the gray values of $P$ neighbors of pixel $q$, and $R$ is the radius of the neighborhood. The neighbors are obtained by equal-sampling in the orbicular neighborhood, and the gray values of them are calculated by bilinear interpolation.

In this paper, we first applied LBP to IKP recognition, and used the uniform LBP patterns to reduce the dimensionality of the patterns, which is proposed by Ojala etc. [7]. After the improvement of the uniform LBP patterns, the pattern is reduced to 59 kinds, which can decrease the interference of high frequency noise. Finally, the histogram is used as the LBP feature vectors

The process of IKP recognition by traditional LBP is shown in Fig. 66.2. First, IKP image in uniform LBP patterns is divided into non-overlapping regions, and then, LBP histogram is computed for each region. Second, each region is given a weight according to the IKP characteristics, and the histograms of regions are concatenated to form the final histogram. Lastly, we use Chi-square distance to measure the similarity of two histograms in feature matching.

## 66.3  IKP Recognition Based on Improved LBP

### 66.3.1  Improved LBP for Feature Extraction

#### 66.3.1.1  Improvement of the Neighbors

The prominent lines in IKP are mostly vertical direction, so this paper selects 8 neighbors in the horizontal direction around the center pixel, shown in Fig. 66.3. Compared with the traditional LBP operator which selects 8 circular neighbors, the proposed method can detect the transition better in the horizontal direction and indicate line feature in the vertical direction more accurately. Therefore, the feature extraction process for IKP can be more effective.

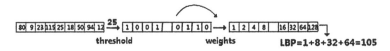

**Fig. 66.3** Illustration of improved LBP operators

In addition, to some prominent lines, the ROI image has many other tiny lines. The robustness of these tiny lines is low, and it will cause interference to IKP recognition. For LBP calculate the order relation for each pixel to its neighbors in the gray scale, it has strong expression in image detail characteristics, and can make a good distinction of different types of texture (such as the expression of eyes and nose in face recognition). However, this characteristic of LBP is a disturbance to the recognition, because it also expresses those undesired tiny lines. And then, it will reduce the accuracy of the identification. Therefore, in order to strengthen the IKP feature of the vertical direction, the first step of our method is Gabor filtering for ROI image in the vertical direction. Second, the ROI image will be filtered by mean filtering, smoothing out the tiny texture (the size of the filter window is $10 \times 10$ by experience). By the above algorithm, the LBP can extract more effective IKP features.

### 66.3.1.2 Improvement of Feature Expression

In traditional LBP algorithm, the local texture pattern is represented by histogram. Such a method may lose some spatial information. To overcome this problem, we adopt a point-to-point matching method. Firstly, we represent the LBP features by 59 binary images, and then compare the binary images with cross-correlation based method which is invariant to shift displacement [9]. The main steps of our algorithm are described as follows:

Step1: Calculate the LBP feature map $I(x, y)$ which has 59 LBP uniform patterns. Each pixel value is an integer $N(N = 1, 2, 3 \ldots 59)$.

Step2: For each $N$, generate a binary image $L_i$ with the following formula:

$$L_n(x, y) = \begin{cases} 1, I(x,y) = n \\ 0, \text{otherwise} \end{cases}, \quad n = 1, 2, 3 \ldots 59 \tag{66.2}$$

In the end, we constitute 59 binary images.

Feature extraction process based on the improved LBP is shown in Fig. 66.4. First, we strengthen the original image by Gabor filtering and mean filtering, and then we get Fig. 66.4c. Second, we extract the LBP feature based on uniform LBP patterns, as is shown in Fig. 66.4d. Finally, 59 binary images are split out as feature vector of the original image. Figure 66.4e is one of the 59 images, and the white points show that their location belongs to the pattern of 52.

Figure 66.5 shows a part of the binary images from different IKP image according to the proposed method $n = 11 \sim 20$. Among them, Fig. 66.5a and b are captured from the same finger of one person, and Fig. 66.5c is from another person, we can see the binary images of the same person have high similarity.

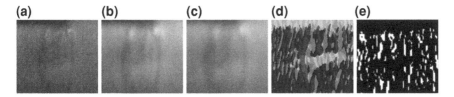

Fig. 66.4 Feature extraction process based on the proposed method. **a** Original image, **b** Gabor filtering, **c** mean filtering, **d** Uniform LBP patterns, **e** Binary image when $n = 52$

Fig. 66.5 Binary images of the improved LBP feature (**a** and **b** are from the same finger's IKP at different times, **c** is from another finger's IKP)

## 66.3.2 Improved LBP for Feature Matching

Cross-correlation-based method is one of the major algorithms in image matching process, for it can solve the problem of translation displacement between the binary images accurately [9]. So we can adopt a cross-correlation-based shape as matching method of IKP.

Let $T(x, y)$ denote a template (grayscale IKP image) registered in the template database, and $L(x, y)$ be a grayscale IKP image which is to be verified. Their binary images are $T_i(x, y)$ and $L_i(x, y)$ respectively $(i = 1, 2, 3 \ldots 59)$. Then the similarity between $L(x, y)$ and $T(x, y)$ can be calculated as follows:

Step1: Calculate the fast Fourier Transform of $T_i(x, y)$ and $L_i(x, y)$, and their product can be defined by $c_i(u, v)$.

$$T_i(u, v) = FFT[T_i(x, y)], \quad L_i(u, v) = FFT[L_i(x, y)] \qquad (66.3)$$

$$c_i(u, v) = T_i(u, v) \cdot T_i(u, v) \qquad (66.4)$$

Step2: Sum all of $c_i(u, v)$ and calculate the inverse fast Fourier transform of the summation.

$$C(u, v) = \sum_{i=1}^{59} c_i(u, v) \qquad (66.5)$$

$$S(T, L) = IFFT[C(u, v)] \qquad (66.6)$$

In the equation above, $S(L, T)$ denotes the similarity between $L(x, y)$ and $T(x, y)$.

Through the above method, the similarity of IKPs from same finger is 6,973; meanwhile, the similarity of the different person is only 3,179. The large difference of them can help us determine an appropriate threshold to do IKP identification. Therefore, our method can complete and improve the IKP identify work.

## 66.4 Experimental Results

### 66.4.1 Database Establishment

In order to evaluate the proposed IKP-based personal authentication algorithm, a database was established. The IKP images were collected from 100 volunteers most of whom were students at the Hebei University. The database will be available in the website of the College of Electronic and Information Engineering, the Hebei University (http://www.ceie.hbu.cn/).

We collected the IKP images on two separate occasions, at an interval of around two months. On each occasion, the subject was asked to provide 10 images of the right hand. In total, the database contains 2,000 images from 100 different subjects. The size of each captured image is 576 × 768, which contains the middle knuckles of the middle and ring fingers. From each image we extracted two ROI sub-images, namely, the middle finger IKP and the ring finger IKP. The following identification experiments are based on the ring finger IKP.

### 66.4.2 Verification

Personal verification, which is a one-to-one matching, involves answering the question "whether this person is whom he or she claims to be". In order to show the performance of the proposed system clearly, the following experiments were conducted. The proposed method, namely the improved LBP method, was compared with the traditional LBP method and the Gabor filter based method [1].

We first evaluated genuine matching scores for all possible combinations of genuine attempts. The number of the attempts was $190 \times 100 = 19,000$. Then, we evaluated impostor matching scores for 200 typical line images (100 images per occasion). The number of attempts was $50 \times 99 \times 4 = 19,800$. Figure 66.6 shows the distributions of the genuine and the imposter scores of the ring finger IKP. It is shown that the distribution curve of genuine matching scores intersects little with that of impostor matching scores. Therefore, the proposed approach can effectively discriminate between finger images.

**Fig. 66.6** Genuine and imposter score distributions obtained using ring IKPs

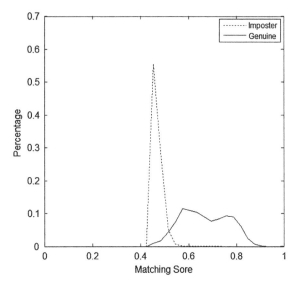

**Fig. 66.7** Comparison of the verification methods with the ring IKPs

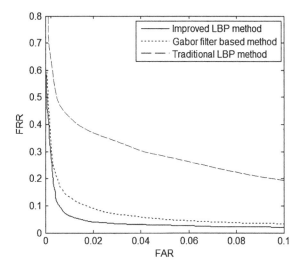

**Table 66.1** ERRs obtained by the different methods

| Verification method | ERR (%) |
|---|---|
| Traditional LBP method | 11.26 |
| Gabor filter based method | 5.06 |
| Improved LBP method | 3.22 |

Figure 66.7 depicts the receiver operating characteristic (ROC) curves of the methods obtained with the ring IKPs. The ROC curve is a plot of the false acceptance rate (FAR) against the false acceptance rate (FRR) at different thresholds on the matching score. It reflects the overall performance of a biometric system. We can see that the proposed method outperforms all of the two conventional methods. The corresponding EER values are listed in Table 66.1. It can be observed from these results that the proposed approach can improve the recognition performance of the system efficiently.

## 66.5 Conclusions

In this paper, we proposed a LBP features based IKP recognition algorithm. Firstly, the neighbors for LBP operator are optimized according to IKP's characteristics. Secondly, 59 binary images are extracted from the original image. Finally, the binary images are matched by using a cross-correlation-based method, which can solve the translation displacement problem accurately. Compared with the traditional LBP, the proposed approach can extract LBP feature more efficiently and robustly. The experimental results show that the proposed method is efficient for IKP recognition.

**Acknowledgments** This work is supported by the National Natural Science Foundation of China (No.60903089, No.60773062, No.61100143, No.60801053), Scientific Research Plan Projects of Hebei Educational Bureau (No. 2008312), and Beijing Natural Science Foundation (No.4082025).

## References

1. Kumar A, Ravikanth C (2009) Personal authentication using finger knuckle surface. IEEE Trans Inf Forensics Secur 4(1):98–109
2. Li Q, Qiu Z-D, Sun D-M (2004) Personal identification using knuckleprint, sinobiometric04. Lecture Notes Comput Sci 3338:680–689 (in Chinese)
3. Ribaric S, Fratric I (2005) A biometric identification system based on eigenpalm and eigenfinger features. IEEE Trans Pattern Anal Mach Intell 27(11):1698–1709
4. Luo R-F, Lin T-S, Wu T (2007) Personal recognition with finger crease pattern. Opto-Electronic Eng 34(6):116–121 (in Chinese)
5. Nanni L, Lumini A (2009) A multi-matcher system based on knuckle-based features. Neural Comput Appl 18(1):87–91
6. Michael G, connie T, Teoh Beng Jin A (2010) An innovative contactless pal print and knuckle print recognition system. Pattern Recogn Lett 31(7):1708–1719
7. Zhu L-Q, Zhang S-Y, Xing R (2009) Automatic personal authentication based on finger phalangeal prints. Acta Automatica Sinica 35(7):875–881
8. Ojala T, Pietikäinen M, Mäenpää T (2002) Multiresolution gray-scale and rotation invariant texture classification with local binary pattern. IEEE Trans Pattern Anal Mach Intell 24(7):971–987
9. Goshtasby A, Gage SH, Bartholic JF (1984) A two-stage cross-correlation approach to template matching. IEEE Trans Pattern Anal Mach Intell 6(3):374–378

# Chapter 67
# Fingerprint Classification Based on Sparse Representation Using Rotation-Invariant Features

**Yong A, Tiande Guo, Xiao Liu and Guangqi Shao**

**Abstract** A new fingerprint classification method is proposed under Galton-Henry classification scheme. We first modified FingerCode to generate rotation-invariant distance. Then, the distances between a fingerprint's FingerCode and templates' are used to represent the fingerprint. On classification step, we put the rotation-invariant features of the training sets together, and solve a sparse representation problem for a query fingerprint. The experiment results show that the proposed feature is robust and the classification method gives an accurate result.

**Keywords** FingerCode · Fingerprint classification · Rotation-invariant features · Sparse representation

## 67.1 Introduction

Fingerprint is one of the most wildly used biometric features due to its stability and uniqueness. Fingerprint classification, as an important step of automatic fingerprint identification system, can greatly improve the matching speed. Nowadays, fingerprint classification is usually based on Galton-Henry classification scheme, which divides the fingerprints into five classes: arch, tented arch, left loop, right loop and whorl, as shown in Fig. 67.1.

When the singularities of a fingerprint are correctly extracted, the fingerprint can be classified by rule-based methods. As a result, many researchers have given

Y. A (✉) · T. Guo · X. Liu · G. Shao
School of Mathematical Sciences, Graduate University of Chinese Academy of Sciences, Yuquan Road 19A, Shijingshang District, Beijing, China
e-mail: ayong08@mails.gucas.ac.cn

W. Lu et al. (eds.), *Proceedings of the 2012 International Conference on Information Technology and Software Engineering*, Lecture Notes in Electrical Engineering 212, DOI: 10.1007/978-3-642-34531-9_67, © Springer-Verlag Berlin Heidelberg 2013

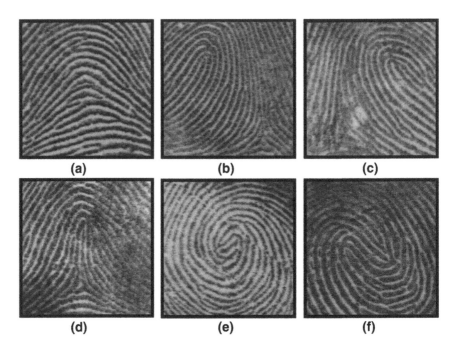

**Fig. 67.1** Fingerprint examples for Galton-Henry classification scheme. **a** Arch, **b** *Left Loop*, **c** *Right Loop*, **d** Tented Arch, **e** Whorl (Plain Whorl) **f** Whorl (*Twin Loop*)

new methods for singularity extraction. Kawagoe and Tojo [1] introduced the Poincare index to find type and position of singularities. In [2], a heuristic algorithm is exploited to find a valid number of singularities. But singularities are hard to extract in low quality fingerprints and part fingerprints.

There are many other features appeared in fingerprint classification methods, and FingerCode [3] is one of the most frequently used feature. In [3], Jain et al. proposed FingerCode which use standard deviation of Gabor filters responses as its content. But the FingerCode itself is not rotation-invariant, which means great differences may occur in fingerprints of the same finger due to different acquire angle.

After preparing the features, kinds of classifiers were adopted by researchers to solve the classification problem, such as k-nearest neighbor (k-NN) [3, 4], support vector machine(SVM) [5], neural network (NN) [3, 5] etc. In [6], Wright et al. proposed a general classification algorithm for object recognition which shows great robustness compared with the methods mentioned above. They put features of sufficient samples together and solve a sparse representation problem for a new sample. Then, the new sample is put into the class with the minimum representation residual. With an appropriate feature, this classification scheme can be used in fingerprint classification.

In this paper, we proposed a new method for fingerprint classification problem. First, a rotation-invariant feature is proposed based on modified FingerCode; then, the classification technique using sparse representation is carried out with the new features.

The rest of this paper is organized as follows. In Sect. 67.2, the new rotation-invariant feature is introduced, and classification method using sparse representation is illustrated in Sect. 67.3. Section 67.4 gives the experiment results of our methods on NIST-4 database. The conclusion is made in Sect. 67.5.

## 67.2 Rotation-Invariant Features

Many features are used in the previous fingerprint classification methods. Singular points, the regions where orientations of ridges change rapidly, are the most common features. If they are extracted accurately, the fingerprint can be simply classified by rules. However, detection of singularities can be difficult due to low quality or partial fingerprints. In [3], a new feature named FingerCode was proposed which located at central point (the north most core point) and took standard deviation of Gabor response of each fan-shaped area as features. Extraction of central point is more robust than extraction of all singularities, especially in part fingerprint. However, the FingerCode itself is not rotation-invariant, and the fingerprints are captured from different angles. As a result, two images of the same finger may have very different representations.

In this section, a new rotation-invariant feature is proposed based on distances between modified FingerCodes. The influence of different angles can be eliminated in distance calculation step. A fingerprint is represented by the distances between its FingerCode and templates' FingerCodes.

### 67.2.1 Modified FingerCode

In this subsection, we give the description of modified FingerCode used in this paper, which is similar with [3]. In [3], the central point of a fingerprint was searched firstly, and secondly a spatial tessellation centered at the point 40 pixels below the central point was drawn as shown in Fig. 67.2a. Thirdly, for each fan-shaped area, 4 Gabor filter is applied. Fourthly, the standard deviations of all filtered fan-shaped images are gathered to make the feature vector.

The modified FingerCode in this paper is different from the original one. First, the center of spatial tessellation is at the central point but not the point 40 pixels below it; second, the orientation at each sector is considered while original FingerCode takes standard deviation of Gabor responses in this sector as content as shown in Fig. 67.2b. These two differences are designed to eliminate the influence of rotation and will be described in Sect. 67.2.2.

More specifically, for a fingerprint image with M * N pixels, let $(x_c, y_c)$ denote the central point, and $O(i,j)$ be the ridge orientation at pixel $(i,j)$. Let K1 and K2

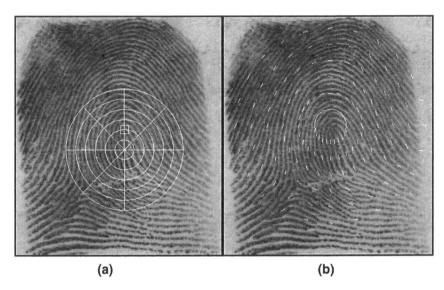

**(a)**                                                                    **(b)**

**Fig. 67.2** **a** Fingercode, **b** modified FingerCode

denote number of angles and number of concentric circles in the spatial tessellation. The modified FingerCode is defined as:

$$mfc = (mfc_1, mfc_2, \ldots, mfc_i, \ldots, mfc_{K1*K2}), \qquad (67.1)$$

Where

$$mfc_i = O(x_i, y_i),$$

$$x_i = b * (T_i + 1) * \cos(A_i),$$

$$y_i = b * (T_i + 1) * \sin(A_i),$$

$$T_i = [i / K1],$$

$$A_i = (i \bmod K1) * 2 * pi / K1.$$

Here, we take $K1 = 24$ angles and $K2 = 6$ concentric circles, and consequently a $24 * 6 = 144$ dimension feature is defined. Besides, b is the difference of neighbor concentric circles and equals to 30 pixels in our experiment. In the rest of paper, we call the modified FingerCode "MFCode".

## 67.2.2 Distance Between Modified FingerCodes

In this subsection, we give the methods to calculate the distance between two MFCodes. The idea is to try every possible rotation to match the two codes, and choose the distance of the most similar match. The following is the illustration.

**Fig. 67.3** An example of MFCode's rotation

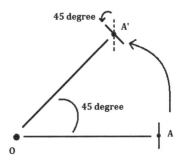

We fix one of the two MFCodes, and rotate another. It should be noticed that, when a MFCode is rotated, its content is changing too. This is because we choose the ridge orientation as content, and it's changing when the fingerprint is rotating. As shown in Fig. 67.3, when a MFCode rotated 45° counterclockwise, the point A moved to A', and A' orientation should rotated 45° counterclockwise.

The distance between two MFCodes mfc1 and mfc2 is defined as:

$$\text{distance}(\text{mfc1}, \text{mfc2}) = \min_{1 \le k \le k1} \Sigma_{1 \le i \le k1 \times k2} \text{oridis}(\text{mfc1}_i, \text{mfc2}_{i(k)} + k \times \pi/K1),$$

$$(67.2)$$

where

$$\text{oridis}(a, \ b) = \begin{cases} |a' - b'|, \text{ if } |a' - b'| \le \frac{\pi}{2} \\ \pi - |a' - b'|, \text{ if } |a' - b'| > \frac{\pi}{2} \end{cases},$$

$$\text{with } a' = a \bmod \pi, \quad b' = b \bmod \pi,$$

$$i(k) = [i \ /K1] \times K1 + (i + k) \bmod K1,$$

Here, oridis (a, b) describes the distance of two ridge orientations, and i(k) denotes the new position of sample point i after rotation step k.

Notice that the effect of rotation is avoided because the best match is chosen in different rotations. However, since the original FingerCode is located at the point 40 pixels down the central point of fingerprint, it is not fixed for images of the same finger with different rotation. As a result, we put MFCode at the central point. Additionally, when a MFCode is rotated, the ridge orientation can be adjusted quickly by adding the angle on it. This is why we change the original FingerCode as mentioned before.

## 67.2.3 Rotation-Invariant Feature

Finally, a new representation of fingerprint is given. Suppose N1 MFCodes (mfc_tmp1, mfc_tmp2, ..., mfc_tmpN1) are randomly selected as templates. When a new fingerprint f is given, the distances between its MFCode mfcf and the templates' MFCodes are calculated using formular (67.2). The collection of these distances makes the new feature of this fingerprint (DisMFC):

DisMFC(f) = (distance(mfcf, mfc_tmp1), distance(mfcf, mfc_tmp1), ..., distance(mfcf, mfc_tmpN1))

This distance feature is used to represent fingerprints, and it is rotation-invariant, for each element of the feature is rotation-invariant distance.

## 67.3 Classification Based on Sparse Representation

In [6], Wright et al. proposed a general classification algorithm for object recognition which suggests more robustness compared with some traditional classification methods, and the algorithm successed in face recognition. They declaimed that if the number of features is sufficiently large and the sparse representation is correctly computed, the choice of features is no longer critical [6]. However, faces can be easily aligned and are not affected by rigid body motion. In fingerprint classification, the situation is different. A large number of fingerprints are needed if the rotation problem is not well handled. However, with the proposed rotation-invariant feature in Sect. 67.2, this general classification algorithm can be applied in fingerprint classification problem. The experiment results in Sect. 67.4 suggest that the combination of rotation-invariant feature and the classification algorithm is accurate.

Given sufficient large training sets $\{S_{i,j}\}$, make a matrix $S = [S_{1,1}\ S_{1,2}\ ...\ S_{t,nt}]$, where $S_{i,j}$ denotes the jth sample of class i and nt denotes the number of samples in class i. Let N2 denote the number of samples. For a new sample y, solve the following optimization problem

$$\min\|x\|_0 \text{s.t.} Ax = y \qquad (67.3)$$

The solution gives a sparse representation of y by A. It is believed that y can be best represented by samples in the class y belongs. So classify y to the class that minimized the residual:

$$\min_i r_i(y) \overset{\text{def}}{=} \|y - A\delta_i(x^*)\|,$$

where, $x^*$ is the solution of problem (67.3), and $\delta_i(x^*)$ is a vector that the entries associated with class i are the entries in x, and other entries are all zero. Actually, if the solution is sparse enough, the solution of (67.4) equals to the following L1-minimization problem [6],

$$\min\|x\|_1 \text{s.t. } Ax = y, \qquad (67.4)$$

which can be solved easier. In the experiment, we use OMP method described in [7] to solve (67.4).

The following algorithm describes the whole fingerprint classification method.

**Algorithm 1:** Fingerprint Classification based on Sparse Representation (FCSR)

*Offline*:

1. Input: a set of training fingerprints.
2. For each fingerprint, extract its MFCode;
3. Randomly select N1 MFCodes as samples;
4. For each fingerprint, calculate the ditances between its MFCode and the samples'. And put them together as the feature of this fingerprint.
5. Output: new features for each fingerprint.

*Online*:

1. Input: a matrix of the new features $S = [S_{1,1} \ S_{1,2} \ ... \ S_{t,nt}]$, N1 MFCode samples selected in the offline step, and a test fingerprint f.
2. Extract the MFCode of f;
3. Calculate the distances between f's MFCode and the N1 samples' as f's new features y.
4. Solve the l1-minimization problem (67.4):
5. Compute the residuals $r_i(y)$.
6. Output: class $(y) = \arg \underset{i}{\text{Min}} \, r_i(y)$.

## 67.4  Experiment

In this section, the proposed method is tested on NIST DB4. The database contains 2,000 fingerprint pairs. The whole 4,000 fingerprints are divided into 5 classes, and each class has about 800 images. Since it is difficult to separate arch and tended arch even for human experts, the two classes are collapsed into one class and results are reported only on four-class classification problem. Moreover, some fingerprints' quality is too low to recognize, so about 1.8 % fingerprints are rejected during the feature extraction step as described in [3].

### 67.4.1  Classification Results

It turns out that our method gives an accuracy of 94.12 % with the parameter N1 = 1600, N2 = 2000 and OMP iterations = 100. As shown in Table 67.1, our method outperforms most methods, and makes a comparable result with the best techniques in [3]. However, in our classification methods, the misclassified fingerprint can be easily added into the samples without training to classify this kind of fingerprints more correctly. Besides, our feature extraction step is faster because only orientation field is used and the Gabor filter is time exhausting. The confusion matrix of our methods is given in Table 67.2.

**Table 67.1** Classification results on NIST DB4

| Methods | Test environment | Classification results (%) |
|---|---|---|
| Candela et al. [8] | 4 classes, second half | 88.6 |
| Yao et al. [5] | 4 classes, second half, 1.8 % rejection | 93.1 |
| Jain et al. [3] | 4 classes, second half, 1.8 % rejection | 94.8 |
| Our methods | 4 classes, whole DB, 1.8 % rejection | 94.12 |

**Table 67.2** Confusion matrix of our methods

| True class | L | R | A&T | W |
|---|---|---|---|---|
| L | 720 | 10 | 39 | 20 |
| R | 5 | 739 | 36 | 13 |
| A&T | 25 | 23 | 1505 | 4 |
| A&T W | 25 | 19 | 12 | 733 |

**Table 67.3** Comparison results on NIST-4

| Methods | Results (%) |
|---|---|
| MFCode + KNN | 87.98 |
| DisMFC + KNN | 91.32 |
| FCSR | 94.12 |

Out results are given on the whorl DB. When a query fingerprint is given, we use all other images of different finger as samples, so the experiment can be carried out on the whorl DB.

As shown in Table 67.3, the rotation-invariant feature combining KNN give a classification result of 91.32 %, which is better than MFCode with KNN. This result suggests that the consideration of rotation is necessary and the proposed feature is more robust. Besides, we can see that FSCR outperforms KNN from the Table, with a result of 94.12 %. In Fig. 67.4, we show the comparison between FCSR and KNN with different parameter K. The KNN classification results are all below 92 %, and FCSR shows more accurate results as illustrated in Fig. 67.6.

The most misclassification in our results occurs between loop type and arch type. There are images of the two types with similar orientation field as shown in Fig. 67.5. Since the key information lays at local area around core point, our method fails on this kind of fingerprints.

## 67.4.2 Parameters Analysis

There are 3 main parameters N1, N2 and OMP iterations in our methods. N1 is the number of samples in feature extraction step, N2 is the number of samples in classification step. When N1 = 2000, N2 = 2000, iterations = 100, we get a reasonable result with 94.02 %. Then, we change each parameter and at the same

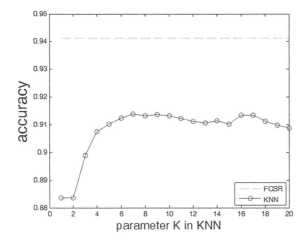

**Fig. 67.4** Comparison between FCSR and KNN with different K

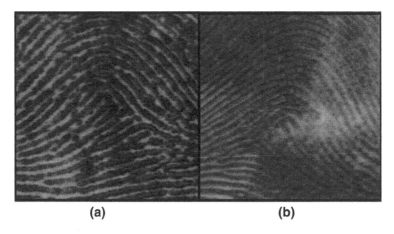

**Fig. 67.5** Misclassified examples **a** *left loop* as arch, **b** *right loop* as arch

time fix other parameters. The results are shown in Fig. 67.6. As N1, N2 or the iteration times grows separately, our result becomes better. Most parameters give good classification results, and it suggests that our method is robust with parameters. When it failed on some fingerprint, we can put the feature of the finger into training set to get better results on this kind of fingerprint.

In Fig. 67.6d, the computation time is shown with different iterations. The experiment is carried out on a computer with 4 3.10 Ghz CPU, and the computation time is acceptable. The most computation time is 0.69 s per image, with parameter N1 = 2,000, N2 = 2,000, iterations = 100.

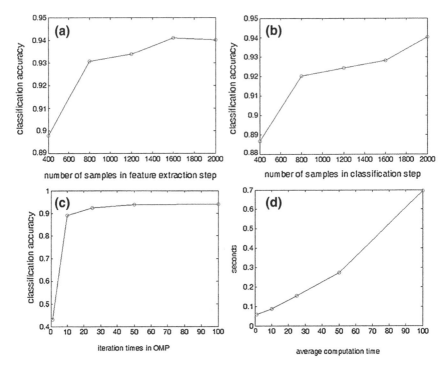

**Fig. 67.6** Results with different parameters. **a** N1, **b** N2, **c** OMP iterations, **d** computation time with different OMP iterations

## 67.5 Conclusions

In this paper, we propose a new fingerprint classification method. To eliminate the influence of rotation, FingerCode is modified to generate rotation-invariant distance. Then, a rotation-invariant feature is given based on the distance with samples. In the classification step, we adopt the method based on sparse representation. The class with the minimum representation residual is the final choice. The experiment results show that the rotation-invariant feature is robust and our classification method is accurate compared with traditional methods.

**Acknowledgments** This work was supported by the National Natural Science Foundation of China under Grants 10831006 and 11101420.

## References

1. Kawagoe M, Tojo A (1984) Fingerprint pattern classification. Pattern Recogn 17:295–303
2. Karu K, Jain AK (1996) Fingerprint classification. Pattern Recogn 29(3):389–404

3. Jain AK, Prabhakar S, Lin H (1999) A multichannel approach to fingerprint classification. IEEE Trans Pattern Anal Mach Intell 21(4):348–359
4. Fitz AP, Green RJ (1996) Fingerprint classification using hexagonal fast fourier transform. Pattern Recogn 29(10):1587–1597
5. Yao Y, Marcialis GL, Pontil M, Frasconi P, Roli F (2001) Combining flat and structured representations for fingerprint classification with recursive neural networks and support vector machines. Pattern Recogn 36(2):253–258
6. Wright J, Yang AY, Ganesh A, Sastry SS, Ma Y (2008) Robust face recognition via sparse representation. IEEE Trans Pattern Anal Mach Intell 31(2):210–227
7. Elad M (2010) Sparse and redundant representations: from theory to applications in signal and image processing. Springer, New York
8. Candela GT, Grother PJ, Watson CI, Wilkinson RA, Wilson CL (1995) PCASYS—a pattern-level classification automation system for fingerprints. Technical Report, NIST TR 5674, Aug 1995

# Chapter 68
# Human Action Recognition for Home Sensor Network

Yingyuan Gu and Chun Yuan

**Abstract** Home sensor network, namely smart home has been developing at an incredible speed. In order to improve the intelligence of home sensor network, we committed our efforts to the research on video-based human action recognition to build a home sensor network, which makes it possible for smart home to interact with users through actions and recognize accidents like falling down through surveillance video automatically. In this paper, we present a survey on video-based human action recognition and address this problem from two major aspects: action representation and recognition approach. A comprehensive overview of this field is provided in this paper. We also analyze the characteristics of home sensor network and propose the challenges in front of all researchers for introduction of action recognition into home sensor network at the end of this survey.

**Keywords** Home sensor network · Human action recognition · Action representation · Smart home

## 68.1 Intoduction

As one of the most promising application of sensor network, smart home system is now developing, which will definitely raise a revolution in lifestyle to benefit billions of families around the world.

Y. Gu (✉) · C. Yuan
F205, Graduate School at Shenzhen, Tsinghua University, Nanshan District, ShenZhen, GuangDong Province, China
e-mail: gyymayw@126.com

W. Lu et al. (eds.), *Proceedings of the 2012 International Conference on Information Technology and Software Engineering*, Lecture Notes in Electrical Engineering 212, DOI: 10.1007/978-3-642-34531-9_68, © Springer-Verlag Berlin Heidelberg 2013

Research groups from MIT, Cisco, Microsoft, IBM, have initiated projects related to smart home for several years. Most existing smart home systems can provide intelligent control of electrical devices such as lighting, curtains, door entry and so on through keypads, touch screens and sensors. However, due to the limitations of response time and technical issues, action recognition still remains to be difficult for application to home sensor network.

Visual applications especially action recognition plays a significant role in the improvement of intelligent home network. Figure 68.1 [1] gives an example architecture for home sensor network with distributed visual processing. This system is mainly oriented at mobile robot in home sensor network. Action recognition is vital in the whole architecture.

Home sensor network in Fig. 68.1 consists of people detection and tracking and action recognition modules at fixed camera node. Action recognition here has a special requirement: real time! As for this topic, related work includes smart surveillance system (S3 system) conducted by IBM [2]. As event based surveillance, S3 system extracts features like trajectory to recognize human action through event triggered mechanism. Although S3 system is good enough for broad environment like airport, it's not suitable for home sensor network. Most early work in this area, such as the system for video surveillance and monitoring (VSAM) by Lipton [3], concentrates on long distance surveillance in broad

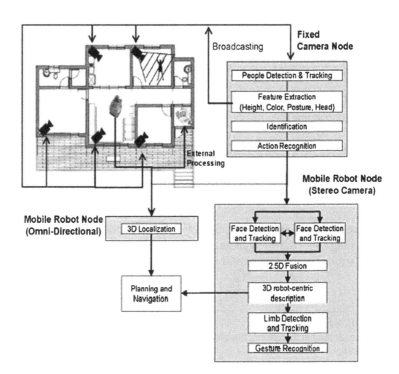

**Fig. 68.1** A home sensor network application [1]

environment. However, for smart home application, short distance surveillance and accurate recognition are required.

We review related work on human action recognition to analyze the suitability for home sensor network in this paper.

## 68.2 Action Recognition

### 68.2.1 Applications of Human Action Recognition

The past decades have witnessed a rapid development of computer vision, as one of the most promising applications of this area, video-based human action recognition has caught the attention of researchers from both industry and academia.

Video-based human action recognition has a wide range of application mainly in three domains:

1. Security and surveillance: Intelligent security and surveillance are often found in occasions requiring high level of security, like banks, supermarkets and garages, human action recognition make it possible for surveillance system to implement real-time detection and recognition of suspicious action.
2. Interactive application: We always hope that computers in future are able to communicate with people in an easier way, for example, by understanding human action including gestures even expressions, users will enjoy a quite different and amazing using experience.
3. Contend-based video retrieval: The explosion of multimedia data especially video data makes it so difficult to find specific video from mass data. Instead of raw video, users want to query the content directly. For instance, someone wants videos including boxing, content-based video retrieval can find those videos with this specific action.

In order to improve the intelligent of home sensor network system, we concentrate on the research of video-base human action recognition for smart home, which make it possible for the system to analyze the surveillance videos automatically and alarm owners for abnormalities like burglary or falling down of aged people.

### 68.2.2 Surveys and general overview

Several related survey papers on human action recognition have appeared over the years. Moeslund and Granum [4] analyzed and concluded the achievements of action recognition before 2001 from four parts: initialization, object tracing, estimation and recognition of human position and induction of the assumptions of that time. Turaga [5] presented a very comprehensive survey of efforts in the past decades to address the problems of representation, recognition and learning of human actions and activities from video and related applications. More recently, Ronald et al. [6] discussed the characteristics and challenges in this field and regarded video-based human action recognition as the combination of feature extraction and subsequent classification of these image representations.

Since action recognition provides a promising solution for the surveillance system and intelligent interaction in home sensor network, we limit our focus on video-based human action recognition for its application in this specific domain.

In human action recognition, the common procedures include extraction of features from video and classification of the action. The environment in which the action performance takes place has great influence on the recognition results. It has been proved harder to localize person in cluttered or dynamic environments. In some occasions, parts of the person might be shielded, which makes localization even harder. Fortunately, application in home sensor network only has to deal with a relatively static environment with messy background full of objects. Considering the characteristic of home sensor network, we have taken the efficiency and robustness of action recognition algorithm into account, that's why we conduct this survey, and compare related work on action recognition from multiple perspectives.

An explicit overview of video-based human action recognition to introduce the related methods suited for home sensor network is provided in this paper. In Sects. 68.1 and 68.2, we outline the characteristics and challenges of the application of action recognition in home sensor network and give a brief introduction of video-based human action recognition system. The rest content is organized as following: we will discuss action recognition from two aspects, action representation in Sect. 68.3 and recognition approach in Sect. 68.4. At last we will give a brief conclusion to indicate the future opportunities and challenges for action recognition in home sensor network.

## 68.3 Action Representation

Action representation refers to the work of extracting data from video to represent action in a reasonable way, which is vital for action recognition. We have to select different action representation according to the action recognition method. For example, trajectory is enough for long-distance surveillance in a broad environment, while 3-Dimention modeling is needed in gesture recognition. Parameswaran et al. [7] proposed four standards to evaluate action representation method: minimalism, completeness, continuity, uniqueness. Generally human action representation is based on appearance or on human body model.

## 68.3.1  Image Based Representation

Different from action representation based on human body model, representation based on appearance represent action by modeling the color or gray information from the image sequences instead of modeling the physical structure of human directly.

Using image information directly to represent action is the simplest way. In early years, Yamato et al. [8] present a simple method with low precision which use mesh feature to analyze human action. They extract person from the image and then divide binary image into meshes, calculate proportion of the pixels of human body over each mesh, which finally represent human action.

We can also represent action by motion information, such as optical flow and trajectories. Optical flow is defined as the apparent motion of individual pixels on the image plane which often regarded as an approximation of the true physical motion projected onto the image plane. Thus optical provides a concise description of both the regions of the image undergoing motion and the velocity of motion. As computation of optical flow is sensitive to noise, optical flow is often regarded as low-level feature to compute mid-level or high level feature. Trajectories of moving person can only provide representation of human action in a broad environment from a long distance, which limit the application of trajectories.

The shape of human silhouette is an intuitive way to represent human action, which give birth to lots of human recognition algorithms based on shape. In this classification, background subtraction, to isolate the moving parts of a scene by segmenting it into background and fore ground, is needed to be completed in the first move. Figure 68.2 shows a set of background subtracted image which easily perceive human's playing tennis. Wang et al. [9] recognize human activities from silhouettes by division of motion subspace and graphical model. Veeraraghaven et al. [10] use marked points on the silhouettes to analyze human action through collection of the limited marked points.

Image based representation is simple and effective, but these features are susceptible to noise and illumination changes, which will influent the recognition significantly.

## 68.3.2  Spatial–Temporal Representation

In Sect. 68.3.1, we give several instances of image models, as a simple solution to action representation, optical flow and other features in image models are

**Fig. 68.2**  Background subtracted images of human playing tennis [8]

generally used to compute middle or high level features. In recent years, spatial–temporal volume has attracted attention of researchers.

A global spatial–temporal representation can be easily obtained by stacking together binary background subtracted images, see in Fig. 68.3 a person waving his hands [5]. Global spatial–temporal representation requires careful background subtraction, which limited its application to fixed camera settings. Limitations of global spatial–temporal representation stimulate the research on local spatial–temporal descriptor. Normally local descriptor is computed based on optical flow or gradient, global representation of human action is organized or calculated through local spatial–temporal descriptor. Figure 68.4 shows the local spatial–temporal feature computed at interest points of human walking [11].

Common local spatial–temporal descriptor includes HOG/HOF [12]. Laptev calculates the gradient and optical flow of the neighborhood points of interest point to represent local motion, after the sequences of images are divided into several blocks, every block is separated into $n_x \times n_y \times n_t$ cells. Compute the histograms of gradient orientations histogram and optical flow of every cell to get descriptor HOG/HOF.

The HOG3D descriptor was proposed by Klaser et al. [13]. It is calculated on the basis of histograms of 3D gradient orientations. Gradients are computed using an integral video representation. Therefore, HOG3D consists of both shape and motion information at the same time. The corresponding descriptor concatenates gradient histograms of all cells and is then normalized. See in Fig. 68.5.

The extended SURF descriptor proposed by Willems et al. [14] extends the image SURF descriptor to videos. Similar to HOG/HOF and HOG3D, the 3D patches are divided into $n_x \times n_y \times n_t$ cells. Each cell is represented by a vector of weighted sums $v = (\sum d_x, \sum d_y, \sum d_t)$ of uniformly sampled responses of the Haar-wavelets dx, dy, dt along the three axes.

**Fig. 68.3** Spatial-temporal object [5]

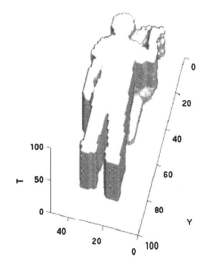

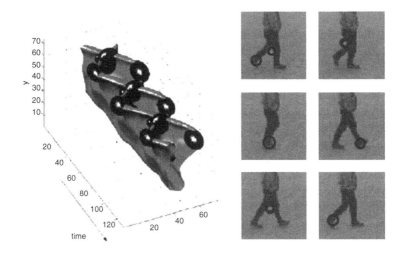

**Fig. 68.4**  Spatial-temporal features computed at interest points [11]

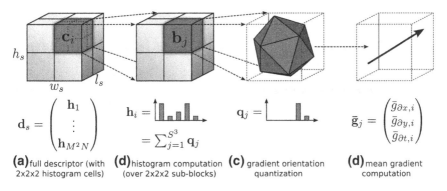

**Fig. 68.5**  Calculation of HOG3D

To perceive the global representation from local spatio-temporal descriptors, Niebles et al. [15] use a bag-of-words model to represent action. The bag-of-words model is learned by extracting spatial–temporal interest points and clustering the features. In recent years, as an emerging method for high dimensional data organization, sparse coding is also applied into the concatenation of local descriptors. Spatial–temporal representation is more robust to non-stationary background.

### 68.3.3 Body Models

Human action representation based on body models is a parametric approach, which recognizes human action with parameterized body model. Body model is applied in recognition of meticulous action like gestures. Compared with image based representation, body models with higher precision indicate the detail of human action distinctly and improve the recognition performance. Body models are simply separated into2D model and 3D model.

Feng et al. [16] proposed a 2D model comprised by ten rectangles, each of which has 5 angles. They use the combination of parameters from present frame and the next frame to represent human action. Another common 2D model, stick figures are proposed by Guo [17]. Marr and Vaina [18] proposed a body model consisting of a hierarchy of 3D cylindrical primitives.

Arie et al. [19] use 3D model to represent human body with 9 cylinders and 1 ball, standing for trunk, head, upper arm, forearm, thigh, shrank. With features calculated by the angle and angular velocity of arms and legs, they project 3D model to 2D plane and decide the action by the pose of the 9 parts.

Human body model represent human action precisely, especially referring to limb movements. By human body model, problems like blocking can be solved easily. But, the high dimension of feature space limits the application of human body. Actually, only a few action recognition systems use 3D body model due to its complexity and the numerous unevaluated parameters.

## 68.4 Recognition Approach

### 68.4.1 Template Matching

Bobick et al. [20] proposed "temporal templates" to model and recognize human action. The first step evolved is background subtraction, followed by an aggregation of a sequence of background subtracted blobs into a single static image using motion energy image (MEI) and motion history image (MHI). MEI gives all images in the sequence equal weight, while MHI gives decaying weight to the images in the sequence with higher weight given to new frames and low weight to older frames (Fig. 68.6).

Thus, MEI represent the scope and intensity of motion and MHI represent the time sequence of motion, together MEI and MHI comprise a template of human action. For classification, they match the template by calculating and comparing the Mahalanobis distance from standard template. MEI and MHI have sufficient discriminating ability for several simple actions such as "bending", "walking". Figure 68.7 shows the template of several simple actions. This approach needs only small scale of calculation but still has to face the problem of robustness for its susceptibility to the changes of time interval.

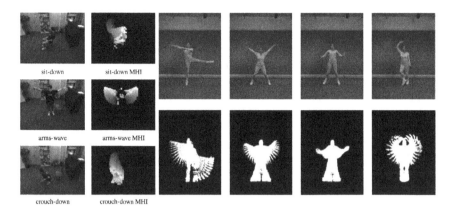

**Fig. 68.6**  Templates for actions: MHI and MEI

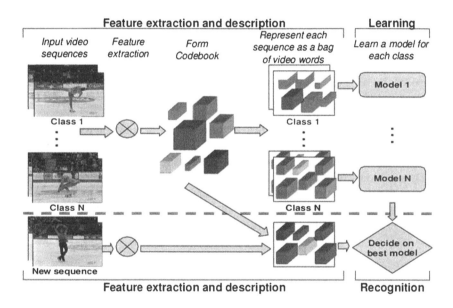

**Fig. 68.7**  Action recognition based on BoW

## 68.4.2  Probabilistic Network

Approaches based on probabilistic network once overwhelmed in the field of action recognition. These approaches take the dynamic procedure of human action into consideration and model diversification on time and space scale using probabilistic methods, making them more robust to scale changes of time and space. Static pose is regarded as a state or a set of states and connected with another pose by probabilistic network, in which the switching between poses is represented by probability. Therefore a traversal of these statuses or sets represents an action. Hidden Markov Models (HMM), a dynamic statistic model based on stochastic process and probability observation first applied in voice recognition successfully followed by development in handwriting recognition and speech signal processing, is the most popular probabilistic network in action recognition.

Since Yamato [8] introduced HMM into human action recognition, HMM and improved models are widely used. The assumption of HMM is that current state of motion only depends on the previous state. HMM is comprised by two sequences of stochastic variables, one of which is a sequence of states can not be observed, another is the sequence of symbols generated by states. State refers to the current attribute which can only be implied by observation, the representation of state.

Human action recognition based on HMMs normally extract the sequence of feature vectors to represent action in the first step, followed by training parameters of HMMs through learning algorithms, finally classify the unknown motion sequence according the trained model.

Generally, human action is not corresponded to the assumption of HMM, the structure of traditional HMM also limits its application to single dynamic process, that's why traditional HMM provides poor performance in recognition of complicated actions. To address this problem, Coupled Hidden Markov Model was proposed by Brand et al. [21] as solution to interactive action recognition. Hierarchical Hidden Markov Model was proposed by Luhr [22] and Nguyen [23] to analyze action for a long time.

In conclusion, HMM is very effective for modeling of temporal data and more robust than template matching. But the application of HMM is limited by its assumption, complicated model and numerous parameters.

Dynamic Bayesian networks [24] construct more flexible and effective model for complex dynamic procedure, leading to successful application in human segmentation and recognition. Other probabilistic networks, for instance conditional random field [25] has also achieved implementation for action models [26].

### 68.4.3 Part-Based Approach

We have introduced some action representations it Sect. 68.2, in fact, these representations can also be separated into local representations and global representation. As for the natural connection between action representation and recognition approach, different representation generates different recognition method. Global representations depend on precise location, background subtraction and tracing, which make recognition based on global representation more susceptible to view, noise, illumination and other factors. To overcome these shortage, part-based recognition approaches based on local action representation first detect spatial–temporal interest point and then calculate local feature to integrate final representation.

**Table 68.1** Comparison between Approaches

|  | Robust to time scale | Robust to space sale | Calculation complexity | Suitability to smart home |
|---|---|---|---|---|
| Template matching | Low | Low | Low | Medium |
| HMM | High | Medium | High | High |
| Part-base approach | Medium | High | High | High |

Consider a video volume as a collection of local parts, thus each parts contains some distinctive motion pattern. Dollar et al. [27] get feature prototypes by k-means clustering of a set of spatial–temporal gradients extracted at interest points from the training data, then the video can be modeled by the distribution of these features.

Among all the part-based recognition approach, the combination of local spatial–temporal feature and bag-of-word (BoW) model is most popular. BoW is a technology to conduct text information retrieval and classification in the area of natural language processing. Niebles et al. [15] introduced BoW into computer vision to represent actions. BoW regards video as a disorder collection of vision key words. They project the 2D image to collections of vision key words, which saves the local features of image as well as compress image representation efficiently. The bag of vision words is learned by extracting spatial–temporal interest points and clustering of the features. Together with support vector machines (SVM) and other machine learning approaches, BoW provides a new solution to action recognition. Figure 68.8 shows the process of action recognition based on local spatial–temporal feature and BoW. Codebook refers to the clustering result.

A new way to get global representation of the input video from local features is sparse coding [28, 29]. Recently, sparse coding has attracted researchers in image and video processing for relatively simple computation and large storage volume. Since Dollor [27] first use sparse coding in image processing, Yang et al. [30] proposed a linear spatial pyramid matching method using sparse coding for image classification which give insights to human action recognition. An action recognition system using sparse coding on local spatial–temporal volumes is implemented by Zhu et al. [31].

As we can see, every kind of recognition approach has its shortages and advantages. We compare three approaches above according to the papers [8, 20, 31], and list results in Table 68.1.

Real time performance is of great importance in home sensor network. Although template matching is not robust enough to time scale and space scale, we still consider it as a possible solution to smart home due to its low calculation complexity. With high recognition accuracy and emerging efficient calculation methods, HMM and part-based approach appear to be much more suitable for smart home.

## 68.5 Conclusion

Advances in human action recognition enable machines to understand and interact with human, thanks to the efforts of all the researchers fascinated by this field. The development of home sensor network give rise to a growing demand for more intelligent and humanized system equipped with excellent action recognition technology. However, present action recognition still faces the challenges of both efficiency and robustness for practical application.

Many approaches assume that video has already been segmented into sequences that contain single action, thus action detection is ignored, which is unacceptable in real time recognition for home sensor network. Although some work addressed this topic [32, 33], it remains a challenge for action recognition in smart home.

Normally, action recognition algorithms are tested on public datasets, for instance, UCF sport dataset, KTH human motion dataset, Hollywood human action dataset. Although most state of art approaches achieve recognition rate of over 80 %, performance in realistic situation appears to be poor for complex and ever-changing real environment.

Besides, most existing work focuses on accuracy rate of recognition more than processing efficiency, while in home sensor network, response time should be regarded as a matter of primary. For instance, an old man passed out at home, smart video surveillance has to respond as soon as possible. Thus, recognition efficiency remains a significant problem in home sensor network.

The problem of multi-view is not discussed in this paper, which is also an important and inevitable problem to be considered in home sensor networks. Preliminary works concerning view-invariant [34–37] problem in human action recognition set the stage for more researchers to engage themselves in this area.

In terms of real-time performance, robustness to real world conditions, complexity of sensor network architecture, action recognition for home sensor network provides opportunities coexisted with challenges in the future development!

## References

1. Kim K, Medioni GG (2008) Distributed visual processing for a home visual sensor network. Application of Computer Vision, pp 1–6
2. Shu C-F, Hampapur A (2005) IBM smart surveillance system (S3): a open and extensible framework for event based surveillance. Advanced video and signal based surveillance, pp 318–323
3. Collins RT, Lipton AJ (2000) A system for video surveillance and monitoring. Internal topical meeting on robotics and remote systems
4. Moeslund T, Granum E (2001) A survey of computer vision-based human motion captures. CVIU 81:231–268
5. Turaga P (2008) Machine recognition of human activities: a survey. Circuits Syst Video Technol 18(11):1473–1488

6. Poppe R (2010) A survey on vision-based human action recognition. Image Vision Comput 28(3):976–990
7. Parameswaran V, Chellappa R (2002) Quasi-invariants for human action representation and recognition. ICPR 2002, pp 307–310
8. Yamto J, Ohya J, Ishii K (1992) Recognizing human action in time-sequential images using hidden markov model. CVPR, pp 379–385
9. Wang L, Suter D (2007) Recognizing human activities from silhouettes: motion subspace and factorial discriminative graphical model. In: Coference on computer vision and pattern recognition
10. Veeraraghavan A, Chowdhury AR (2005) Matching shape sequences in video with applications in human movement analysis. PAMI 27(12):1896–1909
11. Laptev I, Lindeverg T (2003) Space-time interest points. Int Conf Comput Vision 1:432–439
12. Laptev I, Marszalek M, Schmid C, Rozenfeld B (2008) Learning realistic human actions from movies. CVPR
13. Klaser A, Marszalec M, Schmid C (2008) A spatio-temporal descriptor based on 3D-gradients. BMVC
14. Willems G, Tuytelaars T, Van Goll L (2008) An efficient dense and scale-invariant spatio-temporal interest point detector. ECCV
15. Niebles JC, Wang H, Fei LF (2006) Unsupervied learning of human action categories using spatial-temporal words. British Machine Vision Conference, pp 1249–1258
16. Feng X, Perona P (2002) Human action recognition sequence of movelet codewords. 3DPVT, pp 717–723
17. Guo Y, Xu G, Tsuji S (1994) Understanding human motion patterns. Int Conf Pattern Recogn 2:325–329
18. Marr D, Vaina L (1982) Representation and recognition of the movements of shapes. Philos Trans R Soc, pp 501–524
19. Arie JB, Wang Z, Pandit P, Rajaram S (2002) Human activity recognition using multidimensional indexing". IEEE Trans PAMI, 24(8):1091–1104
20. Bobick AF, Davis JW (2001) The recognition of human movement using temporal templates. PAMI 15:257–267
21. Brand M, Oliver N, Pentland A (1997) Coupled hidden markov models for complex action recognition, CVPR, pp 994–999
22. Luhr S, Bui H, Venkatesh S, West GAW (2003) Recognition of human activity through hierarchical stochastic learning. In: Proceedings on pervasive computing and communications, pp 416–422
23. Nguyen NT, Phung DQ, Venkatesh S, Bui H (2005) Learning and detecting activities from movement trajectories using the hierachical hidden Markov model. CVPR, pp 955–960
24. Zhao T, Nevatia R (2003) Bayesian human segmentation in crowed situations. CVPR 2: 459–466
25. Lafferty J, Mccallum A, Pereira F (2001) Conditional random fields: probabilistic models for segmenting and labeling sequence data. ICML, pp 282–289
26. Sminchisescu C, Kanaujia A, Li Z, Metaxas D (2005) Conditional models for contextual human motion recognition. ICCV, pp 1808–1815
27. Dollar P, Rabaud V, Cottrell G, Belongie S (2005) Behavior recognition via sparse spatio-temporal features. Surveillance performance evaluation of tracking surveillance, pp 65–72
28. Lee H, Battle A, Raina R (2005) Efficient sparse coding algorithms. NIPS, 2005
29. Qiu Q, Jiang Z, Chellappa R (2011) Sparse dictionary-based representation and recognition of action attributes. ICCV2011
30. Yang J, Yu K, Gong Y, Huang T (2009) Linear spatial pyramid matching using sparse coding for image classification. CVPR
31. Zhu Y, Zhao X, Fu Y (2010) Sparse coding on local spatial-temporal volumes for human action recognition. ACCV 2010
32. Yuan J, Liu Z, Wu Y (2009) Discriminative sub volume search for efficient action detection. CVPR, pp 2442–2449

33. Ke Y, Sukthankar R, Hebert M (2007) Event detection in crowded videos. ICCV
34. Imran N, Dexter E, Laptev I (2011) View-independent action recognition form temporal self-similarities. Pattern Anal Mach Intell 33:172–185
35. Ogale A, Karapurkar A, Guerra-Filho G, Aloimonos Y (2004) View-invariant identification of pose sequences for action recognition. VACE
36. Natarajan P, Nevatia R (2008) View and scale invariant action recognition using multi view shape-flow models. CVPR, pp 1–8
37. Cherla S, Kulkarni K, Kale A, Ramasubramanian V (2008) Towards fast, view-invariant human action recognition. Computer vision and pattern recognition workshops

# Chapter 69
# Hardware Implementation of Tier1 Coding for JPEG2000

**Shijie Qiao and Yuan Yang**

**Abstract** The tier1 coding is the main compression process in JPEG2000, the coding process is heavy computation and suitable for hardware implementation. This paper presents hardware architecture of the tier1 coding for JPEG2000, the whole architecture contains two coding blocks, one is the bit plane coding and the other is the arithmetic coding. The Verilog HDL modules for the architecture are designed, simulated and synthesized to Altera's FPGA. The result shows that the architectures designed in this paper are correct and efficient for JPEG2000.

**Keywords** JPEG2000 · Tier1 coding · Bit plane coding · Arithmetic coding · FPGA

## 69.1 Introduction

JPEG2000 is a new image coding standard which can get high performances than JPEG standard and supports a rich set of functionalities such as loss and lossless coding, region of interest and rate-distortion scalability [1]. In JPEG2000 coding systems, the image is wavelet transformed and the wavelet coefficients are then coded by tier1 coding [1, 2]. The wavelet transformation and tier1 coding are heavy computation and special hardware should be designed to implement them, such as in papers [3–5].

S. Qiao (✉) · Y. Yang
Department of Electronic Engineering, Xi'an University of Technology,
Xi'an 710048, China
e-mail: shijie_qiao@126.com

W. Lu et al. (eds.), *Proceedings of the 2012 International Conference on Information Technology and Software Engineering*, Lecture Notes in Electrical Engineering 212, DOI: 10.1007/978-3-642-34531-9_69, © Springer-Verlag Berlin Heidelberg 2013

In paper [6] we proposed a SOPC implementation of tier1 coding and code stream organization for JPEG2000. In that system, the tier1 coding is implemented in software. In this paper we proposed a hardware implementation for tier1 coding. The tier1 coding contains two coding blocks, the bit plane coding and arithmetic coding. The architectures for bit plane coding and arithmetic coding are designed and combined together to implement the tier1 coding. The verilog HDL modules for tier1 coding are programmed, simulated and synthesized to Altera's FPGA. The generated programming file is downloaded to FPGA, the Altera's embedded logic analyzer is used to debug the system, and the result shows that the architectures designed in this paper are correct. The hardware for tier1 coding presented in this paper will replace the software implementation of tier1 coding in paper [6].

This paper is organized as follow: the architecture of the tier1 coding is presented in Sect. 69.2. The architecture for bit plane coding is designed in Sect. 69.3. In Sect. 69.4, the architecture for arithmetic coding is proposed. The tier1 coding is implemented with FGPA in Sect. 69.5. Section 69.6 presents the conclusions.

## 69.2 Architecture for Tier1 Coding

The tier1 coding consists of two coding blocks, the bit plane coding and arithmetic coding [1, 2]. In JPEG2000, the wavelet transformed coefficients are partitioned into fixed-size code blocks, and the code blocks are then coded one bit plane at a time, starting from the most significant bit plane to the list significant bit plane. Each bit plane is coded with three passes, i.e. the significant propagation pass (SPP), the magnitude refinement pass (MRP) and the clean up pass (CUP). The basic coding operations include the zero coding (ZC), the sign coding (SC), the magnitude refinement coding (MRC) and the run-length coding (RLC). The symbols CX (context) and D (decision) produced by the bit plane coding are then coded by the arithmetic coding. The arithmetic coding adopted by JPEG2000 is an adaptive binary arithmetic coding, named MQ. The MQ encodes the symbols with MPS or LPS and the compressed data are produced.

The architecture for tier1 coding is showed in Fig. 69.1. The architecture contains three modules, i.e. the bit plane coding, the FIFO and the arithmetic coding. The wavelet coefficients in code blocks are read from memory to coded with the bit plane coding, the CX and D produced by the bit plane coding are

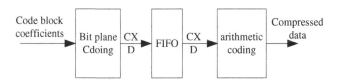

**Fig. 69.1** Architecture for tier1 coding

**Fig. 69.2** Architecture for
bit plane coding

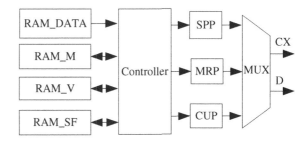

buffered in the FIFO and then send to the arithmetic coding to produce the
compressed data.

In Sects. 69.3 and 69.4, we will give the architectures for bit plane coding and
arithmetic coding. The two architectures are then combined together and synthesized to Altera's FPGA to implement the whole tier1 coding in Sect. 69.5.

## 69.3 Architecture for Bit Plane Coding

The architecture for bit plane coding is showed in Fig. 69.2. The architecture
contains four RAM modules. The coefficients been coding are stored in the
RAM_DATA, the refinement state variables are saved in the RAM_M, the coefficient's states of visited or not are saved in the RAM_V and the RAM_SF saves
the states of significant information. The coefficients are coded by three coding
passes: SPP, MRP, CUP and four basic coding operations, i.e. ZC, SC, MRC and
RLC, the symbols CX and D produce by the coding passes and four basic operations are outputted by the MUX.

The controller is the key module for the bit plane coding. It is implemented by
three state machines, i.e. the READ, WRITE and CODING state machine. The
relationship of the three state machines is showed in the Fig. 69.3.

The READ state machine is responsible for reading data from RAMs.
The CODING state machine controls the three coding passes: SPP, MRP and CUP.
The WRITE state machine is used to write data and information to RAMs.
The three state machines exchange information through the six signals: c_fetch,
c_write, r_ready, w_ready, r_work and w_work. The signals c_fetch and r_ready
are used to exchange information between the state machine READ and CODING.

**Fig. 69.3** Relationship of the
three state machines

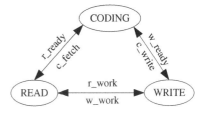

**Fig. 69.4** The CODING
state machine

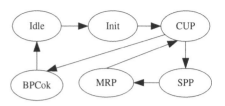

When r_ready is high, it means the data is ready and not fetched by the CODING
state machine, once the data is fetched, the c_fetch signal goes high. The signals
c_write and w_ready are used to inform the WRITE state machine to write data
and information to RAMS. The signals r_work and w_work are used to control the
write and read operations for RAMS.

The CODING state machine is a key control module for bit plane coding. The
diagram of CODING state machine is showed in Fig. 69.4.

The sates in the diagram are described blow:

Idle      Idle state.
Init      Make some initialization.
CUP       Clean up coding pass.
SPP       Significant propagation coding pass.
MRP       Magnitude refinement coding pass.
BPCok     Bit plane coding finished.

## 69.4 Architecture for Arithmetic Coding

The architecture for arithmetic coding is showed in Fig. 69.5. The CX and D
produced by the bit plane coding are buffered in FIFO. The CX_Lookup and
Qe_Lookup modules are used to estimate the probability. The coding module is
used to coding the symbols and output the compressed data CD.

The controller module in this architecture is implemented by state machine. The
state machine for the controller is showed in Fig. 69.6. When the system starts up,
the state machine stays in idle state, when the coding enable signal goes high, the
state machine changes it's state to CX_loopup, the index for probability is looked up
from the CX_table and the values I(CX) and MPS(CX) are returned. In the next
cycle, the state machine changes it's state to Qe_Lookup, in this state, the following

**Fig. 69.5** Architecture for
arithmetic coding

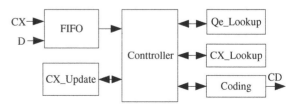

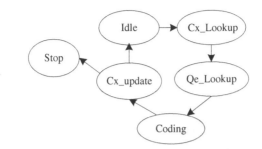

**Fig. 69.6** The state machine of the controller

values are get: Qe, NMPLS, NLPS and switch. In the next cycle, the state machine goes to the state named Coding. The Coding state spends about 15 clock cycles to calculate the interval and implement the normalization and then output the compressed data CD.

## 69.5  FPGA Implementation of the Tier1 Coding

The architectures of the bit plane coding and arithmetic coding are then combined together as showed in Fig. 69.1 to implement the tier1 coding for JPEG2000.

The Verilog HDL module for tier1 coding are designed and simulated. The simulation result shows that the bit streams outputted from the architecture are the same as the bit streams outputted from the C programs. Part of the simulation result is showed in Fig. 69.7.

The architecture of the tier1 coding is then synthesized to Altera's FPGA, The CycloneII device EP2C35F672C8 is selected, and the synthesized results show that the clock of the system can be up to 61.3 MHz. The resources used by the tier1 coding are listed in Table 69.1.

After place and route in Quartus II, the generated programming file is downloaded to the FPGA and tested in system as show in Fig. 69.8.

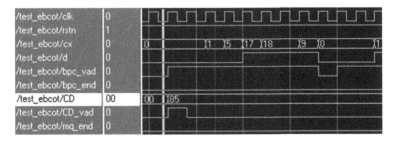

**Fig. 69.7**  Simulation result of the tier1 coding

**Table 69.1** The synthesized results

| Resource type | Used | Available | Utilization (%) |
|---|---|---|---|
| Total logic elements | 3,711 | 33,216 | 11 |
| Total memory bits | 52,224 | 483,840 | 10 |
| Total pins | 56 | 475 | 11 |

**Fig. 69.8** FPGA implementation of tier1 coding

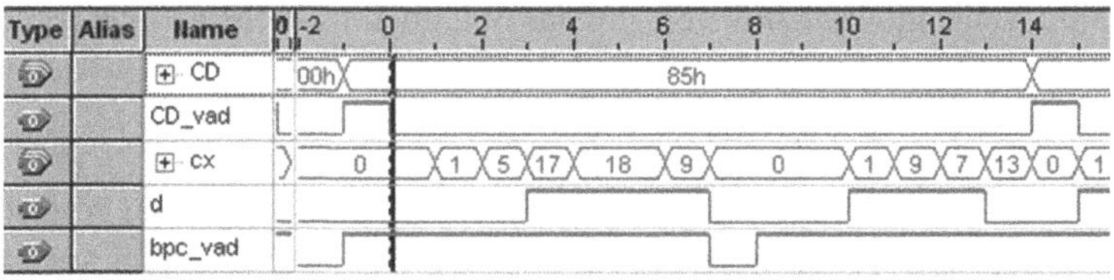

**Fig. 69.9** Waveform captured by signal-tap II

The Altera's embedded logic analyzer, named Signal-Tap II, is used to debug the system, part of the waveform captured by the signal-Tap II is showed in Fig. 69.9, the result shows that the architectures designed for tier1 coding in this paper are correct.

## 69.6 Conclusion

In this paper we proposed a FPGA implementation of tier1 coding for JPEG2000. The tier1 coding contains two coding blocks, the bit plane coding and arithmetic coding. The architectures for bit plane coding and arithmetic coding are designed and combined together to implement the tier1 coding. The Verilog HDL modules for tier1 coding are programmed, simulated and synthesized to Altera's FPGA. The generated programming file is downloaded to FPGA, the Altera's embedded logic analyzer is used to debug the system, and the result shows that the architectures designed in this paper are efficient for tier1 coding.

**Acknowledgments** This work is supported by Science and Technology Planning Project of Xi'an, China (No.CXY1119 (7)) and National Natural Science Foundation of China (No.61102017).

# References

1. ISO/IEC 15444-1 (2002) JPEG2000 image coding systems
2. Taubman D (2000) High performance scalable image compression with EBCOT. IEEE Trans Image Process 9(7):1158–1170
3. Liu LB, Chen N, Meng HY, Zhang L, Wang ZH, Chen HY (2004) A VLSI architecture of JPEG2000 encoder. IEEE J Solid-State Circuits 39(11):2032
4. Mei KZ, Zheng NN, Huang C, Liu YH, Zeng Q (2007) VLSI design of a high-speed and area-efficient JPEG2000 encoder. IEEE Trans Circuits Syst Video Technol 17(8):1065
5. Zhang YZ, Xu C, Wang WT, Chen LB (2007) Performance analysis and architecture design for parallel EBCOT encoder of JPEG2000. IEEE Trans Circuits Syst Video Technol 17(10):1336
6. Qiao SJ, Sain JQ, Gao Y, Yang Y, Wang HJ (2010) SOPC implementation of tier1 coding and code stream organization for JPEG2000. IEEE international conference on intelligent computing and intelligent systems, p 385

# Chapter 70
# Development of a Single-Leaf Disease Severity Automatic Grading System Based on Image Processing

Guanlin Li, Zhanhong Ma and Haiguang Wang

**Abstract** In order to realize accurately calculating and automatically grading of plant disease severity, a single-leaf disease severity automatic grading system based on image processing was developed by using MATLAB GUIDE platform. Using this system, the single-leaf disease severity could be automatically assessed and graded via image development technologies including segmentation processing technologies of plant disease images and related data mining technologies. Structural diagram of the system, algorithms used in the system and realization of the system functions were described. The problems in the current version of the system were discussed and further research on this subject was suggested. The usefulness and adaptability of the system was evaluated using the images of grape downy mildew caused by *Plasmopara viticola*. The results showed that the effectiveness of the system was favorable with high accuracy.

**Keywords** Plant disease · Severity · Automatic grading · Image processing · Computer aided system

## 70.1 Introduction

There are many kinds of plant diseases that can cause severe losses of agricultural production. To ensure the safety of agricultural production and food security, plant diseases should be predicted and be forecasted timely and accurately, and then be controlled effectively. Thus, the surveys of plant diseases should be conducted

G. Li · Z. Ma · H. Wang (✉)
Department of Plant Pathology, China Agricultural University, 100193 Beijing, China
e-mail: wanghaiguang@cau.edu.cn

W. Lu et al. (eds.), *Proceedings of the 2012 International Conference on Information Technology and Software Engineering*, Lecture Notes in Electrical Engineering 212, DOI: 10.1007/978-3-642-34531-9_70, © Springer-Verlag Berlin Heidelberg 2013

to obtain the information of plant disease epidemics. Plant disease severity ($S$), which is an important parameter to measure disease prevalence, is the relative quantity of diseased plant tissue, and is usually expressed as a representative value of disease classification from slight to serious, or area percentage of diseased tissue [1, 2]. Plant disease severity is an important part of the disease surveys. It implies disease level and can be used to predict and forecast plant diseases. It is difficult to carry out an objective and quantitative measurement of plant disease severity [3]. In the current agricultural production, severity is estimated mainly by using naked-eye observation method, which is a subjective assessment according to the experience of the experts, the agricultural technicians or the farmers. However, the estimation results of the same sample obtained by different people can sometimes be very different due to the differences of their knowledge structure and level. Determination of disease severity via this kind of method usually leads to the subjective and arbitrary results. So the objective and accurate estimation of the disease severity cannot be achieved and the results are unable to meet the needs of disease forecasting and disease management. To realize accurately calculating of disease severity, traditionally, disease severity is measured by using grid paper method or paper-weighing method. However, the operation of these methods is complicated and time-consuming, and it is difficult to make extensive use of these methods in the practical agricultural production. Therefore, it is significant to develop a fast, accurate and simple automatic grading system for plant disease severity.

With the development of computer technologies, computers in the studies on plant pathology are playing an increasingly important role. In recent years, it is more convenient and faster to make digital image acquisition and transmission. Digital image processing technologies have been widely used in agriculture field, such as quality detection of agricultural products, monitoring crop growth and manufacture of agricultural robots [4]. The applications of digital image processing technologies in the studies on plant pathology are increasing. For example, it has been used in diagnosis and recognition of plant diseases [5–9]. Computer vision instead of naked-eye observation has made it possible to solve the problems of accuracy and reproducibility in plant disease severity assessment [10]. The suitable image processing algorithms are available to implement automatic classification of plant disease severity.

In this study, a single-leaf disease severity automatic grading system based on digital image processing was developed by using MATLAB GUIDE platform. In the system, image analysis technologies were used to implement disease image processing, lesion segmentation, feature extraction and automatic grading of plant disease severity. The system could be used for disease severity automatic grading of single plant leaf. It could provide a basis for the establishment of a web-based risk assessment and diagnosis system for plant diseases.

## 70.2  General Structure of the System

For the single-leaf disease severity automatic grading system that was established, the input is single-leaf image of plant disease and the output is disease severity. The most important technology in the system is image processing technology, which can be used to extract useful information from the images rapidly and accurately. Image segmentation is one of the key steps of image processing. It refers to segmenting the interested regions from the image [11]. Similarly, segmentation of plant disease color image is to segment the leaf region and the diseased region from the color image of plant disease, respectively.

The general structure of the system contains establishment of plant disease images database, input and display of plant disease images, image segmentation, display of segmented regions, area feature extraction and automatic grading of disease severity. The system was developed in MATLAB 7.6 software environment. Algorithm operations and other related functions were realized using MATLAB as the programming language. The GUI interface of the system was designed using GUIDE tool set. The structural diagram of the system was shown in Fig. 70.1.

## 70.3  Key Technologies of the System

### 70.3.1  K_means Clustering Algorithm

In the single-leaf disease severity automatic grading system, $K$_means clustering algorithm was used for segmentation processing of plant disease images. $K$_means clustering algorithm proposed by Mac Queen in 1967 [12], is a kind of unsupervised real-time clustering algorithm. This algorithm is an indirect hard clustering

**Fig. 70.1** The structural diagram of the single-leaf disease severity automatic grading system based on image processing

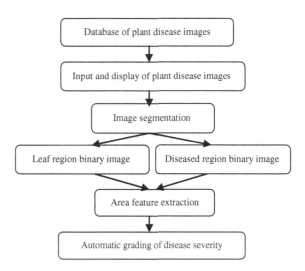

method based on the similarity between the samples. It divides $n$ pixels in the sample space into $k$ clusters with the clustering number $k$ as parameter to achieve high similarity between the pixels in a cluster and low similarity between the clusters. The cluster similarity can be calculated by using the cluster centroid that is the mean of all pixels' value, and the clustering effect can be evaluated using clustering criterion function. The detail procedure of $K\_$means clustering algorithm was described in [13].

The steps of image segmentation for plant disease using $K\_$means clustering algorithm were shown as follows. Firstly, the two initial clustering centers would be selected from the $m \times n$ pixels of plant disease image as the representatives of diseased region and normal region, respectively. The other pixels would be allocated to the most similar cluster according to their similarity with the clustering centers, and two new clusters would be obtained. Then the clustering centers could be calculated from the two new clusters, and the clustering process continues. The process is repeated until the convergence of the clustering criterion function appears. The segmentation result is the two changeless marked clusters.

## 70.3.2 L*a*b* Color Space Transformation

The color space models that can be used for image processing, mainly include *RGB, HSV (HIS), CMYK, XYZ, YUV* and *L*a*b**. Now, most image segmentation techniques of plant diseases are based on *RGB* color space and *HSV* color space, but image segmentation techniques based on other color spaces have rarely been reported. The color of diseased region of plant disease images is too complex to be described with a single color component. The component $a$ and $b$ from *L*a*b** color space are the description of color range, whose color space is larger than *RGB* color space, and they can insinuate all of the color information that *RGB* color space can describe [14]. In terms of the expression of color range, *L*a*b** color space is better than *RGB* color space. In the single-leaf disease severity automatic grading system that was established, image processing of plant disease images was conducted in *L*a*b** color space.

The symptom images of plant diseases acquired by using a common digital camera for the single-leaf disease severity automatic grading system, are described in *RGB* color space model. Since *RGB* color space cannot be directly transformed to *L*a*b** color space, it is needed to transform *RGB* color space to *XYZ* color space firstly, and then transform to *L*a*b** color space from *XYZ* color space. The method and the formula that were used for *L*a*b** color space transformation were shown in [13].

In *L*a*b** color space, all color information is contained in *ab* two-dimension data space. Color clustering can be conducted for image segmentation according to the differences between color pieces [15]. In the single-leaf disease severity automatic grading system, *ab* two-dimension data space was used to be matrix space for color clustering.

### 70.3.3 Calculating and Grading of Disease Severity

In the single-leaf disease severity automatic grading system, pixel statistical method was used to calculate disease severity of diseased leaf. The severity of plant leaf disease is usually measured by the area ratio of diseased region and leaf region. And it is also measured by the ratio of pixels in the matrix space of plant disease image, that is, the ratio between total pixels of diseased region and total pixels of leaf region. The formula for calculating area percentage $(s)$ occupied by diseased region was as follow [16]:

$$s = \frac{A_d}{A_l} \times 100\% = \frac{p \sum\limits_{(x,y) \in R_d} 1}{p \sum\limits_{(x,y) \in R_l} 1} \times 100\% = \frac{\sum\limits_{(x,y) \in R_d} 1}{\sum\limits_{(x,y) \in R_l} 1} \times 100\% \qquad (70.1)$$

in which $s$ is area percentage occupied by diseased region, $A_d$ is the area of diseased region, $A_l$ is the area of leaf region, $p$ is the area occupied by one pixel, $R_d$ is diseased region, and $R_l$ is leaf region.

The numbers of pixels of diseased region and leaf region can be calculated from the segmented binary images using pixel statistical method, respectively. And then the ratio between total pixels of diseased region and total pixels of leaf region can be calculated. Thus, the disease severity $(S)$ can be obtained and the severity level can be figured out according to the grading standards of plant disease severity.

## 70.4 Realization and Functions of the System

### 70.4.1 The Interface of the System

According to the general structure and design scheme of the system, the main functions of the system were implemented by using image processing algorithms with the application of GUIDE tool set in MATLAB 7.6 software environment. The system is composed of the function modules such as image input, image processing (including segmentation of leaf region and diseased region, regional display with primary color and binarization of segmented images) and data output (including area feature extraction and automatic grading of plant disease severity). The GUI interface of the system was as shown in Fig. 70.2.

### 70.4.2 Image Input

Vertical projection images of diseased single leaves can be acquired by using common digital camera. The size of the original images acquired for the system

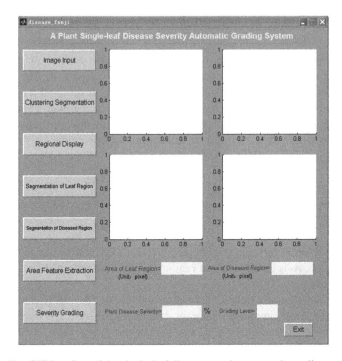

**Fig. 70.2** The GUI interface of the single-leaf disease severity automatic grading system based on image processing

was 2,592 × 1,944 with format of jpg, 24 bitmap. To reduce the operation speed of computer programs, the images were compressed from 2,592 × 1,944 to 800 × 600 in the same proportion without changing the image resolution. Database of plant disease images was established for image processing. The images could be inputted from the image database using the "Image Input" button on the GUI interface of the system, and could be displayed in the image area as shown in Fig. 70.3.

## 70.4.3 Image Processing

Image processing is the core function of the system. In the process, all the steps of image processing algorithms, i.e. clustering segmentation of three clusters, regional display with primary color, segmentation of leaf region, and segmentation of diseased region, are included. The realization of image processing was as shown in Fig. 70.4.

In the system, $K$_means clustering algorithm was used as the main algorithm for image segmentation. On the basis of the color differences of $ab$ two-dimension

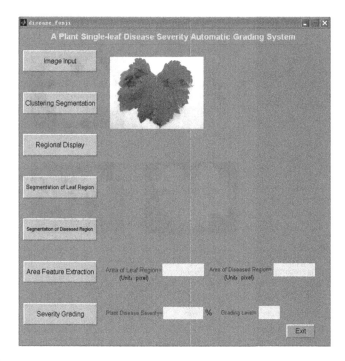

**Fig. 70.3**  Realization of image input for the single-leaf disease severity automatic grading system based on image processing

data space from $L^*a^*b^*$ color space model, iterative color clustering of three clusters is conducted using squared Euclidian distance as the similarity distance and mean square deviation as the clustering criterion function. Thus, the effective segmentation of the background, leaf region and diseased region is realized, and the generated clustering regions can be displayed with primary color. The implementation process of segmentation method was shown in [13]. The segmentation was programmed using $K\_means$ function and some related coefficients set in the Editor window of GUI Interface in MATLAB.

Gray threshold method was used to segment the leaf region. The clustering segmentation image is binarized and filled to get the binary image of leaf region. The segmentation of diseased region is the key step for the system. The three clustering piece is displayed with primary color. The background is displayed with black, whose gray value is zero. And then the segmentation image of diseased region can be obtained. After binarization of the segmentation image, the binary image can be obtained eventually. The processing result was displayed in the image area as shown in Fig. 70.4.

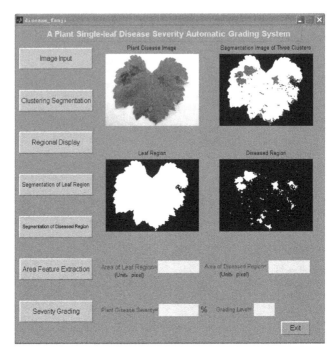

**Fig. 70.4** Realization of image processing for the single-leaf disease severity automatic grading system

## 70.4.4 Data Output

The system for plant single-leaf disease severity automatic grading based on image processing can identify and judge the information of plant disease images, and finally figure out the grading level of disease severity which is usually measured by the area ratio of diseased region and leaf region. Area features are needed to be extracted from the binary image of leaf region and diseased region. In the system, the pixel numbers of the binary images of leaf region and diseased region are calculated using pixel statistical method. The ratio of the pixel numbers of leaf region and diseased region is used to calculate the level of disease severity according to the grading standards of plant disease severity. The processing result was displayed in the data area as shown in Fig. 70.5.

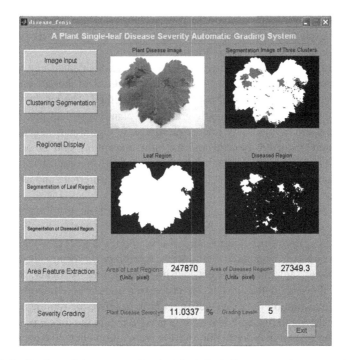

**Fig. 70.5** Realization of data output for the single-leaf disease severity automatic grading system based on image processing

## 70.5 Conclusion and Discussion

A single-leaf disease severity automatic grading system was developed based on image processing by using MATLAB GUIDE platform. The single-leaf vertical projection color images of plant diseases could be treated using the system. The functions including image processing, image segmentation, feature extraction and automatic grading of plant disease severity, and so on, were implemented in the system. It could be used for computer-aided measurement and automatic grading of plant disease severity. On a standard computer, the system can easily be used in combination with a digital camera.

In the single-leaf disease severity automatic grading system based on image processing, $K$\_means clustering algorithm was used as the main algorithm for image segmentation. After $RGB$ color space transformed to $L^*a^*b^*$ color space, iterative color clustering of three clusters was conducted using $ab$ two-dimension matrix space to realize the effective segmentation of the background, leaf region and diseased region, and the generated clustering regions were displayed with primary color. The leaf region and diseased region were segmented after image binarization processing. The pixel numbers of the binary images were calculated using pixel statistical method, and the severity levels of diseased leaves were

674                                                                          G. Li et al.

outputted according to the ratio of the pixel numbers and the grading standards of plant disease severity. So image input, image processing and severity output for plant disease images were realized using the system.

The usefulness and adaptability of the system was evaluated and tested using grape downy mildew caused by *Plasmopara viticola*. And the accuracy of automatic grading was verified using paper-weighing method. The results showed that the system can be used for automatic grading of plant single-leaf disease severity. Using the system, subjectivity and arbitrariness of traditional naked-eye observation method could be avoided and the time-consuming and labor-consuming shortcomings of paper-weighing method could be overcome. The system can provide a rapid, accurate and effective way for the measurement and assessment of plant disease severity.

Because $K$_means clustering algorithm requires high quality images, the effect of complex environment should be controlled in the process of collecting plant disease images. Therefore, it needs further research if the system would be applied in the filed surveys. Compared with other algorithms, $K$_means clustering algorithm has better segmentation effect, but its running time is longer. So it is suggested that the size of the images for processing should be compressed without changing the resolution of the images in order to improve the running speed of the system. For the small diseased leaves, it is needed to add the image pre-processing module to the system in order to improve the recognition effect and the accuracy of automatic grading.

With the development of network technology and agricultural informatization, more and more agricultural technicians and farmers can obtain agricultural technique knowledge from the internet to solve the problems in agricultural production. It is more convenient and easier to use and popularize computer aided system based on web in agricultural production. Web-based system for recognition and severity grading of plant disease, should be developed to meet the needs of agricultural production in the future. When the users upload digital plant disease images to this kind of system, it could provide the information about plant disease types and the severity levels of plant diseases timely for prediction and prevention of plant diseases.

**Acknowledgments** The work was supported by National Key Technology R&D Program (2007BAD57B02) and National Department Public Benefit (Agriculture) Research Foundation (200903035).

# References

1. Xiao YY, Ji BH, Yang ZW, Jiang RZ (2005) Epidemic and forecast of plant disease. China Agricultural University Press, Beijing (in Chinese)
2. Xu ZG (2009) Plant pathology, 4th edn. Higher Education Press, Beijing (in Chinese)
3. James C (1971) A manual of assessment keys for plant disease. American Phytopathological Society, St. Paul

4. Fang RM, Cai JR, Xu L (1999) Computer image processing technology and its application in agricultural engineering. Tsinghua University Press, Beijing (in Chinese)
5. Tucker CC, Chakraborty S (1997) Quantitative assessment of lesion characteristics and disease severity using digital image processing. J Phytopathol 145:273–278
6. Wang YL, Dai XL (2007) The application of neural network and image processing in the expert system of rice's diseases and insects. Microcomput Inf 23:274–275 (in Chinese)
7. Cen ZX, Li BJ, Shi YX, Huang HY, Liu J, Liao NF, Feng J (2007) Discrimination of cucumber anthracnose and cucumber brown speck base on color image statistical characteristics. Acta Horticulturae Sinica 34:1425–1430 (in Chinese)
8. Tan F, Ma XD (2009) The method of recognition of damage by disease and insect based on laminae. J Agric Mechanization Res 28:41–43 (in Chinese)
9. Guan H, Zhang CL, Zhang CY (2010) Grading method of cucumber leaf spot disease based on image processing. J Agric Mechanization Res 29:94–97 (in Chinese)
10. Nilsson HE (1995) Remote sensing and image analysis in plant pathology. Can J Plant Pathol 17:154–166
11. Zhao SL (2009) MATLAB R2008 example tutorial for digital image processing and analysis. Chemical Industry Press, Beijing (in Chinese)
12. Selim SZ, Ismail MA (1984) $K$-means-type algorithm: a generalized convergence theorem and characterization of local optimality. IEEE Trans Pattern Anal Mach Intell 6:81–87
13. Li GL, Ma ZH, Huang C, Chi YW, Wang HG (2010) Segmentation of color images of grape diseases using $K$_means clustering algorithm. Transactions of the CSAE 26(Suppl.2):32–37 (in Chinese)
14. He NB, Du YH (2008) Extraction method of isochromatic's skeleton based on Lab color space. Henan Sci 26:1324–1326 (in Chinese)
15. Zhang Q, Wang ZL (2009) Being proficient in image processing using MATLAB. Publishing House of Electronics Industry, Beijing (in Chinese)
16. Chen ZL, Zhang CL, Shen WZ, Chen XX (2008) Grading method of leaf spot disease based on image processing. J Agric Mechanization Res 27:73–75 (in Chinese)

# Chapter 71
# Pornographic Image Filtering Method Based on Human Key Parts

Ni Pengyu and Huang Jie

**Abstract** Many non-pornographic images containing large exposure of skin area or skin-like area are prone to be detected as the pornographic images. In order to decrease the false positive rate, we propose a novel pornographic filtering method based on human key parts detection in this paper. The method extracts extended Haar-like features which describe local grayscale distribution, and then trains the classifier of human key parts detection with AdaBoost learning algorithm. To further improve the system performance, we extract Histogram of Oriented Gradient features, Texture features based on Gray Level Co-occurrence Matrix and Color Moment features of the human key parts. And the Radial Basis Function Neural Network classifier is trained by these features. The experiments show that this method can detect precisely the human key parts in the images, and can reduce effectively the false positive rate against the non-pornographic images.

**Keywords** Haar-like feature · AdaBoost learning algorithm · Histograms of oriented gradient · Gray level co-occurrence matrix · Color moment · Radial basis function neural network

N. Pengyu (✉) · H. Jie
School of Information Science and Engineering, Southeast University,
210096 Nanjing, China
e-mail: latuo786@sina.com

H. Jie
e-mail: jhuang@seu.edu.cn

W. Lu et al. (eds.), *Proceedings of the 2012 International Conference on Information Technology and Software Engineering*, Lecture Notes in Electrical Engineering 212, DOI: 10.1007/978-3-642-34531-9_71, © Springer-Verlag Berlin Heidelberg 2013

# 71.1 Introduction

With the rapid development of Internet, a large amount of multimedia information is transmitted over the Internet, such as texts, images and videos, etc. It is much easier for users including teenagers to be exposed to sexual contents. Therefore, it is necessary to block pornographic images by a filtering system.

Most of the researches focus on skin detection, which is combined with texture and shape features. In [1], a histogram-based mixture model was used for skin detection and a contour-based algorithm was used for detecting pornographic images. In order to determine adaptively the corresponding skin-color distribution of an image in different lighting conditions, a multilayer feed-forward neural network was used to learn and judge whether the image contained skin [2]. An improved skin model in RGB color space [3] was employed to identify the rough skin regions. Then the useful information of the skin regions was extracted and fed to the SVM classifier to identify whether the image was pornographic or not. In [4], an approach was proposed, which identified skin pixels with the face detection. Based on skin tone information, skin pixels were calculated in the facial region and the remaining body region, and feature vector was prepared. In [5], a pornographic image filtering model was proposed with high-level semantic features, which optimized BoVW model to minimize semantic gap between low-level features and high-level semantic features, and then high-level semantic dictionary was constructed by fusing the context of the visual vocabularies and spatial-related high-level semantic features of pornographic images.

All existing methods mentioned above have a fundamental problem that they do not conduct the detection at the organ level. Many non-pornographic images containing large exposure of skin area or skin-like area are prone to be detected as the pornographic images. So in [6], the skin detection was firstly conducted, and then the nipple detection was performed by using self-organizing map neural network. But the correct nipple detection rate is 65.4 %. In order to increase the nipple detection rate, a method was proposed in [7]. The breast is recognized by virtue of some attributes of the breast, such as ellipse-like shape, the amount of edge pixels and the area of the skin pixels surrounding it. The detection rate and false positive rate of the method is 80.31 and 19.69 % respectively.

In this paper, we train the classifier of human key parts detection with AdaBoost learning algorithm. To further improve the system performance, we extract histogram of oriented gradient (HOG) features, texture features based on gray level co-occurrence matrix (GLCM) and color moment features of the human key parts. A RBF neural network classifier is trained by using these features to reduce effectively the false positive rate against the non-pornographic images.

The rest of this paper is arranged as follows. Section 71.2 introduces briefly the architecture of the pornographic image filtering system. Section 71.3 analyzes the defects of the existing feature extraction method and proposes an improved method. Section 71.4 analyzes and evaluates the AdaBoost algorithm, Radial Basis Function neural network algorithm and C4.5 decision tree algorithm, then proposes the cascaded structure of the AdaBoost classifier and RBF neural network classifier. Experimental results and analysis are presented in Sect. 71.5. Finally, the conclusion of this paper is presented in Sect. 71.6.

## 71.2 The Architecture of the System

The architecture of the pornographic image filtering system is shown in Fig. 71.1.

We train the cascaded AdaBoost classifier of human key parts detection by the extended Haar-like features. The classifier is scanned across the image at multiple scales and locations. Scaling is achieved by scaling the classifier itself, rather than scaling the image. This process makes sense because the features can be evaluated at any scale with the same cost. Multiple locations are obtained by shifting the classifier. To further improve the system performance, we extract Histogram of Oriented Gradient features, Texture features based on Gray Level Co-occurrence Matrix and Color Moment features of the human key parts. The RBF neural network classifier is trained by these features. The human key parts are then cross-checked by the RBF neural network classifier.

In this paper, there are three main contributions as follows:

1. In human key parts detection, the variability of body postures usually causes the deformation of human key parts, thus the original Haar-like features cannot describe effectively the local grayscale distribution. In this paper, the original Haar-like features are extended to describe the deformation more effectively.
2. To detect quickly the candidates of the human key parts by the cascaded AdaBoost classifier. Owing to the limitations of the AdaBoost algorithm and the Haar-like features, we get a high false positive rate during the detection process. We conduct a further detection by using the color features, texture features and shape features.
3. To propose a cascaded structure of the AdaBoost classifier and RBF neural network classifier. A coarse-to-fine strategy is adopted. The human key parts

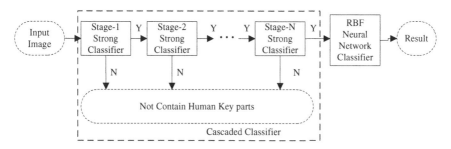

**Fig. 71.1** The architecture of the pornographic image filtering system

are detected first by the cascaded AdaBoost classifier, and then the candidates are cross-checked by the RBF neural network classifier.

## 71.3 Improved Method of Feature Extraction

Haar-like features [8] are reminiscent of Haar basis functions which can be used to describe the local grayscale distribution. LienHart et al. [9] introduce an extended set of Haar-like features, which include edge features, line features and center-surrounded features. We choose five of them to describe normal human key parts in Fig. 71.2a–e. However, the body postures are variable. The variability usually cause the deformation of human key parts, so the shapes of human key parts look like elliptical as shown in Fig. 71.23–6. The computational complexity of the elliptical Haar-like features is high, thus we extend Haar-like features in Fig. 71.2f–i.

Haar-like features just describe the local grayscale distribution. If we just employ Haar-like features, it will cause easily false-positive errors as shown in Fig. 71.3.

In Fig. 71.3a and d, the grayscale distribution and shape features are similar to the human key parts, but the color features and texture features are different. In Fig. 71.3c, the grayscale distribution and texture features are similar to the human key parts, but the shape features and color features are different. But in Fig. 71.3b, the grayscale distribution, color features, shape features and textures features are all similar to the human key parts, so it is difficult to distinguish correctly them.

As for Fig. 71.3a and d, the color features and texture features are employed to distinguish them. In this paper, the gray level co-occurrence matrix $P(i,j|d, \theta)$ of the image is used to compute energy, entropy, contrast, correlation and inverse

**Fig. 71.2** Extended
Haar-like features

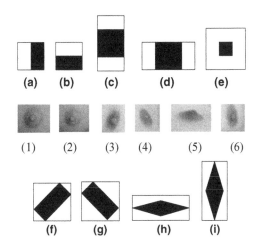

(a)  (b)  (c)  (d)  (e)

(1)    (2)    (3)    (4)    (5)    (6)

(f)    (g)    (h)    (i)

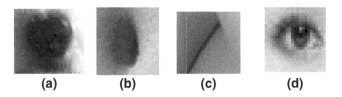

| (a) | (b) | (c) | (d) |

**Fig. 71.3** Haar-like features similar to human key parts

difference moment [10], where $d$ is the distance between two different pixels, and $\theta$ is the angle between the two pixels and the horizontal line:

1. Energy

$$f_1 = \sum_i \sum_j \{P(i,j|d,\theta)\}^2 \qquad (71.1)$$

2. Entropy

$$f_2 = \sum_i \sum_j P(i,j|d,\theta) \log_2 P(i,j|d,\theta) \qquad (71.2)$$

3. Contrast

$$f_3 = \sum_i \sum_j (i-j)^2 P(i,j|d,\theta) \qquad (71.3)$$

4. Correlation

$$f_4 = \frac{\sum_i \sum_j ij P(i,j|d,\theta) - \mu_x \mu_y}{\sigma_x^2 \sigma_y^2} \qquad (71.4)$$

5. Inverse Difference Moment

$$f_5 = \sum_i \sum_j \frac{1}{1+(i-j)^2} P(i,j|d,\theta) \qquad (71.5)$$

When to compute the texture features of the human key parts, the training images are scaled and aligned to a base resolution of 24 × 24 pixels. In this paper, $d$ is set to 1, and the angle is set to 0, 45, 90, and 135° respectively, and then we can get four angular gray level co-occurrence matrices of each image. Hence a set of four values is obtained for each of the preceding 5 measures, and a set of 20 features is comprised.

The color features can be characterized by the color moments [11] and most color distribution information is concentrated in the lower-order moments. The first moment (mean), the second moment (variance) and the third moment (skewness) are taken as features. These features are defined as follows:

$$\mu = \frac{1}{N} \sum_i \sum_j p_{ij} \qquad (71.6)$$

$$\sigma = \left[ \frac{1}{N} \sum_i \sum_j (p_{ij} - \mu)^2 \right]^{1/2} \qquad (71.7)$$

$$s = \left[ \frac{1}{N} \sum_i \sum_j (p_{ij} - \mu) \right]^{1/3} \qquad (71.8)$$

Where $N$ is the total number of the pixels in the image, and $p_{ij}$ is the image pixel in location $(i,j)$.

The RGB model is not well suited for describing a color image from human-perception point of view. Moreover, a kind of color is not simply formed by these primary colors. In contrast, the HSV model is more natural to describe a color image for human visual system. Considering the way human visual system perceives the color object, we compute the color moments in the HSV color space. The image is first scaled and aligned to 24 × 24 pixels, and then it is transferred from RGB to HSV. According to the Eqs. (71.6)–(71.8), the color moments are computed independently for each HSV channel and a set of 9 color features can be obtained.

In Fig. 71.3, the shape features are employed to distinguish Fig. 71.3c from Fig. 71.3a. The shape features can be characterized by the HOG [12] descriptors which can describe the local appearance and shape, so they are usually used for human detection or pedestrian detection [13, 14]. The HOG features are calculated as follows:

1. The image is scaled and aligned to 24 × 24 pixels, and then it is divided into 4 blocks of 16 × 16 pixels. Each block contains 4 cells of 8 × 8 pixels.
2. The image gradient is computed by applying the $[-1, 0, 1]$ and $[1, 0, -1]^T$ filter kernels.
3. The 9 orientation bins are evenly spaced over $[-\frac{\pi}{2}, \frac{\pi}{2}]$, and the votes are accumulated into orientation bins over local spatial regions, namely cells.
4. To reduce aliasing, votes are interpolated trilinearly [15] between the neighboring bin centers in both orientation and position.
5. In order to account for changes in illumination and contrast, the gradient strengths must be locally normalized. The normalization scheme is used as follows:

$$v \leftarrow v \Big/ \sqrt{\|v\|^2 + \varepsilon^2} \qquad (71.9)$$

Where $v$ is the feature vector before normalization, and $\varepsilon$ is a regularization parameter.

6. To obtain a set of 36 features from each block, and to obtain finally a set of 144 HOG features from the 4 blocks of the image.

In this paper, a joint feature is finally obtained by combining the color features, texture features and shape features. And in Fig. 71.3, the false positive errors are decreased effectively by the joint feature.

## 71.4 Optimizing AdaBoost Algorithm

In order to obtain the best filtering effect, we first analyze and compare AdaBoost algorithm [16], Radial Basis Function neural network algorithm and C4.5 decision tree algorithm, and then propose the cascaded structure of the AdaBoost classifier and RBF neural network classifier based on the experimental results.

In this paper, we first obtain several weak classifiers from the set of extended Haar-like features as shown in Fig. 71.2, and the strong classifier takes the form of a perceptron and a weighted combination of weak classifiers. Due to the fact that an overwhelming majority of sub-windows are negative within any single image, the cascaded AdaBoost classifier is employed in this paper. The cascaded classifier attempts to reject as many negatives as possible at the earliest stage.

The RBF neural network is a three-layer feed-forward neural network with a single hidden layer [17, 18]. The RBF neural network with the local generalization abilities and fast convergence speed can overcome the shortcomings of slow convergence and local minimum of back propagation (BP) neutral network. It can solve effectively complex pattern classification problems, which are small-sample and non-linearly separable.

C4.5 decision tree [19], which is an extended version of ID3, is developed to break through the limitations with the ID3. It uses the information gain ratio during the tree building process. The C4.5 can deal with continuous attributes which is not supported by ID3. It also proposes a pruning method which deals with the removal of unwanted branches generated by noise or too small size of training data.

A cascaded AdaBoost classifier is trained by employing the extended Haar-like features. By the joint feature as discussed in Sect. 71.3, the RBF neural network classifier and the C4.5 decision tree classifier are trained respectively. Then the four different classifiers are tested on the same testing set, and the results are shown in Table 71.1.

In Table 71.1, the recall ratio of the cascaded AdaBoost classifier is lower than the RBF neural network classifier. Haar-like features only describe the local grayscale distribution, and each feature is independent. Because of the lack of global consideration of the sample, the number of the false positives is high and the precision ratio is low. The cascaded classifier can reject as many negatives as possible at the earliest stage, so the detection speed is high. The recall ratio of the RBF neural network classifier is the highest and it shares the excellent generality. However, there are a large number of neurons in the classifier and the tested image

**Table 71.1** Testing result for four classifiers

| Classifier | Human key parts number | Correct detection number | False positive number | False negative number | Recall ratio | Precision ratio (%) | Average detection speed (second/frame) |
|---|---|---|---|---|---|---|---|
| AdaBoost | 443 | 417 | 89 | 26 | 94.13 % | 82.41 | 0.94 |
| RBF neural network | 443 | 423 | 42 | 20 | 95.48 % | 90.96 | 8.43 |
| C4.5 decision tree | 443 | 368 | 115 | 75 | 83.06 | 76.19 | 0.36 |

*Recall Ratio* Correct Detection Number/(Correct Detection Number + False Negative number)
*Precision Ratio* Correct Detection Number/(Correct Detection Number + False Positive number)

need to be compared with the center vectors of all of the neurons in the hidden layer. The computational complexity is high, so the detection speed is the lowest. The C4.5 decision tree classifier only selects a small number features and is not globally optimal. It only employs a set of simple rules to classify the images and cannot solve non-linearly separable problems, so it generates a large number of false positives and false negatives, and both the recall ratio and precision ratio are the lowest. But the computational complexity is much lower, so the detection speed is the highest.

Through comparison of the four classifiers, both the detection speed and the recall ratio of the cascaded AdaBoost classifier are high. But it generates many false positives, so the precision ratio is low. The RBF neural network classifier can effectively decrease the false positives. It can achieve high recall ratio and precision ratio, but the detection speed is low. If the cascaded AdaBoost classifier and the RBF neural network classifier can be cascaded, their advantages can be complemented each other. On the one hand, the RBF neural network classifier can reduce effectively the false positives of the cascaded AdaBoost classifier, on the other hand, there are a small number of the candidate human key parts through the cascaded AdaBoost classifier, therefore the RBF neural network classifier doesn't need to scan through the whole image, so we can achieve both high detection accuracy and detection speed.

## 71.5 Experimental Results and Analysis

In this paper, a cascaded AdaBoost classifier is trained firstly. To further improve the system performance, a RBF neural network classifier is trained by employing the joint feature as discussed in Sect. 71.3 and the final pornographic image filtering system is obtained. The detection accuracy and detection speed of the system are to be tested.

The training set of the cascaded AdaBoost classifier is divided into two subsets: Nipple set and Non_Nipple set. The Nipple set has 1,059 images which only contain human key parts and the Non_Nipple set has 1,070 images which do not contain any human key parts. All of the training images are scaled and aligned to 12 × 12 pixels. In this paper, we set the maximum acceptable false positive rate per stage (fp) to 0.7, the minimum acceptable detection rate per stage (det) to 0.99 and the target overall false positive rate (Ftarget) to 0.03. Finally, a cascaded AdaBoost classifier of 10 stages is obtained.

The training set for the RBF neural network classifier is also divided into two subsets: Nipple set and Non_Nipple set. The Nipple set has 1,058 images which only contain human key parts and the Non_Nipple set has 1,058 images which do not contain any human key parts. All of the training images are scaled and aligned to 24 × 24 pixels. As discussed in Sect. 71.3, the joint feature of the image is extracted and the dimension of the feature is 173. The orthogonal least squares learning algorithm which was proposed by Chen [20] is used to train the RBF neural network classifier. In this paper, we set the number of hidden nodes to 12. Finally, a RBF neural network classifier is obtained and the result is shown in Fig. 71.4.

## 71.5.1 Detection Precision

To illustrate that the cascaded structure can reduce effectively the false positives of the cascaded AdaBoost classifier, the cascaded AdaBoost classifier and the pornographic image filtering system are tested on the same testing set which has 200 pornographic images. The result is shown in Table 71.2.

**Fig. 71.4** Result for RBF neural network classifier

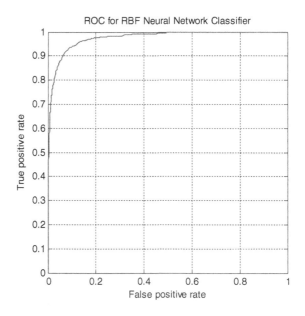

**Table 71.2** Result for detection precision testing

| Classifier | Key parts number | Correct detection number | False positive number | False negative number | Recall ratio | Precision ratio |
|---|---|---|---|---|---|---|
| AdaBoost | 443 | 419 | 89 | 26 | 0.9413 | 0.8241 |
| AdaBoost + RBF | 443 | 410 | 26 | 33 | 0.8347 | 0.9404 |

**Table 71.3** Result for pornographic image detection precision

| Testing set | Pornographic images detected | Correct detection rate (%) | False positive/negative rate (%) |
|---|---|---|---|
| Pornographic images | 176 | 88 | 12 |
| Normal images | 17 | 96.6 | 3.4 |
| Nude images | 28 | 94.4 | 5.6 |

In Table 71.2, the experimental results show that the pornographic image filtering system improves effectively recall ratio when the precision ratio is almost not changed.

To illustrate that the pornographic image filtering system can detect effectively pornographic images, the pornographic image filtering system is tested on the testing set which has 200 pornographic images and 1,000 normal images. The half of the normal images is nude but not pornographic. The result is shown in Table 71.3.

In Table 71.3, the proposed method can achieve excellent performance. Through analysis of the false negatives and false positives, the major reasons are listed following for the false negatives:

1. The images have big revolving angles in plane and out of plane.
2. The human key parts are occluded.
3. The size of the human key parts is too small.

**Table 71.4** Results for pornographic images detection speed

| Classifier | Pornographic images | | | Normal images | | |
|---|---|---|---|---|---|---|
| | Image number (Frame) | Time | (second) | Speed (frame/ second) | Image | |
| number (frame) | Time (second) | Speed | (frame/ second) | | | |
| AdaBoost | 200 | 185.64 | 1.08 | 1,000 | 699.73 | 1.43 |
| AdaBoost + RBF | | 207.47 | 0.96 | | 704.52 | 1.42 |

**Table 71.5** Performance of two different methods

| Method | Correct detection rate (%) | False negative rate (%) | False positive rate (%) | Time (frame/ second) |
|---|---|---|---|---|
| Method [7] | 79.64 | 15.76 | 12.79 | 0.63 |
| Proposed method | 88.37 | 5.78 | 6.52 | 1.08 |

## *71.5.2 Detection Speed*

In order to provide real-time performance, the detection speed of the pornographic image filtering system must be high enough. To illustrate the real-time performance of the system, the system is tested on the same testing set discussed in Sect. 71.5.1. The results are shown in Table 71.4.

In Table 71.4, the detection speed of the system is a bit lower than that of the cascaded AdaBoost classifier. Because the candidate human key parts passed to the RBF neural network classifier are scaled and aligned to 24 × 24 pixels, the dimension of the joint feature is low and the computational complexity is not too high. And there are a small number of candidate human key parts through the cascaded AdaBoost classifier; therefore the processing time of the system is almost the same with the cascaded AdaBoost classifier.

To evaluate the performance of the proposed method, the proposed method and the method in [7] are tested on the same testing set. The results are shown in Table 71.5.

In Table 71.5, the proposed method can reduce effectively the false positives and improve the detection speed. Therefore the method can achieve excellent performance.

## 71.6 Conclusions

In this paper, we propose a novel pornographic image filtering method based on human key parts detection. The method can achieve better performances than the existing methods in both detection precision and detection speed.

Our contributions of this paper include as follows:

1. To extend the Haar-like features which can describe effectively the local grayscale distribution more.
2. To obtain joint features by using color features, texture features and shape features to describe effectively the human key parts.
3. To adopt a coarse-to-fine strategy which can decrease effectively the false positive errors in human key parts detection.

# References

1. Hu W, Wu O, Chen A, Fu Z, Maybank S (2007) Recognition of pornographic web pages by classifying texts and images. IEEE Trans Pattern Anal Mach Intell 29(6):1019–1034
2. Lee J-S, Kuo Y-M, Chung P-C, Chen E-L (2007) Naked image detection based on adaptive and extensible skin color model. Pattern Recogn 40(8):2261–2270
3. Yin H, Huang X, Wei Y (2012) SVM-based pornographic images detection. Softw Eng Knowl Eng AISC 2(115):751–759
4. Sharma J, Pathak VK (2011) Automatic pornographic detection in web pages based on images and text data using support vector machine. Proc Int Conf SocProcS, AISC 131: 473–483
5. Lv L, Zhao C, Lv H, Shang J, Yang Y, Wang J (2011) Pornographic images detection using high-level semantic features. In: 7th International conference on natural computation, pp 1015–1018
6. Fuangkhon P, Tanprasert T (2005) Nipple detection for obscene ictures. In: Proceedings of the 5th International Conference on signal, speech and image processing, Greece, pp 315–320
7. Wei Wei (2008) The Research on network pornographic image filtering based on erotogenic-part detection. Jilin University, Changchun (in Chinese)
8. Viola P, Jones M (2001) Rapid object detection using a boosted cascade of simple features. computer vision and pattern recognition. In: Proceedings of the 2001 IEEE computer society conference on computer vision and pattern recognition, vol 1, pp I-511–I-518
9. Lienhart R, Maydt J (2002) An extended set of haar-like features for rapid object detection. In: Proceedings IEEE conference on image processing, pp 900–903
10. Haralick RM, Shanmugam K, Dinstein I (1973) Textual features for image classification. IEEE Trans Syst Man Cybern 3(6):610–621
11. Stricker MA, Orengo M (1995) Similarity of color images. In: Proceedings of SPIE: storage and retrieval for image and video databases, vol 420, pp 381–392
12. Dalal N, Triggs B (2005) Histograms of oriented gradients for human detection. Proc IEEE Conf Comput Vision Pattern Recognit 1(2):886–893 (San Diego, USA)
13. Gero'nimo D, Lo'pez AM, Sappa AD (2010) Survey of pedestrian detection for advanced driver assistance systems. IEEE Trans Pattern Analysis Machine Intell 31(4):1239–1257
14. Haiyan X, Zhitao X, Fang Z (2011) Study on pedestrian detection method based HOG feature and SVM. Adv Mater Res 268–270:1786–1791
15. Dalal N (2006) Finding people in images and videos. Institute National Polytechnique de Grenoble, France
16. Viola P, Jones MJ (2004) Robust real-time face detection. Int J Comput Vision 57(2):137–154
17. Ahmat Nor NL, Harun S, Mohd Kassim AH (2007) Radial basis function modeling of hourly streamflow hydrograph. J Hydrol Eng 12(1):113–123
18. Zhengrong Y (2006) A model radial basis function neural network for discriminant analysis[J]. IEEE Trans Neural Netw 17(3):604–612
19. Webb AR, Copsey KD (2011) Statistical pattern recognition, 3rd edn. Wiley, Malvern
20. Chen S, Cowan CFN, Grant PM (1991) Orthogonal least squares learning algorithm for radial basis function networks. IEEE Trans Neural Netw 2(2):302–309

# Chapter 72
# Imaging of Transmission Equipment by Saliency-Based Compressive Sampling

Jingjing Zhao, Xingtong Liu, Jixiang Sun and Shilin Zhou

**Abstract** The traditional intelligent inspection system often takes high-resolution images and then compressed through the codec for efficient storage purpose, which leads to the waste of image data and memory resources. The compressive sampling theory showed that under certain conditions, a signal can be precisely reconstructed from only a small set of measurements, however, the reconstruction algorithms are generally very expensive. By studying on the need of imaging of the transmission equipment, we adopt an imaging method based on saliency to balance the reconstruction complexities and the quality of image. The method first uses a low-resolution complementary sensor to obtain the saliency information of the scene, then obtains the saliency map of the imaging scene by the spectral residual approach, and then assigns higher sample rate to the area of transmission equipment and lower sample rate to the background area in compressive imaging. The simulation results show that the image of transmission equipment can be precisely reconstructed from only a small set of measurements.

**Keywords** Compressive sampling · Visual saliency · Intelligent inspection · Transmission equipment · Compressive imaging

## 72.1 Introduction

With the rapid spread of the transmission network, a vast number of overhead transmission equipment deployed in the sparsely populated areas. Therefore, the technology of helicopter/UAV patrol becomes a trend for the intelligent inspection.

J. Zhao (✉) · X. Liu · J. Sun · S. Zhou
School of Electronic Science and Engineering, National University of Defense Technology, 410073 Changsha, People's Republic of China
e-mail: zhaojingjing63@gmail.com

W. Lu et al. (eds.), *Proceedings of the 2012 International Conference on Information Technology and Software Engineering*, Lecture Notes in Electrical Engineering 212, DOI: 10.1007/978-3-642-34531-9_72, © Springer-Verlag Berlin Heidelberg 2013

It first takes images of transmission equipment, then identifies and locates the transmission equipment which is needed repair by analyzing these images. As the first step in intelligent inspection, imaging of the transmission equipment with high quality is of great significance. In generally, the intelligent inspection system takes high-resolution images of equipment, images are first sampled into the digital format at a higher rate and then compressed through the codec for efficient storage purpose. Since many coefficients which carry negligible energy are discarded before coding, much of the acquired information is discarded during this process although the image is fully acquired, which leads to the waste of image data and memory resources.

Recently, a novel sampling theory called as compressive sampling has been developed for simultaneous sampling and compression. It builds on the groundbreaking work by Candes et al. [1] and Donoho [2], who showed that under certain conditions, a signal can be precisely reconstructed from only a small set of measurements. The compressive sampling principle provides the foundation of obvious reduction of sampling rates and computation complexity in digital data acquisitions, it has stirred great excitements both in academia and industries, the compressive imaging is also proposed and developed in the past few years [3, 4]. Since the reconstruction algorithms are generally very expensive, Lu Gan proposed block-based sampling for fast compressive sampling of natural images, where the original image is divided into small blocks and each block is sampled independently using the same measurement operator [5]. Due to the block-by-block processing mechanism, the sampling algorithm has very low complexities, but the quality of reconstructed image is degraded. Ying Yu et al. considered the characteristic of human perception and proposed a saliency-based compressive sampling scheme for image signals to reduce the computational cost of signal recovery algorithms that are able to reconstruct the full-length signal from the small amount of measurement data [6].

For the imaging of transmission equipment by the intelligent inspection system, we prefer to obtain high quality image of the transmission equipment and care less about the quality of the background, therefore, we can assign different sampling rate to different regions based on their salient characteristic. Our work is partially inspired by Ying Yu et al., we used the compressive sampling scheme they proposed and employ a low a low-resolution complementary sensor to obtain the saliency information of the scene. However, we use a method with generality called as spectral residual approach [7] to obtain the saliency map of the imaging scene, thus we can get different kinds of transmission equipment that should be assigned higher sample rate. The spectral residual model is independent of features, categories, or other forms of prior knowledge of the objects, which is suitable for detect different kinds of transmission equipment. Furthermore, the spectral residual approach is fast and simple to construct the corresponding saliency map with low computational complexity.

## 72.2 Salient Transmission Equipment Detection

The intelligent inspection system takes images of different kinds of transmission equipment. In the compressive imaging system, we tend to assign higher sampling rate to salient regions with transmission equipment but lower sampling rate to non-salient background regions, however, the traditional compressive imaging system can't distinguish between transmission equipment and background by itself. When we observe the scene, the equipment automatically and effortlessly "pop-out" from their surroundings, they draw our visual attention because of their saliency [8]. Our vision system can extract the salient regions before performing feature analysis, this is called pre-attention. The candidate object which pops out in the pre-attentive stage is defined as proto object [9]. Hou et al. proposed a front-end method to simulate the behaviour of pre-attentive visual search based on the principle of natural image statistics. They transformed the spectral residual to spatial domain to obtain the saliency map and to locate the proto-objects. We briefly review the spectral residual model in this section [7].

According to the information theory, the image information $H$ (*Image*) can be decomposed into two parts:

$$H(image) = H(innovation) + H(priorknowledge) \qquad (72.1)$$

where $H$ (*innovation*) represents the novel part of the image, which can be seen as the salient information, $H$ (*prior knowledge*) represents the redundant information, which can be seen as statistical invariant properties of our environment [10]. Therefore, the innovational part of an image can be approximate by removing the statistical redundant components. According to the *1/f* law, the innovational part of an image can be defined by spectral residual $R(f)$:

$$R(f) = L(f) - A(f) \qquad (72.2)$$

where $L(f)$ is the log spectrum representation of image amplitude spectrum, $A(f)$ denotes the general shape of log spectra $L(f)$, which is given as prior information. The averaged spectrum $A(f)$ can be approximated by convoluting the input image:

$$A(f) = h_n(f) \times L(f) \qquad (72.3)$$

where $h_n(f)$ is an $n \times n$ smooth matrix defined below:

$$h_n(f) = \frac{1}{n^2} \begin{pmatrix} 1 & 1 & 1 & \cdots & 1 \\ 1 & 1 & 1 & \cdots & 1 \\ \vdots & \vdots & & \ddots & \vdots \\ 1 & 1 & 1 & \cdots & 1 \end{pmatrix} \qquad (72.4)$$

Since the spectral residual contains the innovation of an image, we can obtain the saliency map $S(i)$ which contains primarily the nontrivial part of the scene by using the Inverse Fourier Transform:

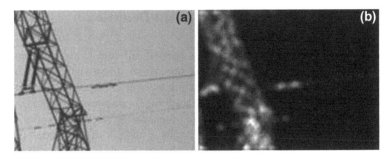

**Fig. 72.1** The original image and saliency map of transmission equipment. **a** Original image. **b** Saliency map

$$S(i) = G(i) \times \mathrm{F}^{-1}[\exp(R(f) + P(f))]^2 \qquad (72.5)$$

where $P(f)$ represents the phase spectrum of the image, $F^{-1}$ denotes the Inverse Fourier Transform, $i$ denotes the pixel in the image. For better saliency effects, we smooth the map with a Gaussian filter $G(i)$. Here, the saliency part can also be interpreted as the location of transmission equipment, which is shown in Fig. 72.1.

## 72.3 Saliency–Based Compressive Imaging of Transmission Equipment

### 72.3.1 Compressive Sampling Theory

Compressive sampling is a new technique for simultaneous data sampling and compression, which enables us to stably reconstruct an image of the scene from fewer measurements than the number of reconstructed pixels. Assume an N-dimensional vector $X$ represents an $N$-pixel digital image. Let

$$X = \Psi\theta = \sum_{i=1}^{N} \theta_i \varphi_i \qquad (72.6)$$

where $\theta = [\theta_1, \theta_2, \cdots\cdots, \theta_N]$ is an $N$-dimensional vector with its coefficient $\theta_i = X^{\mathrm{T}}\varphi_i$, $\Psi = [\varphi_1, \varphi_2, \cdots\cdots, \varphi_N]$ is an $N \times N$ orthonormal basis matrix with $\varphi_i$ as the $i$th column. In a word, $\theta$ is the representation of $X$ in domain $\Psi$. If only $K$ entries of $\theta$ are nonzero, $X$ is called $K$-sparse $(K \ll N)$ in domain $\Psi$. In fact, many signals can be approximated as sparse and the compressive sampling theory is based on this property.

Suppose that we are allowed to take $M$ $(K \ll N)$ linear, non-adaptive measurement of $X$ through the following linear transformation [1, 2]:

$$Y = \Phi X = \Phi\Psi\theta \qquad (72.7)$$

where $Y$ denotes the $M$-dimensional measurement vector of $X$, $\Phi$ is a $M \times N$ linear measurement matrix. It was proved in [1, 2] that when $\Phi$ and $\Psi$ are incoherent, $X$ can be well recovered from $M \geq cKlog(N/K)$ measurements through non-linear optimizations according to the Eq. (72.8), and $c$ is a positive constant.

$$\min_{\theta \in R^N} \|\tilde{\theta}\|_{l_1} \text{ subject to } Y = \Phi\Psi\tilde{\theta} \tag{72.8}$$

## 72.3.2 Sensing Resource Allocation

The main problem of the compressive sampling is that the reconstruction algorithms are generally very expensive, the block-based sampling for fast compressive sampling can reduce the computational cost of signal recovery algorithms, but the quality of reconstructed image is affected by the sample rate. The good reconstruction quality always requires relatively high sampling rate, however, the high sample rate leads to high computational cost of signal recovery. Here, we tend to obtain high quality image of the transmission equipment and care less of the quality of the background, thus we assign higher sensing resource to salient regions with transmission equipment but lower sensing resource to the background.

The block compressive sampling is performed in the manner of block processing, therefore, we need to calculate the saliency value of each image block to assign sensing resource. We employ a low-resolution complementary sensor to acquire a small image and generate a saliency map by using the small image [6]. The sampling controller calculates the number of random measurements for each image block-based on the saliency map, and then controls the block compressive sampling to perform random sampling. Using the measurement data from the block compressive sampling, the signal reconstruction algorithm can recover all the image blocks. The reconstructed blocks are combined to form a full-size image. The framework of the system is shown in Fig. 72.2.

In detail, we first use the low-resolution sensor to obtain a small image of the scene with transmission equipment, then measure the saliency of the scene with spectral residual model, and then resize the saliency map to a full-size image that should be reconstructed, finally, we can get the block saliency $B(k)$ by:

$$B(k) = \frac{1}{L} \sum_{i \in B(k)} S(i) \tag{72.9}$$

where $L$ is the total number of pixels in a block. The number of measurement in block compressive sampling can be assigned by the Eq. (72.10):

$$R(k) = rnd(B(k) \cdot (R_{max} - R_{min}) + R_{min}) \tag{72.10}$$

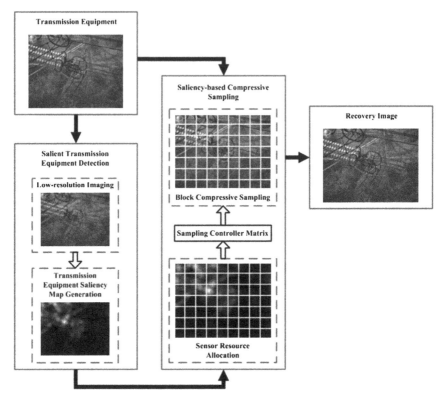

**Fig. 72.2** The framework of the saliency-based compressive imaging system

where $rnd()$ is the rounding function, $R_{Max}$ and $R_{Min}$ are the maximum and minimum of the number of measurements that assigned to the block.

## 72.4 Experiments

As usually done in literature, we use high-resolution images of transmission equipment to simulate the effects that the data were fully acquired, which serves as a reference. We set the block size to $N = 32 \times 32 = 1024$ pixels, which is proved to provide a good trade-off between compressive sampling efficiency and reconstruction complexity [5]. We resize the original image to $64 \times 64$ pixels to simulate small image acquired by low-resolution complementary sensor, and use this small image to get the saliency map. The maximum and minimum of the number of measurements that assigned to each block are 150 and 90. Each block of the original image is compressively sampled with the assigned number of random linear measurements in the wavelet domain, and recovered using orthogonal matching pursuit [11]. At last, all recovery blocks are combined to a full-size image.

**Fig. 72.3** The simulation results of compressive imaging. **a** Reference images. **b** Recovery images with saliency-based compressive sampling

| Table 72.1 The PSNR of simulative experiments | Average sampling rate (%) | PSNR |
|---|---|---|
| The first image | 11.62 | 57.70 |
| The second image | 11.62 | 62.21 |

We have tested the method on different kinds of transmission equipment, parts of reconstruction results are shown in Fig. 72.3, which provide a visual comparison of the recovery images and the fully acquired reference image. The images are about 2048 × 1536 pixels. Since the images are too large to show on the screen, we adjust the image to 10 % of the original image to display. The table 72.1 shows the peak signal-to-noise ratio (PSNR) of the reconstructed image quality, which provide an objective evaluation of the proposed method.

## 72.5 Conclusions

The intelligent inspection system often takes traditional imaging process of data acquisition followed by compression, which leads to the waste of image data. By studying on the mechanism of compressive sampling theory and considering the need of intelligent inspection system, we use an imaging method by saliency-based compressive sampling to image the transmission equipment. The compressive sampling here is performed in the manner of block processing, which is proved to save the computational cost of signal recovery algorithms. We assign higher sample rate to salient blocks with transmission equipment but lower sensing resource to the others. The saliency value of each image block is estimated by the spectral residual approach. One of the advantages of the spectral residual approach is its generality, it doesn't need any prior knowledge for saliency detection. The other advantages of the spectral residual approach is that the computational consumption is parsimonious, which providing a promising solution to real time systems. The experiment results show that the method can save memory resources and reduce computational cost of signal recovery algorithms effectively.

# References

1. Candes E, Romberg J, Tao T (2006) Robust uncertainty principles: exact signal reconstruction from highly incomplete frequency information. IEEE Trans InformTheor 52:489–509
2. Donoho DL (2006) Compressed sensing. IEEE Trans InformTheor 52:1289–1306
3. Romberg J (2008) Imaging via compressive sampling. IEEE Signal Process Mag 25:14–20
4. Duarte MF, Davenport MA, Takhar D, Laska JN, Sun T, Kelly KF, Baraniuk RG (2008) Single-pixel imaging via compressive sampling. IEEE Signal Process Mag 25:83–91
5. Gan L (2007) Block compressed sensing of natural images. In: Proceedings of international conference on digital signal processing, Cardiff, UK
6. Yu Y, Wang B, Zhang L (2010) Saliency-based compressive sampling for image signals. IEEE Signal Process Lett 17:973–976
7. Hou X, Zhang L (2007) Saliency detection: a spectral residual approach. In: Proceedings of IEEE conference on computer vision and pattern recognition, Minneapolis, Minnesota, USA
8. Koch C, Ullman S (1985) Shifts in selective visual attention: towards the underlying neural circuitry. Hum Neurobiol 4:219–227
9. Rensink R (2000) Seeing, sensing, and scrutinizing. Vision Res 40:1469–1487
10. Srivastava A, Lee A, Simoncelli E, Zhu S (2003) On advances in statistical modelling of natural images. J Math Imaging Vis 18:17–33
11. Tropp JA, Gilbert AC (2007) Signal recovery from random measurements via orthogonal matching pursuit. IEEE Trans InformTheor 53:4655–4666

# Chapter 73
# A Noise-Insensitive Algorithm for Pixel Level Image Registration Based on Centroid

Song Feng, Linhua Deng, Jiaben Lin, Hui Deng and Kaifan Ji

**Abstract** Pixel level displacement measurement is the first stage of Coarse-to-Fine approach in high-accuracy image registration. However, the measurement accuracies of well-known techniques drop sharply with increasing of the image noise. We present a noise-insensitive pixel level registration algorithm, which is based on estimating the centroid of cross correlation surface with modified moment method, for low quality images. The experiment of eight standard testing images shows that our proposed algorithm could decrease the minimum requirement of PSNR for pixel level registration, and determine some image displacements which might not be handled by traditional methods.

**Keywords** Image · Registration · Cross · Correlation · Modified · Moment · Pixel level

S. Feng · H. Deng · K. Ji (✉)
Computer Technology Application Key Lab of Yunnan Province, Kunming University of Science and Technology, 650500 Chenggong, Kunming, China
e-mail: jkf@cnlab.net

S. Feng · J. Lin
Key Laboratory of Solar Activity, National Astronomical Observatories, Chinese Academy of Sciences, 100012 Beijing, China

L. Deng
National Astronomical Observatories/Yunnan Astronomical Observatory, Chinese Academy of Sciences, 650011 Kunming, China

L. Deng
Graduate University of Chinese Academy of Sciences, 100049 Beijing, China

W. Lu et al. (eds.), *Proceedings of the 2012 International Conference on Information Technology and Software Engineering*, Lecture Notes in Electrical Engineering 212, DOI: 10.1007/978-3-642-34531-9_73, © Springer-Verlag Berlin Heidelberg 2013

## 73.1 Introduction

Many image processing applications require registering multiple overlaying on the same scene images taken at different times, such as image fusion and super-resolution in remote sensing, biomedical imaging, and astronomical observation and so on. Image correlation technique is a typical area-based matching method in this field, and can be calculated in frequency domain [1, 2]. Over the years, various image registration algorithms based on this idea have been developed, especially in processing subpixel registration [3–10]. For achieving high-accuracy subpixel result, many methods are based on Coarse-to-Fine approach [5]. In the first stage, a pixel level displacement is obtained, and then the image is shifted coarsely. In the second stage, a finer approximation is performed to assess subpixel displacement. There are many related researches on the second stage. However, for pixel level registration, classical techniques such as Cross Correlation (CC) and Phase Correlation (PC) are still used widely.

In some case, for example, in astronomical image processing, the objects are extremely faint and very low contrast and emit light in certain specific wavelengths. Edges of texture are fuzzy and smooth. The Peak Signal-to-Noise Ratio (PSNR) is so low that classical image registration techniques might not obtain the correct result even on pixel level, and registration would fail in the first stage. In this paper, we propose a noise-insensitive pixel level registration algorithm to process this kind of low PSNR images.

## 73.2 Related Work

CC and PC algorithms are two well-known images registration techniques in frequency domain [1, 11–13]. Both of them take Fourier transform of two images first and calculate the cross-power (in CC) or the phase of the cross-power spectrum (in PC), then take inverse Fourier transform to obtain the correlation surface. In frequency domain, the cross-power spectrum is defined as:

$$R(u, v) = F(u, v)G^*(u, v) \qquad (73.1)$$

And the phase of the cross-power spectrum is defined as:

$$R(u, v) = \frac{F(u, v)G^*(u, v)}{|F(u, v)G^*(u, v)|} \qquad (73.2)$$

Where $F(u,v)$ and $G(u,v)$ are Fourier Transform of reference image $f(x,y)$ and register image $g(x,y)$. $G^*$ $(u,v)$ is the complex conjugate of $G(u,v)$. The coordinate of the maximum of the correlation surface $r(x,y)$, which is the inverse Fourier transform of $R(u,v)$, is the estimation of the horizontal and vertical components of shift between two images. Comparing with CC, PC provides a distinct sharp peak at the point of registration whereas CC yields several broad peaks [1]. Although popular, PC techniques have some disadvantages as well. It is more sensitive to noise than direct CC, both for low-pass and high-pass inputs. Sharpening the correlation peaks comes at the expense of increased sensibility to noise of the computed maximum position [11]. Barbara Zitova [1] indicated that in a general case PC could fail in case of multimodal data as well. We tested our images with both CC and PC, and confirmed the earlier results. Therefore, CC was selected as our basic approach for pixel level registration.

## 73.3  Proposed Algorithm

Both CC and PC algorithm are based on detecting the single maximum point. However, our algorithm applies statistics values instead of the single point. The centroid coordinate of CC surface is used to determine the displacement of two images. In astronomical image processing, modified moment is a popular digital centering algorithm and has been widely used in measurement of star positions in digital images [14]. It provides high-accuracy with very high speed. The peak of the CC surface looks like a single star peak, and surrounded by a few of coherent peaks.

In modified moment method, a threshold level is set and only considering those count levels in the data array that are above this threshold in the centering process. Specifically, once the threshold b is determined in the I(x,y) data array, each pixel in the array is calculated according to the following precepts:

$$
\begin{aligned}
I'(x,y) &= I(x,y) - b &&\text{if } I(x,y) > b \\
I'(x,y) &= 0 &&\text{if } I(x,y) < b
\end{aligned}
\tag{73.3}
$$

Then, the centroid of the peak is set equal to the first moment of the marginal distribution.

$$
\begin{aligned}
x_c &= \sum_x x I'(x,y) / \sum_x I'(x,y) \\
y_c &= \sum_y y I'(x,y) / \sum_y I'(x,y)
\end{aligned}
\tag{73.4}
$$

We apply modified moment in the centroid estimation of CC surface. First, select a radius around the maximum of the peak, and set the threshold b by the minimum value inside the circle. Second, calculate each pixel value above the threshold by Eq. (73.3). Third, determine the centroid with the first moment by Eq. (73.4). Fourth, round the centroid coordinate to the nearest integer that equals the pixel level of displacement between two images.

Obviously, the algorithm is based on the assumption that the maximum of the peak is at the same position as the centroid. That means the correlation value above the threshold should be symmetrical in both of horizontal and vertical

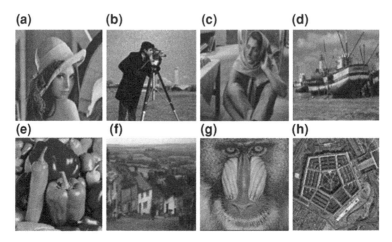

**Fig. 73.1** Eight standard testing images were used in comparison of algorithms. **a** Lena, **b** Camera man, **c** Barbara, **d** Fishing boat, **e** Peppers, **f** Gold hill, **g** Baboon, **h** Pentagon

directions. The assumption is acceptable in the small center area of the cross correlation peak. In our experiment, the radius was set to 3 pixels.

Comparing with picking the maxima value of CC or PC surface, our approach reduces the registration error in mostly case of low PSNR images (<15 dB).

## 73.4 Experimental Setup and Results

Figure 73.1 shows the eight standard testing images (128 × 128) that were employed for our pixel level registration experiment.

Each of them was shifted by a random integer pixel in uniform distribution on the interval [−5, 5] through the x and y directions to obtain pixel level shifted images set. One hundred simulation shifted images were generated from each standard image, and then the White Gaussian Noise (WGN) was added.

Figure 73.2 shows an example of PC and CC surfaces for two Lena images shifted by (3, 2) pixels and PSNR is 5 dB. On the PC surface (left), the maximum point is hard to find. On the CC surface (right), the peak appears but the coordinate of the maximum point is not exactly same as the displacement of two images. Fortunately, after calculating the centroid with modified moment, our algorithm gets the correct answer on CC surface.

Figure 73.3 shows the processing results of the image Lena by PC, CC and the proposed algorithm on different WGN level. Where X axis represents the PSNR in dB, and Y axis represents the percentage of correct registration on specific PSNR level. The minimum requirement of PSNR for achieving 100 % accuracy in registration represents the noise-insensitive ability of an algorithm. Therefore, we

**Fig. 73.2** The example of the PC (*left*) and CC (*right*) surfaces of Lena

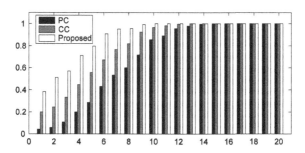

**Fig. 73.3** The processing results of the image LENA with different PSNR by PC, CC and the proposed algorithm

**Table 73.1** The evaluation index of eight standard testing images with processed by three algorithms

|             | PC   | CC   | Proposed |
|-------------|------|------|----------|
| Lena        | 14   | 12   | 9        |
| Camera man  | 14   | 10   | 7        |
| Barbara     | 16   | 14   | 10       |
| Fishing boat| 14   | 11   | 9        |
| Peppers     | 14   | 12   | 8        |
| Gold hill   | 15   | 14   | 14       |
| Baboon      | 13   | 12   | 11       |
| Pentagon    | 9    | 9    | 9        |
| Average     | 13.6 | 11.7 | 9.6      |

choose it as the evaluation index in our comparison. In Fig. 73.3, our proposed algorithm achieves 100 % accuracy at 9 dB, CC at 12 dB, and PC at 14 dB. The minimum requirement of PSNR is decreased by our approach. All processing results of eight images are shown in Table 73.1.

Except the image of 'Pentagon', which we get the same results for all three algorithms, our proposed algorithm shows robustness against random noise comparing with PC and CC. The minimum requirement of PSNR decreases 2 dB in average, and 4 dB in maximum. It means our algorithm could estimate some images displacement which could not be handled by PC or CC.

## 73.5 Conclusions

This paper presents a noise-insensitive technique for pixel level image registration based on calculating the centroid of CC surface by modified moment. The proposed algorithm could decrease the minimum requirement of image PSNR for obtaining correct image translation. The main reasons are that statistics value is calculated instead of a single point, and more information of the correlation surface is involved. Meantime, modified moment provides highly accurate centroid position of CC surface peak. Obviously, the performance depends not only on PSNR, but also the details of images. In some case, for example, the image of 'Pentagon', since it has strongly self-similarity, our algorithm does not show its advantage. However, in most of our testing images, minimum requirement of PSNR is decreased. Our experiment confirms the conclusion of [11] that PC is more noise sensitive than CC as well. Actually, our algorithm could also estimate subpixel shift in image registration, and we will work in this field in the future.

The algorithm will be applied on weak Solar Magnetic Field (SMF) images processing of National Astronomical Observatories, Chinese Academy of Sciences. Hundreds of SMF images are needed to be registered on pixel level and accumulated for increasing the PSNR and decreasing the effects of atmospheric turbulence, wind and the tracking accuracy of the telescope itself in real-time.

**Acknowledgments** We appreciate the support from National Natural Science Foundation of China (11163004, 11003041), and Open Research Program of Key Laboratory of Solar Activity of Chinese Academy of Sciences (KLSA201221, KLSA201205).

## References

1. Zitova B, Flusser J (2003) Image registration methods: a survey. Image Vis Comput 21:977–1000
2. Brown LG (1992) A survey of image registration techniques. ACM Comput Surv (CSUR) 24:325–376
3. Tian Q, Huhns MN (1986) Algorithms for subpixel registration. Comput Vis, Graph, Image Process 35:220–233
4. Zhou F, Yang W, Liao Q (2012) A coarse-to-fine subpixel registration method to recover local perspective deformation in the application of image super-resolution. IEEE Trans Image Process 21:53–66
5. Sousa AMR, Xavier J, Vaz M, Morais JJL, Filipe VMJ (2011) Cross-correlation and differential technique combination to determine displacement fields. Strain 47:87–98
6. Ren J, Jiang J, Vlachos T (2010) High-accuracy subpixel motion estimation from noisy images in Fourier domain. IEEE Trans Image Process 19:1379–1384
7. Hoge WS (2003) A subspace identification extension to the phase correlation method. IEEE Trans Med Imaging 22:277–280
8. Foroosh H, Zerubia JB, Berthod M (2002) Extension of phase correlation to subpixel registration. IEEE Trans Image Process 11:188–200
9. Stone HS, Orchard MT, Chang EC, Martucci SA (2001) A fast direct Fourier-based algorithm for subpixel registration of images. IEEE Trans Geosci Remote Sens 39:2235–2243

10. Guizar-Sicairos M, Thurman ST, Fienup JR (2008) Efficient subpixel image registration algorithms. Opt Lett 33:156–158
11. Manduchi R, Mian GA (1993) Accuracy analysis for correlation-based image registration algorithms. In: Proceedings of the ISCAS, pp 834–837
12. Pratt WK (1974) Correlation techniques of image registration. IEEE Trans Aerosp Electron Syst 10:353–358
13. Kuglin CD, Hines DC (1975) The phase correlation image alignment method. In: Proceedings of the international conference on cybernetics and society, pp 163–165
14. Stone RC (1989) A comparison of digital centering algorithms. Astron J 97:1227–1237

# Chapter 74
# A Human Skin-Color-Preserving Extension Algorithm for Wide Gamut Displays

Xiankui Meng, Gang Song and Hua Li

**Abstract** Gamut extension algorithm is applied in wide-gamut displays to keep hue unaltered and exert a good performance. A skin-color-preserving algorithm based on CIE-Lab space is proposed here. At first the accurate human skin color region is to determined, then a proper algorithm is presented to avoid the skin color distortion and make the normal colors still have good performance comparing to current extension algorithm. Experiment result on theory and practice shows skin colors are extended little and normal colors still have great extension level.

**Keywords** Gamut extension · Gamut mapping · Skin color preserving · Wide gamut display

## 74.1 Introduction

Wide gamut displays (WGD), like LED backlit LCD displays and laser displays, develop so fast since it appeared, which makes it necessary and urgent to have a good algorithm to transform images to WGD from standard gamut displays, like CRT displays. Simply display the image in WGD without transformation will cause color distortion because the primaries are varied in different displays, we can't take full advantage of WGD's wider gamut as well.

Hue preservation and detail preservation are two top objectives to take care of when we formulate gamut mapping [1]. A large many technologies on

X. Meng · G. Song (✉) · H. Li
School of Information Science and Engineering, Shandong University, No. 27 Shanda Nanlu, Jinan, Shandong, People's Republic of China
e-mail: sddxsg@163.com

W. Lu et al. (eds.), *Proceedings of the 2012 International Conference on Information Technology and Software Engineering*, Lecture Notes in Electrical Engineering 212, DOI: 10.1007/978-3-642-34531-9_74, © Springer-Verlag Berlin Heidelberg 2013

transforming an image into a limited gamut, such as a printer gamut, have been proposed, and many of them presented methods of retaining detail information [2, 3]. As kind of an opposite process to gamut compression, gamut extension will not lose detail information, but enhance it to some degree. Even so, we shared some of their theories to finish the work.

We found that few of the color gamut extension algorithms took skin colors into consideration. In these algorithms, all colors will be extended to higher saturation [4], some of the skin colors will overstep the region that all skin colors fall in and look unnatural red after extension to WGD. So in his paper we propose a skin-color-preserving algorithm. Finally, we evaluate the performance of our algorithm in theory and practice.

## 74.2 Algorithm

There contains two steps: first, in order to preserve skin colors, we need to determine the accurate human skin color region; then second, according to the relationship between skin color region and the standard color gamut, a proper algorithm is constructed that can both restrict skin colors and have good performance on global gamut.

We take CRT gamut (sRGB) as the standard gamut and laser TV gamut as the target gamut. And the transformations are done in CIELab space. We take the following processes to achieve the extension: First, we chose the focal point O(white point) in CIELab space and restrict the extension of any pixel C of sRGB gamut to the ray originating in O and shooting in the direction of C, Ray $\overrightarrow{OC}$ intersects sRGB boundary at S, laser TV boundary at D. Figure. 74.1 shows the result of these processes.

Then the extension can be applied by a function related with the foregoing conditions.

### 74.2.1 Human Skin Color Region Determination

Research shows that on a double color difference plane, such as a CbCr plane at a certain Y value, skin colors almost have the same distribution among different ethnic groups, the difference of skin colors mainly concentrates on luminance [5]. Zhengzhen Zhang [5] proposed a series of formulas to describe human skin color distribution in YCgCr [6] and YCgCb [7] space. On CgCr planes skin color region is fitted as a parallelogram described by the following formulas:

$$\begin{cases} Cg \in (85, 135) \\ Cr \in (-Cg + 260, -Cg + 280) \end{cases} \tag{74.1}$$

Fig. 74.1  Color extension
diagram

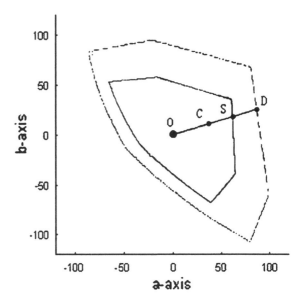

And on CgCb planes the region is fitted as a circle described by the following formula:

$$\frac{(Cg - C\hat{g})^2 + (Cb - C\hat{b})^2}{12.25^2} < = 1 \qquad (74.2)$$

Where $(C\hat{g}, C\hat{b})$ is the center of the circle, $C\hat{g} = 107$, $C\hat{b} = 110$.

Pixels in the region that satisfy condition (74.1) and (74.2) are regarded as human skin colors, contrarily normal colors.

As color gamut extension is easier to be done in a hue-linearized color space, and YCgCr and YCbCr, used as a part of the color image pipeline in video and digital photography systems, are definitely not suitable enough. We need to transform it to a better color space, in our case, CIELab space.

Human skin color region in CIELab space is determined following such steps:

First, sampling in RGB space, then transform the sampling points to YCgCrCb space [5] (combined by YCgCr and YCgCb), retain whichever point that (Cg, Cr, Cb) satisfies condition (74.1) and (74.2);

Second, transform retained sampling points of RGB space to CIELab space, then we can get the enveloping surface of them, Fig. 74.2 shows the skin color region and color gamut of Laser TV and sRGB in CIELab space.

We can see that the distribution of human skin colors is centralized, and only takes a small proportion of the entire sRGB gamut, which is also the top realizability condition of our algorithm. After calculation, we know that the hue angle of skin color ranges from radian 0.2 to radian 1.13, and the color saturation of which ranges below 0.6 in a-b plane at Y = 50.

**Fig. 74.2** Skin color region
and color gamut of Laser TV
and sRGB

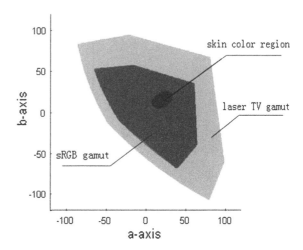

**Fig. 74.2** Skin color region and color gamut of Laser TV and sRGB

## 74.2.2 Human Skin-Color-Preserving Algorithm

Linear compression and nonlinear compression are the main methods used in color gamut mapping algorithm. When transforming to a smaller gamut, nonlinear compression is used mainly to retain the percepted local image information.

We also apply nonlinear extension in certain part of color gamut extension, mainly to prevent human skin colors from extension too much and looks unnatural. We apply nonlinear extension by function $\tilde{f}$ (the mathematical description will be shown later). Figure 74.3 shows the schematic diagram of $\tilde{f}$. The extension is unconspicuous when color saturation ranges below 0.6, which is just the characteristic that we utilize to restrict skin colors. In other parts, linear extension is used to obtain better extension performance and take full advantage of WGD's wider gamut.

The skin color preserving extension function is proposed as Eq. (74.3).

$$C_{out} = \omega_\theta \cdot f_{NL} + (1 - \omega_\theta) \cdot f_L \tag{74.3}$$

$f_L$ is the standard linear extension function. $f_{NL}$ is the sub-nonlinear extension function that consists of two parts: nonlinear extension function $\tilde{f}$ and no-extension part $f_L$, $f_{NL}$ and $\tilde{f}$ are described in Eqs. (74.4, 74.5 and 74.6).

$$f_L = C_{in} \cdot \frac{\overline{OD}}{\overline{OS}} \tag{74.4}$$

$$f_{NL} = \sigma_L \cdot C_{in} + (1 - \sigma_L)\tilde{f} \tag{74.5}$$

$$\tilde{f} = \overline{OD} \cdot \tanh\left(\frac{\overline{OS}}{\overline{OD}} \cdot \tanh^{-1}\left(\frac{C_{in}}{\overline{OS}}\right)\right) \tag{74.6}$$

$C_{in}$ is the distance of the focal point to the color point that needs to be mapped.

**Fig. 74.3** Schematic
diagram of nonlinear
extension function

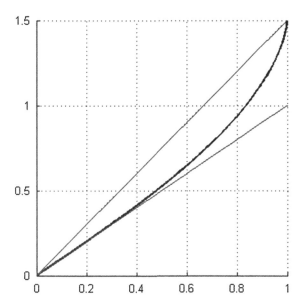

**Fig. 74.4** Graph of function

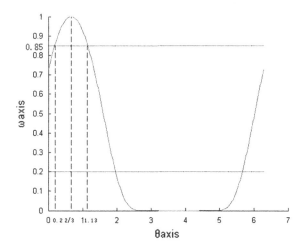

$\theta$ is the hue angle of the color point and $\omega_\theta$, determined by $\theta$, is a scale control coefficient that controls the nonlinearity. As the hue angle of skin color ranges from radian 0.2 to radian 1.13, we construct $\omega_\theta$ presented as Eq. (74.7).

$$\omega_\theta = \exp(-16(\frac{1}{\phi} + \frac{1}{\phi - 2\pi})^2) \qquad (74.7)$$

Where $\phi = (\theta + \frac{2}{3}) \bmod 2\pi$. Figure 74.4 shows the graph of function $\omega_\theta$.

$\omega_\theta$ values greater than 0.85 when $\theta$ ranges from 0.2 to 1.13 and decreases rapidly to 0 in other value range. With it we could apply nonlinear extension on skin colors and approximate linear extension on normal colors.

$\sigma_L$ was introduced because we discovered that the color saturation of skin color does not stay constant at different Y valve.

In regions of high luminance and low luminance, value of skin color saturation almost reaches 1, the nonlinear function presented above could not restrict skin colors from over-extended perfectly. So we introduced the coefficient $\sigma_L$ to improve the restriction effect of skin colors, as shown in Eq. (74.8).

$$\sigma_L = -0.45 \cdot \tanh(-\frac{30}{L} + \frac{300}{(L-50)^2} + \frac{30}{L-100}) + 0.45 \qquad (74.8)$$

When L ranges around 50, we apply nonlinear extension function $\tilde{f}$, and in regions of high luminance and low luminance the colors almost stay unchanged after extension.

## 74.3 Experiments and Results

### 74.3.1 Result Discussion in Theory

The purpose of our algorithm is to restrict skin colors, and still have good performance on the whole gamut. So we compared the distribution of skin colors after extension through our algorithm with linear extension algorithm. In Fig. 74.5 we can see the restriction ability of skin colors of our algorithm is conspicuous and the global gamut extension ability is also satisfying.

### 74.3.2 Images Experiment Result

We selected two typical pictures to evaluate the performance of our algorithm, the first one is a photo of man that contains only colors of human body apart from black, the second one is a picture that contains most colors and used to make a comprehensive evaluation.

As shown in Fig. 74.6, A1 and B1 are the original image, compared to which, the skin colors look unnatural red in A2 and B2 that applied linear extension. A3 and B3 applied skin-color-preserving extension and we can clearly see that the skin colors look more natural than A2 and B2. In both groups of pictures, skin-color-preserving algorithm can achieve better effect in skin colors.

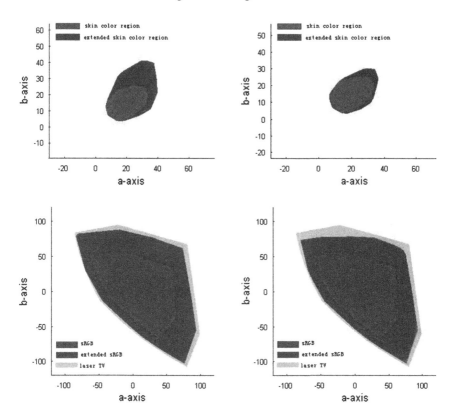

**Fig. 74.5** Comparisons of linear extension and skin-color-preserving extension. (*left*) Linear extension, (*right*) skin-color-preserving extension. (*top*) The extension of skin color region, (*bottom*) the extension of global color space. The *brown* color represents the region before extension, and *blue* color is the region after extension

### 74.3.3 Quality Metrics

As the purpose of the expansion is to exert the color display advantage of wide gamut displays and render more vivid and colorful pictures, we take Color Colorfulness Index (CCI), which is used to present the vividness degree of an image, to evaluate the gamut expansion method, CCI is introduced by Yendrikhovskij [8], it is defined as:

$$C = S_{average} + \sigma \tag{74.9}$$

Where $S_{average}$ is the average saturation of an image, $\sigma$ is the standard deviation of the saturation.

CCI of the images will be increased after applying the proposed method. Table 74.1 shows the CCI of the two testing images shown in Fig. 74.6.

**Fig. 74.6** Application of linear extension and skin-color-preserving extension: (*left*) original pictures, (*middle*) linear extended pictures, (*right*) skin-color-preserving extended pictures

**Table 74.1** CCI of the two testing images

|   | C0 | C1 (linear) | C2 (our method) | Increase ratio | |
|---|---|---|---|---|---|
|   |    |             |                 | C1 (%) | C2 (%) |
| A | 1.32 | 1.45 | 1.38 | 9.8 | 4.5 |
| B | 0.596 | 0.667 | 0.658 | 11.9 | 10.4 |

We can see that our method does not increase CCI of picture A very much, which is just the result that we expected.

## 74.4 Conclusion

In this paper, we proposed a human skin-color-preserving algorithm for color gamut extension. It mainly makes improvement on the region of skin colors. The algorithm can avoid the unnatural red that skin colors look after extension to WGD and keep the optimal extension for normal colors. The research still has great room for improvement because all work we do is from the aspect of artificial calculation. If used, it may need to be transformed to digital calculation.

**Acknowledgments** This work is supported by Shandong Provincial Natural Science Foundation (No. ZR2012FM025). Gang Song is the corresponding author.

# References

1. Giesen J, Schuberth E, Simon K, Zolliker P, Zweifel O (2007) Image-dependent gamut mapping as optimization problem. IEEE Trans Image Process 16(10):2401–2410
2. Zolliker P, Simon K (2007) Retaining local image information in gamut mapping algorithms. IEEE Trans Image Process 16(3):664–672
3. Kimmel R, Shaked D, Elad M, Sobel I (2005) Space-dependent color gamut mapping: a variational approach. IEEE Trans Image Process 14(6):796–803
4. Muijs R, Laird J, Kuang J, Swinkels S (2006) Subjective evaluation of gamut extension methods for wide-gamut displays. In: Proceedings of the 13th international display workshops 1–3:1429–1432, Dec 2006
5. Zhengzhen Z, Yuexiang S (2010) Skin color detecting based on YCgCb and YCgCr color space. Comput Eng Appl 46(34):167–170 (in Chinese)
6. de Dios J, Garcia N (2003) Face detection based on a new color space YCgCr. In: Proceedings of international conference on image processing (3):909–912
7. Xiumei G, Xiuyan Z, Yuliang W, Feng Y, Xianxi L (2008) Research on face detection algorithm based on a novel color space YCgCb. Electron Meas Technol 31(4):79–81 (in Chinese)
8. Yendrikhovskij S, Blommaert F, de Ridder H (1998) Perceptually optimalcolor reproduction. Proc SPIE: Hum Vision Electron Imag III 3299:274–281

# Chapter 75
# A Three-Dimensional CBM Reservoir System Based on Web3D Technology

Jian Wang and Lin Cao

**Abstract** This paper develops a system for better research on the Coal Bed Methane (CBM) reservoir. The system uses the B/S pattern to manage the reservoir data and web3D technology to generate Three-Dimensional (3D) CBM reservoir models. The system provides intuitive structure of CBM reservoir to researchers, while allows researchers to query the reservoir data easily. It's the first time that the 3D model of CBM reservoir is displayed on the internet, so that geological researchers can get more realistic and comprehensive information. The system has a great effect on the research of CBM reservoirs and would be a powerful auxiliary tool in the management of CBM industry.

**Keywords** Web3D · CBM · Reservoir · Three-dimensional

## 75.1 Introduction

CBM is the clean energy in the 21 century, and the resource is abundant in China. CBM extraction, production, and distribution begin with the exploration of such gasses in the ground long before any drilling commences [1]. It requires that

This work was supported in part by the National Science and Technology Major Project under Grant 2011ZX05039-004-02.

J. Wang (✉) · L. Cao
Beijing Information Science and Technology University,
No. 35 North Fourth Ring Road, Beijing, China
e-mail: wangjiandaxia@163.com

W. Lu et al. (eds.), *Proceedings of the 2012 International Conference on Information*
*Technology and Software Engineering*, Lecture Notes in Electrical Engineering 212,
DOI: 10.1007/978-3-642-34531-9_75, © Springer-Verlag Berlin Heidelberg 2013

researchers should have good understanding of the CBM reservoir. However, often located in remote locations, the CBM reservoir has unexpected problems in research. A variety of issue such as significant variation of target size, geographical conditions and exploration equipments, large quantity and dispersed locations of target areas and different levels of research degree impact the researching of CBM reservoir [2]. A comprehensive, intuitive and professional reservoir system for the exploration of CBM resource is required. Currently, there are several systems for CBM reservoir such as CBM WebGIS [3] and CBM reservoir [4] Management Information System (MIS). These systems provide features including information storing, query, and location searching except intuitive display for researchers. And it is why researchers also have difficulties in understanding of reservoir structure. Refer to studying in the oil area, some of oil systems such as 3D stochastic modeling reservoirs [5] and 3D reservoir simulation [6] have provided a display of 3D reservoir and made well effects in intuitively displaying. But these systems are not platform-independent, and the access for users is not simple enough. Therefore, this paper presents a 3D reservoir system which is platform-independent and easily accessible.

## 75.2 Web3D Technologies

As an important part of the information technology, web3D technology has already been used in many areas [7]. CBM reservoir system based on web3D includes the following advantages: Firstly, the system can provide an intuitive display of CBM reservoir and show various data on the 3D model for easy viewing. Secondly, the platform-independent system is based on web so researchers are required only a web browser as researching conditions. Thirdly, the system is able to manage geographical factors of target area systematically and form an integrated database. Lastly, the system can provide powerful spatial query functions for details and convenient means for location searching.

In this article, Java3D and B/S pattern have been chosen as the development tool. Java3D and B/S pattern is widely used in web applications. Compared to other tools, one of the main advantages of Java3D is platform-independent as it's an API extension of java. And the other advantages can be concluded: Firstly, java3D accomplishes higher-level and object-oriented view of 3D graphics by using a scene graph-based 3D graphics model [8]. Programmers can develop 3D applications though they do not have much graphics or multimedia programming experience. Secondly, during runtime, well rendering capability can be used to optimize the scene graph rendering. Lastly, java3D can provide better programming control than VRML due to the powerful Java language [9].

## 75.3  The Architecture of the System

The architecture of CBM reservoir system is showed in Fig. 75.1, which is composed of three main parts: the data layer, the server and the client. Obviously, this is the B/S structure. Users have access to the system through public network and obtain the information of CBM reservoir whenever and wherever.

The web server is responsible for displaying result and handling users' requests through java3D API and JavaScript functions. The correspondence of client side and server side is realized by http. The database server is used to store geographical and geological data of reservoir including wells information, interpret information, laboratory information, desorption information, analysis information, fold information, fault information, subsided column information and so on. In order to integrate the reservoir information well, the system uses Microsoft SQL Server 2008 as development tool, and designs tables in strict accordance with the third paradigm of database designing. The key fields in different tables are not associated with each other, so that the 3D processing is completely independent from data management such as entering, deleting, and modifying.

The application client is in charge of showing the 3D model of CBM reservoir and details. As mentioned earlier, the 3D model of CBM reservoir can be generated by java3D API and embedded in a web page. The architecture of web3D application is showed in Fig. 75.2.

## 75.4  System Function Design and Realization

The main function of the system is to embed 3D model in the browser and show the related information. Concretely, the functions include 3D display, location searching and data operation. The complete framework of the system is showed in Fig. 75.3.

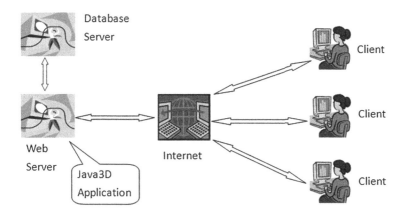

**Fig. 75.1** Architecture of the system

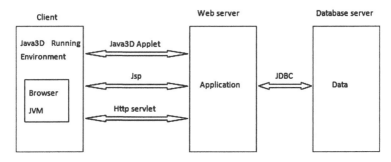

**Fig. 75.2** Architecture of the web3D application

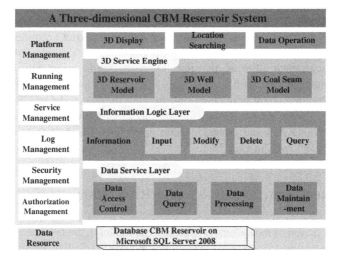

**Fig. 75.3** System framework

## 75.4.1 3D Display

3D display function provides the 3D CBM reservoir models, 3D well models and 3D coal seam models in the browser. All functions are implemented by corresponding JavaBean files.

The method of generating a 3D CBM reservoir model can be described as follows. Firstly, with the geographic sampling data of reservoir in the database, we can convert it to coordinate data adapted to Java3D coordinate system. Secondly, by using the Java3D API, we can generate the local basic shapes of reservoir in the corresponding coordinates. Lastly, we need to color, render and stitch these local shapes and the 3D model could become an initial prototype. The flow chart of how to generate a 3D model of CBM reservoir is showed in Fig. 75.4.

Additionally, with the powerful function of mouse operation offered by Java3D, the interaction of users and the system could be simple. Researchers can view the

**Fig. 75.4** Flow chart of generating a 3D reservoir model

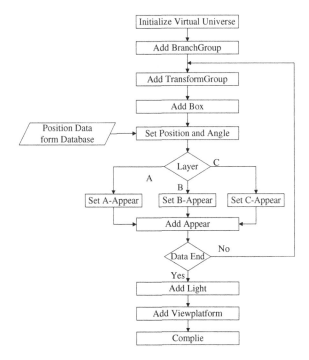

structure of the CBM reservoir from any angle by using the mouse to move, zoom and flip the 3D model. The generation method of 3D well models and 3D coal seam models are essentially similar to the 3D reservoir and it will be not repeated in this article. The 3D reservoir model and the mouse operation are showed in Fig. 75.5.

## 75.4.2 Location Searching

The system can locate the coal seam and display its 3D model when entering the name of a coal seam. Offered the name of a coal seam, the system will look for its respective well and reservoir in reverse and get their data from the database. Then, with the geographical data, the 3D model of the reservoir and well will be generated in order. Next, according to the geographic data of the coal seam, the system can locate the coal seam in the well model and display its detailed information in the page which is showed in Fig. 75.6.

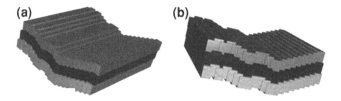

**Fig. 75.5** **a** 3D CBM reservoir model, **b** 3D model is rotated 15 degrees counterclockwise

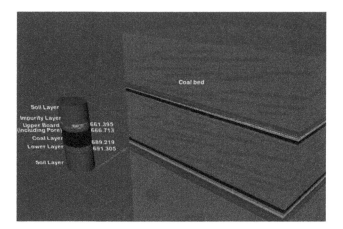

**Fig. 75.6** Location searching result

### 75.4.3 Data Operation

Data operation feature provides the data interface between the user and the system, the user can input, modify, delete, and query all data information. Of course, the premise is that users should get the permission to do these operations because the system provides a login authentication interface and only the authorized users can be allowed. In other words, in addition to the 3D function, the system can be used as an information system. When a user sends a request to the server, the system is able to return the real-time data in the database to the front page by using AJAX technology. So that researchers can view the 3D model and detailed parameter information of the reservoir at the same time. The main page of the system is showed in Fig. 75.7.

## 75.5 Summary and Future Work

The system provides an effective solution for 3D display and data management of the CBM reservoir by using Web3D technology. Several web-based systems mentioned before such as WebGIS [3] and MIS [4] can realize query and storing

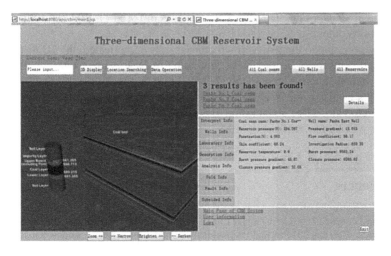

**Fig. 75.7**  Main page of the system

**Table 75.1**  Comparison of several CBM reservoir systems

| Supported feature | WebGIS[a] | MIS[b] | 3D simulation[c] | Web3D system[d] |
|---|---|---|---|---|
| Information storing | Yes | Yes | Yes | Yes |
| Cross platform | Yes | Yes | No | Yes |
| Query | Yes | Yes | No | Yes |
| 3D display | No | No | No | Yes |

[a] WebGIS for CBM reservoir [3]
[b] MIS (Managerment Information System for CBM reservoir) [4]
[c] 3D reservoir simulation [6]
[d] Web3D system in this article

capabilities, but they cannot provide 3D display. Some of the 3D simulation systems [6] are capable of 3D display, but they cannot manage data information and they are not platform-independent. The Web3D system in this article inherits the advantages of others, it has not only realized the information processing feature, but also provided functions including 3D display, interaction between the users and system, location searching and so on. Comparison of several CBM reservoir systems can be concluded in Table 75.1.

In this article, the system combines with Java3D environment and supports distributed architecture, so it solves the problem of platform-independent. At the same time, the 3D construction method of Java3D scene graph makes the design of the virtual scene more intuitive and flexible. That simplifies the design of 3D program and so the construction and controlling of the reservoir model would not be a problem. As a result of the B/S mode combined with the AJAX technology, the system performs very well in information management of the CBM reservoir.

So it is obviously that 3D CBM reservoir system based on Web3D technology is superior to others.

However, due to the reservoir structure is very complicated, the 3D display still exist problems such as adaptively generating of large-scale scene, speed optimization on the internet and so on. Therefore, it needs further research on these problems by using the Web3D technology. Research on computer programming combined with CBM exploration theory to form a complete decision-making system will be the next major work.

# References

1. Zhang J, Tang S, Zhen G, Li Z (2011) The CBM recovery factor prediction of PanZhuang area in QinShui basion. 2011 second international conference of mechanic automation and control engineering (MACE), pp 7799–7805
2. Lymanets A, Chatterji S, Heuser J (2009) The silicon tracker of the CBM experiment at FAIR: detector developments and first in-beam characterizations. Nuclear science symposium conference record (NSS/MIC), pp 1689–1691
3. Wang Y, Zhu X (2011) A coal-bed methane WebGIS based on MapABC Maps API and DWR. IEEE 2nd international conference of computing, control and industrial engineering (CCIE), pp 167–170
4. Huang X, Li X, Wang M, Ling B, Sun J (2012) Research management information system in CBM reservoir. Fault-Block Oil Gas Field 3:307–311 (inChinese)
5. Liu J, Tan X, Chen S, Zhang Y (2009) Fine description of reservoirs by the 3D stochastic modeling in the Daniudi gas field, Ordos Basin. Nat Gas Ind 12:20–22 (in Chinese)
6. Wang Y, Wu Q, Liu Q (2009) Three-dimensional reservoir simulation based on geological exploration data. Energy Technol Manag 1:63–65
7. Chittaro L, Ranon R (2007) Web3D technologies in learning, education and training: Motivations, issues, opportunities. Comput Educ 49:3–18
8. Tian M, Lu X, Zhao Q, Wang W, Ning H (2011) Research and implementation of tunnel three-dimensional modeling algorithm based on java3D. 2nd international conference of artificial intelligence, management science and electronic commerce (AIMSEC), pp 4192–4196
9. Wei B (2010) Applying hibernate to persist Java3D virtual scene in Oracle. 2nd international conference of advanced computer control (ICACC), 2, 551–555

# Chapter 76
# Model and Analysis on Time Complexity for Graph-Based Segmentation

Li Sun, Liu Jia, Lv Caixiai and Li Zheying

**Abstract** Time complexity of an algorithm is closely related to its implement method. In order to make the time complexity analysis more universal in engineering, the Operator Cost Model (OCM) was proposed and used for analyzing the Graph-Based Segmentation Algorithm (GBSA) in this paper. The OCM is to be used for time complexity analysis of GBSA by extracting the cost of operating operators with inherent characteristics that are unrelated to the microprocessor system. Meanwhile, the influence of the control factor $k$ to the operator consumption is also analyzed qualitatively. The relationship between $k$ and OCM was discussed, which provides some help for the application of GBSA in practical engineering.

**Keywords** Graph · Segmentation · Time complexity · Model

## 76.1 Introduction

With the development of computer and information technology, kinds of image segmentation algorithms were proposed [1–3] and have been applied in many information systems. In the applications of image segmentation technologies,

L. Sun (✉)
School of Electronics and Information Engineering, Beijing Jiaotong University,
Beijing, China
e-mail: 10120031@bjtu.edu.cn

L. Jia · L. Caixiai · L. Zheying
Beijing key Lab of Information Service, School of information, Beijing Union University,
Beijing, China
e-mail: zheying@buu.edu.cn

W. Lu et al. (eds.), *Proceedings of the 2012 International Conference on Information Technology and Software Engineering*, Lecture Notes in Electrical Engineering 212, DOI: 10.1007/978-3-642-34531-9_76, © Springer-Verlag Berlin Heidelberg 2013

the algorithm complexity is related with the implementation method and is also the key factor for determining whether the algorithm is applicable [4–7].

In this paper, to deal with the time complexity, the concept of operators is proposed and the Operator Cost Model (OCM) is established which is unrelated to inherent characteristics of the microprocessor system. Based on OCM, the time complexity of the Minimum Spanning Tree (MST) is analyzed for Graph-Based Segmentation Algorithm (GBSA). Furthermore, as to the control factor $k$, the relationship between $k$ and OCM was discussed.

## 76.2 Operators Cost Model

To image process algorithms, the time complexity is an important aspect to measure the performance efficiency [4]. The measuring steps are determined by the algorithm without any relationship with microprocessor. In addition, the execution speed of each operation is related to the microprocessor system. This means that the less operation contents and steps the shorter execution time. With this motivation, Operators Cost Model (OCM) is built for time complexity analysis and is called as the Algorithm Inherent Time Characteristics (AITC).

### 76.2.1 Computational Complexity

To a specified microprocessor, the algorithm time complexity gives the time required for executing operations. Let $N$ be the number of operator types. Then we have operator types $P_1, P_2,..., P_N$. The executing time of $P_i$ is $e_i$, ($i = 1, 2,..., N$). Assuming $A_i$ is the implementing manner and method of computational operations, such as the command structure flow, which influence the consuming time $t_i(A_i)$ of each operator. Then, the total processing time of an algorithm is

$$T_A = \sum_{i=1}^{N} t_i(A_i)e_i \tag{76.1}$$

Equation (76.1) can only analyze the time complexity of algorithms implemented in a specified microprocessor or computer, while cannot represent AITC which is determined by algorithms and irrelevant to the implementation system.

### 76.2.2 Operator Cost Model of Computational Complexity

Based on AITC, each calculating operation (such as arithmetic operations), and/or processing operation (such as the judge transfer), are called operators, which occupy the calculation and logic operation recourses of the microprocessor or computer

**Table 76.1** The impact of $k$ values to AITC and the segmentation result with OCM

| $k$ | $N_A$ | $N_S$ | $N_M$ | $N_D$ | $N_{Rs}$ | $N_{Rc}$ | $f(k)$ | $r$ |
|---|---|---|---|---|---|---|---|---|
| 0 | 158,338 | 459,120 | 459,120 | 2,369 | 153,040 | 11,711,305,822 | 2,369 | 74,431 |
| 10 | 289,468 | 459,120 | 459,120 | 67,934 | 153,040 | 11,711,118,720 | 67,934 | 8,866 |
| 20 | 298,614 | 459,120 | 459,120 | 72,507 | 153,040 | 11,711,066,356 | 72,507 | 4,293 |
| 50 | 304,044 | 459,120 | 459,120 | 75,222 | 153,040 | 11,711,005,508 | 75,222 | 1,578 |
| 150 | 306,092 | 459,120 | 459,120 | 76,246 | 153,040 | 11,710,948,140 | 76,246 | 554 |
| 250 | 306,426 | 459,120 | 459,120 | 76,413 | 153,040 | 11,710,932,754 | 76,413 | 387 |
| 300 | 306,540 | 459,120 | 459,120 | 76,470 | 153,040 | 11,710,926,774 | 76,470 | 330 |
| 500 | 306,668 | 459,120 | 459,120 | 76,534 | 153,040 | 11,710,910,716 | 76,534 | 266 |
| 750 | 306,822 | 459,120 | 459,120 | 76,611 | 153,040 | 11,710,902,286 | 76,611 | 189 |
| 1,500 | 306,944 | 459,120 | 459,120 | 76,672 | 153,040 | 11,710,889,486 | 76,672 | 128 |
| 5,000 | 307,034 | 459,120 | 459,120 | 76,717 | 153,040 | 11,710,861,944 | 76,717 | 83 |

system based on the process of algorithms implementation. The process for realizing an algorithm is to put the arithmetic operations together with the corresponding computing structure and then getting the final results by computing [5]. Therefore, algorithms are the operator consumption systems. The analysis for the algorithm time complexity based on AITC is only concerned of the types of the operators and the number of uses of each operator, but not the process structure, instruction characteristics, and clock speed of the processing system [8].

Assuming that algorithms contain operators, including addition, subtraction, multiplication, division, and function (e.g., calculus, root, basic logic, etc.). Given that the addition and subtraction are basic operations in a microprocessor without considering the other difference, and there are bigger difference among multiplication, division and function, the operators used by an algorithm can be described as

$$\mathbf{O} = \begin{pmatrix} 1 & 1 & P & Q & U \end{pmatrix}^T \tag{76.2}$$

where 1 is the operator cost of the addition and subtraction, $P$, $Q$ and $U$ are the operator cost of the multiplication, division, and function, respectively. The elements in $\mathbf{O}$ depend on computing implementations, such as the look-up Table 76.1 for division.

Let $N_A$, $N_S$, $N_M$, $N_D$ and $N_R$ be the number of uses of operators for addition, subtraction, multiplication, division and function respectively in algorithms. Let $A_d$, $S_d$, $M_d$, $D_d$ and $R_d$ be the cost of the addition operator, subtraction operator, multiplication operator, division operator and function operator respectively. Employing these parameters, the AITC for an algorithm can be expressed as

$$\begin{pmatrix} A_d \\ S_d \\ M_d \\ D_d \\ R_d \end{pmatrix} = \begin{pmatrix} N_A & 0 & 0 & 0 & 0 \\ 0 & N_S & 0 & 0 & 0 \\ 0 & 0 & N_M & 0 & 0 \\ 0 & 0 & 0 & N_D & 0 \\ 0 & 0 & 0 & 0 & N_R \end{pmatrix} \begin{pmatrix} 1 \\ 1 \\ P \\ Q \\ U \end{pmatrix} \tag{76.3}$$

According to the above discussion, set the matrix **N** as the number of uses of the operators for a known algorithm and the matrix **C** as the operators. Then

$$\mathbf{T} = \mathbf{NO} \tag{76.4}$$

where **T** gives the quantity of the operators consumption.

Equations (76.3) or (76.4) is defined as the Operator Cost Model (OCM). Obviously, OCM is determined by algorithm architecture and relevant to the microprocessor structure, the instruction system, and the clock speed.

## 76.3 Graph-Based Image Segmentation

An image is an undirected graph $G = (V, E)$ in GBSA where a vertex $v_i \in V$ corresponds to a pixel in the image, $V$ is the set of elements to be segmented; each edge $e(v_i, v_j) \in E$ connects certain pairs of neighboring pixels and has a weight $w((v_i, v_j))$ which represents the dissimilarity between the two pixels (e.g., the difference in intensity, color, motion, location or some other local attribute). By combining vertices, the segmented image is obtained that consists of connected regions $S(C_1, C_2, \ldots, C_N)$ with similar vertex, where $N$ is the number of regions at last. Based on MST [3] presents the GBSA which employs global information to segment images with a simple criterion.

In the comparison judgment of regions, each component $C \subseteq V$ extracts the feature $Int(C)$ which is the largest weight of the component $MST(C, E)$ and describes internal dissimilarity among the pixels

$$Int(C) = \max(w(e)) \tag{76.5}$$

The minimum weighted edge connecting two neighboring components, $C_1, C_2 \subseteq V$ gives the difference between the two components

$$Dif(C_1, C_2) = \min(w(v_i, v_j)) \tag{76.6}$$

where $v_i \in C_1, v_j \in C_2$. If there is no connection between $C_1$ and $C_2$, $Dif(C_1, C_2) = \infty$.

The region predication decides whether the neighboring $C_1$ and $C_2$ can be merged by comparing the internal difference $Int(C_1, C_2)$ of the two components and the difference between them $Dif(C_1, C_2)$. The judgment condition is

$$D(C_1, C_2) = \begin{cases} true & \text{if } D(C_1, C_2) > MInt(C_1, C_2) \\ false & otherwise \end{cases} \tag{76.7}$$

where $MInt(C_1, C_2)$ is the minimum internal difference between $C_1$ and $C_2$ and

$$MInt(C_1, C_2) = \min(Int(C_1)) + \tau(C_1), Int(C_2) + \tau(C_2) \tag{76.8}$$

$\tau(C)$ is a threshold related with the size of the component to control the degree of merging and described as

$$\tau(C) = \frac{k}{|C|} \tag{76.9}$$

where $k$ is a control factor, $|C|$ is the precise number of pixels in $C$. In fact, $k$ sets a $k$ scale of the segmentation.

To a graph $G = (V, E)$ which denotes an image, there are $n$ vertices and $m$ edges. After the calculation and comparison, the graph (image) will be segmented into several components $S = (C_1, C_2, \ldots, C_r)$. The detailed process of GBSA with MST is

1. Calculate edge weight $w_i$ for each one to form $w(w_1, w_2, \ldots, w_n)$, and then sort it into non-decreasing order.
2. $s^0 = (C_1, C_2, \ldots, C_m)$ is the initial segmentation (original image), and then repeat the step 3 for each edge $e_q = (v_i, v_j)$, $q = 1, 2, \ldots, n$.
3. Assuming that for $e_q = (v_i, v_j)$, $v_i$ and $v_j$ belongs to $C_i^{q-1}$ and $C_j^{q-1}$ respectively, and $C_i^{q-1} \neq C_j^{q-1}$. If $w(e_q) \leq MInt\left(C_i^{q-1}, C_j^{q-1}\right)$, then $S^q$ is obtained by merging $C_i^{q-1}$ and $C_j^{q-1}$. Otherwise, $S^q = S^{q-1}$.

## 76.4 OCM for Graph-Based Segmentation

To time complexity analysis of algorithms, we can build the OCM by confirming the operators and the number of uses of them in GBSA segmentation procedure.

**Edge weight calculation and sorting**

For color images, edge weight measures the Euclidean distance between the two neighboring pixels in RGB or YUV space

$$w((v_i, v_j)) = \sqrt{(R_i - R_j)^2 + (G_i - G_j)^2 + (B_i - B_j)^2} \tag{76.10}$$

During calculating an edge weight, 2 additions, 3 subtractions, 3 multiplications and 1 evolution are accomplished in Eq. (76.10).

We only consider the four neighborhood edges, $e(v_{x+1,y}, v_{x,y})$, $e(v_{x-1,y}, v_{x,y})$, $e(v_{x,y+1}, v_{x,y})$ and $e(v_{x,y-1}, v_{x,y})$ connected pixel $v_{x,y}$. Let the width and height of the image be $w$ and $h$, the number of the edges is $n = 2w \times h - w - h$. That is, Eq. (76.10) would repeat for $n$ times. Therefore, numbers of uses of each operator are

$$N_1 = \begin{bmatrix} 2n & 3n & 3n & 0 & n \end{bmatrix} \tag{76.11}$$

To make the non-decreasing order for the edge $\pi = (w_1, w_2, \ldots, w_n)$ by comparing two elements $w_n$ and $w_{n+1}$, the bubble sort was used here. If $w_n > w_{n+1}$, then $w_n$ exchanges its place with $w_{n+1}$. By that analogy, the largest weight ends up in the last spot. The number of uses of the function operator (comparison operator) is

$$N_2 = \begin{bmatrix} 0 & 0 & 0 & 0 & \frac{n(n-1)}{2} \end{bmatrix} \qquad (76.12)$$

**Components comparison predication**

Before the merging predication, it is necessary to distinguish whether the neighboring pixel $v_i$ and $v_j$, which belong to the edge $e(v_i, v_j)$, are in the same component throughout every edge. The number of uses of comparison operations is $n = 2w \times h - w - h$.

Only if $v_i$ and $v_j$ are located in different component, the predication could be continued. From Eqs. (76.7) and (76.8), we can determine whether the neighboring components can be combined with 2 times comparison. It is known that the degree of segmentation is related to $k$, so we suppose the number of the comparison predication is $g(k)$. During this process the number of uses of the function operator (comparison operator) is

$$\mathbf{N}_3 = \begin{bmatrix} 0 & 0 & 0 & 0 & n + 2g(k) \end{bmatrix} \qquad (76.13)$$

where $g(k) < n$

Two components which satisfy the predication conditions are merged and then $Int(C)$ and $\tau(C)$ are calculated for the new component. Otherwise, do the merging predication with the next edge.

**Region merging and calculation**

Before the segmentation, each pixel is regarded as an independent component, i.e., $Int(C) = 0$, $|C| = 1$. Through the comparison predication, the components with the similar property will be merged and the corresponding merging times are $f(k)$.

To $e(v_i, v_j)$, if $w(e_q) > Int(C_j^{q-1}) + \tau(C_j^{q-1})$ or $w(e_q) > Int(C_i^{q-1}) + \tau(C_i^{q-1})$, $C_i$ and $C_j$ do not meet the merging rules. Meanwhile, since the edges are in non-decreasing order, $w(e_k) > w(e_q), k \geq q + 1$, the merging will not happen anymore, i.e., the edge causing merging is the minimum weight edge between the two components. Thus, according to [9], the edge $e(v_i, v_j)$ is selected for constructing the Minimum Spanning Tree (MST) of the merging component $C_{i+j}$. That is, $w(v_i, v_j)$ is $Int(C)$ of the merging component. Based on Eq. (76.9), 2 additions and 1 division are done in each calculation. Therefore, in the whole merging calculation, the number of uses for operators is

$$\mathbf{N}_4 = \begin{bmatrix} 2f(k) & 0 & 0 & f(k) & 0 \end{bmatrix} \qquad (76.14)$$

In conclusion, operators in GBSA have the addition, subtraction, multiplication, division, and function. The function operator includes evolution and comparison and their individual cost is $U_s$ and $U_c$ respectively. Hence, Eq. (76.1) becomes

$$\mathbf{C} = \begin{bmatrix} 1 & 1 & P & Q & U_s & U_c \end{bmatrix}^T \qquad (76.15)$$

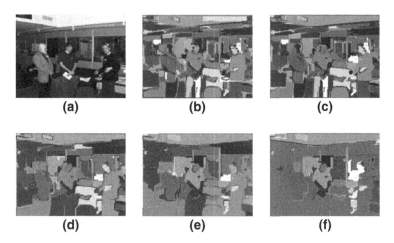

**Fig. 76.1**  Image segmentation results of different $k$ value. **a** Original image, **b** $k = 100$, **c** $k = 150$, **d** $k = 300$, **e** $k = 500$ and **f** $k = 800$

From above the number of uses for operators in each step are $N_1$, $N_2$, $N_3$, and $N_4$. In whole segmentation process, the operators cost can be expressed as

$$
\mathbf{T} = \begin{pmatrix} 2n & 3n & 3n & 0 & n & 0 \\ 0 & 0 & 0 & 0 & 0 & n(n-1)/2 \\ 0 & 0 & 0 & 0 & 0 & n+2g(k) \\ 2f(k) & 0 & 0 & f(k) & 0 & 0 \end{pmatrix} \times \begin{pmatrix} 1 \\ 1 \\ P \\ Q \\ U_s \\ U_c \end{pmatrix}
\tag{76.16}
$$

It can be seen that OCM of GBSA is closely related to the control factor $k$.

## 76.5 Simulation Analyses

In this paper the graph-based segmentation is implemented in the Visual Studio 2005, which is shown as Fig. 76.1 ($320 \times 240$).

It can be seen that the pixels in one component are in the similarity of the color space. Meanwhile, different $k$ values cause different segmentation effect with $r$ sub components (see Fig. 76.1), i.e., $k$ controls the degree of region merging.

Besides, each operator cost has certain variation due to the variation of components merging times $f(k)$ in GBSA. In Table 76.1, $N_A$, $N_S$, $N_M$, $N_D$, $N_{Rs}$, $N_{Rc}$ denote the number of uses of addition, subtraction, multiplication, division, evolution and comparison operator, respectively. It is shown that, with the growing of $k$ value, the number of sub-components decreases significantly. Furthermore, the probability of the merging between two components becomes large with the increasing of $k$ and $f(k)$ during the segmenting. Therefore, the components number $r$ is dropped and $g(k)$ become smaller.

## 76.6 Conclusions

In this paper, it is pointed out that the time complexity of the image processing algorithm is a complicated function that is related to the structure of algorithm, microprocessor and instructions. In fact, algorithm operation has nothing to do with the microprocessor structure, and has its own calculation characteristics. We presented the concept of the algorithm operators and operator cost, besides, built OCM (Operator Cost Model), which has inherent time property (namely, independent of time). Based on OCM, it is convenient to analyze the time complexity of given microprocessor system. Besides, we built the OCM of graph-based segmentation and discuss the influence of $k$ value on the operator cost. The analysis and experiment results show that the execution times of the addition operator and division operator vary with $k$ by exponential relation but other operators cost have little relationship with $k$.

**Acknowledgment** This project is supported by National Natural Science Foundation of China (Grant No. NSFC609976024) and Beijing Municipal commission of Education (PHR.IHLB. 20090513).

## References

1. Comaniciu D, Meer P (2002) Mean shift: a robust approach toward feature space analysis. IEEE Trans Pattern Anal Mach Intell 24(5):603–619
2. Shi J, Malik J (2000) Normalized cuts and image segmentation. IEEE Trans Pattern Anal Mach Intell 22(8):888–905
3. Felzenszwalb PF, Huttenlocher DP (2004) Efficient graph-based image segmentation. Int J Comput Vis 59(2):167–181
4. Keogh E, Chu S, Hart D, Pazzani M (2003) Segmenting time series: a survey and novel approach. In: Data mining in time series databases. World Scientific, Singapore
5. Cormen TH, Leiserson CE, Rivest RL, Stein C (1999) Introduction to algorithms, 2nd edn. The MIT Press, Cambridge, pp 185–196
6. Sarigiannidis P, Papadimitriou G, Pomportsis A (2006) CS-POSA: a high performance scheduling a algorithm for WDM star networks. Photon Netw Commun 11(2):211–227
7. Fan TH, Lee S, Lu HI, Tsou TS, Wang TC, Yao A (2003) An optimal algorithm for maximum-sum segment and its application in bioinformatics. In: Proceedings of the 8th international conference on implementation and application of automata. Lecture notes in computer science, vol 2759. pp 251–257
8. Bentley J (1984) Programming pearls: algorithm design techniques. Commun ACM 27:865–871
9. Nash-Williams C (1961) Edge-disjoint spanning trees of finite graphs. J London Math Soc 36:213–228

# Chapter 77
# Modified Binary Image Thinning Using Template-Based PCNN

**Zuoyong Li, Runhong Wang and Zuchang Zhang**

**Abstract** Existing binary image thinning algorithm using template-based pulse-coupled neural network (PCNN) includes two main stages, i.e., coarse removal and fine removal. The two stages aim to remove those object pixels meeting with 4-pixel template and 3-pixel one, respectively. Unfortunately, the parallelism of PCNN causes unexpected edge disconnection in the pixel-removal process. To solve this problem, a modified image thinning algorithm using local connectivity judgment is proposed in this paper. It adopts an additional local connectivity identification to avoid undesirable edge disconnection caused by removing object pixel and preserve original edge connectivity. The proposed algorithm was compared with the original version on a variety of binary images, and experimental results show its effectiveness.

**Keywords** Pulse-coupled neural network (PCNN) · Binary image thinning · Image skeletonization

## 77.1 Introduction

Binary image thinning (skeletonization) aims to thin a binary image into an edge image with 1-pixel width [1]. Image thinning result is the skeleton of object in an image, which represents the structural features of object by using much less data (object pixels). According to the medial axis transformation [2], image skeleton is

Z. Li (✉) · R. Wang · Z. Zhang
Department of Computer Science, Minjiang University, No. 1 Wenxian road,
Wucheng Office Building room 332, Fuzhou, Fujian, China
e-mail: fzulzytdq@126.com

W. Lu et al. (eds.), *Proceedings of the 2012 International Conference on Information Technology and Software Engineering*, Lecture Notes in Electrical Engineering 212, DOI: 10.1007/978-3-642-34531-9_77, © Springer-Verlag Berlin Heidelberg 2013

usually regarded as the central pixel set of the object. A good image thinning result generally has the following properties [3]: (1) it conforms to human visual perception; (2) it is the median of object; (3) it retains the original connectivity; (4) it has high thinning rate; (5) it has low computational time. Image thinning plays a key role in image processing such as text recognition [4, 5], fingerprint classification [6], and data compression.

In recent years, many algorithms have been developed to extract the skeleton of object in an image. In Ref. [1], image thinning methods are divided into two categories, i.e., parallel algorithms [7] and sequential ones [8]. In addition, some unconventional methods based on neural network [6, 9] are also presented. Here, we only focus on image thinning based on pulse-coupled neural network.

Pulse-coupled neural network (PCNN), a classical category of neural network, has been applied in many fields, such as image processing, object recognition and optimization. In Refs. [9, 10], two PCNN-based image thinning algorithms are developed. Both of them fail to obtain satisfactory result for fingerprint image as they could not overcome ridge spikes. To solve this problem, Ji et al. [6] proposed a template-based PCNN image thinning algorithm. Ji's algorithm is not only suitable for fingerprint image, but also for common binary image. When processing fingerprint image, it utilizes the fingerprint orientation field to constrain the thinning direction of PCNN, which benefits the suppression of ridge spikes. Note that, when dealing with general binary image, Ji's algorithm omits the constrain of fingerprint orientation field. Since PCNN is a parallel neural network (NN), Ji's algorithm is also a parallel one. This ensures its efficiency. Unfortunately, the parallelism of Ji's algorithm will destroy original connectivity and cause unexpected edge disconnection. To resolve the issue, a local connectivity judgment [5] is introduced in this paper. Experimental results on a variety of general binary images show the effectiveness of our algorithm.

## 77.2 Image Thinning Using Template-Based PCNN

In 2007, Ji et al. [6] presented a binary fingerprint image thinning algorithm using template-based pulse-coupled neural network (PCNN). Ji's algorithm is also suitable for general binary images. Since PCNN is a parallel neural network, Ji's algorithm is a parallel algorithm. Following content will brief the thinning algorithm.

Ji's template-based PCNN is a single layer 2D neural network, and its model illustrated in Fig. 77.1. There exists a one-to-one relationship between a neuron and an image pixel. In the above model, some notations are defined as follows: $N_{mn}$ is the neuron located at $m$th row and $n$th column, $\Phi_{ij}$ the linking input from a linking neuron $N_{ij}$ to $N_{mn}$, $W_{ij}$ is the linking weight between $N_{ij}$ and $N_{mn}$; and $X_{mn}$, $U_{mn}$, $\Theta_{mn}$ and $Y_{mn}$ denote the load signal, total activity strength, pulse threshold and the pulse output signal of neuron $N_{mn}$, respectively. Like this traditional PCNN [11], the above model is a 2D iterative neural network.

**Fig. 77.1** Neuron model of
the template-based PCNN

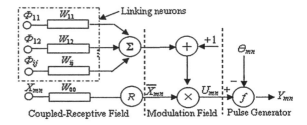

Coupled-Receptive Field   :Modulation Field : Pulse Generator

Ji's image thinning algorithm is composed of two main stages, i.e., pixels' coarse removal and fine removal. The first stage aims at removing (deleting) those object pixels whose local neighborhood meets with 4-pixel templates (patterns) $M_1$, $M_2$ or their rotated versions. $M_1$ and $M_2$ are shown in Eqs. (77.1) and (77.2), and their rotated versions can be obtained via clockwise rotating around central element $\pi/2$, $\pi$ and $3\pi/2$, respectively.

$$M_1 = \begin{bmatrix} -1 & 1 & 1 \\ 0 & 0 & 1 \\ 0 & 0 & -1 \end{bmatrix} \tag{77.1}$$

$$M_2 = \begin{bmatrix} 0 & 0 & 0 \\ 0 & 0 & 0 \\ 1 & 1 & 1 \end{bmatrix} \tag{77.2}$$

In these templates, 0 and 1 denote object pixel and background one, respectively, and $-1$ indicates the pixel that is not to be taken into account as it is negligible for the detection of 4-pixel patterns.

The detailed steps of pixels' coarse removal are as follows:

1. Initialize iterative number $t = 0$, set the load signal $X_{mn}$ to be the gray level of pixel $(m, n)$, and the output signal $Y_{mn}$ (0) as

$$Y_{mn}(0) = f(X_{mn}(0) - 1) = \begin{cases} 1 & if\ X_{mn} = 1, \\ 0 & otherwise. \end{cases} \tag{77.3}$$

2. Set $t = t + 1$, and parallelly calculate each neuron's (pixel's) $U$ value in accordance with following equation

$$U_{mn}(t) = \overline{X}_{mn}(t)[1 + \sum_{i=1}^{3}\sum_{j=1}^{3}\Phi_{ij}(t)W_{ij}], \tag{77.4}$$

where

$$_{ij}(t) = \begin{cases} 1 & if\ M_{ij} = Y_{ij}, 1 \le i, j \le 3, \\ 0 & otherwise, \end{cases} \tag{77.5}$$

$$W_{ij} = \begin{cases} 1 & if \, M_{ij} = 0 \, or \, 1, \, 1 \le i,j \le 3, \\ 0 & otherwise, \end{cases} \tag{77.6}$$

and $\overline{X}_{mn}$ is the reverse value of $X_{mn}$.

3. Set pulse thresholds as

$$\theta_{mn}(t) = \begin{cases} 7 & for \, M_1 \, or \, it's \, rotated \, versions \\ 9 & for \, M_2 \, or \, it's \, rotated \, versions \end{cases} \tag{77.7}$$

4. Determine the output signal $Y_{mn}(t)$ as

$$Y_{mn}(t) = \begin{cases} 1 & if \, U_{mn} \ge \theta_{mn}, \\ 0 & otherwise. \end{cases} \tag{77.8}$$

$Y_{mn}(t)$ will be used as the load signal of neuron $N_{mn}$ in the next iteration.

5. Repeat steps (2–4) until the output signals of all the neurons remain unchanged.

The second stage, fine removal, intends to remove those object pixels meeting with 3-pixel templates $M_3$, $M_4$ or their rotated versions, where $M_3$ and $M_4$ are defined in Eqs. (77.9) and (77.10), and their rotated versions can be obtained via clockwise rotating around central element $\pi/2$, $\pi$ and $3\pi/2$, respectively.

$$M_3 = \begin{bmatrix} -1 & 1 & 1 \\ 0 & 0 & 1 \\ 1 & 0 & -1 \end{bmatrix} \tag{77.9}$$

$$M_4 = \begin{bmatrix} 1 & -1 & 1 \\ 0 & 0 & 0 \\ 1 & 0 & 1 \end{bmatrix} \tag{77.10}$$

The detailed process of pixels' fine removal is as follows:

1. Using the results obtained by the first stage as initial values.
2. Parallelly calculate each neuron's $U$ value via Eq. (77.4).
3. Set pulse thresholds as

$$\theta_{mn}(t) = \begin{cases} 7 & for \, M_3 \, or \, it's \, rotated \, versions \\ 8 & for \, M_4 \, or \, it's \, rotated \, versions \end{cases} \tag{77.11}$$

4. Determine the output signal $Y_{mn}(t)$ as

$$Y_{mn}(t) = \begin{cases} 1 & if \, U_{mn} \ge \theta_{mn}, \\ 0 & otherwise. \end{cases} \tag{77.12}$$

$Y_{mn}$ (*t*) will be used as the load signal of neuron $N_{mn}$ in the next iteration.

5. Repeat steps (2–4) until the output signals of all the neurons stay unchanged.

## 77.3 The Proposed Algorithm

Since Ji's algorithm [6] is parallel, load signal (or state) of each neuron (pixel) will be renewed after a full iteration of all the neurons has been finished. This may cause some unexpected edge disconnection. There is an example in Fig. 77.2. Note that, LX is one pixel's 3 × 3 local neighborhood in a binary image, which is updated after a full iteration of all the neurons. LTX is the neighborhood at the same position, yet with an updated content immediately once a pixel processed. In LX and LTX, 0 and 1 are object pixel and background one, respectively. One can observe that LX is the same as the template obtained by clockwise rotating *M2* around central element $3\pi/2$. Hence, the highlighted central object pixel "0" will be deleted in the coarse removal stage, implying transforming it to background pixel "1". LTX shows that two object pixels confined by dotted circles also should be transformed as background ones in coarse removal. The above transformation of both object pixels is unknown when processing the highlighted central object pixel, as Ji's algorithm is parallel. In this case, the deletion of central pixel will be performed, as its neighborhood LX meets with the rotated version of $M_2$. Central pixel's deletion will cause the disjunction of other object pixels, generating edge disconnection. Similar example for 3-pixel template is shown in Fig. 77.3.

To avoid disjointed edges due to parallelism of Ji's algorithm, a local connectivity judgment [5] is introduced. For an object pixel which is about to delete, its immediately updated local neighborhood LTX is first acquired, and an adjacency matrix constructed after deleting it. If the deletion would not destroy connectivity of other object pixels in its neighborhood, the deletion is reasonable and permitted; otherwise, the deletion canceled. Figure 77.4 exemplifies the situation where each node represents an object pixel. Deletion of $x_5$ in Fig. 77.4a will be prohibited as it causes the disjunction of remainder (i.e., $x_3$, $x_4$ and $x_6$), whereas

**Fig. 77.2** An example causing undesirable edge disconnection in Ji's coarse removal

| LX | | | LTX | | |
|---|---|---|---|---|---|
| 0 | 0 | 1 | 0 | 1 | 1 |
| 0 | 0 | 1 | 1 | 0 | 1 |
| 0 | 0 | 1 | 0 | 0 | 1 |

**Fig. 77.3** An example causing undesirable edge disconnection in Ji's fine removal

| LX | | | LTX | | |
|---|---|---|---|---|---|
| 1 | 0 | 0 | 1 | 1 | 0 |
| 0 | 0 | 1 | 0 | 0 | 1 |
| 1 | 1 | 1 | 1 | 1 | 1 |

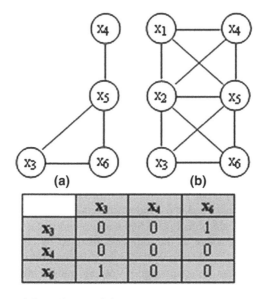

**Fig. 77.4** Non-connectivity and connectivity cases

|     | $x_1$ | $x_2$ | $x_3$ | $x_4$ | $x_6$ |
|-----|-------|-------|-------|-------|-------|
| $x_1$ | 0 | 1 | 0 | 1 | 0 |
| $x_2$ | 1 | 0 | 1 | 1 | 1 |
| $x_3$ | 0 | 1 | 0 | 0 | 1 |
| $x_4$ | 1 | 1 | 0 | 0 | 0 |
| $x_6$ | 0 | 1 | 1 | 0 | 0 |

**Fig. 77.5** Adjacency matrices

deletion of $x_5$ in Fig. 77.4b is acceptable as no disjunction to the remainder (i.e., $x_1$, $x_2$, $x_3$, $x_4$ and $x_6$) incurred. The above judgment is subjective. The objective judgment process is as follows: (1) construct adjacency matrix, and two samples in Fig. 77.5 correspond to the above two cases after deleting $x_5$ and its adhered edges, where 1 denotes the existence of connection between two nodes, 0 otherwise; (2) search adjacency matrix in the following way: start searching a row until first "1" encountered; move to the next row since the presence of a single "1" is enough to guarantee connectivity for the searched row. Similarly, once a row containing only "0" is found, the search should be terminated since this implies prohibition of deleting $x_5$ for the deletion would cause non-connectivity. The additional judgment on local connectivity can avoid the generation of unexpected edge disconnection.

## 77.4 Experimental Results

To evaluate the performance of the proposed method, we have applied it to a variety of binary images. All the images used are of size 200 × 200. The results yielded by our modified algorithm were compared with those obtained by Ji's algorithm [6]. As compared with Ji's algorithm, our improvement is at avoiding the undesirable edge disconnection caused by parallelism of Ji's image thinning process. Hence, improvement of our algorithm is quantitatively evaluated via two following simple and intuitive measures

$$NF = |F_T|, \tag{77.13}$$

$$RF = \frac{|F_T|}{|F_T| + |B_T|}, \tag{77.14}$$

where $B_T$ and $F_T$ are the background and foreground (object) of image thinning result, and $|\cdot|$ cardinality of a set. The first measure is to calculate the number of object pixels (edge pixels) to indicate the degree of edge disconnection. The second measure reflects the disconnection via the ratio of foreground pixels over the whole image pixels. The higher the NF value is, the lower the probability of edge disconnection. Similarly, a higher value of RF means less edge disconnection occurrence (i.e., better edge connectivity) in image thinning result. All experiments are performed on a 3.2 G Pentium PC with 1 G RAM.

In order to demonstrate the effectiveness of the proposed algorithm at avoiding edge disconnection caused by the parallelism in image thinning process based on pulse-coupled neural network [6], two groups of experiments are carried out. The first group is for four images (i.e., Moon, Tank, Sailboat and Airplane) with single object, and the second one for four images (i.e., Potatoes, Block, Bacteria and Rice) with multiple objects. Tables 77.1 and 77.2 list NF and RF values of two methods on these images, respectively. The two tables show that our modified

**Table 77.1** NF values obtained by using different methods for eight images

| Images | Ji's | OUR | Images | Ji's | OUR |
|---|---|---|---|---|---|
| Moon | 33 | 43 | Potatoes | 1,059 | 1,422 |
| Tank | 76 | 91 | Block | 875 | 1,087 |
| Sailboat | 188 | 261 | Bacteria | 1,213 | 1,565 |
| Airplane | 414 | 479 | Rice | 3,137 | 3,731 |

**Table 77.2** RF values obtained by using different methods for eight images

| Images | Ji's | OUR | Images | Ji's | OUR |
|---|---|---|---|---|---|
| Moon | 0.00083 | 0.00108 | Potatoes | 0.02648 | 0.03555 |
| Tank | 0.0019 | 0.00228 | Block | 0.02188 | 0.02718 |
| Sailboat | 0.0047 | 0.00653 | Bacteria | 0.03033 | 0.03913 |
| Airplane | 0.01035 | 0.01198 | Rice | 0.07843 | 0.09328 |

**Fig. 77.6** Image thinning results of moon image: **a** binary image of similar edge structure, **b** Ji's algorithm, **c** the proposed algorithm

**Fig. 77.7** Image thinning results of tank image: **a** binary image of similar edge structure, **b** Ji's algorithm, **c** the proposed algorithm

**Fig. 77.8** Image thinning results of sailboat image: **a** binary image of similar edge structure, **b** Ji's algorithm, **c** the proposed algorithm

**Fig. 77.9** Image thinning results of airplane image: **a** binary image of similar edge structure, **b** Ji's algorithm, **c** the proposed algorithm

**Fig. 77.10** Image thinning results of potatoes image: **a** binary image of similar edge structure, **b** Ji's algorithm, **c** the proposed algorithm

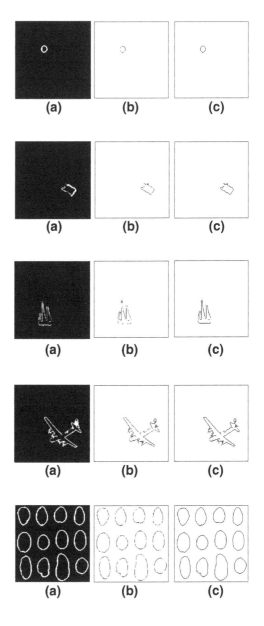

version remains more object pixels (edge pixels) as its NF and RF values are higher than Ji's, showing better edge connectivity. Figures 77.6, 77.7, 77.8, 77.9, 77.10, 77.11, 77.12, and 77.13 give intuitive demonstration. From these images, one can observe that image thinning results obtained by our algorithm preserve original edge connectivity, and obviously avoid undesirable edge disconnection in Ji's results. In our algorithm, we introduced local connectivity judgment to further

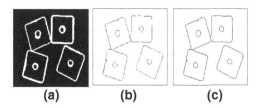

**Fig. 77.11** Image thinning results of block image: **a** binary image of similar edge structure, **b** Ji's algorithm, **c** the proposed algorithm

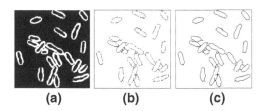

**Fig. 77.12** Image thinning results of bacteria image: **a** binary image of similar edge structure, **b** Ji's algorithm, **c** the proposed algorithm

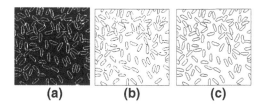

**Fig. 77.13** Image thinning results of rice image: **a** binary image of similar edge structure, **b** Ji's algorithm, **c** the proposed algorithm

**Table 77.3** Running times obtained by using different methods for eight images

| Images | Ji's | OUR | Images | Ji's | OUR |
|---|---|---|---|---|---|
| Moon | 4.906 | 5.094 | Potatoes | 8.703 | 9.313 |
| Tank | 7.781 | 8.204 | Block | 12.313 | 12.89 |
| Sailboat | 4.031 | 4.281 | Bacteria | 16.984 | 18.141 |
| Airplane | 14.656 | 15.422 | Rice | 10.969 | 11.531 |

determine deleting object pixel or not. The judgment will cost some running time. From the comparison listed in Table 77.3, one can conclude that our algorithm is only slightly slower than Ji's algorithm.

## 77.5 Conclusions

Binary image thinning aims to transfer a binary image into an edge image with one pixel width, i.e., extracting the skeleton of object. In Ji's algorithm [6], image thinning is implemented by successively removing those object pixels meeting with 4-pixel template and 3-pixel one. Unfortunately, the parallelism of Ji's algorithm due to its pulse-coupled neural network leads to undesirable edge disconnection in the pixel-removal process. To resolve this issue, a modified version using local connectivity judgment is proposed in this paper. It utilizes an additional operation, namely local connectivity judgment, to avoid unexpected edge disconnection and retain original edge connectivity. The additional judgment has little effect for algorithm efficiency. Experimental results on a variety of binary images demonstrate its superiority.

**Acknowledgments** This work is supported by National Natural Science Foundation of China (Grant Nos. 61,202,318, 61,202,272, 61,202,313), Technology Project of provincial university of Fujian Province (JK2011040), Natural Science Foundation of Fujian Province (2012J01281), Nanjing Institute of Technology Internal Fund (KXJ06037), Guangxi Natural Science Fund of China (No. 2011GXNSFB018070) and Technology Project of Minjiang seedling University (YKY08008, YKY1014).

## References

1. Lam L, Lee SW, Suen CY (1992) Thinning methodologies—a comprehensive survey. IEEE Trans Pattern Anal Mach Intell 14(9):869–885
2. Shih FY, Pu CC (1995) A skeletonization algorithm by maxima tracking on Euclidean distance transform. Pattern Recogn 28(3):331–341
3. Tang YY, You XG (2003) Skeletonization of ribbon-like shapes based on a new wavelet function. IEEE Trans Pattern Anal Mach Intell 25(9):1118–1133
4. Ahmed M, Ward R (2002) A rotation invariant rule-based thinning algorithm for character recognition. IEEE Trans Pattern Anal Mach Intell 24(12):1672–1678
5. Rockett PI (2005) An improved rotation-invariant thinning algorithm. IEEE Trans Pattern Anal Mach Intell 27(10):1671–1674
6. Ji L, Yi Z, Shang L, Pu X (2007) Binary fingerprint image thinning using template-based PCNNs. IEEE Trans Syst Man Cybern B 37(5):1407–1413
7. Lam L, Suen CY (1995) An evaluation of parallel thinning algorithm for character recognition. IEEE Trans Pattern Anal Mach Intell 17(9):914–919
8. Lin J, Chen Z (1995) A Chinese-character thinning algorithm based on global features and contour information. Pattern Recogn 28(4):493–512
9. Gu X, Yu D, Zhang L (2004) Image thinning using pulse coupled neural network. Pattern Recogn Lett 25(9):1075–1084
10. Shang L, Yi Z, Ji L (2007) Binary image thinning using autowaves generated by PCNN. Neural Process Lett 25(1):49–62
11. Johnson JL, Padgett ML (1999) PCNN models and applications. IEEE Trans Neural Netw 10(3):480–498

# Chapter 78
# A Method for Extracting Skeleton of Objects with Fuzzy Boundary

Yongliang Zhang, Ling Li and Yan Yu

**Abstract** This paper proposed a novel method for extracting skeleton of the objects with fuzzy boundary which are possibly aroused by inaccurate segmentation, based on Euclidean distance transform and the curve evolution theory, which integrates the advantages of topology accuracy and good noise elimination effect due to fuzzy boundary. In this paper, firstly, we introduce curve evolution theory for processing the origin objects with fuzzy boundary, then use the proposed method to extract skeleton. Since the distance transformation method will not guarantee the skeleton connectivity, the method firstly calculate the gradient of the distance transform, then obtaining a vector field. We mainly just detect the critical points inside the objects as for each critical point belongs to a local segmentation part of the objects, finally, we use searching the shortest path method to connect these critical points to obtain the whole skeleton, which can reduce data complexity and guarantee connectivity. The results demonstrate that the method is valid on accuracy and complexity.

**Keywords** Skeleton · Euclidean distance transform · Curve evolution · Critical point

Y. Zhang (✉)
College of Information Engineering, Guangdong Jidian Polytechnic,
510515 Guangzhou, China
e-mail: zherac@163.com

L. Li · Y. Yu
Key Laboratory for Health Informatics, Shenzhen Institutes of Advanced Technology,
Chinese Academy of Sciences, 518055 Shenzhen, China

W. Lu et al. (eds.), *Proceedings of the 2012 International Conference on Information Technology and Software Engineering*, Lecture Notes in Electrical Engineering 212, DOI: 10.1007/978-3-642-34531-9_78, © Springer-Verlag Berlin Heidelberg 2013

## 78.1 Introduction

Skeleton is also called medial axis in two dimensions (2D), since Bulm proposed the skeleton concept as a good description form of objects [1], has brought a series of study and research, which is usually described by Grassfire analogy model and maximum inscribed disks model [2]. Skeleton is one of the excellent geometrical characteristic to effectively describe objects because of its topology and shape information consistent with origin objects. Recently it is common used in many disciplines, including medical imaging, objects recognition, image shape retrieval, computer-aided design, path planning [3]. Generally speaking, skeleton of objects described by binary images consists of the conjunction of a series of curves. Up to now, two class algorithms for extracting skeletons appeared, one class is topology thinning methods [3], which will guarantee connectivity, but sensitive to boundary noise and produce some branches with inaccurate skeleton. The other class is based on distance transform [4], main idea is to obtain the distance transform information, advantages are skeleton accurate but without connectivity.

To avoid the above problem, as for the objects with fuzzy boundary brought by inaccurate segmentation [5], in this paper we employ the curve evolution to process the origin objects [6, 7], then propose a novel method inspired by the distance transform to extract the skeleton. Actually distance transform can be regarded as a scalar field, and its associated vector field with important information is the gradient of that. We obtain some critical points according to the local modulus maxima of its gradient, and then connect these critical points by searching shortest path algorithm to keep the invariance of topology [3]. The method in this paper has less computation complexity, at the same time can process the fuzzy boundary which will disturb the accuracy of the skeleton.

In this section, we introduce the curve evolution theory to process the objects with fuzzy boundary, and then present our proposed method: (1) Get the Euclidean Distance Transform (EDT); (2) Calculate the modulus value of the gradient of the objects; (3) Find the critical points and connect them by the shortest searching path to obtain the skeleton.

## 78.2 Curve Evolution Theory

Skeleton is sensitive to noise; small fuzzy boundary will result in large branches, Fig. 78.1. Which make the wrong skeleton and redundant information? Neither thinning method nor distance transform method can avoid this problem. In fact, curve evolution is a polygon simplified course which not only eliminates noise keeping smooth but also reserves important vision parts of object [6]. The curve evolution algorithm is Fig. 78.2. In every evolution step, a pair of line segments on the outline $s1$ and $s2$ merged into one line segment, namely, delete intersection of two line segments, connect the not neighboring points. The formula is below:

**Fig. 78.1** **a** A medial axis in 2D. **b** A medial axis in 2D with fuzzy boundary. **c** A medial surface in 3D

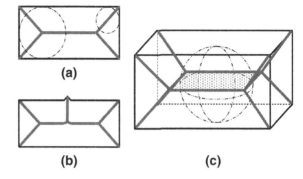

(a)

(b)                    (c)

**Fig. 78.2** Curve evolution with different parameters (**a**) and (**b**) and (**c**) can describe the main shape information while (**c**) and (**d**) lose some main information

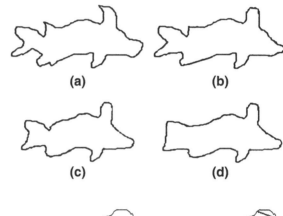

(a)                    (b)

(c)                    (d)

**Fig. 78.3** **a** The origin object with fuzzy boundary. **b** The origin object of (**a**) processing with curve evolution

(a)                    (b)

$$K(s_l, s_2) = \frac{\beta(s_l, s_2)l(s_l)l(s_2)}{l(s_1) + l(s_2)} \qquad (78.1)$$

where $\beta$ ($s_1$, $s2$) is the turn corner of two adjacent line segments $s_1$ and $s_2$, $l$ (.) is the length function normalized responding to the total polygon length. $K$ ($s_1$, $s2$) is contribution parameter reflects contribution degree of the parts consisted of two neighboring line segments to the whole object shape. Figure 78.3 shows (a) the origin boundary, (b) the boundary with curve evolution process; A and B is neighboring vertex, some small convex segment are deleted, which not influence whole topology. The critical factor is the parameter.

## 78.3 Novel Skeleton Extraction Method

### 78.3.1 Calculate the EDT; Compute the Gradient Vector Field of it

We will obtain the Euclidean distance of a binary image. The algorithm is described in [8], the result is in Fig. 78.4b. For 2D image, gradient of the distance and the modulus value of the gradient present as:

$$\nabla DT = (\frac{\partial DT}{\partial x}, \frac{\partial DT}{\partial y}) \tag{78.2}$$

$$|\nabla DT| = \sqrt{(\frac{\partial DT}{\partial x})^2 + (\frac{\partial DT}{\partial y})^2} \tag{78.3}$$

From Fig. 78.4c the gradient modulus value and Fig. 78.4d the local maximum EDT. We can find small modulus value is near to the skeleton position of the objects.

### 78.3.2 Find the Local Modulus Maxima of the EDT

Due to the EDT value on the skeleton points are larger than that of neighboring points (we use 8-neighboring domain), so the points with local modulus maximum EDT value are potential skeleton. Critical points stand on the skeleton are shown in Fig. 78.4e.

### 78.3.3 Find Critical Points, Use Shortest Searching Path to Connect the Critical Point to Obtain Skeleton

According to the definition of local modulus maxima of EDT and transitivity of connected relationship, we can prove the local maximum points connected with the same distance transform values. What's more, a group of connected local maximum points correspond to a convex segment, while less $|\Delta DT|$ instruct the existence of skeleton, so we choose connected local maximum EDT value as the critical point to represent convex segment. On the foundation of finding out the critical points, we use the classical algorithm Dijkstra algorithm to connect the critical points to get the skeleton curves that we want, time complexity is $O(N^2)$.

**Fig. 78.4** The procedure
algorithm process. **a** The
origin objects processed by
curve evolution. **b** The EDT
of (**a**). **c** The modulus value
of gradient of (**b**). **d** Local
maximum EDT. **e** Critical
points are the local minimum
of (**d**) (The exactly position
of critical points)

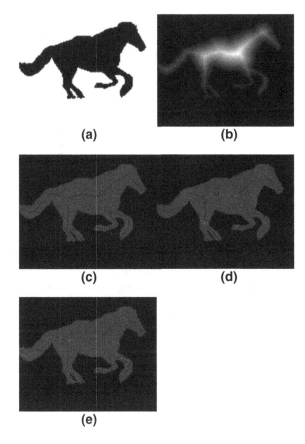

(a)                              (b)

(c)                              (d)

(e)

## 78.3.4  The Description of the Algorithm

The above algorithms in this paper firstly process the fuzzy boundary of origin
objects to get good input for the following skeleton extracting. Then, calculate the
EDT and gradient of the objects, according to the definition regarding maximum
EDT value as source point to search the shortest path from the source point to
other critical points. Finally, according to the sequence of the length of shortest
paths, add them to the skeleton of the objects.

## 78.3.5  Experiment Results with Different Algorithms

Compared with other skeleton extraction methods, thinning method [4], conventional skeleton extracting method [6], and our method, the following three groups
figures will show below in Fig. 78.5. The demonstration results show that our

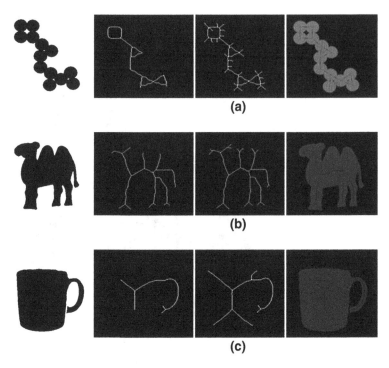

**Fig. 78.5** The first column is the origin objects with fuzzy boundary; the second column is the thinning method in Ref. [4], the third column is distance transform method in Ref. [6], the last column is our method

method proposed in this paper can effectively process objects with fuzzy boundary to obtain good skeleton from our vision habits.

## 78.4 Conclusion and Future Work

This paper according to the distance transform and its gradient of the objects with fuzzy boundary to obtain curve skeleton in two dimension binary images, and the skeleton exactly describe the topology and shape characteristic of objects, and robust to the boundary noise. It can be widely used in object recognition, object retrieval domain. Compared to the current algorithm, this algorithm is easy to implement and have good robustness. What is more, we can use the method in three dimension objects because of it's easily to implement. All those will need further future work.

# References

1. Bulm H (1967) A transformation for extracting new descriptors of shape. In: Walthen-Dunn W (ed) Models for the perception of speech and visual form
2. Bulm H (1973) Biological shape and visual science: part I. Orentical Biol 38:205–287
3. Liu J, Liu W, Wu C, Yuan L (2008) A new method of extracting the objects' curve-skeleton. Acta Automatica Sinica 34(6)
4. Cornea ND, Silver D, Min P (2007) Curve skeleton properties, applications and algorithms. IEEE Trans Vis Comput Graph 13(3)
5. Zhang H, Miao D, Xu F, Zhang H (2008) A novel algorithm for fingerprint skeleton extraction. In: Proceedings of the 7th international conference on machine learning and cybernetics, Kunming, 12–15 July 2008
6. Liu W, Bai X, Zhu G (2006) A skeleton-growing algorithm based on boundary curve evolution. Acta Automatica Sinica 32(2)
7. Xu G, Lei Y (2008) A method of extracting visual main skeleton based on cognition theory. In: Proceedings of the 7th international conference on machine learning and cybernetics, Kunming, 12–15 July 2008
8. Zhu G, Tian J, Wang W (2001) A new method for three dimension distance transform. J Soft 12(3)

# Chapter 79
# Relevance Feedback Based on Particle Swarm Optimization for Image Retrieval

Lijun Cai, Xiaohui Yang, Shuncai Li and Dengfeng Li

**Abstract**  In image retrieval, relevance feedback (RF) is an effective approach to reduce the gap between semantic concepts and low-level visual features, thus it captures user's search intention to some extent. This paper presents two content-based image retrieval strategies with RF based on particle swarm optimization (PSO). The first strategy exploits user indication of positive images. The second one considers not only the positive but also the images indicated as negative. Both two RF strategies are improvements of query point movement by assigning positive and negative images with different weights. These weights are learned by PSO algorithm. Experiments on Corel 5000 database show the competitiveness of our algorithm.

**Keywords**  Image retrieval · Relevance feedback · Particle swarm optimization

## 79.1 Introduction

Large image collections have been created and managed in several applications, such as digital libraries, medicine, and biodiversity information systems [1]. Given the large size of these collections, it is essential to provide efficient and effective mechanisms to retrieve images. This is the objective of the so-called content-based image retrieval (CBIR). The searching process consists of, for a given query image, finding the most similar images stored in the database. Retrieval accuracy of CBIR is essentially limited by the gap between semantic concepts and low-level features.

L. Cai · X. Yang (✉) · S. Li · D. Li
Institute of Applied Mathematics, School of Mathematics and Information Sciences,
Henan University, 475004 Kaifeng, People's Republic of China
e-mail: xhyang@henu.edu.cn

W. Lu et al. (eds.), *Proceedings of the 2012 International Conference on Information Technology and Software Engineering*, Lecture Notes in Electrical Engineering 212, DOI: 10.1007/978-3-642-34531-9_79, © Springer-Verlag Berlin Heidelberg 2013

Relevance feedback (RF) is an online learning technique that engages user and retrieval system in a process of interaction. The strategy asks user to label positive and negative images after previous query loop and dynamically refine retrieval based on feedback information. Therefore, RF is an effective way to reduce the gap. RF is originally developed for information retrieval [2] and is introduced in content-based image retrieval (CBIR) in the 1990s [3]. In addition, it has been shown to provide dramatic performance boost in CBIR.

Frequently-used RF methods include query point movement (QPM) [4], weight updating [3, 5, 6], probability model [7], machine learning [8, 9] and knowledge-based methods [10, 11]. Among these approaches, QPM is developed significantly because of its effectiveness and real-time complexity. The idea is to refine query vector by strengthening the positive images indicated by user and weakening the negative ones. QPM is fulfilled by Rocchio equation [12], in which there are three parameters to be fixed. They are previous query vector weight, positive vector weight and negative vector weight, respectively. These parameters are static and fixed empirically. However, different people may have distinct visual perceptions of the same image. Therefore, static weights may not characterize properly this diversity.

In this paper, two new RF methods for CBIR are proposed. These methods adopt a swarm intelligence optimization algorithm to learn user preference in a query session. Particle swarm optimization (PSO) [13] is a population-based stochastic technique that allows solving complex optimization problems [14]. This technique is based on social behavior of bird flocking or fish schooling to found optimal solutions.

The main contribution of this paper is the proposal of new RF strategies that use PSO to learn the weights corresponding to each feedback images in the QPM framework.

The remainder of the paper is organized as follows. Section 79.2 introduces the background. In Sect. 79.3, our proposed RF frameworks are described in detail. In Sect. 79.4, experiments on Corel 5000 database are performed. Conclusions and future works are given in Sect. 79.5.

## 79.2 Background

This section will introduce the PSO and the motivation of this paper in brief.

### 79.2.1 Particle Swarm Optimization

In the last years, development of optimization algorithms has been inspired and influenced by natural and biological behaviors [15]. In this paper, we investigate the use of a popular stochastic optimization algorithm called PSO to achieve an efficient interactive CBIR algorithm. PSO was introduced by Kennedy and Eberhart [13] in 1995. In the PSO algorithm, the birds in a flock are considered as particles to be flying through a problem space searching for a solution. The solution obtained by the particles is evaluated by a fitness function that provides quantitative value of the solution's utility. During the iterations, the particles move towards the swarm's global best (*gbest*) and the particle's personal best (*pbest*), which are known positions in the solution space. These positions represent the social and the cognitive factor of the swarm and are weighted by two parameters that influence the swarm behavior in the search process.

### 79.2.2 Motivations

QPM tries to improve estimation of optimal query by moving query towards positive examples and away negative ones. It is fulfilled by Rocchio equation

$$\vec{q}_{opt} = \alpha\vec{q}_0 + \beta\frac{1}{|pos|}\sum_{I \in pos}\vec{f}_I - \gamma\frac{1}{|neg|}\sum_{J \in neg}\vec{f}_J. \tag{79.1}$$

where $\vec{q}_{opt}$ is the updated query vector and $\vec{q}_0$ is the original one. *pos* is set of positive images indicated by user, $|pos|$ is the number of *pos*, *neg* is set of negative images, $\vec{f}_I$ is feature vector of image $I$. $\alpha, \beta, \gamma$ are weights, a reasonable choose is $\alpha = 1, \beta = 0.75, \gamma = 0.15$.

From Eq. (79.1), we know that QPM does not consider different importance of feedback images, all positive images have the equal importance, and so are negative ones.

### 79.3 Relevance Feedback Based on Particle Swarm Optimization

This subsection we propose two relevance feedback (RF) strategies based on PSO and QPM. The first strategy, $PSO^+$, exploits only the user indication of positive images. The second one, $PSO^{\pm}$, considers not only the positive but also the images indicated as negative

$PSO^+$ and $PSO^{\pm}$ aims to assign different feedback images with different weights by PSO learning. Considering $\alpha=1$, Eq. (79.1) is modified as

$$\vec{q}_{opt} = \vec{q}_0 + \frac{1}{|pos|}\sum_{I \in pos}\beta_I\vec{f}_I - \frac{1}{|neg|}\sum_{J \in neg}\gamma_J\vec{f}_J. \tag{79.2}$$

We denote $\beta=\{\beta_I, I \in pos\}$, $\gamma=\{\gamma_I, I \in neg\}$.

If we only consider positive images indicated by user, (79.2) is simplified as

**Table 79.1** The algorithm of relevance feedback based on PSO

| Algorithm: relevance feedback based on PSO |
| --- |
| Step 1 User indication of query image $Q$ |
| Step 2 Show initial set of retrieved images according to the similarity with $Q$ (top $L$similar images) |
| Step 3 While user is not satisfied |
| Step 4 User indication of positive images and negative ones among $L$similar images |
| Step 5 Apply PSO to learn the weights of positive and negative images |
| Step 6 The updated query vector $\vec{q}_{opt}$ is obtained by (79.2) or (79.3) |
| Step 7 Rank the database images by comparing the similarity between each image of image database with $\vec{q}_{opt}$ |
| Step 8 Show top $L$ similar images |
| Step 9 end while |

$$\vec{q}_{opt} = \vec{q}_0 + \frac{1}{|pos|} \sum_{l \in pos} \beta_l \vec{f}_l. \tag{79.3}$$

Table 79.1 gives the details of the framework of $PSO^+$ and $PSO^\pm$.

In step 2 and 4, the similarity is obtained by comparing the Euclidean distance between two color histogram belonging to two images. Among the top $L$ similar images, user indicates each image as positive or negative. Then the weights of feedback images are learned

Step 5 is the most important. For $PSO^\pm$, the weights set is $\Omega = \beta \cup \gamma$, and for $PSO^+$, it is $\Omega = \beta$. To find optima parameter solution $\Omega_{opt}$, $\{\Omega_n\}_{n=1}^N$ is treated as the initial population of PSO, $\Omega_n, n = 1, \ldots, N$ are $N$ feasible solutions of optimal parameter. $\Omega_{opt}$ is obtained after generations.

### 79.3.1 Relevance Feedback Based on Positive Images

After the system gives initial search results, user indicates images as positive or negative. First we construct the initial population of PSO, $\{\Omega_n\}_{n=1}^N$. Each $\Omega_n, n \in \{1, \ldots, N\}$ is a $|pos| - $ dim *entional* vector, i.e. $\Omega_n = \{\Omega_{n,1}, \ldots, \Omega_{n,|pos|}\}$, and satisfies $\sum_{i=1}^{|pos|} \Omega_{n,i} = 1$. One $\Omega_n$ corresponds to one $\vec{q}_{opt,n}$ according to (79.3). That is

$$\vec{q}_{opt,n} = \vec{q}_0 + \frac{1}{|pos|} \sum_{i=1}^{|pos|} \Omega_{n,i} \vec{f}_i. \tag{79.4}$$

Each solution $\Omega_n$ is evaluated by fitness function on training set. During the iterations, the solutions move towards the global best and the personal best. The training set and fitness function adopted are introduced briefly following.

Training set $T = \{t_1, \ldots, t_{N_T}\}$, and $T = A \cup B \cup C$. $A, B, C$ are selected randomly from $pos$, $neg$ and unlabeled images, respectively. And the number of $A, B, C$ are $N_A = \mathrm{Min}(N_T/2, N_{pos})$, $N_B = \mathrm{Min}(N_T - N_A, N_{neg})$ and $N_C = N_T - N_A - N_B$. The fitness of $\Omega_n, n \in \{1, \ldots, N\}$ is defined as

$$f(\Omega_n) = \sum_{l=1}^{N} r(st_{\Omega_n}[l]) \cdot \frac{1}{A} (\frac{A-1}{A})^{l-1} \qquad (79.5)$$

where $A = 2, st_{\Omega_n} = \left\{ t_{i_1}, \ldots, t_{i_{N_T}} \right\}$, $\left\{ i_1, \ldots, i_{N_T} \right\}$ is a permutation of $\{1, \ldots, N_T\}$. And the permutation is determined by $d(t_{i_1}, \vec{q}_{opt,n}) \leq d(t_{i_2}, \vec{q}_{opt,n}) \leq \cdots \leq d(t_{i_{N_T}}, \vec{q}_{opt,n})$, $d(t_i, \vec{q}_{opt,n})$ denotes the distance between $t_i$ with $\vec{q}_{opt,n}$.

$$r(st_{\Omega_n}[l]) = \begin{cases} 1, & \text{if } st_{\Omega_n}[l] \in pos \\ 0, & \text{if } st_{\Omega_n}[l] \in neg \end{cases}. \qquad (79.6)$$

After generations, optimum $\tilde{\Omega} = \{\tilde{\Omega}_1, \ldots, \tilde{\Omega}_{|pos|}\}$ is found and $\vec{q}_{opt}$ is obtained by

$$\vec{q}_{opt} = \vec{q}_0 + \frac{1}{|pos|} \sum_{i=1}^{|pos|} \tilde{\Omega}_i \vec{f}_i. \qquad (79.7)$$

Then database images are sorted by comparing the Euclidean distance between color histogram belonging to each image of image database with $\vec{q}_{opt}$.

## 79.3.2 Relevance Feedback Based on Positive and Negative Images

$PSO^{\pm}$ considers not only positive but also negative images. The difference with $PSO^+$ is the generation of initial population $\{\Omega_n\}_{n=1}^{N}$. Each $\Omega_n, n \in \{1, \ldots, N\}$ is a $(|pos|+|neg|) - \dim$ *entional*     vector,     i.e.

$\Omega_n = \{ \Omega_{n,1}, \ldots, \Omega_{n,|pos|}, \ldots, \Omega_{n,|pos|+|neg|} \}$    and    satisfies    $\sum_{i=1}^{|pos|} \Omega_{n,i} = 1$    and

$\sum_{i=|pos|+1}^{|pos|+|neg|} \Omega_{n,i} = 1$.

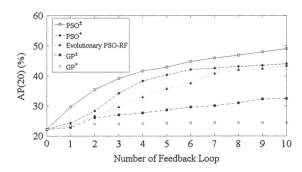

Fig. 79.1 Average precision (*top 20*) of several RF strategies on Corel 5000

## 79.4 Experimental Results

We test our algorithms on Corel 5000 dataset, which is publicly available and widely used. The dataset includes 50 semantic categories with 100 images per category. Feature selection is not in the research scope of this paper, color histogram [16] is adopted throughout the experiments here.

For each category, we select 30 randomly as queries. For each of the queries, 10 iterations of user-and-system interaction are carried out. At each round of feedback, the system examines the top 20 similar images. A retrieved image is considered to be relevant if it belongs to the same category of the query. We use average precision within the top 20 similar images [AP(20)] and $P \times R$ curve (the 10th iteration of feedback) to measure retrieval performance. At the same platform, we compare our methods with other three approaches of the same class, QPM, relevance feedback based on genetic programming ($GP^{\pm}$) [10], Evolutionary PSO-RF [17]. Compared results are shown in Figs. 79.1 and 79.2. It is illustrated in Fig. 79.1 that $PSO^{\pm}$ method's AP(20) after 10 feedback iterations is higher than that of Evolutionary PSO-RF, $GP^{\pm}$ and QPM by 5.65,16.57 and 26.57 %. AP(20) of $PSO^{+}$ is higher than these three approaches by 0.6, 11.52 and 19.52 %. And in Fig. 79.2, the $P \times R$ curve of $PSO^{\pm}$ performs the best. These experimental results show the competitive of our proposed methods.

In PSO learning weights stage, the parameters are predefined as follows. The size of initial population is $N = 60$ and the number of generations is 5. $w = 0.95$, $c_1 = 2$, $c_2 = 2$. It is worth mentioning that all the predefined parameters in this paper are obtained by experiments in terms of AP(20).

All experiments in this paper have been implemented on Intel(R) Core(TM) i5 CPU (2.67 GHz, 2 GB RAM) 32Bit Windows XP, Matlab 7.11 environment. The average execution time on each RF iteration is 0.1891 s for $PSO^{+}$ method, and 0.1954s for $PSO^{\pm}$ method. Therefore, our proposed $PSO^{+}$ and $PSO^{\pm}$ methods are real-time.

**Fig. 79.2**  $P \times R$ curve of several RF strategies

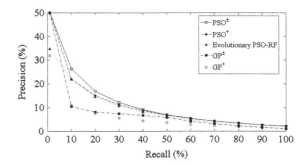

## 79.5  Conclusions

Two effective content-based relevance feedback frameworks, $PSO^{\pm}$ and $PSO^{+}$, which based on particle swarm optimization are proposed. $PSO^{\pm}$ and $PSO^{+}$ strengthen positive images and weaken negative ones with learning weights. We believed that retrieval accuracy will be further improved by considering the contribution of neighbor particles.

**Acknowledgments**  The authors would like to thank the anonymous reviewers and the associate editor for their valuable comments and thoughtful suggestions which improved the quality of the presented work. We also thank Dr. Xiaoting Zhang from Rutgers University for offering Corel 5000 database. This work is supported by the NSF (project nos. 60802061, 61071189).

## References

1. da Torres RS, Falĉao AX (2006) Content-based image retrieval: theory and applications. Revista de Inform'atica Te'orica e Aplicada 13(2):161–185
2. Salton G (1989) Automatic text processing. Addison-Wesley, Reading
3. Rui Y, Huang TS, Ortega M, Mehrotra S (1998) Relevance feedback: a power tool in interactive content based image retrieval. IEEE Trans Circ Syst Video Technol 8(5):644–655
4. Rarza-Yates R, Ribeiro-Neto B (1999) Modern information retrieval. Addison-Wesley, Reading
5. Rui Y, Huang T (2000) Optimizing learning in image retrieval. In: Proceedings of IEEE conference on computer vision and pattern recognition, Hilton Head Island, USA, pp 236–241
6. Zhang YT (2011) Matching algorithm with relevance feedback for brain MRI. In: The 4th international conference on biomedical engineering and informatics, pp 365–370
7. Huang L, Nan JG, Guo L, Lin QY (2012) A bayesian network approach in the relevance feedback of personalized image semantic model. Adv Intell Soft Comput 128(1):7–12
8. Zhao LJ, Tang JK, Yu XJ, Li YZ, Mi SJ, Zhang CW (2012) Content-based remote sensing image retrieval using image multi-feature combination and SVM-based relevance feedback. Recent Adv Comput Sci Inf Eng 124:761–767
9. Wang XY, Chen JW, Yang HY (2011) A new integrated SVM classifiers for relevance feedback content-based image retrieval using EM parameter estimation. Appl Soft Comput 11(2):2787–2804

10. Ferreira CD, Asntos JA, Torres RS, Goncalves MA, Rezende RC, Fan W (2011) Relevance feedback based on genetic programming for image retrieval. Pattern Recogn Lett 32(1):27–37
11. Bulo SR, Rabbi M, Pelillo M (2011) Content-based image retrieval with relevance feedback using random walks. Pattern Recogn 44(9):2109–2122
12. Shao H, Zhang JX, Cui WC, Wu YS (2009) Positive relevance feedback algorithm based on dynamic weight query point movement. Comput Eng Des 30(20):4711–4714
13. Kennedy J, Eberhart R (1995) Particle swarm optimization. In: Proceedings of the 2001 congress on 4th IEEE international conference on neural networks, pp 1942–1948
14. Eberhart RC, Shi Y (2001) Particle swarm optimization: developments, applications and resources. In: Proceedings of 2001 congress on evolutionary computation (IEEE), Seoul, pp 81–86
15. Wilson EO (1975) Sociobiology: the new synthesis. Belknap Press of Harvard University Press, Cambridge
16. Swain M, Ballard D (1991) Color indexing. Int J Comput Vis 7(1):11–32
17. Broilo M, Natale FGB (2010) A stochastic approach to image retrieval using relevance feedback and particle swarm optimization. IEEE Trans Multimedia 12(4):267–277

# Chapter 80
# Improve the Resolution of Medical Image Using POCS Algorithm

Jun Luo and Ying Chen

**Abstract** When we obtain some static low resolution (LR) medical images, the dimension of these images can not satisfy the requirement in some degree, we need to improve the quality of LR image. Firstly, we establish an imaging model, and identify the availability of this model for POCS algorithm, then we use POCS algorithm to reconstruct two high resolution images form 25 low resolution MRI and blood samples individually, in order to compare the ultimate performance of POCS algorithm with other classical interpolation algorithms, we analyze the quality differences of reconstruction images of POCS algorithm and interpolation algorithms, the results reveal that our method can obtain a higher contrast ratio and retain more details than that of the interpolation methods for high resolution image.

**Keywords** Medical image · POCS · Interpolation algorithm · Image reconstruction

## 80.1 Introduction

When we obtain some low resolution (LR) static images, the dimension of imaging elements can not satisfy our requirement in some degree, we need to improve the resolution of these low resolution images by appropriate method, such as super resolution (SR) algorithms [1–3].

J. Luo (✉)
College of Sciences, Huazhong Agricultural University, No.1, Shizishan Street, Hongshan District, Wuhan 430070, Hubei Province, China
e-mail: luojun81@163.com

Y. Chen
Hubei Province Fiber Inspection Bureau, Wuhan 430060, Hubei Province, China
e-mail: cy2047@163.com

W. Lu et al. (eds.), *Proceedings of the 2012 International Conference on Information Technology and Software Engineering*, Lecture Notes in Electrical Engineering 212, DOI: 10.1007/978-3-642-34531-9_80, © Springer-Verlag Berlin Heidelberg 2013

Projection on Convex Set (POCS) is a traditional framework based on set theory which can reconstruct SR image, the POCS algorithm based on some classic space field models as well, and makes use of some prior knowledge, such as data energy, data certainty, data fidelity, data smoothness, etc., then produces a solution among the intersection of all prior knowledge. Therefore, the POCS algorithm can reconstruct a SR image from many low resolution images, and not only restore the details, but also amplify the dimension of low resolution image. There are many applications of POCS algorithm in image or video processing [4], such as image enhancement, restoration, compression and decompression, etc. Meanwhile, the POCS algorithm is robust for any blur type.

Usually, we obtain some LR medical images because of the limitation of imaging condition, so we need to improve the resolution for image analysis and medical diagnosis. In our paper, we will introduce the imaging model briefly for the first, then give some introduction of classic POCS algorithm, and reconstruct two different high resolution medical images by POCS algorithm, finally we compare the ultimate performance of POCS algorithm with other classical interpolation algorithms.

## 80.2 The Model of Imaging

We will introduce some definitions in the following context.

We use symbol $B$ to express the output function of 2D linear shift variant system, and the space-variant PSF is defined in Eq. (80.1):

$$h(m_1, m_2; i_1, i_2) = B\{\delta(m_1 - i_1, m_2 - i_2)\} \tag{80.1}$$

In Eq. (80.1), $\delta$ is impulse response of pixels.

Then we define discrete digital image in Eq. (80.2)

$$f(m_1, m_2) = \sum_{(i_1,i_2)\in S_f} f(i_1, i_2)\delta(m_1 - i_1, m_2 - i_2) \tag{80.2}$$

In Eq. (80.2), the symbol $f(\bullet, \bullet)$ is a sample of discrete image, the $S_f$ is image support field, if $\delta$ stands for blur operator, and add some noise $r(m_1, m_2)$, then we can define blur image by Eq. (80.3)

$$g(m_1, m_2) = \sum_{(i_1,i_2)\in S_f} f(i_1, i_2)h(m_1, m_2; i_1, i_2) + r(m_1, m_2) \tag{80.3}$$

For any image with dimension $M_1 \times M_2$, if we know the PSF at first, then we can obtain equation $f(i_1, i_2)$ of every observed pixel. Therefore, the problem of restoration can be regarded to find a solution of all observed pixels equation. When we consider sub-sample matrix $h_D$, the model of imaging can be defined by Eq. (80.4)

$$g_k = h_D h_{PSF} f + r_k, \quad k = 0, 1, 2 \ldots m \tag{80.4}$$

In Eq. (80.4), sub-sample can be solved by interpolation, however, the reconstruct of the low resolution images is the key problem.

## 80.3 Basic POCS Algorithm

The aim of image amplification is to obtain an original high resolution image from many low resolution images, and one of the most important problems is how to improve the quality of high resolution image. We can use some prior knowledge such as the PSF of imaging model, Gaussian white noise, etc. According to the POCS framework, the unknown signal or image is assumed in a certain Hilbert space, any constraint of prior knowledge or the nearest solution of algorithm will locate in the Hilbert space. So we can define many prior constraints corresponding to many convex sets, and the intersection of these convex sets will contain a super resolution image. Thus, if we can obtain some prior knowledge $C_i$, we will find a non-null intersection $C_0$ which is an intersection of all convex sets, and the original image $f$ will satisfy $f \in C_0 = \bigcap\limits_{i=1}^{m} C_i$, and we can reconstruct the super resolution image in $C_0$ [5, 6].

The POCS algorithm is an iteration and projection process which starts from a given or random initial image in the Hilbert space. Therefore, we can define the projection process as Eq. (80.5).

$$f_{k+1} = T_m T_{m-1} \cdots T_1 \{f_k\}, \quad k = 0, 1 \ldots, m \tag{80.5}$$

In Eq. (80.5), $T_i = (1 - \lambda_i)I + \lambda_i P_i, 0 < \lambda_i < 2$, $\lambda_i$ is a relaxed projection operator which can adjust the convergence rate of iteration. If $\lambda_i = 1$, $T_i$ is equal to $P_i$, and $P_i$ can adjust the step length and direction of projection. In our paper, $\lambda_i = 1$, and the process of projection is defined as Eq. (80.6).

$$f_{k+1} = P_m P_{m-1} \cdots P_1 \{f_k\}, \quad k = 0, 1 \ldots, m \tag{80.6}$$

The projection will cost much time, and then we will obtain a super resolution image as the final solution.

Based on above definitions, we can define many convex sets of image:

$$C_k(m_1, m_2) = \{f(i_1, i_2) : |r_k^{(f)}(m_1, m_2)| \leq \delta_0\}$$

$$r_k^{(f)}(m_1, m_2) = g_k(m_1, m_2) - \sum_{i_1=0}^{M_1-1} \sum_{i_2=0}^{M_2-1} f(i_1, i_2) h_k(m_1, m_2; i_1, i_2), \quad k = 1, 2, \ldots, m$$

$$\tag{80.7}$$

In Eq. (80.7), $f(i_1, i_2)$ is an estimation of ideal SR image, then we use cubic spline interpolation to obtain a basic high resolution image, $h_k(m_1, m_2; i_1, i_2)$ is the PSF of pixel $(i_1, i_2)$.

The projection operator $P$ can adjust the step length and direction of projection, and $P_{(m_1,m_2)}\{f(i_1, i_2)\}$ can be defined as:

$$\hat{f}(i_1, i_2) = P_{(m_1,m_2)}\{f(i_1, i_2)\}$$

$$=f(i_1, i_2) + \begin{cases} \dfrac{r_k^{(\hat{f})}(m_1,m_2)-\delta_0}{\sum\limits_{j_1}\sum\limits_{j_2} h_k^2(m_1,m_2;j_1,j_2)} h_k(m_1,m_2;j_1,j_2) & r_k^{(\hat{f})}(m_1,m_2) > \delta_0 \\[4mm] 0 & -\delta_0 \le r_k^{(\hat{f})}(m_1,m_2) \le \delta_0 \\[4mm] \dfrac{r_k^{(\hat{f})}(m_1,m_2)+\delta_0}{\sum\limits_{j_1}\sum\limits_{j_2} h_k^2(m_1,m_2;j_1,j_2)} h_k(m_1,m_2;j_1,j_2) & r_k^{(\hat{f})}(m_1,m_2) < -\delta_0 \end{cases}$$

$$(80.8)$$

In Eq. (80.8), all parameters and convex sets define a boundary corresponding to high resolution image. $\delta_0$ reflects a prior confidence interval of original image, which is decided by the statistical characteristic of noise process, and for any pixel coordinate $(m_1, m_2)$, the difference between observed image $g_k(m_1, m_2)$ and SR estimation will be decided by $\delta_0$.

Therefore, we can obtain a solution in the intersection $C_0$.

Besides the above constraint of convex sets, we can give another constraint of convex set named $C_A$, which is a range constraint of pixels.

$$C_A = \{y(i_1, i_2) : \alpha \le y(i_1, i_2) \le \beta\}, \quad 0 \le i_1 \le M_1 - 1, \ 0 \le i_2 \le M_2 - 1 \quad (80.9)$$

In Eq. (80.9), $\alpha = 0$ and $\beta = 255$, and the projection operator of $C_A$ is defined in formula (80.10).

$$P_A[x(i_1, i_2)] = \begin{cases} 0 & x(i_1, i_2) < 0 \\ x(i_1, i_2) & 0 \le x(i_1, i_2) \le 255 \\ 255 & x(i_1, i_2) > 255 \end{cases} \quad (80.10)$$

All in all, the POCS framework ensures the monotonicity of convergence, and we can obtain an optimal solution in theory, which will satisfy all constraints of original prior knowledge. However, the intersection $C_0$ contains many solutions, which are equal in theory, so we can not obtain a unique solution every time [7].

## 80.4 Experiments and Analysis

Usually, we obtain some LR medical images because of the limitation of imaging condition, so we need to improve the resolution for image analysis and medical diagnosis. We reconstruct two different high resolution medical images by POCS algorithm, and retain the details of original images at the same time.

In the following experiment, all the original samples are classical which named as "MRI" and "blood" image with 128 × 128 pixels, then we use POCS algorithm to improve the resolution of these images.

## 80.4.1 The Experiment of MRI Image

For the first, we use Eq. (80.4), and consider zero horizontal motion PSF pixels, and then we will obtain 25 low resolution MRI images with 128 × 128 pixels, one of them can be seen in Fig. 80.1a. We use POCS algorithm to obtain a high resolution MRI image 256 × 256 pixels from these low resolution images, the result shows that it is suitable in this imaging condition, which can be seen in Fig. 80.1b. In order to compare the differences between the POCS algorithm and other interpolation algorithms, we use bilinear interpolation, bicubic interpolation and spline interpolation for original low resolution MRI image, which can be seen in Fig. 80.1c, e and g individually.

We use Fig. 80.1b subtract Fig. 80.1c in terms of the values of every corresponding pixels, the result can be seen in Fig. 80.1d, which means that the difference of reconstruction image between the POCS algorithm and bilinear interpolation algorithm, we can observe that the POCS algorithm can provide more details for high resolution MRI image, and we can obtain higher contrast ratio which benefit for image analyzing as well, then we use Fig. 80.1b subtract Fig. 80.1e and g in terms of the values of every corresponding pixels individually, the result can be seen in Fig. 80.1f and h. The results of Fig. 801d, f and h reveal that the quality of reconstruction image using POCS algorithm is better than that of interpolation algorithms mentioned above, which can provide more details and higher contrast ratio for high resolution MRI image.

## 80.4.2 The Experiment of Blood Image

As mentioned in the experiment of MRI image, we use equation (80.4), and consider zero horizontal motion PSF pixels, and then we will obtain 25 low resolution blood images with 128 × 128 pixels, one of them can be seen in Fig. 80.2a. We use POCS algorithm to obtain a high resolution blood image 256 × 256 pixels from these low resolution images, which can be seen in Fig. 80.2b, then we use bilinear, bicubic and spline interpolation for original low resolution blood image, which can be seen in Fig. 80.2c, e and g individually. In order to compare the quality differences of reconstruction image between the POCS algorithm and these interpolation algorithms, we use Fig. 80.2b subtract Fig. 80.2c, e and g in terms of the values of every corresponding pixels, the results

**Fig. 80.1** **a** The original
MRI image with 128 × 128
pixels, **b** high resolution MRI
image with 256 × 256 pixels
reconstructed by POCS
algorithm, **c** MRI image with
256 × 256 pixels
interpolated by bilinear,
**d** Fig. 80.1b subtract
Fig. 80.1c by corresponding
pixels, **e** MRI image with
256 × 256 pixels
interpolated by bicubic,
**f** Fig. 80.1b subtract
Fig. 80.1e by corresponding
pixels, **g** MRI image with
256 × 256 pixels
interpolated by spline,
**h** Fig. 80.1b subtract
Fig. 80.1g by corresponding
pixels

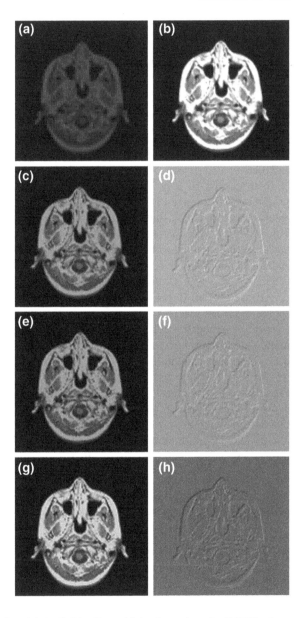

can be seen in Fig. 80.2d, f and h individually, which show that the POCS algorithm can provide more details and higher contrast ratio for high resolution blood image.

**Fig. 80.2  a** The original
blood image with 128 × 128
pixels, **b** high resolution
blood image with 256 × 256
pixels reconstructed by POCS
algorithm, **c** blood image
with 256 × 256 pixels
interpolated by bilinear,
**d** Fig. 80.1b subtract
Fig. 80.1c by every pixels,
**e** blood image with
256 × 256 pixels
interpolated by bicubic,
**f** Fig. 80.1b subtract
Fig. 80.1e by every pixels,
**g** blood image with
256 × 256 pixels
interpolated by spline,
**h** Fig. 80.1b subtract
Fig. 80.1g by every pixels

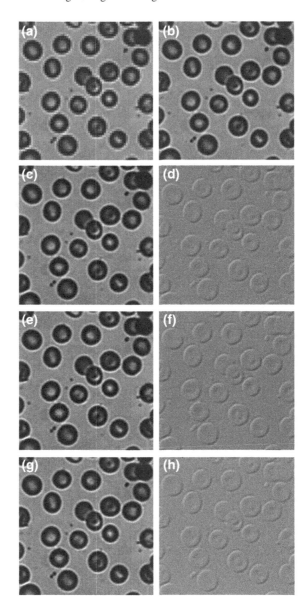

## 80.5  Conclusion

We establish an imaging model, and identify the availability of this model for
POCS algorithm. We use POCS algorithm to reconstruct two high resolution
images form 25 low resolution MRI and blood samples, finally we compare the

ultimate performance of POCS algorithm with three classical interpolation algorithms, the result reveal that our method can obtain a high resolution image and retain more details than the interpolation method mentioned above.

# References

1. Elad M, Feuer A (1997). Restoration of a single super-resolution image from several blurred, noisy and undersampled measured images. IEEE Trans Image Process 6(12):1646–1658
2. Segall CA, Molina R, Katsaggelos AK et al (2002) Reconstruction of high-resolution image frames from a sequence of low-resolution and compressed observations. Process IEEE Int Conf Acoust, Speech, Signal Process 2:1701–1704
3. Tekalp AM, Ozkan MK, Sezan MI (1992) High-resolution image reconstruction from lower-resolution image sequences and space varying image restoration. In: Proceedings of ICASSP, vol 3, San Francisco, CA, pp 169–172
4. Kim Y, Park C-S, Ko S-J (2003) Fast POCS based post-processing technique for HDTV. IEEE Trans Consum Electron 49:1438–1447
5. Ozkan MK, Murat Tekalp A, Ibrahim Sezan M (1994) POCS-based restoration of space-varying blurred images. IEEE Trans Image Process 3:450–454
6. Patti AJ, Altunbasak Y (2001) Artifact reduction for set theoretic super resolution image reconstruction with edge adaptive constraints and higher-order interpolants. IEEE Trans Image Process 10:179–186
7. Wee-Chung Liew A, Yan H, Law N-F (2005) POCS-based blocking artifacts suppression using a smoothness constraint set with explicit region modeling. IEEE Trans Circuits Syst Video Technol 15:795–800

# Chapter 81
# A Survey of JND Models in Digital Image Watermarking

Wei Li, Yana Zhang and Cheng Yang

**Abstract** The Just Noticeable Distortion (JND) model is used to determine the optimum strength for watermark embedding and contribute to provide an imperceptible and robust watermarking scheme. This paper introduces the current JND models in digital watermarking, and simulates the watermarking schemes based on JND model in DCT and DWT domain, the experiment results show that the watermarking schemes based on JND model in DWT domain has better performance than in DCT domain. Meanwhile, we propose a possible research direction of watermarking technique that can better balance the contradiction between robustness and perceptibility.

**Keywords** HVS · JND model · Imperceptibility · Robustness · Prime sketch

## 81.1 Introduction

Digital watermarking is a technique of embedding additional watermark information into digital works while preserving perceptual quality requirement, and the watermark can be detected from the tested data. This technique can be used for various purpose as content copyright protection, content authentication of digital multimedia and so on. Digital watermarking must successfully satisfy trade-offs

W. Li (✉) · Y. Zhang · C. Yang
Information Engineering School, Communication University of China,
No.1 Dingfuzhuang East Street 100024 Chaoyang District, Beijing, China
e-mail: liwei601@126.com

W. Lu et al. (eds.), *Proceedings of the 2012 International Conference on Information Technology and Software Engineering*, Lecture Notes in Electrical Engineering 212, DOI: 10.1007/978-3-642-34531-9_81, © Springer-Verlag Berlin Heidelberg 2013

between imperceptibility, robustness and watermark capacity. Therefore, water-marking algorithm should select the appropriate region to embed watermark information by the highest possible bit rate and the highest possible intensity to resist kinds of attacks on condition that watermark is imperceptible [1, 2]. JND model based on HVS(Human Visual System)provides the effective solution for this problem. Visual threshold represents the maximum image distortion that human eye can tolerate, which is generally a comprehensive reflection of the frequency sensitivity, luminance masking, contrast masking and other character-istics of human vision. Digital watermarking employs JND model to control the embedding position and intensity of watermark, while ensuring the optimal watermarking performance [3].

This paper is organized as followed. In Sect. 81.2, we introduce the basic characteristics of HVS, which will be applied into the construction of JND model. In Sect. 81.3, we present the existing JND models in digital watermarking, including the construction techniques of these models. In Sect. 81.4, we represent the watermarking algorithms based on JND model in DCT and DWT domain in the experiment. In Sect. 81.5, we give the results of the experiment, and evaluate the performance of JND models in the two research fields. Finally, we conclude the advantages and disadvantages of two algorithms, and propose the possible research direction of watermarking technique.

## 81.2 The Basic Characteristics of HVS

The basic characteristics of HVS include the frequency sensitivity, luminance masking, contrast masking and texture masking. Frequency sensitivity determines the human's sensitivity to the different spatial frequency, and we usually represent it by the CSF (contrast sensitivity function). The human eye is most sensitive to changes in the medium-frequency domain, and in the higher and lower frequency domain, the sensitivity will decrease [4]. Luminance masking measures the effect of the detectability threshold of noise in a background environment. The human eye is less sensitive to the noise in those regions of the image where brightness is high or low. Contrast masking refers to the effect of decreasing visual perception of the target signal in the presence of another signal. We can distinguish self masking and neighborhood masking. Self masking is the phenomenon when target signal and masked signal have the same spatial frequencies, orientation and location in an image. Neighborhood masking refers that the complex region can tolerate greater distortion than the smooth region [5]. The human eye is less sensitive to noise in texture region than the smooth region, and the more complex background texture is, the higher perceived noise threshold is, we call this phenomenon as texture masking.

# 81.3 JND Models in Digital Watermarking

Currently the researchers have proposed lots of watermarking technique employing JND models based on the HVS to direct watermark embedding, and it has great significance for enhancing watermark imperceptibility and robustness. Generally, the current JND models have two kinds of categories, one is the JND model in spatial domain which is also called pixel-wise JND model; another one is JND model in transform domain.

## 81.3.1 JND Model in Spatial Domain

The models that were built in the spatial domain to estimate JND profiles for image compression can be found in the paper [6]. Wu et al. [7] propose a pixel wise adaptive JND model, which considers the luminance adaptation factor and the texture masking effect, and the JND threshold of each pixel is shown by the following equation:

$$JND(x,y) = \theta_1(x,y)T_{lum}(x,y) + \theta_2(x,y)T_{tex}(x,y) \tag{81.1}$$

Where $T_{lum}(x,y)$ denotes the luminance adaptation factor, $T_{tex}(x,y)$ refers the texture masking, and the $\theta_1$, $\theta_2$ are the relevant parameters.

## 81.3.2 JND Model in Transform Domain

### 81.3.2.1 JND Model in DCT Domain

However, the spatial JND models do not exploit the HVS comprehensively in comparison with JND model in transform domain. A better JND model is proposed by Ahumada [8], which gives the frequency sensitivity threshold for each DCT coefficient by introducing CSF. Watson et al. [9] give a more effective JND model by considering the luminance masking and contrast masking effect to the base thresholds. Zhang et al. [10] give a new formula for luminance adaptation adjustment and a new contrast masking incorporating block classification. Wei et al. [11] consider Gamma correction which is applied to compensate the luminance adaptation effect for a more accurate result. However, the computational complexity of the model is high, and the efficiency is not high. In those models, Watson JND model [9] is the representative one, which is constructed as follow:

$$t(i,j) = Q(i,j)/2 \tag{81.2}$$

$$t(i,j,k) = t(i,j) \times \left[ F(0,0,k) \Big/ \overline{F(0,0)} \right]^{\alpha} \tag{81.3}$$

$$s(i,j,k) = Max\left\{ t(i,j,k), |F(i,j,k)|^{w(i,j)} t(i,j,k)^{1-w(i,j)} \right\}  \qquad (81.4)$$

where $t(i,j)$ denotes the frequency sensitivity; $t(i,j,k)$ is the luminance masking; $s(i,j,k)$ refers the contrast masking which is the final constitution of JND.

### 81.3.2.2 JND Model in DWT Domain

In 1992, Lewis et al. [12] give a JND model which takes into account the frequency sensitivity, luminance masking effect and texture masking effect. In 1997, Watson et al. [13] determine the visibility thresholds for 9/7 biorthogonal wavelets by using image coding and compression theory. Barni et al. [14] explore the HVS further, construct a JND model which is more consistent with the perceptibility of HVS. Watson et al. [15] discover that the complexity and uncertainty of original image will result in the changes of perception thresholds, which is called entropy masking phenomenon. Akhbari et al. [16] determine different thresholds of perception in different entropy regions by considering perceptual characteristics of HVS and entropy masking characteristics comprehensively. The complexity and uncertainty of image will be greater in the region that image entropy value is large, which will lead the decrease of visual sensitivity in this region, so that the perception threshold in this region increase accordingly. In these models, Barni JND model [14] is the classical one which constitutes as follow:

$$JND_l^s(x,y) = 0.5 \times frequency(l,s) \times L(l,x,y) \times T(l,x,y)^{0.2}  \qquad (81.5)$$

where $frequency(l,s)$ represents the frequency sensitivity of $l$ level, s orientation, $L(l,x,y)$ denotes the luminance masking of $l$ level, and $T(l,x,y)$ refers the texture masking of $l$ level.

## 81.4 Experiment

In this paper, we simulate Watson JND model in DCT domain and Barni JND model in DWT domain, and in the two watermarking schemes, we use the same watermarking embedding, watermarking detection algorithm and watermarking pre-processing method. The difference between these schemes is the watermark embedding, detection domain and the JND models used in watermark embedding and detection processes.

### 81.4.1 Watermark Embedding Process

Figure 81.1 shows a framework of watermark embedding process in DCT and DWT domain. Watermark embedding in DCT domain: we partition the original image into 8*8 nonoverlapping blocks, and calculate the JND threshold of each coefficient, then choose the position (3,2) of each block to embed watermark information. Watermark embedding in DWT domain: we decomposed the original image using three DWT firstly, and calculate the JND threshold of each coefficient, then choose the CH2 region to embed watermark information. In the experiment, we choose intermediate frequency area to embed watermark, because it can balance the contradiction between imperceptibility and robustness.

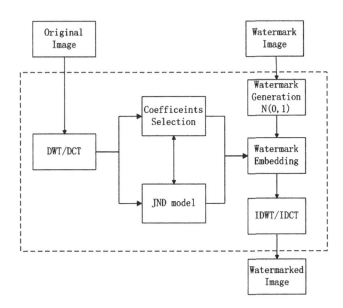

**Fig. 81.1** A framework of watermark embedding process in DCT and DWT domain

## 81.4.2 Watermark Detection Process

Figure 81.2 shows the watermark detection process, which is the inverse process of watermark embedding. We conduct IDCT and IDWT to the watermarked image respectively, find the embedding location and intensity according to the watermark embedding process, and then detect the watermark information.

## 81.5 Result and Analysis

We do experiments according to the algorithms introduced above, get the experiment data, and eventually evaluate performance of the two models on the premise of imperceptibility and robustness.

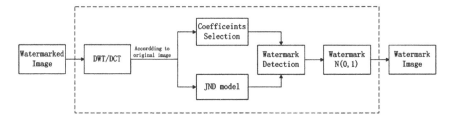

**Fig. 81.2** A framework of watermark detection process in DCT and DWT domain

## 81.5.1 Experiment Environment

We choose matlab programming for simulation experiments, while the original image is Lena image of 256 grayscale (resolution is $512 \times 512$), shown as Fig. 81.3, and the watermark image is the logo of Communication University of china (resolution is $64 \times 64$), shown as Fig. 81.4.

**Fig. 81.3** Original image

**Fig. 81.4** Watermark image

## *81.5.2  Results and Analysis*

A. Imperceptibility tests

In the experiment, we evaluate the imperceptibility by PSNR(Peak Signal to Noise Ratio), The larger this value is, the better watermarked image quality will be. PSNR is described as follows:

$$PSNR = 10\lg \frac{N \times N \times Max(f^2(x,y))}{\sum\limits_{x=1}^{N}\sum\limits_{y=1}^{N}\left((f(x,y) - \hat{f}(x,y))\right)^2} \tag{81.6}$$

In the formular, $f(x,y)$ denotes Pixel value of original image, $\hat{f}(x,y)$ denotes Pixel value of watermarked image, and the size of the image is $N \times N$.

**Fig. 81.5  a** Watermarked image in DCT domain. **b** Watermarked image in DWT domain

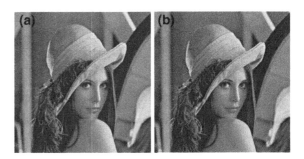

Figure 81.5 shows the watermarked image in DCT and DWT domain,and we cannot distinguish the difference between the original image and Fig. 81.5 from the subjective visual perception. Table 81.1 shows the PSNR value of the two models. As far as we know, the higher PSNR is, the better image visual quality is. So it can be clearly seen that DWT domain has the better imperceptibility then DCT domain.

**Table 81.1**  Imperceptibility experiment

| Num | Algorithm | PSNR/dB |
|---|---|---|
| 1 | Waston JND model in DCT domain | 44.3946 |
| 2 | Barni JND model in DWT domain | 46.3598 |

B. Robustness tests

We do experiments on robustness (adding noise, JPEG compression and rotation), and evaluated the anti- attack capability by BER(Bit Error Rate). The experimental results are shown in the figures below.

**Fig. 81.6** Adding noise
attack

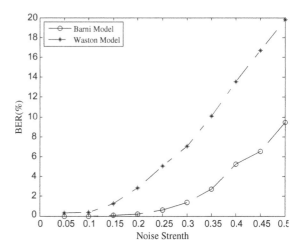

**Fig. 81.7** JPEG compression
attack

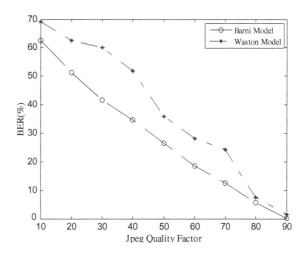

From Fig. 81.8 we could not make a distinction between the two algorithms, but from Figs. 81.6 and 81.7, it is obvious that Barni Model shows high performance when experiencing adding noise and JPEG compression attack. After the experiments we could conclude that the watermarking algorithm based on Barni JND model in DWT domain can better balance the contradiction between robustness and perceptibility.

**Fig. 81.8** Rotation attack

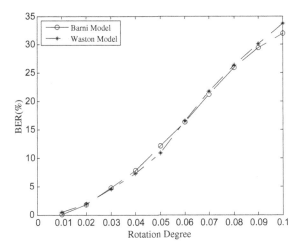

## 81.6 Conclusion

Based on the above discussions, we can see that watermarking algorithm in DWT domain has better performance than in DCT domain, because the DWT has good characteristic of temporal-spatial and direction, and the process of decomposition of original image through DWT is very similar to the characteristic of the human eye perception, therefore, watermarking algorithm in DWT will be the main research direction in future. But the existing JND models in DWT domain do not fully take into account the stratified perception characteristic of HVS, therefore we consider to constitute a JND model based on the content decomposition and stratified perception characteristic. In recent years, some new methods and theories of image analysis and other related areas, particularly the research of primal sketch theory [17], give us a great inspiration to start from the content decomposition of image to explore a more efficient watermarking algorithm that can better balance the contradiction between the robustness and perceptibility.

**Acknowledgments** The work on this paper was supported by National Nature Science Foundation of China (60902061), and the 3rd phase of 211 Project of Communication University of China.

## References

1. Foris P, Levick D (2009) Adaptive digital image watermarking based on combination of HVS models. J RadioEng 18(3):317–323
2. Abdulfetah AA, Sun X, Yang H, Mohammad N (2010) Robust adaptive image watermarking using visual model in DWT and DCT domain. J Inf Technol 9(3):460–466
3. Li W, Yang C, Li C, Yang Q (2012) JND model study in image watermarking. J Intell Soft Comput 129:535–543

4. Ngan KN, Rao KS, Singh H (1986) Cosine transform coding incorporating human visual system model. SPIE fiber'86,Cambridge,MA,USA, pp 165–171
5. FORIŠ P, LEVICKÝ D (2007) Implementations of HVS models in digital image watermarking. J RadioEng 16(1):45–50
6. Chou C-H, Li Y-C (1995) A perceptual tuned subband image coder based on the Measure of just-noticeable-distortion profile. J IEEE Trans Circ Syst Video Technol 5(6):467–476
7. Wu J, Qi F, Shi G (2010) An improved model of pixel adaptive just noticeable difference estimation. In: IEEE international conference acoustics speech and signal processing (ICASSP), pp 2454–2457
8. Ahumada AJ, Peterson HA (1992) Luminance-mode based DCT quantization for color image compression. In: Proceedings of the human vision, visual processing, and digital display III, SPIE Press, San Jose, pp 365–374
9. Watson AB (1993) DCTune:a technique for visual optimization of DCT quantization matrices for individual images. Soc Inf Display Dig Tech Pap XXIV:946–949
10. Zhang X, Lin WS, Xue P (2005) Improved estimation for just-noticeable visual distortion. J Sig Process 85:795–808
11. Wei Z, Ngan KN (2009) Spatio-temporal just noticeable distortion profile for grey scale image/video in DCT domain. J IEEE Trans Circ Syst Video Technol 19(3):337–346
12. Lewis AS, Konwles G (1992) Image compression using the 2-D wavelet transform. J IEEE Trans Image Proeess
13. Watson AB, Yang G, Solomon J, Villasenor J (1997) Visibility of wavelet quantization noise. IEEE Trans Image Process 6(8):1164–1175
14. Barni M, Bartolini F, Piva A (2001) Improved wavelet-based watermarking through pixel-wise masking. J Image Proeess IEEE Trans
15. Watson AB, Borthwick R, Taylor M (1997) Image quality and entropy masking. In: SPIE proceedings, vol 3016. San Diego, California, pp 295–300
16. Akhbari B, Ghaemmaghami S (2005) Watermarking of still images in wavelet domain based on entropy masking model. TENCON, IEEE conference
17. Guo CE, Zhu SC, Wu YN (2003) Towards a mathematical theory of primal sketch and sketchability. In: Proceedings of international conference computer vision

# Chapter 82
# Camouflage Images Based on Mean Value Interpolation

Hui Du and Lianqing Shu

**Abstract** This paper proposes a new algorithm to generate camouflage images. The proposed algorithm starts from converting the foreground and the background images from RGB color space to oRGB color space respectively, and then uses mean value interpolation followed by alpha blending operation on the luma channel. The alpha blending operation is achieved by introducing a parameter that indicates the hidden level of the foreground object. Chroma channels of camouflage images directly come from those of the background image. Our system is efficient because of our CUDA parallel implementation. Experimental results show that the algorithm can effectively and interactively generate high quality camouflage images.

**Keywords** Camouflage images · Mean value coordinates · Parallel computing · CUDA

## 82.1 Introduction

As a kind of entertainment arts, camouflage images (also called hidden images) aim to conceal the foreground object into the background as much as possible while keeping some visual clues of the foreground object for recognizing. Viewers usually have to take some time, or according to a given cue, to identify the foreground object when they view camouflage images. It is not easy to create an interesting camouflage image, which usually is achieved by skilled professional artists. Photoshop is an alternatively tool to create a digital camouflage image.

H. Du (✉) · L. Shu
New Media College, Zhejiang University of Media and Communications, Zhejiang, China
e-mail: huidu1129@163.com

W. Lu et al. (eds.), *Proceedings of the 2012 International Conference on Information Technology and Software Engineering*, Lecture Notes in Electrical Engineering 212, DOI: 10.1007/978-3-642-34531-9_82, © Springer-Verlag Berlin Heidelberg 2013

However, several operation steps are necessary to create a camouflage image, which is out of reach for most casual users.

To address this problem, two tools for generating camouflage images are developed in computer graphics community. Chu et al. [1] used object segmentation and texture synthesis technique to generate a camouflage image for natural scene. Their approach is based on two features of human vision perception: feature search and conjunction search, and can achieve high quality hidden results. Based on the two perception features, their approach removes image clues related to feature search while remaining the clues of the foreground image to conjunction search. Tong et al. [2] introduced an approach for hidden images by using image blending technique. Their approach first uses shape matching to find the place where the foreground object is embedded in the background image, and then uses a modified Poisson seamless cloning technique to generate the hidden result. In their approach, obvious artifacts may emerge when matching edges are not found between the foreground object and the background image.

The composition of camouflage images essentially belongs to the category of image blending. Image seamless cloning is a main technique of image blending and can be classified into three categories, which are the technique used in Photoshop, interpolation technique based on constructing Laplacian pyramid and gradient-based Poisson cloning technique. The basic idea of gradient-based approaches [3–7] is that the gradient field of the cloning region is close to a certain gradient as much as possible. Gradient-based approaches can achieve seamless results by solving a Poisson equation. However, it is difficult to solve Poisson equation quickly when the cloning region is a large size. This becomes the performance bottleneck of the gradient-based approaches. Instead, Farbman et al. [8] proposed a fast image cloning approach based on mean value coordinates. Their approach uses mean value interpolation instead of solving Poisson equation and achieves interactive performance on image cloning.

This paper introduces a camouflage image algorithm based on mean value coordinates. Vision research [9] shows that the luminance of an image provides enough visual clues to recognize an object. we therefore focus on the process of the luminance channel. Our algorithm starts from converting RGB color space to oRGB color space, uses mean value interpolation on the luminance channels of the images to obtain a seamless result, and then adopts alpha blending between the new cloned luminance and the luminance of the background image. Finally, we use chroma channels of the background image in order to faithfully preserve the original color, and convert back oRGB to RGB color space to obtain the final hidden result.

## 82.2 Overview of Camouflage Images Algorithm

Given a foreground source image $S$ and a background image $T$, a user chooses the foreground region $\Omega$ representing the hidden region in the source image by painting stroke, then places the region into the desire location and rotates the region in the background image according to user's desire. Our algorithm automatically embeds and hides the foreground region $\Omega$ into the background image. The user can interactively adjust the hidden level of the region $\Omega$. We now explain our camouflage image algorithm in detail.

## 82.2.1 Color Space Transformation

Bratkova et al. [10] introduced a new color space, the oRGB model. The primaries of this model are based on the three fundamental psychological opponent axes (white-black, red-green, and yellow-blue). The model has three channels-one luma $L$ and two chromes $C_{yb}$, $C_{rg}$, and has some of the advantages of nonlinear perceptual space such as CIE L*a*b* while maintaining a computationally simple transform to and from RGB. Our algorithm starts by converting RGB color space to oRGB color space for both the source and background images. The transformation involves following two steps.

Step 1: Linear transformation. RGB cube is firstly transformed into a parallelepiped using a linear transform and a color space $L'C'C'$ is obtained. The matrix for this transformation is

$$
\begin{bmatrix} L' \\ C'_1 \\ C'_2 \end{bmatrix} = \begin{bmatrix} 0.2990 & 0.5870 & 0.1140 \\ 0.5000 & 0.5000 & -1.0000 \\ 0.8660 & -0.8660 & 0.0000 \end{bmatrix} \begin{bmatrix} R \\ G \\ B \end{bmatrix} \tag{82.1}
$$

Step 2: Nonuniform rotation. The transformation from $L'C'C'$ to oRGB is just a compression or decompression of angles. For points above the yellow-blue axis, the angle in the linear chroma is $\theta = \arctan 2(C'_2, C'_1)$. The new angle in oRGB space, $\theta_o$ is defined as

$$
\theta_o = \begin{cases} (3/2)\theta & \text{if } \theta < \pi/3; \\ \pi/2 + (3/4)(\theta - \pi/3) & \text{if } \pi \geq \theta \geq \pi/3. \end{cases} \tag{82.2}
$$

The point $(C'_1, C'_2)$ is rotated to compute the point $C_{yb}, C_{rg}$ in oRGB.

$$
\begin{bmatrix} C_{yb} \\ C_{rg} \end{bmatrix} = R(\theta_o - \theta) \begin{bmatrix} C'_1 \\ C'_2 \end{bmatrix} \tag{82.3}
$$

The luma channel $L$ is the same as $L'$. After the above transformation, we obtain the luma channels and corresponding chroma channels of the source and background images, respectively.

## 82.2.2 Constrained Mean Value Interpolation

Our algorithm produces the final luma channel by combining mean value interpolation with alpha blending. After users choose a region $\Omega$ by painting stroke, a boundary chain $\partial\Omega$ $(t_0, t_1, \ldots, t_m = t_0)$ with the counterclockwise order is obtained. Mean value cloning firstly computes mean value coordinates $k_i$ of each pixel in the region $\Omega$, and then obtains the cloning result using mean value interpolation. Mean value coordinates of a pixel is defined as

$$\kappa_i = \frac{\omega_i}{\sum_{j=0}^{m-1} \omega_j}, i = 0, 1, \ldots, m - 1 \quad \omega_i = \frac{\tan(\beta_{i-1}/2) + \tan(\beta_i/2)}{\|t_i - p\|} \quad (82.4)$$

where $p$ denotes the pixel in the region, $\beta_i$ is the angle of the triangle $[p, t_i, t_{i+1}]$ at the pixel $p$. Figure 82.1 illustrates the definition of $\beta_i$.

The mean value interpolation $r(p)$ of the pixel $p$ is defined as following formula:

$$r(p) = \sum_{i=0}^{m-1} \kappa_i(p)(L_t(t_i) - L_s(t_i)) \quad (82.5)$$

And the final cloning result is given by

$$L_r(p) = L_s(p) + r(p) \quad (82.6)$$

The texture of $L_r$ in the region $\Omega$ completely comes from the source image $S$ according to formula (82.6). For camouflage images, it is necessary to involve the textures of both the background and foreground images in the hidden region $\Omega$. Therefore, our algorithm uses alpha blending to guarantee that the textures of the background and the foreground object are simultaneously contained. That is, the final luma channel $L$ can be expressed as:

$$L(p) = \alpha L_s(p) + (1 - \alpha)L_t(p) + \sum_{i=0}^{m-1} \alpha \kappa_i(p)(L_t(t_i) - L_s(t_i)) \quad (82.7)$$

where $\alpha \in [0, 1]$ is used to control the hidden level and is specified by the user interactively. The texture of the foreground object is disappeared when $\alpha$ is set to 0, and the texture of the background image is disappeared when $\alpha$ is set to 1.

The main feature of camouflage images is harmonic color between the hidden region and surrounding. We assume that the background image owns harmonic color. The algorithm therefore directly adopts the chroma channels of the background image to those of the camouflage image in order to faithfully preserve the color. Figure 82.2 shows the blending results of a face using different parameter values. We can see that the algorithm preserves the color of the hidden region and avoids discoloration artifacts.

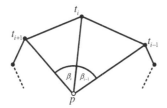

**Fig. 82.1** Angle illustration for mean value coordinates

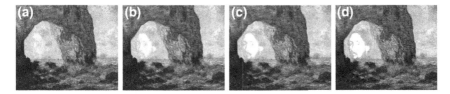

**Fig. 82.2** The blending results of using different parameter values. **a** $\alpha = 0.19$. **b** $\alpha = 0.37$. **c** $\alpha = 0.53$. **d** $\alpha = 0.90$

Once the luma and chroma channels are computed, our approach converts back oRGB color space to RGB color space and produces the final camouflage image.

### 82.2.3 CUDA Parallel Implementation

Formula (82.5) implies that the mean value interpolation of each pixel $p$ in the hidden region $\Omega$ is only related to the boundary coordinates. That is, the interpolation of each pixel is completely independent of other pixels. This feature indicates that it is very suited to use parallel computing to implement mean value cloning.

Recently, NVIDIA Corporation invented a parallel computing platform and programming model-CUDA, which enables dramatic increases in computing performance by using the graphics processing unit (GPU). CUDA programming model considers CPU as the host, GPU as the device. The code of the host is run on CPU and is responsible for copying the data to the GPU memory, the code of the device focuses on parallel process. We implement the mean value cloning by using CUDA technique. To make full use of the performance of GPU, our implementation uses share memory to accelerate the operations of data reading and writing. This further improves the efficiency of the algorithm.

**Table 82.1** The performance of our camouflage images system

| Example | $N\_b$ | $N\_r$ | Running time (s) | Alpha value ($\alpha$) |
|---------|--------|--------|------------------|------------------------|
| Panda   | 408    | 8,456  | 0.087            | 0.4                    |
| Wolf    | 453    | 10,260 | 0.094            | 0.2                    |
| Face    | 492    | 16,583 | 0.107            | 0.18                   |

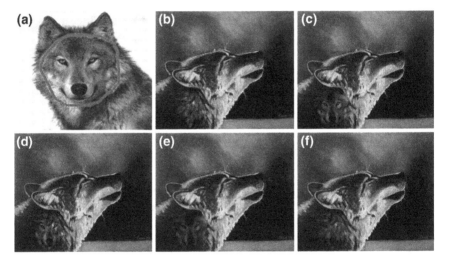

**Fig. 82.3** An example of camouflage image, **a** the source image; **b** the background image. For better recognizing the hidden object, please zoom in the images

**Fig. 82.4** The face of wolf (**a**), is hidden into the background image (**b**). Note discoloration artifacts emerge in the results of original Poisson cloning and mixing gradient cloning

## 82.3 Experimental Results

We use MATLAB to implement our algorithm on a computer with an Intel Core2Duo 2.66 GHz CPU, 4 GB main memory and a graphics card (NVIDIA GeForce GTS250, 1 GB graphics memory). Table 82.1 shows the running time of our experiments and the values of the hidden level parameter specified by the user. The user can interactively manipulate the hidden effect by adjusting the parameter because of our efficient parallel implementation. Note that this time doesn't include the time of painting stroke. $N\_b$ denotes the number of boundary pixels, $N\_r$ represents the number of pixels in the hidden region.

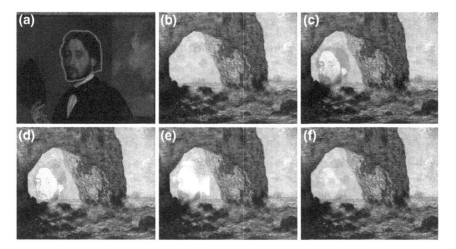

**Fig. 82.5** Another camouflage images example

Figure 82.3 shows a camouflage example of panda. Figure 82.3c is the result of Poisson image cloning. Although Poisson cloning can produce the seamless result, the texture of the result in the hidden region completely comes from the source image which cannot produce the hidden effect. Besides, Poisson cloning may lead to discoloration artifacts. An alternatively method is to use mixing gradient cloning (Fig. 82.3d), but this still produce discoloration artifacts. Figure 82.3e is the result of fast texture transfer [11] followed by Poisson cloning. Figure 82.3f is our result. Since our algorithm uses chroma channels of the background image, discoloration artifacts are avoided. Meanwhile, our algorithm can obtain high quality camouflage images by adjusting the hidden parameter value.

More examples are shown in Figs. 82.4 and 82.5. Figures 82.4a and 82.5a are the source images, Figs. 82.4b and 82.5b are the background images; Figs. 82.4c and 82.5c are the results of Poisson cloning. Figures 82.4d and 82.5d are the results of mixing gradient cloning. Large differences of the luminance and color between the hidden region and the background lead to poor hidden effect, although there is some texture information of the foreground object in the hidden region. Figures 82.4e and 82.5e are the results of texture transfer followed by Poisson cloning. As shown in Figs. 82.4f and 82.5f, our results are visually pleasing.

## 82.4  Conclusions

A new interactive digital camouflage images system is developed. Users can choose the foreground region by painting stroke in the source image, then place the foreground region into the background image and adjust the hidden parameter value according to user's desire. Our system can produce camouflage image without discoloration artifacts. Experimental results show that our algorithm not only produce high quality camouflage images, but also quickly obtain the results because of parallel implementation based on CUDA.

**Acknowledgments** This work is supported by Scientific Research Fund of Zhejiang Provincial Education Department (Y201016221) and Experimental Teaching Demonstration Center of Zhejiang Provincial Animation and Digital Technology.

# References

1. Chu HK, Hsu WH, Niloy JM (2010) Camouflage images. ACM Trans Graph 29(4):51:1–51:8
2. Wolfe JM (1994) Guided search 2.0: a revised model of visual search. Psychon Bull Rev 1(2):202–238
3. Fattal R, Lischinski D, Werman M (2002) Gradient domain high dynamic range compression. ACM Trans Graph 21(3):249–256
4. Pérez P, Gangnet M, Blake A (2003) Poisson image editing. ACM Trans Graph 22(3):313–318
5. Levin A, Zomet A, Peleg S (2004) Seamless image stitching in the gradient domain. In: Proceedings of the 8th European conference on computer vision, pp 377–389
6. Jia J, Sun J, Tang CK, Shum HY (2006) Drag and drop pasting. ACM Trans Graph 25(3):631–637
7. Chen T, Cheng MM, Tan P, Shamir A, Hu SM (2009) Sketch2photo: internet image montage. ACM Trans Graph 28(5):124–134
8. Farbman Z, Hoffer G, Lipman Y, Cohen-Or D, Lischinski D (2009) Coordinates for instant image cloning. ACM Trans Graph 28(3):1–9
9. Palmer S (1999) Vision science: photons to phenomenology. MIT Press, Cambridge
10. Bratkova M, Boulos S, Shirley P (2009) oRGB: a practical opponent color space for computer graphics. IEEE Comput Graph Appl 29(1):186–196
11. Ashikhmin M (2003) Fast texture transfer. IEEE Comput Graph Appl 23(4):38–43

# Chapter 83
# The Simulation of Land Distribution Based on Strategy of Urban Space Development in Nanjing

Zaizhi Zhang, Yizhong Sun and Yi Lu

**Abstract** Due to lack of flexibility, traditional urban planning method is difficult to make proper and timely response to the future scenario of urban development. The distinction that planning objective deviate from the fact becomes more acute In attempt to overcome this problem, this paper proposes a framework for using scenario planning based on strategy of urban space development to simulate land allocation process. The framework consists of three steps: land evaluation, scenario development, scenario simulation. Taking Nanjing City as an example, this study discusses the technical process of this method by exploring the spatial analysis function of GIS. Firstly, land suitability evaluation is undertaken with land assessment. Secondly, the key uncertainties and their driving forces affecting future land-use are identified, the combinations of driver states are used to build scenarios and participate in land allocation model to simulate the future plans. Finally, three land-use layout schemes are generated based on land evaluation and scenario development. The result indicates that the method can seek clues from strategy of urban space development, reflect land allocation scenario rapidly under spatial development strategies, it provides decision support for future land layout and policy.

**Keywords** Scenario simulation · Land-use allocation · Strategy of urban space development · Land assessment and suitability evaluation · Nanjing

Z. Zhang · Y. Sun · Y. Lu (✉)
College of Geographical Science, Key Laboratory of Virtual Geographic Environment,
Nanjing Normal University, Nanjing 210046, China
e-mail: zl_nnu@163.com

W. Lu et al. (Eds.), *Proceedings of the 2012 International Conference on Information Technology and Software Engineering*, Lecture Notes in Electrical Engineering 212, DOI: 10.1007/978-3-642-34531-9_83, © Springer-Verlag Berlin Heidelberg 2013

## 83.1 Introduction

At present, along with the faster urban expansion, uncertainty factors and uncertainty scenarios of urban development increased more and more. However, lack of flexibility in traditional urban planning method makes urban planning not consistent with the actual situation. In the last few years, scenario planning has been increasingly used to analyses urban future developing strategy and simulates land allocation due to their response of the ability in the future. The land allocation model is built to predict land requirement based on BP neural network [1]. Aguilera [2] quantified and analyzed the change of urban space with spatial metrics. In the research of scenario simulation, Barredo and Yang [3, 4] used constraints based CA, Qin et al. [5] made use of UFM, Xu and Lv [6] took advantage of ANN land transfer model, Robert [7] presented a methodology for coupling land-use allocation model, Liu et al. [8] took spatial optimization model and planning information reconstruction model to simulate the process of land allocation and land-use Layout Optimization, Niu et al. [9] utilized multi-criteria decision making method to estimate the final plan in southwest as example.

Although above studies takes nature, space optimization, data precision and public cognitive requirement into consideration, they are still in shortage of the strategy of urban space development. Therefore, this paper proposes a method to simulate land allocation process based on strategy of urban space development. The method is applied to the simulation of land allocation in a fast-growing city-Nanjing.

## 83.2 Scenario Simulation Method

Scenario simulation is based on the result of land-use suitability evaluation, then combined with the study area's policies and regulations, result of future scenario analysis, land-use allocation model to simulate future land-use plans.

### 83.2.1 Land Assessment

According to the demand of urban and rural development, we assess the comprehensive quality of possible land in order to ensure their suitability.

#### 83.2.1.1 Assessment Index System

There are 16 basic and 16 special indexes. Basic indexes are the foundations; the latter are rare condition and specific factors on engineering geology, topography, hydrology and meteorology, ecology, human impact. This paper uses Analytic Hierarchy Process (AHP) method and Delphi Method to enact the weights for assessed factors.

### 83.2.1.2 Dividing of Assessed Unit

Assessed unit is divided by main assessment factor's boundary lines, so natural attribute in one unit is roughly the same. Cartographic overlay analysis is applied on the process of dipartition, the sequence is: (1) Geomorphologic units, engineering geology district, water demarcation lines; (2) Flood line, rupture zones; (3)urbanized areas, protected areas, controlled area.

### 83.2.1.3 Calculate Comprehensive Unit Score

The total effect of basic index and specific index is the comprehensive score, represented by letter P and be calculated by aggregate-value method of weighting

$$P = K \sum_{i=1}^{m} W_i \cdot X_j \tag{83.1}$$

Where P is the comprehensive score, K is the comprehensive influences of special index, m is the number of basic indexes, $W_i$ stands for the weight of index I and $X_i$ stands for its influential score, P values between 0 and 100, the higher is more favorable. What's more, there is a threshold to distinguish construction land from non-construction land. K is calculated as formula 83.2

$$K = 1/ \sum_{j=1}^{n} Y_j \tag{83.2}$$

When n is 0, K equals to 1; N is the number of specific index; $Y_j$ indicates for the score of specific index j. K values are between 0 and 1, with a maximum of 1, the higher the better.

## 83.2.2 Land Suitability Evaluation

Land suitability evaluation is based on the assessment result. It evaluates the land for the purpose of rational utilization. This paper applies analytic hierarchy process method to choose a group of land property as evaluation factors, and the Delphi method is used to measure their weight. Suitability index is calculated b as the suitability value after non-dimensional normalization:

$$S_i = \sum_{j=1}^{j} w_j \cdot e_{ij} \tag{83.3}$$

Where $e_{ij}$ is the score of land i gets under factor j. $W_j$ is the weight of factor j and the sum of all the weight is 1. $S_i$ is the final score of candidate.

## 83.2.3 Land Allocation Model Based on Urban Spatial Development Pattern

Land allocation is the core step of scenario simulation, it transforms allocated land into new urban land as requirement forecasted, according to their district, property and present situation. The steps can be summarized as followed:

Step 1, farmland protect, the range of basic farmland shall not be occupied; Step 2, the key factors are being used to quantified and analyzed the allocation pattern of new land, the priority are added to make the allocation rules as well; Step 3, transform the land which complies with the rules into new increased land, the process takes plot of land as basic unit and the transforming sequence is the value of suitability; Step 4, adjust the plan, merge the small plots of land with same property and geographically nearby, redistribute unreasonable land.

## 83.3 Example Application

### 83.3.1 Profile

Nanjing is an industrial city, the economic center in the middle and lower reaches of Yangtze River, transportation hub of east China. The total area of Nanjing is 6,600 km$^2$, urban area is 4,730.74 km$^2$, 8 districts located in the south of Yangtze river are as large as 782,75 km$^2$. It has a long south-north and narrow east–west distance. Yangtze River is about 95 km long in Nanjing, It has two tributaries–Qin Huai river in the south and Chu river in the north. Water area accounts for 11.4 % of Nanjing, flatland and low-lying land account for 24.08 %.

### 83.3.2 Land Assessment and Suitability Evaluation

Basing on comprehensive score of evaluation unit, the land to be allocated is classified into 4 types—suitable for construction, available for construction, unsuitable for construction and unavailable for construction. According to land suitability evaluation, land suitable for construction and available for construction are classified into constructive land, the other two kinds are non-constructive land.

## 83.3.3 Scenario Construct

This paper focuses attention on strategy of urban space extension. We summed up three typical urban development strategies and corresponding land allocation plans of Nanjing, according to its economic, population and spatial pattern.

Scenario 1: Maintain single center pattern

Nature conservation (N1): the most stringent protection measures are adopted, development around lakes and ecological nature reserves within 1,000 m is forbidden; Farmland protection (A2): no basic farmland and high quality field should be occupied; Allocation priority (P2): living land developed firstly. Land plots in old district can be transformed into new living land; Urban pattern (S1): Maintain the original city center and key regions, gradually expand the outline of them. The proportion of old districts' population will rise to 60 % in the future.

Scenario 2: River-span development

Nature conservation (N1): Adopt a more flexible policy, no development is authorized within 300 m around ecological nature reserves; Farmland protection (A1): protect the basic farmland only; Allocation priority (P1): industrial land has a higher priority; Urban pattern (S2): arrange new land to be distributed in northern shore of Yangtze river priority, focus on developing river-span public transportation, improve the traffic accessibility between main city and Pukou district.

Scenario 3: Develop main city and three vice cities as a group

Nature conservation (N1): no construction is allowed within 500 m around lakes and 800 m around ecological nature reserves; Farmland protection (A2): basic farmland and high quality cultivated field can't be occupied; Allocation priority (P3): pay equal attention to the allocation of living land and industrial land, land located in traditional living district can be transformed into new living land firstly; industrial land is allocated in the districts which have a relative long distance from old district; Urban pattern (S3): till the year 2020, decrease the total population of old district to 45 %,new increased population is scattered at three vice cities.

## 83.3.4 Scenario Simulation Result

We can conclude from simulated results that in scenario one "Maintain single center pattern" (Fig. 83.1a), new living land is concentrated in four riverine districts: Jiangye, Yuhua, Pukou and Qixia; In scenario two "River-span

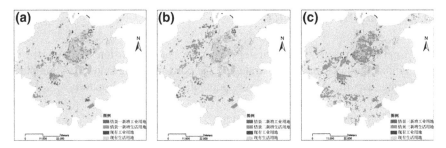

**Fig. 83.1** The simulation of urban land-use of Nanjing under 3 scenarios, 2020. **a** Maintain a single center. **b** River-span development. **c** One old district with three vice cities

development" (Fig. 83.1b), half of new living land is distributed in Pukou district. In scenario three "Develop main city and three vice cities as a group" (Fig. 83.1c), more than 25 % of new living land is distributed in three vice cities, it relieves the population density of old district (Fig. 83.2).

# 83.4 Conclusion and Discussion

## 83.4.1 Conclusion

This paper pointing at the Nanjing space development strategy, firstly, dividing construction and non-construction land from feasible future land plots. Setting up suitability index system to sequence living and industrial land according to suitability result, and then constructing typical futures urban develop scenarios by making up four uncertain factors' future states. Simulation the land allocation consequence under different scenarios based on allocation model. Finally get conclusion that "River-span development" is the most reasonable plan for Nanjing's 2020 overall plan.

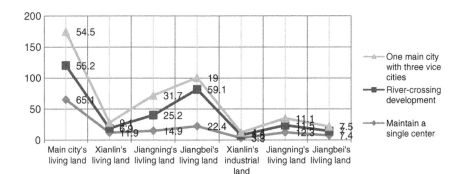

**Fig. 83.2** The amount of newly increased land (km²)

## 83.4.2 Discussion

Although this paper already summarizes the entire process of scenario simulation and verify it in Nanjing, problems still exist as followed:

1. How to select appropriate suitability indexes. The suitability evaluation concentrating too much on distance and ignore the accessibility of target.
2. How to improving the land allocation model. New construction land affect the rest of being allocated land, so it still needs to research how to represent the dynamic allocation process in the future.

**Acknowledgments** This work supported by the Natural Science Foundation of the Jiangsu Higher Education Institutions of China (Grant No.12KJA420001).

## References

1. Chen XJ, Zhang JL (2008) Study on urban land requirement forecast in urbanization. J Shanxi Normal Univ (Nat Sci Ed) 36(3):92–96 (in Chinese)
2. Aguilera F, Valenzuela LM (2001) Land cape. Metrics in the analysis of urban land-use patterns, a case study in a Spanish metropolitan area. Landscape Urban Plan 99:226–238
3. Barredo JI, Kasanko M, McCormick N (2003) Modelling dynamic spatial processes–simulation of urban future scenarios through cellular automata. Landscape Urban Plan 64:145–160
4. Yang XX, Liu YL, Wang XH et al (2007) Land utility planning layout model based on constrained conditions cellular automata. Geom Inf Sci Wuhan Univ 32(12):1164–1168 (in Chinese)
5. Qin XH, Duan XJ, Yang J (2010) Scenario simulation of urban land-use allocation and scheme evaluation based on GIS, a case study of Taicang city. Acta Geogr Sinica 65(9):1121–1129
6. Xu Y, Lv B (2008) Application of land transformation model based on GIS and ANN, a case study of Beijing, China. Acta Scientarum Naturalium Universitatis Pekinensis 44(2):262–270
7. Cromley RG, Hanknk DM (1999) Coupling land use allocation models with raster GIS. Geogr Sys 1:137–153
8. Liu YL, Guo HY, Tang Xu (2011) A land-use planning information reconstruction model for multi-level cognition needs. Geom Inf Sci Wuhan Univ 36(5):556–559 (in Chinese)
9. Niu XY, Song XD, Gao XY (2008) Land-use scenarios, an approach for urban master plans formulation and evaluation. Urban Plan Forum 4:64–69 (in Chinese)

# Chapter 84
# A Fast Mode Selection Algorithm of Intra-Frame Used in Logistics Video Surveillance

Li Ma, Jianbin Song and Xiuying Wang

**Abstract** H.264 adopt intra-prediction algorithm which increase computation complexity of encoder drastically. Thus, a fast mode selection algorithm for H.264 intra-prediction based on the features of DCT coefficients in frequency domain and the correlation of the predictive mode in spatial domain is proposed. This paper estimates the complexity of the block coding, texture of the direction and possible coding mode, and then selects the code block size, narrow mode selection range. Experimental results show, that compared with the other existing fast mode decision algorithm, the proposed algorithm significantly decreases the time consumed by I-frame coding about 64.1 % while the loss of PSNR ratio is negligible.

**Keywords** Video coding · Fast mode decision · Spatial correlation

## 84.1 Introduction

With the development of the network and multimedia technology, video compression technology has been widely used in the logistics video surveillance. In any of modern logistics procedures such as manufacture, transportation,

L. Ma (✉) · X. Wang
College of Automation, Beijing Union University, Beijing 100101, China
e-mail: lima8@126.com

X. Wang
e-mail: zdhtxiu21ying@buu.edu.cn

J. Song
Media Technology Department of Centre Institute, Huawei Corporation, Beijing 100095, China
e-mail: songjianbin@huawei.com

W. Lu et al. (eds.), *Proceedings of the 2012 International Conference on Information Technology and Software Engineering*, Lecture Notes in Electrical Engineering 212, DOI: 10.1007/978-3-642-34531-9_84, © Springer-Verlag Berlin Heidelberg 2013

distribution, warehousing, packaging and so on, video surveillance become more and more widely used requires high compression ratio, good restored image quality and low computational complexity video coding technology. ITU and ISO have formulated a series of video coding standards including the latest new H.264 [1] which is formulated in March 2003 [Joint Video Team (JVT) of ISO/IEC MPEG and ITU-T VCEG, 2003].

H.264 standard introduce the space-based multi-mode intra-prediction algorithm, it uses full search algorithm try to find the minimum cost mode, so it is time-consuming extraordinary. Literatures [2–9] use the characteristics of the spatial or/and frequency domain to preclude some prediction modes. Such algorithms need to make each pixel involved when calculating the image characteristic and the extra computation introduced remains high. Literatures [10–12] makes use of the correlation between the encoding modes, through the mode which has been tested predict the scope of the optimal mode. When the code block has multi-object boundary, such methods will be frequently misjudge the prediction modes in the situation. The optimal mode makes use of the mode which we have tested to identify and it is easy to make the final results into a local optimal value.

In order to increase the performance of logistics video surveillance, speedup the intra-frame coding, a fast mode selection algorithm based on the spatial and frequency domain analysis is proposed in this paper. The algorithm makes use of the energy aggregation characteristics and direction characteristics of the code block's coefficients after discrete cosine transform (DCT). The second section describes of the characteristics of DCT coefficients. The third section makes use of the characteristics of the energy aggregation of DCT coefficients to select the luminance block size. The fourth section make use of the direction characteristics of DCT coefficients to preclude of $16 \times 16$ luminance block and $8 \times 8$ chrominance block to make part of the predication mode. The fifth section makes comparative analysis of the performance of this algorithm and finally, makes a summary.

## 84.2 Characteristics of DCT Coefficients

As the DCT has a good energy aggregation characteristic, directional characteristics and has a corresponding fast algorithm [13, 14], so it has been widely applied in the existing video standards.

### 84.2.1 Energy Aggregation Characteristic

DCT transform has energy aggregation characteristic. In accordance with the DCT energy aggregation characteristic, the reconstruction block use part of mainly DCT coefficient has acceptable quality. So we select part of the DCT coefficients to

**Fig. 84.1** DCT energy
distribution

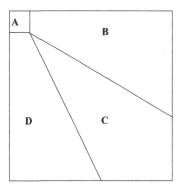

narrow the mode selection range. Namely, we obtain the mathematical variance D, which represents the image complexity, can make use of the AC coefficients through the DCT.

## 84.2.2 Directional Characteristic

DCT coefficients has the direction features, the coefficients in a certain region represents the direction of a certain section of image. As shown in Fig. 84.1, the coefficients of A area (only one coefficient), represents the component of the DC. The coefficients of B area, mainly represents the frequency change of the horizontal direction, C area represent for diagonal direction and D area represent for vertical direction. A large number of experiments and literatures have found that the image DCT coefficients can be used to evaluate the image block's texture direction.

## 84.3  Selection of Luminance Coding Block Size

The luminance micro-block can be divided as a 16 × 16 block or sixteen 4 × 4 blocks in intra-prediction. In general, the simple and flat block is suitable for predicted as 16 × 16 size, while detail-rich block is predicted as 4 × 4 size. We use of the AC coefficients in accordance with formula (84.1) to calculate the complexity D of the image block. The D value represents the degree of the deviation, the higher D value is, the more complicated the image is. Considering formula (84.1) it contains the calculation of the square, so computational complexity is high, in this paper we put the calculation of the square into absolute terms and the simplified formula is shown as formula (84.2).

$$D = \sigma^2 = \sum_{i=2}^{15} Z_i^2 \qquad (84.1)$$

While, $Z = \{Z_i | Z_i$ is dct coefficients as ZIGZAG order $1 \leq i \leq 15\}$

$$d = \sum_{i=2}^{15} |Z_i| \qquad (84.2)$$

The image data has a strong correlation and this paper updates the value of the threshold according to its adjacent block by formula (84.3), by a large number of experiments the initial threshold value $T_i = 1,100$. In order to pre-selecting the encoding block size, we calculated d values firstly. Then we judged by two adaptive updated thresholds $T_1$ and $T_2$, if $d \leq T_1$, $16 \times 16$ blocks size is adopted; if $d > T_2$, $4 \times 4$ blocks size is adopted. If $T_1 < d \leq T_2$, the prediction still use the two kinds of blocks size. Through a large number of experiments, we take $T_1 = 0.8T_i$, $T_2 = 1.2T_i$, the algorithm taking good performance.

$$T_{i+1} = \frac{d_{ll} + d_l + d_{lu} + d_u + d_{ru} + d_{rru} + 4T_i}{10}, \quad i \geq 1, \qquad (84.3)$$

## 84.4 16 × 16 Luminance Block Prediction Mode Selections

For a flat image block, the DC coefficient is a non-zero value, for the vertical texture image block, the value of transformed coefficients showed the vertical distribution and the value of the first line coefficients are non-zero, and the other coefficients are full-zero. Horizontal and diagonal texture image blocks also have their characteristic. Through a large number of experiments, we find that the DCT coefficients of all the image block has direction characteristic and can be distinguish the texture direction by AC coefficients, as shown in Fig. 84.2.

Literature [13, 14] studies have shown that: the energy ratio of the DCT coefficients in vertical and horizontal direction can reflect the changes in the direction of the texture. In the H.264, the $16 \times 16$ intra-prediction modes have three direction prediction modes such as Vertical, Horizontal and Plane and one DC prediction mode. Fast video coding algorithm is an algorithm for the evaluation criteria introduced in the additional computation, therefore, in order to reduce the computational complexity, this paper make use of spatial correlation, obtain the $8 \times 8$ block by sampling $16 \times 16$ block every line and every column, and then make DCT transform of the $8 \times 8$ block, use formula (84.2) to calculate the value d. If the value of d is less than the value of the threshold $T_{DC}$ [through the experimental data, if $T_{DC} = 0.25T_i$, the results is better, and $T_i$ is calculated by using the formula (84.3)], indicating that image block is so flat that we select the DC prediction mode to code, otherwise according to the formula (84.4), we make

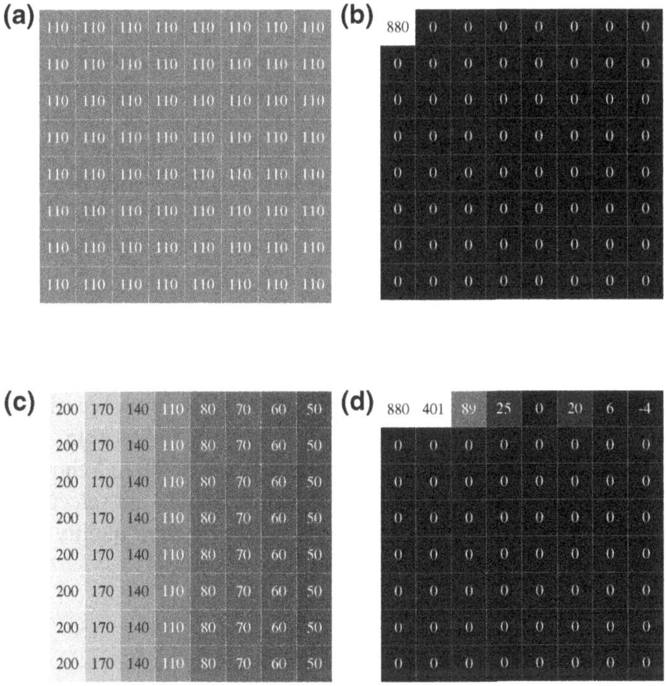

Fig. 84.2   Direction characteristic of DCT. **a** Flat block. **b** Coefficients of flat block. **c** Vertical texture block. **d** Coefficients of vertical texture block

use of the part of the AC coefficients to reduce the mode selection scope, namely, we according to formula (84.5) to determine the candidate prediction.

$$\tan \theta = \frac{\sum_{u=1}^{4} |F(u,0)|}{\sum_{v=1}^{4} |F(0,v)|}, i \geq 1, \tag{84.4}$$

where $F(u,v)$ represents the DCT coefficients, and $\theta$ represents the angle of the image texture between the horizontal direction and the level direction.

$$\text{Mode}_{16\times16} = \begin{cases} \text{Vertical} & d > T_{DC} \text{ and } |\theta| \geq 67.5° \\ \text{Horizontal} & d > T_{DC} \text{ and } |\theta| \geq 22.5° \\ \text{DC} & d \leq T_{DC} \\ \text{Plane} & d > T_{DC} \text{ and } 22.5° \leq |\theta| < 67.5° \end{cases} \tag{84.5}$$

Compared with the luminance, chrominance block contains less information, and is relatively flat. This paper adopts similar method to select the chrominance block prediction mode. For detailed-rich or complex image macro-block, $4 \times 4$ prediction blocks are adopted, the method proposed in literature [12] is used to select the optimum intra mode.

## 84.5 Algorithm Descriptions

Figure 84.3 show the main data flow chart of the proposed algorithm in which the variable Cost16 × 16 indicate that the cost function values of the best mode of the 16 × 16 luminance block, and Cost4 × 4 record the sum of cost function values of sixteen 4 × 4 luminance block within one 16 × 16 luminance block.

## 84.6 Experiments and Analysis

To get the performance of the proposed algorithm, we make experiments on the standard reference software JM16 of H.264. We let the proposed algorithm make comparison with Pan's fast algorithm and Wang's fast algorithm. In the experiments, rate-distortion optimization option id opened, CABAC entropy coding is used, four CIF sequences (Paris, Mobile, Tempete, Stefan) are selected. We set QP as 28, compress 100 frames, record bit-rate, and objective quality and encoding

**Fig. 84.3** Main data flow chart of the proposed

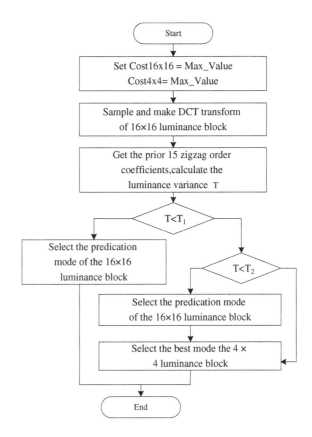

**Table 84.1** Performance when QP = 28

| Content | Seq. | Paris | Mobile | Tempete | Stefan | Avg. |
|---------|------|-------|--------|---------|--------|------|
| ΔPSNR | Pan's | −0.23 | −0.26 | −0.23 | −0.24 | −0.24 |
| | Wang's | −0.02 | −0.04 | −0.02 | −0.02 | −0.03 |
| | Ours | −0.04 | −0.09 | −0.09 | −0.11 | −0.08 |
| BR$_{save}$ | Pan's | 3.21 | 3.17 | 3.51 | 3.71 | 3.40 |
| | Wang's | 2.59 | 1.70 | 2.26 | 2.66 | 2.30 |
| | Ours | 3.43 | 2.16 | 3.33 | 2.02 | 2.74 |
| T$_{save}$ | Pan's | −57.8 | −59.1 | −57.7 | −58.0 | −58.0 |
| | Wang's | −62.5 | −59.6 | −61.0 | −58.5 | −60.4 |
| | Ours | −66.7 | −68.7 | −65.6 | −62.8 | −66.0 |

time, make comparison. This paper gets ΔPSNR, BR$_{save}$, T$_{save}$ in accordance with formula (84.6–84.8), and some experimental results are shown in Table 84.1.

$$T_{save} = \frac{T_{fast} - T_{ref}}{T_{ref}} \times 100\,\% \qquad (84.6)$$

$$\Delta PSNR = PSNR_{fast} - PSNR_{ref} \qquad (84.7)$$

$$BR_{save} = \frac{BR_{fast} - BR_{ref}}{BR_{ref}} \times 100\,\% \qquad (84.8)$$

From the data in Table 84.1 we can see that the bit-rate of the proposed algorithm, is averagely increased about 2.74 % and the PSNR value is reduced about 0.08 dB, while the average encoding time is reduced about 66.0 %. Compared with Wang's algorithm, the quality and bit-rate suitably changed, computational complexity of our algorithm reduced about 5.6 %. Compared with the Pan's algorithm, the quality declines smaller, and the rate increase smaller, but the encoding time of our algorithm reduced about 8 % significantly, and this fully validate the effectiveness of the proposed algorithm.

We set QP as different values (20, 28, and 36), encode 100 frames for different video, record bit-rate, and objective quality and encoding time, compute

**Table 84.2** The performance under different QP of the proposed algorithm

| QP | Content | Paris | Mobile | Tempete | Stefan | Avg. |
|----|---------|-------|--------|---------|--------|------|
| 20 | ΔPSNR | 0.02 | −0.12 | −0.1 | 0.12 | −0.09 |
| | BR$_{save}$ | 3.44 | 2.75 | 3.17 | 1.59 | 2.73 |
| | T$_{save}$ | 63.9 | −65.2 | −64.5 | −64.9 | −64.6 |
| 28 | ΔPSNR | 0.04 | −0.09 | −0.09 | −0.11 | −0.08 |
| | BR$_{save}$ | 3.43 | 2.16 | 3.33 | 2.02 | 2.74 |
| | T$_{save}$ | 66.7 | −68.7 | −65.6 | −62.8 | −66.0 |
| 36 | ΔPSNR | 0.01 | −0.07 | −0.04 | −0.11 | −0.06 |
| | BR$_{save}$ | 3.43 | 2.16 | 3.33 | 2.02 | 2.73 |
| | T$_{save}$ | 61.0 | −61.8 | −61.8 | −62.5 | −61.8 |

$\Delta$PSNR, BR$_{save}$, T$_{save}$. Some experimental results are shown in Table 84.2, from which it can be seen that the proposed method reduces the quality about 0.08 dB, increase the bit-rate about 2.73 %, and reduce the encoding time about 64.1 %. This proposed method has very good speed up performance for different videos compare with the existing algorithms.

## 84.7 Conclusions

To estimate the complexity of the coded image block, textures direction and possibly encoding mode, we make full use of the DCT coefficients' characteristics (energy aggregation, textures direction) and spatial correlation of the coding mode. Compared with the Wang's and Pan's fast intra-prediction algorithm, the proposed algorithm reduced about 64.1 % of the encoding time which speed up the selection effectively while maintain the similar quality almost no drop. The video surveillance which takes advantages of the proposed algorithm has played an important role in modern logistics fields.

## References

1. Joint Video Team (JVT) of ISO/IEC MPEG and ITU-T VCEG (2003) Draft ITU-T recommendation and final draft international standard of joint video specification (ITU-T Rec. H.264/ISO/IEC 14496-10 AVC), JVT-G050
2. Meng B, Au OC (2003) Efficient intra-prediction algorithm in H.264. In: IEEE ICASSP, pp 837–840
3. Yang JH, Yin BC, Sun YF, Zhang N (2006) A block matching based intra frame prediction for H.264/AVC. In: IEEE international conference on multimedia and expo, pp 705–708
4. Fa J et al (2006) A novel fast algorithm for intra mode decision in H.264/AVC encoder. In: IEEE international symposium on circuits and systems, pp 705–708
5. Pan F et al (2005) Fast mode decision algorithm for infra prediction in H.264/AVC. IEEE Trans Circuits Syst Video Technol 15(7):813–822
6. Wang J-C, Wang J-F et al (2007) A fast mode decision algorithm and its VLSI design for H.264/AVC intra-prediction. IEEE Trans Circuits Syst Video Technol 17(10):1414–1422
7. Pan F, Lin X (2003) Fast mode decision for intra prediction. JVT G013 in ISO/IEC JTC1/SC29/WG11 and ITU-T SG16 Q.6, JVT 7th meeting, Pattaya II, Thailand
8. Hwang C, Zhuang SS, Lai SH (2007) Efficient infra mode selection using image structure tensor. In: IEEE international conference on image processing, pp 289–292
9. Jing X, Chau LP (2004) Fast approach for H.264 inter mode decision. Electron Lett 40(17):1050–1052
10. Kim J, Jeong J (2005) Fast intra-mode decision in H.264 video coding using simple directional masks. In: Proceedings of SPIE, vol 5960, pp 1071–1079
11. Kim C, Shih H-H, JayKuo CC (2004). Feature-based intra prediction mode for H.264. In: IEEE international conference on image processing, 2: 769–772
12. Song J, Li B et al (2006) A novel fast intra prediction algorithm applied in H.264/AVC. In: International conference on signal processing proceedings, pp 412–802. ICSP2006. Guilin, China

13. Shen B, Sethi K (1996) Direct feature extraction from compressed images. In: Proceedings
    SPIE storage & retrieval for image and video databases IV, (4), pp 2670–2676
14. Lee S, Kim YM (2000) Fast scene change detection using direct feature extraction from
    MPEG compressed video. IEEE Trans Multimedia 2000 (4), pp 240–254

# Chapter 85
# Research of Image Segmentation Based on Watershed Transformation

Bingren Sun and Sanxing Cao

**Abstract** The watershed transformation is a kind of powerful morphological tool for image segmentation, which can automatically segment images into a series of closed segmentation regions. Fracture image of great amount of information is an important basis for clinical diagnosis. This thesis is about the segmentation to the fracture image by dint of watershed transformation. However, fracture images are often mixed with noise and uneven distribution, direct application of watershed transformation will have a serious over segmentation. Over segmentation phenomenon can be curbed by markers-controlled watershed algorithm in some extent, but this segmentation algorithm is not universal. In this paper, we introduce the morphological direction gradient and marker selection algorithm based the on marker-controlled watershed algorithm. And then we propose an improved watershed algorithm. We evaluate the proposed algorithm by simulation experiment through MATLAB. The experiments' result shows that the improved watershed algorithm can prevent over-segmentation effectively and extract the target bone edge from fracture images accurately.

**Keywords** Watershed transformation · Marker · The image segmentation

## 85.1 Introduction

In the medical field, image segmentation has been known as the cornerstone of the three-dimensional reconstruction for the separation of pathological region [1]: measuring the specific organization, realization of the normal tissue and diseased

B. Sun (✉) · S. Cao
New Media Institute, Communication University of China, Room 1601, The Comprehensive Laboratory Building, No.1, East Street, Dingfuzhang, Caoyang District, Beijing, China
e-mail: sunbingren@gmail.com

W. Lu et al. (eds.), *Proceedings of the 2012 International Conference on Information Technology and Software Engineering*, Lecture Notes in Electrical Engineering 212, DOI: 10.1007/978-3-642-34531-9_85, © Springer-Verlag Berlin Heidelberg 2013

tissue, it also has been used in application research for image—guided surgery, radiation oncology, and treatment assessment and so on. So, image segmentation in medical image processing is of great significance. But medical image is prevalent poor target and background contrast [2], blurred edges, Noisy characteristic. Due to these characteristics of medical images, if the general image segmentation algorithm is directly used on the image segmentation, the effect should be not very satisfactory, so the above characteristics should be fully considered in the actual image segmentation.

The watershed algorithm based on mathematical morphology is an image segmentation method which develops very well in recent years. The watershed segmentation which basic idea is regarding the image as the ups and downs morphological landforms [3], in the image, each point of the pixels just like the altitude of the landforms, the peak corresponding to the maximum value of grayscale images, and valley corresponding to the minimum. Contour edges can be determined by the detection the landforms local minima and its impact of the region. Watershed algorithm for image segmentation method compared to other methods o has benefits of less computation and better segmentation result. But this algorithm starting with the image gradient, by calculating the image gradient values to achieve the image segmentation [4]. Therefore, the watershed transformation will be affected seriously by the impact of noise and quantization error. If watershed algorithm is directly used on the image of the human skeleton, there are very many small regional boundary will be found in the segmented image. These boundaries are due to the presence of noise or other factors, at the same time, the boundary of the object in the image submerged in these cell domains will be unable to distinguish, which has been known as the over-segmentation phenomenon (Fig. 85.1).

Markers controlled watershed segmentation is an algorithm based on the tags, the markers can be divided into two groups: prospect marker and background marker. Prospect markers mark areas of interest, background markers mark other regions. And then gradient modify the gradient image and character by the

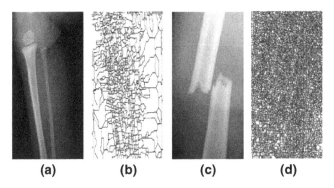

**(a)**          **(b)**          **(c)**          **(d)**

**Fig. 85.1** Result of using watershed algorithm directly: (**a**) original image A; (**b**) segmentation Result of A; (**c**) original image B; (**d**) segmentation Result of B

**Fig. 85.2** Result of using
markers controlled watershed
algorithm: (**a**) original
image A; (**b**) segmentation
Result of A; (**c**) comparison;
(**d**) original image B;
(**e**) segmentation Result of B;
(**f**) comparison

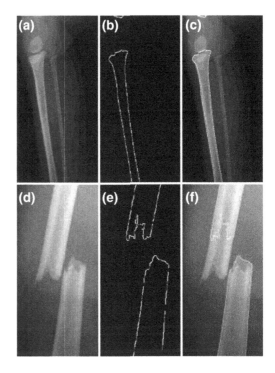

prospect markers and background markers. At last, the watershed transformation
would be done on the modified gradient image. Example is shown in the Fig. 85.2.

It can be seen by the results of Watershed segmentation controlled by markers
that great progress has been made on the segmentation result and over-segmentation phenomenon has been eased. However, at the same time it can be seen from
the edge of segmented image that the results are not good in the areas where grey
value comparison is not obvious. This phenomenon has been known as detail
mishandling.

## 85.2  Improved Watershed Algorithm and Process

During watershed transformation image segmentation process, over-segmentation
phenomenon can be curbed by markers-controlled watershed algorithm in some
extent, but still cannot accurately extract the edge of the target area, and the
versatility is not good, at the same time, for the different characteristics of the
image, the effect of segmentation is different. In this paper, some improvement
measures have been done on the basis of the markers-controlled watershed
transformation which is proposed for the medical fracture image.

For the prospect makers, in image processing, morphological opening-
and-closing operation should been done for the image in order to smooth the image

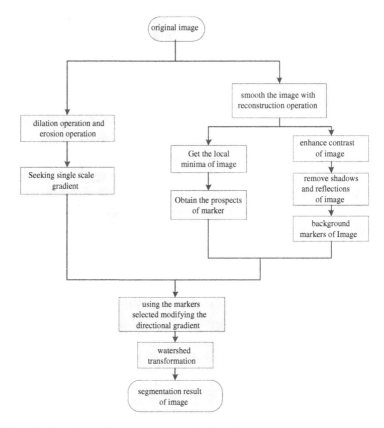

**Fig. 85.3** The flow chart of improved watershed algorithm

and retain the main part of the image and remove small noise in the image [5]. And then extended minimum transformation would be done for the image, through this process the minimum value in the area can be gotten. The minimum value we gotten can be seen as markers for the image, we call these markers prospect makers.

For the background makers, Firstly, image smoothing and the noise removing should be done. And then, hat transformation and Low cap transformation would be done in order to enhance image's contrast, at the same time, background image will be handled by hat reconstruction, open computing reconstruction and closing operation remodelling. At last, background makers would be established after removing shadows and reflective characteristic.

By using dilation and erosion operation [6] in the image processing, image morphology-scale gradient can be got, and then in order to modify the gradient image, the prospect markers and background markers has been used. At last, the image edge can be got after process of watershed transformation on this basis of the labelled gradient that we got (Fig. 85.3).

## 85.3  MATLAB Simulation of Improved Algorithm

Reading image, in order to smooth the image, the open reconfigurable computing and the close reconfigurable computing have been used in the processing, after this, removed the mixed noise in the image, target area in the image displayed more prominently (Fig. 85.4).

Calculating prospect markers, Since the differences exist between the grey value of the bone area, the muscle or other tissue area, Open reconstruction and closed reconstruction operations has been done on the enhanced image. Secondly, ignore the no significance information for the dividing operation, And then according to grey value differences that exist between the area of bone and other regional, at last, the local minima is acquired through expanded smallest transformation in order to obtain prospects markers of the original image (Fig. 85.5).

Calculating background markers, the image is smoothed in order to remove the small details of the structure of the target and background, and then using the hat transformation and low cap transformation transform to enhance image's contrast, through hat reconstruction, open computing remodeling and closing operation to deal with the background image, remove shadows and reflections, at last, the background markers of the image are acquired (Fig. 85.6).

Seeking single scale gradient by using the image morphology, dilation and erosion mathematical operation is used in order to get the single scale gradient (Fig. 85.7).

For the single-scale gradient, using prospect markers and background markers modify the directional gradient. After this, the marked gradient image can be acquired (Fig. 85.8).

For gradient image, watershed transformation is used to extract the region of interest (Fig. 85.9).

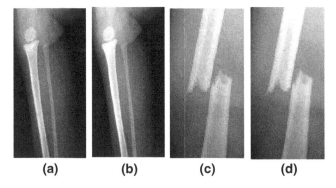

**(a)**            **(b)**            **(c)**            **(d)**

**Fig. 85.4**  Result of smoothing the images: (**a**) original image A; (**b**) image A after smoothing; (**c**) original image B; (**d**) image B after smoothing

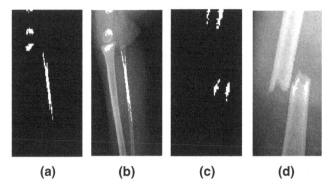

**(a)**          **(b)**          **(c)**          **(d)**

**Fig. 85.5** Result of calculating prospect markers: (**a**) local minima of image A; (**b**) Prospect Markers of Image A; (**c**) local minima of image B; (**d**) Prospect Markers of Image A

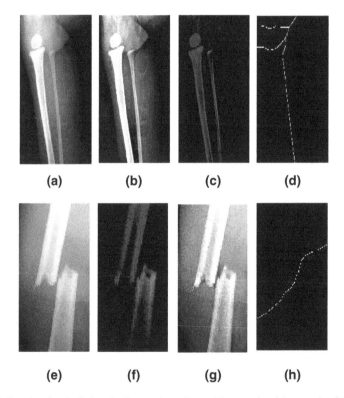

**(a)**          **(b)**          **(c)**          **(d)**

**(e)**          **(f)**          **(g)**          **(h)**

**Fig. 85.6** Result of calculating background markers: (**a**) smooth of image A; (**b**) enhance contrast of image A; (**c**) remove shadows and reflections of image A; (**d**) background markers of Image A; (**e**) smooth of image B; (**f**) enhance contrast of image B; (**g**) Remove shadows and reflections of image B; (**h**) background markers of Image B

**Fig. 85.7**  Result of seeking
single scale gradient by using
the image morphology:
(**a**) Scale gradient of
image A; (**b**) Scale gradient
of image B

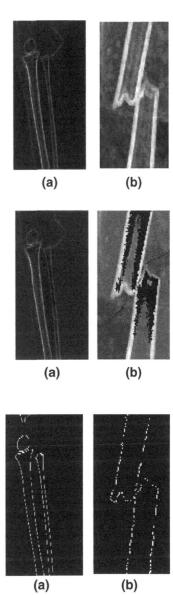

(a)          (b)

**Fig. 85.8**  Result of
modification on gradient
image: (**a**) the modification of
image A; (**b**) the modification
of image B

(a)          (b)

**Fig. 85.9**  Segmentation
result of images:
(**a**) segmentation result of
image A; (**b**) segmentation
result of image B

(a)          (b)

## 85.4  The Contradistinction of Several Different Watershed Algorithms

From the pictures above, we can see that direct application of watershed transformation will have a serious over segmentation, over-segmentation phenomenon
can be curbed by markers-controlled watershed algorithm in some extent, but still
cannot accurately extract the edge of the target area, and the versatility is not good.

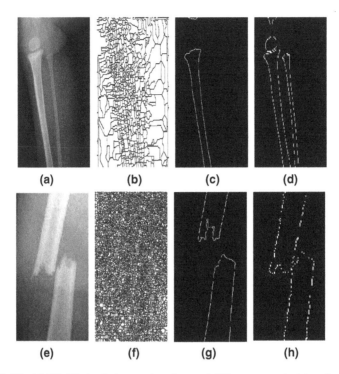

**(a)**        **(b)**        **(c)**        **(d)**

**(e)**        **(f)**        **(g)**        **(h)**

**Fig. 85.10** The MATLAB simulation results of several different watershed transformation for fracture images: (**a**) original image A; (**b**) direct application of watershed transformation for image A; (**c**) the result of markers-controlled watershed algorithm for image A; (**d**) the result of improved watershed algorithm for Image A; (**e**) original image B; (**f**) direct application of watershed transformation for image B; (**g**) the result of markers-controlled watershed algorithm for image B; (**h**) the result of improved watershed algorithm for Image B

The improved watershed algorithm which basis of the markers-controlled watershed transformation can obtain interested region accurately and get the perfect results of image segmentation (Fig. 85.10).

## 85.5 Conclusion

Medical fracture image has prevalence phenomenon like the great contrast gap between background image and the target image, edge blur of the target and big interference of the noise. The markers-controlled watershed algorithm could release the over-segmentation phenomenon in some degree. But the algorithm universal are not well. In this paper, some promotions have been done on the basis of the markers-controlled watershed transformation which is proposed for the medical fracture image. The simulation based on MATLAB and result proved that the improved algorithm could abstract the edge of the bone and realize efficient split of the images.

**Acknowledgments** This work is sponsored by the 382 Talents Plan (G08382304), Chinese National Hi-tech Industrialzation Project(CNGI-09-03-15-1), and the Virtual Library Technology project granted by China Art Science and Technology Institute.

# References

1. Serra J, Vincent L (2010) An overview of morphological filtering. Syst Signal Process 11(2):47–108
2. Sinha D, Dougherty ER (1992) Fuzzy mathematical morphology. J Vision Com-mun Image Represent 3(3):286–302
3. Kim J-B, Kim H-J (2003) Multiresolution-based watersheds for efficient image segmentation. Pattern Recogn Lett 24(3):473–488
4. Zheng W, Yang H (2008) Multiscale reconstruction and gradient algorithm for X-ray image segmentation using watershed. In: The 2nd international conference on bioinformatics and biomedical engineering
5. Zhong W (2009) Watershed algorithm in medical image segmentation. Comput Knowl Technol 12(5):3221–3223 (in Chinese)
6. Su W, Kai C (2005) Medical image segmentation based on mathematical morphology. Comput Appl 25(10):253–258 (in Chinese)

# Chapter 86
# A Type of Block Matching Algorithm Based on Image Edge Extraction

**Kexiang Liu, Chao Chang and Lu Zhao**

**Abstract** This paper introduces a kind of new real-time image stabilization algorithm, the algorithm improves the accuracy and speed of image stabilization effectively, the image edge detection combined with block matching method in the algorithm, and adopted the improved matching criterion in motion estimation. The algorithm can reduce the amount of computation and the error rate of the block matching, and improve the calculation rate and the precision of matching. Through the experimental simulation, the result shows obvious advantages in speed and effect of image stabilization.

**Keywords** Block matching algorithm · Edge detection · Corrosion expansion · Digital image stabilization

## 86.1 Introduction

Digital Image Stabilization is a process which can weaken the unwanted motion of a video, this process can make the video image output steadily. The main component is motion estimation, we can get the motion vector of the relative movement of adjacent frames by motion estimation. In some classical algorithms, block Matching Algorithm (BMA) is adopted widely for less calculating and less complex than other algorithms [1].

In this paper, a kind of real-time digital video stabilization algorithm which is efficient and fast will be introduced. Based on the feature of image center

K. Liu · C. Chang (✉) · L. Zhao
Department of Physics, Xidian University, No.2 TaiBai South Road, Xi'an City, China
e-mail: kxliu@mail.xidian.edu.cn

W. Lu et al. (eds.), *Proceedings of the 2012 International Conference on Information Technology and Software Engineering*, Lecture Notes in Electrical Engineering 212, DOI: 10.1007/978-3-642-34531-9_86, © Springer-Verlag Berlin Heidelberg 2013

migration, the edge of the image in the video will be set to the image feature in the algorithm, and according to the difference of edge information in the image, we select the image block which contains a specified number of edge in the image, for each image block which has selected, we will adopt the improved matching algorithm to search the optimal image block in the reference frame, and then we can obtain the local motion vector and global motion vector.

Through the experimental simulation, the result shows the new algorithm can improve the accuracy of matching, and increase the success rate and the precision of matching, meanwhile, the improved matching algorithm can improve the matching speed, and achieve calculation quickly.

## 86.2 Basic Algorithm of BMA

The current frame of the video is divided into image block, the size of which is constant (M × N pixel), and we suppose that all pixels in the same image block have the same motion, and we only need calculate one motion vector in each image block. For each image block in the current frame, we search for the optimal image block in the specific area of the reference frame by proper algorithm, and consider the image block in the current frame to be moved from the position of the optimal image block [2]. The probable maximum motion vector can be set as $(dx, dy)$, and then the search area will be set as $(M + 2dx) \times (N + 2dy)$, the results in Fig. 86.1.

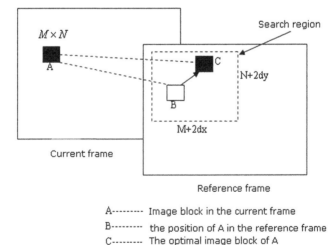

**Fig. 86.1** Algorithm of BMA

The BMA matches blocks according to some rules, such as the Mean Square Error (MSE), the Mean Absolute Difference (MAD), and the Sum of Absolute Difference (SAD) and so on [3].

(1) Mean Square Error (MSE):

$$MSE(i,j) = \frac{1}{MN} \sum_{m=1}^{M} \sum_{n=1}^{N} [f_k(m,n) - f_{k-1}(m+i, n+j)]^2 \qquad (86.1)$$

$(i,j)$ represents the motion vector, $f_k(m,n)$ is the gray value at the point $(m,n)$ in the current frame, and $f_{k-1}(m+i, n+j)$ is the value at the point $(m,n)$ in the reference frame, the block size is $M \times N$, if the value of the $MSE(i_0, j_0)$ is minimum at a point $(i_0, j_0)$, then we consider the point $(i_0, j_0)$ to be the optimal matching point [4].

(2) Sum of Absolute Difference (SAD):

$$SAD(i,j) = \sum_{m=1}^{M} \sum_{n=1}^{N} |f_k(m,n) - f_{k-1}(m+i, n+j)| \qquad (86.2)$$

The relationship between SAD and MAD:

$$SAD(i,j) = M \times N \times MAD(i,j) \qquad (86.3)$$

Ordinary block matching algorithms perform not very well on both matching precision and speed. The speed of calculation will become low usually if they show a good effect, if we improve the speed, the precision will be limited instead.

## 86.3  The Improved Algorithm of BMA

### 86.3.1  The Image Features Extraction and Selected Block

The image feature is capable of exhibiting a region of the image content, processing and extraction of the feature of each frame image will improve the efficiency of the analysis and matching between video frames effectively, one of the most obvious feature in the image is the edge of the image scene. Selecting the image block which contains rich edge information can increase the success rate and matching accuracy. And those image blocks which contain a small amount of edge information, are prone to induce mismatching phenomenon [5].

**Fig. 86.2** Structure of 3 × 3

| | | |
|---|---|---|
| **0** | **0** | **0** |
| **1** | **1** | **1** |
| **0** | **1** | **0** |

**Fig. 86.3** Canny edge image
and morphological
processing result

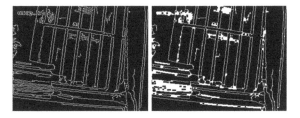

We first smooth each frame of the input image with the structure of 3 × 3 to eliminate noise, and for the result:

Step 1: We process and obtain an edge image by using the canny edge detection algorithm.

Step 2: Expansion operation on the edge image obtained with the structure of 3 × 3 to bridging the Fracture edges.

The breaking edge of the image which after expansion processed is bridged together and forms a complete edge. Edge lines are much more thicker, so that it's difficult to tell the difference between the edge, the results in Fig. 86.2.

Step 3: Etching operation on the image after expansion with the structure of 3 × 3. The results in Fig. 86.3.

As can be seen from the results, Fracture edges are bridged together, so as to ensure complete edge information.

Finally, a threshold operation on the processed image to select the image block qualified [6].

$$S = \begin{cases} 1 & T_2 > R \geq T_1 \\ 0 & T_2 < or\, R < T_1 \end{cases}, \quad R = \sum_{i=1,j=1}^{16} P_{ij} \qquad (86.4)$$

Wherein $T_1, T_2$ is the threshold value, $P_{ij}$ represented edge point within the block, if it is the edge point, $P_{ij}$ is equal to 1, otherwise equal to 0.

Through statistical results of simulation, the following table can be obtained, the results in Table 86.1.

**Table 86.1** Matching efficiency comparison between ordinary matching method and improved matching algorithm

|                            | Total number of blocks | Number of valid samples | Number of mismatching | Mismatching rate |
|----------------------------|-----------|-----------|-----------|-----------|
| Ordinary matching method   | 170       | 170       | 20        | 11.76 %   |
| Improved matching algorithm | 170       | 51        | 0         | 0         |

As can be seen from the above table, the improved matching method using the minimum number of samples, and matching the highest success rate, it proves that edge-based analysis increase matching robustness to exclude the block.

### 86.3.2 Improved Matching Criterion

By improved the *SAD* standards, it is able to reduce the amount of computation and improve the operation efficiency, also does not reduce the accuracy of the matching. Improved *SAD* criterion:

$$SAD(i,j) = \sum_{m}^{M} \sum_{n}^{N} |f_k(m,n) - f_{k-1}(m+i, n+j)| \qquad (86.5)$$

Wherein the value of $m, n$ in the following manner:

$$m = 1, 2, 3, \ldots \ldots M \qquad (86.6)$$

$$n = \begin{cases} 1, 3, 5, \ldots, 2k-1, \ldots, N & m \text{ is odd} \\ 2, 4, 6, \ldots, 2k, \ldots, N & m \text{ is even} \end{cases}, \quad k = 1, 2, 3. \ldots \ldots \qquad (86.7)$$

When the size of the image block ($M \times N$) is $16 \times 16$ pixels, Common *SAD* criterion need to calculate 256 pixels of the block, and criterion for improved *SAD* count only 128 pixels.

The improved *SAD* matching criterion can reduce the number of pixels involved in the calculation of the image block, this method select pixel point at regular intervals is possible to reduce the number of operations, and to improve the speed of the matching operation, and also does not reduce the accuracy of the matching.

## 86.4 Effect Assessment of Image Stabilization

The most intuitive way of effect assessment of image stabilization is comparing the front and rear frame images, if the image does not contain a moving subject, then the two images overlap completely, and it can be identified as the best image stabilization now. However, there are always some differences between two images such

**Fig. 86.4** PSNR for the test image frames

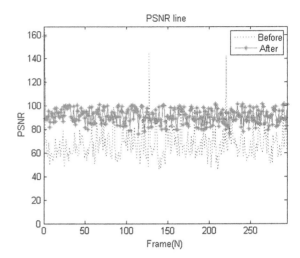

as noise, movement of the main body, perspective effect of lens, which cause minor changes to the image. Commonly PSNR (Power Signal-To-Noise Ratio) is used to assess the effect of image stabilization [7], which Defined as follows:

$$\text{PSNR}(I_1, I_0) = 10 \log \frac{255^2}{\text{MSE}(I_1, I_0)} \tag{86.8}$$

Where MSE (Mean Square Error) is the gray variance of the opposite pixels, it represents the rate of image sequences change, and the extent of it. We define it as follows:

$$\text{MSE}(I_1, I_0) = \frac{1}{(N \times M)} \sum_{i=1}^{i=N} \sum_{j=1}^{j=M} (I_1(i,j) - I_0(i,j))^2 \tag{86.9}$$

Therefore, when the smaller the average squared difference between the two images, the higher the PSNR, the better the effect of image stabilization. Theoretically image completely stable and without any interference, the PSNR is infinite, however, because the image is impossible to match exactly, and there are lots of factors such as noise and a moving subject, the PSNR value does not reach the theoretically infinite [8].It can be seen from the contrast, there is higher PSNR value in the image sequence which be stabilized, the results in Fig. 86.4.

## 86.5 Conclusion

This paper presents a new real-time digital video image stabilization algorithm, by extracting the edge of the image as the region of interest, dividing image block in the region of interest. Through the experimental simulation, improved *SAD* matching criteria for matching operations can improve the computational speed, remove the blocks caused errors effectively, increase matching accuracy.

# References

1. Yang J (2007) The technique of motion estimation based on the block matching. Hunan University. Hunan (in Chinese)
2. Zhang YX, Wang JZ (2010) An improved algorithm of electronic image stability based on block matching. In: Conference on IEEE transactions, pp 1924–1927
3. Chen L (2008) The research of the fast motion estimation algorithm of block matching in the video coding. Xidian University, Xi'an (in Chinese)
4. Liu KX, Qiu QS, Zhang ZZ (2011) A novel fast motion estimation algorithm based on block-matching. In: Conference on IEEE transaction, pp 1402–1405
5. Qiu QS (2012) The study of motion estimation and edge detection for video image. Xidian University, Xi'an (in Chinese)
6. Zong LY (2011) An improved edge detection algorithm based on canny operator. Mod Electron Tech 43(4):104–107 (in Chinese)
7. Qian J (2011). The software design of digital image stabilization. Xidian University, Xi'an (in Chinese)
8. Liu KX, Qian J, Yang RK (2010) Block matching algorithm based on RANSAC algorithm. In: Conference on IEEE transactions, pp 223–227

# Chapter 87
# Non-Photorealistic Tree Creating Based on Stroke and Multipass Rendering

Buying Lai, Xiaoming Wang and Lifei You

**Abstract** This paper proposes a tree-creating model based on stroke and multi-pass rendering, and successfully applies it to non-photorealistic tree rendering; this method enables painters to select an appropriate paintbrush model and its parameters in multipass rendering and to optimize repeatedly the paintbrush placement position till obtaining satisfactory tree morphology, thus to render painting works with distinct hand-drawing style. This method has wide application and reference values in creating non-photorealistic artistic works by using stroke rendering technique.

**Keywords** Non-photorealistic rendering (NPR) · Paintbrush · Multipass rendering · Tree creating

Non-photorealistic rendering (NPR) refers to a kind of technique that generates graphics having hand-drawing style but no photo-like realistic sense by using computer. Its target is not graphic reality, but primarily to express the artistic features of graphics, to simulate artistic works (even including imperfections in the works), or to act as an effective supplement to photorealistic graphics [1]. Utilizing NPR technique to create tree drawing works with various hand-drawing styles has

---

B. Lai (✉)
Department of Computer and Information Engineering, Guangzhou Maritime College,
Guangzhou 510725, China
e-mail: laibuying@163.com

X. Wang (✉)
School of Computer, South China Normal University, Guangzhou 510631, China
e-mail: wangxm@scnu.edu.cn

L. You (✉)
School of Electronic and Information Engineering, South China University of Technology,
Guangzhou 510640, China
e-mail: 185570982@qq.com

W. Lu et al. (Eds.), *Proceedings of the 2012 International Conference on Information*
*Technology and Software Engineering*, Lecture Notes in Electrical Engineering 212,
DOI: 10.1007/978-3-642-34531-9_87, © Springer-Verlag Berlin Heidelberg 2013

become one of research fields focused on by people in recent years. There are two main research interests for NPR: one is to employ an algorithm to artify a realistic input image which acts as the basis and standard so as to get a simulated work similar to the input image and with a hand-drawing style, we call such kind of work image-based artification; the other is to design a computer program conforming to artwork rendering brush stroke and rendering process model based on the artistic features and creation concept of a kind of works of art with hand-drawing style, so as to realize automatic or semi-automatic generation of artistic works, we call such kind of work NPR work creation. Chinese scholars have conducted numerous studies in the non-photorealistic tree rendering field, for example, the adaptive distributions of stroke-based non-photorealistic rendering method proposed by Qian Xiaoyan et al. [2] belongs to the former kind of work; while the tree morphology simulation realized by Chang et al. [3] using the fractal characteristics of plant structure, the plant morphological structure modeling method proposed by Dong et al. [4] from both topological and geometric perspectives, and the tree simulation method based on skeleton customization and particle system model proposed by us [5], etc. belong to the latter kind of work. However, there are few studies on and few achievements about the theoretical methods for creation of or the form and style of non-photorealistic works with various hand-drawing styles.

We put forward a tree-creating model based on stroke and multipass rendering and successfully applied it to non-photorealistic tree rendering; this method enables painters to select appropriate paintbrush model and its parameters in multipass rendering and to optimize repeatedly paintbrush placement position till obtaining satisfactory tree morphology, thus to render painting works with distinct hand-drawing style. This method has wide application and reference values in employing stroke rendering technique to realize non-photorealistic artistic work creation.

## 87.1 Tree-Creating Model Based on Stroke and Multipass Rendering

The generative model based on stroke and multipass rendering originated from the Stroke-Based NPR multipass rendering method proposed by Hertzmann, and the rendering of each layer is accomplished by a set of fixed-size brushes; the paintbrush size keeps decreasing as the number of rendering layers grows, so as to simulate the process that a painter continuously draws details [6]. We defined "one set of fixed-size paintbrushes" as a paintbrush set for one leaf type, and "the process of continuously drawing details" is the very process of rendering (or creating) trunk and branches and multipass rendering of leaf paintbrushes, as shown in Fig. 87.1.

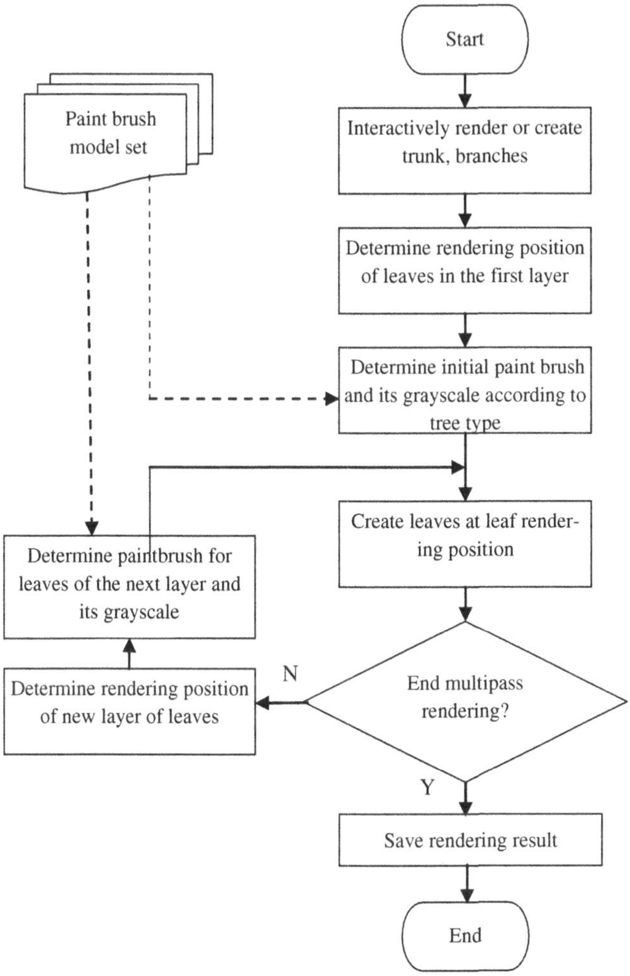

**Fig. 87.1** Tree-creating model based on stroke and multipass rendering

## 87.2 Composition of Stroke and Paintbrush Model Set

The stroke is used to render trunk and branches, and is a basic element of paint-brush. Stroke width and grayscale are selected by the painter upon demand.

The paintbrush is used to create leaves, its model set consists of pre-rendered paintbrush sets corresponding to various leaf types, and each paintbrush set is composed of paintbrushes varying in morphology and size. Each paintbrush is determined by its parameters such as number, paintbrush shape, and paintbrush grayscale:

$$M_p = \{p|p = (n, f, g)\}, \tag{87.1}$$

**Fig. 87.2** Various paintbrush models of paintbrush set for a leaf type

where, number n is the number of paintbrush for different leaf types and paintbrush shapes; paintbrush shape f is pre-designed leaf stroke graphic and a pattern with small area (e.g., 20 × 20 pixels) and with transparent square area as background, embodying the difference in morphology and size of different leaf types; and paintbrush grayscale g is the taken value of paintbrush grayscale parameter. A painter can choose paintbrushes with various morphologies for different leaf types via the numbers according to the practical demand, and decide on the grayscale level of each chosen paintbrush. To note here, since a paintbrush is usually tiny, and the changes in its size and rotation would impact its morphology greatly (a paintbrush typically deforms seriously due to the changes in size and rotation), we did not regard size and rotation angle as paintbrush parameters, instead, we directly rendered various paintbrushes with different size and morphology (e.g., angle) for use. Figure 87.2 shows various paintbrush models of paintbrush set for a leaf type.

## 87.3 Rendering Trunk and Branches

Trunk and branches rendering methods can be divided into interactive real-time rendering and generative rendering.

Interactive real-time rendering means that a painter relies on his/her own drawing ability to adjust stroke width and grayscale at any time, and makes use of various brush strokes to draw on render window freely in real time. The morphological structures of trunk and branches are totally determined by the painter according to the biological characteristics of the tree type to be expressed. The rendering process is repeatable till the rendered work is satisfactory, and the process can be undone for many steps.

**Fig. 87.3** A kind of trunk-and-branches creating method based on skeleton customization and particle system model

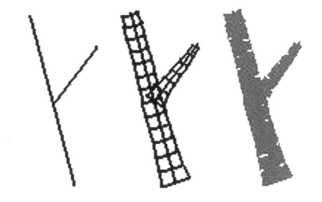

Generative rendering refers to a method for creating trunk and branches with a program according to a pre-designed algorithm. The algorithm is diversified, what shown in Fig. 87.3 is a kind of trunk-and-branches creating method based on skeleton customization and particle system model [5].

## 87.4  Determination of Leaf Rendering Position and Leaf Creating

The rendering position of every layer of leaves (including quantity and distribution morphology) is determined at a fixed point by the painter in an interactive manner, and the position of this point is just the center position that the leaf paintbrush will be pasted to; the leaves in the same layer can be overlaid, and the leaves in different layers can be superposed, too. Generally, the following principles are to be obeyed in layer and superposition rendering of leaves:

(1) Render the farther position first, then the nearer position;
(2) Apply smaller leaves to a farther position and larger leaves to a nearer position; apply smaller grayscale (lighter color) to a farther position and greater grayscale (darker color) to a nearer position;
(3) Apply higher density to a farther position and lower density to a nearer position.

The position a paintbrush is placed determines the leaf distribution morphology and overall shape of a tree, so position optimization becomes the key to a painter' artistic creation, which shall be controlled according to the physiological morphology features of a tree type and the creation thinking of the painter.

The leaf-creating algorithm is very simple, and just to paste the selected paintbrushes to a series of defined leaf position points one by one successively. The pasting algorithm is expressed below:

**Fig. 87.4** Leaf positioning and creating process

$$G = \begin{cases} G_p, \text{when the pixels at respective paintbrush position are opalescent} \\ G_w, \text{when the pixels at respective paintbrush position are transparent} \end{cases}$$

$$(87.2)$$

where $G$ is the grayscale value taken after pasting the pixels at one position onto the render window; $G_p$ is the grayscale value of the pixels at corresponding position of a paintbrush; and $G_w$ is the original grayscale value of the pixels at corresponding position on the render window.

Figure 87.4 shows a process of determining leaf rendering position from trunk and branches and then using the paintbrush in Fig. 87.2 to paste leaves.

Because the leaves rendered in each layer have generally multiple position points, the leaves rendered later are always superposed to those rendered previously; in addition, the leaves rendered in the next layer are always superposed to those rendered in the previous layer, so there comes an effect of multi-layer superposition and leafy profusion eventually.

The painter decides when to end the multipass rendering according to real-time rendering effect. Here, there is neither real image to act as designated standard nor energy function to serve as objective function for evaluating a rendering scheme, the only criterion for rendering effect is the non-photorealistic artistic style and effect a work of art has.

## 87.5 Experimental Results

Here, three non-photorealistic rendering pictures of tree rendered in three passes starting with trunk are given. The trunk and branches in the first and second pictures were hand drawn, whereas the trunk and branches in the third picture was created with program-based generative method. Multipass rendering of all trunk and branches and leaves was done under Windows XP and VC++6.0 environment (Fig. 87.5).

From the results of experimentation, model can simulate the process of art works' creation and drawing, with the features of supporting interactive creative freedom and semi-automatic generation. Compared with other methods' effect, the artwork, which uses model, has the distinct Chinese painting freehand style.

## 87.6 Conclusions

Artistic works with different hand-drawing styles have their own characteristics and techniques in respect of rendering method, but from the perspective of work rendering process, the key is to choose various brush types and brush strokes and to construct an appropriate process model. Usually, a process model conforms to

**Fig. 87.5** Non-photorealistic renderings of tree based on stroke and multipass rendering

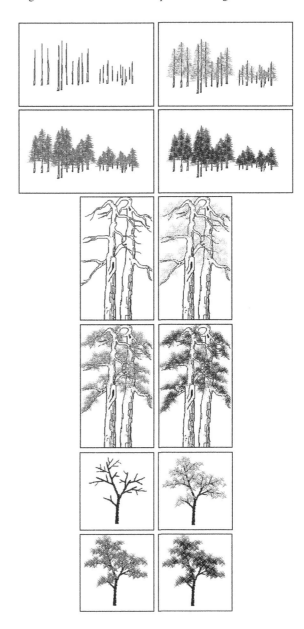

multipass rendering law; whether an optimization algorithm is used or a greedy algorithm is used, there are only two principles: one is to limit the number of strokes (including the number of multipass rendering layers) so that the result looks like a picture rather than a photo; the other is to make the created picture look like fitting the expected hand-drawing style. This study might provide an excellent enlightenment to creating works with various hand-drawing styles by using stroke rendering technique.

## References

1. Bin G (2008) An research of non-photorealistic rendering technology. Microcomput Inf 24(5–3):269–271 (in Chinese)
2. Qian X, Xiao L, Wu H-Z (2006) Adaptive distributions of strokes-based non-photorealistic rendering. J Eng Graph 2:58–63 (in Chinese)
3. Chang J (1995) Fractal feature and simulation of plant structure. Hangzhou University Press, Hangzhou, p 6 (in Chinese)
4. Dong Y, Zhao X, Kang M-Z (2010) New plant morphological structure model. Comp Eng Appl 46(13):191–193 (in Chinese)
5. Wang X, Lin L (2003) Particle system model of tree simulation and its implementation. J South China Normal Univ (Natural Science Edition) 3:49–53 (in Chinese)
6. Hertzmann A (1998) Painterly rendering with curved brush strokes of multiple sizes. In: Proceedings of Siggraph, 98, 453-460

# Chapter 88
# Comparison of Image-Based Measuring Methods for Analysis of Particle Mixing in Rotary Drum

X. Y. Liu and Lei He

**Abstract** Rotating drums are widely used in drying industry to mix granular materials. However, the mixing process is not yet well understood. In the present work, experiments were performed on a 2D rotating drum to investigate the mixing process using image processing techniques. The mixing time is determined by measuring the variance of the color concentration of samples with time, as well as by calculating the contact pixels between different colored balls. The results are then compared to each other and analyzed. It is shown that both methods can describe the mixing process and measured values of the mixing time are comparable, but the method using the variance of the color concentration is more time-consuming. Result of this work is useful for researchers in the choice of image-based measuring tools for particle mixing process in rotary drums.

**Keywords** Rotating drum · Mixing · Granular · Material · Image processing

## 88.1 Introduction

Rotating drums are widely used in chemical, pharmaceutical and metallurgical industries. The particle mixing process has significant influence on the heat transfer efficiency. In previous studies, much effort has been devoted to characterize the mixing dynamics [1–7]. In the work of [8], PEPT method was used to track the motion of a single radioactive tracer particle within a bed of similar particles in a partially filled horizontal rotating drum. PEPT technology is advantageous in that it

X. Y. Liu (✉) · L. He
College of Electrical & Information Engineering, Hunan University,
D-410082 Changsha, China
e-mail: xiaoyanliu2@yahoo.cn

W. Lu et al. (eds.), *Proceedings of the 2012 International Conference on Information Technology and Software Engineering*, Lecture Notes in Electrical Engineering 212, DOI: 10.1007/978-3-642-34531-9_88, © Springer-Verlag Berlin Heidelberg 2013

can track particle inside the bed, but such a measuring technique is rather expensive. In the study of Van Puyvelde et al. 2006, image analysis was used to measure the contact between colored particles on pixel-level [9]. Such image-based measuring method is easy to operate and has the advantage of low cost.

In the present work, particle mixing process in a quasi-2D rotating drum is measured using two different image-based methods, one by measuring the variance of the color concentration of samples with time and the other by calculating the sum contact pixels between differently colored balls with time. The results are compared to each other with the objective to find out which one is more effective and efficient [10].

## 88.2 Experimental

The rotating drum used in the experiments has an inner diameter of 206 mm. It was constructed with steel with one glass plate covered on the front side and another mounted inside the drum. The distance between these two glass plates was about 7 mm (a little higher than the diameter of sample balls). White and yellow plastic balls were used as testing particles (particle diameter 6 mm, white balls: yellow balls = 1:1), as shown in Fig. 88.1. The rotation speed was 8.70 rpm and the fill degree was 0.31.

The particle mixing process was captured by a video camera (Sony, HDR-XR150, 1440 × 1080, 25 fps). These frame images were then analyzed using image processing technology to calculate the variance of the concentration of yellow balls with time and the sum contact pixels between white and yellow balls.

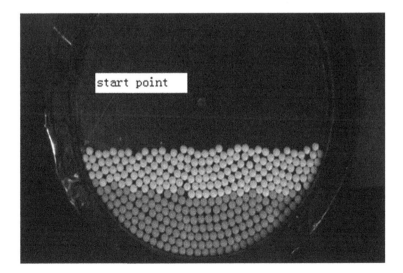

**Fig. 88.1** Initial state

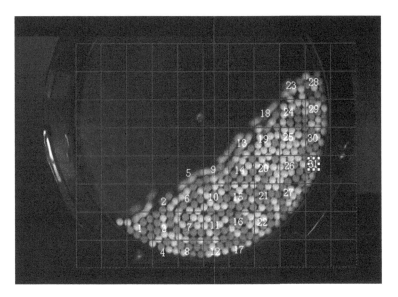

**Fig. 88.2** Particle bed with AOI

The software IPP 6.0 was used to analyze the mixing process. The region of the particle bed was divided into thirty-one area of interesting (AOI) shown in Fig. 88.2, the concentration of yellow balls in each AOI is defined as

$$Cy = Sy / (Sy + Sw) \qquad (88.1)$$

where $S_y$ is the area occupied by yellow balls and $S_w$ is the area of white balls (Fig. 88.3 for example).

With the $C_y$ of each AOI, the concentration variance of yellow balls for the 31AOIs of each image was then calculated. The above process was repeated for all

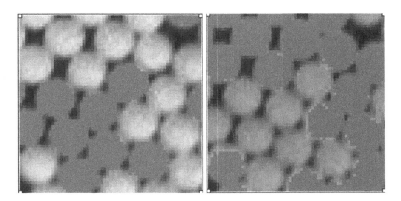

**Fig. 88.3** Area of occupied by *yellow* and *white* balls in one AOI

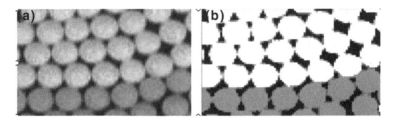

**Fig. 88.4** **a** Picture before be changed. **b** Picture after be changed

images of the mixing process and the change of concentration variance with time can be obtained.

To measure the contact pixels between two different color balls, image processing toolbox of MATLAB was used. To reduce noises in the image, the brightness and contrast of the image needs to be adjusted first by IPP 6.0. It can be seen from Fig. 88.4 that the boundary between balls becomes more clearly,

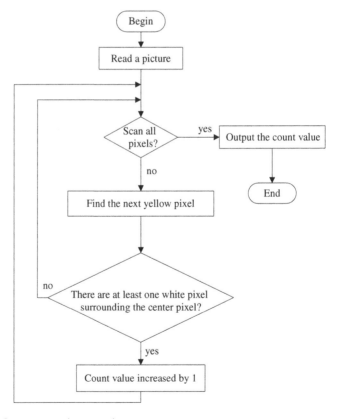

**Fig. 88.5** Image processing procedure

**Fig. 88.6** Variance of the color concentration of yellow ball

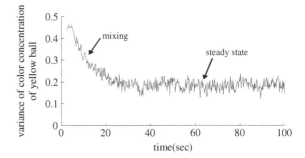

**Fig. 88.7** Contact pixels between two yellow and white balls

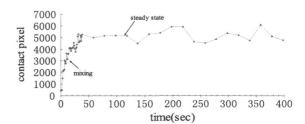

with the RGB value of white (0, 0, 0) and RGB value of yellow (255, 255, 0). This is advantageous for the measurement of the contact pixels.

In image shown in Fig. 88.4b, there are four different colors: white for the white ball, yellow for the yellow ball, black for the background of the drum and green for the disturbance color. The image was then analyzed pixel by pixel using matlab language by counting number of contact pixels between yellow and white balls (Fig. 88.5). For each yellow pixel, if there are at least one white pixel surrounding the center yellow pixel, the value of total contact increased by 1. By analyzing all the images using the above procedure, the change of contact with time can be obtained [10].

## 88.3 Results and Discussion

Figures 88.6 and 88.7 illustrate the change of variance of the concentration of yellow balls with time and the total contact pixels between yellow and white ball with time, respectively. It was shown that different colored balls start to mix when the bed begins to avalanche. With time, the value of variance of the color concentration of yellow balls is reduced and the value of contact pixels is still increased until the steady state is reached. The magnitudes of the mixing time obtained from both curves are (about 30 s), though different measuring methods were used. However, the image processing procedure using the AOIs is more time-consuming.

## 88.4 Conclusion

Experiments were performed on a 2D rotating drum to investigate the mixing process using image processing technology. The mixing rate is determined by measuring the variance of the color concentration of samples with time, as well as by calculating the sum of contact pixels between differently colored balls with time. Results show that both methods are effective to describe the mixing process, but the method by measuring the variance of the color concentration is more time-consuming. Result of this work is useful for researchers in the choice of image-based measuring tools for particle mixing process in rotary drums, and provides experimental data for the further theoretical analysis of mixing process in 2D rotary drum.

**Acknowledgments** This work is supported by State Key Laboratory of Synthetical Automation for Process Industries, and Ministry of Education of China (Program for New Century Excellent Talents in University (NCET-08-0176), Program Nr. [2011]185).

## References

1. Aissa AA, Duchesne C, Rodrigue D (2011) Effect of friction coefficient and density on mixing particles in the rolling regime. Powder Technol 212:340–347
2. Siiria S, Yliruusi J (2011) DEM simulation of influence of parameters on energy and degree of mixing. Particuology 9: 406–413
3. Wightman C, Muzzio FJ (1998) Mixing of granular material in a drum mixer undergoing rotational and rocking motions II. Segregating particles. Powder Technol 98:125–134
4. Sanfratello L, Fukushima E (2009) Experimental studies of density segregation in the 3D rotating cylinder and the absence of banding, Granular Matter 11:73–78
5. Pereira GG, Sinnott MD, Cleary PW, Kurt L, Guy M, Ilija SD (2011) Insights from simulations into mechanisms for density segregation of granular mixtures in rotating cylinders, Granular Matter 13: 53–74
6. Ingram A, Sevile JPK, Parker DJ, Fan X, Forster RG (2005) Axial and radial dispersion in rolling mode rotating drums. Power Technol 158:76–91
7. Liu XY, Xu X, Zhang YY (2011) Experimental study in time features of particle motion in rotating drums. Chem Eng Technol 34:997–1002
8. Parker D, Dijkstra A, Martin T, Seville J (1997) Positron emission particle tracking studies of spherical particle motion in rotating drums. Chem Eng Sci 52:2011–2022
9. Van Puyvelde DR, Young BR, Wilsion MA, Schmidt SJ (2006) Experimental determination of transverse mixing kinetics in rolling drum by image analysis. Powder Technol 106:183–191
10. Van Puyvelde DR (2006) Comparison of discrete elemental modelling to experimental data regarding mixing of solids in the transverse direction of a rotating kiln. Chem Eng Sci 61:4462–4465

# Chapter 89
# Research on the Confidentiality Oriented Image Slicing and Recovering System

**Shiliang Yan and Hua Zhang**

**Abstract** As information technology continues to progress, images, video and other multimedia files are widely transmitted over internet. Security threats like Viruses, Trojans, hackers hinder the application with data especially image exchange. Regarding this problem, an image sharing algorithm is proposed, and the matrix multiplication is used for image slicing. The original image can be recovered only when more than certain number of encrypted slices are collected and processed. The simulation experiment proves that the algorithm proposed can recover the image without loss of quality from qualified slices and any slices less than the threshold can not recover the image.

**Keywords** Image slicing · Image recovering · Information security

## 89.1 Introduction

With the rapid development of information especially network technology, network communication technology become increasingly important for the work and living of people. More and more digital images are transmitted through the

S. Yan (✉) · H. Zhang
Engineering and Technology Center, Southwest University of Science and Technology,
Mianyang, China
e-mail: bmwbenz@163.com

H. Zhang
e-mail: zzhh839@163.com

S. Yan
School of Computer Science and Engineering, University of Electronic Science
and Technology, Chengdu, China

W. Lu et al. (eds.), *Proceedings of the 2012 International Conference on Information*
*Technology and Software Engineering*, Lecture Notes in Electrical Engineering 212,
DOI: 10.1007/978-3-642-34531-9_89, © Springer-Verlag Berlin Heidelberg 2013

network [1, 2], in order to ensure the security of image transmission, the most direct way is to encrypt the image, but it depends entirely on the security of traditional encryption key. If the encryption key is lost or damaged, it is impossible to recover the original image. Some people argued that image segmentation and distributed storage methods can be used to ensure the secrecy of the image.

However, the image clip itself contains rich information, which can be used to restore fragments by the experienced researchers through a few parts of the entire image. In addition, because of the poor fault tolerating capability, some encrypted image slices can not be reconstructed with little slice error, which result in the trouble in image decryption. Therefore, how to encrypt the image during the splitting and rebuild the original image through image slices without data losing has become a challenging problem in the field of image processing.

## 89.2 Related Works

Regarding the problem of image confidentiality protecting for network communication, lots of scholars in this filed have made some achievements. Some of them with representatives can be listed as follows.

Pareek [3] proposed an approach for image encryption based on chaotic logistic maps in order to meet the requirements of the secure image transfer, an external secret key of 80-bit and two chaotic logistic maps are employed, the initial conditions for the both logistic maps are derived using the external secret key by providing different weight age to all its bits. Wu et al. [4, 5] proposed an algorithm encrypting an image through a three stage process. In the first step, a reference Sudoku matrix is generated as the foundation for the encryption and scrambling processes. The image pixels' intensities are then changed by using the reference Sudoku matrix values, and finally the pixels' positions are shuffled using the Sudoku matrix as a mapping process. Zhou et al. [6, 7] presents a concept of image encryption which is based on edge information. The basic idea is to separate the image into the edges and the image without edges, and encrypt them using any existing or new encryption algorithm. With this algorithm, user has the flexibility to encrypt the edges or the image without edges, or both of them.

The achievements mentioned above mainly focus on the image encryption or only proposed some supplement solutions; few of them pay much attention on the image slicing and reconstructing technology. In addition, the fault tolerance design is neglected totally in the solutions developed. To solve these defects, an image sharing algorithm is proposed, and the matrix multiplication is used for image slicing. The original image can be recovered only when more than certain number of encrypted slices are collected and processed. The simulation experiment proves that the algorithm proposed can recover the image without loss of quality from qualified slices and any slices less than the threshold can not recover the image.

## 89.3  Description of System Architecture

In order to achieve image segmentation and restoration, this matrix multiplication based Krain secret sharing ideas, put forward the compressible multi-secret images sharing scheme and image sharing program. The former can be effectively compressed shadow image; learn the secret share of the latter idea can be used multiple times to achieve a multi-image secret sharing, and the program does not produce a shadow image, shadow image is difficult to avoid the allocation and management.

### 89.3.1  Summary of the System Architecture

The input of the system is the image to be shared or protected, the output is the image reconstructed from slices. The image will be divided into n slices, and shared with n separate holders. The slices will be stored distributed, any less than t slices can not leak any information about the original image. Only more than *t* slices are collected, then the image can be recovered. The structure can be described in Fig. 89.1.

### 89.3.2  Components Description

The Image slicing and recovering system is composed of three components, including initializing module, slicing and constructing one.

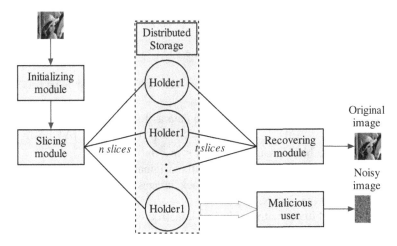

**Fig. 89.1**  Structure of image slicing and recovering system

1. Initializing module is responsible for setting the working environment of the image sharing system. Let D be a secret image distributor, p1, p2... pn for the participants, S is the r × r size of the secret image. D in the finite field GF (251) on the structure of n tm × m-dimensional matrix corresponding to Ai as participants share a secret meet: any t Ai composed tm × tm square for the full rank matrix ($1 \leq i \leq t$).

2. Slicing module is responsible for dividing the given data into n slices. The working step can be described as Algorithm1.

**Algorithm 1** *data dividing*

/*The shadow image block tm × m-dimensional image for the block Sj of 1 / t, and multiplying by the matrix, block any pixel in the image Sj are subject to a secret share of the full replacement of elements Ai*/

Begin

Input image S, output n Slices

Divide S into tm × tm size of the image block Sj, with ($1 \leq j \leq \lceil r / tm \rceil^2$);

According to equation, calculated the slice with vij = Sj × Ai (mod251), vij dimension tm × m, the shadow image of the first j vi block, $1 \leq i \leq n$, $1 \leq j \leq \lceil r / tm \rceil^2$.

End

3. Constructing module is responsible for rebuilding the original image from given number of slices. The working step can be described like Algorithm2.

**Algorithm 2** *data reconstructing*

Begin

Collect any t image slices vi (might take v1... vt), and block the vij, build the matrix

Vj = [v1j, v2j... vtj] = [Sj × A1, Sj × A2... Sj × At] = Sj × [A1, ..., At]

Which $1 \leq i \leq n$, $1 \leq j \leq \lceil r / tm \rceil^2$;

According to equation, calculated temp data as follows:

Sj = Vj × [A1... At]$^{-1}$ (mod251) = Sj × [A1... At] × [A1, ..., At]$^{-1}$ (mod251) Score block image Sj ($1 \leq j \leq \lceil r / tm \rceil^2$);

Block Sj in order to form an image of the original secret image S.

Set the (2,4) threshold, m, plus to block images Sj, {A1,A2,A3,A4} for the domain Z23 on the matrix, respectively.

Ai constitute arbitrary matrix of full rank matrix; calculate the appropriate share of the slice of Vi can be calculated.

V1 and V2 might get used to reconstruct the secret as a share of the reconstruction process is as follows. The final Solution was $Sj = V \times [A1, A2]^{-1}$ (mod23)End

## 89.4 Description of System Workflow

To share the image, some initializing work is needed. Let H (G, x) for the vicariate one-way function, D is the secret image distributor. D in the finite field GF (251) on the structure of n nm $\times$ m dimensional matrix Ai as a participant p1, p2,..., pn the public identity information, and a finite field GF (251) nt constructed on a nm $\times$ m-dimensional matrix B1, B2, ..., Bn-t as a public information; required to satisfy: n matrices Ai consisting of nm $\times$ nm matrix of full rank matrix, and any t Ai and Bk formed nt a nm $\times$ nm matrix for the full rank matrix ($1 \leq i \leq$ n, $1 \leq k \leq$ nt). D xi as the secret choice of n players share the secret of pi ($1 \leq i \leq$ n).

### 89.4.1 Image Dividing

The r $\times$ r size of the shared secret image S can be divided into five steps, the workflow can be described according to Algorithm3.

**Algorithm 3** *image dividing*

Begin

1. divide the secret image S into nm $\times$ nm block size image Sj; select a secret image of the same size with image G (generator image) as public information, will be divided into size nm $\times$ nm block Gj; which $1 \leq j \leq \lceil r / tm \rceil^2$.
2. Calculation of H (Gj, xi), and H (Gj, xi) convert nm $\times$ m-dimensional matrix form vji, the pseudo secret of pi, as participants share, of which $1 \leq i \leq$ n, $1 \leq j \leq \lceil r / tm \rceil^2$.
3. Caculating Uj, Uj $\times$ Ai = vji (mod 251), Uj $\times$ [A1, A2, ..., An] = [vj1, vj2, ..., vjn] (mod 251), and Uj = [vj1, vj2, ..., vjn] $\times$ [A1, A2, ..., An] $-1$ (mod 251), obtain the public information UBjk = Uj $\times$ Bk.
   UBjk is public information U $\times$ Bk of the j-th block, where $1 \leq j \leq$ , $1 \leq k \leq$ nt.
4. Calculation: Sj ' = Sj $\oplus$Uj ($\oplus$denotes XOR) Which $1 \leq j \leq \lceil r / tm \rceil^2$; so that Sj is composed of public image S'.
5. Public UBk, S '(public image) and G (generator image), $1 \leq k \leq$ nt.

End

## 89.4.2 Slices Recovering

The r × r image constructing algorithm can be described in three steps, the workflow can be described like Algorithm4.

**Algorithm 4** *image recovering*

Begin

1. any t participants (we may assume that p1, p2, ..., pt) to generate an image the size of G is divided into sub-nm × nm block Gj; compute H (Gj, xi) and its value into a matrix form vji, where $1 \leq j \leq \lceil r / tm \rceil^2$, $1 \leq i \leq n$.
2. public information UBk into nm × m block size information Uj × Bk, according to *Ai=vji* to solve: Uj × [A1, ..., At, B1, ..., Bn-t] = [vj1, ..., vjt, Uj × B1, ..., Uj × Bn-t] (mod 251) Have Uj = [vj1, ..., vjt, Uj × B1, ..., Uj × Bn-t] × [A1, ..., At, B1, ..., Bn-t] −1 = [Uj × A1, ..., Uj × At, Uj × B1, ..., Uj × Bnt] × [A1, ..., At, B1, ..., Bn-t] −1 (mod 251), Which $1 \leq j \leq \lceil r / tm \rceil^2$.
3. Public image S 'is divided into size nm × nm block Sj', calculated as follows Sj = S'j Uj, Sj in the combination of the secret image S, where $1 \leq j \leq \lceil r / tm \rceil^2$.

End

## 89.4.3 Parameter Selection of the Workflow

1. Karnin and others in secret sharing scheme proposed matrix multiplication, the problem has been made to the detailed proof. nmax is the maximum number of participants, t is the threshold, GF (p) a finite field, m is the secret share of the Ai $(1 \leq i \leq n)$ the number of columns, When t ≤ pm − 1, nmax + 1 − t ≤ pm − 1, When t ≥ pm when, nmax + 1 − t = 1. As long as the threshold t is less than pm, program to the line, dealing with images, p 251 general admission, to meet the requirements.
2. Bivariate one-way function described in the definition: f (r, s) for the bivariate one-way function if and only if the following conditions: the known r and s, f (r, s) easy to calculate; known s and f (r, s), find r in the calculation is not feasible; In the case of unknown s, for any r, is difficult to calculate f (r, s); is known s the case, find a different r1 and r2 satisfy f (r1, s) = f (r1, s) is not feasible; s are known to r and f (r, s), find s in the calculation feasible; For any number of (ri, f [ri, s]) pairs, find f (r, s) is not feasible, in which r ≠ ri $(1 \leq i \leq n)$.

**Fig. 89.2**  The image for sharing

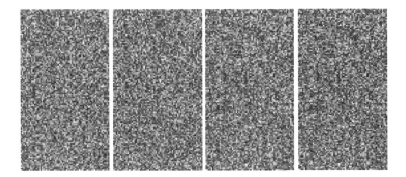

**Fig. 89.3**  The shadow slices divided from original image

## 89.5  Simulation Experiment

According to the technology proposed in this paper, an image slicing and sharing system is developed with matlab7.1; the image for sharing is a $512 \times 512$ Lena color image like Fig. 89.2.

**Fig. 89.4**  The image of recovering from slices

With the image slicing function, the image is divided into four shadow slice, the size of slice is $512 \times 256$ and nothing about original image can be gotten from any shadow slice, the result of slicing can be described like Fig. 89.3.

With the slice recovering function, take slice1 and slice3 as input, rebuild the image, the result can be described as Fig. 89.4. There is no difference from the recovered and the original one, which means that the image can be recovered with no quality loss.

## 89.6 Conclusion and Future Works

With the development of internet, people pay more attentions on the research on the privacy protecting technology for data communicating. Sensitive data leakage will result in serious consequence for the government or enterprise. To solve this problem, this paper proposed an image sharing technology over internet with image dividing and rebuilding, which can reconstruct the original image from slices collected. In the whole process the information of the image can be keep security. In the future we will focus our research on improving the efficiency of the algorithm proposed. In addition, some novel encrypting algorithm will be integrated for function extending.

## References

1. Yan C, Liu X (2009) Research on lossy compression technology about the encrypt coding image. IEEE computer society. In: proceedings of the environmental science and information application technology, ESIAT 2009, Wuhan, China, pp 374–377
2. Acharya B et al (2009) H-S-X cryptosystem and its application to image encryption. IEEE computer society. In: proceedings of the advances in computing, control, and telecommunication technologies, ACT 2009, Raipur, India, pp 720–724
3. Pareek NK, Patidar V, Sud KK (2006) Image encryption using chaotic logistic map. Image Vis Comput 24(9):926–934
4. Wu Y et al (2010) Image encryption using the sudoku matrix. SPIE publications. In: proceedings of the mobile multimedia/image processing, security, and applications 2010, Orlando, United states, doi:10.1117/12.853197
5. Lei GW, Zhuang MJ, Guo DH (2007) STBC-MIMO communication system for image encrypt via CNN. IEEE computer society. In: proceedings of the IEEE international workshop on anti-counterfeiting, security, identification, ASID2010, Xiamen, China, pp 270–274
6. Zhou YC, Panetta K, Agaia S (2009) Image encryption based on edge information. SPIE Publications. In: proceedings of the multimedia on mobile devices 2009, San Jose, United states, doi:10.1117/12.805512
7. Acharya B, Patra SK, Panda G (2008) Image encryption by novel cryptosystem using matrix transformation. IEEE computer society. In: proceedings of the 1st international conference on emerging trends in engineering and technology, ICETET 2008, Nagpur, India, pp 77–81

# Chapter 90
# Stereo-Based Dense Disparity Estimation for Lunar Surface

Yingkui Du, Wei Zheng, Dengke Zhao, Yaonan Wang
and Jianda Han

**Abstract** A stereo-based dense disparity estimation algorithm is proposed to build high quality dense disparity map of lunar surface under special illumination, weak texture and occlusion condition. To avoidance the serious shadow effect effectively, intrinsic image of stereo images are preprocessed. A color similarity probability based belief propagation algorithm (BP) is proposed to solve the depth discontinuous problem of occlusion and obtain an initial dense disparity map. Mean-Shift segmentation algorithm and adaptive threshold optimization are utilized to improve the precision of initial dense disparity map of weak and high similarity texture region in stereo images. Experimental results of the images of standard test library and the stereo images of simulated lunar surface validate that our algorithm is robust to build high quality stereo dense disparity map for Lunar surface.

**Keywords** Lunar surface · Stereo · Disparity map · Mean-shift · BP algorithm

Y. Du (✉) · J. Han
State Key Laboratory of Robotics, Shenyang Institute of Automation, Chinese Academy of Sciences, N0114 Nanta Street 110016 Shenyang, China
e-mail: dyk@sia.cn

W. Zheng · D. Zhao
School of Information Science and Engineering, Shenyang Ligong University,
110016 Shenyang, China

Y. Wang
College of Electrical and Information Engineering, Hunan University,
410082 Changsha, China

W. Lu et al. (eds.), *Proceedings of the 2012 International Conference on Information Technology and Software Engineering*, Lecture Notes in Electrical Engineering 212, DOI: 10.1007/978-3-642-34531-9_90, © Springer-Verlag Berlin Heidelberg 2013

## 90.1 Introduction

Lunar rover is regarded as the most effective technical way of scientific exploring. For the large time delay, the existed deep space exploring rover such as Mars rover are controlled by teleoperation, and the accurate information acquisition of the Lunar surface is very important for the safety of the operation [1, 2]. Contrast to the earth's outdoor condition, Lunar surface is mainly composed of tephra and rocks and the illumination is also greatly different [3]. Accurately reconstruction of the surrounding around Lunar rover is necessary for path planning and scientific analysis. In this paper, we utilize a stereo vision system to obtain solve the problem. The key is to estimate the accurate stereo dense disparity map of the lunar.

The existing dense disparity estimation methods include local method and global method, usually is composed of the four steps include matching cost calculation, cost accumulation, disparity calculation and disparity optimizing [4], but global method is always without the cost accumulation step. Matching cost calculation mainly includes SD, SSD, AD, MAD, NCC, BMC and PFR [5, 6]. Cost accumulation is computed by summing or meaning the matching cost in a fixed window or adaptive moving window area [6, 7]. The global methods have achieved the highest accuracy of dense disparity map in recent years. According to the calculation model, global method can be divided into the method based on Dynamic Programming (DP) [8] and the method based on Markov Random Field (MRF) [9, 10]. The method based on DP method adopts scanning line optimization [11, 12] and minimize the objective function through the calculation of the minimum cost path between two scanning lines. The method based on MRF includes Simulated Annealing (SA) [13], Highest Confidence First (HCF) [14], Graph Cut algorithm (GC) [15, 16] and Belief Propagation (BP) [17, 18]. The main advantage of local methods is low complexity. The type of method is sensitive to illumination, weak texture and occlusion, and is always used to estimate the initial dense disparity map. The global method can improve the accuracy of initial disparity estimation of weak texture and discontinuous boundary area, and the precision of initial estimation is greatly effect on convergence.

Considering the special illumination, weak texture characteristics and occlusions of rocks in Lunar surface, a stereo-based dense disparity estimation algorithm is proposed as shown in Fig. 90.1 to obtain high accurate dense disparity map for the reconstruction of Lunar surface. The main contributions include:

1. According to shadows area of the lunar surface under parallel light illumination, a rapid intrinsic image preprocessing algorithm is utilized to reduce the influence of the shadow area effectively.
2. A belief propagation algorithm based on color similarity probability description is proposed to reduce the influence of occlusion and discontinuous depth. The message is defined by the parallax series that includes color similarity and gradient smoothness of image pixels and is spread across different parallel iterative. Initial dense disparity map is estimated by minimizing energy function.

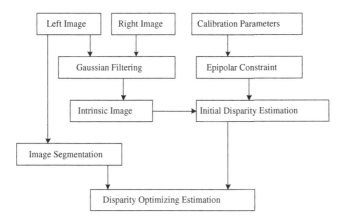

**Fig. 90.1** Dense disparity estimation algorithm flow chart

3. Mean-Shift segmentation algorithm is utilized and an adaptive threshold optimizing method with the constraint of parallax consistency is proposed to improve the accuracy of initial dense disparity map in weak texture and high similarity texture regions.

The paper is organized as follows. In Sect. 90.2, we describe the Illumination of Lunar and the intrinsic image briefly. Then we describe the initial disparity map estimation and optimizing in Sects. 90.3 and 90.4 respectively.

## 90.2 Illumination and Intrinsic Image

The illumination of the lunar surface is parallel light that product serious dark shadows. Intrinsic image is utilized to decompose an image into a lighting map and a reflection map. The reflection map is constant to the illumination conditions changing, so it can be used to suppress the influence of shadow. In this paper, intrinsic image is calculated by the algorithm [19]. The core idea of the algorithm is defined as follows.

$$F_H = \kappa_H f_H + \mu_H \tag{90.1}$$

where $f_H$ is the shadow of a channel, $F_H$ is the linear model parameters with no shadow background $\kappa_H$ and $\mu_H$. The algorithm transforms the original image strictly equal of the shadow area pixel value and the no-shadow area pixel value.

## 90.3 Initial Dense Disparity Map Estimation

In the initial dense disparity estimation, a precision initial dense disparity is necessary for following optimization. Global processing is implemented in a unified framework and is not distinguish error statistics, image noise and occlusion. By defining a global energy minimization function to constrain color consistency and gradient consistent between stereo images, our algorithm can suppress image noise and occlusion effectively in the initial dense disparity estimation.

The left image and right image are denoted as $I_L$ and $I_R$, and $I_L(i,j)$ is the RGB vector of the $(i, j)$ pixel in left image. A Belief Propagation algorithm based on color similarity probability description is proposed to reduce the influence of occlusion and discontinuous depth and get initial dense disparity estimation quickly. The energy function is defined as follows.

$$E = E_{data} + E_{smooth} \tag{90.2}$$

where the $E_{data}$ describes color similarity between image pixels, and the $E_{smooth}$ describes gradient consistency between adjacent image pixels.

The color similarity description probability between the candidates of matching pixels is defined as follows:

$$p(i, j) = \sqrt{p_L^2(i, j) + p_R^2(i, j)} \tag{90.3}$$

$$p_L(i,j) = \frac{\alpha}{\alpha + \|I_L(i, j) - I_R(i', j')\|} \tag{90.4}$$

$$p_R(i, j) = \frac{\alpha}{\alpha + \|I_R(i, j) - I_L(i', j')\|} \tag{90.5}$$

where $\|I_L(i, j) - I_R(i', j')\|$ is the color consistency of the pixels in left and right image, $\alpha$ is a probability weight factor, $I_R(i', j')$ is the candidate matching point that satisfied epipolar constraint $(i', j') = (i, j) + D(i,j)$, the $D(i, j)$ is the disparity value of the candidate matching points.

The energy function $E_{data}$ that describes color similarity between image pixels is defined as:

$$E_{data} = \sum_{p(i,j)\in S} \lambda \min\left(1 - p(i,j), \beta\right) \tag{90.6}$$

where $\lambda$ is a weight coefficient to control weighted data and discontinuous value, $\beta$ is a truncation threshold to filter out some obvious wrong point, $S$ is the pixel sets.

The energy function $E_{smooth}$ describes gradient consistency between adjacent images is defined as:

$$E_{smooth} = \sum_{(i,j)(m,n)\in N} \min\left(\|D(i, j) - D(m, n)\|, \eta\right) \tag{90.7}$$

Minimizing the Eq. (90.2) can estimate the initial dense disparity map. To reduce the influence of occlusion and discontinuous depth effectively, the belief propagation algorithm is utilized to optimize objective function and the message iteration function is defined as follows:

$$m^t_{(i,j)\to(m,n)}\big(s(i,j)\big) = \min_{s(i,j)}\big(E_{smooth}(D(i,j),\,D(m,n))$$
$$+\,E_{data}(D(i,j),\,D(i',j')))$$
$$+\sum_{\substack{(u,v)\in N,\\(u,v)\neq(m,n)}} m^{t-1}_{(u,v)\to(i,j)}(D(i,j)) \tag{90.8}$$

where $m^t_{(i,j)\to(m,n)}$ is the energy of node $(m,n)$, the messages of node $(i,j)$ to transfer to its adjacency node $(m,n)$ in iteration. Each message is calculated in iteration by Eq. (90.9). As the energy is stable, the final confidence is defined.

$$b_{(m,n)}\big(s(m,n)\big) = E_{data}(D(i,j),\,D(i',j'))$$
$$+\sum_{(i,j)\in N} m^{t-1}_{(i,j)\to(m,n)}(s(m,n)), \tag{90.9}$$

## 90.4 Mean-Shift Segmentation and Disparity Optimization

In recent years, feature spatial clustering based segmentation algorithm such as K-Means, Fuzzy C-mean and Mean-Shift has been widely applied in solving computer vision problem [20, 21]. In this paper, the Mean-Shift segmentation algorithm [22] is utilized to segment stereo images into connected region. In each region, a disparity plane is built by a rapid plane voting method and the disparity plane is defined as follows:

$$D(i,j) = a*i + b*j + c \tag{90.10}$$

where $(i,j)$ is the coordinate of pixels, $a,b,c$ is the plane factor.

To solve the plane factor, the candidates of the factor $a$ is computed by partial derivative of all pixels in the region and choose the most votes as the final estimate plane parameters $a$, the solution of the factors $b$ and $c$ are similar. Disparity plane voting algorithm is simple and fast and can remove the outlier effectively.

To get more accurate disparity estimation in each disparity plane, an adaptive threshold function is built to optimize the disparity value by using the mean value replace the original disparity value in every small disparity plane as follows.

$$D(i,j) = \sum_{n=1}^{N} \min(D_n(i,j) - u_n(i,j) * D_n(i,j),\,\varphi) \tag{90.11}$$

where $N$ is the amount of each point in disparity plane, $\varphi$ is a upper limitation of threshold function, $u(i,j)$ is the adaptive threshold function and is defined as.

$$u_n(i,j) = \frac{\frac{1}{N}\sum\limits_{n=1}^{N} D_n(i,j)}{D_n(i,j)} \tag{90.12}$$

**Fig. 90.2** The simulation of Lunar surface. **a** Light source, **b** simulated Lunar surface, **c** stereo collecting system

**Table 90.1** Parameters of the simulated illumination of the Lunar surface

| Light source | Parameters | | | |
|---|---|---|---|---|
| Spherical xenon lamp | Irradiance | Color temperature | Divergence angle | Spectrum |
| | 20,000 Lumen | 6,200 K | 4° | 800–1,000 nm |
| Optical filter | AM | Material | Diameter | Spectrum |
| | 1.5 | JGS2–Quartz | 180 mm | 200–1,200 nm |

## 90.5 Experimental Results

### 90.5.1 Illumination Simulation

There is no atmosphere and scattering on the Lunar surface and the light is parallel incident. But the existing lighting equipment is difficult to simulate the illumination condition in light strength and the spectral characteristics. In this paper, the illumination condition is simulated by using a high-power directional light source as shown in Fig. 90.2 and Table 90.1 to reappear the Lunar surface that is mainly composed of sands and rocks. The illumination simulation is utilized to simulate the shadow distribution situation and identify the efficient of our algorithm.

## 90.6 Experimental Results

In our experiments, the computer parameters include that: CPU-3.40 GHz, Memory-4.00 GB, Programing Platform-VC2010. The stereo vision is composed of two A312fc industrial cameras in 600 mm base-line and the image resolution is 780 × 580 Pixels. In the experiments, our algorithm is tested on the images of standard laboratory and real images of the simulated Lunar surface.

The experimental results of the images of standard laboratory of standard evaluation website (http://vision.middlebury.edu/stereo/) are shown in Figs. 90.3,

**Fig. 90.3** Result of the "Tsukuba" image

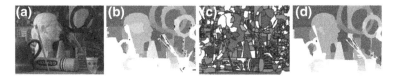

**Fig. 90.4** Result of the "Art" image

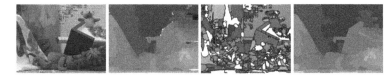

**Fig. 90.5** Result of the "Teddy" image

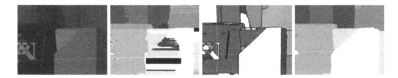

**Fig. 90.6** Result of the "Plastic" image

90.4, 90.5, and 90.6 and the images include Tsukuba, Art, Teddy and Plastic. From left to right, the results are original image, initial dense disparity map, image segmentation and the optimized dense disparity map respectively. The results identify that our algorithm is efficient to the standard images and the accuracy of the initial disparity map is greatly improved.

The experimental results of the real images of the simulated Lunar surface are shown in Figs. 90.7 and 90.8. From left to right, the results are original image, intrinsic image, image segmentation and the optimized dense disparity map respectively. The results validate that our algorithm can performance well on the simulated Lunar surface and is robust to illumination, weak texture and occlusions.

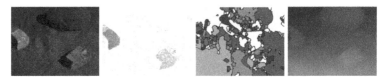

**Fig. 90.7** Result of the image include *sands* and *two rocks*

**Fig. 90.8** Result of the image include only *sands*

## 90.7 Summary

We propose a stereo-based dense disparity map estimation algorithm corresponding to the lunar surface. By computing intrinsic image, the influence of the shadow area is greatly reduced. A color similarity probability description based BP algorithm is proposed to improve the influence of occlusion and discontinuous depth effectively. We build an adaptive threshold optimizing function to improve the accuracy of the initial dense disparity map in weak texture area. Experimental results validate that our algorithm is robust to the special illumination, weak texture and local occlusion of Lunar surface.

**Acknowledgments** This work is supported by Key Program of National Natural Science Foundation of China (61035005, 60835004) and National High Technology Research and Development Program of China (2011AA040202).

## References

1. Lunar surface models. NASA SP-8023
2. Rongxing Li (2004) Rover localization and landing-site mapping technology for the 2003 Mars exploration rover mission. Photogram Eng Remote Sens 70(1):77–90
3. Kaichang D (2008) Photogrammetric processing of rover imagery of the 2003 Mars Exploration Rover mission. ISPRS J Photogram Remote Sens 63(2):181–201
4. Scharstein D, Szeliski R (2002) A taxonomy and evaluation of dense two-frame stereo correspondence algorithms. Int J Comput Vision 47(1):7–42
5. Kanade T, Okutomi M (1994) A Stereo Matching Algorithm with an Adaptive Window: Theory and Experiment. IEEE Trans Pattern Anal Mach Intell 16(9):920–932
6. Bobick AF, Intille SS (1999) Large occlusion stereo. Int J Comput Vision 33(3):181–200
7. Veksler O (2001) Stereo matching by compact windows via mini-mum ratio cycle. Proc Int Conf Comput Vision 1:540–547

8. Ohta Y, Kanade T (1985) Stereo by intra-and inter-scan line search using dynamic programming. IEEE Trans Pattern Anal Mach Intell 7(2):139–154
9. Tardon-Garcia LJ, Portillo-Garcia J, Alberola-Lopez C (1999) Markov random fields and the disparity gradient constraint applied to stereo correspondence. Int Conf Image Process 3:901–905
10. Jiejie Z, Liang W, Jizhou G, Ruigang Y (2010) Spatial-temporal fusion for high accuracy depth maps using dynamic MRFs. IEEE Trans Pattern Anal Mach Intell 32(5):899–909
11. Belhumeur PN (1999) A Bayesian approach to binocular stereopsis. Int J Comput Vision 19(3):237–260
12. Belhumeur PN, Mumford D (1992) A Bayesian treatment of the stereo correspondence problem using half-occluded regions. In CVPR. pp 506–512
13. Barnard ST (1989) Stochastic stereo matching over scale. Int J Comput Vision 3(1):17–32
14. Chou PB, Brown CM (1990) The theory and practice of Bayesian image labeling. Int J Comput Vision 4(3):185–210
15. Boykov Y, Veksler O, Zabih R (2001) Fast approximate energy minimization via graph cuts. IEEE Trans Pattern Anal Mach Intell 23(11):1222–1239
16. Kolmogorov V, Zabih R (2001) Computing visual correspondence with occlusions using graph cuts. Proc Int Conf Comput Vision 2:508–515
17. Sun J et al (2003) Stereo matching using belief propagation. IEEE Trans Pattern Anal Mach Intell 25(7):787–800
18. Felzenszwalb PF, Huttenlocher DP (2006) Efficient belief propagation for early vision. Int J Comput Vision 70(1):41–54
19. Tian J, Tang Y (2011) Linearity of each channel pixel values from a surface in and out of shadows and its applications. Comput Vis Pattern Recogn, 985–992
20. Zhang G, Jia J, Wong TT, Bao H (2009) Consistent depth maps recovery from a video sequence. IEEE Trans Pattern Anal Mach Intell 31(6):974–988
21. Forsyth DA, Ponce J (2002) Computer vision: a modern approach. Prentice Hall, New Jersey
22. Comaniciu D, Meer P (2002) Mean shift: a robust approach toward feature space analysis. IEEE Trans Pattern Anal Mach Intell 24(5):603–619

# Chapter 91
# The Weighted Submodule LDA for Face Recognition

Ye Peng, Shunfang Wang and Longbin Liang

**Abstract** This paper presents an improved algorithm based on submodule Fisherface recognition (SM-Fisherface), which belongs to the most popular subspace algorithm currently. The method first divides the whole face data into multiple modules and analyzes each module separately, which can not only extract more facial feature data, but also capture more local face information and reduce the loss of information compared with no-module-dividing method. Second, we give weights to submodule data in two stages in order to center the sample data accurately in submodule treating stage and reduce the interference caused by external factors such as facial expressions and illumination image in integration stage. Then the recognition strategy for multi-module is proposed, which integrates multiple modules into a whole, and make use of the overall information to determine the final result. Numerical experiments with the YALE face database and FERET face database are given to compare the proposed method with PCA, Fisherface and unweighted SM-fisherface. The conclusion is that the weighted SM-fisherface method has the best recognition rate in the discussed experimental environment.

**Keywords** Face recognition · Submodule · Weight · Fisher linear discriminant analysis

Y. Peng · S. Wang (✉)
School of Information Science and Engineering, Yunnan University,
650091 Kunming, China
e-mail: wangsf_66@hotmail.com

L. Liang
School of Finance, Yunnan University of Finance and Economics,
650221 Kunming, China

W. Lu et al. (eds.), *Proceedings of the 2012 International Conference on Information Technology and Software Engineering*, Lecture Notes in Electrical Engineering 212, DOI: 10.1007/978-3-642-34531-9_91, © Springer-Verlag Berlin Heidelberg 2013

## 91.1 Introduction

With advances in technology and people's safety awareness, identification systems based on biometric, such as face recognition, fingerprint recognition, iris recognition and so on, are getting more and more attention. These biological characteristics are innate, not easily forged and easy to obtain. They can provide a more stable and reliable authentication method. Therefore, biometric-based recognition system has great development space and application prospects, in which face recognition is an important research for its representation and complexity.

There are many face recognition methods, in which PCA and LDA [1] are very common, for they are simple, reliable and they have high recognition rates. The PCA method is to extract small number of features among high dimensional data, so as to describe the data better. But these extracting feature data usually don't have good clustering effects because they make all kinds of data mixed together. Compared with PCA, LDA method improves its clustering ability [2]. The classification idea of LDA is linear discriminant analysis [3].

Some researchers are studying multiple submodule problems of facial recognition [4–6], which mainly includes two research ideas. One consideration is to use the submodule method to expand the number of samples, which partly solve the problem of small sample. Another consideration is to extract more local features from the sub-module, which are more conducive to the image recognition. But how many submodules the face data should be divided into and how face images should be cut and integrated are still open problems waiting for more theoretical and practical studies.

This paper combines LDA method with submodule method, proposes a weighted submodule-Fisherface algorithm to improve the traditional algorithms. In the following sections we give the detailed description of our method.

## 91.2 Submodule FisherFace Algorithm

Fisher linear discriminant analysis function is the most common method in the LDA method and if this method is applied to face recognition field, it is called the Fisherface method. The main purpose of the Fisherface method is not to describe the image precisely, but to construct a projection space of the image data to get a good classification.

### 91.2.1 Fisher Linear Discriminant Criteria Analysis

Fisher criterion is to find an optimal projection direction, so that the projection of the sample data can maintain the largest discrete distance between classes and the smallest discrete distance within classes. It means gathering the same type of samples and separating different types of samples as much as possible, that is to say, maximize the Fisher criterion function. The within-class scatter matrix is evaluated by the distance of the same type data from their sample mean and the between-class scatter matrix is evaluated by the distance of sample means among different types. Suppose a sample contains $n$ d-dimension data. These data belong to two classes of $K_1$ and $K_2$ with the class mean $m_1$ and $m_2$, respectively. Denote the within-class scatter matrix and between-class scatter matrix as $S_w$ and $S_b$, respectively. We have $S_W = \sum_{i=1}^{2} S_i$, $S_i = \sum_{x \in X_i} (x - m_i)(x - m_i)^T$, $i = 1, 2$ and $S_b = (m_1 - m_2)(m_1 - m_2)^T$.

Then our purpose is to find a straight line w, where the two types of data are projected onto, to make the projection be separated as better as possible. Denote $y_j$ as the projected images, j = 1, 2, ..., n, that is, $y_j = w^T x_j$, j = 1, 2, ..., n. The best w can make all $y_{j, j=1, 2, ..., n}$ belong to class $K_1$ or $K_2$. In order to find w, Fisher discriminant criterion function (see [7])

$$J_F(w) = \frac{(\bar{m}_1 - \bar{m}_2)^2}{\bar{S}_1^2 + \bar{S}_2^2} = \frac{w^T S_b w}{w^T S_w w} \qquad (91.1)$$

can be used, where $\bar{S}_i^2 = \sum_{i=1}^{2} (y - \bar{m}_i)^2, i = 1, 2, \quad \bar{m}_i = \frac{1}{n_i} \sum_{y \in Y_i} y, i = 1, 2.$

Following the derivation of [7], maximizing $J_F(w)$ first requires to solve eigenvalues and eigenvectors of matrix $S_w^{-1} S_b$. Then the eigenvector of the largest eigenvalue is the best projecing w.

## 91.2.2 Weighting Idea and SM-Fisherface Algorithm

In the submodule Fisherface (SM-Fisherface) algorithm, according to the geometric characteristics of the human face, the face data is divided into four equal modules by one vertical line and one horizontal line. Suppose the original data set is I and the four parts of I are $I^1$, $I^2$, $I^3$ and $I^4$, respectively. After splitting into sub modules, the overall amount of data has not changed. We analyze each submodule separately and give each submodule certain weight to integrate into the final whole recognition result. In this way, we can extract more facial features than ordinary no-module-dividing method and the face recognition interference caused by illumination, posture and so on can be reduced.

When the facial expression changes, usually the mouth area changes more greatly than the eye area. Therefore, in the recognition process, the data of the eye area should be given larger weight than the mouth area so that the relatively stable area can have a greater effect on the face recognition. We calculate the euclidean distance between the training modules and the testing modules and then integrate all module data for face recognition by giving different weights to different modules.

In our weighting method, weights given to the samples contain two stages. For the first stage, weights to samples is to make the sample center approach the real center as close as possible. According to references [8, 9], the class mean of training samples deviates from the center of this class in small sample size case and adjust the original sample mean is necessary. Suppose the sample means of the four modules $I^1$, $I^2$, $I^3$, $I^4$ are $\varphi^1$, $\varphi^2$, $\varphi^3$, $\varphi^4$, respectively. Centralize each module with $d^j = I^j - \varphi^j$, $j = 1, 2, 3, 4$. Due to the consideration that the farther the distance from the sample mean, the lower the influence to the sample mean, this paper gives small weights to the data far from the sample center and large weights to data near the sample center in each module. That is, the weights can be summarized as $\frac{1}{d^j}$. We use the weighted data to calculate the adjusted sample center $\varphi_q^j$.

For the second stage, weights given to the samples is to make the relatively steady facial area have a greater effect on face recognition. When external factors such as facial expression, pose, illumination and so on change, part of the facial data still remain relatively stable. So it is necessary to give large weights to these steady data to decrease the impact of the external factors. We convert the centralized data with the sample center $\varphi_q^j$, which are column vectors, into N × N square matrixes (N is the dimension of the original image size), which are denoted as $F^j$.

Denote the sub-module of the sample data matrix as $E^j$. Calculate the Euclidean distance between the corresponding vectors of Matrix $E^j$ and $F^j$, which are denoted as $dd_i^j = \left\| E_i^j - F_i^j \right\|^2$, $i = 1, 2, \ldots, N$, where $E_i^j$ and $F_i^j$ indicate the j-th sub-module matrix in the i-th column vector of the original samples and the centralized samples, respectively. If $E_i^j$ is much farther from $F_i^j$, it indicates that this part of data are much easier to be interfered by external factors. We give weights of $\frac{1}{dd_i^j}$ to the corresponding column vector $E_i^j$ to balance these influence caused by the external factors and use data of $\frac{1}{dd_i^j} E_i^j$ to substitute data of $E_i^j$ in recognition.

In the recognition process, in accordance with the distance from small to large order, take the first 25 % of the data as a research object. Add the distances corresponding to the four modules of the same face together, the minimum sum among all training sample is the wanted recognition face.

Calculate within-class scatter matrix $S_w'$ and between-class scatter matrix $S_b'$ of each weighted sub-module. Suppose all training samples include c classes with each class containing n samples.

$$S_W' = \sum_{j=1}^{c} \sum_{X \in I^i} \left( X^j - \varphi_q^j \right)^T \tag{91.2}$$

$$S'_b = \sum_{i=1}^{c} n_i (\varphi_q^j - \varphi)(\varphi_q^j - \varphi)^T \qquad (91.3)$$

where $\varphi = \frac{1}{4n}\sum_{j=1}^{4} n\varphi_q^j$ is the mean of all samples of four sub modules. Project submodule data onto the corresponding projection space $W^j$ and we get the within-class scatter matrix $S_w^j = W^{jT} S'_w W^j$ and the between-class scatter matrix $S_b^j = W^{jT} S'_b W^j$. Calculate the eigenvalues and corresponding eigenvectors of $(S_w^j)^{-1} S_b^j$, make data project onto the corresponding vector space, and then calculate the Euclidean distance between the samples corresponding to submodules. Through studying the obtained four submodule distances of the same face, we can determine their integration method for final face identification. The main steps of the SM-Fisherface algorithm are as follows:

1. In the training step, divide the training samples into four submodules, give the first weights and center the sample data
2. Extract the features from the treated training data and obtain Fisherface projection space W
3. In the testing step, still divide the testing data into four submodules, give the first weights and center the data
4. Project the training data and the testing data onto W, respectively, and calculate the Euclidean distance between the two projection.
5. Use the identification strategy with the second-stage weights to determine the identification results.

## 91.3 Experiment

In this study, the operating environment is win7 system, Intel R CORETM i3 CPU, 2.00 GB RAM with software matlab2010. We do experiments to compare the five algorithms of geometric face, PCA, Fisherface, SM-Fisherface and our weighted SM-Fisherface algorithm. Two popular face databases, YALE [10] face database and FERET [11] face database are used in our experiments.

YALE face database collects grayscale images of 15 subjects. Each subject has 11 images with different facial expressions and picture light. The total number of images is 165. The image size is 100 × 100 with positive pose. Figure 91.1 shows a number of different face selected randomly from the YALE face database.

YALE face database not only includes pictures with happy expression, surprised expression, normal expression and winking, but also includes several pictures with person wearing glasses. The image expressions have significant changes.

**Fig. 91.1** Sample images in
the YALE face database

**Fig. 91.2** Sample images in
the FERET face database

FERET face database collects images of 200 subjects, the size of each image is 80 × 80. Each person has seven images with different postures to form 1,400 pictures in all in database. There are no obvious facial expressions and illumination changes for each person. But each person has different side images with variable angles. Figure 91.2 shows some random faces of different people in FERET database.

As one face is divided into four modules, when the number of training samples is 20, we can get four 10 × 20 PCA projection matrixes, four 9 × 20 LDA projection matrixes in the calculation process.

For different face recognition methods, including geometric face method, the PCA method, the sub-module Fisherface methods without weighting and the proposed weighted SM-Fisherface method, we use different number of test samples such as 20, 50 and 80 to do experiments respectively. For each number of test samples, we repeat 30 times and compute their average value to be the recognition rate. Finally we average three recognition rates to be the final recognition result. The experimental results based on YALE face database and FERET face database are given in Tables 91.1 and 91.2, respectively.

It can be seen from the Table 91.1 that Fisherface, SM-Fisherface and our method are superior to PCA method, which maybe due to PCA method is more sensitive to people's expressions and light than the latter three since YALE face database has obvious illumination and expression changes. But these changing factors have a smaller impact on the latter Fisherface-based recognition methods since Fisher method is based on classification, which can eliminate some changes of illumination, facial expression and other aspects. Compared with Fisherface method, SM-Fisherface is based on submodule, which uses good treatment on the changes of expression, illumination, etc., reduces the impact of these changes to the facial feature recognition rate. Our method combines the weighting idea with SM-Fisherface method, which further improves the recognition rates.

Yale face images are all positive, there is enough information for recognition. Compared with YALE, FERET face database have more side images, but it is still can be seen the same conclusion from Table 91.2 that our weighted SM-Fisherface method performs best in the four considered methods.

**Table 91.1** Recognition rates of five algorithms with YALE database

| Method | 20 samples (%) | 50 samples (%) | 80 samples (%) | Average (%) |
|---|---|---|---|---|
| PCA | 70.0 | 84.0 | 90.0 | 81.3 |
| Fisherface | 75.0 | 86.0 | 93.8 | 84.9 |
| SM-Fisherface | 75.0 | 90.0 | 95.0 | 86.7 |
| Our method | 80.0 | 94.0 | 97.5 | 90.5 |

**Table 91.2** Recognition rates of five algorithms with FERET database

| Method | 20 samples (%) | 50 samples (%) | 80 samples (%) | Average (%) |
|---|---|---|---|---|
| PCA | 70.0 | 80.0 | 85.0 | 78.3 |
| Fisherface | 75.0 | 82.0 | 87.5 | 81.5 |
| SM-Fisherface | 80.0 | 88.0 | 90.0 | 86.0 |
| Our method | 85.0 | 90.0 | 92.5 | 89.2 |

## 91.4 Conclusion

This paper first describes the idea of the submodule Fisherface algorithm and its implementation process. It combines Fisherface and sub-modular methods and thus improve these two methods. Second we consider the weighted SM-Fisherface algorithm, which gives weights to face data for two stages. The first-stage weights are to reduce the dias of the sample center and the second-stage weights are to highlight the importance of key data in recognition. Through experiments, we can see that our method indeed improves the recognition rates.

It is worth figuring out that in the process of giving the second-stage weights, we need to calculate the distance from every vector of each sub-module to the central data. While the final recognition rate is improved, the calculation of this method is a little more complex than the unweighted method. How to decrease the computational complexity of the weighted SM-Fisherface is our future research work.

**Acknowledgments** This research is fully supported by grants from National Natural Science Foundation of China (10901135, 11261068), Special Foundation for Middle and Young Excellent Researchers of Yunnan University and Special Foundation for Middle and Young Excellent Researchers of Kunming.

## References

1. Shi YX, Cai ZX, Wang XW, Benhabib B (2006) Face recognition technology based on improved PCA and Fisher LDA. Mini-Microsystems 27(9):1731–1736
2. Belhumeur PN, Hespanha JP, Kriegman DJ (1997) Eigenfaces vs. fisherfaces: using class specific linear projection. IEEE Trans Pattern Anal Mach Intell 19(7):711–720
3. Lu J, Plataniotis KN, Venetsanopoulos AN (2003) Face recognition using LDA-based algorithms. IEEE Trans Neural Networks 14(1):195–200

4. Kong WZ (2008). Research on learning-based face recognition. Thesis submitted to Zhejiang University for the degree of Doctor of Philosophy
5. Chen B, Wu CD, Zheng JG (2008) A Method of face recognition based on the fusion of multiple feature block bayesian classifiers. Electronic engineering and product world, 10
6. Zhang Y, Wu YQ (2011) New face recognition method based on improved modular PCA. Comput Eng Appl 47(26):216–218
7. Wang HZ (2010) Face recognition based on LDA. The dissertation of master degree for XiDian University
8. Yin HT, Fu P, Meng SW (2006) Face recognition based on adaptively weighted Fisherface. J Optoelectron Laser 17(11):1405–1408
9. Peng Y, Wang SF, Ding HY (2011) An improved method of face recognition combined with wavelet, Fisher face and geometrical characteristics. J Yunnan Univ 33:215–219
10. http://www.face-rec.org/databas
11. Philliips PJ, Moon H, Rizvi SA, Rauss PJ (2000) The FEREAT evaluation methodology for face-recognition algorithms. IEEE Trans Pattern Anal Mach Intell 22(10):1090–1104

# Chapter 92
# A Novel Anti-Vignetting Algorithm for CMOS Image Sensor

**Shengli Zhu, Suying Yao, Jiangtao Xu and Chenfeng Zhong**

**Abstract** In order to eliminate the image vignetting and color aberration caused by the lens, an improved linear approximation algorithm has been proposed in this paper. Firstly a statistical method is adopted to obtain the image central point and the compensation factor curves of RGB three channels which are carried out through the linear extraction. Secondly each RGB channel's attenuation speed is calculated out. Finally the original image is compensated using the obtained attenuation speed. By the software simulation and FPGA verification, the image vignetting can be eliminated effectively and the non-uniform color caused by the lens can be improved significantly. The relative illumination of the image is increased to 97.62 %, and image vignetting phenomenon is disappeared. At the same time, the relative color of the image is increased by 12.8 %, got to 83.14 %. Therefore the image color becomes more uniform. The proposed novel linear approximation algorithm fulfills the requirement of practical applications, and improves image quality effectively.

**Keywords** Vignetting · Linear approximation algorithm · Non-uniform color · Lens correction

S. Zhu (✉) · S. Yao · J. Xu (✉) · C. Zhong
School of Electronic Information Engineering, Tianjin University, Tianjin City, China
e-mail: victorapple@gmail.com

J. Xu
e-mail: xujiangtao@tju.edu.cn

S. Zhu
China International Science and Technology Convention Center, Room 701, Building B, No.12 Yumin Road, Chaoyang District, Beijing, China

W. Lu et al. (eds.), *Proceedings of the 2012 International Conference on Information Technology and Software Engineering*, Lecture Notes in Electrical Engineering 212, DOI: 10.1007/978-3-642-34531-9_92, © Springer-Verlag Berlin Heidelberg 2013

## 92.1 Introduction

In recent years, with rapid development of CMOS image sensor, higher integration of SoC, and die size shrinking, the lens size of CMOS image sensor becomes smaller and smaller. As a result, the trend makes the image vignetting phenomenon more prominent and the image quality cannot be tolerated by customers [1]. The image vignetting is the phenomenon that the pixel brightness declines from image center to image corner as lens view Angle $\omega$ increases, and the optical properties of the lens plays a decisive role in it [2, 3].

The traditional anti-vignetting algorithms require geometric and optical characteristics of the lens, such as LUTs [4], the linear approximation algorithm [5], and etc. These algorithms are simple and implemented easily. However, they do not take into consideration the independence of the three RGB channels of color images and are only suitable for grayscale image processing. Since the lens will cause the color deviation of the image, if the algorithms above are adopted in color image processing, it will result in the uniform colour and worsen the subsequent image processing. In recent years, some new anti-vignetting algorithms had been presented [6], such as the regional anti-halo [7] and Gaussian surface noise reduction method [8], and etc. Compared with the traditional ones, these algorithms are quite complex, not suitable for engineering. In the paper, we proposed a novel linear approximation algorithm to eliminate the vignetting for CMOS image sensors and improve color characteristics. Base on the analysis and optimization for traditional algorithm, the method can reduce complexity and prevent RGB deviation during the anti-vignetting process. Our novel algorithm can provide the protection for the back-end digital image processing.

## 92.2 Cause of Vignetting and Image Color Uniform Character

In the image remote imaging, the cross-sectional area of oblique beam decreases with the increase of the view Angle $\omega$, so that the photon energy received in the CMOS image sensor edge is lower. So the image vignetting occur when the image sensor imaging. Figure 92.1 is the image of the shooting on the white board. Figure 92.2 is the diagonal section of Fig. 92.1. As can be seen from the Fig. 92.2, the pixel point brightness in image edge is significantly less than other pixel point in other image field. Based on optical principle, when the image vignetting occurs, the brightness of the axis's outside pixel point imaging meet [9]:

$$E_\omega = kE_0\cos^4\omega \tag{92.1}$$

where, $E_0$ is the intensity of illumination for axial pixel point; $\omega$ is half the view angle; k is surface vignetting coefficient.

**Fig. 92.1** Image vignetting

**Fig. 92.2** Diagonal section of Fig. 92.1

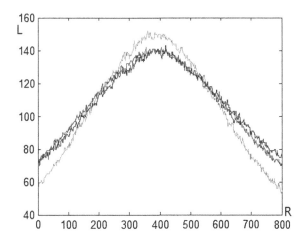

The image vignetting occurs in the image remote imaging by lens, meanwhile there is an impact for color of image. It is known that the light is made up of three kinds of elements RGB. When the beam enters the lens with the view angle $\omega$, the RGB beam will refract in different refractive index, so that the beam position of the receiving RGB beam in the CMOS image sensor produces deviation, which cause the change of the attenuation extent of the RGB beam. The image colour can be seriously distorted if the change of the attenuation extent of the RGB beam is not adjusted and controlled. The image colour deviation caused by the image vignetting can be measured with the image relative colour (RC), as shown in Formula (92.2).

$$\text{Relative Color (RC)} = (\text{Corner} - R/B)/(\text{Center} - R/B) \qquad (92.2)$$

Figure 92.3 shows the colour value of center point and edge point. The relative colour value is 69.57 % according to the above Formula (92.2). Thus it can be seen that the colour deviation caused by Lens is so serious and need to be reduced by all kinds of ways.

Fig. 92.3 Color deviation
analysis

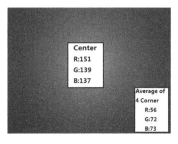

## 92.3 Anti-Vignetting Algorithm

On the basis of linear approximation method, this paper presents an improved algorithm for color images. Firstly, the algorithm is firstly the vignetting image center point position is determined by shooting white board with the CMOS image sensor, and then the RGB compensation factor [10] of the distance RGB three channels relative to the center point is calculated, finally, the vignetting image can be compensated with the related parameters counted.

The procedure can be described as follows. The x-coordinate and y-coordinate of image center pixel point can be counted by the individual summation of the individual rows pixel and table columns pixel in the image. And then the pixels compensation factor is calculated by the Formula (92.3), and the statistics of the pixels compensation factor.

$$K(r) = \frac{I_{ref.max}}{I_{ref}(r)} \quad\quad (92.3)$$

where, $I_{ref.max}$ is the value of brightness center pixel point (i0, j0) in reference image, namely the Luminance maximum value. $I_{ref}(r)$ is the luminance values of pixel point with a distance of r from center pixel point. K(r) is the compensation factor. $r = |i-i0| + |j-j0|$, (i,j) said the coordinate of the pixel point of the reference image.

The result of secondary fitting between the compensation factor and the relative distant from center pixel point is shown as in Fig. 92.4:

The fitting curve shows that the change of the compensation factor is smaller and smaller when the distance r charges in the certain region, so the compensation factor is not affected by r in this region. When r is greater than a specific distance r0, a linear relationship arises between the compensation factor and r. So an approximate estimate way with two straight lines is applied in the paper as shown in Fig. 92.5, the coefficient value of the first part straight line is zero, and the coefficient value of the second part are approximated by oblique line.

Figure 92.1 is analyzed with the above methods and the RGB corresponding parameter can be obtained and shown in Table 92.1.

The original image can be compensated with the statistical parameter in Table 92.1, and the compensation arithmetic is proposed as Formula (92.4).

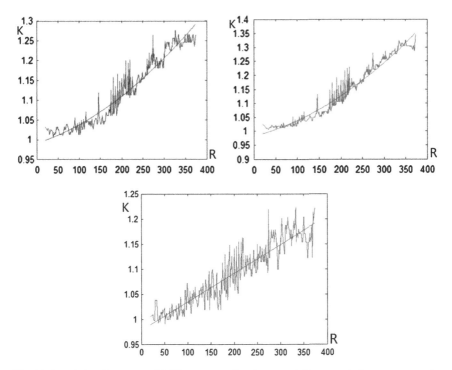

**Fig. 92.4** Relationship curve of RGB compensation factor and distance relative to *center* point

**Fig. 92.5** Approximate
estimate of two *straight lines*

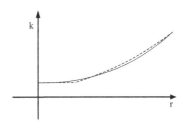

**Table 92.1** Relevant
parameter calculated by
algorithm in paper

| Parameters | Variable | Value |
|---|---|---|
| Center | $(i_0, j_0)$ | (208, 320) |
| Distance without correction | r | 75 |
| Attenuation speed | R | $5.77 \times 10^{-4}$ |
| Attenuation speed | G | $8.11 \times 10^{-3}$ |
| Attenuation speed | B | $2.97 \times 10^{-4}$ |

First of all, the relative distance ($r'$) of every pixel point from center pixel point in the image need be obtained, and the pixel point that the relative distance is greater than $r_0$ is compensated with formula (92.4).

$$E_\omega = E_0(r' - r_0)K_{R/G/B} \qquad (92.4)$$

where, $E_0$ is the intensity of illumination in shaft, $r'$ is the relative distance between one pixel point and center pixel point, $r_0$ is relative distance between the center pixel point and the pixel point that does not need compensation, K is the attenuation rate of RGB.

## 92.4 The Experimental Results

The anti-vignetting algorithm is verified with two images: one is white board picture (Fig. 92.6) and another is the actual picture (Fig. 92.7). The comparison between the anti-vignetting algorithm and linear approximation one is shown in Fig. 92.5. From the results of experiment, the proposed anti-vignetting algorithm can effectively decrease the image vignetting phenomenon and adjust to the image colour simultaneously. Meanwhile the image colour is adjusted so that the image colour is even more pure. The relative intensity of illumination and the relative chromaticity of pixel in Fig. 92.6 image can be calculated and the results are as shown in Table 92.2.

Table 92.2 shows that the anti-vignetting algorithm in the paper is better than the linear approximation one. Although the anti-vignetting effect is nearly the same between the anti-vignetting algorithm and the linear approximation, the relative chroma can be increased about 12.8 %. Therefore our method can guarantee the color uniformity and color accuracy of color image. The experiment results show that the proposed algorithm is more suitable for the real application.

The proposed algorithm is verified by FPGA and the result is shown in Fig. 92.8. The FPGA shooting results that does not use the anti-vignetting algorithm is shown in Fig. 92.8a and it can be seen easily that the vignetting caused by the lens is more serious. According to calculation, the relative intensity of illumination is 47.27 % in Fig. 92.8a and the image vignetting is so serious and the colour deviation also is so obvious at the same time, the relative chroma is 69.57 %. Fig. 92.8b is the image processed with the anti-vignetting algorithm in

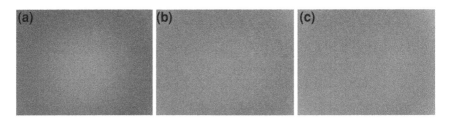

**Fig. 92.6** **a** Raw image. **b** Image based on algorithm in paper. **c** Image based on linear approximation algorithm

**Fig. 92.7**  **a** Raw image. **b** Image based on algorithm in paper

**Table 92.2**  Compare between both algorithms

|  | Relative Illumination (%) | Relative Colorimetric (%) |
|---|---|---|
| Original image | 77.79 | 87.02 |
| Image(this algorithm) | 93.98 | 99.83 |
| Image(linear approximation algorithm) | 94.82 | 89.85 |

the paper, which shows obvious improvement of the image vignetting and the colour deviation. According to calculation, the relative intensity of illumination of the improved image is increased to 97.62 % and the relative chromaticity is increased to 83.14 %.

Figure 92.9 illustrates that the illumination of RGB three channels becomes flat and the image vignetting can be improved. The improved image is color uniformity and can fulfill the human eyes requirements, at a result it is suit to be used in the actual application. Figure 92.10 gives the comparison between two pictures captured in our FPGA platform, in which no anti-vignetting in Fig. 92.10a; on the other hand, the proposed algorithm adopted in Fig. 92.10b. The result shows the algorithm effective.

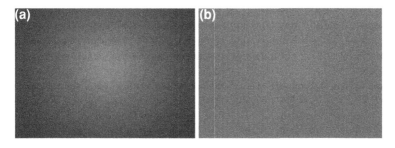

**Fig. 92.8**  **a** Raw image by FPGA. **b** Image based on algorithm in paper by FPGA

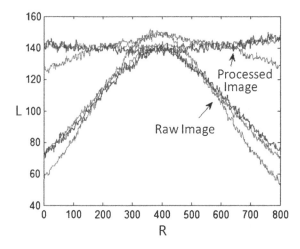

**Fig. 92.9** Illumination compare of diagonal section in Fig. 92.8

**Fig. 92.10** **a** No anti-vigeneting image by FPGA, **b** anti-vigeneting image by FPGA

## 92.5 Conclusions

The paper presents a novel anti-vignetting image algorithm. The proposed algorithm can effectively eliminate image vignetting and improve the image uneven color caused by the lens. By software simulation and FPGA emulation, the method is proven to be easily adopted in the real engineering application. In addition, the linear approximation method is applied in the image vignetting compensation factor curves for the anti-vignetting image algorithm, so this algorithm is more suitable for the simplified fast digital image processing in engineering development.

**Acknowledgments** We would like to acknowledge our funding source for this project—The National Natural Science Foundation of China.

# References

1. Goldman D, Chen J-H (2005) Vignette and exposure calibration and compensation. Proc IEEE Internal Conf Comput Vision 1:899–906
2. Aggarwal M, Hua H, Ahuja N (2001) On cosine-fourth and vignetting effects in real lenses. In: Proceedings of ICCV'01, the eighth IEEE international conference on computer vision 1:472–479
3. Hecht E (2002) Optics, 4th edn. Addison-Wesley, New York
4. Yu W, Chung Y, Soh J (2004) Vignetting distortion correction method for high quality digital imaging. In: Proceedings of the 17th international conference on pattern recognition (ICPR'04) IEEE, Computer society, England, pp 1051–4651
5. Feng Q, Huo JY, Yang HT (2007) A novel technique of image anti-halo. Electron Technol 10:67–70 (in Chinese)
6. He K, Zhao HY, Liu JJ (2007) The method of restoration vignetting in the remote sensing image. Jilin University (Engineering Science), 37(06): 1447–1450 (in Chinese)
7. Zheng Y, Lin S, Kang SB (2006) Single-image vignetting correction. Proceedings of IEEE Conference Computer Vision and Pattern Recognition, June 2006, pp 461–468
8. He K, Tang P-F, Liang R (2009) Vignetting image correction based on gaussian quadrics fitting. In: Fifth international conference on natural computation (ICNC 2009). vol 5, pp 158–161
9. He K (2009) Vignetting image correction based on gaussian quadrics fitting. Electron J 37(1):67–71 (in Chinese)
10. Zheng YJ, Kambhamettu C, Lin S (2009) Single-image optical center estimation from vignetting and tangential gradient symmetry. In: Proceedings of IEEE conference on computer vision and pattern recognition, cvpr, pp 2058–2065

# Chapter 93
# Point Target and Plane Target Imaging of De-Chirped LFM-CW SAR

**Huo He, Hong Wang, Xue gang Wang and Xue lian Yu**

**Abstract** Linear Frequency Modulated Continuous Wave (LFM-CW) SAR is a newly proposed imaging radar system. It combines the technology of LFM-CW and SAR, with the advantages of small cubage, light weight, cost-effective and high resolution, etc. This paper mainly analyses the structure of LFM-SAR system, the theory of de-chirped signal and the process of Range Doppler Algorithm (RDA) in detail. At last, the simulation results prove that LFM-CW SAR has a good spatial resolution.

**Keywords** LFM-CW · SAR · De-chirp · RDA

## 93.1 Introduction

SAR has been a focus for several years because it can generate a high resolution image all time. Traditional SAR is too heavy and too expensive. It is necessary to develop a small cubage, light weight, cost-effective SAR system. LFM-CW SAR can satisfy these requirements [1]. So it is being more and more concerned now. Many countries have been studying in LFM-CW SAR [2–4]. Unlike traditional SAR, the "stop-and-go approximation" is invalid. As the receiver front end adopts the de-chirp receiving system, the receiving signal is mixed with a reference signal, leading a smaller beat frequency bandwidth, so as to reduce the requirements of A/D acquisition equipment and signal processing velocity[5, 6]. So LFM-SAR will be an important development direction of SAR technology.

H. He (✉) · H. Wang · X. g. Wang · X. l. Yu
University of Electronic Science and Technology of China (UESTC), Chengdu, China
e-mail: gracehe1988@gmail.com

W. Lu et al. (eds.), *Proceedings of the 2012 International Conference on Information Technology and Software Engineering*, Lecture Notes in Electrical Engineering 212, DOI: 10.1007/978-3-642-34531-9_93, © Springer-Verlag Berlin Heidelberg 2013

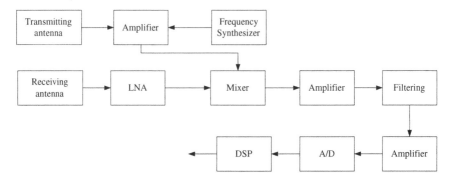

**Fig. 93.1** LFM-CW SAR system structure

**Fig. 93.2** De-chirped signal model

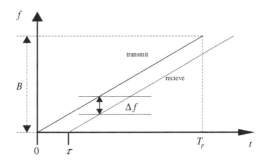

## 93.2 LFM-CW SAR System Structure

The LFM-CW SAR system structure is as Fig. 93.1.

## 93.3 De-chirped Signal Model

The transceiver relationship and beat signal is as Fig. 93.2.
From Fig. 93.2, we can get the beat frequency $f_b$ as:

$$f_b = \Delta f = \frac{B}{T_p}\tau = \frac{B}{T_p}\frac{2R}{C} = \frac{2\alpha}{C}R \qquad (93.1)$$

where $B$ is the bandwidth of transmitted signal, $\alpha = B/T_p$ is the chirp rate, $T_p$ is pulse repetition interval, $C$ is the light speed.

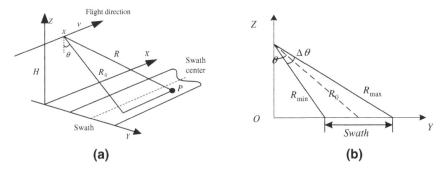

**Fig. 93.3** FMCW SAR image geometry

## 93.4 FMCW SAR Image Geometry

FMCW SAR imaging geometry is shown in Fig. 93.3. $R_{min}$ is the nearest distance and $R_{max}$ is the farthest distance of the swath. We can calculate the bandwidth of the de-chirped signal.

$$B_r = f_{b\max} - f_{b\min} = \frac{2\alpha}{C}(R_{\max} - R_{\min}) \tag{93.2}$$

If the swath is very narrow, according to Nyquist Sampling theory, the range sampling rate $f_s \geq 2B_r$ would also be very small, thus reducing the requirements of A/D acquisition equipment and signal processing velocity as mentioned above.

## 93.5 Range-Doppler Algorithm

### 93.5.1 Echo Model

The received beat signal after de-chirping and mixing is as below:

$$S_{IF}(t', \tau) = \exp\{-j2\pi[f_0(\tau - \tau_{ref}) + \alpha(t' - \tau_{ref})(\tau - \tau_{ref})$$
$$-\frac{1}{2}\alpha(\tau - \tau_{ref})^2]\} \tag{93.3}$$

where $f_0$ is the carrier frequency, $t'$ is the fast time variable on the interval $t[-Tp/2, Tp/2]$, $\tau$ is the time delay, $\tau_{ref} = 2R_{ref}/C$, $R_{ref}$ is the reference distance which is the range between the scene center and the flight line. Expand $\tau$ into its Taylor series at $t' = 0$, ignoring the high-order terms of $t'$, then

$$\tau = \frac{2\sqrt{R_0^2 + (vt' + vt_m)^2}}{C} \cong \tau_0 + At' \tag{93.4}$$

where $\tau_0 = \frac{2R_0}{C} + \frac{v^2 t_m^2}{R_0}$, $A = \frac{2v^2 t_m}{CR_0}$, $t_m$ is slow time variable on the interval $[-Tsar/2, Tsar/2]$, $Tsar$ is the synthetic aperture time. Then,

$$
\begin{aligned}
S_{IF}(t', \tau) =\ & \exp\{-j2\pi[f_0 A t' - \alpha A \tau_0 t' + \alpha(\tau_0 - \tau_{ref})(t' - \tau_{ref})]\} \\
& \cdot \exp[-j2\pi f_0(\tau_0 - \tau_{ref})] \\
& \cdot \exp[j\pi\alpha(\tau_0 - \tau_{ref})^2]
\end{aligned}
\tag{93.5}
$$

### 93.5.2 Range Processing

Range compression can be completed through only once Fourier transform.

$$
\begin{aligned}
S_{IF}(f_r, \tau) =\ & (T_p - \tau_0) \cdot \exp[-j2\pi f_0(\tau_0 - \tau_{ref})] \\
& \cdot \exp[j\pi(\alpha\tau_0^2 - \alpha\tau_{ref}^2)] \\
& \cdot \exp[-j\pi(f_0 A + \alpha\tau_0 - \alpha\tau_0 A - \alpha\tau_{ref} + f_r)(T_p + \tau_0)] \\
& \cdot \operatorname{sin} c[(f_0 A + \alpha\tau_0 - \alpha\tau_0 A - \alpha\tau_{ref} + f_r)(T_p - \tau_0)]
\end{aligned}
\tag{93.6}
$$

The first exponential term represents the azimuth phase history; the second represents Residual Video Phase; the third is the slope term. In FMCW SAR imaging process, the last two exponential terms are usually ignored. Then,

$$
\begin{aligned}
S_{IF}(f_r, \tau) =\ & (T_p - \tau_0) \cdot \exp[-j2\pi f_0(\tau_0 - \tau_{ref})] \\
& \cdot \operatorname{sin} c[(f_0 A + \alpha\tau_0 - \alpha\tau_0 A - \alpha\tau_{ref} + f_r)(T_p - \tau_0)]
\end{aligned}
\tag{93.7}
$$

### 93.5.3 Azimuth Processing

Performing Fourier transform on $S_{IF}(f_r, \tau)$ in azimuth direction, using PSP:

$$
\begin{aligned}
S_{IF}(f_r, f_a) =\ & [T_p - (\frac{2R_0}{C} + \frac{R_0 C f_a^2}{4 f_0^2 v^2})] \\
& \cdot \exp[-j2\pi(\frac{2 f_0 R_0}{C} - \frac{R_0 C f_a^2}{4 f_0 v^2} - f_0 \tau_{ref})] \cdot \operatorname{sin} c\{[T_p - (\frac{2R_0}{C} + \frac{R_0 C f_a^2}{4 f_0^2 v^2})] \\
& \cdot [f_r - \alpha\tau_{ref} + \frac{2\alpha}{C} R_0 - (1 - \frac{2R_0\alpha}{C f_0}) f_a + \frac{\alpha R_0 C}{4 f_0^2 v^2} f_a^2]\}
\end{aligned}
\tag{93.8}
$$

Then we extract the phase information,

$$\theta(f_a) = \exp\left[-j2\pi\left(\frac{2f_0R_0}{C} - f_0\tau_{ref}\right)\right] \cdot \exp\left(j\pi\frac{R_0Cf_a^2}{2f_0v^2}\right) \tag{93.9}$$

We can get that it is a linear frequency signal in azimuth. So we can use the azimuth matched filter to realize the azimuth compression. Before azimuth compression, we need to eliminate the range migration. In Doppler domain, for point target of $R_0$, the corresponding distance caused by range migration is:

$$\Delta R = \frac{C}{2\alpha}\Delta f = -\left(1 - \frac{2R_0\alpha}{Cf_0}\right)\frac{Cf_a}{2\alpha} + \frac{R_0}{8f_0^2v^2}f_a^2 \tag{93.10}$$

In fact, the received signal is often sampled in range and azimuth directions. Migration track is not accurately on the sampling point. Usually we use the interpolation method to solve it as Ref [7]. After range migration, we can get

$$S_{IF}(f_r, f_a) = \left[T_p - \left(\frac{2R_0}{C} + \frac{R_0Cf_a^2}{4f_0^2v^2}\right)\right] \cdot \exp\left[-j2\pi\left(\frac{2f_0R_0}{C} - f_0\tau_{ref}\right)\right]$$
$$\cdot \sin c\left\{\left[T_p - \left(\frac{2R_0}{C} + \frac{R_0Cf_a^2}{4f_0^2v^2}\right)\right] \cdot \left[f_r - \alpha\tau_{ref} + \frac{2\alpha}{C}R_0\right]\right\} \tag{93.11}$$

We can get the azimuth matched filter function as referred in [8]:

$$H(f_a) = \exp\left[j2\pi\left(\frac{2f_0R_0}{C} - \frac{R_0Cf_a^2}{4f_0v^2} - f_0\tau_{ref}\right)\right] \tag{93.12}$$

Then Eq. (93.12) can be changed to

$$S_{IF}(f_r, f_a) = \left[T_p - \left(\frac{2R_0}{C} + \frac{R_0Cf_a^2}{4f_0^2v^2}\right)\right] \cdot \exp\left[-j2\pi\left(\frac{2f_0R_0}{C} - f_0\tau_{ref}\right)\right]$$
$$\cdot \sin c\left\{\left[T_p - \left(\frac{2R_0}{C} + \frac{R_0Cf_a^2}{4f_0^2v^2}\right)\right] \cdot \left[f_r - \alpha\tau_{ref} + \frac{2\alpha}{C}R_0\right]\right\} \tag{93.13}$$

Then the inverse Fourier transform in azimuth of Equation (93.14) is:

$$S_{IF}(f_r, t_m) = (T_p - \tau_0)\sin c\left[(T_p - \tau_0)\left(f_r - \alpha\tau_{ref} + \frac{2\alpha}{C}R_0\right)\right]$$
$$\cdot \exp\left[-j2\pi\left(\frac{2f_0R_0}{C} - f_0\tau_{ref}\right) \cdot \sin c(B_a t_m) \cdot \frac{B_a}{2}\right] \tag{93.14}$$

$B_a = 2v^2T_s/R_0\lambda$ is the Azimuth Doppler bandwidth, $T_s$ is integration time.

**Fig. 93.4** Range imaging result

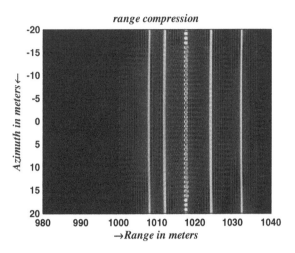

**Fig. 93.5** Range and azimuth imaging result

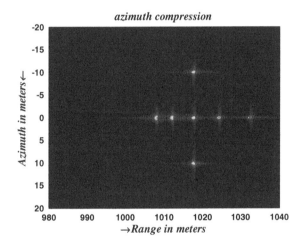

## 93.6 Simulation

The simulation references are as below:

$$f_0 = 15\,\text{GHz};\ T_p = 1\,\text{ms};\ v = 50\,\text{m/s};\ B = 500\,\text{MHz};\ H = 600\,\text{m};$$

## 93.6.1 Point Target

Seven point targets are set in the center of $(1,018\,\text{m}, 0\,\text{m})$, the simulation result is as (Figs. 93.4, 93.5):

Fig. 93.6   Range imaging of plane target

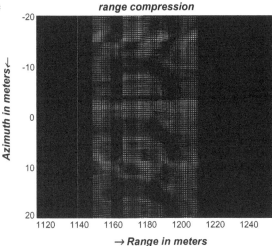

Fig. 93.7   Azimuth imaging of plane target

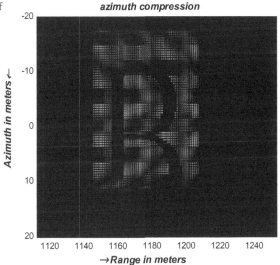

## 93.6.2 Plane Target

Because of no real raw data, the plane target is simulated by a picture of a letter R. Use the gray value of the picture to simulate the RCS of the plane target. The key is to set the pixel coordinate position of the target picture. So in the simulation process, it is required strictly to limit the range and azimuth distance of the pixels, and it must be the integer times of the sampling interval. Thus set the center of the picture in $(1,182\,\text{m}, 0\,\text{m})$, the simulation result is as below (Figs. 93.6, 93.7).

From the simulation result, we can get that Range Doppler algorithm is feasible and LFM-CW SAR has a very high resolution. For the azimuth resolution, we can improve it by using an improved matched filter mentioned in Ref [9].

## 93.7 Conclusion

The signal processing and imaging algorithm of de-chirped LFM-CW SAR has been described in detail. From the simulation result, we can see that LFM-CW SAR has a very high resolution in short distance imaging. For the plane target, it is simulated by the picture pixel. The deficiency is lack of real raw data. If we could get the real raw data, we can prove this algorithm in practical application.

**Acknowledgments** This work is partially supported by the Fundamental Research Funds for the Central Universities (No. ZYGX2010J022) and the National Natural Science foundation of China (No. 61139003).

## Reference

1. Meta A, Hoogeboom P, Ligthart LP (2007) Signal processing for FMCW SAR[J]. IEEE Trans Geosci Remote Sens 45(11):3519–3532
2. Connan G, Griffiths HD, Brennan PV et al (1998) Experimental imaging of internal waves by a mm-wave radar.In: IEEE OCEANS98 conference proceedings, Piscataway, USA, pp 619–623
3. Yamaguchi Y, Mitsumoto M, Sengoku M et al (1994) Synthetic aperture FM-CW radar applied to the detection of objects buried in snowpack. IEEE Trans Geosci Remote Sens 32(1):11–18
4. Giret R, Jeuland H, Enert P (2004) A study of a 3D-SAR concept for a millimeter wave imaging radar onboard an UAV. EuRAD'04, Amsterdam, pp 201–204
5. Shu-min G, Zhu C, Fu kan H (2006) Study on imaging algorithm of de-chirped FM-CW SAR. In: Proceeding of 2006 CIE international conference on radar, Shanghai, China, vol 2, pp 744–747, 16–19 Oct 2006 (in Chinese)
6. ling Zhang Y, wen Qu C, He Y (2007) Research on imaging algorithm of FMCW SAR. J Naval Aeronaut Eng Inst 22(6): 637–640. (in Chinese)
7. Yi Liang, Hong xian Wang, Meng dao Xing. The analysis of FMCW SAR signal and image study. J Electron 1017–1021 (in Chinese)
8. Wei dong Y, Shumei W (2001) Comparison of several interpolation algorithms in range-doppler method. J Electron Inf Technol 23(3):308–312 (in Chinese)
9. ping Hou H, wen Qu C, bing Sun H, gang Song R (2009) Research on FMCW SAR signal characteristic and improved azimuth matched filtering algorithm. In: 2nd Asian-Pacific conference on synthetic aperture radar (in Chinese)

# Chapter 94
# Improvement of Image Decomposition for Cartoon-Texture Based on the VO Model

Qiubo Gong, Mingri Zhu and Nian Wang

**Abstract** There are three improvements of the method for image decomposition based on the VO model proposed by Vese and Osher. One is to introduce an edge detecting function to induct diffusion; one is to use the module of a wavelet transform to instead of the traditional gradient to detect edge; and the other is to update the image during iteration. The improved method overcomes the situation like fuzzy edge and staircase effect in some sense, improves the quality and efficiency of decomposition. The experimental results prove that the improved method protects the edge of cartoon and information of texture effectively.

**Keywords** Image decomposition · Partial differential equation · Wavelet transform · Cartoon · Texture

## 94.1 Introduction

Image decomposition is one of the most important tasks in image processing, the purpose of which is to extract the most meaningful information from the original image. Recently, the models of image decomposition have been widely used in the field of medical image process [1]. And some frequently-used methods have been introduced in the paper [2], including their relative merits. Like image restoration,

Q. Gong (✉) · N. Wang
College of Electronic Engineering and Automation, Guilin University of Electronic Technology, Guilin, Guangxi 541004, China
e-mail: mutourendemeimei@163.com

M. Zhu
College of Beihai Vocational Technology, Guilin University of Electronic Technology, Beihai, Guangxi 536000, China
e-mail: zhumingri@guet.edu.cn

W. Lu et al. (eds.), *Proceedings of the 2012 International Conference on Information Technology and Software Engineering*, Lecture Notes in Electrical Engineering 212, DOI: 10.1007/978-3-642-34531-9_94, © Springer-Verlag Berlin Heidelberg 2013

image decomposition is formulated as an inverse problem. Decomposition of cartoon-texture can be solved by functional minimization and regularization method. In this field, we mention Rudin, Osher and Fatemi [3], Meyer [4], Mumford and Shah [5], Perona and Malik [6], Vese and Osher [7], among many others. Those are all classical models of image decomposition of cartoon-texture. However, models of [3–5] extract the cartoon of images fully but filter out the texture; model of [4] has the texture but its solution is quite difficult; though the VO model can divide the image into cartoon and texture, the quality is not good. This paper takes the VO model as a foundation, chooses afresh the coefficient of diffusion with relation to Euler–Lagrange equation and improves the quality of decomposition, according to the feature of anisotropic transition and the application of wavelet in image processing. Besides, we can improve the efficiency of decomposition by the improved method if we refresh the image immediately during iteration, while choosing the same parameters and iterations of the VO model.

## 94.2 Image Decomposition of VO Model

The VO model was proposed by combining the ROF model for edge with the model of Meyer for texture. The ROF model is introduced as below.

$$u = \arg_{u \in BV(\Omega)} \left\{ \lambda \|f - u\|_{L^2}^2 + \int |\nabla u| \right\} \tag{94.1}$$

The original image $f$ is divided into two different components $u$ and $v$ in this model. In general, $u$ is a cartoon image formed by homogeneous regions and with sharp boundaries, which is expressed by the $BV(\Omega)$ space. And $v$, expressed by $L^2(\Omega)$, is noise or small scale repeated detail, i.e., texture $\lambda > 0$, as a trade-off parameter, balances the two weights of a functional.

Basing on the ROF model, Meyer [4] propose a weak norm $\|.\|_*$ to instead of the $L^2(\Omega)$ to present the oscillation component $v$.

$$G(\Omega) \cong div(L^\infty(\Omega)) = \left\{ v : v = div(\overrightarrow{g}) = \partial_x g_1(x, y) + \partial_y g_2(x, y), \overrightarrow{g} = (g1, g2), g1, g2 \in L^\infty(\Omega) \right\}$$

$$\|v\|_G = \inf_{g=(g_1, g_2)} \left\{ |\sqrt{g_1^2 + g_2^2}\|_{L^\infty}, v = \partial_x g_1(x, y) + \partial_y g_2(x, y) \right\}$$

The decomposition model of Meyer is as followed.

$$\inf_u \left\{ E(u) = |\nabla u| + \lambda \|v\|_*, f = u + v \right\} \tag{94.2}$$

Because of the difficulty of computing the norm $\|.\|_*$, Vese and Osher, following the ideas of Meyer, make a approximation of the norm $L^\infty$ using the $L^p$ of $|\overrightarrow{g}|$ and then propose the VO model, a approximation of functional (94.2).

$$\inf_{u,g1,g2}\left\{G_p(u,g_1,g_2)=|\nabla u|+\lambda\|f-u-div(\overrightarrow{g})\|_{L^2}^2+\mu\|\overrightarrow{g}\|_{L^p}\right\} \qquad (94.3)$$

where $\|\overrightarrow{g}\|_{L^p}=\left[\int\left(\sqrt{g_1^2+g_2^2}\right)^p dxdy\right]^{1/p}$, $\lambda,\mu>0, p\to\infty$

In this model, the first term insures that $u\in BV(\Omega)$, which can remove some noise and small scale detail and maintain the main feature and boundary of the image $f$. The second term is used to make sure the approximation between $f$ and $u+v$ great in degree, while the third term is a penalty of the norm.

## 94.3 Improved Model of Image Decomposition

### 94.3.1 Improvement of Model

In Vese and Osher's numerical calculation [7], the results are quite similar while different values of $p$, with $1\le p\le 10$. The OSV model was deduced by setting $p=2$, a simplification of VO model. Literature [8] presents the multi-scale features using the OSV model. Comparing with the VO model, decomposition for texture is isotropic and the small details are discarded easily. In this paper, we choose $p=1$ for which yields faster calculations per iteration.

$$\inf_{u,g1,g2}\left\{G_p(u,g_1,g_2)=\int|u|_{TV}+\lambda\int|f-u-div(\overrightarrow{g})|^2 dxdy+\mu\int\sqrt{g_1^2+g_2^2}dxdy\right\}$$
$$(94.4)$$

The Eq. (94.4) has the same contents and parameters with (94.3), but the amount of calculation is reduced obviously for its simplification. According to the basic principle of variation method, we can calculate the following Euler–Lagrange equations in case $p=1$.

$$u=f-\partial_x g_1-\partial_y g_2+\frac{1}{2\lambda}div\left(\frac{\nabla u}{|\nabla u|}\right) \qquad (94.5)$$

$$\mu\frac{g_1}{\sqrt{g_1^2+g_2^2}}=2\lambda\left[\frac{\partial}{\partial x}(u-f)+\partial_{xx}^2 g_1+\partial_{xy}^2 g_2\right] \qquad (94.6)$$

$$\mu\frac{g_2}{\sqrt{g_1^2+g_2^2}}=2\lambda\left[\frac{\partial}{\partial x}(u-f)+\partial_{xy}^2 g_1+\partial_{yy}^2 g_2\right] \qquad (94.7)$$

The Eq. (94.5) can be seen as a nonlinear diffusion equation about $u$. It can be deduced that this model is not very good at protecting the edge and texture of images. So we can introduce an edge detecting function $g(s)$ [9, 10] to the right of Eq. (94.5) to protect the details for good. Here is the improved model of decomposition.

$$u = f - \partial_x g_1 - \partial_y g_2 + \frac{1}{2\lambda} g(s) div \left( \frac{\nabla u}{|\nabla u|} \right) \qquad (94.8)$$

The edge detecting function $g(s)$ should meet the conditions: $g(0) = 1$, $g(s)$ is descending and $\lim_{s \to \infty} g(s) = 0$. The improved model insures the isotropic diffusion in flat or smooth field to remove some noise while no diffusion among the normal direction of edge of the given image to protect the details. We choose the classical $g(s)$ in the [6] by Perona and Malik, where $g(s) = \frac{1}{\left(1 + \left(\frac{s}{k}\right)\right)^2}$ and $k$ is the threshold parameter. We can decide the field smooth if $s \leq k$, while edge if $s > k$. In smooth field, we force to diffuse to remove some noise while no diffusion to protect the edge and some important information of the edge field.

Traditional method to detect the edge of an image is using gradient, on which noise may have a bad effect easily. Literature [11] uses the Gauss function to make preprocess with the noise image, which reduces distraction in sense but smoothes the small scale details, causing the extraction not fully. Reference on the literature [12], we can introduce the module of wavelet transform to detect the edge of images.

Before detecting, we transform the image $f(x,y)$ with 2-D wavelet. Assuming that $\psi(x,y)$ is a basic 2-D wavelet, the wavelet transform of $f(x,y)$ with no sampling is like that $W_a f(x,y) = \langle f(i,j), \psi_{a,x,y}(i,j) \rangle$ by considering $\psi_{a,x,y}(i,j) = \frac{1}{a} \psi\left(\frac{i-x}{a}, \frac{i-y}{a}\right)$, where $a \in R^+$ is the scale of transformation. After transform, extract the three high frequency components of $W_a f(x,y)$: $W_a^h f(x,y)$, $W_a^v f(x,y)$, $W_a^d f(x,y)$, which stands for horizontal, vertical and diagonal component respectively. So we define the mode of wavelet transform as follows:

$$M = \left( W_a^h f(x,y)^2 + W_a^v f(x,y)^2 + W_a^d f(x,y)^2 \right)^{1/2} \qquad (94.9)$$

The value of mode will be small in the smooth field, where we implement forced diffusion, while no diffusion or weak diffusion in the field with large value of mode. With doing this, we can improve the quality of decomposition effectively.

### 94.3.2 The Numerical Discretization of the Improved Model

In this paper, we use a semi-implicit finite difference scheme and an iterative algorithm to discretize the (94.6–94.8). The initial guess for iterative algorithm is as follows:

$$u^0 = f; \ g_1^0 = -\frac{1}{2\lambda} \frac{f_x}{|\nabla f|}; \ g_2^0 = -\frac{1}{2\lambda} \frac{f_y}{|\nabla f|}.$$

We note that $G(g_1, g_2) = 1 / \sqrt{g_1^2 + g_2^2}$ to describe in convenience. As mean while, we put each latest iteration results to the next iteration of the application to speed up the processing of decomposition [13].

The discrete forms of our equations are as follows:

$$u_{i,j}^{n+1} = \left( \frac{g(M)}{1 + \frac{1}{2\lambda h^2}(c1 + c2 + c3 + c4)} \right) \left[ u_{i,j}^n - \frac{g_{1,i+1,j}^n - g_{1,i-1,j}^n}{2h} - \frac{g_{1,i,j+1}^n - g_{1,i,j-1}^n}{2h} + \frac{g(M)}{2\lambda h^2} \left( c1 \times u_{i+1,j}^n + c2 \times u_{i-1,j}^n + c3 \times u_{i,j+1}^n + c4 \times u_{i,j-1}^n \right) \right]$$

$$g_{1,i,j}^{n+1} = \left( \frac{2\lambda}{\mu G(g_{1,i,j}^n, g_{2,i,j}^n) + \frac{4\lambda}{h^2}} \right) \left[ \begin{array}{c} \dfrac{u_{i+1,j}^{n+1} - u_{i-1,j}^{n+1}}{2h} - \dfrac{u_{i+1,j}^n - u_{i-1,j}^n}{2h} + \dfrac{g_{1,i+1,j}^n + g_{1,i-1,j}^n}{h^2} \\ + \dfrac{1}{2h^2} \left( \begin{array}{c} 2g_{2,i,j}^n + g_{2,i-1,j-1}^n + g_{2,i+1,j}^n - g_{2,i-1,j}^n \\ -g_{2,i+1,j}^n - g_{2,i,j-1}^n - g_{2,i,j-1}^n \end{array} \right) \end{array} \right]$$

$$g_{2,i,j}^{n+1} = \left( \frac{2\lambda}{\mu G(g_{1,i,j}^n, g_{2,i,j}^n) + \frac{4\lambda}{h^2}} \right) \left[ \begin{array}{c} \dfrac{u_{i+1,j}^{n+1} - u_{i-1,j}^{n+1}}{2h} - \dfrac{u_{i+1,j}^n - u_{i-1,j}^n}{2h} + \dfrac{g_{2,i,j+1}^n + g_{2,i,j-1}^n}{h^2} \\ + \dfrac{1}{2h^2} \left( \begin{array}{c} 2g_{1,i,j}^n + g_{1,i-1,j-1}^n + g_{1,i+1,j+1}^n - g_{1,i-1,j}^n \\ -g_{1,i+1,j}^n - g_{1,i,j-1}^n - g_{1,i,j-1}^n \end{array} \right) \end{array} \right]$$

We introduce the following notations for solving the above equations respectively.

$$c1 = \frac{1}{\sqrt{\dfrac{\left(u_{i+1,j}^n - u_{i,j}^n\right)^2}{h^2} + \dfrac{\left(u_{i,j+1}^n - u_{i,j-1}^n\right)^2}{4h^2}}}$$

$$c2 = \frac{1}{\sqrt{\dfrac{\left(u_{i,j}^n - u_{i-1,j}^n\right)^2}{h^2} + \dfrac{\left(u_{i-1,j+1}^n - u_{i-1,j-1}^n\right)^2}{4h^2}}}$$

$$c3 = \frac{1}{\sqrt{\dfrac{\left(u_{i+1,j}^n - u_{i-1,j}^n\right)^2}{4h^2} + \dfrac{\left(u_{i,j+1}^n - u_{i,j}^n\right)^2}{h^2}}}$$

$$c4 = \frac{1}{\sqrt{\dfrac{\left(u_{i+1,j-1}^n - u_{i-1,j-1}^n\right)^2}{4h^2} + \dfrac{\left(u_{i,j}^n - u_{i,j-1}^n\right)^2}{h^2}}}$$

## 94.4 Numerical Results

In this section, we take the Figs. 94.1 and 94.2 that are textured images to test and verify the decomposition effect of the improved model. At the same time, we also give the results of VO model and model of gradient controlling diffusion coefficients, using the name of gradient model for simplification. In order to increase the observability and comparativity, we extract the edge of figures and note the time of decomposition.

Figures 94.3, 94.4, 94.5, 94.6, 94.7, and 94.8 are the results of decomposition obtained with the three models above mentioned for texture images Figs. 94.1 and 94.2 respectively. In all results, we take $\lambda = 0.2, \mu = 0.002$. The first term is

**Fig. 94.1** Textured image 1

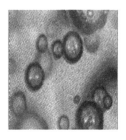

**Fig. 94.2** Textured image 2

cartoon $u$, second is texture $v$, and the third is edge of cartoon in those results. From those figures, we can note that: image $u$ of VO model contains some texture information and $v$ with some structure information, as to say, the decomposition is not complete; While there is much less texture in image $u$ of gradient model, but fuzzy edge and more structure information in image $v$; The two models above can't attain the expected results for image process based on the texture information. Though the effect of decomposition of cartoon $u$ by proposed model is not good as gradient model, better than VO model and the edge is quite obvious and texture is very thorough.

In some cases, the $v$ component is important, especially if it represents texture. Texture could be defined as a repeated pattern of small scale details. And the proposed method is quite useful for extracting features which are based on the texture.

Time comparison of decomposition with the three models is as Tables 94.1 and 94.2, choosing the same parameters.

In conclusion, the difference of execution time with three models is not very obvious from the Tables 94.1 and 94.2, especially between the VO model and gradient model. But the superiority of the improved model can be seen easily.

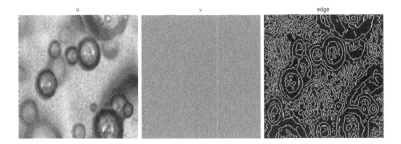

**Fig. 94.3** Decomposition by VO model

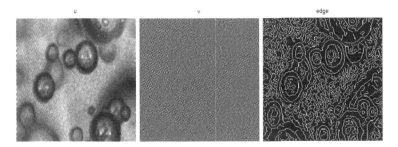

**Fig. 94.4** Decomposition by gradient model

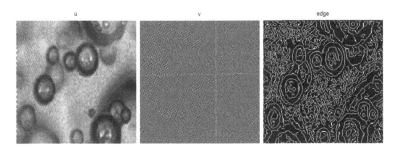

**Fig. 94.5** Decomposition by the proposed model

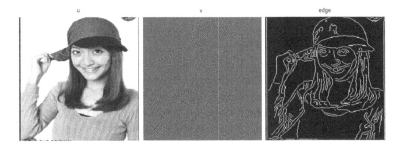

**Fig. 94.6** Decomposition by VO model

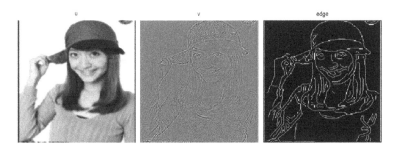

**Fig. 94.7** Decomposition by gradient model

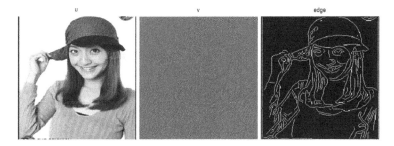

**Fig. 94.8** Decomposition by the proposed model

**Table 94.1** Time comparison of image 1

| Iterations | Proposed model (s) | VO model (s) | Gradient model (s) |
| --- | --- | --- | --- |
| 5 | 0.093698 | 1.262574 | 1.207288 |
| 10 | 1.317637 | 1.410671 | 1.381573 |
| 20 | 1.474170 | 1.524107 | 1.466513 |

**Table 94.2** Time comparison of image 2

| Iterations | Proposed model (s) | VO model (s) | Gradient model (s) |
| --- | --- | --- | --- |
| 5 | 0.915723 | 0.980335 | 1.088586 |
| 10 | 1.005751 | 1.022682 | 1.205024 |
| 20 | 1.043637 | 1.334557 | 1.270748 |

## 94.5 Concluding Remarks

In this paper, an improved model is proposed based on the VO model. It can improve the quality of image decomposition by introducing a function to detect the image edge and using the wavelet transform to decide whether diffusion or not in respective field, according to the feature of the given image. During the processing of decomposition, we refresh the image to the next iteration to reduce the executive time.

The experimental results show that the effect of decomposition is better than other two models, especially for the situation that features are extracted from textured image. Things about how to choose the parameters and wavelet family will be discussed in the future.

# References

1. Yan ZP, Yan GL (2012) Application of image decomposition model to medical image enhancement. Comput Syst Appl 21(2):185 (in Chinese)
2. He J, Ge H, Wang YF (2009) Survey on the methods of image segmentation research. Comput Eng Sci 12(31):58–61 (in Chinese)
3. Rudin L, Osher S, Fatemi E (1992) Nonlinear total variation based noise removal algorithms. Physica D 60:259–268
4. Meyer Y (2001) Oscillating patterns in image processing and nonlinear evolution equations. University Lecture Series, vol 22, pp 1047–3998
5. Mumford D, Shah J (1989) Optimal approximation by piecewise smooth functions and associated variational problems. Comm Pure Appl Math 42(5):577–685
6. Perona P, Malik J (1990) Scale-space and edge-detection using anisotropic diffusion. IEEE on PAMI 12(7):629–639
7. Vese LA, Osher SJ (2003) Modeling textures with total variation minimization and oscillating patterns in image processing. J Sci Comput 19(1–3):553–572
8. Li M, Xu C (2012) A multi-scale Image representation based on OSV decomposition. Acta Electronica Sinica 40(4):769–772
9. Liu F (2006) Diffusion filtering in image processing based on wavelet transform. Sci Chin Ser F 49(4):494–503 (in Chinese)
10. Catte F, Lion PL, Morel JM et al (1992) Image selective smoothing and edge detection by nonlinear diffusion. Siam Numer Anal 29(1):12–193
11. Zhang LN, Li XL, Tang GF (2008) Image decomposition methods based on PDE. Aeronautical Comput Tech 38(6):61–67 (in Chinese)
12. Che LX, Song GX, Ding XH et al (2009) Improved total variation algorithms to remove noise. Acta Photonica Sinica 38(4):1001–1004 (in Chinese)
13. Li NN (2006) An improvement of the algorithm in image decomposition and its applications. East China Normal University, Shanghai (in Chinese)

# Chapter 95
# Application of Binary Image Authentication Algorithm in Digital Watermarking

Wang Chunxian and Li Huishan

**Abstract** A novel fragile watermarking scheme is proposed using a hierarchical mechanism, in which the embedded watermark data are derived both from pixels and blocks. On the receiver side, one can first identify the blocks containing the tampered content, and then use the watermark hidden in the rest blocks to exactly locate the tampered pixels. By combining the advantages of both block-wise and pixel-wise techniques, the proposed scheme is capable of finding the detailed tampered positions even if the modified area is more extensive. Moreover, after localizing the tampered-pixel, the original watermarked version can be perfectly restored using. Experimental results show that the watermark can be blindly extracted, the proposed method can detect any modification to the watermarked image, and verify the ownership while the watermarked image is not manipulated.

**Keywords** Digital watermarking · Image authentication · Chaos encryption · Pixel spread deviation

## 95.1 Introduction

Rapid development and extensive use of computer network technique, communication technique and multimedia technique, especially the rocketing development of Internet, have made the security and protection of network information be a

W. Chunxian (✉)
Engineering Teach Practice Training Center, Tianjin Polytechnic University, Tianjin 300160, China
e-mail: wchunxian@163.com

L. Huishan
Department of Auto Engineering Military Traffic Academy, Tianjin 300161, China
e-mail: lihuishan65@163.com

W. Lu et al. (eds.), *Proceedings of the 2012 International Conference on Information Technology and Software Engineering*, Lecture Notes in Electrical Engineering 212, DOI: 10.1007/978-3-642-34531-9_95, © Springer-Verlag Berlin Heidelberg 2013

problem, which needs to be urgently resolved. The information hiding technique used as the main method for copyright protection and covert communication has been focused on the international information security field. Clear focus on protecting the fidelity, integrity and security of digital content, digital watermarking [1]as an effective scheme can be used in the modern electronically-driven world, especially suitable for fragile watermarking authentication of digital products [2], proof tamper and integrity of the content has aroused great attention.

The fragile watermark is one of the watermarking methods for authentication that has a low robustness toward modifications where even small changes of the content will destroy embedded information. The grayscale or color maps have been used for the fragile digital watermark, in addition, leading watermarking technology providers developed solutions for other emerging applications, such as using watermarks in digital cinema implementations to help law enforcement determine which specific theater a camcorder copy came from.

In this paper, the pixels in binary image are divided into two categories, one is the flippable pixels and another is the non-flippable pixels. In the watermark generation process, the non-flippable pixels are input into a Hash function for generating the authenticating signals which depends on the content of the image, and then the authenticating signals and the image ownership information are encoded with a chaotic sequence to form the watermark. The watermarked image can be obtained by inserting the watermark into the flippable pixels. With the wide range of applications of the binary image, the scholars binary image watermarking techniques were explored. In order to ensure sufficient amount of information embedded, which causes only minor visual differences, a typical algorithm is flip through the images in the spatial domain of individual pixels to embed a watermark. Literature [3] advanced the measure of pixels can be turned way. First of all, to establish the center of an image pixel divide $3 \times 3$ image blocks, the pixels can be turned was evaluated in grades by examining the flip-pixel image block connectivity and smoothness in the change of pixels, which in $3 \times 3$ image block lookup table can was generated from the data. Literature [4] defines the least significant pixel block (Least Significant Pixel Block, LSPB), which can be used to evaluate pixel flip, but only LSPB for the $3 \times 3$ image blocks defined. Literature [5] to overcome these disadvantages, advanced a method of calculating simple and easy to extend for measure of pixels can be turned, called the pixel spread deviation (pixel spread deviation, PSD).

## 95.2 Pixel Spread Deviation and Logistic Mapping

### 95.2.1 Pixel Spread Deviation

In the binary image, as a great visual contrast black and white, while change a pixel embedded in the Information, each pixel neighborhood pixels must be considered, otherwise any inappropriate changes will cause significant traces. In order to measure pixels d is flippable, in the literature [5], the concept of Pixel spread deviation (PSD) was proposed, which distinguishes the connectivity and smoothness of the image blocks.

Firstly, with the centre point d, the image block B with the size of $w \times w$ is object, where $w = 3, 5, 7, 9, \ldots$, All pixels values of the image block B recorded as $B(m, n)$, is for the pixels coordinates, $m = n = 1, 2, \ldots, w$, then the pixels d coordinates are $(m_c, m_c)$, where $m_c = n_c = (w + 1)/2$.

Suppose an average of image block B is $\mu$, then the deviation value of the pixels $B(m, n)$ is $\delta(m, n) = |B(m, n) - \mu|$. For measuring the pixels can be flippable, a weight matrix $W$ can be represented as:

$$W(m, n) = \begin{cases} 1 & m = m_c, n = n_c \\ \dfrac{1}{\sqrt{(m - m_c)^2 + (n - n_c)^2}} & other \end{cases} \tag{95.1}$$

Definition 1 image block B pixel spread (pixel spread, PS) can be formulated as follows:

$$PS = \sum_{m=1}^{w} \sum_{n=1}^{w} \delta(m, n) \cdot \mathbf{W}(m, n) \tag{95.2}$$

Definition 2 the centre point d of the image block B turned, pixel spread is $PS'$, so how the point A can be turned is measured by turning around the image pixel spread deviation (pixel spread deviation, PSD), expressed as:

$$PSD = |PS - PS'| \tag{95.3}$$

## 95.2.2 Logistic Mapping

There's certainty for chaos phenomenon in the nonlinear dynamic system, like stochastic process. This process is non-periodic, not convergence, but bounded, and the initial values is extremely sensitive dependence. To use the characteristic, chaotic mapping can provide the large number of the signal which is non-related or stochastic to be calculated or easy to produce and regenerate.

Despite the fact that Logistic mapping is a kind of very simple chaotic dynamical systems, Logistic map is extensively studied. With the nonlinear differential equations, it can be described as follows:

$$x_{n+1} = \lambda x_n (1 - x_n), \quad \lambda \in [0, 4], \quad x_n \in [0, 1] \tag{95.4}$$

Found: Two chaotic sequences $x_0, x_1, \ldots, x_n$ and $y_0, y_1, \ldots, y_n$ are generated by the two different initial $x_0$ and $y_0$ in Logistic mapping, which cross-correlation is zero. It reflects the Logistic chaotic mapping sensitivity to initial conditions. Where $\lambda = 4$, Logistic chaotic sequence of the mean is $\bar{x} = E\{x\} = 0.5$. The real value chaotic sequence can be translated into a binary "0" and "1" sequence by the threshold function $b_0(x)$.

$$b_0(x) = \begin{cases} 1, & x \geq 0.5 \\ 0 & x < 0.5 \end{cases} \tag{95.5}$$

## 95.3 Binary Image Authentication Watermark Embedding

Using the Hash function and the chaotic mapping, the binary image watermark generated and embedding processed are shown in Fig. 95.1.

### 95.3.1 Watermark Generating and Embedding Procedure

Step 1: divide the original image into non-overlapping blocks $w \times w$, which $w$ is the image block size used in PSD for the calculation of pixel. Using Eq. (95.3), PSD is calculated by each block $w \times w$ in the center point, according to the set threshold $\tau$, for $PSD \leq \tau$ the center point defined a flippable pixels, the others non-flippable pixels. Where $F$ represent the cover flippable pixels in the image $X$, the length of $F$ that is the number of pixels can be flippable denoted $M$.

Step 2: The image $X$ generated the watermark image process is shown in Fig. 95.1. All the flippable pixels point in $X$ are set for zero, to be $\tilde{X}$. In $\tilde{X}$ pixel value is recorded as $V_i, i = 1, 2, \ldots, N$, $N$ is the pixels number. All the pixels $V_i$ input as a Hash function MD5, 128 bits length the authentication information of a image $R$ is obtained.

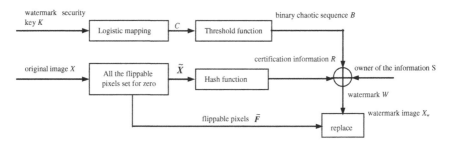

**Fig. 95.1** Watermark generating and embedding

Step 3: Setting $k$ is a security key for the entire watermark for the system, with $k \in (0,1)$. $k$ is required initial value into chaos iterative Eq. (95.4), resulting in the real sequence $C$ of length $M$, then into the Eq. (95.5) the binary chaotic sequence $B$ is obtained.

Step 4: In order to achieve the image owner's certification, the owner of the information $S$ is required embedded in the image. First authentication information $R$ and the owner of the information $S$ are encoded as a length $M$ repeating the information $R'$ and $S'$,then use binary chaotic sequence to encrypt the information and get the watermark information,

$$W = B \oplus R' \oplus S' \qquad (95.6)$$

where, $\oplus$ representation exclusive or.

Step 5: The watermark information $W$ replace the flippable pixels $F$ according to the order of left to right and top to bottom position, to accomplish the embedded watermark. The watermark image $X_w$ has been obtained.

## 95.3.2 Watermark Detection

All flippable pixels $\tilde{F}$ is selected in the watermark image $X_w$ Passing through step 1. By step 2, the image authentication information is obtained, then after step 3 the binary chaotic sequence $\tilde{B}$ is obtained by watermark key $k$, at length according as repeated coding the owner the information $\tilde{S}$ is obtained as follows:

$$\tilde{S} = \tilde{B} \oplus \tilde{R} \oplus \tilde{F} \qquad (95.7)$$

$\tilde{S}$ is decoded to the same size $\bar{S}$ as the original information owner, any pixels of the image tampered will cause the image authentication information changes. Utilizing the unilateralization of Hash function, even though a small change, authentication information would be a completely different. It will induce completely different between the authentication information extraction $\bar{S}$ and the owner original information $S$. If a secret key is wrong, even very small differences in the original secret key, the chaotic mapping is extreme sensitivity to the initial value, it will cause completely different between encryption chaos sequences $B$ and $\tilde{B}$, and resulted that the $\bar{S}$ is differ from the $S$. Only using the correct secret key, without any treatment in the watermarked image can be extracted correctly owner information. The result of image authentication is judged as follows:

1. If the extracted information $\bar{S}$ to reflect the binary image owner information, it is judgment that the binary image has not been tampered with, through certification.

Many wavelet based methods have been proposed in [12]–[18]. In [12], both the host image and the watermark image are transformed into wavelet domain as multiresolution representation. Then the different resolutions of watermark are embedded into corresponding resolutions of host image except the lowest frequency sub-band and higher frequency sub-band. Hence the distortion after watermarking is small. And the watermark can survive after JPEG compression. However, the robustness of common filtering attacks is not discussed in these papers. In [13], the

**(a)**                                              **(b)**

**Fig. 95.2** **a** Binary English image. **b** Ownership image

2. If the extracted information $\bar{S}$ similar to the noise, not to reflect any information related with the image owner, it is judgment that the binary image was tampered with, not through certification.

## 95.4 Experimental Results

To illustrate the effectiveness of this algorithm, Matlab simulation results are given by the algorithm. All simulation is based on the image, for binary images and its owner information image as shown in Figs. 95.2a and 95.2b. Assume watermark key $k = 0.2$, $\lambda = 4$ and threshold $\tau = 0.8$.

### 95.4.1 The Invisibility of the Watermark

The fragile watermark is first important feature is invisible. In order to measure the watermark image and the difference between the original image, using SSIM investigated the visual similarity between the original image and the watermark images [6]. The similarity of the two different images from the image brightness, contrast and structure of the three aspects is investigated by the SSIM. The theoretical and experimental verify it in line with the human visual system, and applies to any two of the same length of signal, defined as follows:

$$SSIM = \frac{(2\mu_x\mu_y + C_1)(2\sigma_{xy} + C_2)}{(\mu_x^2 + \mu_y^2 + C_1)(\sigma_x^2 + \sigma_y^2 + C_2)} \tag{95.8}$$

where, $\mu_x$ and $\mu_y$ are the mean respective of the signals $x$ and $y$, $\sigma_x$ and $\sigma_y$ are the standard deviation respective of the signals $x$ and $y$, $C_1$ and $C_2$ are much smaller than a constant 1. $\sigma_{xy}$ is the estimated correlation coefficient of the signal $x$ and $y$, the discrete region can be expressed as:

**Fig. 95.3** SSIM varies with
the threshold $\tau$

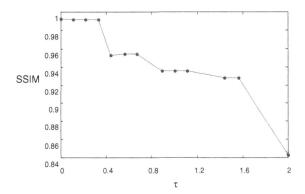

$$\sigma_{xy} = \frac{1}{N-1} \sum_{i=1}^{N} (\mathbf{x}_i - \mu_x)(\mathbf{y}_i - \mu_y) \tag{95.9}$$

Which, $N$ is the length of the signal $x$ and $y$.

As the length of the watermark information is the relevant with the threshold $\tau$, it will affect the SSIM, the changes of the SSIM with threshold $\tau$ should be tested. It can be seen in Fig. 95.3, the SSIM presented with the detection value $\tau$ changes in the overall decline, SSIM value is more close to 1 and the two images are visually more similar. At that time $\tau < 1.2$, SSIM value of large and stable is close to 1.

## 95.4.2 The Integrity Certification of the Binary Image

Binary images of the different English tampering, including deleting, replacing and increasing etc., the integrity of the certification results of the image is shown in Fig. 95.4. Experimental results show that this paper can correctly authenticate the integrity of the image. In the case of the image has not been processed, the owner and the original owner of the images extracted are the same as in Fig. 95.4b, it shows the image through the certification. When the watermarked image has been tampered with, the owner of the image extracted will be similar to the noise, shown in Fig. 4c, that the algorithm has a strong sensitivity of image tamperingit shows. In addition, using the key of k = 0.2001 that a very small difference with the original key, the owner of the information extracted would be similar to noise, shown in Fig. 95.4d, that is only using the watermark key can accurately extract watermark, to achieve the integrity of the binary image and the owner of the two-factor authentication.

**Fig. 95.4 a** Watermarked image without altering. **b** Ownership image with correct key and no-altered image. **c** Ownership image with correct key and altered image. **d** Ownership image with wrong key and altered image

Many wavelet based methods have been proposed in [12]–[18]. In [12], both the host image and the watermark image are transformed into wavelet domain as multiresolution representation. Then the different resolutions of watermark are embedded into corresponding resolutions of host image except the lowest frequency sub-band and higher frequency sub-band. Hence the distortion after watermarking is small. And the watermark can survive after JPEG compression. However, the robustness of common filtering attacks is not discussed in these papers. In [13], the

**(b)**

**(c)**

**(a)**

**(d)**

## 95.5 Conclusion

A new algorithm for the application of digital watermarking binary image integrity verification has been proposed. The image can be flipped pixels as input to the hash function to generate the watermark, and the watermark substitute flipped pixels, to achieve the watermark embedding and blind detection. The algorithm is simple and has good invisibility of the watermark, strong sensitivity of the image tampering. It does not require any additional information to achieve the integrity of the authentication and ownership verification for the binary image. In addition, the owner of the information and the authentication information are encrypted by using of chaotic sequences, even small differences in the key lead to certification information and owner information is radically different from, to ensure the security of the algorithm.

## References

1. Tefas A, Pitas L (2000) Image authentication using chaotic mixing systems. In: Proceedings of 2000 IEEE international conference on circuits and systems: symposium. Geneva: IEEE 1:216–219
2. Ho CK, Li C-T (2004) Semi-fragile watermarking scheme for authentication of JPEG images. In: Proceedings of 2004 IEEE international conference on information technology: coding and computing. Las Vegas, Nevada: IEEE 1:7–11
3. Min W, Bede L (2004) Data hiding in binary image for authentication and annotation. Multimedia, IEEE Transactions on, August 2004. 6(4):528–538
4. Congxu Z, Zhigang C (2006) Sensitive chaotic fragile watermarking technique for binary images verification. Mini-micro systems (1):151–154
5. Zhaohong L, Jianjun H, Song W (2008) Binary document image authentication watermarking technique based on hierarchical structure. Acta automatica sinica 8:841–848
6. Wang Z, Bovik AC (2004) Image quality assessment: from error visibility to structural similarity. IEEE Trans Image Process 13(4):600–612

# Chapter 96
# A Novel Audio Information Hiding Scheme based on rMAC

Litao Yu, Liehuang Zhu, Dan Liu and Yuzhou Xie

**Abstract** We present a novel audio information hiding scheme based on robust message authentication code (rMAC). By combining coefficient quantization based information hiding scheme with rMAC and chaotic encryption, proposed scheme can ensure the content integrity and the confidentiality of the embedded audio as well as secret communication. Experimental results show that our scheme provides highly robust authentication against content preserving degradations. When 30 % noise added into the transporting message, 92.50 % audio communication can also succeed.

**Keywords** Information hiding · Robust message authentication code (rMAC) · Human auditory system (HAS) · High embedding capacity · High robust · Content integrity

L. Yu (✉) · L. Zhu · D. Liu · Y. Xie
Beijing Engineering Research Center of Massive Language Information Processing and Cloud Computing Application, School of Computer Science and Technology, Beijing Institute of Technology, Beijing 100086, China
e-mail: taotaotim@163.com

L. Zhu
e-mail: liehuangz@bit.edu.cn

D. Liu
e-mail: liudanking@bit.edu.cn

Y. Xie
e-mail: xyz910119xyz@163.com

W. Lu et al. (eds.), *Proceedings of the 2012 International Conference on Information Technology and Software Engineering*, Lecture Notes in Electrical Engineering 212, DOI: 10.1007/978-3-642-34531-9_96, © Springer-Verlag Berlin Heidelberg 2013

## 96.1 Introduction

Nowadays, voice communication has been all over around us. Telephone, one of the most representative types of voice communication, has been part of our life. As the development of the Internet, voice communication software based on Internet is springing up recent years. To make sure the safety of the communication, people used only encryption in the past. However, communication security includes not only data security but also traffic security whose essence lies in hiding the very existence of the communication [1]. So people presented the information hiding scheme. This scheme can hide the communication well, but till now all researchers considered just the traffic security but forgetted the data security, including the confidentiality and the integrity of the data. Some people tried to use traditional message authentication code (MAC) to ensure the audio content integrity. However, it is not robust and can't tell the audio content integrity because this code can't care anything about the audio's content.

To solve the problem above, we present a safe audio information hiding scheme based on robust message authentication code (rMAC). This scheme realize secret communication by embedding cryptographic collected audio, which is called secret audio, into base audio which has nothing to do with the secret audio. In the scheme, we use discrete cosine transform (DCT) domain based information hiding scheme based on coefficient quantization. This scheme is high robust and has high embedding capacity. And it can realize blind detection. Also, to make sure our scheme realize data confidentiality, we use selective chaotic encryption. And we present using rMAC to tell the audio content integrity for the first time. The whole scheme can guarantee both the traffic security and the data security.

## 96.2 Related Work

The classification of information hiding methods can be divided into time/spatial domain methods and transformation domain methods. The time/spatial domain methods, such as Tirkel's least significant bit (LSB) [2, 3] and Bender's Patchwork [4] algorithm. Jiang et al. [5] gave an similar patchwork in the wavelet domain. However they are not robust even for some legitimate transformation or compression. The transformation domain methods, such as [6] discrete cosine transform (DCT), [7] discrete wavelet transform (DWT), [8] discrete fourier transform (DFT) methodology are much more robust than the former.

Cox et al. [9] proposed the first transformation domain watermarking method based on spread-spectrum idea using DCT. J. W Huang et al. [10] presented a watermarking method based on two dimensional DCT, and Wu et al. [11] presented another method based on three dimensional DCT. But these methods are hard to realize blind detection, which means during the watermarking detection step, both the original information and watermark are required.

Chen and Wornell et al. [12] firstly gave a theoretical analysis of quantization watermarking and they found that according to the idea of Costa's dirty paper, quantization watermarking can get a relatively big capacity. Akhaee et al. [13] presented a quantization based audio watermarking scheme in a new transform domain.

Jaap Haitsma et al. [14] presented a high robust audio authentication system. Sascha Zmudzinski and Martin Steinebach et al. [15] presented an audio authentication watermarking algorithm based on Jaap's. This algorithm can produce human auditory system (HAS) based authentication code which has fixed length and can have password. Our scheme's audio feature extracting is based on this algorithm. Also others have presented several other features extracting scheme. Saad et al. [16] proposed a scheme using multi-scale feature that exploits the scalability of a structural digital signature in order to achieve a good trade-off between security and image transfer for networked image applications. In [17], the authors presented a robust and efficient signature scheme based on binary authentication tree (BAT), the proposed scheme requires approximately $(k + 1)\log(n/k) + 4k - 2$ time-consuming pairing operations.

## 96.3 rMAC Based Audio Information Hiding Scheme

In this part, we'll introduce the scheme. Firstly, the whole scheme structure will be shown. Then in the next 4 parts, we'll explain the main innovation points of the scheme.

### 96.3.1 Scheme Structure

The structure of the whole scheme is shown in Fig. 96.1. For the original secret audios, we will encrypt it with selective chaotic encryption and embed it into the base audio together with secret audio's rMAC. This flow produces an audio with secret audio embedded, which is shown in Fig. 96.1a.

For an unknowned audio, we can try to extract audio from it. Then we decrypt the extracted audio and calculate its rMAC. This rMAC will be compared with the extracted rMAC' and calculate matching degree, as shown in Fig. 96.1b. It means that the audio content is integrity and credible if the matching degree is close to 1. Otherwise, it means that the audio content has been destroyed if the matching degree is close to 0.5.

In the scheme, we combine coefficient quantization based information hiding scheme, chaotic encryption and rMAC to realize the safe communication.

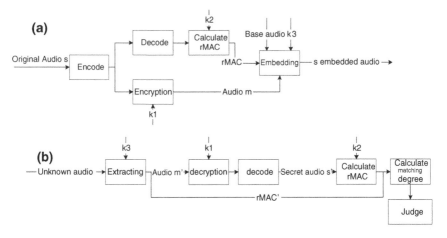

**Fig. 96.1** Structure of the whole scheme

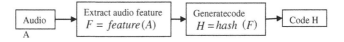

**Fig. 96.2** Generate message authentication code

## 96.3.2 Human Auditory System Based Robust Message Authentication Code

Our message authentication code is generated as in Fig. 96.2.

The generation includes two main parts: the audio feature's extraction and robust message authentication code (rMAC's) generation. For extraction, we use discrete fourier transform (DFT) to get the frequency information of the audio. For a certain quantity of the audio sample, we use DFT to get its frequency domain and calculate every frequency bands's energy sum. These sums are the feature we extract.

To get a robust code, we have to select a good hash function to calculate H. The function we select is as following:

$$H(m) = \begin{cases} 1, & if\ e(t_{m,1}, k_{m,1}) - e(t_{m,2}, k_{m,2}) > 0 \\ 0, & if\ e(t_{m,1}, k_{m,1}) - e(t_{m,2}, k_{m,2}) \le 0 \end{cases}$$

$k_{m,1}, k_{m,2}, t_{m,1}, t_{m,2}$ are coefficients that can be randomly selected as keys. Function $e(t,k)$ is energy function, which return the feature we extract above. $H(m)$ is the m's bit of the result code.

Our rMAC is based on human auditory system (HAS). This means that when the matching degree is between 0.5 and 1, the bigger the matching degree is, the more similar the original audio and the extracted audio is. So the rMAC can correctly reflect audio content integrity.

### 96.3.3 Selected Chaotic Encryption

Chaotic system is sensitive to the initial value, and a small difference in initial value can be enlarged a lot by the system. This phenomenon is called "butterfly effect". As a result, the system can't be predicted. And chaotic sequence has good statistical properties. These advantages makes the chaotic sequence can be used in encryption.

We then learned a lot about the Speex audio encoding scheme and we find the Speex's data contains lots of unimportant data and a little important data. So when using chaotic encryption, we only encrypt the important data. This scheme is very effective and can destroy audio content.

### 96.3.4 Coefficient Quantization Based Safety Audio Information Hiding Scheme

Audio embedding is realized by using discrete cosine transform (DCT). In the DCT domain, we select the coefficients with high energy to quantize. This makes our scheme more robust and secret.

We suppose that: the coefficient to be quantized is $f$; the quantization distance is $p$; the bit to be embedded is $W$; the quantized coefficient is $f'$. The quantization regions are divided in Fig. 96.3.

We divide the regions into two classes, A and B, as shown in Fig. 96.3. When $W$ equals 1, we quantize $f$ as the nearest region A's midpoint. When $W$ equals 0, we quantize $f$ as the nearest region B's midpoint. When trying to extracting $W$, we see where the quantized coefficient $f'$ is. If $f'$ is in region A, then extracted $W$ is 1. Otherwise $W$ is 0.

### 96.3.5 Speex Encoding Scheme with High Quality and Low Bitrate

Speex is a kind of code excited linear prediction (CELP) encoding scheme. CELP encoding contains linear prediction and code excited two parts:

1. Linear prediction is calculated by following formula:

$$y[n] = \sum_{i=1}^{N} a_i x[n-1]$$

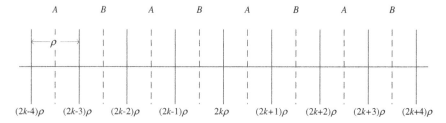

**Fig. 96.3** Quantization regions division

In the formula, x[n] is the nth sample's real value and y[n] is the nth sample's predict value. This formula shows that the linear prediction is using N samples before to predict the current value.

2. Code excited is calculated by following formula:

$$e[n] = p[n] + c[n] = \beta e[n - T] + c[n]$$

In the formula, e[n] is the nth sample's excited. $\beta$ is the improvement and T is the excited period, which is much larger than N in linear prediction. This part is based on the periodicity of the audio wave. c[n] is a static codebook, which is got by experience.

## 96.4 Experimental Evaluations

Our chaotic sequence is the Logistic mapping:

$$x_{k+1} = \mu x_k (1 - x_k), 0 \le \mu \le 4, x_k \in (0, 1)$$

When trying to realize the experiment, we use the miracle to do the calculation, to ensure the precision of the result. And to ensure the randomizing of the sequence, we drop several data in the front of the sequence. We realize encryption by x or the original data and the sequence data. And the decryption is the same.

We set the initial value as 0.10001, which can be set randomly as key. The values generated by the chaotic sequence with 0.10001 as initial value are shown in Fig. 96.4. We can find that when the value is above 0.9 or below 0.1, the values are relatively concentrated. So we set two threshold values to make sure our sequency's random.

In the experiment, we simulate a noisy communication environment. We separately add different noise intensity to the transporting audio and compare the result between bit error rate (BER). Table 96.1 show the experiment result.

The experiment shows that as the noise intensity increasing, the difference between extracted audio and original audio increase too. But they hear similar. Our

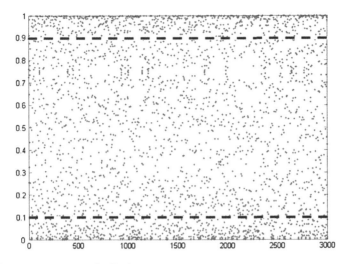

**Fig. 96.4** Chaotic sequence distribution

**Table 96.1** 1,000 times' noisy communication result

| noise intensity (%) | BER | | | | rMAC matching degree | | | |
|---|---|---|---|---|---|---|---|---|
| | Max | min | Average | <0.1 (%) | Max | min | Average | >0.9 (%) |
| 1 | 0 | 0 | 0 | 100 | 1 | 1 | 1 | 100 |
| 10 | 0.3672 | 0 | 0.1086 | 48.60 | 1 | 0.3329 | 0.9945 | 98.70 |
| 30 | 0.3984 | 0.0156 | 0.1615 | 25.30 | 1 | 0.1453 | 0.9611 | 92.50 |

scheme can show this result but BER can't. And our scheme can directly and correctly show the audio content integrity even if the noise is loud.

And if the receivers don't have keys, experiment shows that the audio they extract contains only noise without any content, and the rMAC is close to 0.5.

## 96.5 Conclusions and Future Work

Our information hiding scheme combines rMAC, quantization watermarking and chaotic encryption. These makes our scheme realizes a safety voice communication system, which guarantees both the traffic security and the data security.

In the future, we'll try to improve the embedding capacity more to decrease the voice communication's traffic cost. Currently, our scheme's keys are private keys. We'll try to apply digital signature on our scheme to realize a content integrity authentication algorithm based on public keys.

# References

1. Fabien APP, Ross JA, Markus GK (1999) Information hiding—a survey. In: Proceedings if the IEEE, July 1999, 87(7):1062–1078
2. Tirkel AZ, Rankin GA, Van Schynel RM, Ho WJ, Osborne NR (1993) Electronic watermark. Digital image computing, technology and application DICTA 93. Maquarie University, Sidney pp 666–6673
3. Schydel RG, Tirkel AZ, Osborne CF. A digital watermark. first IEEE international image processing conference. University of Texas, Austin 2:86–90
4. Bender W (1996) Techniques for data hiding. IBM Syst J 35:313–336
5. JiangJ-J, Pun C-M (2010) Digital audio watermarking using an improved patchwork method in wavelet domain. Digital content, multimedia technology and its applications (IDC), 2010 6th international conference on, pp 386–389, 16–18 Aug 2010
6. Cox IJ, Kilian J, Leighton T, Shamoon T (1997) Secure spread spectrum watermarking for multimedia. IEEE Trans Image Process 6(12):1673–1687
7. Tsekeridou S, Pitas I (2001) Embedding self-similar watermarking in the wavelet domain. IEEE international conferences on acoustics technology. Institute of Electrical and Electronics Engineers Inc., Piscataway 4:321–325
8. Solachidis V, Nikolaidis N, Pitas I (2004) Watermarking polygonal lines using fourier descripters. IEEE Comput Graphics Appl 24(3):44–51
9. Cox IJ, Kilian J, Leighton T, Shamoon T (1996) Secure spread spectrum watermarking for images, audio and video. In: Proceedings of the 1996 IEEE international conference in image processing. IEEE, Los Alamitos, CA 6:243–246
10. Huan JW, Shi YQ (2001) Embedding bray level images. The 2001 IEEE international symposium on circuits and systems 5:239–242
11. Wu YH, Guan X, Kankanhalli MS (2001) robust invisible watermarking of volume data using 3D DCT. Comput Graph 1:359–362
12. Chen B, Wornell GW (1999) Provably robust digital watermarking. Processing of the 1999 multimedia systems and applications. Society of Photo-Optical Instrumentation Engineers, Bellingham, 3845:43–54
13. Akhaee MA, Nikooienejad A, Marvasti F (2008) Quantization based audio watermarking in a new transform domain. Telecommunications
14. Haitsma JA, Oostveen JC, Kalker AAC (2001) A highly robust audio fingerprinting system. In: 2nd international symposium of music information retrieval (ISMIR 2001), Indiana University, Bloomington, Indiana, Oct 15–17
15. Zmudzinski S, Steinebach M (2009) Perception-based audio authentication watermarking in the time-frequency domain. Information hiding conference, 2009, LNCS 5806:146–160
16. Saad SM (2009) Design of a robust and secure digital signature scheme for image authentication over wireless channels. Inf Secur, IET 3(1):1–8
17. Jiang Y, Shi M, Shen X, Lin C (2009) BAT: a robust signature scheme for vehicular networks using binary authentication tree. IEEE Trans Wireless Commun 8(4):1974–1983

# Chapter 97
# An Approach to Computer 3D Modeling of Horizon with Complex Faults

Leiyin Jiao, Hongzhuan Lei, Ziliang Yu, Li Luo and Tao He

**Abstract** The 3D modeling of horizon based on complex faults has always been a difficult issue. Adequately considering the barrier effect of faults, the deficiency of data on some horizon subset zones and previous research results, this paper proposes a new modeling method based on fault plane. This method firstly generates fault plane by fault line, then fits horizon based on fault plane data, that is to say, uses fault plane data as reference data to assist to compute when there are deficient data on some subset blocks of horizon. The effect of practical application using this method shows that this method well handles the model of horizon with complicated distribution of faults, which may include normal fault, reverse fault, cross fault or their mixture, and perfectly represents the distribution of horizon.

**Keywords** 3D modeling of horizon · Fault plane · Subset block · Reverse fault · Cross fault

## 97.1 Introduction

Because of the complication of the fault distribution, the research about the 3D modeling of horizon based on faults has always been a difficult issue. The main methods of processing faults are as follows: a method based on blocking, a method based on fault plane, horizon recovery method, fault trajectory method and so on [1], however, any of these methods cannot deal with the problem very well. In

L. Jiao (✉) · H. Lei · Z. Yu · L. Luo · T. He
China University of Mining and Technology, Xue yuan Road Ding 11, 100083 Beijing, China
e-mail: jiaoli666@163.com

W. Lu et al. (eds.), *Proceedings of the 2012 International Conference on Information Technology and Software Engineering*, Lecture Notes in Electrical Engineering 212, DOI: 10.1007/978-3-642-34531-9_97, © Springer-Verlag Berlin Heidelberg 2013

recent years, a segmentation process, $D^m$-splines and the finite element method [2], is used to approximate surfaces with faults; The potential field method was designed to build 3D geological models [3]; Using empirical geological rules to reduce structural uncertainty in seismic interpretation of faults [4]; Treating the faultage as boundary when interpolating the stratum spatial [5]; Using a simple plane to simulate the fault or multiple combined planes to approximate the fault [6], which can simulate the whole fault plane but not the fault plane in some horizon. All of these methods need adequate horizon sample points as the prerequisite, and some of them are very difficult to implement.

In this paper, we propose a novel modeling method based on fault plane. This method is not only competent in the situation of deficient horizon data, but also considers the influence caused by the interception of faults, and it also can automatically establish modeling by computer. The effect of practical application shows that this method works effectively.

## 97.2 Modeling Theory and Flow Chart

### 97.2.1 Modeling Theory

The smooth horizon becomes not smooth under the influence of faults, so the entire fitting of horizon cannot be implemented. If use the way of blocking the horizon into many subset zones, it would be difficult to partition the subset zones, and the situation that there are deficient sample data points in some blocks may appear. Though the traditional method based on fault plane can handle the model of the horizon with faults [7], it needs lots of sample data to build the grid of the fault plane and horizon plane, which is hard to implement in the practical situation, and it will become complex when there are many faults in the horizon.

Based on the above discussion, this paper brings up a new modeling method based on fault plane, the steps of which are as follows:

1. Using the fault line data, fault attribute data and selected fault shape to compute fault throw of every point in the fault line.
2. Generate the intersecting lines of fault and the two sides of horizon according to the fault line and the fault throw computed on step 1 and construct the fault plane of fault in the horizon.
3. Treat the connection of different fault planes according to fault attribute and obtain practical distribution of every fault.
4. Fit the horizon grid data. The search strategy is that the points which are fitted and the sample data points of horizon can not be over fault planes, that is to say, they must be located on the same side of fault plane. If there are deficient even no sample data points searched when fitting grid data points of horizon, then use the reference data to assist to compute.

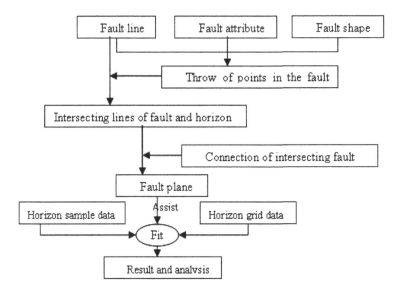

**Fig. 97.1** Flow chart of 3D modeling of horizon with faults

## 97.2.2 Modeling Flow Chart

The modeling flow is as follows: (Fig. 97.1)

## 97.3 Modeling Process

### 97.3.1 Compute the Fault Throw of Points in the Fault Line

The fault line is the intersecting line (or middle line) of fault and the hanging wall (or footwall) of horizon. Based on large number of field study and the theoretic research, the most concordant recognition in the present is that the relationship between the strike length L and the maximum displacement D of faults is as follows [8]:

$$D = cL^n, \quad 0.5 \leq n \leq 2 \tag{97.1}$$

where c is a constant related to material properties.

Hence, this paper has mainly divided the shape of fault plane into shape 'V' (or triangle) and ellipse. According to fault data, the correspondent fault throw of every point in the fault line can be obtained. The concrete computation process is as follows:

Assume that the maximum throw of fault is H, the points in the fault line are $fp_1(x_1, y_1, c)$, $fp_2(x_2, y_2, c)$, ..., $fp_n(x_n, y_n, c)$, c represents a constant (Fig. 97.2c).

Find out the length $s$ of the polygonal line which is obtained by connecting every point together in the fault line and the place of the midpoint $fp_0(x_0, y_0, c)$ of the polygonal line, which is assumed to locate between $fp_k(x_k, y_k, c)$ and $fp_{k+1}(x_{k+1}, y_{k+1}, c)$ (Fig. 97.2c), then the polygonal distance $d_{i,0}$ between a point $fp_i(x_i, y_i, c)$ in the fault line and the midpoint $fp_0(x_0, y_0, c)$ is as follows:

$$d_{i,0} = \begin{cases} \frac{s}{2} - \sum_{m=1}^{i-1} \sqrt{(x_m - x_{m+1})^2 + (y_m - y_{m+1})^2} & , i \leq k \\ \sum_{m=1}^{i-1} \sqrt{(x_m - x_{m+1})^2 + (y_m - y_{m+1})^2} - \frac{s}{2} & , i > k \end{cases} \tag{97.2}$$

$$s = \sum_{i=1}^{n-1} \sqrt{(x_{i+1} - x_i)^2 + (y_{i+1} - y_i)^2} \tag{97.3}$$

The computation formula of the fault throw $h_i$ in the point $fp_i(x_i, y_i, c)$ is as follows:

If the fault plane is triangular (Fig. 97.2a):

$$h_i = H\left(1 - \frac{d_{i,0}}{s/2}\right) \tag{97.4}$$

If the fault plane is ellipse (Fig. 97.2b):

$$\left(\frac{h_i}{H}\right)^2 + \left(\frac{d_{i,0}}{s/2}\right)^2 = 1 \tag{97.5}$$

If the fault is not pinch-out, we make one or two virtual end points in the fault line, and compute their outspread distance accordingly (see Fig. 97.3), the next process is similarly as above discussion.

## 97.3.2 Compute the Intersecting Lines of Fault and Horizon

Fault line may be the intersecting line of fault and the hanging wall (or footwall) of horizon, or the middle line of fault and horizon by fitted using computer. Here we

**Fig. 97.2** Fault plane figure of faults whose two ends are pinch-out **a** Fault plane of triangle **b** Fault plane of ellipse **c** Practicle fault plane

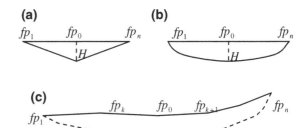

**Fig. 97.3** Measure for fault which are not pinch-out **a** Triangle plane **b** Ellipse plane

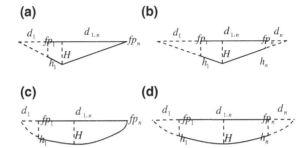

assume that the fault line is the middle line of fault and horizon (Fig. 97.4a), the other condition can be considered similarly, then the intersecting line of fault and the hanging wall, and the intersecting line of fault and footwall of horizon can be computed according to the fault attribute data and the fault line data. The detailed computing process is as follows:

Take the point $f_2$ (Fig. 97.4a) for example, the section figure and plane figure are shown in Fig. 97.4b and c, respectively. From these two figures, we have,

$$(x - x_2)^2 + (y - y_2)^2 = (\frac{h/2}{\tan \alpha})^2 \tag{97.6}$$

$$\frac{y - y_2}{x - x_2} = \tan \beta \tag{97.7}$$

There $\alpha$ is the dip angle of fault, $\beta$ is the trend angle of fault, $h$ is the throw distance of fault. Further more, we know that $|z - z_2| = h/2$. So we can compute

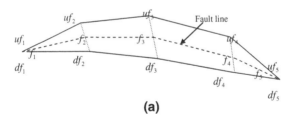

**(a)**

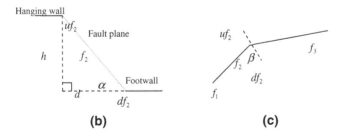

**Fig. 97.4** Compute the intersecting lines of fault and the two sides of horizon **a** Fault line **b** Section figure **c** Plane figure

the intersecting point $uf_2$ and $df_2$ of fault and the two sides of horizon from these formulas above.

Therefore, according to the direction of fault dip, angle of fault dip, the fault line data and its correspondent fault throw, we can compute the intersecting lines of fault and the two sides of horizon. From the compute process, we can see that it is also applicable if it is a reverse fault.

### 97.3.3 Fit Horizon

After computing the intersecting lines of fault and the two sides of horizon, we actually get the fault plane of fault in the horizon. If there exist two or more faults which intersect each other, we need treat the connection of different fault planes and obtain practical distribution of every fault.

Before fitting the horizon, we need choose one appropriate spatial fitting method, such as IDW Method, Multiquadric method, RBF Gauss method, or sequential gaussian simulation method, and so on [9]. Here we take a method called Cross-Validation as the appraise criterion to judge which is the optimum method for interpolating the horizon.

According the result of Cross-Validation, we choose the optimum method, grid the horizon, and take the search strategy of not over the fault plane to fit the grid point of horizon, that is to say, a sample point can be selected to fit the grid point only if it and the grid point are located in some side of the fault plane. If there are deficient sample points in some subset zones of horizon, use the intersecting line points of the generated fault plane as the reference data to assist to compute in the interpolation process.

## 97.4 Application on Practical Examples

### 97.4.1 Example 1

A 7# coal bed of some mine in southwest of CHINA: There are 10 normal faults with different sizes are located in this horizon, interlacing with each other, and one of the faults develops from the others, the distribution of fault is very complex, but sample points of horizon are scarce, even there are no sample points in some subset zones of horizon (see Fig. 97.5a). Taking the new method to compute the model of horizon, the result by the cross-validation method is: the average deviation of the estimated elevation values and the actual values of sample points is − 0.119132, and the standard deviation is 1.6177. It can be speculated from the result of cross-validation that the effect of this method is significant. The 3D figure of horizon with faults is shown in Fig. 97.5b and c.

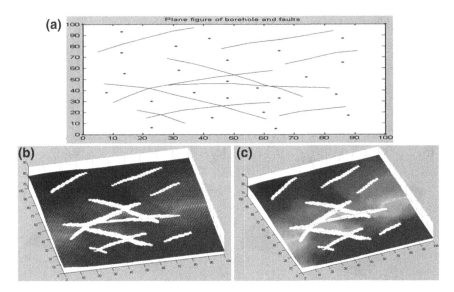

**Fig. 97.5** Example 1 for application of the new modeling method. **a** Planar distribution of borehole points and fault lines. **b** 3D grid drawing of horizon. **c** 3D shadow drawing of horizon

## 97.4.2  Example 2

A 3# coal bed of some mine in northwest of CHINA: There are two large reverse faults in the research zone, several normal faults with interlacing distribution, even some faults are not pinch-out in the research zone. Sample points of the horizon are scarce and relatively centralized, and there are no sample points in some subset zones of horizon (see Fig. 97.6a). Use the new method proposed by this paper to fit the model of horizon, the result by the cross-validation method is: the average deviation of the estimated values and the actual values of sample points is 0.09748, and the standard deviation is 0.1481, and shows that this new method is applicable. Figure 97.6b and c show the grid and shadow figure of the final simulated horizon, respectively.

## 97.5  Conclusion

Interpolation of horizon based on complex faults has always been a difficult issue. On the basis of previous researches, this paper proposes a new method based on fault plane generated by interpolation, which does not only adequately consider the distribution of faults, but also considers the barrier effect of faults, and overcomes the defect of deficient data in some subset zones of horizon. From the effect of application in practical examples, we can see that this method can be used to interpolate the horizon with complicated distribution of faults, which may include

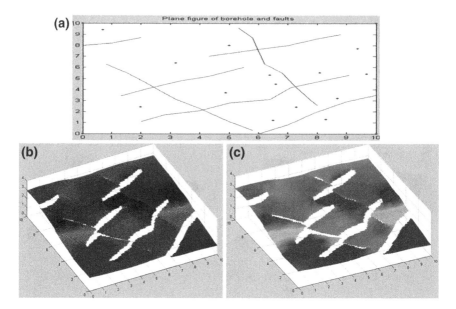

**Fig. 97.6** Example 2 for application of the new modeling method. **a** Planar distribution of borehole points and fault lines. **b** 3D grid drawing of horizon. **c** 3D shadow drawing of horizon

a multiple of normal faults, reverse faults, intersecting faults or their mixture, and perfectly represents the distribution of horizon. Moreover, the fitting error of this method is small, the extent of its automatic design is high.

**Acknowledgments** This work was supported by National Natural Science Foundation of China (Major Program) (50490271) and the National Science and Technology Pillar Program in the Eleventh Five-year Plan Period (2012BAB13B01). The authors are thankful for the help and support from Professor Suping Peng on the subject.

# References

1. Wang J H, Gao HY, Zhou Y (1999) Kriging geological mapping technique. Petroleum Industry Press, pp 250–262 (in Chinese)
2. Gout C, Le Guyader C, Romani L, Saint-Guirons AG (2008) Approximation of surfaces with fault(s) and/or rapidly varying data, using a segmentation process, Dm-splines and the finite element method. Numer Algorithms 48:67–92
3. Calcagno P, Chiles JP, Courrioux G, Guillen A (2008) Geological modeling from field data and geological knowledge Part I. Modeling method coupling 3D potential-field interpolation and geological rules. Phys Earth Planet Inter 171:147–157
4. Brett F, Peter JB, Graham Y, Sandy M (2010) Using empirical geological rules to reduce structural uncertainty in seismic interpretation of faults. J Struct Geol 32:1668–1676
5. Fan YG, Zhang L, Sun YF (2010) The stratum spatial interpolation algorithms with faultage. In: International conference on mechanic automation and control engineering, pp. 5143–5147

6. Wu Q, Xu H (2003) An approach to computer modeling and visualization of geological faults in 3D. Comput Geosci 29:503–509
7. Zhu LF, He Z, Pan X, Wu XC (2006) An approach to computer modeling of geological faults in 3d and an application. J China Univ Min Tech (English edn). Vol 16, No. 4, pp 461–465. (in Chinese) (Dec)
8. Xu SS, Nieto-Samaniego AF, Velasquillo-Martinez LG et al (2011) Factors influencing the fault displacement-length relationship: an example from the Cantarell oilfield, Gulf of Mexico. Geofisica Int 50(3):279–293
9. Mallet JL (2002) Geomodeling. Oxford University Press, New York

# Chapter 98
# Digital Watermark of Static Image Based on Wavelet Transform

Wei Qi, Fan Xia and Yanjuan Wen

**Abstract** Usually a static image is transformed by discrete cosine transform (DCT), texture and edge features mainly concentrated in the high frequency sub-bands LH, HL, and HH. The information on the high-frequency lost easily after a general image processing. In this paper, the watermark information embedded into the low-frequency coefficients in case of less embedded watermark information, then the human eyes is not easy to detect, and the robustness of the watermark greatly enhanced. The experiments show that the algorithm has good imperceptibility and strong robustness. And it has better robustness properties to noise attack, rotation attack and cropping attack.

**Keywords** Digital watermarking · DCT transform · Static image

## 98.1 Introduction

Digital watermarking technology developed quickly in recent years, and became a new hotspot as a new way on digital copyright protection. Owing to the wavelet transform has good time–frequency localization features and the transformation mechanism consistent with the human visual system and the new image compression standard also based on wavelet transform, wavelet transform technique is often applied in the field of digital watermarking in recent years. The reason of embedded watermark in wavelet domain are as follows: to prevent the eliminated of the watermark caused by JPEG lossy compression; to study the watermark

W. Qi (✉) · F. Xia · Y. Wen
Hebei University of Science and Technology, Shijiazhuang City, China
e-mail: qiwei_qiwei@163.com

W. Lu et al. (eds.), *Proceedings of the 2012 International Conference on Information Technology and Software Engineering*, Lecture Notes in Electrical Engineering 212, DOI: 10.1007/978-3-642-34531-9_98, © Springer-Verlag Berlin Heidelberg 2013

embedding location and intensity of the image through the visibility analysis on source coding, and then to realized the watermark embedded in the compressed domain. In addition, using the wavelet multi-resolution analysis can control the distribution of watermark in the host picture accurately and resolve the contradiction between the robustness and visibility of the watermark image.

## 98.1.1 Digital Watermarking

With the rapid development of network technology, multimedia information and information dissemination are also become faster, so the information security is paid more attention. In the early 1990s, digital watermarking and information hiding flourished. Copyright protection of multimedia information (i.e. the digital watermark) is a popular research topic in information security.

Digital watermarking technology is embedded a certain amount of digital information in a digital media (images, video, audio) such as company logos, the company's electronic signature, etc., and to confirm the ownership of the works and as a evidence of the prosecution by illegal infringement to protect the legitimate interests of the works of the owner [1]. Digital watermarking technology contains the watermark information embedding and extraction (detection). The watermark embedding may be considered as transmits a narrowband signal (watermark signal) on a broadband channel (vector image) by use of spread spectrum technology. Although the watermark signal has a certain energy, it's distribute to the frequency of the channel energy is difficult to detect. The watermark detection is a detection of weak signals in a noisy channel [2].

The basic requirements of watermark embedded are: transparency, robustness and security. The methods of watermark embedding are: the airspace embedded and frequency domain embedded. With deeply research, embedded in the frequency domain get more attention by the virtues of its effective of embedded and extracted, but the contradictions between imperceptibility and the quantities of information embedded is always present [3]. To ensure the transparency of visual, we embedded the watermark in the sensitive region of the human eyes, which is embedded into the high frequency component part of the image. But most method of the image processing for high-frequency part of the image has a high damage, such as lossy compression and high frequency filtering. Watermark information is easily lost in the process of image processing. In this way, we can't guarantee the robustness of image watermarking. If you want to get a better robustness, the watermark should be added in the low frequency part of LL, where the human eye is more sensitive [4].

## 98.1.2 The Definition of Discrete Cosine Transform

Discrete Cosine Transform is one method of orthogonal image coding. It is a high accuracy and fast algorithm. Therefore, DCT is often considered as the best algorithm for the signal transformation. Since the image is two-dimensional, the two-dimensional DCT and IDCT are used in the image processing. The digital image $X(m, n)$ is a matrix of $M$ rows and $N$ columns. To weaken or remove the correlation of the image data, image was transferred from the spatial domain to the DCT transform domain by 2D DCT. The definition of DCT is:

$$Y(k, l) = \frac{2}{\sqrt{MN}} c(k)c(l) \sum_{m=0}^{M-1} \sum_{n=0}^{N-1} X(m, n) \cos \frac{(2m + 1)k\pi}{2M} \cos \frac{(2n + 1)l\pi}{2N} \quad (98.1)$$

where

$$c(k) = \begin{cases} 1/\sqrt{2} & k = 0 \\ 1 & k = 1, 2, \ldots, M - 1 \end{cases}$$

$$c(l) = \begin{cases} 1/\sqrt{2} & k = 0 \\ 1 & k = 1, 2, \ldots, N - 1 \end{cases} \quad (98.2)$$

The definition of two-dimensional inverse discrete cosine transform (IDCT) is:

$$X(m, n) = \frac{2}{\sqrt{MN}} \sum_{K=0}^{M-1} \sum_{L=0}^{N-1} c(k)c(l)Y(k, l) \cos \frac{(2m + 1)k\pi}{2M} \cos \frac{(2n + 1)l\pi}{2N} \quad (98.3)$$

## 98.1.3 The Features of Discrete Cosine Transform

After DCT transform, the image has three features: First, the coefficients are all concentrated to 0 (by the meaning of histogram's energy). The dynamic range is very small, which indicated that high-frequency parameter values close to zero by a smaller number of quantization bits. Second, the energy is concentrated on the low-frequency part of the image LL by the DCT transform, that is to say non-zero coefficients together in the upper left, which leading to the coding efficiency is relatively high. Third, DCT transform can not retain specific fine structure of the original image block, so it can't reflect the information of the edge and the contour of the original image. This feature is caused by the lack of locality. Most of the parameters close to zero, only the top left corner on the LL low frequency part is a larger value, The parameter values on the high-frequency and middle frequency are relatively small and close to zero [5].

### 98.1.4 The Strategy of Embedding Watermark

In order to solve the contradiction between watermark visibility and the quantities of the embedded information, in this paper we proposed a DCT domain digital watermarking by chaotic encryption in a human visual masking. First the $64 \times 64$ binary image pretreated by chaotic encryption, then the digital watermark embedded into $512 \times 512$ grayscale images [6]. At the same time taking advantage of the HVS masking characteristics to select the appropriate sub-block of frequency coefficients for watermark embedding, enhanced watermark invisibility and blind detection in the watermark detection process [7].

In this paper, we use a static image as the watermark and studied a blind watermarking algorithm which extracted without original image. Usually a static image is transformed by DCT, texture and edge features concentrated in the high frequency sub-bands LH, HL, and HH. The information on the high-frequency is easy to lose after a general image processing. In this paper, put the watermark information embedded into the low-frequency coefficients in case of embedded less information, then the human eye is not easy to detect, greatly enhancing the robustness of the watermark. The experiments show that the algorithm has good imperceptibility and strong robustness. By attacks, it has better robustness. The process of digital watermarking is shown in Fig. 98.1.

## 98.2 Embedding and Extraction of the Watermark Image and MATLAB Simulation

Embedded digital watermark image is divided into three parts: the transformation of the host image, watermark embedding and watermark detection.

### 98.2.1 Selection of Embedded Position

In order to have better robustness, the watermarked wavelet coefficients should satisfy the following conditions: (1) Wavelet coefficients have a larger perceived capacity, so that the original watermarked image does not cause significant changes of the visual. (2) Wavelet coefficients decomposed should not change by

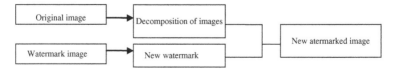

**Fig. 98.1** The Process of digital watermarking

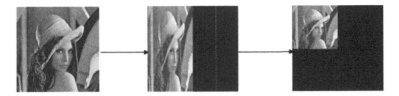

**Fig. 98.2** Wavelet decomposition

too much noise and signal processing, that is to say the energy are well retained in general signal processing and noise. Based on these two requirements, we analyzed the wavelet coefficients qualitative and quantitative distribution. 256 × 256 pixel image decomposed by a DCT transform, which LL is the low frequency component, HL is a high-frequency component, LH a vertical high-frequency components, HH is the diagonal high frequency components, as shown in Fig. 98.2. The energy is concentrated on the low-frequency part of the image, most of the non-zero coefficient of the DCT image together to the upper left, the larger coefficient is indicated that the smaller image of the edge energy concentrated on the other sub-bands: HH, HL, LH and close to zero. So the low-frequency part has a good visual capacity and robustness.

The watermark is embedded into the high frequency part which has a better imperceptibility, but the probability of these sub-band coefficients lost in the quantization is relatively large. So the watermark is embedded into low frequency coefficients, it is difficult for an attacker to get the image without erased the watermark information completely, which can make the robustness enhanced greatly.

## 98.2.2 The Pre-processing of the Watermark Image

### 98.2.2.1 The Extension of the Watermark Image

Since the watermark image W is the binary image W with 64 × 64 pixels, and the original image is 256 × 256 pixels, the original image is transformed by DCT and embedded sub-band in the low-frequency part. The low-frequency part of the original image, by the one-dimensional wavelet decomposed into is 128 × 128 pixels, so extended the watermark image into 128 × 128 pixels, be denoted by W1.

### 98.2.2.2 The Scrambling of the Watermark Image

In fact scrambling is not encryption, it is random treatment the associated contents by a certain scrambling method. The Image scrambling is disrupted each pixel inside an image by an algorithm, but the histogram of the pixels and the total number unchanged. Watermark scrambling eliminate the spatial correlation of the

$$ICE \quad - \quad \frac{ICE\ ICE}{ICE\ ICE} \longrightarrow \qquad \longrightarrow$$

watermark image pixel can improve the watermark robustness against image cropping attacks. In this paper we use Arnold scrambling transformation. Scrambling W1 eight times and eliminating the correlation of neighboring pixels in some extent, be denoted by W2.

### 98.2.2.3 The Encryption of the Watermark Image

Extended and scrambled the watermark image W2 by logistic chaotic sequence to encrypt, the further embedded watermark information to enhance security. Encrypted watermark image be denoted as W3. These processes are shown in Fig. 98.3.

## 98.2.3 The Watermark Image Embedding

(1) Scrambled encryption watermark is embedded into the low-frequency sub-image. Operate on one-dimensional decomposition of the original image low-frequency portion of the watermark value to select the appropriate coefficient. We can obtain embedded 128 × 128 image.
(2) Reconstruct the low-frequency part of the embedded watermark and the other three parts of LH, HL, HH, can get an image I' which have the same size with the original image.

These processes are shown in Fig. 98.4.

## 98.2.4 Blind Extraction of the Watermark

Extracting the watermark is the inverse process of embedded.

(1) Decompose the watermarked image, select the sub-band LL, HL, LH, HH, then extract the watermark.
(2) Compare the size of the 4*4 sub-block to determine the watermark information after DCT transform. The statements in Matlab7.0 are: f $(i, j) = 255$; if f $(i, j) > 0$; f $(i, j) = 0$; if f $(i, j) < 0$.

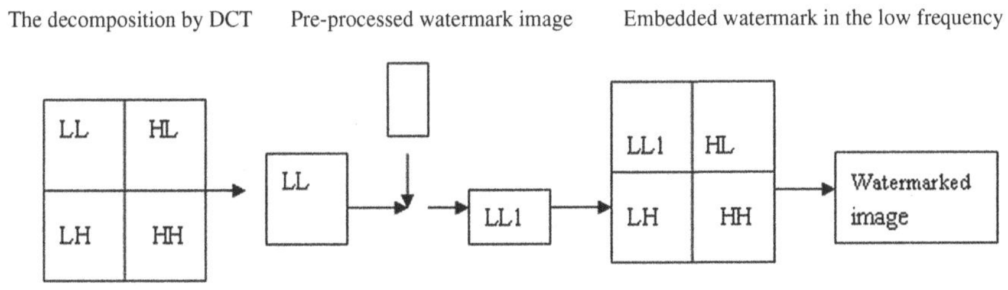

The decomposition by DCT     Pre-processed watermark image     Embedded watermark in the low frequency

**Fig. 98.4** The watermark embedding diagram

(3) Generate the binary sequence m according to x0 = 0.12315, $\mu = 4$ which same as step (2).
(4) Read w to get 0,1 binary sequence corresponding to with each value in the m. After the XOR computation, the results are rewritten back to the N × N image matrix W to achieve chaotic decryption.
(5) Make the watermark anti-Arnold transformation for 8 times, to get the useful watermark finally. It is the inverse process of Fig. 98.3.

## 98.3  The Detection of Watermark Performance

### 98.3.1  Watermark Information Hidden Performance

Embed binary watermark image in the original image, and then extract the watermark. The watermarked image shown in Fig. 98.5a. The extracted watermark shown in Fig. 98.5b. The watermark program has better invisibility in natural images. The visual will not effect by the watermarked image. The extracted watermark information in the lower right corner shown in Fig. 98.5b compared with the information in lower right corner of the original binary watermark shown in Fig. 98.5a, the extracted watermark and original watermark information is consistent without any attack.

### 98.3.2  The Attack Detection

#### 98.3.2.1  Noise Attack

Added Gaussian noise of the mean 0, variance 0.0001 in the watermarked image, the watermark extracted from the image after the noise attack, shown in Fig. 98.6a. It shown that the noise attack has changed the original image. The similarity between extracted watermark image with the original watermark image

**Fig. 98.5** **a** Original image and **b** watermarked image

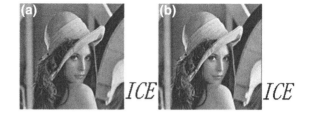

**Fig. 98.6** The extracted watermark after attack

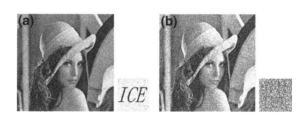

is very high. The following images are: (a) watermarked image after Gaussian noise attack. (b) Watermarked image after salt and pepper noise attack.

### 98.3.2.2 Rotation Attack

Watermarked Lena image rotated ten degrees, taken the watermark shown in Fig. 98.7 with "imrotate" function in matlab7.0. The experiments show that the algorithm is robust to rotation.

### 98.3.2.3 Sharpen Attack

After sharpening attacks on the watermarked image, the watermark extracted from the images, as shown in Fig. 98.8. The watermark detection results show that a tamper occurred between the image content (b) the original watermark image (a).

**Fig. 98.7** The extracted watermark after attack (**a**) Image after rotation attack (**b**) Extracted watermark image

**Fig. 98.8** The extracted
watermark after sharpen
attack

**Fig. 98.9** Cropping image
and extracted watermark

#### 98.3.2.4 Cropping Attack

To test the anti-cropping capacity, we make the shearing attacks on the watermarked image. Cropped Image and extracted the watermark shown in Fig. 98.9. It
can be seen from the Fig. 98.9, the watermarking algorithm has strong robustness
in the cropping processing of the image.

## 98.4 Conclusion

Based on the characteristics of Multi-resolution decomposition of wavelet transform, the binary image watermark embedded in a static image, the simulation
results show that imperceptibility is better and the sharpening destruction is
fragile, and robustness is not strong; but it has high robustness on noise attacks,
rotation attack, cropping attacks. Since the algorithm is calculated in wavelet
transform domain, the characteristics are: simple, easy to detect, easy to implement
and security, so it is a practical watermarking method in reality.

**Acknowledgments** This paper is supported by The Foundation of Shijiazhuang research pro-
ject(11113611A) and Found of HeBei University of Science and Technology (No.XL200868).

# References

1. Hu Y, Chen Z-J (2003) MATLAB application in digital watermarking. Compute Eng 29(7):184–186 (in Chinese)
2. Wu B (2007) Digital watermarking algorithm based on MATLAB. Fujian comput 11:94–100 (in Chinese)
3. Ibrahim K, Osana A (2011) Semi-fragile watermark for sensor data. Int J Multimedia Intell Secur 6(3):156–171
4. Li C-H, Qin Z-Y (2011) Adaptive image watermarking algorithm based on biorthogonal wavelet transform. Hebei Sci Technol 28(2):90–93 (in Chinese)
5. Guo L (2009) A digital watermarking algorithm based on singular value decomposition and inversion of neural networks using multiple wavelet domains [J]. Hebei Sci Technol 23(7):219–221 (in Chinese)
6. Zhang D-F (2009) MATLAB digital image processing. Machinery Industry Press, China (in Chinese)
7. Cui J-T (1995) Introduction to wavelet analysis. Xi'an Jiaotong University Press,Xi'an, p 7 (in Chinese)

# Chapter 99
# Snore Formant Detection Method Based on Software Multi-Filtering

Li Zhang and Lei Xue

**Abstract** Snore is a critical aspect about the sleeping problems. And as a very distinct characteristic in the snore frequency spectrum, detection on snore formant plays a very important role. The paper will introduce a method which is designed by software to ensure the real-time feature detection of snore formant. Our aim is to simplify the algorithm of the frequency spectrum, to save more occupied memory space and finally to realize the real-time detection in the embedded system.

**Keywords** Software multi-filtering · Formant detection · Snore frequency analysis

## 99.1 Introduction

The common method for frequency spectrum analysis is Fast Fourier Transform (FFT). However, owing to the complicated procedure, it is impossible to ensure the real-time proceeding. On the other hand, it occupies too much memory space. Therefore, the paper will introduce a new method, software multi-filtering, for frequency spectrum analysis, especially for the formant detection. The practice showed that the new algorithm applied after the estimating of snore features in

L. Zhang (✉) · L. Xue (✉)
Biomedical Engineering, School of Information and Communication Engineering,
Shanghai University, Shanghai, China
e-mail: zhanglishanghai@yahoo.cn

L. Xue
e-mail: xuelei@shu.edu.cn

W. Lu et al. (eds.), *Proceedings of the 2012 International Conference on Information Technology and Software Engineering*, Lecture Notes in Electrical Engineering 212, DOI: 10.1007/978-3-642-34531-9_99, © Springer-Verlag Berlin Heidelberg 2013

time domain would improve the accuracy of the formant detection. And by series of testing, the design has simply proceeding, good real-time character and small occupied memory space. What's more important, it is efficient for the frequency spectrum, especially the feature extraction of snore formant.

## 99.2 Term Explanation

The paper is centred on the acoustics, so please pay attention to the following explanations.

### 99.2.1 Snore

Snoring can be defined as the voice out of oral and nasal radiation produced by the vibration of the obstruction parts (such as the soft palate, tongue and throat), when the airway obstruction occurs during the sleep [1, 2]. A complete snoring fragment of snoring includes breathe-in, expiratory and transition segment [3].

### 99.2.2 Formant

From the point of physiology, human sound channel can be regarded as a section of the track tube which is uniform. The so-called "Formant" is actually the resonant frequency of the track tube. In fact, in the structure airway, the reason of nasal congestion, the soft palate, tonsil enlargement and so on results in the normal breathing passage not unobstructed, and restriction of airflow caused apnea and hypopnea, thus leading to the formation of formant. From the phonetics, "formant" is the part where energy is relatively concentrated in a frequency band, as shown in Fig. 99.2a. The range lies usually within the 1 kHz. In a certain extent, Snore formant displays the track structure and reflects the resonance characteristics of the system. So the analysis of characteristics has the vital meaning for the understanding of the mechanism of snore generation and airway model establishment [4].

## 99.3 Software Multi-Filtering

On the basis of Sect. 99.2.2, there is no doubt that formant is a very effective characteristic in the frequency domain. The preferred method used by researchers is FFT. Yet, it expends too much time and storage. In another words, it cannot realize the instantaneity and small occupied-space in our whole embedded system. For these reasons, and considering the actual situation, the paper proposes a new algorithm, software multi-filtering.

## 99.3.1 Principle

Generally speaking, signal processing The region of interest (ROI) will be exacted from the signal according to the characteristics of the signal before the proceeding. Furthermore, in view of this section software multi-filtering algorithm can be applied to distinguish the resonant frequency, intensity and relationship.

In reality, "Software multi filtering" is a combination of filtering algorithm based on linear filter method by software. With reference to the actual capacitance, resistance and operational amplifier performances, signal processing program uses virtual simulation of capacitance SoftC, resistance SoftR and operational amplifier SoftOP. These virtual devices own the same working mode and the same electrical characteristics as the practical devices, and are linked in accordance the designed circuit and run virtually, in order to achieve the filtering and extracting the formant.

The default circuit structure can be in all types, such as Butterworth filter, Chebyshev filter and elliptic filter, etc. In this paper, we adopt second order filter model. The Fig. 99.1 illustrates the circuit principle (No.4 and No.8 of the amplifier is connected to the power).

The first level consists of R1, C1 and U1A:

$$\overrightarrow{i_1}(n\tau) = \frac{\overrightarrow{U_i}(n\tau)}{R_1}; \quad \overrightarrow{U_{o1}}(n\tau) = \overrightarrow{U_{o1}}[(n-1)\tau] + \frac{1}{R_1C_1}\overrightarrow{U_i}(n\tau) \qquad (99.1)$$

Similarly, the second lever is composed of R2, C2 and U1B:

$$\overrightarrow{i_2}(n\tau) = \frac{\overrightarrow{U_{o1}}(n\tau)}{R_2}; \quad \overrightarrow{U_{o2}}(n\tau) = \overrightarrow{U_{o2}}[(n-1)\tau] + \frac{\tau}{R_2C_2}\overrightarrow{U_{o1}}(n\tau) \qquad (99.2)$$

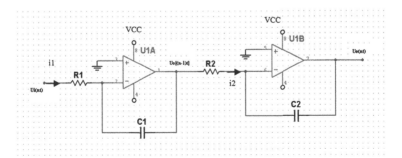

**Fig. 99.1** Second order filter model

Put (99.1) into (99.2), and when $R_1 = R_2 = R$, the model will be:

$$\overrightarrow{U_{o2}}(n\tau) = \overrightarrow{U_{o2}}[(n-1)\tau] + \frac{\tau}{RC}\overrightarrow{U_{o1}}[(n-1)\tau] + \frac{\tau^2}{R^2C^2}\overrightarrow{U_i}(n\tau);$$

To improve the accuracy, we add the correction factor $K_1$ and $K_2$, and the final model will be:

$$\overrightarrow{U_{o2}}(n\tau) = \overrightarrow{U_{o2}}[(n-1)\tau] + K_1\frac{\tau}{RC}\overrightarrow{U_{o1}}[(n-1)\tau] + K_2\frac{\tau^2}{R^2C^2}\overrightarrow{U_i}(n\tau) \qquad (99.3)$$

$$f_c = \frac{1}{RC}, \tau = \frac{1}{f_s} \qquad (99.4)$$

Where $f_c$ is the cut-off frequency and $f_s$ is the sampling rate.

In line with 99.4, when R and C are set to different values, we can get different filter band. And when different power frequency diagram are assembled in the same one, it will generate the multi-filtering power frequency diagram.

Due to the non-physical-restricted feature of software, during the algorithm, we can choose different $SoftR_i$, $SoftC_i$, $SoftOP_i$ (which i = 1, 2,...N) to draw different filtering line ($SoftCutF_i$ represents the cut-off frequency). Thereby, we get the multi-filtering method for formant extraction and analysis.

When choosing $SoftCutF_i$ (which i = 1, 2,...N), it should be better to put the specific distribution of frequency spectrum of into consideration, for example, in the energy-concentrated areas, we can set more $SoftCutF_i$, vice versa.

As the Fig. 99.2b illustrated, the whole band is divided into 10 sub-bands, the cut-off frequency is represented by $SoftCutF_i$ (which i = 1, 2,...N). Then referring to Fig. 99.2a, we can find that the snore formant appears within the range of $SoftCutF_i$. For this reason, the method is effective to detect the distribution of snore formant.

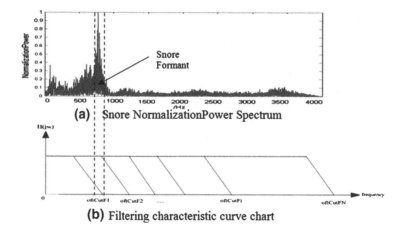

**(a)** Snore NormalizationPower Spectrum

**(b)** Filtering characteristic curve chart

**Fig. 99.2** Snoring statistical spectrum charts

## 99.3.2 Feature Comparation

Fast Fourier transform (FFT) is the most widely used algorithm in the field of digital signal processing. Whereas, compared with the multi-filtering method in the paper, it has the following disadvantages:

1. Cannot fulfill the real-time proceeding in embedded system. Usually, we need to collect N values and then make FFT. However, the FFT of N includes $2 \times \left(\frac{N}{2}\right)^2 + \frac{2}{N}$ complex multiplications and $2 \times \frac{N}{2} \times \left(\frac{N}{2} - 1\right) + N$ complex additions, so the time spending for calculation is magnificent. In the other hand, for FFT, the data refresh rate is required to achieve $\frac{N}{f_s}$ ($f_s$ represents sampling rate) or above, thus affecting the instantaneity of the entire system.
2. Need too much memory space. FFT of N needs N positions to store the values.
3. For pattern recognition system, if the signal's characteristic values are contained in the two nodes, it is possible to lose the vital characteristic information, which affects the accuracy.
4. Demand too cost of hardware resources.
5. In the FFT, the length of data must be determined, yet the voice signal cannot be expected. So it may result in loss of information.

In contrast, multi-filtering method requires less buffer space, do not need to calculate the allowance and simplify the complexity of the algorithm to save the storage space. The detailed results are shown in Table 99.1.

In the aspect of instantaneity, e.g. for the 256-point FFT by 40 k sampling rate, the refresh time is required $\frac{256}{40K}$ s, while in our multi-filtering, the refreshing is real-time.

## 99.4 Snore Formant Detection

So as to detect the snore formant more accurately and efficiently, the detection method is applied after the initial estimation on the time features, which may also save the cost of the system.

## 99.4.1 Detection of Time Features

Time Detection is refer to extract the distinguished feature parameters in the time domain [5]. These parameters includes number of snore, snore time, interval and

**Table 99.1** Comparison of storage space

| Algorithm | Occupied space/KB | Flash space/KB | Ratio (%) |
|---|---|---|---|
| Mutlti-filtering | 159 | 256 | 62 |
| FFT | 182 | 256 | 71 |

so on [6]. Similar to the voice endpoint detection, the common method includes: average short-term rate threshold, short-time energy and average amplitude detection method [7].

After making a preliminary observation and statistics on the real snore, we found that in a short period of time, the signals in time domain has some distinct features. Thus, we select 4 features as the evaluation parameters in time domain. They are: m0: time similarity of breathe-in part; m1: energy similarity of breathe-in part; m2: Uniformity of adjacent expiratory interval; m3: compare time of a single breathe-in part with 1–2 s.

## 99.4.2 Snore Formant Based on Multi-Filtering

Thanks to the time-evaluation, we would like to work with very limited frequency.

The sampling rate of the design is set to 40 kHz. And we divide the whole band into 10 sub-bands. At the same time, considering the snore formant is usually above 800 Hz. So within this range, we put more sub-bands. The result is followed: SB0: 0–200 Hz, SB1: 0–400 Hz, SB2: 0–600 Hz, SB3: 0–800 Hz, SB4: 0–1 kHz, SB5: 0–5 kHz, SB6: 0–10 kHz, SB7: 0–20 kHz, SB8: 0–30 kHz, SB9: 0–40 kHz.

In practice, the short-term-energy-threshold algorithm is combined. Figure 99.3 is the working flow chart.

Where: Xi: the current input; Yi: the current output; Yi-1: the previous output; Y'i-1: the previous output of the former circuit; H_threshold: high threshold, constant; L_threshold: low threshold, constant; Powertmp: energy in short term; Power_filter [1:10]: array, stores the power after 10 filtering; A [1:10]: constant array, stores the filtering factors. B[1:10]: constant array, stores the filtering factors.

## 99.5 Tests

Test condition: TMS 320 F2812 as the core processing chip. Sampling parameters are set to 40 kHz, 12 bit. And the correction factors. In addition, the noise is inevitably in the range of 55–60 dB.

Before the formant test, we also make some pre-tests to confirm the working model is correct. And the results are shown in Table 99.2.

The Table 99.3 demonstrates the test results of the snore sample 1.

According to the above, we can know that the formant of the sample 1 lies in 0–600 Hz.

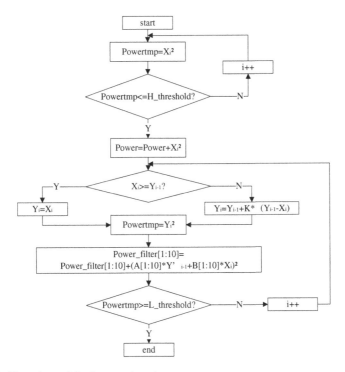

**Fig. 99.3** Flow chart of the formant detecting

**Table 99.2** Pre-tests' results

| Signal fc (Hz) | 200 | 400 | 600 | 800 | 1 K | 5 K | 10 K | 20 K | 30 K | 40 K |
|---|---|---|---|---|---|---|---|---|---|---|
| 512 | 213.91 | 221.44 | 223.10 | 223.90 | 223.51 | 224.66 | 225.56 | 225.55 | 225.96 | 225.84 |
| 1,000 | 219.18 | 229.32 | 230.44 | 231.57 | 233.81 | 235.37 | 235.01 | 235.08 | 233.88 | 233.88 |

**Table 99.3** Power distribution of each sub-band

| power(dB) fc(Hz) | 200 | 400 | 600 | 800 | 1 K | 5 K | 10 K | 20 K | 30 K | 40 K |
|---|---|---|---|---|---|---|---|---|---|---|
| Power1 | 201.56 | 215.34 | 216.83 | 218.03 | 218.52 | 220.59 | 221.47 | 222.14 | 219.40 | 219.56 |
| Power2 | 195.04 | 212.61 | 216.83 | 217.98 | 220.27 | 222.01 | 221.44 | 222.13 | 222.30 | 222.49 |
| Power3 | 201.65 | 215.37 | 216.78 | 217.98 | 218.53 | 220.57 | 221.31 | 222.02 | 222.30 | 222.49 |
| Power4 | 201.73 | 215.37 | 216.81 | 218.03 | 219.78 | 221.55 | 221.33 | 222.01 | 222.40 | 222.59 |
| Power5 | 201.53 | 215.26 | 216.98 | 218.15 | 219.66 | 221.53 | 222.04 | 222.68 | 223.22 | 223.40 |
| avg Power | 200.27 | 214.81 | 217.03 | 218.20 | 219.15 | 221.10 | 221.54 | 222.22 | 222.15 | 222.34 |

## 99.6 Conclusions

The new method, multi-band filtering realizes the snore formant detection in the embedded system. And what's more important, it ensure real-time and low-cost.

## References

1. Lugaresi E, Cirignotta F, Montagna P (1988) Pathogenic aspects of snoring and obstructive apnea syndrome. Schweiz Med Wochenschr 118:1333–1337
2. Liistro G, Stanescu DC, Veriter C, Rodenstein DO, Aubert TG (1991) Pattern of snoring in obstructive sleep apnea patients and in heavy snorers. Sleep 14:517–525
3. Qi ZY, Zhang ZP, Hu HM (2007) Clinical application value of polysomno-graphy instrument (PSG) in obstructive sleep apnea hypopnea syndrome [J]. Contemp Med (118) (in Chinese)
4. Sola-Soler J, Jane R, et al. (2008) Formant frequencies of normal breath sounds of snorers may indicate the risk of obstructive sleep apnea syndrome. In: 30th annual international IEEE EMBS conference, pp 3500–3503
5. Jane R, Sola-Soler J et al. (2000) Automatic detection of snoring signals: validation with simple snorers and OSAS patients. In: Proceedings of the 22nd annual EMBS international conference, pp 3129–3131
6. Yah Liang H, Ming Chou C, Chin Ming C, et al. (2005) In: IEEE international conference on system, man and cybernetics, Hilton Waikoloa Village, USA
7. Yadollahi A, Moussavi Z (2010) Automatic breath and snore sounds classification from tracheal and ambient sounds recordings. Med Eng Phys 32:985–990

# Chapter 100
# Real-Time Simulation of the 3D Explosive Effects

Xin Li, Yue Cao, Ruijiao Tian, Shuai Zhao and Leiting Chen

**Abstract** In order to solve the explosive simulation to realize real-time and realistic, this paper puts forward the real-time explosive simulation method based on the particle system. The basic idea is to use a variety of simple particle effects simulating the aperture of the explosion, splash, and fire. Then according to the characteristics of the explosive model, the simple particles are assembled in one particle system, unified timing to realize the highly realistic explosive special effects.

**Keywords** Motion blending · Time synchronization · Real-time interactive · Visual editing

X. Li (✉) · Y. Cao · R. Tian · S. Zhao · L. Chen
Digital Media Technology Key Laboratory of Sichuan, School of Computer Science and Engineering, University of Electronic Science and Technology of China, ChengDu, China
e-mail: 78707722@qq.com

Y. Cao
e-mail: yuecao@uestc.edu.cn

R. Tian
e-mail: 329675041@qq.com

S. Zhao
e-mail: 446206893@qq.com

L. Chen
e-mail: richardchen@uestc.edu.cn

W. Lu et al. (eds.), *Proceedings of the 2012 International Conference on Information Technology and Software Engineering*, Lecture Notes in Electrical Engineering 212, DOI: 10.1007/978-3-642-34531-9_100, © Springer-Verlag Berlin Heidelberg 2013

## 100.1 Introduction

With the development of computer technology, Computer animation has been integrated into our daily life. The explosion simulation is used more and more in a virtual environment, just like Battlefield simulation, Game, Disaster simulation etc. And the explosion effect simulation also ask high-fidelity and real-time. So, from the aspects of the flexibility, real-time, and realism, this paper proposes a real-time simulation method based on the explosion of particle system. This method stimulates three parts of the aperture of the explosion, splash, Mars respectively. Then through these effective assemblies of simple particle special effects, it forms a strong sense of reality, and good real-time explosive effects.

## 100.2 Related Works and Overview

The computer simulation is one of the hot topics now, especially natural phenomenon such as fire, water, clouds of smoke, fog, which is challenging. But fire, water and some other objects are constantly changing because its shape, form always changes with the dynamics of the time. It is very hard to achieve real simulation with the traditional modeling methods. Reeves was proposed of the particle systems for the first time [1]. Peachey and Fourenier simulated the effect of splash by wind [2, 3], they used ball which is a three-dimensional entity as the basic particles, because the number of particles is very large, so the rendering process need to spend a lot of time.

Recently, is more widely and deeply used to simulate the flow of fuzzy object. Because of the great progress of computer hardware, in 2004, the researchers are dedicated to realize more complicated real-time rendering by using more than one million simple particle [4].Someone others also the first time give the idea that the particle system can be used to deal with a large of growing data and provide interactive controllable frame frequency [5, 6]. In 2006, the researchers spend a lot of time and energy to research how to make the particle system can support large data set [7].

Particle system so far is considered one of the most successful graphics generation algorithms of irregular fuzzy object simulation. This algorithm is that the computer precision has some shortcomings. But, this method could very well simulate the basic characters of the movement of the fluid, which also has very good visual effect. So the computer graphics scholars began to use particle system algorithm to simulate some phenomenon and landscape, for example the flow of flame.

## 100.3 Partical System

### 100.3.1 The Particle Editor

In order to edit particle effect in a very easy way, we firstly design a particle editor, which can enhance the ability of interaction, so that anyone can use it to make great particle effects. The particle editor mainly contains four parts which are emitter management, attribute management, curve editor and particle effect combining (Fig. 100.1).

### 100.3.2 The Basic Theory of the Partial System

Particle system is made of a number of particles called primitive. Every particle has a set of independent properties, including life, color, size, angle, transparency, etc. The whole system is not a static system. With the change of time, the life of the particles will gradually expend and disappear. The new particles will also join into the system ceaselessly. Each particle will experience the process of born, raised, aging and death.

The graph one is a particle system cycle. N is for particle number of the particle effects needed to be rendered. M represents the number of particles in the current special effects particles. We assume that the initial number is 0 (Fig. 100.2)

### 100.3.3 The Particles Attributes of Explosive Special Effects

Explosive effects include three simple particle effects of aperture, splash and flame. The three kinds of particles include life, cycle, color, angle, transparency and size.

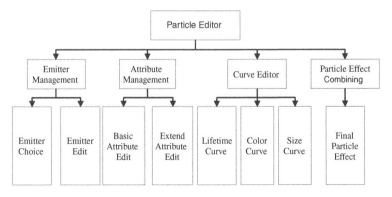

**Fig. 100.1** The structure of particle editor

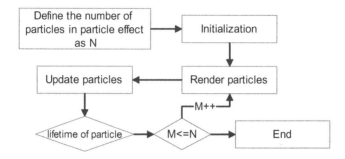

**Fig. 100.2** Particle system process

## 100.4 Explosive Simulation

In order to make the simulation of the explosion vivid and meet the request of real time, we divide following three explosions into three parts: aperture of the explosion, splash, and fire. We further make concrete analysis and stimulate the three important parts of explosions above. Then we assemble these parts together, unit timing and form a vivid and high real-time explosive effects.

1. The simulation of explosive aperture

The aperture of the explosion mainly includes the following factors: (1) the speed of aperture; (2) the color of aperture; (3) the direction of aperture. In order to achieve an explosive aperture with good realistic effect, we need to use a special particle to model. As the aperture of the explosion is not affected by the influence of the space resistance, we abstract its aperture to expand at a high and constant speed with a certain rate. The color of the aperture is a way to express the energy. We will also abstract its energy that diminishes with the time and show the intensity of the energy with the aperture color. The special effects are divided into motion simulation and simulation color, movement simulation is the changes of the SIZE. And the color simulation mainly point at its ALPHA change. We first choose a texture of particle. The picture is as follows (Fig. 100.3);

With the time changes, the character SIZE and ALPHA can be computed as follow formula, we define the start time of explosion as $T(T >= 0)$:

$$SIZE = (FINALSIZE \div LIFE) \times T \tag{100.1}$$

And also the ALPHA is changing with the time, we can use the a very simple formula as follow:

$$ALPHA = BEGINALPHA - (BEGINALPAH \div LIFE) \times T \tag{100.2}$$

LIFE is defined as the lifetime of the aperture particle, T is the time, $0 \le T \le LIFE$.

**Fig. 100.3** The texture of aperture particle

According to the calculation of the above formula, over times, the aperture particle spreads to the surrounding quickly with certain speed and fades out. As shown below: (Fig. 100.4)

2. The simulation of an explosion splash

Explosive splash simulation is composed of Motion simulation and Color simulation. Motion simulation mainly includes Speed simulation and direction simulation. Its main formula is as follows:

$$SPEED = \left( SPEED_{start} - \frac{dis\tan ce}{range} \times SPEED_{start} \right) \times random \qquad (100.3)$$

and random $\in[1.0, 2.0]$.

Thereinto, character $SPEED_{start}$ is defined as initial speed, random is a random number, distance is defined as the distance between the particle and the center of the explosion, range is the range of explosion.

Direction of emission: Direction of emission is divided into X and Y and Z. The formula is as follow:

$$ANGLE = \overline{\left( rand_x, rand_y, rand_z \right)} \qquad (100.4)$$

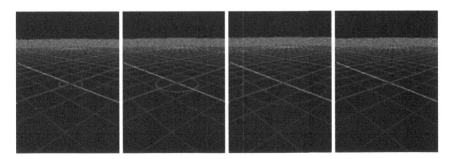

**Fig. 100.4** The effect of the simulation of explosive aperture

Thereinto, $rand_x$, $rand_y$, $rand_z$ are defined as random numbers of X, Y and Z direction, so that every splash particle can have a random direction. And the effect is follow picture: (Fig. 100.5)

3. The simulation of the explosive flame

We use particle system to simulate the explosion. It mainly consists of two main parts: the color simulation and the movement simulation.

1. The color simulation

The color simulation in real-time rendering engine plays a very important role. We mainly use random factors to simulate explosive light effect.

In order to strengthen the authenticity of the explosion of the flame, we need to differentiate the thickness of color. That is to say, we need to ensure consistency of the render color and the color of the explosive particle texture. A simple solution is to read explosion texture map with fading color. The picture is as follows: (Fig. 100.6)

$t_p$ should keep the consistence with the explosional texture P.

In order to simulate that light of fire fade out quickly, we should compute the color of the particle with the formulas as follow:

We assume that the color of the explosional texture is defined as Color = (R, G, B, A), then at the position P of the explosion particle, the color of every frame can be computed by use follow formula:

$$\begin{cases} Color_i.RGB = Color.RGB \times t_p \times FADE_i \\ Color_i.A = Color.RGB \times t_p \times ALPHA_i \end{cases} \tag{100.5}$$

Character i means the i frame, $FADE_i$ and $ALPHA_i$ is defined as the color desalination and the transparency of the i frame, and $FADE_i$, $ALPHA_i \in [0, 1]$.

The desalination and the transparency are into an inverse relationship, So we can determine the value of $FADE_i$ by use follow formula:

$$FADE_i = 1 - \frac{distance}{range} \tag{100.6}$$

**Fig. 100.5** The effect of the simulation of an explosion splash

**Fig. 100.6** The texture of the
explosive flame

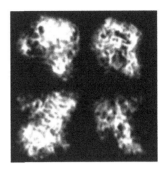

Similarly, we can know the relationship of $ALPHA_i$ and $FADE_i$ is Exponential relationship:

$$ALPHA_i = FADE_i^2 \qquad (100.7)$$

2. The motion simulation

Some properties of particle, like Position, Speed, Size, are used to control the motion of particle, we can simulate these with the simple kinematic formula, As the changes of the time t:

Position spread from the center of a random position to the edge of the explosion;

Speed starts with a high number v, and reduces to 0 quickly.

Size starts with 0, and increases at a fast speed.

## 100.5  Implementation

The above-mentioned three simple particle effects are unified timing and put into a particle system to initialize. They are forming a complete explosive effect. In the first frame, the fire and the splash break out at the same time. Then, they break out strong and fast so the flash come out, in the meantime the aperture appear and disappear in the short time. At last, the fire and splash disappear and the smoke comes out, then disappears. That is a procedure of the simulation of explosion. Its effect is as follows: (Fig. 100.7)

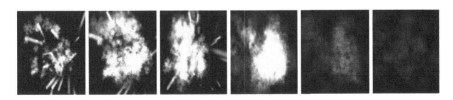

**Fig. 100.7** The effect of the explosion

## 100.6 Conclusion

This article puts forward a method of real-time explosive effect rendering through the research of the explosive effects. This method has the explosive effect with high sense of reality and real-time. The experimental results show that when the explosive splash formula was imported, it can reflect the explosive sense of reality and randomness of explosion. Through the movement simulation and color simulation of explosive flame, we ensure the impact of the explosion. Alas, the introduction of the aperture explosion add vitality to the special effects. Of course more research is needed to further realistic explosive effects.

**Acknowledgments** We want to acknowledge the support provided by the National High-Tech Research and Development Program of China (863 Program), grant NO. 2012AA011503, the Production and Research Project of Guangdong Province and Ministry of Education, grant NO. 2010A090200016, NO.2011A091000003.

## References

1. Reeves WT (1983) Particle systems: a technique for modeling a class of fuzzy objects. Comput Graph 17(3):3592376
2. Peachey D (1986) Modeling waves and surf. Comput Graph 20(4):65274
3. Fournier A, Reeves WT (1986) A simple model of ocean waves. Comput Graph 20(4):75284
4. Latta L (2004) Building a million particle system. Game developers conference. Think Services Game Group, San Francisco, CA, USA
5. Bruckschen R, Kuester F, Hamann B, Joy KI (2001) Real-time out-of-core visualization of particle traces. In: PVG'01: proceedings of the Institute of Electrical and Electronics Engineers 2001 symposium on parallel and large-data visualization and graphics, Institute of Electrical and Electronics Engineers Press, Piscataway, pp 45–50
6. Ellsworth D, Green B, Moran P (2004) Interactive terascale particle visualization. In: VIS'04: proceedings of the Institute of Electrical and Electronics Engineers conference on visualization'04, Institute of Electrical and Electronics Engineers Computer Society, Washington, pp 353–360
7. Gribble CP, Stephens AJ, Guilkey JE, Parker SG (2006) Visualizing particle-based simulation datasets on the desktop. In: Proceedings of the British human computer interaction 2006 workshop on combining visualization

# Chapter 101
# A Texture Image Denoising Model Based on Image Frequency and Energy Minimization

Chanjuan Liu, Xu Qian and Caixia Li

**Abstract** When partial differential equation (PDE) and variation approaches are used in image denoising, its diffusion mechanism only depends on the image gradient, thus, the denoising effect is easily interfered by the noise. It is a difficult problem to suppress influence of the noise, to improve the model's anti-noise performance and to meet the case of suppressing noises while preserving edges and other detail features. This paper first gives the definition of image frequency and then proposes a novel texture image denoising model based on image frequency and energy minimization (NTIEM) on the basis of ROF total variation (TV) model. Meanwhile, in order to ensure the computational stability, we introduce a potential function into the NTIEM model. Theoretical analysis and numerical experiment have shown that compared with other existing approaches the NTIEM model has an obvious antijamming capability and can accurately and subtly describe the image edge area and smooth area. The analyses of experimental results have indicated that the NTIEM method can overcome staircase effect and over-smoothing. Especially for the images with rich texture features, it can remove the noise while preserving significant image details and important characteristics and improve the image peak signal to noise ratio (PSNR).

**Keywords** Texture image · Image frequency · PDE · Energy minimization · Denoising

C. Liu (✉) · X. Qian
School of Mechanical Electronic and Information Engineering, China University of Mining and Technology, Beijing, 100083 Beijing, China
e-mail: luckycj80@sina.com

C. Liu · C. Li
School of Information and Electrical Engineering, Ludong University, 264025 Yantai, China

W. Lu et al. (eds.), *Proceedings of the 2012 International Conference on Information Technology and Software Engineering*, Lecture Notes in Electrical Engineering 212, DOI: 10.1007/978-3-642-34531-9_101, © Springer-Verlag Berlin Heidelberg 2013

## 101.1 Introduction

Most of the image information exists in the parts of edges and detail features, therefore, it is hoped that the denoising methods could not only remove image blurring and noise but also preserve edges and detail features which is also the main task of image denoising. At present, the chief methods of image denoising are stochastic modelling theory, wavelet analysis theory and partial differential equation (PDE) theory. The PDE methods are well established and effective for image restoration. According to its derived equation, the methods of image denoising based on PDE can be divided into two classes. One is procedure-oriented image denoising methods based on the evolution theory in Physics, such as diffusion model, P–M model [1]. The other is object-oriented methods, also called variation denoising theory [2–6], it gets an energy functional from the properties of the image processing targets, and then solves the energy functional to obtain the restored image. By introducing energy function, Rudin et al. [2] proposed a ROF model based on total variation which converted image denoising into a problem of solving functional extreme. But both kinds of the denoising methods use image gradient as the only characteristic quantity to describe image characteristics, which makes the noise with large gradient to be treated as edges and causes fake edges of image, so that affects visual effects.

In order to better describe image detail characteristics, following the ideas of Ref. [7], we gives the definition of image frequency based on local gradient, and then on the basis of ROF model we proposes a novel texture image denoising model based on energy minimization (NTIEM) by using image frequency takes the place of gradient in traditional TV model. If the image has smaller local gradient, then it should be smoother and has lower frequency. Compared with image gradient, image frequency can describe the detailed features more subtly and can distinguish between image edge area and smooth area.

## 101.2 Definition of Image Frequency

In Ref. [7], the author gave the other form of function frequency. We let periodic function $f(x) = \alpha \sin(Tx), x \in [0, 2\pi]$, where positive integer T is the frequency of periodic function $f$, and $\alpha \neq 0$. The frequency of $f(x)$ can also be denoted as:

$$T = \frac{\left[\int\limits_{0}^{2\pi} (\nabla f)^2 dx\right]^{\frac{1}{2}}}{\left[\int\limits_{0}^{2\pi} f^2(x) dx\right]^{\frac{1}{2}}} \tag{101.1}$$

where $\nabla f = \frac{\partial f}{\partial x} = \alpha T \cos(Tx)$.

Following the ideas of Suicheng et al. in [7], here, we define norm as

$$\|f\| = \sqrt{\langle f, f \rangle} \tag{101.2}$$

And the gradient in the point of x can be defined as

$$\nabla f_x = \frac{\partial f}{\partial x} = \left( \frac{\partial f}{\partial x_1}, \frac{\partial f}{\partial x_2}, \cdots, \frac{\partial f}{\partial x_n} \right) \tag{101.3}$$

Therefore, image frequency can be denoted as

$$F(f) = \frac{\|\nabla f\|}{\|f\|}. \tag{101.4}$$

## 101.3  Total Variation Denoising Model

Let the observed function $u_0(x, y)$ denotes the pixel values of a noisy image, and $u(x, y)$ denotes the desired clean image, so $u_0(x, y) = u(x, y) + n(x, y)$, where $n(x, y)$ is the additive noise.

The classical variation denoising algorithm is ROF TV model, which is proposed by Rudin et al. This algorithm seeks an equilibrium state (minimal energy) of an energy functional comprised of the TV norm of the image $u$. They put forward the energy minimization equation in two dimensional continuous frameworks:

$$\min E(u) = \iint_{\Omega} |\nabla u| dx dy \tag{101.5}$$

where $u$ subjects to:

$$\begin{cases} \iint_{\Omega} u(x, y) dx dy = \iint_{\Omega} u_0(x, y) dx dy \\ \frac{1}{|\Omega|} \iint_{\Omega} (u(x, y) - u_0(x, y))^2 dx dy = \sigma^2 \end{cases} \tag{101.6}$$

Suppose the noise is approximated by an additive white Gaussian process of zero-mean and standard deviation $\sigma$. By introducing the Lagrange multiplier $\lambda$, the problem can be converted to a corresponding minimization problem without constraints:

$$\min E(u) = \iint_{\Omega} |\nabla u| dx dy + \frac{\lambda}{2} \iint_{\Omega} |u - u_0|^2 dx dy \tag{101.7}$$

where the Lagrange multiplier $\lambda > 0$ is given.

On the right side of Eq. (101.7), the first term is the image regular (smooth) item, it plays the function of the noise suppression in the minimization process; The second term is fidelity (approximation) item, it mainly plays a role in preserving image edge characters and reducing the image distortion degree. When the value of $\lambda$ is small, the correspondence smooth item plays a more important role which makes the desired image more smooth. However, when $\lambda$ gets bigger, the correspondence fidelity item becomes the dominant part which means smaller diffusion and makes the desired image closer to its initial value, thus the image edges are protected.

The corresponding Euler–Lagrange equation of model (101.7) is:

$$-\nabla \cdot \left( \frac{1}{|\nabla u|} \nabla u \right) + \lambda(u - u_0) = 0 \qquad (101.8)$$

From Eq. (101.8), we note that this approach in essence is an anisotropic diffusion and its diffusion coefficient is equal to $1/\nabla u$. Moreover, from the local coordinate expression we notice that the diffusion operator in TV model only proceeds along the vertical direction (the edge tangent direction) of the image gradient, while without diffusion along the gradient direction. Therefore, the noise can be suppressed and meanwhile image edges and other feature information can be preserved well. However, the edge tangent direction derived from image smooth area does not actually exist. If the diffusion behavior only diffuses along the edge tangent direction in the smooth area, the noise can not be suppressed sufficiently, and it may be easy to cause fake edges and staircase effect.

## 101.4 Texture Image Denoising Model Based on Image Frequency and Energy Minimization

### 101.4.1 NTIEM Model

In order to obtain better denoising effect, we introduce image frequency instead of gradient into the TV model and propose an energy minimization based texture image denoising model (NTIEM).

$$\min E(u) = \iint_\Omega \frac{|\nabla u|}{u} dxdy + \frac{\lambda}{2} \iint_\Omega |u(x,y) - u_0(x,y)|^2 dxdy \qquad (101.9)$$

To ensure the stability of Eq. (101.9) in the process of numerical calculation, we give the improved denoising model below

$$\min E(u) = \iint_\Omega \Phi\left( \frac{|\nabla u|}{u} \right) dxdy + \frac{\lambda}{2} \iint_\Omega |u(x,y) - u_0(x,y)|^2 dxdy \qquad (101.10)$$

$\Phi(\cdot)$ is called potential function, generally it is a non-negative increasing function. The corresponding Euler–Lagrange equation of model (101.10)

$$\frac{\partial E(u)}{\partial u} = -\frac{1}{u} \nabla \cdot \left( \Phi' \left( \frac{|\nabla u|}{u} \right) \frac{\nabla u}{|\nabla u|} \right) - \frac{|\nabla u|}{u^2} \Phi' \left( \frac{|\nabla u|}{u} \right) + \lambda (u - u_0) = 0$$

$$(101.11)$$

According to Eq. (101.11), we can get its gradient decent flow. In order to eliminate the adverse effect of the first term $u^{-1}$ in the process of numerical calculation, we can use the following formula to calculate

$$\frac{\partial u}{\partial t} = \nabla \cdot \left( \Phi' \left( \frac{|\nabla u|}{u} \right) \frac{\nabla u}{|\nabla u|} \right) + \frac{|\nabla u|}{u} \Phi' \left( \frac{|\nabla u|}{u} \right) - \lambda u (u - u_0) \qquad (101.12)$$

Suppose $\eta$ denotes the image gradient direction; $\xi$ denotes image gradient vertical direction. Then we unfold the divergence term $\nabla \cdot \left( \Phi' \left( \frac{|\nabla u|}{u} \right) \frac{1}{|\nabla u|} \cdot \nabla u \right)$, thus we can get the corresponding Euler–Lagrange equation in $(\eta, \xi)$ coordinate system as follow

$$\frac{1}{|\nabla u|} \Phi' \left( \frac{|\nabla u|}{u} \right) u_{\xi\xi} + \frac{1}{u} \Phi'' \left( \frac{|\nabla u|}{u} \right) u_{\eta\eta} - \frac{(\nabla u)^2}{u^2} \Phi'' \left( \frac{|\nabla u|}{u} \right) + \frac{|\nabla u|}{u} \Phi' \left( \frac{|\nabla u|}{u} \right) - \lambda u (u - u_0) = 0$$

$$(101.13)$$

Figure 101.1 shows the curves of potential function $\Phi(s)$ and its first derivative, second derivative

From Eq. (101.13) we note that it has different diffusion coefficients in normal direction and tangent direction, and Fig. 101.1 shows that the first derivative and second derivative of potential function have different change rules. In the area of image edge, that is, the image frequency $|\nabla u|/u$ has a larger value, the value of diffusion coefficient in tangent direction is greater than that in normal direction. Therefore, the noise can be suppressed while image edges and other feature information can be preserved well. When $|\nabla u|/u$ has a smaller value, relative to

**Fig. 101.1** Curves of potential function $\Phi(s)$ and $\Phi'(s), \Phi''(s)$

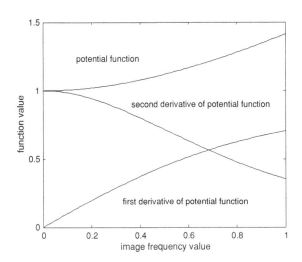

tangent direction, the value of diffusion coefficient in normal direction begins to increase, which means it obtains a stronger diffusion ability.

### 101.4.2 Numerical Implementation of NTIEM

The integrand $F(u)$ in NTIEM is as follow:

$$F = \Phi\left(\frac{|\nabla u|}{u}\right) + \frac{\lambda}{2}(u - u_0)^2 = \Phi\left(\frac{\sqrt{u_x^2 + u_y^2}}{u}\right) + \frac{\lambda}{2}(u - u_0)^2 \qquad (101.14)$$

The solution procedure uses a parabolic equation with time as an evolution parameter, or equivalently, the gradient descent method. For 2-dimension variational problem, this means that we should solve

$$\frac{\partial u}{\partial t} = \frac{\partial}{\partial x}\left(\frac{\partial F}{\partial u_x}\right) + \frac{\partial}{\partial y}\left(\frac{\partial F}{\partial u_y}\right) - \frac{\partial F}{\partial u} \qquad (101.15)$$

To avoid the problem of computational instability when $u = 0$ in the further deducing, here we suppose $u_\varepsilon = u + \varepsilon, 0 < \varepsilon < < 1$, and we substitute $u_\varepsilon$ for $u$, then we have

$$\frac{\partial u}{\partial t} = \frac{\partial}{\partial x}\left(\Phi'\left(\frac{|\nabla u|}{u_\varepsilon}\right)\frac{u_x}{u_\varepsilon|\nabla u|}\right) + \frac{\partial}{\partial y}\left(\Phi'\left(\frac{|\nabla u|}{u_\varepsilon}\right)\frac{u_y}{u_\varepsilon|\nabla u|}\right) + \Phi'\left(\frac{|\nabla u|}{u_\varepsilon}\right)\frac{|\nabla u|}{u_\varepsilon^2}$$
$$- \lambda(u_\varepsilon - u_0)$$

$$(101.16)$$

Similarly, we do the same thing for the function $u(x, y)$ in the following equations. As t increases, we can approach a denoised version of our image. We must compute Lagrange multiplier $\lambda(t)$. In this paper, we choose potential function [8] $\Phi(s) = (1 + s^2)^{1/2} - 1$. We plug $\Phi'\left(\frac{|\nabla u|}{u}\right) = \frac{|\nabla u|}{u\sqrt{1 + \left(\frac{|\nabla u|}{u}\right)^2}}$ into Eq. (101.16) and

integrate $x$, $y$ by parts over $\Omega$, we then have

$$\lambda = \frac{1}{2\sigma^2}\iint_\Omega \frac{uu_x(u_0)_x + uu_y(u_0)_y - u_0(u_x^2 + u_y^2)}{u^2\sqrt{u_x^2 + u_y^2 + u^2}}dxdy \qquad (101.17)$$

**Fig. 101.2** Original images
**a** Goldhill. **b** Barb

(a)                                            (b)

## 101.5 Results and Analysis

In order to verify the effectiveness of the method proposed in this paper, we performed lots of simulation experiments. We used Goldhill and Barb grayscale images as examples (See Fig. 101.2). First, we added different levels of zero-mean Gaussian noise to the original image as input. The size of images was $256 \times 256$ and grayscale was 256. In the simulation experiments, we took peak signal to noise (PSNR) and mean absolute error (MAE) as an objective criterion to the restored image evaluation, and compared the three denoising models: ROF TV model [2], generalized total variation (BS TV) model [5] and the proposed NTIEM model.

Peak signal to noise (PSNR) and mean absolute error (MAE) are defined by:

$$PSNR = 10 \lg \frac{255^2}{\frac{1}{m \times n} \sum_{i=1}^{m} \sum_{j=1}^{n} (\tilde{u}_{ij} - u)^2} \qquad (101.18)$$

$$MAE = \frac{1}{m \times n} \sum_{i=1}^{m} \sum_{j=1}^{n} |\tilde{u}_{ij} - u| \qquad (101.19)$$

where $\tilde{u}_{ij}$ is the restored image, $u$ is the original image without pollution. $m \times n$ is the picture size. Figures 101.3, 101.4, 101.5, and 101.6 show the image visual effect of Goldhill and Barb images before and after noise reduction processing using three approaches separately. Tables 101.1 and 101.2 separately shows the values of PSNR(dB) and MAE using three different approaches under different noise levels.

From Tables 101.1 and 101.2, compared with ROF TV model and BS TV model, the NTIEM model proposed by this paper has achieved better denoising effect under different noise levels. Moreover, from Figs. 101.3, 101.4, 101.5, and 101.6, it has appeared that NTIEM method accurately describes the image smooth areas and edges, overcomes staircase effect, preserves the edges and important detail features of the restored image well, in addition, the results has appeared to

**Fig. 101.3** Noise intensity
$\sigma^2 = 10$, denoising effect of
Goldhill image using three
approaches. **a** Noisy image.
**b** ROF image. **c** BS image.
**d** NTIEM image

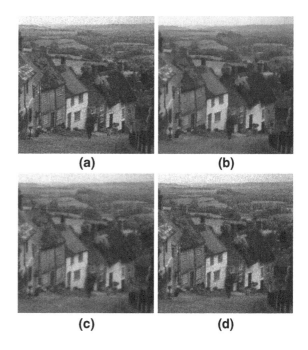

**Fig. 101.4** Noise intensity
$\sigma^2 = 15$, denoising effect of
Goldhill image using three
approaches. **a** Noisy image.
**b** ROF image. **c** BS image.
**d** NTIEM image

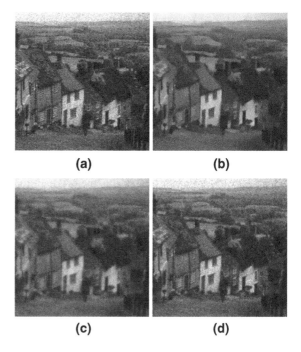

**Fig. 101.5** Noise intensity
$\sigma^2 = 10$, denoising effect of
Barb image using three
approaches **a** Noisy image.
**b** ROF image. **c** BS image.
**d** NTIEM image

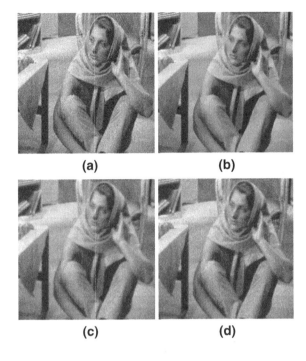

**Fig. 101.6** Noise intensity
$\sigma^2 = 15$, denoising effect of
Barb image using three
approaches **a** Noisy image.
**b** ROF image. **c** BS image.
**d** NTIEM image

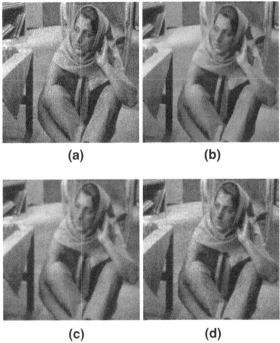

**Table 101.1** The comparing three different models of PSNR(dB)

| $\sigma^2$ | Goldhill | | | Barb | | |
|---|---|---|---|---|---|---|
| | ROF TV | BS TV | NTIEM | ROF TV | BS TV | NTIEM |
| 1 | 48.1563 | 48.3526 | 51.8403 | 48.0162 | 48.4539 | 49.0200 |
| 3 | 38.5973 | 37.6018 | 42.7907 | 38.5824 | 37.7377 | 39.7387 |
| 5 | 34.1469 | 34.4151 | 38.3005 | 34.1502 | 34.6070 | 35.4324 |
| 10 | 28.1283 | 30.5583 | 31.8293 | 28.1283 | 30.3089 | 32.5508 |
| 15 | 24.6084 | 27.6441 | 27.9001 | 24.6074 | 27.6120 | 27.7544 |

**Table 101.2** The comparing three different models of MAE

| $\sigma^2$ | Goldhill | | | Barb | | |
|---|---|---|---|---|---|---|
| | ROF TV | BS TV | NTIEM | ROF TV | BS TV | NTIEM |
| 1 | 0.9311 | 1.1205 | 0.8732 | 0.9089 | 1.2101 | 0.9629 |
| 3 | 2.3063 | 2.5359 | 2.2210 | 2.3124 | 2.5642 | 2.4688 |
| 5 | 3.3234 | 3.6276 | 3.2934 | 3.2890 | 3.6847 | 3.5717 |
| 10 | 4.9957 | 5.5836 | 5.2408 | 4.9103 | 5.6300 | 5.4372 |
| 15 | 6.2931 | 6.9698 | 6.7654 | 6.0509 | 6.8838 | 6.0050 |

be state-of-the-art for those images with rich texture features and low SNR, human eyes can perceive the improvement of image quality intuitively from NTIEM model reconstruction.

## 101.6 Conclusion

On the basis of analysis of TV denoising model, this paper proposes a novel texture image denoising model based on image frequency and energy minimization (NTIEM). The NTIEM model has a strong ability of denoising and can accurately and subtly describe the image edge area and smooth area. The analysis of experimental results have indicated that, compared with other existing approaches, the NTIEM method can overcome staircase effect and over-smoothing, especially for those images with rich texture features, it can remove the noise while preserving significant image details and important characteristics and improve the image peak signal to noise ratio (PSNR). Further more, the restored images are more in line with the visual experience under high noise intensity.

**Acknowledgments** Supported by the National Natural Science Foundation of China (Grant No. 61170161) and Doctoral Foundation of Shandong Province (BS2009DX022).

# References

1. Perona P, Malik J (1990) Scale-space and edge detection using anisotropic diffusion. IEEE Trans Pattern Anal Mach Intell 12(7):629–639
2. Rudin L, Osher S, Fatemi E (1992) Nonlinear total variation based noise removal algorithms. Physica D 60:259–268
3. Gilboa G, Sochen N, Zeevi YY (2003) Texture preserving variational denoising using an adaptive fidelity term. In: Proceedings of VLSM, Nice, France
4. Gilboa G, Sochen N, Zeevi YY (2004) Estimation of optimal PDE-based denoising in the SNR sense, CCIT report 499, Technion
5. Song B (2003) Topics in variational PDE image segmentation, inpainting and Denoising. University of California Los Angeles, USA
6. Zhang H, Peng Q (2006) Adaptive image denoising model based on total variation. Opto-Electron Eng 33(3):50–53 (in Chinese)
7. Gu S, Tan Y, He X (2011) Laplacian smoothing transform for face recognition. Chin Sci 41:257–268 (in Chinese)
8. Charbonnier P, Aubert G, Blanc-Feraud L, Barlaud M (1994) Two deterministic half-quadratic regularization algorithms for computed imaging. In: Proceedings of 1st IEEE international conference on image processing, vol 2, Austin Texas, USA, pp 168–172

# Chapter 102
# Optimal Ellipse Fitting Method Based on Boundary of Least Square Approach

**Wanguo Wang, Zhengfei Xu, Shirong Wang, Zhenli Wang and Wenbo Yang**

**Abstract** An improved ellipse detection algorithm based on least square approach was proposed to enhance the efficiency and accuracy of ellipse detection in digital images. The algorithm get ellipses by lease square based every boundary that obtained by the image edge detection operator. Then, we filter the ellipse by the fitting rate, ellipticity and area of the ellipse. Finally, the compared experiment results indicate that the improved method reduce the time consumption. Application of the algorithm verified the feasibility and effectiveness of the method in the actual image that can fit ellipse with high precision and meter of substation, which can also effectively deal with the extraction of region of ellipse in the image.

**Keywords** Ellipse fitting · Meter dial extraction · Least square approach

## 102.1 Introduction

Pattern recognition has very widely application in industry field, especially in power industry. Meter reading based on image processing is an important application in power system. There are lots of apparatus meters in control room and substation in power system such as oil conservator meter, oil temperature meter,

W. Wang (✉) · Z. Wang
Shandong Electric Power Research Institute, Jinan 250101, China
e-mail: wangwg@powerrobot.org

Z. Xu
Shandong Luneng Intelligence Technology Co., Ltd, Jinan 250002, China

S. Wang · W. Yang
Dali Power Administration of Yunnan, Dali 671000, China

W. Lu et al. (eds.), *Proceedings of the 2012 International Conference on Information Technology and Software Engineering*, Lecture Notes in Electrical Engineering 212, DOI: 10.1007/978-3-642-34531-9_102, © Springer-Verlag Berlin Heidelberg 2013

SF6 switch meter, voltage meter, current meter etc. At the moment, the task of meter monitoring is mostly realized by remote monitoring. The meter reading process is realized by real-time meter monitoring, extracting onsite image and reading them manually. It is crucial for power safety purpose to use robotics and image processing technology to automatically accomplish meter image shooting, locate the meter dial, calculate the reading and record the apparatus status.

Ellipse as an important geometric shape appears quite often in our daily life. In many field, it is required to extract elliptical target. Ellipse extraction is a precondition of sub sequential object recognition and measurement. In order to achieve the region, it is crucial to make sure the robust and accuracy of ellipse extraction. Because of the shooting angle of the camera which the substation patrol robot carries with, the meter dial can be seen as an ellipse in the image. The key to solve the meter reading is how to locate the meter dial fast and accurately.

The comment method of fitting of ellipse based on 3 categories: Hough Transform [1], Invariant Moment [2] and Least Square Method [3]. In these methods, the least square method is a best estimation technology deriving from Maximum Likelihood method when the random error is normally distributed, which makes the sum of square measure error least. Hence, the least square approach is considered as one of the most reliable method of solving a set of unknowns from a set of measurements. Reference [3] uses random theory and voting mechanism to make an improved fitting of ellipse algorithm which could rapidly remove the worst outliers. However, this method has poor performance in complicated environment.

This paper is organized as follows: Sect. 102.2 introduces the general idea of expression of ellipse and least square fitting of ellipse. According to characteristic of fitting of ellipse based on least square, a new iterative process of ellipse fitting based on boundary and the corresponding ellipse shape filtering has been brought in. An improved ellipse detecting algorithm based on boundary has been introduced in Sect. 102.3. In Sect. 102.4, the improved algorithm has been verified by the synthetic image and actual substation image in the experiment. Finally, Sect. 102.5 concludes this paper.

## 102.2 Expression of Ellipse and Fitting of Ellipse

### 102.2.1 Expression of Ellipse

In the 2D coordination, the ellipse can be expressed as two forms. One of is its algebra form, shown as formula (102.1)

$$Ax^2 + Bxy + Cy^2 + Dx + Ey + F = 0 \qquad (102.1)$$

The other one is parametric form, in its polar form expression, the center of ellipse $(x_c, y_c)$, semi-major axis and semi-minor axis $(a, b)$, angle of semi-major

**Fig. 102.1** Ellipse in 2D
coordinate system

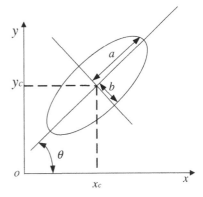

axis $\theta$, any ellipse could be determined by these 5 parameters in 2D plan. The
geometric meaning of the parameters shows in Fig. 102.1. The parameter in two
expression can be transformed using formulas (102.2)–(102.5).

$$x_c = \frac{BE - 2CD}{4AC - B^2} \tag{102.2}$$

$$y_c = \frac{BD - 2AE}{4AC - B^2} \tag{102.3}$$

$$a = 2^* \sqrt{\frac{-2F}{A + C - \sqrt{B^2 + \left(\frac{A-C}{F}\right)^2}}} \tag{102.4}$$

$$b = 2^* \sqrt{\frac{-2F}{A + C + \sqrt{B^2 + \left(\frac{A-C}{F}\right)^2}}} \tag{102.5}$$

$$\theta = \frac{1}{2}\arctan\frac{F}{A - C}. \tag{102.6}$$

## 102.2.2 Square Least Fitting of Ellipse

Assume an ellipse formula shows as formula (102.1), which is represent the two
vector multiplied by the implicit equation

$$f(\alpha, X) = \alpha X = Ax^2 + Bxy + Cy^2 + Dx + Ey + F = 0 \tag{102.7}$$

which $\alpha$ is $(A, B, C, D, E, F)$, coefficient vector, $X_i = \left(x_i^2, x_iy_i, y_i^2, x_i,y_i,1\right)$,
because of the error in the processing of fitting ellipse, $f(\alpha, X_i)$ at point $(x_i, y_i)$ is
non-zero, Assuming the algebra distance $f(\alpha, X_i)$ is from point $(x_i, y_i)$ to formula

$f(\alpha, X)$, according to least square principle, the curve fitting problem could be realized by minimizing sum square of algebra distance.

$$f(A,B,C,D,E,F) = \sum_{i=1}^{n} \left(Ax_i^2 + Bx_iy_i + Cy_i^2 + Dx_i + Ey_i + F\right)^2 \quad (102.8)$$

Through extremum principle, if $f(A, B, C, D, E, F)$ is minimize, then

$$\frac{\partial f}{\partial A} = \frac{\partial f}{\partial B} = \frac{\partial f}{\partial C} = \frac{\partial f}{\partial D} = \frac{\partial f}{\partial E} = \frac{\partial f}{\partial F} = 0 \quad (102.9)$$

From the equation above, the linear function could be obtained, then using solving linear function algorithm (For example, Gaussian Elimination Method), with constraint condition, the coefficient of the function A, B, C, D, E, F could be determined, then the ellipse function could be obtained.

## 102.3 Fitting of Ellipse Based on Boundary

The fitting ellipse algorithm based on least square can only obtain ellipse that have least error, however, it does not consider the matching degree of the result ellipse and original boundaries. Sometimes, the result of algorithm is not acceptable. In such circumstance, it is necessary to evaluate and filter the result fitting ellipse. This paper gives a least square ellipse fitting algorithm based on boundaries.

The matching degree between the original boundary and the fitting ellipse is called fitting rate, which is an important parameter to describe the optimal ellipse that we want to extract. Figure 102.2 depicts boundary that labeled by red curve and fitting ellipse that drawing by imaginary line. In the processing of fitting ellipse, firstly, all the target points of boundary $(E_b)$ need to be went through and calculate the distance $(d)$ between every sample point and fitting ellipse $(E_f)$. If the distance is smaller than threshold $(T_d)$, this sample point is considered as matching points and counting by $P_m$. Once every sample point has been gone through, calculate the total number of edge points $P_e$, the fitting rate can be calculated by

$$\eta = Pm/Pe \quad (102.10)$$

**Fig. 102.2** Boundary and
fitting ellipse

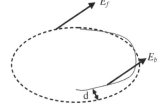

**Fig. 102.3** Algorithm flow
chart

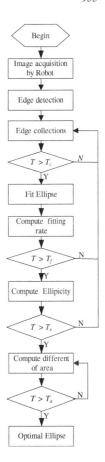

Priori knowledge is important factor for the result. Sometimes, we know roughly the ellipticity that describes the degree of how a fitting ellipse trends to be a circle or the size of ellipse. For getting above parameters, we only set semi-major axis (a) and semi-minor axis (b) as input parameters. Generally, ellipticity is defined as:

$$\rho = b/a \tag{102.11}$$

Meanwhile, the size of the ellipse can be described by its area. So area difference between the ideal ellipse and fitting ellipse is defined as:

$$\Delta Area = |Area_o - Area_f| \tag{102.12}$$

Where $Area_o$ and $Area_f$ represent the area of ideal ellipse and the fitting ellipse, respectively. $Area_o$ could obtain by the ideal semi-major axis and semi-minor axis that are known parameter. The ellipse of the smallest $\Delta Area$ is chosen as optimal ellipse. If the size of ellipse is not what we want, the largest area ellipse is chosen as the best ellipse from all the ellipses.

Algorithm is shown in Fig. 102.3 and the implementation is given as follows:

1. Extracting the image boundary: using edge detect operator of Canny to extract boundary.
2. Deciding the boundary, if the number of boundary points is larger than threshold $T_c$, fitting ellipse by least square algorithm, otherwise re-select the boundary.
3. Calculating the fitting rate and ellipticity according to formulas (102.10) and (102.11)
4. If the fitting rate and ellipticity is larger than threshold $T_f$, $T_e$, respectively, then record the result ellipse $E$.
5. Calculating the area difference between the result ellipse $E$ and the ideal ellipse according to formula (102.12), and update the ellipse of the smallest area if $\Delta Area$ is less than the current ideal ellipse.
6. Repeat step (2)–(5), choose the ellipse with the smallest area difference as the best ellipse.

## 102.4 Experiment and Result

The fitting of ellipse experiment is conducted on a Pentium (R) 2.66 GHz, 1G RAM PC based on Microsoft Visual Studio 2005 platform. Figure 102.4 is composed image and corresponding image after fitting. Figure 102.4a shows all different shapes in composed image, Fig. 102.4b shows the resulting image after fitting, obtaining all ellipses labeled by red curve. Figure 102.5 shows a substation oil conservator image. Figure 102.5b is boundary image after edging detection of Canny, Fig. 102.5c shows the un-filtering fitting ellipses. It can be seen that the oil conservator boundary could also be treated as a fitting ellipses. The correct oil conservator image could be obtained after filtering the fitting ellipse area by controlling ellipticity, fitting rate and the size of ellipse etc.

In composed image, the lower the ellipticity is, the flatter the ellipse and because of that all ellipse shape could be detected in the image. The image that

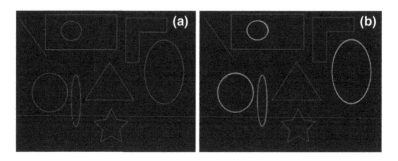

**Fig. 102.4** Composed image testing. **a** Various shapes image. **b** Fitting of ellipse

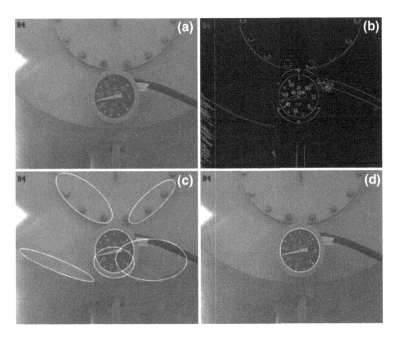

**Fig. 102.5** Image of fitting of ellipse. **a** Image of oil conservator meter. **b** Canny boundary. **c** Ellipse after fitting. **d** Ellipse after selection

is captured by the robot has the changes of view, we normally choose ellipticity to be 0.85 and the fitting rate to be 0.8. Figures 102.6 and 102.7 are two different type meters under different light conditions. The meter dial both could be correctly found through our improved algorithm and labeled by red curve. Meanwhile, Fig. 102.7b show the location of meter's dial. The range of drawing by blue curve is detected by Ref. [3].

Our improved algorithm generally cost 10–25 ms which meets real-time communication requirement. Table 102.1 shows time consumption by using different algorithm. Archive as experiment data, this paper compares Ref. [3]'s algorithm on the execution efficiency, our algorithm cost less time.

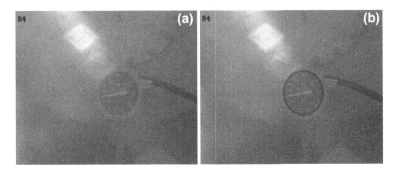

**Fig. 102.6** Image under glaring light. **a** Image of oil conservator meter. **b** Fitting of ellipse

**Fig. 102.7** Switch pressure meter. **a** Image of pressure meter. **b** Fitting of ellipse by different algorithm

**Table 102.1** Time consumption of different algorithm

| Image | Time consumption of Ref. [3]'s algorithm (ms) | Time consumption of this paper's algorithm (ms) |
|---|---|---|
| Image 4 | 28 | 12 |
| Image 5 | 35 | 19 |
| Image 6 | 30 | 18 |
| Image 7 | 50 | 25 |

## 102.5 Conclusion

General least square fitting of ellipse treats all sample points as the actual value to fit ellipse. It costs so much time that it cannot meet the requirement of the robotic meter reading system. The improved least square fitting of ellipse algorithm has proved that it has advantage of time costing and precision. The result indicates that the algorithm can meet the real-time request. It is quite important to locate the dial of meter for robotic reading system.

## References

1. Hough P, Hough PVC (1962) Method and means for recognizing complex patterns. US Patent Vol 3069654
2. Li X, Shi Z (2007) Method of ellipse(circle) recognition based on invariant moments. J Beijing Univ Technol 11:1136–1140 (in Chinese)
3. Gander W, Golub GH, Strebel R (1994) Least-squares fitting of circles and ellipses. BIT numerical mathematics. Springer, Berlin

# Chapter 103
# Research on Shared Ontology Model for Coal Mine Emergency Case

Zhenfeng Hu, Shangheng Yao and Yangtong Liu

**Abstract** As the stable operation in coal production is threaten by a lot kinds of safety accidents seriously, doing research on emergency knowledge in the field of coal mine safety production can provide sever for emergency decision, which is of great importance. This paper designed and developed coal mine emergency case ontology model in order to solve problem of case knowledge sharing and semantic conflicts in the coal mine emergency field. Lastly, this paper constructed coal mine emergency case description based on ontology, taking the Sunjiawan coal mine "2.14" gas explosion accident in Liaoning province as an example.

**Keywords** Coal mine emergency case · Ontology · Knowledge sharing

## 103.1 Introduction

Coal becomes the important energy with the rapid development of national economy in China, but the situation of safe production of coal mine is very serious. The coal mine safety production has become the focus of attention of the whole

Z. Hu (✉) · S. Yao
School of Mechanical Electronic and Information Engineering,
China University of Mining and Technology, Beijing, No. Ding 11,
Xueyuan Road 100083 Haidian District, Beijing, China
e-mail: zfhu2010@163.com

S. Yao
e-mail: yaoshangheng817@yahoo.cn

Y. Liu
School of Materials Science and Engineering, Northwestern Polytechnical University,
No. 127 West Youyi Road 710072 Xi'an, Shannxi Province, China
e-mail: liuyt1001@gmail.com

W. Lu et al. (eds.), *Proceedings of the 2012 International Conference on Information Technology and Software Engineering*, Lecture Notes in Electrical Engineering 212, DOI: 10.1007/978-3-642-34531-9_103, © Springer-Verlag Berlin Heidelberg 2013

society, it is imperative for us to strengthen coal mine safe production emergency management and rescue work.

However, there are still many problems existing in the field of coal mine emergency management and rescue work. For example, there is an over-reliance on paper plans during the process of emergency management disposing. It is hard to implement efficient management on emergency by traditional means. Facing emergency, the traditional way can't meet the need, such as accident information responding timely, rescue teams being available timely, which may delay the opportune time to rescue workers. So, in order to improve emergency capability, it is imperative to establish the basic knowledge system of the emergency rescue in the coal production, solve semantic conflicts and establish coal mine accident knowledge sharing platform.

Ontology, one concept comes from the philosophical field, is introduced in the information science field in the 1990s, which describes the objective existence of the content system in the world. Ontology can describe or express a set of concepts and terminology of one specific knowledge domain, and is a set of standardized description used for domain knowledge sharing and reuse. Ontology, as an important means to describe the semantic model, is the formal specification of the sharing conceptual model, providing application framework and approaches for computer understanding, semantic understanding of knowledge and human–computer interaction [1]. At present, ontology has been widely used in the computer field. By using ontology technology, the coal mine emergency case ontology model can provide the semantic knowledge common understanding of the emergency management process and realize exchanging, sharing, and reusing of the knowledge in the coal mine emergency management field.

## 103.2 Relative Works

There have been few reports about coal mine emergency knowledge model and standardization. Emergency domain knowledge modeling varies according to actual requirements. Wang wen-jun described a new $E^2M$ model based on ABC Ontology model, and listed related concepts of event: event, process, action, situation, state of change, etc. [2]. Reference [3] summarized the emergency domain knowledge model from three aspects: event content, event development and event control. Disaster emergency management model described in Ref. [4] define concept of event object and related behavioral subject by extracting key elements from emergency field, and associated these elements through situation, which provides basic concept interaction for emergency response process. Reference [2] divide Ontology semantic model of emergency event into three levels: event, process, action to integration emergency events in semantic level which provides general information exchange model and vocabulary for integrated emergency response system. The above model designs information interaction model in accordance with emergency event and extracts emergency field key elements. The model defines emergency related field classes and class level from their corresponding perspectives and determines the scope and granularity of the emergency domain ontology, then establish the corresponding knowledge model. However, most of these models mainly emphasis process of emergency response, lacking relevant design of internal elements.

Related concepts between coal mine accident emergency handling and coal mine disaster events have a lot in common, but they have different focuses, so we should model emergency case knowledge from the angle of knowledge representation in emergency field, which is more suitable to the need of emergency field.

## 103.3 Coal Mine Emergency Case Ontology Model

In this paper, eABC ontology is used as upper ontology in coal mine emergency case knowledge expression, and eABC ontology is expanded to form coal mine emergency case ontology model according to the characteristics of coal mine emergency case knowledge expression [5].

### 103.3.1 Construction of Coal Mine Emergency Case Ontology

Coal mine emergency case describe emergency events and their emergency handling process. According to the establishment of ontology concept relationship of Ref. [4]. This model adds handling subject and handling object of emergency events, and divides coal mine emergency cases into five sub-ontology, as is shown in Fig. 103.1 (note of Fig. 103.1: CMEC-coal mine emergency case, CMA-coal mine accident). This ontology model's metadata format uses the Dublin Core Element Set, which is the most widely used element set in the world at present.

*Case subject* Implementing body of emergency response action, it is made up of emergency organization system, and describe the basic component and responsibilities of emergency authorities. It is responsible for the management, scheduling and distribution of emergency resources. It includes emergency management and rescue center, accident Command Center, support and security center, media center and information processing center.

*Case object* Describing environment and specific information of coal mine accident area, it is made up of object environment and object area. Case object mainly embodies the time of disasters event and regional characteristics. Various types of disasters and difference of geological condition will also have a certain effect on case object.

*Coal mine accident* Description of related concepts and events process about coal mine disasters accident, such as event state change of coal mine accident in different periods of time.

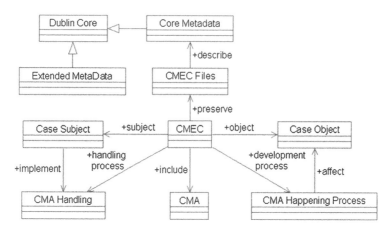

**Fig. 103.1** Coal mine emergency case ontology model

*Coal mine accident happening process* The process takes occurrence, process and the end of accident as its core, define impact factors of emergency response, such as environment, victims, mechanism and materials.

*Coal mine accident emergency handling* It is description of coal mine accident emergency handling process, and is the procedure knowledge representation of emergency rescue activity implemented by case subject. It defines different stages and activity during event handling, and is the core knowledge expression of emergency case.

## 103.3.2 Definition of Coal Mine Emergency Case Ontology

### 103.3.2.1 Definition of Coal Mine Emergency Case Ontology

According to the category of ontology classified by Perez, this paper summarized the five basic elements of ontology, which is based on analysis of coal mine emergency case ontology. These elements are: classes, relations, function, axiom and instances [6]. Classes are called concepts, which refer to any affairs, such as job description, strategy and behavior, Relations refer to interaction between concepts in special field, Function is a special type of relations, Axiom represents real assertion, Instances refer to the specific example of a certain class. Taking the sub-ontology of the model as an example, this paper introduce the five elements of ontology description model.

### 103.3.2.2 The Set of Coal Mine Emergency Case Concept

Sub-ontology of coal mine accidents process modeling process knowledge of emergency rescue events. Because emergency cases are used to recommend knowledge for emergency decisions, it is necessary for us to distinguish this research focuses from coal mine safety science, when describing knowledge of coal mine accidents process. We should pay more attention to elements which has close contact with coal mine accident emergency handling, then we can construct concept model which provides assisted knowledge for emergency response. According to the state of emergency in different stages, coal mine accidents process sub-ontology divide accident process concepts into three concepts groups: accident happening, accident evolution and accident ending, as is shown in Fig. 103.2 (note of Fig. 103.2: CMA-coal mine accident).

*Coal mine accident happening* Knowledge set concerning hidden danger and mechanism of accident occurrence during the process of coal mine accident. Related concept includes accident source, accident occurrence mechanism and accident occurrence condition. Serious accident source is characterized by changing from hidden trouble into accident, reason of accident occurrence are identified by scientific basis, these concepts are the vital event elements during early coal mine accident. Mastering these basic knowledge are good for decision makers to catch the favorable opportunity of emergency handling, and take reasonable and efficient measures to minimize losses.

*Accident evolution process* The entire process of accident occurrence, accident outbreak, it describes key elements of accident process by phases, determines key problems to be solved in each stage of accident process. Continuously changing of the accident and occurrence of derivative accident have influence on emergency measures and decision-making. The core concepts in the process include: human factors, environmental factors, material factors, electrical and mechanical factors, these are the four basic conditions that influence accident occurrence. Environmental factor refers to circumstances influenced by accident, including location,

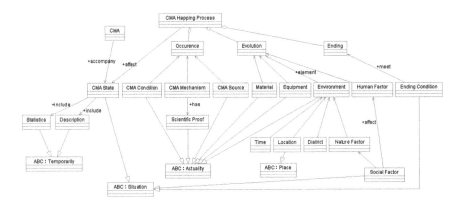

**Fig. 103.2** Coal mine accident happening process concept and relation description

time, geological conditions, regional features, gas, ventilation condition and so on. Natural factor (such as climate, environment) and human factor are affected by social factors. Human factor refer to human behavior that influences the accident process. Electrical and mechanical factors refer to the hidden trouble of equipment. Materials reserves are the factors that affect accident protection efficiency. The four factors are key elements of evolution of the accident. As long as we take effective measures to improve the factors that affect the process of accident. The range of effect and the loss should be reduced to the lowest level.

*The end of accident* During the process of accident, the end is the final step. Its core concept is accident ending conditions. When accident meets the ending conditions, it is bound to cease. Related knowledge need clearly defined in emergency handling.

Coal mine emergency handling sub-ontology models emergency handling process, and describes the emergency handling process of coal mine accident. Coal mine accident has an evolution process from hidden trouble to major accident. To the mine existing hidden danger, the recognition process always follows the process of coal mine emergency event. The handling of coal mine disaster accident should be based on effective prevention, and cope with potential danger by means of hazard monitoring and hidden danger investigation, the paper constructs emergency accident response model according to the feature of accident process, which includes three concepts group: preventive process, response process and the end of process, as is shown in Fig. 103.3 (note of Fig 103.3: CMA-coal mine accident).

*Preventive process* Accident preventive process including emergency drilling, the major hazard source monitoring and risk analyses. Emergency drilling are effective precaution measures, its purpose is to make people master rescue and self-rescue procedures when accident happens. Fire, flood, mineral dust and gas are the main factors that cause coal mine accident, which serious threaten coal mine safety production, so we should take effective measures to implement

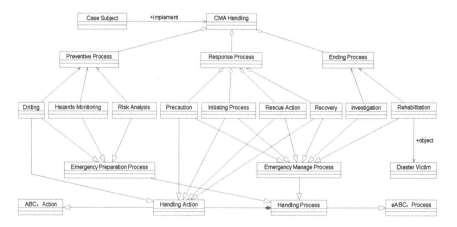

**Fig. 103.3** Coal mine accident emergency handling concept and relation description

supervision to dangerous sources in order to avoid accidents happen. Risk analyses are an important step of emergency plan, and its aim is to give the qualitative or quantitative evaluation results of any accidents that are likely to happen.

*Response process* The basic aspects of response process include warning action, receiving alarming, judging emergency response level, emergency rescue startup, rescue action and the end of emergency rescue. Emergency response process models knowledge according to the key elements of emergency rescue process.

*Ending process* Ending process refers to temporary emergency recovery stage after rescue action. It mainly includes the accident investigation and rehabilitation work. After the emergency response, emergency rescue organizations announces the end of emergency response in accordance with the relevant procedures.

### 103.3.2.3 The Set of Coal Mine Emergency Case Relations

In the coal mine emergency case knowledge description, the relation among concepts has three types: association relation, generalization relation and aggregation relation. Association relation refers to some kind of relationships among the conceptions, including the attribute association and the semantic association. Inheritance relationship refers to the relation between the general and the specific. Aggregation relation refers to the relation between the whole and the part, which comprise a set of elements to a more complex close unit through management.

In specific knowledge expression, association relation is shown in Figs. 103.1 and 103.2, it includes: (1) case subject-implement-coal mine accident handling; (2) the accident cause mechanism-has-scientific basis; (3) the process of coal mine accident-affects-case object; (4) end of accident-meets-the end condition. Generalization relation embodies extensively, as is shown in Fig. 103.3, warning action, emergency startup, rescue action, emergency recovery, accident investigation and rehabilitation are all sub-process of emergency rescue process, the relation between them are son class and father class. Aggregation relation is obvious in the process of accident, as is shown in Fig. 103.2, accident occurrence, accident evolution and accident termination are three sub-process of accident process, the relation between coal mine accident and them is whole and parts. There are any other complex relation in ontology knowledge expression, most of them can be expressed by the three basic relation. Emergency knowledge expression relations sets are made up of these relations together.

### 103.3.2.4 The Set of Coal Mine Emergency Case Functions

Function is a special type of relation, it expresses relation's finite constraints on the basis of case relation sets. Relation's previous $n-1$ elements of relations can sole determining the nth element. Event state evolution, cause of the event and the uncertainty of event situation makes difference in coping actions and decision-making in knowledge representation of emergency case. Clearly representation of emergency case functions sets are the foundation of reasoning about uncertain knowledge. For instance, coal mine safety accidents that have seen 10 or more deaths are identified as major coal mine accident. Description above are function knowledge expression on a specific condition. It is through restricting certain condition of major coal mine accident that constraint result of event level and property. When condition changes, accident condition doesn't fulfill the function, then event level and property should be determined by other functions.

#### 103.3.2.5 The Set of Coal Mine Enterprise Emergency Case Axiom

Axioms are the constraints of concept property value, relation property value or relations among concepts. During the process of coal mine accidents, there are many knowledge description about coal mine accidents, According to the regulations on Coal Mine Accident Investigation and Handling Method issued by Mine Safety Supervision, classification of coal mine accident types and concrete types belongs to category of the coal mine emergency case axiom.

#### 103.3.2.6 The Set of Coal Mine Emergency Case Instances

The instantiated emergency cases concepts, relations and situation can form emergency cases instances sets. For example, Dongfeng coal mine "11.27" coal dust explosion accident in Heilongjiang province, Sunjiawan coal mine "2.14" gas explosion accident in Liaoning province and so on all are instances in case sets.

### 103.4 Application of Coal Mine Emergency Case Ontology Model

Construction of coal mine emergency case ontology model provide good support for exchange, sharing and reuse of case data and case knowledge. Taking Sunjiawan coal mine "2.14" gas explosion accident in Liaoning province as an example, Fig. 103.4 describe some knowledge clips of the accident according to knowledge model that coal mine emergency case ontology model expresses. According to the framework of coal mine emergency case ontology model, Fig. 103.4 extract four key element from "2.14" gas explosion accident: event object-Sunjiawan coal mine accident, event subject-coal mine emergency rescue command center, process of the accident; emergency handling process of accident. In Fig. 103.4, oval represents class of emergency case ontology model, words below represents concrete example, for example, CMEC represents coal mine emergency case, "2.14" gas explosion accident emergency case is the example of the class. Table 103.1.

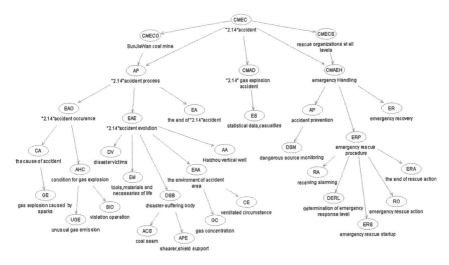

**Fig. 103.4** Sunjiawan coal mine "2.14" gas explosion emergency case in Liaoning province information demonstration

**Table 103.1** Notes of Fig. 103.4

| | |
|---|---|
| CMEC-Coal mine emergency case | APE-The affected production equipment |
| CMECO-Coal mine emergency case object | EAA-The environment of accident area |
| CMAD-Coal mine accident description | GC-Gas concentration |
| CMECS-Coal mine emergency case subject | CE-Circulation environment |
| AP-Accident prevention | AA- Accident area |
| EAO-Explosion accident occurrence | ES-Event state |
| EAE-Explosion accident evolution | CMAEH-Coal mine accident emergency handling |
| EA-The end of accident | AP-Accident prevention |
| CA-The cause of accident | DSM-Dangerous source monitoring |
| GE-Gas explosion | ERP-Emergency rescue process |
| AHC-Accident happening condition | RA-Receiving alarming |
| UGE-Unusual gas emission | DERL-Determination of emergency response level |
| SIO-Staff illegal operation | ERS-Emergency rescue startup |
| DV-Disaster victim | RO-Rescue operations |
| EM-Emergency materials | ERA-The end of rescue action |
| DSB-Disaster-suffering body | ER-Emergency recovery |
| ACS-The affected coal seam | |

Figure 103.4 set up a formal semantic expression system based on Coal Mine Emergency Case knowledge sharing system which standardizes related terms and concepts of emergency cases, and provides convenience for the practical use of domain case knowledge.

## 103.5 The Conclusion

According to the characteristics of coal mine accident, this paper models emergency case based on ontology, and extends coal mine accident happening process and accident emergency handling which are core elements in the model. This paper achieve the goal of describing the emergency case normatively and constructing matching knowledge model.

## References

1. Borst WN (1997) Construction of engineering ontologies for knowledge sharing and reuse. PhD thesis, University of twente, Enschede
2. Wenjun W, Xinpeng L, Yingwei L et al (2005) Study of ontology and application for emergency event model. Comput Eng 31(10):10–44 (in Chinese)
3. Hernandez JZ, Serrano JM (2001) Knowledge-based models for emergency management systems. Expert Syst Appl 20(2):173–186
4. Sotoodeh M (2007) Ontology-based semantic interoperability in emergency management. University of British Columbia, Vancouver
5. Wenjun W, Peng Y, Cunxiang D (2009) Study and application of emergency case ontology model. J Comput App 29(5):1437–1445 (in Chinese)
6. Perez AG, Benjamins VR (1999) Overview of knowledge sharing and reuse components: ontologies and problem-solving methods. In: Proceedings of the IJCAI-99 workshop on ontologies and problem-solving methods (KRR5), Stockholm, pp 1–15

# Chapter 104
# Simplified Skeleton Model Based Hand Gesture Recognition

**Yuan Shi, Qi Wei, Ruijie Liu and Yuli Ge**

**Abstract** There are two ways for 2D graphics recognition in general, which are contour curve description method and graphical Skeleton description method. Graphical Skeleton achieves recognition purpose by analyzing the relationship among the various parts of graphics. However, its performance is unstable, since it is very sensitive to contour noise. This paper adopts the graphical Skeleton description method to identify some commonly used number gestures, and introduces some approaches to optimize it for simplified gesture model.

**Keywords** Hand gesture recognition · Skeleton model · Skeleton thinning · Axial force diagram

## 104.1 Introduction

With the expansion of robot application, there is an increasing number of communications between human being and machines. However, common computer application restraints people in front of the computer, whose displayer, keyboard,

Y. Shi (✉) · Q. Wei · R. Liu · Y. Ge
Dalian Institute of Science and Technology, Dalian Lvshun Economic Development Zone,
Port Road 999-26 116052 Dalian, China
e-mail: 20088041@qq.com

Q. Wei
e-mail: 87284143@qq.com

R. Liu
e-mail: 108730747@qq.com

Y. Ge
e-mail: 254148726@qq.com

W. Lu et al. (eds.), *Proceedings of the 2012 International Conference on Information Technology and Software Engineering*, Lecture Notes in Electrical Engineering 212, DOI: 10.1007/978-3-642-34531-9_104, © Springer-Verlag Berlin Heidelberg 2013

**Fig. 104.1** Simplified model
representation of the hand

and mouse become the most common interactive tools. In recent years, the pervasive computing research has been heated. Its purpose is to liberate people from the front of the computer through ubiquitous computing and networking. As an alternative to traditional interactive tools, the data glove has become a hot research topic, but it also has its limitations. For example, the improper size will affect precision, and expensive price restricts its application. However, the most natural interaction is directly by hand rather than in other ways. In recent years, human face recognition and gesture recognition have become hot research topics in the field of machine vision as well.

Broadly speaking, two methods for image recognition are contour analysis and skeleton analysis. Brantzner proposed a hand model in Article [1], which is shown in Fig. 104.1. The palm of the hand is defined as a rough circle; finger approximately an ellipse, and fingertip approximately a small circle. It separates the hand out of Iuv color space and then uses the gray scale and area information to establish a hand model which is used for recognition. Article [2] also proposes another kind of method to divide the hand. It determines the threshold of skin colour in the YCbCr color space through the sample, and then separates the face and hand out of the background. Horimoto also put forward another gesture recognition method based on feature space in Article [3]. He defines two-dimensional image as one-dimensional vector, and then finds the first i principal components by calculating its covariance matrix, and then match these principal components with specific templates to complete recognition. Overall, the recognition which is based on standard skeleton has better recognition performance. However, the access of standard skeleton means that the algorithm's time complexity increases.

Since Blum proposed the skeleton description for the graph, many scholars have studied skeleton extraction algorithm, and ways to lower sensitivity of skeleton to the contour noise. Dimitrov proposed an effective method to extract the skeleton for standard graphs, which can reduce the influence of contour noise effectively in Article [4]. Siddiqi proposed the pattern recognition method which is based on the impact diagram, mapping graphs to another space in Article [5]. The impact map will define points on the skeleton as different types of impact, thus mapping the skeleton structure levels into a syntax, which will be analyzed to complete recognition. But of course, syntax recognition must be based on the standard skeleton. Eede proposed skeleton pruning in Article [6]. It obtains the standard skeleton for graphs through pruning skeleton bandage branches. The test results show it has good effects. However, it's not necessary for most of the recognition to delete all the pseudo branches. For example, the internal bandage segments can be ignored in the hand model showed in [1]. Based on the definition of the model in [1], this article will simplify the main part of skeleton left to be identified by using the characteristics of impact diagram [4] in order to reduce computation and improve the recognition efficiency for the subsequent calculations. The analysis of the final test can verify the proposed method in this article has good recognition effects in regard to the commonly used number gestures [7].

## 104.2 Description of Algorithm

This paper uses the method of skeleton description for the graphs for recognition. We will identify the samples shown in Fig. 104.2. We refer to the method in [1] using palm and fingers to describe the hand in regard to the hand model. So how to obtain the standard skeleton has become a major problem. According to the definition of the impact diagram, fingers correspond to the third-order impact, namely the point on the segment of the skeleton has a correspond radius which has a constant value. The minimum distance from the point on the skeleton to the boundary can be calculated through the change of graph's distance (DT). According to the prior knowledge, we will define the skeleton point with the largest radius as the center of the palm. Then we distinguish real fingers skeleton branch for recognition through pruning the skeleton branches outside the palm. The following is the detailed description of the algorithm which is divided into four parts.

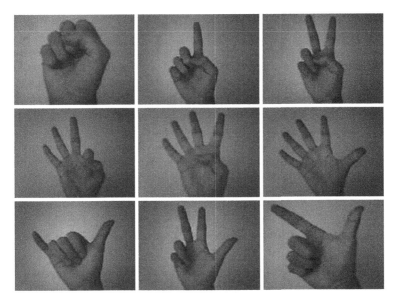

**Fig. 104.2** The sample set of the gestures indicating numbers

**Fig. 104.3** Background
segmentation of (**a**) and
morphological processing in
the smooth region (**b**)

## 104.2.1 Background Segmentation

This paper refers to the method in [2], mapping the sample to the YCbCr color
space for segmentation. The validity of this color space for segmentation is discussed in detail in [2]. In this paper, by analyzing space for skin color samples, the
threshold of Cb is defined as [,] and the Cr threshold value is defined as [,]. For a
single image, segmentation is done by using CbCr dual-threshold value. It can be
seen through the test analysis that this segmentation method can get relatively
ideal segmentation results under normal lighting conditions. However, there are
still relatively large errors in certain areas, as shown in Fig. 104.3a under the
uneven lighting effects. Under such circumstance, we use morphological dilation
algorithm to process the images after the pre-segmentation, thus obtaining a more
satisfactory segmentation result, as shown in Fig. 104.3b.

## 104.2.2 Skeleton Extraction

Skeleton extraction should be done after completing segmentation in the step
above. Later we will use some properties of the shock graph to do skeleton
pruning. Therefore, it is necessary to define the minimum distance from the points
on the skeleton to the boundary, that is, the radius of the biggest inscribed circle
with the points as the center. In order to avoid the trouble of finding biggest
inscribed circle, skeleton extraction algorithm similar to Grassfire is taken, which
is to advance from the border to the center and we should give the skeleton points
radiuses in a timely manner. The following Fig. 104.4a shows the distance
transforms, and Fig. 104.4b shows a skeleton diagram.

## 104.2.3 Simplification of Skeleton Structure

The focus of this article is to refine the skeleton. Due to the segmentation step of
the above, although the morphological algorithm is used, but still there is impact
on the skeleton diagram bound to the outline noise. The skeleton of this time is

**Fig. 103.4** The distance transform diagram of the hand (**a**) and its skeleton diagram (**b**)

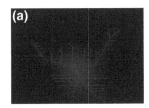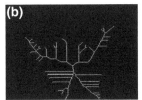

extremely complex, which can be seen from Fig. 104.4b. It is required to simplify in order to facilitate identification. The simplification here will be divided into three steps. The first step is to trim all external bandage branches [5]; the second step is to refine the skeleton after the first step treatment; the third step is to further use the characteristics of the impact diagram to remove the pseudo finger. The following is to introduce the three sections.

### 104.2.3.1 Pruning of External Bandage Branches

Due to the purposes of gesture recognition, we do not aim to achieve complete reconstruction. Instead, we only need to identify the second-order impact fingers corresponds to. Because the contours of the hand are smooth with curves, the external branches of the skeleton tree begin with the first-order impact, and the fingers correspond to the second-order impact. So we can delete all external first-order impact, that is, delete all the outermost branches. First we mark nodes of skeleton tree considering its 8 neighbourhood for each node. A leaf node (red) is marked when there is only a skeleton node in its 8 neighbourhood; a container node (green) is marked when there are two skeleton nodes; a branch node (blue) is marked when there are three or more nodes. As shown in Fig. 104.5a, it is gradually removed from the leaf node to the first branch node of the skeleton tree. These branches correspond to the outermost branch. Figure 104.5b shows the results after deletion in the first step.

### 104.2.3.2 Skeleton Refining

It can be seen from Fig. 104.5b that the simplified diagram still can not meet our requirements. Due to influence of the contour noise on the skeleton, there are still branches to be deleted at this time. In addition, the definition of the branch node

**Fig. 104.5** Marks of the skeleton tree (**a**) and the result after pruning in the first step (**b**)

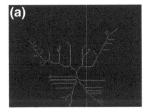

**Fig. 104.6** The order of
neighborhood pixels for the
current skeleton node and the
definition of the
neighborhood matrix

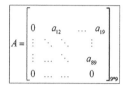

leads to the presence of some pseudo branch nodes, which also need to be removed to eventually complete the single-pixel skeleton description.

Firstly we define the field of matrix. For each skeleton node, we consider its 8 neighbourhood, as shown in Fig. 104.6. For a skeleton node, we will place it in the position 5 and then consider its 8 neighbourhood. We define it adjacent if Pixel 1 and 2 are both the skeleton nodes, otherwise not adjacent; we define Pixel 1 and 3 adjacent as Pixel 1 and 2 adjacent as well as 2 and 3 adjacent, or 1 and 5 adjacent as well as 5 and 3 adjacent. It is seen from the definition above that each node can have eight kinds of adjacency relationship, and for convenience we will define neighbourhood matrix as matrix $a_{ij}$. In this matrix, each element $a_{ij}$ indicates whether Pixel i and j are adjacent. It is 1 if they are adjacent, otherwise 0. Due to the symmetry of the neigh boring relations, we define A as the upper triangular matrix.

The following refining will be discussed on the basis of the neighborhood relations. Any node on the skeleton, whether it can be deleted or not, is defined as:

Def1: if intermittent skeleton branches appear after it is deleted, then it should not be deleted, and if it does not affect the adjacency of other nodes, then it can be deleted.

We use neighborhood matrix to define the definition above, as follows:

Def2: we set the initial neighborhood matrix as $A_0$, then we'll set 0 as the value for Pixel 5 to reconsider this 3 * 3 neighborhood. We set the neighborhood matrix at this time as $A_1$, and then we will set 0 as values for the 5th row and 5th column of $A_0$. If $A_1$ and $A_0$ is equal now, it means if the current node is deleted, it won't affect the other nodes' adjacency, and you can delete it. It can not be deleted if they are not equal. The point should be noted at this time is that deletion should not begin with a leaf node, otherwise the whole tree will be deleted. Thus Single container nodes and single branch nodes should be taken as objects to be deleted. Figure 104.7a shows the structure after pruning the gesture for the number 6 by using the neighborhood matrix in 5(b). It can be seen that till now we obtain the description of a single-pixel finger skeleton.

### 104.2.3.3 Deleting Pseudo Finger Skeleton by Using the Characteristics of Impact Diagram

It can be seen from Fig. 104.7a that the skeleton branches corresponding to the connecting portion of the palm and wrist still needs to be deleted. We can clearly

**Fig. 104.7** A simplified
model of the hand based on
the skeleton

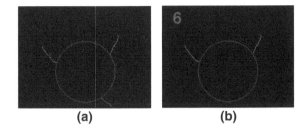

(a)                                    (b)

see that there are differences from skeletons of the fingers and the wrist part. Finger branches correspond to the third-order impact segment, while the wrist branches correspond to first-order impact segment. That is, the value for the radius of the finger skeleton point is basically constant while that of the radius of the wrist skeleton point increases monotonically. We can use the characteristics of the impact to consider radius variations of the skeleton points. We will delete it if it is in the form of monotonously increasing. Figure 104.7b shows the single-pixel finger skeleton and its simplified model which are eventually produced.

### 104.2.4  Gesture Recognition Based on a Simplified Model

We get a simplified skeleton of the relatively simplified model [1] from Fig. 104.7b. Based on this simplified skeleton, we can identify different gestures by analysis of skeleton structure relationships. We first classify by identifying the number of fingers, then further classify by the center angle corresponding to the arc length between the fingers skeleton branch root nodes as the pseudo codes show in Fig. 104.8.

Here we identify the simple number gestures by recognizing the number of the fingers and their structural relationships. If it is possible to identify the direction of the hand, then the fingers will be specifically defined and recognized, thus more hand gestures can be defined.

## 104.3  Test Results

Here we use samples shown in Fig. 104.2 to test the algorithms. Figure 104.7 shows the test results of a group of samples. Figure 104.9 shows the automatic identification results of Fig. 104.2 by using the algorithm above.

We manually segment the hand for collected samples and further use the algorithm given in this article for detection. However, if the wrist part is introduced more than it's required for the segmentation, the second-order impact of skeleton branches the wrist part corresponds to will occur, which will lead to the false detection. The purpose of this article is to introduce an analytical method of

**Fig. 104.8** Pseudo code for
skeleton simplifying
algorithm

```
switch(finger num)
    case 0:  handpose=0;
    case 1:  handpose=1;
    case 2:  switch(jiajiao)
                 case jiajiao<60:  handpose=2;
                 case jiajao>110:  handpose=6;
                 default:  handpose=8;
             end;
    case 3:  switch(max(jiajiao))
                 case max>45:  handpose=7;
                 case max<=45:  handpose=3;
             end;
    case 4:  handpose=4;
    case 5:  handpose=5;
end
```

**Fig. 104.9** The experimental
results for the skeleton
analysis of the sample set in
Fig. 104.2

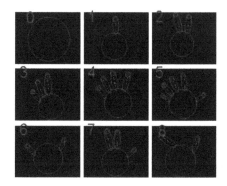

the skeleton based on the simplified model of the hand (Fig. 104.1). It can be seen
from the result of Fig. 104.9 that the algorithm in the article can achieve the goal
of automatic gesture detection.

## 104.4 Conclusion

Skeletons for 2D graphs are simple and intuitive advantages. This article has
conducted in-depth explorations in extraction and simplification of hand skeleton.
According to the definition in the simplified model (Fig. 104.1), we make good
reconstruction and recognition (Fig. 104.9) with the use of the algorithm proposed
in this article. However, it is possible to define more hand gestures because if the
direction of hand can be located, we can identify fingers in detail. This section will
be discussed in further studies. With the development of human–computer interaction and ubiquitous computing technology, it is believed that we will eventually
develop smarter machines in order to conduct more natural interactions and free
human being from the shackles of the traditional computer interaction.

# References

1. Trinder J, John A, Beveren V, Smith P et al (2005) Correlation between ventilation and EEG arousal during sleep onset in young subjects. J Appl Physiol 83:2005–2011
2. Kasper K, Schuster HG (2001) Easily calculable measure for complexity of spatial temporal pattern. Phys Rev Online Arch, 36(2):842–848
3. Viglione SS, Ordon VA, Risch F (1999) A methodology for detecting ongoing changes in the EEG prior to clinical seizures. In: western institute on epilepsy,west Huntington beach, 27–28
4. Williams WJ (1999) Time-frequency analysis of biological signals. IEEE Electr Comput Sci, 12(1):83–86
5. Blanco S et al. (2007) Applying time-frequency analysis to seizure EEG activity. IEEE Eng Med Biol Mag, 16:65–71
6. Williams WJ, Hitten P, Zaveri J (1995) Time-frequency analysis of electrophysiology signals in epilesy. IEEE Trans Biomed Eng 3(2):133–142
7. Richman JS, Moorman JR (2000) Physiological time-series analysis using approximate entropy and sample entropy. AJP Heart Circulatory Physiol 278(6):2039–2049

# Chapter 105
# Ear-Clipping Based Algorithms of Generating High-Quality Polygon Triangulation

**Gang Mei, John C. Tipper and Nengxiong Xu**

**Abstract** A basic and an improved ear-clipping based algorithm for triangulating simple polygons and polygons with holes are presented. In the basic version, the ear with smallest interior angle is always selected to be cut in order to create fewer sliver triangles. To reduce sliver triangles in further, a bound of angle is set to determine whether a newly formed triangle has sharp angles, and edge swapping is accepted when the triangle is sharp. To apply the two algorithms on polygons with holes, 'Bridge' edges are created to transform a polygon with holes to a degenerate polygon which can be triangulated by the two algorithms. Applications show that the basic algorithm can avoid creating sliver triangles and obtain better triangulations than the traditional ear-clipping algorithm, and the improved algorithm can in further reduce sliver triangles effectively. Both of the algorithms run in $O(n^2)$ time and $O(n)$ space.

**Keywords** Polygon triangulation · Ear clipping · Edge swapping

G. Mei (✉) · J. C. Tipper
Institut für Geowissenschaften—Geologie, Albert-Ludwigs-Universität Freiburg, Albert street 23B D-79104 Freiburg im Breisgau, Germany
e-mail: gang.mei@geologie.uni-freiburg.de

J. C. Tipper
e-mail: john.tipper@geologie.uni-freiburg.de

N. Xu
School of Engineering and Technology, China University of Geosciences (Beijing), 100083 Beijing, China

W. Lu et al. (eds.), *Proceedings of the 2012 International Conference on Information Technology and Software Engineering*, Lecture Notes in Electrical Engineering 212, DOI: 10.1007/978-3-642-34531-9_105, © Springer-Verlag Berlin Heidelberg 2013

## 105.1 Introduction

Polygons are very convenient for representing real objects. However, in some cases polygons are too complex. In order to implement polygons faster and easier in applications, usually polygons need to be decomposed into simpler components such as triangles [1, 2], trapezoids [3] or even sub-polygons [4].

In computational geometry, polygon triangulation is the decomposition of a polygonal area into a set of triangles [5, 6], or in other words, to create a set of triangles without non-intersecting interiors whose union is the original polygon.

One way to triangulate a simple polygon is based on a fact that any simple polygon with at least 4 vertices without holes has at least two 'ears', which are triangles with two sides being the edges of the polygon and the third one completely inside it. This fact was proved by Meisters [7]. Meisters proposed a recursively algorithm that consists of searching an ear and cutting it off from current polygon. Removing an ear results in forming a new polygon that still meets the 'two ears' condition and repetitions can be done until there is only one triangle left.

The directly implemented ear clipping method runs in $O(n^3)$ time, with $O(n)$ time spent on checking whether a triangle newly constructed is valid. But in 1990 an efficient technique named 'prune-and-search' brought the time complexity from $O(n^3)$ down to $O(n^2)$ [8]. Also, a simple reorganization of Meisters's algorithm leads to run ear clipping algorithm in time complexity of $O(n^2)$ [9].

There are other triangulation algorithms proposed based on ear clipping, such as Kong, Everett and Toussaint algorithm [10], which adopts the Graham scan to select ears. This algorithm is sensitive to the shape of the polygon and runs in $O(n(r + 1))$ time, where $r$ denotes the number of reflex vertices of the polygon.

A triangle with sharp angle that is also called *silver triangle* is not allowed for its poor shape quality. Based on Rourke's algorithm, Sloan [11] also developed an $O(n^2)$ ear-clipping algorithm. After completely obtaining the triangulation of a polygon, optimization by swapping diagonals is accepted to avoid sliver triangles. Held [12] developed a polygon triangulation package FIST, which is based on ear clipping and can be applied to deal with complex polygons.

The motivation of this paper is to design a new algorithm based on ear clipping to generate high-quality triangulations with fewer sliver triangles. To achieve this, when locate an ear tip, the one with smallest interior angle is always selected and removed. If the ear tip with smallest angle is not chosen firstly, it will be divided into at least two much smaller ones, and several sharp triangles will be formed. To reduce *sliver triangles* in further, edge swapping is adopt during cutting ears rather than after generating polygon triangulation as that done in Sloan's code [11].

In our algorithm, firstly all vertices of a polygon are determined to be convex or reflex according to their interior angles. Secondly, all ear tips will be found by temporarily forming a triangle with each vertex $v_i$ and its two adjacent vertices $v_{i-1}$ and $v_{i+1}$, and then testing whether all reflex vertices are in the triangle $\Delta(v_{i-1}, v_i, v_{i+1})$. If inside, $v_i$ is an ear tip; Otherwise it's not. After indentifying all ear tips, the ear tip $v_i$ with smallest angle is selected, the ear consisted by three vertices ($v_{i-1}$,

$v_i$, $v_{i+1}$) is removed and a triangle $\Delta(v_{i-1}, v_i, v_{i+1})$ can be formed. After removing, ear tip status must be updated for vertices $v_{i-1}$ and $v_{i+1}$. And repetitions can be done until there is only one triangle left.

This paper is organized as follows Sect. 105.2 describes the basic triangulation algorithm for simple polygons and its improved version with edge swapping. Both of the proposed algorithms are extended to the polygons with holes. In Sect. 105.3, tests are made, qualities of resulting triangulations are compared and complexity is analyzed. Finally, Sect. 105.4 concludes the work.

## 105.2 The Proposed Algorithms

### 105.2.1 Basic Algorithm

The ear clipping triangulation algorithm consists of searching an ear and then cutting it off from current polygon. The original version of Meisters's ear clipping algorithm runs in $O(n^3)$ time, with $O(n)$ time spent on checking whether a newly formed triangle is valid. Rourke [9] simply modified and reorganized Meisters's algorithm and made the new version of ear clipping algorithm run in $O(n^2)$ time. The algorithms proposed in this paper are based on Rourke's algorithm.

Given a simple polygon $P$ with $n$ vertices $V(v_0, v_1, \ldots, v_{n-1})$ oriented in count-clockwise (CCW), the basic algorithm proposed in the paper to triangulate simple polygon $P$ is designed into four steps. Pseudo code is listed as Algorithm 1.

Step 1: Compute the interior angles on each vertex of $P$. If the interior angle on a vertex is less than 180°, the vertex is convex; Otherwise, reflex.

Step 2: Find out all ear tips of $P$, and initiate the ear tip status for each vertex according to the following Condition 1 [9, 12, 13].

**Condition 1** Three consecutive vertices $v_{i-1}$, $v_i$, $v_{i+1}$ of $P$ do form an ear if:

1. $v_i$ is a convex vertex;
2. the closure $C(v_{i-1}, v_i, v_{i+1})$ of the triangle $\Delta(v_{i-1}, v_i, v_{i+1})$ does not contain any reflex vertex of $P$ (except possibly $v_{i-1}$, $v_{i+1}$).The closure of a triangle is formed by the union of its interior and its three boundary edges.

Step 3: Select the ear tip $v_i$ which has smallest angle to create a triangle $\Delta(v_{i-1}, v_i, v_{i+1})$, and then delete the ear tip $v_i$, update the connection relationship, angle and ear tip status for $v_{i-1}$ and $v_{i+1}$.

Step 4: Repeat Step 3 until $(n-2)$ triangles are constructed.

Both Step 1 and Step 2 are to initiate status for the original polygon, while Step 3 and Step 4 are the repetition of cutting and updating.

---

**Algorithm 1** Triangulate Simple Polygon (*P*)

---

*Input*: A simple polygon *P* with *n* vertices $V(v_0, v_1, ..., v_{n-1})$
*Output*: A triangulation *T* with $n - 2$ triangles
1: Compute interior angles of each vertex in *P*.
2: Indentify each vertex whether it is an ear tip or not.
3: **while** number of triangles in $T < n - 2$ **do**
4:      Find the ear tip $v_i$ which has the smallest interior angle.
5:      Construct a triangle $\Delta(v_{i-1}, v_i, v_{i+1})$ and add it onto *T*.
6:      Let $v_i$ be no longer an ear tip.
7:      Update connection relationship of $v_{i-1}$ and $v_i$, $v_i$ and $v_{i+1}$, $v_{i-1}$ and $v_{i+1}$.
8:      Compute the interior angles of $v_{i-1}$ and $v_{i+1}$.
9:      Refresh the ear tip status of $v_{i-1}$ and $v_{i+1}$.
10: **end while**

---

## 105.2.2 Improved Algorithm

The basic algorithm tries to avoid creating sliver triangles. However, in some situations, sliver triangles still appear in triangulations. Thus, edge swapping is accepted to avoid sliver triangles. First of all, a bound for limiting interior angle is set. And then, after the ear tip with smallest interior angle is selected to form a new triangle, the new triangle will be checked whether it is sharp: if one of its three angles is smaller than the bound, the triangle is sharp and needs to swap edge with one of its neighbor. Noticeably, the new triangle may have no neighbor triangle because the triangle itself is created earlier than its neighbors.

If a new triangle needs to optimize, firstly find out its biggest interior angle and its opposite edge (the longest edge), and then search between all the generated triangles to see whether there exists a triangle that shares the longest edge with the new created triangle.

If there is one, the two triangles can form a quadrilateral. And then swapping the diagonal of the quadrilateral to see whether the minimum angle of the original pair of triangles is smaller than the minimum one of the new pair of triangles after swapping, if does, which means the new pair of triangles has better quality than the original one, swapping needs to be done; if not, the original triangles must be kept without swapping (Fig. 105.1).

**Fig. 105.1** Edge swapping
**a** before edge swapping,
**b** after edge swapping

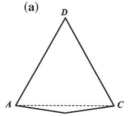 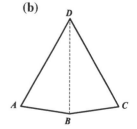

In the procedure of combining the basic algorithm and the edge-swapping optimization, edge swapping just has relationship with the pair of triangles which to be optimized. It does not affect the later updating operations.

### 105.2.3  Extension to Polygon with Holes

The basic and improved algorithms have been described above. However, the two algorithms are only valid for simple polygons and can not be directly applied on polygons with holes. Thus, a pre-processing of creating 'Bridge' edges must be done to transform the polygon with holes into a single polygon.

Creating 'Bridge' edges is widely used to divide a general closed domain into several simply connected, convex sub domains, such as generating Delaunay triangulations or Voronoi diagram in multi-domain polygons, see Tipper [14].

Different from dividing a closed domain, Held [12] adopts 'Bridge' edges to transform a multiply-connected polygonal area into a single polygon. The resulting polygon is not a simple polygon since each 'Bridge' edge appears twice with opposite orientations. These polygons are defined as 'degenerate' polygons by Held. In this paper, creating 'Bridge' edges is also accepted. The algorithm of triangulating polygon with holes can be divided into two stages.

Stage 1: Create several 'Bridge' edges to transform a polygon with holes to a degenerate polygon without holes.

Stage 2: Triangulate the resulting polygon in Step 1 by ear clipping.

Supposing there has a polygon $P$ with $m$ vertices PV($pv_0$, $pv_1$,..., $pv_{m-1}$) which orientate in count-clockwise and a hole $H$ with $n$ vertices HV ($hv_0$, $hv_1$,..., $hv_{n-1}$) orientated in clockwise, the aim is to create 'Bridge' edges to combine polygon $P$ and hole $H$ into a new polygon $P_{new}$.

Firstly, create $m \times n$ segments by a pair of vertices. In the pair of vertices, one is a vertex $pv_i$ from PV ($pv_0$, $pv_1$,..., $pv_{m-1}$) and the other is a vertex $hv_i$ from HV.

Secondly, compute the length of each segment, and then select the shortest segment as the candidate 'Bridge' edge temporarily. Check whether there have any edge from either the polygon $P$ or the hole $H$ intersects the 'Bridge' edge, if not, the 'Bridge' edge is valid; otherwise, invalid and then test the next shortest segment. These selecting and checking will repeat until a valid 'Bridge' is found.

Finally, combine polygon $P$ and hole $H$ into a new polygon $P_{new}$. Because the two vertices of the 'Bridge' edge are added twice, the new polygon $P_{new}$ has $(m + n + 2)$ vertices.

If there is more than one hole in a polygon $P$, just selecting one of the holes as the hole $H$ and creating a 'Bridge' edge to combine $P$ and $H$ into a new polygon $P_{new}$, and then deem $P_{new}$ as the polygon $P$, also select another holes as the hole $H$. This will be repeated until there are no holes left to obtain the final degenerate polygon. After transforming a polygon with holes to a degenerate polygon, the proposed algorithms will be accepted to generate the final triangulation (Fig. 105.2).

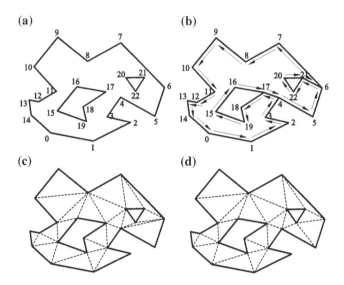

**Fig. 105.2** Transformation of a simple polygon with two holes and its triangulations **a** original polygon, **b** degenerate polygon **c** by basic algorithm, **d** by improved algorithm

## 105.3 Applications and Discussion

### 105.3.1 Tests by Basic Algorithm

In Fig. 105.3a, a simple polygon with 42 vertices is created based on the Chinese word 'Zhi' which means reaching in English [4], and then it is triangulated by traditional version of ear clipping and the basic algorithm proposed in the paper, as shown in Fig. 105.3b, c, respectively. The mentioned traditional version of ear clipping algorithm is the one which locates an ear tip sequentially and does not respect to the special ear tip that has smallest interior angle.

In Table 105.1, the qualities of triangulations are compared according to the minimum angle of each triangle. The minimum angle of a triangle is between 0° and 60°. And this range from 0° to 60° is divided into four equal intervals, 0°–15°, 15°–30°, 30°–45° and 45°–60°. Obviously, the bigger is the minimum angle in a triangle, the better is the triangle. From the comparison listed in Table 105.1, the basic algorithm generates better triangulation than that of traditional ear clipping. This conclusion is also true for a multiply-connected polygonal area, Chinese word 'Xi', presented in Fig. 105.4 and also compared in Table 105.1.

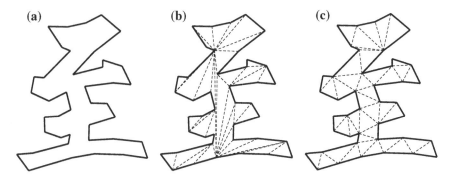

**Fig. 105.3** Chinese word 'Zhi' and its triangulations by traditional and the basic algorithm
**a** word 'Zhi', **b** by traditional, **c** by the basic

**Table 105.1** Minimum angle of triangles in triangulations of 'Zhi' and 'Xi'

| Polygon | Algorithm | Minimum angle | | | | |
|---|---|---|---|---|---|---|
| | | 0°–15° (%) | 15°–30° (%) | 30°–45° (%) | 45°–60° (%) | Average (°) |
| Figure 105.3 | Traditional | 37.50 | 30.00 | 25.00 | 7.50 | 20.98 |
| | Basic | 2.50 | 10.00 | 57.50 | 30.00 | 39.26 |
| Figure 105.4 | Traditional | 55.00 | 30.83 | 11.67 | 2.50 | 16.10 |
| | Basic | 0.00 | 20.00 | 53.33 | 26.67 | 38.34 |

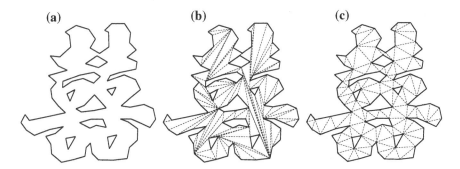

**Fig. 105.4** Chinese word 'Xi' and its triangulations by traditional and the basic algorithm
**a** Chinese word 'Xi', **b** by traditional, **c** by the basic

## 105.3.2 Tests by Improved Algorithm

In Fig. 105.5, a simple polygon with 279 vertices provided by Held [12] is presented, and its triangulations by the improved algorithm with the angle bound set
as 0°, 30° and 60°. According to the quality analysis listed in Table 105.2, when
the angle bound is set as 30°, the algorithm with optimization can improve the

**(a)**                          **(b)**                          **(c)**

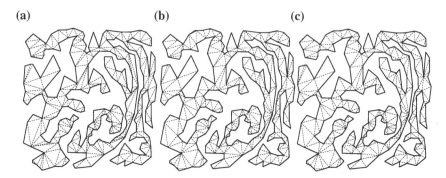

**Fig. 105.5** Triangulations of simple polygon by the improved algorithm **a** bound = 0, **b** bound = 30, **c** bound = 60

**Table 105.2** Minimum angle of triangles in triangulations by the improved algorithm

| Polygon | Algorithm (°) | Minimum angle | | | | |
|---|---|---|---|---|---|---|
| | | 0°–15° (%) | 15°–30° (%) | 30°–45° (%) | 45°–60° (%) | Average |
| Figure 105.5 | 0 | 11.91 | 37.18 | 32.85 | 18.05 | 30.04 |
| | 30 | 5.42 | 37.18 | 37.18 | 20.22 | 32.38 |
| | 60 | 5.42 | 37.18 | 36.10 | 21.30 | 32.68 |
| Figure 105.6 | 0 | 15.05 | 34.95 | 37.63 | 12.37 | 29.31 |
| | 30 | 6.72 | 32.80 | 44.62 | 15.86 | 32.9 |
| | 60 | 6.72 | 32.80 | 43.82 | 16.67 | 33.17 |

**(a)**                          **(b)**                          **(c)**

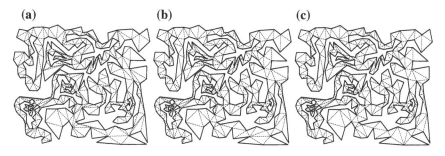

**Fig. 105.6** Triangulations of polygon with holes by the improved algorithm **a** bound = 0, **b** bound = 30, **c** bound = 60

quality of triangulation a lot comparing to that when the angle bound is 0°. However, the quality improvement due to increase the angle bound from 30° to 60° is not so obvious as that from 0° to 30°. In Fig. 105.6, a polygon with nine holes of 374 vertices provided also by Held [12], is triangulated by the improved algorithm. Same conclusions as that of Fig. 105.6 can also be drawn (Table 105.2).

### *105.3.3  Complexity*

In the basic algorithm, the computation of interior angle for all vertices cost $O(n)$ time. And finding all ear tips need $O(n^2)$ time according to Condition 1, although this complexity can be decreased. In the while loop, the most expensive operation is to search the ear tip which has the smallest angle runs in $O(n)$ time. Thus, the while loop spends $O(n^2)$ time on cutting off all ears recursively. Considering this algorithm in whole, it runs in $O(n^2)$ time and $O(n)$ space.

In the improved algorithm, only the procedure of edge swapping is added based on the basic algorithm. So, it is only necessary to analyze the complexity of this part. During edge swapping, finding a suitable neighbor triangle for a newly created triangle costs $O(n)$ time, other operations all run in $O(1)$ time. Hence, only $O(n)$ is spent time on edge swapping and this algorithm with optimization also runs in $O(n^2)$ time and $O(n)$ space.

## 105.4  Conclusion

Two algorithms based on ear clipping are presented in the paper. In the basic algorithm without optimization, the ear tip with smallest interior angle is always selected and then removed. Better triangulations can be generated by the basic algorithm than traditional ear clipping algorithm which cuts ears off sequentially. To avoid creating sliver triangles in further, edge swapping is adopt based on the proposed basic algorithm. In this algorithm with optimization, an angle bound (recommended as 30) is set to determine whether a newly formed triangle needs swapping edge. The optimization by swapping edges is not implemented after generating whole triangulation but during cutting ears to decrease computations. This algorithm with optimization can reduce sliver triangles effectively.

**Acknowledgments** This research was supported by the Natural Science Foundation of China (Grant Numbers 40602037 and 40872183). The author would like to thank Prof. M.Held at Universität Salzburg for providing original polygons' data in Figs. 105.5, 105.6.

## References

1. Chazelle B (1982) A theorem on polygon cutting with applications. 23rd Annual Symposium on foundations of computer science, pp 339–349
2. Chazelle B (1991) Triangulating a simple polygon in linear time. Discrete Comput Geom 6(5):485–524
3. Seidel R (1991) A simple and fast incremental randomized algorithm for computing trapezoidal decompositions and for triangulating polygons. Comput Geom Theory Appl 1(1):51–64

4. Feng H-YF, Pavlidis T (1975) Decomposition of polygons into simpler components: feature generation for syntactic pattern recognition. IEEE Trans Comput 24(6):636–650
5. Berg M, Cheong O, Kreveld M, Mark Overmars M (2008) Computational geometry algorithms and applications. Springer, Berlin
6. Garey MR, Johnson DS, Preparata FP, Tarjan RE (1978) Triangulating a simple polygon. Inform Process Lett 7:175–179
7. Meisters GH (1975) Polygons have ears. Amer Math 82(6):648–651
8. ElGindy H, Everett H, Toussaint G (1993) Slicing an ear using prune-and-search. Pattern Recogn Lett 14(9):719–722
9. O'Rourke J (1998) Computational Geometry in C. Cambridge University Press, Cambridge
10. Kong X, Everett H, Toussaint G (1990) The graham scan triangulates simple polygons. Pattern Recogn Lett 11(11):713–716
11. ftp://ftp.cis.uab.edu/pub/sloan/Software/triangulation/src/
12. Held M (2001) FIST: Fast industrial-strength triangulation of polygons. Algorithmica 30:563–596
13. Toussaint GT (1991) Efficient triangulation of simple polygons. Vis Comput 7:280–295
14. Tipper JC (1991) FORTRAN programs to construct the planar voronoi diagram. Comput Geosci 17(5):597–632

Printed in the United States
By Bookmasters